D1422592

THE NEW ASTROLOGER

MARTIN SEYMOUR-SMITH

Fate . . . is an excellent, but most expensive schoolmaster. In all cases, I would rather trust to a human tutor. Fate, for whose wisdom I entertain all imaginable reverence, often finds in Chance, by which it works, an instrument not over-manageable. At least the latter very seldom seems to execute precisely and accurately what the former had determined.
Goethe, **Wilhelm Meister**.

SIDGWICK & JACKSON
LONDON

TO ROBERT BLY

First published in Great Britain in 1981
by Sidgwick & Jackson Limited
1 Tavistock Chambers, Bloomsbury Way,
London WC1A 2SG

Produced, edited and designed by
Shuckburgh Reynolds Limited
8 Northumberland Place, London W2 5BS

ISBN 0-283-98758-8

Typesetting by SX Composing Ltd, Rayleigh, Essex
Printed and bound in Hong Kong
by Dai Nippon Printing Co. Ltd.

CONTENTS

INTRODUCTION

This is a book about how to do astrology for people of open mind. This is something of a paradox. For while astrology is becoming more and more popular, it is getting an increasingly bad name amongst scientists; and scientists exert much influence. Intelligent people rightly deplore the popular Sun Sign astrology of the newspapers and magazines as superstitious and silly. But they are also hearing, chiefly through television programmes and articles in such newspapers as the *Guardian*, that there is a 'new' and scientific type of astrology for which high claims are made. They also hear, from the more rigid-minded scientists, that these claims are nonsense: they cannot be true. They cannot be true, for example, because gravity is a very weak force which could not effect human beings. This was stated recently and authoritatively on BBC television. Now intelligent people ought to know this: first, that astrologers have not claimed that astrological effect has anything to do with gravity, and, secondly, that it has in any case been shown in the past twenty years that human beings are receptive to *very weak* forces indeed. In other words, the scientist in question did not know anything about astrology. Possibly he has confused it with the Sun Sign astrology of the newspapers, or with very bad, and badly written, mystical books on the subject.

It would be deplorable if astrology became a way of life for everybody. In the first place, we do not know enough about it, and in the second it is so inextricably tied up with the problem of predestination that it would be unwise for anyone to become dependent on it. I have tried to deal with this problem in this book.

What is also not as generally known as it might be is that a good deal of work is now going on, in the realms of astrology, that is deeply thoughtful and in no vulgar sense 'occultish'. It is certainly quite as intellectually respectable (in my view more so) to use astrology as a psychological tool as it is to practice, for example, transcendental meditation.

The plan of the book is as follows. I have begun by giving a brief but reasonably comprehensive history of the important part astrology has played in the past. I have then given an account of some of the more important research that has been done by Michel Gauquelin and others less well known. This demonstrates that a modern scientist, approaching an old subject in order to discredit it, came up with results that confirmed that it was valid at least in part.

I have then devoted a chapter to the astronomical bases of astrology – a chapter that is fully illustrated with diagrams. Then I explain how to construct a birth chart using a pocket calculator. Most people experimenting with astrology use either diurnal logarithms or specially constructed tables in order to do the small amount of mathematics involved in setting up charts and calculating aspects and midpoints. In these days of cheap and efficient calculators, however, this is a waste of time. All the calculations you need, even the ones which look formidable, can be done very simply with an inexpensive calculator. I must emphasise that you do not need to understand spherical trigonometry to calculate such points as the Ascendant and Vertex.

After this I have written a relatively long chapter, entitled 'Factors in Interpretation', an account of how natal astrology (that is, the delineation of character from birth charts) works. In the course of this I have rejected much of the lumber of the old astrology – as being quite unsuitable to our culture – and have substituted some new ideas. But the reader will note that I have kept quite a lot of the old concepts. This is because they work. I have sometimes given an indication of why I believe they work. Chapter Five explains how to interpret a chart, chiefly by example. After examining one chart in full detail, I have taken the charts of a number of well known people of different types, and made interpretations of their charts. These are less detailed, but provide useful illustrations of most of the sorts of configurations with which the astrologer is likely to meet.

I have ended the book with a chapter on synastry and prediction. Synastry, the comparison of two charts with a view to examining the nature of the relationship between the two subjects, is one of the most impressive aspects of astrology. There are four ways of doing it; I have described three of them, and given more detailed instructions about the fourth, which I favour as the most revealing.

I have given my advice on how to approach the difficult and delicate subject of prediction, and I have explained the very various ways in which astrologers do it. I have then shown how and in what spirit I do it.

At the end of the volume is an ephemeris: this is necessarily condensed, but it gives results as accurate as any beginner will need. Preceding it are full instructions on how to use it.

Astrology can never be a science – any more than a humanised psychology can ever be a science. There is too much proper room for disagreement; there are too many mysterious factors in our existence. Despite the hopes and beliefs of the more rigid kinds of scientists – who are wonderfully ingenious people – the mysteries of existence will never be entirely solved. It is a naive and even a de-humanising wish: for then existence would cease, as such. But science has as great a part to play in the 'true voice of feeling' as has any other discipline or art. So I do not apologise for trying to make my astrology as astronomical as possible, and as non-occult – using occult in its most garish and vulgar sense – as possible. This book can be used as the basis of an intelligent parlour-game, or it could be used in the quest for self-knowledge. It is not for me to instruct readers as to how to use it. But it does amount to a compromise between the lurid claims of occultists and the new claims of the behaviouristic astrologers, such as Geoffrey Dean, who believe that such things as love can be measured, quantified. Try it out for yourself, on people you know very well: you will be surprised.

MARTIN SEYMOUR-SMITH

Astrological symbols

♈	Aries
♉	Taurus
♊	Gemini
♋	Cancer
♌	Leo
♍	Virgo
♎	Libra
♏	Scorpio
♐	Sagittarius
♑	Capricorn
♒	Aquarius
♓	Pisces

Symbol	Body/Point
☉	Sun
☽	Moon
☊	Node
☿	Mercury
♀	Venus
♂	Mars
♃	Jupiter
♄	Saturn
♅	Uranus
♆	Neptune
MC	Midheaven
ASC	Ascendant
Vx	Vertex

☌	0°	Conjunction
⚺	30°	Semi-sextile
∠	45°	Semi-square
S	51°	Septile
⚹	60°	Sextile
Q	70°	Quintile
□	90°	Square
△	120°	Trine
⚼	135°	Sesqui-square
±	144°	Bi-quintile
⚻	150°	Quincunx
☍	180°	Opposition

CHAPTER ONE

HISTORY AND EVIDENCE

ASTROLOGY IN THE PAST

ASTROLOGY AND ASTRONOMY BEGAN AS ONE and the same thing. The observation of the Sun and Moon, of the fixed stars, and of the five planets visible to the naked eye (Mercury, Venus, Mars, Jupiter, and Saturn) is as old as man. Our remotest ancestors needed a calendar, and the movements of the celestial bodies provided them with a means of making one. Men also assumed, from the beginning, that the celestial bodies were invested with magical powers and possessed different characteristics. Later they were identified with gods.

The historical origins of astrology are confused. It was being practised in India as long ago as 3000 BC, a fact often ignored. An astrological treatise by the sage Parasara, dated about 3000 BC, still exists. But it is in Sanskrit, no one has ever translated it, and no summary of it in English is remotely comprehensible. All we know is that Parasara used equal houses and measured aspects from sign to sign, regardless of angular distance. This means, despite denials from all quarters, that there must have been some sort of zodiac in existence as early as the fourth millennium. And if Parasara used equal houses, then his zodiac must have consisted of twelve equal 30° signs.

Assyrian astrolabe, used for astrological calculation.

Today there are several zodiacs in use. All, except the constellational zodiac used by astronomers for convenience of reference, have signs of equal 30° width.

The circle of the zodiac was divided into 360° independently in China, Egypt, Babylon, and perhaps elsewhere: the approximation to the 365.2422 days in one year is obvious. 'Zodiac' means 'circle of animals' in Greek, and all the original zodiac signs consisted of animals, although in our own zodiac we have one or two glyphs (such as Libra, the scales) not obviously animal in nature.

Many different zodiacs were invented, all for the purpose of measuring the positions of celestial bodies. Because people did not want to use high numbers, they divided up their 360° into twelve 30° signs, which they named from the shapes they saw in the relevant parts of the sky. Then, instead of saying 278°, they could say 08 Capricorn. Many astrologers seek here, there and everywhere for the original meanings of the modern glyphs. This does not help us, but the names, if not the glyphs, of the modern signs do have some psychological significance.

THE SIDEREAL AND TROPICAL ZODIACS

In this book we shall be working only with the tropical zodiac. But first some preliminary explanation is needed both of the tropical, moving zodiac and of the sidereal, fixed zodiac, which is in fact an abstraction.

The path of the Sun around the Earth (really, of course, the path of the Earth around the Sun) is called the ecliptic, because eclipses of the Sun or Moon occur on it. In the zodiac now familiar to us, the Earth is represented by a dot at the centre, and the great circle divided into twelve signs is the apparent path of the Sun around it. The plane of the ecliptic passes through the centre of the spherical Earth.

In astrology the positions of the planets, the Sun and Moon, and other Points, are almost always measured on the ecliptic; in astronomy and navigation they are measured on the equator. The equator is another great circle, defined by its equidistance between the north and south poles of the Earth, and by the fact that its plane, also, passes through the centre of the Earth.

Now, as a circle has no beginning, it is necessary to invent one. And the most natural beginning for both these great circles, the ecliptic and the equator, is the vernal point, the First Point of Aries, 00 Aries 00. At this point the planes of the ecliptic and the equator intersect at the Spring Equinox, when the Sun's path along the ecliptic crosses the equator, and its declination is zero. (Declination is the Sun's distance above or below the equator measured in degrees, minutes and seconds of arc.)

The zodiacal circle has another natural starting point on or about 23 September, when the Sun again reaches zero declination, at 00 Libra 00. At the First Point of Cancer, Midsummer, the Sun reaches its highest declination, and in the Northern Hemisphere we have our longest day and shortest night. At the First Point of Capricorn it reaches its lowest declination, and we have the longest night and shortest day. These equinoctial and solsticial Points are called the four Cardinal Points: 00 Aries 00, 00 Cancer 00, 00 Libra 00, and 00 Capricorn 00.

If the line connecting the north and south poles, in other words the Earth's axis, were perpendicular to the ecliptic, then we should have no seasons, and the Sun would never have declination relative to the plane of the equator. But the axis is tilted, in a direction almost fixed in space, and the equator is at right angles to this axis. Because of the tilt – known as the obliquity of the ecliptic – we have the seasons.

The obliquity of the ecliptic remains very nearly constant, but not quite. This is because the Earth is not a perfect sphere. The equatorial radius is 3963.208 miles, the polar axis 3949.920 miles. This means that there is a slight bulge at the equator, and that the gravity of the Moon, and to a lesser extent of the Sun as well, causes the Earth's axis to wobble: it describes a cone in space. Therefore, each year when the Sun returns to the vernal point, it does not return to the same place in relation to the fixed stars. The vernal point recedes each year by about 50 seconds of arc, or about one degree of arc every 72 years. Thus our tropical zodiac is moving backwards: in approximately 26,000 years it will have returned to the point where it now is.

This phenomenon is known as the precession of the equinoxes. It is regarded as crucial by sidereal astrologers (as those who insist on using the fixed zodiac are called). The results of this are complicated. Most astrologers use the tropical zodiac, and therefore equate 00 Aries 00 with the vernal point. Certain astrologers, though, will tell you that instead of having been born with your Sun in Aries (according to the tropical zodiac) you were really born with it in Pisces (according to the sidereal zodiac). Most of your other planets will likewise be in other signs. Very few modern astrologers can make sense of these changed positions.

The other consequence of precession is accepted by many more contemporary astrologers. They assert that when the vernal point was in the sign of Taurus, it was the Taurean Age, when it was in the sign of Aries it was the Age of Aries, and so forth. We are now supposed to be moving out of the Age of Pisces into that of Aquarius. This notion forms the basis of a shabby pseudo-philosophy of human history, for which there is no evidence but fancy. It will not be discussed further in this book. None of these so-called Ages can in any case be accurately timed, because no one can show convincingly that the fixed zodiac of the siderealists has any valid continuity.

THE EARLIEST ZODIACS

Until recently it was believed that the first zodiac was a fixed one, based on some high-magnitude, fixed star somewhere near the path of the ecliptic. This now seems very doubtful because the standing stones of north-western Europe and the edifices attached to them were based on the tropical or movable zodiac. We do not know as much as we should like about the peoples who built these first astronomical observatories – so accurate that modern instruments have only surpassed them since 1945 – because they had no writing. No written accounts of their methods or of their intentions remain.

Stonehenge was used for astrological purposes.

One of the most famous examples of one of their observatories, though by no means the earliest, are the standing stones and other features of Stonehenge. Stonehenge incorporated, in the form of holes or posts, highly sophisticated analogue computers for predicting eclipses. They are earlier than any of the comparable monuments of the Middle East or Greece. What is more, Stonehenge's computer, the Aubrey Holes, used the tropical marking points. This means that those who constructed it knew about the precession of the equinoxes thousands of years before the Egyptians. They almost certainly used the tropical zodiac for their astrological purposes. At one time they may have used a fixed zodiac, but it seems very unlikely. We do know, however, that the first Egyptian and Babylonian zodiacs were of the fixed, sidereal type.

The difference in degree between the sidereal and tropical zodiacs at any given time is called the *ayanamsa* (Sanskrit for precession). It is impossible to choose between the 15 or so *ayanamsas* currently propounded by different authorities; they are very close together, and range between 19° and 32°. It is suspicious that each of the alleged 'zero dates' roughly coincides with the period when the first astrological records of the peoples concerned became available. This strongly suggests that the sidereal zodiac is meaningless.

Sidereal zodiacs were clearly used in various parts of the world both before and during the time when the first written astrological records were made. But when they fell into disuse any validity they had disappeared. In India the case is rather different: the sidereal zodiacs have never fallen into disuse and are implicitly believed in by a large number of people; astrologers use a technique akin to harmonics, and for these reasons they may be getting valid results.

The reader will realise that with the rejection of the sidereal zodiac we have decisively rejected the notion that particular constellations of stars exercise particular effects. Yet we seem to be suggesting that 30° segments of the ecliptic, continually moving backwards, along with the vernal point, imply certain modes of psychological expression – modes, moreover, which have a connection with the nature of certain planets. This apparent paradox will not be ignored. It largely explains why a modern school of sidereal astrologers has grown up in the west. But we base our notions of sign meaning on the Sun's annual journey.

THE HISTORY OF ASTROLOGY

Back in about 3000 BC, the Chaldeans of Mesopotamia built their famous *ziggurats*, watch-towers, some of them 300 feet tall, from which their priests observed the movements of the stars and planets. The Chaldeans divided the sky into twelve sections, reflecting the calendrical relationship between the Sun and Moon; they based a profound and beautiful mythology upon the sky. They identified the *bibbus*, 'goats', or planets, wandering among the tranquil and unmoving 'herds' of the fixed stars, and regarded them as interpreters, identified with certain of their most important gods. Venus was Ishstar, Jupiter was Marduk the king of the gods, reddish Mars was Nerval, the god of war, Saturn was the enigmatic Ninurta, the icy god of death, and Mercury was Nabu, the trickster, because it is so hard to observe.

There were many similar systems in other regions, but of all the Middle Eastern peoples the Chaldeans were the most accurate in their measurements. Their myths were adopted and transformed by the Egyptians and the Babylonians, each of whom made their own contributions.

To all these peoples the eclipses were of particular interest, because they were so spectacular and terrifying. It was not long before eclipses were predicted with some accuracy, but personalised birth charts were rare. These were drawn up by priests for Babylonian kings, with whose destinies the future of their country was inextricably interwoven. Otherwise there was little individualisation in the middle of the first millennium BC. As the modern astrologer Michel Gauquelin rightly implies, astrology was not 'democratic' in the days before Alexander the Great, and no one ever imagined that it might become so. Instead it dealt almost entirely with what we might describe as 'worldly' affairs. But it was also a basis for religion.

Over a long period of time astrology was intimately connected with the art of divination by cutting up and studying the entrails of animals, usually the liver or heart. Etruscan entrail-diviners used an elaborate scheme; it clearly has a zodiacal basis, although exactly how it works is impossible to establish. Doubtless the method dates back to the Etruscans' pre-Italian, Middle Eastern past.

The Babylonian universe The dome-shaped Earth is in the centre; around it lies a circular ocean, surrounded by a mountain range which supports the solid dome of the sky. It can be seen how the concept of a celestial sphere came into being.

Certainly the Babylonians made analogies between liver-omens and the night sky: happenings on earth and patterns in heaven were equated in a complex and sophisticated system. This may be seen as childish and unreasonable, but the peoples who used such methods, which were in no way simple, got on as well – if more modestly – as people in the modern world, with its use of reason and its rejection of the unknown.

CHALDEAN ASTROLOGY IN GREECE

In the fifth century BC Chaldean astrology reached Greece. It deeply influenced Plato himself, who identified the gods with the Sun, Moon, planets and stars, calling the stars 'visible gods'.

At the beginning of the third century BC Berosos, a Babylonian priest of Bel Marduk, settled on the Greek island of Kos. In about 280 he published a long history of his country. According to him, the work covered 470,000 years, incorporating a great deal of Babylonian cosmology and astrology. But Berosos' writings were not taken very seriously in Greece at the time. They had to wait until the death of Alexander the Great, until a time of greater uncertainty among the people. Prediction of the future always flourishes in times of uncertainty.

THE SCHOOL OF PYTHAGORAS

Meanwhile, a more astronomical science had developed during the first millennium in Greece, in the pre-Socratic era. It was rather more mystical in its nature than its Middle-Eastern counterpart, but it also possessed more strictly mathematical features. The original view of the soul in Greece – the Homeric view – imagined it as an image of the body, which survived in an apparently wretched condition as a shadow in Hades. The numerological school of Pythagoras in the sixth century BC was the first to assert that the individual soul had any moral importance. And it was Heraclitus, very slightly later in date than Pythagoras, who explicitly linked the soul with the cosmos.

According to Heraclitus the soul was made of fire. If it did not become over-moistened by personal folly and therefore turned to water, it survived to join, eventually, the cosmic fire. Heraclitus found conventional and institutionalised religion false and useless, though it might 'accidentally point to the truth'. For the less obscure and oracular Pythagoras the universe was ordered by number; no doubt he originated the notion of the 'harmony of the spheres' which so inspired Kepler, the seventeenth-century astronomer and astrologer who eventually discovered the true nature of the solar system.

Throughout the Greek enlightenment, the celestial bodies were invested with authoritative power and were regarded as sacred, even though there was still little or no interest in a personalised astrology. The great astronomical effort was instead concentrated on working out a mathematically feasible geocentric (earth-centred) system, which preserved orbital circularity.

A follower of Pythagoras, Philolaus (born c. 470 BC), invented a system which postulated that the Earth was carried on a spoke which circled a fiery centre once every 24 hours. The other planets were situated further out, along other spokes moving at different speeds. The central fire – known as the Watch-Tower of Zeus – could not be seen, partly because Greece was on that part of the Earth that did not face it, but also because, in any case, between the Earth and the central fire, and nearest to it on the spoke, was the counter-Earth. This invisible body balanced up the whole system, and also brought the number of revolving bodies to ten. Ten was the Pythagorean magical number, the sum of the first four integers, the basis of the Pythagorean numerology, the number which embodied 'the whole nature of number'.

Philolaus' system has the merit of simplicity, but entirely ignores the irregular movement of the planets. It is, however, a typical early example of a simple model of the solar system. Later schemes did attempt to account for the irregular movements of the planets – the retrograde motions, stations and other apparent anomalies. Such systems postulated that the planets were situated on the equators of spheres. The geometry was highly convoluted; some believed that the spheres actually existed, others did not. Eventually a mathematician, probably Appollonius of Perga, invented the notion of epicycles to account for the puzzling phenomenon of retrogradation (when the planets appear to go backwards).

THE RATIONALISATION OF EASTERN THOUGHT

After the death of Alexander the Great astrology suddenly became popular, chiefly because Eastern thought, hitherto embodied in myth and symbol, became conceptualised. This meant that metaphorical astrological systems, hitherto inaccessible to the 'intellectuals' of the time, became understandable and appealing. The process of conceptualisation was long and very complex, but in essence Oriental religion became rationalised as it gradually moved westwards, with the help of that abstract, theoretical style of thinking which had been invented by the Greeks and is embodied most obviously in the works of Aristotle. This rationalisation has been called a 'great liberation': what had been bound in symbol was now freed. It has also been described as a terrible descent into the irrational and as a great, and possibly fatal, distortion. For can non-conceptual thought (better defined as 'thought-feeling') really be conceptualised? Whatever the answer, some kind of conceptualisation took place, and it explains why such a great variety of religious systems, many of them extremely puzzling, came into being in the centuries succeeding Alexander the Great. All these religions incorporated astrological elements; when conceptualised they look strangely dreamlike.

ZENO AND THE STOICS

Alexander ended forever the autonomy of the Greek city states; their collapse led to a widespread feeling of insecurity – political, economic and moral. This in turn led to the formulation of new kinds of philosophies. The Sceptics, who have not been given their due for the challenge they posed to other systems, questioned the possibility of man's attaining any knowledge at all. The Epicureans, who were mostly anti-astrological, offered withdrawal from human affairs into hedonism, the pursuit of virtuous pleasure which did *not* include sexual pleasure. The Cynics claimed that happiness was not in man's power, and that he should therefore seek only virtue. The Stoics, the most influential school as far as the history of astrology is concerned, began from the premise put forward by the Cynics: happiness was not in man's power or within his control. Zeno of Citium (335–263 BC), the founder of the Stoic school, took this a step further.

Zeno of Citium

Zeno concentrated on the question of man's powerlessness in the face of his personal fate. He pointed out that good fortune can never be certain: you might win a large sum of money and then drop dead of a heart attack the next day, or you might gain a position of political power only to suffer a paralytic stroke within a few weeks. Such examples show that Zeno and his followers were thinking mainly of external causes, strokes of bad luck, of 'acts of God' – the sort of circumstances which people of that uneasy and unstable time felt they were likely to meet. Zeno built an ethical system out of the attitude towards fate which he thought it desirable for people to cultivate. His system seeks to demonstrate that it is necessary for man to live in harmony with nature. If man can understand how the universe works, then he can live in tune with it: the *logos* (literally 'word', but used by Greek philosophers in the sense of reason or forces) of the universe must be the *logos* of individual man.

The Stoic school lasted until the end of the third century AD, when it faded out, though it reappears in modified form in some medieval thought and, much later, in the philosophy of Spinoza. Zeno's philosophy led inevitably to the development of a very strong strain of fatalism in Stoicism, seen at its most extreme in the learned and enormously influential Posidonius (135–c.50 BC). However, it is quite wrong to assert that Stoicism denied free will. This is simply not the case. Stoicism gave man no power over his destiny, in the sense of external events, but it did give him power over his choice to live in harmony with nature – which embraced his destiny. Living in harmony was virtue, the sole good.

The connection with astrology is obvious. The Stoics were much attracted to both astrology and divination. They believed that the universe was a material organism (everything was material for the early Stoics, including mind), which was subject to an eternal cycle of change. After a very long time everything would be burned up in a huge conflagration and would be turned into divine fire, pure soul. Then the fire would go out, turn wet, and provide a fertile bed for the seeds of reason, which would initiate a new cycle. This theory was elaborated by the fourth-century Nemesius, who said: 'When the planets return, at certain fixed periods of time, to the same relative positions which they had at the beginning, when the cosmos was first constituted, this produces the conflagration and destruction of everything that exists. Then again the cosmos is restored anew. . . . The stars again move in their orbits, each performing its revolution in the former period, without variation.' And, Nemesius added: 'The whole cycle of history would be repeated: all of us will live again exactly as we lived before: there will never be any new thing other than that which has been before down to the minutest detail.'

This belief went back to the pre-Socratic era and was both deeply and religiously felt, especially by Zeno's pupil Cleanthes. It was the Stoic's substitute, as it were, for belief in an after-life. If we feel inclined to dismiss the entire Stoic system as superstitious nonsense, it is as well to remember that the 'big bang' theory postulates just such a pulsating universe, one which contracts and then expands. And plasma, a special state of matter neither gaseous, liquid nor solid, is uncannily like the 'fire' of the pre-Socratics and the Stoics.

It is obvious from what we have seen so far that the religious background of astrology is as respectable as that of any other serious belief-system. It is essential to establish this, since the rehabilitation of astrology in modern times depends as much on neo-Pythagorean ideas as it does on statistics. The Stoical philosophers were certainly all educated and sensible men, both the Greeks and their Roman successors. A great deal of what they wrote is lost, or survives only in the writings of others, but there is no evidence that their attitude towards astrology had anything of the vulgarly 'occult' about it, even if from Posidonius onwards some interest was shown in personalised birth charts. Doubtless those who have detected Chaldean influences in Stoicism are right. Certainly few of the early Stoics were Greek (Zeno was probably Phoenician) and most were Syrian, but this suggests nothing more than that they supplied to philosophy a religious element that was needed at the time.

ARISTARCHUS OF SAMOS AND THE SUN-CENTRED SYSTEM

At this point I must bring in Aristarchus of Samos, a Greek astronomer of the first half of the third century BC. Aristarchus postulated a rotating Earth in circular orbit, with the other planets in similarly circular orbits, around the Sun. In other words, he was among the first to put forward the heliocentric (sun-centred) hypothesis. We do not know the details of his scheme, because most of his writings are lost; we know of it only through a report by Archimedes. It is said that Zeno's pupil Cleanthes wanted Aristarchus charged with impiety, or atheism, for putting forward this heliocentric hypothesis, but the story is suspect. At that time such a charge could not have been made. The modern rationalists' picture of Aristarchus as the great Galileo of ancient times, martyr to superstition, is a dishonest and ignorant caricature. It is true that the heliocentric theory was fatal to the philosophy of such a Stoic as Posidonius, but that is because the details of his complex system depend on a geocentric model.

On the whole the heliocentric hypothesis was rejected by the Greeks for a number of very good reasons. One of these was mathematical, and, as the eminent mathematician and historian Morris Kline has said, this rejection was a step forward, not backward. He points out that the observations made from Alexandria in Aristarchus' own time and earlier clearly showed the impossibility of a system which put the Sun at the centre of a series of planets orbiting it in circles. And indeed such a system is impossible. This makes rubbish of Sir James Jeans' view that Aristarchus leaped 'at one bound to an accurate understanding of the solar system. . . .' He did no such thing; the credit for this belongs to the early seventeenth-century neo-Pythagorean astrologer Johannes Kepler, and then to Newton for explaining how Kepler's laws worked.

The religious element in Stoic thought, at whatever stage of its development, was never based on personalised or predictive astrology, but rather on sacred functions ascribed to the Sun, Moon, planets and stars. The connection between these two kinds of astrology is perfectly obvious, proved by the fact that the one ineluctably led to the other when social conditions were right. But there is a distinction, which is seldom made.

It is not quite properly made even by the late Professor E. H. Dodds, when he writes that Aristarchus' heliocentric hypothesis, killed 'by the influence of the Stoa . . . would have upset both the foundations of astrology and the Stoic religion.' Dodds was a great classical scholar who sought to explain all kinds of irrationality by intelligent application of Freudian concepts. He was a thoroughgoing humanist of the old-fashioned type: for him the collapse of the civilisation of classical Greece was a dreadful tragedy for mankind. In writing his important book *The Greeks and the Irrational* (1951) he hoped to help prevent a similar collapse in our own time. The irrational, he concedes, is 'wonderful' and 'mysterious', but it is also perilous and must be controlled. In other words, Dodds' world-view is a mechanistic one, but he cannot conceive of a universe in which only the laws of logic apply. Nonetheless, he wishes to allow the irrational merely the interesting status of dreams.

Dodds is open-minded as well as learned, but he is unable to envisage the unknown except by absorbing it into logic: he is, ultimately, a worshipper at the shrine of abstract thought and he mourns the fact that even his classical Greek rationalist heroes 'could describe what went on below the threshold of consciousness only in mythological or symbolic language'. With respect, this is a terrible thing to say. Dodds is denying the validity or the viability of a mythological or symbolic language – the language of astrology as well as of art – preferring instead the severe logical algebra of abstract analysis. And, by implication, he is denying that anything irrational can happen outside the human brain. For Dodds there can be no non-mechanistic factor in the functioning of the universe. He would have disagreed with Einstein who, though no believer or adherent of a pseudo-religious system, was prompted by his investigations to make it clear that he could not be sure.

Thus even Dodds is guilty of helping to propagate the legend that early concepts of heliocentricity were suppressed by charlatan astrologers. He also implies that heliocentricity abolishes the possibility of a valid astrology, which is patently untrue: our own position, as humans on Earth, is a geocentric one. And after all even Kepler was inspired by astrological concepts to complete his astronomical work. He saw the merit of both kinds of thought. Dodds was guilty of disingenuousness when he failed to mention that a model postulating a Sun with planets going round it in circular orbits – Aristarchus' model – is mathematically unacceptable, and that this was recognised by various Greek astronomers, many of them Stoics.

The Stoic attitude towards astrology, and its important consequences for later thinking, is connected in most educated and enlightened minds with the superstitious necromancy of charlatans. Yet in fact it began with the Stoics' perfectly natural incorporation of astrology into their religion, which they used to support their ethics. Heliocentricity worried them only because there was no Greek or, subsequently, Roman who was not somehow caught in the 'belief trap' (as one historian of science has called it) that 'none but circular motions suited the motions of the heavenly bodies'. The circle, being perfect, was sacred – as sacred to Aristarchus as to anyone else. On the other hand the Earth as centre of the universe was not a belief trap; there was plenty of speculation on that score. Such speculation failed simply because the hypothesis put forward by Aristarchus and others seemed untenable. It was the Christians – not the Greeks, the astrologers, or even most of the heretics – who would not accept this on metaphysical grounds. Had not God chosen the Earth and its inhabitants, they proclaimed, for His special purpose, and must it therefore not lie at the absolute centre of things? It is curious that Christians come in for so little criticism in comparison to those who practised astrology.

However, let us freely admit that at just about the time when the Stoics, and many other less ethically inclined and more strictly religious sects were coming into being, so also were arising, in huge numbers, rapscallion magicians, astrologers and diviners; and then as now, not more than one out of a thousand of these had genuine intentions. An uneasy populace was in dire need of reassurance, and reassurance was what the itinerant and other prophets (many of them astrologers) were prepared to give – in return, of course, for as large a financial consideration as they could get. Every serious belief has to endure its vulgar and degenerate fringe, and Stoicism had to endure its fake astrologers. The form of Stoic determinism provided a perfect framework for both false and true astrologers. The responsible ones did not abuse the Stoic view, but the mass of charlatans were as impervious to religious or philosophical subtleties as were their customers, whose chief interests lay in their immediate destinies, and who were strung along by the charlatans then, just as they are today.

HIPPARCHUS AND PTOLEMY

The astronomer Hipparchus was the first Greek astronomer to notice the precession of the equinoxes. (We now know that he was rediscovering something that had been known in Europe thousands of years earlier, though unknown to the Babylonians and their neighbours.) He thus re-established the movable zodiac and unwittingly put astrology back onto a course which worked better (in terms of planets in signs) than the astrological systems of those who had employed fixed, sidereal zodiacs.

Hipparchus of Alexandria (19th-century engraving).

Hipparchus died some time after 126 BC, and his ideas were not followed up for some 250 years, when in the second century AD Claudius Ptolemy systematised the work of Hipparchus in his astronomical treatise the *Almagest*. This is rightly described by astronomers in the most admiring terms. As Morris Kline remarks, 'with Ptolemy's completion of Hipparchus' work the evidence for design in the universe was complete to the tenth decimal place'. Ptolemy's system was geocentric and, with its superb fixed-star catalogue, it held sway for more than a thousand years. By that time astrology itself was once again in its heyday, and the Hellenistic Greeks had been practising it in something like its modern form for three centuries. So Ptolemy systematised this, too.

Ptolemy took over the system of epicycles to account for the phenomenon of retrogradation. He perfected this system brilliantly. Briefly and over-simply, he believed that each planet described a loop in its orbit around the earth. These loops, when mathematically described, could be made to account not only for retrogradation and station (when a planet apparently stops and changes direction), but also for changing velocities, including those of the Sun and Moon, neither of which go retrograde. Ptolemy's calculations are pretty nearly correct, and there is no doubt that he was a mathematical genius of the highest order. But he never even considered that the Earth might not lie at the centre of the system. So his theory is an elegant fiction.

Ptolemy also wrote the *Tetrabiblos*, which is the astrological equivalent of the *Almagest*. In it he establishes the moving zodiac, saying: 'The zodiac, being a circle, has no natural beginning, so the sign of the Ram, which begins from the Vernal Equinox, is taken as the beginning of the twelve; and, as if the zodiac were a living being, they make it begin with the excessive moisture of spring, and make the other seasons follow, because all creatures in their first youth have an excess of moisture and, like the spring, are still delicate and growing.'

A few astrologers err in quoting Ptolemy as though the *Tetrabiblos* had the authority of scripture. But, although he was undoubtedly the greatest geographer of antiquity, Ptolemy had of course never heard of the Southern Hemisphere. However, he saved astrology from a certain amount of confusion and – contrary to the opinion of those who have not read him – he was extremely reasonable.

PTOLEMY'S ASTROLOGY

In his astrology Ptolemy allowed that extra-astrological factors have an influence upon

Ptolemy (17th-century engraving).

character and destiny: heredity, race, culture, *mores*. He frankly admitted that only a fool would claim to be able to prognosticate from the planetary positions alone. He allowed that all astrologers make errors. He is both humble and logical, as the fairest of all the historians of astrology, Mark Graubard, points out in *Astrology and Alchemy* (1953).

Ptolemy claimed that knowledge of the future could help to prepare individuals both for the apparently happy and the apparently sad things. More importantly he declared that there 'is divine destiny but there is also mutable fate', as Graubard puts it. He was thus by no means an absolute determinist: 'Not all events are inexorable.' Although Ptolemy's exposition of his science of astrology reads somewhat queerly and fatalistically to us, within the context of his times he was a positive 'liberal' in the matter of determinism. His intention was to create a science of what we would call social psychology, and he based this science on his astronomy, as presented in the *Almagest*.

It is instructive to bear in mind the other great astrological textbook, and the foundation of Hellenistic astrology, when considering Ptolemy's *Tetrabiblos*. The earlier work predates the *Tetrabiblos* by at least 250 years, and is very different. We possess only fragments, but almost certainly it is by one man, though it purports to be by Nechepso, a King of Egypt, and Petosiris, a priest. It claims to be inspired by Hermes Trismegistus and Asclepius, both of whom were god-heroes, the latter of Greek origin, the former a transmutation of the Egyptian god Thoth. It may have been the author of this book who first recorded the meanings of the signs of the zodiac as we know them now, but certainly he was more of a Babylonian-Greek synthesist than he was a master of Egyptian magic: the persistent craze for attributing everything to Egypt is very old indeed. Later on, as we shall see, Hermes Trismegistus was to mislead hundreds, even thousands, of learned men.

By comparison with the Nechepso-Petosiris work, *Tetrabiblos* reads almost like a rationalist-humanist document. But the earlier work contains much valuable information, in particular the descriptions of the zodiacal signs. At all events, as the first systematic statement of Hellenistic astrology, it drew forth criticism. And already the astrologers were making the reply that 'the wise man rules the stars'. And this was 250 years, or thereabouts, before Ptolemy, who said the same thing.

ASTROLOGY AND DETERMINISM

There are three sorts of determinism: philosophical, theological, and fatalistic. The philosophical determinist is concerned only with abstract logic: he has no emotional axe to grind. The theological determinist sees a purpose behind events. The fatalistic determinist emphasises the tragic fact of man's powerlessness in the hands of fate and the inevitability of bad luck. Astrology suffered by getting itself mixed up with the first two kinds of determinism.

Strictly speaking, astrology does not affect the free will/determinism argument at all. But the idea that astrologers have the power to predict that terrible things will happen, seriously worries certain people. Yet astrology is in fact irrelevant to the argument: you cannot prove either free will or determinism from the stars, and modern philosophers do not try.

Besides, few serious astrologers claim that the positions of the heavenly bodies in themselves cause people to have this or that fate or destiny. Such notions persisted only while people thought of the celestial bodies as actual gods.

The Stoics, probably influenced by the Chaldeans, based their astrological beliefs on the notion of correspondences: 'as above, so below' they asserted. This is different from fatalism. The paths of the planets and Sun and Moon reflected the harmony of the cosmos, but they did not cause it, nor did they cause the harmony of nature on Earth. There was an architect of the system; the thinking of the Stoics was not shallow.

But this view, of course, was held only by thoughtful people, and by no means all practising astrologers, or indeed their clients, were thoughtful people. Rome, at the time of its rise, became full of charlatan astrologers – mostly Greek slaves – who were no better than the Sun sign astrologers of our own time. So real astrology did not get a fair hearing, despite Ptolemy's reasonable concessions as to its limitations.

ST. AUGUSTINE'S ATTITUDE TO ASTROLOGY

The first Christians were not especially opposed to astrology: they viewed the biblical Abraham as an astrologer. Like most of the Stoics and Ptolemy himself, they saw in astrology no threat to free will. (We must be careful not to confuse the doctrine of correspondences with that of fatalism. So many people, then as now, do just that.) But as Christianity gathered power and influence, a new view prevailed. This was that astrology may well have been valid before the birth of Christ, but that this holy event had made it wicked. The main point in this argument was that Saturn, Mars and the others had once been pagan gods; the pagans knew no better, but now things were different.

With Augustine (354–430) the argument changes direction. It would be all right, he concedes, if the astrologers admitted that the stars were the 'signs, not causes of . . . effects'. In other words, his position is no different from that adopted by the majority of astrologers. Yet Augustine dealt the severest blow to astrology in the western world. He was not well versed in it, but he had his own personal reasons for opposing it. His arguments against astrology are really red herrings, and in any case are borrowed without exception from earlier writers.

St Augustine (fresco by Botticelli).

Before his conversion Augustine had been a Manichean and gnostic (Manicheism was quasi-Christian; its adherents practise asceticism), and in his youth he had placed great reliance upon astrologers, though without displaying any interest in their techniques. In consulting astrologers Augustine had been going against his Manichean masters. Manicheism condemned astrology on the grounds that the planets (not the stars) were demons which belonged to the *Archons*, the eaters of the souls of man. So Augustine's real anger at astrology in the years after his conversion is reserved for his own youthful folly – mainly at the notion that there might be any cause but God, a notion which astrologers must at least seem to encourage.

He does not go into the question of whether God, in disposing affairs, might not perhaps reflect his will in his remarkable and beautiful direction of the movements of the celestial bodies, although in his remark on 'signs' as distinct from 'causes' he has given away his real belief. Moreover, in this series of arguments Augustine foolishly relied to a great extent on the Roman Cicero. Cicero began as a believer in astrology but, for political reasons, ended up as its opponent: he went so far as to assert that all foreknowledge is impossible. This was so terrible to Augustine that it drove him to prefer the astrologers, since God must have foreknowledge – even if he also allows free will (a paradox which led Augustine into deep theological waters).

Thus, as Mark Graubard remarks, Augustine was not really an opponent of astrology as such. In claiming Augustine as an anti-astrologer modern opponents of astrology are confusing facts invalidating astrology with a disinclination to consult astrologers. In his youth Augustine had been interested in science, and he saw that the observational (astronomical) records of the astrologers were correct. But later he lost his interest in science, and was concerned only to argue for freedom of will: he had to defend his new Christian intellectual position against his former gnostic, emotional one. He was ignorant of astrology – as is every one of its modern opponents without exception – and his attacks on it in the *Confessions* and the *City of God* make it clear that he had not even read Ptolemy or any other astrological treatise.

It must be remembered that Augustine was as much against astronomy as he was against astrology. He thought he saw that science was an enemy of belief; according to his definition of belief, of course, he was right. But his attack on astrology, although leading to its temporary defeat, was ultimately irrelevant to it. Banished for a while from Europe, it was still practised and developed by the non-Christian Arabs, and it suddenly appeared again in the Christian twelfth century.

ASTROLOGY'S REAPPEARANCE IN MEDIEVAL EUROPE

Many of the Arabic writings on astrology are lost, but enough survive to show that their contribution was crucial. Al-Biruni (973–1051) was one of the most important Arab astrologers; he learned Sanskrit and visited India, and it was partly because of him that some Indian ideas were imported into modern astrology.

It was as an Arabic influence that astrology first openly appeared again in Europe, as part of the importation of infidel influences into the West by open-minded men. By the thirteenth century astrology was once again accepted. Those who opposed it did so only on the grounds that practice of it might tend to undermine belief in God or free will. The general atmosphere was once again conducive to all sorts of magic.

The Englishman Michael Scot, who lived early in the thirteenth century and made a number of important translations, was highly thought of by two popes and led an unthreatened life. Yet he was a practising astrologer who wrote freely on all astrological doctrines. There were others like him. Thomas Aquinas himself accepted astrology, an acceptance reflected notably in the works of Dante, whose epic cannot be adequately understood without reference to his astrological beliefs. It is true that another astrologer, Cecco d'Ascoli, was burned at the stake by the Inquisition in 1327 in Florence, but this was because he could not stop himself saying what he really thought; he incurred the enmity of too many holy men. Guido Bonatti, the first astrologer to make use of midpoints (p. 000), did not suffer the same fate. Yet he too was an outspoken man who went so far as to attack clerics for asserting that everything was the result of God's will. 'Of course there must be such a thing as fortune,' he declared.

It was by now generally accepted that God initiated causes through the movements of the celestial bodies, not directly. Only a few pre-Renaissance thinkers denied this, and all of those were what we should call occultists, holding a wide variety of beliefs much more eccentric than astrology.

ASTROLOGY IN THE RENAISSANCE

In the fifteenth and sixteenth centuries there came an excited rediscovery of ancient learning. The essentially nostalgic and paradoxical period of the Renaissance was so called because it regarded itself as making progress through the *rebirth* of ancient ideas. The general attitude underlying the Renaissance thinking was that the present had become corrupt and rotten; the golden age of antiquity was 'the original gold from which the baser metals of

AN IMV S.
ALTIO R INCVBVIT,
SVBIMAGINE.
MVNDI
Astrologia
ptolomeus
zodia cus

Giordano Bruno (in Piazza Campo di Fiori, Rome).

the present and the immediate past were corrupt degenerations', as the writer Frances Yates put it.

The Renaissance saw three main thrusts, three movements which sought to go forward through going backward. Religious reform, which led to the Reformation itself, sought to recapture the truth in the past of the early Christian Church. Humanism rediscovered literature. And magicians attempted also to rediscover the 'pure golden age of magic'. These three movements overlapped in almost all Renaissance writing and thinking. The first two are fully recognised by all educated people; the third is less known and less well understood. Most historians of the period skate nervously over it or ignore it. But it is the magicians, whose purposes have gone largely unacknowledged, with whom we are here concerned, for astrology had a vital place in their thinking. The word 'magician' is not an exaggeration: it is precisely what these men believed they were.

GIORDANO BRUNO AND THE *HERMETICA*

The reformers and the humanists were not too badly mistaken in their datings of the past. But the magicians made a huge error, as Frances Yates has clearly shown in her book *Giordano Bruno and the Hermetic Tradition* (1964). They believed that the magical writings collectively known as the *Hermetica* had been written by the Egyptian priest Hermes Trismegistus in very remote antiquity – long before the existence of, for example, Homer. Some, certainly Giordano Bruno, regarded the *Hermetica* as much more important than the Bible. The same applies to the work known as the *Asclepius*, which is supposed to describe the magical religion of the very ancient Egyptians; it too belongs to the so-called *Corpus Hermeticum*.

Bruno was the most extreme case among the great Italian Renaissance magicians. But he, and those who thought along similar lines, had every reason to believe in the true antiquity of the Hermetic writings. Augustine, and others almost as eminent, had also believed in it. Some early Fathers had used the writings to demonstrate that the truths of Christianity had been prophesied at what they took to be the very beginning of historical time. But in fact this varied collection of writings, much of it in the form of Platonic dialogue, was for the most part produced between 100 and 300 AD, and there is very little, if anything, Egyptian about it at all.

The Hermetic writings are a muddle: veins of gold run through seas of degenerate occult mud. But they are a very interesting muddle, and they tell us a great deal about the state of mind which prevailed in the era in which they were produced. Much of the material, though produced within a pseudo-Egyptian framework, is a synthesis of Platonism, Stoicism and

A Renaissance magician and astrologer, *left*, pictured with Ptolemy (16th-century woodcut).

Neoplatonism; much of it more or less distortedly reformulates ancient beliefs. But there is also a strong gnostic, dualistic flavour about some of the books. Gnosis means knowledge, and the great gnostic movements which arose around the time of Christ – as an alternative to the Pauline version of Christianity – were characterised by a hatred of all matter, which the gnostics regarded as evil. There are various gnostic systems, and every one was denounced as heretical. This was mainly because the gnostics seemed to be denying the absolute power and goodness of God, but also because their thinking was too complex and 'elitist' as a vehicle for the Christian movement, which from the beginning sought to appeal to the masses.

The early Christian Fathers thought that they had destroyed gnosticism, which they regarded with great terror. But it persisted, simply because it represented a perennial attitude to life. Suddenly in the Renaissance gnosticism raised its head, most particularly in the person of Bruno and then in various sects, such as the Cathars, all of which were cruelly persecuted.

The vastly complex astrology of Bruno, which is mixed up with all sorts of other magic, is not a subject that can be dealt with here. Neither is this the place to discuss whether Bruno was a true, fully-fledged gnostic. Let us only claim what all would concede: Bruno was not a Christian in the orthodox Roman Catholic sense of that term in his time.

Bruno believed that he had the power to create a new worldwide religion under the cloak of a purely nominal Catholicism. This religion was unequivocally magical and held that the original truth had become increasingly corrupt throughout history, including Christian history. Had Bruno's ideas prevailed, history would have been changed – perhaps for the better. But that was never likely. Although Bruno was tolerant and eclectic, he could not stop himself from speaking his mind, and he had a violent temper. Because of this and because of a treacherous friend who tempted him back to Rome with the intention of giving him up to the Inquisition, he was rendered powerless. Moreover, his impractical and ardent nature did at times delude him: it was madness to believe that he could achieve what could not be achieved within his environment. His *system* is not incoherent, although it requires enormous application to understand its significance, but (perhaps inevitably in the circumstances) his *presentation* of it was.

COPERNICUS

Bruno did not die as a martyr to the Copernican cause. Frances Yates' book makes that perfectly clear. But he did believe that the 'return' of his magical religion was heralded by the Copernican system. 'The earth moves because it is alive around a sun of Egyptian magic; the planets as living stars perform their courses with her; innumerable other worlds, moving and alive like great animals, people an infinite universe' (Yates).

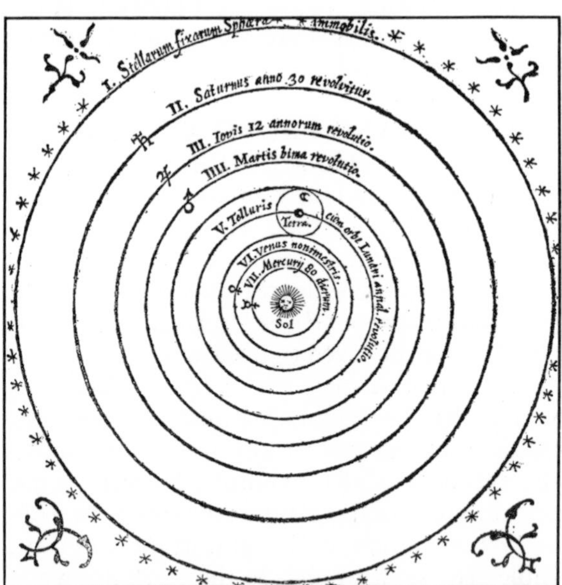

Copernicus' system (facsimile of drawing, dated 1543).

Not many people agreed with Bruno in taking note of the Copernican system, which was not even placed on the Index of Prohibited Books by the Roman Catholic Church until some 75 years after its publication in 1543 (five years before Bruno's birth). The Copernican system is in fact unoriginal and mathematically inferior to the Ptolemaic. After all, Einstein showed that in one sense Ptolemy's system was as legitimate as the heliocentric system, whose nature was first properly described by Johannes Kepler.

JOHANNES KEPLER

It was Kepler who finally took out the epicycles, and placed the planets in elliptical orbits. He worked at it with an almost diabolical persistence, applying himself to the problems caused by one of the most 'difficult' of all the planets, Mars. He based his work on the meticulous observations made by the Dane Tycho Brahe, also an astrologer.

One of Kepler's chief aims in astrology was to separate the wheat from the chaff. Although he was rightly critical of the deceitful and superstitious nature of most astrology (no worse then than it is now). his own astrological work is extremely important. He anticipated serious modern astrology by eventually abandoning the house system (except when forced to do popular astrology for money); by introducing new aspects based on the division of the circle by five; and by his certainty that the planetary positions at birth did influence the character. He anticipated the living French statistician and psychologist Michel Gauquelin by suggesting that individuals in a family tend to be born with the same planets in certain positions. Among his many other accomplishments Kepler was, at his most serious, a great psychological astrologer, who loathed being forced to make predictions.

Johannes Kepler.

ASTROLOGY IN DECLINE IN THE EIGHTEENTH CENTURY

The reader will have noticed that astrology, in the course of its long history, has functioned either as a philosophical basis for a belief-system or as the kind of fortune-telling practised by charlatans with which we are familiar today from newspapers and from the vast majority of popular 'textbooks'. Much serious astrology is fatalistic in flavour. That attitude, which was more suited to times in which there was less individualism than there is now, generally dominated astrology until the twentieth century. Then, amidst a welter of ill-digested and usually ignorant occultism, there developed an interest in character.

The mechanistic universe postulated by Newton led to a collapse of serious astrology in the eighteenth century. Newton himself did not approve of this, for he had originally begun his scientific studies in order to test astrology. As for the popular astrologers they received a severe blow when the satirist Jonathan Swift attacked one of them, a man called Partridge who produced an almanac. Swift prophesied Partridge's death, describing it in detail. The wretched quack was no match for Swift and was forced to protest that he was still alive. For a time even popular astrology suffered, though at no time did it entirely die out.

But, as Kepler insisted, there was a pearl in the dung-heap, and not all the efforts of the mechanists and the charlatans between them could in the end prevent a serious search for this pearl. But it took, and is still taking, a very long time to build up a coherent system, the nature of whose – possibly quite severe – limitations are understood. Until then, we have to draw on the best from an astonishingly durable tradition, which has become badly distorted with the passing of the centuries.

EVIDENCE FOR ASTROLOGY

SINCE WORLD WAR II IMPRESSIVE EVIDENCE, of a scientific kind, has accumulated in favour of astrology. We have already seen that the ancients 'knew' that the positions of the Sun, Moon and planets at birth affected the personality and or destiny. And anyone who has taken the trouble to study astrology properly will also 'know', as I do, that (at the very least) close, hard aspects between celestial bodies in birth charts do manifest in the character. However, it must be admitted that what the ancients 'knew' is not scientific evidence. But the work of the Frenchman Michel Gauquelin is; it is published and therefore available for all to see and it is based on public records. Gauquelin, above all others, has shown that there is a planetary effect on personality.

THE WORK OF MICHEL GAUQUELIN

Gauquelin was born in 1928. As a boy he was inordinately interested in traditional astrology: he planned to write a treatise on it before he had completed his education. He cannot say why he was so fascinated by astrology when he was so young, but I think this may be quite simply explained by the fact, which he would probably deny, that he is a romantic at heart. Gauquelin has proved that the principles or qualities which the peoples of earlier times gave to certain planets – Venus, Mars, Jupiter, Saturn and the Moon – were essentially correct. Yet he himself denies that there is anything in *traditional* astrology at all: he does not believe in signs, or aspects – though it must be added that he has not properly investigated them. He will not do so because he reckons himself to be a scientist, and he does not believe that a scientist should have any truck with 'popular superstition'; in some of his many books he disingenuously confuses the popular Sun-sign pseudo-astrology of newspapers with the work of serious astrologers. But in fact, though he keeps up this front in his books, he is on good terms with many astrologers and he attends astrological congresses. By profession he is a psychologist and a statistician.

Michel Gauquelin

The results of his work, which he has been doing since 1950 (much helped by his wife, Françoise), are published in nineteen volumes to date. Since my account of his work must be brief and simplified, I should point out that in his statistical calculations he makes allowances for all known factors, such as, in particular, that birth times are not random – for example, there are more children born in Paris at 6 a.m., on any given day, than are born at 6 p.m. Had there been anything wrong with Gauquelin's statistical calculations, then his opponents – some of whom display an attitude bordering on the paranoid – would have found it out. They have not done so.

All Gauquelin's work, it must be understood, is based on the diurnal, not the zodiacal, circle: the diurnal circle is the circle described by the Earth as it rotates on its axis. Astrologers use both. They are concerned with the angular relationships between the planets measured on the zodiacal circle at the time of birth, and with planets that are on or near angles, points in the birth chart which are based on diurnal factors. Traditional astrology had always maintained that planets on

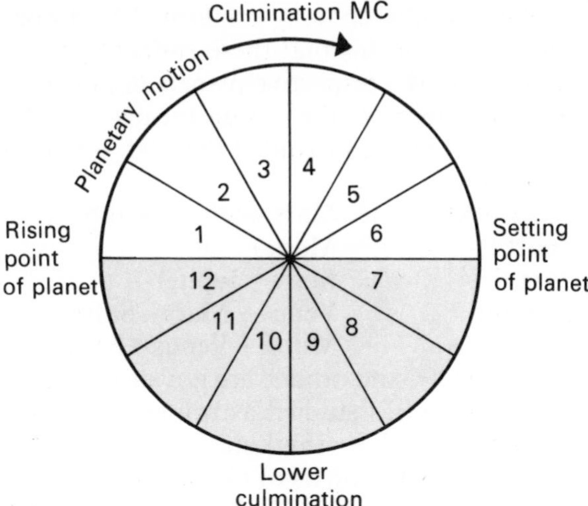

Gauquelin's diurnal sectors Viewed from a fixed point on Earth every planet appears to describe a circle each day. Gauquelin divides the diurnal arc, the time a planet spends above the horizon, and the nocturnal arc, each into six equal sectors.

angles would be dominant in the personality. Gauquelin's findings were in accord with this.

For the work Gauquelin set out to do, knowledge of the time as well as date of birth was essential. His first study included France, Germany, Italy, Belgium and Holland: in all these countries times as well as dates of birth are registered. For his material Gauquelin drew on professional directories. He divided his people (whose times of birth he found from the relevant registry offices) into eminent and non-eminent, using objective (and wholly acceptable) criteria. After a prodigious amount of work (it took nine years) he obtained 16,336 timed births of eminent professionals, and 24,961 of ordinary professionals.

The next thing Gauquelin did was to split up his data: to separate doctors, actors, scientists, sports champions, and so on. Then he had to take each of his births, and place them in the relevant sector (see illustration). Then he had to calculate the expected frequencies for each group, making allowances for the daily cycle of births. Then he had to total up the results for each sector, and see whether the observed frequencies deviated significantly from the expected frequencies. This involved putting the figures through chi-squared and other statistical tests.

Let us take up the story in Gauquelin's own words (1980): 'The statistics led to a bizarre conclusion. It was almost as if, for certain occupations, the presence at birth of a certain planet which had either just risen over the horizon or reached its high point in the sky [i.e. was at the MC, which is identical with the astrological MC] seemed to "provoke" or cause success'.

Thus, of the 3674 scientists 704 were born in sector one (the twelfth astrological house) or in sector four (the ninth astrological house) of Saturn. The odds against this being due to chance are 300,000 to 1. Mars has a similar effect in the charts of outstanding sportsmen: 5,000,000 to 1. Jupiter in the charts of soldiers – eminent ones – could only be where it is at odds of 1,000,000 to 1.* There is a smaller, but similar and definite trend for these planets to be present in the opposite sectors, too.

Gauquelin found that the Moon was significant for writers, Mars for sportsmen and soldiers, Saturn for doctors and scientists, and Jupiter for soldiers, actors, writers. But all these were eminent, or successful, in their

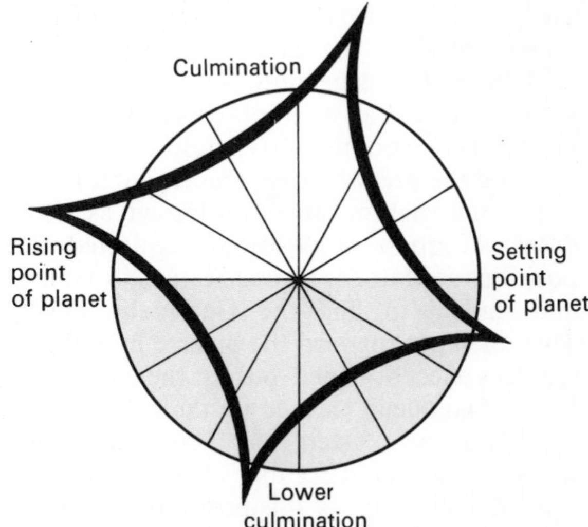

The typical Gauquelin picture The heavy line represents numbers of births. Eminent men tend to be born shortly after a particular planet – different according to profession – has risen or culminated.

*I am aware that it is mathematically unsophisticated to talk about odds in this way; it is more conventional to say that the chance hypothesis is unlikely to a specific degree. However, the 'odds' formulation is correct and more readily intelligible.

professions. The control group, the 'ordinary' professionals, showed no such planetary effect. Eventually he showed that Venus was significant for painters and writers.

However, Gauquelin demonstrated more than this. He found that for successful people of certain professions certain planets actually 'avoided' being in what he called the positions of 'high intensity': sectors 1 and 4, and, to a lesser extent, 7 and 10 (Placidus Houses 12, 9, 7 and 3).

This agreed with tradition except for two facts. First, no significance could be found for the Sun or for Mercury. (Nor could any be found for the invisible planets, but then the old astrologers did not know about these.) Secondly, according to tradition the planets ought to be on or before the midheaven or the ascendant (which is usually very near the rising point), whereas Gauquelin shows that they tend to peak past these points. Anyone who has studied Gauquelin's work will be familiar with the pattern (see illustration).

There are four peaks and four depressions. This is approximately the same for *all* the studies of eminent professionals that Gauquelin has done, but, of course, different planets produce the effect according to the profession. Let us be quite clear: this proof is irrefutable, and all attempts to shoot it down have failed ignominiously, despite attempts to bribe the press (details are available), and to present what in statistics is known as 'dirty data'. A group of positivists collected the positions of Mars for United States sportsmen, and 'failed' to find the Gauquelin effect. They then put forward the bizarre hypothesis that this effect obtained 'only at the latitude of Paris'. Gauquelin cleaned up their data, took out those who were *not* 'eminent', and showed that the effect did, after all, obtain. But the limitations of this proof are obvious: Gauquelin is investigating a fairly crude thing: success. However, it is sensible to keep things simple at the start, and Gauquelin proceeded to take things further. But before this he did something that all statisticians have to do: he repeated his experiments with a different set of data. He got the same results.

Here is a list showing how some of Gauquelin's results actually confirmed tradition. The + sign means that these eminent professionals had the respective planets in positions of high intensity; the – sign means that the planet in question avoided the high intensity positions.

Science/Medicine	Mars + Saturn + Jupiter –
Sport	Mars +
Army	Mars + Jupiter +
Painting	Venus + Mars – Saturn –
Writing	Moon + Venus + Saturn –

These results, and others, are not surprising to anyone who has studied astrology. But most astrologers will be thinking not so much in terms of occupation as of character. After all, even Gauquelin's best results show only about 20 per cent more than the mean: it is obvious that some eminent writers, for example, have Saturn in positions of high intensity – they are 'Saturnine writers'. It did not take Gauquelin long to realise that he was getting his results with certain professions, because these professions attracted people with certain characteristics in common. It seems obvious that there will be some psychological feature that all or nearly all doctors will have in common.

But before I conclude this account of Gauquelin with some details about his later work, I must try to explain why he has failed to get effects for certain planets and for the Sun. There are effects for Sun, Mercury and the outer planets – so we believe. But they may not pertain to anything as simple as groups of successful professionals. It would take a very subtle experiment to show their effect: and these experiments take up much computer time, and cost much money. Yet I am fairly sure that, for example, Neptune would show up in a position of high intensity in a study of alcoholics – though one would have to agree to just what one meant by 'alcoholic'.

Before extending his work to character rather than occupation, Gauquelin followed up a hint that had been made by Kepler, who had suggested that there was a planetary hereditary effect. Briefly, using a sample of 30,000 French parents and children, he found that children tended to have the same planets angular as their parents. The odds against this happening by chance were 100,000 to one. He repeated this experiment and got odds of 37,000 to 1. He found that the effect was strengthened when geomagnetic activity was high.

Gauquelin's work on heredity has been summarised thus: he 'concludes that people differ in their sensitivity to cosmic factors, that they tend to inherit their sensitivity from their parents, and that these different sensitivities manifest as different psychological traits and behaviours'.

From the late 1960s Gauquelin started to incorporate character traits – rather than just success in a given profession – into his work. He made exhaustive lists of the characteristics associated with the different professions; and he went through all the biographies of all 27,000 of his eminent people – and extracted from them every 'trait word' that was there. Whether this was a scientific procedure or not, it was certainly a common-sensical one: the lists of trait words associated with each person represented a sort of consensus of opinion. And, of course, differences were found within professions; the best known is that between introverted and extraverted scientists. For the introverted scientists Saturn tended to be past the angles – for the extraverted, it avoided this position.

More recently Gauquelin found that when people are grouped according to their characters (determined by lists of trait words) the diurnal distribution of the planets in question fluctuated significantly.

It is amazing that, having established that planets in *certain* diurnal positions are significant, Gauquelin has failed to see that planets in *all* diurnal positions are therefore probably significant – although not in as immediately obvious a way as those in 'high intensity' positions. This is why bodies on Placidus cusps are almost certainly significant.

If what Gauquelin believes is entirely right, then aspects – the angular relationships between the planets as viewed from the centre of the Earth, which barely differ from those viewed from the event – are meaningless. But the ancient astrologers – no more 'superstitious' than anyone else, as Gauquelin ought to take the trouble to discover – did not agree. And the work of John Nelson would be very peculiar: for it again supports astrological tradition, though in this case it is in the matter of aspects.

THE PLANETS' INFLUENCE ON SHORT-WAVE RADIO RECEPTION

John H. Nelson is a radio engineer who worked, until his retirement, for RCA. He was not and is not an astrologer. He lectures to astrologers, but will say nothing about astrological effects on personality. He appears to be sympathetic to astrology, since he has allowed his work to be published by astrological publishers. In any case, he solved the problems set him by astrology – even if he refused to call it that.

In 1946 Nelson was commissioned by his employers RCA to attempt an explanation of the phenomenon of short-wave radio disturbance, so that bad conditions might be better forecast. It was known that sunspot conditions affected this, though only sometimes. There was no clear correlation between sunspot activity and short-wave disturbance. Short-wave communication was then of the utmost importance, but no one could predict how well it would work at any one time with better than 60 per cent accuracy. By the time Nelson retired in 1971 he had achieved a predictive accuracy of no less than 93.2 per cent (statistically billions to one against his getting his results by blind guessing). How did he do it?

Using heliocentric planetary positions (the angular relationships between all the planets as measured with the Sun as centre), Nelson began to study possible relationships between the stormy ionospheric conditions, which were known to stop or hinder reception, and planetary positions. He found a connection, continued to work at it, and in effect demonstrated that the planets' positions correlate with radio disturbance through their effect on solar activity. All the planets were involved, including the Earth. No effects have been found for the Moon; it has not been studied.

Now human beings are *not* the Earth's ionosphere. But what was fascinating about Nelson's findings – which he has published only in very piecemeal fashion – was that he discovered (and at first without realizing it) that aspects between planets traditionally regarded by astrologers as 'bad' caused bad reception; ones regarded as 'good' created good reception. Once, when a severe storm was in progress, it suddenly stopped 'as if,' he said, 'a hand had been laid upon it'. All was calm: reception suddenly became perfect. A trine, uncontaminated by any hard aspect, had suddenly formed between two planets. A trine was always regarded as a 'good', 'easy', 'harmonious' aspect.

Nelson's results, his study of the correlation between heliocentric planetary positions and radio activity, his discovery that Mercury was usually the trigger planet, demonstrated that, at least as far as the condition of the ionosphere was concerned, even the most ancient astrologers had been talking good sense. It was now impossible to regard them as superstitious barbarians: they knew things which we have forgotten or chosen to ignore. Nelson's work is ignored by positivistic scientists, who are frightened and embarrassed by 93.2 per cent success in forecasting.

Nelson's work is also important in other ways: he has shown that it is combinations of aspects, rather than single aspects, that are significant, and that certain angles between planets which had not previously been considered are important: $7\frac{1}{2}°$, 15°, 18° and their multiples. He has given astrologers a great deal to think about, and has already brought about improved astrological techniques.

DIESCHBOURG'S WORK ON ASPECTS

Now Nelson's work is open to an obvious objection from the sceptics: human beings are not the condition of the ionosphere, therefore aspects need not affect personality. This is only partly offset by the fact that Nelson's work validated, as much as it was possible to validate, the ancient view of aspects, which had first been investigated with reference to their possible effect on human personality (and destiny). Thus the work of a citizen of Luxembourg, J. Dieschbourg, is particularly significant in this respect. It has not been repeated (it should be, and the data employed should be that published by Gauquelin), nor even published: we are indebted to Geoffrey Dean's *Recent Advances in Natal Astrology* – an important work to which we shall return – for our knowledge of it: Dieschbourg communicated his results to Dean, who has reported on them fully.

Dieschbourg used data which did not contain times of birth. He was therefore able to use only Noon positions. This meant that he could not test the Moon or of course the angles (and that the positions of Mercury and Venus were uncertain). He obtained his data from biographical dictionaries.

He had to use a very large orb (the distance off exactness that is allowed in judging whether there is an aspect or not) in order to get his probability as close to 0.5 as possible. He investigated, in 12,000 cases consisting of eminent professionals (versus a control group), the following aspects: 0° ($11\frac{1}{2}°$ orb), 180° ($10\frac{1}{2}°$), 90° and 120° (10°), 60° ($8\frac{1}{2}°$), 30° and 150° ($2\frac{3}{4}°$). Dieschbourg found military leaders to have more aspects between the Sun and Jupiter than others (20–1 against chance: just significant), and: eminent philosophers and historians, Sun and Neptune (100–1); writers, Mercury and Uranus (500–1); scientists and doctors, Mercury and Uranus again (100–1); painters and sculptors, Venus and Saturn (20–1); social scientists, Venus and Pluto (20–1); workers in science, art and literature, Mars and Jupiter (1000–1).

If these aspects are not due to chance, which some of them can hardly be, then what can they be due to? Such work is expensive; prejudiced scientists ignore it and will not help to fund it, and so it is not yet being done in sufficient quantity. The real correlation – there is no doubt – is between aspects and character; but, as we have seen, there is a correlation between character and occupation.

HOW DOES ASTROLOGY WORK?

It has been suggested that astrologers uniformly believe that astrological effect works by means of gravitation. But this assertion is made by anti-astrologers – and it is without foundation. We do not know much about gravitation, except that it is one of the 'weak' forces of nature. Astrologers do not believe that it is the planets themselves which affect personality. To discover – as Nelson did, by serendipity – a correlation between effects on the Sun and on the planetary angles is one thing; it is quite another to assert that the latter cause the former. There may be, and most probably is, a third factor at work.

It is doubtless best for any astrologer to admit that he has not the least idea how it works. Yet speculation cannot be checked. There are two main theories. One is that there is some cause, leading to an effect. The other is that synchronicity is at work. There should be no conflict here, as I shall explain.

Cause-effect is familiar and easy to explain. The Sun might be affected by the planets, and by other forces, and might then affect human personality. Cause-effect. Quite a few astrologers have believed that the chief effect comes from the Sun, the state of which in that respect may be monitored by a study of the planetary positions (some astrologers do use heliocentric positions in their work – and it is obvious that they are not wasting anyone's time). But whether it is the Sun which 'does the work' or not, is impossible to say. Those who believe in cause-effect must look for a cause, or causes. This is quite natural and proper: there would, one feels, be a cause.

SYNCHRONICITY

The other notion, synchronicity, appears to be mystical; a number of people believe that it was an explanation for all sorts of inexplicable phenomena (ESP, ghosts and so forth) which was invented by C. G. Jung. That is not the case, though Jung's statement of it is quite useful: 'Whatever is born or done this moment of time, has the qualities of this moment of time'. That of course means that there is a law of nature independent of the cause-effect law: thus the pattern of the planets at birth (different for every individual when the angles are taken into account, and in any case different if measured from the event, rather than the Earth's centre) is meaningfully coincidental with the personality of the native.

This is a belief much older than Jung – probably five thousand years older. It underlies the system of Swedenborg, and Baudelaire's very famous sonnet 'Correspondences' is a statement of it. Nature, says Baudelaire (translated more or less literally), is a temple in which the living pillars sometimes babble meaninglessly – we pass through it, through forests of symbols, and these symbols watch us with knowing eyes. Like prolonged echoes which merge together far away into a profound unity, huge as darkness and light, scents, sounds and colours correspond (answer each to each: 'se répondent'). Jung himself called his 'synchronicity' an 'acausal connecting principle'. The pioneer of this investigation into the acausal, however, was the Austrian Paul Kammerer, who spoke of a 'law of series': of 'chance groupings' which could not be dealt with by the laws of probability. As we all know, there can be series of meaningful coincidences which quite simply seem to deny the laws of probability, which are macroscopic. The number of your cloakroom ticket at the theatre is the same as that of your car, and then you are given that number in a lottery. Everyone knows and has experienced this sort of 'run'.

Unfortunately, the literature dealing with 'synchronicity' is rather muddy, Kammerer's work and Arthur Koestler's comments upon it in *The Roots of Coincidence* apart. My own view is that such effects operate *along with* 'cause-effect', which in certain circumstances, such as astrology, is what we should expect. For me, the birth chart is a 'mapping' of the personality, or certain features of it, just as the grooves in a gramophone record are – *if you know what to do with them* – a 'mapping' of a piece of music. They are not by any means that piece of music, but he who denied a relationship between the two would be foolhardy indeed.

The matter of synchronicity, and variations upon it, is one for the individual. Those with imagination (condemned, and rightly, by scientists as 'non-scientific') may like or not like C. G. Jung, but they are unlikely to reject out of hand the notion underlying synchronicity, or whatever they like to call it. The philosophical concept called 'occasionalism' explains, though, why 'synchronistic' explanations need not be in conflict with cause-effect ones. Parallelism, as it is called, maintains that there is no *causal* connection between, say, the attainment of orgasm and the feeling of pleasure that accompanies it. The physical events of our lives only parallel the mental events. Occasionalism is a special instance of parallelism associated with Malebranche (1638–1715): *apparent* causes are what God uses as occasions for creating their *apparent* effects. Thus the feeling of pleasure you get with an orgasm is no more, really, than *an occasion for God to become active*. A variant of this theory, slicing out 'God', maintains that physical and mental events are really two aspects of the same reality. Leibniz suggested that a 'pre-established harmony' existed between the two series (of physical and mental events): mind and body were like two clocks which agreed perfectly.

However, this is a matter for individual taste. Here we can only be concerned with what are at least apparent causes – and there follow a number of odd facts which, taken together, reinforce the view that there are astrological effects.

EYSENCK'S AND MAYO'S STUDY

First, there is the study carried out by H. J. Eysenck and Jeff Mayo. It can very easily be shown that tradition insists that Aries, Gemini, Leo, Libra, Sagittarius and Aquarius (Fire and Air) are extraverted, while the other (Earth and Water) signs are introverted. The study was of Sun placement, so that really it was also an investigation of whether season of birth had any general effect on temperament. Mayo took 1795 births and had them subjected, by Eysenck, to statistical analysis. According to the questionnaires which Mayo had sent out, which established which of the 1795 people were extraverts and which were introverts (friends and relatives contributed), the results agreed with tradition: odds against the chance hypothesis were about 10,000 to 1.

Eysenck was rightly not satisfied, and wanted to repeat the experiment, this time using his own EPI (Eysenck Personality Inventory). This is a questionnaire designed to measure introversion-extraversion and emotionality. What was now being tested was not only the extraversion-introversion correlation, but also the age-old hypothesis that the Water signs are more emotional than the others. In both cases the results were statistically significant. Sagittarius came out as the most extraverted sign (in terms of the Sun's being there), Taurus as the most introverted. The Water signs were more emotional ('neurotic' in Eysenck's terms) than the other signs – with the exception of Aries, which was as emotional as Pisces, which was more emotional than Cancer or Scorpio.

These are interesting results. It must be remembered that they may not be studies of the Sun's position in the zodiac at all – but of birth date. However, this is unlikely, and to some extent these results have been supported by independent tests made by a sociologist, H. J. Cooper, and reported in Playfair and Hills' *The Cycles of Heaven* (1978). A study of cases in which signs are emphasised, versus a control group, would settle the matter.

CYCLES

At this point the reader may feel that all this is very interesting, but *how* could planets exert influence on human beings? By 'rays'? Surely not. By gravitation? This seems impossible. Less unlikely is some form of electro-magnetic force, for it now appears that waves of every kind – very long and very short – are enveloping and affecting us.

Edward R. Dewey is not an astrologer, but in *Cycles: the Mysterious Forces that Trigger Events*, and elsewhere, he has shown that in every sphere of human and animal activity there exist cycles: events recur at regular intervals. There is now a Foundation for the Study of Cycles, and its work proceeds with ever-increasing momentum. There are 9-year cycles in sales of Life Assurance, Wheat Acreage and Ton-Miles of the Canadian Pacific Railway. There are cycles in the behaviour of animal species which match almost exactly with cycles in economic activity. There are, literally, thousands of examples. Sunspot activity correlates most closely to these cycles, though few suggest that sunspot activity causes them. Some periods are avoided – but others, such as 9.6 years, are common. Here are some of the phenomena in which a 9.6 year cycle has been found: coloured fox abundance, Canada; thirteen other Canadian wildlife abundances; barometric pressure, Paris; cotton prices, U.S.A.; financial crises, United Kingdom; and much else. There is a useful summary of some cyclic effects in G. G. Luce's *Body Time* (1973). If some of the work that is being done in this area is slipshod, then it must be emphasised that much of it is not.

As to how astrology works, it is provocative that, as H. Prescott Sleeper pointed out as long ago as 1967, the resonant cavity between the surface of the Earth and the ionosphere has a dominant frequency of about 8 herz. This is the same as the frequency of the human alpha brainwave band. Sleeper thought that the planets might thus have an effect via the Sun: the geomagnetic field might 'provide a fine tuning mechanism for this frequency selection which would set up a direct chain of influence from planet to human brain via the Sun, assuming there to be a link between planetary position and solar flare output [which there is]'.

Geoffrey Dean, though, postulates a theory in which astrological effect is exerted directly on the Earth – though he uses the Sun as a model to show how this might be possible. His work, in the epoch-making *Recent Advances in Natal Astrology* (1977), in which he was assisted by Arthur Mather, is the most important since that of Gauquelin – and we should be pleased rather than angered (as so many astrologers have been) that he is a behaviourist, a positivist and a man who obviously prefers a computer-analysis of character to one by, say, Henry James or Hardy.

THE WORK OF GEOFFREY DEAN

Geoffrey Dean (PhD, DIC, ARCS) is an Englishman and an astrologer. He is also an analytical chemist and science writer, who works in Perth, Western Australia. His extensive work *Recent Advances in Natal Astrology* covers more ground, more scientifically and sensibly, than any other book on this subject ever published. That the approach is as imaginatively impoverished as it is scientifically rigorous is all to the good: there is too much occult mush on the subject.

Dean has been a little misunderstood. It is clear that as an astrologer he is convinced, for himself, that astrology works. He rejects signs and houses (I think), but quite obviously accepts harmonics, which are really no more than the study of resonances (it does seem most likely, though we can't prove it, that astrological effect is obtained by a complex of resonances, probably of an electro-magnetic nature). Dean also accepts aspects, lack of aspects and other astrological manifestations. However, he recognises that what he thinks he knows isn't evidence, and so he has subjected his own beliefs and those of others to a proper scientific scrutiny.

After he has given an account of solar cycles (of which there are a number) and has reviewed the theories put forward to account for them, Dean enters into a discussion of how best the mystery may be resolved, and advances his own hypothesis. It is remarkably convincing and impressive: at the very least a case which needs answering. The hypothesis is somewhat complicated, and I can here give only a very simplified version.

Dean points out that aspects alone cannot explain solar cycles because an 'aspect cannot act in different places at different times'. This is right, because of the phenomenon of latitudinal passage in sunspot formation: 'the first spots of a new cycle appear in a broad band centred on [solar] latitude 30° in both hemispheres. As the cycle progresses they appear progressively closer to the solar equator. . . .' Eventually the leading spots change polarity. The point is that, latitudinally, sunspot cycles are symmetrical.

Now it is a fact that terrestrial cycles, which we now believe are caused by, or correlate with, extra-terrestrial factors (almost certainly planetary ones), also show these latitudinal patterns. As Dean puts it: 'at different latitudes they tend to peak progressively later as they approach the equator. The difference between pole and equator is proportional to cycle length. . . .' We must explain this latitudinal effect before we can say very much about terrestrial cycles. Dean believes he has the answer.

The solar equator is not in the plane of the ecliptic (it cuts it about halfway through the Gemini-Sagittarius axis). Dean has taken some measurements (they are not aspects), in which he takes account of the solar equator, in an attempt to find 'what planetary factor synchronises with the solar equator in tune with the solar cycle'.

The sorts of measurements Dean takes are based on midpoints and parts. Midpoints are simply the two points midway between two bodies in terms of the circle we are dealing with. One point is halfway along the shorter arc – the other halfway along the longer arc, and of course opposite the other point. A part is simply the result of any sum of this kind: A+B –C. Neptune+Jupiter –Earth is a part.

Now Dean knew that the fundamental sunspot period was 22.2 years, although many others have been detected. He found that the cycle of the Jupiter/Neptune midpoint in the plane of the ecliptic seemed to control the solar cycle. He also found that 'there is a remarkable clustering of periods and harmonics at the Jupiter/Neptune period'. Thus (these are examples): Saturn–Uranus $\times \frac{1}{2}$ = 22.68; Mars–SE (Solar Equator) × 12 = 22.57. At least 34 other similar results range from 21.03 to 22.68, a span of 1.65.

By doing this sort of calculation Dean has produced a number of impressive correlations: for example he shows that 'since at least 2000 BC every Neptune/Pluto midpoint square [90°] SE in which Neptune is in opposition to Pluto has coincided with a prolonged period of negligible solar activity'. And he has demonstrated much else. From all this he concludes:

"Between solar minima [negligible solar activity] the Jupiter/Neptune midpoint moves between extremes of solar latitude. . . . the latitude at which spots form is roughly four times the maximum latitude of the midpoint.

"The phenomenon of terrestrial cycles suggests that the effects of the planets on the Sun are duplicated on Earth by an exactly anlogous mechanism, i.e. where the rotating Earth replaces the rotating Sun [the Sun, it ought to be noted, does not rotate uniformly: parts of it rotate at quite different rates – but this does not affect Dean's arguments]. The way in which the planetary forces create cycles is unknown, as is the reason why certain cycles are exhibited by some things and not others.

"Because the ecliptic is at $23\frac{1}{2}$ degrees to the equator the planetary effect should start at a latitude roughly four times higher, i.e. roughly at the poles, and should reach the equator 0.5 cycles later. This is exactly in accordance with the observed latitudinal passage except that the observed lag is 0.7 cycles; the difference can quite easily be explained by the uncertainty in the extrapolation between solar and terrestrial geometry and by the considerable imprecision in the observed data.

"It follows that all cycles which manifest on the Sun should also be found on Earth; however, if the terrestrial response is insensitive to phase then all terrestrial periods will tend to be half the relevant solar periods. If the point of intersection with the rotational plane is important then this allocates significance to equatorial nodes, i.e. to 0 Aries [this is the equatorial node of the Sun]. However the most important point is that the model implies that planets affect the Earth directly and not via the Sun.

"These findings have a number of important implications for astrology: (1) They provide the basis for a plausible model of astrological causation. (2) They may lead to an understanding of how aspects work and why rising planets [as in the work of Gauquelin, where the planet is just after its rising point] are significant. (3) They suggest that rising midpoints, rising parts and other rising configurations may be even more important than rising planets. . . ."

Given that honest investigators have found astrology to work, within certain limitations, Dean's theory certainly needs to be investigated. For we must not be so attached to 'synchronicity' as to suppose that we don't need at least an *apparent* cause.

The judgment of any fair-minded person must now be that there *are* astrological effects.

CHAPTER TWO

THE ASTRONOMICAL BASES OF ASTROLOGY

ASTRONOMY

I SHOULD BE LOTH TO STATE, OF SO MYSTERIOUS a subject as astrology, that its entire basis lay in astronomical fact. But I certainly recommend that the astrology of today should base itself, as far as possible, on astronomy. There is, after all, no shortage of symbolism: the planets are symbols, the signs of the zodiac are symbols, the aspects and planets in the signs are combinations of symbols. Their interpretation must rest, ultimately, on poetic or intuitive judgement, rather than on scientific exactitude – even if Geoffrey Dean, author of the influential *Recent Advances in Natal Astrology*, has referred to the 'dream' of an 'algebraic' astrology and believes that, because computers can do sums much more quickly than we can, so they can judge character and blend together the factors in a birth chart better than we can.

The first astronomers were astrologers, and the calendar was magical. The word 'occult' has unpleasant overtones for some. But after all, it only means 'hidden'. The word 'magician' goes back, eventually, to 'priest'. If we think of magic as mystery, if we bear in mind the Greek philosopher Heraclitus' saying, 'An unapparent relationship is stronger than an apparent one', then we ought not to go far wrong: become too fanciful or too credulous. The mysteries of today are the science of tomorrow, although not all the mysteries will ever become known.

THE GEOCENTRIC POINT OF VIEW

Astrology is almost, although not quite, based on the geocentric point of view: that the Earth is the centre of the universe. Some of the opponents scoff at this: but even the most ill-informed parlour-astrologer knows perfectly well that the Earth is in orbit round the Sun, and not *vice versa*. We need spend no time on this objection.

It is more important to understand that the geocentric viewpoint is not altogether fictional. It is not simply an illusion, a lie, because what is apparent is not altogether a lie. Positivist scientists throughout this century have discovered a series of 'truths', only to discover that most of these were apparent, and that their dream of an 'algebraic truth' has not yet been discovered (nor will it be).

To us it looks as though the Sun goes round the Earth. This creates a natural time measurement, and thus arises our year, which in northern latitudes is very clearly divided into four seasons. We call the movement of Sun, Moon, planets and fixed stars 'apparent motion', because we know that it is the Earth's rotation on its own axis which makes these bodies appear to rise and set.

THE ECLIPTIC AND THE CELESTIAL EQUATOR

The ecliptic, so named because eclipses take place on it, is the Sun's apparent path around the Earth. This path, however, is *not* perpendicular to the north-south axis of the revolving Earth. The equator, on the other hand, *is* at right-angles to the north-south polar axis, and divides the Earth into hemispheres. The equator projected out into space, and called the 'celestial equator', is tilted to the ecliptic at an angle which is always slightly changing, but may be taken for most purposes to be 23.4523 degrees (its value in 1900).*

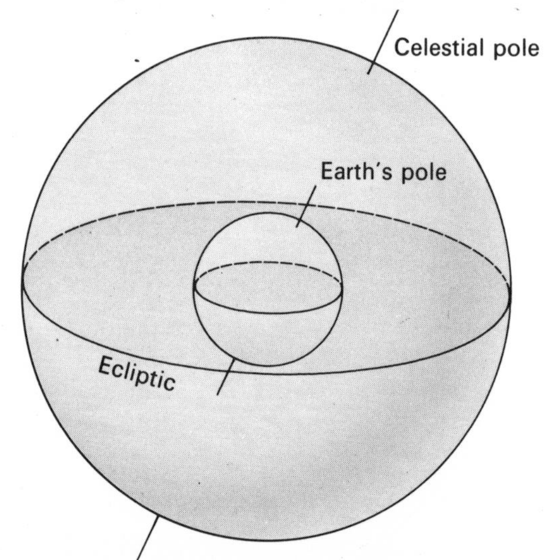

The ecliptic The Sun's apparent path around the Earth, known as the ecliptic, is fundamental to astrology. It is tilted relative to the Earth's equator.

*It may vary each month by ± .003 degrees of arc. For event charts where you have the time to the second and great exactitude is required, the current value should be used, and can be found in Michelson's *The American Ephemeris for the Twentieth Century*.

Heliocentric and geocentric views of the solar system The 'correct' view of the solar system, *right*, is heliocentric, meaning sun-centred. The Sun, *arrowed*, is at the centre and the planets, including Earth, travel around it. The geocentric, or Earth-centred, view of the solar system, *below*, dates of course from antiquity, because this is how the solar system appears when viewed from Earth. The Earth, *arrowed*, is at the centre; the planets and the Sun appear to revolve around it.

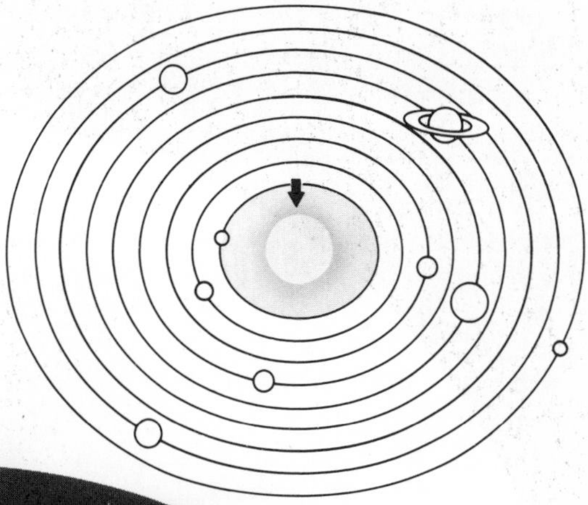

The ecliptic and the celestial equator are great circles. A great circle is created by joining together any two points on a sphere by drawing the shortest possible line between them: the centre of the arc of the circle so formed is the centre of the sphere. The great circles in astrology are drawn on the 'celestial sphere', what used to be called the 'vault of the heavens'; this is the spherical dome which surrounds us, and around which the stars and their celestial bodies appear to move.

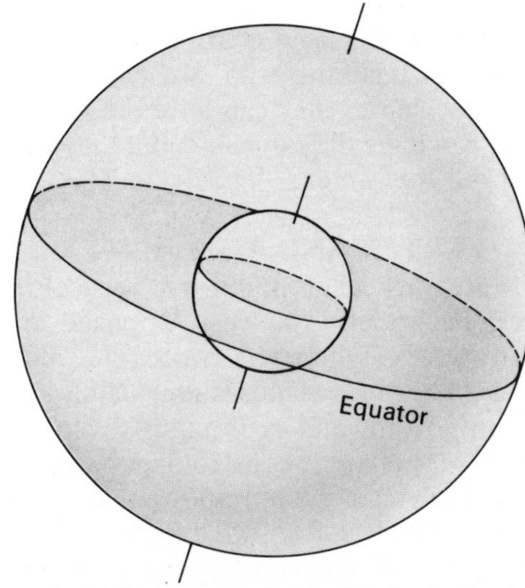

The celestial equator This is simply the Earth's equator projected onto the celestial sphere. Like the other great circles, it can be conceived as a circle or as a disc. It is tilted relative to the ecliptic.

The astrologer's model of the heavens is built up as a series of great circles, of which there are three primary ones and one other very important one called the 'prime vertical'. The three fundamental great circles are the ecliptic, the celestial equator and the horizon. On the celestial sphere we can see the north and south poles of the equator, and their axis, which passes through the centre of the celestial equator at right-angles to it.

The celestial sphere, *left* The notion of a sphere surrounding the Earth, on which all the heavenly bodies travel, is, of course, a fiction. However, this does not invalidate it as a framework for a system of measurement. The five great circles in astrology circumscribe the celestial sphere.

THE HORIZON

The ecliptic and the equator are easy to understand, but more than a few students of astrology go through life without ever quite understanding the exact nature of the third great circle, the horizon. In astrology, we do

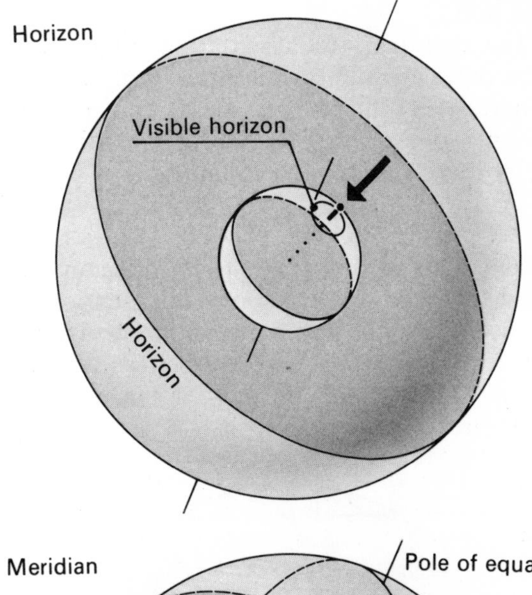

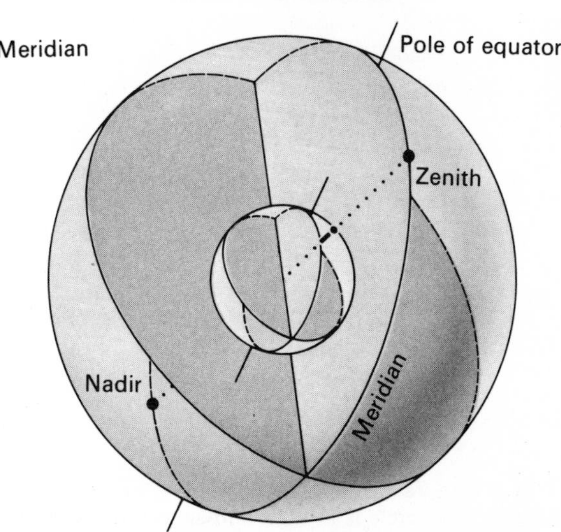

The horizon and the meridian These depend on the place of birth, *arrowed*. The horizon is parallel to the visible horizon with its centre at the centre of the Earth. The meridian joins the poles of the horizon, called zenith and nadir, and the poles of the celestial equator.

not use the visible, or sensible, horizon, but the celestial horizon because it passes round the centre of the Earth. It is simply a circle parallel to the sensible horizon, with its centre the centre of the earth. (For an event taking place at either of the Earth's poles, the horizon will coincide with the equator.) The horizon is determined by the location of the birth, or other event, for which a chart is being drawn. Therefore, unlike the ecliptic and celestial equator, the horizon is unique to the chart in question.

The meridian (italicised to distinguish it from other meridians which are simply lines of longitude) is yet one more great circle. It joins the poles of the horizon (zenith and nadir) and the poles of the celestial equator.

THE PRIME VERTICAL

Gravity cuts at right angles to the horizon: the point in space directly above the location of the event and at right angles to the horizon is the zenith, and that directly below it is the nadir. Joined together these form another great circle, the prime vertical.

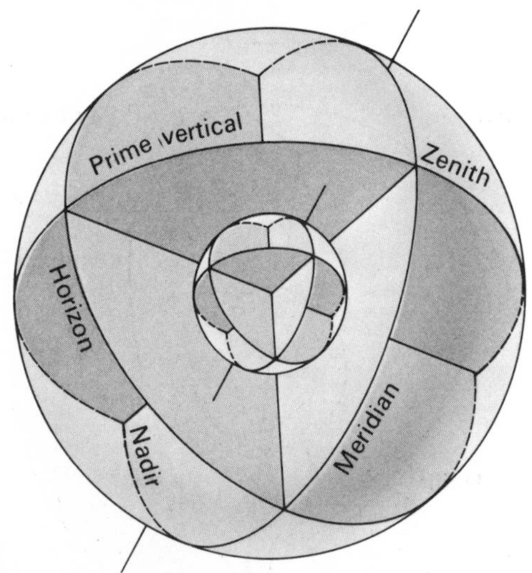

The prime vertical Again dependent on the place of birth, this circle is at right angles to the meridian, joining the zenith and the nadir.

THE MIDHEAVEN

The midheaven, frequently called the MC (*Medium Coeli*), is one of the most important angles in the birth chart. It is an angle because it lies where the ecliptic intersects the meridian (or line of longitude) which passes through the location of the event. The midheaven is the same for everyone born on the same line of longitude at the same time on the same day. Opposite the midheaven, 'under the Earth', is the IC (*Immum Coeli*).

THE ASCENDANT

The ascendant (Asc) is the second important angle in the chart. It is the point where the ecliptic intersects the horizon in the eastern sector (the diagram shows the east as the west: like a birth chart it is the wrong way round). Opposite the ascendant, at the point where the ecliptic meets the horizon in the west is the descendant (Desc).

It is the angles in a chart which give it its absolute individuality: no two charts can be exactly the same: they can have the same MC or they can have the same Asc, but they cannot have both the same.

VERTEX AND ANTIVERTEX

The vertex lies where the prime vertical intersects the ecliptic in the west. Opposite to it is the antivertex, where the two circles meet in the east. The vertical axis is unusual in that its more important end is thought to lie in the west. I alone among astrologers reject the notion that Asc is more important than Desc, or MC than IC: nor do I believe that the western end of the vertical axis is more important than the eastern end. The idea comes from the fact that the Sun rises in the east: dawn is a beginning.

THE TROPICAL ZODIAC

The tropical zodiac runs along the ecliptic, the Sun's apparent path around the Earth. Anyone carefully observing the heavens at night will see that a number of wandering objects appear and re-appear at various irregular intervals within a specific frame of reference, that band of fixed stars which lies some eight degrees north and eight degrees south of the ecliptic. The wanderers (*planetes*, wanderers) are the five visible planets (not counting Sun and Moon). Eight degrees north and south are approximately the highest and lowest celestial latitudes reached by the planets. The band thus formed around the celestial spheres is called the Zodiac. (Pluto, the outermost known planet, is an exception: it strays some 17 degrees from the ecliptic, but it was not discovered until 1930.)

The brighter fixed stars form pictures – the Great Bear and so on – and these pictures have been selected by different peoples at different times to designate constellations, or in astrology the signs of the zodiac. Everyone is familiar with what they imagine is 'their Sign': the sign the Sun appears to be in at the time of their birth.

Nowadays the signs the Sun, Moon and planets are 'in' in a chart no longer correspond with the part of the sky where the 'picture' is

The angles, or personal points The intersections of the three personal great circles – horizon, meridian and prime vertical – with the ecliptic form the all important angles. The midheaven is where the ecliptic meets the meridian above the place of birth. The ascendant is where the ecliptic meets the horizon in the east. The vertex is where the ecliptic meets the prime vertical in the west. Each of these points has its opposite: *immum coeli* (IC), descendant and antivertex, respectively.

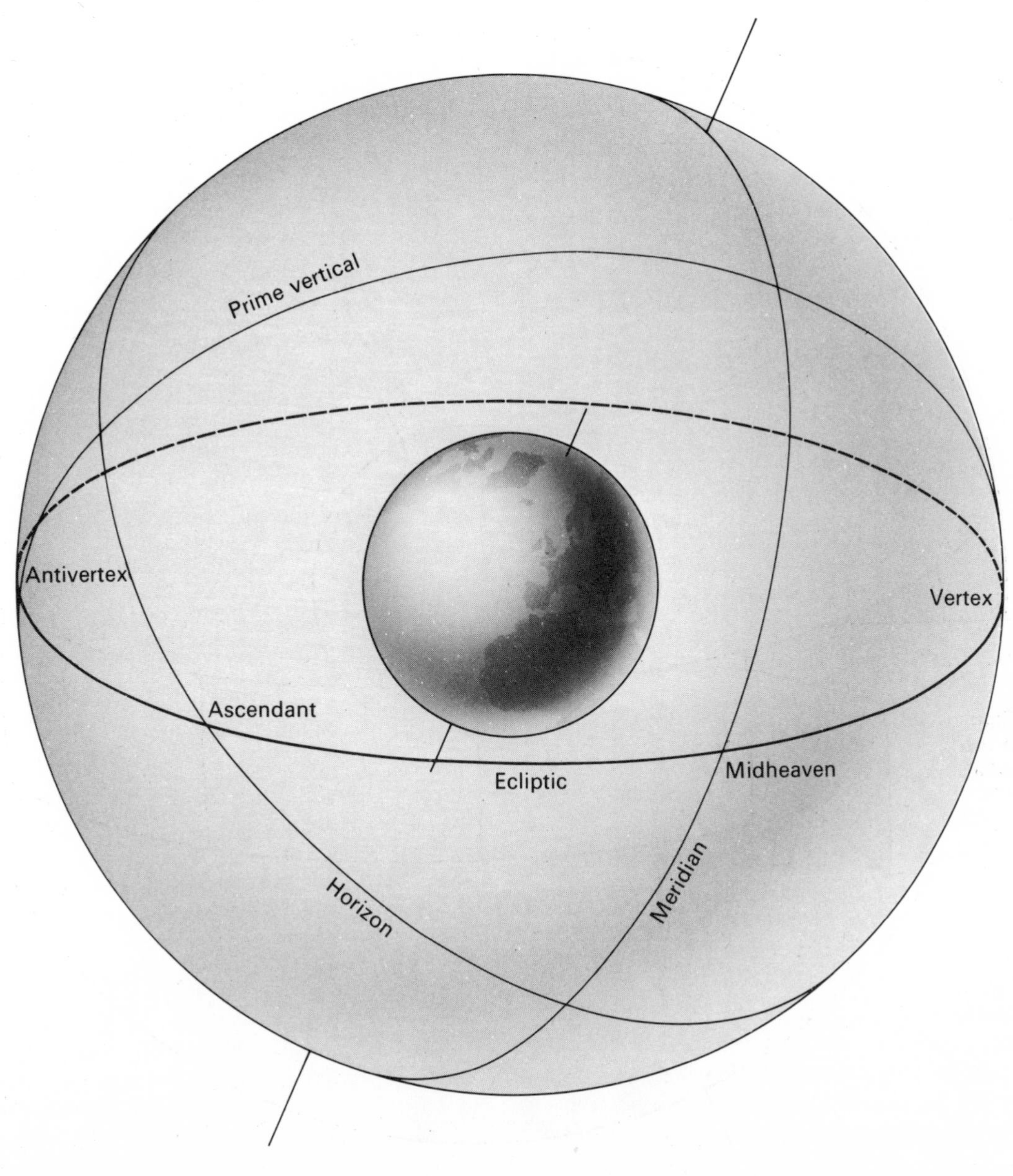

The zodiac The disc formed by the ecliptic, *near right*, is divided into twelve 30° segments radiating from the Earth at its centre. With the exception of Pluto, the planets never stray beyond 8° north or south of the ecliptic. They will always be found within a band 16° deep, *far right*. The twelve 30° segments of this band, *below*, bear the familiar names of the signs of the zodiac, and serve as a grid against which the positions of the planets, Sun, Moon and angles can be plotted.

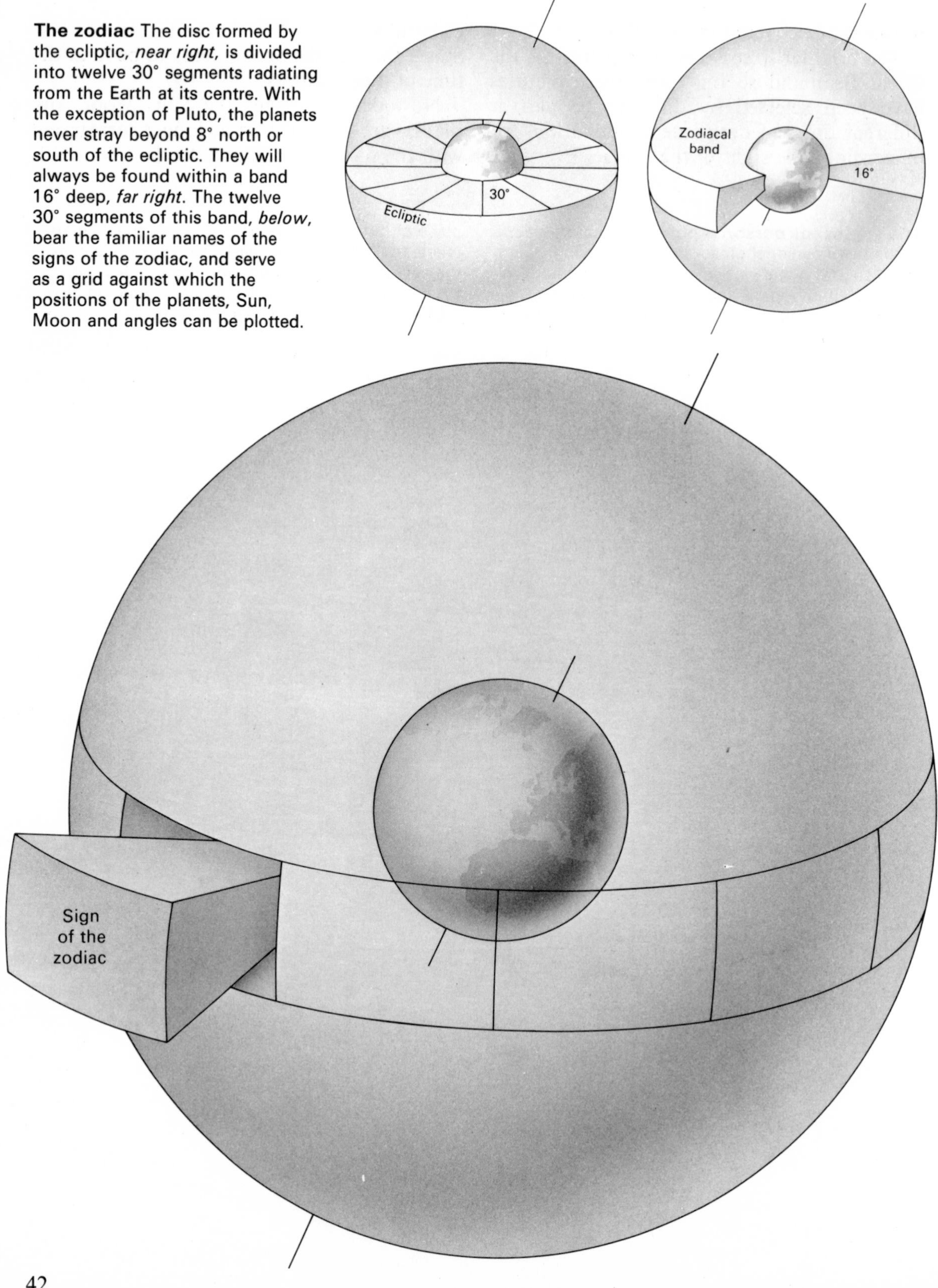

to be found. This is because the first point of Aries, at which the Sun is placed on both the ecliptic and equator simultaneously (the home of the vernal equinox in the northern hemisphere, when the day is equal in time to the night and the Sun has no declination), is 'slipping back' at a rate of about one degree in 72 years. This is owing to the perturbation of the Earth's polar axis, which wobbles. The phenomenon is called precession, and has been known about for a very long time.

The important point, however, is that the tropical zodiac is defined not by the fixed stars and their patterns (few suppose that a constellation in itself has any influence whatever), but by four points: the vernal equinox, when the Sun is at 00 Aries 00; the summer solstice, the Sun at 00 Cancer 00; the autumnal equinox, the Sun at 00 Libra 00; the winter solstice, the Sun at 00 Capricorn 00.*

Certain other points coincide with these four fundamental points. The equatorial nodes of all the planets (where they cross the equator and have no declination) are in Aries, and most of them are very near 00 Aries 00. Three other important points, the galactic centre, the supergalactic centre and the solar apex, are all very near these points. This gives some validity to the four sectors, or quadrants, of the tropical zodiac. The evidence for the twelve zodiacal signs is however, almost solely empirical.

*In the southern hemisphere, where the vernal equinox occurs in September, the tropical zodiac begins at 00 Libra 00.

From zodiac to birth chart A birth chart, *bottom right*, is a map of the sky at the moment of birth, showing the positions of planets, Sun, Moon and angles. In effect, it is the zodiacal band, containing the planets, sliced out of the celestial sphere, *below left*, and turned through 90°, *below right*. Sometimes Pluto is not within the zodiacal band; then, in effect, its perpendicular position relative to the band is plotted.

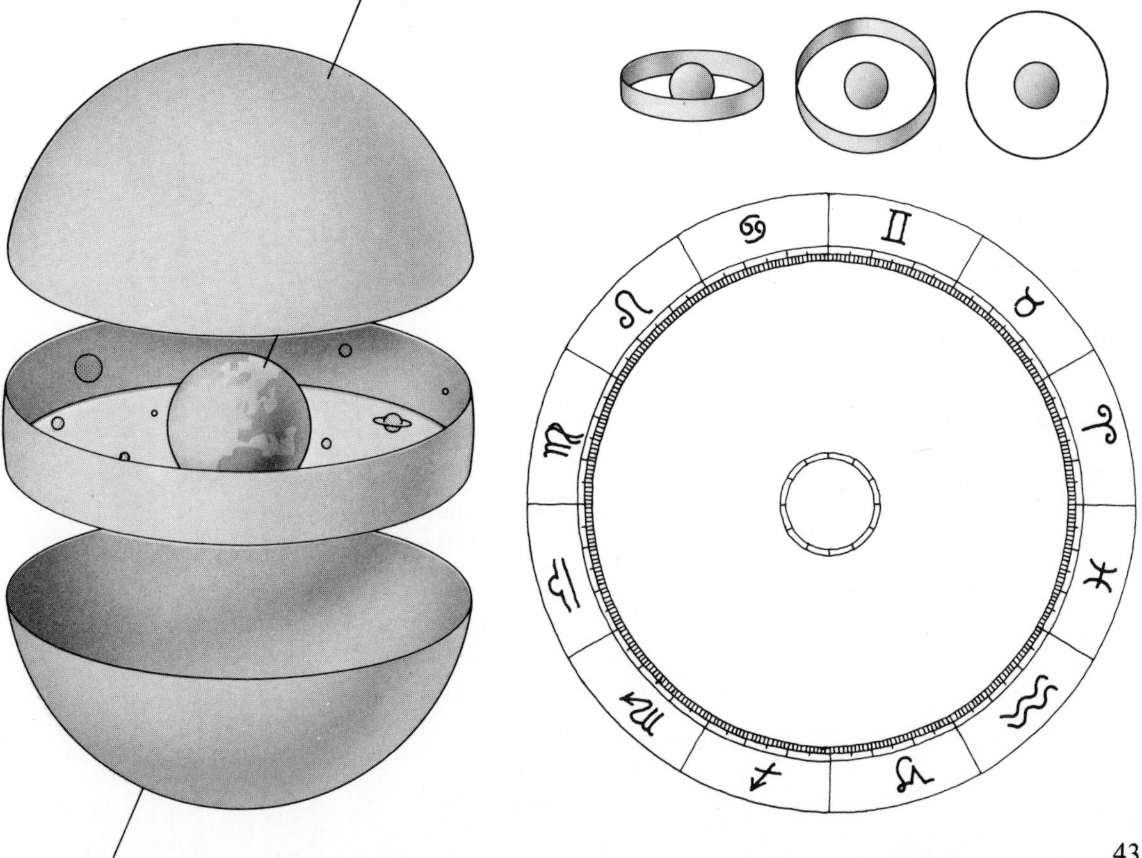

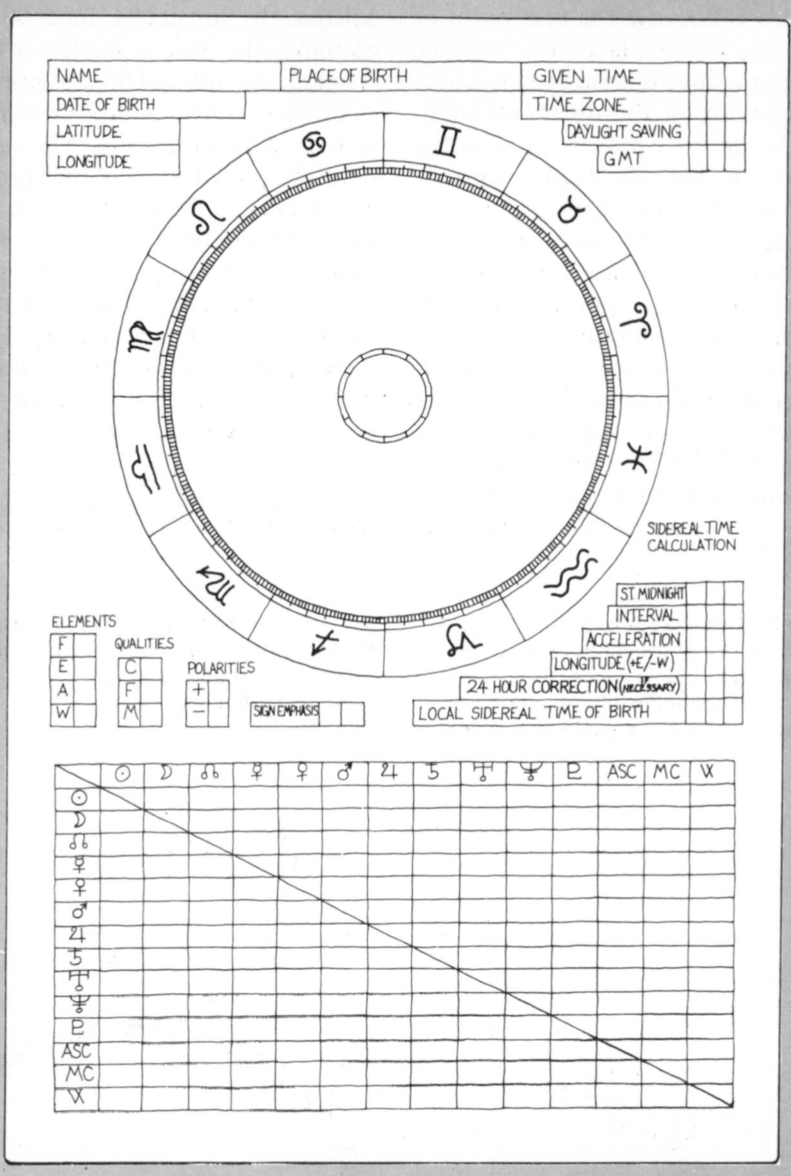

The birth chart Most serious astrologers develop their own chart forms, though blank chart forms can be purchased. This is my preferred lay-out: the chart appears at the top, with data regarding place and time beside it; a grid for recording aspects is underneath. On the chart the order of the signs is always anti-clockwise. The point 00 Cancer appears at the top; this is conventional at EPA, Ebertin's school of astrology, which is the largest and most scientific in Europe. 00 Cancer is the point at which the Sun reaches its highest declination in the northern hemisphere, on midsummer day.

DECLINATION AND RIGHT ASCENSION

Astronomers plot the position of stars, planets and other bodies by projecting terrestrial latitude and longitude out into Space. Terrestrial latitude projected into space is called declination, and this is much used by astrologers. If we described Mars as having a certain declination, we are marking its latitudinal position as though it lay on the surface of the Earth. However astrologers do not normally refer to positions in right ascension, the term given to terrestrial longitude projected into space.

ECLIPTIC LONGITUDE AND CELESTIAL LATITUDE

Ecliptic longitude, the form of longitude generally used by astrologers, is measured from the ecliptic. 0° in ecliptic longitude represents the meridian between the poles of the ecliptic which passes through 00 Aries 00. Measurements are made in degrees eastwards from this point. Celestial latitude records positions in terms of degrees north or south of the ecliptic. It is rarely used, partly because the Sun, whose path defines the ecliptic, never has any celestial latitude and nor do the MC or Asc.

The positions or points in ecliptic longitude, regardless of their latitude or declination, enable the astrologer to determine the angles they make in relation to each other from the geocentric viewpoint. The angles they make in relation to each other in terms of right ascension are close, but not quite the same. These are significant; but it is the ecliptic positions that astrologers must have above all.

ABSOLUTE LONGITUDE

Points on the tropical zodiac can be described in terms of absolute longitude, which is ecliptic longitude expressed solely in degrees 0 to 360, instead of in terms of sign. For example, the point 15 Libra 00 can be expressed simply as 195. This is achieved simply by dividing the tropical zodiac into 360 degrees, and taking 00 Aries 00, the traditional starting point, as 0 degrees. This is called absolute longitude and is extremely useful for calculating aspects and midpoints, two important components of birth charts. The zodiac thus divided can be represented as a straight line, which again facilitates the plotting of aspects.

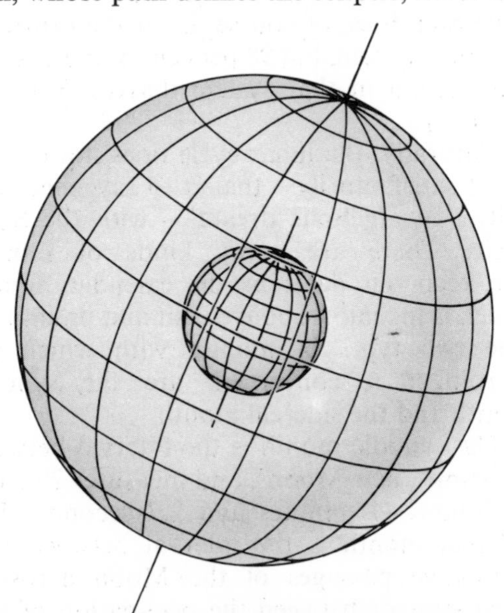

Declination and right ascension Declination is the Earth's latitude projected into space; right ascension is the Earth's longitude similarly projected. Astronomers use these to plot the positions of stars and planets. Astrologers usually use declination with ecliptic longitude.

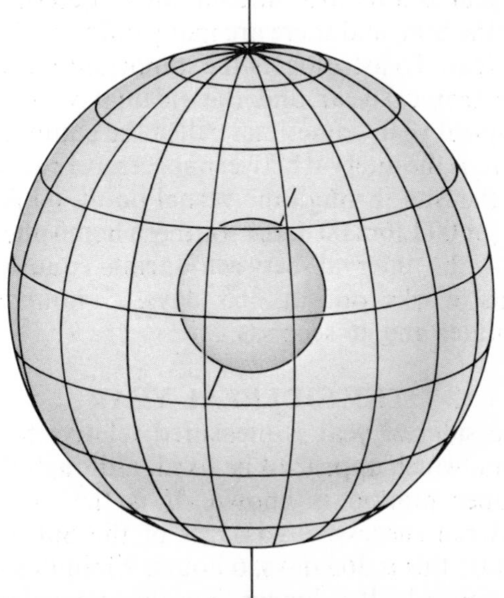

Ecliptic longitude and latitude These are based on the ecliptic, which is treated as the equator of the celestial sphere. 0° in ecliptic longitude is the meridian between the poles of the ecliptic which passes through the point 00 Aries 00. Ecliptic latitude is also known as celestial latitude.

TIME

In life there are many more coordinates than just space and time: we have our own landscapes of experience, and our own speeds of living – slow and fast: and there is our complex response to very low signals (in which most scientists don't believe because these responses are hardly susceptible to measurement). However, space, time and common sense all go together: we cannot explore the more interesting features of our lives through astrology unless we fully understand the basis of time, as well as of space. Accurate time is essential to an accurate chart, although most of us go ahead and draw up the most accurate possible chart if the time of an event is in doubt. If the chart seems inappropriate, we know the error is likely to be to do with time.

In antiquity there were a number of calendars in use. The calendar we use now is not the most accurate that has ever been invented, but it reconciles lunar and solar time fairly well. The Moslems use a solely lunar calendar, with the result that about 33 of their years equal 32 of ours.

THE TROPICAL YEAR

A year is a natural measurement, determined by the Sun, and there are many different forms of year. To astrologers the important ones are the tropical year and the sidereal year. The tropical year, sometimes called the equinoctial year, is the interval between successive passages of the Sun through the vernal point, 00 Aries 00 (or 00 Libra 00 in the southern hemisphere); it is the interval between spring equinoxes. This works out at 365 days, 5 hours, 48 minutes and 46 seconds.

THE SIDEREAL YEAR

The sidereal year is measured relative to the stars, which appear to be fixed, although their proper motion is known. It is the interval between successive passages of the Sun over a star: this is 365 days, 6 hours, 9 minutes and 9.5 seconds. It is longer than the tropical year because of the precession of the equinoxes. According to this method of measuring time, the point 00 Aries 00 is moving backwards by some 50 seconds each year.

Neither the tropical nor the sidereal year is any use as a calendar. You must have an exact number of days in a year. The Gregorian calendar which we now use was introduced in 1752, when it was decreed that the year should begin on January 1st.

MONTHS: THE LUNAR CYCLE

The months are based on the motion of the Moon. It is usual to say that the Moon revolves around the Earth. This is a serious error, and it is important to correct it – especially in a book whose astrology is more Moon-centred than Sun-centred. The Earth and the Moon, always facing each other, revolve around each other, moving round a common point called the barycentre, which is approximately 2922 miles from the Earth's centre, about 1000 miles inside the Earth. The two bodies describe, at a mean interval of 27.32 days, an elliptical orbit. The Moon is a companion planet to the Earth, rather than a satellite: it is very much larger in proportion than any other planet's moon. The two planets are both, of course, subject to the Sun's gravitational pull – but the pull of the Moon has a far greater effect on Earth than that of the Sun. (The Sun does, of course, lie at the centre of the solar system, but 98 per cent of the angular momentum in that system derives from the planets.)

Naturally, the lunar cycle does not correspond satisfactorily – that is to say, mechanically, 'an algebraic dream' – with the Solar cycle. There are many kinds of month. We keep our dates by the calendar month, which is ingenious, convenient and unnatural. The two types of month, with which the astrologer is concerned, are the synodic month and the sidereal month.

The synodic month is the interval between lunations, new Moons, and measures 29 days, 12 hours, 44 minutes and 2.7 seconds. The sidereal month is the interval between two successive passages of the Moon across a fixed star, or between the occupation of any given ecliptic, or equatorial, position and its return to that same position. The sidereal month varies by about 7 hours, but the mean is 27.32 days. There are 13.369 sidereal months in a year, and 12.369 synodic months.

WEEKS: THE MOON'S NODES

The week corresponds roughly to, and originates in, the four phases of the Moon as it moves from lunation to lunation. The Moon and the Sun come into conjunction at lunation, or new Moon; at full Moon the two bodies are in opposition. Conjunction means that Moon and Sun are in the same sector of the sky: the Moon lies on, or close to, a line drawn from Earth to Sun. Opposition means that the Earth lies on a line drawn between Sun and Moon, which are on opposing sides of the heavens.

The Moon's motion is not constant: on some days it travels almost three more ecliptical degrees than on others. This is because it is the barycentre, and not the Moon itself, which orbits the Sun. The Moon's apparent orbit round the Earth is tilted to the ecliptic at a mean angle of five degrees, eight minutes of arc. There are therefore two points at which the Moon's orbit cuts the ecliptic. These are called the Nodes, or Moon's Nodes, and their position in any birth chart is very important. The nodes, or the nodal axis, moves backwards around the zodiac at a rate

The Moon's movements Moon and Earth move around the barycentre, a point about 1000 miles inside the Earth. Viewed from Earth the Moon takes a mean 27.32 days, a sidereal month, to return to the same position relative to a fixed star. In a little more than 29½ days, a synodic month, it returns to the same position relative to the Sun.

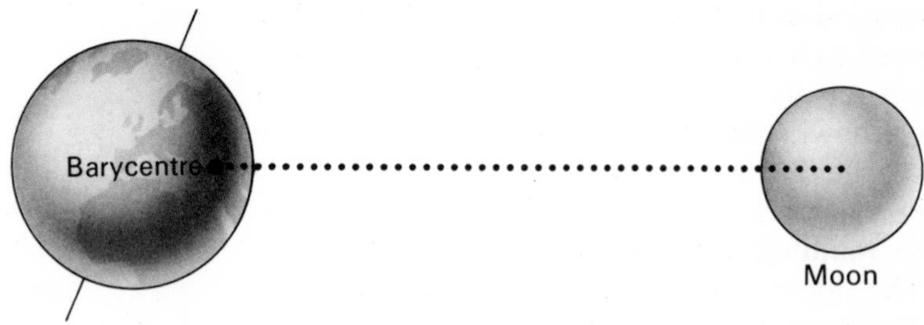

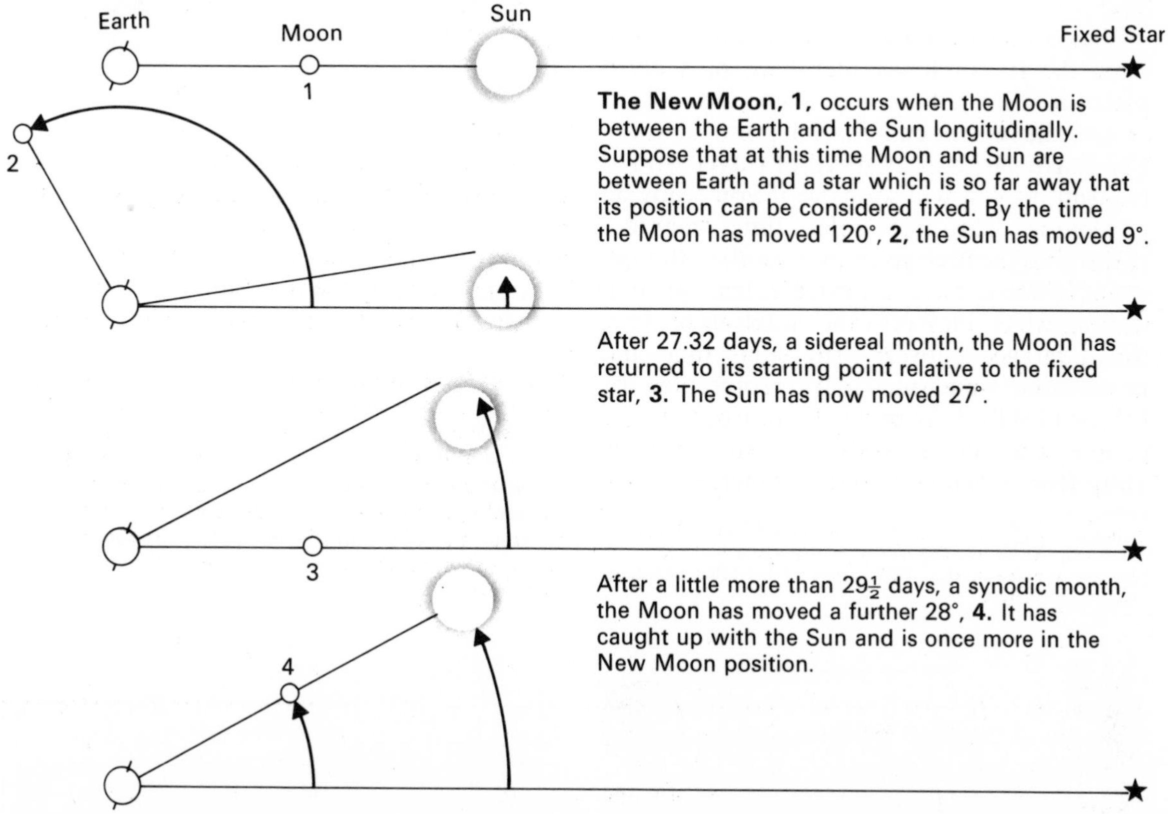

Earth
Moon
Sun
Fixed Star
1

The New Moon, 1, occurs when the Moon is between the Earth and the Sun longitudinally. Suppose that at this time Moon and Sun are between Earth and a star which is so far away that its position can be considered fixed. By the time the Moon has moved 120°, **2,** the Sun has moved 9°.

2

After 27.32 days, a sidereal month, the Moon has returned to its starting point relative to the fixed star, **3.** The Sun has now moved 27°.

3

After a little more than 29½ days, a synodic month, the Moon has moved a further 28°, **4.** It has caught up with the Sun and is once more in the New Moon position.

4

of about 3.18 minutes of arc per day, completing the full circle in about 19 years. The Moon crosses the ecliptic in a northerly direction at the North Node, called *Caput Draconis*, the Dragon's Head; and in a southerly direction at the South Node, *Cauda Draconis*, the Dragon's Tail. As the Moon crosses the Nodes it has no declination: after crossing the North Node it has north declination, which turns to south declination after it crosses the South Node.

DAYS

There are many different sorts of day and many different sorts of time. In astrology we need to know about Sidereal Time (ST) and Universal Time (UT), which is the same as Greenwich Mean Time (GMT). The sidereal, or true, day is one rotation of the Earth on its axis relative to the fixed stars. It lasts 23 hours, 56 minutes, 4.09 seconds of Universal Time. The sidereal day is defined as beginning when 00 Aries 00 crosses the meridian of a given place: it is then 0 hours, 0 minutes, 0 seconds ST.*

Viewed from the Earth, the Sun appears to cross the IC, or lower meridian, of a given place at midnight or 00h. 00m. 00s. ST. It crosses the MC, or culmination point, at noon. The Earth varies in its speed of travel around the Sun, as you will soon see if you study an ephemeris. The true solar time therefore varies; it is the time given by a sundial, though some of these have a device called an analemma, which measures the equation of time, the difference between true solar time and mean solar time (nowadays represented by UT or GMT). It is perfectly appropriate for people who live according to the seasons, away from machinery and commerce, to live according to the true Sun as it casts its shadow on the simple sundial. But this will not do for most of us, and so a mean Sun was invented. This convenient lie is the average of the motions made by the true Sun in the course of a year. We could not do without this fiction,

*Chapter 4 includes a table from which the ST at midnight at Greenwich on any day in any year can be calculated. Using a simple sum the ST of a place on any other meridian can be calculated.

Sidereal and solar days The sidereal day, *left*, is the time the Earth takes to rotate once relative to a fixed star. It lasts 23 hours, 56 minutes, 4.09 seconds of mean solar time (GMT). The solar day, *right*, the time taken by Earth to make one rotation relative to the Sun, varies according to the time of year; its mean is 24 hours.

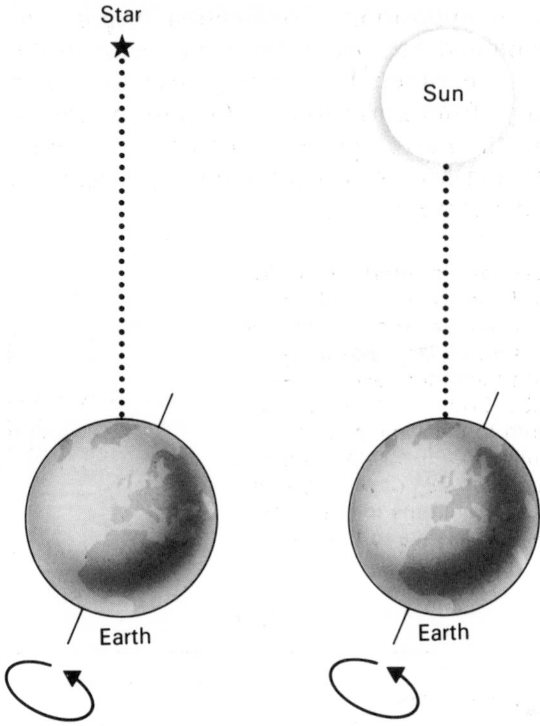

Sidereal and solar times The difference between these times is clearly seen at six-monthly intervals, *below*. When the Sun is between Earth and a given star, it will be noon in both sidereal and solar times at a certain degree of longitude on Earth. Six sidereal months later, when the Earth is directly between the Sun and the same star, sidereal noon at the same longitude will coincide with solar midnight.

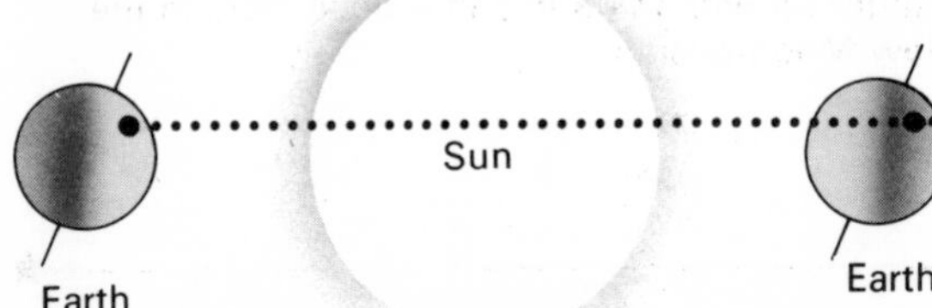

but it must be remembered that the mean Sun is no more than a point travelling at a constant rate, which the true Sun does not do. The equation of time is given in almanacs, such as Whitaker's, for each year, although it does not change much from year to year.

For births before the time when, in a given area, standard time was used – when people took their time from the sundial, or from railway time or from the firing of a cannon at regular intervals – the equation of time must be used to get a more precise time of birth. On four dates each year the two times are identical, but they can be different by as much as 16 minutes. I have used the equation of time in calculating Thomas Hardy's chart, because his parents set their clocks by the sundial (there was no railway at Dorchester then): the angles are therefore slightly different from those given in other books because he was born slightly earlier than is usually thought.

Since ST is slow on mean solar time (by some 3 minutes 46 seconds per day) we have to allow for this when calculating the LST (Local Sidereal Time) of a birth which is necessary for finding the MC, Asc and Vertex. The difference is called the acceleration on the interval (how to calculate it is explained in Chapter 4). This is a diurnal factor, meaning that it depends not on the Sun's apparent position on the ecliptic, but on the position the Earth has reached in its daily rotation on its own axis. This tells us where, for a particular point on Earth, the Sun, Moon and planets are, in terms of rising, culminating, setting or 'under the earth', meaning invisible. These are mundane (worldly) factors.

THE PLANETS: RETROGRADATION

UT, or GMT, not LST, is used to plot the positions of the planets. These are calculated relative to the centre of the Earth: it might be thought that there is a huge difference between the position of a planet viewed from the centre of the Earth and from a point on its surface, but this is not the case. The planets are too far away. For Mercury you will get at most an error of half a minute of arc. Only for the Moon is there an appreciable difference: this occasionally amounts to a degree of arc or slightly more. Not enough research has been done to establish which position is more valid.

In a heliocentric birth chart (where the Sun is the centre of reference)*the planets move directly around the Sun at differing rates at different times. They never move backwards. From the geocentric viewpoint all bodies except the Sun and Moon appear to move backwards at certain times: their motion is then called retrograde. Although these bodies do not actually move backwards, geophysical effects, such as increases in magnetic storms and geomagnetic irregularities, occur at times of station, the moment when a planet 'changes direction'. If a planet is about to turn backwards, it is SR (Stationary Retrograde): if it is about to turn forwards, it is SD (Stationary Direct). For the outer planets – Mars, Jupiter,

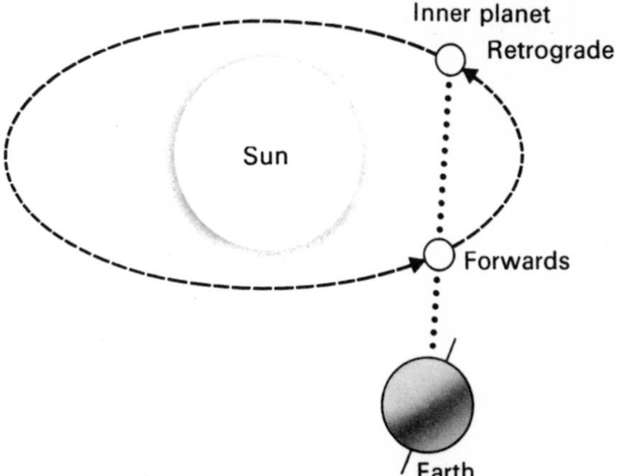

Retrogradation of an inner planet When an inner planet and the Earth are on the same side of the Sun, the planet is seen to travel from left to right, or forwards. When the planet moves 'behind' the Sun, it appears to travel backwards, or retrograde.

Star

Saturn, Uranus, Neptune, Pluto – retrogradation occurs when they are in opposition to the Sun. For the inner planets – Mercury, Venus – it occurs when they are in conjunction with the Sun.

You will see that no account is taken, in an ordinary chart, of the distance of the planets from Earth. Nor, again in ordinary charts, is any importance attached to the planets' declination. They are shown on the chart simply according to their positions in celestial longitude. We know, of course, that, with the exception of Pluto, their declination will be somewhere between 9° north and 9° south; in other words that they lie within the zodiacal band. Astrological information is gathered from a planets' sign position and its aspects.

ASPECTS

If lines are drawn on a birth chart connecting the planets to the Earth, the angles these lines make with one another are called aspects. (I recommend that lines are not actually drawn on a birth chart, because they are a hindrance rather than a help. It is best to use a separate piece of paper, if you need to draw lines. Aspects are usually written in tabular form alongside the chart.)

The aspects which are traditionally considered significant are: conjunction, 0°; sextile, 60°; square, 90°; trine, 120°; and opposition, 180°. (Many others are also significant, and these are discussed in Chapter 4.) Clearly there are always two angles made between planets. Some astrologers make a distinction, but for all general purposes we use the shorter arc: the square is 90°, not 270°; the sextile is 60°, not 300°: and so on.

The angles do not have to be exact to be valid. Only in a few charts will you find, say, an angle of exactly 90°. The difference between the exact angle and the angle in the chart is called orb. Nowadays major aspects are not taken into account if the orb is greater than about 8° on either side. I, in common with most other astrologers, initially use much smaller orbs: the accepted norm is about 5° on either side. As will be seen, it is necessary when interpreting a chart to cut down on this figure as well.

Aspects Lines drawn on a birth chart from the planets to Earth at the centre form angles, or aspects: the most significant are shown below.

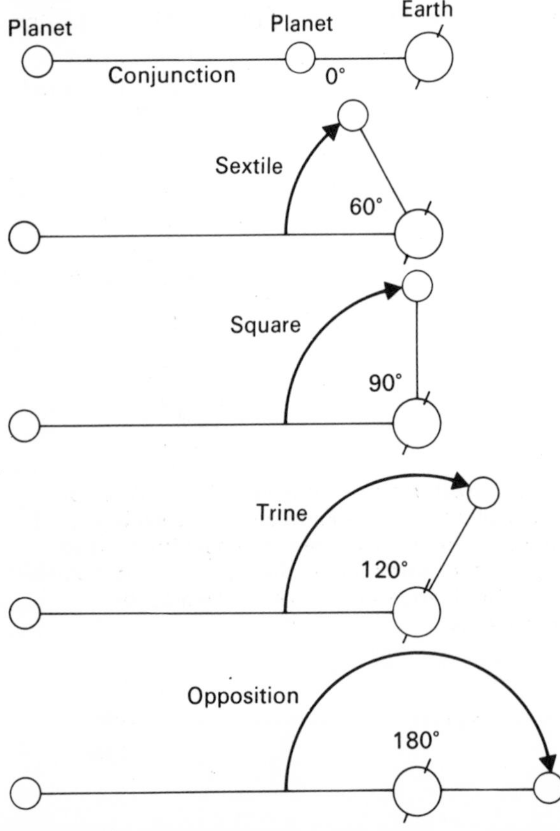

HARMONICS

If you take a cardinal point – 0 of Aries, Cancer, Libra or Capricorn – or the position of a certain planet, or indeed any other point as the beginning of a circle, then the angle between that point and any other body or point can be expressed as a harmonic.

Certain harmonics are significant, in particular the midpoint: this is simply the point halfway between two points. The direct midpoint is the point where the shorter arc between the points is divided; opposite it on the circle is where the longer arc length is divided, the inverse midpoint. Midpoints and other harmonics can be found by measuring them with various devices. But the simplest and most accurate method is to add together the value of the two points in terms of absolute longitude and divide by two.

CHAPTER THREE

BUILDING A BIRTH CHART

STEP-BY-STEP PROCEDURE

THE ADVENT OF CHEAP CALCULATORS HAS made the practice of astrology infinitely simpler – and more accurate. A calculator is an enormous help in constructing a birth chart. It is also useful for calculating aspects and midpoints and for constructing harmonic charts. The machine you choose should be able to perform trigonometrical functions; it should have buttons for sine (sin), cosine (cos) and tangent (tan). However, there is no need for you to understand the principles of spherical trigonometry unless you want to. A machine with one memory is adequate, although most of the machines that have trigonometric functions have more. It is also convenient to have a key which will convert minutes and seconds to decimals and vice versa. Such machines are not much more expensive than others: they are frequently used in schools.

My own choice for astrological work is the Sharpe Elsi Mate PC-1201 Pocket Computer, which is programmable, although I use a Texas Instruments programmable machine with as much ease. There are some 30 machines on the market, ranging in price from £6.00 to £30.00. If you buy from Boots, in particular, you should have no problems with service. They sell a Commodore with one memory: this is adequate although it will not convert minutes and seconds to decimals, and you will have to write down some stages of the longer sums. However, this is a good cheap calculator to begin with. If you have not used a calculator before, persevere with it. All will become clear after you have practised with it for an hour or two.

DECIMALISING MINUTES AND SECONDS

If your machine does not have a button for decimalising minutes and seconds, and vice versa, you can make such calculations with the machine very easily.

To convert to decimal notation: enter the minutes, divide by 60 and add the degrees. If you are working with seconds (which you will do to avoid cumulative error only, because astrologers do not yet work with seconds), then you put in the seconds, divide by 60, add the minutes, divide by 60 again, and then add the degrees.

To convert from decimals: subtract the degrees (and write them down, or you will forget them), and multiply by 60. If the resulting decimal part of the display is .5 or over, round up; otherwise, round down. Some people keep a list of the decimal values of all minute values from 1 to 59 handy; but a cheap spare calculator will do this work for you while you are using your trigonometrical one.

ESTABLISHING BIRTH-TIMES

To set up the chart for a birth – or an event – we need to find two 'times': GMT, the time in general use throughout the United Kingdom from October to March; and LST, Local Sidereal Time (see p. 00). The times of births or events outside the U.K. must be converted to GMT.

The GMT of the birth is used to measure the position of the Sun, Moon, planets and Moon's nodes on the ecliptic. The ecliptic is the Sun's path, so the Sun is always on the ecliptic. In the case of the planets, 'on the ecliptic' really means the point at which a perpendicular dropped from a planet meets the ecliptic.

Sidereal time, ST, is used to determine the positions of the angles, or personal points: the degrees of the rising (Asc) and culminating (MC) signs, and the degree of the sign that is immediately due west of the event (the Vertex).

To establish the GMT of British births is usually easy, although prior to the adoption of GMT in 1884, times may be expressed in LMT, Local Mean Time, or in Sundial Time, or in Railway Time, or in some form of time unknown to us but used by the household in question. A birth recorded before the advent of radio, with its Greenwich time signal, is unlikely to be accurate to within ten minutes either way of GMT, even if the timing was precise in terms of the time the household was using.

It was only towards the end of the nineteenth century that people began to appreciate the convenience of time zones, strips of longitude within which it is agreed that all clocks will run at the same time. All countries recognise Greenwich as 0° longitude, and each country, or part of it, operates on a named time zone, such as EST (parts of America), CET (most of Europe), and so on. Daylight Saving Time, DST, presents another problem. The notion was invented in Germany in 1916: we need to know the dates and times at which the various countries introduced this, and its duration – and whether it was actually observed all over the country.

All the available facts about time are set out in Doris Chase Doane's three books: *Time Changes in the World, Time Changes in Canada and Mexico,* and *Time Changes in America.* Some details are given in other books, but only *The New Waite's Compendium of Astrology* which is inexpensive, approaches the comprehensiveness of Doane.

SETTING UP A BIRTH CHART: STEP-BY-STEP

Later in this chapter I will set up two charts as examples. First, however, here are the steps required to set up a chart:

1 Establish GMT and the true date at birth

The true date may differ from the given date. For example, Shirley Temple Black's time, as given, is 9 p.m. PST 23 April 1928 at Santa Monica, California, U.S.A. This is Pacific Standard Time, and Doane tells us in *Time Changes in America* that no Daylight Saving Time was observed. Pacific Standard Time is 120° West, which is 8 hours slow on Greenwich. We therefore need to add eight hours to find GMT; this means that Shirley Temple was born at 5 a.m. on *24* April 1928. The subject of my first example chart was born two hours and seven minutes after Shirley Temple; he is a very different kind of person: the angles are of course different and at 0614 that day the Moon moved from Gemini into Cancer.

Try to get the most exact time possible: whole hours, quarters and halves are suspicious. For births which took place at at home and which are recorded in suspiciously rounded-off terms you may well be justified in taking off a minute or two: such births are often, but by no means always, timed a little late.

2 Establish Local Sidereal Time (LST) at birth

a) Use the tables over page to calculate the ST at midnight GMT on the day required. Ephemerides giving daily positions also give ST at either midnight or noon GMT. It is easier to work with midnight.
b) Write down the ST for GMT midnight, retaining the seconds to avoid cumulative error. Underneath write the GMT time of birth (*not* the given time if this differs) keeping the figures in columns for hours, minutes and seconds.
c) Each hour of mean time must have 9.86 seconds added in order to convert it to sidereal time, which, as we have seen, is fast on solar time. This is called converting for the 'acceleration on the interval'. Decimalise the GMT time, multiply by 9.86, divide by 60, de-decimalise. Write the result underneath the two times already written down.
d) Add these three sets of figures together. The result will be the ST *at Greenwich* at birth. Do not worry at this point if the result comes to more than 24 hours.
e) To convert this time to Local Sidereal Time, add 4 minutes of time for each degree of longitude to the East of Greenwich. If the birth was West of Greenwich, subtract 4 minutes for each degree. If the result comes to more than 24 hours, subtract 24 hours. You can now, if you wish, round off to the nearest minute: round 1–29 seconds down; 30–59 seconds up. This is the LST at birth.
Note: It is important to locate the birth in terms of latitude and longitude as precisely as possible in order to get an accurate LST and therefore an accurate Ascendant. If a birth took place in a city, try to establish where in that city. The *Times Atlas* lists some districts within cities with their latitudinal and longitudinal co-ordinates. If the district is not listed, find the longitude by looking at the appropriate map in the *Times Atlas*, or at any map which gives precise longitudes.

3 Find the position of the Midheaven (MC)

Decimalise the LST, and multiply it by 15. The answer is the RAMC, the position of the MC on the equator measured in right

Tables for calculating sidereal time at Greenwich midnight First, in the table below, find the ST at midnight (0000) for 1st January of the year in question. Add to this the hours, minutes and seconds given for the appropriate month in the table, right. To this total add the hours, minutes and seconds given for the day required in the table, below right. If the result is more than 24 hours, subtract 24 hours. To take an example: the ST at Greenwich midnight on 13 October 1948 is 6h. 38m. 15s. + 17h. 56m. 19s. + 3m. 56s. (1948 was a leap year) + 47m. 19s. = 25h. 25m. 49s. Subtract 24h. = 1h. 25m. 49s.

Addition for month
(in leap years add 3m. 56s. for all days on and *after* 29 February).

	Hours	Minutes	Seconds
Feb	2	2	13
Mar	3	51	37
Apr	5	54	50
May	7	53	07
Jun	9	55	20
Jul	11	53	36
Aug	13	55	50
Sep	15	58	03
Oct	17	56	19
Nov	19	58	33
Dec	21	56	49

ST at 0000 GMT for 1st January 1900–2000

	Hours	Minutes	Seconds		Hours	Minutes	Seconds		Hours	Minutes	Seconds
1900	6	40	45	**1935**	6	38	52	**1970**	6	40	55
1901	6	39	48	**1936***	6	37	55	**1971**	6	39	58
1902	6	38	50	**1937**	6	40	54	**1972***	6	39	01
1903	6	37	53	**1938**	6	39	57	**1973**	6	42	01
1904*	6	36	55	**1939**	6	38	59	**1974**	6	41	04
1905	6	39	54	**1940***	6	38	02	**1975**	6	40	06
1906	6	38	56	**1941**	6	41	01	**1976***	6	39	09
1907	6	37	59	**1942**	6	40	03	**1977**	6	42	08
1908*	6	37	01	**1943**	6	39	05	**1978**	6	41	10
1909	6	40	01	**1944***	6	38	08	**1979**	6	40	12
1910	6	39	03	**1945**	6	41	07	**1980***	6	39	15
1911	6	38	06	**1946**	6	40	10	**1981**	6	42	14
1912*	6	37	09	**1947**	6	39	12	**1982**	6	41	16
1913	6	40	09	**1948***	6	38	15	**1983**	6	40	19
1914	6	39	12	**1949**	6	41	15	**1984***	6	39	22
1915	6	38	15	**1950**	6	40	18	**1985**	6	42	21
1916*	6	37	18	**1951**	6	39	21	**1986**	6	41	24
1917	6	40	17	**1952***	6	38	24	**1987**	6	40	27
1918	6	39	20	**1953**	6	41	24	**1988**	6	39	30
1919	6	38	23	**1954**	6	40	26	**1989**	6	42	30
1920*	6	37	25	**1955**	6	39	29	**1990**	6	41	33
1921	6	40	24	**1956***	6	38	32	**1991**	6	40	36
1922	6	39	27	**1957**	6	41	31	**1992***	6	39	38
1923	6	38	29	**1958**	6	40	34	**1993**	6	42	38
1924*	6	37	21	**1959**	6	39	36	**1994**	6	41	40
1925	6	40	30	**1960***	6	38	38	**1995**	6	40	43
1926	6	39	33	**1961**	6	41	37	**1996***	6	39	45
1927	6	38	35	**1962**	6	40	40	**1997**	6	42	44
1928*	6	37	38	**1963**	6	39	42	**1998**	6	41	47
1929	6	40	38	**1964***	6	38	45	**1999**	6	40	49
1930	6	39	41	**1965**	6	41	44	**2000**	6	39	51
1931	6	38	44	**1966**	6	40	47				
1932*	6	37	47	**1967**	6	39	50				
1933	6	40	46	**1968***	6	38	53				
1934	6	39	49	**1969**	6	41	52				

***Leap year**

Addition for days

	Hours	Minutes	Seconds
2	0	03	57
3	0	07	53
4	0	11	50
5	0	15	46
6	0	19	43
7	0	23	39
8	0	27	36
9	0	31	32
10	0	35	29
11	0	39	26
12	0	43	22
13	0	47	19
14	0	51	15
15	0	55	12
16	0	59	08
17	1	03	05
18	1	07	01
19	1	10	58
20	1	14	56
21	1	18	51
22	1	22	48
23	1	26	44
24	1	30	41
25	1	34	37
26	1	38	34
27	1	42	30
28	1	46	27
29	1	50	24
30	1	54	20
31	1	58	17

ascension. A simple formula will convert RAMC to MC:

tan–1 (sin RAMC ÷ (cos RAMC cos e))

e is the obliquity of the ecliptic. It varies very slightly, but so slightly that you can use its value for 1900 without your result being affected by more than, at the very most, 1′ of arc. Therefore, unless you feel you must be very precise, you can use these two values always*:

cos e: 0.9174 sin e: 0.3979

To make the calculation, enter sin RAMC, divide it by cos RAMC, and then by cos e; now take tan–1 of the result.

Some calculators have a key marked 'arctan': this means 'tan–1' and can reduce the amount of button-pressing involved in the above calculation. Other calculators have a key marked 'arc' or 'INV': if this is pressed before the 'tan' key, the display will show 'tan–1'. Still other calculators have a key marked 'F' and alternative functions for many of the keys printed just above the keys: on such calculators 'tan' usually has 'arc' printed above it: press 'F', then 'tan–1' and again you will get 'tan–1'.

As you do the equation, store in the calculator's memories, or note down, the values of sin RAMC and cos RAMC.

The answer to this equation may require adjustment, by the addition or subtraction of 180 or 360: the first answer may be a minus number. The MC can never be more than 6° away from the RAMC; it is easy to see how much must be added or subtracted.

Convert the answer to degrees and minutes rounded off from the seconds, and write it down. This is the position of the MC.

4 Find the position of the Ascendant

Like the MC, the Asc can be calculated from the RAMC using another straightforward formula. This method of finding the Asc is 100 per cent accurate:

tan –1 (cos RAMC ÷ – ((sin e tan L) + (cos e sin RAMC)))

You already have the values for sin e and cos e, and sin RAMC and cos RAMC. Tan L is simply the tangent of the latitude of birth. To arrive at a figure for this, enter the latitude in degrees and minutes, decimalise it and press the 'tan' key.

You can write out the formula entering the appropriate figures for each set of letters, and then do the sum. After a little practice you will find this is unnecessary, and that you can enter the figures into the calculator as you make the calculation. It is well worthwhile checking your answer by making the calculation twice. The whole operation, including checking, takes about 60 seconds.

If your calculator is a simple one, you may have to do each part of the sum separately, write down the answers, and complete the equation. The illustrations on pages 57–60 show how to make the calculation all in one.

The result will be a minus or plus quantity decimalised in the display. As with the MC, this may require adjustment by the addition or subtraction of 180 or 360. However, in this case there is no easy reference point, as RAMC is to MC. The table on page 64 gives the Asc for the different MCs at, or near, all latitudes which you are likely to need. Look up the appropriate figure and, if necessary, adjust the answer in your display by adding or subtracting 180 or 360 until it is close to this figure. It will be within 10°.

Convert this figure to degrees, minutes and seconds. Round the seconds up or down and finally convert from absolute longitude to sign form. This is the position of the Asc.

5 Find the position of the Vertex

For this you will use the formula:

tan –1 (cos RAMC ÷ ((sin e cot L) – (cos e sin RAMC)))

Calculators do not give cotangents. However cot L = 1 ÷ tan L; in other words a cotangent is the reciprocal of a tangent, and most calculators do give reciprocals. Simply enter tan L and press the reciprocal button. If your calculator does not give reciprocals, divide 1 by tan L. You will already have the other figures required in this equation.

Again, you may need to add or subtract

*If you want total accuracy you can obtain the exact tilt, monthly, from Michelson's *The American Ephemeris for the 20th Century*.

180 or 360 to or from the result. To find the approximate position of the Vertex, take the RAIC, which is opposite the RAMC (RAMC±180). Find in the table on page 64 the Asc for this RAIC at the co-latitude of the birthplace (90° – latitude of the birthplace). In temperate latitudes in the northern hemisphere it ought not to be more than 60° from the Desc. The Vertex-Antivertex axis can coincide, or more often nearly coincide, with the Asc-Desc axis.

Convert the result to degrees, minutes and seconds. Round the seconds up or down and convert into sign form from absolute longitude. You now have the positions of MC, Asc and Vertex.

6 Find the positions of the planets

The positions of the planets have nothing whatever to do with sidereal time. They are calculated from the true GMT of the birth.

The positions are found by interpolation: that is to say you interpolate the position of a given planet at a given time on a given day from the position of that planet at midnight (or noon, if you have a noon ephemeris) preceding your given time and at midnight succeeding that time. If you are using a condensed ephemeris, where the positions are given less frequently than daily, you interpolate using the positions given for the nearest times before and after the birth time in question. (Full instructions for the use of the condensed ephemeris at the back of this book in this connection are given on p. 207.) Step-by-Step, the procedure is as follows:

a) Convert the GMT of birth to the 24 hour clock (for example, 4.12 p.m. becomes 16.12) and decimalise it (16.12 becomes 16.2)
b) Divide this figure by 24 to discover what fraction of the day has passed by the time of the birth (16.2 ÷ 24 = 0.675). Write this down, or, better, enter it into one of the memories of your calculator.
c) For all planets which are not retrograde (the ephemeris indicates retrogradation) take the position at the midnight (or noon) following the birth and decimalise it.
d) Decimalize the position of the planet at the midnight (or noon) before birth.
e) Subtract the result of d) from the result of c). This gives you the daily motion – the distance covered in the sky, measured in degrees – of the planet on the day of birth.
f) Multiply the daily motion by the fraction found in step b). This gives us the distance the planet has moved between the midnight preceding the birth and the minute of birth itself.
g) Add the figure thus obtained to the position of the planet at the midnight before birth. Convert the answer to degrees and minutes. This is the position of the planet in question.
h) Repeat the process for all planets which are not retrograde.

7 Find the positions of the retrograde planets and the mean node

Some charts (about 8 per cent) have no retrograde planets. However, the mean node is always retrograde. The procedure for finding these positions is a simple reversal of the procedure for non-retrograde positions.

To find the daily motion you *subtract* the *later* position of the planet from the *earlier* position. As before, you multiply the daily motion by the fraction obtained in 6.b). You then *subtract* the result from the earlier position.

Convert your results to degrees and minutes. You now have the positions of all the planets and the mean node.

8 Fill in the chart

Enter all the positions found including MC, Asc and Vertex on a blank chart (see examples).

USING A CALCULATOR

Calculating the Ascendant On this and the following pages each stage of the calculation of the Ascendant for Example Chart I is shown. This appears to be a lengthy procedure: the formula requires the performance of 21 steps. However, after a little practice you will be able to make this calculation in less than 30 seconds. The formula is:

tan−1 (cos RAMC÷ – ((sin e tan L) + (cos e sin RAMC)))

As the sequence of photographs shows, the formula should be entered into the calculator as it is written, with the exception of two steps: tan−1 is entered last of all, steps 20 and 21; the – sign, which follows the ÷ sign is not entered at that point. The effect of this – sign is achieved by step 18, when the +/– key is pressed.

Some calculators have a key marked F, instead of a key marked INV (step 20); pressing F will produce the same result. Other calculators have a key marked arctan: this performs steps 20 and 21 in one jump, so pressing this button alone as step 20 will provide the answer.

Before you begin, you should have written down, or stored in the calculator's memories, values for: cos RAMC and sin RAMC; cos e and sin e; and tan L.

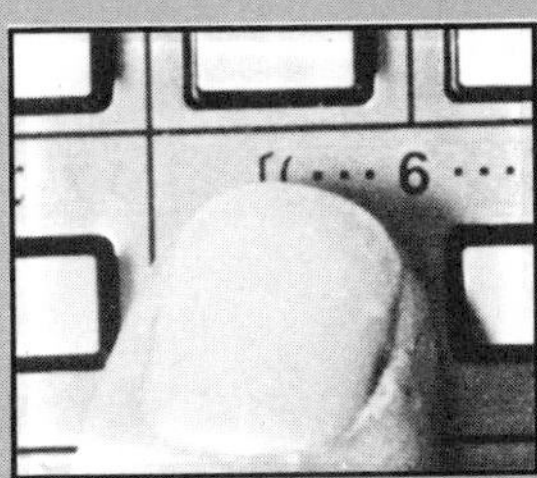

1 Press (

2 Enter .753

3 Press ÷

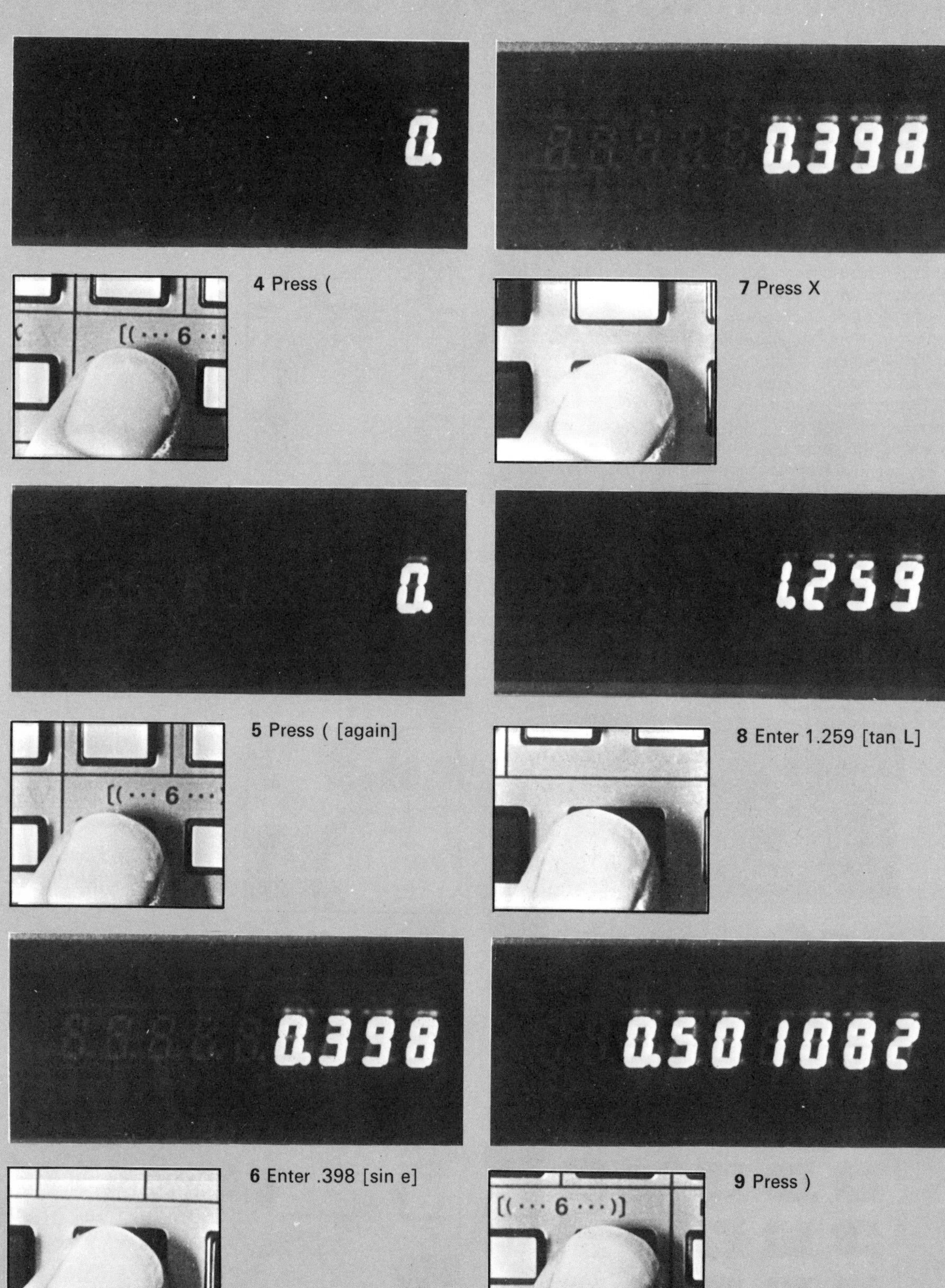

4 Press (

5 Press ([again]

6 Enter .398 [sin e]

7 Press X

8 Enter 1.259 [tan L]

9 Press)

10 Press +

11 Press (

12 Enter .917 [cos e]

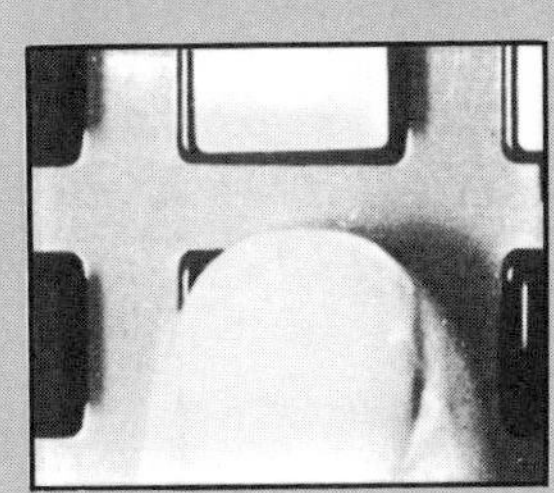

13 Press X

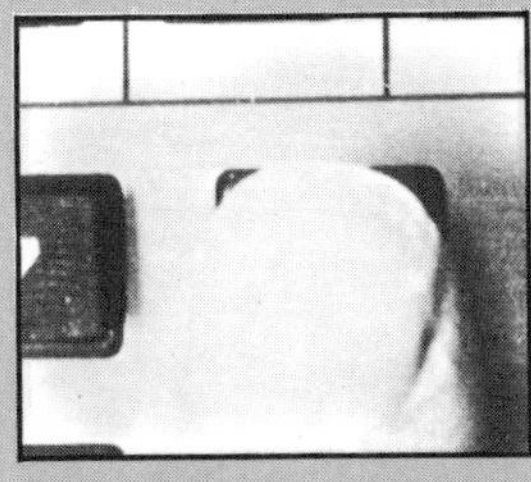

14 Enter .658

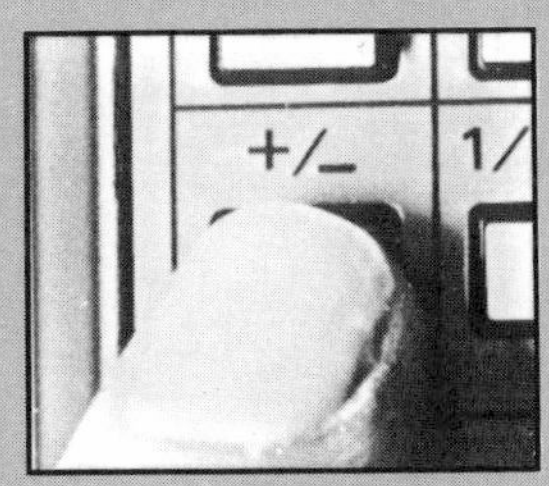

15 Press +/−
[to change the sign of the previous entry: sin RAMC is −0.658]

16 Press)

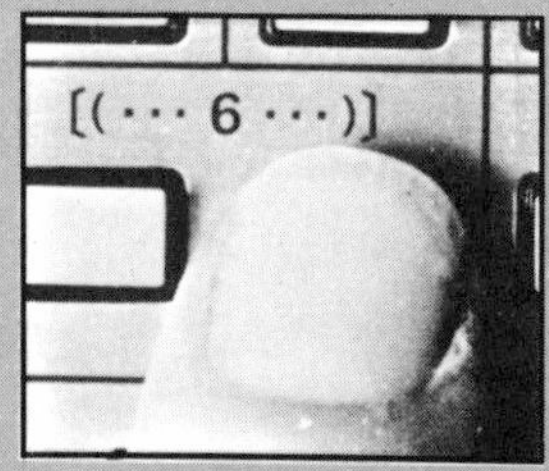

17 Press) [again]

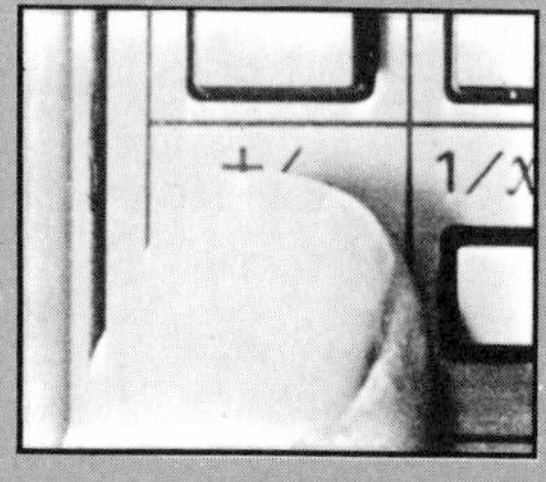

18 Press +/−
[to change sign]

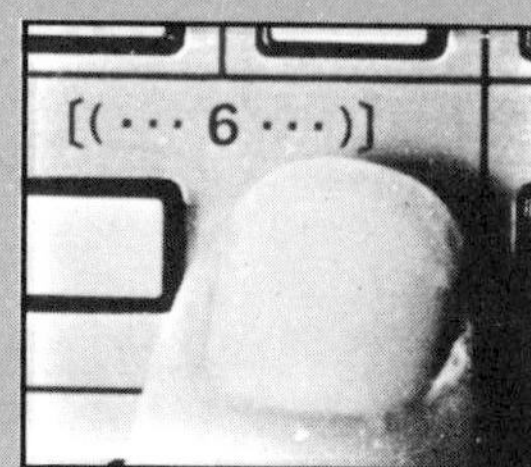

19 Press)

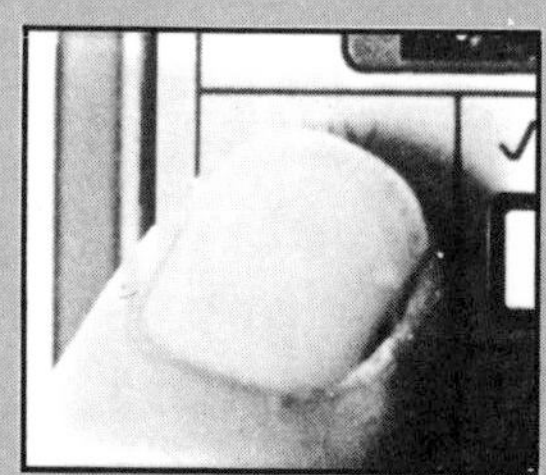

20 Press INV

21 Press tan
[The position of the Ascendant in absolute longitude is now in the display.]

TWO EXAMPLES

My first example is a London birth, a very straightforward chart to construct.

In constructing these charts I use Michelson's *Ephemeris for the Twentieth Century* at midnight. This is because I want to show the accuracy that can be obtained. The condensed ephemeris at the back of this book is more accurate than any other condensed ephemeris, and amply adequate for beginners. Using it, your results will be accurate to within a few minutes of arc. The small margin of error will not affect the work you do with any aspects down to angular separations of 30° (semi-sextile).

EXAMPLE 1

Native born at 0807.5 hours BST on 24 April 1928 at 51N32′44″, 00W04′. The accuracy of the birth time to within half a minute is a lucky fluke: it was timed for an astrologer and two stop watches were used.

GMT

One hour's daylight saving was in use on that date, so I subtract an hour to obtain GMT:

Birth time in GMT: 07h. 05m. 30s.

LST

I discover from the tables that the ST at Greenwich at midnight (00.00) on that day was 14h. 07m. 05s. I do the following sum to discover the LST (Local Sidereal Time) at birth:

	h.	m.	s.
ST at Greenwich at midnight	14	07	05
+ GMT at birth	7	07	30
+ acceleration on the interval (7h. 07m. 30s. × 9.86)		1	10
= ST at Greenwich at birth	21	15	45
− 4′W × 4s			16
= LST at birth	21	15	29

RAMC

I decimalise LST and multiply by 15 to obtain RAMC:

21.25805555 × 15 = 318.8708333

MC

To obtain MC I use the formula: tan −1 (sin RAMC ÷ (cos RAMC cos e)). I know that cos e = .9174. The result is: MC = 316.4123098. This is within 6° of RAMC, so I do not need to add or subtract 180 or 360. (Some calculators, because they are programmed differently, produce a minus answer to this same equation; adding 360 produces the same result.) This figure is in absolute longitude. In sign terms: MC = 16 Aquarius 25.

I now enter into my calculator's memories, making absolutely certain I know which is which, the figures I have discovered for sin RAMC, −.6577587658, and for cos RAMC, .7532286546. I also calculate and record at this point, because I know I shall need them: tan L (latitude), 1.259226079, and cot L, .7941385718. I retain these decimals to this seemingly ridiculous length, because that is how they appear on my calculator display and, since I am entering them directly into the memories, there is no point in correcting them. If you are writing these values down, you can correct them to three decimal places, and still get an extremely accurate result.

ASC

My next step is to look at the table for the position of an Asc for an MC at 16 Aquarius for latitude 50 or 51 N. I find that this Asc should appear in late Gemini, about 17° +, so I know how to correct for it if necessary.

I then calculate the appropriate equation: tan −1 (cos RAMC ÷ − ((sin e tan L) + (cos e sin RAMC))). Using the quantities entered into the memories of my calculator, I get the result 82.26305925: in sign terms 22 Gemini 16.

Just to illustrate the uselessness of writing down the figures to several decimal places, if your calculator lacks memories, here is the equation to just three decimal places:

tan −1 (.753 ÷ − ((.398 × 1.259) + (.917 × −.658)))

The answer to this is also 22 Gemini 16.

VERTEX

To find the Vertex I go through the same process. I check in the tables and find that I expect a point near 10 Scorpio. The equation yields 39.32595152 (absolute longitude). I can see that in this case I must add 180, which gives the Vertex at 9 Scorpio 20.

MOON, SUN, PLANETS AND NODE

I divide the decimalised GMT of the birth, 7.125, by 24 to obtain the fraction of the day that had passed by the time of the birth. The answer is 0.296875. I then use this fraction to interpolate the position of each body and the node. The position of Mars can serve as an example:

Position of Mars at 0000 25 April 1928	13 Pisces 19.6
—Position of Mars at 0000 24 April 1928	12 Pisces 33.7
= Daily motion of Mars during 24 April 1928	45.9
× fraction of day prior to birth	.298765
= Motion of Mars between 0000 24 April 1928 and birth	13.627
+ Position of Mars at 0000 24 April 1928	12 Pisces 33.7
= Position of Mars at birth	12 Pisces 47.327

By this process, reversing it as described for Saturn, Neptune and the node which are retrograde, I get the following positions: Sun, 3 Taurus 51; Moon 0 Cancer 30; Mean node 11 Gemini 36; Mercury 23 Aries 41; Venus 15 Aries 38; Mars 12 Pisces 47; Jupiter 20 Aries 48; Saturn 18 Sagittarius 34 R; Uranus 5 Aries 05; Neptune 26 Leo 26 R; Pluto 15 Cancer 07. (R = retrograde.)

WRITING THE POSITIONS ON A CHART

My primary interest is to show the positions of the bodies and points as they really are. I therefore use a chart form which omits houses. It is an honest geocentric chart which imposes no prejudices on those who look at it. I place the midsummer point of 00 Cancer 00 at the top of every chart; this makes the comparison of charts simple and is standard practice among serious astrologers.

Most British astrologers, almost all of whom work with houses, use a chart which shows the positions artificially: everything is sacrificed in order to show the house positions of Sun, Moon and planets. On such charts the

Example Chart 1

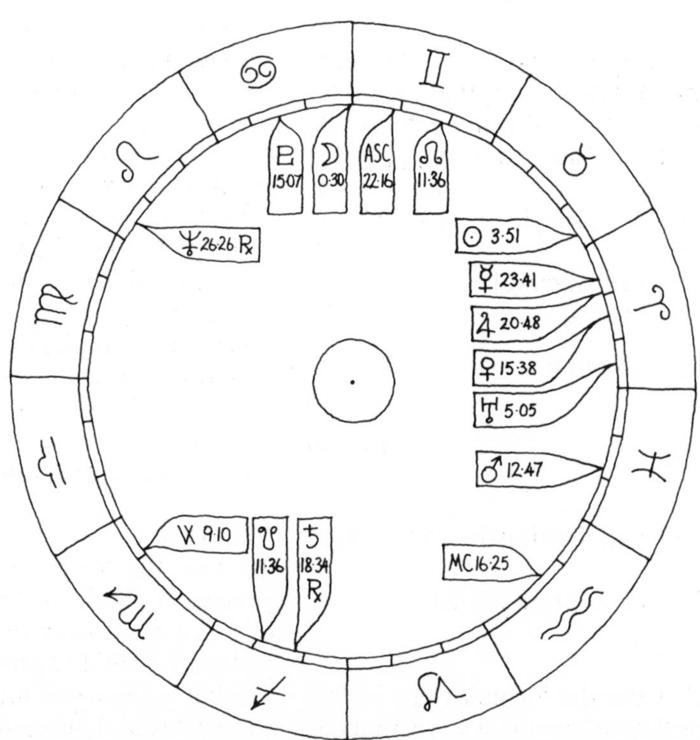

houses, rather than the signs, are divided into equal portions. On the continent of Europe, house systems are also popular, but charts are drawn according to the true (sign) positions and the house cusps are imposed on this. If houses are to be used, I consider this a more useful way to represent them.

EXAMPLE 2

For this example I shall only establish the GMT and go once again through the determination of the LST at birth. The location of the birth makes this slightly complicated.

Native born at 1530 given time on 30 July 1940 in Ottawa, Ontario, Canada (45N27, 75W42).

GMT

Time in Canada during World War II varied from one part of the country to another. Doane's *Time Changes in Canada and Mexico* reveals that since 1895 EST (Eastern Standard

Example Chart 2 This is the full chart form, to my preferred design. It includes spaces for recording: LST at birth; the totals of elements, qualities and polarities (see Chapter 4); and sign emphasis. The top half of the grid below records aspects between bodies and points; the bottom half records the actual angles between every pair of bodies and points.

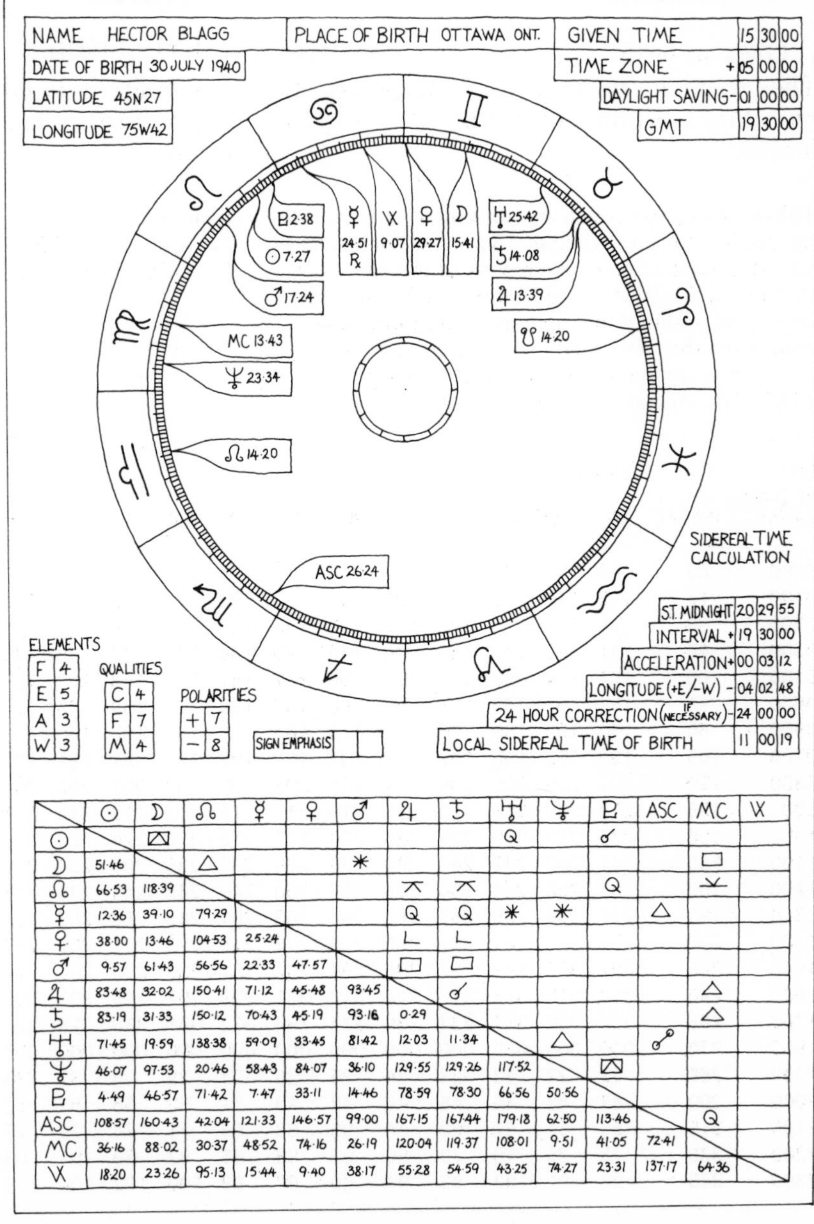

	☉	☽	☊	☿	♀	♂	♃	♄	♅	♆	♇	ASC	MC	Vx
☉		⚼							Q		☌			
☽	51·46		△			✳							□	
☊	66·53	118·39					⊼	⊼			Q		⊻	
☿	12·36	39·10	79·29				Q	Q	✳	✳		△		
♀	38·00	13·46	104·53	25·24			L	L						
♂	9·57	61·43	56·56	22·33	47·57		□	□						
♃	83·48	32·02	150·41	71·12	45·48	93·45		☌					△	
♄	83·19	31·33	150·12	70·43	45·19	93·16	0·29						△	
♅	71·45	19·59	138·38	59·09	33·45	81·42	12·03	11·34		△		☍		
♆	46·07	97·53	20·46	58·43	84·07	36·10	129·55	129·26	117·52		⚼			
♇	4·49	46·57	71·42	7·47	33·11	14·46	78·59	78·30	66·56	50·56				
ASC	108·57	160·43	42·04	121·33	146·57	99·00	167·15	167·44	179·18	62·50	113·46		Q	
MC	36·16	88·02	30·37	48·52	74·16	26·19	120·04	119·37	108·01	9·51	41·05	72·41		
Vx	18·20	23·26	95·13	15·44	9·40	38·17	55·28	54·59	43·25	74·27	23·31	137·17	64·36	

Time), five hours behind GMT, has been observed in the state of Ontario. It further reveals that in Ottawa in 1940 one hour's DST, daylight saving time, was observed between 28 April and the end of that year. GMT of the birth can be calculated as follows:

given time	1530
−DST	0100
	1430
+(Because Ottawa is West of Greenwich) EST	0500
=GMT of birth	1930

The fraction required to interpolate the planetary positions is therefore 19.5 ÷ 24 = 0.8125.

LST

	h.	m.	s.
ST at Greenwich at midnight	20	29	55
+ GMT at birth	19	30	00
+ acceleration on the interval (19.5 × 9.86)		3	12
= ST at Greenwich at birth	40	03	07
− 75.7°W × 4m	4	2	48
	35	00	19
− 24 hours	24	00	00
=LST of birth	11	00	19

RAMC is 11.00.19 × 15 = 165.079. There are no further problems. The chart is shown on page 63.

Table of approximate Ascendants This table is for use in checking whether 180 or 360 needs to be added or subtracted to the results of the formulae for finding Ascendant and Vertex. The Ascendant should be within a few degrees of that indicated here. Take the nearest latitude and interpolate for time. For example, for a birth at latitude 47° at 1145 LST, look at the column for 48°, take three quarters of the difference between the figures given for 1100 and 1200 and add this to the figure given for 1100: approximate Ascendant is 244.

LST of birth/ event	RAMC	Latitude 30°	32°	34°	36°	38°	40°	42°	44°	46°	48°	50°	52°	54°	56°	58°	60°	62°	64°
0000	**00**	103	104	105	106	107	108	110	111	112	114	115	117	119	121	123	125	127	130
0100	**15**	116	117	118	119	120	121	122	123	124	125	126	128	128	130	132	133	135	137
0200	**30**	128	129	130	131	132	132	133	134	135	136	137	138	139	140	142	143	144	146
0300	**45**	141	142	142	143	144	144	145	146	146	147	148	149	149	150	151	152	153	154
0400	**60**	154	154	155	155	156	156	157	157	157	158	158	159	160	160	161	161	162	163
0500	**75**	167	167	167	168	168	168	168	168	169	169	169	170	170	170	170	171	171	171
0600	**90**	180	180	180	180	180	180	180	180	180	180	180	180	180	180	180	180	180	180
0700	**105**	193	193	193	192	192	192	192	192	191	191	191	191	190	189	189	189	188	188
0800	**120**	206	206	205	205	204	204	203	203	203	202	202	201	200	200	199	199	198	197
0900	**135**	219	218	218	217	216	216	215	214	214	213	212	211	210	210	209	208	207	206
1000	**150**	232	231	230	229	228	228	227	226	225	224	223	222	221	220	219	218	216	215
1100	**165**	244	243	242	241	240	239	238	237	236	235	234	232	230	229	228	226	224	223
1200	**180**	257	256	255	254	253	252	250	249	248	246	245	243	241	239	238	235	233	231
1300	**195**	270	269	268	267	266	264	263	261	260	258	256	254	252	250	248	245	242	239
1400	**210**	285	284	282	281	280	278	277	275	273	271	269	267	264	261	258	255	252	248
1500	**225**	301	300	298	297	296	294	292	291	289	286	284	281	278	277	271	267	262	257
1600	**240**	318	318	316	315	314	313	311	309	307	305	303	300	296	292	288	282	275	268
1700	**255**	338	338	337	337	336	335	334	333	331	330	328	326	323	319	314	307	298	285
1800	**270**	000	000	000	000	000	000	000	000	000	000	000	000	000	000	000	000	000	000
1900	**285**	22	22	23	23	24	25	26	27	29	30	32	34	37	41	46	53	62	75
2000	**300**	42	42	44	45	46	47	49	51	53	55	57	60	64	68	72	78	85	92
2100	**315**	59	61	62	63	64	66	68	69	71	74	76	79	82	85	89	93	98	103
2200	**330**	75	76	78	79	80	82	83	85	87	89	91	93	96	99	102	105	109	112
2300	**345**	90	91	92	93	94	96	97	99	100	102	104	106	108	110	112	115	118	121

CHAPTER FOUR

FACTORS IN INTERPRETATION

SIGNS PLANETS AND POINTS

To practise astrology according to strict rules is impossible. Being neither a science in the modern sense, nor an art, it must be treated flexibly and practised in a manner which suits the individual practitioner. However, there are rules and conventions which have to be learned and considered before the astrologer can develop his own approach. This chapter describes the method of interpreting charts which I have developed over several years and which works for me. So that the reader has a full picture of traditional astrology, I also discuss here some widespread practices, for example the use of houses, which I have tried and discarded but with which some readers may well have more success. My intention is not to be dogmatic. If I appear so, this is an inescapable by-product of the process of imparting information.

Although I am in one sense dedicated to the mysterious, I have eschewed the occult, in the sense of the wholly unexplained; I have seen too much rubbish, largely in popular books, to be able to treat this approach to astrology seriously. The reader can be sure that where what I have written seems occult, or strange, it is in fact based either on thoroughgoing scholarship, or, where no scholarship can throw light on the matter, on empirical experience.

THE ZODIACAL SIGNS

The twelve zodiacal signs represent fields of operations, or conditions. They have no influence or power in themselves. The planets, the Moon and the Sun, have power and exercise it in that part of the personality designated by the sign in which they lie.

One demonstrably erroneous, but common, belief about signs should be dealt with straight away. This is the idea that the signs, taken in the order Aries–Pisces, represent a pathway of psychological or mystical development from 'primitive' to 'spiritually evolved'. There is simply no evidence or justification for this. There is no hierarchy of signs: they are, of course, all different, but not one can be said to be in itself better or worse than the others. The signs achieve importance in an individual chart if the celestial bodies lie within them. Each sign has its own intrinsic attributes. These are connected with its rulership; every sign has a planet which rules it and some signs have a second, or co-, ruler. Each sign also has characteristics which it gets from its element, its quality and its polarity.

ELEMENTS, QUALITIES AND POLARITIES

There are four elements: fire, earth, air and water. Three signs are associated with each element; this is why the elements are sometimes known as the triplicities. There are three qualities: cardinal, fixed and mutable. Four signs possess each quality; hence the qualities are also called the quadruplicities. The twelve signs are alternately positive and negative, beginning with Aries, which is positive. These are the signs' polarities. Fire and air signs are positive: earth and water signs are negative.

The 'allocation' of elements and qualities between the signs follows a regular pattern (see illustration): every third sign has the same element; every fourth sign has the same quality. It can be seen that the signs associated with the same elements are in trine with each other: the angles between them are 120°. Squares, angles of 90°, are formed between signs which have the same quality. Signs of the same elements are traditionally thought to be in harmony with one another, while those of the same quality are held to be 'out of sympathy'. This is an over-simplification, but cannot be wholly ignored.

ELEMENTS

The four elements have a long history which precedes their introduction into astrology. In early thought about creation great attention was given to the problem of how reality arose from unreality. Various fundamental things, such as light and darkness, were regarded as the building-blocks of the universe. The fifth-century BC Sicilian Greek philosopher Empedocles said: 'and these things (Fire, Air, Earth and Water) are continually in motion, sometimes becoming One through Love but at others being torn asunder through Disharmony.' Space was at all times filled with these four elements; the only other realities were love

The signs: their polarities, qualities, elements and rulerships

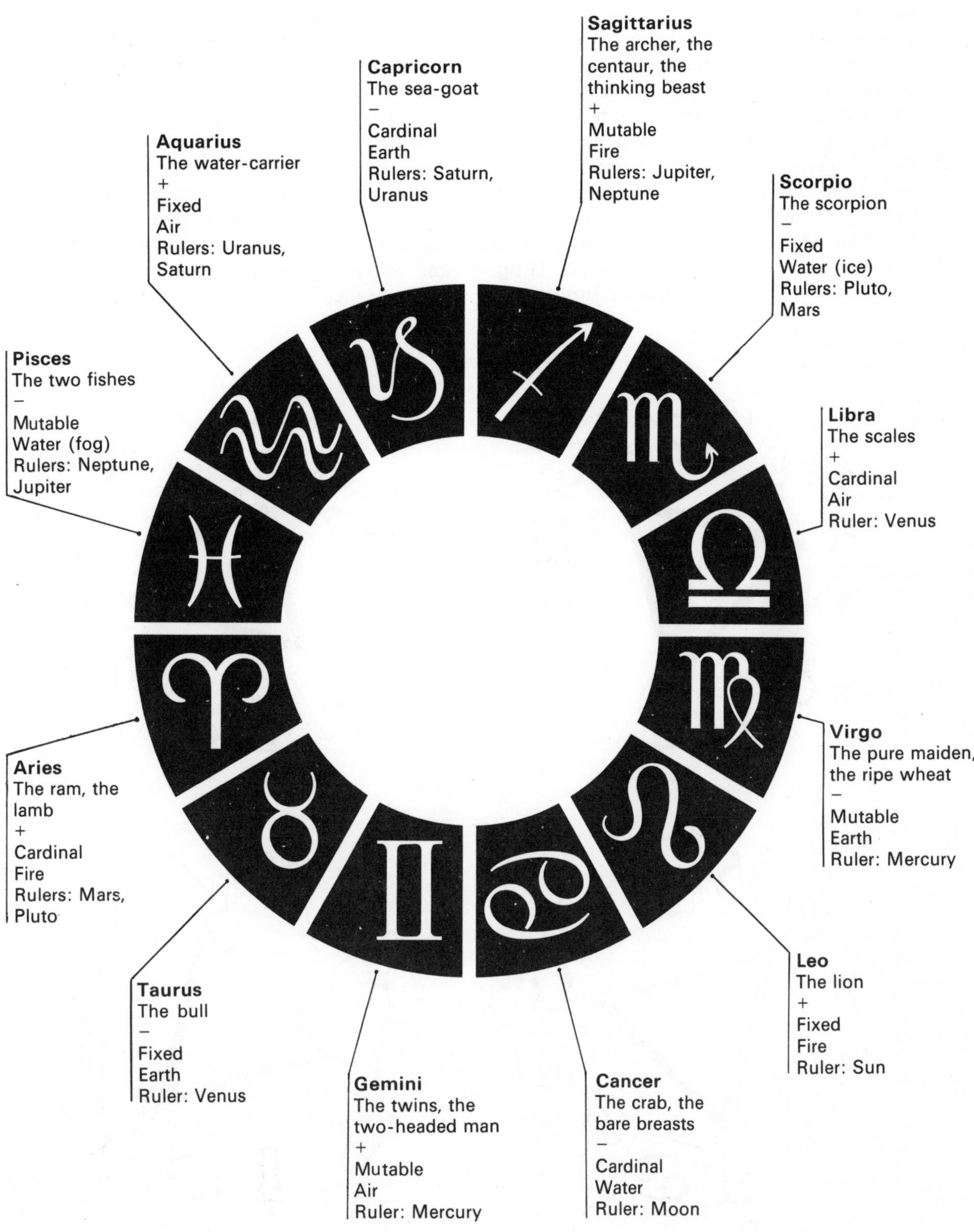

and disharmony. Many systems based on such notions were put forward in the pre-Socratic period in Greece.

Eventually the four elements became the basis of the four humours, four basic types of temperament, of which all men are mixtures. This psychological system (for that is what it is, though it developed from a physiological theory) persisted until the beginning of the seventeenth century. The pathology of Galen (AD 130–200), physician to the Roman Emperor Marcus Aurelius, was based on the four humours. The Greek physician Hippocrates, who lived not long after Empedocles, perhaps believed in and employed them. They still formed an essential part of psychology in Elizabethan England. The humours, in this physiological and psychological sense, were: (a) blood, hot and moist, air; (b) yellow bile, hot and dry, fire; (c) phlegm, cold and moist, water; and (d) black bile, cold and dry, earth. The humours gave off vapours, and these went to the brain and affected it. The balanced man had no one humour dominant. The sanguine man was generous, sensual and happy; the choleric man was angry, revengeful, obstinate and impatient; the phlegmatic man was boring, pale-faced and cowardly; the melancholic

The four elements

man was sentimental, gluttonous, mannered, meditative and lacking in initiative.

This kind of psychology seems on first consideration archaic and useless. However, it must be seen as a formulation. It must not be forgotten that both modern medicine and modern physics are also formulations. The triumph of what is known as the modern scientific method is illusory – impressive, ingenious and remarkable though the work of modern scientists has been.

If you press a physicist to tell you what, for example, an eta-particle (a type of meson) is, he will finally have to tell you that it too is a formulation. He cannot show you one. What he can do is to prove to you that an eta-particle must exist because otherwise certain reactions could not take place. What he might be less likely to admit is that in a few years the whole language of physics may have changed: different formulations will be used.

QUALITIES

Whereas the Elements derive from Greek thought, the Qualities were brought to Europe from India by Arabic astrologers, who partly changed their meaning. In the philosophical system underlying the Indian classic epic the *Bhagavad-Gita*, the *Gunas*, modes, are the primary constituents of nature and of all substances – rather as the elements were for the early Greeks. In early Indian thinking there was no action when the Gunas were in balance; but if they were not – and they seldom were – then evolution began. The Gunas were, in short, passion, dullness and goodness: cardinal, fixed and mutable. This at least serves to bring out the nature of the mutable signs as mediators, reconcilers – and therefore adaptable.

ELEMENTS AND QUALITIES IN SIGNS

By the time that the twelfth-century Sufi master Ibn al'-Arabi was writing, the concept had changed somewhat. Ibn al'-Arabi, who was born in Spain, was a remarkable and learned man, in whose many works there are traces of gnosticism, Moslem orthodoxy, neo-Platonic Christianity and other important streams of thought. For him the qualities are: mobile,

fixed and synthetic. And for him the zodiac began at the vernal equinox: in other words, it was the moving, tropical zodiac. Ibn al'-Arabi gives a description of each sign. These, headed under mobile, fixed and synthetic, are well worth paraphrasing for the still valid characterization he assigns to each. We can begin to see, here, how each of the elements functions in three different ways, and how each of the qualities operates in four different styles. The three signs which share an element (for example: Aries, Leo and Sagittarius, the three Fire signs) always have different qualities (Aries is cardinal, Leo is fixed, Sagittarius is mutable). Thus each of the twelve signs represents a different combination of element and quality. It was the Arabs who made this synthesis between Indian and Greek thought. I have adapted Ibn al'-Arabi's descriptions considerably, and put them into terms suitable for the modern world. Each sign is to be thought of as providing certain conditions, creating circumstances. Remember that the signs are the areas of action, the planets the action itself. This is certainly as 'mystical' or as esoteric as we shall get in this book. There is much more to be said about the signs, but these definitions are of special interest to those of a metaphysical turn of mind (those who wish to link their study of astrology to their mental adventures). The definitions appear below.

Attempts to systematize the elements and qualities along the lines of modern psychology have not been successful. So ought we to abandon a method which, however valid a formulation for many societies in history, including the Elizabethans, is unsuitable for us? Not if we keep it simple – and not if we abandon

Mobile (Cardinal) Signs	Fixed Signs	Synthetic (Mutable) Signs
Aries: fiery, hot, dry. Creates the conditions whereby virtue may be achieved, but only through situations so dangerous that accidents and disasters may too easily occur.	**Taurus**: earthy, cold, dry. Creates the conditions under which the useful and the useless may be built, and is therefore a sign of terror; its danger is that of commitment to greed.	**Gemini**: airy, hot, humid. Creates the conditions in which perfect communications can be achieved. The twins love each other, but the danger is that, insomuch as they hate each other because of their love, so there is disruption of all communication.
Cancer: watery, cold. Creates in the imagination the truest possible representation of the true world, the true and purified nature of the meaning of our dreams; but there is danger of drowning in tears, of excess of feeling spilling into sentimentality.	**Leo**: fiery, hot, dry. Creates the conditions in which generosity may be exercised with wisdom, with understanding of future consequences; its danger is of abandoning generosity for pride in power.	**Virgo**: earthy, cold, dry. Creates the conditions in which physical and mental health may flourish, but its danger lies in its becoming conscious of itself, so leading to illness.
Libra: airy, hot, humid. Creates the equilibrium that can accept and bear change, the mutability of things; but in the need for balance there is a danger of losing balance.	**Scorpio**: icy, cold. Creates an understanding of the depths (those referred to under Capricorn), depression, the notion of eternal damnation; but this understanding may turn active, and create hell for the self and others. It is a sign of terror.	**Sagittarius**: fiery, hot, dry. Creates the conditions under which man may harmonise himself with the nature of which he is part; but its danger is over-excitement owing to this religious understanding.
Capricorn: earthy, cold, dry. Creates the conditions in which the heights and the depths of experience may be assessed and acted upon; but there is a danger of remaining in extremities.	**Aquarius**: airy, hot, humid. Creates the conditions in which immediately useful generosity may be exercised. Its danger is that it may become detached from human feeling by straining its gift.	**Pisces**: misty, cold. Creates the conditions in which understanding of mystery may be accepted; but its danger is that of getting lost in the mistiness of its understanding: it is engulfed in its own essence, leading to men becoming dumb animals.

misleading attempts to 'score points' on the strength of polarities, elements and qualities. The only astrologer to have devised a sensible method of so scoring, Robert Hand in his *Planets in Youth*, adds scores if planets which he considers to be of a fiery, 'feminine' and so forth, nature are near angles or in aspect to the Sun. But this, I have found, leads into further confusion. I have a much simpler method, which puts only as much weight on the strength in charts of elements, qualities and polarities as they warrant.

The fire signs, Aries, Leo and Sagittarius, are inspirational: enthusiastic, impulsive, colourful, direct, honest, innocent, wilful, lacking in control, impatient and incautious. The air signs, Gemini, Libra and Aquarius, are usually called 'mental'. They are rather more difficult to explain than the other Positive group, the fire signs. One can be misled into thinking them 'intellectual', which they are not. They are most usefully distinguished from the fire signs by their concern with the future. The fire signs are concerned with immediate action; the air signs are 'mental' in the sense that they are naturally concerned with consequences. A very stupid man can be highly rational and detached in his approach to his work and his relationships. He can be abstract, too – although not in the manner of a true intellectual who is over-concerned with ideas at the expense of the practical. Everyone, whether clever or not, thinks. So the air signs are 'mental', inasmuch as they tend towards thinking rather than feeling. The water signs are emotional, rooted in the depths of unconscious experience. They understand the unquantifiable, the intangible; indeed, they tend to live by them. They are in every sense the opposite of the air signs. The earth signs are practical and pragmatic. They are aware of the physical, the here-and-now, and for that reason they are as much associated with creativity as with the accumulation of wealth, surplus food, and comforts.

As we have seen, each of the elements functions in three different ways, according to its quality. Cardinality is initiative, pushing-forward, motivation. Fixity stabilizes cardinality: it is resolve, intensity, obstinacy. Mutability reconciles the other two qualities by its adaptiveness, its reconciliatory and mediatory features. So Aries is not just fire but cardinal fire: being both inspirational and initiatory, it is likely to be wild and feverish, but, of course, very strong. And Sagittarius is a different kind of fire: mutable fire. It burns less strongly than that of Aries. Its aspirations are often reconciliatory, although none the less innocent and wilful. When we discuss each sign in detail you will see how useful this system is.

POLARITIES

First, the polarities must be explained. These are obviously related to heat and cold: heat is '+' and cold is '–'. It is helpful to think of the polarities as the two poles of a battery. No current will flow in the absence of either pole. It is important not to take the polarities too seriously. One famous astrologer, Vivian Robson, actually stated that if any woman had more 'positivity' in her chart than 'negativity', then she really ought to be a man. . . . One wonders how many charts this man actually studied. For those who know something of Chinese thought and the *I Ching*, the yin/yang analogy is the right one (yin for '–'; yang for '+').

The best approach to the polarities is to try to understand why fire and air cannot be 'negative', and why earth and water cannot be 'positive'. In that way you may grasp what positivity and negativity really mean in this context. Active/passive or assertive/receptive are less misleading than positive/negative, if only because of the inevitably pejorative connotations of 'negative'. When judging a chart, do not consider the polarities alone (as most chart forms specify) but in conjunction with the elements.

SCORING ELEMENTS, QUALITIES AND POLARITIES

On all chart forms you will find spaces for scoring elements, qualities and polarities. Some astrologers simply count one point for each body in a sign, adding points for the Ascendant and Midheaven signs. In this way they neglect the Vertex. Others score two points for Asc, MC, Sun and Moon, but only in the box listing the elements, ignoring qualities and polarities. Robert Hand alone tries to make allowances for the false picture given: he scores points (again only in the Elements box) if a planet is angular or if it makes a hard major aspect to the Sun. He lists Venus and Saturn as Earth planets; Sun, Mars and possibly Jupiter as Fire planets; Mercury, Uranus (although he thinks this is fiery, too) and possibly Venus as Air planets; and Moon, Neptune and Pluto as Water planets. He admits that this is only a rough guide, and does not claim much for the method. My method is simpler. I do not allow space on the chart for these scores – they are of such minimal importance in the chart itself that they do not deserve to be listed. But, on separate paper, I make the following scores:

For *Qualities*, Cardinal, Fixed and Mutable, I score 1 point for each body and point (including Asc, Desc, MC, IC, North Node, South Node, Vertex and Antivertex) in each sign. There are 18 factors involved, so the scores should total 18.

For *Polarities* I do exactly the same.

For *Elements* I score 5 points for the Moon, 3 points for the Sun and for Asc, MC and Vertex and their three opposites. For the rest including the north and south nodes, I score 1 point. The foregoing scores accrue to the element of the sign the bodies and points are in. The following scores accrue to the elements according to my planetary-element scheme below. I score 5 points for the Sun if it is on an angle (including the Vertex) or conjunct the Moon (orb 2°). I score 5 points for the planets and Moon if they are *before* Asc, Desc, MC or IC (orb 10°); when planets are in this position, they express their principles very strongly and obviously. I score 3 points for planets and Moon in hard major aspect (including quintile) with the Sun or Moon (orb 1°).

The following is my planetary-element scheme. Where a body is split between elements, apportion the score in proportion.

Sun: $\frac{1}{4}$ fire, $\frac{1}{4}$ earth, $\frac{1}{4}$ air, $\frac{1}{4}$ water
Moon: water
Mercury: $\frac{2}{3}$ air, $\frac{1}{3}$ earth
Venus: $\frac{2}{3}$ earth, $\frac{1}{3}$ air
Mars: fire
Jupiter: $\frac{3}{4}$ fire, $\frac{1}{8}$ earth, $\frac{1}{8}$ water
Saturn: $\frac{7}{8}$ earth, $\frac{1}{8}$ air
Uranus: $\frac{1}{2}$ fire, $\frac{1}{2}$ air
Neptune: $\frac{7}{8}$ water, $\frac{1}{8}$ earth
Pluto: $\frac{1}{2}$ water, $\frac{1}{2}$ fire

Admittedly this is complicated, but the more complex planetary-element scheme is applied only to scores for angularity or aspects. This is only done on a scrap of paper, but it is done for a purpose. We are looking for sign emphasis, or sign deficiency, or both. These are entered on the chart; boxes are provided so labelled. Let us take the example of Margaret Thatcher's chart (p. 180).

Polarities: +10, −8 (fairly well balanced).
Qualities: Cardinal 5, Fixed 7, Mutable 6.
Elements: Fire 11.625, Earth 11.385, Air 9, Water 14.

What does this tell us? It indicates that Margaret Thatcher has a slight preponderance of positive over negative, and a similar preponderance of fixed over the other qualities. The elements are not badly balanced, but this is less interesting than the sign that she, so to say, 'needs' in terms of her polarities, qualities, and elements. It is positive fixed water. There is no sign which combines these: Scorpio, the fixed water sign, has negative polarity. Nevertheless, in Scorpio (and her '−' is nearly as strong as her '+') she does have Asc and Saturn. However, the most strongly tenanted sign is Libra, which contains Sun, Mercury and Mars; this is positive, cardinal air. Here there is a problem, for she has a low score for both cardinality and air. She has the Moon in Leo, which helps her realise her fixity through a highly emotional channel. But the water element is badly scattered: Uranus in Pisces with the IC, Asc and Saturn in Scorpio and Pluto in Cancer. Saturn and the Ascendant are in trine to Pluto, but Uranus in Pisces can in no way be said to make up a Grand Trine. So we have learned something:

Sign emphasis: positive fixed water – first two sufficiently realised, water (emotionality) frustrated.

Sign deficiency: negative cardinal air – first realised, second realised in Libra but problematically since the bodies there are nonemotional and weakly placed (Mars in detriment, Sun in 'fall'), air realised Mars, Sun and Mercury in Libra.

What is indicated at this point is that Margaret Thatcher has a problem about her emotionality. Now we would modify this if any other indications (aspects, midpoints, and so forth) went against it.

RULERSHIP

The signs are not accurately described as 'psychological types'. It is better to think of them as twelve distinct forms of human expression. One might divide human expression into two, or into a million, categories. But some degree of simplicity is required, as well as a degree of subtlety: twelve, you will discover, is right. A sign colours the planets which inhabit it, both with its own nature and the nature of its ruler or rulers. Each sign is ruled by a certain planet, and many of the signs also have a sub-ruler, a planet which has a strong influence on the sign, but not as strong as that of the ruler. When a planet is in the sign that it rules, it is said to be in its dignity; when it is in the opposite sign, it is said to be in its detriment. Before the outer planets were known the rulership system was built up with an extraordinary subtlety and beauty. Some might call it poetic magic.

The chart (p. 74) is drawn so that the signs Cancer and Leo come alongside each other at the bottom. The Moon is given rulership over Cancer, the Sun over Leo. We have no way of being certain whether the originators of this system knew that the Earth revolved round the Sun or not (many people knew thousands of years before Copernicus that it did). However, the fact is that for much of the time the Moon and the Sun are the bodies closest to the Earth. (The Moon is always closest, the Sun is next closest whenever Mercury and Venus are behind the Sun viewed from Earth.) You will also notice that, going upwards, the signs are ruled by the same planets – in order of their distance from the Earth from closest to farthest (visible). 'A mere ingenious scheme!', one hears one of those scientists, who know nothing at all of astrology except that it is rubbish, mocking. But that is far from the case. The scheme is perfect, as anyone who understands the qualities of the planets and signs will immediately see. A beautiful diagram, with the Sun at its highest point of declination, the summer solstice (00 Cancer 00), put at what looks like the south of the chart but which is in fact the north (remember that astrological charts show east as west and vice versa, and north as south and vice versa).

As the three new planets were discovered (Uranus in 1781, Neptune in 1846 and Pluto in 1930) serious problems arose for astrologers. It soon became obvious that Pluto was intimately related to Scorpio. It was clear that the principles of Pluto held the same sort of mysteries that the sign Scorpio held in the realm of human expression. Evidently Pluto had to become ruler of Scorpio. But Mars should not be thrown out of the sign: the majority of astrologers have done this and they make a serious error, a mockery of the understanding of the ancients. Mars had to be relegated to sub-ruler (strong, but not as strong as the chief ruler of the sign). Many of the more obvious Scorpio indications, for example fervency, the energy given to profoundly subtle venom, are Martian. Neptune's association with fishy, watery Pisces became rapidly evident. But Jupiter was not displaced from Pisces. Certain of the more obvious Piscean indications were clearly Jovian: true generosity can co-exist with vulgar cultism.

We can now confirm the rulerships given to Neptune and Pluto empirically, but it seems that it was the names of those two planets that first led to their being associated with their signs: an odd coincidence. Uranus presented a greater problem. It was seen quite early that it was a paradoxical planet: it is associated with suddenness, drastic events, revolution, freedom, brotherhood, the public will, fervour tending to fanaticism. Bearing in mind the complex history of the development of the sign Aquarius, it was clear that only this sign could be given to Uranus. But, once again, Saturn was not removed: it became sub-ruler, because there is clearly a 'Saturnine Aquarian' type: cold, technological and well-organised, well able to build on the inspirational inventions of others less precise.

Ancient and modern rulership schemes The ancient rulership scheme, drawn up long before the discovery of the three outer planets, has a perfect simplicity. At the bottom, Sun and Moon, the two bodies for much of the time closest to Earth, rule Leo and Cancer. Moving upwards, in order of their distance from Earth the planets rule two signs each on either side of the zodiac. With the discovery of the outer planets, Sun, Moon, Mercury and Venus retained their sole rulerships. Uranus became ruler of Aquarius, Neptune of Pisces and Pluto of Scorpio; the former rulers remained as sub-rulers. The three outer planets became sub-rulers of Capricorn, Sagittarius and Aries. Thus Uranus rules one of Saturn's signs and sub-rules the other; Neptune rules one of Jupiter's signs and sub-rules the other; and Pluto rules one of Mars' signs and sub-rules the other.

DETRIMENT

A planet in the sign opposite to that which it rules, or sub-rules, is said to be in detriment, or sub-detriment. I attach less importance to planets so placed than most astrologers do. They consider it to be a 'bad' factor in a chart. In fact, Venus in Aries, for example, is not all that 'bad', though it often indicates, depending on other factors, a difficulty with the articulation or demonstration of love.

SUB-RULERSHIP: NEW POSSIBILITIES

It is probable that all the signs, with the exception of Leo and Cancer which clearly belong only to the Sun and Moon respectively, have a ruler and a sub-ruler. The reorganisation of the rulership system brought about by the discoveries of the three outer planets has left only two planets, Venus and Mercury, with two full rulerships. The others rule one sign and sub-rule another. Venus rules Taurus and Libra, Mercury rules Gemini and Virgo. These four signs are not as fully understood as the other eight. To take Virgo as an example: that it belongs to Mercury has always seemed clear in one sense: it is meticulous and orderly, and it figures as rising sign, or in other ways, in the charts of many cunning and thoughtful swindlers and financial crooks. But there is another quality to Virgo: something almost Scorpionic in its penetrativeness.

Clearly two more bodies, or possibly points, would be needed in order to give new rulers to Virgo and Taurus, thereby giving Libra and Gemini sub-rulers for the first time. Most astronomers now believe that there is a planet beyond Pluto; others admit that they do not know. Some astrologers believe that one of the larger asteroids, the belt of small planets which lies between Mars and Jupiter, or even the planetoid Chiron, may rule one of the signs. Another possibility, which I think less likely, is that signs may be associated with the galactic centre, the supergalactic centre or the solar apex. Who knows? But if Virgo has an unknown ruler, then Mercury sub-rules it, and Virgo's ruler sub-rules Gemini. Similarly, if Taurus had a new, as yet unknown, ruler, that planet or point would sub-rule Libra, and Venus would become Taurus' sub-ruler. If these new rulers could be discovered, our understanding of Taurus, Libra, Gemini and Virgo would be greatly enhanced.

EXALTATIONS

In my view exaltations are not very important, but they must be mentioned. The ancients pronounced the planets 'exalted' in certain signs, and 'in fall' in the opposite signs; this idea derived from philosophical concepts peculiar to certain cultures. Sakoian and Acker, two respected contemporary occultist astrologers,

Exaltations

South node
Moon
Saturn
Pluto
Neptune
Jupiter
North node
Moon
Sun
Venus
Mercury
Mars

In fall

base much of their work on ideas of reincarnation and on the notion that Sun is exalted in Aries, Moon in Taurus, Mercury Aquarius, Venus Pisces, Mars Capricorn, Jupiter Cancer, Saturn Libra, Uranus Scorpio, Neptune Cancer, Pluto Leo. In exaltation a planet's power, according to them and others, is released most effectively; the context is that of people who are spiritually 'highly evolved' – 'working their way back on the evolutionary arc of existence to the primary causal principles of life's manifestations'. When a planet is in its dignity, they say, it is placed so as it may express its less 'spiritual' principles easily.

I do not accept any of this. I have never met any 'highly evolved' people; or, if I have, then they will have taken care not to let me know about it. In any case, this is not a language I would use; nor is this book aimed at a readership which would use such language. It could be quite dangerous to assume that one was 'highly evolved', just as it is ridiculous to imagine oneself to be important.

Sakoian and Acker also say that a planet 'in fall' is in a very bad way. I reject this also; as in the question of dignity and detriment, it must always be remembered that a planet is a planet and works according to its principles wherever it is placed. However, the exaltations should not be dismissed. They provide valuable clues to affinities between signs and planets which operate, not at a 'highly evolved' level, but at a high level of sensitivity and self-insight and 'sophistication'. When looking at a chart, don't forget them: occasionally they can explain subtle features of the personality. Sakoian and Acker's set of exaltations is more or less standard, although there is not full agreement, especially about the outer planets. My exaltation scheme (see illustration) differs greatly from standard practice: I exalt Pluto in Virgo, Moon in Scorpio as well as Taurus, and Neptune in Leo. I have devised this scheme from empirical observation.

PLANETS IN SIGNS

I have said this before, but it cannot be emphasized too strongly that signs and planets differ in the following way: while the planets provide the power, the energy and the principles, the signs are areas, circumstances and conditions through which they operate. Think of a planet as a technologically advanced, high-powered model boat, operated by remote control. The boat requires very precise instructions if it is to make a successful voyage from one point to another. It is easier to demonstrate a model boat – let us say it is the planet Venus – successfully when the waters are still, the conditions found in, say, Libra. If the water is rough, say Aries, it is harder to operate the boat.

The analogy must not be carried too far. However, it does show that what is really important is the boat – the planets, Sun and Moon and the points. It shows too that, taken alone without other factors being considered, certain planets operate more 'easily' in some signs than in others. Whether the planets are in 'easy' signs is not 'good' or 'bad' in itself: it depends on other factors and on what a person wants to do, and whether he or she is able to do it, or cares. The analogy must not be taken too far, because more often than not other factors are in evidence. You may find, as I have from experience, that where a planet is in a sign with which it has no special traditional association, other factors are rather likely to be in evidence and to have a strong influence. When the planet is in its dignity, the other factors tend to confirm the meaning of the placement.

The model boat analogy can be taken no further, because, although the signs are clearly fields generated by the Sun's sixth harmonic and are probably marked off in other ways, they can also be considered as fields generated by their rulers so that the rulers may act in their natural fashion.

In a sense the signs are the most 'fatalistic' element in astrology. They can give useful indications as to circumstances towards which the subject of the chart (usually called 'the native') may find him or herself impelled.

In the following pages I give meanings for each sign, planet and point. You will notice that I have personalised them hitherto, and I shall continue to do so. This practice is frowned upon by some, but I choose to ignore the frown. It is obvious that signs, planets and points are not people: the personalisation is a metaphor, and a very useful one in that it makes the meanings considerably clearer. The avoidance of personalisation leads to circumlocution, which can be both misleading and pretentious.

THE MEANINGS OF SIGNS, PLANETS AND POINTS

I inevitably describe here the 'pure type', an almost entirely abstract concept, although a virtually pure type does occasionally turn up: this is most likely to happen where many other factors in the chart reinforce the tendencies indicated by a stellium (four or more planets in a sign).

While I have briefly described here the *principles* of the ways in which any two planets and points can combine, I have not written a full 'cookbook'. The fact that no book of reasonable length could possibly contain every possible combination of chart factors has not been my only deterrent.

I feel that the cookbook approach is an insult to the reader, who if he absorbs the instructions that follow will be able to work out the meanings of factors in charts for himself, and develop his own approach to chart interpretation. Furthermore the cookbook approach is misleading in that it cannot possibly cover every eventuality: after all, everyone's chart is different. For example, there are books which purport to tell you categorically what 'Mars square Jupiter' means. But, consider: Mars can be square Jupiter in cardinals, in mutables, in fixed signs; a cardinal square between the two planets might be between Mars in Aries and Jupiter in Cancer, or vice versa, or between Mars in Cancer and Jupiter in Libra, or vice versa, or between Mars in Libra and Jupiter in Capricorn, or vice versa, etc etc. Without taking into account any other factors, such as whether one or other or both of the planets is angular or aspected closely by a third planet, we have in fact twenty four possible types of squares between these planets. However, that is not the end of the matter: the square may be dissociate, adding several more types of possible square. A square in mutables is, in fact, very different from a fixed square: a square between Virgo and Sagittarius is very different from a square between Gemini and Pisces, although they are both mutable squares. Rather than present the intelligent reader with a bland and categorical generalisation, it is clearly preferable to offer him as many facts as possible, so that he may make his own decision as to the exact meaning of the precise square which confronts him.

Of course, even my simpler and less disingenuous method has its disadvantages. There is unfortunately no alternative to taking each factor in isolation in order to explain it, even though one knows very well that any single factor taken in isolation is meaningless: the whole is greater than the sum of its parts, in characterology as in anything else. Consider a part of the human body, say, the liver. This has a number of functions: it secretes bile, stores glycogen, synthesizes plasma albumen. It is a vital organ, but it cannot be meaningfully described without reference to the functions it performs, and these – as any biologist will tell you – depend on the way other parts of the body function. But biologists can, and do, describe the liver. Then their students, having learned about all the other parts of the body connected to the liver, put the whole together.

It is the only way, and it is thus with 'Mars in Virgo', 'Jupiter in Aries trine the Sun in Leo', 'Mercury in Sagittarius opposition Moon in Taurus (dissociate)' and so forth. Therefore, if readers wish to understand astrology fully, they should not use the following pages just as a cookbook; they should read them discursively as a biology student would a textbook on the human body. It is the only way to get a picture of the whole. The astrologer has to strive to see a chart in its entirety: essentially an intuitive art. It takes time to achieve, but suddenly one realises that one has done it, and that one will be able to do it again.

INTERPRETING SIGNS

ARIES

Absolute longitude 0000–2959. Positive Cardinal Fire. Initiative is expressed aggressively, impulsively and probably very emotively.

Keywords: *competitiveness, blind will, impulsiveness, eliminating-obstacles-without-thought, brutal criminality* or *martyrdom* or (most likely) a mixture of both.

ARIES IS ASSOCIATED WITH THE HEAD AND IS therefore the sign of the psychopath or the genius, or of the psychopathic genius. Those with Aries rising frequently manipulate others with great confidence, obtrusively or otherwise. Those with the Moon in Aries can be so compulsively emotional that their very emotionality may be mistaken for a mannerism: emotional behaviour can become so habitual that the subject is often unaware of it.

In Aries, the energy of Mars is combined with the metamorphic principle of Pluto and gives rise to criminal coarseness or innovativeness of a very high potency. Everything that leads is associated with Aries – the plaintiff in a lawsuit, the primary attacking force in war, the first move in a savage vendetta.

Those with Aries emphasised in their charts will often be very revengeful and, if there are squares to Cancer (the breeding ground of all kinds of emotion), desire for revenge will not fade but will be nursed, rehearsed and finally executed, even after many years. The subject of the chart on page 62 is a good example of this. He has taken ruthless, brooded-over revenges and engaged in impulsive acts of spite and, although in recent years the more violent characteristics shown in his chart have tended to fade, he will probably never succeed in ridding himself of the habit of drawing up lists of people or organisations regarded by him as inhuman – and against whom he will, sooner or later, act. Squares from Aries to Cancer always indicate some kind of violence, even if repressed. They only fail to operate if the bodies or points making up the square are non-violent (Venus–Moon is one example), but this is rare.

When strongly emphasised, Aries can sometimes have a kind of meticulousness. This may at first be easily mistaken for a Virgoan quality. Aries wants to get the job done, but all too often the nature of the job is unknown or useless, even impossible. But if the job is defined, and is intellectual or artistic in nature, the Aries person will rush at it so impulsively that he wastes energy through excessive, even violent attention to detail.

A writer with Mercury in Aries and nothing at all in Virgo might easily acquire a reputation for meticulousness and a desire for accuracy, but also for procrastination, the result of this obsession with detail. Aries is not always wholly heedless, although when it is strongly emphasised it will have to find a channel for heedlessness, for it has a terrible Plutonic objectivity.

One astrologer has said that 'Aries types' are not suitable for intellectual work. This is manifestly untrue. Anthony Powell, the novelist, has Aries rising but no planets there and his Moon is in Libra. There are countless other examples.

Aries, the field projected by Mars (with Pluto) for its enterprises, has to have freedom and has to project itself at all costs.

TAURUS

Absolute longitude 3000–5959. Negative Fixed Earth. Practicality may be felt in non-materialistic and satisfying ways.

Keywords: *creativity, gregariousness, egoism, kindliness, acquisitiveness, egotism, graspingness, affectionateness, enduringness.*

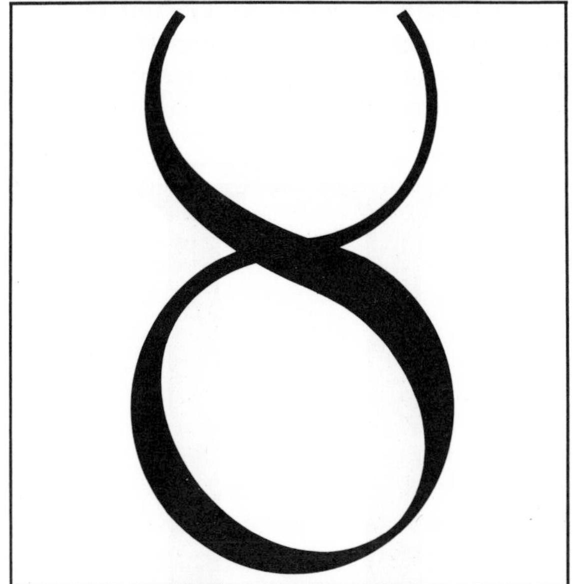

THE SUN IS NOT AS STRONG IN MOST OF THE signs as many astrologers think; but for some reason it is strong not only in Leo, which it rules, but also in Taurus. Hankar, a very original but little-known astrologer, thought it ruled this sign.

Taurus is the field created for its enterprises by an as yet unknown planet or factor with Venus. There can be much of the harmful side of Venus in the sign; idleness, loathsome gluttony, sybaritic sensuality and more.

Taurus is a much more secretly agitated psychological field than it is usually held to be and we see this in the case of Apollinaire (page 177) where it is very strongly emphasised. Ebertin is right in ascribing the qualities of the 'tense introvert' to those with Taurus emphasised; 'introvert' here is used in the sense of someone more interested in what is beneath the surface than in mere events.

Taurus is melancholy, but can be beautifully still when contented. The traditional exaltation of the Moon in Taurus is pregnant with meaning. It is peculiarly poignant. Security is nurtured by the sense of protection carried by the Moon.

There is always reflex action from Scorpio, which means that Taurus has something of the mysterious and penetrative qualities of Scorpio. One may gain insight into the nature of the Taurus–Scorpio axis if one remembers that Scorpio is associated with extreme degeneracy and its opposite; therefore Taurus people can often lapse into a gross materialism that has, if in rather a dull way, the true Scorpionic vileness.

This vileness can of course be wholly externalised, to the point where the subject cannot be considered in any way vile. In the champion tennis player Chris Evert Lloyd, who has Moon, Venus, Saturn and Asc in Scorpio, one sees it coming out in an icy, penetrative skill, put to use in an exacting sport; in the degenerate monarch, Farouk of Egypt, who had it rising with Mars and Moon (on Asc), one sees it at its most bestial. One notes that Freud's Scorpio Asc is balanced by Sun, Mercury, Uranus and Pluto in Taurus; and in the chart of Uri Geller, Moon, Venus and Jupiter are in conjunction in Scorpio.

Chris Evert Lloyd Moon, Venus, Saturn and Asc in Scorpio.

King Farouk Scorpio rising.

It may be thought that I am straying from Taurus to its opposite, but one cannot consider a sign unless one understands its opposite. For example, the multi-murderer Landru (p. 183) had a huge Aries stellium and Pluto (square Mars in Leo) in Taurus, but, despite his gross malevolence, nothing at all in Scorpio.

The same capacity for self-sacrifice may be found in Taurus as in Scorpio, though in Taurus it will usually be more egotistic and attention-seeking. Scorpio can get as near to selflessness as any sign. We have something of this in the example chart (p. 62), where the native certainly makes sacrifices but does so in a most unpleasantly cunning and attention-seeking way: he is unable to stem the histrionic force of the Aries stellium, which is fatal to his chances of achieving virtue.

If the Sun in Taurus is closely afflicted by Saturn, the subject will be neurotically hypersensitive, even to the point that he will scorn praise for fear it may be ironic, if not actually a concealed attack. Such people take things about as hard as anyone can take them – and often the causes of their agonising are trivia, or even creatures of the imagination. A person with the Sun in Taurus afflicted by Saturn and with Moon in Cancer is peculiarly prone to this kind of feeling and the behaviour it generates.

Just as Taurus desperately needs security, so it has empathy for others. This reflects the goodly, Venus, side of the sign as well as the more metaphysical manifestations of the other, as yet unknown, ruler.

Taurus traditionally rules the throat and neck; many people who are said to have nice voices have Taurus involvements.

GEMINI

Absolute longitude 6000–8959. Positive Mutable Air. Adaptability to circumstances or to the facts of the self may be handled with deftness and strategic skill.

Keywords: *duality,* but also *brotherhood* (the paradox at the heart of Gemini: the twins compete, fight and cheat each other, but also wish to love each other beyond human possibility); *communicativeness, slyness, shallow laughter, detachedness* (producing objectivity but a certain coldness).

Other useful keywords for Gemini are Mercurial: *agility, dexterity, impertinence, irreverence, adaptability, talkativeness, apparent inconstancy.*

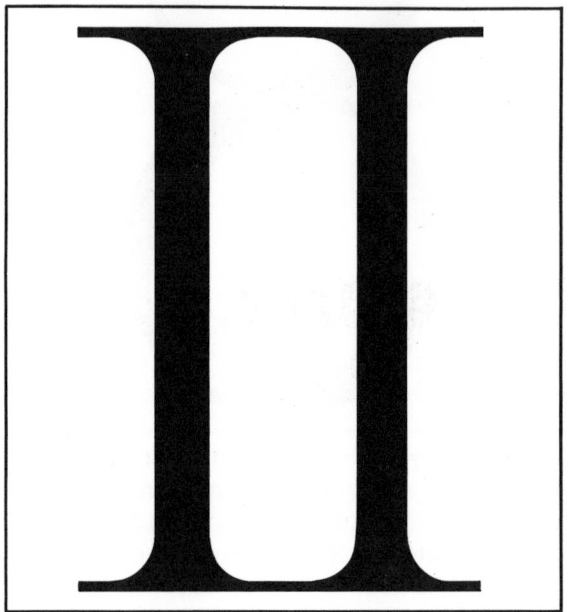

GEMINI IS THE FIELD CREATED BY MERCURY, with another very mysterious and laughingly sinister, but as yet unknown, force, in order to pursue its enterprises. Mercury has rather more importance than any astrologer has been inclined to give it. It is, of course, tied to the Sun (never more than 28° from it geocentrically), but the Sun, as will be seen, is weak and exhausted of astrological power, and Mercury steals a great deal of its strength. It is involved, you will recall, in nearly all radio disturbance patterns as the 'trigger'.

That those with Gemini emphasised are shallow, as has been almost universally asserted, is misleading. The problem for these people is that their natural habit of self-observation makes them seem cold, preoccupied with themselves, disinterested or even uninterested. When this combines with the dissipation of energy which Gemini almost always suffers, it gives the appearance of a slightly hysterical, or at least a shallow, personality. But hysteria is not in fact a Gemini characteristic, although appearance of shallowness is.

Gemini has a reputation for being clever but not robust. This again is misleading. In fact the Gemini mind is tormentedly self-analytical and so seeks relief in light entertainment or even in financial crime. Theodore Dreiser, author of *An American Tragedy*, based his famous trilogy – *The Financier, The Titan* and *The Stoic* – on a real crook. The trilogy demonstrates perfectly the Geminian type, and the protagonist is anything but shallow, though he is not altogether pleasant.

People with Gemini rising or dominant are frequently thought of by others, as often as by themselves, to be enigmatic. Where there is reflex action from Sagittarius in a concrete form (when Sagittarius is occupied or forms the Asc–Desc, MC–IC, VX–AX or nodal axis) then any superficiality is in any case wiped away; this reflex action is generally idealistic and it will be confirmed by other factors in the chart. None of that quality called human warmth comes from Gemini itself, but neither does any actual malice. Financial fraudsters are not usually malicious; they are, or at least the Geminian ones are, entertaining themselves and do not see robbing small investors as ruthless.

If Geminians are not in fact found to be cold as they are usually depicted, then this is often because of the Jovian Fire of Sagittarius; but the cryptic nature of Neptune, watery subruler of the third Fire sign in which it is now placed, should never be discounted. Does it make any aspect to a body or point in Gemini? Is it in Fire, other than Sagittarius? In our example chart (page 62) it is closely applying (orb 10′) to a 75° aspect with the North Node and therefore a 105° aspect to the South Node in Sagittarius, from Leo. These 24H aspects, multiples of 15, are very important: when close, they link planets and/or points together in a peculiar way. They carry the physical 'meaning' of the hard aspect between those two planets/points; thus Neptune in Leo –90– Nodal Axis (Gemini–Sagittarius) would indicate fiery disruptions, attacks on associations or institutions, rageful insomnia, misunderstandings, or, as in this case, because Mars is square to the Nodal Axis, burns and scalds.

The fate of a Geminian who has strongly emotional indications in his or her chart can be harsh, though it is never devoid of colour; the Geminian without much emotionality leads what is sometimes called a 'charmed life', or a scattered, wasted one. He will be less unhappy than his emotional counterpart. The sign itself, like Mercury, which is master of the nervous system, has no emotion at all in itself. Even its humour is heedless and unemotional, or concerned with sexual communication. Traditionally Gemini rules the nervous and respiratory systems and those with the sign emphasised tend to have quick reflexes.

CANCER

Absolute longitude 9000–11959. Negative Cardinal Water. Initiative is expressed emotionally, receptively, protectively, tenaciously and intuitively.

Keywords: *protectiveness* and *self-protectiveness, deviousness*, which may or may not necessarily involve deceit, but may mean simply that the native cannot approach matters directly or crudely and is therefore an exquisitely tactful and intuitive person.

Cancer, to put it mythologically or metaphorically, was the gentle field created by the all-female Moon, when the Sun had reached its midsummer point of highest declination (in the northern hemisphere), in order to express the natural order of all things on earth.

However, the sign is no 'better' than any other, just as mankind is not perfect. The Moon in Cancer is the most immensely powerful of all positions, but not necessarily either for good or for bad. Where it appears in the first degree of Cancer it supplants the ruler of the chart (the planet ruling the Asc), and the aspect relationship between the Moon and this ruler is crucial.

The Cancer-dominated person tends to live out his present in his past, or to nourish the present, protect it and worry at it in order later to be able to cherish it, vile or beautiful, in his memory. One man, a poet I knew well, whose chart was dominated by Cancer, once advised me very sadly: 'Never go back'. He was standing on a wall looking down at a house in which he had lived twenty years before. The reality did not live up to his image of it.

Cancerians often seem to be afflicted by self-pity, but sometimes they are simply worrying over past experience, analysing it to discover if they may have been slighted or abused. The Scottish poet, Norman Cameron, described such people very well when he wrote of himself, 'cronelike in my self-motherhood'.

But while Cancerians can be envious, or shrewish and spiteful, and harbour fearful grudges, they are also almost impossibly loyal and efficient protectors of their loved ones. Often they may misguidedly go too far for they are very jealous.

Like Pisceans, they sometimes become over-sentimental or impossible to deal with due to over-indulgence in alcohol. The Cancerian whose work makes him a public figure is particularly prone to this. He may dislike living near water, but may often find himself forced to, and his home may be affected by serious dampness.

Obviously the Cancerian may be anything

Enoch Powell Moon and Neptune in Cancer.

Leo Tolstoy Asc, Venus and Saturn in Cancer.

emotionally from exquisite in his love for all men and women, to maudlin-sentimental. But the sign offers opportunities for love which can overcome the most serious misfortunes. The past may seem pointless, but the Cancerian knows best that only upon experiences and developments of love may valuable relationships be founded. Cancer is shrewd as long as it is not overwhelmed by sentimental self-analysis.

The Cancerian's tendency to collect things – old bus tickets, for example, and other ephemera relating to the past – is harmless, although it may be untidy. Cancer's humour is probably the subtlest of all the signs. Each sign has its own type of humour, but Cancer's comes nearest to being a humorous way of looking at all things. It laughs at itself and its 'crone-like self-motherhood'.

Reflex action comes from Capricorn, which can supply the passive, sentimental dreamer with enterprise, though not always successfully. The right-wing politician Enoch Powell has Moon and Neptune in Cancer in wide conjunction, but the Moon is opposed from Capricorn by the Asc. Here, wrong-headed enterprise has soured a career. The Birmingham Welshman who might have been a prime minister has become almost a comic 'Irishman', because of his strange but apparently sincere prejudices and his failure to put himself across to enough people.

At other times, Capricorn is very successful in exerting its reflex action. Leo Tolstoy's Asc, Venus and Saturn (the latter bodies conjunct) in Cancer were put to brilliantly versatile work by Mars and Neptune in Capricorn.

LEO

Absolute longitude 1200–14959. Positive Fixed Fire. Enthusiasm for the self and others is expressed in an authoritative and proud way.

Keywords: *ritualism, superstition, pride, self-assertiveness, elitism, self-dramatisation, magnanimity, vivification, egotism, integration.*

LEO RULES THE PHYSICAL HEART AND ALSO what we call 'the heart'; emotion registers as generosity. A heavily-tenanted Leo can be an embarrassment to an ungifted person, leading to the most absurd airs and pretensions. An emphasised Leo does not confer gifts: the native will behave regally, whatever qualities he possesses, and if he does not possess many, or is not satisfied to operate locally – as secretary of the local darts club, or dramatic society, for example – then he may occasionally appear comically pretentious. But the bodies in Leo are usually badly afflicted in these cases.

On the other hand, it is scarcely surprising to learn that Robert Graves, author of *I Claudius* and widely held to be the greatest

Robert Graves Asc, Sun, Moon and Mars in Leo.

love poet of our century, has Asc, Sun, Moon and Mars in this sign. Leo is generous to those whose other chart indications are in his favour, but can be a relentless enemy, especially if any body in the sign is afflicted by Saturn in Scorpio.

It is interesting to compare the Aries–Cancer form of revenge with the Leo–Scorpio type. Both are equally ruthless and spiteful, and neither sticks at lies. However, the Aries–Cancer revenger is usually aware of his 'foul play', especially if he has Gemini connections, in which case he will probably enjoy destroying a person's life or reputation if he cannot learn to stop himself. The Leo revenger, while he does not speak the truth, does genuinely believe the worst, which he contrives to discover and then regally announces to the world; he has the need to feel virtuous. Aries–Cancer is more secretive and will be content with a series of small, nasty acts spread out over years; Leo likes to inflict one big defeat and then stride on, never mentioning the name of the victim again.

The Sun is as strong in Leo as it is in any sign with the exception of Taurus. But the Sun is an enigmatic and weak body nowadays. Those with the Sun and no other body or point in Leo can sometimes experience grave problems. Although they are not pretentious like the ungifted ones with Leo rising or with Leo stelliums, who can at least give expensive parties at which largesse appears to be given, they may sometimes feel fragmented or divorced from themselves, in just the manner that those with unaspected Suns do.

There can be a very useful reflex action from the opposite sign, Aquarius, if the native is peculiarly prone to pomp and circumstance. The Saturn side of Aquarius can well balance overstated pomposity with its cold humanitarianism and natural sense of justice. Aquarius may have its own problems, but it is always in itself just.

The Moon in Leo, along with other factors, can often redress the faults of the sign, but the Moon in Leo by itself can create serious problems. Moon in Leo unaspected may leave the native bewildered and fragmented, since the purely female Moon is placed in the sign of the Sun, which has been incorrectly regarded as the 'masculine principle', a pernicious, and yet almost universal, error.

VIRGO

Absolute longitude 15000–17959. Negative Mutable Earth. Practicality can be achieved with meticulous adaptability. There is something, not as yet fully acknowledged by astrologers, very strange about Virgo. A sign of great beauty, but often of great suffering.

Keywords: *discrimination, analysis, indecision, deviousness* (not in the Cancerian sense, but as the result of a deeply-felt experience that efficiency cannot be achieved by direct methods), *calculation, fussiness, loyalty, tidiness, hypochondria, the cutting out of the useless and wasteful, excessiveness in the matters that are the principle of the sign.*

As a sign, Virgo is perhaps the most misunderstood, although Libra runs it a close second. Virgo is the field created by an unknown planet, with Mercury, as the area in which it may express its somewhat mysterious principles. It is just possible that Mercury itself has qualities not hitherto ascribed to it, but this seems not to be the case, important though the twinkling and elusive body is.

The famous, and by no means unjustified,

reputation of Virgo for being at the same time meticulous and unable to make decisions is certainly a Mercurial function: Mercury can easily be turned by its condition in a chart into a body which sees so much of both sides of a question that it cannot make a decision.

This particular type of indecisiveness will most often occur in a chart in which feeling does not greatly affect thinking, or in which feeling itself is nebulous: it is therefore perhaps as likely to involve Moon–Mercury–Neptune and Pisces configurations as it is to have Virgo emphases.

Nonetheless, the Virgo-dominated person does from time to time experience this sort of indecisiveness, but in these cases I believe that the indecisiveness is reinforced or triggered by the mysterious unknown ruler of Virgo, which also sub-rules Gemini. Gemini, of course, is famous for 'seeing both sides of the question'. The mental direction of Mercury is determined by aspecting planets, but it is also influenced by sign-placement. If Mercury is in Virgo, where tradition has often exalted it, it acts in a decidedly peculiar manner.

But with what, at the profoundest level, is the practicality and efficiency of Virgo concerned? Virgoans are certainly not concerned simply with efficiency for its own sake. In pseudo-astrology, usually based on Sun signs, 'Virgo people' are often portrayed as virginal, dull, fussy, subordinate and over-concerned with hygiene. In fact, Virgo is above all concerned with assimilation as a means to pursue its ends. This assimilation is of all that is valuable in experience, but valuable towards what?

Many swindlers and confidence men have Virgo rising or very heavy Virgo involvements. Most criminologists are agreed that Herbert J. Bennett was convicted of a murder which he did not commit, but he was a deceitful confidence man. He had what amounts to a Virgo stellium: MC with Mercury, Venus and Uranus. The Sun was in Leo, which may have been unfortunate for him, particularly as it was in square to a Moon–Neptune conjunction in Taurus with the Moon applying to this square. Mercury in Virgo was in a fast-applying biquintile to Saturn in Aries, which in this chart was very unfortunately placed. This last gave him considerable power in the exercise of dishonesty and thoroughness in the calculation of it; in fact, a well-structured criminality. The midpoint of the aspect, which very considerably strengthens it, is afflicted by the Moon in an acquisitive Taurus and by Venus in Virgo, which indicates inconstancy, retarded development, a woman who has thoughts of separation, instability in affection, unfaithfulness. Bennett was separated from his life by false evidence.

This is a case in which midpoint-midpoint aspects may be used; the rule is only to bring these in when you cannot explain a curious fate – in this case being hanged unjustly for murder. In this case Mercury/MC forms a grand trine with Asc in Capricorn and Moon–Neptune in Taurus, which indicates in short an over-estimation of self and being misunderstood; being hanged unjustly is an extreme case of this. The grand trine also suggests relationships which change too rapidly: Bennett's wife was cheating him and he was cheating her when she was killed. The whole picture is one of deceit and misunderstanding.

Madame Blavatsky, charlatan, liar and fake spiritualist, had three planets in Virgo (Mercury and a conjunction of Saturn and Mars). A large number of swindlers and politicians of the slippery, clever sort have Virgo rising. But the merely foolish Tsar Nicholas II, who listened to his perverse wife, lost his life due to his crass heedlessness.

In other words, Virgo can get people into certain kinds of misfortune, in part because the sign is wholly antinomian – its moral values are absolutely those of the native. Thus, those of us who have a planet in Virgo will take our own way in the areas of life associated with that planet. The so-called super-ego, that part of conscience formed by training and environment, is rejected by Virgo, though never openly. Rather, Virgo represents the creation of a personal conscience free from the taints of environment. That creation of the private conscience, which is almost impossibly unselfish, may give us one of the keys to the nature of the unknown planet or factor which rules Virgo.

The ruler of Virgo, Witte said, was Hades, a hypothetical planet whose characteristics are 'malefic' in the generally accepted sense. Hades represents dirt, squalor and revulsion. Its principle is 'disintegration', but its function, according to Witte and his followers, is the preservation of life and thought: the manifestation of feelings of disgust, which prompt the individual to remedy the circumstances which cause them. Hades is an unpleasant-sounding planet and we should be glad that it does not exist. Or should we? Its principle is essential to life; it breaks things down. Like a horrific fart, it relieves the farter of perhaps intolerable flatulence. In other words, like any of the planets which are so-called 'malefic', it is 'benefic' as well, but it is dangerous and usually extremely unpleasant in its effects. It is hard to see the 'benefic' side of such a planet, but it is equally hard to see the 'benefic' side of the swarms of bacteria in our intestines. Nevertheless, we need them.

It is clear that those with the Moon in Virgo or Virgo rising, or with heavy Virgo stelliums, are amongst the most puzzling personalities we encounter. Like Scorpio, and to a certain lesser extent Taurus and Capricorn, Virgo is capable of heights or depths, but these are not necessarily obtrusive. The Virgo person is a 'deep one'.

Virgo people are apparently very much preoccupied with protocol, and sometimes they are well behind the times in their view as to what is permissible by way of decorum. This is a matter of practicality. No sign's scorn for protocol is so profound as that of Virgo. Yet at its heart, as perhaps at the heart of every component of astrology, there is a desire for virtue. But Virgo's is secret, intense, cryptic and subject to dangers. Clearly squared, or other, aspects between bodies and points in Virgo–Gemini have to be considered very carefully.

LIBRA

Absolute longitude 18000–20959. Positive Cardinal Air. Initiative may be expressed mentally and harmoniously.

Keywords: *balance, adjustment towards harmoniousness, reconciliation, reciprocation, greed* (because of the Venus influence, Librans often compensate for unhappiness or stress with bouts of gluttony), *indecisiveness* and therefore *fussiness* – not as in Virgo, but because weighing in the mind or feelings is not easy, especially when the principle is justice rather than a semblance of fairness.

LIBRA IS THE FIELD CREATED BY VENUS, WITH the ruler of Taurus, to express its principles most easily and effectively.

It is paradoxical that this graceful and harmonious sign should sometimes be heavily involved in the charts of criminal politicians, such as Hitler, or ambitious and possibly dangerous leaders, such as Douglas MacArthur. It is vital to understand that where there are certain afflictions, what may seem like balance to the Libra-dominated person may not seem at all so to other people: Hitler's Asc is in Libra, parallel to Pluto and in opposition to Mercury in Aries. This is a significant aspect, here indicating total inability to deal with his own or anyone else's emotions or feelings.

One of the great difficulties facing astrologers, myself included, is that while they should speak of signs and planets in a morally neutral way, it is impossible to do so. Undoubtedly

Franz Liszt Sun, Mercury and Midheaven in Libra.

each sign does represent a field of conditions in which the principle of its planet or planets may be exercised in a virtuous manner. But what is virtue? We find that we continually refer to individual charts, nearly always retrodicting instead of predicting, pointing out where things go wrong. This is because, in life, things viewed at least from the highest standards usually do go wrong. It is not always, after all, 'good' to be successful, although it may be if popular success, for its own sake, has not been sought.

Now the 'goodness' of Libra is a rather obvious goodness. The truly harmonious Libran is one who wants to create harmony for its own sake and not for his own. Libra adjusts continually, trying to create equilibrium, but it is sometimes a little inhibited in this and thus its cardinality can give it a certain roughness so that it can be a fierce sign. Hitler's Asc was admittedly badly positioned but his malice also arose to a certain extent from Libran fierceness. There are at least three types of Libran: the decisive Libran, who will probably be a menace; the indecisive Libran, who can be very sweet and often successful in putting things into harmony; and the truly harmonious Libran.

Hitler was a decisive Libran who wanted to 'right the balance' but in an utterly perverse, indeed psychotic manner. Ex-President Carter, who has Sun and Asc in Libra, is an indecisive Libran. Franz Liszt, a paradoxical personality, was wild, restless and exhibitionistic, yet his best music is beautifully balanced and exceedingly generous. Its bases are so often 'redressing a balance' of gratitude, by dealing with the tunes of others – paying homage to them – or with landscapes he loved, as in *Annèes de Pelegrinage*. Liszt had Sun, Mercury and MC in Libra, but his chart, a complex one, contains many subtle and difficult aspects, requiring harmonic analysis; these confirm his essentially Libran nature.

The huge Capricorn stellium of Louis Pasteur (six planets) was undoubtedly balanced to an extent by the fact that he had Libra rising in square to that sign. But truly harmonious Librans are not well known people: in most cases, being well known in itself creates disharmony.

That Libra was a late-comer to the zodiac, as is frequently stated, is incorrect. It is the seventh sign in the Babylonian MULapin tablets, though the Babylonians did not always call it Libra. But that some peoples did call it the 'Horns of the Scorpio' indicates that it may have puzzled them. Its weakness is not that it has principle which is easily displaced into malice, but that its passion for balance and grace can become over-emphasised.

SCORPIO

Absolute longitude 21000–23959. Negative Fixed Water. Emotion may be expressed penetratingly, intensely or coldly.

Keywords: *concentrated power, intensity, refined passion, destruction* (frequently to build anew, in the spirit of its opposite, Taurus), *elimination, disposing of things.*

SCORPIO IS THE FIELD CREATED BY PLUTO, with the violent (rather than defensive) energy of Mars to express its principle of transformation most easily; we need to try to understand Pluto to understand Scorpio.

Scorpio is a notoriously vicious or noble sign, and its properties may have been over-simplified to those who follow crude Sun-sign astrology. The Sun in Scorpio often means nothing at all, though in certain circumstances it can have significance.

Very often, people whose characters would lead you to suppose that they had powerful Scorpio involvements seem to have none at all, or only one planet there. In the latter case it is frequently worth looking closely at that planet's condition overall. The sign itself exercises a very powerful influence over whatever it contains, except that an isolated Sun can be very weak and 'un-Scorpionic'. Scorpio rising is always very powerful, as is MC in Scorpio. The vertical axis passing through Taurus–Scorpio is also highly significant.

Scorpio conflicts with Cancer in that it does the opposite of collecting. Quite often the Scorpio-dominated person has to travel around, even when he or she could settle well, easily and comfortably. Scorpio-dominated people frequently feel themselves burdened with tasks which they do not fully understand, and they frequently stir up trouble for others simply because of their own unease. Sex can be difficult for them (the genitals are traditionally ruled by Scorpio), because they see that it is at one and the same time the negation of the intensely spiritual and yet one of the only ways of reaching the level at which we are able to feel spiritual.

In one case I have encountered, that of a person who combines the expression of pure beauty with the practice of absolute evil and who is typically Scorpionic in nature, only the MC and the North Node are in Scorpio. There is a yod on Neptune in Gemini from N. Node and Sun in Capricorn; although this yod is skew (meaning that the two quincunxes are out of orb) nevertheless Sun/Node exactly opposes Neptune. Also Mars/Neptune is square the MC, and there is a Capricorn stellium. The native is unquestionably paranoiac, though not so severely as to require institutionalisation. All that that person has done has failed, although while the 'beautiful part' deserved better, the 'evil part' brought only grief, unhappiness and waste. Here we see the power of Scorpio MC acting with a Capricorn stellium, for, as has been mentioned, Capricorn is one of the signs which reach abysmal depths and apparently unscalable heights. But while one does see evil, coldness, selfishness and spite in Scorpio-dominated people, one also sees the opposite, and occasionally only the opposite, qualities.

Sometimes the properties of Scorpio do not manifest themselves openly, in which case the

Marie Curie Venus, Mars and Sun in Scorpio.

native leads a turbulent inner life. More frequently, indeed usually, there are other indications in the chart that balance out the extreme difficulties presented by the sign.

As with other strong indications, the whole power of Scorpio may be sublimated into some transformative act. A very obvious example is Madame Curie, who had Venus, Mars and Sun in Scorpio, with an exact square from Neptune in Aries to Uranus in Cancer as well: an undoubtedly difficult chart. All Marie Curie's energies went into that most Plutonic of activities, the discovery of the radioactive substance radium, and she died through her contact with it. She lived an unfortunate life – among other misfortunes her husband died in a street accident – and yet a rewarding and curative one. Asc was in Aquarius squaring the Sun; MC with Mercury in Sagittarius. When one thinks what she could have done with such a chart, one has to be astonished at her will to do good, which was undoubtedly inspired by the elevated powers of Scorpio.

A skew grand trine may have helped her greatly, in part because it was just skew. All three trines which are between Sun–Moon, Sun–Uranus, Moon–Uranus, are separating; but Moon/Uranus = Sun suggests a very strong will, a woman of very great energy and a defier of the perverse side of the masculine principle. Since the Sun is in close opposition to Pluto in Taurus, Pluto is also involved in this configuration, indicating changes that take place quickly, and developments which are important to the public. Pluto is also, of course, the planet that rules the process of radioactivity.

SAGITTARIUS

Absolute longitude 240000–26959. Positive Mutable Fire. Enthusiasm may be expressed inspirationally, idealistically and directly or tactlessly.

Keywords: *extension, expansion, foresight, prophecy, anticipation, apprehensiveness, idealism, pride, reaching-outness.*

SAGITTARIUS IS THE FIELD CREATED BY EXpansive Jupiter. The Sagittarian is always concerned with the future. Those who are teachers of some kind, and many are, are concerned with the future of those they teach, and they tend to view them in an idealistic and protective light. They want to give help, but they are famously blunt; they are forever shooting their ideas, desires and aspirations into the sky. Without helpful features in the chart, they fail to see, or even consider, where their arrows will fall.

However inspired – and the sign is certainly inspirational – Sagittarians can be superbly candid, and can often help greatly on occasions when it would seem at first that they had hurt people's feelings badly. There is humour and sometimes a gift for mimicry, but this humour is not of the subtler kind of Cancer or Taurus, or at all like the sharp wit of Scorpio.

The chief ruler, Jupiter, if it is placed in Capricorn and there are bodies in Sagittarius, can cause serious complications. Margaret Thatcher has Venus and Antivertex in Sagittarius and a very severely afflicted Jupiter in Capricorn. Lindbergh whose adventures cost his baby son his life and who certainly lied at the kidnapper Hauptmann's trial, had Moon, Uranus and Asc in Sagittarius and Jupiter in Capricorn afflicted by Mars/Neptune: this last configuration indicates ill-luck when wealthy among other things.

Sagittarius often knows, without thinking, what people will do. Those with strong Sagittarian involvements can become accurate prophets. This is probably a Neptunian influence, once again. The intuition of the Sagittarian is broad rather than subtle, except in cases where Neptune is significantly placed. (It is interesting that Neptune has been in Sagittarius for some years, and is still there.)

However, Sagittarius is often unerring: it has a gift of precognition that amounts to a superb and helpful, healing empathy. If Cancer knows what people are feeling, Sagittarius knows what they are going to do and often feels helpless to prevent it. Sagittarius, despite its basically harmless and certainly unmalicious tactlessness, is so apprehensive that it is sometimes speechless, powerless and under the spell of its lucid and frequently tormenting precognitions. It can sometimes get into the habit of ignoring them or dreaming them and then dismissing them as 'only bad dreams'. This is particularly true of those with Sagittarius rising, and they can therefore be robbed temporarily of the strategy which is really the function of the rising sign. There is an empirically proven association of Sagittarius with compulsive gamblers. The reasons for this type of gambling are well known: al-

Thatcher Venus and Antivertex in Sagittarius.

Lindbergh Moon, Uranus and Asc in Sagittarius.

though the gambler will usually deny this, he is not trying to make a profit or extend himself, but attempting to be complex and Neptunian, having a desire for punishment and to lose. Gambling is an abuse of the prophetic faculty; if Sagittarius once understands this, it will stop gambling in every sense.

CAPRICORN

Absolute longitude 27000–29959. Negative Cardinal Earth. Initiative may be expressed restrainedly but ambitiously and with great practicality.

Keywords: *getting to the top* or *reaching the depths* (often externalised: Capricornians can end up with 'hopeless' partners), *irresistibleness, ambition, industry, unobtrusiveness, shrewdness, restraint, humour* (a safety valve for the pressure to succeed), *strong concern with sexual expression, dominance within strict limitations, bossiness, direction, management, pragmatism.*

CAPRICORN IS THE VERY HIGHLY STRUCTURED field created by Saturn in which it may exercise its principles; but drastic, sudden Uranus is sub-ruler, and we have here to consider the Saturn–Uranus principle: tension. Capricorn is a tense sign, though tension in the lives of Capricorn-dominated natives may well be externalised. The tension in the life of Pasteur, who had six bodies in the sign, came not from him, but from those ill-willed men who opposed his notions and from the difficulties and dangers he experienced in his experiments with vaccination. His life was tense, though industrious, but he himself was not a violent man. He persisted. Pasteur's Uranus in Capricorn is quintile to the Asc in Libra and is near to a 20H aspect with Mars also in Libra. These 20H aspects seem to convey, among other things, a quiet, persistent facility; one of the multiples of 18° is of course 72°, the quintile itself.

Capricorn is somewhat solitary, frequently finding itself alone. Saturn does, as I have mentioned, possess a sort of grim humour, but this cannot always be a consolation, especially when the influences of Uranus are threatening to undermine what appears to be the Capricornian stability. Oppressive loneliness or a slide towards instability can often be resolved through great industry. The horrors of the depths, the dizziness of the heights, may be stilled by the content of industry.

Yet, of course, the tension of Capricorn, while difficult, can be productive. This may be in an 'evil' direction as with J. Edgar Hoover who had the Sun, Mercury, Venus and Asc in Capricorn. Hoover's Uranus in Scorpio in exact sextile to Venus provides a good illustration of how malevolently the opportunities offered by sextiles may be taken, when they are taken at all. The poet John Dryden, himself an astrologer, derived positive energy from his Capricorn involvement. He had Capricorn rising in exact trine with a Moon–Pluto conjunction in Taurus. His Uranus in Virgo was connected with Saturn in Scorpio by close and applying septile; the two rulers of Capricorn were thus connected in such a way as to create conditions in which the tension between them was able to be intuitively, or inspirationally, dissolved. This aspect could indicate other things, but the predominant consideration here is the fact that it links the ruler and the sub-ruler of the sign together; a Uranian Virgo is a help to practical innovations.

Capricorn has acquired its not wholly deserved reputation for sourness and surliness

J. Edgar Hoover Sun, Mercury, Venus and Asc in Capricorn.

John Dryden Capricorn rising.

Louis Pasteur Six bodies in Capricorn.

from its recognition for the need to bow or kneel (traditionally it rules the knees) before some higher authority, whatever it feels about it. Often such authority will be despised, in which case Capricorn can seem very sour indeed. Capricorn does not necessarily like rationality or structure, but it recognises the need for both; you will find this trait even in those who have only the Sun there.

Capricorn's cardinality and earthiness imply practicality and make it very intolerant of inertia. In those with the sign dominating this energy is not always simply Saturnian industry: it often comes from Uranus.

I have already mentioned that the worst characteristics of Capricorn can be brought out by its containing an afflicted Jupiter. One should not forget Hitler, whose Jupiter in Capricorn was conjunct the Moon. As I have pointed out, a conjunction can on occasion be an affliction – it is a hard aspect – and in Hitler's case the desire to help others which the aspect often indicates became monstrously perverted. Hitler's Jupiter and almost certainly his Moon, by transition of light, are afflicted by Saturn/Pluto: this indicates frigidity, lack of feeling for others, fanaticism and sickness – in this case psychotic sickness. The afflicted Jupiter in Capricorn often also indicates hatred or resentment of the parents, whether conscious or otherwise.

Few of those with Capricorn dominant in their charts will refuse positions of responsibility, whether they are capable of carrying them out or not. Some have positions thrust upon them, domestically or in a wider field. This is a sign which achieves much, and its achievements are usually noted.

AQUARIUS

Absolute longitude 30000–32959. Positive Fixed Air. Adaptability and inventiveness may be expressed with spontaneity and at times extreme, if casually manifested, obstinacy.

Keywords: *gregariousness, association, immediacy, speed, inventiveness, detachedness, stability, scientific rationality* and *creativity* (it is in this sign that modern logical scientism may be modified by human feeling and the recognition of the irrational elements in human life), *intuition, synthesis,* sometimes *cruelty, eccentricity, crankiness, perversity, erraticness, distractedness, rebelliousness.*

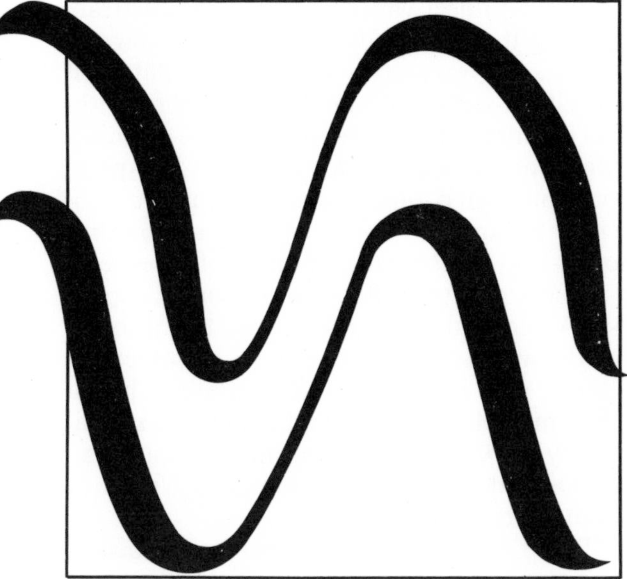

AQUARIUS WAS GENERATED BY URANUS TO express its principles, but, without the structuring powers of Saturn, this could not be achieved; the sign would have 'gone wild'. Aquarius is a difficult sign to understand. The 'modern' aspect of it is not difficult, but the ancient and Saturnian aspect is combined with this and so presents great problems.

Again we see Saturn attempting to control violent impulses, though Uranus is by no means harmful in its own sign. Aquarius is concerned with drastic rearrangement of the old, but at heart it wants to make the old older rather than newer because Aquarius, and others, see what is conventionally considered old to be new. Uranus is progressive, but also dedicated to the truly antique which in our modern world, it must be remembered, is a new phenomenon. This is why the action of Uranus throws out so much false newness, often without knowing why it does so: hence its drastic, electric qualities. Uranus can be an excessive planet as well as a very curious one.

Although, even in 'good' people, Aquarius often seems devoid of feeling, it implicitly assumes the 'I-thou' relationship which is at the heart of true love, but being distracted, it can easily forget to put this into practice; this can be disconcerting. However, aspects to MC and Asc or other bodies in Aquarius, and the presence of Parts or midpoints linked to bodies there, can, and usually does, largely correct this tendency. For example, Venus sextile to an Aquarius MC offers the opportunity to take the roughness out of a Mars in Aries.

Vanessa Redgrave Sun in Aquarius.

The Sun alone in Aquarius can make an eccentric rebel, such as the politically motivated actress Vanessa Redgrave. Traditionally Aquarius rules the ankles and the circulatory system.

PISCES

Absolute longitude 33000–35959. Negative Mutable Water. Flexibility and mercy may be expressed secretly, nebulously and unselfishly.

Keywords: *dissolution* (of structure, of materialistic needs and perhaps of the truth), *nebulousness, universality* (in a mysterious sense, where systems, theories, methodologies are paramount), *inarticulateness* (more properly perhaps, *silence-in-the-interests-of-being-at-oneness*).

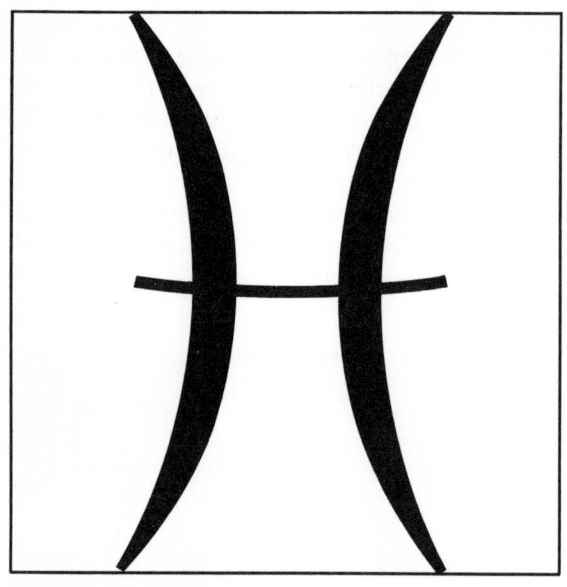

NEPTUNE CREATED PISCES TO EXPRESS ITS principles but needed Jupiter, which for millennia was regarded as its ruler, to counteract its vagueness and extreme refinedness – to lend some kind of stability to the most uncertain, the twelfth, of the twelve signs.

Pisces does not analyse in the way its opposite Virgo does, though the reflex action of its opposite often finds fertile soil for analysis; Pisces literally dissolves. The Pisces-dominated person often appears to be mystical. Pisces has to feel that it exists and so it is something of an actor; it may dissolve its perplexities in drink or drugs, which temporarily dissolve the barriers between the reality and the dream, whose meaning may be lost to the lost Piscean. Mercury in Pisces combust Sun is a good, inelegant linguist.

Pisceans are frequently keen on travel (reflecting the influence of Jupiter), self-effacing, modest, kind, secretive, reticent, hard to pin down and sometimes offhand. They do not often seem to be intense, unless they are very heavy drinkers or drug takers, in which case they quickly become stupefied. They are very often passionately attached to animals, a Neptunian trait.

Squares to Pisces from Sagittarius are often very interesting, having about them a quality of the sub-ruler Jupiter. When Pisces becomes degenerate, it is not only Neptune indicating drugs that is involved; it is also Jupiter which signifies excess.

The Piscean drinker is something to behold, but Pisces in its own unconventional way is impelled to discover no less than the meaning of life, a project which imposes a great strain causing it occasionally to fall for the vulgarly occult. But very often it seeks to fulfil itself in selfless service to another, or others, without counting the cost. In this it can be astonishingly patient. For service to others in a practical manner is one means of gaining a concrete 'meaning' to life, if only a subjective one – and what more can many of us expect?

Pisces receives reflex action from its opposite Virgo. This sign, as I have stated, also has to do with service and can be as selfless as Pisces, but its motives are more analytical than metaphysical, unless it contains a significantly aspected Neptune, in particular an opposition from Pisces from, say, Venus or even Mars.

Pisces need not lack treachery or atrocious vanity wrapped up in nebulousness: we see this, sometimes, with a badly afflicted Sun in Pisces. I know of a distressing example of self-deceit, mediocrity, false grandeur and alcoholism, which involves Sun in Pisces.

INTERPRETING PLANETS

I cannot emphasise two things too strongly: first, that the foregoing descriptions of the signs are not descriptions of the 'types' which may result if the Sun is placed in them; and secondly, that an absolutely pure type is very rare. I chose to use the metaphorical device of personalising the signs, and also the planets which follow, because I wanted to draw the reader's attention to the nature of the sign rather than to anyone in particular who was under its influence. It is for the reader to blend together the indications he finds in individual charts.

Of course, in a chart such as that of Pasteur, there is a very strong Capricorn influence, and this is instructional, although he is by no means a 'pure Capricorn' type. However, the main intention of my descriptions of the signs is to throw anticipatory light upon the planets and to help to show how they work in the various signs. It must never be forgotten that the planets provide the power, even though the signs, the areas in which they operate, are very significant.

Despite the rulership associations between planets and signs, the two must never be identified. Where there is a stellium, or even a single planet, in a sign in close aspect to a planet in another sign, the nature of the planets in both the signs must be considered. 'Mars is always Mars.' This assertion, made by a number of astrologers, is true, but Mars' action is subtly modified by three factors: its position in the diurnal circle (that is, its position in relation to its rising point in terms of the earth's rotation); the aspects made to it in a number of great circles, principally the ecliptic; and its sign placement.

I have spoken of the signs being 'generated' or 'created' by the planets. This is, I hope obviously, metaphorical. But I should add that the Sun's sixth harmonic plays some unknown part in this, since the tropical signs are certainly generated by that harmonic from the Sun's nodes. Each planet can, of course, be said to 'have its own zodiac'. Each has an equatorial node in Aries. We could, if we had time, place all the other planets in a particular planet's zodiac, and we might want to consider in what sign a planet was placed in its own zodiac. The subject is an experimental matter at present.

Only the Lunar zodiac, measured from the position of the north node at birth and used frequently in Hindu astrology, is touched upon here occasionally. Aspects from planet to planet are not affected by its use, but significance is attached to aspects from planets in the Lunar zodiac to planets in the Sun's zodiac. These tend to show how the past will affect the present.

THE SUN

The Sun, most problematic of bodies, is at the centre of the solar system and appears to 'drive it'. Life on earth is undoubtedly owed to it, if not also to other factors of which we are ignorant. Yet it should not be forgotten that 98 per cent of the angular momentum of our system is vested not in the Sun, but in its planets.

Modern pseudo-astrology, and even some serious astrologers, place enormous emphasis on the Sun and its position. Some astrologers can indeed guess people's Sun signs with scores above chance, but it is never stated whether the ones they get right are Suns reinforced by at least Mercury and Venus, and perhaps by other factors. I think this is the explanation, although some of them may be especially sensitive to that basic existential disappointment which everyone carries within them. Aspects to the Sun are important and do manifest themselves in people's characters. Nonetheless, its sign placement is not usually very important. My interpretation of the Sun's meaning is entirely new; it is derived from extensive empirical observation. Astrologers interpret the Sun fairly consistently. It is held to represent self-integration, self-sufficiency and the 'true will to be': the form of the latter can supposedly be judged from the Sun's sign.

It has been stated that a 'weak Sun' indicates a poor and unlucky life. This notion comes from a second-rate American form of astrology which does not concern itself with midpoints. If you have Sun in Libra or Aquarius, seriously afflicted or with no major aspects, don't worry; this interpretation is palpable rubbish.

According to all astrologers (or all that I have read) the Sun represents 'the masculine principle'. Jeff Mayo calls it 'spirit, mind, the living being'; Ebertin describes it as the will to live, the urge to rule, decisiveness. In a chart it represents the subject's basic drives, and the sign it is in shows the nature of them.

All this is based, not unreasonably, on the Sun's obvious importance to us, on its central place in our system, on what we are taught about it. But it ignores the fact that certain activities, or cycles, on both the Sun and the Earth are monitored by extra-solar factors, and that these cycles may be traced through study of the positions of the planets. I do not claim that the planets modify activity on the Sun; I merely make the factual statement that the position of the planets in relation to one another is an index to some cycles and conditions on Sun and Earth alike. This is becoming increasingly evident.

The worst error made by astrologers is their description of the Sun as 'the masculine principle'. The Moon is certainly feminine, all feminine, and in a number of ways it exercises a greater force upon the Earth than does the Sun. But why should the Sun be masculine? Is this not to assert that what gives life to all on Earth is purely masculine? This is a grotesque, indeed an evil notion. For astrologers, myself excepted, the Sun is actually more important than the Moon.

Can we say that the male is *more important* than the female – we, who are born of women? How could the life-giving Sun be purely male? We now know for certain that in the absence of another factor, any baby will be born female; female is the 'natural' sex. This is almost a biological truism – or would be if more biologists were female.

I do not wish to state that the Sun itself is female, nor to make the unhelpful assertion that it is a hybrid. I merely point out that it is as female as it is male. But throughout history, with the exception of a very few mythological systems, the Sun has been seen as a male God or hero.

The most pragmatic view of the Sun in the chart that I can offer is this: that it does indeed represent the drive towards self-integration and the need shared by all human beings to be what they are, to be harmonious. All of us are made up of different and usually conflicting 'selves'. The Sun does indeed represent

Albert Einstein Sun in Pisces.

the will to reconcile these selves. But what does experience show? Few, if any, people achieve this harmony. So, if we view the Sun as in one sense a *point of vulnerability* in the chart, we may gain the most insight.

The man with the Taurean Sun wants security, but he will not get it, at least not fully. The condition of the Sun shows the way in which a person's failure may operate, but it may also show how his partial success might be achieved. Einstein's Pisces Sun (MC was also in the sign) is a good example of this, and, incidentally, of how simplistic Sun-sign astrology fails. Anyone who thinks that Einstein's results, his first and second theories and his other work, are in any way Piscean is badly misled. If Sun-sign astrology were valid, then Einstein's Sun ought to have been in Scorpio or at least Aries, particularly when it is recalled that Linda Goodman, author of *Sun Signs,* the best-selling book on Sun-sign 'astrology', maintains that a person's Sun-sign will be an amazing '80 per cent' accurate. Charles Harvey, on the other hand, has said on television that 'we use the Sun no more than about five per cent in judging charts'. This is a useful correction from a serious researcher.

This notion of taking the Sun's condition (condition being sign-placement, aspects, mid-point-connections, etc) simply as the 'point of vulnerability' should not be overdone. In a crude, self-satisfied person, you would only see its manifestation at deeper levels: emerging in behaviour indicated possibly by aspects to the Sun, such as a square from Mars or Jupiter. The delusion of self-satisfaction is not the same as self-satisfaction. We will not often get admissions, except from the intelligent who recognise that life is a struggle for virtue, or decency, or whatever terminology they prefer, that there is any vulnerability. The person who wants to eliminate all that he imagines he dislikes will not easily see that he fears what he dislikes: that fear could be shown in his Sun position.

To put it a trifle pretentiously, the Sun indicates the 'wound of existence' – that sense of dissatisfaction with the world which most sensitive people feel – and therefore feel with themselves as well. A square from Mars, often producing the 'hair-trigger personality', may be no more, therefore, than an inflammation of that 'wound', or of that sensation of what Paul Tillich called 'existential disappointment'. Clearly, whatever the Sun's condition, the will operates independently of the chart. Therefore, some are more successful than others at overcoming – indeed accepting – this sense of loss.

An astrologer may see ways and means in a chart, but he cannot say whether or not these will be followed. They are frequently related to the puzzling and misunderstood sextile aspect, which means 'opportunities not taken, with consequent sorrow or terror', as often as it means 'opportunities'. If the creative imagination is given a full rein, the effect of the Sun in the chart may be much modified; again, utilised sextiles may play a part in this.

More pragmatically still, the Sun in a chart should be looked upon as the native's chief need (when those needs represented by the much more 'natural' Moon have been excluded) but it is no indication at all of how strongly that need is sought after in life.

Hitler's Sun was in Taurus (p. 178). It lacked major aspects and it made him feel 'inwardly fragmented'. There was, however, a square to the Leo MC (ambition, conflicts with his father) and there was also a very close semi-sextile to Neptune. Taking the rest of his chart into consideration, we can see that he was made psychopathically ill by the failure to realize his chief needs, which were to have security and values or principles.

Thomas Hardy, a good man, had his Sun in Gemini (p. 185), but even here Hardy was hypersensitively vulnerable when his freedom of speech seemed threatened, although he had good reason for his resentments. Apollinaire's Virgo Sun (p. 177) indicates his frustrated need for practicality and efficiency in his life. Ironically, he found this in the army, but he was no killer and hated being one.

It is probably septiles to the Sun which give it the greatest grace, although from which planets and under what conditions is obviously important.

THE MOON

The Moon is not a satellite of the Earth. The two bodies revolve around each other, the time-period of the loop they describe in space as they jointly orbit the Sun providing the most powerful and potent series of prognosticatory information known to astrology. This is known as the Tertiary Moon, and was first discovered (or rediscovered) by the German Troinsky. One day in the ephemeris is taken to represent one of these loops, or to put it in a different way – since most people continue to regard the Moon as a burnt-out satellite of the Earth – one day in the ephemeris measured from time of birth represents one complete circuit of the Moon around the Earth; that is, to when it returns to its radical position.

Keywords: *receptivity* to every feeling manifested by living beings, human or animal; *emotional response* or what used to be called *instinctive habits; the feeling-nature; meditation* (particularly upon the past, but in its relationship to the immediate present); the *female principle* in all its mystery and male-derided wisdom; *changeability* (woman's naturally cyclic nature); *moodiness* (reflecting the subtle, female-driven cycles of nature); *adaptability* (at the depth of one's profoundest emotions); *feelings of protection.*

The Moon, not the Sun, is at the centre of astrology. It is often said that in a woman's chart the Moon represents herself and that in a man's it represents the wife *and* the mother. No case can be made out for any but the first assertion; that the Moon represents wife and mother in male charts is to take too grim a view of life. In a male chart, where the Moon was found to represent wife-mother, the native would be very sick and his wife very unhappy. The truth is that the Moon/Sun midpoint, and its condition, is about as near as you may come to finding the actual wife (or sexual or living partner) in a chart. The condition of Pluto tells us much more about the mother than the Moon does.

It is convenient at this point to state that, so far as any planet can be 'sexed' at all, the 'male' planets are Mars, Jupiter, Uranus and Mercury, while the 'female' planets are Venus, Saturn, Neptune and – emphatically – Pluto. This is a rough and ready guide only; most of the planets can become masculinized, and where something is seriously wrong (dictator, tyrant, psychopath, 'hopeless case') this is often what has happened.

Jeff Mayo is right when he defines the Moon as that which 'actuates . . . life processes, the function necessary for bringing a process into action, for animating psychic processes with active properties.' It is a pity he should add 'The Sun is the source of all life-energy . . .', for astrologically this is not true. In any case, what is life-energy? As human beings, our energy would be inhuman and our rhythms depleted without the Moon. Mayo himself writes: 'Without the Moon, man would be denied vital animation . . .' What more could he say to deny his previous Sun-centred statement?

People who have a powerful Moon – a Moon near a cardinal point, or in Cancer or in Taurus, or in a dominant series of aspects – are essentially nurturing, emotional, sensitive and, when not content, cyclic, in the psychiatric sense that they can go from 'up' to 'down' very quickly. Sometimes they are restless, but they will not be so if they can move with the natural rhythms. The Moon has the power to change unpleasant or squalid environments. Those who cast off difficult pasts do it with the aid of the Moon's condition in their charts.

The Moon will manifest as whatever activity in a person is spontaneous, and it is perhaps as much as one hundred times as obvious in a sign as the Sun is. It is not a part of the function of the Moon to be interested in logic, although it can very usefully humanize those whose charts might otherwise indicate that they placed all their reliance on what they can understand rationally. Although the Moon behaves subtly, it may be looked upon as indicative of the areas of life in which emotional energy is likely to be released. It is, however, so powerful a body that it can quite frequently act against itself by reflex; the native behaves in a manner entirely different from that which his chart suggests.

MERCURY

Mercury is never more than about 28° from the Sun and about 76° from Venus. When it is in a conjunction with the Sun of less than 30′ I consider it to be combust. In these circumstances it will have a strong effect on the native's way of thinking, making him or her intense, strange-seeming and one-sided.

Keywords: *communication, mentality, cunning, co-ordination, consciousness* (Mercury does not act unconsciously at all, although it may act subconsciously), *analysis, adaptability* in the sense of co-ordinating the nervous system, particularly hearing, sight and touch, with the surroundings.

You cannot always derive the level of intelligence from an astrological chart, but the condition of Mercury will reveal a great deal about the type of intelligence a person has, however much of it he may or may not possess. This is why aspects to Mercury are so important. The person with an unaspected Mercury will constantly consider and reconsider, almost in a Virgo manner; this is because there is no strength – no other planet – driving his mentality. But placement in Gemini or other signs can compensate for this, as can septile aspects and other even more subtle ones, such as the 13H series, which tells us about the native's attitude to death and to the feeling of deadness in life.

Those with Mercury in Aries or Gemini gesticulate a great deal; and the planet, unless it is unusually subdued which it sometimes is by Saturn, is naturally very volatile and even merry. Mercury has no emotion, except that it finds great amusement in teasing, in being sceptical, in being slight or flippant; it is certainly, if one may so put it, anti-pompous. Mercury is curious, clever, lucid and fluent, and it becomes frustrated if this last quality is inhibited in some way. It is shrewd, but not, in itself, profound. Writers, though they do not have Mercury in Gemini more than anyone else, almost always have very active Mercuries. Bertrand Russell's unaspected Mer-

Russell Mercury in Gemini, septile to Saturn.

cury has been pointed to as a remarkable factor, but astrologers have missed that it is in septile to Saturn, the perfect aspect for a philosopher who changed his ideas many times in the course of his life.

Mercury co-ordinates sensory experience, although it is not interested in it. It does this together with certain other planets: Saturn, for example, is involved with hearing. In the 125H charts of the blind and deaf statistically significant afflictions to Mercury have been found: in Kepler's 125H chart Mercury is quite closely opposed by Neptune, with a close semi-sextile from Uranus; he had very bad eyesight.

In synastry, the comparison of two charts, Mercury is a vital factor because it helps us judge how two people will think together, or will fail to do so; and it gives clues as to what, if anything, can be done to remedy difficult situations: for example, when people argue constantly, but do not wish to do so.

VENUS

Venus is never more than about 48° from the Sun. It is a planet contributing largely to love, but also to superficiality, greed and possessiveness. It is thus an important factor in judging a person's attitude towards money and possessions.

Keywords: *relatedness, peace and quiet, graceful surroundings, beauty, relaxation, greediness, self-indulgence, wallowing sybaritically in luxury* or *giving out a sense of harmony, arranging affairs pleasantly*.

Venus is the 'laziest' of the planets, although it can easily be, and usually is, energized by other factors in charts, especially by Fire, Mars and Pluto. It cannot be intellectualized. It has some close affinities with the Moon, but the latter cannot energize it even in close, hard aspect, though Moon-Venus squares manifest themselves precisely as romantic, lazy and possessive. The difference between the Moon and Venus is exemplified in Venus' rulership of the Positive Air sign Libra. Libra's urge is to balance polarities and Venus has a specific field of operation in that sign; this suggests that, unlike the Moon, Venus must have potentially 'malefic' qualities, because it will often take violence to balance polarities. But the enemy must come from the unknown sub-ruler.

Venus is cooperative unless afflicted. In the chart on page 62 we have a violent Aries-Cancer Venus-Pluto square, very close: the native is turbulent and can be a trouble-maker of a relentless and malicious kind, but he can equally be very cooperative. The square, though productive of dangerous and self-destructive behaviour, is afflicted in the 32H series by at least the node and this indicates a desire to associate. The result is that, with the square separating, indicating a degree of control over it, the situation is not as difficult as it could be.

Venus in Aries is energized, but not often elegant. Writers and artists who have it there are seldom celebrated for their style, but more often for their roughness and even their luridness and madness. Were the native of our example chart a writer, he would be either morbid, excessively outspoken or highly satirical. Mercury is in Aries, and Venus is energized by Fire from Pluto and connected to the MC by sextile; Venus/MC is linked to Mars/Saturn – this last is a midpoint-midpoint aspect.

Mars-Venus connections are very important: Mars can harden Venus but Venus can also soften Mars, especially in conjunctions in signs where Venus is strong, namely Pisces, Taurus, Cancer and Libra. A conjunction in Scorpio is very difficult and needs to be judged in terms of its orb and condition. Venus/Mars is an important midpoint in terms of sexuality and of attitude towards others.

The Moon is in a significant sense 'beingness'; Venus is less fundamental and even harder to grasp. It is best described as a person's 'passive desire-nature', and it can therefore be unpleasantly selfish as we sometimes see when it is afflicted in Taurus. Hitler's Taurus Venus, which was certainly hardened by its conjunction with Mars, craved not for simple adulation, but for screaming adulation. Here, Taurus failed entirely to modify the malice of the afflicted conjunction.

But even in Hitler's bizarre case, Venus indicates a desire to be cherished (*to cherish* is a function of the Moon), which easily leads to vanity. Venus is usually more 'difficult' in male than in female charts. It represents much of the feminine and indicates how a man might be able to come to terms with the femininity in himself and in his environment.

Venus-Uranus involvements, hard or soft, have for many years been regarded as indicators of homosexuality or sexual deviance, but no serious statistical work has been done on this. My own studies suggest that Venus-Uranus contacts do indicate homosexuality in certain circumstances, but that very unfamiliar harmonics are involved. This may not be simple homosexuality, the physical manifestation of desire for the same sex. It may instead be unconscious or repressed homosexuality.

W. H. Auden alternately felt ashamed of his homosexuality and revelled in it. He never faced the problem in his poetry, but made a clever pretence of doing so. He had a separating conjunction of Venus and Uranus, 4° 23', in Capricorn. Mars, Uranus and Mercury were linked by 11H aspects, indicating excess, and Pluto conjunct Moon was square to Asc/MC. Venus was in a series of septiles between Moon-Pluto and MC, which was in Leo and took an exact semisextile from Neptune in Cancer. Venus was opposed to Neptune, and Venus/Neptune squared Uranus from Aries, indicating in Ebertin's words 'erotic aberrations', 'wrong ways of love'. Because Venus represents the need to evaluate people and things truthfully, the nature of the difficulties caused by the afflictions to it in Auden's chart are fairly clear. But there is always a solution in any chart; unfortunately many people, Auden included, do not find it. He clearly failed to take advantage of the sextiles his Venus made to the Mercury-Saturn conjunction in Pisces; but the moderation Venus in Capricorn can confer would have made an easier way out for him. Unfortunately this manifested itself in his well known and hypocritical insistence on 'good behaviour', a typical example of which was his once saying to a friend, when it was suggested they visit someone, 'I can't see X: he doesn't pay his bills.'

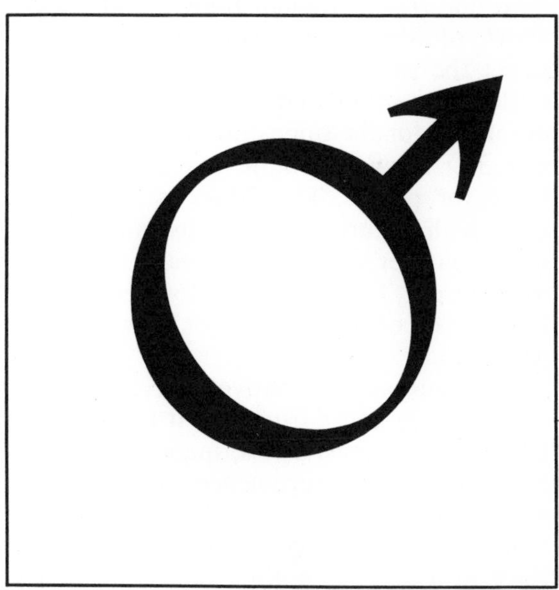

MARS

Mars is badly defined by Henry Weingarten, a well-informed astrologer, when he writes: 'Creative, generative energy which, in a struggle against natural resistance of the Eternal Feminine, masters, penetrates and fertilizes it'. Mars is not male-centred in this sexist sense, but just as the Sun has been masculinized, so has Mars been made male in the wrong, 'macho', way.

Keywords: *energy in attack or defence, heat, lust, aggression, loss* (in an externalised sense: Saturn is more separative), *boldness, direct activity, self-projection, attempts at mastery, self assertion.*

There are people who have violently afflicted Mars who live peaceful lives. Difficulties can arise when there are aspects, usually hard, to Mars from the three outer planets. I have noted in my own work that 11H aspects of Mars with these and other planets can be very difficult; it is as if Mars made 11H almost exclusively excessive. Margaret Thatcher (p. 180) is an example. In her chart, the square from Mars to Pluto is applying but wide (5° 17'), but Mars/Pluto is afflicted by MC and Venus, which are in square, and by the Sun. That reduces the effect of the orb and puts Libran Mars at point-focus of a skew T-square; it squares the menacing Jupiter-Pluto opposition, though Jupiter/Pluto is out of orb of Mars. That Mars does not fully collect the energy of this opposition, which would give it sound and positive energy, is not promising, for the opposition itself (its orb is only 31′) means no more nor less than the desire for power. This Mars is in an 11H series with Saturn and Uranus, and Saturn in on Thatcher's Asc and seems to be wholly externalised: Thatcher does not herself bear the burden of her desire for power – the people do.

Mars is usually combative. It gives courage, independence and daring, but it is also often the cause of offensiveness, impetuosity, egotism, intolerance, turbulence and warmongering.

In the chart on page 62 there is a subdued Mars in Pisces with four bodies in Aries. This sort of placement often leads to trouble, since Mars is frustrated but powerful as dispositor of four bodies – and, when given the chance and the right conditions in Tertiaries or transits, boils up and is ready to make trouble for all the native's enemies. Anyone who does not agree with the native on any matter he regards as important becomes an 'enemy of humanity', especially government officials, such as tax collectors. On occasions the native has made such people the victims of ferocious practical jokes and harassing, scurrilous attacks by letter. This is Mars in Water, letting off steam; the Fire is there to boil it up.

Mars figures in most indications of obvious cases of neuroticism. It needs to be sublimated, its energies channelled into useful and constructive activities. But when we think of it as the 'lesser infortune' or the malefic, we should also remember that its function is to provide the energy that is needed for self-preservation, as well as self-projection.

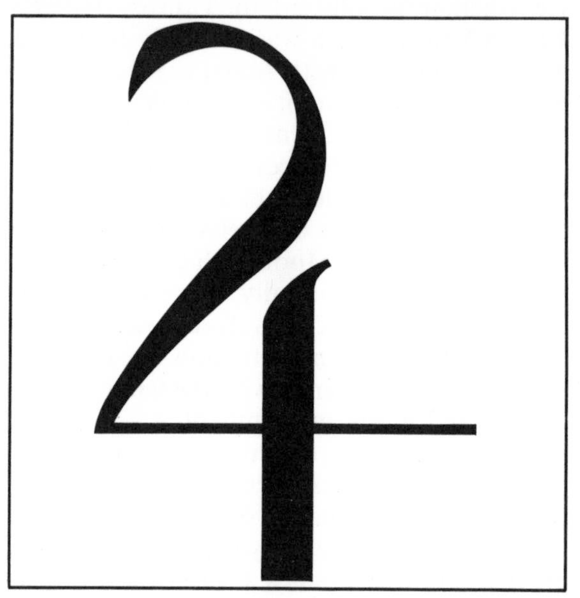

JUPITER

Jupiter is the largest of the planets, the traditional source of good will and creativity. Keywords: *expansion, extension, improvement, increase, jollity, generosity, luck* (in certain circumstances), *self-development, progress, opportunism, power, liberality, conscience, law* (but not the letter of the law), *depth, prophecy* (and at best, *caution*) and above all, *creativity.*

Jupiter, the traditional great benefic, is obviously more pleasant than the traditional great malefic, Saturn. But both are wholly necessary. An afflicted Jupiter and often a Jupiter in a position of high intensity in Gauquelin's sense, can lead people into evil or terrible difficulties or both. A trivial, but instructional, example is that under the influence of Jupiter people tend to become overweight.

Jupiter is the planet of moderation, but it can, under certain conditions, be far more immoderate than the planet of immoderation, Mars. Jupiter, being essentially creative conscience, is very easily corruptible. Hard configurations in which Jupiter is involved, such as true grand trines, can be exceedingly dangerous, creating very unpleasant, indeed horrible, characters. Moon-Jupiter conjunctions, although they ought to be useful, are often very dangerous – the French multi-murderer Landru and Hitler are examples; these conjunctions seem to give a sense of over-importance. There is sympathy and empathy and other pleasant traits, but Moon-Jupiter is dangerous more often than one would expect. To some extent this applies to all the aspects between these two bodies, despite the fact that such aspects add to any protective trait the native may have. Landru seems to have been very protective of his victims' bodies, for few were ever found. Certainly there is nearly always restlessness; Jupiter is the opposite of Venus in that it is very active.

One common mistake of astrologers, who are on the whole conventional in their non-astrological outlooks, is that they tend to equate Jupiter with conventionalised conscience, with the super-ego the state or parents wish to inculcate. Jupiter in that sense is rebellious, though it would not be in a different world. It is in fact true conscience, which is quite indefinable in contemporary conventionalist terms. The decent dropout – in the age of unemployment, when the young are robbed of hope and the old of comfort – is often 'Jupiterian' in finding it necessary to 'do his own thing'. After all, Jupiter meditates, philosophizes and requires the rapidly fading freedoms provided by democracies, so we ought not to be too surprised if we find today what seems like a touch of Uranus in Jupiter. Uranus can be very self-willed and selfish in interpersonal relationships; Jupiter in itself is the opposite: it wants to be generous. But the misused Jupiter of the politician or tycoon is a true malefic; one sees it time and time again in Nazi charts, where it occupies positions of high intensity.

Another common error is the equation of Jupiter with vulgar success. Jupiter can indeed be the most harmlessly vulgar of planets, as Sagittarius can be the most vulgar of signs; but the success Jupiter seeks is integration of the personality and, above all, to be able to give without vanity or self-praise.

The creative conscience of a person, especially a man, is his own imaginative myth-making, the essence of his dreaming, his relation with life itself – not its perversion. This is Jupiter's true function. It does not necessarily involve creativity; response to creativity (poetry, painting, music) is enough, and so is living within one's own mythology.

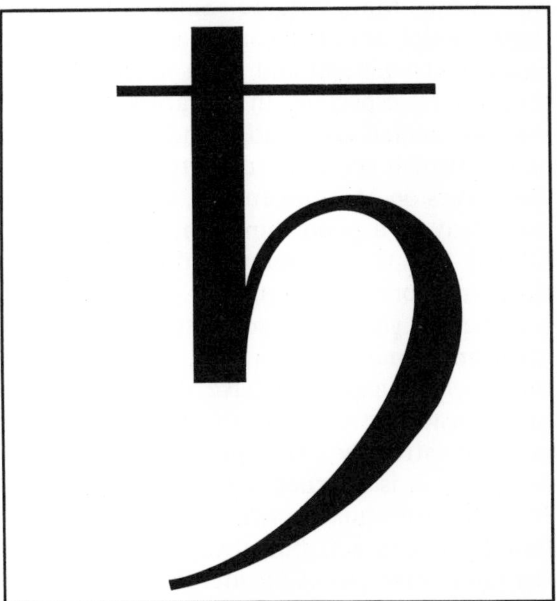

SATURN

Saturn is the second-largest planet; towards the end of 1980 – just before its regular 20-year conjunction with Jupiter – it very amusingly suggested to scientists that their laws of physics might be incorrect, and set many of them to work establishing that the space-probe was wrong.

Keywords: *responsibility, order, limitation, moderation, concentration, practicality, perseverance, sadness, remembrance of things past, separation* (of all kinds), *the enormous joke of death, control,* with the Moon *structured con-*

sciousness, self-denial, sacrifice, coldness, the iciness of living death (hell in its frozen state), *depression, solitude* (that part of us which must live it out alone), *stability, ritual, boredom, the inexorable nature of time, the religious sense* (with Jupiter; the condition of Jupiter-Saturn often indicates the nature of this), *caution, conservation.*

There is good reason to believe that even in the most burdened lives, the Jupiter-Saturn trine is helpful, as most astrologers assert. A Mars-Saturn square has a very bad name among astrologers partly because it is between the two traditional 'malefics' and partly because Hitler had it. It is supposed to indicate cruelty, hardness, brutality, 'blood-lust'. This is by no means inevitable, and Hitler's square was Venus-Mars square Saturn (in fixed signs), which is not the same as Mars square Saturn. The general and most usual effect of this square, especially in mutables, is that it makes a person go in stops and starts, rather as the British economy used to. Saturn puts the brakes on Martian energy, which in some cases may be a good thing, and vitality is inhibited. But the two planets do not have to clash and one manifestation of this square can be to give a person great powers of endurance and perseverance. It is not the most helpful aspect to have, but it can give one characteristic which no other aspect can give so strongly: the power to conquer obstacles. It is instructive to contemplate the Mars-Saturn square; you can see how differently it can act, but always according to the same principles. Consider it in each of the qualities. Of course, you need to look carefully at the condition of each planet. The Mars-Saturn trine is similar but much weaker, and indicates a physically 'stop-start' nature. The sextile can be deadly or brilliantly helpful, depending on whether and how it is used. In these contacts, there is often great bitterness.

Saturn, when in a position of 'Gauquelin' high intensity is said to produce 'introverted scientists', although it produces a number of other kinds of people, as Gauquelin now concedes. Those with Saturn dominant in their charts range from cruel tycoons to witty and cynical creative people.

Paul Getty Saturn in Libra, opposed by Jupiter.

The unhappy tycoon Paul Getty had Capricorn rising, which made Saturn into his chart ruler, which undoubtedly confers planetary strength. Saturn was in Libra, opposed by Jupiter; Asc was in a skew T-Square to it. This indicates a lack of self-confidence: sometimes the native is oversure of himself, at other times he feels worthless. Getty, with MC and three planets in Scorpio, compensated for his lack of confidence by buying objects and people, and then denying the people all he could. His five marriages were famously unhappy, his meanness notorious, his ill luck in losing his two sons great. His well-known face, the paradigmatic physical view of a man who went totally unloved, has the exact look of the Jupiter-Saturn opposition when it is allowed to rampage unchecked. His Sun-Mars square, which could have given him some sparkle, was drenched in the misery of a Saturn which brought him nothing but his cautious operation within the law, though it did bring some good to others through his self-defensive philanthropic devices.

Thomas Hardy (p. 185) had Saturn exactly on his vertex. He did not lack a sense of humour by any means, but was Saturnine in his attitudes towards life. However, Saturn is compulsively realistic about the nature of life, as was Hardy, who has always been unpopular for it. Some comparatively 'easy' Saturn positions can be dull rather than imaginative, though a remedy is usually at hand. Saturn is not a planet that can be said, of itself, to wish to 'live dangerously', but those who have it angular will know what fearful blows it can deliver: how it can be seen to be the destroyer of love, decency and honour; and how events signified by it in tertiaries or transits can appear to bring forth demons.

Saturn wants stability, loyalty, restraint and decently old-fashioned but non-hypocritical honour. It may stop people wreaking revenge, which it regards as wrong. If Mars defends, which it does quite as much as it attacks, then Saturn protects the self by surrounding it with order, which makes Saturn's traditional detriment in Cancer somewhat puzzling.

Saturn in Cancer can be very positive, although it can also indicate over-dependence on the opinion of others. I have the chart of a man who had Saturn conjunct Venus and Sun at the beginning of Cancer, and square to Neptune in Libra; there is also a Leo Asc and a Leo emphasis. Life is very difficult for this man, whose marriage broke up solely because of his inability to admit to his own hypersensitivity and pride.

Saturn is at the least solemn in Mutables, especially in Sagittarius where its placement is, obviously, paradoxical. (How can limitation expand? The answer is that it can well be modified.) However, when it is influenced by the Moon, Saturn makes a great contribution to the saving grace of humour. The Saturnine cynic can on occasions be both wise and witty, and the traditional sadness of the clown or 'funny man' is usually Saturnine. Saturn in 15H aspects with any body or point, most especially the Moon, may indicate that the native regards humour as one of the keys to the meaning of his and perhaps all life.

The conformist Saturn-dominated person (Margaret Thatcher has it on the Asc) is essentially lonely, friendless, over-serious, inhibited and negative. Sometimes we see this concealed by an artificial buoyancy which usually fails to convince.

Saturn rules bureaucracy, the organisation of state, duty and so forth, but we must not make the mistake of imagining that it rules these affairs *as they are* and as the novelist Franz Kafka exposed them; whatever remains good in them, it rules, otherwise it rules them *as they should be*. This is what gives Aquarius its reputation of being 'Utopian' or even 'anarchistic'. Saturn might by its great sorrowful destructive power bring such misfortunes to governments as to destroy their heartless bureaucracies. Saturn, though cold, is not 'inhuman'; there is warmth in laughter – even at the enormous joke that we do not know why we are here – and a fine irony in the fact that Saturn seems to rule scientists. Saturn also rules the 'small' in the 'small is beautiful' sense that has recently become familiar to us: it rules contraction.

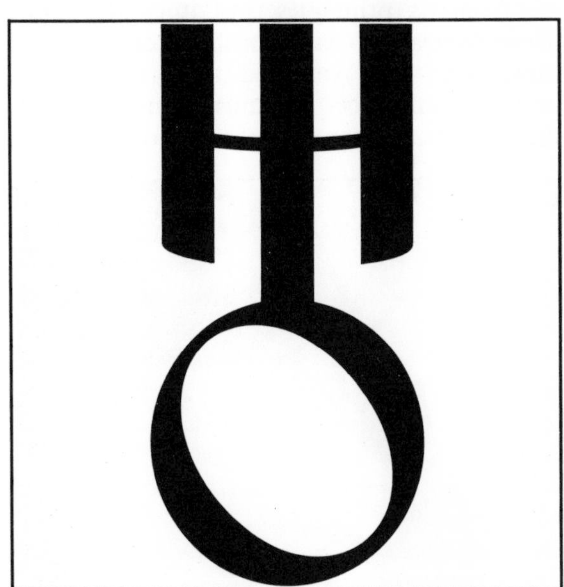

URANUS

Uranus was referred to in the old Ephemerides as Herschel, after its discoverer. The glyph for Uranus conventionally used in Europe is different from that used in this book, which is an older device whose resemblance to a television aerial makes us wonder at the nature of what we call chance.

Keywords: *freedom, independence, change* which may look *innovatory* but which is often an adaptation of new technological factors to nature, *unexpectedness, electricity* and all wave-form energy, *originality, instantaneous fury, extremity, heedlessness, disruption, revolution, unreliability, unpredictability, rhythms, ESP* (in connection with Pluto, Neptune and most usually Mercury), *genius, intuition, eccentricity, deviation, intellect, uninhibitedness, drama, reformation.*

The nature of Uranus, well attested, looks very like the opposite of Saturn. In charts the two can indeed be in conflict. But an understanding of Aquarius, where Saturn maintains control over Uranus, shows how they can work together in balance. If we take Saturn to be working for the natural structure, then we can take Uranus to be working with it by destroying what is unnatural in order to re-form.

Uranus is technological, as we can easily see from its principles, but it is also anti-technological; it will smash machines, and those who have smashed machines did so under its influence. We must remember that the planets, if not ourselves, work for the natural order, an order we cannot pretend to understand much about.

The effects of Uranus in individual charts vary greatly. In the chart of the prudish Mary Whitehouse Uranus opposes Mars. Mrs Whitehouse is intellectually undistinguished and that opposition has led her into waters far too deep for her. She has become, through lack of insight and through a wrong channelling of her lusts (it must be remembered that we all possess lusts), a comic disrupter, an advertiser for the pornographic, the joke of more than a decade among those less disturbed by sex. The black revolutionary Angela Davis, who has been more effective than Mrs Whitehouse in achieving her aims, has Uranus conjunct Mars.

The extraordinarily high energy of Uranus requires sublimation. The person with Moon square to Uranus will need to control his very violent emotions if he is not to get into trouble. In the chart on p. 62, the Moon is square Uranus (wide, but effective: 4° 37′) and the aspect's midpoint is square MC; this gives a proneness to states of great excitement, but does not give the native himself an opportunity to control the energies of the square to

Mary Whitehouse Uranus opposed to Mars.

Angela Davis Uranus conjunct Mars.

sensible or decent use. Release from tension under this configuration is very hard to achieve. It may attract accidents, so that the native is so ill he cannot be tense, or it can lead to misuse of drugs or alcohol. In so tense a chart as this, exhaustion from overwork or catastrophe seems to be the way to relaxation. A Uranus-Jupiter opposition is examined on p. 162.

NEPTUNE

The function of Neptune may best be illustrated by the way in which it was discovered. The whole affair was Neptunian from beginning to end. It was officially discovered in 1846. In fact an astrologer called Lalande saw it twice in 1795 but refused to believe his eyes. This is not in the least surprising. Fifty years after Lalande's sightings astronomers began to worry about the perturbations of Uranus, which they had known for some time could be explained only by the presence of another planet. A number of French and British astronomers were working on the problem, among them Airy, the Astronomer Royal, John Couch Adams and the Frenchman Leverrier. The first to solve the problem was Adams, and he told Airy. The Astronomer Royal not only tucked away the papers in a drawer, but treated Adams with envious discourtesy; he was, however, helpful to Leverrier. An astronomer at Cambridge called Challis was asked to look for the planet in its predicted position in the summer of 1846. He saw it three times, but failed to recognize it. He has been said to have been guilty of 'shocking ineptitude', but this was Neptune. Finally Galle, an astronomer working in Berlin, acting on advice from Leverrier, found the planet in September 1846; it was in Aquarius.

This seems simply a story of success achieved, despite very bad treatment of Adams by both Airy and the French who pretended not to believe that his preliminary work existed. But the story continues. The planet had indeed been discovered, but over a century later it was found that the discovery was in fact due to luck and not at all to the excellent mathematics of two eminent mathematicians; the planetary conditions had happened to be 'kind' to them. They were misguided and yet they still found the planet. The mean distance of the planet is about 30 astronomical units; they thought it was 36 or 37. Its eccentricity of orbit is tiny; they multiplied it by a factor of twelve. They assumed that its longitude of perihelion (Neptune's greatest distance from the Sun) was about 290 when in fact it is 44. They put the value of Neptune's Sun/Mass at between 6670 and 9350, whereas it is 19300. Adams and Leverrier worked independently, yet their figures are very close to each other's and equally far from the truth. The predicted longitude at discovery was the only factor they got right and they ought not to have done so. They were both wrong and right.

All the circumstances surrounding the discovery are totally Neptunian and we should not be surprised to discover that in fact it does not exist, or is opposite where it is supposed to be, were it not for our telescopes.

Keywords: *dissolution, artistry, imagination, unselfishness, refinement* (in the true, not genteel sense), *charity, illusion, delusion, deceit.*

The chief principle of Neptune is dissolution. It dissolves the boundaries between illusion and 'ordinary' common sense reality which are ignored only at peril. It dissolves self-interest and egoism, so that it can represent unselfish impulses and creative imagination.

Equally, though, it can represent self-destructive impulses; illusions, delusions, hallucinations, deceit and treachery. The effects of alcohol and of most drugs, especially those which act on and distort perception and self-perception, are wholly Neptunian. Film-makers, actors and novelists are ruled by Neptune, though they are ruled by other planets as well; their illusory nature is Neptunian.

Neptune plays an essential part, with the Moon, in the understanding of other people and particularly in that feeling one's way into the beings of others which is called 'empathy'. It is fundamental to the process of acceptance of the manifestations of others, particularly the constructive acceptance of their more unpleasant manifestations. Wherever anyone is sensitive and wherever anyone is compassionate, Neptune is involved. Neptune makes for love of animals, especially the Cardinal square between it and Venus. It is also involved with Pluto and usually Uranus in all 'paranormal' matters.

The negative features of Neptune are by no means always immediately visible. Neptune is an exceedingly sinister planet though it cannot be called 'malefic'; being so intimately connected with the good and the beautiful, it would be sinister. It plays its part in madness, credulousness, treachery, fraud and lying, but it must be remembered that lying can be destructive, as in politics, or constructive, as in poetic or creative lying. Neptune always features in cases of paranoia and delusions of grandeur. It is also involved in escapism, vulgarity and vagueness.

Neptune and Uranus in certain combinations, especially if Mars is involved as well, usually indicate a tendency to hysteria. Persistently self-deluded people have Neptune in difficult positions, though this is not always easy to see. Neptune-Sun in conjunction is very difficult, especially in Virgo.

Ultimately Neptune and its influence have to be understood through the study of individual charts. In certain cases it can mimic other planets; in Mary Whitehouse's case, it mimics a decent Venus, while the true Venus wallows in the search for the sexually suggestive. Neptune gives rise to a difficult question: to what extent, if at all, does its unrealistic nature point to the existence of a greater reality?

Examination of the Neptunes of lucid, genuinely creative men and women tells us a lot about the planet.

In Georges Simenon's chart (p. 190) Neptune is unaspected, but in a close undecimal series with Moon and Asc. Now Simenon has never announced his intention of doing anything; he is not that kind of man. So we can eliminate the 'misguided' interpretation that often applies and turn to the other: 'intuitively very gifted'. The undecimal series between Neptune, Moon and Asc may well, in the light of what has been said about 11H, be related to many of the problems Simenon deals with in his novels and which reflect those in his own life. Simenon's Neptune is uncomplicated, but in many charts of men and women who are known liars and swindlers, Neptune seems problematical. This is what we would expect.

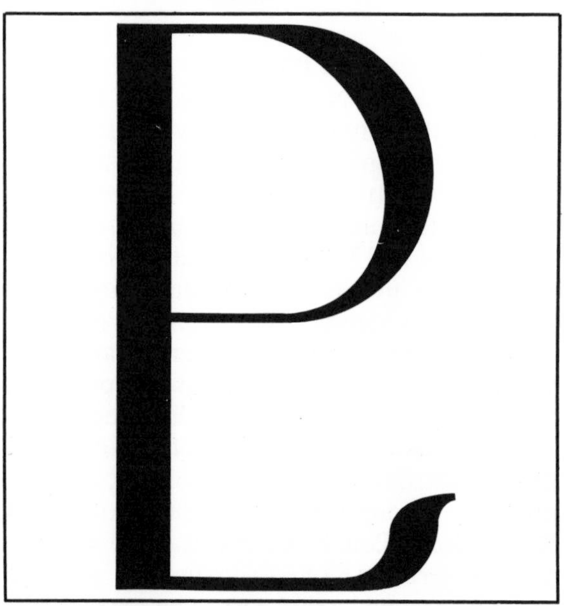

PLUTO

It is appropriate, nature being enigmatic and paradoxical, that Pluto should be so small a planet. Astronomically, not much is known about it; it shows up in the largest telescopes as a dot like a star rather than a disc like other planets. It has a large moon, recently discovered. The eccentricity of its orbit is much larger than that of any of the other planets: it lies at an inclination of 17° to the ecliptic.

Pluto functions *subversively* and *invisibly* to *transform* by *elimination* or *metamorphosis*. Its connection with the sign of Scorpio is particularly obvious. There is still a great deal to be learned about Pluto in charts, but in general it may be said that Pluto in the chart shows how power of any kind will be exercised.

Most people find themselves at some time or another in a position to wield power over others, and, of course, power can be directed inwards. Any close Pluto square or conjunction is likely to manifest itself strongly in the personality, but the manifestations tend to be enigmatic. Nonetheless, we can learn much about the planet's effect by studying these particular hard aspects.

In the chart of the psychopath Jim Jones (p. 186) the opposition between Saturn and Pluto in Cardinals is rather wide, but it is given special significance by the T-square formed by the conjunction between the Moon, Venus and Uranus. The conjunction between Pluto and Jupiter is fairly close, and Jupiter is in very close square to the Moon. This is a chart in which Pluto displays decidedly 'malefic' features. Pluto is usually involved in the charts of criminals, both those who are breaking the law and those who are politically corrupt.

Higher civil servants who are over-assiduous in carrying out their instructions, whatever these may be (the Eichmann syndrome), often have unaspected Mercury-Pluto trines, while their counterparts in the underworld tend to have squares. Mars-Pluto squares indicate over-assertion, Venus-Pluto squares a desire to dominate perhaps with sadistic impulses, and Moon-Pluto squares emotional over-intensity. In many people these tendencies are successfully sublimated; in others they are the cause of very serious trouble.

Pluto always compels and it can either compel to high, virtuous achievement, or to villainous behaviour within or outside the law. Pluto has many of the qualities that we have already ascribed to Jupiter – conscience, creativity, religiosity – but Pluto violently intensifies those qualities. Thus Pluto-Jupiter contacts, particularly hard ones, are always potentially dangerous. They are likely to be very good or very bad, even in people whose ideas and personalities are commonplace rather than merely neutral.

Aspects between Pluto and the planets from Saturn outwards are significant when very close. Saturn-Pluto can be sinister, signifying violence and, as Ebertin suggests, 'hard labour and cruelty'. Uranus-Pluto is, obviously enough, revolutionary and given to drastic and sudden action. Neptune-Pluto is an extremely enigmatic combination. It is the most likely indicator of a 'strange' personality capable of paranormal activity, whether consciously or not. Some of those who had the conjunction which took place in 1891-2 really close (within 30′) were very strange in this way, although not usually well-known outside small circles of people; the Moon softens the effects of this rare conjunction.

THE ASTEROIDS

The asteroids, of which there are many hundreds, have been proposed as having astrological effect. I have found no indication that the more popular ones – Ceres and Vesta – for which there are ephemerides, do have an effect. I therefore ignore them in this book.

THE PERSONAL POINTS

It remains to discuss the significance of certain points, also known as angles because they lie where two great circles intersect: the Ascendant (Asc) and the Descendant (Desc); the Midheaven (MC) and the *Imum Coeli* (IC); the Vertex and Antivertex; and the Moon's nodes. Not enough work has been done on such points as the Co-Vertex (the Vertex for the co-latitude, i.e. 90 – Latitude) and the Co-Ascendant (the Asc for the same) to make them worthy of discussion. The East Point (where the Horizon and Prime Vertical intersect in the East) is likely to be significant, but in exactly what way we do not as yet know.

I shall therefore confine myself to the Moon's nodes and the three main axes, the last of which, Vertex-Antivertex – the axis true East-West of birth – has received very little consideration elsewhere, save from certain American astrologers.

THE ASCENDANT-DESCENDANT AXIS

Gauquelin's proof, crude though it may be in psychological terms, that some planets just before angles are significant in character-formation, is irrefutable. As yet the proof only applies to the Asc and MC axes, but it does finally confirm what has been known for at least seven thousand years, that the angles are important.

All astrologers – except Sun-sign pseudo-practitioners – find angles significant, and anyone who has correlated aspects of personality to rising, or Asc, sign would confirm this.

In my view the Asc sign is an indication of what is best called a person's strategy, their way of manipulating the environment, dealing with people, handling life. This formulation avoids the illogic of calling it both the lens through which we view the world and the way others see us. I dismiss this view of the Asc sign, because the link between the notions is too tenuous. One's strategy, one's way of managing, is by no means the equivalent of the way one sees the world, although the two are more or less intimately connected. It is the Sun that seems to bring out the power of the Asc sign; in other words sunrise births are highly significant, just as new Moon births seem to be. Karl Marx was born at an eclipse whose path included most of Russia and its Moslem empire. The nearer the Sun is to the Asc in the same sign, the stronger the effect. Aspects to the Asc itself can change matters very considerably; so can bodies in the sign, whether technically conjunct (5°) the Asc or not.

The Asc sign undoubtedly has an effect on physique; I can myself guess certain rising signs, especially Aries and Leo, with scores very significantly above chance. So can many other astrologers and with higher scores than mine. Physical appearance plays a part in this, but it is more the bearing and facial expression. Sometimes, where I have guessed the sign wrongly, I find that the Moon, a stellium or very occasionally the Sun with Venus and Mercury, is in the sign I have chosen.

If the Asc means personal strategy or 'the mask I wear', what does its opposite, the Desc, mean? Usually this is subsumed under the definition of the Seventh House, of which in most house systems it is the cusp: 'other people, partners, open (not secret) enemies'.

Now, if there is an opposition to Asc or Desc (or MC, IC, Vertex or Antivertex), there will be a conjunction to the other point on the axis. If there is a square to one of them, there will be a square to the point at the opposite side of the axis. If there is a sextile or trine, then there will be the opposite, a trine or a sextile respectively, to the other point, although the sextile might be too wide-orbed to be valid. If there is a quintile, there will also be a 108° aspect in the 20H series.

All astrologers ignore the effect of septiles and undecimals (11H) to the Desc, and to the IC, Vertex and Antivertex. Doubtless, as-

Karl Marx New Moon and Sun in conjunction.

pects generated by other similar harmonics have an effect, but apart from 13H, which has something to do with death, we know very little about such aspects.

In the chart on p. 62 there is a bi-septile, close, from Uranus to the Desc. With this type of aspect there is no kindred one to Asc. In the case of the bi-septile in question to the Desc, the aspect to the Asc is 76° 53′: the nearest harmonic aspect to this is 22/103 and I do not think that any astrologer yet knows what that means. But it is a prime, and doubtless has a meaning. However, the bi-septile, Uranus to the Desc, is highly significant in the native's life. His relationships with others are exceedingly odd, drastic and changeable (Uranus is afflicted by the Moon). He is upset by the drastic excitability of others and of himself. So that certainly here, the traditional meaning of the Desc can be confirmed.

This example and many others, in any chart, show clearly that the Desc is concerned with other people. In what way? The Desc shows both what we experience from others, and our weakness of strategy, the ways in which we habitually fail to deal efficiently with our lives. It indicates an area of failure to understand and therefore, perhaps, some intolerance.

Jim Jones' Desc does have an undecimal to Saturn and a semisquare from the Sun; but sensitivity, protectiveness and subtlety of approach were manifestations which he consistently failed to understand.

The native just mentioned who has his Uranus bi-septile to his Desc has Saturn in conjunction to this. Desc and Saturn are in Sagittarius, and fire-trines are formed by the ruler in Aries to both of them. One would thus expect him to have a great sympathy with the idealism, prophetic propensities and tactlessness of Sagittarius, but Saturn on the Desc usually indicates a good deal of cynicism.

He himself denies any idealism and states that he dislikes it intensely; his wife says that his trouble is that he is too idealistic. Can we tell from the chart who is right? Certainly his cynicism is often experienced by genteel people as very offensive, as a mechanical tendency to ascribe the most appalling motives to respectable, well-thought-of people. But is this an act? I would suggest that both the native and his wife are right, and so here we see just to what measure the general effect of the Desc can be modified by an aspect, in this case from Saturn. We have a native who is certainly tactless in the Sagittarian manner, and who enjoys making unpleasant prophecies about public people whom he dislikes, but there is in him a certain blankness towards Sagittarian idealism – he tends to sneer at the very word.

MIDHEAVEN AXIS

There is great disagreement among astrologers over the meaning of the Midheaven (MC) Axis, and the IC, or at least aspects to it, is shamefully neglected. Traditionally, the MC represents career, attainment, 'honours', status, 'aim in life'. These are all outward characteristics. Ebertin, however, states that the MC indicates the inner life, or 'spiritual awareness'. Others, with much evidence to support them, find that there seems to be less difference between the MC and the Asc than has previously been supposed.

This, psychologically, is just what we might expect, for if the Asc indicates the *persona* – the mask through which roles are played – and the MC indicates the hidden life, then these two are so closely connected as to be difficult to separate, whether in principle or in practice. Your strategy is how you get things; your 'inner self' requires outward expression or fulfilment for the reason that it exists in the world and is related intimately to it.

Ebertin is close to the truth. The sign on the MC and all aspects to it, while one of the most difficult astrological factors to interpret, indicates 'goal-consciousness'. However, the MC does not in itself indicate anything about the unconscious desires. This function is shown primarily by the Moon, and also by Neptune, Pluto and the IC. The MC sign tells us how a person feels, consciously or subconsciously, to him or herself, which is very important. The Moon on the Asc might well indicate a strategy employing great empathy with others, which may or may not imply true empathy; the Moon on MC would be more likely to indicate someone who feels true empathy for others, whether he or she shows it or not. Clearly, the MC will very often indicate what a person does, how he behaves and its condition will indicate how he or she does it – and why.

It may not be without significance that the Asc is mathematically derived from the RAMC (which is simply the MC measured in right ascension). Some astrologers think that the angle separating these two points – they are often near to ecliptic sextile, trine or square – is significant; this is a mistake. What is significant is that in diurnal terms – and they are wholly diurnal factors – they are in square by definition (p. 41). There is thus 'difficulty' between them, despite their connections. One would expect this. It is never easy to fulfil oneself.

But what of the IC? The usual definition, which cheerfully includes the grave, is 'roots, foundation' and therefore of course a person's domestic inclinations. The IC is certainly a 'domestic' point, giving indications of the private conditions under which a person lives. Logically we might expect to treat the IC rather as we treated the Desc, as in certain respects an opposite point in that the latter reveals weaknesses or areas of intolerance. But nature is not wholly logical in the way in which positivists use logic, and this approach proves unfruitful. The IC does not appear to indicate areas of 'ego-weakness' at all. The IC rather complements the MC by indicating the unconscious foundations of the inner self (MC) in terms of its outward-thrusting nature. Thus, the MC alone is only an oblique guide to the secret self. At its simplest, it could be, 'I want to be a bus conductor because I like to be polite and to keep order and I enjoy punching paper and making allowances for people who insult and poke me with sharp objects and I don't want any money and I like to defend London Transport because I want to express my loyalty to an unpopular cause.'

More likely is: 'I want to be my own boss because I can fulfil myself best in that way; I will therefore be a decorator and save on tax and be my own master. I like being praised and I really can do a good job for cash on the nail – no bills, no receipts.'

The IC gives the reasons for the MC indications (in other words, one sign is feeding its opposite); it may even be slightly more indicative. It will show what kind of private circumstances – normally domestic in the wide sense, though they could involve a roving life spent in hotels, or movement from brothel to brothel, or life as a tramp – a person requires to fulfil his ambitions.

It is obviously very significant if the Moon, Neptune or Pluto are on the IC; if they are on the MC, then there may possibly be some form of imbalance; the native could try vainly to reject what are in all senses his 'roots'. But this is by no means inevitable; other indications should be looked for in the chart.

In the chart on page 62 the Venus trine to the IC, which is in Fire, is closer and more important than the corresponding Venus sextile to the MC. This person will probably yearn for harmony in his private circumstances, but in public he will be regarded by some as a nuisance, a disrupter, a spoilsport. He cares less about the latter, perhaps, and more about the former. There is in fact a grand trine, though admittedly not a wholly planetary one, between the IC, Venus and Saturn. This is the chart of someone who works, not always unaggressively, at home. Notice the 7H series linking Sun and Mars to the IC. The chart is in fact loaded with septiles: between Jupiter and the North node and between Pluto and Saturn, as well as those already mentioned.

In this chart the MC is in Aquarius and the IC in Leo. Analysing this one would begin by saying: that the native's goals were, at least at the beginning of his life, somewhat 'Utopian'; that he cast himself as a rebel; that he felt distinctly 'cool' about his public position; that he would be humanitarian, although perhaps in a mechanical or doctrinaire manner. This set of attitudes, held perhaps a little insecurely because Aquarius is not always a secure sign, would be based in a stronger and altogether more innate desire to hold court on his own ground, to be deferred to.

We must always look at the rulers. In the chart in question, Uranus (ruler of Aquarius) is in Aries, a very self-willed sign; and the Sun (ruler of Leo) is in Taurus, indicating a dependence on feelings of security. The sub-ruler of Aquarius, Saturn, is well placed in Sagittarius.

You should, from this and other examples given elsewhere in this book, be able to work out the effect of MC-IC axes. Above all, do not make the mistake of ignoring this axis at the expense of the Asc-Desc axis. Remember that it is fruitless to consider the rising sign alone as an indication of 'how others see you'. That might be the case, but it is unlikely; the matter usually depends on a multitude of other factors.

VERTEX AND ANTIVERTEX

This is the true East-West axis through the birth-place. Very little work has been done on it. It was pioneered, so far as we know, by a very eccentric American astrologer, Johndro, who called the Eastern end of this axis, now known as the Antivertex, the 'Electric Ascendant'.

Johndro used a number of electromagnetic arguments – now mostly shown to have been invalid – to support his contention that the conventional Asc indicated 'volitional life, free choice' and that his Electric Asc, the Antivertex, indicated 'involuntary actions, no choice, fate'. Later a better astrologer, Charles Jayne, persuaded him that it was the Vertex rather than its opposite which produced the results, and this is why the Vertex gets greater attention nowadays.

The conventional interpretation of the Vertex has remained very close to Johndro's explanation of the Antivertex: 'things over which one has no control'. This is suggestive but by no means precise enough to be helpful. Your character as a whole, after all, is something over which you have limited control.

There is very little real evidence to support the significance of the Vertex, but that is because not enough work has been done on it. I have satisfied myself that conjunction transits of the radical Vertex (oppositions to the Antivertex) by heavy planets correlate in a very impressive number of instances with important changes in life. To what extent these are any more 'fated' than other changes I cannot say: I do not think they are, since I believe that character, in the sense of what one is, attracts circumstances. In radical charts planets on, or opposite, or in quintile or septile to, the Vertex play a particularly important part in the life: a fine example is Thomas Hardy's Saturn (p. 185). The Antivertex is no less important, in my view.

As we have seen, the Desc has something to do with other people, in a particular way; so has the Vertex, but in another way. I believe that this axis (I will not pretend that I understand the difference between the two ends more than any other astrologer does) indicates the kind of people who will cause important changes which will have an external as well as an internal effect. I know a person who suddenly and unpredictably became completely obsessed with astrology. At that time Uranus, the planet associated with astrologers and astrology, was transiting conjunct his Vertex. Saturn was exactly quintile Margaret Thatcher's Vertex when the American advertising agency, Saatchi and Saatchi, successfully sold her to the British electorate: in transits, quintiles often indicate gaining of power, and her regime is, of course, Saturnine to many people.

The sign nature of the Vertex-Antivertex axis is likely to be of significance: it hints at the kind of people who will interest and therefore influence the native. This should not be confused with one of the functions of the Moon's nodes: the North node's sign often shows the kind of people for whom the native will search, the South node's sign the kind he will avoid. This is an indication of behaviour which will frequently fade out early in life, while there is an element of true need in the Vertex-Antivertex indications. One can often find a reflection of one's true disposition.

THE MOON'S NODES

Until the beginning of this century, the Moon's nodes were taken little, or frequently no, notice of in Western astrology. But in

Indian astrology they have long been regarded as of the utmost importance. Even today Indian astrologers seldom use more than the visible planets, but they always use the Dragon's Head (North node) and the Dragon's Tail (South node). They also use a zodiac

which takes the North node as its starting point. The British astrologer Ronald Davison, the doyen of the occult astrologers, uses this zodiac in all the charts to which he devotes special study. He regards the cross-aspects between this lunar zodiac and the radical positions as indicating 'how the legacy of the past affects the life-pattern of the present'. I concur with this, but, unlike Davison, I do not think of the past in terms of 'past lives': I think of it simply as the past in the present life.*

Since it is very often the case that the more dramatic or obvious features of radical charts tend to fade out in later life – between the ages of 30 and 40 – these cross-aspects between planets in the lunar zodiac and those in the tropical zodiac become interesting in the charts of middle-aged people.

Ebertin over-influenced by his 90° circle which puts all points in opposition into conjunction, denies that there is any difference between the Dragon's Head and its Tail. He interprets the principle as 'Association or Alliance' and, according to the condition of the node in terms of midpoints, asserts that it indicates either the need to communicate with others, or antisocial behaviour, or both.

*To obtain the positions in this lunar zodiac you treat the position of the North node as 00 Tropical Aries 00; therefore all you need to do is to add the position of the North node in degrees of absolute longitude to the positions, again in absolute longitude, of the other bodies and points (when the answer is over 360, subtract 360). For example, if the North node is at 38° and Mars is at 270°, you add 38° to 270°, and find that Mars is at 308° in the lunar zodiac. You then note all its cross aspects to the radical chart, and continue in the same way with all other points on the chart.

The usual interpretation may be summed up as follows: the North node is a point of intake, gain, 'benefit without conscious effort'; the South node is a point of loss, indicating areas in life where sacrifice is demanded without reward. The North node, it is asserted, is Jupiterian and lucky; the South node is Saturnian and 'unlucky'.

Certainly the distinction between the two holds good and the traditional interpretations are on the right lines. The North node seems to indicate the sort of people the native searches for or gets on with; the South node those he avoids. The two points can be important in synastry. An aspect from an afflicted planet in one chart to a node in the other indicates help from the latter in matters connected with the afflicted planet in the former's chart.

I doubt, however, if the North node is 'luckier' than the South node unless the native is grossly materialistic. The gains can be mental as well as material. It is the South node that is a point of release, and release is surely necessary to everyone at some time.

The nodal axis obviously has a lunar quality, which is why the interpreter should always consider it in terms of unconscious, habitual and instinctive behaviour. The Moon close to its own node makes for an extremely emotional nature: such people are seldom reticent and they do not suffer the consequences of repressing their feelings. Those with Moon conjunct North node express their emotions towards others in a manner indicated by the sign involved; those with Moon conjunct South node can, unless there are quite strong counter-indications, make use of others in a selfish way.

If the Moon is square to the nodal axis, thus becoming the point-focus of the natural opposition, the effect depends greatly on the Moon's condition in other respects. Any planet or point square to the nodal axis is significant. Those with Mars square nodes, for example, invariably carry the burden of thinking that their own views are always 'right' – and this is dangerous when it is not balanced by an attempt at objectivity. It is a feature of the chart on page 62.

ASPECTS

An aspect between two or more planets or points is the angular distance between them, measured by the shorter of the two arcs.

MAJOR ASPECTS

The traditional aspects used in astrology through the ages, and by the vast majority of astrologers now, are: conjunction (0°), sextile (60°), square (90°), trine (120°) and opposition (180°). Each of these aspects, called the major aspects, is allowed an orb. An exact aspect is very rare; astrologers call this partile.

One school of Indian astrology – and Ptolemy himself – measured aspects simply in terms of signs. If signs were trine, the planets contained in them were trine; if they were square, the planets in them were square, and so on. Trines, of course, usually fall in signs of the same element; squares and oppositions usually fall in signs of the same quality but of different elements. The squares were considered 'bad' because signs of the same quality are disharmonious; the trines good because signs of the same element are harmonious.

There is a certain justification for this, both theoretical and empirical, but it represents a very serious over-simplification. The method I present here takes account of most of the new work that has been done on aspects, orbs and harmonics and provides a base for study.

MINOR ASPECTS

The minor aspects eventually allowed by most, though not all, astrologers are semisextile (30°) sesquisquare and sesquiquadrate (45° and 135°) and quincunx (150°). The exceedingly powerful quintile (72°), though introduced by Kepler himself, has been ignored, to the great detriment of astrology, until revived in modern times, mainly by Addey and Robert Hand in America and by the German Walter Koch and the Swiss H. J. Walter.

Quintiles, though their orb is small, are unquestionably major aspects, and in this respect the method presented here differs from any other.

PLANES OF MEASUREMENT

Aspects are normally measured in the ecliptic circle, regardless of latitude. Planets are rarely in exact aspect in absolute terms, since they would have to be on a common plane.

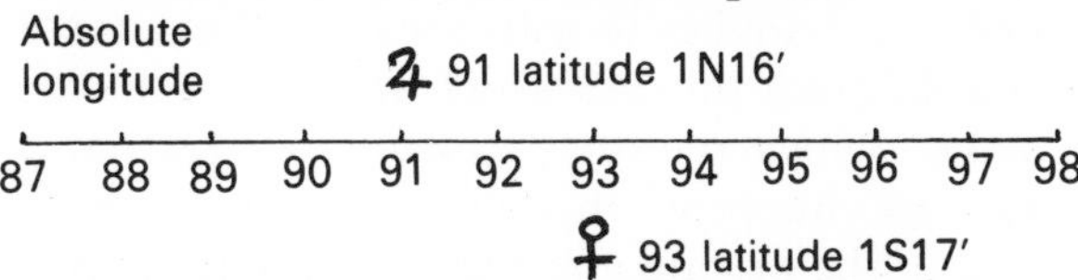

Venus-Jupiter conjunction The planets are separated by 2° in absolute longitude, thereby forming a conjunction. Latitude is ignored in all aspect measurement, although with a conjunction the difference in latitude can be little more than 2°.

Aspects in right ascension (RA) are clearly very important, especially for rectification and for retrodiction and prediction: these are aspects measured on the celestial equator. Where you are puzzled by an aspect that either manifests, or does not manifest, when it is wide or close respectively, you should check its orb in RA.* There are other reference planes, and these doubtless have significance: the plane of the horizon, that of the prime vertical, that of any great circle. But they are beyond the scope of this book, since they involve quite complex formulae. I shall, then, always be speaking of aspects in the ecliptic circle unless I state otherwise.

However, before discussing aspects in more detail, I must introduce the subjects of harmonics and midpoints, since these are the bases of modern aspect-theory. Indeed, it is not too much to assert that wave theory is the basis of the aspects themselves.

HARMONICS

Harmonics are waves of one sort or another: the waves produced by the plucking of a string, by radio signals and so on. Light waves, radio waves, X-rays and innumerable other types of waves are generated by electro-magnetic forces. Human beings are sensitive to signals of this kind, of incredibly low intensity. The planets give every appearance of generating waves from their positions in the zodiacal circle, and this is probably the way, or part of the way, in

*To find RA from the ecliptic position, use the formula:
tan − 1 (cos E sin EL − sin E tan CL/cos EL).
E: Obliquity of the ecliptic.
EL: Ecliptic Longitude.
CL: Celestial Latitude, the perpendicular distance of a planet from the ecliptic (given in ephemerides).

which astrology works. However, I do not believe that straightforward scientific cause and effect applies to astrology; I believe there is a different process which we do not understand, which parallels cause and effect: this process 'happens' in music, painting, poetry and in the private and personal myth-making which I mentioned as being a function of Jupiter and called the creative conscience.

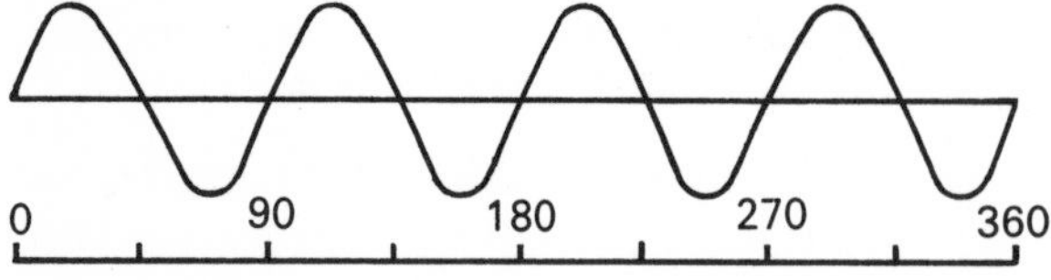

4H: the fourth harmonic This is called 4H because four complete waves fill the 360° circle: therefore the length of each wave is 90°. Planets at 90° to one another are in square, or 4H aspect.

A wave has a length, an amplitude and a phase. In a circle – and in astrology we are dealing with the 360 degrees of the circle, and nothing else – the fourth harmonic, 4H as I have called it throughout this book, divides the circle into four, so we know that its length would be 90°.

AMPLITUDE

Amplitude is the power of a wave: if you strike a tuning-fork very softly then you will generate waves of a lower amplitude than if you strike it very hard. A fictitious and over-simplified astrological example is a useful way to explain amplitude. This is my own invention, and bears no relation to reality; but it does illustrate the sort of effect that some astrologers are seeking to obtain in their search for astrological factors which correlate members of certain professions or categories.

Consider 9720 Welsh tax inspectors all of whom have been convicted of thefts from their mothers' purses. Each birth is accurately timed, so that each ecliptic Sun position is known. We might expect 27 (9720 ÷ 360) Suns on each degree of the 360° circle; if this were so, a graph with degrees of the circle as one axis and the number of births as the other, would be a straight line showing 27 births for each degree. A statistician would expect some deviation from a precise norm; on a graph this would produce a randomly wavy line which does not stray far from 27. Laboriously, then, we list all the positions and plot them as a graph (see below). We discover something unexpected: that peaks and troughs of these totals regularly rise and fall between 14 and 40 in the scale, 27.7 being the mean.

A wave's amplitude The amplitude of this wave, which measures the distribution of ecliptic sun positions at birth of the fictitious Welsh tax inspectors, is 13. Its peak is 40, which is 13 greater than the mean, 27.

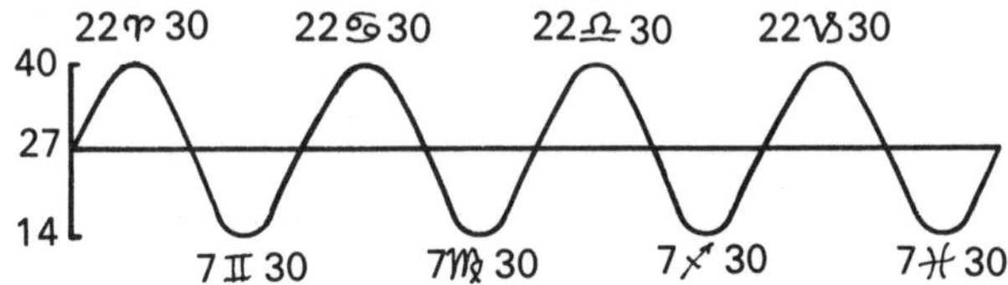

There is a pattern here, and it tells us something about *these* Welsh tax inspectors. The wave length is obviously 4, meaning that we are dealing with 4H. 40 is 13 more than the mean, 27, so 13 is the amplitude. It can be expressed as a percentage of the mean, 48.1 per cent. In any real case this would be astonishingly high; but this is only an example. What do we discover from it? First, that the Sun distribution for 9720 Welsh tax inspectors who have been convicted of theft from their mothers' purses shows a clear and unambiguous 4H pattern. They tend to be born on or about certain dates of the year, and to 'avoid' others. If required, this could be analysed in terms of signs: the first peak comes at 22 Aries 30. There are four peaks and they are in Cardinal signs. We know that *more* Welsh tax inspectors who have been convicted of the crime mentioned have their Suns at $22\frac{1}{2}$° of Cardinals, and that less have them at $7\frac{1}{2}$° of Mutables.

A wave has an ascending and a descending node. The ascending node is the point at which it starts to rise above the mean, in astrology the point where it crosses the ecliptic on its way up. The Sun's ascending node is at 00 Tropical Aries 00, and the signs are the result if its 6H is generated from that point. A wave starts to fall at its descending node.

PHASE

A wave also has phase (see illustration). Harmonic astrologers use the term phase in a slightly different way from wave theorists. The phase of an astrological harmonic is the point in the 360° circle where the peak occurs. As Addey puts it, astrologers 'treat the length of each wave *whatever its length might be in other respects* as being 360° in extent'.

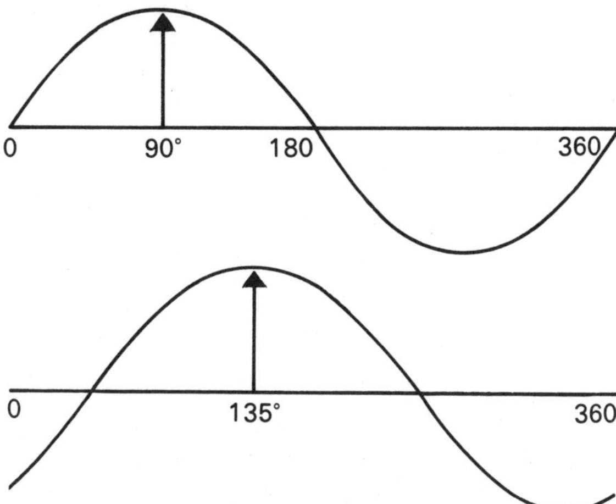

A wave's phase The top wave has a phase of 90°, because this is where its peak falls in the 360° circle. Likewise the lower wave has a phase of 135°: that its ascending node does not coincide with the beginning of the circle is not relevant to astrologers.

HARMONICS AND THE WORK OF GAUQUELIN

I described in Chapter One how Michel Gauquelin, a French statistician, studied the positions of the Moon, Venus, Mars, Jupiter and Saturn in the diurnal circle in the births of various groups of professionals – sports champions, doctors, scientists, and so on; how he rightly changed his mind, and decided that the planetary effect was on character and not necessarily on profession; how he made laborious lists of 'trait words' from thesauruses, relating to character traits, and found the same effects as he had found for the professions. This is a clumsy form of research, but it has an undeniable if crude validity.

The typical Gauquelin picture looks like a fourth harmonic effect with, in terms of absolute longitude, bigger peaks just before the Asc and MC than before Desc and IC. Working with Gauquelin's scrupulously full accounts of his results, the British astrologer John Addey found that other harmonics often applied: thirds, fifths and sixths, for instance. Addey further pointed out that if planets have a special effect in what may be called the 'Gauquelin positions', the ones the Frenchman has found for professions, then they must of course have significance, perhaps of a subtler sort, in every other position in the diurnal circle.

Gauquelin's work on harmonics is significant because it shows that, if full and intelligent harmonic analyses of groups of people are made along his lines, then we shall eventually gain clues about the significance of *all* the positions of each body in the diurnal circle. We shall undoubtedly find that aspects, probably both ecliptic and diurnal (and in equatorial, prime vertical, horizon and other circles), affect such positions.

Each planet retains its characteristics; but its position in the diurnal circle and the aspects made to and from it subtly modify those principles. This is akin to sign influences on planets: Mars will always be Mars, but it can't work in Pisces in the same way as it works in Virgo or any other sign.

HARMONICS AND ASPECTS

Harmonics explain why some aspects, the major aspects, are more powerful, and have a wider orb, than other aspects. If we assume that the zodiac is generating white noise, which indicates nothing significant, then we may assume that an aspect is a signal, and that the closer it is the stronger it is. The traditional notion that conjunctions, trines, squares and oppositions are the strongest of these signals is confirmed by harmonics. At 0°, or 360°, the strength is infinite: this is simply the fundamental harmonic. The next strongest, in order, are: opposition, trine, square, quintile, sextile. But what does 'strongest' mean? Simply that there are more harmonics at 90° than at 45°, that there are even more at 120° and even more still at 180°. The diagrams show that 90° aspects, or squares, are generated by the fourth harmonic, 4H, which embraces the 8H, 12H, 16H and so on up to 45/180; there are 45

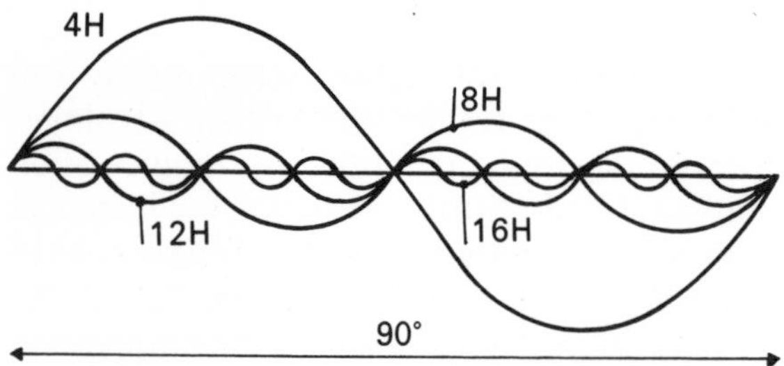

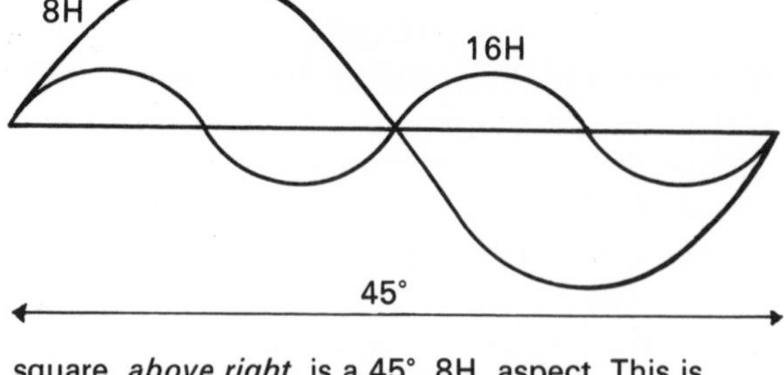

An aspect's strength A square, *above left*, which is a 90°, or 4H, aspect, is reinforced by the sub-harmonics of 4H, namely 8H, 12H, 16H and so on up to 180H – 45 sub-harmonics in all. A semi-square, *above right*, is a 45°, 8H, aspect. This is weaker than a square because it has only 22 sub-harmonics, 16H, 24H, 32H and on up to 180H.

harmonics in all at 90°. So the division of the circle into four is much reinforced by the sub-harmonics of the fourth harmonic. 45° aspects, or semi-squares, are generated by the eighth harmonic, 8H, and its subharmonics, 16H, 24H, 32H etc; in all there are 22 harmonics at 45°. It is clear then, that a square is 'stronger' than a semi-square. However, there are 90 harmonics at 180°, opposition, and 60 at 120°, trine.

In their *Astrologers' Guide to the Harmonics* James and Ruth Williamsen give the nearest harmonics to *any* specific arc length between 2° and 359°: if, say, your Uranus and your Sun do not make a conventional aspect, you can discover what their harmonic relationship is. The Williamsens state:

> Harmonics *correspond* to arclengths between any two points in the 360° circle. The 'points' may be cosmic bodies – planets, fixed stars, or whatever. They may also be more abstract . . . midheaven or ascendant, East Point, Vertex, 0° Aries, etc. However, harmonics themselves are *not* arclengths. They are proportions or ratios describing the inter-relationship between a whole cycle or repeating process and some part of it. . . . The word 'harmonics' in our usage . . . should be thought of as deriving its meaning from two sources. First, it is a shortened word for referring to what are known as 'harmonics of cosmic periods'. Briefly, these are the cycles, subcycles and supercycles which together determine the geometry of the changing spatial relationships between cosmic bodies as they move relative to one another in the heavens. There is a harmony here . . . .

Even more to the point:

> . . . the word 'harmonics' betrays the essential similarity between the mathematics and geometry of astrological harmonics and that of the harmonics of modern science. These latter are often represented by wave forms and are described in terms of amplitudes, periods and phase angles. They are the subject matter of, for example, cybernetics, acoustics, electromagnetic theory and oceanography. Incidentally, but not at all accidentally, the musical concept of harmony equally embodies the same basic ideas which underlie harmonics in the astrological and scientific senses.

ORBS FOR ASPECTS

The strictly logical harmonic approach appears to lead to an indisputable hierarchy, and so to an apparently foolproof way of deciding how great an orb to allow to each aspect: 0 and 180 the greatest, then 120, and so on. But this hierarchy is in empirical fact anything but indisputable. Our knowledge tells us that squares, and hard aspects in general, manifest much more obviously than trines and soft aspects. Hard aspects result from division of the circle by 2, 4, 8, 16, 32, 64, 128. All the rest are soft. But we must have some way of judging orbs, and this hierarchy is the only practical basis even though we deviate from it: it has the virtue of giving us a general guide, from which we may make quite deliberate departures.

In order to treat orbs in this mechanistic, hierarchical manner, we would have to give the conjunction, and therefore the opposition, an orb of 10°, which is in fact twice what most serious astrologers would allow. This is because we should otherwise get orbs for the other aspects that are too small even for the most fanatic astrologer. Logically, then, the orbs for the major aspects should be: 0° (conjunction) and 180° (opposition), orb 10°; 120° (trine), $10 \div 3 = 3° 20'$; 90° (square), $10 \div 4 = 2\frac{1}{2}°$; 72° (quintile), $10 \div 5 = 2°$; 60° (sextile), $10 \div 6 = 1° 40'$.

These results are fairly realistic, but practice has proved that it is necessary to allow 5° to conjunction, opposition, square and trine. Some allow 5° to the sextile, but this is unjustified and has led to some of the most serious errors perpetrated in astrology: the orb given above is almost exactly right for most sextiles. The correct orb for the quintile and bi-quintile (144°) is about 1° in most circumstances. Although what we are looking for is the definite signal generated against a background of white noise, the principle of orb is not that it 'cuts out', but that, like an old soldier, it simply fades away.

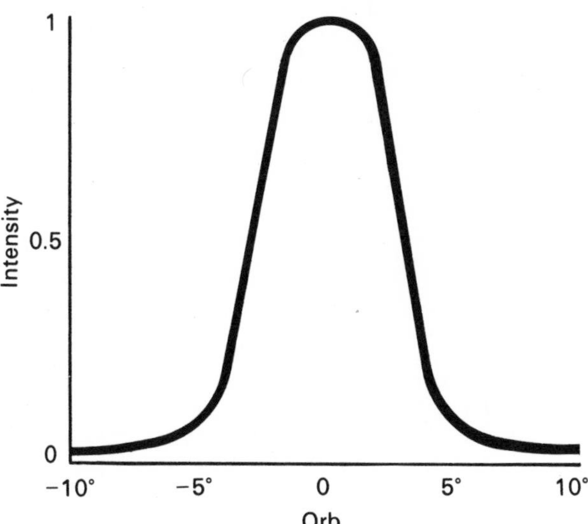

An aspect's intensity drops markedly over 5° of orb, and then gradually fades away.

Working from Nelson's data (see illustration), Geoffrey Dean very properly infers the following measures of intensity for the hard aspects: conjunction, square and opposition.

orb	0°	1°	2°	3°	6°	12°
intensity	1	.5	.3	.2	.1	.05

The reason, then, that we use 5° is merely practical. Judging hard aspects at roughly one-tenth their potential intensity is about as far as we can go without danger of confusion, of seeing too many trees too soon and missing the wood. Occasionally we come across a chart which has no close major aspects at all: then we use minor aspects, some of which must be close, and we note which harmonic tends to dominate the chart.

Orb is ultimately a matter of time, of aspect balanced against aspect. If we call the harmonically very powerful aspects major, the harmonically quite powerful ones strong minor, and the others minor, then we have, very approximately, three categories of orb: respectively, 5°, 1–2°, $\frac{1}{2}°$.

ORBS FOR SLOW-MOVING PLANETS

Astrologers nowadays tend to allow the 5° orb only to the fast-moving bodies: they give the full orb to the two inferior planets, Mercury and Venus – both of which move faster than the Sun, and to the Sun and Moon; they give about 4° to Mars and possibly Jupiter, and 3° to the rest. Their case is that an aspect between, say, Saturn and Pluto lasts for many months: this aspect therefore affects everyone in the same way and therefore we must discount it.

Such thinking is illogical. First, no aspect acts alone, even if it is a 'duet' (Dean's word for a major aspect between two bodies that lacks any other major aspects): even a duet has to be seen in the context of the chart. Since every chart is different so the long-lasting aspect must blend quite differently into it. The same applies to the heavy bodies which stay for years in the same sign: they mean something different in each chart. We don't simply list each feature of a chart along with its meaning, and then leave it at that. Secondly, as Dean has pointed out, aspects between outer planets may manifest, but they may be hard to pick out because everyone shares them. This is a worthwhile point, though it still tends to assume that aspects manifest on their own, which they do not. The sextile between Neptune and Pluto which will operate until the end of this century at varying orbs cannot possibly be the 'same' for everyone: their charts are different, so it fits into their charts differently. In any case, remembering the likely effect of micro-harmonics (harmonics less than $7\frac{1}{2}°$: 48H), that 'sextile' is going to be subtly different for everyone. Hitler has these two planets only 3° 49′ apart, but, it may be argued, millions of people had this conjunction. That is not the case. Millions had a sinister applying conjunction of orb less than 5°, but only those born on the day Hitler was born had the planets 3° 49′ apart: this was separating from 94H (very closely), and applying, quite closely, to 95H. There could easily be significance in this.

For these and other reasons I give all the planets the same orb, but I pay special attention when the heavy planets are in exact, or near to exact major or strong minor (1–12H) aspect. Clearly we do look for the way in which the heavy planets are aspected by the lighter, faster ones, but we should not neglect the significance of aspects between the heavy planets: the relationships between these change slightly all the time, and these relationships are significant in individual charts.

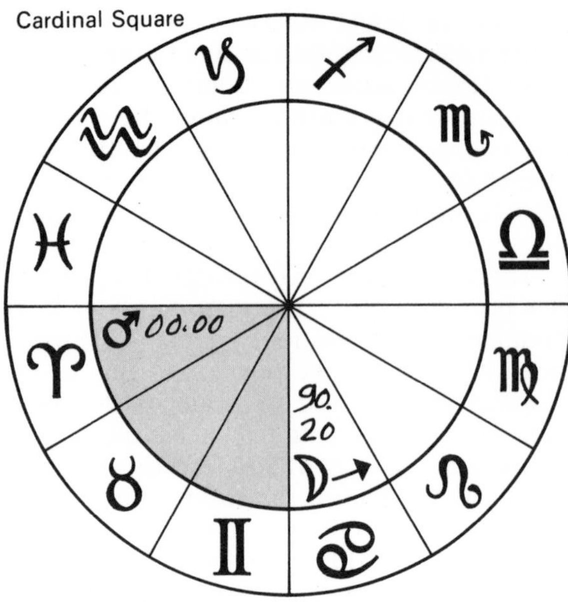

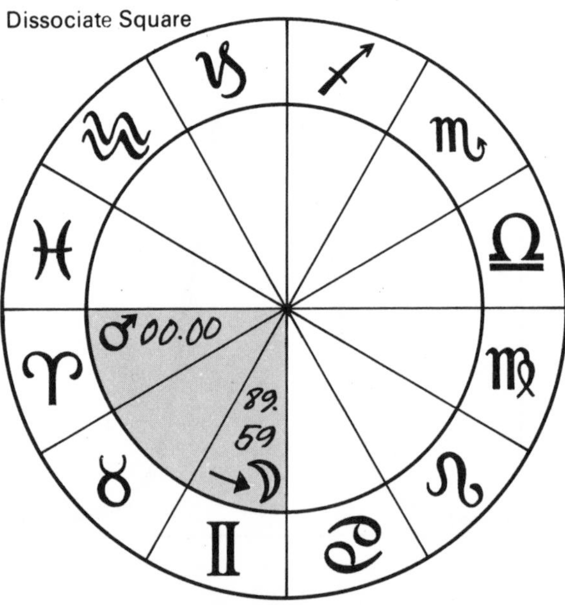

A separating, dexter, cardinal square, *top* The square is cardinal because Moon and Mars are both in cardinal signs. The faster body, the Moon, is moving away from the exact angle: the square is therefore separating. The square is dexter because the faster body makes the aspect against the order of the signs. **An applying, dexter, dissociate square,** *above* The square is dissociate because the bodies are in signs of different quality It is applying because the Moon is moving towards the exact angle. It is dexter as in the top diagram.

ORB FOR THE MOON

The Moon moves much faster than any other body: its mean speed is approximately eight-and-a-half times that of Mercury. Since orbs are really a matter of time, it is to be expected that the Moon should be allowed a wider orb of influence when applying to an aspect, especially to a major aspect. I have found this to be so. What seem to be wide-orbed applying Moon aspects, especially dexter ones, can be unexpectedly powerful. An excellent example is the Moon-Uranus square in the chart on p. 62. However, it is advisable to be cautious in such cases.

DISSOCIATE ASPECTS, APPLYING AND SEPARATING, DEXTER AND SINISTER

With major aspects – 0°, 60°, 72°, 90°, 120°, 180° – we should look to see if they are dissociate, applying or separating, dexter or sinister (see illustrations). An aspect is regarded as being 'thrown' from the faster to the slower body. It is easy to see whether the faster has passed the point of exact aspect or not. If it has not, then it is applying. If it has, then it is separating. When one or both bodies are retrograde, you need to look in the ephemeris to see if the aspect is ever made. An aspect that is read from faster to slower in order of the signs, in other words to the left, is *sinister*; one that reads against the order of the signs, to the right, is *dexter*.

DEXTER AND SINISTER

The dexter-sinister distinction goes back to very early astrology. It should be noted that it is based on whether the two bodies involved are moving towards opposition or conjunction. If they are moving towards opposition then the aspect is dexter, and vice versa. Ptolemy regarded the dexter aspect as much more powerful than the sinister. We do not yet have enough evidence to say what the distinction is, only that there is one and that it is to do with psychology rather than power. I regard the dexter aspect as being more difficult for the person concerned.

APPLYING AND SEPARATING

There is more agreement about the applying/separating distinction, and this is mentioned in modern books much more often. Since the applying aspect is building up to a peak, it seems obvious that it is more powerful and that it should therefore be allowed a wider orb. There is some evidence that suggests that this is so, but other evidence goes against this. The most sensible modern thinking is that the applying aspect implies more tension, less control; that seems to me to be right for most, though not all, charts. Two examples illustrate this. First, the sinister separating Venus-Pluto square in the chart on p. 62. The native is certainly 'erotic', is certainly very willingly more moved by unconscious than by conscious forces – and certainly in his early life he went, many times, for 'gratification at all costs'. But the last characteristic has faded out and he has been able to work out the conflicts indicated by this square quite constructively. (Very strong manifestations in the radical chart do tend, in general, to fade out as the native gets older – and those indicated by close but separating aspects fade out earlier, and present less difficulty.) T. E. Lawrence had the same aspect a little wider, but dexter applying. Does not this explain much about his self-destructive impulses, his immature need to work out an infantile masochistic fantasy by paying to have himself flogged?

TRANSITION OF LIGHT

In the chart on p. 62 there is a stellium in Aries, involving Mercury, Venus, Jupiter and Uranus. Mercury and Jupiter are in conjunction (orb 2° 53′). Jupiter and Venus are separated by 5° 10′, just 10′ over the recommended orb for conjunctions. However, where a conjunction is part of a stellium there is a strong case for extending the orb – certainly by as little as 10′, so we also have a Jupiter-Venus conjunction. Mercury and Venus are separated by 8° 3′. Can they be said to be in conjunction either because they are in the stellium, or by transition of light?

Transition of light, sometimes called translation of light, works like this. Since Mercury is in aspect with Jupiter and Venus is in aspect with Jupiter, Mercury might be said to be in aspect with Venus, because Jupiter 'carries' the 'light'. However, transition of light is by no means a rule which should be mindlessly followed: the surrounding factors, especially midpoints, should be considered. Here Uranus is also in Aries and has something in common with, a background influence on, the other bodies, but it is very plainly not in conjunction with them. However, the extent of the stellium is 18° 36′, which is a vigintile aspect (20H); this strengthens the power of the stellium. Further, the Mercury/Uranus midpoint is applying to Venus at orb 1° 15′, thereby linking Mercury and Venus in another way. Taking these factors with the transition of light, we could say that Mercury and Venus are weakly conjunct.

However, in this instance and in many other instances of transition of light, there are other links between the two bodies which are more significant than a weak conjunction. The Mercury/Venus midpoint is rapidly applying to conjunction with Jupiter; with all three bodies in Aries this implies very close friendships. Mercury and Venus are also only 3′ separating from a 45H aspect, which is an excessively soft aspect implying that the two bodies, representing thought and desire, are well disposed to one another. If we take into account that they are working through Jupiter – representing conscience, constructiveness, expansion as well as authoritariansim – we get a notion of Aries toughness being softened a little. Further softening is suggested by Mercury trine Neptune, which will try to refine the already Aries-tough Venus, which is being savaged by Pluto and in trine to the cynicism and gloom of Saturn. Clearly then transition of light could be said to apply here, although the other indications reduce the significance of the aspect.

The same chart provides a less convincing example of transition of light. Mercury is in trine with Neptune, and Jupiter is in trine with Saturn; and, as we have seen, Mercury is in conjunction with Jupiter which is in conjunction with Venus. It might be argued that there is a grand trine between Venus-Jupiter-Mercury, Saturn and Neptune.

INTERPRETING ASPECTS

One delineates a chart, as I show in the examples (pp. 152–190) by pursuing similar indications, often those indications which show specific contradictions in the character. But one has, nevertheless, to be able to see chart factors in isolation before one can blend them. Aspects are vital chart factors, as are sign positions and midpoint connections. Clearly the meaning of any separate aspect is modified by the presence of another aspect. For example, the effect of the Venus square Pluto in the chart on p. 62 is modified considerably by Mars being trine Pluto, by Venus and Mars being in a very close undecimal relationship, and by Venus and Mars being undecimal to Neptune.

This predictable effect of one aspect on another connected one is what made Nelson's results from his study of the planets' effect on short-wave radio disturbance so extraordinary. Radio weather is a crude thing compared to human psychology, but Nelson's work does show that trines and squares, hard and soft aspects, angles of 18° and its multiples, have an effect. Astrologers should take more note of his findings, for while these confirm that the old astrologers were interpreting facts, not fictions, they also help to correct many modern misinterpretations. For example, most astrologers would consider that, in the chart on p. 62, the Venus-Pluto square was 'improved' by the Mars-Pluto trine – in the sense that the 'harmony' of the latter would help to resolve the difficulties made by the former. Nelson found, however, that it was isolated, meaning unaspected, trines, and multiple soft aspects unconnected to hard aspects, which indicated quiet weather. Thus the Mars-Pluto trine, hooked up to the Venus-Pluto square, suggests difficulty rather than ease: the possible ease of the Mars-Pluto connection is destroyed by the Venus-Pluto one. However, Venus is trine to Saturn and applying (sinister) to conjunction with Jupiter. Clearly, then, we must judge charts in terms of patterns as well as of individual aspects. Having said that, squares and to a certain extent 8H aspects do tend to manifest very strongly, whether they are isolated or part of a pattern.

The modern tendencies are to use small orbs and, either to disregard soft aspects altogether, or to disregard the nature (hard or soft) of the aspect in favour of attention to the principle of the combination. To use small orbs is sensible, so long as this is not taken to an extreme. Disregarding soft aspects is mistaken but understandable, since the hard aspects, which are said to indicate 'events', do manifest more obviously than the soft, which are said to indicate 'states'. This is near to the truth, but what leads to action or behaviour unless it is a state? We cannot afford to be too unsubtle. Giving more attention to combinations of aspects, than to the nature of individual aspects, produces the best results. Most astrologers now acknowledge that Carter was right when, in his famous and still unbettered *The Astrological Aspects*, he noted that study of actual charts suggested that there was not such a great difference between the so-called harmonious and inharmonious aspects as one would suppose.

I put it like this. Trines, the major soft aspects, uncontaminated by any hard aspects are likely to indicate ease and happiness and even relief from conditions indicated by hard aspects elsewhere in the chart. Many astrologers say that trines simply indicate luck. This is quite wrong: consider the chart of the murderer Landru (p. 183) – luck for whom? One can say, however, that when the possessor of a trine is lucky, then very often the nature of his or her luck is to be found in the trine.

I have said that a trine denotes ease, but there are, of course, many kinds of ease. We can only assess the kind of ease if we take the nature of the bodies involved into account, and the general tenor of the chart. Thus to take a random example, the Mercury-Neptune principle is sensitivity, nervousness, refinement, cunning, imagination. Are we then to suppose that the hard connection is more cunning than the soft, that the native with the square is likely to be a swindler while the one with the trine is likely to be a poet? To a certain extent, yes: the native with the hard aspect will have more difficulties from, and will make more difficulties for others through, his sensitivity and his imagination. But he might be a more gifted poet or actor or novelist or confidence man or politician than the native with the trine.

OBSCURE ASPECTS

There is obviously an unlimited quantity of aspects, as I have shown in my consideration of the harmonic approach. Does every aspect indicate something? Is, for example, the 69H series as valid, and does it act in exactly the same way, as the 4H series? We know a great deal about the 4H series, which includes square and opposition, and nothing whatsoever about the 69H, which consists of multiples of 5° 13′ 2.6″, which for practical purposes should be rounded off to 5° 13′. If our attention were drawn to 69H, this would be because we should note, in the course of harmonic analysis of a number of charts, that it predominated in the charts of certain types of people or in those of a certain profession – it could indicate, for example, larceny in tax officials.

Now some harmonics might mean nothing at all; but that is perhaps unlikely. What they might do, though, is to mean something that is at present and, perhaps eternally, inaccessible to enquiry: the condition of the pyramidal tract on hot days, let us say. The manifestations of such harmonics cannot be seen, or cannot be seen at all easily. What is certain, however, is this: while the logical approach to orbs described above is justified, some harmonics, or aspects, have wider orbs than others, and sometimes these orbs are much greater than we expect. Dexter applying aspects seem effective over slightly wider orbs than others.

It is also certain that some aspects operate on a different level from others. Thus 11H manifests itself rather obviously while 7H is much less obvious, though it can be spectacular, as in the case of Winston Churchill's Sun-Mars septile.

The aspects I discuss fully below, apart from the fundamental (the conjunction), are based on 2, 3, 4, 5, 6, 7, 8, 9, 10, 11 and 12H; I also mention 13, 15 and 20H, and the quincunx.

Each low harmonic has, of course, its subharmonics – thus, if 7 is important, then so must be 14, 21, 28 and so on. For those who wish to go further, I can only recommend the Williamsens' *Guide to the Harmonics*, since there is not space in this book to supply some 100 pages of mathematical information without which nothing more can be done.

THE MEANINGS OF THE ASPECTS

CONJUNCTION: *0°. Harmonic: Fundamental. Orb 5°.*

The conjunction joins the principles of two bodies or points together. If the bodies/points are in different signs, or if the bodies are not obviously friendly, for example Moon-Mars, then there will be friction. Much depends on whether the conjunction is aspected or not. If it is unaspected, by which I mean that it does not receive or throw a sextile, quintile, square, opposition or trine, then it operates largely alone, although minor aspects can explain something of how it works. They can indicate that help, or disaster, may come in spasms, or once, or never; and for subtle people they indicate ways and means of making the two bodies cooperate. For although the conjunction is a hard aspect, it carries with it the promise that cooperation can be achieved. This by no means suggests that it will be: Landru's chart provides an example of failure in this respect. In just the same way, while a square indicates a difficulty, it also promises the capacity to overcome it. But that that promise will be fulfilled is not guaranteed.

Judgement of a conjunction, then, depends on the nature of the two bodies involved; then on the sign, or signs, occupied; then on midpoint involvements; then on orb; then on the applying/separating, dexter/sinister distinction: application implies less control, dexter difficulty – so that applying sinister and separating dexter are interesting and worthy of study.

Usually the conjunction manifests itself as an unconscious ('instinctive') mode of behaviour; it will not be as obvious, however, as the Moon in its sign, or as a close square. The one-time British and European heavyweight

Henry Cooper Sun-Mars conjunction in Taurus

champion boxer Henry Cooper has a Sun-Mars conjunction in Taurus, applying sinister, orb 4° 13′. This is altogether highly appropriate, except that the orb is rather wide. Sun-Mars aspects imply fighters, ambitiousness, determination, power, egoism, exhibitionism. Cooper, the best true heavyweight that Britain has produced in this century, sublimated his fighting instincts entirely into his profession. The conjunction being in Taurus helped him to avoid the usual temptations open to successful boxers, which spoiled the career of John Conteh and so many others. The midpoint of the conjunction is semisquare the Pisces Venus, which is itself at the Saturn/Uranus midpoint. These configurations imply a constructive and artistic attitude and a certain complementary distaste for ill-willed violence. Cooper was no brawler, but a fine aesthetic boxer of cunning and skill (Gemini rising). At the same time there is the need to resolve tension by quick separations: knock-outs – Cooper's left hook was famous, and gave Ali, at his peak, more trouble than any other punch he received. Venus is itself in a fairly close double-applying septile aspect to Neptune, which suggests a much more refined nature than one would normally associate with a very tough cockney boxer: this is confirmed by Cooper's sensible, apolitical stands on certain humane issues. All this tends to resolve any difficulty that might arise from the orb of the conjunction being rather too wide for so successful a boxer: it is applying sinister, supplying enough killer instinct, but modulated. The sign a conjunction is in colours it considerably: here we have the cautious side of Taurus combined with the 'fury when roused' side.

Conjunctions with points must be judged rather differently. Thomas Hardy's Saturn-Vertex conjunction indicates circumstances and attitude of mind. Margaret Thatcher's Asc-Saturn conjunction in Scorpio, not a pleasant combination except in thoughtful or creative people, indicates misery for the many, but this can only be inferred from the rest of the chart. This aspect is widely seen as indicating a tendency to evade facts, lack of self-awareness, unpleasant manner, extreme conservatism, 'questionable moral qualities' (Harding); but it will depend, of course, on the rest of the chart and particularly on the aspects to Asc and Saturn. All this shows that it is necessary to discover in what ways conjunctions may be modified.

Some have asserted that conjunctions are weakened by the bodies being in different signs: this is untrue, but their nature is changed and one has to consider the relationship between the two signs. Henry Cooper also has a dissociate conjunction between Uranus in Aries and Mercury at the beginning of

Astrology today

PLANTING BY THE PLANETS

by Diana Hunt

Many books have been written about the special affinity between a plant and a Sun sign. Yet though Taureans may be super rose growers and Taurus on the Midheaven brings Leo to the Ascendant, we all know people who grow fantastic roses yet are not necessarily born under Taurus or Leo.

Virgoans are said to have green fingers. Aquarians, we read, are supposed to grow the best lilac and to have the lucky touch with flowering shrubs and trees. But in my opinion that does not mean that an Aries subject can't plant winter jasmine or rhododendrons successfully. In fact, astrologers vary a great deal in their theories about which plants belong to which Sun sign.

I am inclined to think that the flowers or shrubs you love best will grow for you regardless of any old almanac which gives you totally different ones for your Sun sign. You'll lavish care and attention on your favourite plant, possibly talk to it—and this will, I am sure, create a reaction in your plant. It will grow for you.

I believe, though, that the Moon, which makes the tide rise and fall, has a certain influence on the time of your planting, feeding, spraying and looking after your garden.

You should plant during phases when the Moon is waxing (growing bigger), beginning with the New Moon and going on during the next fortnight. Always plant flowers, shrubs and trees during the waxing Moon—everything in fact which grows strongly above the soil. Go on planting those up to the time of the Full Moon.

Root crops and bulbs, though, are an exception. They should be planted during the week which starts at the Full Moon. That means onions and flower bulbs of all kinds, potatoes, carrots, turnips, radishes, etc.

But don't plant these during the week which starts at the time of the Last Quarter Moon.

It sounds dead simple but it isn't quite as easy to follow.

The best garden in my district belongs to a tall, white-haired lady in her 70s. Her carnations look like jewels; her forget-me-nots are shaded from palest blue to almost gentian, and she manages to cultivate wild cyclamen—in a London garden! She was born under Capricorn, by the way, and has done her growing by the Moon for years.

The other day in passing I heard her telling a neighbour: 'Gemini, Leo and Virgo are barren.'

'My dear, my sister is a Gemini and has four children,' protested her neighbour.

'I am speaking of Moon phases, not of people,' said the tall lady. 'When the Moon is in these signs don't plant, don't separate plants, but weed, fight the pests or cut off branches which you don't want to grow.

'Sagittarius, Aquarius and Aries are semi-barren (again I'm talking of Moon phases, not people). So many Aries subjects have green fingers, and Sagittarians are great at growing things they like to eat—strawberries or asparagus or courgettes. Still, when the Moon is in one of those signs prepare the soil, weed, get a soil analysis made, or cut the grass. But don't plant or transplant!

'A good time for planting is when the Moon is in a semi-ferial phase in Capricorn, Taurus or Libra. But the very best phase is the week before the Full Moon and the days when Lunar is in Cancer, Scorpio or Pisces—the very fertile signs.'

Her neighbour and I listened spellbound. The super-gardener laughed. 'One last taboo. Don't put seeds in, don't plant or re-pot your houseplants on the days of the First Quarter and the Last Quarter Moon. These are, from the gardener's point of view, tricky phases. And if you have to work in the garden during the New Moon or the Full Moon—I try to avoid this—work on your own. You're almost bound to argue with your companion.'

These rules appear to be tempting. For her they do work. I'll try them out and I'll let you know next year if my garden is like the one we see in the seed catalogues!

VIRGO ♍

THE BUSY, KINDLY PERFECTIONIST

by DIANA HUNT

POSITION IN THE ZODIAC	SIXTH SIGN
CORRESPONDING TO	AUGUST 22 TO SEPTEMBER 22
PRINCIPLE	SERVICE
ELEMENT	EARTH
QUALITY	MUTABLE
PLANETARY RULER	MERCURY
SYMBOL	THE MAIDEN

If you were born under Virgo your friends (and you have many) think you are the most sympathetic person on Earth. Your boss finds you invaluable, reliable, highly efficient and punctual. Your mum says you work too much and don't have enough fun. And all of them come to you when they are troubled, sick or things have gone seriously wrong.

Since Virgo is a feminine sign and its symbol a maiden with free-flowing hair carrying the fruits of the harvest let's turn our astrological spotlight first on the lady of the sign. If she reads these lines she'll give us a gentle smile, an honest glance and say politely that we are just a trifle wrong about her character.

For while compassionate, kind-hearted and willing to help right and left she is a critical lady and a perfectionist. She will declare that she doesn't want to be constantly busy only she has a lot to do—what with her job, a man and two kids, not to mention the dog, cat, hamster and gerbil—and other people she could mention leave work undone so she just has to do it, doesn't she?

My Virgoan friends, whom I love dearly, will nurse me when I have 'flu, stuff me with herbal tea and undiluted honey and get me well again. Four weeks later it will be said that my illness was my fault—after all I never dress warmly enough, smoke too much, eat the wrong food—and while I'm still very grateful, these tirades about my wrong-doings depress me. Yes, a Virgoan friend is wonderful when you're down and a confidence-shatterer when you are up again.

Ms Virgo is order personified. Her desk, her home, her well-groomed person are models of cleanliness and tidiness to all of us less well organised humans. Passing cars just don't splash mud on to her white coat; they keep it for us. Hair shining, nails beautifully lacquered, the lady really can find last year's bank statements in a jiffy. And she pays her gas bill on the dot. She hates messes or chaos.

She would wish that her emotions were equally in order. Alas, they are often far from well-organised and controlled. This girl, who knows so well how to handle any difficult task in her career, handles her love life far from efficiently.

Like the rest of us, she may fall for a man who wants a quick adventure while she longs for stability and emotional security. And with her obsessional helpfulness she will try her utmost to help him find true values, find the right perspective of their relationship, making it go on in harmony and bliss.

When she also gently points out that he smokes, drinks and flirts too much he'll run like a scalded cat. And our Virgo will blame herself for having made him unhappy — for self-criticism is another of her characteristics.

Some Virgo ladies find sex threatening and too bewildering. Abandoning their self-control when passion storms through their veins is a terrifying experience. Only a man who can give this unselfish woman the emotional security she needs will make her a happy and willing partner.

Mr Virgo is a practical fellow. He trusts his excellent brains, his gifted hands and is slightly sceptical (perhaps a little afraid) of strong emotions. A good logical talker, he is a fine organiser. In his career life he is

Taurus, indicating self-will and a good brain in the chosen profession: the sudden left hook.

Clearly, unaspected conjunctions are likely to manifest more strongly. The general characteristic of the conjunction is that the two (or three, or even four) bodies blend together, and express themselves in a manner that comes so naturally to the native that he may well be unaware of it. Venus would soften Mars; but Mars would harden Venus. Hitler had Venus-Mars, double-applying dexter, very close in Taurus. Since Taurus is Venus' sign, one might have presumed that Venus would be stronger than Mars, and so soften it. But this was by no means the case. Clearly this is a good example of Venus functioning as ragingly acquisitive rather than as harmonious: one must always allow for the possibility that this planet will function not at all as a 'benefic' but as its opposite.

13H *27° 41′ 33″ and multiples. Orb: 45′–1°*
This is a complex aspect, but claims that it gives indications of a person's attitude both to death and to spiritual deadness (when the emotion is blunted either by physiological derangements in the brain or by extreme stress) seem to stand up. I have looked at the chart of Van Gogh (p. 171) from this point of view.

SEMISEXTILE: *30°. Harmonic: 12H. Orb 50′, but this minor aspect can manifest, if there are several 12H connections, up to 1° applying.*

The semisextile has been neglected at the expense of the quincunx (150°), which operates at a slightly wider orb but is only more important inasmuch as it functions as part of 'yod' configurations (p. 133). The semisextile aspect was once called, with exquisite vagueness, 'slightly beneficial'. It is not. It denotes strain, and at close orbs very severe strain, between the two bodies or points involved. Astrologers very frequently ignore the almost zero-orb sinister applying semisextile between Sun and Neptune in Hitler's chart. This functioned as malevolently as any square: it is an excellent illustration of how the very close minor aspect can be as strong as the major aspect.

As Addey remarks, the semisextile being 3 × 4H (12H), combines the 'difficulty-effort-achievement' characteristics of 4H with the 'enjoyment' characteristics of 3H. This is what justifies our adopting, as a keyword, the 'strain' feature of the aspect, but, although strain is probably the main effect of semisextiles, it is not the only way in which they manifest. As always, this will depend on the bodies/points involved, and on the presence or absence of other connecting aspects. Mercury semisextile Uranus can simply indicate sharpness of tongue, but won't that cause strain somewhere?

UNDECIMAL: *32.727272° (rounds off to 32° 44′, but multiples must be calculated from the decimal, and then rounded) and multiples. Harmonic: 11H. Orb: ½°, or 1° if there are more than two such aspects.*

As the reader will already have inferred, aspects are in one important sense harmonics. If in a chart Uranus and Jupiter are separated by an arclength of 32° 44′, then the majority of conventional astrologers would say that they are in semisextile aspect (30°). More sophisticated astrologers would not consider this to be an aspect, for in modern terms 2° 44′ is an enormous and misleading orb to allow for the semisextile. If there is no semisextile here, then is there anything? There is, in fact, an undecimal (11H) aspect, for 360 ÷ 11 = 32° 43′ 38″. That arclength and its multiples form part of the 11H series, which is highly significant. In practice, where the exact aspect runs into seconds of arc, we round off to the nearest minute. The only quick way to detect an undecimal is to set up the 11H chart, a matter of three minutes on a calculator (see p. 134).

The undecimal is a very powerful but wholly neglected aspect which, although technically not hard, can act in a manner very similar to the genuinely hard aspects. 11H aspects manifest in a very definite way and they indicate excess. They also, according to Williamsen, describe a 'person's ability to integrate diversities and dualisms'. These interpretations are reconcilable: the tension of 'double-bind' situations, which can be external

– where you are trapped by feelings of obligation or duty, but cannot entirely please one or more people – or internal – the tug between scepticism and faith – is likely to lead to a type of stress which in its turn will lead to excess in one form or another. 11H aspects in a chart show the type of excess; the 11H chart will show the way to overcome it.

I have found 11H aspects, and the 11H chart, invaluable in interpretation.

SEMIQUINTILE: *36°. Harmonic: 10. Orb ¾–1°.*

This is a subharmonic of 5H, and I have found it indicative of the interpersonal difficulties which arise from the exercise of any kind of power or talent, whether for good or evil. It is more difficult than 15H (24° and multiples), but is frequently suggestive of useful ways of relating to people. 108°, called the tre-decile, has a similar meaning. These aspects should never be neglected, and they are by no means neutral. They appear as oppositions in the 5H chart, and the signs, or houses, across which such aspects fall are helpful indications of the areas of life in which the difficulties will be found.

NOVILE: *40°, 80°, 160°. Harmonic: 9. Orb 1°.*

There is some evidence, which I have found to be corroborated, that 80° is an arclength at which no aspects seem to operate effectively; there are complex mathematical reasons for this. The Navamsa chart, as the 9H chart is called in Hindu astrology, is very important; it is probably more important than the aspect itself. Two planets in novile indicate that in any kind of work that the native finishes the two principles involved will be seen to work well together. A house decorator who had Mars and Venus in close novile would perhaps produce an energetically graceful result, a peculiarly well and appropriately decorated bedroom for lovers, for example.

The 9H chart is supposed to show the nature of the marriage partner. It seems more often to show the nature of anything that the native achieves. It will show the nature of the marriage partner only if he or she has proved compatible; otherwise it will show the nature of the person who would prove so, whether he or she has come into the native's life or not. It is very useful in discovering the kind of person the native really needs, as distinct from the kind of person he thinks he needs.

SEMISQUARE, SESQUIQUADRATE: *45°, 135°. Harmonic: 8. Orb 1–1¼°.*

These are very like squares, and can be as powerful if very close. Ebertin uses them as though they were identical with squares, and, though this is a dubious procedure, he does not seem to go very wrong with it: this is probably because his astrology is event-oriented, and is therefore concerned with transits and directions. There is little doubt that in terms of things that happen – from accidents to wins on the pools – the semisquares and sesquiquadrates are more indicative than the trines or sextiles. But in the radical chart, where we are interested in states as much as we are in 'destiny', the trines and sextiles are as significant.

There is a useful way to find these aspects. First, think in terms of Cardinal, Fixed, Mutable. Look at the position of the body or point which you are examining for an 8H aspect. Measure 45° from it forwards in the zodiac (this is most easily done in absolute longitude with a calculator). You will find a degree in a Cardinal, Fixed or Mutable sign which will aspect the body/point in 8H; there may not be a body or point at this degree. But look at the other three points in square (i.e. at the same degrees in signs of the same quality): are any of these occupied? Take the chart on p. 62: suppose we want to see if the Sun is afflicted by an 8H aspect, having easily assured ourselves that nothing squares or opposes it. Absolute longitude of Sun is 33° 51′. Add 45 = 78° 51′ = 18 Gemini 51. There is nothing there at all. But look quickly around to see if it is squared or opposed. It is: by Saturn in Sagittarius: a 135° aspect, separating, dexter.

As it happens this is one of the most difficult aspects in astrology: a Sun in Taurus afflicted by Saturn. Natives with this aspect take things much too hard for their own good. Those close to them have to learn to manage this quasi-pathological sensitivity, and to try to understand that it stems in part from frustrated idealism: these people expect too much from others, even though they may deny it. A very close square between Sun in Taurus and Saturn is even more drastic; but this dexter sesquiquadrate is very disturbing to the native. However, the aspect would be more difficult if Saturn were in any other of the Mutables: Sagittarius is a useful placement for it.

In the same chart: is anything in 8H aspect to the Moon? 90° 30′ + 45 = 135° 30′: there is nothing at 15 Leo 30, but MC is at 16 Aquarius 25. A quick check reveals that there are no other 8H aspects in this chart.

A few astrologers have alleged special distinctions between the two 8H aspects, but, while I accept that such are likely to exist, I have not been able to find them. It is therefore practical to treat them in the same way as squares, but their intensity falls off very rapidly indeed after about 20′. Thus, the Sun-Saturn aspect in the chart in question is much stronger than the Moon-MC one; and the Moon-Uranus square, which is unaspected, is much more powerful than Moon-MC, though somewhat modulated by the MC connection. If a chart has no squares, but a number of 8H aspects all of which have a widish orb (say 1–1¼°), then these will probably act as powerfully, in concert, as a square.

SEPTILE: *51.42857° and multiples, called bi-septile and tri-septile respectively. In practice the aspects are called exact at 51° 26′, 102° 51′ and 154° 48′. Harmonic: 7. Orb: 1°.* There must be a distinction between these three aspects, but, once again, this has not yet been discovered. Septiles work on a different level from other low harmonic aspects. They show the potential the native has to rise to occasions: to bring something extra out of him- or herself, and perhaps to add something extra to a situation which lacks it. In 1939 Great Britain lacked a politician capable of waging war; the exception was Winston Churchill. He had Sun-Mars in septile. He was able to lead the nation, and to embody its will in a manner similar to Queen Elizabeth I at the time of the Armada. Churchill was thus, in this respect, receptive to inspiration of a Sun-Mars type.

Sir Winston Churchill Sun-Mars septile

As Addey says, the septile does not indicate inspiration, but receptivity to it. He has found a better term than inspiration, one under which ‘inspiration’ may confidently be subsumed, the state of being ‘switched on’. He thus suggests that John Ruskin's sexual masochism is shown in his chart by the septile between Mars and Saturn: he suggests that Ruskin could only be ‘switched on’ if his lover was cruel to him, cruelty being one feature of the Mars-Saturn principle. The septile is thus valuable in judging the sexual psychology and in demonstrating the nature of a person's creativity – creativity, it must be remembered, extends to dreams and games as well as to more obvious things like stews, books, instruments of death or torture and paintings.

The septile, which describes inner states in terms of what conditions a person *needs* in order to operate with the greatest effectiveness, may well work in the following way. Take the strongest major aspect(s) in the chart, preferably squares. These indicate difficulties which can produce achievement if met and resolved constructively. Churchill has Mercury-Uranus in double-applying dexter square in fixed signs, suggesting: impulsiveness; a desire to escape the dull and everyday; a potentially very effective self-control, because the aspect in itself is so very wild that the native could hardly survive without controlling himself; an enjoyment of the power to challenge conventional thinking. Churchill clearly needed a context in which he could operate this square without violating his own conscience. He prepared for such conditions in an inspired way, taking up an anti-fascist position long before other politicians did. When the time came, he was the obvious, the only, choice – even though the occasion was a failure initiated by none other than himself. In other words, the septiles can show how the squares in particular, though the other hard aspects come into it, can be resolved.

The 7H chart describes a person's capacity to achieve creativity, just as the 5H chart describes the sort of creativity he or she aspires to. The 6H chart, one of the most puzzling of all, but one of the most indicative, describes how people reach their goals: it is therefore a failure chart, since a sense of failure characterizes all human creative enterprises – nothing is wholly successful.

SEXTILE: *60°. Harmonic: 6. Orb: $1\frac{1}{2}$°–2°.* The sextile is the most easily misunderstood aspect, although its nature is generally agreed upon. It is usually said that it is like the trine but that it requires effort, and that it is therefore the aspect of opportunity. This is perfectly true. But many astrologers spoil their interpretations by too easily assuming that the opportunities offered are first good, and secondly properly taken. Some sextiles, such as Moon-Venus, are easy to 'use': so easy that they don't in fact get used at all. Others, such as Mars-Saturn or Mercury-Neptune are very difficult to use indeed. They are frequently either bungled – the way they are bungled may be seen from the condition of the two bodies in the chart: midpoint involvements, sign placement, other aspects – or evaded so unconsciously, but conscientiously, that they become, so to say, eyesores in the character. And sometimes they are overused, as in the case of Lindbergh's Mars-Moon sextile which tells us almost all that was unpleasant about him.

Thus the sextile is very often a malicious aspect: sometimes it will appear in the charts of those who by circumstance are not able to take up the opportunities offered. It must be remembered that the sextile is, above all, a Sun aspect, and that the Sun exhausts itself in generating the zodiac, and so to a certain extent marks a point of failure in the chart. The 6H chart is therefore the chart of failure, although usually only from the very highest standards. Thus the sextile can be a useful or a positively dangerous aspect. Sextiles do often manifest as well managed achievements of character and the 6H chart can at least be turned from a failure chart into a warning chart.

The best way to deal with sextiles is to judge them from the tenor of the rest of the chart. The chart will tell you if an opportunity offered by a sextile ought to be taken up or not: whether it is promising or threatening. Sextiles to the points, though, are generally very useful; whatever planet makes them, they present good opportunities. In the chart on p. 62 the Asc-Desc and MC-IC axes are ringed with sextiles and trines: Mercury and Jupiter to Asc, which means that both these planets are trine Desc, and Venus and Saturn to MC, which means that these two trine the IC. In that chart Desc takes a close septile from Uranus, and the IC close septiles from Sun and Mars. A great deal would be missed in this chart if these trines and septiles were neglected, yet most astrologers hardly bother about Desc or IC, insisting that the other ends of the axes are the most important. This is a serious error. For example: Henry Cooper's MC is very closely trined by Jupiter, as one might expect, but is the exceedingly close sextile to the IC less important? It indicates, among many other things, the opportunity to make money to spend on his 'home base' – and this opportunity has been taken. The opportunities offered by sextiles to personal points usually are taken, in fact.

QUINTILE: *72°*. **BI-QUINTILE:** *144°*.
Harmonic: 5. Orb 1°–2°.

The intensity of the quintile is very great at orbs of up to 1°, but falls off sharply after that. This series of aspects, with its sub-harmonics (especially 15H and 20H), has been very seriously neglected. The aspect was introduced, with the 8H aspects, by Kepler. Quintile and bi-quintile connections describe the capacity a person has for integrating his faculties in action: to put it more simply, they show not what he ought to be good at so much as what he most certainly *can* be good at, even if that is positively evil. The bodies involved in a quintile should be looked at, initially, as 'malefics': they should be seen in their most sinister light. This is because the quintiles indicate power, and so in the first instance we should take, so to say, the gloomiest view. But the quintile is not a malefic aspect in itself, any more than is any other aspect. A trine shows which principles flow easily together; a quintile, the Pluto aspect *par excellence*, shows which principles act together in a compulsive and external way. A trine might show no more than a state of mind, though this cannot be neglected: states lead to actions, or to inertia. A quintile between the same two bodies would indicate something either compulsive or something achieved.

The quintiles between Neptune-Vertex and Sun-Pluto in the chart on p. 62 are useful illustrations. The first is between a body and a point, in this case a point that is rather more mysterious than the other personal points, but which certainly seems to tell us something about the circumstances that will attend the native. That quintile suggests that throughout his life the native will have to deal with Neptunian matters – imagination, deception, madness, the sea – on all levels. A quintile aspect between a body and a personal point brings out the nature of the body, suggesting that in the life that body will predominate in some way or another. The Sun-Pluto quintile indicates compulsion to create, arrogance, the need to be able to speak as an authority, a violent and contradictory emotional life, difficulties in relaxing. All this functions, one would suggest, as near-compulsive behaviour in the native, almost out of his control.

The 5H chart indicates, as we should expect, facility. People who tend to explode into the world in a fluent or cacophonous manner are likely to have charts loaded with quintiles: Mozart and Hitler are examples. In 5H charts

The young Mozart A chart with many quintiles

we can look for such indications as 'harmoniousness' more confidently than we can in radical charts: if we don't find it, we may well begin to fear misfortune for someone. An important clue to the nature of the quintile is its undeniable power in synastry: here it shows sexual attraction, the capacity of two people to enjoy each other physically, especially if the Mars and the Venus of each chart are connected by quintile. This gives a precise indication of the kind of power that the quintile carries: it is a power that is coloured by sexuality, or that has at least the quality of a strong sexual urge. The quintile tells us a great deal about the way in which sexual energy is used.

SQUARE: *90°. Harmonic: 4. Orb 5°, sometimes extending to 6° especially if the orb in RA is closer than the one in ecliptic longitude.*

The squares in a chart are the most easy aspects to see, which is not to say that they are the most important. They indicate severe difficulty in the integration of two principles, but the difficulties are so severe that more often than not they become resolved and are turned into strengths of achievement or character, though these need not be in any way virtuous, or helpful to anyone but the native. This is why some of the more 'raw' features of the radical chart tend to 'fade out' as the native gets older; the trines and soft aspects become more important, for they tend to persist.

Certain squares, especially if isolated, seem to indicate persisting features of character rather than potential achievement. The Mars-Mercury square, in particular, is usually of this nature. It is often found, in mutables, in those who have mood disorders which lead them into nervous difficulties; such people are frequently over-argumentative or bad tempered, but they are persistent workers who, whatever other indications may be present in the chart as a whole, make quick and efficient decisions. This is one of the most easily recognisable of all squares. William Blake, T. E. Lawrence and Mrs. Gandhi all have this aspect, close.

All squares, however, need to be judged in the light of the chart as a whole. I have illustrated the powerful effects of a close applying square in the case of Arthur (p. 152), and shown how it blends in with, and is to some extent modified by, the rest of the chart. Of all the harmonics, 4H probably manifests itself most obviously. These aspects operate at a concrete level. They affect behaviour directly and as nearly unequivocally as any other indications in astrology except for the Moon sign. We look for them and for the oppositions, first of all when judging a chart.

TRINE: *120°. Harmonic: 3. Orb 5°.*

This is the soft aspect *par excellence*; but it is soft, meaning 'easy', 'harmonious' and giving the personality a quietness in some area of

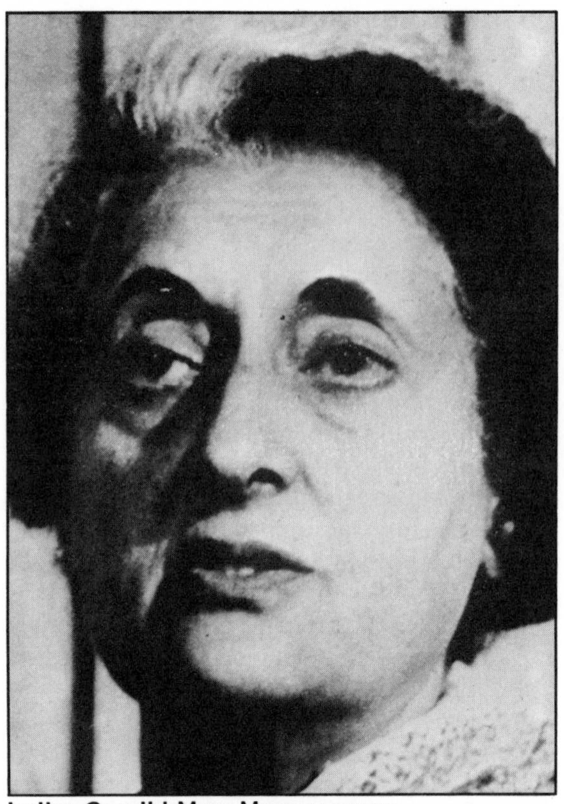

Indira Gandhi Mars-Mercury square

T. E. Lawrence Mars-Mercury square

life, only when the bodies involved are obviously friendly, or when the trine is comparatively isolated in terms of major aspects. A true grand trine (three planets in trine, where each planet is at the midpoint, orb 2°, of the other two) is clearly something quite different, as the case of Landru (p. 183) illustrates. But however 'contaminated' a trine may be by other aspects connected to it, those bodies that are in close trine do have a potential in the personality for cooperation, although this cooperation may not benefit anyone at all, let alone the native. Rupert Brooke's rather wide Venus-Neptune trine gave his verse an ephemerally popular, but feeble, sort of sensuality; Robert Graves' close double-applying square between the same bodies explains why he is so great a love poet and much else about him.

Rupert Brooke and **Robert Graves** Venus-Neptune trine and square respectively

There is no doubt that the trines can lead to weakness and indolence, whereas the squares tend to produce tension and work. The trine is sometimes then the aspect of the idler and the parasite, but as often it indicates smooth working in some area. It would be unfair to say that those astrologers who ascribe 'luck' to the trine are wholly misguided: some trines do persistently suggest that those who possess them do have luck. The Jupiter-Saturn trine, which it will be noted is in traditional terms the 'great benefic' in harmonious aspect with the 'greater infortune', denotes difficulties but, as one sees time and time again, the chance to emerge from these by the skin of the teeth. 'Someone or something will come to (their) rescue,' one American astrologer remarked.

The 3H chart, which is not often used, reveals the subject's potential for synthesis. This is another way of saying that we look to our trines to see in what manner our oppositions might be resolved. It is interesting, particularly in view of what I have said about sextiles, that the sextile appears as an opposition in 3H. This demonstrates that interpersonal problems are created by the need for synthesis, a need which everyone has in some degree. The trines in a chart are therefore more difficult to interpret than other major aspects: they are more psychologically subtle, because they pertain directly to internal psychological balance. These are the states of mind which lie behind the more obvious manifestations of behaviour. No doubt, this is why sextiles in the radical chart so often seem to indicate nothing: in order to discover what they mean, we have to look at the 3H chart.

QUINCUNX: *150°. 12H. Orb: 1–1½°.* The quincunx has received a great deal of attention in recent years. It is an important aspect, and is rather like it looks: skew, strained, like an opposition but obviously not one. The effects of these aspects to points or between bodies is very noticeable; and I wonder if this has not brought about a corresponding neglect of the semisextile. Both aspects are 12H aspects. The quincunx has more to do with health, mental and physical, than the semisextile, and is a little like the opposition inasmuch as it concerns interpersonal rather than wholly 'internal' matters. It shows what a person will, or will not, do for others, and how much this costs him; it indicates what a person believes are his obligations, and his feelings about carrying them out. People can get ill if they starve themselves of the input gained from others or if they refuse, or cannot find a way, to reciprocate the affections of others.

There is a very close quincunx between Mercury and Pluto (from Sagittarius to Cancer) in the chart of the Indian crypto-dictator Mrs. Gandhi; it explains a great deal about her now rather obvious unhappiness in her job: the astrologer can see that she feels the loss of her son was a punishment. She was early conditioned, very probably against her own instincts, to take on huge responsibilities; this made her obsessional about everyone's responsibilities, and this in turn led to her deteriorating into a nepotic and arrogant despot who wore the uneasy but desperate mask of one who knew what was best for all: she could not leave anything to others, or trust others. This particular quincunx is a peculiarly obsessive aspect, causing her to act with great callousness, and without understanding, towards anyone who fails in her eyes.

Not all quincunxes will manifest in such a straightforwardly unpleasant way; indeed, the problem indicated by any quincunx is soluble by relating decently to others, so that even a Mercury-Pluto quincunx can, in some charts, indicate just and sensitive behaviour. In Mrs. Gandhi's case, Mercury is closely opposed by Jupiter, and a not very skew T-Square is formed by Mars from Virgo; clearly the quincunx does not help any more than a Virgo Mars can. No quincunx is really intense in effect beyond about $1\frac{1}{2}°$ orb.

OPPOSITION: *180°. Harmonic: 2. Orb: 5–7°.*

This is a hard aspect, but is usually less drastic and a little less obvious than the square. The opposition involves difficulties in relationship to the environment, mainly relationships with other people or with what they represent or seem to represent. The opposition, it has been well said, causes 'alienation in relationships'; there is 'raging conflict and controversy' set up between the two planets, or rather between the principles they represent. Let us take a rather obvious example: Richard Nixon's widish (5° 22′) but double applying dexter Sun-Neptune opposition. This indicates a fear of confronting people directly, as exemplified by the ultimately stupid and unnecessary underground tactics which led to Watergate and to Nixon's disgrace. However unsuitable Nixon might have been, had he acted decisively over the matter of Watergate, he need never have met his deserts. The opposition makes the native feel more uneasy than the square because other people are directly involved, but astrologers are probably right in seeing this aspect as somewhat easier to resolve than the square: the action of other people, when they are positive and constructive, as they often are, can help.

A close trine and sextile to each end of the opposition indicates fairly easy, often effortless, means of resolution. The chart on p. 62 has an opposition from Saturn to Asc, which also means a conjunction to Desc. The Mercury-Jupiter conjunction trines Saturn-Desc and sextiles Asc. Now Saturn is never 'easy' in any life, but it can be rewarding. Such a configuration strongly suggests that idleness would destroy the native and that any idling he actually does is harmful to him. His salvation, if he has one, lies in unrelenting work. He will view things cynically, be over-severe on himself and on others, and his manner will often be teasing, mocking or perhaps simply austere.

In Arthur's chart (p. 155) we have a different kind of opposition: between two bodies. Such very close oppositions have the effect of slicing the chart in two, and they can be traumatic, but only if they have an orb of less than about 1°.

In the 2H chart the oppositions are, of course, conjunct, while the squares become oppositions and the 8H aspects become squares. Here we are looking at the character from the point of view of difficulties in relating either, as I have said, to people or to what they appear to represent: we view the conjunctions, and the sign they fall in, in the harmonic chart, as indicative of the specific difficulties. Why the signs they fall in, treated as houses, should help in interpretation, I cannot tell; but they undoubtedly do.

CONFIGURATIONS

There are certain patterns formed by planets and points, which appear frequently in birth charts; all of these are explicable in terms of midpoints. Most common are: the T-square, the grand cross, the yod (or Finger of Fate or Finger of God), and the grand trine. These can also exist in what I call skew form, in which case they are less powerful, though never to be neglected. To be true, or genuine, the midpoints involved must not exceed an orb of 2°, or 3° at the very outside. Thus, a true T-square has two planets, A and B, opposing each other, with C square to both – and A/B = C must be in orb 2–3°; otherwise the T-square is a skew T-square. Similarly a grand cross, which is two sets of oppositions square to each other, is skew if the orb of the square is greater than 2–3°. When considering a grand trine, we do not allow transition of light: each of the three planets must be in orb 2–3°; in a skew grand trine one only of the three planets may be in an orb of 5°, or 6° at the outside.

In a T-square the planet at point focus – in square to the opposition – will resolve the problems generated by the opposition. A true grand cross is quite rare: it is a very difficult configuration to live with. The native will either be extremely dynamic or crazy, but other indications in the chart may, of course, help to reduce the level of tension. A yod consists of two quincunxes to a single planet; the native will slide from one direction to another in matters concerning the planet at point-focus. A grand trine is a hard aspect, despite the fact that a trine is decidedly soft. Sometimes the native will lack the energy to solve the problems generated by the three midpoints.

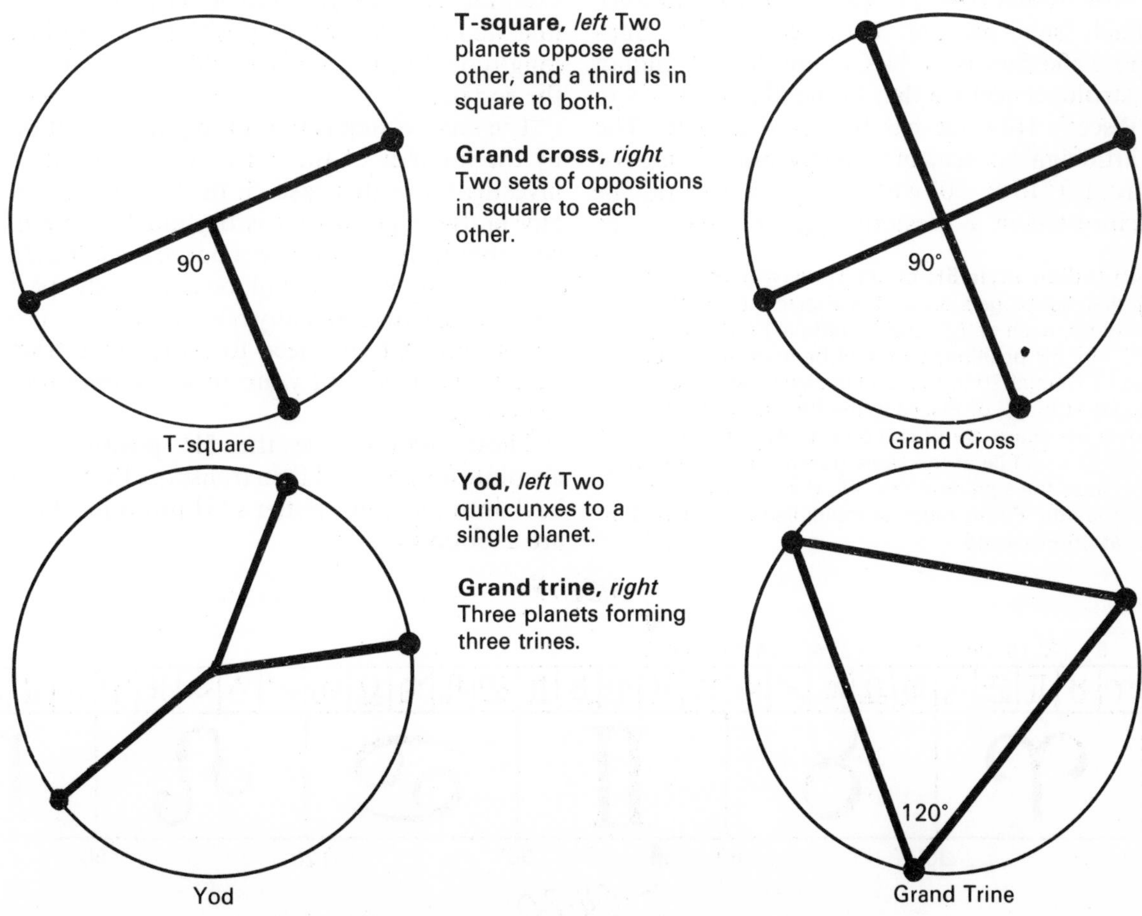

T-square, *left* Two planets oppose each other, and a third is in square to both.

Grand cross, *right* Two sets of oppositions in square to each other.

Yod, *left* Two quincunxes to a single planet.

Grand trine, *right* Three planets forming three trines.

BUILDING HARMONIC CHARTS

The principle behind harmonic charts is best explained by reference to Indian astrology, of which there are many forms. In most of them the astrologer presents his client, who is very often the father of a new baby, with the radical chart and fifteen others (2–15H). Although these are not judged in the same way as we judge harmonic charts, since each is supposed to show an important aspect of the destiny, they are nonetheless harmonic charts. How do they set them up? Nowadays they may use calculators, just as we do, but this is unlikely: the work one does in setting up something from which one is going to obtain information is important in attaining a receptive state of mind; their method is highly appropriate and shows us what in fact a harmonic chart is.

5H can serve as an example: it is based on 72° of the circle. Indian astrologers therefore envisage the whole zodiac divided into five 'little zodiacs' of 72° each (see illustration). Each 'sign' has only 6° instead of 30°. Suppose the Sun is at 11 Gemini 20. An Indian astrologer will see that in the 5H chart it is in 'Pisces'. How far has it moved into it? The 'little sign' consists of 6°, so the Sun has moved from 0° to 5° 20′ within it. How can this be expressed in a Western-style 5H chart? The 'little sign' has been collapsed from 30° into 6°, in other words reduced to a fifth of its size. So we must multiply the 5° 20′ that the Sun has moved into Pisces by five. The answer is 26 Pisces 40: this is the Sun's position in 5H.

This principle applies to all harmonic charts: 9H is based on nine 'little zodiacs' of 40° each, so that each 'little sign' must measure $40 \div 12 = 3° \ 20'$. Some harmonic charts, like the important 7H, are very hard to calculate in this way because the 'little signs' can only be close approximations: $360 \div 7$ produces the recurring decimal 51.428571428571, which is hard to draw. This is approximately 51° 25′ 42.857″, which in practice we round off to 51° 26′.

You can, of course, set up charts in the Indian way by drawing a series of 'little zodiacs' from which you can read off the appropriate positions, but it is easier to use a calculator. The 5H chart of Adolf Hitler can serve as an example (his radical chart is on p. 178). The first step is to list all the positions in absolute longitude. Start at 00 Aries 00, and go round the zodiac.

The second step is to multiply each position by the number of the harmonic you want to investigate: in this case, 5. In the case of 5H, any body or point that is beyond 12 Gemini will obviously multiply to a figure over 360. In the case of 50H, it will be any body past 7 Aries 12, with 100H any body past 3 Aries 36 and so on. All you need to do is to subtract successive 360s until your answer comes into the range 0–360.

These figures give the 5H positions in absolute longitude; I then transpose the figures back into the signs. Hitler's 5H positions then, are as follows:

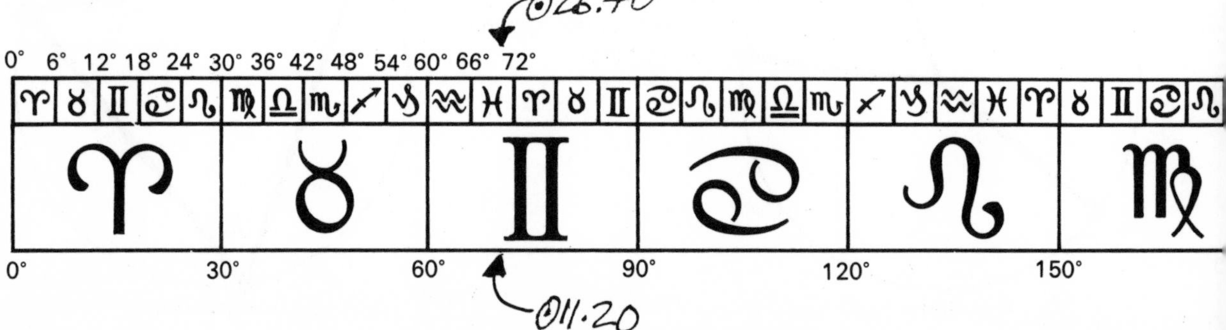

An Indian-style 5H chart To draw a 5H chart Indian astrologers divide the zodiac into 5 little zodiacs, each of 72°; these contain 12 signs of just 6°. The 5H positions can then be read off: a Sun at 11 Gemini 20 in the radical chart can be seen to be at 5° 21′ of Pisces in the 5H chart. Western-style 5H charts are drawn on one 360° zodiac. The Sun will be at the same position in Pisces, but, because the sign contains 30°, the Sun's position in the little Pisces must be multiplied by 5. The Sun is at 26 Pisces 45.

Mercury: 25 40 × 5 = 8 Leo 20
Sun: 30 48 × 5 = 4 Virgo 00
Mars: 46 25 × 5 = 22 Scorpio 05
Venus: 46 42 × 5 = 23 Scorpio 30
Vertex: 55 41 × 5 = 8 Capricorn 25
Neptune: 60 51 × 5 = 4 Aquarius 15
Pluto: 64 35 × 5 = 22 Aquarius 55
At this point I have to start subtracting:
Node: 106 05 × 5 = 530.416 (the calculator is operating in the decimal mode) − 360 = 20 Virgo 25
MC: 122 57 × 5 = 614.75 − 360 = 14 Sagittarius 45
Saturn: 133 27 × 5 = 667.25 − 360 = 7 Aquarius 15
Uranus: 199 30 × 5 = 997.5 − 720 = 7 Capricorn 30
Asc: 205 10 × 5 = 1025.83 − 720 = 5 Aquarius 50
The Moon and Jupiter necessitate 3 × 360 deducted:
Moon: 2 Aquarius 50
Jupiter: 11 Aquarius 15

This method can be used to set up all harmonic charts, even very high ones. It should be noted that we don't have to calculate the opposite ends of the angular or nodal axes: these are preserved. The few astrologers who use these charts tend generally to set them up from the new Asc, using the Equal House method (p. 142), or sometimes from the MC on the radical chart using the same method. I set them up on the 'natural' zodiac, using Aries as House I, Taurus as House II, and so on. This would be regarded as perverse by some; I do it for no other reason than that it works in the context of the meaning of the harmonic. Equal House measured from Asc or from MC in the harmonic chart simply does not work, and there is no reason why it should. If that Asc is 1° out, then it is 5° out in the 5H chart, 50° out in 50H etc.

A 5H chart brings the bodies in 5H (quintile) aspect in the radical chart into conjunction, and will show 10H aspects as oppositions, 15H as trines, 20H as squares, 25H as quintiles and so on. It will preserve only very close radical aspects (an orb of 1° is turned into one of 5° in a 5H chart).

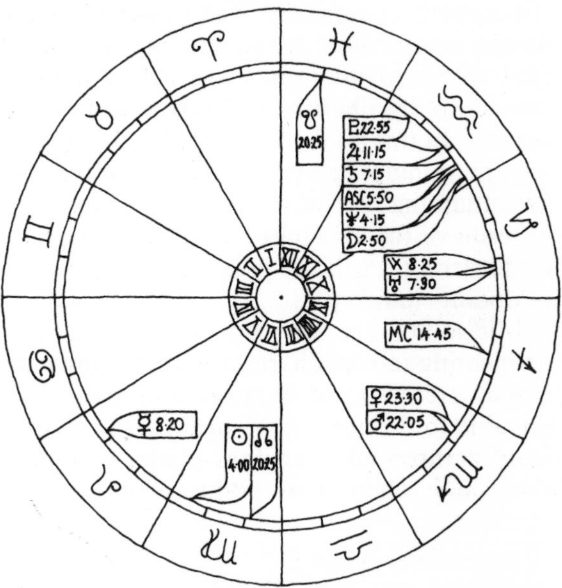

In Hitler's 5H chart notice that the gruesome conjunction in Aquarius (House XI of friends, hopes, wishes, group enterprises) spans only 8° 15′ in the harmonic chart: this means that there are no less than ten related quintiles in the radical chart of orb less than 1° 39′: radical orb is calculated from the 5H chart by dividing by 5. Everything is relevant in these charts; they are essential to the deep analysis of people well known to the astrologer.

0° 210° 240° 270° 300° 330° 360°

MIDPOINTS

A midpoint is the point exactly between two bodies/points. It is found by adding together the absolute longitude of the bodies and then dividing by two. The answer you get may give you the farther midpoint or the nearer midpoint; you can easily tell which, by inspection. The direct midpoint is the nearer midpoint, the result of dividing the shorter arc-distance between the two bodies/points. In practice, the point opposite, the farther midpoint, is – if occupied or transited – as powerful as the nearer one. Points in square or 8H aspect (45°, 135°) to midpoints are called indirect midpoints by Ebertin, and this is technically correct. In this book, however, I call points in square to midpoints (there are two of these to any midpoint) direct, because they are direct in terms of the 4H chart and because they are quite strong. I call the points in 8H aspect to midpoints indirect.

Midpoints are an aid to judging and delineating radical charts; they are significant if they are occupied by a body or point. We are able to deduce a good deal that is specific from a three- or even four-planet combination, and where two bodies/points are in traditional aspect, or nearly so, a planet at the nearer or farther midpoint strengthens that aspect, and allows us to give it a greater orb.

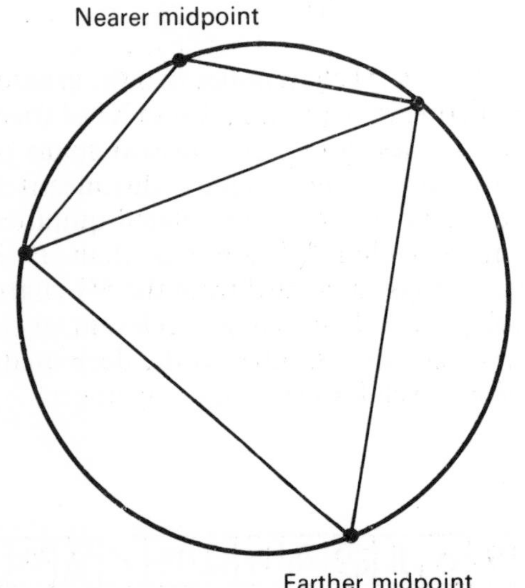

Midpoints There are two midpoints between every pair of bodies/points in the chart. The nearer midpoint is midway along the shorter arc between the two bodies/points. The farther midpoint is directly opposite, midway along the longer arc.

In the chart on p. 62 the Moon is at 00 Cancer 30 and Mercury is at 23 Aries 41. To find the midpoint, add the two absolute longitudes together and divide by two:

Moon	90 30
Mercury	23 41
2/	114 11
	57 06

Note that we round off the answer upwards. We always write Moon/Mercury when we want to indicate the midpoint between these two bodies, occupied or not. An oblique stroke, or solidus, between any two bodies or points indicates the midpoint.

SQUARES TO MIDPOINTS

The nearer Moon/Mercury midpoint is at 27 06 of a fixed sign. To find any squares, look to see if there is anything within 2° of this in any fixed sign. Neptune is in a double-separating square to this midpoint, orb 40′. This is close, and I therefore call it a direct midpoint. This is not a near or far midpoint, but it is so close a square that it makes the hard contact between the Moon and Mercury (an applying dexter 32H aspect of 66° 49′, orb 49′) operative in the character.

Moon/Jupiter is also square Neptune, but is double-applying, and very fast-moving. The orb is 47′: could this make the albeit weak quintile, between Moon and Jupiter, valid? The angle between them is 69° 42′, and the fast-moving Moon will in four hours cover the 2° 18′ to reach the exact aspect. Is it beginning to pick up power? This is a good example of the kind of question that has to be left to the individual astrologer. He or she should look at the Moon-Jupiter principle, then at the rest of the chart, and consider whether any feature of the principle fits into the general picture. Here, in my judgement at least, one does: excess of emotion and the tendency to overreact.

8H ASPECTS TO MIDPOINTS

Again taking the chart on p. 62, we see that

Moon + Neptune = 236° 56′ ÷ 2 = 118° 28′, which is 28° of a cardinal sign. There is nothing near this in any cardinal sign. We therefore look to see if there are any 8H (45°) aspects to the midpoint by adding 45° to the midpoint position. This brings us to 13° of a Mutable and, sure enough, we immediately see that Mars is only 38′ away from this point, though the aspect is separating from the planet.

These midpoint connections, which are based exclusively on hard aspects, are written either Moon/Jupiter – 90 – Neptune or Moon/Jupiter = Neptune. The = sign stands for either 0, 45, 90, 135 or 180.

FURTHER ASPECTS TO MIDPOINTS

Alfred Witte, a very eccentric German astrologer who in pre-war Germany developed a system of interpreting charts which is based mostly on midpoints, believed that the 16H ($22\frac{1}{2}°$) aspects were as strong as the 2, 4 and 8H. I concur, except that in almost every case I find that the $22\frac{1}{2}°$ aspect is little more than confirmatory, though it enriches the portrait. In very detailed work, however, one must consider aspects in 16, 32 and 64H. There is a sharp fall in important new information at 16H; but 32 and 64H give us a good deal of interesting secondary information. 128H (2° 48′ 45″ and multiples) is valid, but must be restricted to orbs of about 5′ applying and 3′ separating. In practice, you should not work with more than what I call the direct midpoints, at least to begin with, though the indirect 8H ones are indispensable in subtle analysis.

INTERPRETING MIDPOINTS

An occupied midpoint gives us a very specific piece of information, because we can combine the three principles indicated by the planets or points involved. It is important to take into account whether a midpoint is applying or separating and the nature of the sign in which the midpoint falls.

With the help of the many examples given in this book, and with the brief keyword guide I give of the two-planet/point principles (pp. 145–148), the reader will easily be able to interpret occupied or aspected midpoints. For example: Mercury-Neptune keywords are *imagination, intuition, lying, swindling, confusion, fantasy, fiction.* What should we expect then of Mercury/Neptune = Mars? The Martian energy could well bring the swindling or the fantasies into actuality. This could be a successful writer or a successful swindler. Certainly purposeful thinking of an imaginative sort is indicated, but the condition of the particular Mars involved must be considered. Mercury/Neptune = Saturn, on the other hand suggests depressed, conscientious or cynical thinking. Ebertin interprets this midpoint configuration as 'morbid sensitiveness', while Witte, always more daring but more interesting, states 'collection mania; to use mental products of others'. As always, and as I illustrate in my delineation of Arthur's chart, we are guided by an accumulation of similar detail and by intuition.

There are two useful books about midpoints: Ebertin's very famous *The Combination of Stellar Influences,* and *Rules for Planetary Pictures* by Witte and Lefeldt. Ebertin uses rather stark and moralistic language, but gives a short general interpretation of every aspect between two planets/points (the Vertex is excluded), and every possible combination of three planets/points, making 1117 interpretations in all. *Rules for Planetary Pictures* is the properly authorised revised version of Witte's first *Rules*, and it is a surprising, and often uncannily precise book. It is an essential book for all imaginative astrologers: both crazier and less commercial than the valuable *Combinations of Stellar Influences*, it is a more exciting and more endearing book to consult and it often brings astonishingly accurate results.

PARTS/RETROGRADATION

Until quite recently many of the more sensible astrologers tended to dismiss the points known as Arabic Parts as being over-superstitious. The most familiar Arabic Part is *Pars Fortuna*, or the Part of Fortune. Fortuna, as it is usually called, is found by adding together the absolute longitude of the Asc and Moon, and subtracting that of the Sun. 360 is added or subtracted from the result, if this is necessary to bring it into the range 0–360. Fortuna, by sign position, by aspects to it, and by midpoint involvement, is said to indicate the means by which a person may make adjustment between his inner and his outer needs. Very surprisingly, this seems to be true of all charts.

We should probably have dropped these parts, particularly since their correct calculation requires an accurate birth-time, if it had not been realised from study of harmonics and midpoints that they were calculated on similar principles. Furthermore, in the form Planet A + Planet B – Planet C, they have been shown by Dean to play a crucial role in the sunspot cycle when heliocentric planetary aspects are taken in the plane of the solar ecliptic.

Rising Parts, in other words parts in the 'twelfth house', could, Dean suggested, be as crucial in birth charts as rising midpoints and planets. I have found that to be the case.

RETROGRADATION

Planets do not really go backwards, any more than you go backwards when a train travelling more quickly than yours passes you. They merely appear to go backwards and to become stationary for short periods as they are viewed from Earth (see p. 49). Geophysical effects have been noted, by Nelson and others, at those times when planets 'go stationary'. The heavy planets remain stationary for a day or two; the faster ones for only a few hours.

I have found the interpretations of the American astrologer Thyrza Escobar to be, with certain modifications, empirically accurate. These interpretations are based on the notion that if a planet is retrograde then its principle is forced inwards: the principle does not appear overtly, but is still basic to the personality. Put another way, retrograde planets are stronger than direct ones. This is generally true, but it is necessary, as always, to blend this in with the rest of the chart. Where a retrograde planet is in a close aspect with the Moon, for example, observers will probably be able to detect its powerful effect. So that, although Escobar says that the retrograde effect means that the planet's principle will 'be more active than is apparent to others', this need not always be the case. T. P. Davis, an accomplished and serious-minded American astrologer, has suggested that retrogradation indicates that full expression of the principle of the planet must be found in relationships with others. This would seem to contradict Escobar's view, but in fact it does not. Retrogradation indicates an area of conflict, but one that is surely familiar to many people: that inner needs can only be fulfilled in personal relationships.

Only eight per cent of charts have no planets retrograde. It is argued that the outer planets are retrograde for a great deal of the time, so that they cannot all have the same effect. This is wooden thinking; as I have explained regarding aspects between the heavy planets, they manifest differently in every chart.

The effects of retrograde planets may be put briefly as follows:

Mercury: broods, keeps reconsidering, but to a purpose only if the condition of Mercury permits.

Venus: nostalgic, secret affections, keeps creating emotional hierarchies in the mind.

Mars: private activity, tendency to keep trying to make the abstract concrete.

Jupiter: religiously and/or philosophically inclined whatever the native thinks of himself.

Saturn: cynical outlook whatever he or she thinks.

Uranus: independent, but this may be frustrated.

Neptune: more idealistic than he or she thinks.

Pluto: obsessed by power, or a great reorganiser, or a subdued personality.

These interpretations should be blended into the chart as a whole. Obviously the aspects to the planets, and particularly two retrograde planets in close aspect, creating a combined effect, will be important.

HOUSES

Almost all astrologers use houses: Ebertin and Geoffrey Dean are notable exceptions. I do not reject houses, but they do clog up an already difficult subject and they add to the number of factors we need to consider. In our present state of knowledge, how useful are they? Or, are they in fact a hindrance?

There are some twenty house systems in current use, and as many more as anyone cares to invent. If I could find a system that worked comprehensively, I should use it whether it added to the number of factors that needed to be taken into consideration or not.

The famous astrologer Charles Carter pointed out many years ago that 'we cannot draw a clear line between that portion of the nativity (birth chart) which works out in terms of character and that which is shown in destiny'. This large admission amply explains why Carter, for all of his long working life, tirelessly experimented with a variety of house systems in his search for that 'clear line'. No astrologer has tried out so many so honestly and open-mindedly.

What he said sums up one of the two main difficulties about the houses. Yet, we still find astrologers who assert – with absolute certainty – that whereas the planets in the signs show the character, the planets in the houses show the destiny. Apart from such meaningless claptrap as 'the astrological houses indicate how the vibratory pattern established by the planets and the signs . . . relate to the auric field of the Earth itself', we are told by occultist astrologers that the houses 'relate to everyday life-on-earth activities'. The idea is this: you interpret the character from the sign position, and the circumstances of life from the houses and their occupants and rulers. But Carter knew long ago that this simply did not work out.

There are twelve houses just as there are twelve signs of the zodiac. There are twelve signs because that is the closest possible approximation to the natural number of months in a solar year, the month being measured by the interval between lunations. Signs are generated by the sixth harmonic of the Sun, a wave beginning at its ascending equatorial node, which is at 00 Aries 00. The houses are more personal than the signs, because they almost always begin from a very personal point in the zodiac. By far the most usual point to begin numbering houses from is the Ascendant (which is, of course, different for everyone), though there are systems which number them from the Sun (the Solar houses) both at its exact degree on the ecliptic and at the beginning of the sign it occupies, from the MC, from the Antivertex, from the Vertex, and from certain other points. The solar houses, which are measured in 30° segments numbered from 1 to XII going around the zodiac counter-clockwise, are not, properly, personal; but they are very popular with a few astrologers, especially lazy ones.

You will find astrologers telling you that the houses, unlike the zodiacal positions of the planets, are based on the diurnal factor. So they are, for the MC, the Asc and the Vertex are all found by taking into account the diurnal motion of the Earth: its daily rotation on its axis. (The so-called solar houses are not really houses at all, because they are not based on this factor.) What astrologers don't say, and I think it would be useful to them if they did, is that the houses are a personal zodiac superimposed on the natural zodiac. The sign Aries is a mode of expression involving energy, high spirits, impulsiveness, and so on. In traditional astrology the first house, based upon Aries, is not, however, a mode of expression; it is a 'sphere of life'. This is a risky jump, from mode of expression to sphere of life, and I see no reason for it.

The natural zodiac starts at Aries, but, since I was born at a certain time and place (with a particular latitude and longitude), my first house begins at a particular point on the ecliptic, which in many house systems will be the position of my Ascendant. Assume my Ascendant is at 26 Libra 00, then my chart ruler, or ruling planet, is Venus, because Venus rules the sign of Libra. On nearly all systems of houses using the Ascendant as first cusp my first house extends well into the sign of Scorpio, ruled by Pluto and Mars, but even if the cusp of the first house were situated at 29 Libra 59, my first house would still be ruled by Venus, and that would thus still be called my chart ruler. This despite the fact that all but one minute of the space of the first house would be taken up by the sign of Scorpio. If on a certain system (and there are many) the first house extended into Sagittarius – and we shall soon discover how that might happen – then Pluto-Mars would also be a ruler of the first house: the sign of Scorpio would be 'intercepted'. However, if on another system – such as Equal House, which simply takes the Ascendant as cusp one and then goes round the zodiac dividing it into segments of 30° – the house ends in Scorpio, then, although Pluto and Mars rule the cusp of the second house, which contains only a very small proportion of Scorpio, they do not rule the first house: this in spite of the fact that this house is nearly all taken up by the sign of Scorpio. It all seems very arbitrary and illogical, and it doesn't work in a clear-cut way. The only way, in this case, in which Pluto or Mars could be a ruler of the first house would be if it were actually occupied by either of these planets.

The accidental rulers – as they are called – of a house, then, are the ruler or rulers of any sign intercepted, and the planets which occupy the house, if any. The last are usually reckoned to be the strongest influence. The 'essential' ruler or rulers of a house are simply the ruler or rulers of the sign the house represents. Thus the essential ruler of the paradigmatic first house is Mars, or Mars and Pluto if you take Aries to be co-ruled by these two planets. The essential ruler of the sixth house is Mercury, because that is the Virgo house, and so on. The positions of the essential rulers by sign, house and aspect are supposed to indicate the disposition of the native toward the matters in life represented by that house. For example, if your fourth house (the Cancer house) is ruled by Pluto and Mars because its cusp lies in Scorpio, then your attitude towards your home and to the other things signified by the fourth house will be indicated by the position of the Moon and its aspects because the Moon is the essential ruler of Cancer; and your actual destiny in those matters can – so most astrologers claim – be predicted, to a certain reasonable degree of precision, by the positions of Mars and Pluto and of the occupants, if any, of the house.

Despite the difficulties of this method, some of which I have described, I should be loath to deny it any efficacy at all, though I am very strongly inclined to believe that – given the almost infinite variety of interpretations possible – intuition and some form of psi-factor are involved when correct results are obtained.

HOUSES AS A PERSONAL ZODIAC

But the real merit in the idea of houses is that of a personal zodiac superimposed on the natural one. The matter is not usually put in this way, but when houses are employed in a delineation that is what is in fact being done. My approach to a house system, and I think it is more immediately useful, would be as follows: your Ist house starts at, say, 8 Virgo 00, and so your energy, your spirit of initiative and so on is Virgoan in nature. Such a system would take account only of the signs, or combinations of signs, that occur along with each house. The amount of each sign that is involved in each house would, of course, be significant, and the effect of any planet in the sign would be judged in terms of the house. Any question of 'rulers' of the houses would be disregarded, and the traditional meaning of the signs – 'mode of expression' – would not be arbitrarily changed to 'sphere of life'.

I have said that I favour a simplified form of house system. Why then, in a book which advocates an original mix of astrological systems, do I not offer the reader a method of interpretation based upon such a house system? There are two main reasons: first, the difficult question of determining a starting point; secondly, the widely held, but erroneous, view that house systems should be measured in terms of time rather than space, which casts severe doubts on the validity of many of the house systems.

A STARTING POINT FOR A HOUSE SYSTEM

On the question of a starting point: it is perfectly true that the Ascendant (the symbol of the rising Sun) is a very important point in the chart, and it is understandable why it has been chosen in almost every house system as the marking point for the first cusp. It is the only point in the chart which is within a few degrees of where every planet rises on the day in question. The implied analogy with 00 Aries 00 and the vernal point seems right. However, is the Ascendant really valid as a starting point for a system from which so much is to be inferred?

This must depend on what the true significance of the Ascendant really is. There is much difference of opinion on this. Mayo, for example, insists that the Ascendant indicates what kind of character a person possesses: many American astrologers see the Sun as indicating just this. Hand says of the Ascendant, or rather of its sign, that it is 'indicative of the way you react to the world around you'. Certain astrologers assert that the Ascendant is simultaneously how others see you and 'the window through which you see the world'. I have not found any of these interpretations to work (my interpretation is given on p. 110). In my view only Ebertin comes near to the truth: he calls the Ascendant the *persona*, the mask under which the native thinks he presents himself to the world, while the MC is the 'inner self'. If it is true that the Ascendant is only a mask, then is it really a suitable point to represent the vernal point, the point of sunrise and the beginning of life, the cusp of the Ist house?

Other points have been proposed as starting points for house systems, but they are based on theory rather than empirical observation. This is what is wrong, and is one reason why I do not suggest a house system.

TIME OR SPACE AS A BASIS

My second reason is more complicated. Let me begin by quoting from the section on houses in Marcia Moore's and Mark Douglas's massive tome *Astrology*. It is fairly representative of the treatment given to the subject in many astrological textbooks.

> The houses depict the circumstances of life . . . houses are based on cycles of the day . . . each house represents (according to the commonly used Placidian system) the number of degrees of the zodiac which pass over the horizon in one twelfth of a day, or two hours . . . houses show specific areas of everyday experience . . . There is considerable controversy as to how these houses should be partitioned, since the divisions can be made in time or space. However, since astrology is fundamentally a science of time, many astrologers find it logical to think in terms of twelve, two-hour phases rather than in terms of spatial divisions of the vault of the heavens.

This is misleading: houses can be conceived as dividing time or space, and the initial intention is significant. But all house systems in fact divide time *and* space, or neither. Moore and Douglas go on, in a single paragraph, to mention three or four types of house systems, which they do not explain clearly. Now this, in the context of the literature of astrology, is extraordinarily generous with regard to its treatment of space. Yet it omits fundamental facts of which no one who is setting out to set up charts showing houses should be in ignorance.

PLACIDUS HOUSES

First, although the system of the seventeenth-century monk Placidus de Tito is based on the notion of time, it is in fact no more time-based than any space system. That is because in astrology, indeed in astronomy as well, time can be expressed as space, and vice versa. Opponents of the Placidus system have made a great deal of this – too much, perhaps, because since the basis of the Placidian conception is time, and time alone, so it might possess the 'time-dynamic' results that are claimed for it.

Moore and Douglas should also have mentioned that there are three other time-based systems – by 'time-based' I mean only that the astrologer who invented them wants to use time and not space as his basic concept. They are the first-century system of Alcabitius, and two twentieth-century systems, that of Polich and Page, known as the topocentric system, and that of Walter Koch, the Koch birthplace system. Placidus, Alcabitius and Koch trisect semi-arcs, or quadrants.

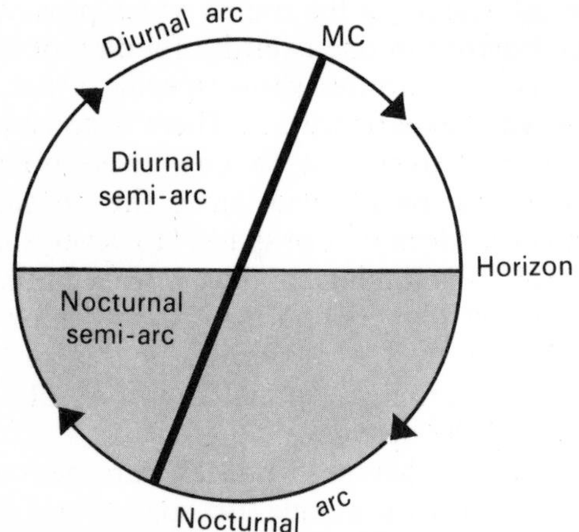

The Sun's semi-arcs The Sun's diurnal arc is the portion of the Sun's travel on a given day, during which it is above the horizon: its travel from Asc to Desc. Its nocturnal arc describes its travel below the horizon. The MC-IC axis divides these arcs into four semi-arcs, or quadrants.

Placidus and Koch fail in the polar regions (above latitude 67½°) because at certain times of the year some parts of the ecliptic do not rise and cannot be included in the chart. Of course, if you do not try to divide up the circle in terms of time, then you avoid this problem altogether. However, this does not prove that Placidus and Koch do not work in other regions.

ALCABITIUS HOUSES

Alcabitius has been unduly neglected: it is the only trisection system that does not fail in the polar regions. Unlike Placidus or Koch, it is a projection and not an intersection system. Alcabitius projects the points obtained by trisection of the quadrant onto the ecliptic by means of the great hour circles (lines of ecliptic longitude) which pass through the poles. Strangely no modern account of empirical experiment with this system exists.

THE KOCH BIRTHPLACE SYSTEM

The modern Koch system, on the other hand, has been subjected to a great deal of empirical testing, and it is used by Hand and a dozen other of the best astrologers. Koch claims that the intermediate cusps (those between the four points of the quadrant, i.e. II, III, V, VI, VIII, IX, XI, and XII) are 'calculated on the basis of the birthplace itself'. The spherical trigonometry involved is complicated, but it seems to me that, however high-pitched Koch's claims sound, they are essentially correct. To put it very briefly Koch's system incorporates oblique ascension – the diurnal factor which lies at the basis of all proper house systems, rather than half-baked compromises such as Equal House – into his method more thoroughly than does any other. Even Ebertin, who does not use houses, accepts that the cusps Koch's system generates are significant. I have used the method and accept this also, but, like Ebertin, I am not convinced that these significant cusps generate a reliable system of houses in the sense that because Venus is 'in' II it has a certain meaning.

THE EQUAL HOUSE SYSTEM

Perhaps the earliest system of all is Equal House. This was recommended by Parasara, and it may have been Ptolemy's method, though he does not say so. It has the merit of simplicity. You find the Ascendant, and then mark off each house at a distance of 30°

Equal House early went out of favour. It is hard to take its cusps seriously as cusps; they are merely aspect-points to the Ascendant and one suspects that Nature does not work quite so neatly. Equal House illogically ignores the MC as a cusp and it ignores the obliquity of the ecliptic, being based only on a single diurnal factor. Undoubtedly the current popularity of Equal House is very largely due to the ease with which charts can be set up; it is much easier than setting up Placidus charts. However, I have never, in my own work, found Equal House to offer anything useful whatsoever.

THE CAMPANUS AND REGIOMONTANUS SYSTEMS

Most of the other house systems are static systems, based on space. The two best known are Campanus (thirteenth century) and the Regiomontanus system of Johannes Muller (fifteenth century), which is really a revival of an Arabic method invented, or at least used, by Ibn Ezra as early as the eleventh century.

Traditional meanings of the houses

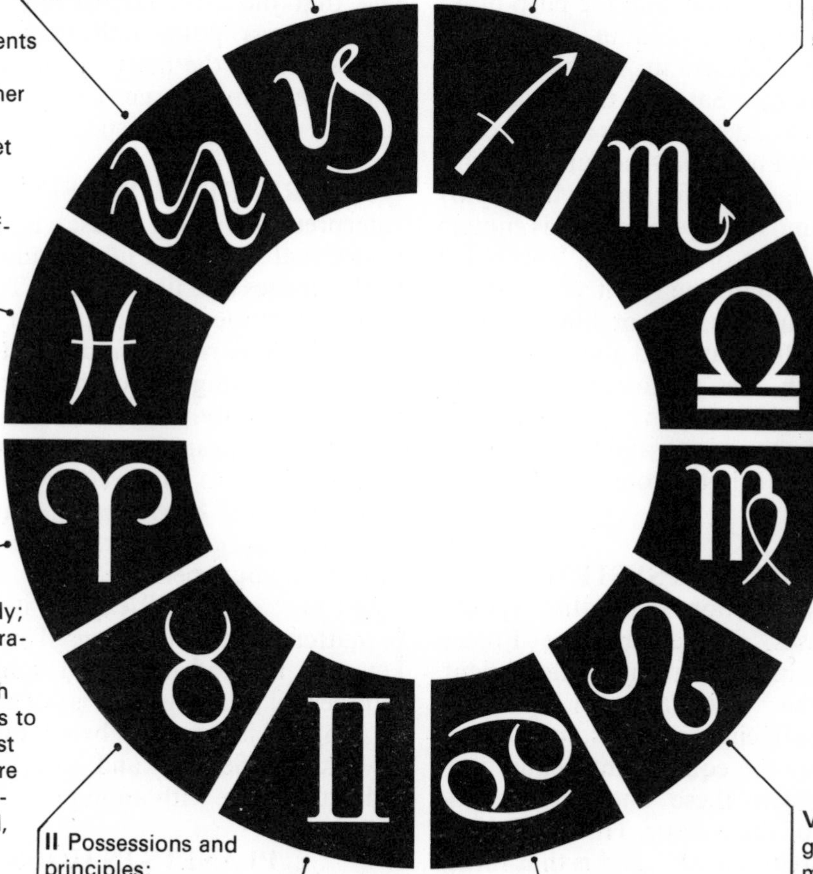

I Physical body; health; temperament; 'a lens through which everything has to pass'; the most obvious feature of the disposition; keyword, 'I am'; self-awareness.

II Possessions and principles; personal material resources; moral values; ability to earn money.

III Relations and communications; brothers and sisters; writing of all sorts: books, letters, bills, bureaucratic forms, treaties; education; 'everyday thinking'.

IV The domestic scene, but also the grave; land owned by the native's family; private life; according to some authorities, the father; the beginning and the end of life.

V Joys; pleasures; gambling; love making; children (and the children of the mind – Shakespeare's plays or Stalin's 'ideas'); objects of the instinctive affections: pets and tycoons' playgirls. Serious affliction of ruler or bodies in this house can indicate profligacy.

VI Work; toil; service; methodology; sacrifice. Supposed on no good evidence to be an 'unfortunate' house.

VII 'The other party to all our bargains' (Carter); open enemies, such as tax inspectors, or, if you are a criminal, the police.

VIII In earlier times the house of death, now usually referred to more politely as the house of 'joint resources'; wills; joint cash; the meat trade; regeneration; sex.

IX Religion; long journeys; exploration of mind and of places; inspiration; prophecy; dreams; conscience in the highest sense; wisdom.

X Status; success; according to some authorities, the mother – according to others, the father; native's 'base of operation' in society; ambition.

XI Hopes; wishes; friends; spiritual aspirations; group creative expression.

XII Confinements in hospital, prison and other institutions; betrayal; secret enemies; ambushes; loss; limitation; self-sacrifice.

Campanus trisects the quadrants of the prime vertical and projects the points he obtains from its pole onto the ecliptic. The Campanus houses are extremely irregular in size. Indeed, it is very common to find *doubly* intercepted houses, houses which contain parts of two signs and two whole signs within them. While this cannot be held against the method, it does lead to considerable complexity. For example, we might find the cusp of X in Virgo, then both Libra and Scorpio within the house, and the cusp of XI in Sagittarius. Suppose that in addition to this we have four planets in X. The essential ruler is, of course, Saturn: that does not change. But the accidental rulers are Mercury, Venus and Mars-Pluto *and* the four occupants of the house. Judgement, for those who employ houses – and almost everyone does – is enough to tax the mightiest of intellects. You could the more easily obtain the result you wanted.

Regiomontanus cusps do not differ so much from those of Placidus, and the size of the houses is much less distorted than with Campanus. In this system the equator is divided into equal portions, and the points are projected onto the ecliptic from the pole of the prime vertical.

THE MORINUS SYSTEM

I must briefly mention one other system. Morinus Houses, devised by the French astrologer Morin, are latitude-independent, and neither the Ascendant nor the MC, except under freak circumstances, form cusps. Morinus divides the equator into equal portions and projects these onto the ecliptic from the pole of the ecliptic. His first cusp is in ecliptic square to the MC, and is thus rather near, though not identical to, the East Point. He simply finds the RA of the first cusp, and then divides the equator into equal 30° segments.

Obviously if you want to use an Equal House system, Morinus is preferable to the simple division of the ecliptic, since it at least recognises that houses are based on diurnal motion; it divides the equator, and is projected from a significant pole. The method ignores latitude, but Morinus sacrificed this factor in order to introduce another equally important one: that in a mundane figure, a figure based on the positions of the bodies in terms of the Earth's daily rotation, the Ascendant is always square to the MC. His system is a sort of rough approximation to this in ecliptic terms. I have found, rather to my surprise, that this system can give extraordinary results when used in the charts of political figures. The true Ascendant and MC are entered on the chart and treated in the normal way; but I find that the artificial Ascendant should be treated as a point indicating the political disposition of the native; it is quite different in nature from the true Ascendant, and is best thought of as a first cusp.

INTERPRETATION USING HOUSES

Interpretation using houses is simple if the traditional 'sphere of life' meanings are given to the houses (see illustration). This simplicity of interpretation accounts to a great extent for the popularity of house systems and the common glossing over of the doubts surrounding their validity.

To take an example, what can we say about Venus in Aries in XI? *Feeling* will express itself *impulsively* and *assertively* in matters relating to *group objectives*. Or, if we want to be awkward, but perhaps more truthful, we could say: *greed* will express itself *ruthlessly* in matters relating to *groups*. This is the classic keyword method used, and taught, by large numbers of astrologers. It is not a bad method, so long as it is remembered that you must always be flexible and continually blend indications one with another.

PLANETS IN HOUSES

A few astrologers, especially those who use Campanus, take the middle of the house to be the point of most power within it, and judge bodies accordingly; this is still common in India, but is dying out in Western astrology. Normally, a planet is judged to be especially 'strong' when it is very near to a house cusp, or, in certain cases, when it makes an exact aspect to a cusp.

TWO-PLANET PRINCIPLES

There follow keywords as guides to the meanings of combinations of any two of the following: Moon, Mercury, Venus, Sun, Mars, Jupiter, Node, Saturn, Uranus, Neptune, Pluto, Asc and MC. Since Asc and MC represent the two sides of a single personality, the two points differ less in charts than is claimed: I have therefore combined Asc and MC. I have excluded the Vertex because, while it and the Antivertex do quite obviously refer to what the native attracts to him in the way of life circumstances, not enough work has yet been done on these angles to justify the giving of even the most flexible principles.

I must reiterate that, while the nature (hard, soft, dexter, applying, etc) of the aspect between two bodies/points does affect the way they interact, the fact that they are linked at all takes precedence over this. This applies even to a square, which, although it manifests itself very obviously in the personality, is not really stronger than a trine.

My keywords give an indication of the basic psychological factors generated by the various combinations. As can be seen from my stage-by-stage delineation of 'Arthur's' chart (pp. 152–165), an interpretation builds up as you go along. You get the feel of the way these combinations will be expressed, and, of course, the nature of the actual aspect will help you. No-one will exhibit all the qualities indicated here: we judge which they exhibit, and how, by confirmation from the rest of the chart.

When using these keywords, one is bound to make moral, or moral-sounding judgements – whether one likes it or not – but it is a great mistake to look at the aspects of charts in a moralistic way. The keyword 'deception' under Mercury-Neptune does not imply moral censure, suggesting that all those with such contacts are 'deceivers' of themselves and/or others: they could be actors, novelists, politicians, playwrights, film-makers, illusionists, swindlers – or they might simply be people who have to deal with the unreal, even the boringly unreal such as advertising products which do not live up to the claims made for them. It is necessary always to be flexible, to take heed of the character, the personality, that is emerging.

Moon-Mercury: emotional thinking; nervous; protective; home-bound; loquacious; tells lies.
Moon-Sun: sensual, subject to difficult circumstances (conjunction, orb $\frac{1}{2}$°); life swings between 'good' and 'bad' times.
Moon-Venus: sentimental; lazy; acquisitive of objects for home; wallows in pretty lust; devoted; moody.
Moon-Mars: opinionated; active thinker; angry when bored; bully; impulsive; volatile.
Moon-Jupiter: generous; glutton; religious feelings; modest; has empathy; social; wasteful.
Moon-Node: concerned with or affected by friendships and associations; emotional; social/anti--social; cooperative; love-ins/separations.
Moon-Saturn: conscientious about others; passion for tidiness; shy; sensitive; sad; depressed; controlled; solitary.
Moon-Uranus: drastic domestically; original; strange; receptive to the mysterious; enigmatic; independent; wild; curious; sinister libertarian.
Moon-Neptune: needs love-life to conform with inner vision, thus frustrated; poetic; imaginative; filthy; refined; delicate; vulgar.
Moon-Pluto: transformative; emotional about money; fanatic; acts from subconscious motives; can be unstable.
Moon-Asc or MC: temperamental; adaptable/infuriated – often a wobble between these; restless; apparently inconsistent; moody; subjective; poetic.

Mercury-Venus: grace/conceit; elegant/vain; charm/absurd mannerisms; nicely insincere in small matters; fluent; lazy; mocking; bawdy.
Mercury-Sun: very peculiar (conjunction, orb up to 1°); obscure; anxious; wrapped up in thoughts; absent-minded.
Mercury-Mars: critical; aggressive; argumentative; subject to bouts of nervous illness; irascible; nervous; malicious; goes too far in speech – mind races ahead of itself; very efficient if allowed to be boss.
Mercury-Jupiter (usually a very helpful aspect): talker, many ideas; idle; gossip; literary; sensible; witty; malicious; reclusive; modest/arrogant and excessive; conjunction is powerful in Fire.
Mercury-Node: associative/unassociative; commercial; literary friends; uses others with naked mischievousness/helps others greatly in important affairs; exploits animals by such activities as show-jumping,

circuses, racing, exhibiting, etc.
Mercury-Saturn: logical; cynical and enjoys it; humorous in a disconcerting way; melancholy; puritanical; blunt; seldom genteel or conventional unless a trapped, diligent functionary who switches off all analysis of self; can be wise but feels captive of circumstances; creative.
Mercury-Uranus: original; curious, sometimes trivially so; extreme; nervous; can be irritating to all; astute; intuitive unless wholly superficial; bizarre humour; ironic; strange.
Mercury-Neptune: deception; fiction; acting; swindler; mental processes can be blocked by imaginings, leading to tragedy – can be an aspect of the 'tragic genius'; often hard to understand when trying to communicate; intuitive grasp of matters; wrong judgements leading to chaos; not naturally efficient; has empathy; joker.
Mercury-Pluto: powerful and/or criminal thinking; salesman; persuader; may be literary or creative; obsessive; will be helpless and hopeless if the aspect is close and is not expressed in context of power; critical; transformer of thought into action.
Mercury-Asc or MC: agile-minded; slick; self-critical; cunning or shrewd; nervous underneath; can be wily con-man; can be snowed under with verbal or written agreements or just meaningless paper.

Venus-Sun: lazy; priapic – grunts in the fantastic sensual sty while mouthed by adored adorers; good manners; may tend to want to break into dance, thus restless; graceful; sybaritic/a charming mover in flash suits; wants wealth and enjoys ease.
Venus-Mars: sexual passion; desires lustful luxury in zestful bursts; may be over-indulgent; exhibitionist; pushy; enigmatic; paradoxical; excessive; can be energetically kind or lazily cruel.
Venus-Jupiter: extravagant; over-indulgent of self and others; lazy glutton; excessive; foully/naturally charming; political or religious conventionalist; reactionary; warm-hearted; happy; wise from the overblown couch loaded with grapes and liquor; sends others charmingly to do errands; merry; pompous; can be very aesthetic; often slow but can be sure; intelligent.
Venus-Node: tactful; social/anti-social; lazy about social obligations; charming; affectionate; mask of politeness/true courtesy.
Venus-Saturn: sour; cannot express love-feelings; can be a cold lover and feel frustrated by inability to express self fully; strict; relentless; mean; will throw back gifts or compliments with cynical ill grace; can feel very uneasy in presence of others – men with this aspect often think they are throwing off foul smells in the direction of vivacious women, and they sometimes are; can be sadistic; a very useful aspect in any chart despite the difficulties because it indicates self-discipline, wisdom, great devotion to the loved one(s); difficulties often fade out early, giving way to great privately expressed warmth.
Venus-Uranus: excited and/or drastic love relationships; sexual assaults, usually playful but possibly criminal; perversity outside 'normal' bounds; unusual tastes in all things; sarcastic; wobbles between laziness and violent activity; likes to enjoy life; anti-puritanical; tense; hidden sex-secrets; with Mercury can mean hidden lust.
Venus-Neptune (a very powerful contact in any chart): imagination is captivated by love-visions; delicately tortured by own lusts; can be lazy or self-indulgent about providing self with necessities, preferring luxuries; curious about all relationships; has empathy; sexual mystic; loves mystery; would rather be unhappily in love than not in love at all.
Venus-Pluto: lascivious day-dreams; desire-nature prompted by instincts; will happily be 'immoral'; wants to be a love-transformer; may search for sexual experience in the gutters of life; fated love; this aspect has to function or the native will be a cripple, but it can be sublimated so that the sexual side is entirely subsumed.
Venus-Asc or MC: desires harmony and is unhappy when he/she cannot get it; hates a bad atmosphere; successful strategies based on ideas of possession; affectionate; needs security; arranges for others to do the work, if possible; tendency to inertia.

Sun-Mars: ambitious; extra drive towards being 'real self'; trigger-personality; aggressive; wants to be popular; will smash others in pursuit of aims; excitable; vigorous fighter; wants to be on top; a 'controversial' person.
Sun-Jupiter: confident; can be authoritarian; generous; extravagant; can ruin prospects with others by over-confidence; entertains too lavishly; wants to be famous, or admires fame uncritically; may be able to persuade people to follow his lead; wants to enjoy a colourful and pleasing life; can be insufferably selfish (conjunction, close); extreme.

Sun-Node: needs to show off his friends; name-dropper; can be ridiculous or very shrewd in choice of friends; superior attitude; wants to be in the public eye either at national or local level; patronising; sometimes ruins his associations with others by being pompous, especially if Sun is in Leo.
Sun-Saturn: a difficult life, but native might well accept this gladly if he can attain wisdom, for this very powerful aspect gives the capacity for understanding at a profound level, though not all grasp the chance; the pattern of the life, at least when studied retrospectively, is seen to be stubborn, obstinate and determined – these people cannot be fundamentally changed except by themselves; pessimistic; cynical; cruel joker; ruthlessly truthful; slow but sure; a private person; hates authority; can be very selfish indeed.
Sun-Uranus: self-willed; eccentric; true needs emerge spasmodically; noisy person – may be absurd or a genius; anti-authoritarian; tense; subject to accidents.
Sun-Neptune: brings out basic needs in an imaginative or, perhaps, crooked way; solves difficulties through deception; dreamy; intuitive; neurotic or slightly, but harmlessly, mad; weak; feeble; ill; lives vicariously through his and others' dreams; existence haunted by dreams; 'paranormal' gifts; may be charismatic.
Sun-Pluto: tense; strained; authoritative; believes himself to know more than he does; brutally honest; creative; sets high standards for everyone; ruthless; relentless; can live in a daze; may have authoritarian mentality or act as changing influence in others' lives.
Sun-Asc or MC: arrogant; selfish; authoritarian; energetic; individualistic; may want fame; conjunction emphasises sign occupied.

Mars-Jupiter: lives dangerously – thinks he/she is lucky; creative; capacity to make well-judged decisions; adventurous; open; exaggerates; may be materialistic/very religious; if male, may love his children very greatly; pushes his employers aside over-impulsively; often lovable.
Mars-Node: native is always 'right' with regard to others; cooperative/uncooperative – with the hard aspects there can be a wobble between these; brutal; enthusiastic then cools off; excitable exhibitionist; wants to be loved and admired.
Mars-Saturn: a difficult life; may be cruel; a stop-go person; endures much patiently; bitter and cynical and world-weary/harsh joker; moody; controlled; varies between high and low opinion of self; capable of bursts of high energy; this very powerful aspect can confer wisdom or destroy the native – or he may be a nonentity, preferring not to cope with his constructive/destructive impulses.
Mars-Uranus: impatient; quickly-efficient – can mend things rapidly; suddenly cruel; intolerant; rebellious; original; assertive; nuisance to authorities; independent; acts on impulse; choleric.
Mars-Neptune: may be alcoholic or drug-taker/likes harmless pills; very dramatic/histrionic; lies like truth; actor; surrounds self with aura of mystery; poetic; suffers nightmares when waking and sleeping; enigmatic; an exciting person; weak in face of life's demands; confused but often inspired; obsessive.
Mars-Pluto: unwise to trifle with him/her; vengeful; violent; instrument of the Id; reckless; brutal in pursuit of truth/transformative lusts; powerful; extreme; dangerous and likes to be; supremely arrogant; killer.
Mars-Asc or MC: fiery; energetic; fighter; aggressive strategist; uses threats; often in disputes; may use physical violence.

Jupiter-Node: commercial; likes clubs/societies; gets advantage from associations without trying; can do jobs requiring much knowledge; polymath; may be reclusive and unable to cope with others or with groups.
Jupiter-Saturn: lucky; paradoxical; patient; mean in certain or all respects; looks after self – or something seems to do it for him/her; optimist-pessimist – almost always a wobble between these attitudes; faithful; will punish relentlessly, if need be waiting for very long periods – even decades – those who ill use his/her loved ones; believes in retribution, even if intellectually disinclined.
Jupiter-Uranus: fiery; pious/devoted to his/her religious view, even if not conventional; optimistic; grateful; loves knowledge and freedom; tactless; possessed of a sharp lust capable of being well satisfied; understands relaxation; intuitive; clairvoyant.
Jupiter-Neptune: a peculiar person; gambler in some area of life; rich imagination; confused about conventional attitudes to money and success; histrionic; may wobble between gluttony and self-starvation; wasteful of mental resources; natives with these connections, close, can suffer from mystery-illnesses.
Jupiter-Pluto: wants power either in materialistic or artistic sense; native feels driven, even though he or she may be

commonplace or mediocre; nags, fusses and threatens; despot; can be a menace to the community if without imagination. This aspect must be used in such a way as to improve quality of character, or it is malefic. Despite its dangers, it can be a useful aspect in the hands of imaginative or merciful people.
Jupiter-Asc or MC: generous ambitious; genial; may be careless; excessive or over-lavish; materialistic; slimily seeks prizes, praise, honour, and promotion – therefore unpopular at work; pleasant; pompous; can be idiotic as in the case of some dignitaries.

Node-Saturn: cautious in making associations; refuses to join clubs or societies but may found and dominate them; cuts fools down to size fast if intelligent and and perceptive; surly; good organizer; often hated and resented but loved and admired in old age; does better later in life.
Node-Uranus: restless and lonely; eager to share experiences with others; nightmares; short intense associations – sexual 'one-night stands'; disruptive/very cooperative – likely to wobble between these; excited.
Node-Neptune: isolated; 'unreliable' because artistic or mind taken up with matters more important than office or work affairs; swindler; deceiver; show-off; magician.
Node-Pluto: seeks fame; a transformer; wants to be influential; may be explosive; may lust after men, women and children.
Node-Asc or MC: keen on group activities/anti-social; may lead a community with good/disastrous results; is driven to associate at all levels; wastes energy.

Saturn-Uranus: violent alternation of moods; enigmatic; paradoxical; tense; irascible; persevering; provocative; *femme fatale*/gigolo; willpower fluctuates; a difficult life.
Saturn-Neptune: introspective suffering; treachery – either the native is treacherous or he suffers from it; creative; stern analyst of dreams and fantasies; weak; sick person; neurasthenic; slow degeneration of everything – ruin; courage; a peculiar person; poetic; a difficult life.
Saturn-Pluto: low occultism/great knowledge of the strange; paradoxical – practicality struggles with the impossible; fear; savage puritanism; cruelty; saintliness/criminality; liar; self-deceiver/relentless self-analyst.
Saturn-Asc or MC: a difficult life; carries a burden/imposes one; marries older person/has many older friends; finds it hard to articulate; may have a repulsive manner; severe self-critic/preening over-confidence; inhibited – public life brings many difficulties; this aspect requires imaginative handling.

Uranus-Neptune: sharp terrible nightmares that may seem more real than waking life; intuitive; very imaginative; chaotic personality; a very difficult life.
Uranus-Pluto: creative; innovatory; brutal – will drastically eliminate the unnecessary in his/her vision; visionary; authoritarian/libertarian; paradoxical; not easy to live with.
Uranus-Asc or MC: vigorous and drastic; can be violent in speech and/or action; eccentric; anti-conventionalist.

Neptune-Pluto: mysterious personality; explorer of the fantastic; adept in paranormal matters; very imaginative; chaotic personality; very violent – or may be recipient of mistakenly-directed violence; often unaware of what he/she is doing in the world – can be blindly ignorant of this throughout life; eccentric.
Neptune-Asc or MC: impressionable; confused; can be charismatic; traitor; coloured by surroundings but retains own individuality; chaotic personality; may be psychopathic; with Mars indicates arsonist.

Pluto-Asc or MC: powerful; authoritarian; transformative; chaotic; may make unpleasant changes in their environment after getting power by fraud (trine); bully; treads on the susceptibilities of others.

CHAPTER FIVE

INTERPRETING A BIRTH CHART

EXAMINING THE PLANETS

IF A CHART IS TO BE EXAMINED THOROUGHLY, rather than cursorily, the condition of each factor within it – the planets, Sun, Moon and points – must be determined. The condition of a planet includes what aspects it makes and what aspects it receives. These must be listed, and then they must be studied in the context of the whole chart to reveal the patterns they fall into.

ANALYSING A PLANET'S SIGN AND RULERSHIP

First, we note which sign the planet is in. This is important because it determines the basic manner in which the energy represented by the planet will function. This is written as follows (the chart on p. 62 will serve as an example):

Mars/Pisces (Jupiter Aries, MR; Neptune Leo)

A planet in a sign operates through that sign, but it is also modified by the positions of that sign's ruler, or rulers. Pisces' rulers are Jupiter and Neptune. In the chart in question Jupiter is in Aries, which puts Mars and Jupiter in mutual reception (MR), and Neptune is in Leo. The rulerships are noted in brackets, as above.

Mars in Pisces means that energy is subdued, dispersed in the sense that it vanishes into nebulousness. The subject does not lack energy, but he will have to combat the tendency to waste it. He will be intensely (Mars) emotional (Pisces); he will be temperamental, and possibly unstable, generous, or kindly.

The placements of the two rulers modify the general picture. Jupiter, being in Aries, means that there is some energy to be expended. Because Mars and Jupiter are in mutual reception, Mars is 'given back' some of its Aries nature, which it needs in Pisces. Neptune in Leo is more difficult to interpret: the subject may well waste some of his energy in speculation or in histrionics. Certainly he will use energy in playing out a role. Jupiter and Neptune are called the dispositors of Mars. At the same time we note that there is a stellium in Aries: Mars, in fact disposits four planets in Aries. This gives it more strength than it might otherwise have in Pisces, and shows a certain indefatigability. We may suspect that this tirelessness lies in the realm of the emotions, Pisces being a highly emotional sign. A summary of the placement of Mars may be written as follows:

Mars/Pisces (Jupiter Aries, MR; Neptune Leo; d. Uranus, Venus, Jupiter, Mercury – Aries)

'd' stands for disposits: we add 'Aries' because those planets could be in Scorpio.

LISTING A PLANET'S ASPECTS

Next we list the aspects Mars makes. The bodies are taken in order of their mean speed with the points, Asc, MC, VX added at the end in that order. Conjunctions, semi- and sesquisquares, sextiles, squares, trines and oppositions must be listed, and I suggest you also list all multiples of 5H, 9H, 10H, 11H, 12H (this includes the semi-sextile and quincunx) 15H and 20H. Mars' condition can now be set down as follows:

Mars/Pisces (Jupiter Aries, MR Neptune Leo; d. Uranus, Venus, Jupiter, Mercury – Aries; 108 Moon, 7H Sun, 11H Venus (close), 90 Saturn (wide by 5°47′, applying), $22\frac{1}{2}$ Uranus, 11H Neptune (exact), 120 Pluto, 120 VX (Skew-Grand Trine in Water: Mars-Pluto-Vertex).

At this point I suggest that you simply list the aspects and do not ponder them too deeply.

LISTING A PLANET'S MIDPOINTS

The final thing we need to do is list the axes in which Mars is involved as a midpoint. I have found that the 45- and 135-relationships, as well as the conjunctions, squares and oppositions, are often very strong. However, one can cut down initial work by including only the direct mid-points (conjunctions and oppositions), and the squares (as strong, but technically indirect).

The German astrologer Ebertin uses and markets a dial which finds midpoints by measurement. Nonetheless, when you have found a midpoint, you still have to calculate it, to make sure of its orb and to discover whether it is applying or separating. It is therefore preferable, in my view, to list all the midpoints systematically, and draw diagrams

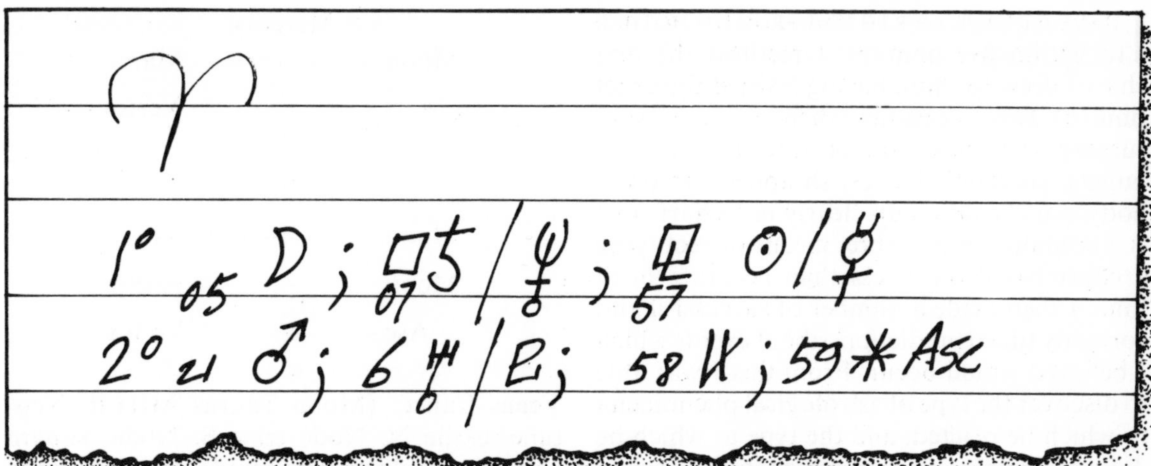

for each planet and point, showing their involvements. This is a little laborious to begin with, but it only needs to be done once. You begin by taking the Moon, the fastest travelling body, and investigating its relationship with every other body and point. When you have listed all the planets which fall within an orb of 2° (you can put a ? after all those which exceed $1\frac{1}{2}$°; include them only if they fit into the general picture) of the Moon and all the other bodies and points, you can go on to Mercury (eliminating, of course, the Moon), and so on through all the factors. I personally take twelve sheets of lined paper (one for each sign), with at least thirty lines (one for each degree) on each, and enter all the information for each degree of each sign. You put in a planet or point where there is one; you enter all the points at which each body is aspected, with the nature of the aspect, and you enter the position of each midpoint. Two lines might look like the facsimile above.

In this case Mars is involved in just one configuration: Pluto/Vertex. This is the only direct midpoint, or midpoint by square. The average chart has only some 17 direct midpoints so, bearing in mind that there are 13 planets and points to be considered, this is not very surprising.

My completed tabulation of the 'condition' of Mars looks like the facsimile below.

I then do the same for the other bodies and points.

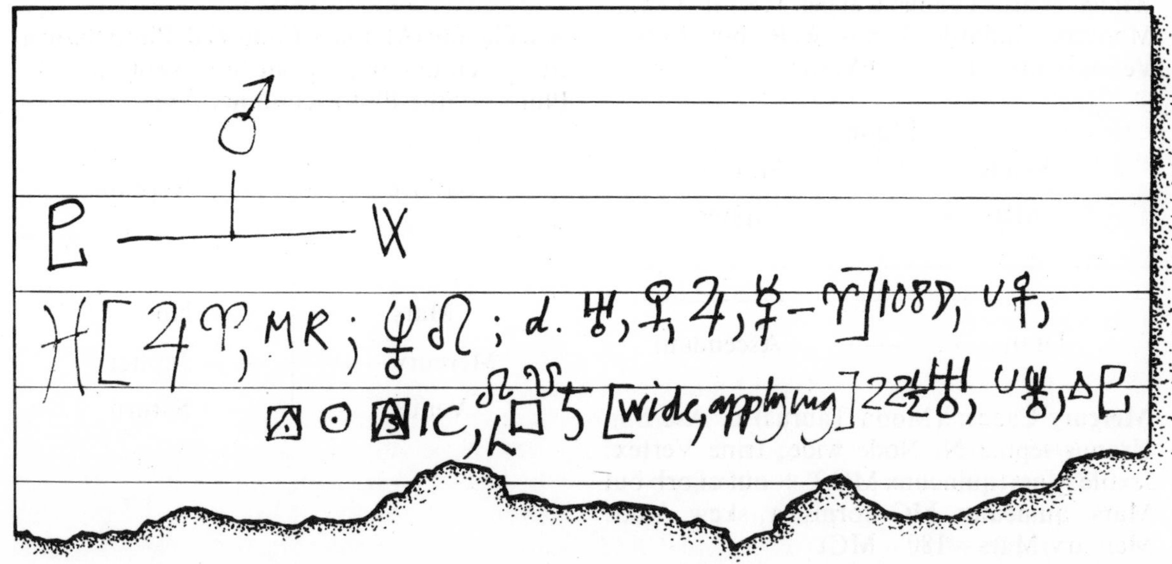

A DETAILED EXAMPLE

I HAVE ARTHUR'S BIRTH TIME FROM HIS MOTHER to within five minutes. I rectified the first chart I drew for him, having learned the exact time of two occasions when he underwent surgery. The insertion of foreign objects – bullets, surgeon's knives, shrapnel – into the body usually shows up clearly in a chart: this is a common, if macabre, means of rectifying a chart based on a less than accurate birth time. I then made a number of successful and correctly timed predictions about events which I believed would occur. From this I was able to discover the type of astrological phenomena to which he reacted, and the type to which he did not. People vary very much in their sensitivity to certain approaches to chart delineation.

I used Primary Directions and Tertiary Progressions (p. 201), and was then able to erect a wholly accurate chart.

ASSEMBLING THE DATA

Having drawn the chart, I tabulate the condition of the planets as described above and draw a diagram to indicate the midpoints. The direct midpoints and the points in square to the direct points, which I consider to be as significant as the direct midpoints, appear above the double line. Below the double line, I have listed the points in semi-square to the direct points.

Moon Taurus (Venus Cancer MR) d. Venus, Mercury; quintile Venus wide but Moon/Venus – 90 – Mars; 180 Vertex

Moon

Venus	Saturn
Mars	Jupiter
═══	═══
Uranus	Ascendant

Mercury Cancer (Moon Taurus) d. Asc Sun Uranus/septile N. Node wide; trine Vertex; sextile Mars (quincunx MC 2°+ out of orb but Mars quincunx MC forms a skew Yod: Mercury/Mars – 180 – MC)

Mercury

Moon	Mars
Mars	Vertex
═══	═══
Moon	Sun
Moon	Asc
Asc	Vertex

Venus Cancer (Moon Taurus MR) d. Neptune/sextile N. Node trine S. Node; square Neptune v. close; semisextile Asc; quincunx Desc; septile MC

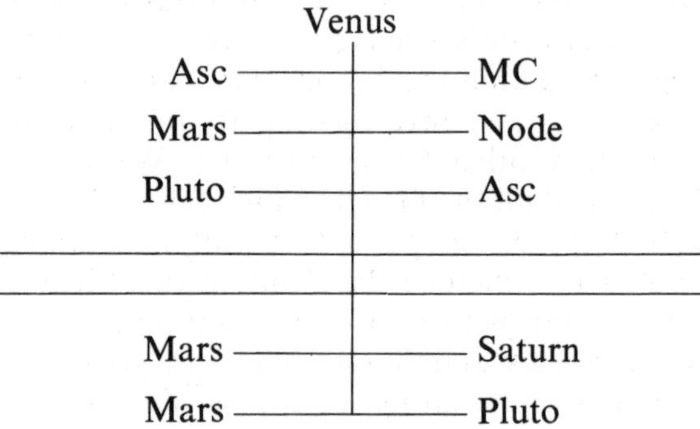

(Note that because the Venus–Neptune square is close, the Neptune picture will be almost identical, especially if we treat points square to direct midpoints as of equal power.)

Sun Gemini (Mercury Cancer) d. Pluto Saturn/trine Neptune widish but Sun/Neptune – 0 – Pluto; sextile Pluto; conjunct Asc

Sun

Saturn	Neptune
═══	═══
Mars	Node
Mercury	Jupiter
Venus	Saturn

Mars Virgo (Mercury Cancer)/quincunx MC

Mars	
Moon	Venus
Neptune	MC
Mercury	Pluto
Mercury	MC

Jupiter Sagittarius/opposition Uranus (3′)

Jupiter	
Moon	Saturn
Mercury	Sun
Venus	Sun
Node	MC
Saturn	Vertex
Venus	Mars
Neptune	Asc

(Note that the Uranus condition will be identical owing to the close opposition.)

Nodes N. Node Taurus S. Node Scorpio/square Pluto

N. Node	
Sun	Neptune
Saturn	MC
Venus	Sun
Venus	Asc

Saturn Leo (Sun Taurus) d. MC (with Uranus)/septile Uranus septile Neptune (widish but Uranus/Neptune–0–Saturn) UNASPECTED

Saturn	
Uranus	Neptune
Moon	Mars
Venus	Jupiter
Uranus	Jupiter
Jupiter	Neptune

(Note that the conjunction of 4° 48′ with Pluto is too wide to count as aspected in this special sense: there is no special occupied midpoint between Saturn and Pluto.)

Uranus Gemini (Mercury Cancer) co-d. MC/bi-septile Neptune

Uranus	
Moon	Saturn
Mercury	Sun
Venus	Sun
Node	MC
Saturn	Vertex
Venus	Mars
Neptune	Asc

Neptune Libra (Venus Cancer)/trine MC

Neptune	
Asc	MC
Mars	Node
Pluto	Asc
Mars	Pluto
Mars	Saturn

Pluto Leo (Sun Taurus)/ sextile Asc trine Desc

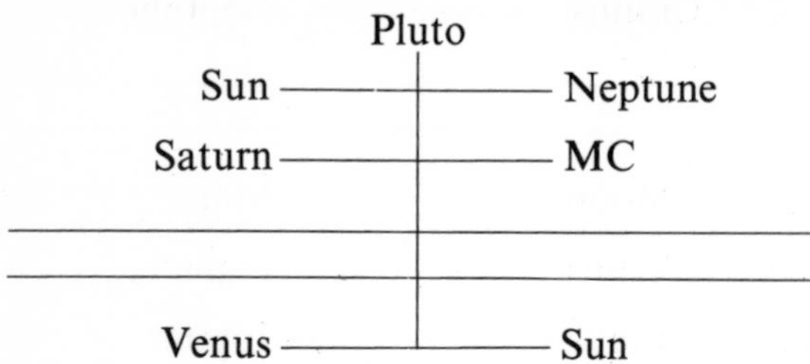

MC Aquarius (Uranus Gemini Saturn Leo)/ opposition Composite Degree*

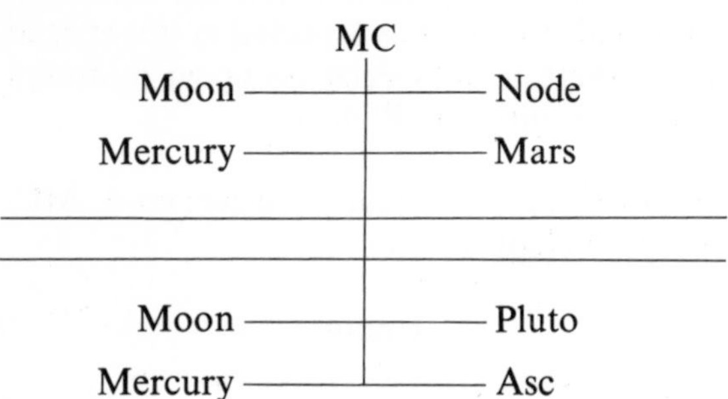

Asc Gemini (Mercury Cancer)

Asc

Neptune — Pluto

Mercury — Saturn

Sun — Mars

Node — Uranus

Vertex axis Scorpio–Taurus (Mars Virgo Pluto Leo; Venus Cancer)

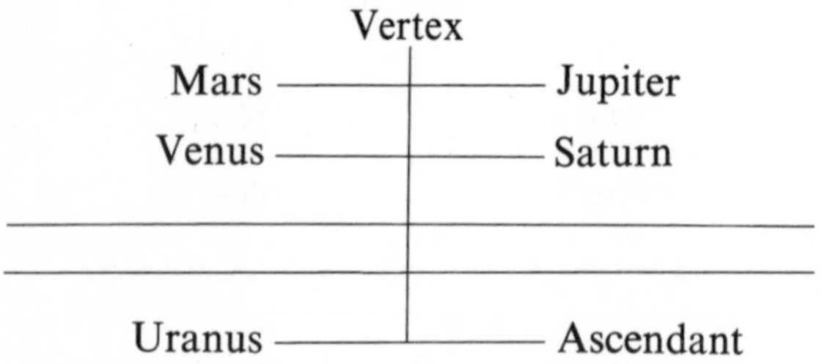

*The Composite Degree is a point which has a significance in terms of destiny. To find it, add up the Sun, Moon and planets in absolute longitude, and divide by ten.

INTERPRETING THE CHART

The first step is always to take the indications made by each planet, luminary and point in their signs; then to proceed to examine further features of their 'condition'.

THE MOON

The Moon is in Taurus (its traditional exaltation), and in quintile with Venus which is retrograde in Cancer, and with which it is therefore in mutual reception. The quintile is wide, but made stronger because the midpoint of the two bodies is in applying square to Mars.

The moon in Taurus indicates a sympathetic personality: enduring, persevering, loving song and rhythm. There is a love of comfort which in this case should be as aesthetically pleasing as possible owing to the mutual reception with Venus. To those astrologers who reject the quintile as a major aspect (and they all do) this Moon is unaspected. Since the orb of the aspect, 1° 59′, is very wide indeed, even though it is strengthened by the Mars connection, it is certainly worth looking at the characteristics of an unaspected Moon: they may play some part in this personality. This suggests that the native is extremely sensitive, possibly hypersensitive, and we should expect him to be assailed suddenly by drastic emotions, which have to be endured until they pass. This is a man whom one would expect to 'switch on' and then, often for no apparent reason, 'switch off': to retreat into himself and take cold solace in musical (Taurus) activity. This feature of his personality is given very great emphasis by the fact that his Moon lies exactly opposite the Vertex, the most 'fatalistic' point in the chart (except for the Composite Degree, which is in this case at 7 Leo on the IC). The interpretation of this position must be that the values represented by the Moon (receptiveness, the natural un-self-conscious self, mutability, domesticity) are the *raison d'être* of the native. If the Vertex is the group function that is forced upon one, then the Antivertex (upon which the Moon stands) is, among other things, the secret reactions of a person to these enforced circumstances. The Moon is itself secret.

Against this it must be pointed out that the

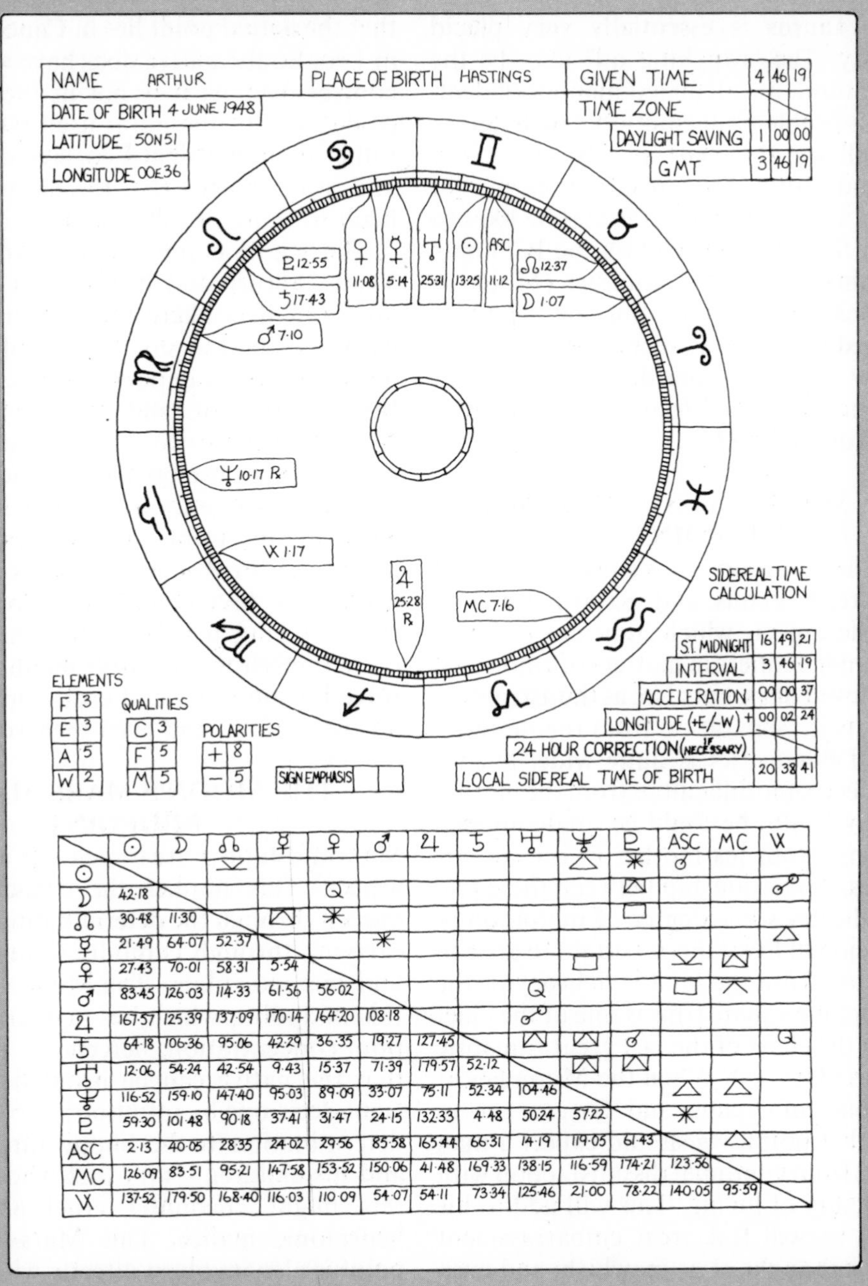

	☉	☽	☊	☿	♀	♂	♃	♄	♅	♆	♇	ASC	MC	Vx
☉			⚺							△	✶	☌		
☽	42·18				Q						⚼			☍
☊	30·48	11·30		⚼	✶						□			
☿	21·49	64·07	52·37			✶								△
♀	27·43	70·01	58·31	5·54						□		⚺	⚼	
♂	83·45	126·03	114·33	61·56	56·02				Q			□	⚻	
♃	167·57	125·39	137·09	170·14	164·20	108·18			☍					
♄	64·18	106·36	95·06	42·29	36·35	19·27	127·45		⚼	⚼	☌			Q
♅	12·06	54·24	42·54	9·43	15·37	71·39	179·57	52·12		⚼	⚼			
♆	116·52	159·10	147·40	95·03	89·09	33·07	75·11	52·34	104·46			△	△	
♇	59·30	101·48	90·18	37·41	31·47	24·15	132·33	4·48	50·24	57·22		✶		
ASC	2·13	40·05	28·35	24·02	29·56	85·58	165·44	66·31	14·19	119·05	61·43		△	
MC	126·09	83·51	95·21	147·58	153·52	150·06	41·48	169·33	138·15	116·59	174·21	123·56		
Vx	137·52	179·50	168·40	116·03	110·09	54·07	54·11	73·34	125·46	21·00	78·22	140·05	95·59	

Arthur's birth chart The top, right hand, half of the grid shows the aspects between bodies and points. The bottom, left hand, half lists the actual angles between every pair of bodies and points.

Moon in Taurus is essentially very placid emotionally. The 'switching off' may be the native's natural, uncalculated manner of dealing with his problems of emotional turbulence. As we shall see, the chart as a whole is very strongly indicative of a capacity to earn a lot of money; my interpretation is that he likes to do so, but that, with his CD on the IC, home and meaningful material comfort (Moon in Taurus) mean more to him: thus, he is entirely uninterested in money as such.

We now have to consider three further factors concerning the Moon: two direct midpoints and one indirect.

THE MOON'S VENUS/SATURN MIDPOINT

Here we have Moon = Venus/Saturn and Mars/Jupiter.* Venus and Saturn are in a semiquintile aspect, which indicates a power and single-mindedness in matters of emotional loyalty to loved ones, but also, as the astrologer Ebertin puts it, 'separation from the mother'. The orb of this aspect is quite wide, but we should expect some difficulties from the mother in this native's life: he could be single-minded in separating from his mother in certain circumstances. A relationship between these two planets indicates some degree of inhibition in the expression of love: this is certain to arise in Arthur's case from the fanatic delicacy of the Venus–Neptune square (this is one of the chief features in the chart of the last great romantic poet, Robert Graves). When the Moon lies at the midpoint of Venus and Saturn, or in square to that point, we should expect a man who suffers from continual dissatisfaction with his own quality of loving. This will add to his inhibition: he will feel great embarrassment in case he is thought of as mawkish, and even his sexual performance could be affected in certain circumstances by the fanatic delicacy derived from the Venus–Neptune square.

The Venus/Saturn midpoint itself is separating – the Moon has passed it – and the orb is wide; moreover it is 'dissociate' in the sense that the actual point lies in Cancer rather than in Leo. So the native does have a great deal of control over it; it is not as ineluctable as it could be. But the point itself lying in Cancer rather than in ardent Leo, sign of procreation and pride, means that the native finds it difficult to think or talk about his inhibition.

The whole combination, involving Moon, Venus, Saturn and Neptune, is a very poetic one, and it is likely therefore that what the native has had to say that is truly meaningful on the subject is in poetry or in creative prose. But the idealism and purity of the Venus–Neptune square would not allow him to be prolific, or to use poetry as a method of publicity: he is poetic, but would find it deeply embarrassing to be an official poet. (Such an inclination in Robert Graves is overcome by his having Ascendant, Sun, Moon and Mars in Leo.) Thus it is likely that Arthur will express himself in a creative manner in order to solve his amorous and erotic problems – but not very often, and even then very reticently.

THE MOON'S MARS/JUPITER MIDPOINT

Mars and Jupiter are in a closely applying 108° aspect. This implies the capacity to enjoy oneself through the determination to do so: by carrying through carefully thought out, wise and energetic plans. The Moon is applying to this midpoint, which lies in Scorpio (penetration, concentration, fierceness), and indicates that the native can be inspired to make the right decisions by intuition; also that he has a determination to be happy through women and his children – and that whoever opposes this might encounter cruel and relentless Scorpionic malice. This Mars–Jupiter midpoint is also involved directly with the Vertex, which being in Scorpio and opposing the Moon of course gives it extra power. There is likely, then, to be a successful vocation, a successful marriage, and many successful enterprises. But there will also be a savage rebelliousness which suddenly rears itself, a drastic (Uranus opposes Jupiter) flooding-in, at times, of exaggerated hostility, a hastiness, an immoderation. This may be why the native has to 'switch off', as I have suggested that he

*At this point I adopt the quicker and easier practice of substituting = for the particular midpoint relationship, which anyone can in any case work out for himself.

does. Would he, if he did not do so, go out of control? I would confidently assert that he has on a few occasions performed ruthlessly revengeful acts, when he has felt that his personal relationships have been threatened. Such a threatener he would gladly eliminate (Pluto is square to the Moon's nodes) without conscience. But he can control this, usually by his 'switching off'.

There may be a sense of a tragedy too deep to endure: the fact that the idealism of his Venus–Neptune square is in one sense not in accord with reality. Venus and Jupiter are associated with the colours blue and purple respectively, and Aquarius, the sign of Arthur's MC and of the true self, is also associated with a sky-blue. While he does not dislike the colour range covered by blue, it is so in accord with his own restless nature (further indicated by Gemini rising, Sun and Uranus in Gemini, close opposition Jupiter–Uranus) that it disturbs him, seeming to threaten the certainty (because of its conjunction with the Antivertex) of his Moon-oriented nature. Taking the Moon in Taurus in conjunction with this, I would suggest that he sometimes listens to, or plays, blues music, feeling the savage monotony of *blue* murder.

I must point out that the Mars/Jupiter midpoint is in an $11\frac{1}{4}°$ aspect with the south node and therefore a $168\frac{3}{4}°$ one with the north node. The orb is 3′. This is a valid hard aspect – it is, furthermore, double applying – and, with such a very small orb, is likely to be highly significant. This indicates a capacity, and a wish, to cooperate well with others. The native is, as the Venus–Neptune square would suggest, in the first instance well disposed. The reader must keep in mind that, whereas squares in general represent obstacles to be overcome, difficulties from the solution of which meaningful answers may arise, oppositions represent external conflicts: all things being equal, the mind is often more clouded with idealism than in the case of the square. Conjunctions, unless aspected (preferably by septile or quintile), leave the native more helpless. The soft aspects lack that sense of 'divine discontent', which the astrologer Charles Carter so often rightly and poetically attributed to these hard aspects between Venus and Neptune.

THE THREE DOMINATING CONFIGURATIONS

It will have been noted that much of the discussion has been carried on in the light of the dominating square, in this case Venus–Neptune: this is inevitable. But it must not be forgotten that there are two other dominating configurations (ignoring for the moment planetary groupings): the only slightly skew-yod on the MC from Mercury and Mars, and, above all, the opposition from Uranus to Jupiter, which slashes the chart into two halves. Continually, throughout our discussions of all charts, we find ourselves referring to the background of the dominating close major aspects.

THE MOON'S URANUS/ASCENDANT MIDPOINT

As to the indirect involvement of the Moon: this is with Uranus and the Ascendant. If we regard the Ascendant as 'frozen' in the chart, as I do, then, although this is a wide orb, it is nonetheless applying. This is a powerful aspect (the semi- and sesquiquadrates carry 22 harmonics); there are more involvements tied in, Vertex, Venus, Mars, and Neptune with a slightly wider but nonetheless valid orb. The aspects made by what is in effect the Venus–Neptune square and by the Vertex are rather more powerful than the one made by Mars (the former each carry 11 harmonics, the latter only 5). Uranus–Ascendant denotes, above all, alertness, restlessness, excitability, the tendency to attract tense, sometimes ranting, people. This is reinforced by the fact that both factors are in Gemini. The Vertex connection also reinforces this in the way that one would expect, as I described when dealing with the significance of the Moon's being on the Antivertex. The Moon's involvement here simply confirms what we have already learned, but such confirmation is very important, since it is by a series of emphases that we build up character-portraits. Venus' involvement indicates a strong tendency to 'allow things to happen' in the romantic field: the native may admit to having to be on his guard against too sudden and drastic attachments, but his erotic curiosity is enormous. Neptune's part is to confirm something already established: that the native suffers from hypersensitivity and fierce feelings of slight. Mars' involvement bears out the tendency to feel, and sometimes exhibit, physical violence: this is a man who might attack someone who had slighted his beloved but not himself.

It will be noted that nearly all these 16H, 32H and 64H aspects serve as confirmation, but sometimes as embellishments, of what the more obvious features of the chart tell us.

MERCURY

The condition of Mercury must always be given special attention. It is a guide to the mentality: the way of thinking, the level of mental agility and the analytical powers. It is connected above all with the faculties of speech and, together with Saturn, of hearing, both in the purely physical sense* and in the sense of grasp of a subject. Mercury governs not only all kinds of communications, but also ambivalence, particularly with regard to nature: the manipulation of the environment in every sense.

Here we have Mercury in Cancer, with the Moon, its dispositor, in Taurus. Like the Moon itself, it is almost unaspected in the special sense used in this book: all it has of note is a sextile to Mars of orb 1° 56′. Most astrologers, knowing that Mercury was faster than Mars and approaching it, would take this sextile to be applying. It is not, however, for while Mars continues on the ecliptic at a rate of just less than half a degree a day, Mercury goes retrograde at 7 Cancer 16: it never 'catches up'. Mercury must be allowed a touch of both its unaspected characteristics and its retrograde ones. Unaspected Mercury suggests that the native is an intellectual, that he leans very conspicuously upon the rational. Obviously in a man we have already labelled as extremely emotional, this would create a conflict. But Mercury is, even if only just, aspected. Its sextile to Mars indicates acuteness, curiosity, friendliness, agility and responsiveness in two senses: gratitude for kindness, savage fury for any kind of treachery. This sextile also indicates a supreme lack of timidity about saying what he thinks. The tendency to rely on reason is mitigated by this, and by the fact that Mercury is in Cancer, which indicates that the emotions tend to rule the thoughts and, as in so many people, crass sentimentality has to be resisted.

Mercury in Cancer also indicates a good memory. It means that the native, however rebellious, will have absorbed a great deal from his family as a child. If this man's family lacked enlightenment, or was divided, or inarticulate, then he will have spent many years ridding himself of their influence upon him. Unless his family is a remarkably enlightened one, it is probable that, on occasion, he has attacked it with ruthless severity. However, his attachment remains, and he will therefore alternate between a stiff taciturnity (resentment at the sentimental family-orienting power of Mercury in Cancer) and a genial fulfilment of duty. The Moon being on the Antivertex and the general tenor of the chart already being established as one that is very woman-oriented, we may guess that any family conflict primarily concerns the mother. Venus is often, among other things, the mother in a chart. Here Venus is semisquare the midpoint of Mars/Saturn which indicates troublesome separations.

What weight should be accorded to the Mercury–Venus conjunction? It is wide by my standards, but it cannot be entirely without effect: it is not as if Mercury and Venus were separated from each other by a large area of the sign. It helps the native to win people over to his point of view, reinforces his looking for comfortable and tasteful surroundings, and gives him the capacity to be graceful in manner. But conjunction between these two planets is never a strong indication. I would guess that his capacity to impress enables him to use tricks of charm and to simulate liking for those from whom he wants something, probably his employers.

Mercury also has a trine to the vertex that is too wide to count for much, and a septile to the north node of orb 1° 11′, separating. What

*The deaf and the blind invariably have a severely afflicted Mercury in 125H.

power this has is in the area of personal friendships. The aspect being from Cancer to Taurus has a Moon–Venus quality, so that we might say that the native always manages to keep himself 'switched on' through a friend, even if he has switched off in his familial relationships.

MERCURY'S MIDPOINTS

The midpoints in which Mercury is involved are particularly important in judging the mentality. Midpoints can have a strong, sometimes adverse, influence. For example, in the chart on p. 62 it can be seen that, although Mercury is in conjunction with Jupiter, an always useful contact in itself, Mercury is, to use Ebertin's word, somewhat 'sickened', because it stands opposite the midpoint of Saturn/Neptune. In fact the conjunction itself is sickened, its own midpoint being very close indeed to the Saturn/Neptune farther midpoint. This implies a character much given to despair, lacking in self-confidence about work, cynical about others' motives, and concerned about status in the eyes of others.

Is Arthur's Mercury menaced in a similar way? It stands in the direct midpoints of Moon/Mars and Mars/Vertex, and in the indirect midpoint of the very personal configuration, Asc/Vertex.

The first configuration shows that the native frequently thinks about changing or improving his home, which for him is his centre of operations. The centre of this home must be, as Ebertin puts it, a 'woman doing intellectual work'. Sometimes she is very angry. The native's brain is very active and he attracts people who want to have very heated arguments with him. He may more frequently than other people encounter situations at work which cause him anger, although, as we have seen, he will have deliberate techniques for controlling this if it is wasteful of energy.

Mercury standing at the direct midpoint of Mars/Vertex indicates that, whether Arthur wants to or not, he will encounter circumstances in both the private and public, or work, areas of his life in which there will be disputes. These will often cause him serious difficulties. The involvement with the Ascendant/Vertex midpoint simply emphasizes Mercury in his chart: he will use to the full in his life all the capacities conferred by an emotionally invested thoughtfulness, and he will take peculiar emotional pleasure in cleverly outmanoeuvring his employers over money, but only if he considers that they make it too easily.

VENUS

So Mercury in this chart is, as some astrologers put it, 'in good shape'. What of Venus? Its mutual reception with the Moon has already been discussed. The indication is of a basically peaceful person who wants to be happy and left alone by 'the world'. The strain on Arthur is manifested by the square to Neptune, which is both close and applying. The retrograde Venus drives the characteristics of acquisitiveness, appreciation of others, gratitude to others at profound levels, nostalgia and feeling of love ineluctably back into the innermost core of the native. There is, too, the tendency towards metaphysical and psychological self-probing. The square between Neptune and Venus is rendered especially poignant when one notices two things: that, by reason of its retrogradation alone, Arthur's Neptune is very much more idealistic than is apparent from a casual glance at the chart; that his Neptune possesses an irresistible curiosity (Gemini rising, Uranus–Gemini, Uranus MC ruler) about the unconscious processes, even an unusually poetic awareness of them.

Arthur cannot help evaluating, re-evaluating, and re-evaluating yet again, creating vicious circles of solitary nostalgia which may every so often lead him into the temptation of escaping them by wild and crudely 'animal' actions (Uranus opposition Jupiter, with other indication of this sort already mentioned). He cannot escape the quest for perfection: he is therefore a man dedicated only to the impossibilities of what we call art, which includes poetry and music, and of love.

Venus in Cancer gives, again, a yearning for the comforts of home and a strong desire to depend on the beloved: a desire which is continually undermined, if only at the 'metaphysical' level – the level of the impossible perfection demanded by the square to Neptune – by small doubts which act on the native like barbed in-turned knives, causing him to experience great fury with himself. As always with Cancer, much of this goes on in the subconscious or even unconscious mind.* The strong intuitive awareness of this, caused by retrograde Neptune and other indications, is at times a torment to the native, who needs must devote himself to mystery and love-as-salvation.

THE VENUS–NEPTUNE RELATIONSHIP

It will be noted further that Venus disposits Neptune, thus lending Neptune, the planet of secrets, delusions, refinement and regrets, a Venus–Cancer quality. The obstacles and difficulties caused by this cardinal square, Venus–Neptune, from water to air are somewhat paradoxical. It is the quest for perfection, to some extent inhibited in action by the Water-Air involvement, which spurs the native on. Whereas a square is an obstacle and therefore a challenge, an opposition is a signal that some kind of compromise must be reached between inner needs and external demands. Is there a relevant opposition? The Venus/Neptune midpoint is not involved in any conjunction, square, opposition or semisquare with any factor. This justifies us in examining the axis by Witte's method of using the hard angles down to $11\frac{1}{4}°$ and even half that: these are valid if the orbs are kept well down, but only in such cases as this might they do more than confirm other judgements. Only Mars is involved: in a separating aspect to the midpoint of $11\frac{1}{4}°$, orb $12\frac{1}{2}'$. This is close enough to be valid. It merely strengthens the square, gives it a little more meticulous energy: the midpoint is in proud and unyielding Leo, so the Virgo Mars may calm this down somewhat.

VENUS' TRINE TO THE SOUTH NODE

The trine to the south node is interesting inasmuch as it is close enough to involve the north node in a sextile relationship with the planet.* This configuration gives the native the opportunity to achieve good timing in his more impersonal friendships, such as relationships at work, and the ability to relieve tensions involving the affections or the desire for possessions. He will sometimes achieve release by drinking until he is quite drunk; he will recover from this state, through vomiting, more quickly than most people – and so feel better. But the ease with which greed (Venus) leads to such release does tempt him to indulge himself in the consumption of rich delicacies and favourite foods, which cause him digestive anguish until he can be sick. This is a man, I suggest, who might guzzle the whole of his family's weekend food supplies late on Friday night, and show no shame, so natural to him is his violent gluttony, which he exercises in a cool manner, not at all evasively.

VENUS' QUINCUNX TO THE DESCENDANT

The quincunx to the Desc and the corresponding semisextile to the Asc indicate that at times compromises which have to be made for the sake of getting money or other conveniences from employers cause some strains at home. The orb is only 4′, so this is very strong. Is there a clue to the nature of these compromises and the strains they lead to? The midpoint of Venus/Asc (or of course Desc) is semisquare to the nodes; this gives the native empathy and reinforces the other indications of this, so the strains will probably be modified. But there is no indication yet of the sort of strains. I think this is likely to be found in the Jupiter–Uranus opposition, which is extremely close. The wanderlust this opposition can promote is smothered by the home-oriented indications, and the tendency to religious bias it suggests is countered by Gemini scepticism. However, the wanderlust tendency here seems to be externalised: the native might have travel forced upon him. The Jupiter–Uranus opposition is across the

*The subconscious holds information immediately available to consciousness, such as the tickling of one's moustache. The unconscious holds secret and frequently dangerous information unavailable, in ordinary circumstances, to the mind.

*We allow up to 5° for the trine but we do not allow the principle of transition of light to put the other point into sextile. We allow no more than 2° for this.

Gemini–Sagittarius axis, as is the Asc–Desc axis, and this does bring travel into the life (Mercury and Jupiter rule the signs involved). Further, both Jupiter and Uranus are on the direct midpoint Mercury/Sun, indicating respectively 'travel' and 'new adjustments'. Jupiter is double applying to the farther midpoint, and Uranus itself is applying to it. The strains produced by such absences would probably be no more than have already been indicated. The septile from Venus to the MC indicates that the native is motivated by the notion of love for an individual, and that he can at times act in an inspired manner in relation to it.

VENUS' MIDPOINT INVOLVEMENTS

Further heavy emphasis on Venus is given by the fact that it stands square to the midpoint of Asc/MC. This configuration indicates little more than that Venus plays the essential part in Arthur's life, and is further evidence of why the Jupiter–Uranus opposition is modified and transformed by the Venus–Neptune square.

The other direct midpoints in which Venus is involved are Mars/Node (in applying conjunction), and Pluto/Asc (orb 55′, again direct). This means that Mars/Node = Pluto/Asc, which makes Venus, and all points in cardinals at 11° 08′, an important place when it is transited by heavy planets, or when they reach there in progressions or directions.

The Mars/Node midpoint indicates that the native is inclined to form some associations for his own ends, but it also indicates a desire for intense sexual intimacy. Both inclinations have already been seen. Can they be reconciled or explained? This, for once, is simple: Gemini rising with Sun almost on the ascending degree implies, not the rare phenomenon of 'multiple personality', as is sometimes suggested, but a conscious division between two areas of life, as well as seeing both sides of the question. The one habit of exploitation does not corrupt the personal relationship, although a man with a Venus–Neptune square might be tormented by the notion that it did, since his goal is perfection.

The involvement of Venus with the Pluto/Asc midpoint is coloured by Pluto being in a sextile to the Asc – a potentially malefic aspect, offering the dangerous opportunity to control and master the environment – but the trine from Pluto to the Desc means that the relations with others can flow easily and meaningfully, and the Venus involvement will work usefully.

THE SUN

The Sun, I have suggested, can most usefully be seen as a point of failure, but this is to judge charts from high standards, and is of interest only to those who wish to analyse themselves in 'metaphysical' terms. We need not make too much of it. Arthur's Sun is strengthened by being so close to its rising point; the native will see his 'failure' as an awareness of himself at almost all times. His sense of detachment, which is involuntary, will occasionally worry him in that he will feel himself to be 'cold'. But Mercury in Cancer gives natural warmth to his feeling, and he will discover, or by now has discovered, that detachment is not necessarily a cold attribute. The trine of the Sun to Neptune would be fairly weak with a separating orb of 3° 17′, but we observe that the midpoint of the two bodies is applying to Pluto and this strengthens the aspect. This is a difficult aspect to judge, but generally indicates a person of imaginative disposition; and also a person who is interested in all things to do with the sea. Pluto at the midpoint tends to make Arthur transform his sufferings into wounds: it is as if, once his hypersensitive susceptibilities have been slighted in some way, he takes the opportunity to inflict violent wounds upon himself, retreating into tragic silence. The Sun is in sextile to Pluto – and, as I have stated before, the sexile is by no means the 'benefic' aspect it is made out to be.

There are no direct midpoints involving the Sun. In general the configurations in which it is involved confirm what we have already learned.

MARS

Mars signifies will-power and energy, both aggressive and defensive. It may involve timidity, as well, in certain placements, but the habit of describing these placements as indicating a weak Mars should be resisted. Timidity is not a fault. The sign-placement in Virgo indicates sensitivity, discretion, humour. The chart as we have analysed it so far gives little sign of discretion in manner: on the contrary, we have seen indications of a rough and candid approach. But there is discretion in this Mars placement, and of course the very strong indications of personal loyalty and, deliberately to employ an old-fashioned word, honour, imply discretion in personal affairs. Mars in Virgo indicates a deliberate concentration of energies – useful in one who suffers from the inevitable Gemini tendency to scatter his energies – and a capacity to withdraw feeling from necessary arrangements. Mars always makes itself felt very strongly in a chart, so that this indication of an ability to be straightforwardly practical and critical is very positive. The coldness of Mars is modified here by Mercury in Cancer. However, there can be a tendency to be nervous and irritable at home, and Mars in Virgo suggests once again that the native tends to suffer his turbulent feelings through his stomach: digestive difficulties owing to the terrible hurling of titbits into himself. Ebertin interestingly mentions that Mars in Virgo can sometimes lead to 'frequent trips abroad' in connection with the vocation. He mentions a case of a man who travelled a great deal, and who had Mars in Virgo and Mars trine Moon. In Arthur's chart the aspect to the Moon is applying to 126°, orb only 3′: an important and powerful aspect in 20H.

MARS' MIDPOINT INVOLVEMENTS

The direct midpoints with which Mars is involved are Moon/Venus (square from Gemini) and Neptune/MC (square from Sagittarius). The first picture implies passion, a passionate wife and the fact that actions are caused by feelings. But, while this may be the case with this man, it must be remembered that Mars is in Virgo and that the midpoint is considerably cooled by occurring in Gemini, which imparts a controlled and, again, 'metaphysical' approach. The second picture indicates a swindler! This, in the matter of his employment, the native could well be. Otherwise, it emphasizes his desire for unreality, his refusal to accept that his employment is unreal, which means, phenomenologically, that there is a sense in which in his existence it is not unreal.

JUPITER

Jupiter in Sagittarius is in its dignity, where it imparts a religious sense. All things being equal, which they seldom are, it can indicate a person who seeks some specific esoteric channel for his beliefs. The opposition to Uranus in Arthur's chart reverses this effect, throwing him into rebellion against – one would suggest – all established systems. The opposition is idealistic, further reinforcing the Venus–Neptune square, but, since it involves Uranus, it is also dangerous. However, the axis across which it occurs, Sagittarius–Gemini (Fire–Air), is not so dangerous. It is a mutable, adaptable, opposition. Unconventional violence will certainly manifest at times, but there is coolness and control. The opposition gives the strongest indication of the blunt, apparently harsh, candid manner; the capacity to create disharmony from time to time. The aspect here is, moreover, very mental: the ardour of Fire is unhappy not to encounter with immediacy (Uranus) the experience (Air) of perfection, but to encounter instead corruption or at the least obstacles.

Both planets are involved in the same midpoint aspects, and there are an unusual number of direct ones: Moon/Saturn, Mercury/Sun, Venus/Sun, Node/MC, Saturn/Vertex. These suggest: tension and release from it; separations through journeys; a high valuation of quiet times, either alone or with close friends; optimism and a desire to expand personal knowledge and to integrate it; an unconventional approach; a desire for happiness, or perfection, in love, which is somewhat threatened by self-will; happy gatherings with close friends but also a sudden overwhelming desire to be alone, reflecting the violent 'switching' of mood associated with Gemini. Jupiter's involvement with the Saturn/Vertex midpoint reinforces the Moon's involvement with the same midpoint, building Arthur's inner life, so to say, into his outer life: externalising his whole chart in the sense that the 'being attracts the life'.

THE MOON'S NODES

The North node attracts experiences which will build up to a point at which some kind of release is required, and that point of release is indicated by the condition of the south node. Arthur's nodal axis is Taurus–Scorpio. We have seen that Venus trines the South node closely enough to sextile the North, and have discussed its effects already. More important is that there is a kind of T-Square involved here: Pluto is in very close square to the nodal axis, which means that Pluto mediates between acceptance, willing response and release. On the most physical level, the native is often sick, and this gives him release not only from his gluttony but also from any powerful tensions building up within him. Also he may, if only temporarily, throw up friendships or associations if they prove too much for him. We have discussed the effect of the configuration Sun/Neptune = Pluto, which strengthens the trine between the Sun and Neptune; Pluto, being square to the nodes, further reinforces it. Quite often the configuration can indicate weakness in relationships with others, but the tenor of the chart is all against this. It is rather that the native does feel very weak in regard to his position with certain people – possibly his parents, particularly the mother, in this case – but Pluto has the effect of reforming, transforming or eliminating whatever makes him uneasy. The perfection he seeks, it seems, cannot be there – is out of the question – and so he alternates between hostility and a mechanically dutiful attitude.

The nodes in Saturn/MC give empathy and compassion; the septile to the north node from Mercury in Cancer (orb 1° 11′ separating) helps him to be usefully thoughtful to those in distress: he may often do what is best for them by intuition. He would know, for example, when to leave someone alone.

SATURN

The condition of Saturn has to do with work, organisation, concentration, caution, the burdens of time, inhibitions and usually, alas, some aspect of our misfortune. Arthur's Saturn is in Leo. It is here thought of as being in detriment because it co-rules Aquarius; but I have found no cases where Saturn functions badly in Leo, save for some over-inflated public figures. Rather it is reliable, loyal and gives a person a proud simplicity of nature, the sort of qualities once called nobility and justice.

It is interesting to see, as one builds up the analysis of a chart, how the portrait of the native – contradictions included – tends to fall into a piece. For Saturn in Leo also suggests some inhibition, lack of sexual confidence – this last in the sense that the performance is a performance and therefore not perfect.

SATURN'S INVOLVEMENT WITH URANUS AND NEPTUNE

Saturn is genuinely unaspected, but its one direct midpoint is extremely interesting. Saturn divides, and therefore strengthens, a bi-septile aspect between Uranus and Neptune. That is a very interesting aspect in itself, inasmuch as it ties together two of the planets which feature in the two dominant aspects in the chart, Venus–Neptune and Uranus–Jupiter. We should consider the possible meaning of the Uranus–Neptune aspect at this point. The septile relates to things that inspire people, and in particular to inspiration in the affairs associated with the planets in question. Saturn is of course septile to both the others: there is therefore a series of three septiles.

Ebertin defines the Uranus–Neptune principle as 'the elimination of the waking consciousness', and as 'inner illumination'. Adding Saturn gives: 'depression' and 'pessimism'. However, this is to ignore the septile relationship between the three planets. The whole configuration is associated with 'psychic states' or inexplicable experiences. Here is a man who is poetically* inspired by unhappiness, which by definition he does not like. Saturn is, however, coloured by the Gemini Sun, and therefore has humour. Yet, I would assert that, when under stress, this man feels haunted by creatures from beyond the grave, that doors

*I use 'poetic' to describe that principle in life which defies science in its life-denying modern sense: the type of science which claims 'science will discover all'; 'love is chemistry alone'; 'Shakespeare is explicable in terms of the known laws of physics'.

open where no man's hand may be seen, that the dark blue sea (Neptune) sweeps into the room suddenly (Uranus) and that all seems organised and well (Saturn). The unhappy man is paradoxically happy, and talks to the dead in whose continued existence he is unlikely to 'believe', if he thinks about them consciously.

There is some disagreement about the effects of unaspected Saturn. I find the interpretation 'erratic self-control' most usually applies. However, the septile relationships add to this information. The orb of the bi-septile between the two outer planets, Uranus and Neptune, is wide: 1° 55′, though double-applying and of course strengthened by the Saturn midpoint: Saturn is applying to it, and the orb here is very small, 11′. Thus the emphasis goes on the condition of Saturn, which controls the aspect between the outer planets. Saturn–Neptune is undoubtedly indicative of a physical response to emotional difficulties, and we have the Sun square to the Saturn–Neptune midpoint in Virgo. This gives the physical reaction a certain deliberative quality; it can be used as a strategy in order to eliminate the emotional problem. The Saturn–Neptune relationship also suggests that Arthur can help others, and the septile indicates that this help can be inspired; in other words, that the right thing can be done intuitively. This confirms an earlier finding.

As for Saturn–Uranus, this indicates tension, but also endurance and perseverance which the septile would bring out. Saturn–Uranus is also connected with the removal of internal parts of the body. It may be that Arthur has had, or will have, something removed in order to relieve some kind of tension. Because Neptune is involved in the configuration, this may be done erroneously.

URANUS

Uranus is emotionally labile, curious, drastic, tense, innovatory, technological, air-fire, all-embracing inasmuch as while it is scientific in the modern sense it is also mystical in the ancient sense. There are reasons for suggesting that it dominates this chart, not the least of which is that in Volguine's scheme, which seems to work, it scores highest. Its septile to Saturn is paradoxical in the sense that it represents a union of two principles: the orthodox and the unorthodox. The conventional chart-ruler is Mercury, and Mercury is strong in the chart. But Uranus, as the stronger of the two rulers of Aquarius, rules the MC, which represents the true self: what Ebertin calls 'ego-consciousness and spiritual awareness'. The chief reason for suggesting that Uranus dominates the chart, though, is that its principles sum up most aptly what we think we have discovered about Arthur, who seems to blend in a unique (Uranus) manner the old and the new (Aquarius).

NEPTUNE AND PLUTO

Neptune in Libra indicates a strange relationship with the public, and an idealistic attitude to love; there is also the danger of disappointment through seeing people in a falsely romantic light. If, as the chart indicates, the relationship with the mother is poor, then great strain can be imposed by the idealised romanticism of Neptune in Libra. The trine of Neptune to MC gives grace and refinement in a real, rather than a Victorian, sense.

Neptune's real importance in this chart arises from its square to Venus, which has already been dealt with at length. Pluto has been discussed adequately in connection with its close square to the nodal axis.

THE MC

The MC is the focus of a skew-yod, because it is at the inverse midpoint of a Mercury–Mars sextile. There are also, of course, Mercury–MC and Mars–MC quincunxes. The orb from Mercury is rather wide, but the sextile is in orb (1° 56′) and the midpoint is applying. The sextile itself indicates decisiveness and directness, and is not more than strong confirmation of Arthur's sharp-minded and brutal frankness.

There are two possible interpretations of the yod on the MC, although they are not irreconcilable. One is that each of the planets forming the sextile represents a choice: that the native must take one course or another. The other, the 'Finger of God' or 'Finger of Fate' interpretation, puts the emphasis on the focal planet or point, suggesting that it is being 'pointed at'. The pattern Mercury/Mars = MC indicates, simply, a thoughtful fighter, a determined person, but the sextile aspect emphasizes this ever further. This is a determined and ruthless man, although the definition of ruthlessness must be modified in view of the other chart indications: there will be no ruthlessness towards people the native loves. The Venus–Neptune square in cardinals is an 'all or nothing' square: either the people are acceptable to Arthur or they are not.

The Mercury–MC quincunx is an indication of tension, experienced in early years, between Arthur's own spontaneous ideas and those imparted by his parents. This ties in with what we have learned already. Early in life there is an enormous conflict between self-expression and conformist utterance.

The Mars–MC quincunx confirms an earlier inference: as Hand puts it, 'mixed feeling about authority figures'; I would add, 'particularly parents'. The yod indicates then, that the native is determined to find himself. He has specific ideas about the self, believes that each person's self is unique, and he would probably reject all teaching, *all* the processes which form the 'superego', were he not restrained by his powers of reason. He is extraordinarily self-willed, although, as we have seen, this does not preclude dedicating himself to the service of someone else. However, he may still tend to veer between the harshly meticulous (Mars Virgo) expression of his will, and the softer (Mercury Cancer) approach. It is interesting that his CD is opposite the MC, at what is called the 'reaction point' opposite the focal planet of a yod. Transits, and most particularly bodies and points, progressed to the CD in Tertiary Progressions, which are easily the most potent for this Moon-oriented man, will indicate critical times of self-appraisal, which we know to be a habit of the native.

The MC in Aquarius indicates Utopian ideals, a tendency to scatter energy but a capacity to put things together in a creative and useful manner.

THE ASCENDANT

The Ascendant is the mask the native wears: his strategy. It is in Gemini, which is cunning but often divided. The MC-ruler, Uranus, is also in Gemini, septile to its co-ruler, Saturn, which is in Leo. The MC ruler is square to the Neptune/Pluto midpoint: a very mysterious picture suggesting paranormal experiences, especially ones relating to people who are 'there' when they are not in logical fact there at all. It suggests, in Witte's words, 'to be missing'. 'To be missing' is to be 'switched off'.

SUMMARY

In delineating Arthur's chart I have tried to avoid the 'universally valid', although that is impossible to avoid altogether: if something is universally valid, then it is going to crop up. What one can do, as I have here, is to try to relate the universally valid to the specific.

Here, then, is a man who combines what respectable society would condemn as criminality – if he robbed a bank he would reproach himself only if he was caught – with extreme loyalty and perfectionism. Arthur is an extremely tense man, whose interests are wide but basically metaphysical in the widest sense. I would suggest that he is frustrated because he cannot work for himself, but recognizes that this would not be a commercial proposition and so accepts it. He therefore exploits his employers to the utmost. This one half of his life is as divorced as he can possibly make it from his private life, which is dedicated to perfecting an imperfectible romantic project.

FOURTEEN PERSONALITIES

In the following pages I study the charts of some well-known people, either looking at their charts' more interesting features or making a quick examination of the whole. I have chosen these charts because, together, they provide examples of most of the more serious problems encountered in astrology. Many of them are difficult but interesting because they show a person who is functioning at a low level of awareness. It is very important to remember that no chart ever states that the native *will* behave in such and such a way;

SIGMUND FREUD

Freud was the founder of the psychoanalytic movement, which he proceeded to dominate in a paternalistic and sometimes ruthless way. But the Freud of the movement differs greatly from Freud the thinker and writer. His lesser known writings show that he became increasingly interested in religion and in such matters as the paranormal (he was a member of the Society for Psychical Research), although he always stayed inside the rationalist framework. He remained loyal to his Jewish origins to the end of his life, and left Vienna in the late 1930s after being raided by the Gestapo.

The first thing to be noticed about Freud's chart is that the Gemini Moon is right on the Vertex. This is appropriate for the man who brought sex out into the open and who made the suggestion that supposedly rational behaviour and thinking was motivated by unconscious (Moon) conflicts. Moon in Gemini is also appropriate for a man who intellectualised emotion in his work. Sun in Taurus is in applying sinister conjunction to Uranus, also in Taurus; this is in a fairly tight dexter sextile to Neptune in its own sign of Pisces. The Sun is otherwise unaspected. Taurus is the sign of sensuality, as well as of principles and values; there is a stellium here, and the Libran Mars is backing out of a juicy quincunx to the angular Pluto, in very tight separating semisquare to Neptune. The Moon is in an applying dexter square to the dream planet, nicely in middle of its own sign. Jupiter, also in its own sign, has recently begun to slide past a sinister square to Saturn. Venus is pushing relentlessly into sextile with only if he displays a total lack of self-awareness will the person with a difficult chart fulfil its worst indications. (This is so, however, in the cases of Hitler and the murderer Landru.)

Readers may have seen some of these charts elsewhere with slightly different planetary positions and angles. Each chart is based on the most up-to-date research, some on data unknown to previous astrologers. We will first look at the charts of Freud and Jung, the two most famous proto-psychiatric thinkers of the modern age.

Saturn: this aspect is building up power.

There is an uneasy and difficult dissociate opposition: Mars, while pulling back desperately from the Pluto quincunx (suggesting overwork, a strong but inhibited libido, financial stress and a transformative, sublimating personality), is going into opposition to Jupiter, here suggesting a need to dominate others. Asc/MC, always a very important point, is at 28 Virgo and is squared by the controlling, truthful and pessimistic – or at least realistic – Saturn. Asc is at Saturn/Neptune (illness: Freud was of course a doctor), Pluto at Moon/Neptune (dreams).

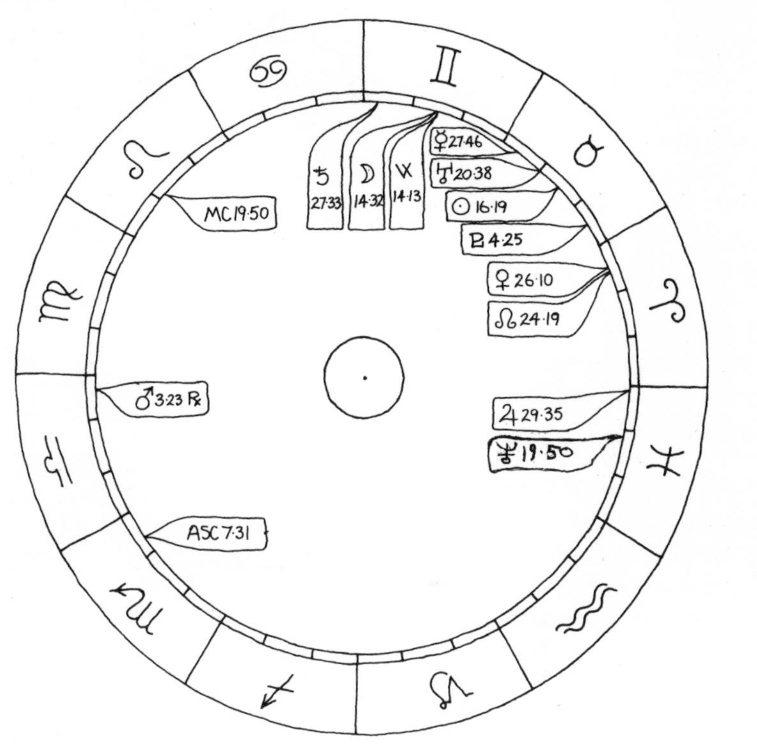

Freud's chart is full of opportunities – opportunities that were taken, at the expense of the inner need expressed by the strong Taurus Sun, which is just past the square to Mars/Neptune, at 15 Leo. The 6H opportunity/failure chart is extremely interesting, as the radical map has a number of true sextiles. Pluto opposite Asc indicates a demanding man, and a man who wants to effect transformations: it is appropriate that the planet of sublimation should be the angular one in this chart, since sublimation can be briefly defined as the channelling of dangerous impulses into useful ones. Pluto energises the Moon–Neptune square in mutables, being near its midpoint; the square indicates powerful and memorable dreams (which we know Freud had) and imaginings about mother/wife (the heart of his work). Pluto at the midpoint indicates a dynamic sensitivity, a 'changeable fearsome mood'.

Asc at Saturn/Neptune suggests very keen suffering; the adroit Gemini Saturn punishing Asc/MC in proper, protocol-loving Virgo points to Freud's seriousness, just as his Scorpio Asc gives him a penetrative strategy. The cautious, Taurus-like, conservative Jupiter–Saturn square stood him in good stead: he had explosive material to publish, and any wildness in him would have meant scandal, and thus oblivion for what he felt to be the truth.

CARL JUNG

Jung, a younger man than Freud, was at first his close associate, but relations between the two men were broken off after a quarrel, which upset Freud far more than Jung. Jung's therapeutic method is called analytical psychology; it is a mystical system, using all the Freudian notions, but desexualising them and putting them in a Grimm Brothers setting.

Although safe in neutral Switzerland during the 1930s, Jung accepted high office in the 'restructured' psychoanalytical movement, now purged of Jews and Jewish thought and run by a cousin of Göring's. Jung denounced Jewishness, comparing the Jews to women, but he was neither anti-semitic nor Nazi. However, he himself came near to saying that he was 'without principle' and an opportunist: he was just waiting for a chance to get back at Freud without whom his own commercially successful and very popular system could not have come into being. Anthropologists still acknowledge a certain debt to Freud, who is taken seriously as a thinker; no anthropologist is interested in Jungian thinking, which is fuzzy, unscholarly, and badly organised. Jung's early work is undoubtedly brilliant, it must be said, and some of his objections to Freud's more dogmatic notions are cogent; likewise his analysis of individuals is often highly astute.

In Jung's chart the Sun, not the Moon, has just separated from the fixed square to Neptune, dexter; Saturn is backing into yet another fixed dexter square with Pluto; the Moon has not long passed the fixed square to Uranus. Mars slices the 'lucky' Jupiter–Saturn trine into two halves: it is applying to the midpoint, indicating discontent and sour driving ambition. Asc/MC at 00 Capricorn – suggesting fame – is semi-squared by Uranus. The

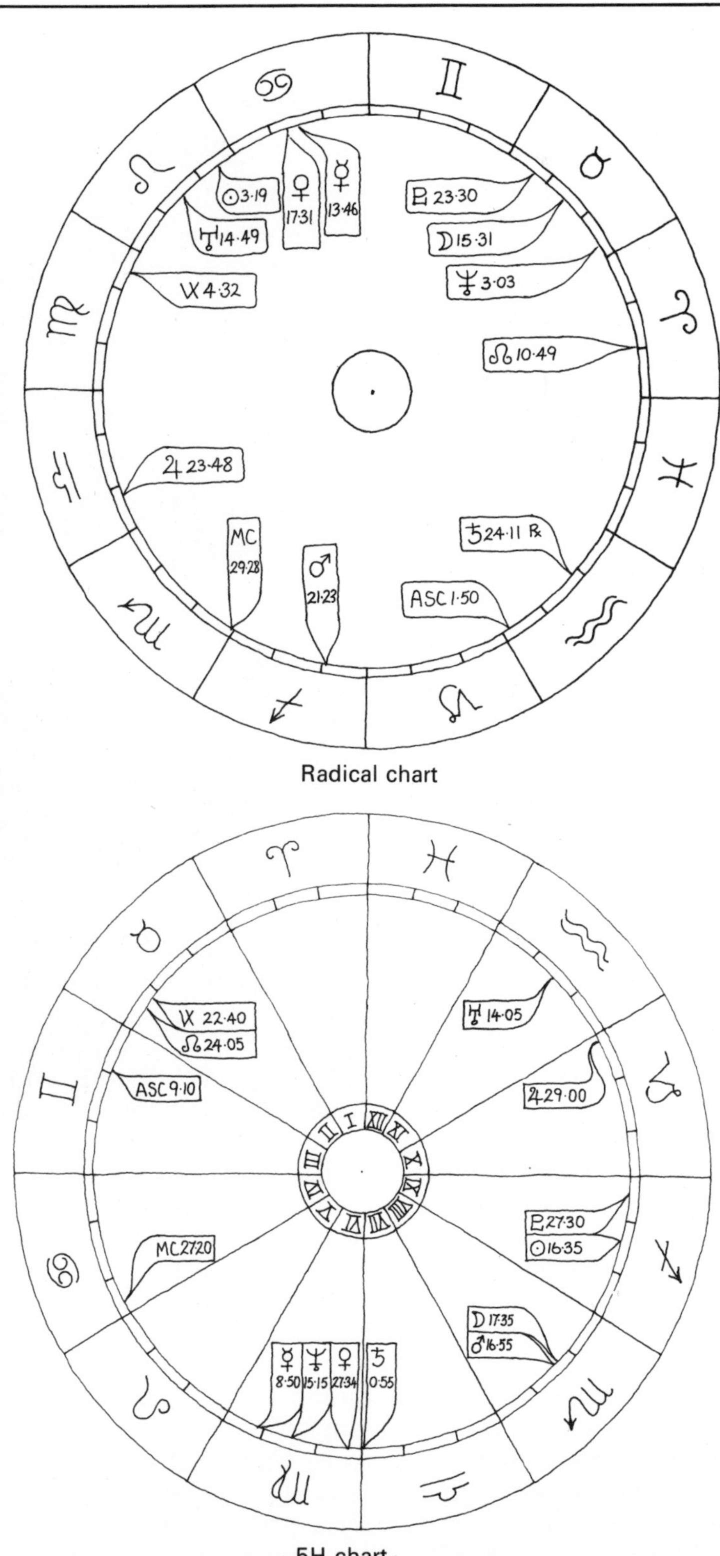

Radical chart

5H chart

picture is of a hasty and determined man, willing and able to make scenes. Jung was as domineering as Freud, though frightened of the over-demanding older man. But let us look at Jung's 5H chart, which indicates his intellectual strengths and capacity for power.

Here Moon is on Mars (signifying a powerful will) in the house of others' money. The Neptune–Sun square is preserved in mutables: the suggestion is of healing where there is no real sickness (Neptune in Virgo) by remodelling the patient's character on lines suggested by the native (Sagittarius Sun activated by tricks about 'constructive' dreams). The cool quincunx from Uranus in its own sign to the bullish Neptune seems to cock a snook at Jung's own attractively muddled and mystical ideology: it indicates people who want nothing to do with mystery but prefer large bank balances. Jung managed to get away with both mystery and cash, while also grasping the opportunities afforded by the Sun–Uranus sextile. Asc is in the third house of communications, squared by Mercury from the house of sickness and hypochondria. The Vertex axis almost coincides with the Nodal axis across the cash-houses, and Jupiter, here suggesting expansion, is on the IC – Jung always lived in great luxury.

VINCENT VAN GOGH

We next look at the chart of a different kind of man: the painter Van Gogh. Mystery still surrounds Van Gogh: it is not at all clear why he committed suicide, and different descriptions of his death disagree as to where he shot himself and in what part of his body. It is not clear either whether he was technically 'mad', or from what he suffered. It is likely that he had some kind of epilepsy.

Certainly in his lifetime Van Gogh failed to gain popularity as an artist, although he worked for a time with Gauguin, who recognised his worth but was unable to help him personally. Posthumously he became one of the most popular painters of all time, although certain critics feel that he has been overrated, possibly because they are frightened by the extreme violence of his vision. We know what we do about him largely because his brother Theo, an art dealer, supported him both morally and financially, and Van Gogh wrote his brother one of the most important and interesting series of letters in existence.

The truth about Van Gogh seems to be that he suffered, all his life, from the most acute disappointment and panic reactions. He was definitely not schizophrenic, though he was subject to acute agitated depression, and to attacks of mania; he may have been the victim of alcoholic poisoning. His personality was unstable, but possibly this was to be expected given the unhappy deal he had in life and in love. As his brother said, he might have avoided madness had he had someone to love him. Certainly Van Gogh was not a lucky man. Most painters of his genius find a rich patron or a dealer to finance them; Van Gogh had no success in this respect. His letters, along with his paintings and drawings, show that he was dedicated to loving sincerely and living truthfully, and that he was by no means unconcerned with society, or merely egocentric. He wanted to help the sick as much as he wanted to paint. When he tried to put the precepts of Christ into practice he was certainly being extreme, but he was not suffering from religious mania. He admitted that he was risking his life for his work. And was his violent resentment at the commercial use of art really mad? All in all, he was a man of exquisite sensitivity and very high values, and his is a chart which we should view as 'used': this does not mean that Van Gogh was interested in astrology, merely that he had great insight into his own personality.

The chart provides an excellent, though cruel, example of how the Sun indicates failure, if only at the highest level. The Sun was always regarded as exalted in Aries, and it is to this exaltation that Van Gogh, with his impossible aspirations, wanted his life to conform: Aries is not only the ram, but also the lamb. Van Gogh was deeply influenced by his childhood and by the faith of his parents (his father was a priest). This is an unaspected Sun, providing a

remarkable example of the characteristics suggested by Dean as accompanying this condition: the native feels inwardly fragmented and identifies with an inner self, but finds no way of integrating his abilities with this strong feeling of identification. Van Gogh did seem to feel that his inner self was floating somewhere out of his reach, but still in the realms of reality: he would have liked to be more practical as lover, helper of the sick, and minister of God. But he found it impossible. His wild gesture of cutting off his ear and sending it in a box to a prostitute reflects this feeling. We should not simply dismiss this act as mad: in Van Gogh, it is full of meaning.

Moon–Jupiter are in majestic trine to Mercury, which is as sharp in Fire as they are; here we see the aspiring Van Gogh, confirmed by the Sagittarius–Gemini Vertex axis. However, heavy and mystical Pisces involvements (including Venus) threaten the picture as a whole: Mars catches the Jupiter square, and the Moon must be afflicted, if only through Jupiter. But Jupiter's safety and nobility, in its own sign of wisdom and philosophical serenity, are thus menaced. The MC is in quite close square to the Moon while Neptune is angular in the Gauquelin sense. The Mars–Venus conjunction in Pisces is strange and the squares to both from the Moon-enhanced Jupiter are disturbing: finances are forever perilous, the emotions are always near boiling-point, the kindliness is extreme.

Neptune is isolated, unaspected, though in its own sign: the native is imaginative and sensitive to an agonised degree and very creative, but he cannot be creative without regarding his creations as part and parcel of man's whole life. Pluto too is unaspected and therefore raging, ensuring that the native is subject to sudden compulsive acts which he can understand only after he has performed them, when they can be captured in his paintings. The Moon is moving fast towards the sesquiquadrate to Uranus, which, astonishingly, is yet another unaspected planet. In such cases we find that parts of the native function as if independently of the rest, leaving him to try and integrate the pieces. Saturn too is unaspected, since the sextile between it and Neptune has an orb of 3°45′: more fools they who, in the light of this chart, allow such enormous orbs to this aspect.

Van Gogh's 13H chart is remarkable for what it tells us about betrayal and the native's attitude to death and to the spiritual deadness which so many of us equate with death. The Asc is in the first house, the MC (for the true self) is flung into the house of mental and physical exploration. The Node is also in the first house, conjunct

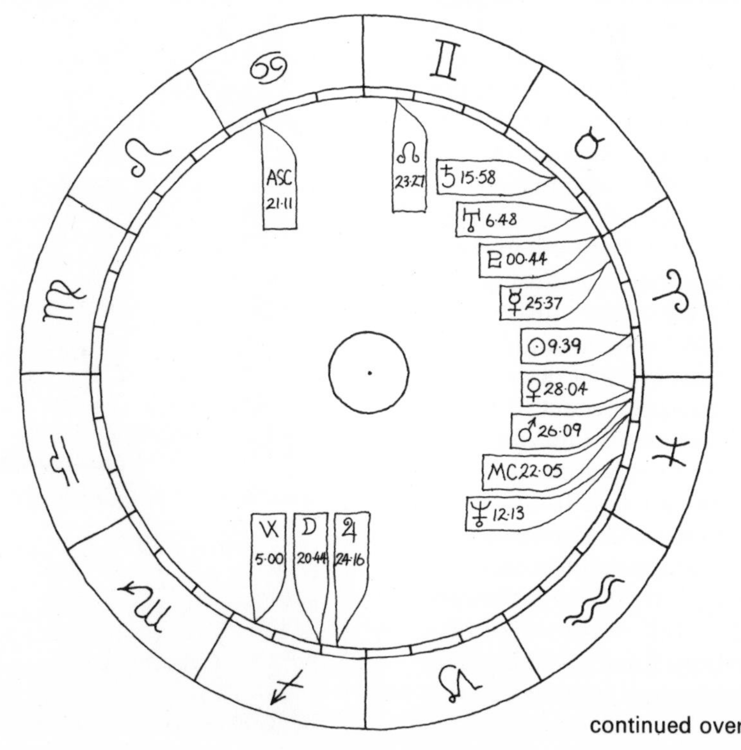

continued over

Van Gogh continued

Asc. Mercury and Venus are conjunct in Pisces, suggesting death, secrets, and ultimate meanings. In the creative Leo house the Sun conjoins Neptune, but in the Cancer house of home the Moon is poignantly afflicted by Uranus. There is freedom, but no peace, no true home. Saturn from the house of death serenely trines the Sun–Neptune conjunction. Pluto in the house of values and of money is squared by Neptune (the radical orb in 52H is 3′), indicating a creator of powerful images, an artist. In fact there is a very tight fixed T-square, which is frequently the case in a harmonic appropriate to a remarkable life: it lies between Mars–Neptune, which oppose each other, and Pluto at point-focus. The radical orbs are negligible. Somehow or other the native has to solve the problem of his religious fervour (Mars–Neptune) towards others (Mars in the fifth house, Neptune in the ninth): metamorphosing Pluto is just about the most explosive way he could go about it. He may perhaps be said to have done it, for at the very end of his life Van Gogh wrote to his brother that his reason had 'half-foundered' owing to his devotion to his work, and he added 'well, that's all right'. So his letters show a full awareness of his position. It may well be that in one sense, as shown in this chart, he fulfilled himself.

RICHARD NIXON

Richard Nixon, the disgraced politician, is the only president of the United States ever to have been forced to resign. We have already looked at certain features of his chart. Attention is usually first drawn to the appropriate Sun–Neptune opposition, though this is wide. It shows a man who will either be altruistic in the extreme, or one – like Nixon – who will exploit and use crooked friends. But the close conjunction of Mars, Mercury and Jupiter at the end of Sagittarius and beginning of Capricorn is as interesting as the Sun–Neptune opposition. The Mercury–Jupiter conjunction is not in itself an aspect to cause much trouble, but it seems that Mars has hardened it. This view is given greater credence by the fact that Nixon's chart is cleft by the Mars–Pluto opposition which is really much closer, more important, and more malicious than the Sun–Neptune one. We see here an exact similarity to part of Thatcher's chart (Jupiter in Capricorn opposed by Pluto), but although the orb is wider the triple conjunction is much more troublesome.

Basically we have three very difficult inter-personal problems to deal with: Pluto opposing Mars, Mercury and

Jupiter. This would splinter the chart of a much more resilient native than this small-time Virgo lawyer. Virgo here means a strategy of the con-man type, including a good deal of straight-forward, guilty handwashing and scrubbing. The famous five o'clock shadow (presumably dealt with in the end by electrolysis) is an appropriate metaphor. If Nixon grew a beard, he would feel that he had something to conceal, whereas he has probably never felt that he really *needed* to conceal anything. It simply comes naturally to him to conceal everything. Mercury–Pluto indicates difficulties with lies and propaganda, dangerous for someone whose profession involves playing about with half-truths. Jupiter–Pluto, just as in Thatcher's chart, suggests the urge to re-establish the values of the past. Mars–Pluto is either dictatorial, or determined to get to the bottom of problems.

In this chart Mercury has slickly intervened, to make Nixon seem less ambitiously authoritarian than he is. (He is not in fact malicious, except when crossed.) The Moon is in septile aspect to both Neptune and Mars, a useful configuration which would be of the greatest significance in a creative person but which, in a disgraced president, is likely to tell us more about the underlying sexual motives. I would suggest that Nixon has successfully kept a tendency to sado-masochism under wraps: he may never have faced it consciously, but nevertheless it created the pattern of his career. Early success was accompanied by dirty tricks, then an unsavoury reputation and failure, followed by success, and then by total failure. Even today he is trying to climb back to success; beyond admitting that he mishandled Watergate he does not feel ashamed of anything.

One final point about this chart: the Aquarian Moon, almost on the Vertex, appears to be a problem. However, several factors resolve this: the Moon in Aquarius is always problematical, since it can indicate great secrecy and/or great openness; in this chart it is unaspected; occasionally in a chart it can indicate the public. The Moon in Aquarius can signify helplessness: the emotions are helpless, replaced by a sort of violent obstinacy. The unaspected Moon has been connected with cold-blooded murders, but it more commonly indicates a person whose emotions are outside his control. And it was of course the public for whom Nixon had to make his last gesture. In his chart the Moon has not long passed the mid-point of Mars/Node: this, if considered to be just in orb, would indicate how passionately Nixon wished to be loved, how he overstepped the mark due to bad judgement, and how ultimately he was destroyed by public opinion.

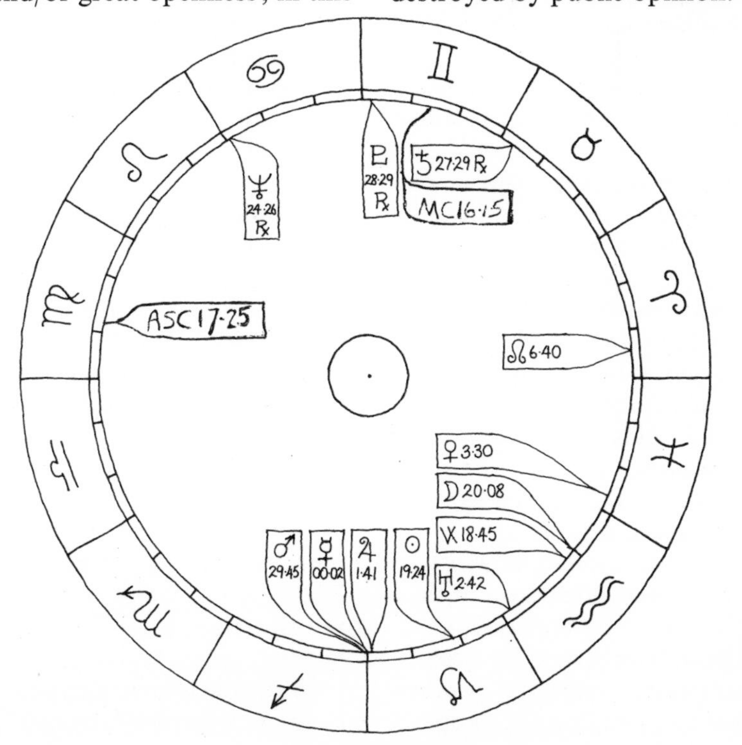

BILLY GRAHAM

The next chart is that of a devoutly Christian friend of Richard Nixon's, who has frightened or otherwise mesmerised thousands into going to church, at least for a few months.

In Billy Graham's chart Pluto is almost exactly square to Asc/MC, which could not be more appropriate for an evangelist, since it indicates a fascinating personality and the desire to interfere with and transform the lives of other people. Neptune, suggesting illusions, is almost exactly angular, within 3° of, the IC. This man, even according to many Christians, is no more than a pedlar of dreams. Certainly his missions, though they bring him fame and success at the time when he undertakes them, have not so far been ultimately successful: studies have shown that the people he converts don't continue to 'believe'. Graham is a fundamentalist with a crude message. The secret of his personal success is that he over-simplifies everything: this is right, that is wrong. He is undoubtedly sincere, but the quality of his message is poor. He is wholly lacking in subtlety, and does not appeal to people of an intellectual or critical cast of mind.

Jupiter, signifying religion in all its forms, is in a quintile to his Vertex (the orb is just the prescribed 2°), and this is appropriate: Graham is switched on, and switches others on, by his violent and efficient preaching (Mars is in an exact Fire trine with Saturn, suggesting hell). The Node is backing into a semisquare aspect with Mars/Saturn; Graham associates with people who are hypnotised, by him or by cheap ideas, into believing that they are sick for God and righteousness. Neptune is in an applying 20H aspect with the Node, giving the native a talent for deluding others, or for making them believe in his dreams. He has the very poetic and aspiring Venus–Neptune square, with the Moon square to Venus/Neptune: this is externalised, for the usual meaning of this configuration is that the native is easily led, whereas it is clear that Graham easily leads. Neptune opposes the MC, so that Venus is given the burden of resolving the conflict, of sticking the two halves of the sliced chart together. If the native is not an artist, or one who finds expression in personal myth-making, then this aspect indicates that he is deluded or deluding: Venus is of course 'God's' love – and cash. I do not know whether this messenger chosen by God lives comfortably or ascetically, but he probably doesn't want for a dime.

The exact Mercury–Saturn square in fixed signs rather gives the lie to the notion that these contacts suggest taciturnity – or does it? A comparison between Graham and the native of the chart on page 62 is instructive. That native has a trine between Mercury and Saturn and, while the orb is 7′ over the prescribed 5°, there is an Aries stellium with Jupiter mediating; Uranus tends to strengthen the aspect slightly by semisquaring the midpoint. This native is one of the most talkative people it is possible to come across. Furthermore, although the trine is wide and separating, he has little control over his talkativeness. But in his case, as in Graham's, Mercury is the chart ruler, and it is in Aries conjunct Jupiter. However, this native does have a characteristic that is close to taciturnity: he is a bad speaker and for much of his life he was inhibited when speaking in public: he dislikes being talkative, feels guilty about it, and what he says to others is frequently melancholy and cynical. In Graham's case we have a man who is in fact somewhat taciturn and stern when he is off the rostrum; in any case Mercury, irresistibly penetrating in Scorpio, is energised by the semisextile from Mars.

Unquestionably, Graham exercises power over masses of people. In this he resembles Hitler, but it would of course be absurd to suggest that his influence is as evil as Hitler's; or indeed to argue that his influence was evil at all. We have looked at Hitler's exceedingly difficult 5H; what of Graham's? Are there any resemblances? In the first place, there is no 'messy' conjunction in Graham's chart in any sign, let alone Aquarius. There is a not too badly skewed Grand Trine in Earth between Sun, Jupiter and Neptune (this last planet is needed to enrich the dreams of Graham's audience). Graham takes great care of himself or, to put it another way, is eminently practical. Neptune is in the tenth house for profession. The Saturn–Node opposition (radical orb in 10H, 41′) is resolved by Neptune: the basic gloom of Graham's message – that sinners go to hell – is nicely obscured by his big-brother image and rough-hewn film-star looks. But the roots of his teaching almost certainly involve a belief in hellfire.

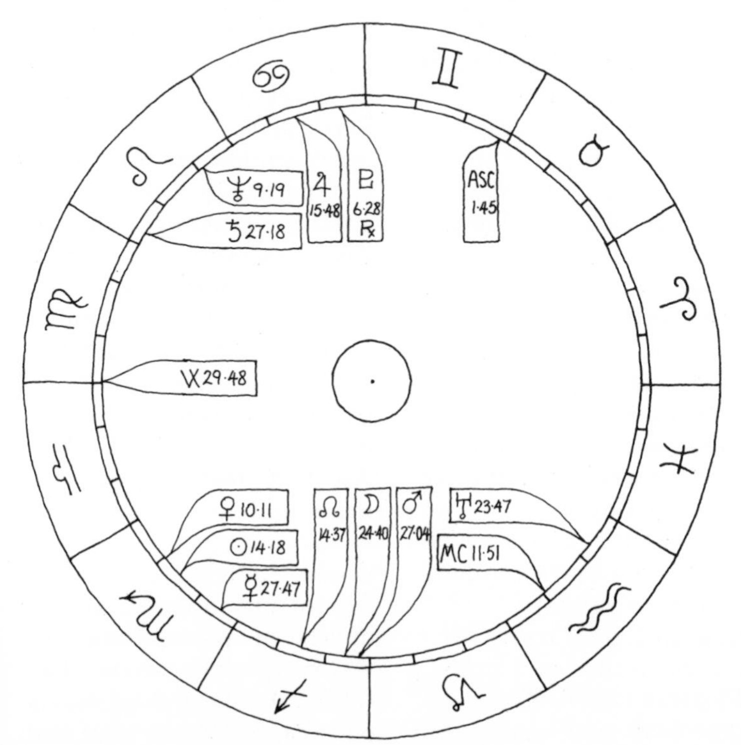

Graham is disingenuous about this. If he handled his chart at a proper level, or rather if his insights into himself were more refined, then he would have to rethink his message or else admit to himself that he lacked integrity. This is shown by the Grand Cross which Mercury completes from Cancer. Energy flows uselessly around this power chart, and is wasted. Asc is appropriately in the house of friends, masses of people, hopes and wishes: as I have remarked, Graham is sincere. The true self, MC, is in the house of home – or the grave. We therefore conclude that this 5H is not of the Hitler kind, but more like that of a successful professional actor. Jupiter, indicating religion, has here been flung into the house of service to others – perhaps Graham does do more good, if only for a short time, than he does harm.

GUILLAUME APOLLINAIRE

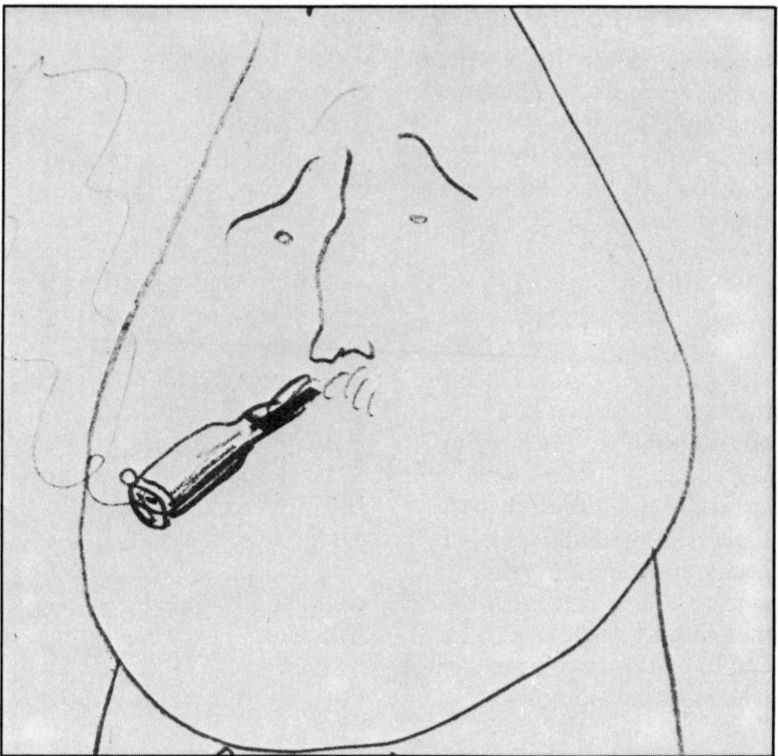

We will now take a look at the chart of the Rome-born, French-speaking, Polish–Swiss poet Guillaume Apollinaire (real name, Kowstrowski). This man lived his life on a much higher level of self-awareness than the American evangelist. He was complex and mysterious, always attracting trouble and notoriety, which he liked less than his friends thought he did and less than he pretended.

Apollinaire was the son of a Swiss officer in the Italian army who did not marry his mother. She was a courtesan, so that at one time Apollinaire was reputed to be the son of the Pope – not impossible as his mother worked in the Vatican. One of the greatest poets of modern times, Apollinaire was an innovator and a highly influential art critic: in one sense he invented cubism. He coined the word surrealism, wrote some amusing pornography, and led a wholly bohemian existence. He was a close friend of Picasso's and had some influence on him. He knew everyone of any importance in the artistic and literary worlds of Paris in the years before World War I. When the Mona Lisa was stolen he was arrested as a suspect, although in fact he had nothing to do with the theft. He joined the army and saw much action before eventually being wounded in the head and trepanned. He died at the end of the war, a victim of the Spanish influenza. Crowds in the street outside shouted 'Down with Guillaume' as he lay dying. They were referring to the German Kaiser, but Apollinaire thought they meant him.

Apollinaire's time of birth may be incorrectly recorded: Gauquelin has accepted it as correctly registered, but there is reason to doubt the accuracy of the report, which was not made by his mother. However, by Primary Directions it does rectify to this: a given time of 5 am, LMT, 0410 GMT, Rome, 26 August 1880, and I accept this as likely. The chief features of the chart are two stelliums in Earth signs. A stellium always means complexity of character, not specifically intellectual complexity, though that is the case here. Apollinaire's Leo Asc is appropriate, as is his Taurus MC. Fundamentally he was a man who cherished the highest values (Taurus) while life conspired to bring him into the limelight. The Asc is squared by Pluto and trined by Saturn, and the two planets are themselves in a double-applying semisextile: Apollinaire showed a great interest in ancient things and was very nervous about the future. At first sight it seems odd that he should have such a preponderance of Earth – indicating practicality – in his chart, despite there being some Fire to energise it; the truth is that he was misunderstood by his friends, who laughed at the difficult situations into which he got himself. He himself worried about them. By the end of his life he was increasingly seeking out practicality. He was an efficient soldier.

His Virgo characteristics emerge in the form and technique of his poems, which, although very unconventional, are never 'free'. There is a persistent Virgoan urge in a man who writes a poem about a car in the shape of a car, rain in the shape of rain and so forth. Virgo is also, of course, deeply subversive beneath its love of protocol. Many con-men have heavy Virgo involvements – and in his early days Apollinaire was a con-man, for example when it came to hotel bills, which he saw no reason to pay if he could avoid it.

Mars is in very close bi-quintile to Saturn: creative power is needed to resolve the famous conflict between these two planets, with their stop-go action. This power is seen in Apollinaire's major poetry. Uranus is at Sun/Venus, exactly describing his troubled and spasmodic love-life, which did end, however, in what appeared to be a permanent and happy relationship. Pluto is in bi-quintile to the Node, demonstrating the transformative effect Apollinaire had on all his artistic and literary friends; the Node is also trined by the Virgo Sun.

The chart lacks Air, and it would lack Water if it were not that the Moon and Neptune are strongly angular. This helps us to understand what Air means. It does *not* mean intellectual ability, of which Apollinaire had his fair share (though his mind did not work along strictly logical lines). Air is abstract, and those with a preponderance of Air can detach themselves from concrete experience. This Apollinaire could not do. He was in a state of perpetual excitement about his experience, but at the same time bewildered. His extreme restlessness and the chaos forced upon him by his life circumstances (including the attentions of his bizarre and embarrassing mother) are indicated by the close Moon–Mercury square. The Moon is not very far past the conjunction with Neptune either, again suggesting 'a peculiar person with strange ideas who is misunderstood,' as Ebertin puts it; and Witte adds 'not quite clearly conscious' which aptly characterises the poet – at least until the time of his army service when, to the surprise of his friends, he operated with great efficiency. This chart obviously justifies the view that a stellium indicates complexity, and that two indicate even greater complexity.

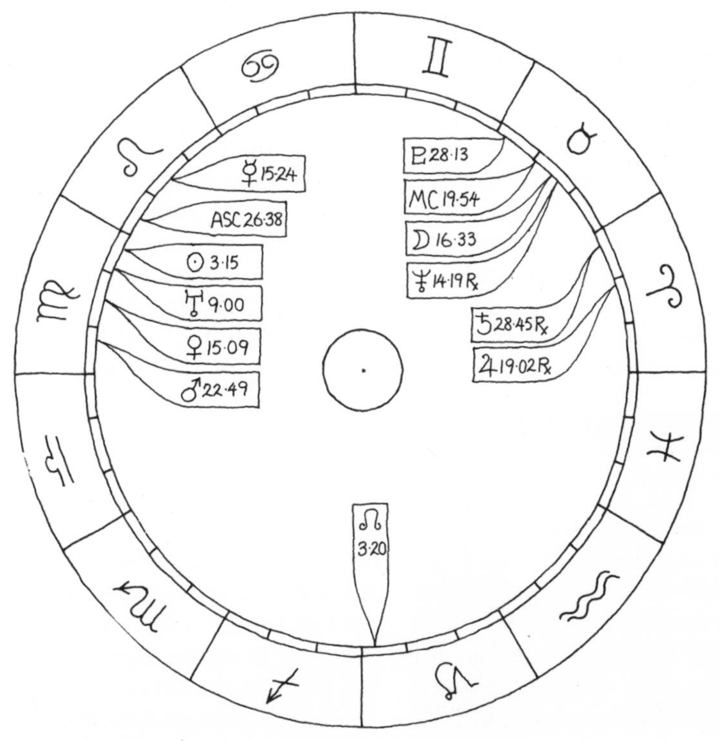

ADOLF HITLER

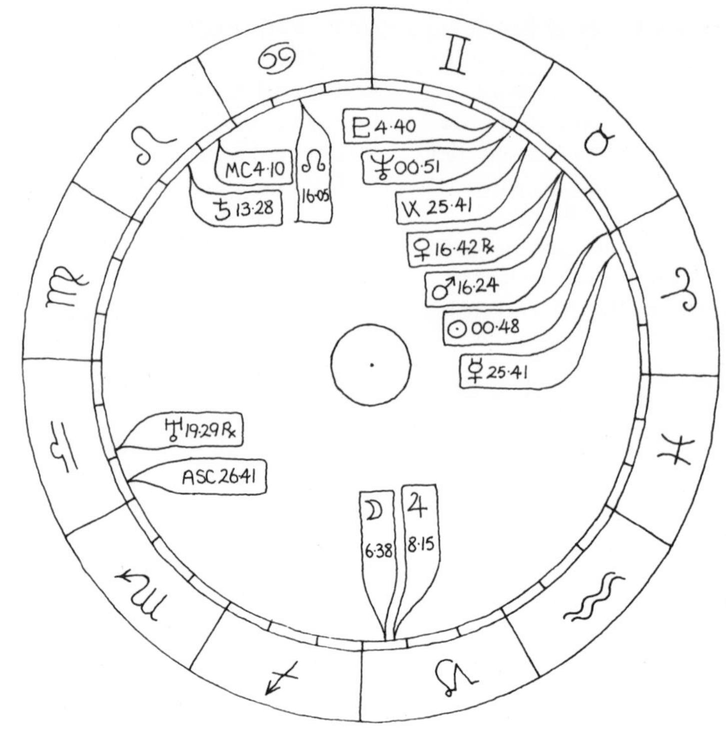

Obviously the chart of Hitler has been the subject of much discussion. We must remember that – like any other chart – it does not point ineluctably to Hitler's destiny.

We have already looked at the 5H chart on p. 135. The radical chart is shorter of major aspects than the average; it has been said that the sesquiquadrate between Uranus and Pluto 'is exactly descriptive of Hitler but would normally be disregarded because it applies to many other charts'. This is foolish and illogical: the orb in this map is 5′ – an orb *not* shared by 'many' charts; nor does the sesquiquadrate blend with other factors in the same way as it does in other charts. In any case, both planets = Sun/Moon. So we have combinations indicating the following characteristics: a ruthless person, highly capable of leadership; someone charismatic, able to arouse the masses; someone drastic, autocratic, inflexible in attitude; a person confronting a life full of conflicts, a ruptured soul, and huge separations (meaning Hitler's policies towards the Jews). The enterprising Capricorn Moon (signifying the public, the masses) is in a powerful quintile aspect to Neptune (suggesting deception) in the sign of communications: the native has the ability to deceive the people. Asc joins this quintile series, reinforcing a rhetorical strategy.

In the 5H chart the Mars–Venus conjunction is in the Scorpio house of death, in shuddering square to transformative Pluto in the house of group enterprises, or clubs (N.D.A.S.P.); this is the house which carries what Addey calls Hitler's 'messy' conjunctions, or quintiles. Asc/MC is semisquare Sun; MC is at Mars/Uranus; Mercury opposes Asc; the native must win or die. The Mars–Venus conjunction is at Sun/Neptune, enormously strengthening the already very powerful semisextile (orb 3′ applying) between the two: if not poetic – out of the question here – then the native is psychopathic. (Some people with strong Sun–Neptune contacts are both.) He is also sexually perverse and inhibited, with a sexuality so disturbed as to be a menace to others. Hitler merely operated on a scale vastly larger than that of the ordinary sex-criminal, although there were some odd perverse episodes in his earlier life. Moon/Neptune = MC suggests a man who lives in a dream, frustrated because he cannot penetrate the secrets of femininity.

CHARLES BAUDELAIRE

Another poet with a huge stellium – this time a single one spreading over two signs – is Charles Baudelaire. His Node at 11 Pisces 51 begins a stellium which ends with the Sun at 19 Aries 21 – a range of 37°30′ carrying one point and no less than seven planets. We have Mercury–Pluto at the end of Pisces, in conjunction, followed by Mars, Venus, Jupiter, Saturn and Sun, all in Aries. There are slamming, dangerous cardinal squares from Capricorn and Cancer, and Asc in Virgo is on the nodal axis, splitting the chart; Mars/Venus is very heavily punished by the exact Uranus–Neptune conjunction from Capricorn. This is one of the most difficult charts in astrology.

Baudelaire's response was transmitted in chaotic, uneven, but often very powerful and imaginative poetry. The man's philosophical ideas were puerile in the extreme, but his best poetry is full of a deadly wisdom. And what of those born at about the same time? If they were not psychopathic murderers, they were certainly nonentities: no one could stand this chart and amount to anything without extreme suffering. It is a chart which repays the most intensive study. Although difficult, it is very instructive about the application of such notions as transition of light, sign emphasis, and other techniques. The mixture of Pisces and Aries is impressive evidence for signs, since it is appropriate to the poet's personality and to the circumstances into which he was born.

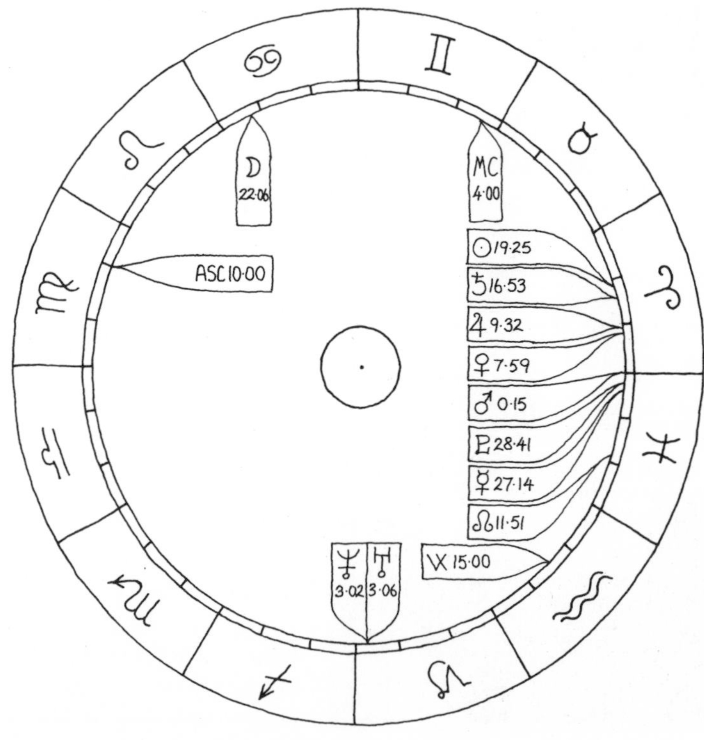

MARGARET THATCHER

The radical chart of Mrs Margaret Thatcher has been wholly misused, and explains why Scorpio has such a bad name. According to opinion polls, Thatcher is one of the most unpopular prime ministers of recent times. Like Hitler, she has Jupiter in Capricorn – a bad position for statesmen, dictators and politicians. It is to this position that she owes the failure of her unoriginal policies: Jupiter in Capricorn is never in itself original, though it borrows and uses the ideas of others, sometimes fanatically. Offensive and obstinate, Thatcher has been unsuccessful in politics, save in the cause of furthering her own career. In certain other areas – as a forewoman on a shop floor, for instance – she could have been successful, though not widely loved.

Radical chart

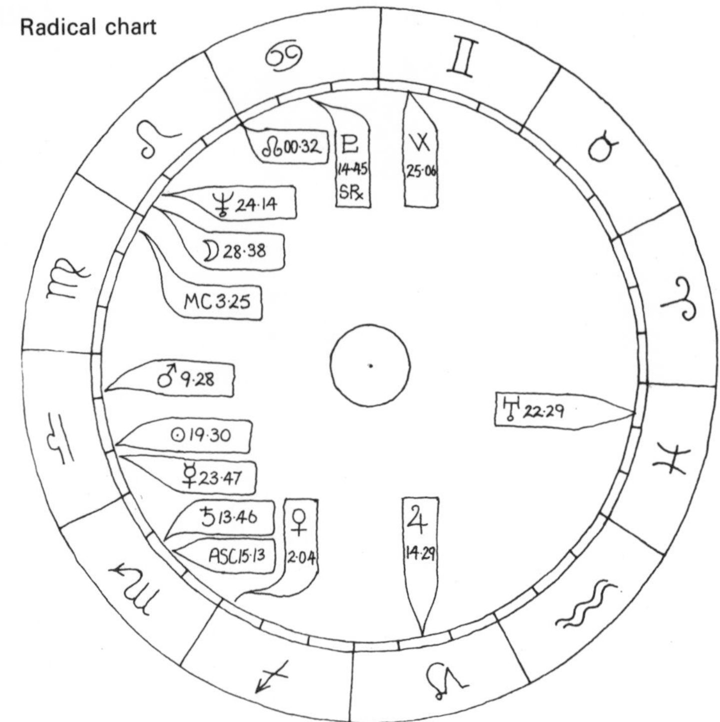

As a girl Thatcher was severely disciplined by her father. Jupiter in Capricorn indicates a secret hatred of the father. Saturn–Asc has meant loneliness for her from youth. Few remember her at Oxford: she was, one says, 'never there'. She could relate to others only by nagging or bossing them, and so she found herself isolated. The Jupiter–Pluto opposition, just dexter, applying, has made her passionately impatient to return to a time when, after revenging herself on her feared father, she might once again love him: a time of simple balanced budgets, an England untainted by the feared foreigners, with the opportunity for retribution such as she suffered as a child. Her first act upon gaining power was to try and bring back the rope. Perhaps because she has intellectual defects, she cannot end what she starts and so takes severe punishment. That she will always seek out this pattern, initiated by the loved, hated father, is indicated by the plangent Mercury–Uranus quincunx, which forms part of a deadly yod on drowned Uranus: Neptune is in sharp dexter sextile to Mercury, and

Mercury/Neptune = Uranus. Let us follow the implications of this complex and threatening picture before examining Thatcher's opportunity/failure chart, the 6H.

The Mercury–Neptune sextile, an opportunity malevolently grasped, gives the capacity to lie about fantasies, in this case fantasies of some earlier golden age. Jupiter in Capricorn and stationary Pluto in Leo also suggest strong daydreams of royalty. Thatcher has the ability to appear sincere. Her broken election pledges will not seem to her to be broken: they will seem to her to be the insolent public's refusal to conform to her programme. She feels guilty at not doing what she can for others, yet, no matter what she says, her programme is designed to withdraw all aid. The Mercury–Neptune sextile sickens this guilt, causing her to make promises which she knows she will not keep (as shadow environment minister, she promised to abolish rates). Pelettier describes this in his book on aspects: 'you create for yourself painful responsibilities that are usually unnecessary... You spread yourself so thin and expect to accomplish so much'. The Mercury–Neptune sextile needs an accomplished mind if it is to be used successfully.

The yod on the Pisces Uranus suggests an ultimate state of pure abstraction for this unhappy woman: perhaps daydreaming of monetarism in some expensive institution, lecturing a blank wall for disobedience. This end is preceded by a violent oscillation between professed principles: weeks of unyielding obstinacy followed by sudden socialistic acts, such as her surrender to the miners in the winter of 1980. Opposite Uranus lies Fortuna, creating a twice-fractured chart.

In Margaret Thatcher's 6H chart, the failure chart, the house of communication, so important for a politician, is empty. Its ruler Mercury is in the house of pleasure conjunct Neptune. What would be right for an artist is wrong for a statesman, whose thought is flawed by artificiality and lies, even if the Sun in Cancer suggests sensitivity.

In this failure chart the Node is squared by Asc, indicating the euphoric and autocratic manner which makes it impossible for the native to gain cooperation. Thatcher's fanaticism is clear from the bizarre conjunction in the fifth house: we find intense enthusiasm combined with a horror of home memories; there is also the danger of victimisation, a difficulty in sacrificing subjective desires, a further pressure to nag, an inability to ease suffering, and an obsession with possessing and retaining public attention.

This 6H chart would be a fascinating one in a creative person: it would show how he might marshal his forces. But the 'material' for a politician is other people: colleagues and public.

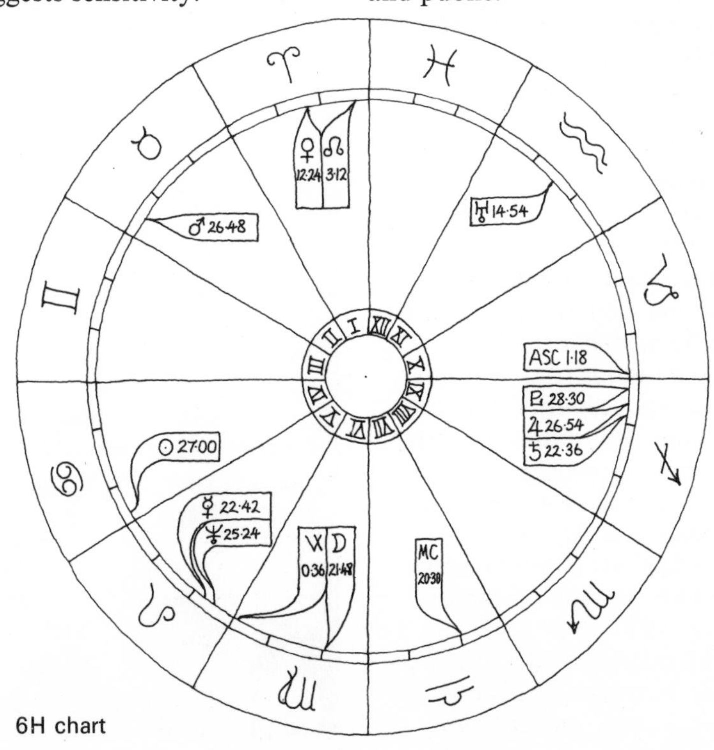

6H chart

HENRI DESIRÉ LANDRU

The radical chart of the French murderer Landru is something of a contrast to Margaret Thatcher's. Landru is usually described as meticulous and determined in his project of murdering at least ten women and a child for relatively small sums of money. In reality he wanted to be meticulous, but failed. The reason for his initial success was the administrative confusion generated by World War I, of which he took deliberate advantage. Soon after the war ended, he was caught. As a young man he had served various sentences for foolish, petty crimes; on these occasions he was always caught through his own carelessness. He liked to think that he was a well-dressed, personable man, but in fact he was somewhat repulsive to look at. His successful murders were the result of persistence.

The only real mystery about Landru concerns the way in which he disposed of his victims' bodies. Parts of them he burned in a stove, an exhibit at his trial. But this does not account for all the victims. It is almost certain that, using his logical mind, he disposed of most of the bodies in a cemetery.

The chart is astonishing to look at. Apart from the huge stellium in Aries and the very exact Grand Trine, we also immediately observe the way Venus – indicating money – is lying on his Antivertex, and how Uranus afflicts so much of the chart, from Cancer. Node = Asc/Pluto, suggesting an urge to form new and unusual associations! And Sun/Neptune squares MC, suggesting a negative outlook.

But we must not let the obvious detail make us miss the fact that the greedy Taurus Asc is in close quintile to Saturn, which is unusually merry in Sagittarius (Landru could never accept that he caused suffering) and is one of the points of the Grand Trine. Saturn is also in a septile aspect to Uranus (orb 48′), which hints at disturbed sexuality: Landru seems to have picked up his women when he was bored, because they 'turned him on'. Undoubtedly he enjoyed orgasmic release as and after he killed them.

The Cancer Uranus opposes MC and afflicts the Venus–Neptune conjunction in fiery and impetuous Aries; it is also in close semisextile to the roaring Leo Node. The Venus–Neptune conjunction in Aries indicates extreme vulgarity (a characteristic of Landru's) and a lazy but spasmodic use of the sensual (reinforced by the Taurus Asc, and the fact that Venus is chart ruler – a greedy Venus, deluded by

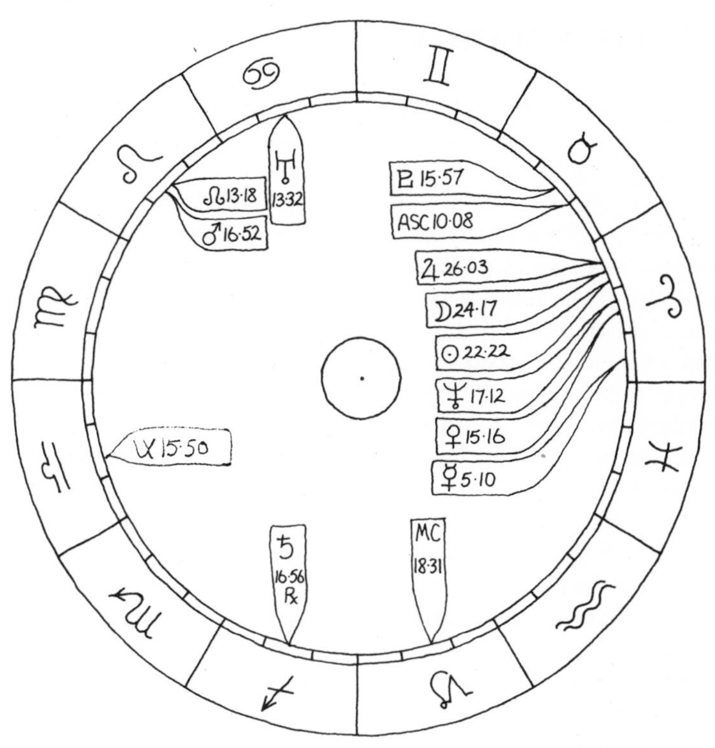

Neptune into thinking that murder saves work and time). The square from Uranus to the conjunction shows abysmal taste, delusions about get-rich-quick schemes and a strange sexual nature. Ruthlessness is seen in the very close Mars–Pluto square in fixed signs. The semi-sextile to the Node from Uranus indicates Landru's disruptiveness. The huge stellium in Aries suggests an impulsiveness and impetuosity – quite lacking in Landru! Their absence is explained by the great power of the Asc in Taurus, a sign which is exceedingly cautious as well as greedy; Landru's strategy was undoubtedly cautious. His rituals with his victims when he had enticed them to his villa were bizarre in the extreme and carefully mimicked 'impetuosity'.

Here it is interesting to comment on the style of the native's 'objectivity'. This quality is often rightly ascribed to Aries, and here we meet an extreme example. At best an emphasised Aries indicates an inability to see the other person's point of view, even where there are other, contrary indications in the chart. As we know, Landru never had any sense of anyone else's point of view, and was clearly very puzzled that the authorities wanted to try him at all. He would probably not have been at all surprised – although already an experienced petty criminal – if the government had congratulated him on his ingenuity and decorated him. Repulsive though he was, he managed to obtain a leading lawyer to conduct his defence, and succeeded in enlisting the sympathy of a large number of women who closely resembled his victims.

Of all the elements in Landru's chart it is the Grand Trine which fascinates most, particularly as it is so close: Venus–Neptune trine Mars trine Saturn, so that Venus/Mars = Saturn, Venus/Saturn = Mars, Mars/Saturn = Venus, Neptune/Mars = Saturn, Neptune/Saturn = Mars, and Mars/Saturn = Neptune. All these are indications of separation and delusion. The Grand Trine itself shows a monumental obstinacy: its effect is less like that of three trines than of three oppositions (six, if the whole process is repeated with Neptune instead of Venus – but the Venus–Neptune conjunction is best considered as just one aspect). In the 3H chart all these bodies end up, significantly, in Taurus, here surely indicating sensual greed rather than personal values. Landru was once legally married, and he did not kill his wife or any of his children. But the Uranus–MC opposition meant that he could not stay for long at home. The Venus–Neptune conjunction (at point-focus) does not suggest any resolution of this difficulty, except of the most catastrophic kind.

THOMAS HARDY

In Thomas Hardy's chart Saturn is exactly on the Vertex, as befits a writer with such apparently gloomy views about fate. From his youth Hardy was popular and successful; he has always had a high reputation and his books have sold well. But he never felt that he had been understood, nor would he change, even though his living might well have seemed to depend on it. He was the enemy of gentility, and offended many of his readers. However, his sales continued to be good, and he lived comfortably in a rather nasty house of his own design (he had originally been a mediocre architect). His first marriage was unhappy for most of its duration, and he reproached himself for this after his first wife's death.

Hardy's fate resembled that of Van Gogh and Apollinaire at least in as much as he was seriously misunderstood, ultimately even by his first wife, with whom he was for some years in rapturous love. He has even been misunderstood by his biographers. He still comes in for the most ferocious attacks: he was mean, for instance, or his outlook was reprehensibly un-Christian. He is only grudgingly accepted by academics. Yet the beauty of his prose and poetry is such that he is universally read and his sales show no signs of abating, even in an age of deteriorating standards.

In his chart only Saturn is angular, and this is singularly appropriate, for Hardy is well known to all for his melancholy. His poetry is melancholy, and his life was mostly melancholy. He could be sour to fools. There is a preponderance of Mutable Fire in his chart, yet only Saturn on the Vertex lies in Sagittarius. In such cases – where there is sign-preponderance but the sign has no stellium – there is often frustration. The native is idealistic, religious-minded and aspiring, but destined to be disappointed. Disappointment is indeed one of the keys to Hardy's life, although ultimately subsumed under his enormous compassion and beauty of spirit.

The Asc is in Leo, explaining how Hardy managed to resist the attacks of his critics and of the circulating libraries (what these would buy and not buy was important to the novelist of Hardy's day, who depended upon them financially). Mars is at Asc/MC, and is MC ruler. The Moon is in Cancer in exact Water trine to Jupiter in Scorpio, indicating a generous spirit and empathy. Hardy may have been 'close' in money matters, but his work speaks for itself, with its

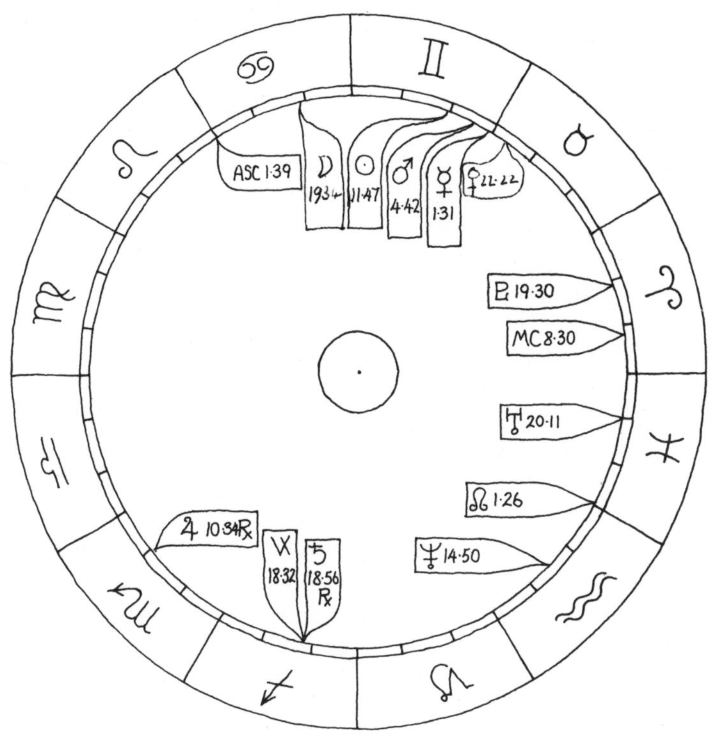

overwhelming outgoingness and desire to share emotional experience. The Mars-Saturn opposition across mutables is not close enough to act as more than a background influence on mood: Hardy worked very steadily indeed, whereas people with these in strong hard aspect are often stop-go. The Mercury–Mars conjunction, applying, gave him obstinacy, and the square of this conjunction to the nodal axis made his relationship with his public uneasy: he could be sarcastic about the hands that fed him, even on occasion seeming inclined to bite them. Certainly he thought little of reviewers.

The Saturn–Uranus square is quite close, confirming his great determination, his eccentricity and love of privacy. Asc semi-square Sun/Saturn confirms the Saturnine nature of his life and personality. The Moon is in septile to the South Node, and Uranus is in 8H to Moon/Node. The Moon in Cancer is sensitive and protective, while the South Node in Virgo indicates generosity of feeling: here is one of the mainsprings of Hardy's imaginative work, one of the motives which inspired him. Uranus involved with this aspect indicates understanding and love of women, for which Hardy is famous.

7H charts do not indicate, even if loaded with conjunctions and other close major aspects, that the natives are creative in the sense of actually producing writings or paintings or music. They first show the sexual nature and secondly the kind of personal myths or dreams of which the natives are capable. There are many ways in which a person may be creative. In Hardy's 7H the strength of V, the house of creativity, is immediately noticeable. Asc stays there, joined by Sun and Pluto in loose but powerful conjunction. This grouping is harshly squared by the close Venus–Neptune conjunction in II, showing the romantic and nostalgic, which were what most affected Hardy. Saturn shows up once more, in very close trine (21H, radical orb 8′) to Asc: Hardy's attitude to life was well integrated in his novels and poems.

There is one energising T-square: Moon-Node across the Pisces–Virgo axis is resolved by Mercury in the versatile house of communications, its own house. The Moon is very appropriately placed in Pisces. Mars and Venus in this chart are themselves in septile (thus in radical 49H: the orb is in fact only 49″ and so virtually exact). This is astonishingly appropriate in the chart of such a renowned love poet, who was famously unhappy in, and yet could only thrive on, love. Square to Venus/Mars in the radical chart lies the nodal axis: the orb is 24″ and the axis is sliding back to the midpoint, which is itself moving forwards.

JIM JONES

Jim Jones was the leader of an organisation which, although always religiously crude, began by trying to do good. It attacked corruption in local government, helped the very poor, and denounced the excesses of capitalism. Jones, an American from Indiana, began as a fundamentalist left-winger. But soon he began to assert himself in a disturbing way: members of his organisation who disagreed with him were dealt with by violence (some possibly even murdered) and he also became sexually promiscuous with both women and men. He turned to drugs and by the time of his suicide was hopelessly dependent on narcotics. His financial dealings were crooked, and he kept much more from the contributions he received than he gave out to those he was pledged to help. His organisation was forced to move to California to escape prosecution, and then to the Guyana of dictator and election-rigger Forbes Burnham (whose part in the notorious Guyana massacre has not yet been investigated). By now there were a number of defectors from the organisation, but when a US senator visited the settlement to try and find out what was happening there, he and some of his companions were murdered. After this, Jones ordered all his followers to kill themselves by drinking cyanide; those who refused were forced to drink it and comparatively few escaped with their lives. Jones then killed himself.

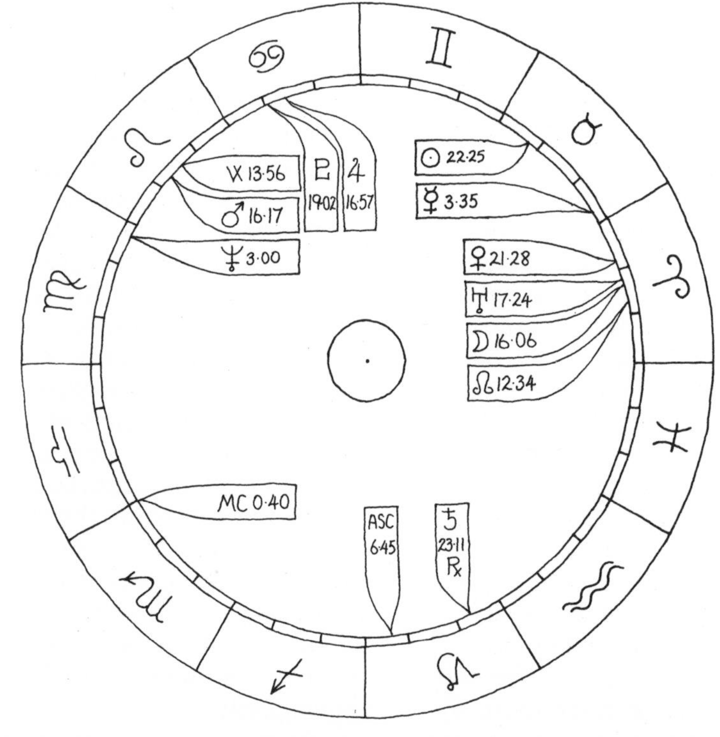

In sum, we are looking at the chart of an undereducated man who began with the sincere wish to help others, but who was soon intoxicated by the power which he found his charismatic personality could easily bring him. He quickly became degenerate and corrupt, ending as a dangerously insane killer, though one who always kept the support of at least some of his unhappy followers.

His chart is a very striking one (there is a slight doubt about the angles, because Indiana time at the date of Jones' birth was chaotic, with communities choosing to go on whatever time they liked). The Stationary Direct Neptune in Virgo is one of the chart's dominant features. It is not a good placement for this planet, yet here it is given special emphasis by the fact that it is almost without apparent motion. It is semi-square Pluto (loosely) and sesquiquadrate Uranus (orb 36′ applying). But more important is the not so very skew Grand Trine it forms with Mercury and Asc. Many astrologers refuse to consider any configuration as valid if a point (Asc, Vertex, MC, Node) rather than a body is involved. This seems foolish,

though we have to accept that the nature of the configuration is going to be different. This Grand Trine is a highly deceptive one: Neptune/Asc = Mercury (this is close), Mercury/Asc = Neptune (wide). These indicate: to be notorious, to tell lies, to, in Witte's words, 'discuss unclear matters', to perpetrate evil talk, to respond to a situation where people 'say no', to 'commit fraud with others' (Witte again), and to go in for 'malicious scheming' (Ebertin). This is almost too appropriate to be credible, but at least it suggests that the time I have taken for Jones' birth is about right, although he could have been born a little earlier. My work with Primary Directions gives him an Asc of about 3 Capricorn, which is of course even better; but apart from the final catastrophe I have not been able to obtain times.

In this chart the Saturn/Neptune midpoint, assuredly malefic if anything in astrology is, falls in Scorpio and squares the Vertex: it suggests that Jones' unfortunate followers will experience sickness, weakness, lies, death and tragedy. There is a hard (64H) aspect between Saturn and Neptune, although its orb is as much as 26′ and it is separating (we must remember that in the 64H chart this would show up as separation of 26 × 64 = 27°44′). The angular planets are Venus and Jupiter, which are in a wide, separating, sinister square. Closer and more important are the Moon–Uranus conjunction and the exact square of this to Jupiter in Cardinals (indicating violent overstrain of emotions, generosity, and a fanatic religious zeal – easily turned to something else by Uranus). It seems as though Jones may have surrendered to the involvement of Uranus in this square, for the drastic planet is also involved in the wider Venus–Pluto square. Indeed, both Venus and Pluto are tied up in conjunctions, though they are a little wide. The square to Uranus from the Capricorn Saturn is 5° 45′ off orb, but is double applying (in fact this aspect is only 9′ off a 64H aspect), and at a point where the power of the square could be given extra strength. There is nothing to suggest Jones' dependence on drugs in this chart, except that Neptune is very closely square to Asc/MC, and that in the 11H chart Neptune is flung into this very same Asc/MC midpoint position, at 3 Sagittarius, square its own radical placing.

JIM CLARK

This is the chart of a record-breaker. The racing driver Jim Clark was killed at an early age. According to the most authoritative sources, his death was not the result of carelessness on his part, but of bad luck.

For this man strategy consists in winning motor-races, and the exact Fire trine from Asc to Jupiter in his chart suggests this immediately. The sad Sun–Saturn conjunction in soulful Pisces underlines the fact that so many of those who engage in dangerous pursuits do it 'to grow a soul', as a writer once put it. Mars is exactly square to the nodal axis: aggression finds its outlet in team-spirit, absolutely necessary to a racing driver. The warm Leo Moon moves into a Fire trine with Mars, powerful and dexter: instinct runs well with energy, but there is a vigilance that needs to be released.

But the chart is slit into two by the treacherous and doleful Sun–Neptune opposition

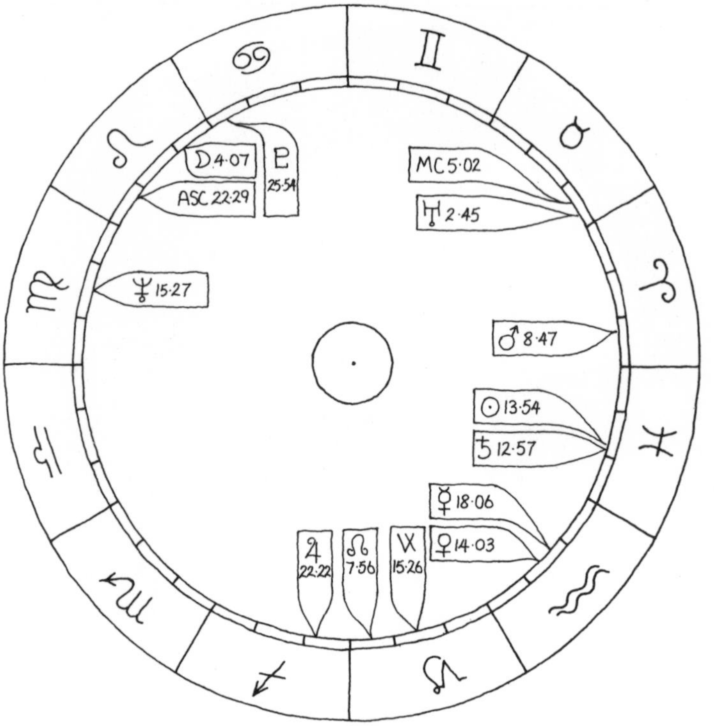

Radical chart

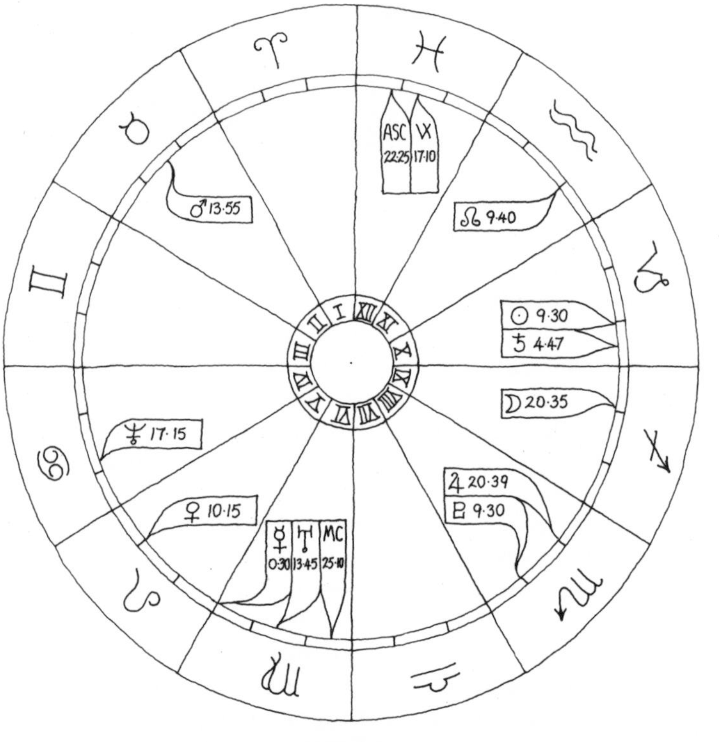

5H chart

across the Pisces–Virgo axis; both Sun and Saturn apply to the exact dexter aspect, which is building up. This shows us that beneath his confident exterior Jim Clark was fearful – of failure, of loss of nerve, and of competition. Neptune is not always very happy in Virgo, where its mistiness is attacked by the classifying passion of the sign. Somebody or something could let the native down: Clark died because there was something wrong with his car. The angular Uranus, suggesting technology, is in quite close fixed square to the Moon: the winner of races is likely to be very much his own master. This is energising, but the real energy in this chart is seen in 5H, where the facility-giving 15H aspects are shown as trines.

These Grand Trines (in harmonic charts not potentially malefic) speak for themselves. In a 5H chart we can allow a reasonable orb, since we know that a radical orb of only 2° becomes 10° in the chart. The 5H chart is a power and a facility chart; its trines show facility and pleasure. In that of so successful a driver as Clark we should expect to find a T-square, this being the energising aspect *par excellence*. We are not disappointed: the Mars–Pluto opposition (radical orb 53′ off the 108°, 10H aspect) is resolved by Venus, as pleasure, at point-focus in V, the house of pleasure and creativity.

GEORGE SIMENON

The life of Belgian novelist Georges Simenon has not been quite as catastrophic as that of Van Gogh, but it has not been without its peculiarities and difficulties. Simenon's wife became ill and lived in institutions for many years, having caused him great worry for a long period of time. Simenon is of course most famous as the inventor of Inspector Maigret, although his best work does not feature the Paris detective. Although he set out to write popular novels, he finds himself admired as an absolutely serious novelist by the majority of academic critics, one of whom has called him superior to Balzac. Simenon himself has wisely taken little notice of this admiration. He wrote each of his novels – which are really long short stories – in a very short time, more or less locking himself up to do it. He gave up writing some years ago because of dizziness and bad nerves. (For Simenon the creative act is closely bound up with health.) He is celebrated for his supreme compassion, for his ability to evoke atmosphere, and for his understanding of all sorts and kinds of people. His brand of objectivity is both lofty and sympathetic.

Simenon's radical chart has the Moon in Virgo: the Moon in this sign is much warmer than is often believed, though it does indicate a practical, tidy and methodical nature, all of which characteristics apply to Simenon. It is in a wide (4°47′) but applying and dexter opposition to the compassionate Pisces Venus, itself in Water trine to the Asc in Scorpio (suggesting strategy and penetration of motive). This opposition does not split the chart any more than the closely angular Jupiter at the IC does. The Moon–Venus aspect indicates popularity with the public, which after a short hard struggle Simenon easily obtained and held, at the expense of serious emotional crises in his private life.

Uranus near the Antivertex suggests an easy escape from conventionalist thinking (essential for a

continued over

Simenon continued

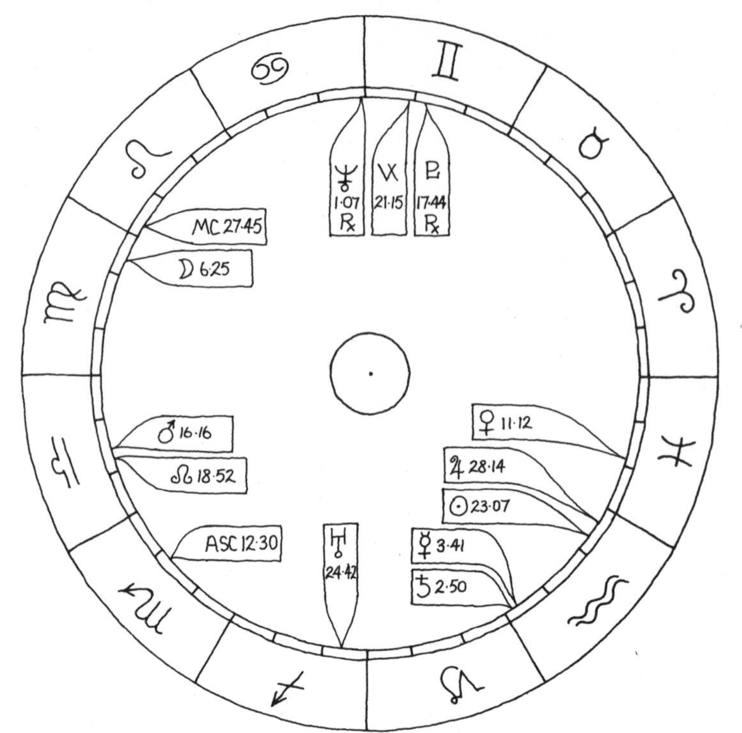

serious writer). Jupiter is in an interesting dissociate trine to Neptune, Air to Water, orb 2°53′, sinister double-applying. When this becomes exact eleven days after Simenon's birth it does so in Water: Jupiter has entered Pisces. This trine is a peculiarly refined and creative one, and shows that Simenon's popularity is well deserved. Even though he is keenly sensitive to the disgusting and the evil, he is able to effect a withdrawal of moral prurience in his work, and in so doing confers on his readers an understanding of actions most people would regard as unmitigatedly evil. It is an acknowledged part of this author's achievement that he is able, without making crime glamorous, to demonstrate why people commit crimes.

The Sun lies exactly opposite Mars/Neptune in Simenon's chart. This is a good example of externalisation, where the native experiences the meaning of the configuration through a manifestation in others rather than in his own characteristics. Here we see Simenon's wife, sick, weak, ill, unable to withstand the pressure and obviously causing much unhappiness. Venus squares the other 'sickness' axis, Mars/Saturn – signifying, in Ebertin's words, 'illness of and separation from female persons'. (Witte adds 'insensibility', a possibly apt description in this case.)

The stellium in Aquarius is split into two conjunctions (there are three altogether in this chart: Mars–Node, Mercury–Saturn, and Sun–Jupiter, the last slightly wide). In itself the split stellium suggests humanitarian understanding rather than coldness (the Pisces Venus, tied up with the Moon, saves the disposition from being over-surgical). Mars–Node involvements can make people very disruptive, but the skew Grand Trine (by no means as deadly as the true form of this configuration) between Mars–Node, Pluto and the Aquarian Sun softens the conjunction to a mere liking for solitude and privacy. Not very much is known about Simenon's private life, for he has not sought publicity. The Pluto–Mars trine, close, dexter, and double-applying, does, however, indicate toughness: it is not advisable to trifle with anyone with such a contact. Opposite Mars/Pluto there lies the Mercury–Saturn conjunction suggesting taciturnity, overworked nerves, indefatigability and industry. Simenon has written a record number of books; no one has count of all of them, since many early ones were written under pseudonyms, which he has forgotten. The Sun–Jupiter conjunction, though wide, is exactly appropriate, and confirms other features of the chart: great creativity and record achievements. We can see that in this chart the energy is generated by the conjunctions.

CHAPTER SIX

CHART COMPARISON AND PREDICTION

COMPARING TWO CHARTS

THE ASTROLOGICAL TECHNIQUE OF CHART comparison is known as synastry. By far its most common use is to investigate the compatibility or otherwise of lovers. But the charts of friends, business associates, and so on, can also be compared.

Of all the branches of astrology, synastry yields the most impressive results. An Australian psychiatrist, Furze-Morrish, made a study of two groups of married couples, the first compatible, the second incompatible. He used a random group as control. According to the British astrologer, Geoffrey Dean, the results 'show a consistent tendency for compatible relationships to coincide with a predominance of harmonious aspects' (aspects between one chart and another). Furze-Morrish confirmed these results with another study, ending up with odds against chance of about 1000 to 1. The harmonious aspects were sextiles and trines, the inharmonious, squares and oppositions. Minor aspects were not tested. Unfortunately Furze-Morrish does not state the orb he used, and this is a serious omission: it is easy to arrange orbs that fit the required results.

But if Furze-Morrish was scrupulous in his use of orbs, then what he found about marriage was very roughly similar to what John Nelson found about radio weather in heliocentric charts: that aspects traditionally believed harmonious are indeed so. However, this does not mean that those couples with many inharmonious aspects between their charts are doomed to incompatibility or divorce. There is no real harm in a preponderance of very inharmonious (hard) aspects – as long as neither partner in a relationship wants a quiet life above all else. But there must be some harmonious aspects between friendly planets, or there will be no basis for a relationship. On the other hand two charts linked by numerous trines may mean a dull partnership.

Astrologers can give remarkably accurate accounts of what causes conflict between people, and they can point to ways in which such conflicts can be resolved. There is no area of astrology in which the meaning of aspects is more evident.

There are now several methods of synastry, though the established one of simply comparing two charts remains both the simplest and the most effective. But two newer methods should be mentioned. In each case only one chart is involved.

TIME – MIDPOINT CHARTS

In the first method the midpoint in time is taken between the two births. A chart for that time is then erected, using the latitude either of the place where the couple reside, or the latitude midway between the two places where they were born. The mean latitude and the mean MC are used with either Koch or Placidus houses. The resulting chart is said to indicate the nature of the relationship.

I have not had great success with these time-midpoint charts. However, that may simply mean that I am not comfortable with them.

There is an interesting and suggestive book by R. C. Davison called *Synastry*, which describes this method in detail.

COMPOSITE CHARTS

The other new method is called the composite chart, and Robert Hand has devoted a long book to it called *Planets in Composite*. This is probably the most popular method at the moment, and everyone who uses it seems to use Koch houses.

The composite chart consists of the midpoints between the planets in the two charts. Where they are more than 150° apart, both midpoints are entered, though the nearer is regarded as stronger. The MC is calculated by adding both MCs together and dividing the shorter arc-length by two. An Asc and a Vertex are then calculated from that MC using the latitude 'where the relationship is taking place'. Most astrologers also enter the 'derived' Asc and the 'derived' Vertex. The same rules apply for finding these as for finding the positions of the planets: the midpoints of the two Vertices and the two Ascendants are taken.

The Composite chart must not be misunderstood: it is not the chart of a person or even of two people, but the chart of their relationship. I find that these charts are meaningful though their interpretation calls for great psychological subtlety. Some astrologers interpret them as giving the meaning of the relationship, others the purpose. I find it preferable to interpret them as indicating the direction the relationship is likely to take. Thus, I might say that such-and-such a couple can achieve nirvana, or that they would be successful in a literary, or a musical, or any other sort of enterprise.

CHART COMPARISON

The most interesting and fruitful work in synastry still lies in chart-comparison. In this field most astrologers use either Equal house or Placidus; I find signs, aspects and midpoints quite enough. Ebertin has extended the chart-comparison method by bringing in midpoints. Clearly an unoccupied midpoint in one chart may be occupied by a planet or a point in the other, and as clearly this means something. It is best, however, to start by simply comparing the charts; later on the direct midpoints may be introduced, and later still the indirect ones.

I shall confine my discussion here to marriage and/or love partnerships. When two charts are to be compared, the first step must be to look at them individually. From this examination it is possible to tell what kind of aims and needs each partner has or does not have.

The interpretations of the aspects between charts are much the same as in radical charts, except that what is involved is not a combination of elements in one personality, but an interchange between two people. It is important to allow for this. Furthermore, the notions of harmony and disharmony are rather more important then they are in radical charts.

In at least one sense comparison of two charts helps to throw light on each individual chart. If a harmonious aspect is made from, say, Jupiter to a planet in another chart, then this Jupiter can reveal in what circumstances a person who is not usually easygoing in any way might *be* easygoing; if that aspect is to, say, Mars, then that Mars can suggest in what circumstances a lazy person might be energetic.

Some astrologers use orbs as large as 5° for synastry. These may have some background effect, but they are quite useless for any kind of precise work. Lynne Palmer, who has written the most comprehensive book on the subject, *Astrological Compatibility*, uses an absolutely rigid orb of 1°. According to her, an orb of 60′ and the aspect is all right, 61′ and it is invalid. This is obviously too rigid: 1° is right, but – like everything else in astrology – not absolutely right. There are circumstances in which the orb should be very slightly extended, but we probably ought not to go much above 70′ except in very special cases.

FREDERICK BYWATERS AND EDITH THOMPSON

As an example of chart-comparison I shall take the charts of two people who were hanged for murder, Frederick Bywaters and Edith Thompson. Mrs Thompson entered into an affair with her lodger Bywaters, a seaman eight years her junior. After he had ceased to be her lodger she wrote him several highly indiscreet letters in which she stated (histrionically and falsely) that she had tried in various ways to get rid of her husband. Although Bywaters did not believe these letters, he was certainly affected by them: at 0012 GMT, on 4 October 1922, when drunk, he attacked and killed Edith Thompson's husband with a knife, while Thompson and his wife were on their way back to their Ilford home from Ilford station after visiting the theatre.

Edith Thompson had been wholly unaware of Bywaters' intentions. However, the Crown successfully argued that she had deliberately incited Bywaters to the crime. In fact, like Flaubert's Madame Bovary, Edith Thompson lived in a vulgar but by no means untouching dream-world, and had no real murderous intentions whatsoever. But, because she told the truth in the witness-box, she was hanged along with her lover, to the disgust of the civilised world. Furthermore, the trial judge made it clear that her real crime was to have been caught at adultery.

The charts are laid out in the usual way for comparison: Edith Thompson's is inside the circle, Bywaters' is outside. (It does not take much experience to judge the charts indi-

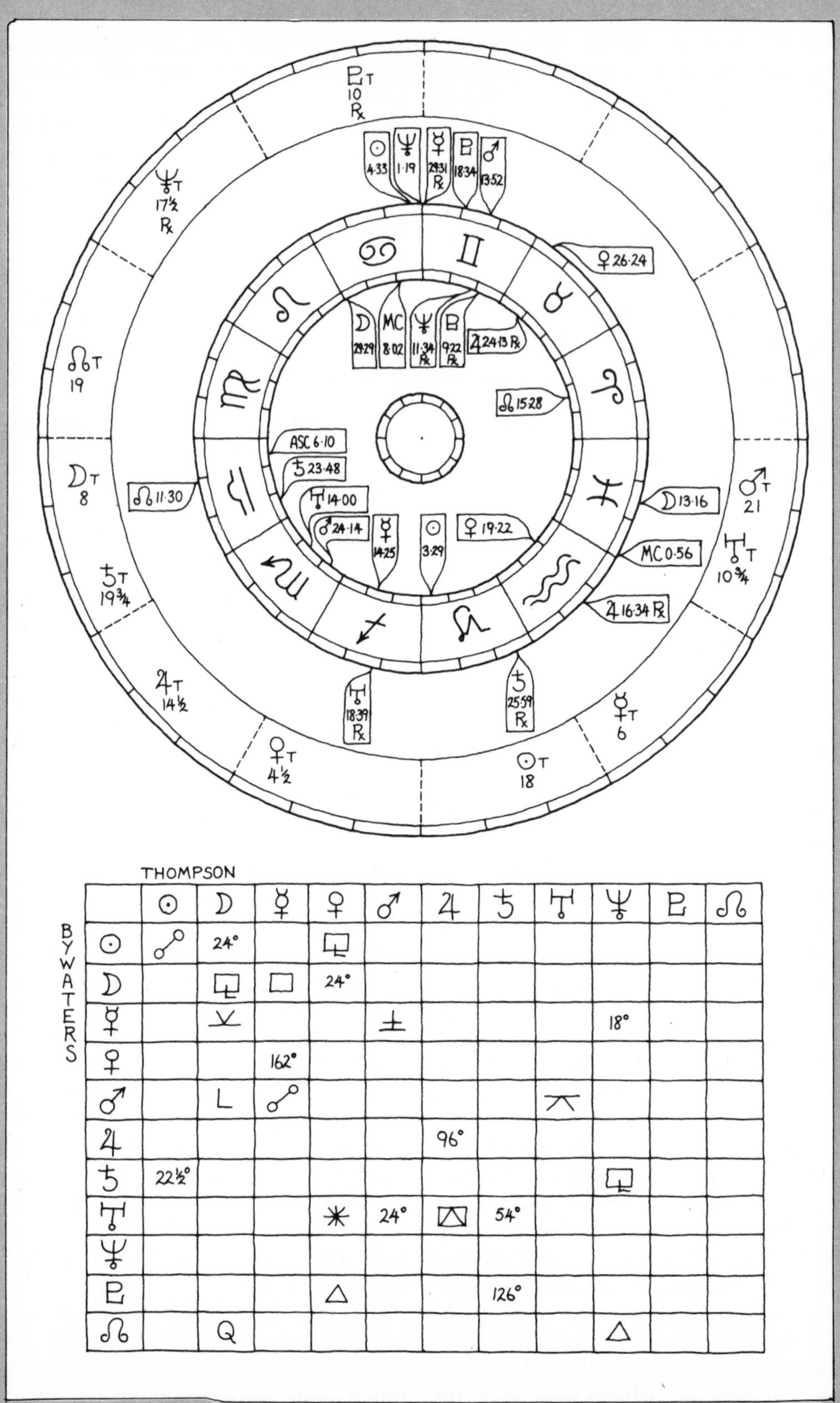

BYWATERS \ THOMPSON	☉	☽	☿	♀	♂	♃	♄	♅	♆	♇	☊
☉	☍	24°		⚼							
☽		⚼	□	24°							
☿		⚺			⊥				18°		
♀			162°								
♂		∟	☍					⚻			
♃						96°					
♄	22½°								⚼		
♅				✳	24°	⊿	54°				
♆											
♇				△			126°				
☊		Q							△		

vidually in this format.) Bywaters' chart is speculative, though the birth date is correct, so the angles and Moon position should be treated with caution: his chart has been calculated for sunrise, which is statistically slightly more likely to be correct, as there are more births around sunrise than noon.

I have deliberately selected two charts not correct to a real degree of certainty (though Thompson's is fairly well attested): they are typical of what the astrologer frequently has to work with. The major rectification here is that Bywaters' Moon was in closer square to Thompson's Neptune: his birth could have taken place some 45 minutes earlier. I have not listed the square, though it certainly operated.

Comparison chart: Thompson and Bywaters, *left* Thompson's chart is inside the inner band; Bywaters' is outside this band. The transits of their execution are on the outer band.

THE CHARTS INDIVIDUALLY

The two charts are individually very difficult. Thompson has Sun, North Node Moon and Pluto in septile, making her highly sexed, unlikely to allow conventions to get in her way. Mercury opposes Neptune, always dangerous: she was a day-dreamer, confused and prone to false communication. (This last point proved to be her downfall: the Crown could have done nothing against her without her letters.) There is quite a close skew T-square on Venus, which has the very difficult task of resolving a Mars-Jupiter opposition. Venus is altogether too wildly hopeful in Aquarius for this, especially since it is applying to an Air trine with Saturn. This trine is quite inappropriate

Edith Thompson and Frederick Bywaters

to the rest of the chart, which is so violently sliced that it is hanging in slashed strips: Sun-MC, Mercury-Neptune, Mercury-Pluto, Mars-Jupiter. Moreover Venus is extremely heavily sickened by being at the farther midpoint of Saturn/Neptune, suggesting painful love; transiting Neptune, meaning drugs, was right on the near midpoint as the warders dragged the semi-conscious Thompson to the scaffold. We can see from her chart as from her life that Thompson was devoted and loyal (she tried to shield Bywaters until tricked by the police). But, with her Mars-Jupiter opposition as well as all her other difficulties, she was impatient, prone to terrible exaggeration, liable to fits of thoughtlessness, and eager for immediate freedom – while too unsophisticated to achieve it.

Bywaters' chart is not so suggestive of self-damage as Thompson's. While she did no more than write some fantastic and very stupid letters, Bywaters committed murder on an impulse, the flames of which he fanned with drink. He was dangerously unstable, though not evil. Certainly he damaged himself, but he asked for it much more than his lover did. He did not go to his death with the stink of psychotic injustice in his nostrils, as she did; he behaved decently and reckoned he had it coming to him.

Bywaters' chart is also fractured, though not as badly as the more sensitive Thompson's. He has the Sun conjunct Neptune, which is never easy, but though it is dexter, it is not applying. His Uranus is sent mad by Pluto, for this deadly opposition is building up power and the two planets are within 5′ of opposing each other. This is explosive, disruptive, and just the kind of aspect to cause a man to stab someone suddenly and without warning. The aspect also gives a man immense sexual potency – appreciated in this case by Edith Thompson. Mars is within orb of a conjunction with Pluto, which does not help, as well as being in a very close, applying square with the sensitive Pisces Moon, indicating action before thought, a violent temper and vicious moods. It is interesting that, like Thompson, Bywaters has the Venus-Saturn trine, but in Earth signs. Jupiter is also trining the Mars-Pluto conjunction, but the Node in Libra forms a skew grand trine which menaces it: Mars at the Jupiter/Node midpoint means a happy partner, but in close hard aspect to this axis stand both Moons and Thompson's Mercury. The happiness of the partner is a menacing, prolonged, orgasmic ecstasy. As Bywaters went to the gallows transiting Neptune was semisquare Sun/Neptune – identical to Thompson's Saturn/Neptune.

ASPECTS BETWEEN THE CHARTS

Had these two not met, it is unlikely that either would have been hanged for murder. Bywaters had a desperate and brooding temper, which caused the deaths of both the shipping-clerk Percy Thompson and his wife; but the comparison of his chart with Edith Thompson's shows that he was very specially affected by her, even though he denied being incited to murder by her letters.

There are a number of close hard aspects between the two charts which I have not listed on the aspect grid, but which are of as much interest as the more obvious, listed connections. Neither have I listed a number of obviously relevant aspects in 9H. There is also a very interesting feature combining the two charts: a resonance, or lack of it, hovering around 18H – to be exact, 7/18 (140°).

However, the grid as I have filled it clearly shows how each affected the other, and I have hardly needed to stray outside the 1° orb. It is immediately noticeable that the two Suns are opposed: this is a 'fateful' aspect between charts, also indicating two people who are irresistibly drawn together. The orb on these charts is 1° 4′, fitting in very well with my rectification of Bywaters' birth time, which I believe to have been earlier than here given.

Bywaters' sensitive, tenacious love-nature was agitated by Thompson's Sun, Moon and Venus. As in the case of the Moon-Sun aspect, I have here put in the sub-harmonics of 5H, which indicate what the two did well together, and whether it was bad or good for them in the long run. His emotional receptivity was brought out into the open by her weak but shrewd Capricorn Sun. Curiously enough, he admired her facility in book-keeping; the idea of efficiently satisfying the strong sexual needs of this efficient and attractive book-keeper kept his lust on the boil, and her communications to him disturbed him in such a way that he could not have enough of her (his Mercury is semisextiled by her Moon). Each partner's Mars is powerfully affected: his by an opposition from her Mercury (meaning that his mentality was excited by her words and her pleasure), and hers is in bi-quintile to his Mercury. This means that the couple gained immense physical and mental pleasure from each other.

There is no conventionally understood aspect between her Mars and his Venus, or between his Mars and her Venus, as we might expect. But Bywaters' Venus is near to an opposition to Thompson's Mars, across the dangerous Scorpio-Taurus axis and close to her own Mars-Jupiter opposition. His Mercury is a willing tool of her Neptune, as is her own Mercury. In the conventional astrologer's book, his Neptune would be unaffected by any planet of hers, whereas in fact there is a bi-quintile from her Mars (orb 1° 20′). Between such people we can only interpret this at a very deep sexual level, when it indicates fanaticism, catastrophe, crime, crisis, and the sharp ecstasy of repeated sexual climax.

Bywaters' Uranus, the planet most responsible for the crime, is much agitated by Thompson's planets. It is sextiled by her Venus – suggesting that conventionality should be thrown to the winds in favour of exciting opportunity – and in harmony with her Mars. But what is Mars-Uranus harmony but perfect simultaneous orgasm? In all other areas Bywaters' Uranus makes trouble and must be controlled, as where it is in tri-septile to Thompson's Jupiter (orb 1° 17′). Again looked at sexually, this represents the orgasm itself. The 20H contact between this Uranus and Thompson's Saturn can only make for further furious tension. When we remember that Bywaters' Uranus is crazed by his own Pluto, we see how very nearly inevitable this murder was.

Bywaters' Mercury was retrograde at birth, and he began forming his wild plan as he woke at 6.14 in the early morning of 3 October 1922. At that very moment Mercury went retrograde at 00 Scorpio 11, building up power to re-square Edith Thompson's very late Cancer Moon and to sesquisquare his own Moon; the subtle planet was also backing into an Air trine with its retrograde self in the radical chart. The transiting mean Node was in almost exact semisquare with this Mercury, thus squaring the radical Mercury. The transiting Venus was right on Thompson's Mars: an erotic transit, but in this case a hideous parody of the pleasures she had enjoyed with the deluded murderer whom she had unintentionally misled.

The Moon was on Bywaters' Moon, building to a quincunx with the transiting Neptune, which stood at 17½ Leo (almost the exact point to which it had returned by the time the trap opened and Bywaters was sent to his death), midway between Edith Thompson's Saturn and Neptune. Mars was at 12½ Capricorn, in a quincunx to Thompson's Neptune, building to a further sextile with her Uranus, after it had caught Bywaters' own Mars in a further quincunx and sextiled his Moon. Jupiter, signifying excess, had not long passed Thompson's Saturn and was coming into square with Bywaters'. This, it seems, was pulling closer those aspects between the charts which were not exact enough.

We should note the two sad and ironic trines between these charts: Bywaters' Pluto, Thompson's Venus; his Node, her Neptune; his Mars quincunx, her Uranus. In the context of the comparison between charts, these are murderous trines, added to which his Mars-maddened Pisces Moon has the enforced task of resolving her deadly Mercury-Neptune opposition. With the Moon enraged by Mars, no resolution could take place, and so the stink of blood permeated the air in that Ilford street that midnight.

As the couple hanged, the transiting Saturn sextiled his Pluto-crazed Uranus and completed a Grand Trine in Air between his radical Pluto and her radical Venus.

PREDICTION

I DO NOT RECOMMEND PREDICTION, BUT PEOPLE are fascinated by it and seemingly cannot do without it. Astrologers are always being asked such questions as 'When will my wife/husband die?', and 'When will I have money?', 'What are my prospects for finding a nice girl?', 'Will I be promoted?', and 'When will I be lucky'?

The future is indeed an open book. But we shall never learn to read every line of every page. And in one sense the future is already the past. Who has not felt that a series of events has happened before, and that in living through them he or she is doing no more than conforming to his or her pattern? We say: 'I hope things will be better for me tomorrow.' We know very well that tomorrow things will look as uncertain as today. To have a tiny degree of certainty only increases that general terror in which we all live.

Yet the desire for certainty means that prediction and predictive techniques are always in demand. Astrologers call prediction 'future trends'; for paltry sums they will reveal these for the next year, two years, ten years, or whatever. These sums are not enough for such work to be properly done, even if it were acceptable in the first place. But it is not acceptable, for the only acceptable thing is to tell interested people of the opportunities they may be able to grasp. And this can be done from the radical chart as well as it can by any other method.

An astrologer is predicting when he interprets a chart. He is saying that this person is like this, like that, and so he is saying something, however vague, about the future. He is doing this by giving a character to that person. But if he is careful, and says only what he thinks the native should avoid and what opportunities he should seize, then the element of prophecy can be virtually eliminated.

THE DANGERS OF PREDICTION

It is not unreasonable to make predictions about criminals, celebrities or politicians: they are not paying us, and they are public people who want to be talked about. But there are many people who have not sought the limelight: we should be careful as to what we say about their futures, if indeed we say anything at all. If we feel that we owe sports people and actors something for entertaining us, then we should not make predictions about them. Obviously, however, there is less danger in predicting the outcome of a sports fixture than there is in broadcasting a prophecy that someone will be shot and killed.

The difficulty is this. Everyone is encouraged by being told about the good things that might happen to them, but no one finds it helpful to be told about the possible bad things. Many people who read the 'stars' in their daily newspapers will go and enact whatever trash they have read. One young building worker read that he would quarrel with his girl. He went out that evening convinced of this. Not only did he quarrel with her, he killed her. Subconsciously he was determined to 'fulfil his fate'. The writer of the trash in the newspaper might well claim that he had stopped many other people 'born under Virgo' or whatever from quarrelling by 'warning' them. But whatever the conscious mind says, a prophecy can effect behaviour and so actually influence the future.

THE QUESTION OF FATE

Another related difficulty about prediction is that we may unwittingly cause someone to miss a great chance by pointing to some future problem. Suppose we see a very bad turn of events approaching, and we tell the person concerned about it. Now the difficulties may be quite easily avoidable, so that the threatened person can see the context and can act to avoid immediate suffering. He may naturally feel impelled to do so. But it may well be that had he undergone the suffering, he would have found improvement in his life as a consequence – simply because he was forced into a new set of circumstances more suitable for him. A man might avoid the sack, when the sack would have helped him to find a better life. Many people will tell you that they owe their good fortune, or at least their material comfort, to events that at the time seemed unfortunate. Yet who is so omnipotent as to give advice on these matters? Who dares to say: 'Take the sack, you will be happier later on.'

In the last chapter I discussed the charts of Edith Thompson and Frederick Bywaters. We might ask whether, even after they had met, these two could have escaped their fates. The obvious answer is that they could have done, by ending their relationship, by running away together, or just by behaving more sensibly. I believe that.

But simultaneously I believe that those particular people had fallen into a trap: they were re-enacting something that had in one sense already happened. Innocent, simple, and foolish though they were, in their love-pangs lay the seeds of the death of Percy Thompson. It was ordained. A moment of awareness might have helped the couple to avoid the extremest grossness of what was ordained, which they would then have experienced on another level; lacking that moment of awareness, they could not escape.

Let me explain further. A piece of music exists as a whole series of sounds coming to our ears. It exists as a series of notes on pieces of ruled paper. It has existed in the composer's head, as a series of complex impulses. On a record it consists of a specific pattern in the grooves. No one would deny that all of these 'mappings' of the music are valid; the piece is not just the sound we hear.

Similarly, our lives are mapped in many mysterious ways, mostly unknown to us. One of these 'mappings' is the radical chart. This radical chart is being acted upon, all the time, by the continued movements of the Sun, Moon and planets (transits). The pattern itself, if we could grasp it, *is* ineluctable. There is no more an escape from it than there is an escape from death. But it is a neutral pattern. It carries within it only the residue of the true self, unweighted by such relative notions as 'good' or 'bad'. We are thus ruled by our true natures, by which too frequently we are held prisoner; but we might be free if we chose to try.

It is therefore true to say of Bywaters and Thompson that they were indeed fated to experience what they experienced. But they could have experienced it in a different way and at a different level. Knowledge and sophistication would not have helped them here; the quality of their hearts would.

Astrologers constantly see the surrender of people to the grossest in themselves; but gross is not bad, any more than refined is good. Each fate has all qualities, from gross to refined. My examples deal almost exclusively with public people, those who project themselves into the world and who want to exercise power over others. They often become the rather obvious victims of the grossness of their fates. In fact, we can all choose how we experience our fates, though the choice is difficult.

For those who still want to attempt prediction, there are three categories of technique; in practice they are often combined.

TRANSITS

Transits are the current movements of the planets. In their courses they make aspects to the radical positions. The Moon travels round every radical chart in an average time of 27.32 days. The Sun travels round it in a year. Saturn travels round it every 30 years, Uranus every 84 years. Neptune and Pluto only traverse a part of any radical chart.

The transits to a chart can reasonably be claimed as actually part of it, until the death of the native. But some are very fast, for instance those of the Moon, Sun, inner planets, and even Mars. These are therefore all judged together as a complex of effects. The transits of the heavier planets, from Jupiter outwards, are judged as more critical in the life.

Many astrologers nowadays, following Witte and Ebertin, take no notice of soft aspects in transit. They use only 2H, 4H and 8H aspects – oppositions, squares and semisquares. This is justified, for it is undoubtedly these hard aspects that bring about the events, the concrete manifestations. If we study our own transits, however, we often find that the hard aspects alone, to planets and to direct midpoints, signally fail to produce events. They are quite unreliable for use in prediction. It is different when we are making an investigation after the event; in such cases we use some type of progression in conjunction with transits. I put down the failure of the hard aspects to the fact that some events occur at a subconscious level or, literally, elsewhere (we know about them only later).

Transits by trine and sextile often go entirely unnoticed, perhaps because we are all so bad at grasping opportunities. They are certainly much more difficult to follow. I believe they represent not just states of mind, but unconscious states that will later emerge into consciousness. Transits by quintile give urges, which may or may not be acted upon. These urges can be useful, or dangerous, or both. Transits by septile are generally discernible in the sexual feelings, but will pass unnoticed unless they link up with series of septiles in the chart (at an orb of less than 1°).

ACCOUNTING FOR PRECESSION

A few astrologers take precession into account when interpreting transits. In so doing they are not rejecting the tropical zodiac. It is simply that as the first point of Aries is sliding backwards, owing to precession, so all our radical positions must be sliding forward in the tropical zodiac. Fortunately there is an easy and accurate way to advance our positions year by year, if so desired.

Suppose my Venus is at 4 Pisces 24, and I am 24 years old. To advance this to allow for precession I multiply my age by five, and divide the result by six; then I add the final result, in minutes of arc, to the radical position. Thus 24 times five divided by six equals 20; and so at age 24 this Venus will be advanced to 4 Pisces 44. There is nothing magical about this: it is just a piece of luck that 5/6 of the age almost exactly coincides with the rate of precession in minutes of arc.

Transits to the precessed positions rather than the radical ones are favoured by good astrologers such as Hand. My view is that charts are susceptible to both, that the results are different, and that only experimentation can show which 'work' most obviously in specific charts. It is best to start with the radical positions: if everything seems to be happening a little later than it should, you can switch to the use of precessed positions.

CALCULATING TRANSITS

There is no such thing as an effective orb in transits. This is because no transit exists on its own, though one by a heavy planet may dominate. It is necessary to do a sum to find when a complex of transits is going to reach its peak. Taking the planets from Mars outwards only, we allow an orb of 5° for Mars, 4° for Jupiter, and 3° for the rest, taking into account only the three hard aspects – conjunction, opposition, and square. We then calculate how far each planet is from exactness. Aspects that are approaching exactness are treated as minus, those that are past it as plus. We omit all the planets that are not in the orbs mentioned, and then divide by the number of planets we have had to use. If the answer is a minus quantity then the transit has yet to peak, if it is plus then it has peaked.

Because this is only a very approximate way of doing things, it is possible to miss much. For example, many simultaneous minor aspects may have the force of a square, and so may many septiles or quintiles. We can vary the technique by bringing in any grand trines. Transits by sextile should be omitted at first, though eventually they should be incorporated into the whole picture.

If this experiment is carried out, I cannot too strongly recommend that some past period of the relevant life is taken, and not a point in the future. Preferably it should be a period when a series of definite events occurred (such as a wedding, a divorce, an arrest, or a mugging). The transit situation is then examined in retrospect.

INTERPRETING TRANSITS

When a planet transits a radical planet, it imparts to the radical planet some of its 'principle'. My radical Venus transited by Mars and also by Uranus may make me feel suddenly and drastically in need of sex, to the point of indiscretion. But Venus transiting my Uranus (especially if it goes stationary on it, so that it stays longer than it normally would) will soften it, and make it gentler, less drastic or just lazy. It all depends on the condition of the planet in the radical chart. When planets transit the natal chart in the same configurations as they are in the natal chart, they may be particularly potent.

In considering transits we must not forget transiting midpoints. These have to be calculated by hand, for although there are now ephemerides for them, they are hard to find. Transiting midpoints are unlike the transiting bodies: they seem to time events much more exactly. They can be used on radical, progressed and directed charts.

DIRECTIONS

In directions every body and every point is directed by a 'key' – most profitably the same Sun-MC key (MCC) that directs the angles only in progressions (see below). All the bodies remain in the same angular relationship, so that only aspects to midpoints and to radical positions count. Ebertin works exclusively with directions, using this key. (He adds the distance travelled by the progressed Sun (see below) to Asc, while other astrologers derive a proper Asc from the directed MC, using the latitude of birth. Both these Ascs are significant, but the latter, which is derived astronomically is more personal and more useful.) Ebertin makes it clear that if something is certain to happen, the directed body should be 'excited' by hard transits.

There are other ways of directing charts. The true astronomical Asc arc for each year can be found and added to all bodies. This will reveal something about changing strategies. Or the Vertex arc can be found in the same way, so that all the bodies are directed by it. In each of the two latter cases the Sun-MC should be left as it would be astronomically. A point should never be directed by artificial means, even though Ebertin does occasionally get results from his Sun-directed Asc. All bodies *could* be directed by the distance Mars – or any other planet – travels in one year. In all these cases only the transits and the aspects to radical bodies count: the angularities between the radical bodies are preserved.

There are also 'symbolic directions', which involve directing the bodies by various mystical numbers. They have never seemed to me to yield any information.

PROGRESSIONS

There are three main types of progression: Secondary, Tertiary and Minor. All of these are based on rational equations of time to time, though not one is rationally explicable.

Secondary Progressions are based on the belief that one day in the ephemeris is equal to one year in the life: for example, the progressed chart for the twenty-fourth day of the life indicates the events of the twenty-fourth year. Tertiary Progressions are based on the notion that one day in the ephemeris is equal to one tropical month in the life (27.32 days, the mean time that it takes the Moon to return to its radical position). Minor Progressions are based on the supposition that one tropical month in the ephemeris is equivalent to one year in the life.

The progressed Sun is used to move all bodies in a directed chart (see above).

DETERMINING ANGLES

In all these systems it is necessary to determine the angles, or personal points, and that of course is done from the MC. There are a number of ways of finding this, and each one leads to quite different results by the time the native reaches about 30. The most popular method is as follows: Calculate the shorter arc distance between the Sun and the MC on the radical chart. Consider the example chart on p. 62. There the Sun is at 33° 51′, MC at 316° 25′. The shorter arc distance between them is $33° 51' - 316° 25' + 360° = 77° 26'$. This is what Chester Kemp calls the MC Constant (MCC). Here, it needs a minus sign in front of it, because MC is 'behind' the Sun on the zodiacal circle; so we should note on the chart that the MCC = –77° 26′. Whatever chart we use, the MC of that chart is going to be 77° 26′ from where the Sun is. (We preserve the radical relationship between the Sun and the MC in all progressed charts.)

SECONDARY PROGRESSIONS

These are based on the belief that a day in the ephemeris is equivalent to a year in the life. They are very popular; and easy to do.

Suppose you want to find the Secondary Progressions for the twenty-fourth year of your life: one easy way is to construct a chart for the hour of your birth on the twenty-fourth day after it. You would use GMT, but have no need of ST because you would use the MCC to calculate the MC. However, an even easier way saves you the trouble – principally the interpolation of the position of each planet – of working out this chart.

If the positions given in the ephemeris for the time of birth on the twenty-fourth day after birth relate to the twenty-fourth year of the life, from twenty-fourth to twenty-fifth birthday, then the positions given for midnight on the twenty-fourth day relate to a year which begins on a day some time before the twenty-fourth birthday and ends on a day some time before the twenty-fifth. The day in question is known as the Adjusted Calculation Date (ACD). Once you have it for any person, you can use it to find Secondary Progressions for any year of their life, simply by reading off the midnight positions for the appropriate day in the ephemeris.

The ACD is derived from the time of birth, and is calculated by equating time to space. The Sun travels 360° around the ecliptic in one year. If a day equals a year, we can say, equating time to space, that a day equals 360°. An hour therefore equals 15°, and a minute 15′. Take the now familiar man (p. 62) who was born at 7.07 a.m. GMT. 7 hours = 105°, 7 minutes = 1° 45′: total = 106° 45′. Subtract this from the Sun's position in the radical chart: 33° 51′–106° 45′+360° = 17 Capricorn 06. (360° must be added if there is a minus result.) Look in the ephemeris to find on what day in the year preceding the birthday the sun transited 17 Capricorn 06. The ACD is January 9th.

The movements of the Sun and planets between the twenty-fourth and twenty-fifth days after birth relate to the whole of that year: in this case 9 January 1952 to 9 January 1953. If we were reading from a noon ephemeris, then we would subtract 7h 7m from 12h (4h 53m), find the degree equivalent in absolute longitude (73° 15′) and add it to the Sun's position to obtain our point of reference (33° 51′ + 73° 15′ = 105° 06′ or 15 Cancer 06). We would have a period beginning later than the birthday.

In the Secondary Progressions only the faster planets move much: the outer planets merely complete aspects, or pass them. The chart is read both for aspects to the radical chart, and in its own right. And the new chart is susceptible to transits. Transits to progressed charts are very important, and are too often missed.

MINOR PROGRESSIONS

These are valuable for timing events, and for rectification of birth times. A tropical month in the ephemeris is equal to a year in the life. Let us take as example a man whose radical Moon is at 12 Libra 08. He was born on 17 March 1900 at 16.00. It is now 7 July 1981. Assume we want today's minor progressions.

We shall make use of a day-number chart, which is useful in many connections.

January	0	July	181
February	31	August	212
March	59	September	243
April	90	October	273
May	120	November	304
June	151	December	334

This gives us the number of days prior to the first of each month. We should add one extra day for all months after February in leap years. To the month number we add the date of the month.

Our native's eighty-first birthday was on day 59 + 17. 7 July is day 181 + 7. (181+7) – (59+17) = 156. So the native has lived 156/365 of his current (82nd) year.

Now we must find out when his 81st Lunar Return (in the lunar cycle) occurs in the ephemeris. The mean time taken for a tropical return is 27.32 days. So we multiply 81 by 27.32; the answer, rounded up, is 2213. 2213 days is six years 23 days.

We turn to the ephemeris for 1906: day 59+17+23 = 9 April. The Moon should be transiting near or in Libra on that day. In fact, it starts in 14 Libra. We have come very near indeed to the place in the ephemeris we want. (The longer the time, the closer the mean 27.32 will bring us to exactitude.)

We go back a little in the ephemeris, to 8 April 1906, and calculate the exact time that the Moon is at the radical position, 12 Libra 08. Then we go forward and find when it is next there, about 27.32 days later. To find these times, we take the Moon's motion for the day, which will be B (the later position) minus A (the earlier position). Now we take 12 Libra 08–A, and divide it by B–A. We multiply the fraction by 24 and the answer gives us the time we want. (Since the Moon often changes signs in the course of a day, it is safest to work in absolute longitude.) We find the other, later time in the same manner.

So it is now possible to calculate the exact duration, in days, hours, minutes and seconds, of that particular tropical month. It will be quite near 27.32, but not exactly that.

To obtain the Minor Progressions chart for 0000 7 July 1981, we multiply the result we just obtained by 156/365. We then add that number of days, hours, minutes and seconds to the time of the first Lunar Return we calculated, and set up a chart for that time, at birth latitude. We find the MC by use of the MCC, and we calculate an Asc for the latitude of his birthplace.

This is a chart for the Progressed Minor Moon, and it should give us indications about this native's prospects. We look at the chart in its own right, tabulating the aspects. We look at it in relation to the radical chart, again tabulating the aspects. We note, in particular, if there are any planets on the new angles, or if any radical angles have planets on them. We look at the transits to both charts.

TERTIARY PROGRESSIONS

Tertiary Progressions are easily the most valuable and fascinating in astrology. They are a trifle difficult, although once they are exactly understood, it is impossible to go wrong. A day equals a tropical month in the life.

Tertiaries are quite slow enough to be the most potent of all progressions, and they involve the Moon, the prime astrological mover. For Tertiary Progressions it is worth finding an ACD. We do the same for the Moon as we have done for the Sun in the Secondaries. Again referring to the example chart on page 62, we find that the time (using the midnight ephemeris) is equal to the same space: 106° 49′. So, if we want to take our positions straight out of the ephemeris, the Tertiary Moon must be at 90° 30′–105° 49′+360° = 14 Pisces 43. This gives us a date shortly before the native's birthday from which to measure the tropical months.

But suppose we have not done the Tertiary Progressions for this man before. How shall we know what day to take out of the ephemeris for the particular date we want to investigate? Say we want to know what happened to our native on Friday 18 May 1973 at 2.55 BST at 51N31, 00W28. (Let it be noted that this is an exercise in retrodiction, and not prediction.) At this time the man was 45 years and 24 days old. He was born on 24 April 1928.

How many revolutions of the zodiac has the Moon made since his birth? (As in the case of the Minor Progressions, we shall have to find the exact spot, 14 Pisces 43, by inspection.) The number of Lunar months in a year is 365.25/27.32 = 13.369327 (the ratio always used for all TPs). 45 × 13.369327 = about 602 days. Using the table of day numbers we add these to his birth date and get 6 December 1929.

But we must find out to precisely which date these midnight positions refer. We do not have to be as precise as we did with the Minors, because the Sun will only move about a degree in the lunar month; the MC cannot change very much, and we can see from the ephemeris what aspects if any, mutual and to the radical chart, will become exact. What we are looking for is a time when the Moon will be at 14 Pisces 43. The Moon before his birth passed through 14 Pisces on 17 April 1928: day 107 of 1928.

From 17 April 1928 until 17 April 1973 the native has lived for 45 × 365 days, plus 12 extra days for the 12 leap years. That amounts to 601.647 revolutions – as we have already established another way. We ought then to find the 602nd some time after 17 April 1973; about .647 of 27.32 days after, or about 17½ days.

Let us look 17½ days after 17 April 1973. The Moon on 4 May 1973 is in Taurus. We are a little late. We have to go back a few days, to 28 April, when the Moon passes through 14 Pisces. And so we have established that the positions for 0000, 6 December 1929 refer to 23 April 1973.

The Moon next passes through the TP degree on 26 May, too late for 18 May, the date which we want to investigate. However, we do now know that positions at 0000 for 7 December will refer to 26 May and the ensuing lunar month, and so we can now keep track of the TP positions. This is better than using confusing prepared tables.

One single day in the ephemeris, 6 December 1929, includes the day we are interested in. If we wanted absolute precision we should have to fractionalise the day in question as we did with the Minors for our 81-year-old native. But is it necessary? Hardly. We can see, over a mere day as distinct from the period of 27.32 days, just what we want to see. So we will draw the TP chart and surround it with the radical chart of the event, which will include an MC, an Asc and a Vertex. Our chart for the TP Moon will not be difficult: we read out the positions from an ephemeris for 0000 hrs 6 December 1929, find the Sun position, 253° 34′, and subtract the MCC, 77° 26′, from it: the MC is at 25 Virgo 58. The RAMC is given by the formula: cos e × sin EL ÷ cos EL. Cos e is .9174 as always. EL is ecliptic longitude. The RAMC is 26 Virgo 06. So Asc for 51N30 is therefore 00 Sagittarius 19. This is Asc for the TP chart. The Vertex is 27 Gemini 02.

The position of the TP Moon for 18 May would be about 15 Aquarius: this is the only body which moves appreciably in one day. It is in quincunx to the radical Pluto, and in sextile to the radical Venus, as well as being very near to the radical MC. It is thus going

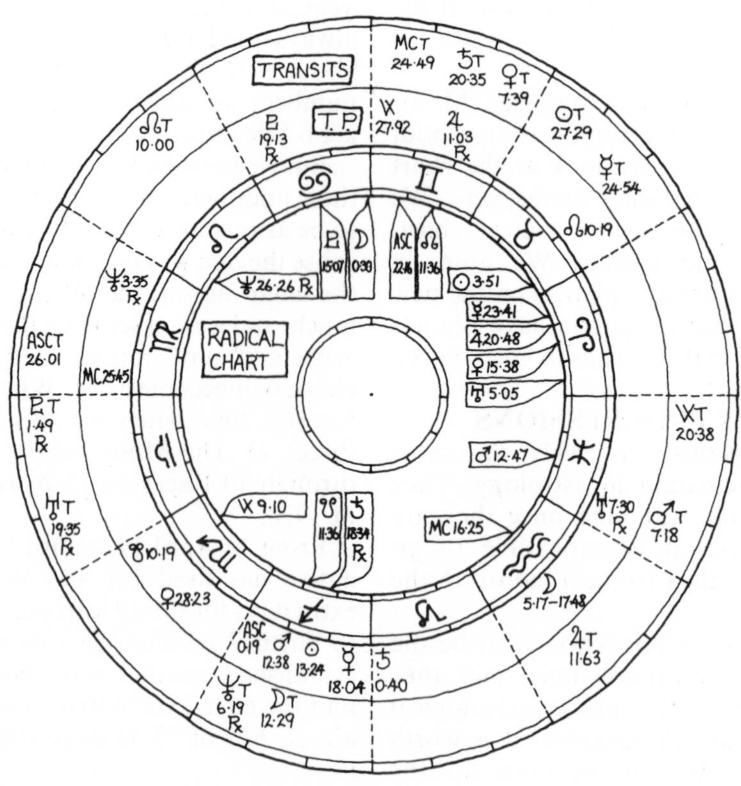

Tertiary Progressions and Transits for 18 May 1973 at 2.55 BST The radical chart is at the centre. The Tertiary Progressions (T.P.) are immediately outside the zodiacal band. Outside them are the Transits.

into sesquisquare with its radical position.

The charts here drawn up refer to an event from which the native does not remember benefitting in any way: he was the victim of an attack by two drunken men which resulted in concussion, broken teeth, and the loss of certain valuables. Other parts of the native's life at that time were fairly pleasant.

Let us pause to look at the radical chart. The cardinal points here are important: the Moon is within 28′ of one, and Venus/Mars is within 53′ of one. This means that the Moon and MC are at Venus/Mars, which are in a close undecimal. Further, the violence-brutality midpoint Mars/Pluto – in an applying dexter trine contaminated by the Venus-Pluto square – is in 8H to the cardinal points. It is 16′ further away from them than Venus/Mars is, but must be regarded as afflicting Moon and MC. The native is subject to accidents: severe scalding, broken bones, sudden falls.

EXAMINING THE TERTIARY PROGRESSIONS

Let us look at the TP chart. We can take the Moon as being about midway in Aquarius, and all the other bodies moved on (or back) according to their respective rates; the distances will be almost negligible. Mars is building up to a dangerous conjunction with the Sun (the radical aspect is septile). The MC is pushing into a position where it will put a strain on the radical Neptune (semisextile). Mars is square to the radical Mars, while the transiting Mars is going into a semisquare to the radical Mercury: the TP Mercury approaches the radical Saturn.

Saturn is at the cardinal point 00 Capricorn, important in this progression: it opposes the radical Moon, and stands in aspect to Mars/Pluto and Venus/Pluto. Further, the Mars/Pluto of the TP chart is also attacking the cardinal point (and therefore the TP Saturn as well as radical Moon and MC, and the transiting Pluto itself). The transiting Mars/Pluto is at the TP Mercury and the radical Saturn, suggesting debate and hindrance to plans. The radical Sun, in 8H to Saturn, is also involved.

The TP Mars/Uranus – suggesting bloody injury – equals the radical Mars/Uranus, while the transiting Mars/Uranus attacks the cardinal points just as Mars/Pluto, TP and radical, do.

The TP Neptune is stone still, affecting the radical Saturn at an orb of 1′ from the 105° contact (7/24H). The transiting Nodes are in square to the TP Nodes. The transiting Asc (of the event) is right on the MC of the TP chart. Transiting Pluto will square the TP Saturn; both are threatened by Mars/Pluto, TP and radical. The cardinal points, involving the radical Moon and the deadly Mars-Pluto midpoint, are menaced, though the TP Asc trines 00 Aries 00. We should also observe that the transiting Moon is right on the TP Mars, square the radical Mars. Transiting Uranus punishes the TP Pluto (orb 22′, double applying) by a cardinal square: this suggests a drastic act performed by denizens of the underworld posing as other than they are (Neptune SR quintile the transiting Saturn, which is approaching the radical Asc). The radical Neptune is trapped at the square of the transiting Sun/Mercury. Witte says 'Author. Not clear, rambling, impractical thinking. Sluggish. Swindle. Fraud.' This precisely describes the affair. There is quite a close T-square between transiting Uranus opposing radical Jupiter with TP Pluto at point focus.

The better aspects of the native's existence at that time are shown in the TP chart, as they are in the transits. But the foregoing was retrodiction. Certainly some danger can be seen in the TP chart, and an astrologer might have given the native some warning. But would he have taken any notice? Unlikely. The native does not believe in astrology.

EPHEMERIS
1900-2000

USING THE EPHEMERIS

THIS EPHEMERIS GIVES POSITIONS FOR GMT (UT) midnight from 1900 to 2000 inclusive. Positions for the Sun and Moon are given daily; positions for Mercury, Venus and Mars are given two-daily; positions for Jupiter and Saturn are given four-daily; positions for Uranus, Neptune and Pluto are given six-daily; the position of the mean node of the Moon is given once monthly.

To find the positions of the Sun and Moon at any given time proceed as instructed in step 6 on page 56.

The procedure for finding the positions of the other bodies is exactly similar in principle, but interpolation must be based on longer periods. If the birth or event does not fall on an exact hour, use minutes: 24 hours = 1440 minutes; 48 hours = 2880 minutes; 96 hours (4 days) = 5760 minutes; 144 hours (6 days) = 8640 minutes. With a calculator, the finding of the necessary fraction is very easy. You will need to use absolute longitude in the case of the Moon and in the cases of any other bodies which change sign over the period in question.

To find the exact position of the Moon's mean node, which is always retrograde, multiply $3.18'$ by the day number of the month concerned, and *subtract* from the position given for the 1st of that month. Remember that this sum is in minutes, *not* degrees of arc.

Example: birth at 03.27 7 January 1917. The fraction required will be: for Sun and Moon $207 \div 1440$; for Mercury, Venus and Mars $207 \div 2880$; for Jupiter and Saturn $3087 \div 5760$; for Uranus, Neptune and Pluto $207 \div 8640$. The position of the node will be found by *subtracting* 7×3.18 *minutes of arc* (do the multiplication sum, and then divide by 60, which will give you the value in degrees) from the position given for 1 January 1917. You should obtain the following positions: Moon 3 Cancer 27; Sun 16 Capricorn 16; Mercury 4 Aquarius 46; Venus 19 Sagittarius 40; Mars 28 Capricorn 08; Jupiter 25 Aries 56; Saturn 28 Cancer 01R; Uranus 17 Aquarius 51; Neptune 3 Leo 58R; Pluto 3 Cancer 08R; Node 20 Capricorn 00 (R signifies retrograde). None of these positions is more than $2'$ less accurate than the positions to be obtained from a daily ephemeris. It would be very unusual for this condensed ephemeris to be less accurate than 3–5 minutes of arc.

♈	Aries
♉	Taurus
♊	Gemini
♋	Cancer
♌	Leo
♍	Virgo
♎	Libra
♏	Scorpio
♐	Sagittarius
♑	Capricorn
♒	Aquarius
♓	Pisces

☉	Sun
☽	Moon
☊	Node
☿	Mercury
♀	Venus
♂	Mars
♃	Jupiter
♄	Saturn
♅	Uranus
♆	Neptune
MC	Midheaven
ASC	Ascendant
VX	Vertex

Sun

January

	1st	2nd	3rd	4th	5th	6th	7th	8th	9th	10th	11th	12th	13th	14th	15th	16th
1900	10 ♑ 09 11	10 12	12 13	13 14	14 15	15 16	16 17	17 18	19 19	20 20	21 21	22 22	23 23	24 24	25 25	26
1901	09 ♑ 55 10	56 11	57 12	58 13	59 15	00 16	01 17	02 18	04 19	05 20	06 21	07 22	08 23	09 24	10 25	12
1902	09 ♑ 39 10	40 11	42 12	43 13	44 14	45 15	46 16	47 17	49 18	50 19	51 20	52 21	53 22	54 23	56 24	57
1903	09 ♑ 24 10	25 11	27 12	28 13	29 14	30 15	31 16	32 17	34 18	35 19	36 20	37 21	38 22	39 23	40 24	41
1904	09 ♑ 09 10	11 11	12 12	13 13	14 14	15 15	16 16	17 17	19 18	20 19	21 20	22 21	23 22	24 23	25 24	27
1905	09 ♑ 56 10	57 11	58 12	59 14	00 15	01 16	03 17	04 18	05 19	06 20	07 21	08 22	10 23	11 24	12 25	13
1906	09 ♑ 41 10	42 11	43 12	44 13	46 14	47 15	48 16	49 17	50 18	51 19	52 20	53 21	55 22	56 23	57 24	58
1907	09 ♑ 26 10	27 11	28 12	29 13	30 14	31 15	33 16	34 17	35 18	36 19	37 20	38 21	40 22	41 23	42 24	43
1908	09 ♑ 11 10	12 11	13 12	14 13	15 14	17 15	18 16	19 17	20 18	21 19	22 20	24 21	25 22	26 23	27 24	28
1909	09 ♑ 58 10	59 11	60 13	01 14	02 15	03 16	04 17	05 18	07 19	08 20	09 21	10 22	11 23	12 24	13 25	14
1910	09 ♑ 42 10	44 11	45 12	46 13	47 14	48 15	49 16	51 17	52 18	53 19	54 20	55 21	56 22	57 23	59 24	60
1911	09 ♑ 28 10	29 11	30 12	31 13	32 14	34 15	35 16	36 17	37 18	38 19	39 20	40 21	42 22	43 23	44 24	45
1912	09 ♑ 13 10	14 11	16 12	17 13	18 14	19 15	20 16	21 17	22 18	23 19	25 20	26 21	27 22	28 23	29 24	30
1913	09 ♑ 59 11	00 12	02 13	03 14	04 15	05 16	06 17	08 18	09 19	10 20	11 21	12 22	13 23	15 24	16 25	17
1914	09 ♑ 45 10	46 11	47 12	48 13	49 14	51 15	52 16	53 17	54 18	55 19	56 20	58 21	59 22	00 24	01 25	02
1915	09 ♑ 30 10	31 11	32 12	33 13	34 14	35 15	37 16	38 17	39 18	40 19	41 20	42 21	43 22	45 23	46 24	47
1916	09 ♑ 15 10	16 11	17 12	18 13	19 14	21 15	22 16	23 17	24 18	25 19	26 20	28 21	29 22	30 23	31 24	32
1917	10 ♑ 02 11	03 12	04 13	05 14	06 15	07 16	08 17	10 18	11 19	12 20	13 21	14 22	15 23	16 24	17 25	18
1918	09 ♑ 46 10	48 11	49 12	50 13	51 14	52 15	53 16	54 17	56 18	57 19	58 20	59 22	00 23	01 24	03 25	04
1919	09 ♑ 32 10	33 11	34 12	35 13	36 14	37 15	39 16	40 17	41 18	42 19	43 20	44 21	45 22	47 23	48 24	49
1920	09 ♑ 17 10	18 11	19 12	20 13	21 14	23 15	24 16	25 17	26 18	27 19	28 20	29 21	31 22	32 23	33 24	34
1921	10 ♑ 03 11	04 12	05 13	06 14	08 15	09 16	10 17	11 18	12 19	13 20	15 21	16 22	17 23	18 24	19 25	20
1922	09 ♑ 48 10	50 11	51 12	52 13	53 14	54 15	55 16	56 17	58 18	59 19	60 21	01 22	02 23	03 24	04 25	05
1923	09 ♑ 33 10	34 11	36 12	37 13	38 14	39 15	40 16	41 17	42 18	44 19	45 20	46 21	47 22	48 23	49 24	50
1924	09 ♑ 18 10	19 11	20 12	22 13	23 14	24 15	25 16	26 17	28 18	29 19	30 20	31 21	32 22	33 23	35 24	36
1925	10 ♑ 05 11	06 12	07 13	08 14	09 15	10 16	12 17	13 18	14 19	15 20	16 21	17 22	18 23	19 24	21 25	22
1926	09 ♑ 49 10	51 11	52 12	53 13	54 14	55 15	56 16	57 17	59 18	60 20	01 21	02 22	03 23	04 24	06 25	07
1927	09 ♑ 34 10	36 11	37 12	38 13	39 14	40 15	41 16	43 17	44 18	45 19	46 20	47 21	48 22	49 23	51 24	52
1928	09 ♑ 20 10	21 11	22 12	23 13	24 14	26 15	27 16	28 17	29 18	30 19	31 20	32 21	33 22	35 23	36 24	37
1929	10 ♑ 06 11	07 12	08 13	09 14	11 15	12 16	13 17	14 18	15 19	16 20	18 21	19 22	20 23	21 24	22 25	23
1930	09 ♑ 51 10	53 11	54 12	55 13	56 14	57 15	59 16	60 18	01 19	02 20	03 21	04 22	05 23	06 24	07 25	09
1931	09 ♑ 37 10	38 11	39 12	40 13	41 14	42 15	43 16	45 17	46 18	47 19	48 20	49 21	50 22	51 23	53 24	54
1932	09 ♑ 22 10	23 11	24 12	25 13	26 14	27 15	29 16	30 17	31 18	32 19	33 20	35 21	36 22	37 23	38 24	39
1933	10 ♑ 08 11	10 12	11 13	12 14	13 15	14 16	15 17	17 18	18 19	19 20	20 21	21 22	22 23	23 24	24 25	25
1934	09 ♑ 54 10	55 11	56 12	57 13	58 14	59 16	00 17	02 18	03 19	04 20	05 21	06 22	07 23	08 24	10 25	11
1935	09 ♑ 39 10	40 11	41 12	42 13	43 14	45 15	46 16	47 17	48 18	49 19	50 20	52 21	53 22	54 23	55 24	56
1936	09 ♑ 24 10	25 11	27 12	28 13	29 14	30 15	31 16	32 17	33 18	35 19	36 20	37 21	38 22	39 23	40 24	41
1937	10 ♑ 10 11	11 12	12 13	14 14	15 15	16 16	17 17	18 18	19 19	21 20	22 21	23 22	24 23	25 24	26 25	28
1938	09 ♑ 55 10	57 11	58 12	59 14	00 15	01 16	02 17	04 18	05 19	06 20	07 21	08 22	09 23	10 24	11 25	13
1939	09 ♑ 40 10	42 11	43 12	44 13	45 14	46 15	47 16	48 17	49 18	51 19	52 20	53 21	54 22	55 23	56 24	57
1940	09 ♑ 25 10	26 11	27 12	29 13	30 14	31 15	32 16	33 17	34 18	36 19	37 20	38 21	39 22	40 23	41 24	43
1941	10 ♑ 12 11	13 12	14 13	15 14	17 15	18 16	19 17	20 18	21 19	22 20	23 21	24 22	26 23	27 24	28 25	29
1942	09 ♑ 57 10	58 11	59 13	00 14	01 15	02 16	03 17	05 18	06 19	07 20	08 21	09 22	10 23	12 24	13 25	14
1943	09 ♑ 42 10	43 11	44 12	45 13	46 14	47 15	49 16	50 17	51 18	52 19	53 20	54 21	56 22	57 23	58 24	59
1944	09 ♑ 27 10	28 11	29 12	31 13	32 14	33 15	34 16	35 17	36 18	37 19	39 20	40 21	41 22	42 23	43 24	44
1945	10 ♑ 14 11	15 12	16 13	17 14	18 15	19 16	21 17	22 18	23 19	24 20	25 21	26 22	27 23	29 24	30 25	31
1946	09 ♑ 59 11	00 12	01 13	03 14	04 15	05 16	06 17	07 18	08 19	10 20	11 21	12 22	13 23	14 24	15 25	16
1947	09 ♑ 44 10	45 11	47 12	48 13	49 14	50 15	51 16	52 17	53 18	55 19	56 20	57 21	58 22	59 24	00 25	01
1948	09 ♑ 29 10	30 11	31 12	33 13	34 14	35 15	36 15	37 17	38 18	40 19	41 20	42 21	43 22	44 23	45 24	47
1949	10 ♑ 16 11	17 12	18 13	19 14	20 15	22 16	23 17	24 18	25 19	26 20	27 21	29 22	30 23	31 24	32 25	33
1950	10 ♑ 00 11	01 12	03 13	04 14	05 15	06 16	07 17	08 18	09 19	11 20	12 21	13 22	14 23	15 14	16 25	17
1951	09 ♑ 45 10	46 11	48 12	49 13	50 14	51 15	52 16	53 17	55 18	56 19	57 20	58 21	59 23	00 24	01 25	03
1952	09 ♑ 31 10	32 11	33 12	34 13	36 14	37 15	38 16	39 17	40 18	41 19	42 20	43 21	45 22	46 23	47 24	53
1953	10 ♑ 17 11	18 12	19 13	21 14	22 15	23 16	24 17	25 18	26 19	27 20	29 21	30 22	31 23	32 24	33 25	34
1954	10 ♑ 02 11	03 12	05 13	06 14	07 15	08 16	09 17	11 18	12 19	13 20	14 21	15 22	16 23	17 24	19 25	20
1955	09 ♑ 48 10	49 11	50 12	51 13	52 14	53 15	55 16	56 17	57 18	58 19	59 21	00 22	01 23	02 24	04 25	05
1956	09 ♑ 33 10	34 11	35 12	36 13	37 14	38 15	39 16	41 17	42 18	43 19	44 20	45 21	46 22	48 23	49 24	50
1957	10 ♑ 19 11	20 12	22 13	23 14	24 15	25 16	26 17	27 18	29 19	30 20	31 21	32 22	33 23	34 24	35 25	36
1958	10 ♑ 04 11	05 12	07 13	08 14	09 15	10 16	11 17	12 18	13 19	15 20	16 21	17 22	18 23	19 24	20 25	21
1959	09 ♑ 49 10	50 11	51 12	53 13	54 14	55 15	56 16	57 17	59 18	60 20	01 21	02 22	03 23	04 24	05 25	07
1960	09 ♑ 35 10	36 11	37 12	38 13	40 14	41 15	42 16	43 17	44 18	45 19	46 20	48 21	49 22	50 23	51 24	51
1961	10 ♑ 21 11	22 12	23 13	24 14	25 15	27 16	28 17	29 18	30 19	31 20	32 21	33 22	35 23	36 24	37 25	38
1962	10 ♑ 06 11	07 12	08 13	09 14	10 15	12 16	13 17	14 18	15 19	16 20	17 21	19 22	20 23	21 24	22 25	23
1963	09 ♑ 51 10	52 11	53 12	54 13	56 14	57 15	58 16	59 18	00 19	01 20	02 21	03 22	05 23	06 24	07 25	08
1964	09 ♑ 36 10	37 11	38 12	39 13	40 14	42 15	43 16	44 17	45 18	46 19	47 20	49 21	50 22	51 23	52 24	53
1965	10 ♑ 22 11	23 12	24 13	26 14	27 15	28 16	29 17	30 18	31 19	33 20	34 21	35 22	36 23	37 24	38 25	39
1966	10 ♑ 07 11	08 12	10 13	11 14	12 15	13 16	14 17	15 18	16 19	17 20	19 21	20 22	21 23	22 24	23 25	24
1967	09 ♑ 52 10	53 11	54 12	56 13	57 14	58 15	59 17	00 18	01 19	03 20	04 21	05 22	06 23	07 24	08 25	10
1968	09 ♑ 38 10	39 11	40 12	41 13	42 14	44 15	45 16	46 17	47 18	48 19	49 20	50 21	52 22	53 23	54 24	55
1969	10 ♑ 24 11	25 12	26 13	28 14	29 15	30 16	31 17	32 18	33 19	34 20	36 21	37 22	38 23	39 24	40 25	41
1970	10 ♑ 10 11	11 12	12 13	13 14	14 15	16 16	17 17	18 18	19 19	20 20	21 21	23 22	24 23	25 24	26 25	27
1971	09 ♑ 55 10	56 11	58 12	59 14	00 15	01 16	02 17	03 18	04 19	06 20	07 21	08 22	09 23	10 24	11 25	12
1972	09 ♑ 40 10	41 11	42 12	44 13	45 14	46 15	47 16	48 17	49 18	50 19	52 20	53 21	54 22	55 23	56 24	57
1973	10 ♑ 26 11	28 12	29 13	30 14	31 15	32 16	34 17	35 18	36 19	37 20	38 21	39 22	41 23	42 24	43 25	44
1974	10 ♑ 12 11	13 12	14 13	15 14	16 15	17 16	18 17	20 18	21 19	22 20	23 21	24 22	25 23	26 24	27 25	29
1975	09 ♑ 56 10	57 11	58 12	59 14	01 15	02 16	03 17	04 18	05 19	06 20	08 21	09 22	10 23	11 24	12 25	13
1976	09 ♑ 41 10	43 11	44 12	45 13	46 14	47 15	49 16	50 17	51 18	52 19	53 20	54 21	55 22	56 23	58 24	59
1977	10 ♑ 28 11	29 12	30 13	31 14	32 15	33 16	35 17	36 18	37 19	38 20	39 21	40 22	41 23	43 24	44 25	45
1978	10 ♑ 13 11	14 12	15 13	16 14	17 15	19 16	20 17	21 18	22 19	23 20	24 21	26 22	27 23	28 24	29 25	30
1979	09 ♑ 58 11	59 12	00 13	01 14	03 15	04 16	05 17	06 18	07 19	08 20	09 21	11 22	12 23	13 24	14 25	15
1980	09 ♑ 43 10	44 11	45 12	46 13	47 14	49 15	50 16	51 17	52 18	53 19	54 20	55 21	57 22	58 23	59 25	00
1981	10 ♑ 29 11	30 12	32 13	33 14	34 15	36 16	36 17	37 18	39 19	40 20	41 21	42 22	43 23	44 24	45 25	47
1982	10 ♑ 15 11	16 12	17 13	18 14	19 15	20 16	21 17	22 18	24 19	25 20	26 21	27 22	28 23	29 24	30 25	31
1983	09 ♑ 59 11	01 12	02 13	03 14	04 15	05 16	06 17	07 18	09 19	10 20	11 21	12 22	13 23	14 24	16 25	17
1984	09 ♑ 45 10	46 11	47 12	48 13	49 14	51 15	52 16	53 17	54 18	55 19	56 20	58 21	59 22	60 24	01 25	02
1985	10 ♑ 31 11	32 12	33 13	34 14	36 15	37 16	38 17	39 18	40 19	41 20	42 21	44 22	45 23	46 24	47 25	48
1986	10 ♑ 16 11	17 12	18 13	19 14	21 15	22 16	23 17	24 18	25 19	26 20	28 21	29 22	30 23	31 24	32 25	33
1987	10 ♑ 01 11	02 12	04 13	05 14	06 15	07 16	08 17	09 18	11 19	12 20	13 21	14 22	15 23	16 24	14 25	18
1988	09 ♑ 47 10	48 11	49 12	50 13	51 14	52 15	53 16	54 17	56 18	57 19	58 20	59 22	00 23	01 24	02 25	04
1989	10 ♑ 33 11	34 12	35 13	36 14	38 15	39 16	40 17	41 18	42 19	44 20	45 21	46 22	47 23	48 24	49 25	50
1990	10 ♑ 18 11	19 12	21 13	22 14	23 15	24 16	25 17	26 18	28 19	29 20	30 21	31 22	32 23	33 24	34 25	35
1991	10 ♑ 03 11	04 12	06 13	07 14	08 15	09 16	10 17	11 18	12 19	14 20	15 21	16 22	17 23	18 24	19 25	20
1992	09 ♑ 49 10	50 11	51 12	52 13	53 14	54 15	56 16	57 17	58 18	69 20	00 21	02 22	03 23	04 24	06 25	06
1993	10 ♑ 35 11	36 12	37 13	39 14	40 15	41 16	42 17	43 18	44 19	45 20	47 21	48 22	49 23	50 24	51 25	52
1994	10 ♑ 20 11	21 12	23 13	24 14	25 15	26 16	27 17	28 18	29 19	31 20	32 21	33 22	34 23	35 24	36 25	37
1995	10 ♑ 05 11	07 12	08 13	09 14	10 15	11 16	12 17	14 18	15 19	16 20	17 21	18 22	19 23	20 24	22 25	23
1996	09 ♑ 50 10	52 11	53 13	54 13	56 14	56 15	57 16	58 17	60 19	01 20	02 21	03 22	04 23	05 24	06 25	07
1997	10 ♑ 36 11	37 12	39 13	40 14	41 15	42 16	43 17	45 18	46 19	47 20	48 21	49 22	50 23	52 24	53 25	54
1998	10 ♑ 21 11	23 12	24 13	25 14	26 15	27 16	28 17	30 18	31 19	32 20	33 21	34 22	35 23	36 24	37 25	38
1999	10 ♑ 06 11	07 12	09 13	10 14	11 15	12 16	13 17	14 18	15 19	17 20	18 21	19 22	20 23	21 24	22 25	23
2000	09 ♑ 52 10	53 11	54 12	55 13	56 14	57 15	59 16	60 18	01 19	02 20	03 21	04 22	06 23	07 24	08 25	09

	17th	18th	19th	20th	21st	22nd	23rd	24th	25th	26th	27th	28th	29th	30th	31st
1900	26 27	27 29	28 30	29 31	00♒32	01 33	02 34	03 35	04 36	05 37	06 38	07 39	08 40	09 42	10♒42
1901	26 13	27 14	28 15	29 16	00♒17	01 18	02 19	03 20	04 21	05 22	05 24	07 24	08 25	09 26	10♒27
1902	25 58	26 59	28 00	29 01	00♒02	01 03	02 04	03 05	04 06	05 07	06 08	04 09	08 10	09 11	10♒12
1903	15 42	26 44	27 45	28 46	29 47	00♒48	01 49	02 50	03 51	04 52	05 53	06 43	07 55	08 56	09♒57
1904	25 27	26 29	27 30	28 31	29 32	00♒33	01 34	02 35	03 36	04 37	05 38	06 39	07 40	08 42	09♒42
1905	26 14	27 15	28 16	29 17	00♒18	01 19	02 20	03 31	04 22	05 23	06 24	07 25	08 26	09 27	10♒28
1906	25 59	27 00	28 01	29 02	00♒03	01 04	02 05	03 06	04 07	05 08	06 09	07 10	08 11	09 12	10♒13
1907	25 44	26 45	27 46	28 47	29 49	00♒50	01 51	02 52	03 53	04 54	05 55	06 56	07 56	08 57	09♒58
1908	25 29	26 30	27 31	28 32	29 33	00♒34	01 35	02 36	03 37	04 38	05 39	06 40	07 42	08 42	09♒43
1909	26 16	27 17	28 18	29 19	00♒20	01 21	02 22	03 23	04 24	05 25	06 26	07 27	08 28	09 29	10♒30
1910	26 01	27 02	28 03	29 04	00♒05	01 06	02 07	03 08	04 09	06 10	06 11	07 12	08 13	09 14	10♒15
1911	25 46	26 47	27 28	28 49	29 50	00♒51	01 52	02 53	03 54	04 55	05 56	06 57	07 58	08 59	10♒00
1912	25 31	26 32	27 34	28 35	29 36	00♒37	01 38	02 39	03 40	04 41	05 42	06 43	07 44	08 45	09♒46
1913	26 18	27 19	28 20	29 21	00♒22	01 23	02 24	03 25	04 26	05 27	06 28	07 29	08 30	09 31	10♒32
1914	26 03	27 04	28 05	29 06	00♒07	01 08	02 09	03 10	04 11	05 12	06 13	07 14	08 15	09 16	10♒17
1915	25 48	26 49	27 50	28 51	29 52	00♒43	01 55	02 56	03 57	04 58	05 59	06 59	08 00	09 01	10♒02
1916	25 33	26 34	27 35	28 36	29 37	00♒38	01 39	02 40	03 41	04 42	05 43	06 44	07 45	08 46	09♒47
1917	26 20	27 21	28 22	29 23	00♒24	01 25	02 26	03 27	04 28	05 29	06 30	07 31	08 32	09 33	10♒34
1918	26 05	27 06	28 07	29 08	00♒09	01 10	02 11	03 12	04 12	05 14	06 15	07 16	08 17	09 18	10♒19
1919	25 50	26 51	27 52	28 53	29 54	00♒55	01 56	02 57	03 58	04 59	06 00	07 01	08 02	09 03	10♒04
1920	25 35	26 36	27 37	28 38	29 39	00♒41	01 42	02 43	03 44	04 45	05 46	06 47	07 48	08 49	09♒50
1921	26 21	27 22	28 23	29 25	00♒26	01 27	02 28	03 29	04 30	05 31	06 32	07 33	08 34	09 34	10♒35
1922	26 06	27 08	28 09	29 10	00♒11	01 12	02 13	03 14	04 15	05 16	06 17	07 18	08 19	09 20	10♒21
1923	25 52	26 53	27 54	28 55	29 56	00♒57	01 58	02 59	04 00	05 01	06 02	07 03	08 04	09 05	10♒06
1924	25 37	26 38	26 39	28 40	29 41	00♒42	01 43	02 44	03 45	04 46	05 47	06 48	07 49	08 50	09♒51
1925	26 23	27 24	28 25	29 26	00♒27	01 28	02 29	03 30	04 31	05 32	06 33	07 34	08 35	09 36	10♒37
1926	26 08	27 09	28 10	29 11	00♒12	01 13	02 14	03 15	04 16	05 17	06 18	07 19	08 20	09 21	10♒22
1927	25 53	26 54	27 55	28 56	29 57	00♒58	01 59	03 00	04 01	06 02	06 03	07 04	08 05	09 06	10♒07
1928	25 38	26 39	27 40	28 41	29 42	00♒43	01 44	02 46	30 47	04 48	05 49	06 50	07 51	08 52	09♒52
1929	26 24	27 26	28 27	29 28	00♒29	01 30	02 31	03 32	04 33	05 34	06 35	07 36	08 37	09 37	10♒38
1930	26 10	27 11	28 12	29 13	00♒14	01 15	02 16	03 17	04 18	05 19	06 20	07 21	08 22	09 23	10♒24
1931	25 55	26 56	27 57	28 58	29 59	01♒00	02 01	03 02	04 03	05 04	06 05	07 06	08 07	09 08	10♒09
1932	25 40	26 41	27 42	28 43	29 44	00♒45	01 47	02 48	03 49	04 50	05 50	06 51	07 52	08 53	09♒54
1933	26 27	27 28	28 29	29 30	00♒31	01 32	02 33	03 34	04 35	05 36	06 37	07 38	08 39	09 40	10♒41
1934	26 12	27 13	28 14	29 15	00♒16	01 17	02 18	03 19	04 20	05 21	06 22	07 23	08 24	09 25	10♒26
1935	25 57	26 58	27 59	29 00	00♒01	01 02	02 03	03 04	04 05	05 06	06 07	07 08	08 09	09 10	10♒11
1936	25 42	26 43	27 45	28 46	29 47	00♒48	01 49	02 50	03 51	04 52	05 53	06 54	07 55	08 56	09♒57
1937	26 29	27 30	28 31	29 32	00♒33	01 34	02 35	03 36	04 37	05 38	06 39	07 40	08 41	09 42	10♒43
1938	26 14	27 15	28 16	29 17	00♒18	01 19	02 20	03 21	04 22	05 23	06 24	07 25	03 26	09 27	10♒28
1939	25 59	27 00	28 01	29 02	00♒03	01 04	02 05	03 06	04 07	05 08	06 09	07 10	08 11	09 12	10♒13
1940	25 44	26 45	27 46	28 27	29 48	00♒29	01 50	02 51	03 52	04 53	05 54	06 55	07 56	08 57	09♒58
1941	26 30	27 31	28 32	29 33	00♒34	01 35	02 36	03 37	04 38	05 39	06 40	07 42	08 42	09 43	10♒44
1942	26 15	27 16	28 17	29 18	00♒19	01 20	02 21	03 22	04 24	05 25	06 25	07 26	08 27	09 28	10♒29
1943	26 00	27 01	28 02	29 03	00♒04	01 05	02 06	03 07	04 08	05 09	06 10	07 11	08 12	09 13	10♒14
1944	25 45	26 46	27 47	28 48	29 50	00♒51	01 52	02 53	03 54	04 55	05 56	06 57	07 58	08 59	10♒00
1945	26 32	27 33	28 34	29 35	00♒36	01 37	02 38	03 39	04 40	05 41	06 42	07 43	08 44	09 45	10♒46
1946	26 17	27 18	28 19	29 20	00♒21	01 22	02 24	03 25	04 26	05 27	06 28	07 28	08 29	09 30	10♒31
1947	26 02	27 03	28 05	29 06	00♒07	01 08	02 09	03 10	04 11	05 12	06 13	07 14	08 15	09 16	10♒17
1948	25 48	26 49	27 50	28 51	29 52	00♒53	01 54	02 55	03 56	04 57	05 58	06 59	08 00	09 01	10♒02
1949	26 34	27 35	28 36	29 37	00♒38	01 39	02 40	03 41	04 42	05 43	06 44	07 45	08 46	09 47	10♒48
1950	26 19	27 30	28 21	29 22	00♒23	01 24	02 25	03 26	04 27	05 29	06 30	07 30	08 31	09 32	10♒33
1951	26 04	27 05	28 06	29 07	00♒08	01 09	02 10	03 11	04 12	05 13	06 14	07 15	08 16	09 17	10♒18
1952	25 49	26 50	27 51	28 52	29 53	00♒54	01 55	02 56	03 58	04 59	06 00	07 34	08 02	09 03	10♒03
1953	26 35	27 37	28 38	29 39	00♒40	01 41	02 42	03 43	04 44	05 45	06 46	07 47	08 48	09 49	10♒50
1954	26 21	27 22	28 23	29 24	00♒25	01 26	02 27	03 28	04 29	05 30	06 31	07 32	08 33	09 34	10♒35
1955	26 06	27 07	28 08	29 09	00♒10	01 11	02 12	03 13	04 14	05 14	06 16	07 17	08 18	09 19	10♒20
1956	25 51	26 52	27 53	28 54	29 55	00♒56	01 58	02 59	03 59	05 01	06 02	07 02	08 03	09 04	10♒05
1957	26 37	27 38	28 40	29 41	00♒42	01 43	02 44	03 45	04 56	05 47	06 48	07 49	08 50	09 51	10♒52
1958	26 22	27 23	28 25	29 26	00♒27	01 28	02 29	03 30	04 31	05 32	06 33	07 34	08 35	09 36	10♒37
1959	26 08	27 09	28 10	29 11	00♒12	01 13	02 14	03 15	04 16	05 17	05 18	07 19	08 20	09 21	10♒22
1960	25 53	26 54	27 55	28 56	29 57	00♒58	02 00	03 01	04 02	05 03	06 04	07 05	08 06	09 07	10♒08
1961	26 39	27 40	28 41	29 42	00♒44	01 45	02 46	03 47	04 48	05 49	06 50	07 51	08 52	09 52	10♒53
1962	26 24	27 25	28 26	29 27	00♒28	01 29	02 30	03 31	04 32	05 33	06 34	07 35	08 36	09 37	10♒38
1963	26 09	27 10	28 11	29 12	00♒13	01 14	02 15	03 17	04 18	06 19	06 20	07 21	08 22	09 23	10♒24
1964	25 54	26 55	27 56	28 58	29 59	01♒00	02 01	03 02	04 03	05 04	06 05	07 06	08 07	09 08	10♒08
1965	26 40	27 42	28 42	29 44	00♒46	01 46	02 47	03 48	04 49	05 50	06 51	07 52	08 53	09 54	10♒54
1966	26 25	27 27	28 28	29 29	00♒30	01 31	02 32	03 33	04 34	05 35	06 36	07 37	08 38	09 39	10♒40
1967	26 11	27 12	28 13	29 14	00♒15	01 16	02 17	03 18	04 19	05 20	06 21	07 22	08 23	09 25	10♒25
1968	25 56	26 57	27 58	28 59	00♒00	01 01	02 02	03 03	04 04	05 05	06 06	07 07	08 08	09 09	10♒10
1969	26 42	27 43	28 45	29 46	00♒47	01 48	02 49	03 50	04 51	05 52	06 53	07 54	08 55	09 56	10♒57
1970	26 28	27 29	28 30	29 31	00♒32	01 33	02 34	03 35	04 36	05 37	06 38	07 39	08 40	09 41	10♒42
1971	26 13	27 14	28 15	29 17	00♒18	01 19	02 20	03 21	04 22	05 23	06 23	07 24	08 26	09 27	10♒28
1972	25 58	27 00	28 01	29 02	00♒03	01 04	02 05	03 06	04 07	05 08	06 09	07 10	08 11	09 12	10♒13
1973	26 45	27 46	28 47	29 48	00♒49	01 50	02 51	03 52	04 53	05 54	06 55	07 56	08 57	09 58	10♒59
1974	26 30	27 31	28 32	29 33	00♒34	01 35	02 36	03 37	04 38	05 39	06 40	07 41	08 42	09 43	10♒44
1975	26 14	27 16	28 17	29 18	00♒19	01 20	02 21	03 22	04 23	05 24	06 25	07 26	08 27	09 28	10♒29
1976	26 00	27 01	28 02	29 03	00♒04	02 05	02 06	03 07	04 08	05 09	06 10	07 11	08 12	09 13	10♒14
1977	26 46	27 47	28 48	29 49	00♒50	01 41	02 42	03 53	04 54	05 55	06 56	07 57	08 58	09 59	11♒00
1978	26 31	27 32	28 33	29 34	00♒35	01 36	02 37	03 38	04 39	05 40	06 41	07 42	08 43	09 44	10♒45
1979	26 16	27 17	28 18	29 19	00♒20	01 21	02 22	03 24	04 25	05 26	06 27	07 28	08 29	09 30	10♒31
1980	26 01	27 02	28 03	29 04	00♒06	01 07	02 08	03 09	04 10	05 11	06 12	07 13	08 14	09 15	10♒16
1981	26 48	27 49	28 50	29 51	00♒52	02 53	02 54	03 55	04 56	05 57	06 58	07 59	08 00	10 01	11♒02
1982	26 33	27 34	28 35	29 36	00♒37	01 38	02 39	03 40	04 41	05 42	06 43	07 44	08 45	09 46	10♒47
1983	26 18	27 19	28 20	29 21	00♒22	01 23	02 24	03 25	04 26	05 27	06 28	07 29	08 30	09 31	10♒32
1984	26 03	27 04	28 05	29 06	00♒07	01 08	02 09	03 11	04 12	05 13	06 14	07 15	08 16	09 17	10♒17
1985	26 49	27 50	28 51	29 52	00♒54	01 55	02 56	03 57	04 58	05 59	07 00	08 01	09 02	10 03	11♒04
1986	26 34	27 36	28 37	29 38	00♒39	01 40	02 41	03 42	04 43	05 44	06 45	07 46	08 47	09 48	10♒49
1987	26 19	27 21	28 22	29 23	00♒24	01 25	02 26	03 27	04 28	05 29	06 30	07 31	08 32	09 33	10♒34
1988	26 05	27 06	28 07	29 08	00♒09	01 10	02 11	03 12	04 13	05 14	06 15	07 16	08 17	09 18	10♒19
1989	26 51	27 52	28 54	29 55	00♒56	01 57	02 58	03 59	05 00	06 01	07 02	08 03	09 04	10 04	11♒05
1990	26 36	27 37	28 38	29 40	00♒41	01 42	02 43	03 44	04 45	05 46	06 47	07 48	08 49	09 50	10♒51
1991	26 22	27 23	28 24	29 25	00♒26	01 27	02 28	03 29	04 30	05 31	06 32	07 33	08 34	09 35	10♒36
1992	26 07	27 08	28 09	29 10	00♒11	01 12	02 13	03 14	04 15	05 16	06 17	07 18	08 19	09 20	10♒21
1993	26 53	27 54	28 55	29 56	00♒58	01 59	03 00	04 01	05 02	06 03	07 04	08 06	09 06	10 07	11♒08
1994	26 39	27 40	28 41	29 42	00♒43	01 44	02 45	03 46	04 47	05 48	06 49	07 50	08 51	09 52	10♒53
1995	26 24	27 25	28 26	29 27	00♒28	01 29	02 30	03 31	04 32	05 33	06 34	07 35	08 36	09 37	10♒38
1996	26 09	27 10	28 11	29 12	00♒13	01 14	02 15	03 16	04 17	05 18	06 19	07 20	08 21	09 22	10♒23
1997	26 55	27 56	28 57	29 58	00♒59	02 00	03 01	04 02	05 03	06 04	07 05	08 06	09 07	10 08	11♒09
1998	26 40	27 41	28 42	29 43	00♒44	01 45	02 46	03 47	04 48	05 49	06 50	07 51	08 52	09 53	10♒54
1999	26 25	27 26	28 27	29 28	00♒29	01 30	02 31	03 32	04 33	05 34	06 35	07 36	08 37	09 38	10♒39
2000	26 10	27 11	28 12	29 13	00♒14	01 15	02 16	03 17	04 18	05 19	05 20	07 21	08 22	09 23	10♒24

Sun

February

	1st	2nd	3rd	4th	5th	6th	7th	8th	9th	10th	11th	12th	13th	14th	15th	16th
1900	11♒43	12 43	13 44	14 45	15 46	16 47	17 48	18 48	19 49	20 50	21 50	22 51	23 52	24 52	25 53	26 53
1901	11♒28	12 29	13 29	14 30	15 31	16 32	17 33	18 34	19 34	20 35	21 36	22 36	23 37	24 38	25 38	26 39
1902	11♒13	12 14	13 14	14 15	15 16	16 17	17 18	18 19	19 19	20 20	21 21	22 22	23 22	24 23	25 23	26 24
1903	10♒58	11 59	12 60	14 00	15 01	16 02	17 03	18 04	19 04	20 05	21 06	22 06	23 07	24 08	25 08	26 09
1904	10♒43	11 44	12 45	13 46	14 46	15 47	16 48	17 49	18 49	19 50	20 51	21 52	22 52	23 53	24 54	25 54
1905	11♒29	12 30	13 31	14 31	15 32	16 33	17 34	18 35	19 35	20 36	21 37	22 38	23 38	24 39	25 39	26 40
1906	11♒14	12 15	13 16	14 17	15 18	16 18	17 19	18 20	19 21	20 21	21 22	22 23	23 23	24 24	25 24	26 25
1907	10♒59	12 00	13 01	14 02	15 03	16 03	17 04	18 05	19 06	20 07	21 07	22 08	23 08	23 09	24 09	25 10
1908	10♒44	11 45	12 46	13 47	14 48	15 49	16 50	17 50	18 51	19 52	20 53	21 53	22 54	23 56	24 55	25 56
1909	11♒31	12 32	13 32	14 33	15 34	16 35	17 36	18 36	19 37	20 38	21 38	22 39	23 40	24 40	25 41	26 42
1910	11♒16	12 17	13 17	14 18	15 19	16 20	17 21	18 22	19 22	20 23	21 24	22 24	23 25	24 26	25 26	26 27
1911	11♒01	12 02	13 03	14 04	15 05	16 05	17 06	18 07	19 08	19 08	20 08	21 09	21 09	22 10	23 10	24 11
1912	10♒47	11 48	12 49	13 49	14 50	15 51	16 52	17 52	18 53	19 54	20 55	21 55	22 56	23 57	24 57	26 59
1913	11♒33	12 34	13 35	14 35	15 36	16 37	27 38	18 39	19 39	20 40	21 41	22 42	23 42	24 43	25 43	26 44
1914	11♒18	12 19	13 20	14 21	15 22	16 22	17 23	18 24	19 45	20 25	21 26	22 27	23 27	24 28	25 29	26 29
1915	11♒03	12 04	13 05	14 06	15 07	16 07	17 08	18 09	19 10	20 10	21 11	21 12	23 13	24 13	25 14	26 15
1916	10♒48	11 49	12 50	13 51	14 52	15 53	16 53	17 54	18 55	19 56	20 57	21 57	22 58	23 59	24 59	25 60
1917	11♒35	12 36	13 36	14 37	15 38	16 39	17 40	18 40	19 41	20 42	21 42	22 43	23 44	24 44	25 45	26 46
1918	11♒20	12 21	13 21	14 22	15 23	16 24	17 25	18 26	19 26	20 27	21 28	22 28	23 29	24 30	25 30	26 31
1919	11♒05	12 06	13 07	14 08	15 08	16 09	17 10	18 11	19 12	20 12	21 13	22 14	23 14	24 15	25 16	16 16
1920	10♒50	11 51	12 52	13 53	14 54	15 55	16 55	17 56	18 57	19 58	20 58	21 59	22 60	24 00	25 01	26 02
1921	11♒36	12 37	13 38	14 39	15 40	16 41	17 41	18 42	19 43	20 44	21 44	22 45	23 46	24 46	25 47	26 48
1922	11♒22	12 23	13 23	14 24	15 25	16 26	17 27	18 27	19 28	20 29	21 30	22 30	23 31	24 31	25 32	26 33
1923	11♒07	12 08	13 08	14 09	15 10	16 11	17 12	18 12	19 13	20 14	21 15	22 15	23 16	24 17	25 17	26 18
1924	10♒52	11 53	12 54	13 55	14 55	15 56	16 57	17 58	18 59	19 59	21 00	22 01	23 01	24 02	25 03	26 03
1925	11♒38	12 39	13 40	14 41	15 42	16 42	17 43	18 44	19 45	20 45	21 46	22 47	23 47	24 48	25 48	26 49
1926	11♒23	12 24	13 25	14 25	15 26	16 27	17 28	18 29	19 29	20 30	21 31	22 32	23 32	24 33	25 34	26 34
1927	11♒08	12 09	13 10	14 11	15 11	16 12	17 13	18 14	19 15	20 15	21 16	22 17	23 17	24 18	25 19	26 19
1928	10♒53	11 54	12 55	13 56	14 57	15 58	16 58	17 59	18 60	20 01	21 01	22 02	23 03	24 03	25 04	26 05
1929	11♒39	12 40	13 41	14 42	15 43	16 44	17 44	18 45	19 46	20 47	21 47	22 48	23 49	24 49	26 50	26 51
1930	11♒25	12 26	13 27	14 27	15 28	16 29	17 30	18 31	19 31	20 32	21 33	22 33	23 34	24 35	25 35	26 36
1931	11♒10	12 11	13 12	14 13	15 13	16 14	17 15	18 16	19 17	20 17	21 18	22 19	23 19	24 20	25 21	26 21
1932	10♒55	11 56	12 57	13 58	14 59	15 60	17 00	18 01	19 02	20 03	21 04	22 04	23 05	24 06	25 06	26 07
1933	11♒42	12 43	13 44	14 44	15 45	16 46	17 47	18 48	19 48	20 49	21 50	22 50	23 51	24 52	25 52	26 53
1934	11♒27	12 28	13 29	14 29	15 30	16 31	17 32	18 33	19 33	20 34	21 35	22 36	23 36	24 37	25 38	26 38
1935	11♒12	12 13	13 14	14 15	15 16	16 16	17 17	18 18	19 19	20 20	21 20	22 21	23 22	24 22	25 23	26 24
1936	10♒58	11 59	12 60	14 00	15 01	16 02	17 03	18 04	19 04	20 05	21 06	22 06	23 07	24 08	25 08	26 09
1937	11♒44	12 45	13 45	14 46	15 47	16 48	17 49	18 49	19 50	20 51	21 52	22 52	23 53	24 54	25 54	26 55
1938	11♒29	12 30	13 31	14 31	15 32	16 33	17 34	18 35	19 35	20 36	21 36	22 38	23 38	24 39	25 39	26 40
1939	11♒14	12 15	13 16	14 16	15 17	16 18	17 19	18 20	19 20	20 21	21 22	22 23	22 23	24 24	25 25	26 25
1940	10♒59	11 60	13 00	14 01	15 02	16 03	17 04	18 05	19 05	20 06	21 07	22 08	23 08	24 09	25 10	26 10
1941	11♒45	12 46	13 47	14 48	15 49	16 49	17 50	18 51	19 52	20 52	21 53	22 54	23 54	24 55	25 56	26 56
1942	11♒30	12 31	13 32	14 33	15 33	16 34	17 35	18 36	19 37	20 37	21 38	22 39	23 39	24 40	25 41	26 41
1943	11♒15	12 16	13 17	14 18	15 19	16 19	17 20	18 21	19 22	20 23	21 23	22 24	23 25	24 25	25 26	26 26
1944	11♒01	12 02	13 02	14 03	15 04	16 05	17 06	18 06	19 07	20 08	21 09	22 09	23 10	24 11	25 11	26 12
1945	11♒47	12 48	13 49	14 50	15 50	16 51	17 52	18 53	29 53	20 54	21 55	22 56	23 56	24 57	25 58	26 58
1946	11♒32	12 33	13 34	14 35	15 36	16 37	17 37	18 38	19 39	20 40	21 40	22 41	23 42	24 43	25 43	26 43
1947	11♒18	12 19	13 19	14 20	15 21	16 22	17 23	18 23	19 24	20 25	21 26	22 26	23 27	24 28	25 28	26 29
1948	11♒03	12 04	13 05	14 05	15 06	16 07	17 08	18 09	19 10	20 10	21 11	22 12	23 12	24 13	25 14	26 14
1949	11♒49	12 50	13 51	14 52	15 53	16 54	17 54	18 55	19 56	20 57	21 57	22 58	23 59	24 59	26 00	27 00
1950	11♒34	12 35	13 35	14 36	15 37	16 38	17 39	18 39	19 40	20 41	21 42	22 42	23 43	24 44	25 44	26 45
1952	11♒19	12 20	13 21	14 21	15 22	16 23	17 24	18 25	19 26	20 26	21 27	22 28	23 28	24 29	26 30	26 30
1952	11♒04	12 05	13 06	14 07	15 08	16 09	17 10	18 10	19 11	20 12	21 12	22 13	23 14	24 14	25 15	26 16
1953	11♒50	12 51	13 52	14 53	15 54	16 55	17 55	18 56	19 57	20 58	21 58	22 59	23 60	25 00	26 01	27 02
1954	11♒36	12 37	13 38	14 38	15 39	16 40	17 41	18 42	19 42	20 43	21 44	22 45	23 45	24 46	25 46	26 47
1955	11♒21	12 22	13 23	14 24	15 25	16 25	17 26	18 27	19 28	20 28	21 29	22 30	23 30	24 31	25 32	26 32
1956	11♒06	12 07	13 08	14 09	15 10	16 10	17 11	18 12	19 13	20 14	21 14	22 15	23 16	24 16	25 17	26 18
1957	11♒53	12 54	13 54	14 55	15 56	16 57	17 58	18 58	19 59	20 60	22 01	23 01	24 02	25 02	26 03	27 04
1958	11♒38	12 39	13 39	14 40	15 41	16 42	17 43	18 43	19 44	20 45	21 46	22 46	23 47	24 47	25 48	26 49
1959	11♒23	12 23	13 24	14 25	15 26	16 27	17 28	18 29	19 29	20 30	21 31	22 32	23 32	24 33	25 34	26 34
1960	11♒09	12 09	13 10	14 11	15 12	16 13	71 14	18 14	19 15	20 16	21 17	22 17	23 18	24 19	25 19	26 20
1961	11♒54	12 55	13 56	14 57	15 58	16 58	17 59	19 00	20 01	21 02	22 02	23 03	24 04	25 04	26 05	27 06
1962	11♒39	12 40	13 41	14 42	15 43	16 44	17 44	18 45	19 46	29 47	21 47	22 48	23 49	24 49	25 50	26 51
1963	11♒24	12 25	13 26	14 27	15 28	16 29	17 29	18 30	19 31	20 32	21 32	22 33	23 34	24 34	25 35	26 36
1964	11♒09	12 10	13 11	14 12	15 13	16 14	17 14	18 15	19 16	21 17	21 18	22 18	23 19	24 20	25 20	26 21
1965	11♒55	12 56	13 57	14 58	15 59	16 60	18 01	19 01	20 02	21 03	22 03	23 04	24 05	25 05	26 06	27 07
1966	11♒41	12 42	13 42	14 43	15 44	16 45	17 46	18 46	19 47	20 48	21 48	22 49	23 50	24 50	25 51	26 52
1967	11♒26	12 27	13 27	14 28	15 29	16 30	17 31	18 32	19 32	20 33	21 34	22 35	23 35	24 36	25 37	26 37
1968	11♒11	12 12	13 13	14 14	15 15	16 16	17 17	18 17	19 18	20 19	21 20	22 20	23 21	24 22	25 22	26 23
1969	11♒58	12 58	13 59	15 00	16 01	17 02	18 02	19 03	20 04	21 05	22 05	23 06	24 07	25 07	26 08	27 09
1970	10♒06	11 04	12 01	12 59	13 56	14 53	15 51	16 48	17 46	18 43	19 40	20 38	21 35	22 32	23 30	24 27
1971	09♒53	10 50	11 48	12 45	13 43	14 40	15 37	16 35	17 32	18 30	19 27	20 24	21 22	22 19	23 16	24 13
1972	11♒14	12 15	13 16	14 16	15 17	16 18	17 19	18 20	19 20	20 21	21 22	22 23	23 23	24 24	25 25	26 25
1973	12♒00	13 01	14 02	15 03	16 04	17 04	18 05	19 06	20 07	21 07	22 08	23 09	24 10	25 10	26 11	27 11
1974	11♒45	12 46	13 47	14 48	15 48	16 49	17 50	18 51	19 52	20 52	21 53	22 54	23 54	25 55	25 56	26 56
1975	11♒30	12 30	13 31	14 32	15 33	16 34	17 35	18 35	19 36	20 37	21 38	22 38	23 39	24 40	25 40	26 41
1976	11♒15	12 16	13 17	14 18	15 19	16 19	17 20	18 21	19 22	20 23	21 23	22 24	23 25	24 25	25 26	26 26
1977	12♒01	13 02	14 03	15 04	16 04	17 05	18 06	19 07	20 08	21 08	22 09	23 10	24 10	25 11	26 12	27 12
1978	11♒46	12 47	13 48	14 49	15 50	16 50	17 51	18 52	19 53	20 54	21 54	22 55	23 56	24 56	25 57	26 58
1979	11♒31	12 32	13 33	14 34	15 35	16 36	17 37	18 37	19 38	20 39	21 40	22 40	23 41	24 41	25 42	26 43
1980	11♒16	12 17	13 18	14 19	15 20	16 21	17 21	18 22	19 23	20 24	21 25	22 25	23 26	24 27	25 27	26 28
1981	12♒03	13 04	14 04	15 05	16 06	17 07	18 08	18 09	20 09	21 10	22 11	23 11	24 12	25 13	26 13	27 14
1982	11♒48	12 49	13 50	14 50	15 51	16 52	17 53	18 54	19 54	20 55	21 56	22 56	23 57	24 58	25 58	26 59
1983	11♒33	12 34	13 35	14 36	15 36	16 37	17 38	18 39	19 40	20 40	21 41	22 42	23 42	24 43	25 44	26 44
1984	11♒18	12 19	13 20	14 21	15 22	16 23	17 24	18 24	19 25	20 26	21 27	22 27	23 28	24 29	25 29	26 30
1985	12♒05	13 05	14 06	15 07	16 08	17 09	18 09	19 10	20 11	21 12	22 12	23 13	24 14	25 14	26 15	27 16
1986	11♒49	12 50	13 51	14 52	15 53	16 54	17 55	18 55	19 56	20 57	21 58	22 58	23 59	24 60	26 00	27 01
1987	11♒35	12 36	13 37	14 38	15 38	16 39	17 40	18 41	19 42	20 42	21 43	22 44	23 44	24 45	25 46	26 46
1988	11♒20	12 21	13 22	14 23	15 24	16 24	17 25	18 26	19 27	20 27	21 28	22 29	23 30	24 30	25 31	26 31
1989	12♒06	13 07	14 08	15 09	16 10	17 11	18 12	19 12	20 13	21 14	22 15	23 15	24 16	2 17	26 17	27 18
1990	11♒52	12 53	13 53	14 54	15 55	16 56	17 57	18 58	19 58	20 59	21 60	23 00	24 01	25 02	26 02	27 03
1991	11♒37	12 38	13 39	14 40	15 40	16 41	17 42	18 43	19 43	20 44	21 45	22 46	23 46	24 47	25 48	26 48
1992	11♒22	12 23	13 24	14 25	15 26	16 27	17 28	18 28	19 29	20 30	21 31	22 31	23 32	24 33	25 33	26 34
1993	12♒09	13 09	14 10	15 11	16 12	17 13	18 13	19 14	20 15	21 16	22 16	23 17	24 18	25 18	26 19	27 20
1994	11♒54	12 54	13 55	14 56	15 57	16 58	17 59	18 59	20 00	21 01	22 02	23 02	24 03	25 04	26 04	27 05
1995	11♒39	12 40	13 41	14 42	15 43	16 43	17 44	18 45	19 46	20 47	21 47	22 48	23 49	24 49	25 50	26 50
1996	11♒24	12 25	13 26	14 27	15 28	16 28	17 29	18 30	19 31	20 31	21 32	22 33	23 34	24 34	25 35	26 35
1997	12♒10	13 11	14 12	15 13	16 13	17 14	18 15	19 16	20 17	21 17	22 18	23 19	24 20	25 20	26 21	27 21
1998	11♒55	12 56	13 57	14 58	15 58	16 59	18 00	19 01	20 02	21 02	22 03	23 04	24 04	25 05	26 06	27 06
1999	11♒40	12 41	13 42	14 42	15 43	16 44	17 45	18 46	19 46	20 47	21 48	22 49	23 49	24 50	25 51	26 51
2000	11♒25	12 26	13 27	14 28	15 29	16 29	17 30	18 31	19 32	20 33	21 34	22 34	23 36	24 36	25 36	26 37

Year	17th	18th	19th	20th	21st	22nd	23rd	24th	25th	26th	27th	28th	29th
1900	27 54	28 54	29 55	00♓55	01 56	02 56	03 57	04 57	05 57	06 58	07 58	08♓58	
1901	27 39	28 40	29 40	00♓41	01 41	02 42	03 42	04 43	05 43	06 43	07 44	08♓44	
1902	27 25	28 25	29 26	00♓26	01 26	02 27	03 27	04 28	05 28	06 28	07 28	08♓29	
1903	27 09	28 10	29 10	00♓11	01 11	02 12	03 12	04 13	05 13	06 13	07 14	08♓14	
1904	26 55	27 55	28 56	29♓56	00 57	02 57	02 58	03 58	04 59	05 59	06 59	07 59	08♓00
1905	27 41	28 41	29 41	00♓42	01 42	02 43	03 43	04 43	05 44	06 44	07 44	08♓45	
1906	27 26	28 26	29 27	00♓27	01 28	02 28	03 28	04 29	05 29	06 30	07 30	08♓30	
1907	27 11	28 12	29 12	00♓13	01 13	02 14	03 14	04 14	05 15	06 15	07 15	08♓15	
1908	26 56	27 57	28 57	29♓58	00 58	01 59	02 59	03 59	05 00	06 00	07 00	08 01	09♓01
1909	27 42	28 43	29 43	00♓44	01 44	02 45	03 45	04 45	05 46	06 46	07 46	08♓47	
1910	27 28	28 28	29 29	00♓29	01 29	02 30	03 30	04 31	05 31	06 31	07 32	08♓32	
1911	27 13	28 13	29 14	00♓14	01 15	02 15	03 16	04 16	05 16	06 17	07 17	08♓17	
1912	26 59	27 59	29 00	00♓00	01 01	02 01	03 02	04 02	05 02	06 03	07 03	08 03	09♓03
1913	27 45	28 46	29 46	00♓46	01 46	02 47	03 47	04 48	05 48	06 48	07 48	08♓49	
1914	27 30	28 30	29 31	00♓31	01 32	02 32	03 33	04 33	05 33	06 34	07 34	08♓34	
1915	27 15	28 16	29 16	00♓17	01 17	02 18	03 18	04 18	05 19	06 19	07 19	08♓20	
1916	27 00	28 01	29 01	00♓02	01 02	01 03	03 03	04 03	05 04	06 04	07 04	08 05	09♓05
1917	27 46	28 47	29 47	00♓48	01 48	02 49	03 49	04 49	05 50	06 50	07 50	08♓51	
1918	27 32	28 32	29 33	00♓33	01 32	02 34	03 34	04 35	05 35	06 35	07 36	08♓36	
1919	27 17	28 17	29 18	00♓18	01 19	02 19	03 19	04 20	05 20	06 21	07 21	08♓21	
1920	27 02	28 03	29 03	00♓04	01 04	02 05	03 05	04 06	05 06	06 06	07 07	08 07	09♓07
1921	27 48	28 49	29 49	00♓50	01 50	02 50	03 51	04 51	05 51	06 52	07 52	08♓52	
1922	27 33	28 34	29 34	00♓35	01 35	02 36	03 36	04 36	05 37	06 37	07 37	08♓38	
1923	27 19	28 19	29 20	00♓20	01 21	02 21	03 22	04 22	05 22	06 23	07 23	08♓23	
1924	27 04	28 04	29 05	00♓05	01 06	02 06	03 07	04 07	05 07	06 08	07 08	08 08	09♓09
1925	27 50	28 50	29 51	00♓51	01 52	02 52	03 52	04 53	05 53	06 54	07 54	08♓54	
1926	27 35	28 35	29 36	00♓36	01 37	02 37	03 38	04 38	05 38	06 39	07 39	08♓39	
1927	27 20	28 20	29 21	00♓21	01 22	02 22	03 23	04 23	05 23	06 24	07 24	08♓24	
1928	27 05	28 06	29 06	00♓07	01 07	02 08	03 08	04 09	05 09	06 09	07 10	08 10	09♓10
1929	27 51	28 52	29 52	00♓53	01 53	02 53	03 54	04 54	05 54	06 55	07 55	08♓55	
1930	27 36	28 37	29 37	00♓38	01 38	02 39	03 39	04 39	05 40	06 40	07 40	08♓41	
1931	27 21	28 22	29 23	00♓24	01 24	02 24	03 25	04 25	06 26	06 26	07 26	08♓27	
1932	27 07	28 08	29 08	00♓09	01 09	02 10	03 10	04 11	05 11	06 11	07 11	08 12	09♓12
1933	27 53	28 54	29 54	00♓55	01 55	02 56	03 56	04 56	05 57	06 57	07 57	08♓58	
1934	27 39	28 39	29 40	00♓40	01 41	02 41	03 42	04 42	05 42	06 43	07 43	08♓43	
1935	27 24	28 25	29 25	00♓26	01 26	02 26	03 27	04 27	05 28	06 28	07 28	08♓28	
1936	27 10	28 10	29 11	00♓11	01 12	02 12	03 13	04 13	05 13	06 14	07 14	08 14	09♓15
1937	27 56	28 56	29 57	00♓57	01 58	02 58	03 58	04 59	05 59	06 59	08 00	09♓00	
1938	27 41	28 41	29 42	00♓42	01 42	02 43	03 43	04 44	05 44	06 44	07 45	08♓45	
1939	27 26	28 26	29 27	00♓27	01 28	02 28	03 29	04 29	05 30	06 30	07 30	08♓30	
1940	27 11	28 11	29 12	00♓12	01 13	02 13	03 14	04 14	05 14	06 15	07 15	08 15	09♓16
1941	27 57	28 57	29 58	00♓58	01 59	02 59	03 59	05 00	06 00	07 01	08 01	09♓01	
1942	27 42	28 42	29 43	00♓43	01 44	02 44	03 45	04 45	05 45	06 46	07 46	08♓46	
1943	27 27	28 28	29 28	00♓29	01 29	02 29	03 30	04 30	05 31	06 31	07 31	08♓31	
1944	27 12	28 13	29 13	00♓14	01 14	02 15	03 15	04 16	05 16	06 17	07 17	08 17	09♓17
1946	27 59	28 59	00 00	01♓00	02 01	03 01	04 02	05 02	06 02	07 03	08 03	09♓03	
1946	27 44	28 44	29 45	00♓45	01 46	02 46	03 47	04 47	05 47	06 48	07 48	08♓48	
1947	27 29	28 30	29 31	00♓31	01 32	02 32	03 32	04 33	05 33	06 34	07 34	08♓34	
1948	27 15	28 16	29 16	00♓17	01 17	02 17	03 18	04 18	05 19	06 19	07 19	08 19	09♓20
1949	28 01	29 01	00♓02	01 02	02 03	03 03	04 04	05 04	06 04	07 05	08 05	09♓05	
1950	27 46	28 46	29 47	00♓47	01 48	02 48	03 49	04 49	05 49	06 50	07 50	08♓50	
1951	27 31	28 31	29 32	00♓32	01 33	02 33	03 34	04 34	05 34	06 35	07 35	08♓35	
1952	27 16	28 17	29 17	00♓18	01 18	02 19	03 19	04 20	05 20	06 20	07 21	08 21	09♓21
1953	28 02	29 03	00 03	01♓04	02 04	03 05	04 05	05 05	06 06	07 06	08 06	09♓07	
1954	27 48	28 48	29 49	00♓49	01 49	02 50	03 50	04 51	05 51	06 51	07 52	08♓52	
1955	27 33	28 33	29 34	00♓35	01 35	02 35	03 36	04 36	05 37	06 37	07 37	08♓38	
1956	27 18	28 19	29 19	00♓20	01 20	02 21	03 21	04 22	05 22	06 22	07 23	08 23	09♓23
1957	28 04	29 05	00 05	01♓06	02 06	03 06	04 07	05 07	06 08	07 08	08 08	09♓09	
1958	27 49	28 50	29 50	00♓51	01 51	02 52	03 52	04 53	05 53	06 53	07 54	08♓54	
1959	27 36	28 35	29 36	00♓36	01 37	02 37	03 37	04 38	05 38	06 39	07 39	08♓39	
1960	28 21	29 21	00 22	01♓22	02 23	03 23	04 24	05 24	06 24	07 25	08 25	09♓25	09♓25
1961	28 06	29 07	00 07	01 08	02 08	03 09	04 09	06 09	06 10	07 10	08 10	09♓11	
1962	27 51	28 52	29♓52	00♓53	01 53	02 54	03 54	04 54	05 55	06 55	07 55	08♓55	
1963	27 36	28 37	29 37	00♓38	01 38	02 39	03 39	04 40	05 40	06 40	07 41	08♓41	
1964	27 21	28 22	29 23	00♓23	01 24	02 24	03 25	04 25	05 25	06 26	07 26	08 26	09♓26
1965	28 07	29 08	00 08	01♓09	02 09	03 09	04 10	05 10	06 11	07 11	08 11	09♓11	
1966	27 52	28 53	29 53	00♓54	01 54	02 55	03 55	04 56	05 56	06 56	07 57	08♓57	
1967	27 38	28 38	29 39	00♓39	01 40	02 40	03 41	04 41	05 41	06 42	07 42	08♓42	
1968	27 23	28 24	29 24	00♓25	01 25	02 26	03 26	04 27	05 27	06 27	07 28	08 28	09♓28
1969	28 09	29 10	00 10	01♓11	02 11	03 12	04 12	05 13	06 13	07 13	08 13	09♓14	
1970	27 55	28 56	29 56	00♓57	01 57	02 57	03 58	04 58	05 58	06 59	07 59	08♓59	
1971	27 40	28 41	29 42	00♓42	01 43	02 43	03 43	04 44	05 44	06 45	07 45	08♓45	
1972	27 26	28 27	29 27	00♓28	01 28	02 29	03 29	04 29	05 30	06 30	07 30	08 31	09♓31
1973	28 12	29 12	00♓13	01 13	02 14	03 14	04 15	05 15	06 15	07 16	08 16	09♓16	
1974	27 57	28 57	29 58	00♓58	01 59	02 59	04 00	05 00	06 01	07 01	08 01	09♓02	
1975	27 42	28 42	29 43	00♓43	01 44	02 44	03 45	04 45	05 45	06 46	07 46	08♓46	
1976	27 27	28 28	29 28	00♓29	01 29	02 29	03 30	04 30	05 31	06 31	07 31	08 32	09♓32
1977	28 13	29 13	00 14	01♓14	02 15	03 15	04 16	05 16	06 16	07 17	08 17	09♓17	
1978	27 58	28 59	29 59	01♓00	02 00	03 00	04 01	05 01	06 02	07 02	08 02	09♓02	
1979	27 43	28 44	29 44	00♓45	01 45	02 46	03 46	04 57	05 47	06 47	07 48	08♓48	
1980	27 29	28 29	29 30	00♓30	01 31	02 31	03 32	04 32	05 32	06 33	07 33	08 33	09♓34
1981	28 14	29 15	00 15	01 16	02 16	03 17	04 17	05 18	06 18	07 18	08 18	09 19	
1982	27 59	29 00	00 01	01 01	02 02	03 02	04 03	05 03	06 03	07 04	08 04	09 04	
1983	27 45	28 46	29 46	00♓47	01 47	02 48	03 48	04 48	05 49	06 49	07 49	08♓50	
1984	27 31	28 31	29 32	00♓32	01 33	02 33	03 33	04 34	05 34	06 35	07 35	08 35	09♓35
1985	28 16	29 17	00 17	01♓18	02 18	03 19	04 19	05 20	06 20	07 20	08 21	09♓21	
1986	28 02	29 02	00 03	01♓03	02 04	03 04	04 04	05 05	06 05	07 05	08 06	09♓06	
1987	27 47	28 47	29 48	00♓48	01 49	02 49	03 50	04 50	05 51	06 51	07 51	08♓52	
1988	27 32	28 33	29 33	00♓34	01 34	02 35	03 35	04 36	05 36	06 36	07 37	08 37	09♓37
1989	28 18	29 19	00 19	01♓20	02 20	03 21	04 21	05 21	06 22	07 22	08 22	09♓23	
1990	28 03	29 04	00 04	01♓05	02 05	03 06	04 06	05 07	06 07	07 07	08 08	09♓08	
1991	27 49	28 49	29 50	00♓50	01 51	02 51	03 52	04 52	05 53	06 53	07 53	08♓54	
1992	27 34	28 35	29 35	00♓36	01 36	02 37	03 37	04 38	05 38	06 38	07 39	08 39	09♓39
1993	28 20	29 21	00 21	01♓22	02 22	03 23	04 23	05 23	06 24	07 24	08 25	09♓25	
1994	28 06	29 06	00 07	01♓07	02 08	03 08	04 08	05 09	06 09	07 09	08 10	09♓10	
1995	27 51	28 51	29 52	00♓52	01 53	02 53	03 54	04 54	05 55	06 55	07 55	08♓56	
1996	27 36	28 37	29 37	00♓38	01 38	02 39	03 39	04 40	05 40	06 40	07 41	08 41	09♓41
1997	28 22	29 23	00 23	01♓23	02 24	03 24	04 25	05 25	06 25	07 26	08 26	09♓26	
1998	28 07	29 07	00 08	01♓08	02 09	03 09	04 10	05 10	06 10	07 11	08 11	09♓11	
1999	27 52	28 52	29 53	00♓54	01 54	02 54	03 55	04 55	05 56	06 56	07 56	08♓57	
2000	27 37	28 38	29 38	00♓39	01 39	02 40	03 40	04 41	05 41	06 41	07 42	08 42	09♓42

Sun

March

	1st	2nd	3rd	4th	5th	6th	7th	8th	9th	10th	11th	12th	13th	14th	15th	16th
1900	09 ♓ 58	10 59	11 59	12 59	13 59	14 59	15 59	16 59	17 59	18 59	19 59	20 59	21 59	22 58	23 58	24 58
1901	09 ♓ 44	10 44	11 44	12 44	13 45	14 45	15 45	16 45	17 44	18 44	19 44	20 44	21 44	22 44	23 44	24 44
1902	09 ♓ 29	10 29	11 29	12 29	13 30	14 30	15 30	16 30	17 30	18 30	19 30	20 30	21 30	22 29	23 29	24 29
1903	09 ♓ 14	10 14	11 15	12 15	13 15	14 15	15 16	16 15	17 15	18 15	19 15	20 15	21 15	22 14	23 14	24 14
1904	09 ♓ 60	11 00	12 00	13 00	14 00	15 00	16 00	17 00	18 00	19 00	20 00	21 00	21 60	22 60	23 60	24 60
1905	09 ♓ 45	10 45	11 45	12 45	13 46	14 46	15 46	16 46	17 46	18 46	19 46	20 45	21 45	22 45	23 45	24 45
1906	09 ♓ 30	10 31	11 31	12 31	13 31	14 31	15 31	16 31	17 31	18 31	19 31	20 31	21 30	22 30	23 30	24 30
1907	09 ♓ 16	10 16	11 16	12 16	13 16	14 16	15 16	16 16	17 16	18 16	19 16	20 16	21 16	22 16	23 16	24 16
1908	10 ♓ 01	11 01	12 02	13 02	14 02	15 02	16 02	17 02	18 02	19 02	20 02	21 02	22 02	23 01	24 01	25 01
1909	09 ♓ 47	10 47	11 47	12 47	13 47	14 47	15 47	16 47	17 47	18 47	19 47	20 47	21 47	22 47	23 47	24 46
1910	09 ♓ 32	10 32	11 32	12 32	13 33	14 33	15 33	16 33	17 33	18 33	19 33	20 33	21 32	22 32	23 32	24 32
1911	09 ♓ 18	10 18	11 18	12 18	13 18	14 18	15 18	16 18	17 18	18 18	19 18	20 18	21 18	22 18	23 18	24 17
1912	10 ♓ 04	11 04	12 04	13 04	14 04	15 04	16 04	17 04	18 04	19 04	20 04	21 04	22 04	23 03	24 03	25 03
1913	09 ♓ 49	10 49	11 49	12 49	13 50	14 50	15 50	16 50	17 50	18 50	19 50	20 49	21 49	22 49	23 49	24 49
1914	09 ♓ 34	10 35	11 35	12 35	13 35	14 35	15 35	16 35	17 35	18 35	19 35	20 35	21 35	22 34	23 34	24 34
1915	09 ♓ 20	10 20	11 20	12 20	13 20	14 20	15 21	16 21	17 21	18 21	19 20	20 20	21 20	22 20	23 20	24 20
1916	10 ♓ 05	11 05	12 05	13 06	14 06	15 06	16 06	17 06	18 06	19 06	20 06	21 06	22 06	23 05	24 05	25 05
1917	09 ♓ 51	10 51	11 51	12 51	13 51	14 51	15 51	16 51	17 51	18 51	19 51	20 51	21 51	22 51	23 50	24 50
1918	09 ♓ 36	10 36	11 36	12 36	13 36	14 37	15 37	16 37	17 37	18 37	19 37	20 37	21 36	22 36	23 36	24 36
1919	09 ♓ 21	10 22	22 22	12 22	13 22	14 22	15 22	16 22	17 22	18 22	19 22	20 22	21 22	22 22	23 22	24 21
1920	10 ♓ 07	11 08	12 08	13 08	14 08	15 08	16 08	17 08	18 08	19 08	20 08	21 08	22 07	23 07	24 07	25 07
1921	09 ♓ 52	10 53	11 53	12 53	13 53	14 53	15 53	16 53	17 53	18 53	19 53	20 53	21 53	22 53	23 52	24 52
1922	09 ♓ 38	10 38	11 38	12 38	13 38	14 39	15 39	16 39	17 39	18 39	19 39	20 38	21 38	22 38	23 38	24 37
1923	09 ♓ 23	10 24	11 24	12 24	13 24	14 24	15 24	16 24	17 24	18 24	19 24	20 24	21 24	22 24	23 23	24 23
1924	10 ♓ 09	11 09	12 09	13 09	14 09	15 10	16 10	17 10	18 10	19 10	20 09	21 09	22 09	23 09	24 09	25 09
1925	09 ♓ 54	10 55	11 55	12 55	13 55	14 55	15 55	16 55	17 55	18 55	19 55	20 55	21 54	22 54	23 54	24 54
1926	09 ♓ 39	10 40	11 40	12 40	13 40	14 40	15 40	16 40	17 40	18 40	19 40	20 40	21 40	22 40	23 40	24 39
1927	09 ♓ 24	10 25	11 25	12 25	13 25	14 25	15 25	16 25	17 25	18 25	19 25	20 25	21 25	22 25	23 25	24 25
1928	10 ♓ 10	11 11	12 11	13 11	14 11	15 11	16 11	17 11	18 11	19 11	20 11	21 11	22 10	23 10	24 20	25 20
1929	09 ♓ 55	10 56	11 56	12 56	13 56	14 56	15 56	16 56	17 56	18 56	19 56	20 56	21 56	22 56	23 56	24 55
1930	09 ♓ 41	10 41	11 41	12 42	13 42	14 42	15 42	16 42	17 42	18 42	19 42	20 42	21 41	22 41	23 41	24 41
1931	09 ♓ 27	10 27	11 27	12 27	13 27	14 27	15 27	16 27	17 27	18 27	19 27	20 27	21 27	22 27	23 27	24 26
1932	10 ♓ 12	11 12	12 13	13 13	14 13	15 13	16 13	17 13	18 13	19 13	20 13	21 13	22 13	23 13	24 12	25 12
1933	09 ♓ 58	10 58	11 58	12 59	13 59	14 59	15 59	16 59	17 59	18 59	19 59	20 58	21 58	22 58	23 59	24 57
1934	09 ♓ 43	10 43	11 44	12 44	13 44	14 44	15 44	16 44	17 44	18 44	19 44	20 44	21 44	22 43	23 43	24 43
1935	09 ♓ 29	10 29	11 29	12 29	13 29	14 29	15 29	16 29	17 29	18 29	19 29	20 29	21 30	22 30	23 30	24 30
1936	10 ♓ 15	11 15	12 15	13 15	14 15	15 15	16 15	17 15	18 15	19 15	20 15	21 15	22 15	23 15	24 14	25 14
1937	10 ♓ 00	11 00	12 00	13 00	14 00	15 01	16 01	17 01	18 01	19 01	20 01	21 01	22 00	23 00	24 00	25 00
1938	09 ♓ 45	10 45	11 46	12 46	13 46	14 46	15 46	16 46	17 46	18 46	19 46	20 46	21 46	22 46	23 45	24 45
1939	09 ♓ 31	10 31	11 31	12 31	13 31	14 31	15 31	16 31	17 31	18 31	19 31	20 31	21 31	22 31	23 31	24 31
1940	10 ♓ 16	11 16	12 16	13 16	14 16	15 17	16 17	17 17	18 17	19 17	20 17	21 16	22 16	23 16	24 16	25 16
1941	10 ♓ 01	11 02	12 02	13 02	14 02	15 02	16 02	17 02	18 02	19 02	20 02	21 02	22 02	23 01	24 01	25 01
1942	09 ♓ 46	10 47	11 47	12 47	13 47	14 47	15 47	16 47	17 47	18 47	19 47	29 47	21 27	22 27	23 47	24 46
1943	09 ♓ 32	10 32	11 32	12 32	13 32	14 32	15 33	16 33	17 33	18 33	19 33	29 33	21 32	22 32	23 32	24 32
1944	10 ♓ 28	11 18	12 18	13 18	14 18	15 18	16 18	17 18	18 18	19 18	29 18	21 18	22 18	23 18	24 17	25 27
1945	10 ♓ 03	11 03	12 04	13 04	14 04	15 04	16 04	17 04	18 04	19 04	20 04	21 04	22 04	23 04	24 04	25 03
1946	09 ♓ 49	10 49	11 49	12 49	13 49	14 49	15 49	16 50	17 50	18 49	19 49	20 49	21 49	22 49	23 49	24 48
1947	09 ♓ 34	10 35	11 35	12 35	13 35	14 35	15 35	16 35	17 35	18 35	19 35	20 35	21 35	22 35	23 34	24 34
1948	10 ♓ 20	11 20	12 20	13 20	14 20	15 21	16 21	17 21	18 21	19 21	20 21	21 20	22 20	23 20	24 20	25 20
1949	10 ♓ 06	11 06	12 06	13 06	14 06	15 06	16 06	17 06	18 06	19 06	20 06	21 06	22 06	23 06	24 06	25 05
1950	09 ♓ 50	10 51	11 51	12 51	13 51	14 51	15 51	16 51	17 51	18 51	19 51	20 51	21 51	22 51	23 50	24 50
1951	09 ♓ 35	10 36	11 37	12 36	13 36	14 36	15 36	16 37	17 17	18 17	19 37	20 36	21 36	22 36	23 36	24 36
1952	10 ♓ 22	11 22	12 22	13 22	14 22	15 22	16 22	17 22	18 22	19 22	20 22	21 22	22 22	23 22	24 21	24 21
1953	10 ♓ 97	11 07	12 07	13 07	14 07	15 07	16 07	17 07	18 07	19 07	20 07	21 07	22 07	23 07	24 07	25 07
1954	09 ♓ 52	10 52	11 53	12 53	13 53	14 53	15 53	16 53	17 53	18 53	19 53	20 53	21 53	22 53	23 52	24 52
1955	09 ♓ 38	10 38	11 38	12 38	13 39	14 39	15 39	16 39	17 39	18 39	19 39	20 39	21 38	22 38	23 38	24 38
1956	10 ♓ 23	11 24	12 24	13 24	14 24	15 24	16 25	17 24	18 24	19 24	29 24	21 24	22 24	23 24	24 24	25 23
1957	10 ♓ 09	11 09	12 09	13 09	14 10	15 10	16 10	17 10	18 10	19 10	20 10	21 10	22 09	23 09	24 09	25 09
1958	09 ♓ 54	10 54	11 55	12 55	13 55	14 55	15 55	16 55	17 55	18 55	19 55	20 55	21 55	22 54	23 54	25 54
1959	09 ♓ 39	10 40	11 40	12 40	13 40	14 40	15 40	16 40	17 40	18 40	19 40	20 40	21 40	22 40	23 40	25 40
1960	10 ♓ 26	11 26	12 26	13 26	14 26	15 26	16 26	17 26	18 26	19 26	20 26	21 26	22 26	23 26	24 25	25 25
1961	10 ♓ 11	11 11	12 11	13 11	14 11	16 11	16 11	17 11	18 11	19 11	20 11	21 11	22 11	23 11	24 11	25 11
1962	09 ♓ 56	10 56	11 56	12 56	13 56	14 57	15 57	16 57	17 57	18 57	19 57	20 57	21 57	22 56	23 56	24 56
1963	09 ♓ 41	10 42	11 42	12 42	13 42	14 42	15 42	16 42	17 42	18 42	19 42	20 42	21 42	22 42	23 41	24 41
1964	10 ♓ 27	11 27	12 27	13 27	14 27	15 27	16 27	17 27	18 27	19 27	20 27	21 27	22 27	23 27	24 27	25 26
1965	10 ♓ 12	11 12	12 12	13 12	14 12	15 12	16 13	17 13	18 13	19 13	20 12	21 12	22 12	23 12	24 12	25 12
1966	09 ♓ 57	10 57	11 58	12 58	13 58	14 58	15 58	16 58	17 58	18 58	19 58	20 58	21 58	22 57	23 57	24 57
1967	09 ♓ 42	10 43	11 43	12 43	13 43	14 43	15 43	16 43	17 43	18 43	19 43	20 43	31 43	22 43	23 43	24 43
1968	10 ♓ 29	12 29	12 29	13 29	14 29	15 29	15 29	17 29	18 29	19 29	20 29	21 29	22 29	23 29	24 28	25 28
1969	10 ♓ 14	11 14	12 14	13 14	14 15	15 15	16 15	17 15	18 15	19 15	20 15	21 14	22 14	23 14	24 14	25 14
1970	10 ♓ 00	11 00	12 00	13 00	14 00	15 00	16 00	17 01	18 01	19 01	20 00	21 00	22 00	23 00	24 00	25 00
1971	09 ♓ 46	10 46	11 46	12 46	13 46	14 46	15 46	16 46	17 46	18 46	19 46	20 46	21 46	22 46	23 46	24 45
1972	10 ♓ 31	11 31	12 31	13 32	14 32	15 32	16 32	17 32	18 32	19 32	20 32	21 32	22 32	23 32	24 31	25 31
1973	10 ♓ 16	11 17	12 17	13 17	14 17	15 17	16 17	17 17	18 17	19 17	20 17	21 17	22 17	23 17	24 17	25 16
1974	10 ♓ 02	11 02	12 02	13 02	14 02	15 03	16 03	17 03	18 03	19 03	20 02	21 02	22 02	23 02	24 02	25 02
1975	09 ♓ 46	10 47	11 47	12 47	13 47	14 47	15 47	15 47	17 47	18 47	19 47	20 47	21 47	22 47	23 47	24 47
1976	10 ♓ 32	11 32	12 32	13 33	14 33	15 33	16 33	17 33	18 33	19 33	20 33	21 33	22 32	23 33	24 32	25 32
1977	10 ♓ 18	11 18	12 18	13 18	14 18	15 18	16 18	17 18	18 18	19 18	20 18	21 18	22 18	23 18	24 17	25 17
1978	10 ♓ 93	11 03	12 03	13 03	14 03	15 03	16 03	17 03	18 03	19 03	20 03	21 03	22 03	23 03	24 03	25 03
1979	09 ♓ 48	10 49	11 49	12 49	13 29	14 29	15 29	16 49	17 49	18 49	19 49	20 49	21 49	22 49	23 49	24 48
1980	10 ♓ 34	11 34	12 34	13 34	14 34	15 34	16 34	17 34	18 34	19 34	20 34	21 34	22 34	23 34	24 34	25 33
1981	10 ♓ 19	11 19	12 19	13 20	14 20	15 20	16 20	17 20	18 20	19 20	20 20	21 20	22 20	23 19	24 19	25 19
1982	10 ♓ 04	11 05	12 05	13 05	14 05	15 05	16 05	17 05	18 05	19 05	20 05	21 05	22 05	23 05	24 04	25 04
1983	09 ♓ 50	10 50	11 50	12 50	13 50	14 51	15 51	16 51	17 51	18 51	19 51	20 51	21 50	22 50	23 50	24 50
1984	10 ♓ 36	11 36	12 36	13 36	14 36	15 37	16 37	17 37	18 37	19 37	20 37	21 36	22 36	23 36	24 36	25 36
1985	10 ♓ 21	11 21	12 22	13 22	14 22	15 22	16 22	17 22	18 22	19 22	20 22	21 22	22 21	23 21	24 21	25 21
1986	10 ♓ 06	11 06	12 07	13 07	14 07	15 07	16 07	17 07	18 07	19 07	20 07	21 07	22 07	23 07	24 07	25 06
1987	09 ♓ 50	10 52	11 52	12 52	13 53	14 53	15 53	16 53	17 53	18 53	19 53	20 53	21 53	22 53	23 52	24 52
1988	10 ♓ 37	11 37	12 38	13 38	14 38	15 38	16 38	17 38	18 38	19 38	20 38	21 38	22 38	23 38	24 38	25 37
1989	10 ♓ 23	11 23	12 23	13 23	14 24	15 24	16 [illegible]	17 [illegible]	18 24	19 24	20 24	21 24	22 23	23 23	24 23	25 23
1990	10 ♓ 08	11 09	12 09	13 09	14 09	15 09	16 09	17 09	18 09	19 09	20 09	21 09	22 09	23 09	24 09	25 08
1991	09 ♓ 54	10 54	11 54	12 54	13 54	14 54	15 55	16 55	17 55	18 55	19 55	20 54	21 54	22 54	23 54	24 54
1992	10 ♓ 40	11 40	12 40	13 40	14 40	15 40	16 40	17 40	18 41	19 40	20 40	21 40	22 40	23 40	24 40	25 40
1993	10 ♓ 25	11 25	12 25	13 26	14 26	15 26	16 26	17 26	18 26	19 26	20 26	21 25	22 25	23 25	24 25	25 25
1994	10 ♓ 10	11 10	12 11	13 11	14 11	15 11	16 11	17 11	18 11	19 11	20 11	21 11	22 11	23 11	24 11	25 10
1995	09 ♓ 56	10 56	11 56	12 56	13 57	14 57	15 57	16 57	17 57	18 57	19 57	20 57	21 57	22 57	23 57	24 57
1996	10 ♓ 42	11 42	12 42	13 42	14 42	15 42	16 42	17 42	18 42	19 42	20 42	21 42	22 42	23 42	24 41	25 41
1997	10 ♓ 27	11 27	12 27	13 27	14 27	15 27	16 27	17 27	18 28	19 28	20 27	21 27	22 27	23 27	24 27	25 27
1998	10 ♓ 12	11 12	12 12	13 12	14 13	15 13	16 13	17 13	18 13	19 13	20 13	21 13	22 12	23 12	24 12	25 12
1999	99 ♓ 87	10 57	11 57	12 57	13 47	14 58	15 58	16 58	17 58	18 58	19 58	20 58	21 57	22 57	23 57	24 57
2000	10 ♓ 42	11 43	12 43	13 43	14 43	15 43	16 43	17 43	18 43	19 43	20 43	21 43	22 43	23 43	24 43	25 42

	17th	18th	19th	20th	21st	22nd	23rd	24th	25th	26th	27th	28th	29th	30th	31st
1900	25 58	26 57	27 57	28 56	29 56	00♈55	01 55	02 54	03 54	04 53	05 53	06 52	07 52	08 51	09♈50
1901	15 43	26 43	27 42	28 42	29 42	00♈41	01 41	02 40	08 40	04 39	05 38	06 38	07 37	08 36	09♈36
1902	25 29	26 28	27 28	28 28	29 27	00♈27	01 26	02 26	03 25	04 24	05 24	06 23	07 22	08 22	09♈21
1903	15 14	26 13	27 13	28 13	29 12	00♈12	01 11	02 11	03 10	04 10	05 09	06 09	07 08	08 07	09♈07
1904	25 59	26 59	27 58	28 58	29 58	00♈57	01 57	02 56	03 56	04 55	05 54	06 54	07 53	08 52	09♈51
1905	25 44	26 44	27 44	28 43	29 43	00♈42	02 42	02 41	03 41	04 40	05 39	06 39	07 38	08 37	09♈37
1906	25 29	26 29	27 29	28 28	29 28	00♈28	01 27	02 27	03 26	04 26	05 25	06 24	07 24	08 23	99♈22
1907	25 15	26 15	27 15	28 14	29 14	00♈14	01 13	02 13	03 12	04 11	05 11	06 10	07 09	08 08	09♈08
1908	26 00	27 00	28 00	28 59	29 59	00♈48	01 58	02 57	03 57	04 56	05 56	06 55	07 54	08 54	09♈53
1909	25 46	26 46	27 45	28 45	29 45	00♈44	01 44	02 43	03 43	04 42	05 41	06 41	07 40	08 39	09♈39
1910	25 32	26 31	27 31	28 31	29 30	00♈30	01 29	02 29	03 28	04 27	05 27	06 26	07 25	08 25	09♈24
1911	25 17	26 17	27 16	28 16	29 16	00♈15	01 15	02 14	03 14	04 13	05 12	06 12	07 11	08 11	09♈10
1912	26 03	27 02	28 02	29 02	00♈01	01 01	02 00	03 00	03 49	04 59	05 58	06 57	07 57	08 56	09♈55
1913	25 48	26 48	27 48	28 47	29 47	00♈46	01 46	02 45	03 45	04 44	05 43	06 43	07 42	08 41	09♈41
1914	25 34	26 33	27 33	28 33	29 32	00♈32	01 31	02 31	03 30	04 30	05 29	06 29	07 28	08 27	09♈26
1915	25 19	26 19	27 19	28 19	29 18	00♈18	01 17	02 17	03 16	04 16	05 15	06 14	07 14	08 13	09♈12
1916	26 05	27 04	28 04	29 03	00♈03	01 03	02 02	03 02	04 01	05 00	06 00	06 59	07 58	08 58	09♈57
1917	25 50	26 50	27 49	28 49	29 49	00♈48	01 48	02 47	03 47	04 46	05 45	06 45	07 44	88 43	09♈43
1918	25 36	26 35	27 35	28 35	29 34	00♈34	01 33	02 33	03 32	04 32	05 31	06 30	07 30	08 29	09♈28
1919	25 21	26 21	27 20	28 20	29 20	00♈19	01 19	02 18	03 18	04 17	05 16	06 16	07 15	08 14	09♈14
1920	26 06	27 06	28 06	29 05	00♈05	01 05	02 04	03 04	04 03	05 02	06 02	07 01	08 00	09 00	09♈59
1921	25 52	26 52	27 51	28 51	29 50	00♈50	01 49	02 49	03 48	04 48	05 47	06 46	07 46	08 45	09♈44
1922	25 37	26 37	27 36	28 36	29 36	00♈35	01 35	02 34	03 34	04 33	05 33	06 32	07 31	08 31	09♈30
1923	25 23	26 23	27 22	28 22	29 22	00 21	01 21	02 20	03 20	04 19	05 19	06 18	07 17	08 16	09♈16
1924	26 08	27 08	28 07	29 07	00♈07	01 06	02 06	03 05	04 05	05 04	06 03	07 03	08 02	09 01	10♈00
1925	25 53	26 53	27 53	28 52	29 52	00♈52	01 51	02 51	03 50	04 50	05 49	06 48	07 48	08 47	09♈46
1926	25 39	26 39	27 38	28 38	29 38	00♈37	01 37	02 36	03 36	04 35	05 34	06 34	07 33	08 32	09♈32
1927	25 24	26 24	27 24	28 23	29 23	00♈22	01 22	02 21	03 31	04 20	05 20	06 19	07 18	08 18	09♈17
1928	26 10	27 09	28 09	29 09	00 08	01 08	02 07	03 07	04 06	05 06	06 05	07 04	08 04	09 03	10♈10
1929	25 55	26 55	27 54	28 54	29 54	00♈53	01 53	02 52	03 52	04 51	05 50	06 50	07 49	08 48	09♈47
1930	25 40	26 40	27 40	28 39	29 39	00♈38	01 38	02 38	03 37	04 36	05 36	06 35	07 35	08 34	09♈33
1931	25 26	26 26	27 26	28 24	28 26	00♈25	01 24	02 24	03 23	04 23	05 22	06 21	07 21	08 20	09♈19
1932	26 12	26 12	27 11	28 11	99♈19	91 19	92 98	93 98	94 97	95 96	95 96	96 95	97 95	98 95	19♈94
1933	25 57	26 57	27 57	28 56	29 56	00♈55	01 55	02 54	03 54	04 53	05 53	06 52	07 51	08 51	09♈50
1934	25 43	26 43	27 42	28 42	29 41	00♈41	01 41	02 40	03 40	04 39	05 38	06 38	07 37	08 36	09♈35
1935	25 28	26 28	27 28	28 27	29 27	00♈27	01 26	02 26	03 25	04 24	05 24	06 23	07 23	08 22	09♈21
1936	26 14	27 14	28 13	29 13	00♈13	01 12	02 12	03 11	04 11	05 10	06 09	07 09	08 08	09 07	10♈07
1937	26 00	26 59	27 59	28 59	29 58	00♈58	01 57	02 57	03 56	04 55	05 55	06 54	07 53	08 53	09♈52
1938	25 45	26 44	27 44	28 44	29 43	00♈43	01 42	02 42	03 41	04 41	05 40	06 40	07 39	08 38	09♈38
1939	25 30	26 30	27 30	28 29	29 92	00♈29	01 28	02 28	03 27	04 27	05 26	06 25	07 25	08 24	09♈23
1940	26 15	27 15	28 15	29 14	00♈14	01 13	02 13	03 12	04 12	05 11	06 11	07 10	08 09	09 09	10♈08
1941	26 01	27 00	28 00	29 00	29 59	00♈59	01 58	02 58	03 57	04 57	05 56	06 55	07 55	08 54	09♈54
1942	25 46	26 46	27 45	28 45	29 45	00♈44	01 44	02 43	03 43	04 42	05 42	06 41	07 40	08 40	09♈39
1943	25 32	26 31	27 31	28 31	29 30	00♈30	01 29	02 29	03 28	04 28	05 27	06 26	07 26	08 25	09♈24
1944	26 17	27 16	28 16	29 16	00♈15	01 15	02 14	03 14	04 13	05 13	06 12	07 12	08 11	09 10	10♈10
1945	26 03	27 03	28 02	29 02	00♈01	01 01	02 00	03 00	03 59	04 59	05 58	06 57	07 57	08 56	09♈55
1946	25 48	26 48	27 48	28 47	29 47	00♈46	01 46	02 45	03 45	04 44	05 44	06 43	07 42	08 42	09♈41
1947	25 34	26 34	27 33	28 33	29 33	00♈32	01 32	02 31	03 31	04 30	05 30	06 29	07 28	08 28	09♈27
1948	26 19	27 19	28 19	29 18	00♈18	01 17	02 17	03 16	04 16	05 15	06 15	07 14	08 13	09 13	10♈12
1949	26 05	27 05	28 04	29 04	00♈03	01 03	02 03	03 02	04 01	05 01	06 00	07 00	07 59	08 58	09♈58
1950	25 50	26 50	27 49	28 49	29 49	00♈48	01 48	02 47	03 47	04 46	05 46	06 45	07 44	08 44	09♈43
1951	15 36	26 35	27 35	28 35	29 34	00♈34	01 33	02 33	03 32	04 32	05 31	06 30	07 30	08 29	09♈28
1952	26 21	27 20	28 20	29 20	00♈19	01 29	02 18	03 18	04 17	05 17	06 16	07 16	08 15	09 14	10♈13
1953	26 06	27 06	28 06	29 05	00♈05	01 05	02 04	03 04	04 03	05 02	06 02	07 01	08 00	09 00	09♈59
1954	25 52	26 52	27 51	28 51	29 50	00♈50	01 49	02 29	03 48	04 48	05 47	06 47	07 46	08 45	09♈44
1955	25 38	26 37	27 37	28 37	29 36	00♈36	01 35	02 35	03 34	04 34	05 33	06 33	07 32	08 31	09♈31
1956	26 23	27 23	28 22	29 22	00♈22	01 21	02 21	03 20	04 20	05 29	06 18	07 18	08 17	09 16	10♈15
1957	26 08	27 08	28 08	29 07	00♈07	01 06	02 06	03 05	04 05	05 04	06 04	07 03	08 02	09 02	10♈01
1958	25 54	26 53	27 53	29 53	29♈52	00 52	01 51	02 51	03 50	04 50	05 49	06 49	07 48	08 47	09♈47
1959	25 39	26 39	27 39	28 38	29 38	00♈37	01 37	02 36	03 36	04 35	05 35	06 34	07 33	08 33	09♈32
1960	26 25	27 25	28 24	29 24	00♈23	01 23	02 22	03 22	04 21	05 21	06 20	07 20	08 19	09 18	10♈18
1961	26 10	27 10	28 10	29 09	00♈09	01 09	02 08	03 08	04 07	05 06	06 06	07 05	08 04	09 04	10♈03
1962	25 56	26 55	27 55	28 55	29 54	00♈54	01 53	02 53	03 52	04 52	05 51	06 50	07 50	08 49	09♈48
1963	25 41	26 41	27 40	28 40	29 40	00♈39	01 39	02 38	03 38	04 37	05 37	06 36	07 36	08 35	09♈34
1964	26 26	27 26	28 26	29 25	00♈25	01 24	02 24	03 23	04 23	06 22	06 22	07 21	08 20	09 19	10♈19
1965	26 11	27 11	28 11	29 10	00♈10	01 09	02 09	03 08	04 08	05 07	06 07	07 06	08 05	09 05	10♈04
1966	25 57	26 56	27 56	28 56	29 55	00♈55	01 54	02 54	03 53	04 53	05 52	06 52	07 51	08 50	09♈50
1967	25 42	26 42	27 42	28 41	29 41	00♈41	01 40	02 40	03 39	04 39	05 38	06 37	07 37	08 36	09♈35
1968	26 28	27 27	28 27	29 27	00♈26	01 26	02 26	03 25	04 24	05 24	06 23	07 23	08 22	09 21	10♈21
1969	26 13	27 13	28 13	29 12	00♈12	01 12	02 11	03 11	04 10	05 10	06 09	07 08	08 08	09 07	10♈06
1970	25 59	26 59	27 59	28 58	29 58	00♈58	01 57	02 57	03 56	04 55	05 55	06 54	07 54	08 53	09♈52
1971	25 45	26 45	27 45	28 44	29 44	00♈43	01 43	02 43	03 42	40 42	05 41	06 40	07 40	08 39	09♈38
1972	26 31	27 30	28 30	30 00	00♈29	01 29	02 28	03 28	04 27	05 27	06 27	07 25	08 25	09 24	10♈23
1973	26 16	27 16	28 16	29 15	00♈15	01 14	02 14	03 13	04 13	05 12	06 12	07 11	08 10	09 10	10♈09
1974	26 01	27 01	28 01	29 00	00 D 00	01♈00	01 59	02 59	03 58	04 58	05 57	06 57	07 56	08 55	09♈54
1975	25 47	26 46	27 46	28 46	29 45	00♈45	01 44	02 44	03 43	04 43	05 42	06 42	07 41	08 40	09♈39
1976	26 32	27 31	28 31	29 31	00♈30	01 30	02 29	03 29	04 28	05 28	06 27	07 26	08 26	09 25	10♈24
1977	26 17	27 17	28 16	29 17	00♈16	01 15	02 15	03 14	04 14	05 13	06 13	07 12	08 11	09 11	10♈10
1978	26 03	27 02	28 02	29 02	00♈01	01 01	02 00	03 00	03 59	04 59	05 58	06 57	07 57	08 56	09♈55
1979	25 48	26 48	27 47	28 47	29 47	00♈46	01 46	02 45	03 45	04 44	05 44	06 43	07 43	08 42	09♈41
1980	26 33	27 33	28 33	29 32	00♈32	01 31	02 30	03 30	04 30	05 29	06 29	07 28	08 27	09 27	10♈26
1981	26 19	27 18	28 18	29 18	00♈17	01 17	02 16	03 16	04 15	05 15	06 14	07 13	08 13	09 12	10♈11
1982	26 04	27 04	28 03	29 03	00♈03	01 02	02 20	03 01	04 01	05 00	06 00	06 59	07 58	08 58	09♈57
1983	25 50	26 49	27 49	28 49	29 48	00♈48	01 48	02 47	03 47	04 46	05 45	06 45	07 44	08 43	09♈43
1984	26 35	27 35	28 35	29 34	00♈34	01 33	02 33	03 32	04 32	05 31	06 31	07 30	08 29	09 29	10♈28
1985	26 21	27 20	28 20	29 20	00♈19	01 19	02 18	03 18	04 17	05 17	06 16	07 16	08 15	09 14	10♈14
1986	26 06	27 06	28 06	29 05	00♈05	01 04	02 04	03 03	04 03	05 02	06 02	07 01	08 00	08 59	09♈59
1987	25 52	26 51	27 51	28 51	29 50	00♈50	01 50	02 49	03 49	04 48	05 48	06 47	07 46	08 46	09♈45
1988	26 37	27 37	28 36	29 36	00♈36	01 35	02 35	03 34	04 34	05 33	06 33	07 32	08 31	09 31	10♈30
1989	26 23	27 22	28 22	29 22	00♈21	01 21	02 20	03 20	04 19	05 29	06 18	07 17	08 17	09 16	10♈15
1990	26 08	27 08	28 07	29 07	00♈07	01 06	02 06	03 05	04 05	05 04	06 04	07 03	08 03	09 02	10♈01
1991	25 54	26 53	27 53	28 53	29 52	00♈52	01 52	02 51	03 51	04 50	05 49	06 49	07 48	08 47	09♈47
1992	26 39	27 39	28 39	29 38	00♈38	01 37	02 37	03 36	04 36	05 35	06 35	07 34	08 33	09 33	10♈32
1993	26 24	27 24	28 24	29 24	00♈23	01 23	02 22	03 22	04 21	05 21	06 20	07 20	08 19	09 18	10♈17
1994	26 10	27 10	28 10	29 09	00♈09	01 08	02 08	03 07	04 07	05 06	06 06	07 05	08 04	09 04	10♈03
1995	25 56	26 56	27 55	28 55	29 54	00♈54	01 54	02 53	03 53	04 52	05 51	06 51	07 50	08 50	09♈49
1996	26 41	27 41	28 40	29 40	00♈40	01 39	02 39	03 38	04 38	05 37	06 37	07 36	08 35	09 35	10♈35
1997	26 26	27 26	28 26	29 25	00♈25	01 25	02 24	03 24	04 23	05 22	06 22	07 21	08 21	09 20	10♈19
1998	26 12	27 11	28 11	29 11	00♈10	01 10	02 09	03 09	04 08	05 08	06 07	07 07	08 06	09 05	10♈05
1999	25 57	26 57	27 56	28 56	29 56	00♈55	01 55	02 54	03 54	04 53	05 53	06 52	07 51	08 51	09♈50
2000	26 42	27 42	28 42	29 41	00♈41	01 40	02 40	03 39	04 39	05 38	06 38	07 37	08 36	09 36	10♈35

Sun

April

	1st	2nd	3rd	4th	5th	6th	7th	8th	9th	10th	11th	12th	13th	14th	15th	16th
1900	10 ♈ 49	11 28	12 27	13 26	14 46	15 45	16 44	17 43	18 41	19 40	20 39	21 38	22 37	23 35	24 34	25 33
1902	10 ♈ 35	11 34	12 33	13 32	14 31	15 30	16 29	17 28	18 27	19 26	20 25	21 24	22 22	23 21	24 20	25 19
1902	10 ♈ 20	11 19	12 18	13 18	14 17	15 16	16 15	17 14	18 13	19 12	20 11	21 09	22 08	23 07	24 06	25 04
1903	10 ♈ 06	11 05	12 04	13 03	14 02	15 01	16 00	16 59	17 58	18 57	19 56	20 55	21 54	22 52	23 51	24 50
1904	10 ♈ 51	11 50	12 49	13 48	14 47	15 45	15 45	17 44	18 43	19 52	20 41	21 40	22 38	23 37	24 36	25 34
1905	10 ♈ 36	11 35	12 35	13 33	14 32	15 31	16 30	17 29	18 28	19 26	20 26	21 25	22 24	23 23	24 21	25 20
1906	10 ♈ 21	11 21	12 20	13 19	14 18	15 17	16 16	17 15	18 14	19 13	20 12	21 10	22 09	23 08	24 07	25 04
1907	19 ♈ 07	12 06	12 05	13 05	14 04	15 03	16 02	17 01	18 00	19 00	20 00	20 57	21 55	22 54	23 53	24 52
1908	10 ♈ 52	11 51	12 50	13 49	14 49	15 48	16 47	17 46	18 44	19 43	20 42	21 41	22 40	23 40	25 37	25 36
1909	10 ♈ 38	11 37	12 36	13 35	14 35	13 33	16 32	17 31	18 30	19 30	20 28	21 27	22 25	23 25	24 23	25 22
1910	10 ♈ 23	11 22	12 21	13 21	14 20	15 19	16 18	17 17	18 16	19 15	20 14	21 12	22 11	23 10	24 09	25 08
1911	10 ♈ 09	11 08	12 07	13 07	14 06	15 05	16 04	17 03	18 02	19 01	19 59	20 58	21 57	22 56	23 55	24 53
1912	10 ♈ 54	11 53	12 53	13 52	14 51	15 50	16 29	17 28	18 47	19 45	20 44	21 43	22 42	23 41	24 39	25 38
1913	10 ♈ 40	11 39	12 38	13 37	14 36	15 35	16 34	17 33	18 32	19 32	20 30	21 29	22 28	23 27	24 25	25 24
1914	10 ♈ 26	11 25	12 24	13 23	14 22	15 21	16 20	17 19	18 18	19 17	20 16	21 15	22 13	23 12	24 11	25 10
1915	10 ♈ 11	11 11	12 10	13 09	14 08	15 07	16 06	17 05	18 04	19 03	20 02	21 01	22 00	23 00	23 57	24 56
1916	10 ♈ 56	11 44	12 55	13 54	14 53	15 52	16 51	17 50	18 49	19 48	20 26	21 25	22 44	23 43	24 42	25 40
1917	10 ♈ 42	11 41	12 40	13 39	14 38	15 37	16 36	17 35	18 34	19 33	20 32	21 31	22 29	23 28	24 27	25 26
1918	10 ♈ 27	11 26	12 26	13 25	14 24	15 23	16 22	17 21	18 20	19 29	20 18	21 16	22 15	23 14	24 13	25 12
1919	10 ♈ 13	11 12	12 11	13 10	14 10	15 09	16 08	17 07	18 06	19 05	20 03	21 02	22 01	23 00	24 00	24 57
1920	10 ♈ 58	11 57	12 56	13 44	14 54	15 53	16 52	17 51	18 50	19 49	20 48	21 47	22 46	23 44	24 43	25 42
1921	10 ♈ 43	11 43	12 42	13 41	14 40	15 39	16 38	17 37	18 36	19 35	20 34	21 33	22 32	23 30	25 30	25 28
1922	10 ♈ 29	11 28	12 27	13 27	14 26	15 25	16 24	17 23	18 22	19 20	20 19	21 18	22 27	23 26	24 14	25 13
1923	19 ♈ 15	11 14	12 13	13 12	14 11	15 10	16 09	17 08	18 07	19 06	20 05	21 04	22 03	23 02	24 01	25 00
1924	11 ♈ 00	12 00	13 00	13 57	14 56	15 55	16 54	17 53	18 52	19 51	20 50	21 49	22 48	23 46	24 45	25 44
1925	19 ♈ 45	11 45	12 44	13 43	14 42	15 41	16 40	17 39	18 38	19 37	20 35	21 34	22 33	23 32	24 31	25 29
1926	10 ♈ 31	11 30	12 29	13 28	14 28	15 26	16 25	17 24	18 23	19 22	20 21	21 20	22 29	23 28	24 26	25 15
1927	10 ♈ 16	11 16	12 15	13 14	14 13	15 12	16 11	17 10	18 09	19 08	20 07	21 06	22 05	23 03	24 02	25 01
1928	11 ♈ 01	12 01	13 00	14 00	15 00	16 00	17 00	18 00	19 00	20 00	20 51	21 50	22 01	23 48	24 47	25 45
1929	10 ♈ 47	11 46	12 45	13 44	14 43	15 42	16 41	17 40	18 39	19 38	20 37	21 36	22 35	23 33	24 32	25 31
1930	10 ♈ 32	11 32	12 31	13 30	14 29	15 28	16 27	17 26	18 25	19 24	10 23	21 22	22 20	23 19	24 28	25 16
1931	10 ♈ 18	11 18	12 17	13 16	14 15	15 14	16 13	17 12	18 11	19 10	21 09	21 08	22 06	23 05	24 04	25 03
1932	11 ♈ 03	12 02	13 02	14 01	15 00	15 59	16 58	17 57	18 56	19 55	20 54	21 53	22 51	23 50	24 49	25 47
1933	10 ♈ 49	11 48	12 47	13 47	14 46	15 45	16 44	17 43	18 42	19 40	20 39	31 38	22 37	23 36	24 34	25 33
1934	10 ♈ 35	11 34	12 33	13 32	14 31	15 30	16 29	17 28	18 27	19 26	20 25	21 24	22 23	23 22	24 20	25 19
1935	10 ♈ 20	11 20	12 29	13 18	14 17	15 16	16 15	17 14	18 13	19 12	20 11	21 10	22 09	23 07	24 06	25 05
1936	11 ♈ 96	12 95	13 94	14 03	15 02	16 01	17 00	17 59	18 58	19 57	20 56	21 55	22 53	23 52	25 51	25 50
1937	10 ♈ 51	11 50	12 49	13 49	14 48	15 47	16 46	17 45	18 44	19 42	20 41	21 40	22 39	23 38	24 37	25 35
1938	10 ♈ 37	11 36	12 35	13 34	14 33	15 32	16 32	16 30	18 29	19 28	20 27	21 26	22 25	23 24	24 22	25 21
1939	10 ♈ 23	11 22	12 21	13 20	14 19	15 18	16 17	17 16	18 15	19 14	20 13	21 12	22 11	23 09	24 08	25 07
1940	11 ♈ 07	12 06	13 05	14 04	15 04	16 03	17 02	18 01	18 00	19 59	20 57	21 56	22 55	23 54	24 53	25 51
1941	10 ♈ 53	11 52	12 51	13 50	14 49	15 48	16 47	17 46	18 45	19 44	20 43	21 43	22 40	23 39	24 38	25 37
1942	10 ♈ 38	11 37	12 36	13 35	14 34	15 33	16 32	17 31	18 30	19 29	20 28	21 27	22 26	23 25	24 24	25 22
1945	10 ♈ 24	11 23	12 22	13 21	14 20	15 29	16 18	16 16	18 16	19 15	20 14	21 13	22 12	23 11	24 09	25 08
1944	11 ♈ 09	12 08	13 07	14 06	15 05	16 04	16 03	18 02	19 01	20 00	20 59	21 58	22 57	23 55	24 54	25 53
1945	10 ♈ 54	11 54	12 53	13 52	14 51	15 50	16 49	17 48	18 47	19 46	20 45	21 44	22 42	23 41	24 40	25 39
1946	10 ♈ 40	11 39	12 38	13 38	14 37	15 36	16 35	17 34	18 33	19 32	20 31	21 29	22 28	23 27	24 26	25 24
1947	10 ♈ 26	11 25	12 25	13 24	14 23	15 22	16 21	17 20	18 19	19 18	20 17	21 15	22 14	23 13	24 12	25 10
1948	11 ♈ 11	12 10	13 09	14 08	15 07	16 07	17 06	18 05	19 03	20 02	21 01	22 00	22 59	23 58	24 57	25 55
1949	10 ♈ 57	11 56	12 55	13 54	14 53	15 52	16 51	17 50	18 49	19 48	20 47	21 46	22 45	23 43	24 42	25 41
1950	10 ♈ 42	11 41	12 40	13 39	14 39	15 38	16 37	17 36	18 34	19 33	20 32	21 31	22 30	23 29	24 28	25 26
1951	10 ♈ 28	11 27	12 26	13 25	14 24	15 23	16 22	17 21	18 20	19 19	20 18	21 17	22 16	23 15	24 14	25 12
1952	11 ♈ 13	12 12	13 11	14 10	15 09	16 08	17 07	18 06	19 05	20 04	21 03	22 02	23 00	23 59	24 58	25 57
1953	10 ♈ 58	11 57	12 56	13 44	14 55	15 54	16 53	17 52	18 51	19 50	20 49	21 48	22 46	23 45	24 44	25 42
1954	10 ♈ 44	11 43	12 42	13 41	14 40	15 39	16 38	17 37	18 36	19 35	20 34	21 33	22 32	23 31	24 28	25 28
1955	10 ♈ 30	11 29	12 28	13 27	14 26	15 25	16 24	17 23	18 22	19 21	20 20	21 29	22 18	23 17	24 16	25 14
1956	11 ♈ 15	12 14	13 13	14 12	15 11	16 10	17 09	18 08	19 07	20 06	21 05	22 04	23 03	24 01	25 00	25 59
1957	11 ♈ 00	11 59	12 59	13 58	14 57	15 56	16 55	17 54	18 53	19 52	20 51	21 49	22 28	23 47	24 46	25 44
1958	10 ♈ 46	11 45	12 44	13 43	14 42	15 41	16 40	17 39	18 38	19 37	20 36	21 35	22 34	23 33	24 31	25 30
1959	10 ♈ 31	11 31	12 30	13 29	14 28	15 27	16 26	17 25	18 24	19 23	20 22	21 21	22 20	23 19	24 17	25 16
1960	11 ♈ 17	12 16	13 15	14 14	15 13	16 12	17 11	18 10	19 09	20 08	21 07	22 06	23 05	24 03	25 02	26 01
1961	11 ♈ 02	12 01	13 00	14 00	14 59	15 58	16 57	17 56	18 55	19 54	20 52	21 51	22 50	23 49	24 48	25 46
1962	10 ♈ 48	11 47	12 46	13 45	14 44	15 43	16 42	17 41	18 40	19 39	20 38	21 37	22 36	23 35	24 33	25 32
1963	10 ♈ 33	11 33	12 32	13 31	14 30	15 29	16 28	17 27	18 26	19 25	20 24	21 23	22 22	23 20	24 19	25 18
1964	11 ♈ 18	12 17	13 16	14 15	15 14	16 13	17 12	18 11	19 10	20 09	21 08	22 07	23 06	24 05	25 03	26 02
1965	11 ♈ 03	12 02	13 02	14 01	15 00	15 59	16 58	17 57	18 56	19 55	20 54	21 52	22 51	23 50	24 49	25 47
1966	10 ♈ 49	11 48	12 47	13 46	14 45	15 44	16 43	17 42	18 41	19 40	20 39	21 38	22 37	23 36	24 34	25 33
1967	10 ♈ 34	11 34	12 33	13 32	14 31	15 30	16 29	17 28	18 27	19 26	20 25	21 24	22 23	23 22	24 21	25 19
1968	11 ♈ 20	12 19	13 18	14 17	15 16	16 15	17 14	18 13	19 12	20 11	21 10	22 09	23 08	24 06	25 05	26 04
1969	11 ♈ 05	12 04	13 04	14 03	15 02	16 01	17 00	17 59	18 58	19 57	20 56	21 54	22 53	23 52	24 51	25 50
1970	10 ♈ 51	11 51	12 50	13 49	14 48	15 47	16 46	17 45	18 44	19 43	20 42	21 41	22 40	23 38	24 37	25 36
1971	10 ♈ 38	11 37	12 36	13 35	14 34	15 33	16 32	17 31	18 30	19 29	20 29	21 27	22 26	23 25	24 23	25 22
1972	11 ♈ 22	12 22	13 21	14 20	15 19	16 18	17 17	18 16	19 15	20 14	21 13	22 12	23 10	24 09	25 08	26 07
1973	11 ♈ 08	12 07	13 06	14 06	15 05	16 04	17 03	18 02	19 01	20 00	20 59	21 57	22 56	23 55	24 54	25 52
1974	10 ♈ 54	11 53	12 52	13 51	14 50	15 49	16 48	17 47	18 46	19 45	20 44	21 43	22 42	23 41	24 39	25 38
1975	10 ♈ 39	11 38	12 38	13 36	14 35	15 34	16 33	17 32	18 31	19 30	20 29	21 28	22 28	23 26	24 25	25 24
1976	11 ♈ 24	12 23	13 22	14 21	15 20	16 19	17 18	18 17	19 16	20 15	21 14	22 13	23 12	24 10	25 09	26 08
1977	11 ♈ 09	12 08	13 07	14 06	15 06	16 05	17 04	18 03	19 01	20 00	20 59	21 58	22 57	23 56	24 55	25 53
1978	10 ♈ 54	11 54	12 53	13 52	14 51	15 50	16 49	17 48	18 47	19 46	20 45	21 44	22 43	23 42	24 40	25 39
1979	19 ♈ 40	11 40	12 39	13 38	14 37	15 36	16 35	17 34	18 33	19 32	20 31	21 30	22 29	23 27	24 26	25 25
1980	11 ♈ 25	12 24	13 23	14 22	15 22	16 21	17 20	18 19	19 18	20 16	21 15	22 14	23 13	24 12	25 22	26 09
1981	11 ♈ 11	12 10	13 09	14 08	15 07	16 06	17 05	18 04	19 03	20 02	21 01	22 00	22 59	23 58	24 56	25 55
1982	10 ♈ 56	11 56	12 55	13 54	14 53	15 52	16 51	17 50	18 49	19 48	20 47	21 46	22 44	23 43	24 42	25 41
1983	10 ♈ 42	11 41	12 40	13 39	14 38	15 38	16 37	17 36	18 35	19 34	20 33	21 31	22 30	23 29	24 28	25 27
1984	11 ♈ 27	12 26	13 25	14 25	15 24	16 23	17 22	18 21	19 20	20 19	21 18	22 16	23 15	24 14	25 13	26 11
1985	11 ♈ 13	12 12	13 11	14 10	15 09	16 08	17 07	18 06	19 05	20 04	21 03	22 02	23 01	23 59	24 58	25 57
1986	10 ♈ 58	11 57	12 57	13 56	14 54	15 54	16 53	17 52	18 51	19 50	20 49	21 48	22 47	23 45	24 44	25 43
1987	10 ♈ 44	11 43	12 43	13 42	14 41	15 40	16 39	17 38	18 37	19 36	20 35	21 34	22 33	23 31	24 30	25 29
1988	11 ♈ 29	12 28	13 27	14 26	15 25	16 25	17 24	18 22	19 21	20 20	21 19	22 18	23 17	24 16	25 15	26 13
1989	11 ♈ 14	12 14	13 13	14 12	15 11	16 10	17 09	18 08	19 07	20 06	21 05	22 04	23 03	24 02	25 00	25 59
1990	11 ♈ 00	12 00	12 59	13 58	14 57	15 56	16 55	17 54	18 53	19 52	20 51	21 50	22 49	23 47	24 46	25 45
1991	10 ♈ 46	11 45	12 44	13 44	14 43	15 42	16 41	17 40	18 39	19 38	20 37	21 35	22 34	23 33	24 32	25 31
1992	11 ♈ 31	12 30	13 29	14 29	15 28	16 27	17 26	18 25	19 24	20 23	21 22	22 21	23 29	24 28	25 27	26 15
1993	11 ♈ 17	12 16	13 15	14 14	15 13	16 12	17 11	18 10	19 09	20 08	21 07	22 06	23 05	24 04	25 02	26 01
1994	11 ♈ 02	12 01	13 00	14 00	14 59	15 58	16 57	17 56	18 55	19 54	20 53	21 52	22 50	23 49	24 48	15 47
1995	10 ♈ 48	11 47	12 47	13 46	14 45	15 44	16 43	17 42	18 41	19 40	20 39	21 38	22 37	23 35	24 34	25 33
1996	11 ♈ 33	12 32	13 31	14 30	15 29	16 28	17 27	18 26	19 25	20 24	21 23	22 22	23 21	24 21	25 18	26 17
1997	11 ♈ 18	12 17	13 17	14 16	15 15	16 14	17 13	18 12	19 11	20 10	21 09	22 08	23 07	24 05	25 04	26 03
1998	11 ♈ 04	12 03	13 02	14 01	15 01	16 00	16 59	17 58	18 57	19 56	20 54	21 53	22 52	23 51	24 50	25 48
1999	10 ♈ 49	11 48	12 48	13 47	14 46	15 45	16 44	17 43	18 42	19 41	20 40	21 39	22 38	23 37	24 35	25 34
2000	11 ♈ 34	12 33	13 32	14 32	15 31	16 30	17 29	18 28	19 27	20 26	21 25	22 24	23 22	24 21	25 20	26 19

Year	17th	18th	19th	20th	21st	22nd	23rd	24th	25th	26th	27th	28th	29th	30th
1900	26 31	27 30	28 29	29 27	00♉26	01 24	02 23	03 21	04 20	05 18	06 16	07 15	08 13	09♉11
1901	26 17	27 16	28 15	29 13	00♉12	01 10	02 09	03 07	04 06	05 04	06 02	07 01	07 59	08♉57
1902	26 03	27 02	28 00	28 59	29 57	00♉56	01 54	02 53	03 51	04 50	05 48	06 46	07 45	08♉43
1903	25 49	26 47	27 46	28 44	29 43	00♉42	01 40	02 39	03 37	04 35	05 34	06 32	07 30	08♉29
1904	26 33	27 32	28 30	29 29	00♉28	01 26	02 25	03 23	04 21	05 20	06 18	07 16	08 15	09♉13
1905	26 19	27 17	28 16	29 14	00♉13	01 11	02 10	03 08	04 07	05 05	07 03	07 02	08 00	08♉58
1906	26 04	27 03	28 01	29 00	29 58	00♉57	01 55	02 54	03 52	04 51	05 49	06 48	07 46	08♉44
1907	25 50	26 49	27 48	28 46	29 45	00♉43	01 41	02 40	03 39	04 37	05 35	06 34	07 32	08♉30
1908	26 35	27 33	28 32	29 30	00♉29	01 27	02 26	03 24	04 23	05 21	06 19	07 18	08 16	09♉14
1909	26 20	27 19	28 18	29 16	00♉15	01 13	02 12	03 10	04 09	05 07	06 05	07 04	08 02	09♉00
1910	26 06	27 05	28 03	29 02	00♉01	00 59	01 58	02 56	03 54	04 53	05 51	06 49	07 48	08♉46
1911	25 52	26 51	27 49	28 48	29 46	00♉45	01 43	02 42	03 40	04 39	05 37	06 35	07 34	08♉32
1912	26 37	27 35	28 34	29 33	00♉31	01 30	02 28	03 27	04 25	05 23	06 22	07 20	08 18	09♉17
1913	26 23	27 21	28 20	29 18	00♉17	01 15	02 14	03 12	04 11	05 09	06 07	07 06	08 04	09♉02
1914	26 08	27 07	28 06	29 04	00♉03	01 01	02 00	02 58	03 57	04 55	05 53	06 52	07 50	08♉48
1915	25 55	26 53	27 52	28 51	29 49	00♉48	01 46	02 45	03 43	04 41	05 50	06 38	07 36	08♉35
1916	26 39	27 37	28 36	29 35	00♉33	01 32	02 30	03 29	04 27	05 25	06 24	07 22	08 20	09♉19
1917	26 24	27 23	28 22	29 20	00♉19	01 17	02 16	03 14	04 13	05 11	06 10	07 08	08 06	09♉04
1918	26 10	27 09	28 08	29 06	00♉05	01 03	02 02	03 00	03 58	04 57	05 55	06 54	07 52	08♉50
1919	25 56	26 55	27 53	28 52	29 50	00♉49	01 47	02 46	03 44	04 43	05 41	06 39	07 38	08♉36
1920	26 41	27 39	28 38	29 36	00♉35	01 34	02 32	03 30	04 29	05 27	06 26	07 24	08 22	09♉20
1921	26 26	27 25	28 24	29 22	00♉21	01 19	02 18	03 16	04 14	05 13	06 11	07 09	08 08	09♉06
1922	26 12	27 10	28 09	29 08	00♉06	01 05	02 03	03 02	04 00	04 59	05 57	06 55	07 54	08♉52
1923	25 58	26 57	27 55	28 54	29 52	00♉52	01 50	02 48	03 46	04 45	05 43	06 41	07 40	08♉38
1924	26 42	17 41	28 40	29 38	00♉37	01 35	02 34	03 32	04 30	05 29	06 27	07 25	08 24	09♉22
1925	26 28	27 27	28 25	29 24	00♉22	01 21	02 19	03 18	04 16	05 25	06 13	07 11	08 10	09♉08
1926	26 14	27 13	28 11	29 10	00♉08	01 07	02 05	03 04	04 02	05 01	05 59	06 57	07 55	08♉54
1927	25 59	26 58	27 57	28 55	29 54	00♉52	01 51	02 49	03 48	04 46	05 45	06 43	07 41	08♉40
1928	26 44	27 43	28 41	29 40	00♉38	01 37	02 35	03 34	04 32	05 31	06 29	07 27	08 26	09♉24
1929	26 30	27 28	28 27	29 25	00♉24	01 22	02 21	03 19	04 18	05 16	06 14	07 13	08 11	09♉09
1930	26 15	27 14	28 12	29 11	00 10	31 10	02 07	02 06	04 03	05 02	06 00	06 59	07 59	08♉55
1931	26 01	27 00	27 59	28 57	29 56	00♉55	01 53	02 51	03 50	04 48	05 47	06 45	07 43	08♉42
1932	26 46	27 45	28 43	29 42	00♉40	01 39	02 37	03 36	04 34	05 32	06 31	07 29	08 27	09♉26
1933	26 32	27 30	28 29	29 28	00♉26	01 25	02 23	03 22	04 20	05 18	06 17	07 15	08 13	09♉12
1934	26 18	27 16	28 15	29 14	00♉12	01 11	02 09	03 08	04 06	06 04	06 03	07 01	07 59	08♉58
1935	26 04	27 02	28 01	28 59	29 58	00♉56	01 55	02 53	03 52	04 50	05 49	06 47	07 45	08♉44
1936	26 48	27 47	28 46	29 44	00♉43	01 41	02 40	03 38	04 37	05 35	06 33	07 32	08 30	09♉28
1937	26 34	27 33	28 31	29 30	00♉28	01 27	02 25	03 24	04 22	05 21	06 19	07 17	08 16	09♉14
1938	26 20	27 18	28 17	29 16	00♉14	01 13	02 11	03 10	04 08	05 06	06 05	07 03	08 01	09♉00
1939	26 06	27 04	28 03	29 02	00♉00	00 59	01 57	02 56	03 54	04 53	05 51	06 49	07 48	08♉46
1940	26 50	27 49	28 47	29 46	00♉44	01 43	02 41	03 40	04 38	05 36	06 35	07 33	08 31	09♉30
1941	26 35	27 34	28 33	29 31	00♉30	01 28	02 27	03 25	04 24	05 22	06 20	07 19	08 17	09♉15
1942	26 21	27 20	28 18	29 17	00♉16	01 14	02 13	03 11	04 09	05 08	06 06	07 05	08 03	09♉01
1943	26 07	27 05	28 04	29 03	00♉01	01 00	01 58	02 57	03 55	04 53	05 52	06 50	07 49	08♉47
1944	26 51	27 50	28 49	29 47	00♉46	01 44	02 43	03 41	04 40	05 38	06 36	07 35	08 33	09♉31
1945	26 37	27 36	28 35	29 33	00♉32	01 30	02 29	03 27	04 26	05 24	06 22	07 21	08 19	09♉17
1946	26 23	27 22	28 20	29 19	00♉17	01 16	02 14	03 13	04 11	05 10	06 08	07 06	08 05	09♉03
1947	26 09	27 08	28 07	29 05	00♉04	01 02	02 01	02 59	03 58	04 56	05 55	06 53	07 51	08♉50
1948	26 54	27 53	28 51	29 50	00♉48	01 47	02 45	03 44	04 42	05 40	06 39	07 37	08 35	09♉34
1949	26 40	27 38	28 37	29 35	00♉34	01 32	02 31	03 29	04 28	05 26	06 25	07 23	08 21	09♉20
1950	26 25	27 24	28 22	29 21	00♉20	01 18	02 17	03 15	04 14	05 12	06 10	07 09	08 07	09♉05
1951	26 11	27 10	28 08	29 07	00♉05	01 04	02 02	03 01	03 59	04 58	05 56	06 54	07 52	08♉51
1952	26 55	27 54	28 53	29 52	00♉50	01 48	02 48	03 45	04 44	05 42	06 41	07 39	08 37	09♉35
1953	26 41	27 40	28 38	29 37	00♉36	01 34	02 33	03 31	04 49	05 28	06 26	07 24	08 23	09♉21
1954	26 27	27 25	28 24	29 23	00♉21	01 20	02 18	03 17	04 15	05 13	06 12	07 10	08 09	09♉07
1955	26 13	27 12	28 10	29 09	00♉07	01 06	02 05	03 03	04 01	06 00	05 58	06 57	07 55	08♉53
1956	26 58	27 56	28 55	29 53	00♉52	01 40	02 49	03 47	04 46	05 44	06 42	07 41	08 39	09♉37
1957	26 43	27 42	28 40	29 39	00♉37	01 36	02 34	03 33	04 31	05 30	06 28	07 26	08 25	09♉23
1958	26 29	27 27	28 26	29 25	00♉23	01 22	02 20	03 19	04 17	05 16	06 14	07 12	08 11	09♉09
1959	26 15	27 13	28 12	29 11	00♉09	01 08	02 06	03 05	04 03	05 01	06 00	06 58	07 56	08♉54
1960	26 59	27 58	28 57	29 55	00♉54	01 52	02 51	03 49	04 48	05 46	06 44	07 43	08 41	09♉39
1961	26 45	27 44	28 42	29 41	00♉40	01 38	02 37	03 35	04 33	05 32	06 30	07 29	08 27	09♉25
1962	26 31	27 29	28 28	29 27	00♉25	01 24	02 22	03 21	04 19	05 17	06 16	07 14	08 12	09♉11
1963	26 17	27 15	28 14	29 12	00♉11	01 10	02 08	03 07	04 05	05 04	06 02	07 00	07 59	08♉57
1964	27 01	28 00	28 58	29 57	00♉55	01 54	02 52	03 51	04 49	05 48	06 46	07 44	08 42	09♉41
1965	26 46	27 45	28 43	29 42	00♉40	01 39	02 37	03 36	04 34	05 33	06 31	07 30	08 28	09♉27
1966	26 32	27 31	28 29	29 28	00♉26	01 25	02 23	03 22	04 20	05 19	06 17	07 16	08 14	09♉12
1967	26 18	27 17	28 15	29 14	00♉12	01 11	02 09	03 08	04 06	05 05	06 03	07 01	08 00	08♉58
1968	27 03	28 01	29 00	29 59	00♉57	01 55	02 54	03 52	04 51	05 49	06 47	07 46	08 44	09♉43
1969	26 48	27 47	28 46	29 44	00♉43	01 41	02 40	03 38	04 37	05 35	06 34	07 32	08 30	09♉28
1970	26 35	27 33	28 32	29 30	00♉29	01 28	02 26	03 24	04 23	05 21	06 20	07 18	08 16	09♉15
1971	26 21	27 19	28 18	29 17	00♉15	01 14	02 12	03 11	04 09	05 08	06 06	07 04	08 03	09♉01
1972	27 05	28 04	29 03	00♉01	01 00	01 58	02 57	03 55	04 54	05 52	06 50	07 49	08 47	09♉45
1973	26 51	27 50	28 48	29 47	00♉45	01 44	02 42	03 41	04 39	05 38	06 36	07 34	08 33	09♉31
1974	26 37	27 35	28 34	29 33	00♉31	01 30	02 28	03 27	04 25	05 24	06 22	07 21	08 19	09♉17
1975	26 22	27 21	28 20	29 18	00♉17	01 15	02 14	03 12	04 11	05 09	06 08	07 06	08 04	09♉02
1976	27 07	28 05	29 04	00♉02	01 01	01 59	02 58	03 56	04 55	05 53	06 52	07 50	08 48	09♉47
1977	26 52	27 51	28 50	29 48	00♉46	01 45	02 44	03 42	04 40	05 39	06 37	07 36	08 34	09♉32
1978	26 38	27 36	28 35	29 34	00♉32	01 31	02 29	03 28	04 26	05 24	06 23	06 21	08 19	09♉18
1979	26 24	27 22	28 21	29 20	00♉18	01 27	02 15	03 14	04 12	05 11	06 09	07 07	08 06	09♉04
1980	27 08	28 07	29 05	00♉04	01 03	02 01	03 00	04 00	04 56	05 55	06 53	07 51	08 50	09♉48
1981	26 54	27 52	28 51	29 49	00♉48	01 46	02 45	03 43	04 42	05 40	06 39	07 37	08 35	09♉34
1982	26 39	27 38	28 37	29 35	00♉34	01 32	02 31	03 30	04 28	05 26	06 25	07 23	08 21	09♉20
1983	26 25	27 24	28 23	29 21	00♉20	01 18	02 17	03 15	04 14	05 12	06 11	07 09	08 07	09♉06
1984	27 10	28 09	29 07	00♉06	01 04	02 03	03 01	04 00	04 58	05 57	06 55	07 53	08 52	09♉50
1985	26 56	27 54	28 53	29 52	00♉50	01 49	02 47	03 46	04 44	05 43	06 41	07 39	08 38	09♉36
1986	26 42	27 40	28 39	29 38	00♉36	01 35	02 33	03 32	04 30	05 28	06 27	07 25	08 23	09♉23
1987	26 28	27 26	28 25	29 24	00♉22	01 21	02 19	03 18	04 16	05 15	06 13	07 11	08 10	09♉08
1988	27 12	28 11	29 09	00♉08	01 07	02 05	03 04	04 02	05 00	05 59	06 57	07 36	08 34	09♉52
1989	26 58	27 56	28 55	29 54	00♉52	01 51	02 49	03 48	04 46	05 44	06 43	07 41	08 39	09♉38
1990	26 43	27 42	28 41	29 39	00♉38	01 37	02 35	03 34	04 32	05 30	06 29	07 27	08 26	09♉24
1991	26 29	27 28	28 27	29 25	00♉24	01 23	02 21	03 20	04 18	05 16	06 15	07 13	08 12	09♉10
1992	27 14	28 13	29 11	00♉10	01 08	02 07	03 05	04 04	05 02	06 01	06 59	07 57	08 56	09♉54
1993	27 00	27 58	28 57	29 56	00♉54	01 53	02 51	03 50	04 48	05 47	06 45	07 43	08 42	09♉40
1994	26 46	27 44	28 43	29 41	00♉40	01 39	02 37	03 35	04 34	05 32	06 31	07 29	08 27	09♉26
1995	26 32	27 30	28 29	29 27	00♉26	01 25	02 23	03 22	04 20	05 18	06 17	07 15	08 14	09♉12
1996	27 16	28 15	29 13	00♉12	01 10	02 09	03 07	04 06	05 04	06 03	07 01	07 59	08 58	09♉56
1997	27 02	28 00	28 59	29 57	00♉56	01 54	02 53	03 51	04 50	05 48	06 47	07 45	08 43	09♉42
1998	26 47	27 46	28 44	29 43	00♉42	01 40	02 39	03 37	04 36	05 34	06 33	07 31	08 29	09♉28
1999	26 33	27 31	28 30	29 29	00♉27	01 26	02 25	03 23	04 21	05 20	06 18	07 17	08 15	09♉13
2000	27 17	28 16	29 14	00♉13	01 12	01 10	03 09	04 07	05 05	06 04	07 02	08 01	08 59	09♉57

Sun

May

Year	1st	2nd	3rd	4th	5th	6th	7th	8th	9th	10th	11th	12th	13th	14th	15th	16th
1900	10 ♉ 09	11 08	12 06	13 04	14 02	15 00	15 58	16 56	17 54	18 52	19 50	20 48	12 46	22 43	23 42	24 39
1901	09 ♉ 55	10 53	11 52	12 50	13 48	14 46	15 44	16 42	17 41	18 38	19 36	20 34	21 32	22 30	23 27	24 25
1902	09 ♉ 41	10 39	11 37	12 36	13 34	14 32	15 30	16 28	17 26	18 24	19 22	20 20	21 18	22 16	23 14	24 11
1903	09 ♉ 27	10 25	11 23	12 22	13 20	14 18	15 16	16 14	17 12	18 10	19 08	20 06	21 04	22 02	22 59	23 57
1904	10 ♉ 11	11 09	12 07	13 06	14 04	15 02	16 00	16 58	17 56	18 53	19 52	20 60	21 48	22 45	23 43	24 41
1905	09 ♉ 57	10 55	11 53	12 51	13 49	14 47	15 45	16 43	17 42	18 39	19 37	20 35	21 33	22 31	23 29	24 27
1906	09 ♉ 42	10 42	11 39	12 37	13 35	14 33	15 31	16 29	17 27	18 25	19 23	20 21	21 19	22 17	23 15	24 12
1907	09 ♉ 28	10 27	11 25	12 23	13 21	14 19	15 17	16 15	17 13	18 11	19 09	20 07	21 05	22 03	23 01	23 59
1908	10 ♉ 13	11 11	12 09	13 07	14 05	15 03	16 01	16 59	17 57	18 55	19 53	20 51	21 49	22 47	23 45	24 43
1909	09 ♉ 58	10 57	11 55	12 53	13 51	14 49	15 47	16 45	17 43	18 41	19 39	20 37	21 35	22 33	23 31	24 28
1910	09 ♉ 44	10 42	11 41	12 39	13 37	14 35	15 33	16 31	17 29	18 27	29 25	20 23	21 21	22 19	23 17	24 15
1911	09 ♉ 30	10 29	11 27	12 25	13 23	14 21	15 19	16 17	17 15	18 13	19 11	20 09	21 07	22 05	23 03	24 01
1912	10 ♉ 15	11 13	12 11	13 09	14 07	15 05	16 03	17 01	17 59	18 57	18 55	20 53	21 51	22 49	23 47	24 45
1913	10 ♉ 01	10 59	11 57	12 55	13 53	14 52	15 49	16 47	17 46	18 44	19 41	20 39	21 37	22 35	23 33	24 31
1914	09 ♉ 47	10 45	11 43	12 41	13 39	14 37	15 35	16 35	17 31	18 29	19 27	20 25	21 23	22 21	23 19	24 17
1915	09 ♉ 33	10 31	11 29	12 27	13 25	14 24	15 22	16 20	17 18	18 16	19 14	20 12	21 10	22 08	23 05	24 03
1916	10 ♉ 17	11 15	12 13	13 11	14 10	15 08	16 06	17 04	18 02	19 00	19 58	20 56	21 54	22 51	23 49	24 47
1917	10 ♉ 03	11 01	11 59	12 57	13 55	14 53	15 51	16 49	17 47	18 45	19 43	20 41	21 39	22 37	23 35	24 33
1918	09 ♉ 48	10 47	11 45	12 43	13 41	14 39	15 37	16 35	17 33	18 31	19 29	20 27	21 25	22 23	23 21	24 19
1919	09 ♉ 34	10 33	11 31	12 29	13 27	14 25	15 23	16 21	17 19	18 17	19 15	20 13	21 11	22 09	23 07	24 05
1920	10 ♉ 19	11 17	12 15	13 13	14 11	15 09	16 07	16 05	18 03	19 01	19 59	20 57	21 55	22 53	23 51	24 49
1921	10 ♉ 04	11 02	12 01	12 59	13 57	14 55	15 53	16 51	17 49	18 47	19 45	20 43	21 41	22 39	23 37	24 35
1922	09 ♉ 50	10 48	11 47	12 45	13 43	14 41	15 39	16 37	17 35	18 33	19 31	20 29	21 27	22 25	23 23	24 20
1923	09 ♉ 36	10 34	11 33	12 21	13 29	14 27	15 25	16 23	17 21	18 19	19 17	20 15	21 13	22 11	23 09	24 07
1924	10 ♉ 20	11 18	12 17	13 15	14 13	15 11	16 09	17 07	18 05	19 03	20 21	20 59	21 57	22 55	23 53	24 51
1925	10 ♉ 06	11 04	12 03	13 01	13 59	14 57	15 55	16 53	17 51	18 49	19 47	20 45	21 43	22 40	23 38	24 36
1926	09 ♉ 52	10 50	11 48	12 46	13 45	14 43	15 41	16 39	17 37	18 35	19 33	20 31	21 29	22 27	23 25	24 22
1927	09 ♉ 38	10 36	11 34	12 33	13 31	14 29	15 27	16 25	17 23	18 21	19 19	20 17	21 15	22 13	23 11	24 08
1928	10 ♉ 22	11 20	12 18	13 17	14 15	15 13	16 11	17 09	18 07	19 05	20 03	21 01	21 59	22 56	23 54	24 52
1929	10 ♉ 08	11 06	12 04	13 02	14 00	14 58	15 56	16 55	17 53	18 51	19 49	20 47	21 44	22 42	23 40	24 38
1930	09 ♉ 54	10 52	11 50	12 48	13 46	14 44	15 42	16 41	17 39	18 36	19 34	20 32	12 30	22 28	23 26	24 24
1931	09 ♉ 40	10 38	11 36	12 34	13 32	14 31	15 29	16 27	17 25	18 23	19 21	20 19	21 17	22 15	23 12	24 10
1932	10 ♉ 24	11 22	12 20	13 18	14 17	15 15	16 13	17 11	18 09	19 07	20 05	21 03	22 01	22 59	23 56	24 54
1933	10 ♉ 10	11 08	12 06	13 05	14 03	15 00	15 59	16 57	17 55	18 53	19 51	20 49	21 46	22 44	23 42	24 40
1934	09 ♉ 56	10 54	11 52	12 50	13 49	14 47	15 45	16 43	17 41	18 39	19 37	20 35	21 33	22 31	23 29	24 26
1935	09 ♉ 42	10 40	11 38	12 37	13 35	14 33	15 31	16 29	17 27	18 25	19 23	20 21	21 19	22 17	23 15	24 13
1936	10 ♉ 26	11 25	12 23	13 21	14 19	15 17	16 15	17 13	18 11	19 09	20 07	21 05	22 03	23 01	23 59	24 56
1937	10 ♉ 12	11 10	12 08	13 07	14 05	15 03	16 01	16 59	17 57	18 55	19 53	20 51	21 49	22 47	23 45	24 42
1938	09 ♉ 58	10 36	11 54	12 53	13 51	14 49	15 47	16 45	17 43	18 41	19 39	20 37	21 35	22 33	23 31	24 28
1939	09 ♉ 44	10 42	11 41	12 39	13 37	14 35	15 33	16 31	17 29	18 27	19 25	20 23	21 21	22 19	23 17	24 15
1940	10 ♉ 29	11 26	12 24	13 22	14 21	15 19	16 17	17 15	18 13	19 11	20 09	21 07	22 05	23 03	24 01	24 58
1941	10 ♉ 14	11 12	12 10	13 08	14 06	15 04	16 03	17 01	17 59	18 57	19 54	29 52	21 50	22 48	23 46	24 44
1942	09 ♉ 59	10 58	11 56	12 54	13 52	14 50	15 48	16 46	17 44	18 42	19 40	20 38	21 26	22 34	23 32	24 30
1943	09 ♉ 45	10 43	11 42	12 40	13 38	14 36	15 34	16 32	17 30	18 28	29 26	20 24	21 22	22 20	23 18	24 16
1944	10 ♉ 30	11 28	12 26	13 24	14 22	15 20	16 18	17 16	18 14	19 12	20 10	21 08	22 06	23 04	24 02	24 59
1945	10 ♉ 15	11 13	12 12	13 10	14 08	15 06	16 04	17 02	18 00	18 58	19 56	20 54	21 52	22 50	23 48	24 46
1946	10 ♉ 01	11 00	11 58	12 56	13 54	14 52	15 50	16 48	17 46	18 44	19 42	20 40	21 38	22 36	23 34	24 32
1947	09 ♉ 48	10 46	11 44	12 42	13 40	14 39	15 37	16 35	17 33	18 31	19 29	20 27	21 25	22 22	23 20	24 18
1948	10 ♉ 32	11 30	12 28	13 26	14 24	15 23	16 21	17 19	18 16	18 15	29 13	21 11	22 98	23 95	24 94	25 92
1949	10 ♉ 18	11 16	12 14	13 12	14 11	15 09	16 07	17 05	18 03	19 01	19 59	20 57	21 54	22 52	23 50	24 48
1950	10 ♉ 03	11 02	12 00	12 58	13 56	14 54	15 52	16 50	17 48	18 46	19 44	20 42	21 40	22 38	23 36	24 34
1951	09 ♉ 49	10 48	11 46	12 44	13 42	14 40	15 38	16 36	17 35	18 33	19 31	20 29	21 27	22 24	23 22	24 20
1952	10 ♉ 34	11 32	12 30	13 28	14 26	15 24	16 22	17 21	18 19	19 16	20 14	21 12	22 10	23 08	24 06	25 04
1953	10 ♉ 19	11 17	12 16	13 14	14 12	15 10	16 08	17 06	18 04	19 02	20 00	20 58	21 56	22 54	23 52	24 50
1954	10 ♉ 05	11 03	12 02	13 00	13 58	14 56	15 54	16 52	17 50	18 48	19 46	20 44	21 42	22 50	23 38	24 36
1955	09 ♉ 52	10 50	11 48	12 56	13 44	14 42	15 40	16 38	17 36	18 34	19 32	20 30	21 28	22 26	23 24	24 22
1956	10 ♉ 35	11 34	12 32	13 30	14 28	15 26	16 24	17 22	18 20	19 28	20 16	21 14	22 12	23 10	24 08	25 06
1957	10 ♉ 21	11 20	12 18	13 16	14 14	15 12	16 10	17 08	18 06	19 04	20 02	21 00	21 58	22 56	23 54	24 52
1958	10 ♉ 07	11 05	12 04	13 02	14 00	14 58	15 56	16 54	17 52	18 50	19 48	20 46	21 44	22 42	23 40	24 38
1959	09 ♉ 53	10 51	11 49	12 48	13 46	14 44	15 42	16 40	17 38	18 36	19 34	20 32	21 30	22 28	23 26	24 24
1960	10 ♉ 38	11 36	12 34	13 32	14 30	15 28	16 27	17 25	18 23	19 21	20 18	21 16	22 14	23 12	24 10	25 08
1961	10 ♉ 23	11 21	12 20	13 18	14 16	15 14	16 12	17 10	18 08	19 06	20 04	21 02	22 00	22 58	23 56	24 54
1962	10 ♉ 09	11 07	12 05	13 04	14 01	15 00	15 58	16 56	17 54	18 52	19 50	20 48	21 46	22 44	23 42	24 40
1963	09 ♉ 55	10 54	11 51	12 50	13 48	14 46	15 44	16 42	17 40	18 38	19 36	20 34	21 32	22 30	23 28	24 26
1964	10 ♉ 39	11 37	12 35	13 34	14 32	15 30	16 28	17 26	18 24	19 22	20 20	21 18	22 16	23 14	24 12	25 09
1965	10 ♉ 24	11 23	12 21	13 19	14 17	15 15	16 13	17 11	18 09	19 07	20 05	21 03	22 01	22 59	23 58	24 55
1966	10 ♉ 10	11 09	12 07	13 05	14 28	15 01	15 59	16 57	17 55	18 53	19 51	20 49	21 47	22 45	23 43	24 41
1967	09 ♉ 56	10 55	11 53	12 51	13 49	14 47	15 45	16 43	17 41	18 39	19 37	20 35	21 33	22 31	23 29	24 27
1968	10 ♉ 41	11 39	12 37	13 35	14 34	15 32	16 30	17 28	18 26	19 24	20 22	21 20	22 17	23 15	24 13	25 11
1969	10 ♉ 27	11 25	12 23	13 21	14 19	15 17	16 15	17 13	18 11	19 09	20 07	21 05	22 03	23 01	23 59	24 57
1970	10 ♉ 13	11 11	12 09	13 07	14 06	15 04	16 02	17 00	17 58	18 56	19 54	20 52	21 50	22 48	23 46	24 44
1971	09 ♉ 59	10 58	11 56	12 54	13 52	14 50	15 48	16 46	17 45	18 42	19 40	20 38	21 36	22 34	23 32	24 30
1972	10 ♉ 43	11 42	12 40	13 38	14 36	15 34	16 32	17 30	18 28	19 26	20 24	21 22	22 20	23 18	25 16	25 14
1973	10 ♉ 29	11 28	12 26	13 24	14 22	15 20	16 18	17 16	18 14	19 12	20 10	21 08	22 06	23 04	24 02	25 00
1974	10 ♉ 15	11 14	12 12	13 10	14 08	15 06	16 04	17 02	18 00	18 58	19 56	20 54	21 52	22 50	23 48	24 46
1975	10 ♉ 01	10 59	11 57	12 55	13 54	14 52	16 50	16 48	17 46	18 44	19 42	20 40	21 38	22 36	23 34	24 32
1976	10 ♉ 45	11 43	12 41	13 39	14 38	15 36	16 34	17 32	18 30	19 28	20 26	21 24	22 22	23 20	24 17	25 15
1977	10 ♉ 30	11 29	12 27	13 25	14 23	15 21	16 19	17 17	18 15	19 13	20 11	21 09	22 07	23 05	24 03	25 01
1978	10 ♉ 16	11 14	12 12	13 11	14 09	15 07	16 05	17 03	18 01	18 59	19 55	20 58	21 53	22 51	28 49	24 47
1979	10 ♉ 02	11 02	11 59	12 57	13 55	14 53	15 51	16 49	17 47	18 45	19 43	20 41	12 39	22 37	23 35	24 33
1980	10 ♉ 46	11 44	12 43	13 41	14 39	15 37	16 35	17 33	18 31	19 29	20 27	21 25	22 23	23 21	24 19	25 17
1981	10 ♉ 32	11 30	12 28	13 27	14 25	15 23	16 21	17 19	18 17	19 15	20 13	21 11	22 09	23 07	24 05	25 02
1982	10 ♉ 18	11 16	12 14	13 13	14 11	15 09	16 07	17 05	18 03	19 01	19 59	20 57	21 55	22 53	23 51	24 48
1983	10 ♉ 04	11 02	12 00	12 58	13 57	14 55	15 53	16 51	17 49	18 47	19 45	20 53	21 41	22 39	23 37	24 35
1984	10 ♉ 48	11 46	12 45	13 43	14 41	15 39	16 37	17 35	18 33	19 31	20 29	21 27	22 25	23 23	24 21	25 19
1985	10 ♉ 34	11 32	12 31	13 29	14 27	15 25	16 23	17 21	18 19	19 17	20 15	21 13	22 11	23 09	24 07	25 04
1986	10 ♉ 20	11 18	12 16	13 15	14 13	15 11	16 09	17 07	18 05	19 03	20 01	20 59	21 57	22 55	23 53	24 51
1987	10 ♉ 06	11 05	12 03	13 01	13 59	14 57	15 55	16 54	17 52	18 50	19 48	20 45	21 43	22 41	23 39	24 37
1988	10 ♉ 50	11 49	12 47	13 45	14 43	15 41	17 39	17 37	18 35	19 33	20 31	21 29	22 27	23 26	24 23	25 21
1989	10 ♉ 36	11 34	12 32	13 31	14 29	15 27	16 25	17 23	18 21	19 19	20 17	21 15	22 13	23 11	24 09	25 07
1990	10 ♉ 22	11 20	12 19	13 17	14 15	15 13	16 11	17 09	18 07	19 05	20 03	21 01	21 59	22 57	23 55	24 53
1991	10 ♉ 08	11 06	12 04	13 03	14 01	14 59	15 57	16 55	17 53	18 51	19 49	20 47	21 45	22 43	23 41	24 39
1992	10 ♉ 52	11 51	12 49	13 47	14 45	15 43	16 41	17 39	18 37	19 35	20 33	21 31	22 29	23 27	24 25	25 23
1993	10 ♉ 38	11 36	12 35	13 33	14 31	15 29	16 27	17 25	18 23	19 21	20 19	21 17	22 15	23 13	24 11	25 09
1994	10 ♉ 24	11 22	12 20	13 18	14 17	15 15	16 13	17 11	18 09	19 07	20 05	21 03	22 01	22 59	23 57	24 56
1995	10 ♉ 10	11 08	12 07	13 05	14 03	15 01	15 59	16 57	17 55	18 53	19 51	20 49	21 47	22 45	23 43	24 41
1996	10 ♉ 54	11 52	12 51	13 49	14 47	15 45	16 43	17 41	18 39	19 37	20 35	21 33	22 31	23 29	24 27	25 25
1997	10 ♉ 40	11 38	12 36	13 34	14 33	15 31	16 29	17 27	18 25	19 23	20 21	21 19	22 17	23 15	24 13	25 10
1998	10 ♉ 26	11 24	12 22	13 21	14 19	15 17	16 15	17 13	18 11	19 09	20 07	21 05	22 03	23 01	23 59	24 56
1999	10 ♉ 11	11 10	12 08	13 06	14 04	15 02	16 00	16 59	17 57	18 55	19 53	20 51	21 49	22 47	23 44	24 42
2000	10 ♉ 55	11 53	12 52	13 50	14 48	15 46	16 44	16 43	18 41	19 39	20 38	21 35	22 32	23 30	24 28	25 26

	17th	18th	19th	20th	21st	22nd	23rd	24th	25th	26th	27th	28th	29th	30th	31st
1900	25 37	26 35	27 33	28 30	29 28	00♊26	01 23	02 21	03 19	04 16	05 14	06 12	07 09	08 07	09♊04
1901	25 37	26 34	27 19	28 16	29 14	00♊12	01 10	02 07	03 06	04 02	05 00	05 58	06 55	07 53	08♊50
1902	25 09	26 07	27 05	28 03	29 00	29 58	00♊56	01 53	02 51	03 48	04 46	05 44	06 41	07 39	08♊36
1903	24 55	25 53	26 51	27 48	28 46	29 44	00♊41	01 39	02 37	03 34	04 32	05 30	06 27	07 25	08♊22
1904	25 39	26 37	27 35	28 32	29 30	00♊28	01 25	02 23	03 21	04 18	05 16	06 13	07 11	08 08	09♊06
1905	25 25	26 22	27 20	28 18	29 16	00♊13	01 11	02 08	03 06	04 04	05 01	05 59	06 56	07 54	08♊51
1906	25 10	26 08	27 05	28 04	29 01	29 59	00♊57	01 54	02 52	03 50	04 47	05 45	06 42	07 40	08♊38
1907	24 57	25 55	26 52	27 50	28 48	29 45	00♊43	01 41	02 38	03 36	04 34	05 31	06 29	07 26	08♊24
1908	25 40	26 38	27 36	28 34	29 31	00♊29	01 27	02 24	03 22	04 19	05 17	06 15	07 12	08 10	09♊07
1909	25 26	26 24	27 22	28 20	29 17	00♊15	01 13	02 10	03 08	04 06	05 03	06 01	06 58	07 56	08♊53
1910	25 13	26 10	27 08	28 06	29 04	00♊01	00 59	01 56	02 54	03 52	04 49	05 47	06 44	07 42	03♊39
1911	24 59	25 56	26 54	27 52	28 50	29 47	00♊45	01 43	02 40	03 38	04 36	05 33	06 31	07 28	08♊26
1912	25 43	26 40	27 38	28 36	29 34	00♊31	01 29	02 27	03 24	04 22	05 20	06 17	07 15	08 12	09♊10
1913	25 29	26 26	27 24	28 22	29 20	00♊17	02 15	02 13	03 10	04 08	06 05	06 03	07 00	07 58	08♊55
1914	25 15	26 12	27 10	28 08	29 06	00♊03	01 01	01 59	02 56	03 54	04 52	05 49	06 47	07 44	08♊42
1915	25 01	25 59	26 57	27 55	28 52	29 50	00♊48	01 45	02 43	03 41	04 38	05 36	06 33	07 31	08♊28
1916	25 45	26 43	27 40	28 38	29 36	00♊33	01 31	02 29	03 26	04 24	06 22	06 19	07 17	08 14	09♊12
1917	25 30	26 28	27 26	28 24	29 22	00♊19	01 17	02 15	03 12	04 10	05 08	06 05	07 03	08 00	08♊58
1918	25 17	26 14	27 12	28 10	29 08	00♊05	07 03	02 01	02 58	03 56	04 54	05 51	06 49	07 46	08♊44
1919	25 03	26 00	26 58	27 56	28 54	29 51	00♊59	01 47	02 44	03 42	04 39	05 37	06 35	07 32	08♊30
1920	25 46	26 44	27 42	28 40	29 38	00♊35	01 33	02 31	03 28	04 26	05 23	06 21	07 18	08 16	09♊13
1921	25 32	26 30	27 28	28 26	29 23	00♊21	01 19	02 16	03 14	04 11	05 09	06 07	07 04	08 02	08♊59
1922	25 18	26 16	27 14	28 11	29 09	00♊07	01 05	02 02	03 00	03 57	04 55	05 53	06 50	07 48	08♊45
1923	25 05	26 02	27 00	27 58	28 56	29 63	00♊51	01 49	02 46	03 44	04 42	05 39	06 37	07 34	08♊32
1924	25 48	26 46	27 44	28 41	29 39	00♊37	01 34	02 32	03 30	04 27	05 25	06 23	07 20	08 18	09♊15
1925	25 34	26 32	27 30	28 27	29 25	00♊23	01 20	02 18	03 16	04 13	05 11	06 09	07 06	08 04	09♊01
1926	25 20	26 18	27 16	28 14	29 11	00♊09	01 07	02 04	03 02	04 00	04 58	05 55	06 52	07 50	08♊47
1927	25 06	26 04	27 02	27 59	28 57	29 55	00♊53	01 50	02 48	03 46	04 43	05 41	06 38	07 36	08♊33
1928	25 50	26 48	27 46	28 43	29 41	00♊39	01 36	02 34	03 32	04 29	05 27	06 25	07 22	08 20	09♊17
1929	25 36	26 34	27 31	28 29	29 27	00♊25	01 22	02 20	03 17	04 15	05 13	06 10	07 08	08 05	09♊03
1930	25 22	26 19	27 17	28 15	29 13	00♊10	01 08	02 06	03 03	04 01	04 59	05 56	06 54	07 51	08♊49
1931	25 08	26 06	27 04	28 02	28 59	29 57	00♊55	01 52	02 50	03 48	04 45	05 43	06 40	07 38	08♊35
1932	25 52	26 50	27 48	28 45	29 43	00♊41	01 38	02 36	03 33	04 31	05 29	06 26	07 24	08 21	09♊19
1933	25 38	26 36	27 33	28 31	29 29	00♊27	01 24	02 22	03 20	04 17	05 15	06 12	07 10	08 08	09♊05
1934	25 24	26 22	27 20	28 18	29 15	00♊13	01 11	02 08	03 06	04 04	05 01	05 59	06 56	07 54	08♊51
1935	25 10	26 08	27 06	28 04	29 01	29 59	00♊57	01 54	02 52	03 50	04 47	05 45	06 42	07 40	08♊38
1936	25 54	26 52	27 50	28 48	29 45	00♊43	01 41	02 38	03 36	04 34	05 31	06 29	07 26	08 24	09♊21
1937	25 40	26 38	27 36	28 34	29 31	00♊29	01 26	02 24	03 22	04 19	05 17	06 15	07 12	08 10	09♊07
1938	25 26	26 24	27 22	28 19	29 17	00♊15	01 13	02 10	03 08	04 05	05 03	06 01	06 58	07 56	08♊53
1939	25 12	26 10	27 08	28 06	29 04	00♊01	00 59	01 57	02 54	03 52	04 50	05 47	06 45	07 42	08♊40
1940	25 56	26 54	27 52	28 49	29 47	00♊45	01 42	02 40	03 38	04 35	05 33	06 30	07 28	08 25	09♊23
1941	25 42	26 39	27 37	28 35	29 33	00♊30	01 28	02 26	03 23	04 21	05 19	06 16	07 14	08 11	09♊09
1942	25 28	26 26	27 23	28 21	29 19	00♊16	01 14	02 12	03 09	04 07	05 05	06 02	07 00	08 57	08♊55
1943	25 14	26 11	27 09	18 07	29 05	00♊02	01 00	01 58	02 55	03 53	04 51	05 48	06 46	07 43	08♊41
1944	25 57	26 55	27 53	28 51	29 48	00♊46	01 44	02 41	03 39	04 37	05 34	06 32	07 29	08 27	09♊25
1945	25 43	26 42	27 39	28 37	29 35	00♊32	01 30	02 28	03 25	04 23	05 21	06 18	07 16	08 13	09♊11
1946	25 30	26 27	27 25	28 23	29 21	00♊18	01 16	02 14	03 11	04 09	05 07	06 04	07 02	07 59	08♊57
1947	25 16	26 14	27 12	28 09	29 07	00♊05	01 03	02 00	02 58	03 56	07 53	05 51	06 48	07 46	08♊43
1948	26 00	26 58	27 56	28 53	29 51	00♊49	01 46	02 44	03 41	04 39	05 37	06 34	07 32	08 29	09♊27
1949	25 46	26 44	27 41	28 39	29 37	00♊34	01 32	02 30	03 27	04 25	05 23	06 20	07 18	08 15	09♊13
1950	25 32	26 30	27 27	28 25	29 23	00♊21	01 18	02 16	03 14	04 11	05 09	06 06	07 04	08 01	08♊59
1951	25 18	26 16	27 13	28 11	29 09	00♊07	01 04	02 02	03 00	03 57	04 55	05 52	06 50	07 47	08♊45
1952	26 02	26 59	27 57	28 55	29 53	00♊50	01 48	02 46	03 43	04 41	05 39	06 36	04 34	08 31	09♊29
1953	25 48	26 45	27 43	28 41	29 39	00♊36	01 34	02 32	03 29	04 27	05 24	06 22	07 20	08 17	09♊15
1954	25 33	26 31	27 29	28 27	29 24	00♊22	01 20	02 18	03 15	04 13	05 10	06 08	07 06	08 03	09♊01
1955	25 20	26 18	27 15	28 13	29 11	00♊09	01 06	02 04	03 02	03 59	04 57	05 55	06 52	07 50	08♊47
1956	26 04	27 02	27 59	28 57	29 55	00♊52	01 50	02 48	03 45	04 43	05 40	06 38	07 36	08 33	09♊31
1957	26 49	26 47	27 45	28 43	29 40	00♊38	01 36	02 33	03 31	04 29	05 26	06 24	07 21	08 19	09♊17
1958	25 36	26 33	27 31	28 29	29 27	00♊24	01 22	02 20	03 17	04 15	05 13	06 10	07 08	08 05	09♊03
1959	25 22	26 20	27 17	28 15	29 13	00♊10	01 08	02 06	03 03	04 01	04 59	05 56	06 53	07 51	08♊49
1960	26 06	27 03	28 01	28 59	29 57	00♊54	01 52	02 50	03 47	04 45	05 43	06 40	07 38	08 35	09♊33
1961	26 51	26 49	27 47	28 45	29 43	00♊40	01 38	02 36	03 33	04 31	05 28	06 26	07 24	08 21	09♊19
1962	25 37	26 35	27 33	28 31	29 28	00♊26	01 24	02 21	03 19	04 17	05 14	06 12	07 09	08 07	09♊05
1963	25 24	26 21	27 19	28 17	29 15	00♊12	01 10	02 08	03 05	04 03	05 01	05 58	06 56	07 54	08♊51
1964	26 07	27 05	28 03	29 01	29 58	00♊56	01 54	02 51	03 49	04 47	05 44	06 42	07 39	08 37	09♊34
1965	25 53	26 40	27 48	28 46	29 44	00♊41	01 39	02 37	03 34	04 32	05 29	06 27	07 25	08 22	09♊20
1966	25 39	26 37	27 34	28 32	29 30	00♊28	01 25	02 23	03 21	04 18	05 16	06 14	07 11	08 09	09♊06
1967	26 25	26 23	27 21	28 18	29 16	00♊14	01 11	02 09	03 07	04 04	05 02	05 59	06 57	07 55	08♊52
1968	26 09	27 07	28 04	29 02	30 00	00♊57	01 55	02 53	03 50	04 48	05 46	06 43	07 41	08 38	09♊36
1969	25 55	26 53	27 50	28 48	29 46	00♊44	01 41	02 39	03 37	04 34	05 32	06 29	07 27	08 25	09♊22
1970	25 41	26 39	27 37	28 35	29 32	00♊30	01 28	02 25	03 23	04 21	05 18	06 16	07 13	08 11	09♊09
1971	25 28	26 26	27 23	28 21	29 19	00♊17	01 14	02 12	03 10	04 07	05 05	06 03	07 00	07 58	08♊55
1972	26 12	27 10	28 07	29 05	00♊03	01 00	01 58	02 56	03 53	04 51	05 49	06 46	07 44	08 41	09♊39
1973	25 58	26 55	27 53	28 51	29 49	00♊46	01 44	02 42	03 39	04 37	05 34	06 32	07 30	08 27	09♊25
1974	25 44	26 41	27 39	28 37	29 35	00♊33	01 30	02 28	03 26	04 23	05 21	06 19	07 16	08 14	09♊11
1975	25 29	26 27	27 25	28 23	29 21	00♊18	01 16	02 14	03 11	04 09	05 06	06 04	07 02	08 00	08♊57
1976	26 13	27 11	28 09	29 06	00♊04	01 02	01 59	02 57	03 55	04 52	05 50	06 48	07 45	08 43	09♊40
1977	25 59	26 56	27 54	28 52	29 50	00♊48	01 45	02 43	03 41	04 38	05 36	06 33	07 31	08 28	09♊26
1978	25 45	26 42	27 40	28 38	29 36	00♊33	01 31	02 29	03 26	04 24	05 21	06 19	07 17	08 14	09♊12
1979	25 31	26 28	27 26	28 24	29 22	00♊19	01 17	02 15	03 13	04 10	05 08	06 05	07 03	08 01	08♊58
1980	26 14	27 12	28 10	29 08	00♊06	01 03	02 01	02 59	03 56	04 54	05 51	06 49	07 46	08 44	09♊41
1981	26 00	26 58	27 56	28 54	29 51	00♊49	01 47	02 44	03 42	04 39	05 37	06 35	07 32	08 30	09♊27
1982	25 46	26 44	27 42	28 40	29 37	00♊35	01 33	02 31	03 28	04 26	05 24	06 21	07 19	08 16	09♊14
1983	25 32	26 30	27 28	28 26	29 24	00♊21	01 19	02 17	03 14	04 12	05 10	06 07	07 05	08 02	09♊00
1984	26 16	27 14	28 12	29 10	00♊07	01 05	02 03	03 00	03 58	04 66	05 53	06 51	07 48	08 46	09♊44
1985	26 02	27 00	27 58	28 56	29 53	00♊51	01 49	02 47	03 44	04 42	05 39	06 37	07 35	08 32	09♊30
1986	25 49	27 46	27 44	28 42	29 40	00♊37	01 35	02 33	03 30	04 28	05 26	06 23	07 21	08 18	09♊16
1987	25 35	26 33	27 30	28 28	29 26	00♊24	01 21	02 19	03 17	04 14	05 12	06 10	07 07	08 05	09♊02
1988	26 19	27 16	28 14	29 12	00♊10	01 07	02 05	03 03	04 00	04 58	05 56	06 53	07 51	08 48	09♊46
1989	26 04	27 02	28 00	28 58	29 55	00♊53	01 51	02 48	03 46	04 44	05 41	06 39	07 36	08 34	09♊32
1990	25 51	27 48	27 46	28 44	29 42	00♊39	01 37	02 35	03 32	04 30	05 28	05 25	07 23	08 21	09♊18
1991	25 37	26 35	27 32	28 30	29 28	00♊26	01 23	02 21	03 19	04 16	05 14	06 11	07 09	08 07	09♊04
1992	26 21	27 18	28 16	29 14	00♊12	01 09	02 07	03 05	04 02	05 00	05 57	06 55	07 53	08 50	09♊48
1993	26 06	27 04	28 02	29 00	29 58	00♊55	01 53	02 51	03 48	04 46	05 44	06 41	07 39	08 36	09♊34
1994	25 53	26 50	27 48	28 46	29 44	00♊41	01 39	02 37	03 34	04 32	05 30	06 27	07 25	08 22	09♊20
1995	25 39	26 36	27 34	28 32	29 30	00♊27	01 25	02 23	03 21	04 18	05 16	06 13	07 11	08 09	09♊06
1996	26 22	27 20	28 18	29 16	00♊14	01 11	02 09	03 07	04 04	06 02	05 59	06 57	07 55	08 52	09♊50
1997	26 08	27 07	28 04	29 02	29 59	00♊57	01 55	02 52	03 50	04 48	05 45	06 43	07 40	08 38	09♊35
1998	25 54	26 52	27 50	28 48	29 45	00♊43	01 41	02 38	03 36	04 34	05 31	06 29	07 27	08 24	09♊22
1999	25 50	26 38	27 36	28 34	29 31	00♊29	01 27	02 25	03 22	04 20	05 17	06 15	07 13	08 10	09♊08
2000	26 24	27 22	28 19	29 17	00♊15	01 13	02 10	03 08	04 06	05 03	06 01	06 58	07 56	08 53	09♊51

Sun

June

	1st	2nd	3rd	4th	5th	6th	7th	8th	9th	10th	11th	12th	13th	14th	15th	16th
1900	10 ♊ 02	10 59	11 57	12 54	13 51	14 49	15 46	16 44	17 41	18 38	19 36	20 33	21 30	22 28	23 25	24 22
1901	09 ♊ 48	10 45	11 42	12 40	13 37	14 35	15 32	16 29	17 25	18 24	19 21	20 19	21 16	22 13	23 11	24 08
1902	09 ♊ 34	10 31	11 29	12 26	13 23	14 21	15 18	16 16	17 13	18 11	19 08	20 05	21 03	22 00	22 57	23 54
1903	09 ♊ 20	10 17	11 15	12 12	13 10	14 07	15 05	16 02	16 59	17 57	18 54	19 51	20 49	21 46	22 43	23 40
1904	10 ♊ 03	11 01	11 58	12 56	13 53	14 50	15 48	16 45	17 43	18 40	19 37	20 35	21 32	22 29	23 27	24 24
1905	09 ♊ 49	10 46	11 44	12 41	13 39	14 36	15 34	16 31	17 29	18 26	19 23	20 21	21 18	22 15	23 12	24 10
1906	09 ♊ 35	10 32	11 30	12 27	13 25	14 22	15 20	16 17	17 14	18 12	19 09	20 06	21 04	22 01	22 58	23 56
1907	09 ♊ 21	10 19	11 16	12 14	13 11	14 08	15 06	16 03	17 01	17 58	18 55	19 53	20 50	21 48	22 45	23 42
1908	10 ♊ 05	11 02	12 00	12 57	13 55	14 52	15 49	16 47	17 44	18 42	19 39	20 36	21 33	22 31	23 28	24 25
1909	09 ♊ 51	10 48	11 46	12 43	13 41	14 38	15 35	16 33	17 30	18 27	19 25	20 22	21 20	22 17	23 14	24 11
1910	09 ♊ 37	10 34	11 32	12 29	13 27	14 24	15 22	16 19	17 17	18 14	19 11	20 09	21 06	22 03	23 01	23 58
1911	09 ♊ 23	10 21	11 18	12 16	13 13	14 11	15 08	16 05	17 03	18 00	18 57	19 55	20 52	21 49	22 27	23 44
1912	10 ♊ 07	11 04	12 02	12 59	13 57	14 54	15 52	16 49	17 46	18 44	19 41	20 38	21 36	22 33	23 30	24 28
1913	09 ♊ 53	10 50	11 48	12 45	13 53	14 40	15 38	16 35	17 33	18 30	19 27	20 25	21 22	22 19	23 17	24 14
1914	09 ♊ 30	10 37	11 34	12 32	13 29	14 27	15 24	16 21	17 19	18 16	19 13	20 11	21 08	22 05	23 03	24 00
1915	09 ♊ 26	10 23	11 21	12 18	13 16	14 13	15 10	16 08	17 05	18 03	19 00	19 57	20 55	21 52	22 49	23 47
1916	10 ♊ 09	11 07	12 04	13 02	13 59	14 57	15 54	16 51	17 29	18 26	19 43	20 41	21 38	22 35	23 33	24 30
1917	09 ♊ 55	10 53	11 50	12 48	13 45	14 42	15 40	16 37	17 34	18 32	19 29	20 26	21 24	22 21	23 18	24 16
1918	09 ♊ 41	10 39	11 36	12 34	13 31	14 28	15 26	16 23	17 21	18 18	19 15	20 13	21 10	22 08	23 05	24 02
1919	09 ♊ 27	10 25	11 22	12 20	13 17	14 15	15 12	16 09	17 07	18 04	19 02	19 59	20 56	21 54	22 51	23 48
1920	10 ♊ 11	11 08	12 06	13 03	14 01	14 58	15 55	16 53	17 50	18 47	19 45	20 42	21 39	22 37	23 34	24 31
1921	09 ♊ 57	10 54	11 52	12 49	13 47	14 44	15 41	16 39	17 36	18 34	19 31	20 28	21 26	22 23	23 20	24 18
1922	09 ♊ 43	10 41	11 38	12 35	13 33	14 30	15 28	16 25	17 22	18 20	19 17	20 14	21 12	22 09	23 06	24 03
1923	09 ♊ 29	10 27	11 24	12 22	13 19	14 16	15 14	16 11	17 09	18 06	19 03	20 01	20 58	21 55	22 53	23 50
1924	10 ♊ 13	11 10	12 08	13 05	14 03	15 00	15 57	16 55	17 52	18 49	19 47	20 44	21 41	22 39	23 36	24 33
1925	09 ♊ 59	10 56	11 54	12 51	13 48	14 46	15 43	16 41	17 38	18 35	19 33	20 30	21 27	22 25	23 22	24 19
1926	09 ♊ 45	10 42	11 40	12 37	13 35	14 32	15 29	16 27	17 24	18 22	19 19	20 16	21 14	22 11	23 08	24 06
1927	09 ♊ 31	10 28	11 26	12 23	13 21	14 18	15 16	16 13	17 11	18 08	19 05	20 03	21 00	21 57	22 54	23 52
1928	10 ♊ 15	11 12	12 09	13 07	14 04	15 02	15 59	16 56	17 54	18 51	19 49	20 46	21 43	22 41	23 38	24 35
1929	10 ♊ 00	10 58	11 55	12 53	13 50	14 48	15 45	16 42	17 40	18 37	29 35	20 32	21 29	22 27	23 24	24 21
1930	09 ♊ 46	10 44	11 41	12 39	13 36	14 34	15 31	16 29	17 26	18 23	19 21	20 18	21 15	22 13	23 10	24 07
1931	09 ♊ 33	10 30	11 28	12 25	13 23	14 20	15 17	16 15	17 12	18 10	19 07	20 04	21 02	21 59	22 56	23 54
1932	10 ♊ 16	11 14	12 11	13 09	14 06	15 04	16 01	17 00	18 00	18 53	19 51	20 48	21 45	22 43	23 40	24 34
1933	10 ♊ 03	11 00	11 58	12 55	13 52	14 50	15 47	16 45	17 42	18 39	19 37	20 34	21 31	22 28	23 26	24 23
1934	09 ♊ 49	10 46	11 44	12 41	13 39	14 36	15 33	16 31	17 28	18 26	19 23	20 20	21 18	22 15	23 12	24 10
1935	09 ♊ 35	10 33	11 30	12 28	13 25	14 22	15 20	16 17	17 15	18 12	19 09	20 07	21 04	22 01	22 59	23 56
1936	10 ♊ 19	11 16	12 14	13 11	14 09	15 06	16 03	17 01	17 58	18 55	19 53	20 50	21 47	22 45	23 42	24 39
1937	10 ♊ 05	11 02	12 00	12 57	13 54	14 52	15 49	16 47	17 44	18 42	19 39	20 36	21 34	22 31	23 28	24 26
1938	09 ♊ 51	10 48	11 46	12 43	13 41	14 38	15 36	16 33	17 30	18 28	19 25	20 22	21 20	22 17	23 14	24 12
1939	09 ♊ 37	10 34	11 32	12 30	13 27	14 24	15 22	16 19	17 17	18 14	19 11	20 09	21 06	22 03	23 01	23 58
1940	10 ♊ 20	11 18	12 15	13 13	14 10	15 08	16 05	17 03	18 00	18 57	19 55	20 52	21 49	22 47	23 44	24 41
1941	10 ♊ 06	11 04	12 01	12 59	13 56	14 54	15 51	16 48	17 46	18 43	19 40	20 38	21 35	22 33	23 30	24 37
1942	09 ♊ 52	10 50	11 47	12 45	13 42	14 40	15 37	16 34	17 32	18 29	19 27	20 24	21 21	22 18	23 16	24 13
1943	09 ♊ 38	10 36	11 33	12 31	13 28	14 26	15 23	16 21	17 18	18 15	19 13	20 10	21 07	22 05	23 59	24 57
1944	10 ♊ 22	11 19	12 17	13 14	14 12	15 09	16 07	17 04	18 01	18 59	19 56	20 53	21 51	22 48	23 45	24 42
1945	10 ♊ 08	11 06	12 03	13 01	13 58	14 55	15 53	16 50	17 48	18 45	19 42	20 40	21 37	22 34	23 32	24 29
1946	09 ♊ 54	10 52	11 49	12 49	13 44	14 42	15 39	16 37	17 34	18 31	19 29	20 26	21 23	22 21	23 18	24 15
1947	09 ♊ 41	10 38	11 36	12 33	13 31	14 28	15 26	16 23	17 20	18 18	19 15	20 12	21 10	22 07	23 04	24 02
1948	10 ♊ 24	11 22	12 19	13 17	14 14	15 12	16 09	17 06	18 04	19 01	19 59	20 56	21 53	22 51	23 48	24 45
1949	10 ♊ 11	11 08	12 05	13 03	14 00	14 58	15 55	16 53	17 50	18 47	19 45	20 42	21 39	22 37	23 34	24 31
1950	09 ♊ 56	10 54	11 51	12 49	13 46	14 44	15 41	16 38	17 36	18 33	19 31	20 28	21 25	22 23	23 20	24 17
1951	09 ♊ 43	10 40	11 38	12 35	13 33	14 30	15 27	16 25	17 22	18 20	19 17	20 14	21 12	22 09	23 06	24 04
1952	10 ♊ 26	11 24	12 21	13 19	14 16	15 14	16 11	17 08	18 06	19 03	20 00	20 58	21 55	22 52	23 50	24 47
1953	10 ♊ 12	11 10	12 07	13 05	14 02	14 59	15 57	16 54	17 52	18 49	19 46	20 44	21 41	22 38	23 36	24 33
1954	09 ♊ 58	10 56	11 53	12 51	13 48	14 46	15 43	16 40	17 38	18 35	19 33	20 30	21 27	22 25	23 22	24 19
1955	09 ♊ 45	10 42	11 40	12 37	13 35	14 32	15 29	16 27	17 24	18 21	19 19	20 16	21 14	22 11	23 08	24 05
1956	10 ♊ 28	11 26	12 23	13 20	14 18	15 15	16 13	17 10	18 08	19 05	20 02	21 00	21 57	22 54	23 52	24 49
1957	10 ♊ 14	11 12	12 09	13 07	14 04	15 01	15 59	16 56	17 54	18 51	19 48	20 46	21 43	22 40	23 37	24 35
1958	10 ♊ 00	10 58	11 55	12 53	13 50	14 48	15 45	16 42	17 40	18 37	19 34	20 32	21 29	22 27	23 24	24 21
1959	09 ♊ 46	10 44	11 41	12 39	13 36	14 34	15 31	16 29	17 26	18 23	19 21	20 18	21 15	22 13	23 10	24 07
1960	10 ♊ 30	11 28	12 25	13 23	14 20	15 18	16 15	17 12	18 10	19 07	20 04	21 02	21 59	22 56	23 53	24 51
1961	10 ♊ 16	11 14	12 11	13 08	14 06	15 03	16 01	16 58	17 56	18 53	19 50	20 48	21 45	22 42	23 40	24 37
1962	10 ♊ 02	11 00	11 57	12 55	13 52	14 50	15 47	16 44	17 42	18 39	19 37	20 34	21 31	22 28	23 26	24 23
1963	09 ♊ 49	10 46	11 44	12 41	13 38	14 36	15 33	16 31	17 28	18 25	19 23	20 20	21 17	22 15	23 12	24 09
1964	10 ♊ 32	11 29	12 27	13 24	14 22	15 19	16 16	17 14	18 11	19 09	20 06	21 03	22 01	22 58	23 55	24 53
1965	10 ♊ 17	11 15	12 12	13 10	14 07	15 05	16 02	17 00	17 57	18 54	19 52	20 49	21 46	22 44	23 41	24 38
1966	10 ♊ 04	11 01	11 59	12 56	13 53	14 51	15 48	16 46	17 43	18 40	19 38	20 35	21 32	22 30	23 27	24 24
1967	09 ♊ 50	10 047	11 45	12 42	13 40	14 37	15 34	16 32	17 29	18 27	19 24	20 21	21 19	22 16	23 13	24 11
1968	10 ♊ 34	11 31	12 28	13 26	14 23	15 21	16 18	17 16	18 13	19 10	20 08	21 05	22 02	22 59	23 57	24 54
1969	10 ♊ 20	11 17	12 14	13 12	14 09	15 07	16 04	17 02	17 59	18 56	19 54	20 51	21 48	22 46	23 43	24 40
1970	10 ♊ 06	11 04	12 01	12 59	13 56	14 53	15 51	16 48	17 46	18 43	19 40	20 38	21 35	22 32	23 30	24 27
1971	09 ♊ 53	10 50	11 48	12 45	13 43	17 40	15 37	16 35	17 32	18 30	19 27	20 24	21 22	22 19	23 16	24 13
1972	10 ♊ 36	11 34	12 31	13 28	14 26	15 23	16 21	17 18	18 16	19 13	20 10	21 08	22 05	23 02	24 00	24 57
1973	10 ♊ 22	11 20	12 17	13 15	14 12	15 10	16 07	17 04	18 02	18 59	19 57	20 54	21 51	22 48	23 46	24 43
1974	10 ♊ 09	11 06	12 04	13 01	13 58	14 56	15 53	16 51	17 48	18 45	19 42	20 40	21 37	22 35	23 32	24 29
1975	09 ♊ 54	10 52	11 49	12 47	13 44	14 42	15 39	16 36	17 34	18 31	19 29	20 26	21 23	22 21	23 18	24 15
1976	10 ♊ 38	11 35	12 33	13 30	14 28	15 25	16 22	17 20	18 17	19 15	20 12	21 09	22 07	23 04	24 01	24 58
1977	10 ♊ 23	11 21	12 18	13 16	14 13	15 11	16 08	17 05	18 03	19 00	19 58	20 55	21 52	22 50	23 47	24 44
1978	10 ♊ 09	11 07	12 04	13 02	13 59	14 57	15 54	16 52	17 49	18 46	19 44	20 41	21 38	22 36	23 33	24 30
1979	09 ♊ 56	10 53	11 51	12 48	13 46	14 43	15 40	16 38	17 35	18 33	19 30	20 27	21 25	22 22	23 19	24 16
1980	10 ♊ 39	11 36	12 34	13 31	14 29	15 26	16 24	17 21	18 18	19 16	20 13	21 10	22 08	23 05	24 03	25 00
1981	10 ♊ 25	11 22	12 20	13 17	14 15	15 12	16 10	17 07	18 04	19 02	19 59	20 57	21 54	22 51	23 48	24 46
1982	10 ♊ 11	11 09	12 06	13 04	14 01	14 59	15 56	16 53	17 51	18 48	19 45	20 43	21 40	22 37	23 35	24 32
1983	09 ♊ 57	10 55	11 52	12 50	13 47	14 45	15 42	16 39	17 37	18 34	19 32	20 29	21 26	22 24	23 21	24 18
1984	10 ♊ 41	11 39	12 36	13 33	14 31	15 28	16 26	17 23	18 21	19 18	20 15	21 13	22 09	23 07	24 04	25 02
1985	10 ♊ 27	11 25	12 22	13 20	14 17	15 14	16 12	17 09	18 07	19 04	20 01	20 59	21 56	22 53	23 51	24 48
1986	10 ♊ 13	11 11	12 08	13 06	14 03	15 01	15 58	16 55	17 53	18 50	19 48	20 45	21 42	22 40	23 37	24 34
1987	10 ♊ 00	10 57	11 55	12 52	13 50	14 47	15 45	16 42	17 39	18 37	19 34	20 31	21 29	22 26	23 23	24 21
1988	10 ♊ 43	11 41	12 38	13 36	14 33	15 31	16 28	17 25	18 23	19 20	20 17	21 15	22 12	23 10	24 07	25 04
1989	10 ♊ 29	11 27	12 24	13 22	14 19	15 17	16 14	17 11	18 09	19 06	20 04	21 01	21 58	22 56	23 53	24 50
1990	10 ♊ 16	11 13	12 11	13 08	14 06	15 03	16 00	16 58	17 55	18 52	19 50	20 47	21 44	22 42	23 39	24 36
1991	10 ♊ 02	10 59	11 57	12 54	13 51	14 49	15 46	16 44	17 42	18 39	19 36	20 33	21 31	22 28	23 25	24 23
1992	10 ♊ 45	11 43	12 40	13 38	14 35	15 33	16 30	17 27	18 25	19 22	20 20	21 17	22 14	23 11	24 09	25 06
1993	10 ♊ 31	11 29	12 26	13 24	14 21	15 19	16 16	17 13	18 11	19 08	20 05	21 03	22 00	22 57	23 55	24 51
1994	10 ♊ 17	11 15	12 12	13 10	14 07	15 05	16 02	17 00	17 57	18 54	19 52	20 49	21 46	22 44	23 41	24 38
1995	10 ♊ 04	11 01	11 59	12 56	13 54	14 51	15 49	16 46	17 43	18 41	19 38	20 35	21 33	22 30	23 27	24 25
1996	10 ♊ 47	11 45	12 42	13 39	14 37	15 34	16 32	17 29	18 26	19 24	20 21	21 19	22 16	23 13	24 11	25 08
1997	10 ♊ 33	11 30	12 28	13 25	14 23	15 20	16 18	17 15	18 13	19 10	20 07	21 05	22 02	22 59	23 57	24 54
1998	10 ♊ 19	11 17	12 14	13 12	14 09	15 07	16 04	17 01	17 59	18 56	19 54	20 51	21 48	22 45	23 43	24 40
1999	10 ♊ 05	11 03	12 00	12 58	13 55	14 52	15 50	16 47	17 45	18 42	19 39	20 37	21 34	22 32	23 29	24 26
2000	10 ♊ 49	11 46	12 44	13 42	14 39	15 36	16 33	17 31	18 28	19 26	20 23	21 20	22 18	23 15	24 12	25 09

	17th	18th	19th	20th	21st	22nd	23rd	24th	25th	26th	27th	28th	29th	30th
1900	25 20	26 17	27 14	28 11	29 08	00♏ 06	01 03	02 00	02 57	03 55	04 52	05 49	06 46	07♏ 43
1901	25 05	26 03	27 00	27 57	28 55	29 52	00♏ 49	01 46	02 43	03 41	04 38	05 35	06 32	07♏ 29
1902	24 52	25 49	26 46	27 44	28 41	29 38	00♏ 35	01 32	02 30	03 27	04 24	05 21	06 18	07♏ 16
1903	24 38	25 35	26 32	27 30	28 27	29 24	00♏ 21	01 19	02 16	03 13	04 10	05 08	06 05	07♏ 02
1904	25 21	26 19	27 16	28 13	29 10	00♏ 08	01 05	02 02	02 59	03 56	04 54	05 51	06 48	07♏ 45
1905	25 07	26 04	27 02	27 59	28 56	29 53	00♏ 50	01 48	02 45	03 42	04 39	05 37	06 34	07♏ 31
1906	24 52	25 50	26 47	27 45	28 42	29 39	00♏ 37	01 34	02 31	03 28	04 25	05 23	06 20	07♏ 17
1907	24 39	25 37	26 34	27 31	28 28	19 26	00♏ 23	01 20	02 17	03 15	04 12	05 09	06 06	07♏ 03
1908	25 23	26 20	27 17	28 14	29 12	00♏ 09	01 06	02 03	03 01	03 58	04 55	05 52	06 49	07♏ 47
1909	25 09	26 06	27 03	28 00	28 58	29 55	00♏ 52	01 50	02 47	03 44	04 41	05 38	06 36	07♏ 33
1910	24 55	25 52	26 50	27 47	28 44	29 42	00♏ 39	01 36	02 33	03 30	04 27	05 25	06 22	07♏ 19
1911	24 41	25 39	27 36	27 33	28 30	29 28	00♏ 25	01 22	02 19	03 17	04 14	05 11	06 08	07♏ 06
1912	25 25	26 22	27 20	28 17	29 14	00♏ 11	01 08	02 06	03 03	04 00	04 57	05 55	06 52	07♏ 59
1913	25 11	26 08	27 06	28 03	29 00	29 57	00♏ 54	01 52	02 49	03 46	04 43	05 41	06 38	07♏ 35
1914	24 57	25 54	26 52	27 49	38 46	29 44	00♏ 41	01 38	02 35	03 33	04 30	05 27	06 24	07♏ 21
1915	24 44	25 41	26 38	27 36	28 33	29 30	00♏ 27	01 25	02 22	03 19	04 16	05 13	06 11	07♏ 08
1916	25 27	26 24	27 22	28 19	29 16	00♏ 13	01 11	02 08	03 06	04 02	04 59	05 57	06 54	07♏ 51
1917	25 13	26 10	27 08	28 05	29 02	30 00	00♏ 57	01 54	02 51	03 48	04 46	05 43	06 40	07♏ 37
1918	24 59	25 57	26 54	27 51	28 48	29 46	00♏ 43	01 40	02 37	03 35	04 32	05 29	06 26	07♏ 23
1919	24 45	25 43	26 40	27 37	28 34	29 32	00♏ 29	01 26	02 23	03 21	04 18	05 15	06 12	07♏ 10
1920	25 29	26 26	27 23	28 21	29 18	00♏ 15	01 12	02 10	03 07	04 04	05 01	05 58	06 56	07♏ 53
1921	25 15	26 12	27 09	28 07	29 04	00♏ 01	00 58	01 55	02 53	03 50	04 47	05 44	06 41	07♏ 39
1922	25 01	25 58	26 55	27 53	28 50	29 47	00♏ 44	01 42	02 39	03 36	04 33	05 31	06 28	07♏ 25
1923	24 47	25 45	26 42	27 39	28 36	29 34	00♏ 31	01 28	02 25	03 23	04 20	05 17	06 14	07♏ 11
1924	25 31	26 28	27 25	28 22	29 20	00♏ 17	01 14	02 11	03 08	04 06	05 03	06 00	06 57	07♏ 54
1925	25 16	26 14	27 11	28 08	29 06	00♏ 03	01 00	01 57	02 55	03 52	04 49	05 56	06 43	07♏ 41
1926	25 03	26 00	26 58	27 55	28 52	29 49	00♏ 47	01 44	02 41	03 38	04 35	05 33	06 30	07♏ 27
1927	24 49	25 46	26 44	27 41	28 38	29 35	00♏ 33	01 30	02 27	03 24	04 21	05 19	06 16	07♏ 13
1928	25 32	26 30	27 27	28 24	29 22	00♏ 19	01 16	02 13	03 11	04 08	05 05	06 02	06 59	07♏ 57
1929	25 19	26 16	27 13	28 10	29 08	00♏ 05	01 02	01 59	02 56	03 54	04 51	05 48	06 45	07♏ 42
1930	25 04	26 02	26 59	27 56	28 54	29 51	00♏ 48	01 45	02 43	08 40	04 37	05 34	06 32	07♏ 29
1931	24 51	25 48	26 46	27 43	28 40	29 37	00♏ 35	01 32	02 29	03 26	04 24	05 21	06 18	07♏ 15
1932	25 34	26 32	27 29	28 26	29 23	00♏ 21	01 18	02 15	03 12	04 09	05 07	06 04	07 01	07♏ 58
1933	25 20	26 18	27 15	28 12	29 09	00♏ 07	01 04	02 01	02 59	03 56	04 53	05 50	06 47	07♏ 45
1934	25 07	26 04	27 02	27 59	28 56	29 53	00♏ 51	01 48	02 45	03 42	04 39	05 37	06 34	07♏ 31
1935	24 53	25 50	26 48	27 45	28 42	29 39	00♏ 37	01 34	02 31	03 28	04 26	05 23	06 20	07♏ 17
1936	25 37	26 34	27 31	28 29	29 26	00♏ 23	01 20	02 17	03 15	04 12	05 09	06 06	07 04	08♏ 01
1937	25 22	26 20	27 17	28 15	29 12	00♏ 09	01 06	02 04	03 01	03 58	04 55	05 52	06 50	07♏ 47
1938	25 09	26 06	27 03	28 01	28 58	29 55	00♏ 52	01 50	02 47	03 44	04 41	05 39	06 36	07♏ 33
1939	24 55	25 52	26 50	27 47	28 44	29 42	00 39	01 36	02 33	03 31	04 28	05 25	06 22	07♏ 19
1940	25 39	26 36	27 33	29 30	29 28	00♏ 25	01 22	02 29	03 16	04 14	05 11	06 08	07 05	08♏ 02
1941	25 24	26 22	27 19	28 16	29 13	00♏ 11	01 08	02 05	03 02	04 00	04 57	05 54	06 52	07♏ 49
1942	25 11	26 08	27 05	28 02	29 00	29 57	00♏ 54	01 51	02 49	03 46	04 43	05 40	06 37	07♏ 35
1943	24 57	25 54	26 51	27 48	28 46	29 43	00♏ 40	01 37	02 35	03 32	04 29	05 26	06 23	07♏ 21
1944	25 40	26 37	27 34	28 32	29 29	00♏ 26	01 23	02 21	03 18	04 15	05 12	06 10	07 07	08♏ 04
1945	25 26	26 24	27 21	28 18	29 15	00♏ 13	01 10	02 07	03 04	04 02	04 59	05 56	06 53	07♏ 50
1946	25 12	26 10	27 07	28 04	29 01	29♏ 59	00 56	01 53	02 50	03 48	04 45	05 42	06 39	07♏ 37
1947	24 59	25 56	26 54	27 51	28 48	29♏ 45	00 43	01 40	02 37	03 34	04 32	05 29	06 26	07♏ 23
1948	25 42	26 40	27 37	28 34	29 31	00♏ 29	01 26	02 23	03 20	04 17	05 15	06 12	07 09	08♏ 06
1949	25 28	26 26	27 23	28 20	29 17	00♏ 15	01 12	02 09	03 06	04 04	05 01	05 58	06 55	07♏ 53
1950	25 15	26 12	27 09	28 06	29 04	00♏ 01	00 58	01 55	02 53	03 50	04 47	05 44	06 41	07♏ 39
1951	25 01	25 58	26 55	27 53	28 50	29 47	00♏ 44	01 42	02 39	03 36	04 33	05 30	06 28	07♏ 25
1952	25 44	26 41	27 39	28 36	29 33	00♏ 31	01 28	02 25	03 22	04 20	05 17	06 14	07 11	08♏ 08
1953	25 30	26 28	27 25	28 22	29 19	00♏ 17	01 14	02 11	03 08	04 06	05 03	06 00	06 57	07♏ 54
1954	25 16	26 14	27 11	28 08	29 05	00♏ 03	01 00	01 57	02 54	03 52	04 49	05 46	06 43	07♏ 41
1955	25 03	26 00	26 57	27 55	28 52	29 49	00♏ 46	01 44	02 41	03 38	04 35	05 33	06 30	07♏ 27
1956	25 46	26 43	27 41	28 38	29 35	00♏ 32	01 30	02 27	03 24	04 21	05 18	06 16	07 13	08♏ 10
1957	25 32	26 29	27 27	28 24	29 21	00♏ 18	01 16	02 13	03 10	04 07	05 04	06 02	06 59	07♏ 56
1958	25 18	26 16	27 13	28 10	29 08	00♏ 05	01 02	01 59	02 57	03 54	04 51	05 48	06 45	07♏ 43
1959	25 05	26 02	26 59	27 56	28 54	29 51	00♏ 48	01 45	02 43	03 40	04 37	05 34	06 32	07♏ 29
1960	25 48	26 45	27 43	28 40	29 37	00♏ 34	01 32	02 29	03 26	04 23	05 21	06 18	07 15	08♏ 12
1961	25 34	26 32	27 29	28 26	29 23	00♏ 21	01 18	02 15	03 12	04 09	05 07	06 04	07 01	07♏ 58
1962	25 20	26 18	27 15	28 12	19 09	00♏ 07	01 04	02 01	02 58	03 55	04 53	05 50	06 47	07♏ 44
1963	25 07	26 04	27 01	27 58	28 56	29 53	00♏ 50	01 48	02 45	03 42	04 39	05 36	06 34	07♏ 31
1964	25 50	26 47	27 44	28 42	29 39	00♏ 36	01 33	02 31	03 28	04 25	05 22	06 19	07 17	08♏ 14
1965	25 35	26 33	27 30	28 27	29 24	00 22	01 19	02 16	03 13	04 11	05 08	06 05	07 02	08♏ 00
1966	25 22	26 19	27 16	28 14	29 11	00 08	01 05	02 03	03 00	03 57	04 54	05 52	06 49	07♏ 46
1967	25 08	26 04	27 03	28 00	28 57	29 54	00♏ 52	01 49	02 46	03 43	04 40	05 38	06 35	07♏ 32
1968	25 51	26 49	27 46	28 43	29 40	00♏ 38	01 35	02 32	03 29	04 27	05 24	06 21	07 18	08♏ 16
1969	25 38	26 35	27 32	28 30	29 27	00♏ 24	01 21	02 19	03 16	04 13	05 10	06 07	07 05	08♏ 02
1970	25 24	26 22	27 19	28 16	29 13	00♏ 11	01 08	02 05	03 02	03 59	04 57	05 54	06 51	07♏ 48
1971	25 11	26 08	27 05	28 03	29 00	29 57	00♏ 54	01 52	02 49	03 46	04 43	05 41	06 38	07♏ 35
1972	25 54	26 52	27 49	28 46	29 43	00♏ 41	01 38	02 35	03 32	04 29	05 27	06 24	07 21	08♏ 18
1973	25 40	26 38	27 35	28 32	29 29	00♏ 27	01 24	02 21	03 18	04 15	05 13	06 10	07 07	08♏ 04
1974	25 27	26 24	27 21	28 19	29 16	00♏ 13	01 10	02 08	03 05	04 02	04 59	05 57	06 54	07♏ 51
1975	25 13	26 10	27 07	28 04	29 02	29 59	00♏ 56	01 53	02 51	03 48	04 45	06 42	06 39	07♏ 37
1976	25 56	26 53	27 50	28 47	29 45	00♏ 42	01 39	02 36	03 34	04 31	05 28	06 25	07 23	08♏ 20
1977	25 42	26 39	27 36	28 34	29 31	00♏ 28	01 25	02 23	03 20	04 17	05 14	06 11	07 09	08♏ 06
1978	25 28	26 25	27 22	28 20	29 17	00♏ 14	01 11	02 08	03 06	04 03	05 00	05 57	06 54	07♏ 52
1979	25 14	26 11	27 08	28 06	29 03	00♏ 00	00 57	01 55	02 52	03 49	04 46	05 44	06 41	07♏ 38
1980	25 57	26 54	27 52	28 49	29 46	00♏ 43	01 41	02 38	03 35	04 32	05 30	06 27	07 24	08♏ 21
1981	25 43	26 40	27 38	28 35	29 32	00♏ 29	01 26	02 24	03 21	04 18	05 15	06 13	07 10	08♏ 07
1982	25 29	26 27	27 24	28 21	29 19	00♏ 16	01 13	02 10	03 08	04 05	05 02	05 59	06 56	07♏ 54
1983	25 16	26 13	27 10	28 08	29 05	00♏ 02	00 59	01 56	02 54	03 51	04 48	05 45	06 43	07♏ 40
1984	25 59	26 56	27 53	28 51	29 48	00♏ 45	01 42	02 40	03 37	04 34	05 31	06 29	07 26	08♏ 23
1985	25 45	26 43	27 40	28 37	29 34	00♏ 32	01 29	02 26	03 23	04 21	05 18	06 15	07 12	08♏ 09
1986	25 32	26 29	27 26	28 23	29 21	00♏ 18	01 15	02 12	03 10	04 07	05 04	06 01	06 58	07♏ 56
1987	25 18	26 15	27 13	28 10	29 07	00♏ 04	01 02	01 59	02 56	03 53	04 51	05 48	06 45	07♏ 42
1988	26 01	26 59	27 56	28 53	29 51	00♏ 48	01 45	02 42	03 40	04 37	05 34	06 31	07 28	08♏ 26
1989	25 47	26 45	27 42	28 39	29 36	00♏ 34	01 31	02 28	03 25	04 23	05 20	06 17	07 14	08♏ 11
1990	25 34	26 31	27 28	28 26	29 23	00♏ 20	01 17	02 15	03 12	04 09	05 06	06 04	07 01	07♏ 58
1991	25 20	26 17	27 15	28 12	29 09	00♏ 06	01 03	02 01	02 58	03 55	04 53	05 50	06 47	07♏ 44
1992	26 03	27 01	27 58	28 55	29 52	00♏ 50	01 47	02 44	03 41	04 38	05 36	06 33	07 30	08♏ 27
1993	25 49	26 50	27 44	28 41	29 39	00♏ 36	01 33	02 30	03 28	04 25	05 22	06 19	07 16	08♏ 14
1994	25 36	26 33	27 30	28 27	29 25	00♏ 22	01 19	02 16	03 14	04 11	05 08	06 05	07 02	08♏ 00
1995	25 22	26 19	27 16	28 14	29 11	00♏ 08	01 05	02 30	03 00	03 57	04 54	05 52	06 49	07♏ 46
1996	26 05	27 02	28 00	28 57	29 54	00♏ 52	01 49	02 46	03 43	04 40	05 38	06 35	07 32	08♏ 29
1997	25 51	26 48	27 46	28 43	29 40	00♏ 37	01 35	02 32	03 29	04 26	05 23	06 21	07 18	08♏ 15
1998	25 37	26 35	27 32	28 29	29 26	00♏ 24	01 21	02 18	03 16	04 13	05 10	06 07	07 05	08♏ 02
1999	25 24	26 21	27 18	28 15	29 13	00♏ 10	01 07	02 04	03 02	03 59	04 56	05 53	06 50	07♏ 48
2000	26 07	27 04	28 01	28 58	29 56	00♏ 53	01 50	02 47	03 45	04 42	05 39	06 36	07 34	08♏ 31

Sun

July

	1st	2nd	3rd	4th	5th	6th	7th	8th	9th	10th	11th	12th	13th	14th	15th	16th
1900	08♋41	09 38	10 35	11 32	12 29	13 27	14 24	15 21	16 18	17 15	18 13	19 10	20 07	21 04	22 01	22 59
1901	08♋27	09 24	10 21	11 18	12 15	13 12	14 10	15 07	16 04	17 01	17 58	18 56	19 53	20 50	21 47	22 45
1902	08♋13	09 10	10 07	11 05	12 02	12 59	13 56	14 53	15 51	16 48	17 45	18 42	19 40	20 37	21 34	22 31
1903	07♋59	08 56	09 54	10 51	11 48	12 45	13 42	14 39	15 37	16 34	17 31	18 28	19 25	20 23	21 20	22 17
1904	08♋42	09 39	10 37	11 34	12 31	13 28	14 25	15 23	16 20	17 17	18 14	19 11	20 09	21 06	22 03	23 00
1905	08♋28	09 25	10 23	11 20	12 17	13 14	14 12	15 09	16 06	17 03	18 00	18 58	19 55	20 52	21 49	22 46
1906	08♋14	09 12	10 09	11 06	12 03	13 00	13 57	14 55	15 52	16 49	17 46	18 43	19 41	20 38	21 35	22 32
1907	08♋01	08 58	09 55	10 52	11 49	12 47	13 44	14 41	15 38	16 35	17 33	18 30	19 27	20 24	21 22	22 19
1908	08♋44	09 41	10 38	11 36	12 33	13 30	14 27	15 24	16 22	17 19	18 16	19 13	20 10	21 07	22 05	23 02
1909	08♋30	09 27	10 24	11 21	12 19	13 16	14 13	15 10	16 07	17 05	18 02	18 59	19 56	20 53	21 51	22 48
1910	08♋16	09 13	10 11	11 08	12 05	13 02	14 00	14 57	15 54	16 51	17 48	18 46	19 43	20 40	21 37	22 35
1911	08♋03	08 00	09 57	10 54	11 52	12 49	13 46	14 43	15 40	16 38	17 35	18 32	19 29	20 26	21 23	22 21
1912	08♋46	09 43	10 40	11 38	12 35	13 32	14 29	15 26	16 24	17 20	18 18	19 15	20 12	21 10	22 07	23 04
1913	08♋32	09 29	10 27	11 24	12 21	13 18	14 16	15 13	16 10	17 07	18 04	19 02	19 59	20 56	21 53	22 50
1914	08♋19	09 16	10 13	11 10	12 07	13 05	14 02	14 59	15 56	16 53	17 50	18 48	19 45	20 42	21 39	22 37
1915	08♋05	09 02	10 00	10 57	11 54	12 51	13 48	14 45	15 43	16 40	17 37	18 34	19 32	20 29	21 26	22 23
1916	08♋48	09 46	10 43	11 40	12 37	13 34	14 32	15 29	16 26	17 23	18 20	19 18	20 12	21 12	22 08	23 06
1917	08♋34	09 32	10 29	11 26	12 23	13 20	14 18	15 15	16 12	17 09	18 06	19 03	20 01	20 58	21 55	22 52
1918	08♋21	09 18	10 15	11 12	12 09	13 07	14 04	15 01	15 58	16 56	17 53	18 50	19 47	20 45	21 42	22 39
1919	08♋07	09 04	10 01	10 58	11 56	12 53	13 50	14 47	15 44	16 42	17 39	18 36	19 33	20 30	21 28	22 25
1920	08♋50	09 47	10 44	11 42	12 39	13 36	14 33	15 30	16 27	17 25	18 22	19 19	20 16	21 14	22 11	23 08
1921	08♋36	09 33	10 30	11 28	12 25	13 22	14 19	15 16	16 14	17 11	18 08	19 05	20 03	21 00	21 57	22 54
1922	08♋22	09 19	10 17	11 14	12 11	13 08	14 05	15 02	16 00	16 57	17 54	18 51	19 48	20 46	21 43	22 40
1923	08♋08	09 06	10 03	11 00	11 57	12 54	13 52	14 49	15 46	16 43	17 40	18 38	19 35	20 32	21 29	22 27
1924	08♋52	09 49	10 46	11 43	12 41	13 38	14 35	15 32	16 29	17 27	18 24	19 21	20 18	21 15	22 13	23 10
1925	08♋38	09 35	10 32	11 29	12 27	13 24	14 21	15 18	16 15	17 12	18 10	19 07	20 04	21 01	21 59	22 56
1926	08♋24	09 21	10 18	11 16	12 13	13 10	14 07	15 05	16 02	16 59	17 56	18 53	19 51	20 48	21 45	22 42
1927	08♋10	09 07	10 05	11 02	11 59	12 56	13 54	14 51	15 48	16 45	17 42	18 40	19 37	20 34	21 31	22 28
1928	08♋54	09 51	10 48	11 45	12 42	13 40	14 37	15 34	16 31	17 28	18 26	19 23	20 20	21 17	22 15	23 12
1929	08♋40	09 37	10 34	11 31	12 29	13 26	14 23	15 20	16 17	17 15	18 12	19 09	20 06	21 04	22 01	22 58
1930	08♋26	09 23	10 20	11 18	12 15	13 12	14 09	15 06	16 04	17 01	17 58	18 55	19 52	20 50	21 47	22 44
1931	08♋12	09 09	10 07	11 04	12 01	12 58	13 55	14 53	15 50	16 47	17 44	18 42	19 39	20 36	21 33	22 31
1932	08♋56	09 53	10 50	11 47	12 44	13 42	14 39	15 36	16 33	17 31	18 28	19 25	20 22	21 19	22 17	23 14
1933	08♋42	09 39	10 36	11 33	12 31	13 28	14 25	15 22	16 19	17 16	18 14	19 11	20 08	21 05	22 02	23 00
1934	08♋28	09 25	10 23	11 20	12 17	13 14	14 11	15 09	16 06	17 03	18 00	18 57	19 55	20 52	21 49	22 46
1935	08♋15	09 12	10 09	11 06	12 03	13 01	13 58	14 55	15 52	16 49	17 47	18 44	19 41	20 38	21 35	22 33
1936	08♋58	09 55	10 52	11 49	12 47	13 44	14 41	15 38	16 35	17 33	18 30	19 27	20 24	21 21	22 19	23 16
1937	08♋44	09 41	10 38	11 36	12 33	13 30	14 27	15 24	16 22	17 19	18 16	19 13	20 11	21 08	22 05	23 02
1938	08♋30	09 27	10 25	11 22	12 19	13 16	14 13	15 11	16 08	17 05	18 02	18 59	19 57	20 54	21 51	22 48
1939	08♋17	09 14	10 11	11 08	12 05	13 03	14 00	14 57	15 54	16 51	17 49	18 46	19 43	20 40	21 37	22 35
1940	09♋00	09 57	10 54	11 51	12 49	13 46	14 43	15 40	16 37	17 35	18 32	19 29	20 26	21 24	22 21	23 18
1941	08♋46	09 43	10 40	11 37	12 35	13 32	14 29	15 26	16 23	17 20	18 18	19 15	20 12	21 09	22 06	23 04
1942	08♋32	09 29	10 26	11 23	12 21	13 18	14 15	15 12	16 09	17 07	18 04	19 01	19 58	20 56	21 53	22 50
1943	08♋18	09 15	10 12	11 10	12 07	13 04	14 01	14 58	15 56	16 53	17 50	18 47	19 45	20 42	21 39	22 36
1944	09♋01	09 58	10 56	11 53	12 50	13 47	14 44	15 41	16 39	17 36	18 33	19 30	20 27	21 25	22 22	23 19
1945	08♋48	09 45	10 42	11 39	12 36	13 34	14 31	15 28	16 25	17 22	18 20	19 17	20 14	21 11	22 09	23 06
1946	08♋34	09 31	10 28	11 26	12 23	13 20	14 17	15 14	16 12	17 09	18 06	19 03	20 00	20 58	21 55	22 52
1947	08♋20	09 18	10 15	11 12	12 09	13 06	14 03	15 01	15 58	16 55	17 52	18 49	19 47	20 44	21 41	22 38
1948	09♋03	10 01	10 58	11 55	12 52	13 50	14 47	15 44	16 41	17 38	18 36	19 33	20 30	21 27	22 25	23 22
1949	08♋50	09 47	10 44	11 41	12 39	13 36	14 33	15 30	16 27	17 25	18 22	19 19	20 16	21 13	22 11	23 08
1950	08♋36	09 33	10 30	11 27	12 25	13 22	14 19	15 16	16 13	17 11	18 08	19 05	20 02	21 00	21 57	22 54
1951	08♋22	09 19	10 17	11 14	12 11	13 08	14 05	15 03	16 00	16 57	17 54	18 51	19 49	20 46	21 43	22 40
1952	09♋06	10 03	11 00	11 57	12 54	13 52	14 49	15 46	16 43	17 40	18 37	19 35	20 32	21 29	22 26	23 24
1953	08♋52	09 49	10 46	11 43	12 40	13 38	14 35	15 32	16 29	17 26	18 24	19 21	20 18	21 15	22 13	23 10
1954	08♋38	09 35	10 32	11 30	12 27	13 24	14 21	15 18	16 16	17 13	18 10	19 07	20 04	21 02	21 59	22 57
1955	08♋24	09 21	10 19	11 16	12 13	13 10	14 07	15 05	16 02	16 59	17 56	18 53	19 51	20 48	21 45	22 42
1956	09♋07	10 04	11 02	11 59	12 56	13 53	14 51	15 48	16 45	17 42	18 39	19 37	20 34	21 31	22 28	23 26
1957	08♋53	09 51	10 48	11 45	12 42	13 39	14 37	15 34	16 31	17 28	18 25	19 23	20 20	21 17	22 14	23 11
1958	08♋40	09 37	10 34	11 31	12 29	13 26	14 23	15 20	16 17	17 15	18 12	19 09	20 06	21 03	22 01	22 58
1959	08♋26	09 23	10 20	11 17	12 15	13 12	14 09	15 06	16 04	17 01	17 58	18 55	19 52	20 50	21 47	22 44
1960	09♋10	10 07	11 04	12 01	12 58	13 55	14 53	15 50	16 47	17 44	18 41	19 39	20 36	21 33	22 30	23 27
1961	08♋55	09 53	10 50	11 47	12 44	13 41	14 39	15 36	16 33	17 30	18 28	19 25	20 22	21 19	22 16	23 14
1962	08♋42	09 39	10 36	11 33	12 30	13 28	14 25	15 22	16 19	17 17	18 14	19 11	20 08	21 05	22 03	23 00
1963	08♋28	09 25	10 22	11 20	12 17	13 14	14 11	15 08	16 06	17 03	18 00	18 57	19 54	20 52	21 49	22 46
1964	09♋11	10 08	11 05	12 03	13 00	13 57	14 54	15 52	16 49	17 46	18 43	19 40	20 38	21 35	22 32	23 29
1965	08♋57	09 54	10 51	11 48	12 46	13 43	14 40	15 37	16 34	17 32	18 29	19 26	20 23	21 21	22 18	23 15
1966	08♋43	09 40	10 38	11 35	12 32	13 29	14 26	15 24	16 21	17 18	18 15	19 12	20 10	21 07	22 04	23 01
1967	08♋29	09 26	10 24	11 21	12 18	13 15	14 13	15 10	16 07	17 04	18 02	18 59	19 56	20 53	21 50	22 48
1968	09♋13	10 10	11 07	12 04	13 02	13 59	14 56	15 53	16 50	17 48	18 45	19 42	20 39	21 36	22 34	23 31
1969	08♋59	09 56	10 53	11 50	12 48	13 45	14 42	15 39	16 36	17 34	18 31	19 28	20 25	21 23	22 20	23 17
1970	08♋46	09 43	10 40	11 37	12 34	13 32	14 29	15 26	16 23	17 21	18 18	19 15	20 12	21 09	22 07	23 04
1971	08♋32	09 29	10 27	11 24	12 21	13 18	14 15	15 13	16 10	17 07	18 04	19 01	19 59	20 56	21 53	22 50
1972	09♋15	10 13	11 10	12 07	13 04	14 01	14 59	15 56	16 53	17 50	18 48	19 45	20 42	21 39	22 36	23 34
1973	09♋02	09 59	10 56	11 53	12 51	13 48	14 45	15 42	16 39	17 37	18 34	19 31	20 28	21 25	22 23	23 20
1974	08♋48	09 45	10 43	11 40	12 37	13 34	14 31	15 28	16 26	17 23	18 20	19 17	20 14	21 12	22 09	23 06
1975	08♋34	09 31	10 28	11 25	12 23	13 20	14 17	15 14	16 12	17 09	18 06	19 03	20 00	20 58	21 55	22 52
1976	09♋17	10 14	11 12	12 09	13 06	14 03	15 00	15 58	16 55	17 52	18 49	19 46	20 44	21 41	22 38	23 35
1977	09♋03	10 00	10 57	11 55	12 52	13 49	14 46	15 43	16 41	17 38	18 35	19 32	20 30	21 27	22 24	23 21
1978	08♋49	09 46	10 43	11 41	12 38	13 35	14 32	15 30	16 27	17 24	18 21	19 18	20 16	21 13	22 10	23 07
1979	08♋35	09 33	10 30	11 27	12 24	13 21	14 19	15 16	16 13	17 10	18 07	19 04	20 02	20 59	21 56	22 53
1980	09♋18	10 15	11 13	12 10	13 07	14 04	15 01	15 59	16 56	17 53	18 50	19 48	20 45	21 42	22 30	23 37
1981	09♋04	10 02	10 59	11 56	12 53	13 50	14 48	15 45	16 42	17 39	18 36	19 34	20 31	21 28	22 25	23 22
1982	08♋51	09 48	10 45	11 42	12 39	13 37	14 34	15 31	16 28	17 26	18 23	19 20	20 17	21 14	22 12	23 09
1983	08♋37	09 34	10 31	11 29	12 26	13 23	14 20	15 17	16 15	17 12	18 09	19 06	20 04	21 01	21 58	22 55
1984	09♋20	10 18	11 15	12 12	13 09	14 06	15 04	16 01	16 58	17 55	18 52	19 50	20 57	21 44	22 41	23 38
1985	09♋07	10 04	11 01	11 58	12 55	13 53	14 50	15 47	16 44	17 41	18 39	19 36	20 33	21 30	22 28	23 24
1986	08♋53	09 50	10 47	11 44	12 42	13 39	14 36	15 33	16 31	17 28	18 25	19 22	20 20	21 17	22 14	23 11
1987	08♋40	09 37	10 34	11 31	12 28	13 26	14 23	15 20	16 17	17 14	18 11	19 09	20 06	21 03	22 00	22 57
1988	09♋23	10 20	11 17	12 14	13 11	14 09	15 06	16 03	17 00	17 57	18 55	19 52	20 49	21 46	22 44	23 41
1989	09♋09	10 06	11 03	12 00	12 58	13 55	14 52	15 49	16 47	17 44	18 41	19 38	20 35	21 33	22 30	23 27
1990	08♋55	09 53	10 50	11 47	12 44	13 41	14 39	15 36	16 33	17 30	18 27	19 25	20 22	21 19	22 16	23 13
1991	08♋41	09 39	10 36	11 33	12 30	13 27	14 25	15 22	16 19	17 16	18 13	19 11	20 08	21 05	22 02	23 00
1992	09♋25	10 22	11 19	12 16	13 14	14 11	15 08	16 05	17 02	18 00	18 57	19 54	20 51	21 48	22 46	23 43
1993	09♋11	10 08	11 05	12 02	13 00	13 57	14 54	15 51	16 48	17 46	18 43	19 40	20 37	21 34	22 32	23 29
1994	08♋57	09 54	10 51	11 48	12 46	18 43	14 40	15 37	16 35	17 32	18 29	19 26	20 24	21 21	22 18	23 15
1995	08♋43	09 41	10 38	11 35	12 32	13 29	14 27	15 24	16 21	17 18	18 15	19 13	20 10	21 07	22 04	23 01
1996	09♋26	10 24	11 21	12 18	13 15	14 12	15 10	16 07	17 04	18 01	18 58	19 56	20 53	21 50	22 47	23 45
1997	09♋12	10 10	11 07	12 04	13 01	13 58	14 56	15 53	16 50	17 47	18 45	19 42	20 39	21 36	22 33	23 31
1998	08♋59	09 56	10 53	11 51	12 48	13 45	14 42	15 39	16 36	17 34	18 31	19 28	20 25	21 22	22 20	23 17
1999	08♋45	09 42	10 39	11 36	12 34	13 31	14 28	15 25	16 22	17 20	18 17	19 14	20 11	21 09	22 06	23 03
2000	09♋28	10 25	11 22	12 20	13 17	14 14	15 11	16 09	17 06	18 03	19 00	19 57	20 55	21 52	22 49	23 46

	17th	18th	19th	20th	21st	22nd	23rd	24th	25th	26th	27th	28th	29th	30th	31st
1900	23 56	24 53	25 50	26 48	27 45	28 42	29 39	00♌ 37	01 34	02 31	03 29	04 36	05 24	06 21	07♌ 18
1901	23 42	24 39	25 37	26 34	27 31	28 28	29 26	00♌ 23	01 20	02 18	03 25	04 12	05 10	06 07	07♌ 04
1902	23 28	24 26	25 23	26 20	27 17	28 15	29 12	00♌ 09	01 06	02 04	03 02	03 58	04 56	05 54	06♌ 51
1903	23 14	24 12	25 09	26 06	27 03	28 01	28 58	29 55	00♌ 53	01 50	02 47	03 45	04 42	05 39	06♌ 37
1904	23 58	24 55	25 52	26 50	27 47	28 44	29 41	00♌ 39	01 35	02 33	03 31	04 28	05 25	06 23	07♌ 20
1905	23 44	24 41	25 38	26 35	27 33	28 30	29 27	00♌ 24	01 22	02 19	03 16	04 14	05 11	06 09	07♌ 06
1906	23 30	24 27	26 24	26 21	27 19	28 16	29 13	00♌ 11	01 08	02 05	03 03	04 00	04 57	05 55	06♌ 52
1907	23 16	24 13	25 11	26 08	27 05	28 02	29 00	29 57	00♌ 54	01 51	02 49	03 46	04 43	05 41	06♌ 38
1908	23 59	24 56	25 54	26 51	27 48	28 45	29 43	00♌ 40	01 37	02 35	03 32	04 29	05 27	06 24	07♌ 22
1909	23 45	24 43	25 40	26 37	27 34	28 32	29 29	00♌ 26	01 24	02 21	03 18	04 16	05 13	06 10	07♌ 08
1910	23 32	24 29	25 26	26 24	27 21	28 18	29 15	00♌ 13	01 10	02 07	03 05	04 02	04 59	05 57	06♌ 54
1911	23 18	24 15	25 12	26 10	27 07	28 04	29 02	29 59	00♌ 56	01 54	02 51	03 48	04 46	05 43	06♌ 40
1912	24 01	24 59	25 56	26 53	27 51	28 48	29 45	00♌ 42	01 40	02 37	03 34	04 32	05 29	06 26	07♌ 24
1913	23 48	24 45	25 42	26 39	27 37	28 34	29 31	00♌ 29	01 26	02 23	03 20	04 18	05 15	06 13	07♌ 10
1914	23 34	24 31	25 28	26 26	27 23	28 20	29 18	00♌ 15	01 12	02 10	03 07	04 04	05 02	05 59	06♌ 56
1915	23 21	24 18	25 15	26 12	27 10	28 07	29 04	00♌ 01	00 59	01 56	02 53	03 51	04 48	06 45	06♌ 43
1916	24 04	25 01	25 58	26 55	27 53	28 50	29 47	00♌ 45	01 42	02 39	03 36	04 34	05 31	06 29	07♌ 26
1917	23 50	24 47	25 44	26 42	27 39	28 36	29 33	00♌ 31	01 28	02 25	03 23	04 20	05 17	06 15	07♌ 12
1918	23 36	24 33	25 31	26 28	27 25	28 23	29 20	00♌ 17	01 14	02 12	03 09	04 06	05 04	06 01	06♌ 58
1919	23 22	24 19	25 17	26 14	27 11	28 08	29 06	00♌ 03	01 00	01 58	02 55	03 52	04 50	05 47	06♌ 45
1920	24 05	25 03	26 00	26 57	27 54	28 52	29 49	00♌ 46	01 44	02 41	03 38	04 36	05 33	06 30	07♌ 28
1921	23 51	24 49	25 46	26 43	27 40	28 38	29 35	00♌ 32	01 30	02 27	03 24	04 22	05 19	06 17	07♌ 14
1922	23 37	24 35	25 32	26 29	27 26	28 24	29 21	00♌ 18	01 16	02 13	03 10	04 08	05 05	06 02	07♌ 00
1923	23 24	24 21	25 18	26 16	27 13	28 10	29 07	00♌ 05	01 02	01 59	02 57	03 54	04 51	05 49	06♌ 46
1924	24 07	25 04	26 02	26 59	27 56	28 53	29 51	00♌ 48	01 45	02 42	03 40	04 37	05 35	06 32	07♌ 29
1925	23 53	24 50	25 48	26 45	27 42	28 39	29 37	00♌ 34	01 31	02 29	03 26	04 23	05 21	06 18	07♌ 15
1926	23 40	24 37	25 34	26 31	27 29	28 26	29 23	00♌ 20	01 28	02 15	03 12	04 10	05 07	06 04	07♌ 02
1927	23 26	24 23	25 20	26 17	27 15	28 12	29 09	00♌ 07	01 04	02 01	02 59	03 56	04 53	05 51	06♌ 48
1928	24 09	25 06	26 04	27 01	27 58	28 55	29 53	00♌ 50	01 47	02 45	03 42	04 39	05 37	06 34	07♌ 31
1929	23 55	24 53	25 50	26 47	27 44	28 42	29 39	00♌ 36	01 33	02 31	03 28	04 25	05 23	06 20	07♌ 17
1930	23 41	24 38	25 36	26 33	27 30	28 28	29 25	00♌ 22	01 20	02 17	03 14	04 12	05 09	06 06	07♌ 04
1931	23 28	24 25	25 22	26 20	27 17	28 14	29 11	00♌ 09	01 06	02 03	03 01	03 58	04 55	05 53	06♌ 50
1932	24 11	25 08	26 05	27 03	28 00	28 57	29 55	00♌ 52	01 49	02 46	03 44	04 41	05 39	06 36	07♌ 33
1933	23 57	24 54	25 51	26 49	27 46	28 43	29 41	00♌ 38	01 35	02 33	03 30	04 27	05 25	06 22	07♌ 19
1934	23 44	24 41	25 38	26 35	27 33	28 30	29 27	00♌ 25	01 22	02 19	03 16	04 14	05 11	06 08	07♌ 06
1935	23 30	24 27	25 24	26 22	27 19	28 16	29 13	00♌ 11	01 08	02 05	03 03	04 00	04 57	05 55	06♌ 52
1936	24 13	25 10	26 08	27 05	28 02	29 00	29 57	00♌ 54	01 52	02 49	03 46	04 44	05 41	06 38	07♌ 36
1937	23 59	24 57	25 54	26 51	27 48	28 46	29 43	00♌ 40	01 38	02 35	03 32	04 30	05 27	06 24	07♌ 22
1938	23 45	24 43	25 40	26 37	27 34	28 32	29 29	00♌ 26	01 24	02 21	03 18	04 16	05 13	06 11	07♌ 08
1939	23 32	24 29	25 26	26 24	27 21	28 18	29 16	00♌ 13	01 10	02 07	03 05	04 02	04 59	05 57	06♌ 54
1940	24 15	25 12	26 10	27 07	28 04	29 01	00 00	00♌ 57	01 53	02 51	03 48	04 45	05 43	06 40	07♌ 37
1941	24 01	24 58	25 55	26 53	27 50	28 47	29 45	00♌ 42	01 39	02 37	03 34	04 31	05 29	06 26	07♌ 03
1942	23 47	24 45	25 42	26 39	27 37	28 34	29 31	00♌ 28	01 26	02 23	03 20	04 18	05 15	06 12	07♌ 10
1943	23 33	24 31	25 28	26 25	27 22	28 20	29 17	00♌ 14	01 11	02 09	03 06	04 03	05 01	05 58	06♌ 56
1944	24 16	25 14	26 11	27 08	28 06	29 03	00♌ 00	00 57	01 55	02 52	03 49	04 47	05 44	06 42	07♌ 39
1945	24 03	25 00	25 58	26 55	27 52	28 49	29 47	00♌ 44	01 41	02 39	03 36	04 33	05 31	06 28	07♌ 25
1946	23 49	24 46	25 44	26 41	27 38	28 35	29 33	00♌ 30	01 27	02 25	03 22	04 19	05 17	06 14	07♌ 12
1947	23 36	24 33	25 30	26 27	27 25	28 22	29 19	00♌ 17	01 14	02 11	03 09	04 06	05 03	06 01	06♌ 58
1948	24 19	25 16	26 14	27 11	28 08	29 05	00♌ 03	01 00	01 57	02 54	03 52	04 49	06 47	06 44	07♌ 41
1949	24 05	25 02	26 00	26 57	27 54	28 51	29 49	00♌ 46	01 43	02 41	03 38	04 35	05 33	06 30	07♌ 28
1950	23 51	24 49	25 46	26 43	27 40	28 38	29 35	00♌ 32	01 30	02 27	03 24	04 21	05 19	06 16	07♌ 14
1951	23 38	24 35	25 32	26 29	27 26	28 24	29 21	00♌ 18	01 16	02 13	03 10	04 08	05 05	06 02	07♌ 00
1952	24 21	25 18	26 15	27 13	28 10	29 07	00♌ 04	01 02	01 59	02 56	03 54	04 51	05 49	06 46	07♌ 43
1953	24 07	25 04	26 02	26 59	27 56	28 53	29 51	00♌ 48	01 45	02 43	03 40	04 37	05 35	06 32	07♌ 29
1954	23 53	24 50	25 48	26 45	27 42	28 39	29 37	00♌ 34	01 31	02 29	03 26	04 23	05 21	06 18	07♌ 16
1955	23 40	24 37	25 34	26 31	27 29	28 26	29 23	00♌ 21	01 18	02 15	03 12	04 10	05 07	06 05	07♌ 51
1956	24 23	25 20	26 17	27 15	28 12	29 09	00♌ 06	01 04	02 01	02 58	03 56	04 53	06 50	06 48	07♌ 45
1957	24 09	25 06	26 03	27 00	27 58	28 55	29 52	00♌ 50	01 47	02 44	03 42	04 39	05 36	06 34	07♌ 31
1958	23 55	24 52	25 50	26 47	27 44	28 42	29 39	00♌ 36	01 33	02 31	03 28	04 25	05 23	06 20	07♌ 17
1959	23 41	24 39	25 36	26 33	27 30	28 28	29 25	00♌ 22	01 29	02 17	03 14	04 11	05 09	06 06	07♌ 03
1960	24 25	25 22	26 19	27 16	28 14	29 11	00♌ 08	01 06	02 03	03 00	03 58	04 55	05 52	06 50	07♌ 47
1961	24 11	25 08	26 06	27 03	28 00	28 57	29 55	00♌ 52	01 49	02 47	03 44	04 41	05 38	06 36	07♌ 33
1962	23 57	24 54	25 51	26 49	27 46	28 43	29 41	00♌ 38	01 35	02 32	03 30	04 27	05 25	06 22	07♌ 19
1963	23 43	24 40	25 38	26 35	27 32	28 30	29 27	00♌ 24	01 22	02 19	03 16	04 14	05 11	06 08	07♌ 06
1964	24 27	25 24	26 21	27 18	28 16	29 13	00♌ 10	01 07	02 05	03 02	03 59	04 57	05 54	06 51	07♌ 49
1965	24 12	25 09	26 07	27 04	28 01	28 58	29 56	00♌ 53	01 50	02 48	03 45	04 42	05 40	06 37	07♌ 35
1966	23 59	24 56	25 53	26 50	27 48	28 45	29 42	00♌ 40	01 37	02 34	03 32	04 29	05 26	06 24	07♌ 21
1967	23 45	24 42	25 39	26 37	27 34	28 31	29 28	00♌ 26	01 23	02 20	03 18	04 15	05 12	06 10	07♌ 07
1968	24 28	25 25	26 22	27 20	28 17	29 14	00♌ 12	01 09	02 06	03 04	04 01	04 58	05 56	06 53	07♌ 51
1969	24 14	25 12	26 09	27 06	28 04	29 01	29 58	00♌ 55	01 53	02 50	03 47	04 45	05 42	06 39	07♌ 37
1970	24 01	24 58	25 56	26 53	27 50	28 47	29 45	00♌ 42	01 39	02 36	03 34	04 31	05 28	06 26	07♌ 23
1971	23 47	24 45	25 42	26 39	27 36	28 34	29 31	00♌ 28	01 26	02 23	03 20	04 18	05 15	06 12	07♌ 10
1972	24 31	25 28	26 26	27 23	28 20	29 17	00♌ 15	01 12	02 09	03 06	04 04	05 01	05 58	06 56	07♌ 53
1973	24 17	25 14	26 11	27 09	28 06	29 03	00♌ 00	00 58	01 55	02 52	03 50	04 47	05 45	06 42	07♌ 39
1974	24 03	25 01	25 58	26 55	27 53	28 50	29 47	00♌ 45	01 42	02 39	03 36	04 34	05 31	06 28	07♌ 26
1975	23 49	24 47	25 44	26 41	27 38	28 36	29 33	00♌ 30	01 27	02 25	03 22	04 19	05 17	06 14	07♌ 11
1976	24 32	25 30	26 27	27 24	28 21	29 19	00♌ 15	01 13	02 11	03 08	04 05	05 03	06 00	06 57	07♌ 55
1977	24 19	25 16	26 13	27 10	28 08	29 05	00♌ 02	01 00	01 57	02 54	03 51	04 49	05 46	06 44	07♌ 41
1978	24 05	25 02	25 59	26 56	27 54	28 51	29 48	00♌ 45	01 43	02 40	03 37	04 35	05 32	06 29	07♌ 27
1979	23 51	24 48	25 45	26 42	27 40	28 37	29 34	00♌ 32	01 29	02 26	03 24	04 21	05 18	06 16	07♌ 13
1980	24 34	25 31	26 28	27 26	28 23	29 20	00♌ 17	01 15	02 12	03 09	04 07	05 04	06 01	06 59	07♌ 56
1981	24 20	25 17	26 14	27 11	28 09	29 06	00♌ 03	01 00	01 58	02 55	03 52	04 50	05 47	06 45	07♌ 42
1982	24 06	25 03	26 01	26 58	27 55	28 53	29 50	00♌ 47	01 44	02 42	03 39	04 36	05 34	06 31	07♌ 29
1983	23 52	24 50	25 47	26 44	27 41	28 39	29 36	00♌ 33	01 31	02 28	03 25	04 22	05 20	06 17	07♌ 14
1984	24 36	25 33	26 30	27 27	28 25	29 22	00♌ 19	01 16	02 14	03 11	04 08	05 06	06 03	07 01	07♌ 58
1985	24 22	25 19	26 17	27 14	28 11	29 08	00♌ 06	01 03	02 00	02 58	03 55	04 52	05 50	06 47	07♌ 44
1986	24 08	25 06	26 03	27 00	27 57	28 55	29 52	00♌ 49	01 46	02 44	03 41	04 38	05 36	06 33	07♌ 30
1987	23 55	24 52	25 49	26 46	27 44	28 41	29 38	00♌ 36	01 33	02 30	03 28	04 25	05 22	06 20	07♌ 17
1988	24 38	25 35	26 33	27 30	28 27	29 25	00♌ 22	01 19	02 16	03 14	04 11	05 08	06 06	07 03	08♌ 00
1989	24 24	25 21	26 19	27 16	28 13	29 10	00♌ 08	01 05	02 02	03 00	03 57	04 54	05 52	06 49	07♌ 46
1990	24 11	25 08	26 05	27 02	28 00	28 57	29 54	00♌ 52	01 49	02 46	03 44	04 41	05 38	06 36	07♌ 33
1991	23 57	24 54	25 51	26 49	27 46	28 43	29 40	00♌ 38	01 35	02 32	03 30	04 27	05 24	06 22	07♌ 19
1992	24 40	25 37	26 34	27 32	28 29	29 26	00♌ 24	01 21	02 18	03 15	04 13	06 10	07 08	07 05	08♌ 02
1993	24 26	25 23	26 21	27 18	28 15	29 13	00♌ 10	01 07	02 05	03 02	03 59	04 57	05 54	06 51	07♌ 49
1994	24 12	25 10	26 07	27 04	28 01	28 59	29 56	00♌ 53	01 51	02 48	03 45	04 42	05 40	06 37	07♌ 35
1995	23 59	24 56	25 53	26 50	27 48	28 45	29 42	00♌ 39	01 37	02 34	03 31	04 29	05 26	06 23	07♌ 21
1996	24 42	25 39	26 36	27 34	28 31	29 28	00♌ 26	01 23	02 20	03 17	04 15	05 12	06 09	07 07	08♌ 04
1997	24 28	25 25	26 22	27 20	28 17	29 14	00♌ 11	01 09	02 06	03 03	04 01	04 58	05 55	06 53	07♌ 50
1998	24 14	25 11	26 09	27 06	28 03	29 00	29 58	00♌ 55	01 52	02 50	03 47	04 44	05 42	06 39	07♌ 37
1999	24 00	24 58	25 55	26 52	27 49	28 47	29 44	00♌ 41	01 38	02 36	03 33	04 30	05 28	06 25	07♌ 22
2000	24 43	25 41	26 38	27 35	28 32	29 30	00♌ 27	01 24	02 22	03 19	04 16	05 14	06 11	07 08	08♌ 06

Sun

August

Year	1st	2nd	3rd	4th	5th	6th	7th	8th	9th	10th	11th	12th	13th	14th	15th	16th
1900	08♌16	09 13	10 11	11 08	12 06	13 03	14 00	14 58	15 56	16 53	17 51	18 48	19 46	20 43	21 41	22 39
1901	08♌02	08 59	09 56	10 54	11 51	12 49	13 46	14 44	15 41	16 39	17 36	18 34	19 32	20 29	21 27	22 25
1902	17♌48	08 45	09 43	10 40	11 38	12 35	13 33	14 30	15 28	16 25	17 23	18 21	19 18	20 16	21 13	22 11
1903	07♌34	08 32	09 29	10 26	11 23	12 21	13 19	14 16	15 14	16 11	17 09	18 06	19 04	20 02	20 59	21 57
1904	08♌17	09 15	10 12	11 10	12 07	13 05	14 02	15 00	15 57	16 55	17 52	18 50	19 48	20 45	21 43	22 41
1905	08♌03	09 01	09 58	10 56	11 53	12 51	13 48	14 46	15 43	16 41	17 38	18 36	19 34	20 31	21 29	22 26
1906	07♌50	08 47	09 44	10 42	11 39	12 37	13 34	14 32	15 29	16 27	17 24	18 22	19 19	20 17	21 15	22 12
1907	07♌36	08 33	09 30	10 28	11 25	12 23	13 20	14 18	15 15	16 13	17 10	18 08	19 06	20 03	21 01	21 59
1908	08♌19	09 16	10 14	11 11	12 09	13 06	14 04	15 01	15 59	16 56	17 54	18 52	19 49	20 47	21 44	22 42
1909	08♌05	09 02	10 00	10 57	11 55	12 52	13 50	14 47	15 45	16 42	17 40	18 37	19 35	20 33	21 30	22 28
1910	07♌51	08 49	09 46	10 44	11 41	12 39	13 36	14 34	15 31	16 29	17 26	18 24	19 22	20 19	21 17	22 15
1911	07♌38	08 35	09 33	10 30	11 27	12 25	13 22	14 20	15 17	16 15	17 12	18 10	19 08	20 05	21 03	22 00
1912	08♌21	09 19	10 16	11 13	12 11	13 08	14 06	15 03	16 01	16 58	17 56	18 54	19 51	20 49	21 47	22 44
1913	08♌07	09 05	10 02	11 00	11 57	12 55	13 52	14 50	15 47	16 45	17 42	18 40	19 38	20 35	21 33	22 31
1914	07♌54	08 51	09 49	10 46	11 43	12 41	13 38	14 36	15 33	16 31	17 28	18 26	19 24	20 21	21 19	22 17
1915	07♌40	08 37	09 35	10 32	11 30	12 27	13 25	14 22	15 20	16 17	17 15	18 12	19 10	20 08	21 05	22 03
1916	08♌24	09 21	10 18	11 16	12 13	13 11	14 08	15 06	16 03	17 01	17 58	18 56	19 54	20 51	21 49	22 46
1917	08♌10	09 07	10 04	11 02	11 59	12 57	13 54	14 52	15 49	16 47	17 44	18 42	19 39	20 37	21 35	22 32
1918	07♌56	08 53	09 51	10 48	11 46	12 43	13 41	14 38	15 36	16 33	17 31	18 28	19 26	20 24	21 21	22 19
1919	07♌42	08 39	09 37	10 34	11 32	12 29	13 27	14 24	15 22	16 19	17 17	18 14	19 12	20 09	21 07	22 05
1920	08♌25	09 22	10 20	11 17	12 15	13 12	14 10	15 07	16 05	17 02	18 00	18 58	19 55	20 53	21 51	22 48
1921	08♌11	09 09	10 05	11 03	12 01	12 58	13 56	14 53	15 51	16 49	17 46	18 44	19 41	20 39	21 37	22 34
1922	07♌57	08 55	09 52	10 50	11 47	12 44	13 42	14 39	15 37	16 34	17 32	18 30	19 27	20 25	21 22	22 20
1923	07♌43	08 41	09 38	10 36	11 33	12 30	13 28	14 25	15 23	16 21	17 18	18 16	19 13	20 11	21 09	22 06
1924	08♌27	09 24	10 22	11 19	12 17	13 14	14 12	15 09	16 07	17 04	18 02	18 59	19 57	20 54	21 52	22 50
1925	08♌13	09 10	10 08	11 05	12 03	13 00	13 57	14 55	15 52	16 50	17 48	18 45	19 43	20 40	21 38	22 36
1926	07♌59	08 57	09 54	10 51	11 49	12 46	13 44	14 41	15 39	16 37	17 34	18 32	19 29	20 27	21 25	22 22
1927	07♌45	08 43	09 40	10 38	11 35	12 33	13 30	14 28	15 25	16 23	17 20	18 18	19 15	20 13	21 10	22 08
1928	08♌29	09 26	10 24	11 21	12 18	13 16	14 13	15 11	16 08	17 06	18 04	19 01	19 59	20 56	21 54	22 52
1929	08♌15	09 12	10 10	11 07	12 05	13 02	14 00	14 57	15 55	16 52	17 50	18 48	19 45	20 43	21 40	22 38
1930	08♌01	08 59	09 56	10 53	11 51	12 48	13 46	14 43	15 41	16 38	17 36	18 33	19 31	20 29	21 26	22 24
1931	07♌47	08 45	09 42	10 40	11 37	12 34	13 32	14 29	15 27	16 25	17 22	18 20	19 17	20 15	21 13	22 10
1932	08♌31	09 28	10 26	11 23	12 21	13 18	14 16	15 13	16 11	17 08	18 06	19 03	20 01	20 59	21 56	22 54
1933	08♌17	09 15	10 12	11 09	12 07	13 04	14 01	14 59	15 56	16 54	17 52	18 49	19 47	20 44	21 42	22 40
1934	08♌03	09 01	09 58	10 55	11 53	12 50	13 48	14 45	15 43	16 41	17 38	18 36	19 33	20 31	21 29	22 26
1935	07♌50	08 47	09 44	10 42	11 39	12 37	13 34	14 32	15 29	16 27	17 24	18 22	19 19	20 17	21 15	22 12
1936	08♌33	09 30	10 28	11 25	12 23	13 20	14 18	15 15	16 13	17 10	18 08	19 05	20 03	21 01	21 58	22 56
1937	08♌19	09 16	10 14	11 11	12 09	13 06	14 04	15 01	15 59	16 56	17 54	18 52	19 49	20 47	21 45	22 42
1938	08♌05	09 03	10 00	10 58	11 55	12 53	13 50	14 48	15 45	16 43	17 40	18 38	19 35	20 33	21 30	22 28
1939	07♌51	08 49	09 46	10 44	11 41	12 39	13 36	14 31	15 31	16 29	17 26	18 23	19 21	20 19	21 17	22 14
1940	08♌35	09 32	10 30	11 27	12 25	13 22	14 20	15 17	16 15	17 12	18 10	19 07	20 05	21 03	22 00	22 58
1941	08♌21	09 18	10 16	11 13	12 11	13 08	14 05	15 03	16 00	16 58	17 56	18 53	19 51	20 48	21 46	22 44
1942	08♌07	09 04	10 02	10 59	11 57	12 54	13 52	14 49	15 47	16 44	17 42	18 39	19 37	20 35	21 32	22 30
1943	07♌53	08 50	09 48	10 45	11 43	12 40	13 38	14 35	15 33	16 30	17 28	18 25	19 23	20 21	21 18	22 16
1944	08♌36	09 34	10 31	11 29	12 26	13 23	14 21	15 18	16 16	17 13	18 11	19 09	20 06	21 04	22 02	22 59
1945	08♌23	09 20	10 18	11 15	12 12	13 10	14 08	15 05	16 03	17 00	17 58	18 55	19 53	20 51	21 48	22 46
1946	08♌09	09 06	10 04	11 01	11 59	12 56	13 54	14 51	15 49	16 46	17 44	18 41	19 39	20 37	21 34	22 32
1947	07♌55	08 53	09 50	10 47	11 45	12 42	13 40	14 37	15 35	16 32	17 30	18 27	19 25	20 23	21 20	22 18
1948	08♌39	09 36	10 33	11 31	12 28	13 26	14 23	15 21	16 19	17 16	18 14	19 11	20 09	21 06	22 04	23 02
1949	08♌25	09 22	10 20	11 17	12 15	13 12	14 10	15 07	16 05	17 02	18 00	18 57	19 55	20 52	21 50	22 48
1950	08♌11	09 08	10 06	11 03	12 01	12 58	13 55	14 53	15 51	16 48	17 46	18 43	19 41	20 39	21 36	22 34
1951	07♌57	08 55	09 52	10 49	11 47	12 44	13 42	14 39	15 37	16 34	17 32	18 30	19 27	20 25	21 22	22 20
1952	08♌41	09 38	10 35	11 33	12 30	13 28	14 25	15 23	16 20	17 18	18 15	19 13	20 10	21 08	22 06	23 03
1953	08♌27	09 24	10 22	11 19	12 16	13 14	14 11	15 09	16 07	17 04	18 02	18 59	19 57	20 55	21 52	22 50
1954	08♌13	09 10	10 08	11 05	12 03	13 00	13 58	14 55	15 53	16 50	17 48	18 45	19 43	20 41	21 38	22 36
1955	07♌59	08 57	09 54	10 51	11 49	12 46	13 44	14 41	15 39	16 36	17 34	18 31	19 29	20 27	21 24	22 22
1956	08♌42	09 40	10 37	11 35	12 32	13 30	14 27	15 25	16 22	17 20	18 17	19 15	20 13	21 10	22 08	23 06
1957	08♌29	09 26	10 23	11 21	12 18	13 16	14 13	15 11	16 08	17 06	18 03	19 01	19 58	20 56	21 54	22 51
1958	08♌15	09 12	10 10	11 07	12 04	13 02	13 59	14 57	15 54	16 52	17 50	18 47	19 45	20 42	21 40	22 38
1959	08♌01	08 58	09 56	10 53	11 51	12 48	13 46	14 43	15 41	16 38	17 36	18 33	19 31	20 28	21 26	22 24
1960	08♌45	09 42	10 39	11 37	12 34	13 32	14 29	15 27	16 24	17 22	18 19	19 17	20 14	21 12	22 10	23 07
1961	08♌31	09 28	10 25	11 23	12 20	13 18	14 15	15 13	16 10	17 08	18 05	19 03	20 01	20 58	21 56	22 54
1962	08♌17	09 14	10 11	11 09	12 07	13 04	14 02	14 59	15 57	16 54	17 52	18 49	19 47	20 44	21 42	22 40
1963	08♌03	09 00	09 57	10 55	11 53	12 50	13 47	14 45	15 42	16 40	17 37	18 35	19 33	20 30	21 38	22 26
1964	08♌46	09 44	10 41	11 38	12 36	13 33	14 31	15 28	16 26	17 24	18 21	19 19	20 16	21 14	22 12	23 09
1965	08♌32	09 29	10 27	11 24	12 22	13 19	14 17	15 14	16 12	17 09	18 07	19 04	20 02	20 59	21 57	22 55
1966	08♌18	09 16	10 13	11 11	12 08	13 05	14 03	15 00	15 58	16 55	17 53	18 51	19 48	20 46	21 44	22 41
1967	08♌04	09 02	09 59	10 57	11 54	12 52	13 49	14 47	15 44	16 42	17 39	18 37	19 34	20 32	21 30	22 27
1968	08♌48	09 45	10 43	11 40	12 38	13 35	14 33	15 30	16 28	17 25	18 23	19 20	20 18	21 15	22 13	23 11
1969	08♌34	09 31	10 29	11 26	12 24	13 21	14 19	15 16	16 14	17 11	18 09	19 07	20 04	21 02	21 59	22 57
1970	08♌21	09 18	10 16	11 13	12 10	13 08	14 05	15 03	16 01	16 58	17 56	18 53	19 51	20 48	21 46	22 44
1971	08♌07	09 05	10 02	10 59	11 57	12 54	13 52	14 49	15 47	16 44	17 42	18 39	19 37	20 34	21 32	22 30
1972	08♌50	09 48	10 45	11 43	12 40	13 38	14 35	15 33	16 30	17 28	18 25	19 23	20 21	21 18	22 16	23 14
1973	08♌37	09 34	10 32	11 29	12 27	13 24	14 21	15 19	16 16	17 14	18 12	19 09	20 07	21 04	22 02	23 00
1974	08♌23	09 21	10 18	11 15	12 13	13 10	14 08	15 05	16 03	17 00	17 58	18 55	19 53	20 51	21 48	22 46
1975	08♌09	09 06	10 04	11 01	11 59	12 56	13 54	14 51	15 49	16 46	17 44	18 41	19 39	20 36	21 34	22 32
1976	08♌52	09 49	10 47	11 45	12 42	13 39	14 37	15 34	16 32	17 29	18 27	19 25	20 22	21 20	22 17	23 15
1977	08♌38	09 36	10 33	11 30	12 28	13 25	14 23	15 20	16 18	17 15	18 13	19 11	20 08	21 06	22 04	23 01
1978	08♌24	09 22	10 19	11 16	12 14	13 11	14 09	15 06	16 04	17 02	17 59	18 57	19 54	20 52	21 50	22 47
1979	08♌10	09 08	10 05	11 03	12 00	12 57	13 55	14 52	15 50	16 47	17 45	18 42	19 40	20 38	21 35	22 33
1980	08♌52	09 51	10 48	11 46	12 43	13 41	14 38	15 36	16 33	17 31	18 28	19 26	20 24	21 21	22 19	23 17
1981	08♌39	09 37	10 34	11 32	12 29	13 27	14 24	15 22	16 19	17 17	18 14	19 12	20 09	21 07	22 05	23 02
1982	08♌26	09 23	10 21	11 18	12 16	13 13	14 10	15 08	16 05	17 03	18 00	18 58	19 56	20 53	21 51	22 49
1983	08♌12	09 09	10 07	11 04	12 02	12 59	13 57	14 54	15 52	16 49	17 47	18 44	19 42	20 39	21 37	22 35
1984	08♌55	09 53	10 50	11 47	12 45	13 43	14 40	15 38	16 35	17 33	18 30	19 28	20 25	21 23	22 21	23 18
1985	08♌42	09 39	10 37	11 34	12 31	13 29	14 26	15 24	16 21	17 19	18 16	19 14	20 12	21 10	22 07	23 05
1986	08♌28	09 25	10 23	11 20	12 18	13 15	14 13	15 10	16 08	17 05	18 03	19 00	19 58	20 56	21 53	22 51
1987	08♌14	09 12	10 09	11 07	12 04	13 02	13 59	14 56	15 54	16 51	17 49	18 46	19 44	20 42	21 39	22 37
1988	08♌58	09 55	10 53	11 50	12 47	13 45	14 42	15 40	16 37	17 35	18 33	19 30	20 28	21 25	22 23	23 21
1989	08♌44	09 41	10 39	11 36	12 34	13 31	14 29	15 26	16 24	17 21	18 19	19 16	20 14	21 12	22 09	23 07
1990	08♌31	09 28	10 25	11 23	12 20	13 18	14 15	15 13	16 10	17 08	18 05	19 03	20 00	20 58	21 55	22 53
1991	08♌16	09 14	10 11	11 09	12 06	13 04	14 01	14 59	15 56	16 54	17 51	18 49	19 46	20 44	21 42	22 39
1992	09♌00	09 57	10 55	11 52	12 50	13 47	14 45	15 42	16 40	17 37	18 35	19 32	20 30	21 27	22 25	23 23
1993	08♌46	09 43	10 41	11 38	12 36	13 33	14 31	15 28	16 26	17 23	18 21	19 18	20 16	21 13	22 11	23 09
1994	08♌32	09 29	10 27	11 24	12 22	13 19	14 17	15 14	16 12	17 09	18 07	19 04	20 02	21 00	21 57	22 55
1995	08♌18	09 16	10 13	11 11	12 08	13 05	14 03	15 00	15 58	16 55	17 53	18 50	19 48	20 46	21 43	22 41
1996	09♌01	09 59	10 56	11 54	12 51	13 49	14 46	15 44	16 41	17 39	18 36	19 34	20 31	21 29	22 27	23 24
1997	08♌47	09 45	10 42	11 40	12 37	13 35	14 32	15 30	16 27	17 25	18 22	19 20	20 17	21 15	22 13	23 10
1998	08♌34	09 31	10 29	11 26	12 24	13 21	14 18	15 16	16 13	17 11	18 08	19 06	20 04	21 01	21 59	22 56
1999	08♌20	09 17	10 15	11 12	12 09	13 07	14 04	15 02	15 59	16 57	17 54	18 52	19 50	20 47	21 45	22 43
2000	09♌03	10 01	10 58	11 55	12 53	13 50	14 48	15 45	16 43	17 40	18 38	19 36	20 33	23 31	22 28	23 26

	17th	18th	19th	20th	21st	22nd	23rd	24th	25th	26th	27th	28th	29th	30th	31st
1900	23 36	24 34	25 32	26 30	27 27	28 25	29 23	00♍ 21	01 19	02 17	03 15	04 13	05 11	06 09	07♍ 07
1901	23 23	24 20	25 18	26 16	27 13	28 11	29 09	00♍ 07	01 05	02 03	03 01	03 59	04 57	05 54	06♍ 52
1902	23 09	24 06	25 04	26 02	27 00	27 57	28 55	29 53	00♍ 51	01 49	02 47	03 45	04 43	05 41	06♍ 39
1903	22 55	23 52	24 50	25 48	26 46	27 43	28 41	29 39	00♍ 37	01 35	02 33	03 31	04 29	05 27	06♍ 25
1904	23 38	24 36	25 34	26 31	27 29	28 27	29 25	00♍ 23	01 21	02 18	03 16	04 14	05 12	06 10	07♍ 08
1905	23 24	24 22	25 20	26 17	27 15	28 13	29 11	00♍ 09	01 06	02 04	03 02	04 00	04 58	05 56	06♍ 54
1906	23 10	24 08	25 06	26 03	27 01	27 09	28 57	29 55	00♍ 53	01 50	02 48	03 46	04 44	05 42	06♍ 40
1907	22 56	23 54	24 52	25 49	26 47	27 45	28 43	29 41	00♍ 38	01 36	02 34	03 32	04 30	05 28	06♍ 26
1908	23 40	24 37	25 35	26 33	27 31	28 29	29 26	00♍ 24	01 22	02 20	03 18	04 16	05 14	06 12	07♍ 10
1909	23 26	24 23	25 21	26 19	27 17	28 15	29 12	00♍ 10	01 08	02 06	03 04	04 02	05 00	05 58	06♍ 56
1910	23 12	24 10	25 08	26 05	27 03	28 01	29 00	29 56	00♍ 54	01 52	02 50	03 48	04 46	05 44	06♍ 42
1911	22 58	23 56	24 54	25 51	26 49	27 47	28 45	29 43	00 40	01 38	02 36	03 34	04 32	05 30	06♍ 28
1912	23 42	24 40	25 37	26 35	27 33	28 31	29 29	00♍ 26	01 24	02 22	03 20	04 18	05 16	06 14	07♍ 12
1913	23 28	24 26	25 24	26 21	27 19	28 17	29 15	00♍ 13	01 10	02 08	03 06	04 04	05 02	06 00	06♍ 58
1914	23 14	24 12	25 10	26 07	27 05	28 03	29 01	30 00	00♍ 57	01 55	02 53	03 51	04 48	05 46	06♍ 44
1915	23 01	23 58	24 56	25 54	26 52	27 49	28 47	29 45	00♍ 43	01 41	02 39	03 36	04 34	05 32	06♍ 30
1916	23 44	24 42	25 40	26 37	27 35	28 33	29 31	00♍ 29	01 26	02 24	03 22	04 20	05 18	06 16	07♍ 14
1917	23 30	24 28	25 26	26 23	27 21	28 19	29 17	00♍ 15	01 13	02 11	03 08	04 06	05 04	06 02	07♍ 00
1918	23 17	24 14	26 12	26 10	27 08	28 05	29 03	00♍ 01	00 59	01 57	02 55	03 53	04 50	05 48	06♍ 47
1919	23 02	24 00	24 58	25 56	26 53	27 51	28 49	29 47	00♍ 45	01 43	02 41	03 39	04 36	05 34	06♍ 33
1920	23 46	24 44	25 41	26 39	27 37	29 35	29 33	00♍ 30	01 28	02 26	03 24	04 22	05 20	06 18	07♍ 16
1921	23 32	24 30	25 27	26 25	27 23	28 21	29 18	00♍ 16	01 14	02 12	03 10	04 08	05 06	06 04	07♍ 02
1922	23 18	24 15	25 13	26 11	27 09	28 07	29 04	00♍ 02	01 00	01 58	02 56	03 54	04 52	05 50	06♍ 48
1923	23 04	24 02	24 59	25 57	26 55	27 53	28 50	29 48	00♍ 46	01 44	02 42	03 40	04 38	05 36	06♍ 34
1924	23 47	24 45	25 43	26 41	27 38	28 36	29 34	00♍ 32	01 30	02 28	03 26	04 24	05 22	06 20	07♍ 18
1925	23 33	24 31	25 29	26 27	27 25	28 22	29 20	00♍ 18	01 16	02 14	03 12	04 10	05 08	06 06	07♍ 04
1926	23 20	24 18	25 15	26 13	27 11	28 09	29 06	00♍ 04	01 02	02 00	02 58	03 56	04 54	05 52	06♍ 50
1927	23 06	24 03	25 01	25 59	26 57	27 54	28 52	29 50	00♍ 48	01 46	02 44	03 42	04 40	05 38	06♍ 36
1928	23 49	24 47	25 45	26 43	27 41	28 38	29 36	00♍ 34	01 32	02 30	03 28	04 26	05 24	06 22	07♍ 20
1929	23 36	24 33	25 31	26 29	27 27	28 24	29 22	00♍ 20	01 18	02 16	03 14	04 12	05 10	06 08	07♍ 06
1930	23 21	24 19	25 17	26 15	27 13	28 10	29 09	00♍ 06	01 04	02 02	03 00	03 58	04 56	05 54	06♍ 52
1931	23 08	24 06	25 03	26 01	26 59	27 57	28 55	29 53	00♍ 50	01 48	02 46	03 44	04 42	05 40	06♍ 38
1932	23 52	24 49	25 47	26 45	27 42	28 40	29 38	00♍ 36	01 34	02 32	03 30	04 28	05 26	06 24	07♍ 22
1933	23 37	24 35	25 33	26 31	27 29	28 26	29 24	00♍ 22	01 20	02 18	03 16	04 14	05 12	06 10	07♍ 08
1934	23 24	24 22	25 19	26 17	27 25	28 13	29 11	00♍ 08	01 06	02 04	03 02	04 00	04 58	05 56	06♍ 54
1935	23 10	24 08	25 05	26 03	27 01	27 59	28 56	29 54	00♍ 52	01 50	02 48	03 46	04 44	05 42	06♍ 40
1936	23 54	24 51	25 49	26 47	27 45	28 42	29 40	00♍ 38	01 36	02 34	03 32	04 30	05 28	06 26	07♍ 24
1937	23 40	24 38	25 35	26 33	27 31	28 29	29 26	00♍ 24	01 22	02 20	03 18	04 16	05 14	06 12	07♍ 10
1938	23 26	24 24	25 21	26 19	27 17	28 15	29 12	00♍ 10	01 08	02 06	03 04	04 02	05 00	05 58	06♍ 56
1939	23 12	24 10	25 07	26 05	27 03	28 01	28 59	29 56	00♍ 54	01 52	02 50	03 48	04 46	05 44	06♍ 42
1940	23 56	24 53	25 51	26 49	27 46	28 44	29 42	00♍ 40	01 38	02 36	03 34	04 31	05 29	06 27	07♍ 26
1941	23 41	24 39	25 37	26 35	27 32	28 30	29 28	00♍ 26	01 24	02 22	03 20	04 18	05 16	06 14	07♍ 12
1942	23 28	24 26	25 23	26 21	27 19	28 17	29 14	00♍ 12	01 10	02 08	03 06	04 04	05 02	06 00	06♍ 58
1943	23 14	24 11	25 09	26 07	27 04	28 02	29 00	29 58	00♍ 56	01 54	02 51	03 49	04 47	05 45	06♍ 43
1944	23 57	24 55	25 52	26 50	27 48	28 46	29 44	00♍ 42	01 39	02 37	03 35	04 33	05 31	06 29	07♍ 27
1945	23 44	24 41	25 39	26 37	27 35	28 32	29 30	00 28	01♍ 26	02 24	03 22	04 20	05 17	06 15	07♍ 14
1946	23 29	24 27	25 25	26 23	27 20	28 18	29 16	00 14	01♍ 12	02 10	03 08	04 06	05 04	06 02	07♍ 00
1947	23 16	24 13	25 11	26 09	27 07	28 04	29 02	00 00	00♍ 58	01 56	02 54	03 52	04 50	05 48	06♍ 46
1948	23 59	24 57	25 55	26 53	27 50	28 48	29 46	00 44	01♍ 42	02 39	03 37	04 35	05 33	06 31	07♍ 29
1949	23 45	24 43	25 41	26 39	27 36	28 34	29 32	00 30	01♍ 28	02 26	03 24	04 22	05 20	06 18	07♍ 16
1950	23 32	24 29	25 27	26 25	27 23	28 20	29 18	00♍ 16	01 14	02 12	03 10	04 08	05 05	06 03	07♍ 01
1951	23 18	24 15	25 12	26 11	27 08	28 06	29 04	00♍ 02	01 00	01 58	02 55	03 53	04 51	05 49	06♍ 47
1952	24 01	24 59	25 56	26 54	27 52	28 50	29 48	00♍ 46	01 44	02 41	03 39	04 37	05 35	06 33	07♍ 31
1953	23 48	24 45	25 43	26 41	27 39	28 36	29 34	00♍ 32	01 30	02 28	03 26	04 23	05 21	06 10	07♍ 17
1954	23 33	24 31	25 29	26 27	27 24	28 22	29 20	00♍ 18	01 16	02 14	03 12	04 10	05 08	06 06	07♍ 04
1955	23 20	24 17	25 15	16 13	27 11	28 08	29 06	00♍ 04	01 02	01 00	02 58	03 56	04 54	05 52	06♍ 50
1956	24 03	25 01	25 59	26 56	27 54	28 52	29 50	00♍ 48	01 45	02 43	03 41	04 39	05 37	06 35	07♍ 33
1957	23 49	24 47	25 44	26 42	27 40	28 38	29 36	00♍ 33	01 31	02 29	03 27	04 25	05 23	06 21	07♍ 19
1958	23 35	24 33	25 31	26 29	27 26	28 24	29 22	00♍ 20	01 18	02 16	03 13	04 11	05 09	06 07	07♍ 05
1959	23 21	24 19	25 17	26 14	27 12	28 10	29 08	00♍ 05	01 03	02 01	02 59	03 57	04 55	05 53	06♍ 51
1960	24 05	25 03	26 01	26 58	27 56	28 54	29 52	00♍ 50	01 47	02 45	03 43	04 41	05 39	06 37	07♍ 35
1961	23 51	24 49	25 47	26 45	27 42	28 40	29 38	00♍ 36	01 34	02 31	03 29	04 27	05 25	06 23	07♍ 20
1962	23 37	24 35	25 33	26 30	27 28	28 26	29 24	00♍ 22	01 19	02 17	03 15	04 13	05 11	06 09	07♍ 07
1963	23 23	24 21	25 19	26 16	27 14	28 12	29 10	00♍ 08	01 06	02 03	03 01	03 59	04 57	05 55	07♍ 53
1964	24 07	25 05	26 02	27 00	27 58	28 56	29 53	00♍ 51	01 49	02 47	03 45	04 43	05 41	06 38	07♍ 37
1965	23 52	24 50	25 48	26 46	27 43	28 41	29 39	00♍ 37	01 35	02 33	03 31	04 29	05 27	06 25	07♍ 23
1966	23 39	24 37	25 34	26 32	27 30	28 28	29 26	00♍ 23	01 21	02 19	03 17	04 15	05 13	06 11	07♍ 09
1967	23 25	24 23	25 20	26 18	27 16	28 14	29 11	00♍ 09	01 07	02 05	03 02	04 01	04 59	05 57	06♍ 55
1968	24 08	25 06	26 04	27 02	27 59	28 57	29 55	00♍ 53	01 51	02 59	03 47	04 45	05 43	06 41	07♍ 39
1969	23 55	24 53	25 50	26 48	27 46	28 44	29 41	00♍ 39	01 37	02 35	03 33	04 31	05 29	06 27	07♍ 25
1970	23 42	24 39	25 37	26 34	27 32	28 30	29 28	00♍ 25	01 23	02 21	03 19	04 17	50 15	06 13	07♍ 11
1971	23 27	24 25	25 23	26 21	27 18	28 16	29 14	00♍ 12	01 10	02 08	03 05	04 03	05 01	05 59	06♍ 57
1972	24 11	25 09	26 07	27 04	28 02	29 00	29 58	00♍ 56	01 53	20 51	03 49	04 47	05 45	06 43	07♍ 41
1973	23 57	24 55	25 53	26 50	27 48	28 46	29 44	00♍ 42	01 39	02 37	03 35	04 33	05 31	06 29	07♍ 27
1974	23 44	24 41	25 39	26 37	27 35	28 32	29 30	00♍ 28	01 26	02 24	03 22	04 20	05 18	06 16	07♍ 14
1975	23 29	24 27	25 25	26 23	27 20	28 18	29 16	00♍ 14	01 11	02 09	03 07	04 05	05 03	06 01	06♍ 59
1976	24 13	25 10	26 08	27 05	28 04	29 01	29 59	00♍ 57	01 55	02 53	03 51	04 49	05 47	06 45	07♍ 43
1977	23 59	24 57	25 54	26 52	27 50	28 48	29 46	00♍ 43	01 41	02 39	03 37	04 35	05 33	06 31	07♍ 29
1978	23 45	24 42	25 40	26 38	27 36	28 33	29 31	00♍ 29	01 27	02 25	03 23	04 21	05 19	06 17	07♍ 15
1979	23 31	24 28	25 26	26 24	27 22	28 19	29 17	00♍ 15	01 13	02 11	03 09	04 07	05 05	06 03	07♍ 01
1980	24 14	25 12	26 10	27 07	28 05	29 03	00♍ 01	00 59	01 56	02 54	03 52	04 50	05 48	06 46	07♍ 44
1981	24 00	24 58	25 55	26 53	27 51	28 49	29 46	00♍ 44	01 42	02 40	03 38	04 36	05 34	06 32	07♍ 30
1982	23 46	24 44	25 42	26 39	27 37	28 35	29 33	00♍ 31	01 29	02 26	03 24	04 22	05 20	06 18	07♍ 16
1983	23 32	24 30	25 28	26 25	27 23	28 21	29 19	00♍ 17	01 14	02 12	03 10	04 08	05 06	06 04	07♍ 02
1984	24 16	25 14	26 11	27 09	28 07	29 05	00♍ 02	01 00	01 58	02 56	03 54	04 52	05 50	06 48	07♍ 46
1985	24 02	25 00	25 58	26 56	27 53	28 51	29 49	00♍ 47	01 45	02 43	03 40	04 38	05 36	06 34	07♍ 32
1986	23 49	24 46	25 44	26 42	27 39	28 37	29 35	00♍ 33	01 31	02 28	03 26	04 24	05 22	06 20	07♍ 18
1987	23 35	24 32	25 30	26 28	27 25	28 23	29 21	00♍ 19	01 17	02 15	03 13	04 10	05 08	06 06	07♍ 04
1988	24 18	25 16	26 14	27 12	28 09	29 07	00♍ 05	01 03	02 01	02 59	03 56	04 54	05 52	06 50	07♍ 48
1989	24 04	25 02	26 00	26 58	27 55	28 53	29 51	00♍ 49	01 47	02 45	03 42	04 40	05 38	06 36	07♍ 34
1990	23 55	24 49	25 46	26 44	27 42	28 40	29 37	00♍ 35	01 33	02 31	03 29	04 27	05 25	06 23	07♍ 21
1991	23 37	24 35	25 32	26 30	27 28	28 26	29 23	00♍ 21	01 19	02 17	03 15	04 13	05 11	06 09	07♍ 07
1992	24 20	25 18	26 16	27 13	28 11	29 09	00♍ 07	01 05	02 03	03 00	03 58	04 56	05 54	06 52	07♍ 50
1993	24 07	25 04	26 02	27 00	27 58	28 55	29 53	00♍ 51	01 49	02 47	03 45	04 43	05 41	06 39	07♍ 37
1994	23 53	24 50	25 48	26 46	27 43	28 41	29 39	00♍ 37	01 35	02 32	03 30	04 28	05 26	06 24	07♍ 22
1995	23 38	24 36	25 34	26 32	27 29	28 27	29 25	00♍ 23	01 21	02 18	03 16	04 15	05 12	06 10	07♍ 08
1996	24 23	25 20	26 18	27 15	28 13	29 11	00♍ 09	01 07	02 04	03 02	04 00	04 58	05 56	06 54	07♍ 52
1997	24 08	25 06	26 03	27 01	27 59	28 57	29 54	00♍ 52	01 50	02 48	03 46	04 44	05 42	06 40	07♍ 38
1998	23 54	24 52	25 50	26 47	27 45	28 43	29 41	00♍ 39	01 36	02 34	03 32	04 30	05 28	06 26	07♍ 24
1999	23 40	24 38	25 36	26 33	27 31	28 29	29 27	00♍ 24	01 22	02 20	03 18	04 16	05 14	06 12	07♍ 10
2000	24 24	25 21	26 19	27 17	28 14	29 12	00♍ 10	01 08	02 06	03 04	04 02	05 00	05 58	06 56	07♍ 54

Sun

September

	1st	2nd	3rd	4th	5th	6th	7th	8th	9th	10th	11th	12th	13th	14th	15th	16th
1900	08♍05	09 03	10 01	10 59	11 57	12 56	13 54	14 52	15 50	16 49	17 47	18 45	19 44	20 42	21 41	22 39
1901	07♍51	08 49	09 47	10 45	11 43	12 41	13 39	14 38	15 36	16 34	17 33	18 31	19 30	20 28	21 27	22 25
1902	07♍37	08 35	09 33	10 31	11 29	12 28	13 26	14 24	15 22	16 21	17 19	18 17	19 16	20 14	21 13	22 11
1903	07♍23	08 21	09 19	10 17	11 15	12 13	13 12	14 10	15 08	16 06	17 05	18 03	19 01	20 00	20 58	21 57
1904	08♍06	09 04	10 02	11 01	11 59	12 57	13 55	14 54	15 52	16 50	17 49	18 47	19 46	20 44	21 42	22 41
1905	07♍52	08 51	09 49	10 47	11 45	12 43	13 41	14 40	15 38	16 36	17 35	18 33	19 31	20 30	21 28	22 27
1906	07♍38	08 36	09 34	10 33	11 31	12 29	13 27	14 25	15 24	16 22	17 20	18 19	19 17	20 16	21 14	22 13
1907	07♍24	08 22	09 20	10 18	11 17	12 15	13 13	14 11	15 10	16 08	17 06	18 05	19 03	20 02	21 00	21 58
1908	08♍08	09 06	10 04	11 03	12 01	12 59	13 57	14 55	15 34	16 52	17 50	18 49	19 47	20 46	21 44	22 43
1909	07♍54	08 52	09 50	10 48	11 46	12 45	13 43	14 41	15 39	16 38	17 36	18 35	19 33	20 31	21 30	22 28
1910	07♍40	08 38	09 36	10 35	11 33	12 31	13 29	14 28	15 26	16 24	17 23	18 21	19 19	20 18	21 16	22 15
1911	07♍26	08 24	09 23	10 21	11 19	12 17	13 15	14 13	15 12	16 10	17 08	18 07	19 05	20 03	21 02	22 00
1912	08♍10	09 08	10 06	11 04	12 03	13 01	13 59	14 57	15 56	16 54	17 52	18 51	19 49	20 48	21 46	22 45
1913	07♍56	08 55	09 53	10 51	11 49	12 47	13 45	14 44	15 42	16 40	17 39	18 37	19 35	20 34	21 32	22 31
1914	07♍43	08 41	09 39	10 37	11 35	12 33	13 31	14 30	15 28	16 26	17 24	18 23	19 21	20 20	21 18	22 17
1915	07♍28	08 26	09 25	10 23	11 21	12 19	13 17	14 16	15 14	16 12	17 11	18 09	19 07	20 06	21 04	22 03
1916	08♍13	09 11	10 09	11 07	12 05	13 03	14 02	15 00	15 58	16 56	17 55	18 53	19 51	20 50	21 48	22 47
1917	07♍58	08 56	09 55	10 53	11 51	12 49	13 47	14 45	15 44	16 42	17 40	18 39	19 37	20 36	21 34	22 33
1918	07♍45	08 43	09 41	10 39	11 37	12 35	13 34	14 31	15 30	16 28	17 27	18 25	19 24	20 22	21 21	22 19
1919	07♍31	08 29	09 27	10 25	11 23	12 21	13 19	14 18	15 16	16 14	17 12	18 11	19 09	20 08	21 06	22 05
1920	08♍14	09 12	10 10	11 08	12 07	13 50	14 03	15 01	16 00	16 58	17 56	18 55	19 53	20 52	21 50	22 49
1921	08♍00	08 58	09 56	10 55	11 53	12 51	13 49	14 47	15 46	16 44	17 42	18 41	19 39	20 38	21 36	22 35
1922	07♍46	08 44	09 42	10 40	11 38	12 37	13 35	14 33	15 31	16 30	17 28	18 26	19 25	20 23	21 22	22 20
1923	07♍32	08 30	09 28	10 26	11 24	12 22	13 21	14 19	15 17	16 15	17 14	18 12	19 11	20 09	21 08	22 06
1924	08♍16	09 14	10 12	11 10	12 08	13 07	14 05	15 03	16 01	17 00	17 58	18 56	19 55	20 53	21 52	22 50
1925	08♍02	09 00	09 58	10 56	11 54	12 52	13 50	14 49	15 47	16 45	17 44	18 42	19 40	20 39	21 37	22 36
1926	07♍48	08 46	09 44	10 42	11 40	12 39	13 37	14 35	15 33	16 32	17 30	18 28	19 27	20 25	21 24	22 22
1927	07♍34	08 32	09 30	10 28	11 26	12 25	13 23	14 21	15 19	16 17	17 16	18 14	19 12	20 11	21 09	22 08
1928	08♍18	09 16	10 14	11 12	12 10	13 08	14 07	15 05	16 03	17 01	18 00	18 58	19 57	20 55	21 54	22 52
1929	08♍04	09 02	10 00	10 58	11 56	12 55	13 53	14 51	15 49	16 48	17 46	18 44	19 43	20 41	21 40	22 38
1930	07♍50	08 48	09 46	10 44	11 42	12 41	13 39	14 37	15 35	16 34	17 32	18 30	19 29	20 27	21 25	22 24
1931	07♍36	08 34	09 32	10 30	11 28	12 26	13 25	14 23	15 21	16 19	17 18	18 16	19 15	20 13	21 12	22 10
1932	08♍20	09 18	10 16	11 14	12 12	13 11	14 09	15 07	16 05	17 04	18 02	19 01	19 59	20 57	21 56	22 54
1933	08♍06	09 04	10 02	11 00	11 58	12 56	13 55	14 53	15 51	16 49	17 48	18 46	19 45	20 43	21 41	22 40
1934	07♍52	08 50	09 48	10 46	11 44	12 43	13 41	14 39	15 37	16 36	17 34	18 32	19 31	20 29	21 28	22 26
1935	07♍38	08 36	09 34	10 32	11 30	12 29	13 27	14 25	15 23	16 22	17 20	18 18	19 17	20 15	21 13	22 12
1936	08♍22	09 20	10 18	11 16	12 14	13 12	14 11	15 09	16 07	17 06	18 04	19 02	20 01	20 59	21 58	22 56
1937	08♍08	09 06	10 04	11 02	12 00	13 00	13 57	14 55	15 53	16 52	17 50	18 49	19 47	20 45	21 44	22 42
1938	07♍54	08 52	09 50	10 48	11 46	12 45	13 43	14 41	15 39	16 38	17 36	18 34	19 33	20 31	21 30	22 28
1939	07♍40	08 38	09 36	10 34	11 32	12 30	13 29	14 27	15 25	16 23	17 22	18 20	19 18	20 17	21 15	22 14
1940	08♍24	09 22	10 20	11 18	12 16	13 14	14 13	15 11	16 09	17 08	18 06	19 04	20 03	21 01	22 00	22 58
1941	08♍10	09 08	10 06	11 04	12 02	13 00	13 58	14 57	15 55	16 53	17 51	18 50	19 48	20 47	21 45	22 44
1942	07♍56	08 54	09 52	10 50	11 48	12 46	13 44	14 43	15 41	16 39	17 38	18 36	19 35	20 33	21 31	22 30
1943	07♍42	08 40	09 38	10 36	11 34	12 32	13 30	14 29	15 27	16 25	17 24	18 22	19 20	20 19	21 17	22 15
1944	08♍25	09 23	10 21	11 20	12 18	13 16	14 14	15 12	16 11	17 09	18 07	19 06	20 04	21 03	22 01	23 00
1945	08♍12	09 10	10 08	11 06	12 04	13 02	14 00	14 59	15 57	16 56	17 54	18 52	19 51	20 49	21 48	22 46
1946	07♍58	08 56	09 54	10 52	11 50	12 48	13 47	14 45	15 43	16 41	17 40	18 38	19 36	20 35	21 33	22 32
1947	07♍44	08 42	09 40	10 38	11 36	12 34	13 32	14 30	15 29	16 27	17 25	18 24	19 22	20 21	21 19	22 18
1948	08♍27	09 26	10 24	11 22	12 20	13 18	14 17	15 15	16 13	17 11	18 10	19 08	20 07	21 05	22 03	23 02
1949	08♍14	09 12	10 10	11 08	12 06	13 04	14 02	15 01	15 59	16 57	17 56	18 54	19 52	20 51	21 49	22 48
1950	07♍59	08 57	09 56	10 54	11 52	12 50	13 48	14 46	15 45	16 43	17 41	18 40	19 38	20 37	21 35	22 34
1951	07♍45	08 44	09 42	10 40	11 38	12 36	13 34	14 33	15 31	16 29	17 27	18 26	19 24	20 23	21 21	22 19
1952	08♍29	09 27	10 26	11 24	12 22	13 20	14 18	15 16	16 15	17 13	18 11	19 10	20 08	21 07	22 05	28 04
1953	08♍15	09 14	10 12	11 10	12 08	13 06	14 04	15 03	16 01	16 59	17 58	18 56	19 55	20 53	21 51	22 50
1954	08♍02	09 00	09 58	10 56	11 54	12 52	13 51	14 49	15 47	16 45	17 44	18 42	19 40	20 39	21 37	22 36
1955	07♍48	08 46	09 44	10 42	11 40	12 38	13 36	14 34	15 33	16 31	17 29	18 28	19 26	20 25	21 23	22 21
1956	08♍31	09 29	10 28	11 26	12 24	13 22	14 20	15 19	16 17	17 15	18 14	19 12	20 10	21 09	22 07	23 06
1957	08♍17	09 15	10 13	11 12	12 10	13 08	14 06	15 04	16 03	17 01	17 59	18 58	19 56	20 54	21 53	22 51
1958	08♍03	09 01	09 59	10 58	11 56	12 54	13 52	14 50	15 49	16 47	17 45	18 44	19 42	20 41	21 39	22 38
1959	07♍49	08 47	09 45	10 43	11 42	12 40	13 38	14 36	15 34	16 33	17 31	18 29	19 28	20 26	21 25	22 23
1960	08♍33	09 31	10 29	11 28	12 26	13 24	14 22	15 20	16 19	17 17	18 15	19 14	20 12	21 10	22 09	23 07
1961	08♍19	09 17	10 15	11 14	12 12	13 10	14 08	15 06	16 05	17 03	18 01	19 00	19 58	20 57	21 55	22 54
1962	08♍05	09 03	10 01	11 00	11 58	12 56	13 54	14 52	15 51	16 49	17 47	18 46	19 44	20 42	21 41	22 39
1963	07♍51	08 49	09 47	10 45	11 43	12 42	13 40	14 38	15 36	16 35	17 33	18 31	19 30	20 28	21 26	22 25
1964	08♍35	09 33	10 31	11 29	12 27	13 26	14 24	15 22	16 21	17 19	18 17	19 16	20 14	21 13	22 11	23 09
1965	08♍21	09 19	10 17	11 15	12 13	13 11	14 10	15 08	16 06	17 04	18 03	19 01	19 59	20 58	21 56	22 55
1966	08♍07	09 05	10 03	11 01	11 59	12 57	13 56	14 54	15 52	16 50	17 49	18 47	19 46	20 44	21 42	22 41
1967	07♍53	08 51	09 49	10 47	11 45	12 43	13 42	14 40	15 38	16 36	17 35	18 33	19 31	20 30	21 28	22 27
1968	08♍37	09 35	10 33	11 31	12 29	13 27	14 26	15 24	16 22	17 20	18 19	19 17	20 15	21 14	22 12	23 11
1969	08♍23	09 21	10 19	11 17	12 15	13 13	14 12	15 10	16 08	17 07	18 05	19 03	20 02	21 00	21 59	22 57
1970	08♍09	09 07	10 05	11 04	12 02	13 00	13 58	14 56	15 55	16 53	17 51	18 50	19 48	20 46	21 45	22 43
1971	07♍55	08 53	09 51	10 49	11 48	12 46	13 44	14 42	15 40	16 39	17 37	18 35	19 34	20 32	21 31	22 29
1972	08♍39	09 37	10 35	11 34	12 32	13 30	14 28	15 26	16 25	17 23	18 21	19 20	20 18	21 17	22 15	23 14
1973	08♍25	09 23	10 22	11 20	12 18	13 16	14 14	15 12	16 11	17 09	18 07	19 06	20 04	21 02	22 01	22 59
1974	08♍12	09 10	10 08	11 06	12 04	13 02	14 00	14 59	15 57	16 55	17 53	18 52	19 50	20 49	21 47	22 46
1975	07♍57	08 55	09 53	10 51	11 49	12 48	13 46	14 44	15 42	16 41	17 39	18 37	19 36	20 34	21 33	22 31
1976	08♍41	09 39	10 37	11 35	12 33	13 32	14 30	15 28	16 26	17 25	18 23	19 21	20 20	21 18	22 16	23 15
1977	08♍27	09 25	10 23	11 21	12 19	13 17	14 16	15 14	16 12	17 11	18 09	19 07	20 06	21 04	22 03	23 01
1978	08♍13	09 11	10 09	11 07	12 05	13 03	14 02	15 00	15 58	16 57	17 55	18 53	19 52	20 50	21 48	22 47
1979	07♍59	08 57	09 55	10 53	11 51	12 49	13 47	14 45	15 44	16 42	17 40	18 39	19 37	20 35	21 34	22 32
1980	08♍42	09 40	10 38	11 36	12 35	13 33	14 31	15 29	16 28	17 26	18 24	19 23	20 21	21 20	22 18	23 17
1981	08♍28	09 26	10 24	11 22	12 21	13 19	14 17	15 15	16 14	17 12	18 10	19 08	20 07	21 05	22 04	23 02
1982	08♍14	09 12	10 10	11 08	12 07	13 05	14 03	15 01	15 59	16 58	17 56	18 54	19 53	20 51	21 50	22 48
1983	08♍00	08 58	09 56	10 54	11 52	12 51	13 49	14 47	15 45	16 44	17 42	18 40	19 39	20 37	21 36	22 34
1984	08♍44	09 42	10 40	11 38	12 37	13 35	14 33	15 31	16 29	17 28	18 26	19 24	20 23	21 21	22 20	23 18
1985	08♍30	09 28	10 26	11 24	12 23	13 21	14 19	15 17	16 16	17 14	18 12	19 11	20 09	21 07	22 06	23 04
1986	08♍16	09 14	10 12	11 11	12 09	13 07	14 05	15 03	16 02	17 00	17 58	18 57	19 55	20 53	21 52	22 50
1987	08♍02	09 01	09 59	10 57	11 55	12 53	13 51	14 49	15 48	16 46	17 44	18 42	19 41	20 39	21 38	22 36
1988	08♍46	09 44	10 43	11 41	12 39	13 37	14 35	15 34	16 32	17 30	18 28	19 27	20 25	21 24	22 22	23 21
1989	08♍32	09 31	10 29	11 27	12 25	13 23	14 21	15 20	16 18	17 16	18 15	19 13	20 11	21 10	22 08	23 07
1990	08♍19	09 17	10 15	11 13	12 11	13 09	14 08	15 06	16 04	17 02	18 01	18 59	19 57	20 56	21 54	22 53
1991	08♍05	09 03	10 01	10 59	11 57	12 55	13 53	14 52	15 50	16 48	17 47	18 45	19 43	20 42	21 40	22 39
1992	08♍49	09 47	10 45	11 43	12 41	13 39	14 37	15 36	16 34	17 32	18 31	19 29	20 27	21 26	22 24	23 23
1993	08♍35	09 33	10 31	11 29	12 27	13 25	14 23	15 22	16 20	17 18	18 16	19 15	20 13	21 12	22 10	23 09
1994	08♍20	09 18	10 16	11 15	12 13	13 11	14 09	15 07	16 06	17 04	18 02	19 01	19 59	20 58	21 56	22 54
1995	08♍06	09 04	10 02	11 01	11 59	12 57	13 55	14 53	15 51	16 50	17 48	18 46	19 45	20 43	21 41	22 40
1996	08♍50	09 48	10 46	11 44	12 42	13 41	14 39	15 37	16 35	17 34	18 32	19 30	20 29	21 27	22 26	23 24
1997	08♍36	09 34	10 32	11 30	12 28	13 27	14 25	15 23	16 21	17 20	18 18	19 16	20 15	21 13	22 12	23 10
1998	28♍45	09 20	10 18	11 16	12 15	13 13	14 11	15 09	16 07	17 06	18 04	19 02	20 01	20 59	21 57	22 56
1999	08♍08	09 06	10 04	11 02	12 00	12 58	13 56	14 55	15 53	16 51	17 50	18 48	19 46	20 45	21 43	22 42
2000	08♍52	09 50	10 48	11 46	12 44	13 42	14 41	15 39	16 37	17 35	18 34	19 32	20 30	21 29	22 27	23 26

	17th	18th	19th	20th	21st	22nd	23rd	24th	25th	26th	27th	28th	29th	30th
1900	23 38	24 36	25 35	26 34	27 32	28 31	29 30	00♎29	01 27	02 26	03 25	04 24	05 23	06♎22
1901	23 24	24 22	25 21	26 19	27 18	28 17	29 16	00♎14	01 13	02 12	03 11	04 10	05 09	06♎08
1902	23 10	24 08	25 07	26 05	27 04	28 03	29 02	00♎00	00 59	01 58	02 57	03 56	04 55	05♎54
1903	22 55	23 54	24 52	25 51	26 50	27 48	28 47	29 46	00♎45	01 44	02 42	03 41	04 40	05♎39
1904	23 40	24 38	25 37	26 35	27 34	28 33	29 31	00♎30	01 29	02 28	03 27	04 26	05 24	06♎23
1905	23 25	24 24	25 22	26 21	27 20	28 18	29 17	00♎16	01 15	02 14	03 12	04 11	05 10	06♎09
1906	23 11	24 10	25 08	26 07	27 06	28 04	29 03	00♎02	01 01	01 59	02 58	03 57	04 56	05♎55
1907	22 57	23 56	24 54	25 53	26 51	27 50	28 49	29 47	00♎46	01 45	02 44	03 43	04 42	05♎41
1908	23 41	24 40	25 38	26 37	27 36	28 34	29 33	00♎32	01 31	02 30	03 29	04 27	05 26	06♎25
1909	23 27	24 26	25 24	26 23	27 22	28 20	29 19	00♎18	01 17	02 15	03 14	04 13	05 12	06♎11
1910	23 13	24 12	25 10	26 09	27 08	28 06	29 05	00♎04	01 02	02 01	03 00	03 59	04 58	05♎57
1911	22 59	23 57	24 56	25 55	26 53	27 52	28 51	29 49	00♎48	01 47	02 46	03 45	04 44	05♎43
1912	23 43	24 42	25 40	26 39	27 38	28 36	29 35	00♎34	01 33	02 32	03 30	04 29	05 28	06♎27
1913	23 29	24 28	25 26	26 25	27 24	28 22	29 21	00♎20	01 19	02 18	03 16	04 15	05 14	06♎13
1914	23 15	24 14	25 12	26 11	27 10	28 08	29 07	00♎06	01 05	02 04	03 02	04 01	05 00	05♎59
1915	23 01	24 00	24 58	25 57	26 56	27 54	28 53	29 52	00♎50	01 49	02 48	03 47	04 46	05♎45
1916	23 45	24 44	25 43	26 41	27 40	28 39	29 37	00♎36	01 35	02 34	03 33	04 31	05 31	06♎30
1917	23 31	24 30	25 28	26 27	27 26	28 25	29 23	00♎22	01 21	02 20	03 19	04 17	05 16	06♎15
1918	23 18	24 16	25 15	26 13	27 12	28 11	29 09	00♎08	01 07	02 06	03 04	04 03	05 02	06♎01
1919	23 03	24 02	25 00	25 59	26 57	27 56	28 55	29 54	00♎52	01 51	02 50	03 49	04 48	05♎47
1920	23 47	24 46	25 45	26 43	27 42	28 41	29 39	00 38	01 37	02 36	03 34	04 33	05 32	06♎31
1921	23 33	24 32	25 30	26 29	27 28	28 26	29 25	00 24	01 22	02 21	03 20	04 10	05 18	06♎17
1922	23 19	24 17	25 16	26 14	27 13	28 12	29 11	00 09	01 08	02 07	03 06	04 05	05 04	06♎03
1923	23 05	24 03	25 02	26 00	26 59	27 58	28 56	29 55	00♎54	01 53	02 51	03 50	04 49	05♎48
1924	23 49	24 47	25 46	26 44	27 43	28 42	29 40	00♎39	01 38	02 37	03 36	04 35	05 34	06♎33
1925	23 34	24 33	25 32	26 30	27 29	28 28	29 26	00♎25	01 24	02 23	03 22	04 21	05 19	06♎18
1926	23 21	24 19	25 18	26 16	27 15	28 14	29 12	00♎11	01 10	02 09	03 08	04 06	05 05	06♎04
1927	23 06	24 05	25 03	26 02	27 01	27 59	28 58	29 57	00♎56	01 54	02 53	03 52	04 51	05♎50
1928	23 51	24 49	25 48	26 47	27 45	28 44	29 43	00♎41	01 40	02 39	03 38	04 37	05 36	06♎35
1929	23 37	24 35	25 34	26 32	27 31	28 30	29 29	00♎27	01 26	02 25	03 24	04 23	05 22	06♎21
1930	23 23	24 21	25 20	26 18	27 17	28 16	29 14	00♎13	01 12	02 11	03 10	04 09	05 08	06♎07
1931	23 09	24 07	25 06	26 04	27 03	28 02	29 00	29 59	00♎58	01 57	02 55	03 54	04 53	05♎52
1932	23 53	24 51	25 50	26 49	27 47	28 46	29 45	00♎43	01 42	02 41	03 40	04 39	05 38	06♎37
1933	23 39	24 37	25 36	26 34	27 33	28 32	29 31	00♎29	01 28	02 27	03 26	04 25	05 24	06♎23
1934	23 25	24 23	25 22	26 21	27 19	28 18	29 17	00♎15	01 14	02 13	03 12	04 11	05 09	06♎08
1935	23 10	24 09	25 07	26 06	27 05	28 03	29 02	00♎01	01 00	01 59	02 57	03 56	04 55	05♎54
1936	23 55	24 53	25 52	26 51	27 49	28 48	29 47	00♎45	01 44	02 43	03 42	04 41	05 40	06♎39
1937	23 41	24 39	25 38	26 37	27 35	28 34	29 33	00♎31	01 30	02 29	03 28	04 27	05 26	06♎25
1938	23 27	24 25	25 24	26 22	27 21	28 20	29 18	00♎17	01 16	02 15	03 14	04 13	05 12	06♎10
1939	23 12	24 11	25 10	26 08	27 07	28 05	29 04	00♎03	01 02	02 00	02 59	03 58	04 57	05♎54
1940	23 57	24 55	25 54	26 52	27 51	28 50	29 48	00♎47	01 46	02 45	03 44	04 43	05 41	06♎40
1941	23 42	24 41	25 39	26 38	27 37	28 35	29 34	00♎33	01 32	02 31	03 29	04 28	05 27	06♎26
1942	23 28	24 27	25 26	26 24	27 23	28 21	29 20	00♎19	01 18	02 16	03 15	04 14	05 13	06♎12
1943	23 14	24 12	25 11	26 10	27 08	28 07	29 06	00♎04	01 03	02 02	03 01	04 00	04 59	05♎58
1944	23 58	24 57	25 55	26 54	27 53	28 51	29 50	00 49	01 48	02 47	03 45	04 44	05 43	06♎42
1945	23 45	24 43	25 42	26 40	27 39	28 38	29 36	00♎35	01 34	02 33	03 32	04 30	05 29	06♎28
1946	23 30	24 29	25 27	26 26	27 25	28 23	29 22	00♎21	01 20	02 18	03 17	04 16	05 15	06♎14
1947	23 16	24 15	25 13	26 12	27 11	28 09	29 08	00♎07	01 05	02 04	03 03	04 02	05 01	06♎00
1948	24 00	24 59	25 58	26 56	27 55	28 54	29 52	00♎51	01 50	02 49	03 47	04 46	05 45	06♎44
1949	23 46	24 45	25 43	26 42	27 41	28 39	29 38	00♎37	01 36	02 35	03 33	04 32	05 31	06♎30
1950	23 32	24 31	25 29	26 28	27 27	28 25	29 24	00♎23	01 21	02 20	03 19	04 18	05 17	06♎16
1951	23 18	24 16	25 15	26 14	27 12	28 11	19 10	00♎08	01 07	02 06	03 05	04 04	05 03	06♎01
1952	24 02	25 01	25 59	26 58	27 57	28 55	29 54	00♎53	01 52	02 51	03 49	04 48	05 47	06♎46
1953	23 48	24 47	25 46	26 44	27 43	28 41	29 40	00♎39	01 38	02 36	03 35	04 34	05 33	06♎32
1954	23 34	24 33	25 31	26 30	27 29	28 27	29 26	00♎25	01 23	02 22	03 21	04 20	05 19	06♎18
1955	23 20	24 19	25 17	26 16	27 14	28 13	29 12	00♎11	01 09	02 08	03 07	04 06	05 05	06♎04
1956	24 04	25 03	26 01	27 00	27 59	28 57	29 56	00♎55	01 54	02 52	03 51	04 50	05 49	06♎48
1957	23 50	24 48	25 47	26 46	27 44	28 43	29 42	00♎41	01 39	02 38	03 37	04 36	05 35	06♎34
1958	23 36	24 35	25 33	26 32	27 30	28 29	29 28	00♎27	01 25	02 24	03 23	04 22	05 21	06♎20
1959	23 22	24 20	25 19	26 17	27 16	28 14	29 13	00♎12	01 11	02 09	03 08	04 07	05 06	06♎05
1960	24 06	25 05	26 03	27 02	28 00	28 59	29 58	00♎57	01 56	02 54	03 53	04 52	05 52	06♎50
1961	23 52	24 51	25 49	26 48	27 47	28 45	29 44	00♎43	01 41	02 40	03 39	04 38	05 37	06♎36
1962	23 38	24 36	25 35	26 34	27 32	28 31	29 30	00♎28	01 27	02 26	03 25	04 24	06 23	06♎22
1963	23 24	24 22	25 21	26 19	27 18	28 17	29 15	00♎14	01 13	02 12	03 10	04 09	05 08	06♎07
1964	24 08	25 06	26 05	27 04	28 02	29 01	00 00	00♎58	01 57	02 56	03 55	04 54	05 53	06♎52
1965	23 53	24 52	25 50	26 49	27 48	28 46	29 45	00♎44	01 43	02 41	03 40	04 39	05 38	06♎37
1966	23 40	24 38	25 37	26 35	27 34	28 33	29 31	00♎30	01 29	02 28	03 26	04 25	05 24	06♎23
1967	23 25	24 24	25 22	26 21	27 20	28 18	29 17	00♎16	01 14	02 13	03 12	04 11	05 10	06♎09
1968	24 09	25 08	26 07	27 05	28 04	29 03	00♎01	01 00	01 59	02 58	03 57	04 56	05 55	06♎53
1969	23 56	24 54	25 53	26 51	27 50	28 49	29 47	00♎46	01 45	02 44	03 43	04 41	05 40	06♎39
1970	23 42	24 40	25 39	26 37	27 36	28 35	29 33	00♎32	01 31	02 30	03 29	04 28	05 26	06♎25
1971	23 28	24 26	25 25	26 23	27 22	28 21	29 19	00♎18	01 17	02 16	03 14	04 13	05 12	06♎11
1972	24 12	25 11	26 09	27 08	28 07	29 05	00♎04	01 03	02 01	03 00	03 59	04 58	05 57	06♎56
1973	23 58	24 56	25 55	26 54	27 52	28 51	29 50	00♎48	01 47	02 46	03 45	04 44	05 43	06♎42
1974	23 44	24 43	25 41	26 40	27 39	28 37	29 36	00♎35	01 33	02 32	03 31	04 30	05 29	06♎28
1975	23 30	24 28	25 27	26 25	27 24	28 22	29 21	00♎20	01 19	02 17	03 16	04 15	05 14	06♎13
1976	24 13	25 12	26 11	27 09	28 08	29 07	00♎05	01 04	02 03	03 02	04 01	05 00	05 59	06♎57
1977	24 00	24 58	25 57	26 55	27 54	28 53	29 51	00♎50	01 49	02 48	03 47	04 45	05 44	06♎43
1978	23 45	24 44	25 42	26 41	27 40	28 38	29 37	00♎36	01 34	02 33	03 32	04 31	05 30	06♎29
1979	23 31	24 29	25 28	26 27	27 25	28 24	29 23	00♎21	01 20	02 19	03 18	04 17	05 16	06♎14
1980	24 15	25 14	26 12	27 11	28 10	29 08	00♎07	01 06	02 04	03 03	04 02	05 01	06 00	06♎59
1981	24 01	24 59	25 58	26 56	27 55	28 54	29♎52	00 51	01 50	02 49	03 48	04 47	05 46	06♎45
1982	23 47	24 45	25 44	26 42	27 41	28 40	29♎39	00 37	01 36	02 35	03 34	04 33	05 31	06♎30
1983	23 33	24 31	25 30	26 28	27 27	28 25	29♎24	00 23	01 22	02 20	03 19	04 18	05 17	06♎16
1984	24 17	25 15	26 14	27 12	28 11	29♎10	00 08	01 07	02 06	03 05	04 04	05 03	06 02	07♎01
1985	24 03	25 02	26 00	26 59	27 57	28 56	29♎55	00 54	01 52	02 51	03 50	04 49	05 48	06♎47
1986	23 49	24 47	25 46	26 45	27 43	28 42	29♎40	00 39	01 38	02 37	03 36	04 34	05 33	06♎32
1987	23 35	24 33	25 32	26 30	27 29	28 28	29♎26	00 25	01 24	02 23	03 22	04 20	05 19	06♎18
1988	24 19	25 18	26 16	27 15	28 14	29♎12	00 11	01 10	02 09	03 07	04 06	05 05	06 04	07♎03
1989	24 05	25 04	26 02	27 01	27 59	28 58	29♎57	00 56	01 54	02 53	03 52	04 51	05 50	06♎49
1990	23 51	24 50	25 48	26 47	27 46	28 44	29♎43	00 42	01 41	02 39	03 38	04 37	05 36	06♎35
1991	23 37	24 36	25 34	26 33	27 31	28 30	29♎29	00 27	01 26	02 25	03 24	04 23	05 21	06♎20
1992	24 21	25 20	26 18	27 17	28 16	29♎14	00 13	01 12	02 11	03 09	04 08	05 07	06 06	07♎05
1993	24 07	25 06	26 04	27 03	28 02	29 00	29♎59	00 58	01 57	02 55	03 54	04 53	05 52	06♎51
1994	23 53	24 51	25 50	26 49	27 47	28 46	29♎45	00 43	01 42	02 41	03 40	04 38	05 37	06♎35
1995	23 38	24 37	25 35	26 34	27 33	28 31	29♎30	00 29	01 28	02 26	03 25	04 24	05 23	06♎22
1996	24 23	25 21	26 20	27 19	28 17	29♎16	00 15	01 13	02 12	03 11	04 10	05 09	06 08	07♎06
1997	24 09	25 07	26 06	27 04	28 03	29♎01	00 00	00 59	01 58	02 56	03 55	04 54	05 53	06♎52
1998	23 54	24 53	25 52	26 50	27 49	28 48	29♎46	00 45	01 44	02 43	03 41	04 40	05 39	06♎38
1999	23 40	24 39	25 37	26 36	27 34	28 33	29♎32	00 31	01 29	02 28	03 27	04 26	05 24	06♎23
2000	24 24	25 23	26 21	27 20	28 19	29♎17	00 16	01 15	02 14	03 12	04 11	05 10	06 09	07♎08

Sun

October

Year	1st	2nd	3rd	4th	5th	6th	7th	8th	9th	10th	11th	12th	13th	14th	15th	16th
1900	07♎21	08 20	09 19	10 18	11 17	12 17	13 16	14 15	15 14	16 14	17 13	18 12	19 12	20 11	21 11	22 10
1901	07♎06	08 06	09 05	10 04	11 03	12 02	13 01	14 00	15 00	15 59	16 58	17 58	18 57	19 57	20 54	21 56
1902	06♎53	07 52	08 51	09 50	10 49	11 48	12 47	13 47	14 46	15 45	16 44	17 44	18 43	19 48	20 42	21 42
1903	06♎38	07 37	08 36	09 35	10 34	11 34	12 33	13 32	14 31	15 30	16 30	17 29	18 28	19 28	20 27	21 27
1904	07♎22	08 21	09 21	10 20	11 19	12 18	13 17	14 17	15 16	16 15	17 15	18 14	19 13	20 13	21 12	22 12
1905	07♎08	08 07	09 07	10 06	11 05	12 04	13 03	14 02	15 02	16 01	17 00	18 00	18 59	19 58	20 58	21 57
1906	06♎54	07 53	08 52	09 51	10 50	11 49	12 49	13 48	14 47	15 46	16 46	17 45	18 44	19 44	20 43	21 43
1907	06♎40	07 39	08 38	09 37	10 36	11 35	12 34	13 33	14 33	15 32	16 31	17 31	18 30	19 30	20 29	21 29
1908	07♎24	08 23	09 23	10 22	11 21	12 20	13 19	14 18	15 18	16 17	17 16	18 16	19 15	20 14	21 14	22 13
1909	07♎10	03 09	09 08	10 07	11 06	12 05	13 05	14 04	15 03	16 02	17 02	18 01	19 01	20 00	21 00	21 59
1910	06♎56	07 55	08 54	09 53	10 52	11 52	12 52	13 50	14 49	15 49	16 48	17 47	18 47	19 46	20 46	21 45
1911	06♎42	07 41	08 40	09 39	10 38	11 37	12 36	13 35	14 35	15 34	16 33	17 33	18 32	19 31	20 31	21 30
1912	07♎26	08 25	09 24	10 23	11 23	12 22	13 21	14 20	15 20	16 19	17 18	18 18	19 17	20 17	21 16	22 16
1913	07♎12	08 11	09 10	10 10	11 09	12 08	13 07	14 06	15 06	16 05	17 04	18 04	19 03	20 02	21 02	22 01
1914	06♎58	07 57	08 56	09 55	10 54	11 54	12 53	13 52	14 52	15 50	16 50	17 49	18 49	19 48	20 47	21 47
1915	06♎44	07 43	08 42	09 41	10 40	11 39	12 38	13 38	14 37	15 36	16 36	17 35	18 34	19 34	20 33	21 33
1916	07♎29	08 28	09 27	10 26	11 25	12 24	13 23	14 23	15 22	16 21	17 21	18 20	19 19	20 19	21 18	22 18
1917	07♎14	08 13	09 12	10 11	11 10	12 10	13 09	14 08	15 07	16 07	17 06	18 05	19 05	20 04	21 04	22 03
1918	07♎00	07 59	08 58	09 57	10 56	11 56	12 55	13 54	14 53	15 53	16 52	17 51	18 51	19 50	20 50	21 49
1919	06♎46	07 45	08 44	09 43	10 42	11 41	12 40	13 40	14 39	15 38	16 37	17 37	18 36	19 36	20 35	21 34
1920	07♎30	08 29	09 28	10 27	11 27	12 26	13 25	14 24	15 24	16 23	17 22	18 22	19 21	20 21	21 20	22 20
1921	07♎16	08 15	09 14	10 13	11 13	12 12	13 11	14 10	15 09	16 09	17 08	18 07	19 07	20 06	21 06	22 05
1922	07♎02	08 01	09 00	09 59	10 58	11 57	12 56	13 55	14 55	15 54	16 53	17 53	18 52	19 51	20 51	21 50
1923	06♎47	07 46	08 45	09 44	10 43	11 42	12 42	13 41	14 40	15 49	16 39	17 38	18 38	19 37	20 36	21 36
1924	07♎32	08 31	09 30	10 29	11 28	12 27	13 27	14 26	15 25	16 24	17 24	18 23	19 22	20 22	21 21	22 21
1925	07♎17	08 16	09 15	10 14	11 14	12 13	13 12	14 11	15 10	16 10	17 09	18 08	19 08	20 07	21 07	22 06
1926	07♎03	08 02	09 01	10 00	11 00	11 59	12 58	13 57	14 57	15 56	16 55	17 55	18 54	19 53	20 53	21 52
1927	06♎49	07 48	08 47	09 46	10 45	11 45	12 44	13 43	14 42	15 41	16 41	17 40	18 39	19 39	20 38	21 38
1928	07♎34	08 33	09 32	10 31	11 30	12 29	13 28	14 27	15 27	16 26	17 26	18 25	19 24	20 24	21 23	22 23
1929	07♎20	08 19	09 18	10 17	11 16	12 15	13 14	14 14	15 13	16 12	17 12	18 11	19 10	20 10	21 09	22 09
1930	07♎06	08 05	09 04	10 03	11 02	12 01	13 00	13 59	14 58	15 58	16 57	17 56	18 56	19 55	20 55	21 54
1931	06♎51	07 50	08 49	09 48	10 47	11 46	12 46	13 45	14 44	15 43	16 43	17 42	18 41	19 41	20 40	21 40
1932	07♎36	08 35	09 34	10 33	11 32	12 32	13 31	14 30	15 29	16 29	17 28	18 27	19 27	20 26	21 26	22 25
1933	07♎22	08 21	09 20	10 19	11 18	12 17	13 16	17 15	15 15	16 14	17 13	18 13	19 12	20 12	21 11	22 11
1934	07♎07	08 06	09 05	10 05	11 04	12 03	13 02	14 01	15 01	16 00	16 59	17 59	18 58	19 58	20 57	21 56
1935	06♎53	07 52	08 51	09 50	10 49	11 49	12 48	13 47	14 46	15 45	16 45	17 44	18 43	19 43	20 42	21 42
1936	07♎38	08 37	09 36	10 35	11 34	12 33	13 32	14 32	15 31	16 30	17 29	18 29	19 28	20 28	21 27	22 27
1937	07♎24	08 23	09 22	10 21	11 20	12 19	13 18	14 18	15 17	16 16	17 15	18 15	19 14	20 14	21 13	22 13
1938	07♎09	08 08	09 08	10 07	11 06	12 05	13 04	14 03	15 02	16 02	17 01	18 00	19 00	19 59	20 59	21 58
1939	06♎55	07 54	08 53	09 52	10 51	11 50	12 49	13 49	14 48	15 47	16 46	17 45	18 45	19 45	20 44	21 44
1940	07♎39	08 39	09 38	10 37	11 36	12 35	13 34	14 34	15 33	16 32	17 31	18 31	19 30	20 30	21 29	22 29
1941	07♎25	08 24	09 23	10 22	11 21	12 21	13 20	14 19	15 18	16 17	17 17	18 16	19 16	20 15	21 14	22 14
1942	07♎11	08 10	09 09	10 08	11 07	12 06	13 06	14 05	15 04	16 03	17 03	18 02	19 01	20 01	21 00	22 00
1943	06♎57	07 56	08 55	09 54	10 53	11 52	12 51	13 50	14 50	15 49	16 48	17 48	18 47	19 46	20 46	21 45
1944	07♎41	08 40	09 39	10 38	11 37	12 37	13 36	14 35	15 34	16 32	17 33	18 32	19 32	20 31	21 31	22 30
1945	07♎27	08 26	09 25	10 25	11 24	12 23	13 22	14 21	15 21	16 20	17 29	18 19	19 18	20 18	21 17	22 17
1946	07♎13	08 12	09 11	10 10	11 09	12 09	13 08	14 07	15 06	16 05	17 05	18 04	19 03	20 03	21 02	22 02
1947	06♎59	07 58	08 57	09 56	10 55	11 54	12 53	13 52	14 52	15 51	16 50	17 49	18 49	19 48	20 48	21 47
1948	07♎43	08 42	09 41	10 41	11 40	12 39	13 38	14 37	15 37	16 36	17 35	18 35	19 34	20 34	21 33	22 32
1949	07♎29	08 28	09 27	10 26	11 25	12 25	13 24	14 23	15 22	16 22	17 21	18 20	19 20	20 19	21 18	22 18
1950	07♎15	08 14	09 13	10 12	11 11	12 10	13 09	14 08	15 08	16 07	17 06	18 06	19 05	20 05	21 04	22 04
1951	07♎00	08 00	08 59	09 58	10 57	11 56	12 55	13 54	14 54	15 53	16 52	17 51	18 51	19 50	20 50	21 49
1952	07♎45	08 44	09 43	10 42	11 41	12 41	13 40	14 39	15 38	16 37	17 37	18 36	19 36	20 35	21 35	22 34
1953	07♎31	08 30	09 29	10 28	11 27	12 27	13 26	14 25	15 24	16 24	17 23	18 22	19 22	20 21	21 21	22 20
1954	07♎17	08 16	09 15	10 14	11 13	12 12	13 12	14 11	15 10	16 09	17 09	18 08	19 07	20 07	21 06	22 06
1955	07♎03	08 02	09 01	10 00	10 59	11 58	12 57	13 56	14 55	15 55	16 54	17 53	18 53	19 52	20 52	21 51
1956	07♎47	08 46	09 45	10 44	11 44	12 43	13 42	14 41	15 41	16 40	17 39	18 39	19 38	20 37	21 37	22 36
1957	07♎33	08 32	09 31	10 30	11 29	12 28	13 27	14 27	15 26	16 25	17 25	18 24	19 23	20 23	21 22	22 22
1958	07♎19	08 18	09 17	10 16	11 15	12 13	13 13	14 12	15 12	16 11	17 10	18 10	19 09	20 08	21 08	22 07
1959	07♎04	08 03	09 02	10 01	11 00	11 59	12 59	13 58	14 57	15 56	16 56	17 55	18 54	19 54	20 53	21 53
1960	07♎49	08 48	09 47	10 46	11 45	12 44	13 44	14 43	15 42	16 41	17 41	18 40	19 39	20 39	21 38	22 38
1961	07♎35	08 34	09 33	10 32	11 31	12 30	13 29	14 29	15 28	16 27	17 27	18 26	19 25	20 25	21 24	22 24
1962	07♎21	08 20	09 19	10 18	11 17	12 16	13 15	14 14	15 14	16 13	17 12	18 11	19 11	20 10	21 10	22 09
1963	07♎06	08 05	09 04	10 03	11 02	12 01	13 00	14 00	14 59	15 58	16 57	17 57	18 56	19 56	20 55	21 55
1964	07♎51	08 50	09 49	10 48	11 47	12 46	13 45	14 45	15 44	16 43	17 43	18 42	19 41	20 41	21 40	22 40
1965	07♎36	08 35	09 34	10 33	11 32	12 32	13 31	14 30	15 29	16 28	17 28	18 27	19 26	20 26	21 25	22 25
1966	07♎22	08 21	09 20	10 19	11 18	12 17	13 16	14 16	15 15	16 14	17 14	18 13	19 12	20 12	21 11	22 11
1967	07♎08	08 07	09 06	10 05	11 04	12 03	13 02	14 02	15 01	16 00	16 59	17 59	18 58	19 57	20 57	21 56
1968	07♎52	08 51	09 51	10 50	11 49	12 48	13 47	14 46	15 45	16 45	17 44	18 43	19 43	20 42	21 42	22 41
1969	07♎38	08 37	09 36	10 35	11 35	12 34	13 33	14 32	15 31	16 31	17 30	18 29	19 29	20 28	21 28	22 27
1970	07♎24	08 23	09 23	10 22	11 21	12 20	13 19	14 18	15 18	16 17	17 16	18 15	19 15	20 14	21 14	22 13
1971	07♎10	08 09	09 08	10 07	11 06	12 05	13 04	14 04	15 03	16 02	17 01	18 01	19 00	20 00	20 59	21 58
1972	07♎55	08 54	09 53	10 52	11 51	12 50	13 49	14 49	15 48	16 47	17 47	18 46	19 45	20 45	21 44	22 44
1973	07♎41	08 40	09 39	10 38	11 37	12 36	13 35	14 35	15 34	16 33	17 32	18 32	19 31	20 30	21 30	22 29
1974	07♎27	08 26	09 25	10 24	11 23	12 22	13 21	14 20	15 19	16 19	17 18	18 17	19 17	20 16	21 16	22 15
1975	07♎12	08 11	09 10	10 09	11 08	12 07	13 06	14 06	15 05	16 04	17 03	18 03	19 02	20 02	21 01	22 00
1976	07♎56	08 55	09 55	10 54	11 53	12 52	13 51	14 50	15 49	16 49	17 48	18 47	19 47	20 46	21 46	22 45
1977	07♎42	08 41	09 40	10 39	11 38	12 38	13 37	14 36	15 35	16 35	17 34	18 33	19 33	20 32	21 32	22 31
1978	07♎28	08 27	09 26	10 25	11 24	12 23	13 22	14 22	15 21	16 20	17 20	18 19	19 18	20 18	21 17	22 16
1979	07♎13	08 12	09 11	10 10	11 10	12 09	13 08	14 07	15 06	16 05	17 05	18 04	19 03	20 03	21 02	22 02
1980	07♎58	08 57	09 56	10 55	11 54	12 53	13 53	14 52	15 51	16 50	17 50	18 49	19 49	20 48	21 47	22 47
1981	07♎44	08 43	09 42	10 41	11 40	12 39	13 38	14 37	15 37	16 36	17 35	18 35	19 34	20 33	21 33	22 32
1982	07♎29	08 28	09 27	10 26	11 25	12 25	13 24	14 23	15 22	16 21	17 21	18 20	19 19	20 19	21 18	22 18
1983	07♎15	08 14	09 13	10 12	11 11	12 10	13 09	14 09	15 08	16 07	17 06	18 06	19 05	20 05	21 04	22 03
1984	08♎00	08 59	09 58	10 57	11 56	12 55	13 54	14 53	15 53	16 52	17 51	18 50	19 50	20 49	21 49	22 48
1985	07♎46	08 45	09 44	10 43	11 42	12 41	13 40	14 39	15 38	16 38	17 37	18 36	19 36	20 35	21 35	22 34
1986	07♎31	08 30	09 29	10 28	11 28	12 27	13 26	14 25	15 24	16 24	17 23	18 22	19 22	20 21	21 21	22 20
1987	07♎17	08 16	09 15	10 14	11 13	12 12	13 12	14 11	15 10	16 09	17 08	18 08	19 07	20 06	21 06	22 05
1988	08♎02	09 01	10 00	10 59	11 58	12 57	13 56	14 56	15 55	16 54	17 54	18 53	19 52	20 52	21 51	22 51
1989	07♎48	08 47	09 46	10 45	11 44	12 43	13 42	14 42	15 41	16 40	17 40	18 39	19 38	20 37	21 37	22 36
1990	07♎34	08 33	09 32	10 31	11 30	12 29	13 28	14 27	15 27	16 26	17 25	18 24	19 24	20 23	21 23	22 22
1991	07♎19	08 18	09 17	10 16	11 16	12 15	13 14	14 13	15 12	16 12	17 11	18 10	19 10	20 09	21 08	22 08
1992	08♎04	09 03	10 02	11 01	12 00	12 59	13 59	14 58	15 57	16 56	17 56	18 55	19 54	20 54	21 53	22 53
1993	07♎50	08 49	09 48	10 47	11 46	12 45	13 44	14 44	15 43	16 42	17 41	18 41	19 40	20 40	21 39	22 39
1994	07♎35	08 34	09 33	10 32	11 32	12 31	13 30	14 29	15 28	16 28	17 27	18 26	19 26	20 25	21 25	22 24
1995	07♎21	08 20	09 19	10 18	11 17	12 16	13 15	14 14	15 14	16 13	17 12	18 12	19 11	20 10	21 10	22 09
1996	08♎05	09 04	10 03	11 03	12 02	13 01	14 00	14 59	15 58	16 58	17 57	18 57	19 56	20 55	21 55	22 54
1997	07♎51	08 50	09 49	10 48	11 47	12 47	13 46	14 45	15 44	16 43	17 43	18 42	19 41	20 41	21 40	22 40
1998	07♎37	08 36	09 35	10 34	11 33	12 32	13 31	14 31	15 30	15 29	17 28	18 28	19 27	20 26	21 26	22 25
1999	07♎22	08 21	09 20	10 19	11 19	12 18	13 17	14 16	15 15	16 15	17 14	18 13	19 13	20 12	21 11	22 11
2000	08♎07	09 06	10 05	11 04	12 03	13 02	14 02	15 01	16 01	16 59	17 59	18 58	19 57	20 57	21 56	22 56

	17th	18th	19th	20th	21st	22nd	23rd	24th	25th	26th	27th	28th	29th	30th	31st
1900	23 10	24 09	25 09	26 09	27 08	28 08	29 08	00♏ 08	01 08	02 07	03 07	04 07	05 07	06 07	07♏ 07
1901	22 55	23 55	24 55	25 54	26 54	27 54	28 53	29 53	00♏ 53	01 53	02 53	03 52	04 52	05 42	06♏ 52
1902	22 41	23 41	24 40	25 40	26 39	27 39	28 39	29 39	00♏ 38	01 38	02 38	03 38	04 38	05 38	06♏ 38
1903	22 26	23 26	24 26	25 25	26 25	27 25	28 24	29 24	00♏ 24	01 24	02 24	03 24	04 24	05 23	06♏ 23
1904	23 11	24 11	25 11	26 10	27 10	28 10	29 09	00♏ 09	01 09	02 09	03 09	04 09	05 09	06 08	07♏ 09
1905	22 57	23 57	24 56	25 56	26 55	27 55	28 55	29 55	00♏ 55	01 54	02 54	03 54	04 54	05 54	06♏ 54
1906	22 42	23 42	24 42	25 41	26 41	27 41	28 41	29 40	00♏ 04	01 40	02 40	03 40	04 40	05 40	06♏ 40
1907	22 28	23 28	24 27	25 27	26 26	27 26	28 26	29 25	00♏ 25	01 25	02 25	03 25	04 25	05 25	06♏ 25
1908	23 13	24 13	25 12	26 12	27 12	28 11	29 11	00♏ 11	02 11	02 11	03 11	04 11	05 10	06 10	07♏ 11
1909	22 59	23 48	24 58	25 58	26 57	27 57	28 57	29 57	00♏ 56	01 56	02 56	03 56	04 56	05 56	06♏ 56
1910	22 45	23 44	24 44	25 43	26 43	27 43	28 42	29 42	00♏ 42	01 42	02 42	03 42	04 41	05 41	06♏ 41
1911	22 30	23 29	24 29	25 29	26 28	27 28	28 28	29 28	00♏ 27	01 27	02 27	03 27	04 27	05 27	06♏ 27
1912	23 15	24 15	25 14	26 14	27 14	28 13	29 13	00♏ 13	01 13	02 13	03 12	04 12	05 12	06 12	07♏ 12
1913	23 01	24 00	25 00	26 00	26 59	27 59	28 59	29 59	00♏ 58	01 58	02 58	03 58	04 58	05 58	06♏ 58
1914	22 47	23 46	24 46	25 45	26 45	27 45	28 45	29 44	00♏ 44	01 44	02 44	03 44	04 44	05 44	06♏ 44
1915	22 32	23 32	24 31	25 31	26 31	27 30	28 30	29 30	00♏ 29	01 29	02 29	03 29	04 29	05 29	06♏ 29
1916	23 17	24 17	25 16	26 16	27 16	28 16	29 15	00♏ 15	01 15	02 15	03 15	04 15	05 15	06 15	07♏ 15
1917	23 03	24 02	25 02	26 02	27 01	28 01	29 01	00♏ 01	01 00	02 00	03 00	04 00	05 00	06 00	07♏ 00
1918	22 49	23 48	24 48	25 47	26 47	27 47	28 46	29 46	00♏ 46	01 46	02 46	03 46	04 45	05 45	06♏ 45
1919	22 34	23 34	24 33	25 33	26 32	27 32	28 32	29 32	00♏ 32	01 31	02 31	03 31	04 31	05 31	06♏ 31
1920	23 05	24 04	25 04	26 04	27 03	28 03	29 03	00♏ 02	01 02	02 02	03 02	04 02	05 02	06 02	07♏ 02
1921	22 50	23 50	24 49	25 49	26 49	27 48	28 48	29♏ 48	00 48	01 48	02 47	03 47	04 47	05 47	06♏ 47
1922	22 35	23 35	24 35	25 34	26 34	27 34	28 33	29 33	00♏ 33	01 33	02 32	03 32	04 32	05 32	06♏ 32
1923	23 20	24 20	25 19	26 19	27 19	28 19	29 18	00 18	01♏ 18	02 18	03 18	04 18	05 18	06 18	07♏ 18
1924	23 06	24 05	25 05	26 05	27 04	28 04	29 04	00♏ 04	01 04	02 03	03 03	04 03	05 03	06 03	07♏ 03
1925	22 52	23 51	24 51	25 51	26 50	27 50	28 50	29♏ 49	00 49	01 49	02 49	03 49	04 49	05 48	06♏ 48
1926	22 37	23 37	24 36	25 36	26 36	27 35	28 35	29 35	00♏ 35	01 34	02 34	03 34	04 34	05 34	06♏ 34
1927	23 22	24 22	25 22	26 21	27 21	28 21	29 20	00 20	01♏ 20	02 20	03 20	04 20	05 19	06 19	07♏ 19
1928	23 08	24 08	25 07	26 07	27 07	28 06	29 06	00♏ 06	01 06	02 05	03 05	04 05	05 05	06 05	07♏ 05
1929	22 54	23 53	24 53	25 53	26 52	27 52	28 52	29♏ 51	00 51	01 51	02 51	03 51	04 51	05 51	06♏ 51
1930	22 39	23 39	24 39	25 38	26 38	27 38	28 37	29 37	00♏ 37	01 37	02 36	03 36	04 36	05 36	06♏ 36
1931	22 39	23 39	24 39	25 38	26 38	27 38	28 37	29 37	00♏ 37	01 37	02 36	03 36	04 36	05 36	06♏ 36
1932	23 25	24 24	25 24	26 23	27 23	28 23	29 22	00♏ 22	01 22	02 22	03 22	04 22	05 22	06 22	07♏ 22
1933	23 10	24 10	25 09	26 09	27 09	28 08	29 08	00♏ 08	01 08	02 08	03 08	04 07	05 07	06 07	07♏ 07
1934	22 56	23 56	24 55	25 55	26 54	27 54	28 54	29 54	00♏ 53	01 53	02 53	03 53	04 53	05 53	06♏ 53
1935	22 41	23 41	24 40	25 40	26 40	27 39	28 39	29 39	00♏ 39	01 39	02 38	03 38	04 38	05 38	06♏ 38
1936	23 26	24 26	25 26	26 25	27 25	28 25	29 24	00♏ 24	01 24	02 24	03 24	04 24	05 23	06 23	07♏ 23
1937	23 12	24 12	25 11	26 11	27 11	28 10	29 10	00♏ 10	01 09	02 09	03 09	04 09	05 09	06 09	07♏ 09
1938	22 59	23 57	24 57	25 56	26 56	27 56	28 55	29 55	00♏ 55	01 55	02 55	03 55	04 55	05 55	06♏ 55
1939	22 43	23 43	24 42	25 42	26 42	27 41	28 41	29 41	00♏ 40	01 40	02 40	03 40	04 40	05 40	06♏ 40
1940	23 28	24 28	25 27	26 27	27 27	28 26	29 26	00 26	01 26	02 25	03 25	04 25	05 25	06 25	07 25
1941	23 14	24 13	25 13	26 12	27 12	28 12	29 12	00♏ 11	01 11	02 11	03 11	04 11	05 11	06 11	07♏ 11
1942	22 59	23 59	24 59	25 58	26 58	27 57	28 57	29 57	00♏ 57	01 56	02 56	03 56	04 56	05 56	06♏ 56
1943	22 45	23 44	24 44	25 43	26 43	27 43	28 42	29 42	00♏ 42	01 42	02 42	03 42	04 42	05 42	06♏ 42
1944	23 30	24 29	25 29	26 29	27 28	28 28	29 28	00♏ 28	01 27	02 27	03 27	04 27	05 27	06 27	04♏ 27
1945	23 16	24 16	25 15	26 15	27 14	28 14	29 14	00♏ 14	01 13	02 13	03 13	04 13	05 13	06 13	07♏ 13
1946	23 01	24 01	25 00	26 00	27 00	27 59	28 59	29 59	00♏ 59	01 59	02 59	03 58	04 58	05 58	06♏ 58
1947	22 47	23 46	24 46	25 46	26 45	27 45	28 45	29 44	00♏ 44	01 44	02 44	03 44	04 44	05 44	06♏ 43
1948	23 32	24 32	25 31	26 31	27 30	28 30	29 30	00♏ 30	01 29	02 29	03 29	04 29	05 29	06 29	07♏ 29
1949	23 17	24 17	25 17	26 16	27 16	28 16	29 16	00♏ 15	01 15	02 15	03 15	04 15	05 15	06 15	07♏ 15
1950	23 03	24 03	25 02	26 02	27 02	28 01	29 01	00♏ 01	01 00	02 00	03 00	04 00	05 00	06 00	07♏ 00
1951	22 49	23 48	24 48	25 47	26 47	27 47	28 46	29 46	00♏ 46	01 46	02 46	03 45	04 45	05 45	06♏ 45
1952	23 34	24 33	25 33	26 32	27 32	28 32	29 32	00♏ 31	01 31	02 31	03 31	04 31	05 31	06 31	07♏ 31
1953	23 20	24 19	25 19	26 18	27 18	28 18	29 17	00♏ 17	01 17	02 17	03 17	04 16	05 16	06 16	07♏ 16
1954	23 05	24 05	25 04	26 04	27 03	28 03	29 03	00♏ 03	01 02	02 02	03 02	04 02	05 02	06 02	07♏ 02
1955	22 51	23 50	24 50	25 49	26 49	27 49	28 49	29 48	00♏ 48	01 48	02 48	03 48	04 47	05 47	06♏ 47
1956	23 36	24 35	25 35	26 35	27 34	28 34	29 34	00♏ 33	01 33	02 33	03 33	04 33	05 33	06 33	07♏ 33
1957	23 21	24 21	25 20	26 20	27 20	28 19	29 19	00♏ 19	01 19	02 19	03 18	04 18	05 18	06 18	07♏ 18
1958	23 07	24 07	25 06	26 06	27 05	28 05	29 05	00♏ 05	01 04	02 04	03 04	04 04	05 04	06 04	07♏ 04
1959	22 52	23 52	24 51	25 51	26 50	27 50	28 50	29 50	00♏ 49	01 49	02 49	03 49	04 49	05 49	06♏ 49
1960	23 37	24 37	25 36	26 36	27 36	28 36	29 35	00♏ 35	01 35	02 35	03 35	04 35	05 35	06 34	07♏ 34
1961	23 23	24 23	25 22	26 22	27 22	28 21	29 21	00♏ 21	01 21	02 20	03 20	04 20	05 20	06 20	07♏ 20
1962	23 09	24 08	25 08	26 07	27 07	28 07	29 06	00♏ 06	01 06	02 06	03 06	04 06	05 06	06 05	07♏ 05
1963	22 54	23 45	24 53	25 53	26 53	27 52	28 52	29 52	00♏ 51	01 51	02 51	03 51	04 51	05 51	06♏ 51
1964	23 39	24 39	25 38	26 38	27 38	28 37	29 37	00♏ 37	01 37	02 36	03 36	04 36	05 36	06 36	07♏ 36
1965	23 24	24 24	25 23	26 23	27 23	28 22	29 22	00♏ 22	01 22	02 22	03 22	04 21	05 21	06 21	07♏ 21
1966	23 10	24 10	25 09	26 09	27 09	28 08	29 08	00♏ 08	01 08	02 07	03 07	04 07	05 07	06 07	07♏ 07
1967	22 56	23 55	24 55	25 54	26 54	27 54	28 53	29 53	00♏ 53	01 53	02 53	03 53	04 52	05 52	06♏ 52
1968	23 41	24 40	25 40	26 40	27 39	28 39	29 39	00♏ 39	01 38	02 38	03 38	04 38	05 38	06 38	07♏ 38
1969	23 27	24 26	25 26	26 26	27 25	28 25	29 25	00♏ 24	01 24	02 24	03 24	04 24	05 24	06 24	07♏ 24
1970	23 13	24 12	25 12	26 11	27 11	28 11	29 10	00♏ 10	01 10	02 10	03 10	04 10	05 09	06 09	07♏ 09
1971	22 58	23 58	24 57	25 57	26 56	27 56	28 56	29 56	00♏ 55	01 55	02 55	03 55	04 55	05 55	06♏ 55
1972	23 43	24 43	25 43	26 42	27 42	28 41	29 41	00♏ 41	01 41	02 41	03 40	04 40	05 40	06 40	07♏ 40
1973	23 29	24 28	25 28	26 28	27 27	28 27	29 27	00♏ 26	01 26	02 26	03 26	04 26	05 26	06 26	07♏ 26
1974	23 15	24 14	25 14	26 14	27 13	28 13	29 13	00♏ 12	01 12	02 12	03 12	04 12	05 11	06 11	07♏ 11
1975	23 00	23 59	24 59	25 59	26 58	27 58	28 58	29 57	00♏ 57	01 57	02 57	03 57	04 56	05 56	06♏ 56
1976	23 45	24 44	25 44	26 43	27 43	28 43	29 43	00♏ 42	01 42	02 42	03 42	04 42	05 42	06 42	07♏ 42
1977	23 31	24 30	25 30	26 29	27 29	28 29	29 28	00♏ 28	01 28	02 28	03 28	04 27	05 27	06 27	07♏ 27
1978	23 16	24 15	25 15	26 15	27 14	28 14	29 14	00♏ 13	01 13	02 13	03 13	04 13	05 13	06 13	07♏ 13
1979	23 01	24 01	25 00	26 00	27 00	27 59	28 59	29 59	00♏ 59	01 58	02 58	03 58	04 58	05 58	06♏ 58
1980	23 47	24 46	25 46	26 45	27 45	28 45	29 44	00♏ 44	01 44	02 44	03 44	04 43	05 43	06 43	07♏ 43
1981	23 32	24 31	25 31	26 30	27 30	28 30	29 30	00♏ 29	01 29	02 29	03 29	04 29	05 29	06 29	07♏ 29
1982	23 17	24 17	25 17	26 16	27 16	28 16	29 15	00♏ 15	01 15	02 15	03 14	04 14	05 14	06 14	07♏ 14
1983	23 03	24 02	25 02	26 02	27 01	28 01	29 01	00♏ 00	01 00	02 00	03 00	04 59	05 59	05 59	05♏ 59
1984	23 48	24 47	25 47	26 47	27 46	28 46	29 46	00♏ 45	01 45	02 45	03 45	04 45	05 45	06 45	07♏ 45
1985	23 34	24 33	25 33	26 33	27 32	28 32	29 32	00♏ 31	01 31	02 31	03 31	04 31	05 31	06 31	07♏ 30
1986	23 19	24 19	25 19	26 18	27 18	28 17	29 17	00♏ 17	01 17	02 16	03 16	04 16	05 16	06 16	07♏ 16
1987	23 05	24 04	25 04	26 04	27 03	28 03	29 03	00♏ 02	01 02	02 02	03 02	04 02	05 02	06 02	07♏ 02
1988	23 50	24 50	25 50	26 49	27 49	28 49	29 48	00♏ 48	01 48	02 48	03 47	04 47	05 47	06 47	07♏ 47
1989	23 36	24 35	25 35	26 35	27 34	28 34	29 34	00♏ 33	01 33	02 33	03 33	04 33	05 33	06 33	07♏ 33
1990	23 22	24 21	25 21	26 21	27 20	28 20	29 20	00♏ 19	01 19	02 19	03 19	04 19	05 19	06 18	07♏ 18
1991	23 07	24 07	25 07	26 06	27 06	28 05	29 05	00♏ 05	01 05	02 04	03 04	04 04	05 04	06 04	07♏ 04
1992	23 52	24 52	25 51	26 51	27 51	28 50	29 50	00♏ 50	01 50	02 50	03 49	04 49	05 49	06 49	07♏ 49
1993	23 38	24 38	25 37	26 37	27 37	28 36	29 36	00♏ 36	01 36	02 35	03 35	04 35	05 35	06 35	07♏ 35
1994	23 24	24 23	25 23	26 22	27 22	28 21	29 21	00♏ 21	01 21	02 20	03 20	04 20	05 20	06 20	07♏ 20
1995	23 09	24 08	25 08	26 07	27 07	28 07	29 06	00♏ 06	01 06	02 06	03 06	04 06	05 05	06 05	07♏ 05
1996	23 54	24 53	25 53	26 53	27 52	28 52	29 52	00♏ 51	01 51	02 51	03 51	04 51	05 51	06 51	07♏ 51
1997	23 39	24 39	25 38	26 38	27 38	28 37	29 37	00♏ 37	01 37	02 36	03 36	04 36	05 36	06 36	07♏ 36
1998	23 25	24 24	25 24	26 24	27 23	28 23	29 23	00♏ 22	01 22	02 22	03 22	04 22	05 22	06 22	07♏ 22
1999	23 10	24 10	25 10	26 09	27 09	28 08	29 08	00♏ 08	01 08	02 07	03 07	04 07	05 07	06 07	07♏ 07
2000	23 55	24 55	25 54	26 54	27 54	28 53	29 53	00♏ 53	01 53	02 52	03 52	04 52	05 52	06 52	07♏ 52

Sun

November

Year	1st	2nd	3rd	4th	5th	6th	7th	8th	9th	10th	11th	12th	13th	14th	15th	16th
1900	08 ♏ 07	09 07	10 07	11 08	12 08	13 08	14 08	15 08	16 09	17 09	18 09	19 10	20 10	21 10	22 11	23 11
1901	07 ♏ 52	08 52	09 53	10 53	11 53	12 53	13 53	14 54	15 54	16 54	17 55	18 55	19 55	20 56	21 56	22 57
1902	07 ♏ 38	08 38	09 38	10 38	11 39	12 39	13 39	14 39	15 39	16 40	17 40	18 40	19 41	20 41	21 42	22 42
1903	07 ♏ 23	08 23	09 24	10 24	11 24	12 24	13 24	14 24	15 25	16 25	17 25	18 25	19 26	20 26	21 27	22 27
1904	08 ♏ 09	09 09	10 09	11 09	12 09	13 09	14 10	15 10	16 10	17 10	18 11	19 1'1	20 12	21 12	22 13	23 13
1905	07 ♏ 54	08 54	09 54	10 55	11 55	12 55	13 55	14 55	15 56	16 56	17 56	18 57	19 57	20 57	21 58	22 58
1906	07 ♏ 40	08 40	09 40	10 40	11 40	12 40	13 40	14 40	15 41	16 41	17 41	18 42	19 42	20 43	21 43	22 44
1907	07 ♏ 25	08 25	09 25	10 25	11 25	12 25	13 26	14 26	15 26	16 26	17 27	18 27	19 27	20 28	21 28	22 29
1908	08 ♏ 11	09 11	10 11	11 11	12 11	13 11	14 11	15 12	16 12	17 12	18 13	19 13	20 13	21 14	22 14	23 15
1909	07 ♏ 56	08 56	09 56	10 56	11 56	12 56	13 57	14 57	15 57	16 58	17 58	18 58	19 59	20 59	22 00	23 00
1910	07 ♏ 42	08 42	09 42	10 42	11 42	12 42	13 42	14 43	15 43	16 43	17 44	18 44	19 44	20 45	21 45	22 46
1911	07 ♏ 27	08 27	09 27	10 27	11 27	12 28	13 28	17 28	15 28	16 28	17 29	18 29	19 29	20 30	21 30	22 31
1912	08 ♏ 12	09 12	10 12	11 13	12 13	13 13	14 13	15 13	16 14	17 14	18 14	19 15	20 15	21 16	22 16	23 17
1913	07 ♏ 58	08 58	09 58	10 58	11 59	12 59	13 59	14 59	16 00	17 00	18 00	19 00	20 01	21 01	22 02	23 02
1914	07 ♏ 44	08 44	09 44	10 44	11 44	12 44	13 44	14 44	15 45	16 45	17 45	18 46	19 46	20 47	21 47	22 47
1915	07 ♏ 29	08 29	09 29	10 29	11 29	12 29	13 30	14 30	15 30	16 31	17 31	18 31	19 32	20 32	21 32	22 33
1916	08 ♏ 15	09 15	10 15	11 15	12 15	13 15	14 16	15 16	16 16	17 16	18 17	19 17	20 17	21 18	22 18	23 19
1917	08 ♏ 00	09 00	10 00	11 00	12 00	13 01	14 01	15 01	16 01	17 02	18 02	19 02	20 03	21 03	22 04	23 04
1918	07 ♏ 46	08 46	09 46	10 46	11 46	12 46	13 46	14 47	15 47	16 47	17 48	18 48	19 48	20 49	21 49	22 50
1919	07 ♏ 31	08 31	09 31	10 31	11 31	12 32	13 32	14 32	15 32	16 32	17 33	18 33	19 33	20 34	21 34	22 35
1920	08 ♏ 16	09 16	10 16	11 16	12 17	13 17	14 17	15 17	16 18	17 18	18 18	19 19	20 19	21 20	22 20	23 21
1921	08 ♏ 02	09 02	10 02	11 02	12 02	13 03	14 03	15 03	16 03	17 04	18 04	19 04	20 05	21 05	22 06	23 06
1922	07 ♏ 47	08 47	09 47	10 47	11 47	12 48	13 48	14 48	15 48	16 49	17 49	18 49	19 50	20 50	21 51	22 51
1923	07 ♏ 32	08 32	09 32	10 32	11 33	12 33	13 33	14 33	15 33	16 34	17 34	18 35	19 35	20 35	21 36	22 36
1924	08 ♏ 18	09 18	10 18	11 18	12 18	13 18	14 19	15 19	16 19	17 19	18 20	19 20	02 20	21 21	22 21	23 22
1925	08 ♏ 03	09 03	10 03	11 03	12 03	13 03	14 04	15 04	16 04	17 05	18 05	19 05	20 06	21 06	22 07	23 07
1926	07 ♏ 49	08 49	09 49	10 49	11 49	12 49	13 49	14 50	15 50	16 50	17 51	18 51	91 51	20 52	21 52	22 53
1927	07 ♏ 34	08 34	09 34	10 34	11 35	12 35	13 35	14 35	15 35	16 36	17 36	18 36	19 37	20 37	21 37	22 38
1928	08 ♏ 19	09 19	10 20	11 20	12 20	13 20	14 20	15 21	16 21	17 21	18 22	19 22	20 22	21 23	22 23	23 24
1929	08 ♏ 05	09 05	10 05	11 06	12 06	13 06	14 06	15 06	16 07	17 07	18 07	19 08	20 08	21 08	22 09	23 09
1930	07 ♏ 51	08 51	09 51	10 51	11 51	12 51	13 51	14 52	15 52	16 52	17 52	18 53	19 53	20 54	21 54	22 54
1931	07 ♏ 36	08 36	09 36	10 36	11 36	12 37	13 37	14 37	15 37	16 38	17 38	18 38	19 39	20 39	21 40	22 40
1932	08 ♏ 22	09 22	10 22	11 22	12 22	13 23	14 23	15 23	16 23	17 24	18 24	19 24	20 25	21 25	22 25	23 26
1933	08 ♏ 07	09 07	10 07	11 08	12 08	13 08	14 08	15 08	16 09	17 09	18 09	19 10	20 10	21 10	22 11	23 11
1934	07 ♏ 53	08 53	09 53	10 53	11 53	12 53	13 54	14 54	15 54	16 54	17 55	18 55	19 56	20 56	21 56	22 57
1935	07 ♏ 38	08 38	09 38	10 38	11 39	12 39	13 39	14 39	15 39	16 40	17 40	18 40	19 41	20 41	21 41	22 42
1936	08 ♏ 23	09 23	10 24	11 24	12 24	13 24	14 24	15 24	16 25	17 25	18 25	19 26	20 26	21 27	22 27	23 28
1937	08 ♏ 09	09 09	10 09	11 09	12 10	13 10	14 10	15 10	16 11	17 11	18 11	19 12	20 12	21 12	22 13	23 13
1938	07 ♏ 55	08 55	09 55	10 55	11 55	12 55	13 55	14 55	15 56	16 56	17 56	18 57	19 57	20 57	21 58	22 58
1939	07 ♏ 40	08 40	09 40	10 40	11 40	12 40	13 40	14 41	15 41	16 41	17 42	18 42	19 42	20 43	21 43	22 44
1940	08 ♏ 25	09 25	10 26	11 26	12 26	13 26	14 26	15 26	16 27	17 27	18 27	19 28	20 28	21 28	22 29	23 29
1941	08 ♏ 11	09 11	10 11	11 11	12 11	13 11	14 11	15 12	16 12	17 12	18 12	19 13	20 13	21 14	22 14	23 14
1942	07 ♏ 56	08 56	09 56	10 56	11 56	12 57	13 57	14 57	15 57	16 58	17 58	18 58	19 59	20 59	22 00	23 00
1943	07 ♏ 42	08 42	09 42	10 42	11 42	12 42	13 42	14 42	16 43	16 43	17 43	18 44	19 44	20 44	21 45	22 45
1944	08 ♏ 27	09 27	10 27	11 27	12 27	13 27	14 28	15 28	15 28	16 28	17 28	18 29	19 29	20 30	21 30	22 30
1945	08 ♏ 13	09 13	10 13	11 13	12 13	13 14	14 14	15 14	16 14	17 15	18 15	19 15	20 16	21 16	22 17	23 17
1946	07 ♏ 58	08 58	09 59	10 59	11 59	12 59	13 59	14 59	16 00	17 00	18 00	19 00	20 01	21 01	22 02	23 02
1947	07 ♏ 43	08 44	09 44	10 44	11 44	12 44	13 44	14 44	15 45	16 45	17 45	18 46	19 46	20 46	21 47	22 47
1948	08 ♏ 29	09 29	10 29	11 29	12 30	13 30	14 30	15 30	16 31	17 31	18 31	19 32	20 32	21 32	22 33	23 33
1949	08 ♏ 15	09 15	10 15	11 15	12 15	13 15	14 15	15 16	16 16	17 16	18 16	19 17	20 17	21 18	22 18	23 18
1950	08 ♏ 00	09 00	10 00	11 00	12 00	13 00	14 00	15 01	16 01	17 01	18 02	19 02	20 02	21 03	22 03	23 04
1951	07 ♏ 45	08 45	09 46	10 46	11 46	12 46	13 46	14 46	15 47	16 47	17 47	18 46	19 48	20 48	21 49	22 49
1952	08 ♏ 31	09 31	10 31	11 31	12 31	13 31	14 31	15 32	16 32	17 32	18 33	19 33	20 33	21 34	22 34	23 35
1953	08 ♏ 16	09 16	10 17	11 17	12 17	13 17	14 17	15 18	16 18	17 18	18 18	19 19	20 19	21 20	22 20	23 21
1954	08 ♏ 02	09 02	10 02	11 02	12 02	13 03	14 03	15 03	16 03	17 03	18 04	19 04	20 04	21 05	22 05	23 06
1955	07 ♏ 47	08 47	09 47	10 47	11 48	12 48	13 48	14 48	15 48	16 49	17 49	18 49	19 50	20 50	21 51	22 51
1956	08 ♏ 33	09 33	10 33	11 33	12 33	13 34	14 34	15 34	16 34	17 35	18 35	19 35	20 36	21 36	22 37	23 37
1957	08 ♏ 18	09 18	10 18	11 19	12 19	13 19	14 19	15 19	16 19	17 20	18 20	19 20	20 20	21 21	22 22	23 22
1958	08 ♏ 04	09 04	10 04	11 04	12 04	13 04	14 04	15 05	16 05	17 05	18 05	19 06	20 06	21 07	22 07	23 08
1959	07 ♏ 49	08 49	09 49	10 49	11 49	12 49	13 50	14 50	15 50	16 50	17 51	18 51	19 51	20 52	21 52	22 53
1960	08 ♏ 34	09 35	10 35	11 35	12 35	13 35	14 35	15 35	16 36	17 36	18 36	19 37	20 37	21 37	22 38	23 39
1961	08 ♏ 20	09 20	10 20	11 20	12 20	13 21	14 21	15 21	16 21	17 22	18 22	19 22	10 23	21 23	22 24	23 24
1962	08 ♏ 05	09 06	10 06	11 06	12 06	13 06	14 06	15 06	16 07	17 07	18 07	19 07	20 08	21 08	22 09	23 09
1963	07 ♏ 51	08 51	09 51	10 51	11 51	12 51	13 51	14 51	15 52	16 52	17 52	18 53	19 53	20 53	21 54	22 54
1964	08 ♏ 36	09 36	10 36	11 37	12 37	13 37	14 37	15 37	16 38	17 38	18 38	19 39	20 39	21 39	22 40	23 40
1965	08 ♏ 21	09 21	10 22	11 22	12 22	13 22	14 22	15 22	16 23	17 23	18 23	19 23	20 24	21 24	22 25	23 25
1966	08 ♏ 07	09 07	10 07	11 07	12 07	13 07	14 07	15 07	16 08	17 08	18 08	19 09	20 09	21 10	22 10	23 11
1967	07 ♏ 52	08 52	09 53	10 53	11 53	12 53	13 53	14 53	15 54	16 54	17 54	18 55	19 55	20 55	21 56	23 57
1968	08 ♏ 38	09 38	10 38	11 38	12 38	13 39	14 39	15 39	16 39	17 39	18 40	19 40	20 41	21 41	22 41	23 42
1969	08 ♏ 24	09 24	10 24	11 24	12 24	13 24	14 24	15 25	16 25	17 25	18 26	19 26	20 26	21 27	22 27	23 28
1970	08 ♏ 09	09 10	10 10	11 10	12 10	13 10	14 10	15 10	16 11	17 11	18 11	19 12	20 12	21 12	22 13	23 13
1971	07 ♏ 55	08 55	09 55	10 55	11 55	12 55	13 55	14 55	15 56	16 56	17 56	18 57	19 57	20 57	21 58	22 58
1972	08 ♏ 40	09 40	10 40	11 41	12 41	13 41	14 41	15 41	16 42	17 42	18 42	19 43	20 43	21 43	22 44	23 44
1973	08 ♏ 26	09 26	10 26	11 26	12 26	13 26	14 27	15 27	16 27	17 27	18 28	19 28	20 28	21 29	22 29	23 29
1974	08 ♏ 11	09 11	10 11	11 11	12 12	13 12	14 12	15 12	16 12	17 13	18 13	19 13	20 14	21 14	22 15	23 15
1975	07 ♏ 56	08 56	09 56	10 57	11 57	12 57	13 57	14 57	15 58	16 58	17 58	18 59	19 59	20 59	22 00	23 00
1976	08 ♏ 42	09 42	10 42	11 42	12 42	13 42	14 42	15 43	16 43	17 43	18 44	19 44	20 44	21 45	22 45	23 46
1977	08 ♏ 27	09 27	10 27	11 27	12 28	13 28	14 28	15 28	16 28	17 29	18 29	19 29	20 30	21 30	22 31	23 21
1978	08 ♏ 13	09 13	10 13	11 13	12 13	13 13	14 13	15 14	16 14	17 14	18 14	19 15	20 15	21 15	22 16	23 16
1979	07 ♏ 58	08 58	09 58	10 58	11 58	12 58	13 58	14 59	15 59	16 59	17 59	19 00	20 00	21 00	22 01	23 01
1980	08 ♏ 43	09 43	10 43	11 44	12 44	13 44	14 44	15 44	16 44	17 45	18 45	19 45	20 46	21 47	22 47	23 47
1981	08 ♏ 29	09 29	10 29	11 29	12 29	13 29	14 30	15 30	16 30	17 30	18 31	19 31	20 31	21 32	22 32	23 32
1982	08 ♏ 14	09 14	10 14	11 14	12 14	13 14	14 15	15 15	16 15	17 15	18 16	19 16	20 16	21 17	22 17	23 18
1983	07 ♏ 59	08 59	09 59	11 00	12 00	13 00	14 00	15 00	16 01	17 01	18 01	19 02	20 02	21 02	22 03	23 03
1984	08 ♏ 45	09 45	10 45	11 45	12 45	13 45	14 56	15 46	16 46	17 46	18 47	19 47	20 47	21 48	22 48	23 49
1985	08 ♏ 30	09 31	10 31	11 31	12 31	13 31	14 31	15 31	16 32	17 32	18 32	19 33	20 33	21 33	22 34	23 34
1986	08 ♏ 16	09 16	10 16	11 16	12 16	13 17	14 17	15 17	16 17	17 18	18 18	19 18	20 18	21 19	22 19	23 20
1987	08 ♏ 02	09 02	10 02	11 02	12 02	13 02	14 02	15 02	16 02	17 03	18 03	19 03	20 04	21 04	22 04	23 05
1988	08 ♏ 47	09 47	10 47	11 47	12 47	13 48	14 48	15 48	16 48	17 49	18 49	19 49	20 50	21 50	22 51	23 51
1989	08 ♏ 33	09 33	10 33	11 33	12 33	13 33	14 34	15 34	16 34	17 34	18 35	19 35	20 35	21 36	22 36	23 36
1990	08 ♏ 18	09 18	10 18	11 18	12 19	13 19	14 19	15 19	16 19	17 20	18 20	19 20	20 21	21 21	22 21	23 22
1991	08 ♏ 04	09 04	10 04	11 04	12 04	13 04	14 04	15 05	16 05	17 05	18 06	19 06	20 06	21 07	22 07	28 06
1992	08 ♏ 49	09 49	10 49	11 50	12 50	13 50	14 50	15 50	16 51	17 51	18 51	19 51	20 52	21 52	22 53	23 53
1993	08 ♏ 35	09 35	10 35	11 35	12 35	13 35	14 36	15 36	16 36	17 36	18 37	19 37	20 37	21 38	22 38	23 39
1994	08 ♏ 20	09 20	10 20	11 20	12 20	13 21	14 21	15 21	16 21	17 22	18 22	19 22	20 23	21 23	22 23	23 24
1995	08 ♏ 05	09 05	10 05	11 05	12 06	13 06	14 06	15 06	16 06	17 06	18 07	19 07	20 07	21 08	22 08	23 09
1996	08 ♏ 51	09 51	10 51	11 51	12 51	13 51	14 51	15 52	16 52	17 52	18 53	19 53	20 53	21 54	22 54	23 55
1997	08 ♏ 36	09 36	10 36	11 36	12 36	13 37	14 37	15 37	16 37	17 38	18 38	19 38	20 38	21 39	22 39	23 40
1998	08 ♏ 22	09 22	10 22	11 22	12 22	13 22	14 22	15 22	16 22	17 23	18 23	19 23	20 24	21 24	22 24	23 25
1999	08 ♏ 07	09 07	10 07	11 07	12 07	13 07	14 07	15 08	16 08	17 08	18 08	19 09	20 09	21 10	22 10	23 10
2000	08 ♏ 52	09 52	10 52	11 52	12 53	13 53	14 53	15 53	16 53	17 54	18 54	19 54	20 55	21 55	22 55	23 56

	17th	18th	19th	20th	21st	22nd	23rd	24th	25th	26th	27th	28th	29th	30th
1900	24 12	25 13	26 13	27 14	28 14	29 15	00♐16	01 16	02 17	03 18	04 19	05 19	06 20	07♐21
1901	23 57	24 58	25 58	27 00	28 00	29 00	00♐01	01 01	02 02	03 03	04 04	50 04	06 05	07♐06
1902	23 42	24 43	25 43	26 44	27 45	28 45	29 46	00♐47	01 47	02 48	03 49	04 49	05 50	06♐51
1903	23 28	24 28	25 29	26 29	27 30	28 31	29 31	00♐32	01 33	02 33	03 34	04 35	05 36	06♐36
1904	24 14	26 14	26 15	27 15	28 16	29 16	00♐17	01 18	02 18	03 19	04 20	05 21	06 21	07♐22
1905	24 00	24 59	26 00	27 00	28 01	29 02	00♐02	01 03	02 04	03 04	04 05	05 06	06 07	07♐08
1906	23 44	24 45	25 45	26 46	27 46	28 47	29 48	00♐48	01 49	02 50	03 50	04 51	05 52	06♐53
1907	23 29	24 30	25 30	26 31	27 31	28 32	29 33	00♐33	01 34	02 35	03 35	04 36	05 37	06♐38
1908	24 15	25 16	26 16	27 17	28 17	29 18	00♐19	01 19	02 20	03 21	04 22	05 23	06 23	07♐24
1909	24 01	25 01	26 02	27 02	28 03	29 04	00♐04	01 05	02 06	03 06	04 07	05 08	06 08	07♐09
1910	23 46	24 47	25 47	26 48	27 48	28 49	29 49	00♐50	01 51	02 52	03 52	04 53	05 54	06♐55
1911	23 31	24 32	25 32	26 33	27 34	28 34	29 35	00♐36	01 36	02 37	03 38	04 39	05 39	06♐40
1912	24 17	25 18	26 18	27 19	28 19	29 10	00♐21	01 21	02 22	03 23	04 24	05 24	06 25	07♐26
1913	24 03	25 03	26 04	27 04	28 05	29 05	00♐06	01 07	02 07	03 08	04 09	05 10	06 11	07♐11
1914	23 48	24 49	25 29	26 50	27 50	38 51	29 52	00♐52	01 53	02 54	03 54	04 55	05 56	06♐57
1915	23 33	24 34	25 34	26 35	27 36	28 36	29 37	00♐37	01 38	02 39	03 39	04 40	05 41	06♐42
1916	24 19	25 20	25 20	27 21	28 22	29 22	00♐23	01 24	02 24	03 25	04 26	05 27	06 27	07♐28
1917	24 05	25 05	26 06	27 06	28 07	29 08	00♐08	01 09	02 10	03 10	04 11	05 12	06 12	07♐13
1918	23 50	24 50	25 51	26 52	27 52	28 53	29 53	00♐54	01 55	02 55	03 56	04 57	05 58	06♐58
1919	23 35	24 36	25 36	26 37	27 37	28 38	29 39	00♐39	01 40	02 41	03 42	04 42	05 43	06♐44
1920	24 21	25 22	26 22	27 23	28 23	29 24	00♐25	01 25	02 26	03 27	04 27	05 28	06 29	07♐30
1921	24 06	25 07	26 08	27 08	28 09	29 09	00♐10	01 11	02 11	03 12	04 13	05 14	06 14	07♐15
1922	23 52	24 52	25 53	26 53	27 54	28 54	29 55	00♐56	01 57	02 57	03 58	04 59	05 59	07♐00
1923	23 37	24 37	25 38	26 38	27 39	28 39	29 40	00♐41	01 41	02 42	03 43	04 44	05 44	06♐45
1924	24 22	25 23	26 23	27 24	28 25	29 25	00♐26	01 27	02 27	03 28	04 29	05 30	06 30	07♐31
1925	24 08	25 08	26 09	27 09	28 10	29 10	00♐11	01 12	02 12	03 13	04 14	05 15	06 15	07♐15
1926	23 53	24 53	25 54	26 55	27 55	28 56	29 56	00 57	01 58	02 58	03 59	05 00	06 01	07♐01
1927	23 38	24 39	25 39	26 40	27 40	28 41	29 42	00♐42	01 43	02 44	03 45	04 45	05 46	06♐47
1928	24 24	25 25	26 25	27 26	28 27	29 27	00♐28	01 28	02 29	03 30	04 31	05 31	06 32	07♐33
1929	24 10	25 10	26 11	27 11	28 12	29 13	00♐13	01 14	02 14	03 15	04 16	05 17	06 18	07♐18
1930	23 55	24 56	25 56	26 57	27 57	28 58	29 59	00♐59	02 00	03 00	04 01	05 02	06 03	07♐04
1931	23 40	24 41	25 41	26 42	27 43	28 43	29 44	00♐44	01 45	02 46	03 46	04 47	05 48	06♐49
1932	24 26	25 27	26 27	27 28	28 29	29 29	00♐30	01 31	02 31	03 32	04 33	05 34	06 34	07♐35
1933	24 12	25 12	26 13	27 14	28 14	29 15	00♐15	01 16	02 17	03 18	04 18	05 19	06 20	07♐21
1934	23 57	24 58	25 58	26 59	27 59	29 00	00♐01	01 01	02 02	03 03	04 03	05 04	06 05	07♐06
1935	23 43	24 43	25 43	26 44	27 45	28 45	29 46	00♐47	01 47	02 48	03 49	04 50	05 50	06♐51
1936	24 28	25 29	26 29	27 30	28 31	29 31	00♐32	01 32	02 33	03 34	04 35	05 35	06 36	07♐37
1937	24 14	25 14	26 15	27 15	28 16	29 16	00♐17	01 18	02 18	03 19	04 20	05 21	06 21	07♐22
1938	23 59	24 59	26 00	27 00	28 01	29 02	00♐02	01 03	02 04	03 04	04 05	05 06	06 07	07♐07
1939	23 44	24 45	25 45	26 46	27 46	28 47	29 47	00♐48	01 49	02 49	03 50	04 51	05 52	06♐51
1940	24 30	25 30	26 31	27 31	28 32	29 33	00♐33	01 34	02 35	03 35	04 36	05 37	06 38	07♐39
1941	24 15	25 16	26 16	27 17	28 17	29 18	00♐19	01 19	02 20	03 21	04 21	05 22	06 23	07♐24
1942	24 00	25 01	26 01	27 02	28 03	29 03	00♐04	01 04	02 05	03 06	04 06	05 07	06 08	07♐09
1943	23 46	24 46	25 47	26 47	27 48	28 48	29 49	00♐50	01 50	02 51	03 52	04 53	05 53	06♐54
1944	24 31	25 32	26 33	27 33	28 34	29 34	00♐35	01 36	02 36	03 37	04 38	05 39	06 39	07♐40
1945	24 18	26 18	26 19	27 19	28 20	29 20	00♐21	01 22	02 22	03 23	04 24	05 24	06 25	07♐26
1946	24 03	25 03	26 04	27 04	28 05	29 05	00♐06	01 07	02 07	03 08	04 09	05 10	06 11	07♐11
1947	23 48	24 48	25 49	26 49	27 50	28 51	29 51	00♐52	02 53	02 53	03 54	04 55	05 55	06♐56
1948	24 34	25 34	26 35	27 35	28 36	29 37	00♐37	01 38	02 39	03 39	04 40	05 41	06 42	07♐42
1949	24 19	25 19	26 20	27 21	28 21	29 22	00♐23	01 23	02 24	03 25	04 25	05 26	06 27	07♐28
1950	24 04	25 05	26 05	27 06	28 06	29 07	00♐07	01 08	02 09	03 09	04 10	05 11	06 12	07♐12
1951	23 49	24 50	25 50	26 51	27 52	28 52	29 53	00♐53	01 54	02 55	03 56	04 56	05 57	06♐58
1952	24 35	25 36	26 36	27 37	28 38	29 38	00♐39	01 40	02 40	03 41	04 42	05 42	06 43	07♐44
1953	24 21	25 21	26 22	27 23	28 23	29 24	00♐24	01 25	02 26	03 26	04 27	05 28	06 29	07♐29
1954	24 06	25 07	26 07	27 08	28 08	29 09	00♐10	01 10	02 11	03 12	04 12	05 13	06 14	07♐15
1955	23 51	24 52	25 53	26 53	27 54	28 54	29 55	00♐56	01 56	02 57	03 58	04 58	05 59	07♐00
1956	24 37	25 38	26 38	27 39	28 40	29 40	00♐41	01 42	02 42	03 43	04 44	05 44	06 45	07♐46
1957	24 23	25 23	26 24	27 24	28 25	29 25	00♐26	01 27	02 28	03 28	04 29	05 30	06 31	04♐31
1958	24 08	25 09	26 09	27 10	28 10	29 11	00♐11	01 12	02 13	03 13	04 14	05 15	06 16	07♐16
1959	23 53	24 53	25 54	26 55	27 55	28 56	29 56	00♐57	01 58	02 58	03 59	05 00	06 01	07♐00
1960	24 39	25 39	26 40	27 41	28 41	29 42	00♐43	01 43	02 44	03 45	04 45	05 46	06 47	07♐48
1961	24 24	25 25	26 25	27 26	28 27	29 27	00♐28	01 28	02 29	03 30	04 31	05 31	06 32	07♐33
1962	24 10	25 10	26 11	27 11	28 12	29 12	00♐13	01 14	02 14	03 15	04 16	05 16	06 17	07♐18
1963	23 55	24 55	25 56	26 56	27 57	28 58	29 58	00♐59	02 00	03 00	04 01	05 02	06 02	07♐03
1964	24 41	25 41	26 42	27 42	28 43	29 44	00♐44	01 45	02 46	03 46	04 47	05 48	06 48	07♐49
1965	24 26	25 26	26 27	27 27	28 28	29 28	00♐29	01 30	02 30	03 31	04 32	05 33	06 34	07♐34
1966	24 11	25 12	26 12	27 13	28 13	29 14	00♐15	01 15	02 16	03 17	04 17	05 18	06 19	07♐19
1967	23 57	24 57	25 58	26 58	27 59	28 59	00 00	01♐00	02 01	03 02	04 03	05 03	06 04	07♐05
1968	24 42	25 43	26 43	27 44	28 45	29 45	00♐46	01 47	02 47	03 48	40 49	05 50	06 50	07♐51
1969	24 28	25 29	26 29	27 30	28 30	29 31	00♐32	01 32	02 33	03 34	04 34	05 35	06 36	07♐36
1970	24 14	25 14	26 15	27 15	28 16	19 16	00♐17	01 18	02 18	03 19	04 20	05 21	06 21	07♐22
1971	23 59	24 59	26 00	27 00	28 01	29 02	00♐02	01 03	02 04	03 04	04 05	05 06	06 06	07♐07
1972	24 45	25 45	26 46	24 46	28 47	29 48	00♐48	01 49	02 50	03 50	04 51	05 52	06 52	07♐53
1973	24 30	25 30	26 31	27 32	28 32	29 33	00♐33	01 34	02 35	03 36	04 36	05 37	06 38	07♐39
1974	24 16	25 16	26 17	27 17	28 18	29 18	00♐19	01 20	02 20	03 21	04 22	05 22	06 23	07♐24
1975	24 01	25 01	26 01	27 02	28 03	29 03	00♐04	01 04	02 05	03 06	04 06	05 07	06 08	07♐09
1976	24 46	25 47	25 47	27 48	28 48	29 49	00♐50	01 50	02 51	03 52	04 53	05 53	06 54	07♐55
1977	24 32	25 32	26 33	27 33	28 34	29 34	00♐35	01 36	02 36	03 37	04 38	05 38	06 39	07♐40
1978	24 17	25 17	26 18	27 18	28 19	29 19	00♐20	01 21	02 21	03 22	04 23	05 24	06 24	07♐25
1979	24 02	25 02	26 03	27 03	28 04	29 05	00♐05	01 06	02 07	03 07	04 08	05 09	06 10	07♐10
1980	24 48	25 48	26 49	27 50	28 50	29 51	00♐51	01 52	02 53	03 53	04 54	05 55	06 56	07♐56
1981	24 33	25 33	26 34	27 35	28 35	29 36	00♐36	01 37	02 38	03 38	04 39	05 40	05 41	07♐42
1982	24 18	25 29	26 29	27 20	28 21	29 21	00♐22	01 22	02 23	03 24	04 24	05 25	06 26	07♐27
1983	24 04	25 04	26 05	27 05	28 06	29 06	00♐07	01 07	02 08	03 09	04 09	05 10	06 11	07♐12
1984	24 49	25 50	26 50	27 51	28 51	29 52	00♐53	01 53	02 54	03 55	04 56	05 56	06 57	07♐58
1985	24 35	25 35	26 36	27 36	28 37	29 38	00♐38	01 39	02 40	03 40	04 41	05 42	06 42	07♐43
1986	24 20	25 21	26 21	27 22	28 22	29 23	00♐23	01 24	02 25	03 25	04 26	05 27	06 28	07♐28
1987	24 05	25 06	26 06	27 07	28 08	29 08	00♐09	01 10	02 10	03 11	04 12	05 12	06 13	07♐14
1988	24 52	25 52	26 53	27 53	28 54	29 54	00♐55	01 56	02 56	03 57	04 58	05 58	06 59	08♐00
1989	24 37	25 37	26 38	27 38	28 39	29 40	00♐40	01 41	02 42	03 42	04 43	05 44	06 45	07♐45
1990	24 22	25 23	26 23	27 24	28 25	29 25	00♐26	01 26	02 27	03 28	04 29	05 29	06 30	07♐31
1991	24 08	25 08	26 09	27 09	28 10	29 11	00♐11	01 12	02 12	03 13	04 14	05 14	06 15	07♐16
1992	24 54	25 54	26 55	27 55	28 56	29 56	00♐57	01 58	02 58	03 59	05 00	06 01	07 00	08♐02
1993	24 39	25 40	26 40	27 41	28 41	29 42	00♐43	01 43	02 44	03 45	04 45	05 46	06 47	07♐48
1994	24 24	25 25	26 25	27 26	28 26	29 27	00♐28	01 28	02 29	03 30	04 30	05 31	06 32	07♐33
1995	24 09	25 10	25 10	27 11	28 11	29 12	00♐13	01 13	02 14	03 15	04 15	05 16	06 17	07♐18
1996	24 55	25 56	26 56	27 57	28 57	29 58	00♐59	01 59	03 00	04 01	05 01	06 02	07 03	08♐03
1997	24 40	25 41	26 41	27 42	28 42	29 43	00♐43	01 44	02 45	03 45	04 46	05 47	06 48	07♐49
1998	24 25	25 26	26 26	27 27	28 28	29 28	00♐29	01 30	02 30	03 31	04 32	05 32	06 33	07♐34
1999	24 11	25 11	26 12	27 12	28 13	29 14	00♐14	01 15	02 15	03 16	04 17	05 17	06 18	07♐19
2000	24 56	25 57	26 57	27 58	28 59	29 59	01♐00	02 00	03 01	04 02	05 03	06 03	07 04	08♐05

Sun

December

	1st	2nd	3rd	4th	5th	6th	7th	8th	9th	10th	11th	12th	13th	14th	15th	16th
1900	08 ♐22 09	23 10	24 11	24 12	25 13	26 14	27 15	28 16	29 17	30 18	31 19	32 20	33 21	34 22	35 23	36
1901	08 ♐07 09	08 10	08 11	09 12	10 13	11 14	12 15	13 16	14 17	15 18	16 19	17 20	18 21	19 22	20 23	21
1902	07 ♐52 08	53 09	54 10	55 11	55 12	56 13	57 14	58 15	59 17	00 18	01 19	02 20	03 21	04 22	05 23	06
1903	07 ♐37 08	38 09	39 10	40 11	41 12	41 13	42 14	43 15	44 16	45 17	46 18	47 19	48 20	49 21	50 22	51
1904	08 ♐23 09	24 10	25 11	26 12	27 13	27 14	28 15	29 16	30 17	31 18	32 19	33 20	35 21	36 22	37 23	38
1905	08 ♐09 09	09 10	10 11	11 12	12 13	13 14	14 15	15 16	16 17	17 18	18 19	19 20	20 21	21 22	22 23	23
1906	07 ♐53 08	54 09	55 10	56 11	57 12	58 13	59 15	00 16	01 17	02 18	03 19	04 20	05 21	06 22	07 23	08
1907	07 ♐38 08	39 09	40 10	41 11	42 12	43 13	44 14	45 15	46 16	47 17	48 18	49 19	50 20	51 21	52 22	53
1908	08 ♐25 09	26 10	27 11	28 12	28 13	29 14	30 15	31 16	32 17	33 18	34 19	35 20	36 21	37 22	38 23	39
1909	08 ♐10 09	11 10	12 11	13 12	14 13	14 14	15 15	16 16	17 17	18 18	19 19	20 20	21 21	22 22	23 23	25
1910	07 ♐55 08	56 09	57 10	58 11	59 13	00 14	01 15	02 16	03 17	04 18	05 19	06 20	07 21	08 22	09 23	10
1911	07 ♐41 08	42 09	43 10	43 11	44 12	45 13	46 14	47 15	48 16	49 17	50 18	51 19	52 20	53 21	54 22	55
1912	08 ♐27 09	28 10	28 11	29 12	30 13	31 14	32 15	33 16	34 17	35 18	36 19	37 20	38 21	39 22	40 23	41
1913	08 ♐12 09	13 10	14 11	15 12	16 13	17 14	18 15	19 16	20 17	20 18	21 19	22 20	23 21	24 22	26 23	27
1914	07 ♐57 08	58 09	59 11	00 12	01 13	02 14	03 15	04 16	04 17	05 18	06 19	07 20	08 21	09 22	11 23	12
1915	07 ♐43 08	43 09	44 10	45 11	46 12	47 13	48 14	49 15	50 16	51 17	52 18	53 19	54 20	55 21	56 22	57
1916	08 ♐29 09	30 10	31 11	32 12	33 13	33 14	34 15	35 16	36 17	37 18	38 19	39 20	40 21	41 22	42 23	43
1917	08 ♐14 09	15 10	16 11	17 12	17 13	18 14	19 15	20 16	21 17	22 18	23 19	24 20	25 21	26 22	27 23	29
1918	07 ♐59 09	00 10	01 11	02 12	03 13	04 14	05 15	06 16	07 17	08 18	09 19	10 21	11 21	12 22	13 23	14
1919	07 ♐45 08	46 09	46 10	47 11	48 12	49 13	50 14	51 15	52 16	53 17	54 18	55 19	56 20	57 21	58 22	59
1920	08 ♐30 09	31 10	32 11	33 12	34 13	35 14	36 15	37 16	38 17	39 18	40 19	41 20	42 21	43 22	44 23	45
1921	08 ♐16 09	17 10	18 11	19 12	20 13	21 14	21 15	22 16	23 17	24 18	25 19	26 20	27 21	28 22	29 23	30
1922	08 ♐01 09	02 10	03 11	04 12	04 13	05 14	06 15	07 16	08 17	09 18	10 19	11 20	12 21	13 22	14 23	15
1923	07 ♐46 08	47 09	48 10	48 11	49 12	50 13	51 14	52 15	53 16	54 17	55 18	56 19	57 20	58 21	59 23	00
1924	08 ♐32 09	33 10	34 11	35 12	36 13	37 14	37 15	38 16	39 17	40 18	41 19	42 20	43 21	44 22	45 23	46
1925	08 ♐17 09	18 10	19 11	20 12	20 13	21 14	22 15	23 16	24 17	24 18	26 19	27 20	28 21	29 22	30 23	31
1926	08 ♐02 09	03 10	04 11	05 12	06 13	07 14	08 15	09 16	09 17	10 18	11 19	12 20	13 21	14 22	16 23	17
1927	07 ♐48 08	49 09	49 10	50 11	51 12	52 13	53 14	54 15	55 16	56 17	56 18	58 19	59 21	00 22	01 23	02
1928	08 ♐34 09	34 10	35 11	36 12	37 13	38 14	39 15	40 16	41 17	42 18	43 19	44 20	45 21	46 22	47 23	48
1929	08 ♐19 09	20 10	21 11	22 12	23 13	24 14	25 15	26 16	27 17	27 18	28 19	29 20	30 21	31 22	32 23	34
1930	08 ♐04 09	05 10	06 11	07 12	08 13	09 14	10 15	11 16	11 17	12 18	13 19	14 20	15 21	16 22	17 23	19
1931	07 ♐50 08	50 09	51 10	52 11	53 12	54 13	55 14	56 15	57 16	58 17	59 19	00 20	01 21	02 22	03 23	04
1932	08 ♐36 09	37 10	38 11	39 12	40 13	41 14	41 15	42 16	43 17	44 18	45 19	46 20	47 21	48 22	49 23	50
1933	08 ♐21 09	22 10	23 11	24 12	25 13	26 14	27 15	27 16	28 17	29 18	30 19	31 20	32 21	33 22	35 23	36
1934	08 ♐07 09	07 10	08 11	09 12	10 13	11 14	12 15	13 16	14 17	15 18	16 19	17 20	18 21	19 22	20 23	21
1935	07 ♐52 08	53 09	54 10	55 11	55 12	56 13	57 14	58 15	59 17	00 18	01 19	02 20	03 21	04 22	05 23	06
1936	08 ♐38 09	39 10	39 11	40 12	41 13	42 14	43 15	44 16	45 17	46 18	47 19	48 20	49 21	50 22	51 23	52
1937	08 ♐23 09	24 10	25 11	26 12	27 13	27 14	28 15	29 16	30 17	31 18	32 19	33 20	34 21	35 22	36 23	37
1938	08 ♐08 09	09 10	10 11	11 12	12 13	12 14	13 15	14 16	15 17	16 18	17 19	18 20	19 21	20 22	21 23	22
1939	07 ♐53 08	54 09	55 10	56 11	57 12	57 13	58 14	59 16	00 17	01 18	02 19	03 20	04 21	05 22	06 23	07
1940	08 ♐38 09	40 10	41 11	42 12	43 13	44 14	45 15	46 16	47 17	48 18	49 19	50 20	51 21	52 22	53 23	54
1941	08 ♐25 09	25 10	26 11	27 12	28 13	29 14	30 15	31 16	32 17	33 18	34 19	35 20	36 21	37 22	38 23	39
1942	08 ♐10 09	10 10	11 11	12 12	13 13	14 14	15 15	16 16	17 17	18 18	19 19	20 20	21 21	22 22	23 23	24
1943	07 ♐55 08	56 09	57 10	58 11	58 12	59 14	00 15	01 16	02 17	03 18	04 19	05 20	06 21	07 22	08 23	09
1944	08 ♐41 09	42 10	43 11	43 12	44 13	45 14	46 15	47 16	48 17	49 18	50 19	51 20	52 21	53 22	54 23	55
1945	08 ♐27 09	28 10	29 11	29 12	30 13	31 14	32 15	33 16	34 17	35 18	36 19	37 20	38 21	39 22	40 23	41
1946	08 ♐12 09	13 10	14 11	15 12	16 13	16 14	17 15	18 16	19 17	20 18	21 19	22 20	23 21	24 22	25 23	26
1947	07 ♐57 08	58 09	59 11	00 12	00 13	01 14	02 15	03 16	04 17	05 18	06 19	07 20	08 21	09 22	10 23	11
1948	08 ♐43 09	44 10	45 11	46 12	47 13	48 14	49 15	50 16	51 17	52 18	53 19	54 20	55 21	56 22	57 23	58
1949	08 ♐29 09	29 10	30 11	31 12	32 13	33 14	34 15	35 16	36 17	36 18	37 19	38 20	39 21	41 22	42 23	43
1950	08 ♐13 09	14 10	15 11	16 12	17 13	18 14	18 15	19 16	20 17	21 18	22 19	23 20	24 21	25 22	26 23	28
1951	07 ♐59 08	00 10	00 11	01 12	02 13	03 14	04 15	05 16	06 17	07 18	08 19	09 20	10 21	11 22	12 23	13
1952	08 ♐45 09	46 10	46 11	47 12	48 13	49 14	50 15	51 16	52 17	53 18	54 19	55 20	56 21	57 22	58 23	59
1953	08 ♐30 09	31 10	32 11	33 12	34 13	35 14	36 15	37 16	38 17	39 18	40 19	41 20	42 21	43 22	44 23	45
1954	08 ♐16 09	16 10	17 11	18 12	19 13	20 14	21 15	22 16	23 17	24 18	24 19	25 20	26 21	27 22	28 23	30
1955	08 ♐01 09	01 10	02 11	03 12	04 13	05 14	06 15	07 16	08 17	09 18	10 19	11 20	12 21	13 22	14 23	15
1956	08 ♐47 09	48 10	49 11	50 12	05 13	51 14	52 15	53 16	54 17	55 18	56 19	57 20	58 21	59 23	00 24	01
1957	08 ♐32 09	33 10	34 11	35 12	36 13	36 14	37 15	38 16	39 17	40 18	41 19	42 20	43 21	44 22	45 23	46
1958	08 ♐17 09	18 10	19 11	20 12	21 13	21 14	22 15	23 16	24 17	25 18	26 19	27 20	28 21	29 22	30 23	31
1959	08 ♐02 09	03 10	04 11	05 12	06 13	07 14	08 15	09 16	10 17	10 18	11 19	12 20	13 21	14 22	15 23	16
1960	08 ♐48 09	49 10	50 11	51 12	52 13	53 14	54 15	55 16	56 17	57 18	58 19	59 21	00 22	01 23	02 24	03
1961	08 ♐34 09	34 10	35 11	36 12	37 13	38 14	39 15	40 16	41 17	42 18	43 19	44 20	45 21	46 22	47 23	48
1962	08 ♐19 09	20 10	21 11	21 12	22 13	23 14	24 15	25 16	26 17	27 18	28 19	29 20	30 21	31 22	32 23	33
1963	08 ♐04 09	05 10	06 11	06 12	07 13	08 14	09 15	10 16	11 17	12 18	13 19	14 20	15 21	16 22	17 23	18
1964	08 ♐50 09	51 10	52 11	53 12	54 13	55 14	56 15	56 16	57 17	58 18	59 20	00 21	01 22	03 23	04 24	05
1965	08 ♐35 09	36 10	37 11	38 12	39 13	39 14	40 15	41 16	42 17	43 18	44 19	45 20	46 21	47 22	48 23	49
1966	08 ♐20 09	21 10	22 11	23 12	24 13	24 14	25 15	26 16	27 17	28 18	29 19	30 20	31 21	32 22	33 23	34
1967	08 ♐06 09	07 10	07 11	08 12	09 13	10 14	11 15	12 16	13 17	14 18	15 19	16 20	17 21	18 22	19 23	20
1968	08 ♐52 09	53 10	54 11	54 12	55 13	56 14	57 15	58 16	59 18	00 19	01 20	02 21	03 22	04 23	05 24	06
1969	08 ♐37 09	38 10	39 11	40 12	41 13	42 14	43 15	44 16	45 17	46 18	47 19	48 20	49 21	50 22	51 23	52
1970	08 ♐23 09	24 10	25 11	26 12	26 13	27 14	28 15	29 16	30 17	31 18	32 19	33 20	34 21	35 22	36 23	37
1971	08 ♐08 09	09 10	10 11	11 12	11 13	12 14	13 15	14 16	15 17	16 18	17 19	18 20	19 21	20 22	21 23	22
1972	08 ♐54 09	55 10	56 11	57 12	58 13	59 15	00 16	00 17	01 18	02 19	03 20	05 21	06 22	07 23	08 24	09
1973	08 ♐39 09	40 10	41 11	42 12	43 13	44 14	45 15	46 16	47 17	47 18	48 19	49 20	50 21	51 22	52 23	53
1974	08 ♐25 09	25 10	26 11	27 12	28 13	29 14	30 15	31 16	32 17	33 18	34 19	35 20	36 21	37 22	38 23	39
1975	08 ♐10 09	10 10	11 11	12 12	13 13	14 14	15 15	16 16	17 17	18 18	19 19	20 20	21 21	22 22	23 23	24
1976	08 ♐56 09	56 10	57 11	58 12	59 14	00 15	01 16	02 17	02 18	04 19	05 20	06 21	07 22	08 23	09 24	10
1977	08 ♐41 09	42 10	42 11	43 12	44 13	45 14	46 15	47 16	48 17	49 18	50 19	51 20	52 21	53 22	54 23	55
1978	08 ♐26 09	27 10	28 11	29 12	29 13	30 14	31 15	32 16	33 17	34 18	35 19	36 20	37 21	38 22	39 23	40
1979	08 ♐11 09	12 10	13 11	13 12	14 13	15 14	16 15	17 16	18 17	19 18	20 19	21 20	22 21	23 22	24 23	25
1980	08 ♐57 09	58 10	59 12	00 13	01 14	02 15	02 16	03 17	04 18	05 19	06 20	07 21	08 22	09 23	11 24	12
1981	08 ♐42 09	43 10	44 11	45 12	46 13	47 14	48 15	49 16	50 17	50 18	52 19	52 20	53 21	54 22	55 23	56
1982	08 ♐27 09	28 10	29 11	30 12	31 13	32 14	33 15	34 16	34 17	35 18	36 19	37 20	38 21	39 22	41 23	42
1983	08 ♐13 09	13 10	14 11	15 12	16 13	17 14	18 15	19 16	20 17	21 18	22 19	23 20	24 21	25 22	26 23	27
1984	08 ♐59 10	00 11	00 12	01 13	02 14	03 15	04 16	05 17	06 18	07 19	08 20	09 21	10 22	11 23	12 24	13
1985	08 ♐44 09	45 10	46 11	46 12	47 13	48 14	49 15	50 16	52 17	52 18	53 19	54 20	55 21	56 22	57 23	58
1986	08 ♐29 09	30 10	31 11	32 12	33 13	34 14	35 15	35 16	36 17	37 18	38 19	39 20	40 21	41 22	42 23	43
1987	08 ♐15 09	15 10	16 11	17 12	18 13	19 14	20 15	21 16	22 17	22 18	23 19	24 20	25 21	26 22	27 23	29
1988	09 ♐01 10	02 11	03 12	03 13	04 14	05 15	06 16	07 17	08 18	09 19	10 20	11 21	12 22	13 28	14 24	15
1989	08 ♐46 09	47 10	48 11	49 12	50 13	51 14	51 15	52 16	53 17	54 18	55 19	56 20	57 21	58 22	59 24	00
1990	08 ♐31 09	32 10	33 11	34 12	35 13	36 14	37 15	37 16	38 17	39 18	40 19	41 20	42 21	43 22	44 23	45
1991	08 ♐17 09	18 10	18 11	19 12	20 13	21 14	22 15	23 16	24 17	25 18	26 19	27 20	28 21	29 22	30 23	31
1992	09 ♐03 10	04 11	05 12	06 13	06 14	07 15	08 16	09 17	10 18	11 19	12 20	13 21	14 22	15 23	16 24	17
1993	08 ♐48 09	49 10	50 11	51 12	52 13	53 14	53 15	54 16	55 17	56 18	57 19	58 20	59 22	00 23	01 24	03
1994	08 ♐33 09	34 10	35 11	36 12	37 13	38 14	39 15	40 16	41 17	42 18	43 19	44 20	45 21	46 22	47 23	48
1995	08 ♐18 09	19 10	20 11	21 12	22 13	23 14	24 15	24 16	25 17	26 18	27 19	28 20	29 21	30 22	31 23	32
1996	09 ♐04 10	05 11	06 12	07 13	08 14	09 15	10 16	11 17	11 18	12 19	13 20	15 21	16 22	17 23	18 24	19
1997	08 ♐49 09	50 10	51 11	52 12	53 13	54 14	55 15	56 16	57 17	58 18	58 19	59 21	00 22	01 23	02 24	03
1998	08 ♐35 09	35 10	36 11	37 12	38 13	39 14	40 15	41 16	41 17	42 18	43 19	44 20	45 21	46 22	47 23	48
1999	08 ♐20 09	21 10	21 11	22 12	23 13	24 14	25 15	26 16	27 17	28 18	29 19	30 20	31 21	32 22	33 23	34
2000	09 ♐06 10	07 11	08 12	08 13	09 14	10 15	11 16	12 17	13 18	14 19	15 20	16 21	17 22	18 23	19 24	20

Year	17th	18th	19th	20th	21st	22nd	23rd	24th	25th	26th	27th	28th	29th	30th	31st
1900	24 37	25 38	26 40	27 41	28 42	29 43	00♑ 44	01 45	02 46	03 48	04 49	05 50	06 51	07 52	08♑ 53
1901	24 22	25 24	26 25	27 26	28 27	29 28	00♑ 29	01 30	02 31	03 32	04 33	05 35	06 36	07 37	08♑ 38
1902	24 07	25 08	26 09	27 10	28 12	29 13	00♑ 14	01 15	02 16	03 17	04 18	05 20	06 21	07 22	08♑ 23
1903	23 52	24 54	25 55	26 56	27 57	28 58	29 ♑59	01♑ 00	02 01	03 03	04 04	05 05	06 06	07 07	08♑ 08
1904	24 39	25 40	26 41	27 42	28 43	29 44	00♑ 45	01 46	02 47	03 49	04 50	05 51	06 52	07 53	08♑ 54
1905	24 24	25 25	26 26	27 27	28 28	29 29	00♑ 30	01 32	02 33	03 34	04 35	05 36	06 37	07 39	08♑ 40
1906	24 09	25 10	26 11	27 12	28 13	29 14	00♑ 16	01 17	02 18	03 19	04 20	05 21	06 22	07 23	08♑ 25
1907	23 54	24 55	25 56	26 57	27 58	28 59	00♑ 00	01 01	02 03	03 04	04 05	05 06	06 07	07 08	08♑ 10
1908	24 40	25 41	26 42	27 44	28 45	29 46	00♑ 47	01 48	02 49	03 50	04 52	05 53	06 54	07 55	08♑ 56
1909	24 26	25 27	26 28	27 29	28 30	29 31	00♑ 32	01 33	02 34	03 36	04 37	05 38	06 39	07 40	08♑ 41
1910	24 11	25 12	26 13	27 14	28 15	29 16	00♑ 17	01 18	02 20	03 21	04 22	05 23	06 24	07 26	08♑ 27
1911	23 56	24 57	25 58	26 59	28 01	29 02	00♑ 03	01 04	02 05	03 06	04 07	05 09	06 10	07 11	08♑ 12
1912	24 42	25 44	26 45	27 46	28 47	29 48	00♑ 49	01 50	02 51	03 52	04 54	05 55	06 56	07 57	08♑ 58
1913	24 28	25 29	26 30	27 31	28 32	29 33	00♑ 34	01 35	02 36	03 38	04 39	05 40	06 41	07 42	08♑ 44
1914	24 13	25 14	26 15	27 16	28 17	29 18	00♑ 19	01 21	02 22	03 23	04 24	05 25	06 26	07 27	08♑ 29
1915	23 58	24 59	26 00	27 01	28 02	29 03	00♑ 04	01 06	02 07	03 08	04 09	05 10	06 11	07 12	08♑ 13
1916	24 44	25 45	26 47	27 48	28 49	29 50	00♑ 51	01 52	02 53	03 55	04 56	05 57	06 58	07 59	09♑ 00
1917	24 30	25 31	26 32	27 33	28 34	29 35	00♑ 36	01 37	02 38	03 40	04 41	05 42	06 43	07 44	08♑ 45
1918	24 15	25 16	26 17	27 18	28 19	29 20	00♑ 21	01 22	02 23	03 25	04 26	05 27	06 28	07 29	08♑ 30
1919	24 00	25 01	26 02	27 03	28 04	29 05	00♑ 06	01 08	02 09	03 10	04 11	05 12	06 13	07 15	08♑ 16
1920	24 46	25 47	26 48	27 49	28 51	29 52	00♑ 53	01 54	02 55	03 56	04 57	05 58	06 59	08 01	09♑ 02
1921	24 31	25 32	26 33	27 35	28 36	29 37	00♑ 38	01 39	02 40	03 41	04 42	05 44	06 45	07 46	08♑ 47
1922	24 16	25 17	26 19	27 20	28 21	29 22	00♑ 23	01 24	02 25	03 26	04 28	05 29	06 30	07 31	08♑ 32
1923	24 01	25 02	26 04	27 05	28 06	29 07	00♑ 08	01 09	02 10	03 11	04 12	06 14	06 15	07 16	08♑ 17
1924	24 47	25 49	26 50	27 51	28 52	29 53	00♑ 54	01 55	02 56	03 58	04 59	06 00	07 01	08 02	09♑ 04
1925	24 33	25 34	26 35	27 36	28 37	29 38	00♑ 39	01 40	02 41	03 43	04 44	05 45	06 46	07 47	08♑ 48
1926	24 18	25 19	26 20	27 21	28 22	29 23	00♑ 24	01 25	02 26	03 27	04 29	05 30	06 31	07 32	08♑ 33
1927	24 03	25 04	26 05	27 06	28 07	29 08	00♑ 09	01 11	02 12	03 13	04 14	05 15	06 16	07 18	08♑ 19
1928	24 49	25 50	26 51	27 53	28 54	29 55	00♑ 56	01 57	02 58	03 59	05 00	06 01	07 03	08 04	09♑ 05
1929	24 35	25 36	26 37	27 38	28 39	29 40	00♑ 41	01 42	02 43	03 44	04 46	05 47	06 48	07 49	08♑ 50
1930	24 20	25 21	26 22	27 23	28 24	29 25	00♑ 26	01 27	02 29	03 30	04 31	05 32	06 33	07 34	08♑ 36
1931	24 05	25 06	26 07	27 08	28 09	29 10	00♑ 11	01 13	02 14	03 15	04 16	05 17	06 18	07 19	08♑ 20
1932	24 51	25 52	26 54	27 55	28 56	29 57	00♑ 58	01 59	03 00	04 01	05 03	06 04	07 05	08 06	09♑ 07
1933	24 37	25 38	26 39	27 40	28 41	29 42	00♑ 43	01 45	02 46	03 47	04 48	05 49	06 50	07 51	08♑ 52
1934	24 22	25 23	26 24	27 25	28 26	29 27	00♑ 28	01 30	02 31	03 32	04 33	05 34	06 35	07 36	08♑ 38
1935	24 07	25 08	26 09	27 10	28 11	29 13	00♑ 14	01 15	02 16	03 17	04 18	05 20	06 21	07 22	08♑ 23
1936	24 53	25 54	26 56	27 57	28 58	29 59	01♑ 00	02 01	03 02	04 03	05 04	06 06	07 07	08 08	09♑ 09
1937	24 38	25 39	26 41	27 42	28 43	29 44	00♑ 45	01 46	02 47	03 48	04 49	05 51	06 52	07 53	08♑ 54
1938	24 23	25 24	26 25	27 27	28 28	29 29	00♑ 30	01 31	02 32	03 33	04 35	05 36	06 37	07 38	08♑ 39
1939	24 09	25 10	26 11	27 12	28 13	29 14	00♑ 15	01 16	02 17	03 18	04 19	05 21	06 22	07 23	08♑ 24
1940	24 55	25 56	26 57	27 58	28 59	00♑ 00	01 01	02 02	03 04	04 05	05 06	06 07	07 08	08 09	09♑ 11
1941	24 40	25 41	26 42	27 43	28 44	29 45	00♑ 47	01 48	02 49	03 50	04 51	05 52	06 53	07 54	08♑ 56
1942	24 25	25 26	26 27	27 28	28 29	29 30	00♑ 31	01 33	02 34	03 35	04 36	05 37	06 38	07 39	08♑ 40
1943	24 10	25 11	26 12	27 13	28 14	29 15	00♑ 17	01 18	02 19	03 20	04 21	05 22	06 24	07 25	08♑ 26
1944	24 56	25 57	26 59	28 00	19 01	00♑ 02	01 03	02 04	03 05	04 07	05 08	06 09	07 10	08 11	09♑ 12
1945	24 42	25 43	26 44	27 45	28 46	29 48	00♑ 49	01 50	02 51	03 52	04 53	05 54	06 55	07 57	08♑ 58
1946	24 27	26 28	26 29	27 30	28 32	29 33	00♑ 34	01 35	02 36	03 37	04 38	05 40	06 41	07 42	08♑ 43
1947	24 12	25 14	26 15	27 16	28 17	29 18	00♑ 19	01 20	02 21	03 22	04 23	05 25	06 26	07 27	08♑ 28
1948	24 59	26 00	27 01	28 02	29 03	00♑ 04	01 05	02 06	03 08	04 09	05 10	06 11	07 12	08 13	09♑ 15
1949	24 44	25 45	26 46	27 47	28 48	29 49	00♑ 50	01 52	02 53	03 54	04 55	05 56	06 57	07 58	08♑ 00
1950	24 29	25 30	26 31	27 32	28 33	29 34	00♑ 35	01 36	02 37	03 38	04 40	05 41	06 42	07 43	08♑ 44
1951	24 14	25 15	26 16	27 17	28 18	29 19	00♑ 20	01 22	02 23	03 24	04 25	05 26	06 27	07 28	08♑ 30
1952	25 00	26 01	27 02	28 04	29 05	00♑ 06	01 07	02 08	03 09	04 10	05 11	06 13	07 14	08 15	09♑ 16
1953	24 46	25 47	26 48	27 49	28 50	29 51	00♑ 52	01 53	02 54	03 55	04 57	05 58	06 59	08 00	09♑ 01
1954	24 31	25 32	26 33	27 34	28 35	29 36	00♑ 37	01 38	02 39	03 41	04 42	05 43	06 44	07 45	08♑ 46
1955	24 16	25 17	26 18	27 19	28 20	29 21	00♑ 22	01 24	02 25	03 26	04 27	05 28	06 29	07 30	08♑ 31
1956	25 02	26 03	27 04	28 05	29 07	00♑ 08	01 09	02 10	03 11	04 12	05 13	06 14	07 16	08 17	09♑ 18
1957	24 47	25 48	26 49	27 51	28 52	29 53	00♑ 54	01 55	02 56	03 57	04 59	06 00	07 01	08 02	09♑ 03
1958	24 33	25 34	26 35	27 36	28 57	29 38	00♑ 39	01 40	02 41	03 42	04 43	05 45	06 46	07 47	08♑ 48
1959	24 18	25 19	26 20	27 21	28 22	29 23	00♑ 24	01 25	02 26	03 27	04 29	05 30	06 31	07 32	08♑ 33
1960	25 04	26 05	27 06	28 07	29 08	00♑ 09	01 11	02 12	03 13	04 14	05 15	06 16	07 17	08 19	19♑ 20
1961	24 49	25 50	26 51	27 52	28 53	29 54	00♑ 56	01 57	02 58	03 59	05 00	06 01	07 02	08 03	09♑ 05
1962	24 34	25 35	26 36	27 37	28 38	29 39	00♑ 40	01 42	02 43	03 44	04 45	05 46	06 47	07 49	08♑ 50
1963	24 19	25 20	26 21	27 22	28 24	29 25	00♑ 26	01 27	02 28	03 29	04 30	05 31	06 32	07 34	08♑ 35
1964	25 06	26 07	27 08	28 09	29 10	00♑ 11	01 12	02 13	03 14	04 15	05 17	06 18	07 19	08 20	09♑ 21
1965	24 50	26 51	26 52	27 53	28 55	29 56	00♑ 57	01 58	02 59	04 00	05 01	06 03	07 04	08 05	09♑ 06
1966	24 36	25 37	26 38	27 39	28 40	29 41	00♑ 42	01 43	02 44	03 45	04 47	05 48	06 49	07 50	09♑ 51
1967	24 21	25 22	26 23	27 24	28 25	29 26	00♑ 27	01 28	02 30	03 31	04 32	05 33	06 34	07 35	08♑ 37
1968	25 07	26 08	27 09	28 10	29 12	00♑ 13	01 14	02 15	03 16	04 17	05 18	06 20	07 21	08 22	09♑ 23
1969	24 53	25 54	26 55	27 56	28 57	29 58	00♑ 59	02 00	03 04	03 05	04 06	05 07	06 08	07 08	09♑ 08
1970	24 38	25 39	26 40	27 41	28 42	29 44	00♑ 45	01 46	02 47	03 48	04 49	05 50	06 52	07 53	08♑ 54
1971	24 23	25 24	26 25	27 26	28 28	29 29	00♑ 30	01 31	02 32	03 33	04 35	05 36	06 37	07 38	08♑ 39
1972	25 10	26 11	27 12	28 13	29 14	00♑ 15	01 16	02 17	03 18	04 20	05 21	06 22	07 23	08 24	09♑ 25
1973	24 55	25 56	26 57	27 58	28 59	00 00	01♑ 01	02 02	03 03	04 05	05 07	06 07	07 08	08 09	09♑ 10
1974	24 40	25 41	26 42	27 43	28 44	29 45	00♑ 46	01 47	02 49	03 50	04 51	05 52	06 53	07 54	08♑ 55
1975	24 25	25 26	26 27	27 28	28 29	29 30	00♑ 31	01 32	02 33	03 35	04 36	05 37	06 38	07 39	08♑ 40
1976	25 11	26 12	27 13	28 14	29 15	00♑ 16	01 17	02 19	03 20	04 21	05 22	06 23	07 24	08 26	09♑ 27
1977	24 56	25 57	26 58	27 59	29 00	00♑ 02	01 03	02 04	03 05	04 06	05 07	06 08	07 09	08 10	09♑ 12
1978	24 41	25 42	26 43	27 44	28 45	29 46	00♑ 47	01 49	02 50	03 51	04 52	05 53	06 54	07 56	08♑ 57
1979	24 26	25 27	26 28	27 29	28 30	29 32	00♑ 33	01 34	02 35	03 36	04 37	05 38	06 39	07 41	08♑ 42
1980	25 13	26 14	27 15	28 16	29 17	00♑ 18	01 19	02 20	03 21	04 22	05 24	06 25	07 26	08 27	09♑ 28
1981	24 57	25 59	27 00	28 01	29 02	00♑ 03	01 04	02 50	03 06	04 08	05 09	06 10	07 11	08 12	09♑ 13
1982	24 43	25 44	26 45	27 46	28 47	29 48	00♑ 49	01 50	02 52	03 53	04 54	05 55	07 56	07 57	08♑ 58
1983	24 28	25 29	26 30	27 31	28 32	29 33	00♑ 34	01 35	02 37	03 38	04 39	05 40	06 41	07 42	08♑ 43
1984	25 14	26 15	27 16	28 17	29 18	00♑ 19	01 21	02 22	03 23	04 24	05 25	06 26	07 28	08 29	09♑ 30
1985	24 59	26 00	27 01	28 03	29 04	00♑ 05	01 06	02 07	03 08	04 09	05 10	06 11	07 13	08 14	09♑ 15
1986	24 44	25 45	26 46	27 48	28 49	29 50	00♑ 51	01 52	02 53	03 54	04 55	05 57	06 58	07 59	09♑ 00
1987	24 30	25 31	26 32	27 33	28 34	29 35	00♑ 36	01 37	02 39	03 40	04 41	05 42	06 43	07 44	08♑ 45
1988	25 16	26 17	27 18	28 20	29 21	00♑ 22	01 23	02 24	03 25	04 26	05 27	06 28	07 30	08 31	09♑ 32
1989	25 01	26 02	27 03	28 04	29 06	00♑ 07	01 08	02 09	03 10	04 11	05 12	06 14	07 15	08 16	07♑ 17
1990	24 47	25 48	26 49	27 50	28 51	29 52	00♑ 53	01 54	02 55	03 57	04 58	05 59	07 00	08 01	09♑ 02
1991	24 32	25 33	26 34	27 35	28 36	29 37	00♑ 38	01 40	02 42	03 42	04 43	05 44	06 45	07 46	08♑ 47
1992	25 18	26 19	27 20	28 21	29 23	00♑ 24	01 25	02 26	03 27	04 28	05 29	06 31	07 32	08 33	09♑ 34
1993	25 04	26 05	27 06	28 07	29 08	00♑ 09	01 10	02 11	03 12	04 14	05 15	06 16	07 17	08 18	09♑ 19
1994	24 49	25 50	26 51	27 52	28 53	29 54	00♑ 55	01 56	02 57	03 58	05 00	06 01	07 02	08 03	09♑ 04
1995	24 33	25 34	26 36	27 37	28 38	29 39	00♑ 40	01 41	02 42	03 43	04 45	05 46	06 47	07 48	08♑ 49
1996	25 20	26 21	27 22	28 23	29 24	00♑ 25	01 26	02 27	03 29	04 30	05 31	06 32	07 33	08 34	09♑ 35
1997	25 04	26 06	27 07	28 08	29 09	00♑ 10	01 11	02 12	03 13	04 14	05 16	06 17	07 18	08 19	09♑ 20
1998	24 50	25 51	26 52	27 53	28 54	29 55	00♑ 56	01 57	02 58	04 00	05 01	06 02	07 03	08 04	09♑ 05
1999	24 35	25 36	26 37	27 38	28 39	29 40	00♑ 41	01 42	02 44	03 45	04 46	06 47	06 48	07 49	08♑ 50
2000	25 21	26 22	27 23	28 24	29 25	00♑ 26	01 28	02 29	03 30	04 31	05 32	06 33	07 34	08 36	09♑ 37

Moon

January

Year	1st	2nd	3rd	4th	5th	6th	7th	8th	9th	10th	11th	12th	13th	14th	15th	16th
1900	01♑25	16 42	01♒35	16 22	01♓08	15 45	00♈09	14 15	28 03	11♉33	24 46	07♊45	20 30	03♋04	15 28	27 43
1901	18♉19	02♊24	16 23	00♋24	13 52	27 15	10♌22	23 10	05♍40	17 55	29 56	11♎50	23 39	05♏30	17 28	29 38
1902	02♎06	14 19	26 17	08♏07	19 53	01♐40	13 33	25 34	07♑45	20 09	02♒45	15 33	28 33	11♓43	25 06	08♈39
1903	02♒19	14 18	26 22	08♓34	20 57	03♈36	16 34	29 55	13♉43	27 60	12♊43	27 48	13♋06	28 26	13♌37	28 27
1904	08♊30	22 59	07♋49	22 53	07♌59	22 59	07♍43	22 07	06♎09	19 48	03♏07	16 09	28 55	11♐29	23 53	06♑08
1905	10♏20	24 11	07♐54	21 27	04♑47	17 52	00♒41	13 13	25 29	07♓32	19 26	01♈14	13 02	24 55	06♉58	19 16
1906	21♓43	03♈54	15 53	27 45	09♉36	21 31	03♊32	15 43	28 06	10♋43	23 32	06♌35	19 50	03♍17	16 54	00♎42
1907	22♋45	04♌48	16 58	29 19	11♍54	24 44	07♎53	21 24	05♏18	19 36	04♐14	19 08	04♑10	19 13	04♒07	18 44
1908	29♏07	13♐38	28 29	13♑35	29 45	13♒52	28 45	13♓18	27 27	11♈11	24 31	07♉28	20 06	02♊29	14 38	26 39
1909	02♉37	16 11	29 31	12♊37	25 32	08♋14	20 44	03♌04	15 13	27 14	09♍09	21 01	02♎53	14 50	26 56	09♏15
1910	11♍30	23 41	05♎40	17 32	29 21	11♏14	23 14	05♐27	17 56	00♑43	13 49	27 14	10♒55	24 50	08♓54	23 03
1911	13♑01	25 19	07♒28	20 28	03♓19	16 24	29 42	13♈15	27 04	11♉11	25 35	10♊13	25 01	09♋52	24 37	09♌09
1912	19♉28	03♊60	18 57	04♋12	19 35	04♌54	19 57	04♍36	18 45	02♎25	15 36	28 22	10♏28	22 50	05♐01	16 56
1913	24♎32	07♏29	20 52	03♐43	16 23	28 53	11♑13	23 24	05♒27	17 22	19 12	10♓59	22 47	04♈40	16 45	29 05
1914	01♓12	13 14	25 06	06♈54	18 43	00♉38	12 46	25 09	07♊53	20 58	04♋24	18 11	02♌14	16 28	00♍48	15 10
1915	03♋36	16 08	28 50	11♌43	24 47	08♍03	21 32	05♎14	49 10	93♏19	17 40	02♐11	16 45	01♑17	15 41	29 50
1916	10♏40	25 14	10♐08	25 17	10♑31	25 39	10♒32	25 03	09♓08	22 45	05♈56	18 43	01♉10	13 22	25 23	07♊17
1917	16♈12	29 25	12♉20	24 59	07♊24	19 38	01♋43	13 40	25 33	07♌21	19 09	00♍59	12 52	24 54	07♎07	29 36
1918	20♌47	02♍48	14 42	26 34	08♎28	20 28	02♏39	16 05	27 52	11♐00	24 33	08♑30	22 48	07♒21	22 04	06♓49
1919	13♐39	06♑23	19 23	02♒38	16 08	29 49	13♓41	27 39	11♈44	25 51	10♉02	24 12	08♊22	22 27	06♋26	20 13
1920	02♉05	16 26	02♊06	16 01	01♋03	16 05	00♌55	15 27	29 34	13♍12	26 21	09♎05	21 27	03♏31	15 25	27 12
1921	07♎44	10 45	03♏26	15 49	28 00	10♐03	21 59	03♑53	15 45	27 37	09♒30	21 25	03♓25	15 32	27 49	10♈18
1922	10♒48	22 44	04♓33	16 21	28 10	10♈07	22 16	04♉44	17 34	00♊53	14 40	28 55	13♋35	28 32	13♌36	28 37
1923	13♊47	16 52	10♋16	23 55	07♌47	21 48	05♍53	20 01	04♎08	18 14	02♏18	16 19	00♐15	14 05	27 46	11♑16
1924	23♎51	08♏10	22 45	07♐32	22 22	07♑09	21 43	05♒57	19 57	03♓11	16 10	28 46	11♈04	23 08	05♉03	26 55
1925	28♓23	11♈23	24 02	06♉24	18 34	00♊34	12 28	24 19	06♋09	17 59	29 53	11♌52	23 57	06♍11	18 38	01♎19
1926	00♌46	12 36	24 23	06♍12	18 05	00♎08	12 25	25 01	07♏59	21 23	05♐14	19 32	04♑14	19 13	04♒21	19 29
1927	03♐53	17 05	00♑39	14 33	28 43	13♒04	27 32	12♓01	26 25	10♈42	24 48	08♉42	22 24	05♊52	19 07	02♋10
1928	16♈14	00♉27	14 48	29 12	13♊37	27 57	12♋07	26 04	09♌42	23 00	05♍57	18 34	00♎52	12 56	24 51	06♏41
1929	19♍05	02♎04	14 39	26 54	08♏54	20 45	02♐32	14 18	26 07	08♑02	20 05	02♒16	14 38	27 11	09♓54	22 50
1930	20♑52	02♒43	14 35	26 29	08♓27	20 34	02♈52	15 26	28 22	11♉43	25 32	09♊51	24 37	09♋46	25 07	10♌29
1931	23♉35	07♊01	20 54	05♋12	19 49	04♌37	19 28	04♍14	18 47	03♎04	17 03	00♏45	14 11	27 22	10♐21	23 08
1932	08♎37	22 42	06♏51	21 00	05♐09	19 12	03♑06	16 46	00♒09	13 12	25 56	08♓20	20 28	02♈25	14 14	26 02
1933	09♓12	22 03	04♈32	16 43	28 42	10♉35	22 26	04♊18	16 15	28 20	10♋35	22 59	05♌33	18 19	01♍15	14 23
1934	11♋17	23 07	04♌59	16 54	28 55	11♍06	23 31	06♎13	19 16	02♏45	16 40	01♐02	15 48	00♑52	16 06	01♒18
1935	13♏51	27 26	11♐28	25 54	10♑38	25 35	10♒35	25 30	10♓13	24 39	08♈44	22 29	05♉52	18 57	01♊44	14 17
1936	01♈02	15 13	29 19	13♉17	27 06	10♊45	24 12	07♋25	20 24	03♌09	15 39	27 56	10♍02	21 59	03♎52	15 44
1937	29♌03	11♍54	24 25	06♎38	18 38	00♏31	12 20	24 11	06♐08	18 15	00♑35	13 09	25 59	09♒05	22 25	05♓58
1938	01♑21	13 14	25 13	07♒20	19 35	02♓02	14 41	27 34	10♈44	24 13	08♉04	22 16	06♊49	21 39	06♋41	21 46
1939	03♉59	17 33	01♊36	16 07	01♋03	16 15	01♌34	16 48	01♍46	16 21	00♎29	14 08	27 21	10♏12	22 43	05♐01
1940	23♍40	07♎47	21 41	05♏20	18 48	02♐04	14 12	28 08	10♑53	23 26	05♒48	17 58	29 59	11♓52	23 39	05♈27
1941	19♒06	01♓47	14 09	26 14	08♈08	19 56	01♉44	13 38	25 42	08♊00	20 36	03♋30	16 42	00♌12	13 55	27 49
1942	21♊38	03♋42	15 52	28 10	10♌38	23 15	06♍03	19 04	02♎20	15 54	29 56	13♏58	28 28	13♐12	28 04	22♑56
1943	24♎33	08♏14	22 24	07♐02	22 02	07♑16	22 35	07♒45	22 40	07♓11	21 15	04♈52	18 03	00♉52	13 22	25 38
1944	15♓29	29 40	13♈35	27 13	10♉34	23 41	06♊33	19 12	01♋39	13 55	26 01	07♌59	19 51	01♍39	13 27	25 17
1945	08♌52	21 23	03♍39	15 43	27 39	09♎32	21 25	03♏24	15 33	27 57	10♐38	23 39	07♑01	20 44	04♒43	18 57
1946	11♐41	23 47	06♑04	18 33	01♒16	14 12	27 21	10♓44	24 19	08♈07	22 06	06♉16	20 34	04♊59	19 27	03♋52
1947	15♈42	29 22	13♉26	27 54	12♊43	27 48	13♋01	28 11	13♌09	27 45	11♍55	25 36	08♎48	21 34	03♏58	16 05
1948	07♍26	21 45	05♎38	19 08	02♏14	15 02	27 35	09♐55	22 06	04♑10	16 09	28 04	09♒56	21 48	03♓40	15 35
1949	28♑53	11♒18	23 29	05♓30	17 22	29 10	11♈00	22 56	05♉03	17 29	00♊16	13 28	27 08	11♋13	25 39	10♌21
1950	01♊25	13 44	26 19	09♋10	22 16	05♌36	19 08	02♍48	16 36	00♎30	14 29	28 33	12♏42	26 53	11♐05	25 15
1951	07♎03	20 42	04♏45	19 10	03♐56	18 58	04♑05	19 07	03♒55	18 21	02♓20	15 51	28 53	11♈32	23 51	05♉56
1952	28♒42	12♓57	26 47	10♈11	23 14	05♉57	18 24	00♊40	12 46	24 45	06♋39	18 31	00♌20	12 10	24 02	05♍59
1953	19♋12	01♌22	13 22	25 14	07♍02	18 50	00♎42	12 42	24 57	07♏31	20 27	03♐49	17 37	01♑51	16 26	01♒16
1954	21♏23	03♐50	16 34	29 35	12♑54	26 29	10♒18	24 18	08♓25	22 37	06♈51	21 03	05♉12	19 15	03♊11	16 58
1955	28♓54	12♈42	26 48	11♉08	25 41	10♊22	25 06	09♋45	24 14	08♌26	22 16	05♍43	18 46	01♎26	13 47	25 53
1956	19♌27	03♍51	17 47	01♎15	14 16	26 54	09♏13	21 17	03♐12	15 00	26 47	08♑34	20 25	02♒20	14 22	26 32
1957	09♑18	21 20	03♒16	15 09	27 00	08♓52	20 47	02♈50	15 06	27 38	10♉33	23 53	07♊42	22 00	06♋45	21 50
1958	10♉54	23 25	06♊18	19 34	03♋15	17 17	01♌35	16 04	00♍37	15 07	29 29	13♎41	27 40	11♏27	25 03	08♐28
1959	21♍11	05♎00	18 59	03♏08	17 26	01♐51	16♑18	00 42	14 57	28♒56	12 35	25♓51	08 44	21♈15	03 27	15 26
1960	10♒16	24 35	08♓23	21 43	04♈35	17 05	29 18	11♉19	23 13	05♊03	16 54	28 48	10♋48	22 54	05♌07	17 28
1961	29♊49	11♋46	23 38	05♌28	17 16	29 06	11♍02	23 06	05♎24	18 01	01♏01	14 28	28 25	12♐50	27 41	12♑50
1962	00♏40	13 22	26 27	09♐57	23 51	08♑07	22 40	07♒22	22 06	06♓47	21 18	05♈35	19 38	03♉24	16 55	00♊10
1963	13♓08	27 11	11♈19	25 31	09♉45	23 57	08♊06	22 06	05♋54	19 27	02♌44	15 42	28 22	10♍46	22 56	04♎56
1964	00♌30	14 40	28 25	11♍44	24 39	07♎11	19 26	01♏28	13 21	25 10	06♐59	18 53	00♑53	13 03	25 25	07♒59
1965	20♐07	01♑55	13 42	25 31	07♒24	19 22	01♓28	13 45	26 14	09♈00	22 06	05♉34	19 26	03♊44	18 25	03♋25
1966	20♈39	03♉20	16 25	29 57	13♊56	28 22	13♋10	28 13	18♌21	28 24	13♍13	27 42	11♎47	25 27	08♏45	21 42
1967	05♍38	19 54	04♎06	18 11	02♏10	16 01	29 44	13♐19	26 44	09♑58	22 60	05♒47	18 20	00♓38	12 44	24 40
1968	20♑57	04♒60	18 38	01♓51	14 39	27 04	09♈12	21 07	02♉56	14 43	26 34	08♊34	20 45	03♋11	15 53	28 50
1969	10♊17	22 08	04♋02	15 60	28 02	10♌10	22 25	04♍50	17 25	00♎15	13 22	26 51	10♏42	25 58	09♐37	24 34
1970	10♎42	23 26	06♏37	20 17	04♐27	19 05	04♑05	19 19	04♒34	19 42	04♓31	18 58	03♈00	16 36	29 49	12♉41
1971	27♒31	11♓55	26 11	10♈18	24 15	07♉59	21 33	04♊54	18 03	00♋59	13 42	26 11	08♌28	20 33	02♍30	14 20
1972	11♋37	25 18	08♌39	21 37	04♍16	16 36	28 43	10♎40	22 33	04♏26	16 23	28 29	10♐48	23 23	06♑13	19 22
1973	00♐33	12 23	24 16	06♑15	18 21	00♒37	13 04	25 43	08♓35	21 41	05♈04	18 44	02♉41	16 55	01♊24	16 04
1974	01♈17	14 09	27 23	11♉04	25 11	09♊45	24 40	09♋50	25 06	10♌18	25 16	09♍52	24 02	07♎43	20 56	03♏45
1975	19♌11	03♍57	18 30	02♎44	16 38	00♏12	13 28	26 27	09♐12	21 45	04♑08	16 22	28 28	10♒28	22 23	04♓15
1976	01♑06	15 30	28 37	11♒28	24 02	06♓20	18 25	00♈19	12 09	23 59	05♉54	17 50	00♊21	13 02	26 07	09♋34
1977	10♉16	02♊08	14 08	26 18	08♋41	21 28	04♌07	17 08	00♍20	13 43	27 16	10♎60	24 54	08♏59	23 14	07♐38
1978	22♍15	05♎07	18 20	01♏58	16 03	00♐35	15 30	00♑31	16 00	01♒13	16 09	00♓42	14 45	28 18	11♈23	24 03
1979	10♒45	25 38	10♓12	24 23	08♈11	21 37	04♉43	17 33	00♊09	12 34	24 49	06♋56	18 57	00♌51	12 42	24 31
1980	23♊09	06♋15	19 06	01♌40	14 00	26 07	08♍02	19 52	01♎39	13 30	25 30	07♏42	20 13	03♐06	16 23	00♑05
1981	10♏06	22 05	04♐13	16 33	29 06	11♑54	24 56	08♒12	21 40	05♓19	19 07	03♈05	17 09	01♉20	15 34	29 50
1982	13♓18	26 23	09♈46	23 33	07♉43	22 08	06♊55	21 52	06♋52	21 47	06♌29	20 52	04♍50	18 22	01♎28	14 11
1983	01♌33	16 35	01♍20	15 40	29♎35	13 03	26♏07	08 49	21♐14	03 25	15 26	27♑19	09 09	20♒56	02 44	14 35
1984	14♐07	26 48	09♑18	21 37	03♒47	15 49	27 44	09♓36	21 27	03♈21	15 23	27 37	10♉09	23 02	06♊20	20 06
1985	29♈42	11♉40	23 50	06♊15	18 58	02♋02	15 27	29 09	13♌07	27 15	11♍28	25 43	09♎56	25 04	08♏06	22 02
1986	05♍04	18 21	01♎50	15 34	29 34	13♏49	28 18	12♐59	27 44	12♑47	26 59	11♒14	25 07	08♓32	21 32	04♈08
1987	22♑27	07♒37	22 25	06♓45	10 35	03♈56	16 50	29 22	11♉38	23 42	05♊38	17 30	29 21	11♋14	23 09	05♌08
1988	05♊00	17 31	29 52	12♋03	24 07	06♌04	16 55	29 43	11♍31	23 23	05♎23	17 37	00♏11	13 09	26 35	10♐31
1989	19♎11	01♏14	13 32	26 09	09♐08	22 29	06♑12	20 13	04♒28	18 52	03♓18	17 43	02♈02	16 13	00♉14	14 06
1990	26♒33	10♓02	23 42	07♈35	21 40	05♉55	20 20	04♊49	19 17	03♋39	17 49	01♌42	15 14	28 24	11♍13	23 43
1991	13♋14	28 13	12♌52	27 07	10♍55	24 16	07♎12	19 46	02♏02	14 05	26 00	07♐50	19 38	01♑29	13 24	25 25
1992	26♏09	08♐23	20 27	02♑24	14 16	26 05	07♒52	19 41	01♓33	13 33	25 42	08♈06	20 48	03♉51	17 19	01♊14
1993	08♈55	21 02	03♉22	16 02	29 04	12♊30	26 22	10♋37	25 12	09♌59	24 51	09♍39	24 17	08♎39	22 42	06♏26
1994	18♌17	02♍11	16 12	00♎17	14 25	28 32	12♏40	26 45	10♐46	24 40	08♑25	21 59	05♒17	18 18	01♓01	13 27
1995	03♑46	18 38	03♒14	17 27	01♓14	14 33	27 24	09♈52	22 02	03♉59	15 47	27 34	09♊23	21 18	03♋22	15 38
1996	16♉42	28 45	10♊43	22 37	04♋29	16 22	28 15	10♌12	22 12	04♍18	16 33	29 00	11♎42	24 44	08♏10	22 02
1997	28♍44	10♎49	23 09	05♏51	19 00	02♐37	16 44	01♑17	16 11	01♒16	16 22	01♓20	16 02	00♈23	14 21	27 57
1998	09♒59	24 08	08♓19	22 30	06♈38	20 44	04♉44	18 39	02♊28	16 07	29 36	12♋51	25 51	08♌35	21 03	03♍17
1999	24♊58	09♋33	23 51	07♌47	21 19	04♍26	17 09	29 33	11♎42	23 39	05♏32	17 23	29 19	11♐21	23 34	06♑00
2000	07♏18	19 19	01♐13	13 04	24 53	06♑43	18 36	00♒34	12 38	24 52	07♓16	19 54	02♈49	16 03	29 38	13♉36

	17th	18th	19th	20th	21st	22nd	23rd	24th	25th	26th	27th	28th	29th	30th	31st
1900	09♌49	21 29	03♍44	15 36	27 28	09♎23	21 25	03♏38	16 08	29 00	12♐17	26 01	10♑15	24 54	09♒53
1901	12♐04	24 51	07♑59	21 30	05♒21	19 28	03♓47	18 10	02♈33	16 51	01♉01	15 03	28 54	12♊37	26♊10
1902	22 24	06♉22	20 33	04♊55	19 47	04♋03	18 37	03♌02	17 11	00♍59	14 23	27 22	09♎58	22 14	04♏15
1903	12♍51	26 44	10♎07	23 02	05♏35	17 50	29 53	11♐47	23 38	05♑28	17 21	29 16	11♒18	23 25	05♓40
1904	18 14	00♒14	12 08	23 57	05♓45	17 33	29 25	11♈27	23 41	06♉14	19 11	02♊36	16 30	00♋54	15♋44
1905	01♊54	14 55	28 20	12♋08	26 17	10♌41	25 16	09♍54	24 28	08♎55	23 11	07♏14	21 04	04♐40	18♐02
1906	14 39	28 45	12♏58	27 15	11♐35	25 52	10♑02	24 00	07♒43	21 08	04♓13	16 58	29 26	11♈39	23♈40
1907	02♓59	16 48	00♈10	13 07	25 42	07♉59	20 02	01♊57	13 46	25 36	07♋28	19 25	01♌31	13 47	26♌14
1908	08♋33	20 23	02♌11	14 00	25 51	07♍46	19 49	02♎01	14 27	27 10	10♏12	23 38	07♐29	21 46	06♑26
1909	21 54	04♐55	18 22	02♑15	16 34	01♒14	16 09	01♓09	16 06	00♈51	15 18	29 24	13♉08	26 30	09♊34
1910	07♈14	21 23	05♉30	19 32	03♊30	17 22	01♋07	14 43	28 07	11♌18	24 14	06♍54	19 18	01♎28	13♎27
1911	23 21	07♍07	20 25	03♎18	15 47	27 57	09♏54	21 43	03♐29	15 18	27 14	09♑21	21 41	04♒14	17♒02
1912	28 47	10♑38	22 30	04♒25	16 23	28 26	10♓36	22 54	05♈24	18 08	01♉11	14 35	28 25	12♊41	27♊22
1913	11♉46	24 53	08♊30	22 37	07♋12	22 10	07♌20	22 33	07♍39	22 28	06♎55	20 58	04♏36	17 52	00♐48
1914	29 29	13♎42	27 49	11♏47	25 37	09♐17	22 47	06♑05	19 10	02♒01	14 37	27 00	09♓09	21 08	02♈59
1915	13♒40	27 07	10♓11	22 53	05♈17	17 26	29 24	11♉17	23 09	05♊05	17 10	29 25	11♋55	24 39	07♌40
1916	19 06	00♋56	12 48	24 44	06♌46	18 56	01♍16	13 48	26 33	09♎33	22 50	06♏26	20 22	04♐36	19♐08
1917	02♏25	15 37	29 15	13♐21	27 52	12♑45	27 54	13♒08	28 19	13♓16	27 52	12♈03	25 46	09♉02	21♉55
1918	12 29	05♈58	20 12	04♉09	17 48	01♊11	14 18	27 12	09♋53	22 24	04♌44	16 56	29 01	10♍59	22♍52
1919	03♌47	17 03	00♍02	12 42	25 04	07♎12	19 09	00♏59	12 49	24 43	06♐46	19 03	01♑39	14 36	27♑54
1920	08♐58	20 47	02♑43	14 48	27 05	09♒33	22 13	05♓05	18 08	01♈22	14 48	28 27	12♉18	26 23	10♊42
1921	23 06	06♉16	19 52	03♊55	18 27	03♋24	18 38	04♌00	19 17	04♍18	18 55	03♎02	16 39	29 47	12♏30
1922	13♍28	28 00	12♎11	26 01	09♏30	22 41	05♐36	18 17	00♑47	13 08	25 20	07♒23	19 20	01♓12	13♓00
1923	24 31	07♒29	20 11	02♓35	14 45	26 44	08♈34	20 22	02♉12	14 09	26 20	08♊48	21 37	04♋49	18♋25
1924	28 47	10♊44	22 49	05♋05	17 33	00♌14	13 08	26 15	09♍33	23 03	06♎44	20 35	04♏36	18 47	03♐04
1925	14 18	27 38	11♏21	25 28	09♐58	24 47	09♑48	24 53	09♒54	24 41	09♓08	23 10	06♈45	19 54	02♉39
1926	04 28	19 11	03♈31	17 27	00♉58	14 06	26 54	09♊24	21 40	03♋46	15 44	27 36	09♌25	21 14	03♍03
1927	15 00	27 39	10♌05	22 20	04♍26	16 25	28 18	10♎10	22 04	04♏04	16 17	28 46	11♐35	24 49	08♑29
1928	18 31	00♐27	12 33	24 53	07♑29	20 24	03♒38	17 09	00♓55	14 52	28 57	13♈05	27 14	11♉21	25♉27
1929	06♈00	19 25	03♉06	17 05	01♊22	15 56	00♋42	15 35	00♌27	15 09	29 32	13♍32	27 04	10♎09	22♎49
1930	25 40	10♍30	24 53	08♎46	22 10	05♏08	17 43	00♐02	12 08	24 06	06♑00	17 51	29 43	11♒36	23♒31
1931	05♑45	18 12	00♒29	12 36	24 35	06♓28	18 16	00♈03	11 53	23 51	06♉03	18 34	01♊28	14 51	28♊44
1932	07♉54	19 55	02♊10	14 43	27 37	10♋52	24 27	08♌20	22 26	06♍41	20 59	05♎17	19 32	03♏42	17♏45
1933	27 44	11♎18	25 06	09♏09	23 26	07♐55	22 31	07♑08	21 39	05♒58	20 00	03♓39	16 56	29 49	12♈22
1934	16 20	01♓02	15 20	29 10	12♈34	25 32	08♉08	20 27	02♊33	14 30	26 21	08♋11	20 00	01♌53	13♌51
1935	26 38	08♋48	20 50	02♌45	14 36	26 24	08♍12	20 03	02♎00	14 07	26 28	09♏07	22 07	05♐33	19♐26
1936	27 41	09♏46	22 04	04♐40	17 37	00♑57	14 41	28 47	13♒12	27 49	12♓31	27 12	11♈45	26 05	10♉10
1937	19 43	03♈35	17 35	01♉42	15 52	00♊04	14 16	28 27	12♋32	26 28	10♌12	23 39	06♍48	19 38	02♎10
1938	06♌45	21 28	05♍28	19 40	03♎03	15 59	28 30	10♏42	22 40	04♐30	16 16	28 03	09♑55	21 55	04♒05
1939	17 08	29 08	11♑04	22 57	04♒49	16 41	28 35	10♓32	22 34	04♈44	17 06	29 45	12♉43	26 06	09♊57
1940	17 19	29 22	11♉40	24 19	07♊24	20 57	04♋58	19 26	04♌14	19 14	04♍15	19 09	03♎49	18 09	02♏08
1941	11♍49	25 54	09♎59	24 05	08♏11	22 14	06♐15	20 12	04♑00	17 39	01♒03	14 12	27 04	09♓37	21♓55
1942	27 39	12♒05	26 09	09♓46	22 57	05♈45	18 11	00♉21	12 20	24 12	06♊04	17 58	29 58	12♋08	24♋29
1943	07♊43	19 40	01♋32	13 22	25 12	07♌03	18 58	00♍59	13 07	25 26	07♎59	20 48	03♏58	17 30	01♐26
1944	07♎15	19 25	01♏51	14 38	27 49	11♐27	25 33	10♑03	24 54	09♒58	25 06	10♓09	24 59	09♈29	23♈36
1945	03♓20	17 46	02♈11	16 31	00♉42	14 43	28 32	12♊08	25 32	08♋43	21 42	04♌28	17 02	29 25	11♍36
1946	18 11	02♌18	16 08	29 37	12♍46	25 32	08♎00	20 10	02♏09	14 00	25 50	07♐42	19 42	01♑54	14 21
1947	28 00	09♐48	21 34	03♑21	15 13	27 11	09♒17	21 32	03♓58	16 34	29 22	12♈23	25 39	09♉12	23 02
1948	27 37	09♈48	22 14	04♉58	18 07	01♊43	15 48	00♋22	15 22	00♌38	16 01	01♍18	16 19	00♎54	15 01
1949	25 09	09♍55	24 32	08♎56	23 03	06♏53	20 27	03♐47	16 53	29 48	12♑32	25 06	07♒30	19 43	01♓47
1950	09♑17	23 07	06♒41	19 56	02♓50	15 24	27 40	09♈42	21 34	03♉23	15 12	27 08	09♊16	21 39	04♋22
1951	17 51	29 42	11♊33	23 28	05♋28	17 36	29 54	12♌22	24 59	07♍48	20 48	04♎00	17 26	01♏07	15♏03
1952	18 04	00♎21	12 54	25 46	09♏02	22 45	06♐56	21 32	06♑29	21 40	06♒55	22 03	06♓56	21 26	05♈29
1953	16 14	01♓10	15 58	00♈31	14 46	28 40	12♉14	25 28	08♊25	21 06	03♋33	15 50	27 57	09♌56	21♌49
1954	00♋33	13 56	27 05	09♌58	22 37	05♍01	17 13	29 15	11♎10	23 02	04♏56	16 56	29 07	11♐34	24♐20
1955	07♏49	19 39	01♐28	13 21	25 22	07♑34	20 00	02♒41	15 37	28 47	12♓12	25 49	09♈36	23 32	07♉34
1956	08♓52	21 23	04♈08	17 08	00♉28	14 08	28 10	12♊34	27 19	12♋18	27 25	12♌30	27 22	11♍55	26♍01
1957	07♌07	22 23	07♍29	22 14	06♎34	20 26	03♏51	16 52	29 33	11♐58	24 11	06♑15	18 14	00♒09	12♒02
1958	21 42	04♑46	17 39	00♒20	12 29	25 06	07♓11	19 08	00♈58	12 45	24 34	06♉31	18 41	01♊10	14♊02
1959	27 17	09♉04	20 55	02♊53	15 03	27 29	10♋13	23 15	06♌34	20 08	03♍54	17 49	01♎49	15 52	29♎57
1960	29 58	12♍39	25 31	08♎39	22 03	05♏46	19 49	04♐12	18 52	03♑44	18 39	03♒30	18 07	02♓23	16 14
1961	28 08	13♒23	28 26	13♓08	27 24	11♈14	24 37	07♉36	20 16	02♊39	14 49	26 50	08♋44	20 36	02♌25
1962	13 10	25 58	08♋32	20 55	03♌07	15 10	27 05	08♍55	20 43	02♎32	14 26	26 29	08♏47	21 23	04♐23
1963	16 50	28 43	10♏38	22 42	04♐58	17 29	00♑20	13 30	27 01	10♒50	24 55	09♓11	23 33	07♈58	22 19
1964	20 46	03♓47	17 01	00♈28	14 08	28 01	12♉06	26 22	10♊46	25 15	09♋45	24 11	08♌26	22 27	06♍09
1965	18 36	03♌50	18 55	03♍43	18 07	02♎01	15 26	28 24	10♏58	23 12	06♐13	17 04	28 51	10♑37	22♑26
1966	04♐23	16 50	29 07	11♑15	23 18	05♒16	17 10	29 02	10♓53	22 46	04♈43	16 49	29 07	11♉42	24♉38
1967	06♈30	18 18	00♉10	12 12	24 28	07♊04	20 03	03♋29	17 21	01♌36	16 09	00♍52	15 37	00♎17	14♎45
1968	12♌00	25 24	08♍57	22 39	06♎28	20 23	04♏25	18 32	02♐44	16 59	01♑13	15 22	29 22	13♒07	26♒33
1969	09♑41	24 49	09♒46	24 25	08♓38	22 22	05♈37	28 27	00♉55	13 06	25 06	06♊59	18 49	00♋42	12♋38
1970	25 16	07♊38	19 50	01♋53	13 50	25 43	07♌33	19 22	01♍12	13 06	25 06	07♎16	19 40	02♏22	15 27
1971	26 07	07♎56	19 52	02♏00	14 24	27 09	10♐18	23 53	07♑54	22 18	07♒00	21 53	06♓49	21 40	06♈19
1972	02♒47	16 26	00♓18	14 20	28 28	12♈40	26 52	11♉03	25 10	09♊12	23 06	06♋49	20 21	03♌39	16 42
1973	00♋50	15 35	00♌12	14 34	28 37	12♍16	25 31	08♎23	20 53	03♏06	15 05	26 57	08♐46	20 36	02♑33
1974	16 12	28 23	10♐22	22 14	04♑02	15 48	27 37	09♒29	21 27	03♓32	15 45	28 09	10♈46	23 38	06♉50
1975	16 06	27 59	09♈58	22 06	04♉30	17 13	00♊21	13 56	28 00	12♋33	27 28	12♌40	27 57	13♍07	28♍02
1976	23 24	07♌33	21 55	06♍24	20 53	05♎17	19 32	03♏37	17 31	01♐13	14 45	28 07	11♑19	24 20	07♒09
1977	22 08	06♑37	21 00	05♒10	19 01	02♓30	15 35	28 16	10♈37	22 42	04♉36	16 25	28 13	10♊07	22♊11
1978	06♉23	18 30	00♊27	12 18	24 09	06♋01	17 58	29 59	12♌07	24 22	06♍46	19 20	02♎04	15 03	28♎17
1979	06♍19	18 11	00♎10	12 21	24 48	07♏36	20 50	04♐33	18 46	03♑25	18 27	03♒42	18 59	04♓08	19♓00
1980	14 10	28 32	13♒08	27 50	12♓30	27 04	11♈27	25 37	09♉31	23 10	06♊34	19 44	02♋39	15 22	27♋52
1981	14♊03	28 10	12♋08	25 51	09♌18	22 27	05♍18	17 50	00♎08	12 13	24 09	06♏02	17 55	29 54	12♐03
1982	26 33	08♏41	20 37	02♐28	14 16	26 07	08♑03	20 07	02♒21	14 47	27 26	10♓18	23 23	06♈43	20♈14
1983	26 29	08♓31	20 41	03♈02	15 40	28 35	11♉52	25 33	09♊39	24 10	09♋03	24 11	09♌26	24 37	09♍35
1984	04♋19	18 56	03♌52	18 57	04♍01	18 56	03♎33	17 49	01♏40	15 09	28 16	11♐06	23 41	06♑04	18♑18
1985	05♐51	19 33	03♑06	16 29	29 39	12♒36	25 17	07♓44	19 56	01♈57	13 49	15 38	07♉27	19 23	01♊32
1986	16 23	28 24	10♉15	22 02	03♊51	15 46	27 51	10♋08	22 41	05♌28	18 30	01♍45	15 11	28 46	12♎29
1987	17 12	29 22	11♍40	24 08	06♎49	19 47	03♏05	16 45	00♐50	15 20	00♑11	15 17	00♒27	15 32	00♓22
1988	24 56	09♑47	24 54	10♒09	25 20	10♓17	24 55	09♈07	22 55	06♉19	19 21	02♊05	14 34	26 52	08♋59
1989	27 46	11♊16	24 33	07♋38	20 29	03♌07	15 31	27 43	09♍44	21 37	03♎26	15 14	27 06	09♏08	21♏24
1990	05♎56	17 58	29 52	11♏44	23 39	05♐40	17 52	00♑17	12 58	25 56	09♒11	22 41	06♓24	20 19	04♈22
1991	07♒35	19 54	02♓25	15 09	28 07	11♈20	24 51	08♉40	22 46	07♊10	21 47	06♋33	21 21	06♌05	20♌38
1992	15 35	00♋21	15 26	00♌40	15 56	01♍01	15 48	00♎10	14 05	27 31	10♏31	23 08	05♐27	17 31	29♐27
1993	19 51	02♐59	15 52	28 33	11♑02	23 23	05♒34	17 38	29 37	11♓30	23 21	05♈13	17 08	29 11	11♉27
1994	25 38	07♈37	19 29	01♉18	13 10	25 09	07♊22	19 53	02♋45	16 00	29 38	13♌36	27 49	12♍13	26♍39
1995	28 06	10♌47	23 40	06♍45	20 00	03♎26	17 03	00♏51	14 51	29 02	13♐25	27 55	12♑28	26 58	11♒18
1996	06♐23	21 09	06♑15	21 33	06♒51	21 57	06♓41	20 59	04♈46	18 03	00♉55	13 24	25 37	07♊38	19♊33
1997	11♉13	24 12	06♊56	19 27	01♋48	14 00	26 05	08♌03	19 56	01♍45	13 33	25 22	07♎17	19 21	01♏40
1998	15 18	27 11	08♎59	20 48	02♏42	14 48	27 10	09♐52	22 56	06♑25	20 18	04♒30	18 58	03♓34	18♓14
1999	18 38	01♒31	14 38	27 57	11♓28	25 10	09♈01	23 01	07♉09	21 23	05♊40	19 57	04♋10	18 16	02♌09
2000	27 56	12♊35	27 29	12♋31	27 32	12♌23	26 56	11♍07	24 52	08♎11	21 05	03♏37	15 51	27 52	09♐45

Moon

February

Year	1st	2nd	3rd	4th	5th	6th	7th	8th	9th	10th	11th	12th	13th	14th	15th	16th
1900	25♒04	10♓15	25 17	10♈00	24 20	08♉14	21 42	04♊48	17 34	00♋05	12 24	24 33	06♌36	18 35	00♍30	12 23
1901	09♋34	22 48	05♌50	18 40	01♍17	13 40	25 50	07♎50	19 42	01♏30	13 20	25 16	07♎24	19 49	02♏37	15 50
1902	16♏06	27 54	09♐43	21 38	03♑45	16 05	28 42	11♒35	24 44	08♓08	21 43	05♈27	19 18	03♉15	17 16	01♊20
1903	18♓03	00♈36	13 22	16 22	09♉41	23 21	07♊23	21 48	06♋32	21 30	06♌34	21 33	06♍19	20 43	04♎41	18 10
1904	00♌52	16 10	01♍26	16 29	01♎12	15 30	29 21	12♏47	25 50	08♐32	20 59	03♑12	15 16	27 13	09♒06	20 55
1905	01♑10	14 05	26 47	09♒17	21 35	03♓42	15 40	27 31	09♈19	21 06	02♉59	15 00	27 16	09♊50	22 46	06♋08
1906	05♉35	17 27	29 22	11♊24	23 37	06♋05	18 51	01♌54	15 17	28 57	12♍52	26 58	11♎12	25 30	09♏47	24 01
1907	08♍53	21 45	04♎52	18 11	01♏46	15 36	29 40	13♐57	28 26	13♑02	27 40	12♒14	26 38	10♓46	24 34	07♈59
1908	21♑27	06♒39	21 53	07♓00	21 49	06♈15	20 11	03♉39	16 40	29 17	11♊35	23 39	05♋32	17 21	29 08	10♌56
1909	22♊22	04♋56	17 20	29 35	11♌42	23 44	05♍40	17 34	29 25	11♎18	23 14	05♏18	17 34	00♐06	13 00	26 20
1910	25♎18	07♏07	18 58	00♐58	13 11	25 43	08♑37	21 55	05♒38	19 43	04♓05	18 38	03♈14	17 47	02♉12	16 24
1911	00♓03	13 16	26 39	10♈12	23 54	07♉45	21 45	05♊53	20 09	04♋31	18 55	03♌15	17 25	01♍21	14 57	28 11
1912	12♋23	27 36	12♌50	27 54	12♍39	25 58	10♎47	24 06	06♏59	29 30	01♐43	13 44	25 38	07♑28	19 19	01♒13
1913	13♐28	25 54	08♑10	20 17	02♒17	14 12	26 02	07♓51	19 39	01♈29	13 26	25 31	07♉51	20 29	03♊30	16 57
1914	14♈47	26 35	08♉30	20 35	02♊57	15 39	28 45	12♋16	26 12	10♌30	25 06	99♍52	24 41	09♎27	24 02	08♏24
1915	20♌56	04♍26	18 08	02♎01	16 01	00♏07	14 18	28 29	12♐41	26 49	10♑52	24 45	08♒27	21 55	05♓06	18 01
1916	03♑53	18 45	03♒37	18 21	02♓50	16 58	00♈42	14 01	26 55	09♉28	21 43	03♊44	15 37	27 26	09♋16	21 10
1917	04♊26	16 42	28 45	10♋40	22 30	04♌18	16 06	27 57	09♍52	21 53	04♎02	16 21	28 53	11♏41	24 47	08♐14
1918	04♎43	16 36	28 34	10♏41	23 03	05♐43	18 48	02♑19	16 18	00♒45	15 35	00♓40	15 50	00♈56	15 47	00♉17
1919	11♒33	25 31	09♓41	24 00	08♈21	22 40	06♉53	20 58	04♊55	18 44	02♋24	15 55	29 17	12♌28	25 27	08♍12
1920	28♊12	09♋49	24 28	09♌01	23 21	07♍22	20 59	04♎11	16 57	29 23	11♏30	23 25	05♐14	17 02	28 53	10♑54
1921	24♏53	07♐02	18 00	00♑52	12 43	24 34	06♒28	18 25	00♓29	12 38	24 55	07♈21	19 59	02♉50	16 00	29 29
1922	24♓47	06♈37	18 33	00♉41	13 04	25 49	09♊01	22 41	06♋51	21 30	06♌30	21 44	07♍01	22 10	07♎02	21 32
1923	02♌23	16 38	01♍06	15 39	00♎13	14 42	29 02	13♏12	27 08	10♐52	24 22	07♑39	20 43	03♒34	16 11	28 36
1924	17♐25	01♑46	16 03	00♒10	14 03	27 39	10♓56	23 52	06♈29	18 49	00♉56	12 53	24 46	06♊39	18 37	00♋44
1925	15♉04	27 13	09♊12	21 03	02♋52	14 42	26 35	08♌36	20 46	03♍05	15 37	28 20	11♎18	24 29	07♏55	21 37
1926	14♍56	26 54	09♎01	21 19	03♏53	16 45	29 59	13♐38	27 43	12♑14	27 06	12♒14	17 30	12♓41	27 40	12♈17
1927	22♑35	07♒04	21 51	06♓47	21 45	06♈34	21 09	05♉24	19 18	02♊51	16 04	29 01	11♋43	24 14	06♌34	18 47
1928	09♊28	23 26	07♋17	21 01	04♌34	17 54	01♍00	13 49	26 22	08♎39	20 43	02♏38	14 27	26 17	08♐11	20 17
1929	05♏07	17 10	29 01	10♐48	22 36	04♑28	16 29	28 41	11♒06	23 45	06♓37	19 42	02♈57	16 23	29 59	13♉44
1930	05♓31	17 36	29 48	12♈11	24 46	07♉39	20 53	04♊31	18 35	03♋06	18 00	03♌10	18 27	03♍38	18 34	03♎05
1931	13♋06	27 52	12♌57	28 08	13♍17	28 12	12♎49	27 03	10♏52	24 19	07♐25	20 13	02♑47	15 09	27 21	09♒25
1932	01♐40	15 27	29 04	12♑31	25 45	08♒45	21 30	04♓01	16 17	28 22	10♈17	22 06	03♉54	15 45	27 45	09♊58
1933	24♈37	06♉40	18 35	00♊27	12 21	24 21	06♋30	18 51	01♌27	14 18	27 24	10♍44	24 18	08♎03	21 58	06♏00
1934	25♌56	08♍10	20 34	03♎11	16 02	29 10	12♏36	26 22	10♐28	24 54	09♑35	24 26	09♒21	24 12	08♓51	23 11
1935	03♑45	18 28	03♒31	18 43	03♓56	19 00	03♈46	18 09	02♉05	15 33	28 37	11♊18	23 42	05♋51	17 50	29 43
1936	23♉58	07♊30	20 46	03♋48	16 37	29 15	11♌43	24 00	06♍10	18 11	00♎07	12 00	23 51	05♏46	17 48	00♐02
1937	14♎25	26 26	08♏19	20 09	01♐59	13 57	26 07	08♑33	21 18	04♒24	17 52	01♓39	15 41	29 53	14♈10	28 28
1938	16♒25	28 58	11♓42	24 37	07♈43	21 02	04♉33	18 17	02♊16	16 30	00♋57	15 34	00♌16	14 56	29 26	13♍39
1939	24♊17	09♋04	24 12	09♌32	24 54	10♍03	24 52	09♎13	23 04	06♏25	19 19	01♐52	14 07	26 10	08♑06	19 57
1940	15♏47	29 07	12♐11	25 00	07♑38	20 05	02♒22	14 31	26 32	08♓26	20 16	02♈03	13 51	25 43	07♉44	19 59
1941	03♈49	15 53	27 42	09♉30	21 24	03♊28	15 46	28 25	11♋25	24 49	08♌34	22 39	06♍59	21 27	05♎59	20 28
1942	07♌01	19 47	02♍44	15 54	29 16	12♎50	26 35	10♏30	24 36	08♐52	23 13	07♑37	21 59	06♒15	20 18	04♓05
1943	15♐46	00♑28	15 25	00♒31	15 37	00♓32	15 10	29 25	13♈13	26 34	09♉31	22 05	04♊22	16 25	28 19	10♋09
1944	07♉19	20 18	03♊36	16 15	28 38	10♋50	22 52	04♌48	16 39	28 27	10♍16	22 07	04♎02	16 04	28 15	10♏41
1945	23♍39	05♎34	17 27	29 19	11♏16	23 22	05♐42	18 21	01♑23	14 50	28 42	12♒59	27 37	12♓27	27 23	12♈15
1946	27♑06	10♒08	23 29	07♓05	20 55	04♈53	18 57	03♉04	17 12	01♊19	15 24	29 26	13♋23	27 13	10♌55	24 25
1947	07♊12	21 39	06♋23	21 16	06♌12	21 02	05♍37	19 49	03♎36	16 54	29 45	12♏13	24 23	06♐19	18 08	29 54
1948	28♎38	11♏47	24 33	07♐00	19 13	01♑15	13 11	25 04	06♒55	18 47	00♓41	12 38	24 39	06♈46	19 02	01♉30
1949	13♓43	25 32	07♈19	19 04	01♉01	13 06	25 27	08♊10	21 19	04♋57	19 05	03♌40	18 36	03♍44	18 53	03♎54
1950	17♋25	00♌49	14 31	28 28	12♍36	26 50	11♎07	25 22	09♏33	23 39	07♐39	21 32	05♑17	18 52	02♒14	15 24
1951	29♏15	13♐40	28 15	12♑55	27 32	12♒01	26 13	10♓05	23 34	06♈39	19 22	01♉46	13 55	25 53	07♊46	19 38
1952	19♈05	02♉15	15 02	27 29	09♊41	21 42	03♋36	15 25	27 15	09♌05	20 00	03♍00	15 08	27 25	09♎54	22 36
1953	03♍39	15 27	27 16	09♎10	21 11	03♏25	15 54	28 44	11♐57	25 37	09♑44	24 17	09♒11	24 19	09♓32	24 41
1954	07♑28	20 59	04♒53	29 07	03♓37	18 15	02♈55	17 30	01♉55	16 07	00♊03	13 44	25 09	10♋19	23 17	06♌03
1955	21♉42	05♊54	20 09	04♋23	18 34	02♌39	16 32	00♍10	13 30	26 30	09♎11	21 34	03♏42	15 39	27 29	09♐18
1956	09♎38	22 47	05♏29	17 50	29 54	11♐47	23 34	05♑20	17 09	29 04	11♒08	23 22	05♓47	18 23	01♈11	14 10
1957	23♒54	05♓46	17 41	29 39	11♈44	23 59	06♉28	19 17	02♊28	16 06	00♋13	14 48	29 49	15♌05	00♍28	15 44
1958	27♊21	11♋09	25 23	10♌01	24 54	09♍53	24 49	09♎34	24 02	08♏11	21 59	05♐29	18 41	01♑39	14 24	26 58
1959	14♏03	28 08	12♐13	26 14	10♑09	23 56	07♒31	20 50	03♓52	16 35	29 01	11♈12	23 11	05♉01	16 50	28 41
1960	29♓38	12♈37	25 13	07♉31	19 34	01♊30	13 21	25 13	07♋10	19 14	01♌28	13 53	26 30	09♍19	22 21	05♎34
1961	14♌15	26 07	08♍04	20 07	02♎19	14 44	27 24	10♏23	23 44	07♐29	21 39	06♑12	21 04	06♒08	21 17	06♓19
1962	17♐48	01♑40	15 85	00♒39	15 36	00♓42	15 47	00♈43	15 22	29 39	13♉33	27 04	10♊12	23 00	05♋32	17 50
1963	06♉34	20 40	04♊35	18 19	01♋52	15 12	28 19	11♌14	23 56	06♍26	18 43	00♎51	12 50	24 44	06♏36	18 30
1964	19♍29	02♎27	15 03	27 22	09♏26	21 20	03♐09	14 59	26 54	08♑59	21 18	03♒53	16 45	29 55	13♓21	27 02
1965	04♒20	16 21	28 30	10♓49	23 18	05♈59	18 52	01♉59	15 23	29 05	13♊06	27 26	12♋05	26 57	11♌55	26 51
1966	08♊01	21 52	06♋14	21 03	06♌12	21 33	06♍54	22 02	06♎50	21 09	05♏00	18 22	01♐18	13 54	26 14	08♑21
1967	28♎59	12♏57	26 39	10♐07	23 22	06♑25	29 16	01♒57	14 28	26 47	08♓57	20 57	02♈49	14 37	26 24	08♉15
1968	09♓38	22 23	04♈28	16 57	28 53	10♉43	22 31	04♊24	16 25	28 40	11♋13	24 05	07♌17	20 48	04♍36	18 36
1969	24♋42	06♌53	19 14	01♍45	14 26	27 18	10♎22	23 39	07♏12	21 00	05♐05	19 25	03♑59	18 39	03♒22	17 58
1970	28♏57	12♐55	27 20	12♑09	27 15	12♒30	27 43	12♓44	27 25	11♈41	25 30	08♉52	21 50	04♊26	16 45	28 51
1971	20♈42	04♉45	18 29	01♊53	14 59	27 49	10♋25	22 48	05♌01	17 05	29 01	10♍53	22 42	04♎30	16 21	28 19
1972	29♌30	12♍03	24 22	06♎29	18 27	00♏21	12 13	24 10	06♐15	18 33	01♑09	14 05	27 24	11♒05	25 08	09♓28
1973	14♑38	26 56	09♒27	22 14	05♓15	18 31	01♈59	15 39	29 29	13♉27	27 32	11♊44	25 59	10♋16	24 33	08♌44
1974	20♉17	04♊09	18 24	03♋01	17 55	03♌02	18 10	03♍11	17 55	02♎15	16 06	29 28	12♏22	24 53	07♐04	19 01
1975	12♎33	26 37	10♏15	23 27	06♐18	18 51	01♑10	13 20	25 22	07♒20	19 14	01♓07	12 59	24 51	06♈47	18 48
1976	19♒46	02♓10	14 22	26 23	08♈16	20 04	01♉52	13 44	25 48	08♊07	20 47	03♋53	17 26	01♌27	15 53	00♍38
1977	04♋28	17 02	29 54	13♌03	26 27	10♍05	23 52	07♎47	21 46	05♏49	19 54	04♐01	18 07	02♑13	16 14	00♒09
1978	11♏51	25 45	10♐00	24 34	09♑23	24 21	09♒17	24 03	08♓31	22 36	06♈14	19 25	02♉11	14 37	26 47	08♊46
1979	03♈28	17 30	01♉05	14 16	27 05	09♊36	21 52	03♋58	15 56	27 49	09♌39	21 28	03♍19	15 12	27 11	09♎17
1980	10♌11	22 19	04♍18	16 11	28 00	09♎48	21 39	03♏38	15 48	28 15	11♐03	24 15	07♑54	22 00	06♒30	21 19
1981	24♐26	07♑06	20 05	03♒24	17 03	00♓58	15 06	29 23	13♈45	28 06	12♉24	26 34	10♊36	24 27	08♋07	21 35
1982	04♉00	17 59	02♊11	16 33	01♋02	15 35	00♌06	14 30	28 42	12♍34	26 06	09♎16	22 03	04♏30	16 40	28 38
1983	24♍11	08♎19	21 58	05♏08	17 53	00♐16	12 23	24 18	06♑07	17 53	29 40	11♒31	23 28	05♓32	17 45	00♈07
1984	00♒25	12 26	24 22	06♓15	18 07	29 58	11♈53	23 53	06♉04	18 30	01♊16	14 26	28 04	12♋12	26 48	11♌49
1985	13♊57	26 45	09♋57	23 36	07♌38	22 01	06♍37	21 19	06♎00	20 32	04♏52	18 57	02♐47	16 22	29 45	12♑56
1986	26♎20	10♏18	24 23	08♐34	22 50	07♑08	21 24	05♒32	19 27	03♓04	16 22	29 17	11♈52	24 08	06♉11	18 03
1987	14♓48	28 46	12♈15	25 17	07♉55	20 14	02♊18	14 14	26 06	07♋57	19 50	01♌50	13 56	25 11	08♍35	21 08
1988	21♋00	02♌55	14 47	26 36	08♍25	20 16	02♎12	14 16	26 32	09♏05	21 58	05♐16	19 01	03♑14	17 53	02♒53
1989	03♐58	16 55	00♑17	14 05	28 17	12♒50	17 36	12♓29	27 21	12♈95	26 34	10♉47	24 40	08♊14	21 30	04♋29
1990	18♈30	02♉42	16 53	01♊03	15 10	29 10	13♋01	26 42	10♌09	23 22	06♍29	19 01	01♎28	13 41	25 44	07♏39
1991	04♍52	18 44	02♎12	15 15	27 55	10♏15	22 21	04♐16	16 05	27 54	09♑46	21 46	03♒56	16 20	28 57	11♓49
1992	11♑16	23 03	04♒51	16 41	28 35	10♓35	10 35	22 43	05♈01	17 30	00♉13	13 13	26 32	10♊14	24 19	08♋47
1993	24♉00	06♊55	20 17	04♋07	18 27	08♌12	18 16	03♍30	18 44	03♎45	18 26	02♏42	16 32	29 56	12♐57	25 39
1994	11♎04	25 22	09♏31	23 31	07♐19	20 58	04♑28	17 47	00♒56	13 54	26 39	09♓11	21 03	03♈36	15 33	27 23
1995	25♒21	09♓02	22 20	05♈13	17 43	29 56	11♉54	23 45	05♊32	17 23	29 21	11♋32	23 57	06♌38	19 37	02♍51
1996	01♋24	13 15	25 09	07♌07	19 10	01♍20	13 38	26 05	08♎42	21 32	04♏37	18 01	01♐45	15 51	00♑19	15 04
1997	14♏17	27 19	10♐48	24 47	09♑15	24 07	09♒17	24 33	09♓47	24 46	09♈26	23 40	07♉27	20 49	03♊49	16 28
1998	02♈49	17 16	01♉32	15 33	29 20	12♊53	26 11	09♋16	22 06	04♌44	17 10	29 25	11♍29	23 26	05♎17	17 05
1999	15♌47	29 07	12♍08	24 50	07♎15	19 26	01♏27	13 21	25 13	07♐09	19 12	01♑28	13 58	26 47	09♒54	23 21
2000	25♐42	08♑24	21 27	04 52	18♒38	02 40	16♓53	01 13	15 33	29♈51	14 02	28♉06	12 02	25♊49	09 29	22♋59

Year	17th	18th	19th	20th	21st	22nd	23rd	24th	25th	26th	27th	28th	29th
1900	24 15	06♎08	18 05	00♏08	12 20	24 47	07♐32	10 41	04♑16	18 21	02♒55	17♒53	
1901	29 31	13♒38	28 07	12♓51	27 41	12♈30	27 10	11♉35	25 44	09♊34	23 08	06♋26	
1902	15 28	29 38	13♋28	27 53	11♌51	25 37	09♍07	22 18	05♎10	17 42	29 57	11♏59	
1903	01♏13	13 53	26 13	08♐18	20 14	02♑05	13 56	25 51	07♒51	29 00	02♓19	14♓48	
1904	02♌44	14 34	26♍26	08 25	20♎31	02 50	15 25	28♏19	11 37	25♐20	09 29	24 04	08♑59
1905	29 57	04♌12	18 48	03♍41	18 42	03♎43	18 35	03♏12	17 30	01♐26	14 59	28♐12	
1906	08♐09	22 10	06♑01	19 42	03♒12	16 29	29 32	12♓21	24 57	07♈19	19 30	01♉31	
1907	21 01	03♉41	16 01	28 07	10♊02	21 52	03♋41	15 36	27 38	09♌52	22 21	05♍06	
1908	22 48	04♍46	16 51	29 06	11♎29	24 03	06♏50	19 53	03♐13	16 53	00♑54	15 16	29♑58
1909	10♑08	24 26	09♒11	24 17	09♓34	24 51	09♈58	24 44	09♉04	22 56	06♊21	29♊21	
1910	00♊24	14 10	27 44	11♋06	24 18	07♌19	20 09	02♍47	15 14	29 29	09♎32	21♎29	
1911	11♎21	23 32	05♏44	17 43	29 34	11♐22	23 13	05♑12	17 24	29 51	12♒36	25♒40	
1912	13 13	25 19	07♓33	19 56	02♈29	15 12	28 08	11♉18	24 45	08♊29	22 33	06♋56	21♋34
1913	00♋54	15 19	00♌08	15 16	00♍33	15 48	00♎52	15 35	29 54	13♏45	27 10	10♐10	
1914	22 28	06♐15	19 44	02♑56	15 53	28 36	11♒05	23 24	05♓32	17 33	29 26	11♈15	
1915	00♈39	13 01	25 11	07♉11	19 04	00♊57	12 52	24 56	07♋13	19 45	02♌37	15♌59	
1916	03♌12	15 25	27 50	10♍29	23 21	06♎28	19 47	03♏19	17 03	00♐58	15 03	29 17	13♑37
1917	22 06	06♑21	20 59	05♒56	21 04	06♓16	21 20	06♈07	20 30	04♉24	17 48	00♊46	
1918	14 23	28 03	11♊20	24 15	06♋54	19 20	01♌35	13 43	25 44	07♍42	19 36	01♎29	
1919	20 43	03♎00	15 05	27 00	08♏50	20 38	02♐31	14 32	26 49	09♑25	22 26	05♒53	
1920	23 07	05♒34	18 18	01♓17	14 31	27 38	11♈35	25 20	09♉12	23 10	07♊13	21 20	05♋31
1921	13♊21	27 37	12♋14	27 09	12♌13	27 17	12♍12	26 48	10♎59	24 43	07♏59	20♏49	
1922	05♏35	19 13	02♐26	15 19	27 53	10♑13	22 23	04♒24	16 18	28 09	09♓58	21♓47	
1923	10♓49	22 52	02♈47	16 37	28 24	10♉14	22 11	04♊19	16 44	29 29	12♋30	26♋14	
1924	13 04	25 39	08♌33	21 44	05♍14	18 59	02♎57	17 04	01♏19	15 35	19 51	14♐02	28♐08
1925	05♐35	19 47	04♑12	18 47	03♒27	18 07	02♓39	16 56	00♈57	14 34	27 48	10♉39	
1926	26 27	10♉08	23 22	06♊09	18 36	00♋46	12 45	24 36	06♌23	18 11	00♍00	11♍55	
1927	00♍52	12 52	24 48	06♎40	18 32	00♏26	12 25	24 35	06♐58	19 42	02♑49	16♑23	
1928	02♑39	15 22	28 27	11♒57	25 50	10♓02	24 28	09♈00	23 33	07♉59	22 16	06♊22	20♊15
1929	27 39	11♊44	25 58	10♋20	24 47	09♌12	23 31	07♍37	21 25	94♎51	16 54	99♏34	
1930	17 09	00♏42	13 47	26 28	08♐49	20 55	02♑52	14 44	26 34	08♒26	20 22	02♓24	
1931	21 23	03♓16	15 05	26 53	08♈41	20 34	02♉34	14 46	27 15	10♊04	23 19	07♋03	
1932	22 30	05♋24	18 42	02♌25	16 32	00♍58	15 37	00♎23	15 09	29 48	14♏15	28 27	12♐23
1933	20 08	04♐19	18 32	02♑44	16 52	00♒53	14 44	28 21	11♓43	24 48	07♈35	20♈06	
1934	07♈08	20 39	03♉45	16 48	48 51	10♊58	22 54	04♋44	16 33	28 24	10♌21	22♌28	
1935	11♌32	23 20	05♍09	17 01	28 59	11♎03	23 16	05♏41	18 20	01♐16	14 33	28♐13	
1936	12 33	25 25	08♑43	22 29	06♒43	21 21	06♓19	21 26	06♈33	21 30	06♉09	20 26	04♊17
1937	12♉43	26 51	10♊53	24 47	08♋33	22 12	05♌41	19 01	02♍08	15 02	27 41	10♎06	
1938	27 28	10♎53	23 52	06♏27	18 42	00♐43	12 34	24 22	06♑11	18 06	00♒12	12♒32	
1939	01♒48	13 40	25 35	07♓34	19 39	01♈51	14 10	26 41	09♉24	22 24	05♊43	19♊24	
1940	02♊34	15 33	28 59	12♋56	27 21	12♌12	27 21	12♍36	27 49	12♎48	27 28	11♏43	25♏32
1941	04♏52	19 05	03♐08	16 59	00♑37	14 03	27 16	10♒15	23 01	05♓34	17 54	00♈03	
1942	17 33	00♈40	13 27	25 55	08♉09	20 10	02♊05	13 58	25 53	07♋54	20 07	02♌34	
1943	21 57	03♌48	15 45	27 48	10♍01	22 25	05♎01	17 49	00♏52	14 10	27 43	11♐33	
1944	23 23	06♐26	19 53	03♑47	38 06	02♒49	17 52	03♓05	18 20	03♈26	18 13	02♉36	16♉31
1945	26 56	11♉19	25 23	09♊06	22 29	05♋35	18 25	01♌03	13 31	25 49	07♍59	20♍03	
1946	07♍40	20 39	03♎21	15 47	27 57	09♏56	21 47	03♐36	15 28	27 28	09♑41	22 13	
1947	11♑43	23 39	05♒45	18 02	00♓33	13 16	26 13	09♈20	22 39	06♉07	19 46	03♊36	
1948	14 13	27 16	10♊43	24 35	08♋55	23 40	08♌45	24 01	09♍18	24 22	09♎06	23 23	07♏11
1949	18 39	03♏02	17 02	00♐39	13 56	26 53	09♑35	22 04	04♒22	16 31	28 33	10♓29	
1950	28 19	10♓58	23 22	05♈33	17 33	29 25	11♉13	23 02	04♊58	17 04	29 27	12♋10	
1951	01♋34	13 38	25 52	08♌19	21 01	13♍57	17 09	00♎33	14 10	27 58	11♏55	25♏59	
1952	05♏35	18 51	02♐25	16 25	00♑42	15 18	00♒28	15 04	30 00	14♓46	29 17	13♈27	27♈11
1953	09♈35	24 09	08♉17	21 58	05♊14	18 05	00♋37	12 54	24 58	06♌54	18 45	00♍34	
1954	18 37	01♍02	13 16	25 23	07♎22	19 16	01♏08	13 00	24 58	07♐06	19 28	02♑10	
1955	21 12	03♑15	15 32	28 07	11♒02	24 17	07♓53	21 45	05♈50	20 02	04♉18	18♉32	
1956	27 20	10♉44	24 41	08♊13	22 21	06♋43	21 29	06♌02	20 47	05♍25	19 49	03♎52	17♎29
1957	00♎44	15 18	29 22	12♏57	26 03	08♐56	21 09	03♑18	15 17	27 11	09♒02	20♒53	
1958	09♒21	21 36	03♓41	15 39	27 31	09♈19	21 06	02♉55	14 52	27 00	09♊24	22♊11	
1959	10♊39	22 51	05♋19	18 08	01♌19	14 53	28 46	12♍57	27 18	11♎46	26 15	10♏39	
1960	19 00	02♏38	16 27	00♐28	14 40	29 00	13♑26	27 52	12♒14	26 27	10♓24	24 04	07♈22
1961	21 07	05♈34	19 35	03♉09	16 17	29 01	11♊26	23 35	05♋33	17 25	29 13	11♌03	
1962	29 58	11♌57	23 51	05♍42	17 30	29 20	11♎12	23 09	05♏16	17 34	00♐07	13♐00	
1963	00♐32	12 44	25 14	08♑03	21 17	05♒57	19 01	03♓28	18 11	03♈03	17 55	02♉40	
1964	10♈53	24 52	08♉57	23 03	07♊11	21 17	05♋23	19 25	03♌22	17 12	00♍51	14 16	27♍25
1965	11♍36	26 01	10 01	23 33	06♏37	19 15	01♐33	13 35	25 26	07♑13	19 01	00♒52	
1966	20 21	02♒16	14 08	26 00	07♓53	19 47	01♈45	13 48	25 58	08♉19	20 53	03♊46	
1967	20 13	02♊26	14 58	27 55	11♋19	25 13	09♌35	24 21	09♍22	24 30	09♎34	24♎25	
1968	02♎45	16 58	01♏11	15 23	29 32	13♐36	27 34	11♑25	25 07	08♒39	21 58	05♓02	17♓51
1969	02♓21	16 25	00♈06	13 24	26 18	08♉51	21 06	03♊09	15 04	26 56	08♋50	20♋49	
1970	10♋48	22 40	04♌29	16 18	28 10	10♍06	22 09	04♎20	16 41	29 16	12♏05	25♏12	
1971	10♏26	22 47	05♐26	18 28	01♑55	15 49	00♒10	14 54	29 56	15♓08	00♈19	15♈20	
1972	24 00	08♈37	23 13	07♉42	22 00	06♊04	19 53	03♋26	16 46	29 52	12♌45	25 28	07♍59
1973	22 46	06♍34	20 05	03♎17	16 08	28 40	10♏55	22 56	04♐49	16 38	28 29	10♑26	
1974	00♑51	12 37	24 24	06♒16	18 15	00♓23	12 41	25 09	07♈49	20 40	03♉43	16♉59	
1975	00♉57	13 18	25 56	08♊56	22 21	06♋15	20 38	05♌29	20 39	06♍01	21 22	06♎30	
1976	15 33	00♎29	15 17	29 52	14♏09	28 06	11♐45	25 07	08♑13	21 06	03♒47	16 17	28♒38
1977	13 53	27 22	10♓34	23 28	06♈04	18 22	00♉27	12 22	24 11	06♊00	17 54	29♊59	
1978	20 39	02♋30	14 24	26 24	08♌32	20 50	03♍19	16 00	28 53	11♎58	25 16	08♏46	
1979	21 35	04♏06	16 55	00♐05	13 39	27 38	12♑01	26 46	11♒47	26 55	12♓03	26♓59	
1980	06♓20	21 25	06♈25	21 11	05♉38	19 43	03♊24	16 43	29 42	12♋22	24 48	07♌02	19♌06
1981	04♌52	17 55	00♍46	13 23	25 48	08♎02	20 05	02♏02	13 55	25 47	07♐45	19♐51	
1982	10♐29	22 18	04♑10	16 09	28 20	10♒46	23 28	06♓27	19 43	03♈14	16 58	00♉51	
1983	12 40	25 26	08♉24	21 39	05♊12	19 04	03♋17	17 49	02♌37	17 36	02♍37	17♍30	
1984	27 06	12♍28	27 42	12♎39	27 11	11♏15	24 49	07♐58	20 43	03♑11	15 25	27 29	09♒27
1985	25 55	08♒44	21 22	03♓48	16 04	28 09	10♈05	12 55	03♉42	15 30	27 24	09♊30	
1986	29 52	11♊42	23 38	05♋46	28 09	00♌51	13 52	27 12	10♍50	24 41	08♎42	22♎51	
1987	03♎52	16 48	29 58	13♏22	27 02	10♐59	25 14	09♑43	24 23	09♒08	23 51	08♓23	
1988	18 05	03♓21	18 28	03♈19	17 48	01♉49	15 24	28 33	11♊19	23 46	05♋59	18 00	09♋37
1989	17 13	29 43	12♌02	24 11	06♍13	18 07	29 58	11♎46	23 36	05♏29	17 31	27♏43	
1990	19 32	01♐26	13 26	25 38	08♑04	20 49	03♒56	17 25	01♓16	15 26	29 50	14♈23	
1991	24 55	08♈15	21 47	05♉30	19 23	03♊25	17 34	01♋49	16 08	00♌28	14 46	28♌56	
1992	08♌39	23 49	08♍57	23 51	08♎23	22 28	06♏04	19 11	01♐52	14 11	26 15	08♑08	19♑55
1993	08♑06	20 21	02♒28	14 29	26 26	08♓20	20 12	02♈04	13 57	25 54	07♉58	20♉12	
1994	09♉10	22 00	02♊58	15 09	27 38	10♋32	23 51	07♌39	21 52	06♍27	21 15	06♎09	
1995	16 20	29 59	13♎48	27 43	11♏43	25 46	09♐52	24 00	08♑09	22 15	06♒17	20♒09	
1996	00♒00	15 00	29 54	14♓34	28 51	12♈42	26 06	09♉04	21 40	03♊57	16 01	26 56	09♋48
1997	28 52	11♋04	23 06	05♌01	16 53	28 42	10♍31	22 22	04♎17	16 19	28 30	10♏53	
1998	28 54	10♏49	22 53	05♐12	17 49	00♑50	14 16	28 08	12♒26	27 06	12♓01	27♓03	
1999	07♓06	21 06	05♈16	19 34	03♉54	18 12	02♊26	16 32	00♋30	14 17	27 54	11♌19	
2000	21 22	05♌58	20 29	04♍49	18 54	02♎38	15 59	28 57	11♏34	23 52	05♐55	17 59	29♐38

Moon

March

Year	1st	2nd	3rd	4th	5th	6th	7th	8th	9th	10th	11th	12th	13th	14th	15th	16th
1900	03 ♓ 08	18 30	03 ♈ 46	18 46	03 ♉ 21	17 27	01 ♊ 04	14 13	26 59	09 ♋ 25	21 38	03 ♌ 40	15 37	27 30	09 ♍ 22	21 14
1901	19 ♋ 31	02 ♌ 24	15 06	27 37	09 ♍ 58	22 09	04 ♎ 12	16 07	27 56	09 ♏ 44	21 33	03 ♐ 28	15 34	27 56	10 ♑ 40	23 50
1902	23 ♏ 52	05 ♐ 41	17 31	29 28	11 ♑ 37	24 01	06 ♒ 45	19 49	03 ♓ 14	16 58	00 ♈ 58	15 09	29 27	13 ♉ 47	28 05	12 ♊ 19
1903	27 ♓ 28	10 ♈ 20	23 23	06 ♉ 40	20 09	03 ♊ 53	17 51	02 ♋ 03	16 27	00 ♌ 59	15 35	00 ♍ 08	14 31	28 40	12 ♎ 28	25 55
1904	24 ♌ 08	09 ♍ 21	24 28	09 ♎ 20	23 51	07 ♏ 55	21 33	04 ♐ 44	17 31	29 58	12 ♑ 10	24 10	06 ♒ 02	17 51	20 39	11 ♓ 29
1905	11 ♑ 06	23 44	06 ♒ 08	18 21	00 ♓ 24	12 21	24 12	06 ♈ 01	17 49	29 39	11 ♉ 34	23 37	05 ♊ 51	18 22	01 ♋ 12	14 25
1906	13 ♉ 25	25 18	07 ♊ 11	19 11	01 ♋ 23	13 50	26 36	09 ♌ 47	23 20	07 ♍ 17	21 36	06 ♎ 10	20 54	05 ♏ 39	10 19	04 ♐ 48
1907	18 ♍ 07	01 ♎ 23	14 54	28 36	12 ♏ 28	26 27	10 ♐ 31	24 39	08 ♑ 50	23 01	07 ♒ 11	21 17	05 ♓ 16	19 04	01 ♈ 37	15 53
1907	14 ♒ 54	29 57	14 ♓ 58	29 48	14 ♈ 18	28 22	11 ♉ 58	25 05	07 ♊ 46	10 06	02 ♋ 10	14 03	25 51	07 ♌ 38	19 28	01 ♍ 26
1909	02 ♋ 02	14 26	26 38	08 ♌ 42	20 40	02 ♍ 35	14 28	26 21	08 ♎ 14	20 10	02 ♏ 10	14 17	26 35	09 ♐ 06	21 55	05 ♑ 08
1910	03 ♏ 19	15 07	26 57	08 ♐ 54	21 05	03 ♑ 35	16 27	29 47	13 ♒ 36	27 51	12 ♓ 30	27 24	12 ♈ 25	27 22	12 ♉ 09	26 38
1911	09 ♓ 02	22 38	06 ♈ 28	20 26	04 ♉ 29	18 36	02 ♊ 43	16 51	00 ♋ 57	15 00	28 59	12 ♌ 51	26 34	10 ♍ 04	23 19	06 ♎ 17
1012	06 ♌ 22	21 13	05 ♍ 00	20 33	04 ♎ 46	18 35	01 ♏ 58	14 57	27 33	09 ♐ 52	21 56	03 ♑ 52	15 44	27 36	09 ♒ 33	21 37
1913	22 ♐ 49	05 ♑ 11	17 20	29 20	11 ♒ 13	23 02	04 ♓ 50	16 39	28 32	10 ♈ 30	22 35	04 ♉ 50	17 17	00 ♊ 00	13 01	26 24
1914	23 ♈ 03	04 ♉ 53	16 47	28 49	11 ♊ 10	23 47	06 ♋ 47	20 12	04 ♌ 04	18 22	03 ♍ 04	18 03	03 ♐ 12	18 20	03 19	18 ♑ 01
1915	29 ♌ 24	13 ♍ 18	27 28	11 ♎ 51	26 19	10 ♏ 49	25 14	09 ♐ 31	23 37	07 ♑ 31	21 11	04 ♒ 39	17 54	00 ♓ 56	13 46	26 24
1916	28 ♑ 01	12 ♒ 26	26 46	10 ♓ 57	24 53	08 ♈ 31	21 49	04 ♉ 44	17 20	29 37	11 ♊ 40	23 34	05 ♋ 23	17 13	29 09	11 ♌ 16
1917	13 ♊ 19	25 33	07 ♋ 33	19 24	01 ♌ 11	12 48	24 48	06 ♍ 44	18 48	01 ♎ 01	13 24	25 57	08 ♏ 41	21 38	04 ♐ 48	18 14
1918	13 ♎ 21	25 15	07 ♏ 14	19 21	01 ♐ 40	14 15	27 13	10 ♑ 35	24 27	08 ♒ 48	23 36	08 ♓ 45	25 05	09 ♈ 25	24 32	09 ♉ 18
1919	19 ♒ 46	04 ♓ 04	18 39	03 ♈ 25	18 12	02 ♉ 55	17 25	01 ♊ 40	15 39	29 21	12 ♋ 48	26 01	09 ♌ 02	21 51	04 ♍ 30	16 57
1920	29 ♋ 44	03 ♌ 55	18 00	01 ♍ 55	15 36	28 58	12 ♎ 01	24 43	07 ♏ 07	19 15	01 ♐ 12	13 02	24 51	06 ♑ 44	18 47	01 ♒ 03
1921	03 ♐ 18	15 29	27 29	09 ♑ 23	21 13	03 ♒ 06	15 02	27 06	09 ♓ 18	21 40	04 ♈ 13	16 57	29 52	13 ♉ 00	26 21	09 ♊ 57
1922	03 ♈ 37	15 31	27 33	09 ♉ 45	22 11	04 ♊ 55	18 01	01 ♋ 32	15 30	29 54	14 ♌ 42	29 46	14 ♍ 59	00 ♎ 10	15 11	29 52
1923	10 ♌ 16	24 42	09 ♍ 26	24 22	09 ♎ 22	24 17	09 ♏ 01	23 27	07 ♐ 33	21 17	04 ♑ 40	17 44	00 ♒ 31	13 02	25 21	07 ♓ 31
1924	12 ♑ 05	25 54	09 ♒ 32	22 58	06 ♓ 10	19 09	01 ♈ 53	14 23	26 40	08 ♉ 46	20 43	02 ♊ 37	14 29	26 25	08 ♋ 31	20 50
1925	23 ♉ 08	05 ♊ 21	17 20	29 12	11 ♋ 01	22 52	04 ♌ 49	16 56	29 16	11 ♍ 52	24 43	07 ♎ 50	21 11	04 ♏ 46	18 31	02 ♐ 24
1926	23 ♍ 55	06 ♎ 03	18 21	00 ♏ 48	13 28	26 22	09 ♐ 33	23 03	06 ♑ 55	21 08	05 ♒ 43	20 34	05 ♓ 37	20 43	05 ♈ 41	20 22
1927	00 ♒ 28	15 00	29 57	15 ♓ 09	00 ♈ 26	15 38	00 ♉ 33	15 04	29 09	12 ♊ 46	25 58	08 ♋ 48	21 20	03 ♌ 39	15 47	27 49
1928	03 ♋ 56	17 26	00 ♌ 45	13 54	26 52	09 ♍ 38	22 13	04 ♎ 35	16 45	28 45	10 ♏ 37	22 26	04 ♐ 14	16 07	28 12	10 ♑ 32
1929	12 ♏ 55	25 00	06 ♐ 54	18 43	00 ♑ 32	12 27	24 31	06 ♒ 50	19 26	02 ♓ 19	15 30	28 57	12 ♈ 37	25 28	10 ♉ 27	24 30
1930	14 ♓ 33	26 50	09 ♈ 16	21 52	04 ♉ 39	17 41	00 ♊ 58	14 34	28 29	12 ♋ 44	27 18	12 ♌ 04	26 48	11 ♍ 50	16 32	10 ♐ 57
1931	21 ♋ 15	05 ♌ 54	20 55	06 ♍ 09	21 26	06 ♎ 35	21 28	05 ♏ 58	20 02	03 ♐ 39	16 50	29 40	12 ♑ 10	24 25	06 ♒ 29	18 26
1932	26 ♐ 01	09 ♑ 23	22 28	05 ♒ 20	17 57	00 ♓ 23	12 38	24 43	06 ♈ 40	18 32	00 ♉ 20	12 08	24 00	06 ♊ 00	18 11	00 ♋ 39
1933	02 ♉ 22	14 27	26 23	08 ♊ 16	20 10	02 ♋ 09	14 18	26 42	09 ♌ 23	22 25	05 ♍ 47	19 29	03 ♎ 30	17 44	02 ♏ 08	16 35
1934	04 ♍ 45	17 15	29 59	12 ♎ 56	26 07	09 ♏ 31	23 08	06 ♐ 57	20 57	05 ♑ 07	19 26	03 ♒ 51	18 19	02 ♓ 45	17 04	01 ♈ 10
1935	12 ♑ 18	26 46	11 ♒ 36	26 42	11 ♓ 54	27 04	12 ♈ 01	26 36	10 ♉ 43	24 22	07 ♊ 31	20 15	02 ♋ 38	14 44	26 39	08 ♌ 28
1936	17 ♊ 45	00 ♋ 51	13 39	26 12	08 ♌ 34	20 46	02 ♍ 52	14 52	26 49	08 ♎ 42	20 34	02 ♏ 27	14 23	26 25	08 ♐ 37	21 04
1937	22 ♎ 17	04 ♏ 18	16 10	27 58	09 ♐ 48	21 44	03 ♑ 53	16 20	29 08	12 ♒ 22	26 02	10 ♓ 07	24 32	09 ♈ 11	23 55	08 ♉ 38
1938	25 ♒ 05	07 ♓ 56	21 00	04 ♈ 18	17 48	01 ♉ 26	15 13	29 06	13 ♊ 06	27 11	11 ♋ 22	25 37	09 ♌ 52	24 04	08 ♍ 08	21 59
1939	03 ♋ 30	17 59	02 ♌ 48	17 51	02 ♍ 59	18 01	02 ♎ 48	17 12	01 ♏ 09	14 38	27 40	10 ♐ 18	22 38	04 ♑ 43	16 39	28 31
1940	08 ♐ 57	21 59	04 ♑ 43	17 11	29 26	11 ♒ 31	23 30	05 ♓ 23	17 12	29 01	10 ♈ 49	22 41	04 ♉ 38	16 43	29 02	11 ♊ 36
1941	12 ♈ 02	23 54	05 ♉ 43	17 31	29 24	11 ♊ 27	23 42	06 ♋ 18	19 16	02 ♌ 39	16 28	00 ♍ 41	15 16	00 ♎ 05	15 02	29 58
1942	15 ♌ 17	28 18	11 ♍ 37	25 12	09 ♎ 01	23 02	07 ♏ 11	21 24	05 ♐ 40	19 53	04 ♑ 02	18 06	02 ♒ 01	15 47	29 21	12 ♓ 43
1943	25 ♐ 39	10 ♑ 00	24 33	09 ♒ 13	23 57	08 ♓ 35	23 03	07 ♈ 14	21 04	04 ♉ 30	17 32	00 ♊ 11	12 31	24 36	06 ♋ 31	18 20
1944	29 ♉ 57	12 ♊ 56	25 33	07 ♋ 51	29 54	01 ♌ 29	13 38	25 26	07 ♍ 14	19 06	01 ♎ 02	13 06	25 17	07 ♏ 38	20 10	02 ♐ 56
1945	02 ♎ 01	13 55	25 47	07 ♏ 39	19 35	01 ♐ 39	13 55	26 28	09 ♑ 24	22 45	06 ♒ 36	20 55	05 ♓ 41	20 46	06 ♈ 01	21 15
1946	05 ♒ 06	18 23	02 ♓ 04	16 05	00 ♈ 02	14 49	29 19	13 ♉ 46	28 06	12 ♊ 16	26 15	10 ♋ 03	23 41	07 ♌ 08	20 24	03 ♍ 30
1947	17 ♊ 36	01 ♋ 48	16 08	00 ♌ 36	15 06	29 32	13 ♍ 48	27 47	11 ♎ 26	24 41	07 ♏ 32	20 02	02 ♐ 14	14 13	26 04	07 ♑ 52
1948	20 ♏ 29	03 ♐ 21	15 51	28 04	10 ♑ 05	21 59	03 ♒ 50	15 41	27 34	09 ♓ 32	21 36	03 ♈ 48	16 07	28 36	11 ♉ 16	24 09
1949	22 ♓ 20	04 ♈ 08	15 55	27 45	09 ♉ 40	21 46	04 ♊ 06	16 45	29 48	13 ♋ 18	27 17	11 ♌ 45	26 36	11 ♍ 45	27 02	12 ♎ 16
1950	25 ♋ 16	08 ♌ 46	22 40	06 ♍ 55	21 27	06 ♎ 08	20 52	05 ♏ 32	20 04	04 ♐ 22	18 26	02 ♑ 13	15 44	28 59	11 ♒ 59	24 45
1951	10 ♐ 09	24 22	08 ♑ 37	22 49	06 ♒ 57	20 56	04 ♓ 42	18 15	01 ♈ 30	14 27	27 07	09 ♉ 31	21 41	03 ♊ 41	15 36	27 28
1852	10 ♉ 29	23 23	05 ♊ 55	18 09	00 ♋ 10	12 02	23 51	05 ♌ 40	17 33	29 34	11 ♍ 45	25 07	06 ♎ 42	19 31	02 ♏ 33	15 29
1953	12 ♍ 23	24 13	06 ♎ 07	18 07	00 ♏ 15	12 33	25 04	07 ♐ 51	10 58	04 ♑ 27	18 20	02 ♒ 39	17 20	02 ♓ 21	17 32	02 ♈ 45
1954	15 ♑ 15	28 47	12 ♒ 47	27 14	12 ♓ 02	27 04	12 ♈ 10	27 11	11 ♉ 58	26 24	10 ♊ 26	24 05	07 ♋ 21	20 19	03 ♌ 00	15 29
1955	02 ♊ 43	16 48	00 ♋ 47	14 39	28 24	12 ♌ 01	25 29	08 ♍ 45	21 48	04 ♎ 36	17 09	29 27	11 ♏ 33	23 29	05 ♐ 18	17 07
1956	00 ♏ 41	13 27	25 51	07 ♐ 58	19 53	01 ♑ 42	13 30	25 22	07 ♒ 22	19 34	01 ♓ 59	14 39	27 35	10 ♈ 44	24 05	07 ♉ 36
1957	01 ♓ 46	14 43	26 44	08 ♈ 50	21 04	03 ♉ 27	16 03	28 53	12 ♊ 02	25 33	09 ♋ 28	23 48	08 ♌ 30	23 29	08 ♍ 38	23 46
1958	05 ♋ 25	19 07	03 ♌ 20	17 59	C3 ♍ 00	18 12	03 ♎ 26	18 31	03 ♏ 19	17 45	01 ♐ 46	15 22	28 36	11 ♑ 28	24 04	06 ♒ 26
1959	24 ♏ 57	09 ♐ 05	23 02	06 ♑ 48	20 22	03 ♒ 43	16 52	29 47	12 ♓ 28	24 56	07 ♈ 11	19 15	01 ♉ 11	13 01	24 49	06 ♊ 40
1960	20 ♈ 20	02 ♉ 58	15 19	27 26	09 ♊ 24	21 17	03 ♋ 10	15 08	27 14	09 ♌ 33	22 07	04 ♍ 58	18 05	01 ♎ 30	15 10	29 03
1961	22 ♌ 55	04 ♍ 54	17 01	29 18	11 ♎ 46	24 26	07 ♏ 20	20 29	03 ♐ 54	17 36	01 ♑ 34	15 49	00 ♒ 19	14 58	29 44	14 ♓ 28
1962	26 ♐ 15	09 ♑ 56	24 04	08 ♒ 37	23 32	08 ♓ 41	23 57	09 ♈ 08	24 05	08 ♉ 39	22 47	06 ♊ 26	19 37	02 ♋ 24	14 51	27 01
1963	17 ♉ 10	01 ♊ 23	15 15	28 49	12 ♋ 04	25 03	07 ♌ 49	20 23	02 ♍ 48	15 03	27 11	09 ♎ 13	21 09	03 ♏ 02	14 54	26 47
1964	10 ♎ 17	22 51	05 ♏ 08	17 13	29 07	10 ♐ 56	22 46	04 ♑ 41	16 48	29 10	11 ♒ 52	24 57	08 ♓ 24	22 14	06 ♈ 21	20 41
1965	12 ♒ 53	25 03	07 ♓ 26	20 01	02 ♈ 49	15 29	28 59	12 ♉ 21	25 53	09 ♊ 36	23 32	07 ♋ 39	21 57	06 ♌ 25	20 57	05 ♍ 29
1966	17 ♊ 01	00 ♋ 42	14 50	29 25	14 ♌ 23	29 37	14 ♍ 55	00 ♎ 07	15 02	29 32	13 ♏ 33	27 05	10 ♐ 08	22 48	05 ♑ 09	17 16
1967	08 ♏ 57	23 08	06 ♐ 55	20 22	03 ♑ 29	16 29	28 56	11 ♒ 20	23 35	05 ♓ 41	17 41	29 34	11 ♈ 23	23 10	04 ♉ 58	16 50
1968	00 ♈ 24	12 42	24 47	06 ♉ 43	18 33	00 ♊ 21	12 14	24 14	06 ♋ 29	19 02	01 ♌ 56	15 14	28 56	12 ♍ 59	27 21	11 ♎ 56
1969	02 ♌ 57	15 17	27 50	10 ♍ 37	23 38	06 ♎ 54	20 22	04 ♏ 03	17 53	01 ♐ 53	15 59	00 ♑ 12	14 27	28 43	12 ♒ 56	27 03
1970	08 ♐ 38	22 26	06 ♑ 35	21 04	05 ♒ 49	20 45	05 ♓ 44	20 37	05 ♈ 18	19 39	03 ♉ 36	17 07	00 ♊ 12	12 54	25 16	07 ♋ 23
1971	00 ♉ 03	14 23	28 17	11 ♊ 44	24 47	07 ♋ 28	19 52	02 ♌ 03	14 04	25 58	07 ♍ 48	29 36	01 ♎ 26	13 18	25 14	07 ♏ 17
1972	20 ♍ 20	02 ♎ 31	14 35	26 31	08 ♏ 24	20 16	02 ♐ 11	14 13	26 28	09 ♑ 00	21 53	05 ♒ 12	18 58	03 ♓ 12	17 49	02 ♈ 44
1973	22 ♑ 36	05 ♒ 01	17 45	00 ♓ 49	14 13	27 55	11 ♈ 51	25 57	10 ♉ 09	24 22	08 ♊ 33	22 41	06 ♋ 43	20 41	04 ♌ 32	18 16
1974	00 ♊ 28	14 13	28 14	12 ♋ 31	27 03	11 ♌ 46	26 34	11 ♍ 19	25 53	10 ♎ 08	23 59	07 ♏ 23	20 22	02 ♐ 56	15 11	27 11
1975	21 ♎ 16	05 ♏ 34	19 22	02 ♐ 41	15 35	28 07	10 ♑ 23	22 27	04 ♒ 23	16 16	28 07	09 ♓ 59	21 53	03 ♈ 51	15 53	28 02
1976	10 ♓ 49	22 51	04 ♈ 46	16 37	28 23	10 ♉ 10	22 02	04 ♊ 04	16 20	28 57	11 ♋ 57	25 26	09 ♌ 25	23 53	08 ♍ 43	23 50
1977	12 ♋ 19	24 57	07 ♌ 56	21 18	05 ♍ 00	19 00	03 ♎ 14	17 36	02 ♏ 02	16 27	00 ♐ 47	14 59	29 02	12 ♑ 55	26 37	10 ♒ 06
1978	22 ♏ 28	06 ♐ 23	10 30	04 ♑ 48	19 14	03 ♒ 43	18 11	02 ♓ 31	16 39	00 ♈ 30	14 00	27 09	09 ♉ 57	22 26	04 ♊ 39	16 41
1979	11 ♈ 37	25 51	09 ♉ 38	22 59	04 ♊ 54	18 27	00 ♋ 44	12 47	24 41	06 ♌ 30	18 18	00 ♍ 09	12 04	24 05	06 ♎ 16	18 37
1980	01 ♍ 03	12 55	24 45	06 ♎ 34	18 24	00 ♏ 19	12 20	24 32	06 ♐ 57	19 40	02 ♑ 44	16 13	00 ♒ 09	14 31	29 16	14 ♓ 20
1981	02 ♑ 12	14 51	27 53	11 ♒ 19	25 10	09 ♓ 25	23 59	08 ♈ 45	23 36	08 ♉ 23	22 58	07 ♊ 19	21 20	05 ♋ 03	18 28	01 ♌ 36
1982	14 ♉ 51	28 56	13 ♊ 02	27 10	11 ♋ 18	25 24	09 ♌ 27	23 24	07 ♍ 12	20 47	04 ♎ 06	17 08	29 51	12 ♏ 17	24 28	06 ♐ 26
1983	02 ♎ 07	16 20	00 ♏ 05	13 22	26 12	08 ♐ 39	20 48	02 ♑ 44	14 32	16 19	08 ♒ 08	20 03	02 ♓ 08	14 24	16 51	09 ♈ 31
1984	21 ♒ 21	03 ♓ 13	15 05	26 58	08 ♈ 53	10 52	02 ♉ 58	15 12	27 39	10 ♊ 22	23 26	06 ♋ 54	10 51	05 ♌ 15	20 04	05 ♍ 13
1985	21 ♊ 52	04 ♋ 37	17 48	01 ♌ 28	15 36	00 ♍ 11	15 04	00 ♎ 08	15 12	00 ♏ 08	14 48	29 08	13 ♐ 06	26 42	09 ♑ 59	22 58
1986	07 ♏ 02	21 14	05 ♐ 23	19 30	03 ♑ 33	16 29	01 ♒ 19	14 59	28 27	11 ♓ 41	24 39	07 ♈ 21	19 47	01 ♉ 59	13 59	25 52
1987	22 ♓ 39	06 ♈ 33	10 03	03 ♉ 08	15 51	28 14	10 ♊ 24	22 22	04 ♋ 15	16 07	28 03	10 ♌ 06	22 19	04 ♍ 43	17 22	00 ♎ 14
1988	11 ♌ 44	23 33	05 ♍ 23	17 16	29 14	11 ♎ 19	23 34	06 ♏ 01	18 42	01 ♐ 39	14 55	28 33	12 ♑ 33	26 53	11 ♒ 33	26 27
1989	12 ♐ 15	25 06	08 ♑ 21	22 02	06 ♒ 11	20 44	05 ♓ 38	20 45	05 ♈ 57	21 02	05 ♉ 54	20 24	04 ♊ 30	18 09	01 ♋ 23	14 15
1990	28 ♈ 58	13 ♉ 29	27 51	12 ♊ 01	25 57	09 ♋ 39	23 08	06 ♌ 22	19 24	02 ♍ 15	14 53	27 21	09 ♎ 39	21 47	03 ♏ 47	15 42
1991	12 ♍ 54	26 36	09 ♎ 59	23 01	05 ♏ 42	18 05	00 ♐ 13	12 09	23 59	05 ♑ 48	17 42	29 44	12 ♒ 01	24 35	07 ♓ 27	20 40
1992	01 ♒ 41	13 30	25 25	07 ♓ 27	19 39	02 ♈ 01	14 33	27 17	10 ♉ 12	23 19	06 ♊ 41	20 17	04 ♋ 11	18 22	02 ♌ 50	17 31
1993	02 ♊ 42	15 31	28 44	12 ♋ 24	26 35	11 ♌ 14	26 16	11 ♍ 35	26 57	12 ♎ 12	27 09	11 ♏ 40	25 41	09 ♐ 13	22 18	05 ♑ 00
1994	20 ♎ 59	05 ♏ 39	20 03	04 ♐ 09	17 56	01 ♑ 27	14 42	27 43	10 ♒ 32	23 09	05 ♓ 36	17 53	00 ♈ 01	12 00	23 52	05 ♉ 40
1995	03 ♓ 49	17 12	00 ♈ 16	13 02	25 29	07 ♉ 40	19 40	01 ♊ 31	13 20	25 11	07 ♋ 11	19 23	01 ♌ 51	14 40	27 49	11 ♍ 20
1996	21 ♋ 40	03 ♌ 36	15 39	27 50	10 ♍ 13	22 46	05 ♎ 31	18 27	01 ♏ 36	14 58	28 33	12 ♐ 21	26 23	10 ♑ 37	25 01	09 ♒ 32
1997	23 ♏ 33	06 ♐ 32	19 54	03 ♑ 42	17 54	02 ♒ 31	17 26	02 ♓ 34	17 44	02 ♈ 47	17 35	02 ♉ 00	16 00	29 33	12 ♊ 40	25 24
1998	12 ♈ 04	26 56	11 ♉ 31	25 46	09 ♊ 39	23 09	06 ♋ 17	19 07	01 ♌ 41	14 01	26 11	08 ♍ 13	20 08	01 ♎ 59	13 49	25 38
1999	24 ♌ 31	07 ♍ 31	20 16	02 ♎ 49	15 09	27 18	09 ♏ 18	21 13	03 ♐ 05	15 00	27 01	09 ♑ 14	21 44	04 ♒ 34	17 48	01 ♓ 26
2000	11 ♑ 27	23 22	05 ♒ 26	17 43	00 ♓ 16	13 05	26 11	09 ♈ 33	23 08	06 ♉ 54	20 48	04 ♊ 49	18 54	03 ♋ 02	17 11	01 ♌ 21

	17th	18th	19th	20th	21st	22nd	23rd	24th	25th	26th	27th	28th	29th	30th	31st
1900	03♎09	15 08	27 11	09♏21	21 39	04♐10	16 56	00♑02	13 30	27 23	11♒43	26 27	11♓43	26 42	11♈53
1901	07♒29	12 38	06♓12	21 08	06♈15	21 24	06♉26	21 11	05♊35	19 35	03♋14	16 31	29 28	12♌09	24♌37
1902	26 27	10♋28	24 19	08♌02	21 33	04♍51	17 57	00♎47	13 23	25 45	07♏55	19 54	01♐46	13 36	25♐26
1903	08♏59	21 41	04♐06	16 15	28 14	10♑08	22 00	03♒56	16 00	28 15	10♓43	23 26	06♈24	19 39	03♉07
1904	23 24	05♈25	17 35	29 55	12♉26	25 13	08♊15	21 34	05♋12	19 10	03♌26	18 00	02♍46	17 39	02♎32
1905	28 05	12♌12	26 44	11♍38	26 47	12♎02	27 13	12♏10	26 46	10♐55	24 36	06♑52	40 42	03♒13	15♒27
1906	19 01	02♑56	16 35	29 57	13♒03	25 57	08♓38	21 09	03♈30	15 42	27 46	09♉44	21 37	03♊29	15♊21
1907	28 51	11♉29	23 50	05♊56	17 52	29 42	11♋32	23 26	05♌30	17 49	00♍26	13 25	26 45	10♎25	24♎23
1908	13 32	15 50	08♎19	20 59	03♏51	16 54	00♐08	13 35	27 15	11♑08	25 16	09♒38	24 10	08♓51	23♓30
1909	18 46	02♒53	17 28	02♓26	17 41	03♈01	18 15	03♉11	17 43	01♊47	15 20	28 26	11♋09	23 32	05♌41
1910	10♊48	24 37	08♋07	21 19	04♌15	16 59	29 31	11♍52	24 04	06♎08	18 05	29 57	11♏45	23 33	05♐23
1911	18 57	01♏22	13 32	25 30	07♐22	19 11	01♑03	13 02	25 15	07♒44	20 34	03♓46	17 20	01♈15	15♈27
1912	03♓52	16 18	28 57	11♈59	24 53	08♉11	21 41	05♊23	19 16	03♋19	17 32	01♌51	16 14	00♍37	14♍54
1913	10♋10	24 19	08♌51	23 40	08♍42	23 47	08♎48	23 34	08♏00	22 02	05♐37	18 45	01♑30	13 55	26♑03
1914	02♐21	16 17	29 47	12♑54	25 41	08♒10	20 25	02♓30	14 27	26 19	08♈08	19 56	01♉45	13 38	25♉37
1915	08♈50	21 06	03♉12	15 10	27 03	08♊55	20 49	02♋50	15 03	27 33	10♌24	23 39	07♍21	21 29	05♎59
1916	23 37	06♍15	19 11	02♎26	15 58	29 45	13♏42	27 46	11♐54	26 02	10♑10	24 16	08♒19	22 18	06♓10
1917	01♑56	15 57	00♒17	14 53	29 41	14♓35	29 27	14♈08	28 29	12♉25	25 54	08♊56	21 33	03♋49	15♋51
1918	23 38	07♊27	20 49	03♋45	16 21	28 40	10♌48	22 48	04♍42	16 35	28 28	10♎21	22 17	04♏16	16♏21
1919	29 15	11♎23	23 21	05♏14	17 02	28 49	10♐41	22 41	04♑55	17 29	00♒27	13 52	27 47	12♓09	26♓55
1920	13 37	26 30	09♓44	23 17	07♈07	21 10	05♉21	19 38	03♊55	18 10	02♋20	16 25	00♌23	14 12	27♌52
1921	23 48	07♋54	22 14	06♌45	21 23	06♍01	20 32	04♎51	18 51	02♏30	15 45	28 39	11♐12	23 28	05♑31
1922	14♏09	27 59	11♐23	24 21	06♑57	19 16	01♒21	13 17	25 07	06♓55	19 43	00♈25	12 32	24 36	06♉05
1923	19 32	01♈26	13 17	25 05	06♉54	18 46	00♊44	12 52	25 14	07♋55	20 57	04♌25	18 19	02♍40	17♍24
1924	03♌26	16 24	29 45	13♍30	27 37	12♎02	26 40	11♏22	26 03	10♐36	24 55	08♑59	22 46	06♒17	19♒33
1925	16 25	00♑31	14 42	28 54	13♒08	27 19	11♓25	25 22	09♈05	22 32	05♉40	18 28	00♊58	13 11	25♊11
1926	04♉39	18 28	01♊49	14 42	27 11	09♋22	21 19	03♌09	14 56	26 44	08♍38	20 39	02♎50	15 12	26♎45
1927	09♍46	21 41	03♎34	15 26	27 20	09♏18	21 20	03♐31	15 55	28 35	11♑36	25 03	08♒57	23 20	08♓09
1928	23 13	06♒20	19 54	03♓57	18 24	03♈10	18 06	03♉03	17 53	02♊29	16 47	00♋45	14 24	27 46	10♌51
1929	08♊35	22 42	06♋50	20 56	05♌00	18 59	02♍49	16 29	29 54	13♎02	25 53	08♏26	20 43	02♐47	14♐42
1930	24 59	08♏35	21 46	04♐33	16 59	29 10	11♑09	23 03	04♒54	16 48	28 48	10♓56	23 15	05♈46	18♈29
1931	00♓17	12 05	23 53	05♈44	17 38	29 38	11♉46	24 06	06♊41	19 32	02♋44	16 19	00♌18	14 41	29♌24
1932	13 27	26 40	10♌19	24 25	08♍56	23 47	08♎51	23 59	09♏01	23 51	08♐21	22 27	06♑09	19 27	02♒24
1933	01♐01	15 21	29 33	13♑33	27 21	10♒57	24 20	07♓31	20 30	03♈16	15 50	28 12	10♉23	22 26	04♊21
1934	14 59	28 28	11♉35	24 20	06♊46	18 56	00♋53	12 44	24 33	06♌25	18 26	00♍39	13 07	25 53	08♎58
1935	20 14	02♍03	13 55	25 55	08♎02	20 18	02♏45	15 22	28 10	11♐12	24 29	08♑04	21 56	06♒08	20♒39
1936	03♑50	17 01	00♒39	14 47	29 24	14♓24	29 40	15♈01	00♉14	15 10	29 42	13♊44	27 18	10♋26	23♋11
1937	23 12	07♊34	21 39	05♋30	19 05	02♌26	15 35	28 32	11♍18	23 53	06♎17	18 31	00♏35	12 30	24♏20
1938	05♎32	18 46	01♏39	14 12	26 28	08♐30	20 23	02♑12	14 03	26 01	08♒10	20 34	03♓17	16 19	29♓41
1939	10♒22	22 15	04♓15	16 22	28 37	11♈03	23 39	06♉26	19 26	02♊38	16 06	29 49	13♋49	28 03	12♌32
1940	24 32	07♋51	21 37	05♌50	20 28	05♍26	20 37	05♎50	20 57	05♏38	20 17	04♐20	17 56	01♑05	13♑52
1941	14♏46	29 19	13♐34	27 29	11♑02	24 16	07♒12	19 52	02♓19	14 34	26 40	08♈39	20 32	02♉21	14♉09
1942	25 51	08♈44	21 22	03♉57	15 59	28 00	09♊56	21 48	03♋42	15 43	27 54	10♌22	23 08	06♍17	19♍50
1943	00♌09	12 03	24 04	06♍17	18 43	01♎25	14 22	27 34	10♏59	24 37	08♐25	22 21	06♑24	20 33	04♒47
1944	15 58	29 19	13♑00	27 04	11♒31	26 17	11♓17	26 25	11♈29	26 20	10♉50	24 53	08♊26	21 31	04♋11
1945	06♉17	20 59	05♊15	19 05	02♋28	15 28	28 09	10♌35	22 50	04♍56	16 56	28♎63	10 47	22♏39	04♏32
1946	16 25	29 07	11♎37	23 54	05♏59	17 55	29 45	11♐33	23 23	05♑22	17 34	00♒05	12 59	26 20	10♓09
1947	19 43	01♒43	13 54	26 20	09♓04	22 04	05♈21	18 52	02♉35	16 27	00♊26	14 28	28 34	12♋42	16♋50
1948	07♊17	20 43	04♋29	18 36	03♌03	17 46	02♍40	17 36	02♎26	17 02	01♏16	15 06	28 29	11♐27	24♐02
1949	27 16	11♏57	26 12	10♐02	23 25	06♑25	19 04	01♒27	13 36	25 37	07♓30	19 20	01♈08	12 57	24♈48
1950	07♓18	19 40	01♈51	13 52	25 47	07♉37	29 25	01♊15	13 11	25 16	07♋36	20 14	03♌15	16 42	00♍35
1951	09♋24	21 28	03♌44	16 16	29 06	12♍17	25 48	09♎38	23 43	08♏00	22 23	06♐48	21 10	05♑25	19♑31
1952	29 17	12♐59	26 53	10♑59	25 16	09♒40	24 10	08♓40	23 06	07♈22	21 22	05♉02	18 21	01♊17	13♊52
1953	17 60	02♉36	16 56	00♊48	14 11	27 06	09♋38	21 52	03♌52	15 43	27 31	09♍18	21 08	03♎04	15♎06
1954	27 47	09♍58	22 01	04♎01	15 56	27 49	09♏40	21 34	03♐32	15 39	27 58	10♑35	23 34	06♒59	20♒53
1955	28 59	11♑02	23 20	05♒57	18 58	02♓25	16 17	00♈31	15 01	29 41	14♉22	28 59	13♊24	27 36	11♋34
1956	21 17	05♊05	19 01	03♋04	17 14	01♌29	15 47	00♍04	14 16	28 16	12♎01	25 26	08♏30	21 13	03♐38
1957	08♎42	23 18	07♏29	21 11	04♐25	17 15	29 43	11♑54	23 54	05♒48	17 39	29 30	11♓26	23 28	05♈38
1958	18 37	00♓39	12 35	24 27	06♈15	18 03	29 52	11♉46	23 46	05♊57	18 23	01♋08	14 16	27 50	11♌51
1959	18 38	00♋47	13 13	26 00	09♌10	22 40	06♍47	21 11	05♎52	20 45	00♏40	20 30	05♐00	19 02	09♑36
1960	13♏06	27 16	11♐29	25 43	09♑55	24 02	08♒04	21 57	05♓40	19 11	02♈28	15 31	28 18	10♉50	23♉08
1961	29 04	13♈26	27 27	11♉05	24 19	07♊09	19 38	01♋49	13 48	25 40	07♌28	19 19	01♍15	13 21	25♍40
1962	09♌00	20 52	02♍41	14 28	26 18	08♎12	20 11	02♏17	14 32	26 58	09♐35	22 29	05♑40	19 11	03♒05
1963	08♐47	20 56	03♑21	16 05	29 14	12♒51	26 57	11♓31	26 27	11♈38	26 52	11♉59	26 49	11♊16	25♊18
1964	05♉07	19 33	03♊55	18 09	02♋13	16 07	29 51	13♌26	26 50	10♍04	23 07	05♎58	18 35	00♏59	13♏11
1965	19 54	04♎04	17 55	01♏22	14 25	27 05	09♐26	21 30	03♑24	15 13	27 03	08♒57	21 02	03♓20	15♓54
1966	29 13	11♒05	22 56	04♓48	16 43	28 43	10♈49	23 03	05♉25	17 57	00♊42	13 42	26 58	10♋35	24♋33
1967	28 50	11♊02	23 32	06♋24	19 41	03♌27	17 42	02♍24	17 25	02♎39	17 54	03♏01	17 51	02♐81	16♐19
1968	26 36	11♏16	25 51	10♐15	24 25	08♑20	22 00	05♒24	18 33	01♓28	14 09	26 38	08♈56	21 03	03♉02
1969	10♓59	24 41	08♈07	21 14	04♉04	16 36	28 53	10♊58	22 55	04♋48	16 42	28 41	10♌51	23 14	05♍54
1970	19 19	01♌09	12 57	24 47	06♍44	18 48	01♎03	13 30	26 10	09♏04	22 11	05♐31	19 05	02♑53	16♑54
1971	19 29	01♐52	14 31	27 28	10♑46	24 28	08♒36	23 08	08♓01	23 10	08♈24	23 35	08♉30	23 03	07♊08
1972	17 48	02♉50	17 42	02♊17	16 29	00♋19	13 46	26 53	09♌43	22 19	04♍44	17 00	29 08	11♎11	23♎09
1973	01♍51	15 16	28 28	11♎26	24 08	06♏34	18 46	00♐46	12 38	24 27	06♑17	18 14	00♒24	12 51	25♒41
1974	09♑02	20 49	02♒39	14 34	26 39	08♓57	21 29	04♈15	17 15	00♉28	13 51	27 25	11♊07	24 58	08♋57
1975	10♉19	22 47	05♊28	18 28	01♋48	15 32	29 41	14♌15	29 09	14♍17	29 28	14♎32	29 19	13♏42	27♏38
1976	09♎03	24 11	09♏07	23 42	07♐54	21 42	05♑05	18 08	00♒53	13 22	25 40	07♓47	19 47	01♈40	13♈30
1977	23 23	06♓27	19 17	01♈53	14 16	25 26	08♉27	20 20	02♊09	13 58	25 52	07♋55	20 13	02♌50	15♌49
1978	28 36	10♋29	22 24	04♌26	16 37	29 03	11♍44	24 41	07♎56	21 26	05♏10	19 06	03♐10	17 20	01♑33
1979	01♏09	13 55	26 55	10♐11	23 44	07♑34	21 43	06♒07	20 44	05♓30	20 18	05♈01	19 32	03♉45	17♉36
1980	29 34	14♈48	29 52	14♉37	28 57	12♊49	26 13	09♋11	21 47	04♌05	16 10	28 05	09♍56	21 44	03♎32
1981	14 31	27 12	09♍44	22 05	04♎18	16 24	28 24	10♏18	22 10	04♐02	15 58	28 02	10♑19	22 54	05♒51
1982	18 18	00♑07	11 58	23 59	06♒13	18 44	01♓37	14 52	28 30	12♈26	26 38	20♉58	25 22	09♊44	24♊00
1983	22 22	05♉25	18 39	02♊04	15 41	29 30	13♋32	27 46	12♌13	26 47	11♍23	25 55	10♎15	24 17	07♏57
1984	20 31	05♎48	20 53	05♏35	19 49	03♐34	16 50	29 41	12♑10	24 24	06♒25	18 20	00♓11	12 02	23♓55
1985	05♒43	18 14	00♓36	12 47	24 51	06♈47	18 38	00♉26	12 13	24 02	05♊58	18 03	00♋24	13 05	26♋11
1986	07♊41	19 31	01♋28	13 36	25 59	08♌43	21 48	05♍18	19 10	03♎21	17 48	02♏23	17 01	01♐37	16♐04
1987	13 20	26 40	10♏12	23 55	07♐49	21 52	06♑02	20 17	04♒35	18 53	03♓06	17 10	01♈02	14 38	27♈56
1988	11♓27	26 26	11♈15	25 57	09♉56	23 40	06♊57	19 50	02♋21	14 34	26 35	08♌27	20 15	02♍04	13♍56
1989	26 48	09♌05	21 11	03♍09	15 01	26 51	08♎40	20 30	02♏24	14 23	26 29	08♐46	21 17	04♑04	17♑12
1990	27 34	09♐27	21 25	03♑33	15 56	28 39	11♒45	25 18	09♓18	23 44	08♈29	23 28	08♉29	23 25	08♊06
1991	04♈11	17 58	01♉57	16 04	00♊14	14 25	28 33	12♋39	26 40	10♌37	24 27	08♍10	21 43	05♎05	18♎12
1992	02♍20	17 11	01♎53	16 19	00♏23	14 01	27 12	09♐57	22 20	04♑26	16 21	28 10	09♒58	21 50	03♓50
1993	17 24	29 34	11♒34	23 29	05♓21	17 13	29 05	11♈00	22 59	05♉03	17 14	29 35	12♊09	24 59	08♋09
1994	17 27	29 16	11♊13	23 21	05♋48	18 37	01♌53	15 38	29 52	14♍32	29 31	14♎41	29 51	14♏51	29♏35
1995	25 10	09♎14	23 30	07♏52	22 15	06♐35	20 51	04♑58	18 57	02♒46	16 24	29 50	13♓03	26 02	08♈47
1996	24 04	08♓31	22 48	06♈50	20 32	03♉52	16 51	29 29	11♊50	23 57	05♋55	17 48	29 42	11♌39	23♌45
1997	07♋48	19 57	01♌55	13 46	25 35	07♍23	19 15	01♎12	13 17	25 31	07♏56	20 34	03♐25	16 32	29♐56
1998	07♏30	19 27	01♐33	13 51	26 25	09♑19	22 37	06♒20	20 30	05♓05	20 01	05♈12	20 27	05♉26	20♉30
1999	15 29	29 52	14♈31	29 18	14♉05	28 44	13♊11	27 21	11♋13	24 47	08♌04	21 06	03♍57	16 35	29♍04
2000	15 28	29 32	13♍27	27 12	10♎41	23 54	06♏47	19 22	01♐40	13 44	25 38	07♑28	19 17	01♒13	13♒19

Moon

April

	1st	2nd	3rd	4th	5th	6th	7th	8th	9th	10th	11th	12th	13th	14th	15th	16th
1900	26♈54	11♉34	25 48	09♊33	22 50	05♋42	18 12	00♌25	12 27	24 21	06♍13	18 05	29 59	11♎59	24 05	06♏29
1901	06♍53	19 02	02♎02	12 56	24 46	06♏35	18 23	00♐15	12 12	24 21	06♑44	19 26	02♒31	16 03	00♓02	14 29
1902	07♑23	19 31	01♒55	14 38	27 45	11♓16	25 10	09♈26	23 59	08♉42	23 29	08♊12	22 46	07♋06	21 11	04♌58
1903	16♉49	00♊41	14 42	28 49	13♋01	27 16	11♌28	25 37	09♍41	23 35	07♎18	20 46	03♏57	16 52	29 31	11♐54
1904	17♎16	01♏45	15 53	29 37	12♐55	25 49	08♑21	20 34	02♒35	14 27	26 15	08♓04	19 57	01♈59	14 11	26 36
1905	27♒29	09♓23	21 13	03♈01	14 49	26 40	08♉35	20 36	02♊46	15 06	27 38	10♋27	23 35	07♌05	20 59	05♍17
1906	27♊19	09♋27	21 50	04♌32	17 39	01♍13	15 15	29 44	14♎36	29 42	14♏51	29 55	14♐43	29 11	13♑13	26 51
1907	08♏33	22 51	07♐10	21 28	05♑40	19 46	03♒43	17 33	01♓15	14 48	28 11	11♈23	24 21	07♉06	19 34	01♊50
1908	08♈03	22 21	06♉19	19 52	03♊00	15 44	28 07	10♋13	22 08	03♌57	15 46	27 40	09♍42	21 57	04♎25	17 10
1909	17♌41	29 35	11♍27	23 18	05♎13	17 10	29 13	11♏23	23 39	06♐06	18 45	01♑39	14 52	28 26	12♒23	26 43
1910	17♐21	29 31	11♑59	24 47	08♒02	21 46	05♓58	20 37	05♈36	20 47	05♉59	21 04	05♊51	20 17	04♋18	17 55
1911	29♈52	14♉22	28 54	13♊22	27 42	11♋52	25 49	09♌35	23 07	06♍25	19 29	02♎20	14 58	27 23	09♏36	21 40
1912	29♍02	12♎55	26 31	09♏47	22 43	05♐20	17 41	29 48	11♑46	23 40	05♒34	17 32	29 39	11♓58	24 33	07♈25
1913	08♒02	19 51	01♓39	13 27	25 20	07♈20	19 29	01♉48	14 19	27 03	10♊00	23 13	06♋41	20 24	04♌24	18 38
1914	07♊45	20 05	02♋39	15 33	28 49	12♌31	26 38	11♍11	26 06	11♎16	26 32	11♏44	26 42	11♐17	25 25	09♑03
1915	20♎47	05♏44	20 41	05♐29	20 01	04♑15	18 07	01♒39	14 51	27 48	10♓30	23 01	05♈23	17 35	29 41	11♉41
1916	19♓55	03♈29	16 49	29 54	12♉42	15 13	07♊28	19 30	01♋24	13 13	25 02	06♌58	19 06	01♍31	14 16	27 24
1917	27♋43	09♌31	21 19	03♍13	15 15	27 29	09♎55	22 34	05♏26	18 30	01♐45	15 11	28 47	12♑34	26 31	10♒39
1918	28♏34	10♐58	23 35	06♑31	19 48	03♒30	17 39	02♓14	16 10	02♈21	17 35	02♉43	17 34	02♊00	15 59	29 28
1919	11♈56	27 04	12♉08	26 59	11♊32	25 43	09♋31	22 58	06♌05	18 55	01♍30	13 53	26 06	08♎11	20 09	02♏01
1920	11♍19	24 34	07♎34	20 19	02♏49	15 05	27 10	09♐05	20 56	02♑46	14 39	26 41	08♒57	21 31	04♓26	17 45
1921	17♑27	29 20	11♒14	23 13	05♓21	17 41	00♈15	13 04	26 09	09♉27	23 00	06♊45	20 40	04♋42	18 52	03♌05
1922	19♉14	01♊52	14 45	27 54	11♋23	25 12	09♌21	23 48	08♍31	23 24	08♎20	23 11	07♏50	22 09	06♐06	29 36
1923	02♎27	17 40	02♏54	17 57	02♐42	17 03	00♑48	14 25	27 26	10♒06	22 28	04♓37	16 35	28 27	10♈16	22 04
1924	01♓35	15 24	28 02	10♈30	22 48	04♉57	16 59	28 54	10♊46	22 38	04♋32	16 35	28 50	11♌23	24 18	07♍39
1925	07♋03	18 52	00♌44	12 42	24 53	07♍21	20 08	03♎17	16 45	00♏33	14 34	28 46	13♐02	27 18	11♑32	25 40
1926	10♏29	23 24	06♐31	29 50	03♑22	17 09	01♒10	15 27	29 58	14♓38	29 22	14♈02	28 30	12♉40	26 26	09♊46
1927	23♓18	08♈38	23 56	09♉01	23 45	08♊01	21 48	05♋06	17 59	00♌31	12 47	24 51	06♍48	18 41	00♎33	12 26
1928	23♌42	06♍22	18 50	01♎08	13 17	25 18	07♏12	19 02	00♐49	12 38	24 32	06♑36	18 54	01♒33	14 35	28 06
1929	26♐32	08♑22	20 18	02♒23	14 44	27 24	10♓24	23 46	07♈30	21 32	05♉48	20 13	04♊42	10 10	03♋32	17 47
1930	01♉25	14 34	27 55	11♊29	25 16	09♋14	23 23	07♌40	22 04	06♍30	20 54	05♎10	19 13	02♏59	16 27	29 33
1931	14♍23	29 29	14♎34	29 29	14♏06	28 20	12♐07	25 28	08♑24	20 57	03♒13	15 15	27 08	08♓57	20 44	02♈34
1932	15♒02	27 25	09♓35	21 37	03♈31	15 22	27 11	09♉00	20 51	02♊46	14 49	27 02	09♋28	22 13	05♌18	18 48
1933	16♊13	28 06	10♋03	22 10	04♌31	17 12	00♍15	13 44	27 38	11♎57	26 36	11♏27	26 22	11♐12	25 51	10♑12
1934	22♎19	05♏56	19 45	03♐44	17 48	01♑55	16 03	00♒10	14 16	28 19	12♓18	26 11	09♈53	23 23	06♉38	19 35
1935	05♓25	20 20	05♈16	20 05	04♉38	18 47	02♊29	15 43	28 32	10♋57	23 05	05♌01	16 50	28 38	10♍29	22 26
1936	05♌39	17 52	29 56	11♍54	23 48	05♎41	17 34	29 28	11♏24	23 26	05♐33	17 50	00♑20	13 06	26 12	09♒43
1937	06♐07	17 56	29 52	11♑59	24 23	07♒09	20 22	04♓03	18 12	02♈47	17 40	02♉44	17 48	02♊44	17 25	01♋45
1938	13♈21	27 15	11♉20	25 31	09♊46	24 00	08♋12	22 20	06♌23	20 19	04♍05	17 42	01♎05	14 15	27 10	09♏48
1939	27♌09	11♍51	26 29	10♎57	25 08	08♏59	22 27	05♐31	18 14	00♑38	12 47	24 46	06♒39	18 32	00♓28	12 31
1940	26♑18	08♒30	20 30	02♓23	14 11	25 59	07♈48	19 42	01♉41	13 49	26 06	08♊36	21 20	04♋20	17 39	01♌18
1941	25♉59	07♊54	19 57	02♋12	14 43	27 35	10♌51	24 32	08♍41	23 15	08♎11	23 19	08♏33	23 41	08♐34	23 06
1942	03♎44	17 59	02♏29	17 07	01♐47	16 22	00♑47	14 58	28 53	12♒33	25 57	09♓08	22 06	04♈52	17 27	29 51
1943	19♒02	03♓18	17 30	01♈35	15 28	29 05	23♉24	25 23	08♊02	20 23	02♋29	14 24	26 14	08♌03	19 58	02♍02
1944	16♋30	28 33	10♌26	22 14	04♍01	15 52	27 49	09♎54	22 09	04♏35	17 11	29 59	12♐58	26 09	09♑34	23 13
1945	16♏27	28 26	10♐32	22 48	05♑19	18 10	01♒25	15 07	29 18	13♓56	28 58	14♈14	29 35	14♉47	29 41	14♊09
1946	24♓24	08♈59	24 49	08♉44	23 36	08♊17	22 42	06♋49	20 37	04♌07	17 21	00♍21	13 08	25 44	08♎08	20 23
1947	10♌58	25 02	08♍00	22 48	06♎23	19 42	02♏43	15 26	27 51	10♐01	22 01	03♑53	15 42	27 35	09♒35	21 49
1948	06♑20	18 25	00♒20	12 12	24 04	06♓01	18 04	00♈16	12 39	25 14	08♉02	21 02	04♊15	17 40	01♋19	15 11
1949	06♉44	18 47	01♊00	13 26	26 09	09♋10	22 35	06♌23	20 36	05♍11	20 05	05♎10	20 18	05♏20	20 06	04♐32
1950	14♍54	29 35	14♎32	29 38	14♏42	29 37	14♐16	28 33	12♑26	25 55	09♒02	21 49	04♓20	16 37	28 44	10♈43
1951	03♒27	27 10	00♓42	14 02	27 09	10♈04	22 46	05♉14	17 32	29 40	11♊39	23 02	05♋24	17 19	09 21	11♌35
1952	26♊09	08♋11	10 04	01♌53	13 43	25 39	07♍45	10 05	02♎41	15 35	28 46	12♏13	25 53	09♐45	23 45	07♑29
1953	27♎17	09♏37	22 07	04♐48	17 42	00♑50	14 16	28 00	12♒04	26 28	11♓09	26 03	11♈03	25 59	10♉42	25 03
1954	05♓17	20 08	05♈18	20 27	05♉51	20 58	04♊40	19 55	03♋42	17 02	29 57	12♌33	24 54	07♍03	19 04	01♎01
1955	25♋17	08♌47	22 04	05♍09	18 03	00♎46	13 17	25 37	07♏46	19 46	01♐38	13 26	25 14	07♑06	19 07	01♒23
1956	15♐26	27 43	09♑33	21 23	03♒17	15 20	27 36	10♓10	23 01	06♈12	19 41	03♉26	17 23	01♊28	15 39	29 51
1957	17♈57	00♉26	13 05	25 56	09♊01	22 20	05♋54	19 46	03♌55	18 19	02♍55	17 39	02♎22	16 58	01♏20	15 23
1958	26♌19	11♍09	26 16	11♎30	26 41	11♏40	26 20	10♐35	24 23	07♑44	20 42	03♒17	15 36	27 41	09♓37	21 27
1959	17♑19	00♒43	13 49	26 38	09♓13	21 35	03♈46	15 49	27 46	09♉37	21 26	03♊15	15 07	27 05	09♋14	21 37
1960	05♊16	17 14	29 07	11♋00	22 57	05♌03	17 22	29 59	12♍56	26 16	09♎59	24 02	08♏23	22 55	07♐32	22 08
1961	08♎12	21 00	04♏02	17 19	00♐48	14 29	28 20	12♑19	26 26	10♒38	24 55	09♓14	23 31	07♈43	21 45	05♉33
1962	17♒23	02♓02	16 58	02♈05	17 14	02♉13	16 54	01♊10	14 57	28 15	11♋07	23 35	05♌45	17 42	29 32	11♍19
1963	08♋53	22 04	04♌54	17 28	29 49	12♍01	24 05	06♎04	18 00	29 53	11♏45	23 39	05♐34	17 36	29 46	12♑09
1964	25♏12	07♐04	18 53	00♑41	12 35	24 41	07♒02	19 45	02♓53	16 29	00♈30	14 55	29 37	14♉28	29 19	14♊03
1965	28♓45	11♈52	25 14	08♉28	22 33	06♊26	20 24	04♋27	18 34	02♌43	16 53	01♍02	15 07	29 03	12♎48	26 17
1966	08♌42	23 30	08♍23	23 21	08♎17	23 02	07♏29	21 31	05♐06	18 16	01♑02	13 28	25 38	07♒38	19 31	01♓22
1967	29♐54	13♑05	25 54	08♒25	20 41	02♓46	14 43	26 35	08♈23	20 11	02♉00	13 53	25 51	07♊58	20 17	02♋51
1968	14♉54	26 43	08♊32	20 24	02♋25	14 37	27 06	09♌57	23 11	06♍41	20 58	05♎28	20 18	05♏19	20 23	05♐22
1969	18♍54	02♎13	15 51	29 57	13♏56	28 14	12♐36	26 58	11♑16	25 26	09♒28	23 19	06♓59	20 28	03♈43	16 47
1970	01♒06	15 29	29 59	14♓33	29 04	13♈28	27 39	11♉30	25 01	08♊08	20 53	03♋18	15 27	27 24	09♌14	21 03
1971	20♊44	03♋52	16 34	28 56	11♌02	22 57	04♍47	16 34	28 23	10♎15	22 13	04♏19	16 33	28 56	11♐30	24 16
1972	05♏03	16 55	28 47	10♐42	22 44	04♑56	17 24	00♒12	13 25	27 06	11♓17	25 56	10♈58	26 13	11♉32	26 42
1973	08♓54	22 33	06♈35	20 56	05♉29	20 08	04♊44	19 13	03♋30	17 34	01♌25	15 02	28 27	11♍41	24 43	07♎33
1974	23♋05	04♌19	21 39	06♍01	20 19	04♎28	18 24	02♏00	15 16	28 10	10♐43	22 59	05♑01	16 54	28 44	10♒35
1975	11♐05	24 06	06♑43	29 02	01♒08	13 04	24 56	06♓47	18 40	00♈38	12 43	24 56	07♉17	19 49	02♊32	15 28
1976	25♈18	07♉06	18 56	00♊52	12 57	25 16	07♋51	20 48	04♌10	17 59	02♍15	16 56	01♎57	17 09	02♏23	17 29
1977	29♌12	13♍01	27 13	11♎44	26 30	11♏22	26 13	10♐56	25 26	09♑38	23 31	07♒05	20 20	03♓19	16 02	28 31
1978	15♑46	29 57	14♒04	28 04	11♓55	25 35	09♈01	22 14	05♉10	17 51	00♊17	12 30	24 32	06♋28	18 20	00♌15
1979	01♊02	14 03	26 41	09♋01	21 05	02♌59	14 48	26 37	08♍29	20 30	02♎41	15 05	27 44	10♏37	23 44	07♐05
1980	15♎24	27 20	09♏21	21 31	03♐50	16 20	29 05	12♑07	25 28	09♒12	23 20	07♓50	22 41	07♈46	22 57	08♉03
1981	19♒15	03♓07	17 28	02♈14	17 17	02♉30	17 39	02♊36	17 13	01♋26	15 12	28 34	11♌35	24 17	06♍46	19 03
1982	08♋09	22 08	05♌58	29 40	03♍12	16 34	29 46	12♎45	25 31	08♏03	20 21	02♐27	14 23	26 13	08♑01	19 52
1983	21♏13	04♐04	16 33	28 45	10♑43	22 34	04♒23	16 15	28 14	10♓25	22 50	05♈31	18 28	01♉40	15 06	25 43
1984	05♈52	17 54	00♉02	12 18	24 44	07♊21	20 11	03♋19	16 46	00♌34	14 45	29 17	14♍05	29 04	14♎05	28 58
1985	09♌44	23 46	08♍16	23 09	08♎18	23 33	08♏44	23 41	08♐18	22 31	06♑18	19 39	02♒39	15 18	27 42	09♓53
1986	00♑21	14 23	28 11	11♒44	25 03	08♓06	20 56	03♈33	15 58	28 11	10♉14	22 10	04♊01	15 50	27 40	09♋37
1987	10♉56	23 37	06♊02	18 13	00♋13	12 08	24 01	05♌57	18 01	00♍17	12 48	25 36	08♎45	22 12	05♏57	29 57
1988	25♍56	08♎04	20 24	02♏56	15 41	28 39	11♐51	25 17	08♑57	22 52	06♒59	21 19	05♓49	20 24	05♈00	19 31
1989	00♒43	14 39	29 01	13♓46	28 50	14♈04	29 18	14♉21	29 05	13♊23	27 12	10♋32	23 26	05♌57	18 10	00♍10
1990	22♊28	06♋28	20 06	03♌23	16 22	29 07	11♍38	24 00	06♎14	18 20	00♏21	12 17	24 10	06♐02	17 55	29 53
1991	01♏03	13 38	25 57	08♐03	19 59	01♑48	13 37	25 30	07♒34	19 52	02♓30	15 32	28 58	12♈47	26 57	11♉22
1992	16♓00	28 24	11♈02	23 53	06♉56	20 12	03♊38	17 13	00♋59	14 53	28 58	13♌11	27 31	11♍55	26 19	10♎36
1993	21♋42	05♌40	20 04	04♍52	19 56	05♎08	20 18	05♏14	19 50	03♐59	17 39	00♑52	13 40	26 07	08♒18	20 19
1994	13♐57	27 55	11♑30	24 43	07♒37	20 15	02♓39	14 52	26 56	08♈53	20 45	02♉34	14 21	26 09	08♊02	20 01
1995	21♈17	03♉34	15 40	27 37	09♊28	21 17	03♋08	15 07	27 18	09♌45	22 33	06♍44	19 20	03♎20	17 42	02♏19
1996	06♍03	18 35	01♎23	14 27	27 47	11♏22	25 09	09♐07	23 13	07♑23	21 37	05♒50	20 00	04♓06	18 04	01♈53
1997	13♑38	27 39	11♒57	26 31	11♓15	26 06	10♈54	25 34	09♉58	24 00	07♊38	20 51	03♋40	16 08	28 19	10♌17
1998	05♊01	19 06	02♋42	15 52	28 38	11♌05	23 16	05♍16	17 09	28 59	10♎47	22 37	04♏30	16 28	28 33	10♐46
1999	11♎23	23 33	05♏36	17 34	29 27	11♐18	23 12	05♑11	17 22	29 47	12♒33	25 44	09♓23	23 31	08♈05	23 00
2000	25♒42	08♓24	21 27	04♈52	18 38	02♉40	16 53	01♊13	15 33	29 51	14♋02	28 06	12♌02	25 49	09♍29	22 59

	17th	18th	19th	20th	21st	22nd	23rd	24th	25th	26th	27th	28th	29th	30th
1900	18 42	01♐14	13 58	26 56	10♑09	23 39	07♒28	21 37	06♓03	20 44	05♈34	20 25	05♉09	19♉39
1901	29 19	14♈25	29 39	14♉50	29 49	14♊28	28 43	12♋32	25 55	08♌55	21 33	03♍55	16 05	28♍04
1902	18 27	01♍40	14 37	27 20	09♎50	22 09	04♏18	16 19	28 13	10♐04	21 53	03♑45	15 42	27♑49
1903	24 04	06♑05	17 59	29 53	11♒49	23 53	06♓10	18 42	01♈34	14 46	28 20	12♉13	26 22	10♊42
1904	09♉14	22 06	05♊12	18 32	02♋04	15 48	29 44	13♌51	28 06	12♍29	26 56	11♎24	25 46	09♏59
1905	19 59	04♎59	20 10	05♏23	20 27	06♐12	19 32	03♑23	16 44	29 39	12♒09	24 22	06♓21	18♓12
1906	10♒06	23 02	05♓41	18 07	00♈23	12 31	24 33	06♉30	18 24	00♊16	12 07	24 01	05♋59	18♋06
1907	13 53	25 47	07♋36	19 24	01♌17	13 21	25 40	08♍20	21 24	04♎55	18 50	03♏08	16 43	02♐26
1908	00♏09	13 22	26 48	10♐23	24 08	08♑01	22 00	06♒05	20 16	04♓30	18 46	02♈59	17 05	01♉00
1909	11♓23	26 20	11♈24	26 27	11♉18	25 49	09♊55	23 35	06♋47	19 35	02♌03	14 14	26 15	08♍09
1910	01♌08	14 00	26 36	08♍57	21 06	03♎08	15 03	26 34	08♏42	20 31	02♐22	14 17	26 21	08♑36
1911	03♐35	15 26	27 15	09♑07	21 07	03♒18	15 45	28 33	11♓44	15 12	09♈22	23 47	08♉29	23♉22
1912	10 35	04♉03	17 47	01♊44	15 51	00♋04	14 20	28 36	12♌48	26 54	10♍53	24 43	08♎22	21♎49
1913	03♍06	17 43	02♎27	17 07	01♏40	15 59	29 59	13♐35	27 48	09♑37	22 05	04♒16	16 14	28♒05
1914	22 14	04♒59	17 25	29 34	11♓31	23 22	05♈10	16 57	28 47	10♉41	22 42	04♊50	17 06	29♊34
1915	23 36	05♊27	17 19	29 12	11♋12	23 22	05♌47	18 33	01♍44	15 23	29 32	14♎08	29 07	14♏20
1916	10♎56	24 50	09♏02	23 26	07♐56	22 26	06♑51	21 07	05♒11	19 05	02♓48	16 19	29 41	12♈51
1917	24 57	09♓23	23 52	08♈19	22 38	06♉42	20 27	03♊49	16 48	29 25	11♋43	23 47	05♌41	17♌30
1918	12♋31	25 11	07♌31	19 39	01♍36	13 29	25 22	07♎14	19 10	01♏12	13 20	25 37	08♐03	20♐39
1919	13 51	25 38	07♐28	19 22	01♑24	13 39	26 12	09♒06	22 26	06♓13	20 28	05♈08	20 08	05♉20
1920	01♈27	15 32	29 55	14♉32	29 14	13♊57	28 34	13♋00	27 11	11♌07	24 45	08♍08	21 14	04♎06
1921	17 20	01♍34	15 44	29 46	13♎37	27 15	10♏37	23 42	06♐30	19 01	01♑17	13 22	25 20	07♒13
1922	02♑41	15 22	27 44	09♒50	21 45	03♓35	15 22	27 13	09♈10	21 15	03♉32	16 02	28 45	11♊43
1923	03♉53	15 46	27 43	09♊48	22 01	04♋27	17 07	00♌05	13 25	27 08	11♍16	25 49	10♎42	25♎51
1924	21 28	05♎44	20 25	05♏24	20 31	05♐36	20 30	05♑06	19 19	03♒08	16 34	29 39	12♓27	25♓00
1925	09♒43	23 38	07♓26	21 07	04♈38	17 58	01♉05	13 58	26 36	08♊59	21 08	03♋06	14 57	26♋45
1926	22 42	05♋14	17 27	29 27	11♌18	23 07	04♍57	16 55	29 03	11♎24	23 59	06♏49	19 53	03♐10
1927	24 21	06♏20	18 25	00♐36	12 57	25 28	08♑13	21 16	04♒40	18 26	02♓37	17 11	02♈03	17♈07
1928	24♓21	06 20	18♈25	00 36	12♉57	25 28	08♊14	21 16	04♋40	18 26	02♌37	17 11	02♍03	17♍07
1929	12♌05	26 32	11 22	26♍28	11 39	26♎47	11 42	26♏17	10 28	24 16	07♐40	20 42	03♑26	15♑55
1930	12♐20	24 49	07♑03	19 05	01♒00	12 53	24 49	06♓50	19 03	01♈29	14 11	27 11	10♉28	24♉02
1931	24 30	26 32	08♉45	21 08	03♊44	16 33	29 36	12♋56	26 31	10♌24	24 32	08♍56	23 31	08♎14
1932	02♍44	17 06	01♎52	16 57	02♏12	17 27	02♐32	17 17	01♑37	15 29	28 52	11♒49	24 23	06♓39
1933	24 14	07♒55	21 18	04♓23	17 14	29 53	12♈20	24 39	06♉50	18 53	00♊51	12 44	24 35	06♋27
1934	02♊15	14 38	26 47	08♋44	20 34	02♌23	14 15	26 17	08♍33	21 08	04♎04	17 23	01♏05	15♏07
1935	04♎34	16 52	29 23	12♏07	25 03	08♐10	21 28	04♑57	18 37	02♒29	16 33	00♓48	15 13	29♓44
1936	23 41	08♓05	22 53	08♈00	23 15	08♉28	23 28	08♊07	22 18	06♋01	19 15	02♌06	14 34	26♌48
1937	15 43	29 23	12♌37	25 36	08♍19	20 49	03♎09	15 18	27 20	09♏16	21 06	02♐55	14 42	26♐33
1938	22 12	04♐23	16 23	28 16	10♑06	21 57	03♒55	16 04	28 29	11♓14	24 21	07♈51	21 44	05♉57
1939	24 44	07♈10	19 50	02♉44	15 54	29 17	12♊53	26 41	10♋39	24 44	08♌56	23 12	07♍28	21♍43
1940	15 19	29 39	14♍17	29 08	14♎06	29 02	13♏49	28 20	12♐28	26 11	09♑28	22 20	04♒50	17♒03
1941	07♑12	20 52	04♒05	16 55	29 26	11♓41	23 44	05♈40	17 31	29 19	11♉08	22 59	04♊53	16♊53
1942	12♉06	24 12	06♊10	18 04	29 55	11♋48	23 46	05♌55	18 19	01♍03	14 12	27 47	11♎51	26♎20
1943	14 21	26 58	09♎55	23 12	06♏48	20 41	04♐45	18 56	03♑10	17 24	01♒34	15 39	29 39	13♓33
1944	07♒08	21 19	05♓46	20 25	05♈11	19 56	04♉34	18 55	02♊54	16 27	29 34	12♋16	24 38	06♌43
1945	28 09	11♋40	24 44	07♌26	29 49	01♍59	14 00	25 55	07♎47	19 39	01♏33	13 30	25 30	07♐37
1946	02♏29	14 27	26 18	08♐06	19 54	01♑45	13 43	25 54	08♒23	21 14	04♓32	18 18	02♈33	17♈13
1947	04♓19	17 08	00♈19	13 51	27 42	11♉49	26 08	10♊32	24 58	09♋22	23 39	07♌48	21 47	05♍35
1948	29 15	13♌30	27 53	12♍21	26 50	11♎13	25 25	09♏22	23 01	06♐19	19 16	01♑54	14 14	26♑22
1949	18 32	02♑05	15 12	27 55	10♒19	22 27	04♓24	16 14	28 02	09♈50	21 42	03♉40	15 46	28♉02
1950	22 36	04♉26	16 15	28 04	09♊57	21 55	04♋03	16 22	28 58	11♌53	25 11	08♍55	23 06	07♎42
1951	24 05	06♍57	20 13	03♎55	18 01	02♏29	17 13	02♐04	16 55	01♑38	16 06	00♒16	14 07	27♒39
1952	21 55	06♒03	20 12	04♓18	18 23	02♈22	16 12	29 52	13♉17	26 24	09♊14	21 45	04♋01	16♋03
1953	08♊58	22 26	05♋26	18 01	00♌17	12 18	24 10	05♍57	17 46	29 40	11♎42	23 54	06♏18	18♏53
1954	12 55	24 47	06♏40	18 35	00♐33	12 36	24 47	07♑09	19 46	02♒42	16 02	29 48	14♓01	28♓40
1955	13 58	26 58	10♓26	24 22	08♈46	23 29	08♉27	23 30	08♊28	23 14	07♋43	21 50	05♌37	19♌03
1956	14♋04	28 14	12♌20	26 21	10♍15	23 59	07♎32	20 52	03♏56	16 44	29 16	11♐34	23 39	06♑35
1957	29 02	12♐18	25 11	07♑44	19 59	02♒03	13 59	25 51	07♓45	19 44	01♈51	14 10	26 41	09♉26
1958	03♈15	15 03	26 54	08♉49	20 51	03♊02	15 24	28 00	10♋51	24 01	07♌30	21 21	05♍34	20♍06
1959	04 19	17♌23	00 53	14♍49	29 12	13 58	29♎01	14 12	29♏23	14 23	29♐04	13 22	27♑13	10♒38
1960	06 36	20♑53	04 56	18♒44	02 17	15♓36	28 42	11 37	24♈19	06 50	19♉11	01 22	13♊25	25♊21
1961	19 03	02♊13	15 02	27 31	09♋44	21 44	03♌35	15 24	27 15	09♍14	21 26	03♎53	16 39	29♎45
1962	23 08	05♎01	17 01	29 10	11♏29	23 59	06♐39	19 30	02♑33	15 50	29 21	13♒09	27 13	11♓35
1963	24 50	07♒54	21 23	05♓21	19 48	04♈41	19 53	05♉13	20 29	05♊32	20 12	04♋25	18 08	01♌24
1964	28 34	12♋48	26 45	10♌24	23 47	06♍55	19 51	02♎34	15 05	27 26	09♏38	21 40	03♐35	15♐24
1965	09♏29	22 22	04♐56	17 14	29 18	11♑13	23 04	04♒55	16 51	28 58	11♓19	23 59	06♈59	20♈19
1966	13 16	25 15	07♈22	19 38	02♉05	14 44	27 36	10♊40	23 57	07♋28	21 12	05♌10	19 21	03♍42
1967	15 43	28 56	12♌34	26 36	11♍03	25 50	10♎52	26 01	11♏07	26 03	10♐39	24 51	08♑36	21♑55
1968	20 07	04♑33	18 37	02♒17	15 35	28 32	11♓11	23 36	05♈49	17 52	29 49	11♉41	23 31	05♊20
1969	29 37	12♉14	24 39	06♊52	18 55	00♋51	12 44	24 37	06♌34	18 42	01♍04	13 45	26 49	10♎18
1970	02♍55	14 55	27 07	09♎34	22 18	06♏19	18 36	02♐08	15 51	29 44	13♑44	27 49	11♒56	26♒05
1971	07♑16	20 33	04♒08	18 03	02♓19	16 55	01♈47	15 47	01♉48	16 39	01♊13	15 21	29 02	12♋14
1972	11♊33	26 00	09♋59	23 31	06♌37	19 23	01♍51	14 06	26 12	08♎12	20 07	02♏01	13 53	25♏46
1973	20 12	02♏39	14 54	16 59	08♐55	20 45	02♑33	14 22	26 18	08♒27	20 53	03♓41	16 56	00♈38
1974	22 33	04♓43	17 07	29 49	12♈49	26 07	09♉42	23 30	07♊29	21 34	05♋44	19 55	04♌06	18♌15
1975	28 38	12♋05	25 48	09♌50	24 08	08♍42	23 25	08♎12	22 55	07♏26	21 40	05♐32	19 01	02♑05
1976	02♐18	16 44	00♑44	14 18	27 26	10♒11	22 38	04♓49	16 50	28 43	10♈32	22 19	04♉08	16♉00
1977	10♈50	22 58	04♉58	16 52	28 43	10♊31	22 22	04♋16	16 20	28 36	11♌09	24 02	07♍20	21♍04
1978	12 16	24 28	06♍55	19 42	02♎50	16 20	00♏12	14 23	28 47	13♐20	27 54	12♑24	26 46	10♒55
1979	20 39	04♑23	18 17	02♒20	16 30	00♓47	15 08	29 30	13♈48	27 59	11♉56	25 37	08♊58	21♊58
1980	22 54	07♊23	21 23	04♋54	17 47	00♌35	12 53	24 56	06♍49	18 37	00♎25	12 16	24 12	06♏16
1981	01♎12	13 14	26 12	07♏07	19 00	00♐52	12 46	24 43	06♑48	19 05	01♒37	14 29	27 47	11♓32
1982	01♒52	14 05	26 38	09♓34	22 56	06♈44	20 57	05♉30	20 15	05♊04	19 49	04♋24	18 45	02♌59
1983	12♊29	26 23	10♋22	24 27	08♌35	22 47	06♍59	21 09	05♎13	19 07	02♏47	16 09	29 13	11♐57
1984	13♏35	27 50	11♐38	25 00	07♑57	20 32	02♒49	14 53	26 49	08♓41	20 33	02♈28	14 30	26♈40
1985	21 54	03♈49	15 39	27 27	09♉14	21 04	02♊59	15 01	27 13	09♋38	22 20	05♌23	18 50	02♍41
1986	21 43	04♌04	16 44	29♍47	13 15	27♎09	11 28	26♏08	11 03	26 04	11♐05	25 55	10♑29	24♑42
1987	04♐08	18 26	02♑47	17 06	01♒20	15 26	29 24	13♓12	26 49	10♈13	23 26	06♉25	19 10	01♊42
1988	03♉51	17 54	01♊36	14 55	27 51	10♋25	22 41	04♌42	16 35	28 24	10♍13	22 09	04♎15	16♎33
1989	12 03	23 51	05♎39	17 29	29 24	11♏25	23 33	07♐00	18 17	00♑56	13 48	26 55	10♒21	24♒07
1990	11♑59	24 19	06♒57	19 58	03♓27	17 24	01♈51	16 43	01♉53	17 10	02♊24	17 24	02♋01	16♋12
1991	25 56	10♊31	26 01	09♋23	23 32	07♌29	21 14	04♍47	18 08	01♎18	14 17	27 04	09♏39	22♏01
1992	24 42	08♏30	21 57	05♐03	17 46	00♑10	12 18	24 15	06♒06	17 56	29 50	11♓54	24 10	06♈43
1993	02♓12	14 03	25 55	07♈50	19 50	01♉58	14 13	26 38	09♊14	22 01	05♋03	18 20	01♌55	15♌48
1994	02♋13	14 39	27 26	10♌36	24 13	08♍17	22 48	07♎41	22 50	08♏04	23 14	08♐11	22 48	04♑00
1995	17 07	01♐56	16 42	01♑16	15 36	29 38	13♒22	26 47	09♓54	22 46	05♈24	17 49	00♉03	12♉09
1996	15 29	28 51	11♉57	24 47	07♊21	19 41	01♋48	13 47	25 50	07♌34	19 31	01♍37	13 57	26♍33
1997	22 08	03♍56	15 46	27 42	09♎47	22 03	04♏33	17 17	00♐15	13 27	26 52	10♑29	24 18	08♒16
1998	23 09	05♑46	18 39	01♒50	15 24	29 21	13♓43	28 27	13♈28	28 38	13♉49	28 49	13♊29	27♊42
1999	08♉08	23 18	08♊20	23 05	07♋28	21 26	04♌59	18 10	01♍02	13 38	26 01	08♎16	20 22	02♏24
2000	06♎29	29 27	02♏21	15 02	27 28	09♐40	21 41	03♑34	15 22	27 11	09♒06	21 12	03♓36	16♓20

Moon

May

	1st	2nd	3rd	4th	5th	6th	7th	8th	9th	10th	11th	12th	13th	14th	15th	16th
1900	03♊48	17 33	00♋53	13 48	26 23	08♌40	20 44	02♍41	14 33	26 26	08♎24	20 29	02♏43	15 09	27 48	24♐39
1901	09♎57	21 46	03♏35	15 24	27 17	09♐16	21 22	03♑40	16 10	28 56	12♒02	25 29	09♓19	23 32	08♈06	24 25
1902	10♒11	22 51	05♓53	19 20	03♈14	17 33	02♉14	17 12	02♊18	17 23	02♋19	16 57	01♌14	15 06	28 34	11♍39
1903	25♊10	09♋37	24 01	08♌17	22 22	06♍16	19 57	03♎26	16 42	29 46	12♏38	25 17	07♐45	20 01	02♑08	23 57
1904	23♏56	07♐34	20 51	03♑45	16 18	28 34	10♒35	22 29	04♓18	16 08	28 04	10♈12	22 31	05♉12	18 09	24♊41
1905	29♓58	11♈46	23 37	05♉33	17 37	29 49	12♊11	24 43	07♋27	20 23	03♌33	17 01	00♍47	14 52	29 17	13♎58
1906	00♌27	13 05	26 06	09♍34	23 31	07♎57	22 49	08♏01	23 21	08♐39	23 42	08♑24	22 38	06♒24	19 42	02♓36
1907	17♐11	01♑50	16 18	00♒31	14 29	28 12	11♓40	24 54	07♈56	20 47	08♉25	15 52	28 08	10♊14	22 11	04♋02
1908	14♉38	27 58	10♊57	23 36	05♋57	18 03	29 59	11♌50	23 41	05♍36	17 41	30 00	12♎36	25 31	08♏45	24 43
1909	20♍01	01♎54	13 51	25 55	08♏07	20 29	03♐01	15 45	28 41	11♑50	25 14	08♒53	22 48	06♓59	21 23	05♈57
1910	21♑05	03♒54	17 04	00♓40	14 42	29 09	13♈58	29 01	14♉12	29 20	14♊17	28 54	13♋07	26 53	10♌14	23 10
1911	08♊19	23 11	07♋51	22 15	06♌19	20 02	03♍25	16 28	29 15	11♎47	24 .07	06♏16	18 18	00♐14	12 05	23 55
1912	05♏03	18 02	00♐47	13 18	25 36	07♑42	19 40	01♒34	13 27	25 25	07♓31	19 51	02♈29	15 28	28 50	12♉35
1913	09♓53	21 44	03♈41	15 48	18 08	10♉44	23 35	06♊41	20 01	03♋34	17 18	01♌11	15 11	29 19	13♍31	27 47
1914	12♋14	25 09	08♌21	21 54	05♍50	20 08	04♎47	19 44	04♏50	19 57	04♐55	19 34	03♑48	17 34	00♒50	13 39
1915	29♏37	14♐45	29 36	14♑03	28 04	11♒38	24 48	07♓27	20 09	02♈28	14 38	26 40	08♉38	20 32	02♊24	14 16
1916	25♈49	08♉35	21 08	03♊29	15 37	27 35	09♋26	21 13	03♌02	14 57	27 04	09♍28	22 13	05♎25	19 04	03♏09
1917	29♌21	11♍18	23 25	05♎46	18 23	01♏17	14 27	27 54	11♐33	25 22	09♑19	23 22	07♒29	21 38	05♓48	19 57
1918	03♑28	16 32	29 53	13♒33	27 34	11♓54	26 30	11♈20	26 14	11♉04	25 44	10♊04	24 01	07♋33	20 40	03♌25
1919	20♉33	05♊38	20 26	04♋52	18 52	02♌27	15 37	28 25	10♍55	23 11	05♎15	17 11	29 02	10♏51	22 39	04♐30
1920	16♎44	29 10	11♏25	23 31	05♐29	17 21	29 11	11♑01	22 56	04♒58	17 12	29 43	12♓35	25 50	09♈31	23 39
1921	19♒07	01♓07	13 17	25 41	08♈23	21 24	04♉45	18 27	02♊26	17 39	01♋01	15 26	29 50	14♌09	28 19	12♍20
1922	24♊53	08♋18	21 55	05♌44	19 46	03♍58	18 20	02♎48	17 19	01♏48	16 09	00♐16	14 06	27 34	10♑39	23 22
1923	11♏05	26 15	11♐10	25 42	09♑47	23 21	06♒27	19 08	01♓28	13 33	25 28	07♈17	19 03	00♉52	12 45	24 44
1924	07♈23	19 36	01♉42	13 42	25 38	07♊31	19 22	01♋14	13 09	25 11	07♌25	19 54	02♍44	16 00	29 44	13♎57
1925	08♌35	20 34	02♍45	15 15	28 07	11♎25	25 08	09♏14	23 39	08♐16	22 58	07♑37	22 08	06♒27	20 32	04♓22
1926	16♐38	00♑16	14 02	27 57	11♒59	26 08	10♓23	24 41	08♈59	23 12	07♉16	21 05	04♊36	17 46	00♋35	13 05
1927	02♉13	17 12	01♊54	16 13	00♋05	13 30	26 29	09♌05	21 24	03♍29	15 26	27 18	09♎10	21 05	03♏05	15 12
1928	28♍11	10♎17	22 15	04♏08	15 58	27 46	09♐35	21 28	03♑26	15 34	27 56	10♒35	23 35	06♓59	20 50	05♈06
1929	28♑21	10♒26	22 45	05♓23	18 23	01♈47	15 36	29 49	14♉22	29 09	14♊03	28 56	13♋40	28 11	12♌23	26 16
1930	07♊50	21 50	05♋58	20 11	04♌26	18 40	02♍51	16 55	00♎52	14 39	28 15	11♏38	24 47	07♐42	20 20	02♑45
1931	23♎00	07♏40	22 09	06♐19	20 08	03♑32	16 32	29 10	11♒28	23 32	05♓25	17 14	29 02	10♈56	22 57	05♉10
1932	18♓42	00♈36	12 26	24 13	06♉02	17 53	29 50	11♊53	24 04	06♋25	18 57	01♌44	14 47	28 11	11♍56	26 05
1933	18♋23	00♌27	12 45	25 21	08♍20	21 46	05♎42	20 06	04♏55	20 01	05♐16	20 27	05♑25	20 02	04♒14	18 00
1934	29♏23	13♐48	28 16	12♑41	26 59	11♒08	25 07	08♓57	22 36	06♈05	19 23	02♉30	15 25	28 06	10♊34	22 48
1935	14♈16	28 43	12♉57	26 54	10♊28	23 39	06♋26	18 52	01♌03	13 01	24 52	06♍41	18 35	00♎36	12 50	25 18
1936	08♍50	20 45	02♎37	14 29	26 23	08♏21	20 25	02♐36	14 55	27 24	10♑05	23 00	06♒12	19 43	03♓34	17 47
1937	08♑31	20 39	03♒03	15 47	28 55	12♓30	26 33	11♈02	25 54	11♉02	26 15	11♊23	26 19	10♋55	25 06	08♌52
1938	20♉25	05♊03	19 43	04♋21	18 51	03♌08	17 11	00♍59	14 30	27 46	10♎47	23 33	06♏07	18 29	00♐40	12 43
1939	05♎52	19 52	03♏39	17 12	00♐27	13 24	26 04	08♑28	20 38	02♒39	14 34	26 27	08♓24	20 28	02♈44	15 17
1940	29♒03	10♓54	22 42	04♈30	16 23	28 23	10♉33	22 55	05♊30	18 18	01♋20	14 36	28 05	11♌48	25 44	09♍52
1941	29♊01	11♋20	23 52	06♌41	19 50	03♍22	17 20	01♎42	16 28	01♏33	16 47	02♐01	17 04	01♑47	16 04	29 52
1942	11♏10	26 12	11♐17	26 15	10♑58	25 20	09♒20	22 56	06♓11	19 08	01♈50	14 19	26 38	08♉49	20 53	02♊52
1943	27♓21	10♈59	24 28	07♉45	20 47	03♊34	16 05	28 21	10♋24	22 18	04♌07	15 55	27 49	09♍54	22 15	04♎57
1944	18♌38	00♍27	12 17	24 10	06♎13	18 26	00♏53	13 35	26 30	09♐38	22 58	06♑28	20 08	03♒57	17 55	02♓01
1945	19♐51	02♑15	14 52	27 46	10♒59	24 35	08♓26	23 01	07♈46	22 48	07♉57	23 01	07♊53	22 24	06♋29	20 06
1946	02♉11	16 20	02♊29	14 29	16♋29	02 12	16♌34	00 32	14 06	27♍19	10 12	22♎48	05 11	17 23	29♏26	11 22
1947	19♍10	02♎33	15 42	28 37	11♏18	23 46	06♐01	18 06	00♑02	11 54	23 44	05♒37	17 37	29 49	12♓18	25 07
1948	08♒20	20 13	02♓07	14 05	26 11	08♈30	21 03	03♉53	16 59	00♊22	14 01	27 53	11♋55	26 04	10♌17	24 31
1949	10♊30	23 11	06♋06	19 16	02♌43	16 27	00♍28	14 49	29 19	14♎02	28 50	13♏36	28 13	12♐35	26 35	10♑12
1950	22♎40	07♏51	23 07	08♐18	23 13	07♑44	21 48	05♒24	18 32	01♓17	13 41	25 51	07♈49	19 41	01♉29	13 18
1951	10♓54	23 53	06♈40	19 15	01♉40	13 56	26 04	08♊05	20 00	01♋52	13 43	25 36	07♌35	19 47	02♍14	15 02
1952	17♋56	09♌45	21 35	03♍31	15 40	28 05	10♎50	23 58	07♏28	21 18	05♐25	19 43	04♑07	18 31	02♒50	17 03
1953	01♐41	14 40	27 50	11♑12	24 45	08♒30	22 29	06♓40	21 03	05♈34	20 10	04♉43	19 07	03♊15	17 01	00♋24
1954	13♈41	28 55	14♉11	29 19	14♊08	28 32	12♋27	25 54	08♌55	21 33	03♍54	16 01	27 59	09♎53	21 44	03♏37
1955	02♍12	15 03	27 41	10♎07	22 23	04♏30	16 29	28 22	10♐11	21 59	03♑47	15 41	27 44	10♒00	22 34	05♓30
1956	17♑27	29 17	11♒11	23 15	05♓32	18 07	01♈03	14 21	28 02	12♉04	26 23	10♊54	25 31	10♋08	24 40	09♌03
1957	22♉26	05♊40	19 07	02♋47	16 38	00♌39	14 48	29 03	13♍21	27 39	11♎54	26 02	09♏58	23 41	07♐07	20 14
1958	04♎53	19 51	04♏51	19 45	04♐25	18 45	02♑40	16 09	29 12	11♒52	24 13	06♓18	18 12	00♈01	11 49	23 38
1959	23♒39	06♓18	18 41	00♈51	12 51	24 45	06♉35	18 23	00♊13	12 05	24 01	06♋04	18 17	00♌42	13 22	26 21
1960	07♋13	19 05	01♌00	13 04	25 20	07♍54	20 51	04♎13	18 04	02♏20	17 00	01♐55	16 58	01♑58	16 46	01♒17
1961	13♏10	26 52	10♐48	24 53	09♑04	23 15	07♒26	21 34	05♓38	19 37	03♈30	17 16	00♉53	14 19	27 31	10♊27
1962	26♓11	10♈58	25 48	10♉32	25 04	09♊15	23 01	06♋21	19 14	01♌45	13 58	25 57	07♍48	19 37	01♎28	13 25
1963	14♌16	26 48	09♍04	21 10	03♎08	15 02	16 54	08♏46	20 41	02♐38	14 41	26 49	09♑07	21 37	02♒21	17 24
1964	27♌12	09 00	20 54	02♍59	15 19	28♎00	11 05	24♏38	08 40	23 08	07♐59	23 02	08♑11	23 14	08 04	22♒34
1965	03♉59	17 56	02♊17	16 26	00♋49	15 11	29 31	13♌43	27 48	11♍42	25 26	08♎57	22 16	05♏20	18 10	00♐46
1966	18♍11	02♎43	17 12	01♏33	15 41	29 30	13♐00	26 08	08♑55	21 23	03♒37	15 39	27 34	09♓27	21 22	03♈24
1967	04♒49	17 21	29 36	11♓38	23 31	05♈20	17 07	28 56	10♉50	22 51	05♊01	17 22	29 54	12♋41	25 42	09♌00
1968	17♊10	29 05	11♋08	23 20	05♌48	18 33	01♍41	15 13	29 12	13♎38	28 27	13♏33	28 48	14♐02	29 04	13♑46
1969	24♎12	08♏29	23 03	07♐49	22 39	07♑23	21 57	06♒15	20 14	03♓56	17 19	00♈28	13 22	26 05	08♉37	20 59
1970	10♓15	24 23	08♈28	22 27	08♉15	19 50	03♊08	16 08	28 48	11♋11	23 20	05♌16	17 07	28 55	10♍48	22 51
1971	25♋00	07♌25	19 32	01♍27	13 17	25 05	06♎55	18 53	00♏59	13 16	25 44	08♐23	21 15	04♑17	17 31	00 56
1972	07♐42	19 41	01♑47	14 02	26 31	09♒18	22 26	06♓00	20 02	04♈31	19 24	04♉34	19 52	05♊05	20 03	04♋39
1973	14♈48	29 22	14♉13	29 12	14♊11	29 01	13♋37	27 53	11♌49	25 25	08♍42	21 43	04♎29	17 02	29 24	11♏37
1974	02♍20	16 20	00♎12	13 53	27 22	10♏36	23 34	06♐15	18 41	00♑53	12 53	24 47	08♒37	18 30	00♓28	12 37
1975	14♑47	27 10	09♒19	21 18	03♓11	15 03	26 59	09♈01	21 13	03♉36	16 13	29 04	12♊08	25 27	08♋58	22 42
1976	27♉57	10♊03	22 18	04♋45	17 28	00♌28	13 48	27 29	11♍32	25 57	10♎40	25 36	10♏37	25 37	10♐26	24 56
1977	05♎15	19 50	04♏46	19 53	05♐04	20 09	04♑58	19 26	03♒28	17 05	00♓17	13 07	25 38	07♈54	19 59	01♉57
1978	24♒50	08♓32	22 00	05♈15	18 17	01♉08	13 47	26 15	08♊32	20 39	02♋39	14 33	26 24	08♌17	20 16	02♍26
1979	04♋36	16 57	29 02	10♌57	22 46	04♍36	16 30	28 35	10♎54	23 30	06♏25	19 39	03♐11	16 57	00♑55	15 01
1980	18♏29	00♐51	13 24	26 08	09♑03	22 11	05♒35	19 14	03♓12	17 27	01♈59	16 45	01♉37	16 28	01♊08	15 31
1981	25♓47	10♈29	25 34	10♉51	26 11	11♊20	26 11	10♋35	24 31	07♌59	21 02	03♍43	16 06	18 17	10♎19	22 16
1982	16♌37	00♍08	13 25	26 29	09♎20	21 59	04♏27	16 44	28 52	10♐50	22 42	04♑30	16 18	28 09	10♒08	22 20
1983	24♐23	06♑34	18 33	00♒25	12 15	24 09	06♓10	18 24	00♈55	13 44	26 53	10♉22	24 09	08♊11	22 23	06♋41
1984	09♉01	21 32	04♊15	17 10	00♋19	13 41	27 18	11♌09	25 14	09♍32	24 00	08♎34	23 08	07♏36	21 53	05♐54
1985	16♍58	01♎38	16 35	01♏43	16 53	01♐55	16 41	01♑04	15 02	28 33	11♒38	24 20	06♓42	18 50	00♈57	12 37
1986	08♒33	22 02	05♓09	16 58	00♈31	12 50	24 59	07♉00	18 55	00♊46	12 36	24 25	06♋18	18 16	00♌23	12 43
1987	14♊02	26 10	08♋09	20 03	01♌56	13 51	25 53	08♍08	20 40	03♎32	16 48	00♏29	14 34	28 59	13♐38	28 24
1988	29♎08	11♏58	25 05	08♐27	22 03	05♑49	19 43	03♒44	17 50	01♓59	16 10	00♈22	14 32	28 37	23♉34	26 19
1989	08♓15	22 44	07♈31	22 31	07♉35	22 34	07♊18	21 39	05♋33	18 58	01♌57	14 29	26 44	08♍44	20 36	02♎24
1990	29♋55	13♌13	26 08	08♍45	21 07	03♎18	15 22	27 20	09♏15	21 08	03♐00	14 54	26 50	08♑51	21 01	03♒22
1991	04♐11	16 12	28 04	09♑53	21 41	03♒33	15 35	27 53	10♓31	23 33	07♈02	20 59	05♉22	20 04	04♊58	19 55
1992	19♈33	02♉40	16 05	29 44	13♊35	27 34	11♋39	25 48	09♌58	24 08	08♍17	22 22	06♎21	20 11	03♏49	17 13
1993	00♍00	14 29	29 11	13♎59	28 48	13♏28	27 53	11♐57	25 37	08♑53	21 45	04♒17	16 32	18 35	10♓30	22 23
1994	20♑45	04♒05	17 00	29 36	11♓54	24 00	05♈57	17 58	29 35	11♉23	23 12	05♊06	17 07	29 16	11♋36	24 10
1995	24♉07	05♊59	17 49	29 38	11♋30	23 29	05♌39	18 03	00♍47	13 53	27 25	11♎23	25 48	10♏34	15 36	10♐45
1996	09♎30	22 48	06♏28	20 28	04♐44	19 10	03♑42	18 12	02♒36	16 51	00♓53	14 42	28 19	11♈42	24 53	07♉52
1997	22♒23	06♓39	21 00	05♈25	19 49	04♉07	18 14	02♊06	15 38	28 48	11♋37	24 06	06♌18	18 17	00♍08	11 57
1998	11♋27	24 42	07♌31	19 48	02♍07	14 05	25 55	07♎43	19 31	01♏25	13 24	25 31	07♐47	20 13	02♑50	15 37
1999	14♏21	26 14	08♐06	19 39	01♑54	13 54	26 04	08♒28	21 10	04♓16	17 49	01♈51	16 22	01♉18	16 31	01♊50
2000	28♓00	13♈11	28 21	13♉20	18 00	12♊18	26 10	09♋36	22 39	05♌21	17 46	29♍57	11 58	23♎51	03 41	17 29

	1st	2nd	3rd	4th	5th	6th	7th	8th	9th	10th	11th	12th	13th	14th	15th	16th
1900	23 45	07♑03	20 34	04♒18	18 14	02♓21	16 37	00♈59	15 24	29 48	14♉05	28 11	12♊03	25 36	08♋49	
1901	07♉59	23 03	08♊01	22 44	07♋06	21 04	04♌35	17 40	00♍22	12 44	24 51	06♎48	18 38	00♏26	12♏15	
1902	24 24	06♎53	19 09	01♏14	13 12	25 05	06♐55	18 45	00♑36	12 31	24 32	06♒42	19 04	01♓41	14♓38	
1903	26 00	07♒53	19 48	01♓50	14 05	26 37	09♈31	22 48	06♉32	20 41	05♊12	19 59	04♋52	19 44	04♌27	
1904	14 54	28 39	12♋33	26 35	10♌40	24 48	08♍56	23 04	07♎10	21 12	05♏08	18 56	02♐33	15 54	28♐59	
1905	28 52	13♏50	28 43	13♐23	27 42	11♑34	24 59	07♒57	20 31	02♓45	14 45	26 37	08♈25	20 15	02♉09	
1906	15 11	27 30	09♈38	21 39	03♉34	15 27	27 18	09♊11	21 05	03♋03	15 07	27 19	09♌43	22 22	05♍22	
1907	15 48	27 36	09♌28	21 31	03♍49	16 27	29 30	13♎01	27 00	11♏26	26 13	11♐13	26 18	11♑18	26♑05	
1908	06♐07	20 08	04♑18	18 33	02♒50	17 05	01♓17	15 24	29 23	13♈14	26 54	10♉22	23 35	06♊34	19♊17	
1909	20 36	05♉14	19 44	04♊00	17 57	01 32	14♋44	27 35	10♌05	22 20	04♍23	16 19	28 12	10♎06	22♎07	
1910	05♍45	18 02	00♎07	12 02	23 53	05♏41	17 30	29 22	11♐20	23 25	05♑40	18 06	00♒46	13 42	26♒55	
1911	05♑45	17 39	29 40	11♒51	24 16	07♓00	20 05	03♈36	17 33	01♉57	16 43	01♊46	16 58	02♋08	17♋07	
1912	26 42	11♊06	25 41	10♋21	24 58	09♌27	23 44	07♍46	21 32	05♎03	18 19	01♏23	14 14	26 55	09♐24	
1913	12♎03	26 18	10♏28	24 27	08♐12	21 39	04♑46	17 32	00♒00	12 11	24 10	06♓01	17 50	29 42	11♈42	
1914	26 06	08♓15	20 11	02♈01	13 48	25 37	07♉31	19 33	01♊44	14 04	20 36	09♋18	22 11	05♌17	18♌36	
1915	26 08	08♋04	20 06	02♌17	14 42	27 26	10♍31	24 04	08♎05	22 34	07♏29	22 41	08♐02	23 18	08♑19	
1916	17 37	02♐23	17 16	02♑10	16 56	01♒28	15 43	29 40	13♓19	26 40	09♈46	22 39	05♉18	17 46	00♊03	
1917	04♈04	18 05	01♉56	15 35	28 58	12♊04	24 51	07♋21	19 36	01♌39	13 33	25 23	07♍15	19 13	01♎22	
1918	15 49	27 59	09♍59	21 53	03♎45	15 40	27 40	09♏49	22 08	04♐39	17 22	00♑18	13 27	26 50	10♒26	
1919	16 25	28 26	10♑37	22 59	05♒37	18 33	01♓49	15 29	29 32	13♈58	28 44	13♉43	28 49	13♊52	28♊44	
1920	08♉10	23 00	08♊01	23 06	08♋05	22 51	07♌17	21 20	04♍58	18 14	01♎09	13 47	26 09	08♏20	20♏23	
1921	26 08	09♎46	23 10	06♏23	19 23	02♐11	14 46	27 09	09♑21	21 24	03♒20	15 13	27 06	09♓04	21♓13	
1922	05♒46	17 54	29 50	11♓40	23 29	05♈21	17 23	29 37	12♉06	24 52	07♊57	21 17	04♋52	18 39	02♌35	
1923	06♊51	19 07	01♋32	14 08	26 57	09♌59	23 17	06♍54	20 51	05♎09	19 45	04♏37	19 37	04♐36	19♐25	
1924	28 39	13♏43	29 00	14♐20	29 30	14♑21	28 47	12♒44	26 14	09♓20	22 03	04♈30	16 44	28 48	10♉47	
1925	17 58	01♈21	14 31	27 29	10♉16	22 50	05♊13	17 25	29 26	11♋20	23 08	04♌55	16 45	28 42	10♍52	
1926	25 18	07♌19	19 12	01♍02	12 55	24 55	07♎07	19 34	02♏19	15 22	28 45	12♐23	26 17	10♑19	24♑29	
1927	27 27	09♐52	22 28	05♑16	18 16	01♒31	15 02	28 50	12♓53	27 13	11♈45	26 25	11♉08	25 45	10♊10	
1928	19 45	04♉45	19 55	05♊06	20 08	04♋55	19 19	03♌18	16 50	29 56	12♍41	25 06	07♎17	19 16	01♏09	
1929	09♍49	23 02	05♎58	18 38	01♏05	13 21	25 28	07♐27	19 21	01♑12	13 02	24 54	06♒50	18 56	01♓14	
1930	14 57	26 59	08♒54	20 47	02♓42	14 44	26 57	09♈25	22 13	06♉24	18 57	02♊52	17 06	01♋34	16♋09	
1931	17 37	00♊18	13 15	26 26	09♋50	23 27	07♌13	21 09	05♍13	19 24	03♎40	17 59	02♏19	16 35	00♐42	
1932	10♎36	25 28	10♏33	26 43	10♐48	25 37	10♑04	24 02	07♒31	20 32	03♓08	16 25	27 27	09♈19	21♈07	
1933	01♓20	14 19	27 00	09♈26	21 41	03♉48	15 49	27 45	09♊39	21 30	03♋22	15 15	27 13	09♌19	21♌36	
1934	04♋51	16 45	28 34	10♌22	22 13	04♍14	16 30	29 05	12♎04	25 30	09♏23	23 40	08♐16	23 04	07♑56	
1935	08♏03	21 04	04♐20	17 50	01♑32	15 22	29 20	13♒23	27 31	11♓41	25 53	10♈03	24 10	08♉09	21♉57	
1936	02♈18	17 05	02♉00	16 56	01♊43	16 14	00♋24	14 08	27 27	10♌22	22 55	05♍11	17 15	29 11	11♎04	
1937	22 13	05♍12	17 50	00♎13	12 23	24 23	06♏17	18 07	29 55	11♐44	23 36	05♑33	17 38	29 53	12♒23	
1938	24 38	06♑29	18 19	00♒11	12 09	24 17	06♓40	19 22	02♈26	15 55	29 50	14♉10	28 51	13♊47	28♊50	
1939	28 07	11♉17	24 48	08♊36	22 40	06♋55	21 17	05♌40	20 00	04♍14	18 20	02♎15	16 00	29 34	12♏55	
1940	24 11	08♎39	23 12	07♏46	22 14	06♐31	20 32	04♑11	17 28	00♒22	12 54	25 09	07♓10	19 02	00♈50	
1941	13♒10	26 02	08♓31	20 43	02♈42	14 33	26 21	08♉09	19 59	01♊55	13 57	25 07	08♋26	20 55	03♌35	
1942	14 46	26 38	08♋29	20 22	02♌20	14 27	26 48	09♍28	22 31	06♎03	20 04	04♏34	19 29	04♐41	20♐00	
1943	18 02	01♏32	15 26	29 40	14♐10	28 47	13♑25	27 58	12♒21	26 31	10♓28	24 12	07♈42	21 01	04♉07	
1944	16 22	29♈17	11 58	24 26	06♉42	18 49	00♊48	12 40	24♋31	06 22	18♌17	00 22	12 41	25♍17	08♍14	
1945	03♌17	16 03	28 30	10♍41	22 41	04♎36	16 28	28 20	10♏17	22 19	04♐29	16 47	29 16	11♑55	24♑48	
1946	05♐02	16 50	28 40	10♑34	22 37	04♒52	17 22	00♓11	13 24	27 03	11♈09	25 39	10♉31	25 38	10♊49	
1947	08♈20	21 57	05♉58	20 21	05♊00	19 49	04♋40	19 27	04♌03	18 23	02♍25	16 07	29 30	12♎35	25♎25	
1948	08♍44	22 53	06♎56	20 51	04♏36	18 08	01 27	14♐30	27 18	09♑50	22 09	04♒16	16 14	28 08	10♓01	
1949	23 23	06♒11	18 37	00♓47	12 44	24 35	06♈22	18 13	00♉09	12 15	24 34	07♊07	19 54	02♋56	16♋11	
1950	25 07	07♊01	18 59	01♋06	13 20	25 46	08♌24	21 19	04♍32	18 07	02♎06	16 29	01♏14	16 16	01♐27	
1951	28 16	11♎58	26 09	10♏47	25 45	10♐56	26 09	11♑12	25 57	10♒19	24 16	07♓48	20 57	03♈46	16♈20	
1952	01♓07	15 02	28 48	12♈24	25 51	09♉06	22 09	04♊59	17 35	29 57	12♋06	24 04	05♌55	17 43	29♌32	
1953	13 23	25 59	08♌16	20 19	02♍13	14 03	25 54	07♎51	19 58	02♏19	14 54	27 46	10♐52	24 13	07♑46	
1954	15 33	27 33	09♐39	21 52	04♑14	16 48	29 34	12♒37	25 58	09♓40	23 43	08♈08	22 50	07♉45	22♉44	
1955	18 53	02♈43	17 02	01♉44	16 45	01♊56	17 07	02♋09	16 53	01♌15	15 13	28 45	11♍53	24 41	07♎12	
1956	23 12	07♍08	20 48	04♎12	17 22	00♏18	13 00	25 29	07♐47	19 55	01♑54	13 47	25 38	07♒29	19♒23	
1957	03♑04	15 35	27 52	09♒57	21 54	03♓48	15 42	27 42	09♈52	22 16	04♉56	17 56	01♊14	14 52	28♊47	
1958	05♉34	17 38	29 53	12♊20	24 59	07♋53	20 59	04♌20	17 55	01♍45	15 47	00♎03	14 29	29 03	13♏40	
1959	09♍43	23 29	07♎41	22 18	07♏16	22 28	07♐44	22 53	07♑47	22 16	06♒16	19 47	02♓51	15 30	27♈49	
1960	15 26	29 13	12♓38	25 44	08♈34	21 11	03♉36	15 53	28 02	10♊04	22 01	03♋54	15 45	27 36	09♌31	
1961	23 06	05♋30	17 40	29 38	11♌28	23 17	05♍08	17 07	29 20	11♎51	24 45	08♏02	21 44	05♐47	20♐08	
1962	25 33	07♏52	20 25	03♐11	16 11	29 22	12♑45	26 17	10♒00	23 53	07♓55	22 06	06♈25	20 49	05♉14	
1963	00♓50	14 40	28 55	13♈34	28 31	13♉39	28 48	13♊48	28 30	12♋47	26 37	10♌00	22 57	05♍32	17♍50	
1964	06♌43	20 28	03♍50	16 53	29 38	12♎08	24 26	06♏34	18 34	00♐28	12 18	24 06	05♑54	17 46	29♑43	
1965	13 08	25 19	07♑20	19 13	01♒04	12 55	24 52	06♓58	19 19	01♈58	14 59	28 24	12♉12	26 25	10♊55	
1966	15 35	28 00	10♉40	23 37	06♊50	20 19	04♋01	17 56	01♌59	17 09	00♍23	14 37	28 49	12♎58	26♎59	
1967	22 35	06♍29	20 41	05♎09	19 50	04♏38	19 29	04♐13	18 45	02♑57	16 46	00♒09	13 07	25 43	08♓00	
1968	28 02	11♒50	25 11	08♓06	20 39	02♈56	14 59	26 55	08♉44	20 33	02♊22	14 13	26 09	08♋10	20♋20	
1969	03♊12	15 17	27 16	09♋10	21 01	02♌52	14 48	26 53	09♍12	21 50	04♎52	18 21	02♏19	16 44	01♐34	
1970	05♎07	17 42	00♏38	13 56	27 35	11♐32	25 42	10♑01	24 22	08♒41	22 56	07♓03	21 03	04♈55	18♈39	
1971	14 35	28 27	12♓33	26 52	11♈23	26 01	10♉39	25 11	09♊30	23 28	07♋04	20 14	03♌01	15 26	27♌35	
1972	18 47	02♌27	15 39	28 27	10♍56	23 09	05♎12	17 07	29 00	10♏52	22 46	04♐42	16 44	28 52	11♑08	
1973	23 40	06♐37	17 28	29 16	11♑03	22 54	04♒51	17 00	29 25	12♓11	25 22	09♈00	23 06	07♉38	22♉32	
1974	25 05	07♈50	20 57	04♉26	18 17	02♊26	16 49	01♋21	15 56	00♌29	14 54	29 09	13♍12	27 00	10♎34	
1975	06♌36	20 41	04♍54	19 12	03♎32	17 52	02♏07	16 12	00♐05	13 41	26 59	09♑59	22 39	05♒03	17♒14	
1976	09♑04	22 45	06♒00	18 50	01♓19	13 30	25 24	07♈20	19 08	00♉56	12 48	24 47	06♊55	19 14	01♋46	
1977	13 49	25 39	07♊28	19 18	01 12	13♋11	25 18	07♌36	20 08	02♍58	16 09	29 44	13♎45	28 12	13♏02	
1978	14 51	27 37	10♎47	24 24	08♏28	22 56	07♐43	22 42	07♑41	22 33	07♒11	21 28	05♓25	19 00	02♈16	
1979	29 10	13♒19	27 28	11♓34	25 37	09♈36	23 29	07♉14	20 49	04♊10	17 16	00♋05	12 37	24 53	06♌57	
1980	29 30	13♋03	26 08	08♌49	21 09	03♍14	15 08	26 57	08♎47	20 41	02♏43	14 56	27 21	09♐59	22♐50	
1981	04♏09	16 01	27 54	09♐49	21 48	03♑52	16 04	28 26	11♒02	23 56	07♓10	20 49	04♈54	19 24	04♉16	
1982	04♓51	17 45	01♈06	14 54	29 11	13♉51	28 48	13♊54	28 59	13♋53	18 32	12♌49	26 44	10♍17	23♍30	
1983	21 02	05♌21	19 37	03♍45	17 46	01♎37	15 17	28 44	11♏58	24 57	07♐42	20 12	02♑29	14 35	26♑32	
1984	19 35	02♑54	15 51	28 29	10♒49	22 56	04♓54	16 47	28 41	10♈38	22 45	05♉02	17 33	00♊20	13♊23	
1985	24 24	06♉12	18 03	30 00	12♊04	24 18	06♋43	19 21	02♌13	15 22	28 48	12♍34	26 38	11♎00	25♎37	
1986	25 19	08♍16	21 37	05♎24	19 38	04♏17	19 17	04♐29	19 44	04♑52	19 43	04♒11	18 11	01♓43	14♓49	
1987	13♑09	27 46	12♒09	26 17	10♓07	23 40	06♈57	20 00	02♉51	15 30	27 59	10♊18	22 28	04♋31	16♋27	
1988	09♊47	22 57	05♋48	18 20	00♌35	12 36	24 29	06♍18	18 08	00♎05	12 15	24 40	07♏26	20 32	03♐59	
1989	14 13	26 07	08♏08	20 18	02♐40	15 12	27 55	10♑49	23 55	07♒13	20 44	04♓29	18 29	02♈44	17♈12	
1990	16 00	28 58	12♓20	26 10	10♈27	25 12	10♉16	25 32	10♊49	25 55	10♋42	25 03	08♌55	22 19	05♍17	
1991	04♋48	19 28	03♌52	17 57	01♍42	15 09	28 18	11♎13	23 54	06♏23	18 41	00♐50	12 50	24 44	06♑33	
1992	00♐21	13 12	25 46	08♑04	20 10	02♒07	13 59	25 50	07♓45	19 50	02♈08	14 44	27 40	10♉57	24♉37	
1993	04♈16	16 14	28 20	10♉37	23 05	05♊47	18 42	01♋52	15 14	28 50	12♌38	26 27	10♍46	25 02	09♎24	
1994	07♌01	20 10	03♍41	17 35	01♎51	16 28	01♏21	16 23	01♐26	16 22	01♑02	15 22	29 15	12♒42	15♒43	
1995	25 52	10♑48	25 25	09♒39	23 27	06♓50	19 50	02♈30	14 54	27 06	09♉07	21 03	02♊54	14 44	26♊33	
1996	20 39	03♊14	15 38	27 51	09♋54	21 51	03♌43	15 35	27 31	09♍35	21 52	04♎28	17 27	00♏51	14♏42	
1997	23 48	05♎47	17 59	00♏25	13 10	26 13	09♐34	23 12	07♑01	21 01	05♒05	19 13	03♓22	17 29	01♈35	
1998	28 38	11♒53	25 24	09♓13	23 21	07♈48	22 31	07♉23	22 19	07♊07	21 41	05♋53	19 38	02 56	15♌48	
1999	17 05	02♋04	16 40	00♌48	14 28	27 42	10♍32	23 04	05♎22	17 28	29 28	11♏23	23 16	05♐08	17♐02	
2000	11♏23	23 47	06♐01	18 04	29 59	11♑49	23 36	05♒25	17 20	29 26	11♓48	24 31	07♈39	21 15	05♉18	

Moon

June

Year	1st	2nd	3rd	4th	5th	6th	7th	8th	9th	10th	11th	12th	13th	14th	15th	16th
1900	21♋43	04♌18	16 37	28 43	10♍41	22 35	04♎28	16 27	28 35	10♏56	23 32	06♐26	19 37	03♑06	16 50	00♒48
1901	24♏09	06♐09	18 19	00♑40	13 12	25 58	08♒58	22 12	05♓42	19 29	03♈31	17 49	02♉20	17 00	01♊44	16 26
1902	27♓58	11♈43	25 55	10♉32	25 29	20♊40	25 55	11♋04	25 57	10♌26	24 27	08♍00	21 06	03♎48	16 11	28 19
1903	18♌55	03♍04	16 53	00♎23	13 36	26 33	09♏17	21 51	04♐14	16 29	28 36	10♑37	22 32	04♒24	16 15	28 09
1904	11♑46	24 15	06♒29	18 30	00♓22	12 11	24 01	05♈59	18 10	00♉37	13 25	26 35	10♊08	24 02	08♋11	22 32
1905	14♉13	26 26	08♊52	21 30	04♋19	17 21	00♌34	13 58	27 33	11♍21	25 21	09♎34	23 57	08♏29	23 03	07♐33
1906	18♍44	02♎33	16 49	01♏30	16 31	01♐45	17 00	02♑05	16 52	01♒13	15 07	28 32	11♓31	24 09	06♈28	18 35
1907	10♒34	24 42	08♓28	21 54	05♈00	17 50	00♉25	12 48	25 00	07♊04	19 00	00♋51	12 39	24 25	06♌14	18 09
1908	01♋44	13 59	26 02	07♌56	19 47	01♍38	13 33	25 38	07♎57	20 35	03♏33	16 55	00♐39	14 45	29 08	13♑44
1909	04♏16	16 37	29 11	12♐01	25 06	08♑25	21 58	05♒43	19 39	03♓44	17 55	02♈10	16 27	00♉42	14 52	28 54
1910	10♓28	24 20	08♈33	23 04	07♉50	22 44	07♊40	22 30	07♋06	21 22	05♌14	18 40	01♍40	14 18	26 37	08♎41
1911	01♌47	16 03	29 52	13♍15	26 14	08♎51	21 12	03♏21	15 20	27 14	09♐04	20 54	02♑44	14 38	26 37	08♒43
1912	21♐44	03♑54	15 56	27 52	09♒44	21 36	03♓32	15 36	27 54	10♈30	23 29	06♉54	20 46	05♊06	19 48	04♋45
1913	23♈55	06♉25	19 14	02♊23	15 51	29 37	13♋36	27 43	11♌56	26 09	10♍20	24 27	08♎31	22 28	06♏20	20 04
1914	02♍10	15 59	00♎06	14 28	29 05	13♏51	28 39	13♐21	27 49	11♑56	25 39	08♒56	21 47	04♓16	16 27	28 25
1915	22♑58	07♒08	20 50	04♓05	16 55	29 26	11♈41	23 46	05♉43	17 36	29 27	11♊19	23 14	05♋11	17 13	29 23
1916	12♊11	24 10	06♋03	17 51	29 37	11♌25	24 21	05♍27	17 50	00♎33	13 42	27 18	11♏23	25 54	10♐46	25 52
1917	13♎45	26 28	09♏31	22 55	06♐39	20 40	04♑55	19 19	03♒46	18 13	02♓34	16 48	00♈52	14 45	28 25	11♉52
1918	24♒15	08♓16	22 28	06♈49	21 16	05♉44	20 08	04♊23	18 24	02♋08	15 33	28 37	11♌21	23 47	05♍59	18 00
1919	13♋17	27 26	11♌09	24 26	07♍18	19 49	02♎02	14 03	25 56	07♏45	19 33	01♐23	13 20	25 24	07♑38	20 02
1920	02♐19	14 11	26 01	07♑51	19 44	01♒41	13 46	26 01	08♓30	21 18	04♈27	18 01	02♉01	16 27	01♊17	16 23
1921	03♈36	16 19	29 25	12♉56	26 53	11♊12	25 50	10♋39	25 30	10♌15	24 48	09♍05	23 03	06♎42	20 03	03♏10
1922	16♌37	00♍42	14 50	28 59	13♎08	27 15	11♏17	25 13	08♐59	22 31	05♑46	18 42	01♒21	13 42	25 48	07♓44
1923	03♑55	18 01	01♒39	14 48	27 33	09♓55	22 01	03♈56	15 46	27 34	09♉26	21 24	03♊32	15 50	28 20	11♋01
1924	22♉41	04♊33	16 25	28 17	10♋13	22 12	04♌19	16 36	29 07	11♍56	25 08	08♎45	22 49	07♏21	22 16	07♐26
1925	23♍21	06♎13	19 31	03♏17	17 30	02♐07	17 01	02♑02	17 03	01♒55	16 31	00♓47	14 43	28 18	11♈34	24 32
1926	08♒43	22 57	07♓10	21 20	05♈25	19 22	03♉10	16 46	00♊10	13 18	26 10	08♋47	21 08	03♌17	15 16	27 08
1927	24♊19	08♋05	21 29	04♌30	17 10	29 32	11♍40	23 38	05♎32	17 25	29 22	11♏26	23 40	06♐07	18 47	01♑42
1928	12♏58	24 46	06♐36	18 30	00♑30	12 39	24 58	07♒30	20 17	03♓21	16 44	00♈27	14 31	28 56	13♉37	28 30
1929	13♓48	26 44	10♈03	23 48	08♉00	22 36	07♊32	22 40	07♋51	22 55	07♌44	22 10	06♍11	19 45	02♎54	15 42
1930	00♌46	15 17	29 38	13♍46	27 40	11♎20	24 45	07♏57	20 57	03♐45	16 22	28 48	11♑04	23 10	05♒09	17 04
1931	14♐37	28 15	11♑33	24 30	07♒07	19 25	01♓29	13 23	25 13	07♈02	18 58	01♉04	13 25	26 04	09♊02	22 19
1932	02♉55	14 46	25 43	08♊49	21 03	03♋27	16 02	28 48	11♌46	24 56	08♍22	22 03	06♎03	20 20	04♏53	29 38
1933	04♍10	17 05	00♎26	14 14	28 32	13♏17	28 23	13♐42	29 01	14♑10	28 59	13♒21	27 16	10♓42	23 43	06♈22
1934	22♑43	07♒20	21 41	05♓46	19 33	03♈03	16 18	29 19	12♉06	24 42	07♊06	19 19	01♋23	13 19	25 09	06♌56
1935	05♊31	18 47	01♋45	14 24	26 47	08♌55	20 53	02♍45	14 36	26 30	08♎34	20 50	03♏23	16 15	29 28	13♐01
1936	22♎57	04♏54	16 58	29 10	11♐34	24 08	06♑56	19 56	03♒10	16 38	00♓19	14 14	28 21	12♈40	27 06	11♉36
1937	25♒09	08♓15	21 44	05♈37	19 54	04♉33	19 28	04♊34	19 40	04♋39	19 22	03♌42	17 37	01♍06	14 09	26 49
1938	13♋50	28 41	13♌15	27 28	11♍17	24 44	07♎49	20 35	03♏06	15 23	27 31	09♐31	21 26	03♑17	15 07	26 58
1939	26♏04	09♐00	21 44	04♑14	16 32	18 40	10♒39	22 33	04♓25	16 21	28 24	10♈40	23 13	06♉07	19 26	03♊10
1940	12♈40	24 37	06♉44	19 04	01♊41	14 35	27 46	11♋11	24 50	08♌39	22 36	06♍38	20 44	04♎53	19 03	03♏14
1941	16♌29	29 39	13♍07	26 55	11♎04	25 34	10♏22	25 22	10♐25	25 22	10♑03	24 21	08♒12	21 35	04♓30	17 02
1942	05♑14	20 13	04♒50	18 59	02♓41	15 57	28 51	11♈26	23 46	05♉56	17 58	29 54	11♊48	23 40	05♋31	17 24
1943	17♉02	29 45	12♊15	24 33	06♋40	18 37	00♌28	12 15	24 03	05♍56	18 00	00♎20	13 01	26 06	09♏40	23 40
1944	21♎36	05 24	19 36	04♏11	19 02	04♐01	19 01	03♑52	18 29	02♒45	16 40	00 12	13♓23	26 16	08♈53	21 16
1945	07♒54	21 16	04♓55	18 51	03♈05	17 33	02♉13	16 58	01♊41	16 15	00♋34	14 33	28 09	11♌21	24 10	06♍40
1946	25♊57	10♋51	25 26	09♌36	23 20	06♍38	19 32	02♎06	14 23	26 28	08♏24	20 14	02♐03	13 51	25 42	07♑38
1947	08♏00	20 22	02♐35	14 39	26 36	08♑28	20 19	02♒09	14 03	26 04	08♓16	20 42	03♈27	16 35	00♉08	14 08
1948	21♓59	04♈06	16 47	29 05	12♉03	25 24	09♊07	23 11	07♋30	22 00	06♌33	21 05	05♍30	19 44	03♎44	17 32
1949	29♋39	13♌19	27 09	11♍09	25 17	09♎32	23 52	08♏15	22 37	06♐52	20 57	04♑46	18 15	01♒23	14 10	26 36
1950	16♐36	01♑35	16 13	00♒25	14 07	27 20	10♓07	22 32	04♈39	16 36	28 26	10♉13	22 02	03♊56	15 57	28 05
1951	28♈42	10♉54	22 59	04♊58	16 53	28 45	10♋36	22 28	04♌23	16 24	28 35	11♍00	23 45	06♎54	20 30	04♏35
1952	11♍48	23 36	06♎02	18 50	02♏03	15 43	29 48	14♐14	28 55	13♑43	18 30	13♒10	27 37	11♓48	25 43	09♈22
1953	21♑30	05♒21	19 20	03♓25	17 34	01♈46	15 59	00♉11	14 18	28 15	11♊58	25 26	08♋34	21 23	03♌54	16 10
1954	07♊38	22 19	06♋41	20 37	04♌08	17 14	29 57	12♍21	24 30	06♎29	18 23	00♏15	23 09	24 09	06♐16	18 33
1955	19♎28	01♏33	13 31	25 22	07♐11	18 59	00♑49	12 43	24 42	06♒52	19 13	01♓51	14 47	28 05	11♈48	25 55
1956	01♓26	13 42	26 14	09♈08	22 25	06♉08	20 16	04♊47	19 35	04♋34	19 35	04♌29	19 10	03♍31	17 31	01♎08
1957	12♋54	27 10	11♌30	25 50	10♍07	24 17	08♎18	22 10	05♏52	19 22	02♐40	15 45	28 37	11♑15	23 40	05♒53
1958	28♏15	12♐41	26 52	10♑43	24 12	07♒17	19 59	02♓21	14 27	26 23	08♈12	20 01	01♉53	13 54	26 08	08♊35
1959	09♈54	20 49	03♉38	15 26	27 15	09♊07	21 05	03♋10	15 23	27 46	10♌19	23 04	06♍05	19 24	03♎03	17 03
1960	21♌33	03♍47	16 17	29 10	12♎29	26 16	20♏34	26 18	20♐23	25 40	10♑56	26 02	10♒48	25 09	09♓02	22 30
1961	04♑39	19 14	03♒47	18 12	02♓27	16 30	00♈21	13 59	27 26	10♉40	23 43	06♊34	19 12	01♋38	13 51	25 53
1962	19♉33	03♊42	17 35	01♋09	14 20	27 10	09♌40	21 52	03♍53	15 46	27 36	09♎29	21 30	03♏43	16 10	28 53
1963	29♍55	11♎52	23 45	05♏37	17 31	29 29	11♐34	23 47	06♑08	18 40	01♒24	14 22	27 34	11♓04	24 52	08♈59
1964	11♒51	24 13	06♓53	19 55	03♈22	17 16	01♉37	16 20	01♊22	16 32	01♋43	16 44	01♌28	15 49	29 44	13♍14
1965	25♊38	10♋27	25 14	09♌53	24 20	08♍30	22 21	05♎54	19 08	02♏07	14 50	27 20	09♐39	21 48	03♑50	15 45
1966	10♏52	24 34	08♐02	21 15	04♑12	16 53	29 19	11♒31	23 33	05♓29	17 22	29 17	11♈19	23 32	06♉01	18 49
1967	20♓02	01♈55	13 43	25 31	07♉24	19 25	01♊36	14 01	26 39	09♋31	22 38	05♌58	19 30	03♍13	17 08	01♎12
1968	02♌38	15 09	27 55	10♍59	24 24	08♎13	22 26	07♏03	22 00	07♐09	22 22	07♑28	22 17	06♒41	20 36	04♓02
1969	16♐39	01♑50	16 56	01♒48	16 20	00♓27	14 10	27 29	10♈28	23 10	05♉39	17 56	00♊06	12 09	24 07	06♋01
1970	02♉13	15 37	28 49	11♊48	24 32	07♋02	19 18	01♌21	13 15	25 04	06♍52	18 44	00♎46	13 04	25 41	08♏42
1971	09♍33	21 24	03♎14	15 08	27 10	09♏23	21 50	04♐32	07 30	00♑41	14 06	27 42	11♒26	25 19	09♓20	23 27
1972	23♑34	06♒13	19 06	02♓17	15 49	29 44	14♈00	28 37	13♉29	28 29	13♊29	28 19	12♋51	27 00	10♌44	24 01
1973	07♊39	22 50	07♋56	22 48	07♌19	21 27	05♍10	18 30	01♎27	14 06	26 30	08♏41	20 42	02♐37	24 27	26 15
1974	23♎53	06♏57	19 48	02♐25	14 50	27 04	09♑08	21 04	02♒56	14 47	26 39	08♓38	20 47	03♈11	15 55	29 01
1975	29♒14	11♓09	23 02	04♈59	17 03	29 19	11♉51	24 40	07♊48	21 15	04♋59	18 57	03♌06	17 22	01♍41	15 58
1976	14♋30	27 28	10♌41	24 08	07♍49	21 46	05♎56	20 20	04♏53	19 33	04♐12	18 46	03♑07	17 10	00♒50	14 06
1977	28♏10	13♐26	28 40	13♑41	28 22	12♒35	26 19	09♓34	22 24	04♈52	17 03	29 02	10♉54	22 43	04♊31	16 21
1978	15♈14	27 59	10♉32	22 54	05♊08	17 15	29 15	11♋10	23 02	04♌53	16 45	28 52	10♍50	23 12	05♎55	19 01
1979	18♌50	00♍39	12 28	24 23	06♎29	18 51	01♏34	14 40	28 09	12♐01	26 11	10♑35	25 06	09♒37	24 04	08♓22
1980	05♑52	19 07	02♒32	16 08	29 54	13♓52	27 59	12♈17	26 42	11♉09	25 35	09♊53	23 57	07♋42	21 05	04♌06
1981	19♉22	04♊33	19 40	04♋31	19 01	03♌03	16 38	29 46	12♍21	24 47	07♎07	19 08	01♏02	12 54	24 47	06♐42
1982	06♒24	19 02	01♓26	13 40	25 45	07♈42	19 34	01♉23	13 10	24♊59	06 53	18♋56	01 10	13♌41	26 32	09♍48
1983	08♎24	20 15	02♏08	14 10	26 24	08♐54	21 44	04♑58	18 35	02 35	16♒55	01 30	16♓15	01 01	15 42	00♈13
1984	26♊42	10♋15	24 01	07♌58	22 04	06♍14	20 28	04♎43	18 55	03♏03	17 03	00♐54	14 31	27 54	11♑01	23 51
1985	10♏26	25 19	10♐10	24 50	09♑13	23 14	06♒49	19 59	02♓45	15 10	27 18	09♈14	21 04	02♉51	14 41	26 37
1986	27♓33	09♈57	22 07	04♉06	15 59	27 49	09♊38	21 27	03♋20	15 18	27 22	09♌35	21 59	04♍37	17 31	00♎46
1987	28♋19	10♌09	22 03	04♍03	16 15	28 44	11♎34	24 51	08♏35	22 48	07♐26	22 24	07♑32	22 39	07♒37	22 16
1988	17♐45	01♑47	15 59	00♒16	14 34	28 49	12♓59	27 03	11♈00	24 50	08♉31	22 03	05♊24	18 32	01♋26	14 04
1989	01♉51	16 33	01♊12	15 40	29 50	13♋38	27 01	09♌58	22 34	04♍50	16 52	28 45	10♎35	22 27	04♏25	16 32
1990	17♍55	00♎14	12 22	24 22	06♏16	18 08	00♐00	11 55	23 54	05♑57	18 07	00♒26	12 57	25 42	08♓43	22 05
1991	18♑21	00♒09	12 03	24 06	06♓23	18 59	01♈58	15 24	29 17	13♉38	28 23	13♊24	28 34	13♋42	28 39	13♌20
1992	08♊35	22 50	07♋15	21 47	06♌18	20 45	05♍05	19 13	03♎09	16 51	00♏19	13 32	26 32	09♐18	21 50	04♑11
1993	23♎47	08♏08	22 22	06♐24	20 10	03♑39	16 49	29 39	12♒11	24 28	06♓33	18 30	00♈23	12 17	24 17	06♉27
1994	08♓21	20 40	02♈44	14 38	26 27	08♉14	20 03	01♊58	14 01	26 13	08♋37	21 13	04♌03	17 06	00♍25	13 58
1995	08♋25	20 20	02♌23	14 34	26 59	09♍40	22 40	06♎04	29 54	04♏10	18 52	03♐53	19 07	04♑24	19 32	04♒22
1996	28♏58	13♐35	28 27	13♑25	28 18	13♒01	27 26	11♓32	25 17	08♈42	21 50	04♉42	17 23	29 52	12♊12	24 23
1997	15♈38	29 37	13♉30	27 13	10♊44	24 00	06♋59	19 40	02♌04	14 13	26 11	08♍02	19 50	01♎42	13 42	25 56
1998	28♌17	10♍28	22 27	04♎18	16 07	27 58	09♏56	22 03	04♐20	16 51	29 33	12♑28	25 34	08♒51	22 20	05♓59
1999	28♐57	10♑58	23 04	05♒20	17 48	00♓32	13 36	27 04	10♈58	25 18	10♉02	25 04	10♊16	25 27	10♋27	25 08
2000	19♉49	04♊37	19 38	04♋42	19 41	04♌25	18 51	02♍56	16 39	00♎01	13 04	25 50	08♏23	20 43	02♐53	14 54

	17th	18th	19th	20th	21st	22nd	23rd	24th	25th	26th	27th	28th	29th	30th
1900	14 55	29 08	13♓24	27 39	11♈51	25 58	09♉57	23 48	07♊27	20 54	04♋08	17 06	29 50	12♌19
1901	00♋59	15 16	29 13	12♌45	25 53	08♍38	21 02	03♎10	15 06	26 56	08♏44	20 36	02♐35	14♐45
1902	10♏17	22 08	03♐57	15 47	27 38	09♑34	21 36	03♒45	16 02	28 31	11♓12	24 09	07♈25	21♈02
1903	10♓10	22 23	04♈52	17 42	00♉58	14 43	28 56	13♊36	28 37	13♋48	29 00	14♌02	28 45	13♍05
1904	06♌57	21 22	05♍42	19 55	03♎59	17 53	01♏37	15 12	28 36	11♐49	24 50	07♑37	20 10	02♒29
1905	21 53	05♑57	19 40	02♒59	15 55	28 29	10♓45	22 47	04♈40	16 31	28 23	10♉21	22 30	04♊52
1906	00♉32	12 25	24 16	06♊09	18 04	00♋04	12 11	24 26	06♌50	19 25	02♍15	15 20	28 45	12♎30
1907	00♍13	12 31	25 08	08♎07	21 33	05♏26	19 47	04♐31	19 34	04♑46	19 57	04♒59	19 43	04♓05
1908	28 25	13♒06	27 41	12♓05	26 14	10♈08	23 46	07♉07	20 12	03♊03	15 40	28 05	10♋19	22♋24
1909	12♊46	26 23	09♋43	22 46	05♌32	18 01	00♍16	12 19	24 15	06♎09	18 03	00♏04	12 16	24♏42
1910	20 35	02♏24	14 12	26 03	08♐01	20 09	02♑28	14 59	27 43	10♒42	23 53	07♓18	20 57	04♈48
1911	20 58	03♓26	16 08	29 10	12♈33	26 21	10♉34	25 12	10♊10	25 20	10♋35	25 42	10♌32	24♌58
1912	19 49	04♌49	19 37	04♍06	18 13	01♎57	15 20	18 25	11♏13	23 48	06♐12	18 28	00♑36	12♑37
1913	03♐39	17 02	00♑10	13 04	25 41	08♒02	20 09	02♓06	13 56	25 45	07♈37	19 37	01♉52	14♉26
1914	10♈16	22 06	03♉58	15 57	28 06	10♊27	23 02	05♋50	18 52	02♌06	15 31	29 06	12♍51	26♍46
1915	11♌43	24 14	07♍01	20 08	03♎36	17 29	01♏47	16 27	01♐25	16 32	01♑39	16 37	01♒16	15♒30
1916	11♑02	26 06	10♒56	25 27	09♓35	23 19	06♈41	19 41	02♉24	14 52	27 06	09♊11	21 09	03♋00
1917	25 05	08♊04	20 49	03♋20	15 39	27 46	09♌45	21 37	03♍27	15 19	27 16	09♎24	21 47	04♏28
1918	29 55	11♎49	23 45	05♏48	18 01	00♐29	13 13	26 14	09♑32	23 07	06♒55	20 55	05♓03	29♓16
1919	02♒40	15 31	28 36	11♓58	25 36	09♈31	23 43	08♉10	22 49	07♊35	22 21	07♋02	21 29	05♌37
1920	01♋38	16 50	01♊51	16 31	00♍44	14 29	27 47	10♎39	23 11	05♏25	17 28	29 23	11♐14	23♐03
1921	16 02	28 42	11♐13	23 33	05♑45	17 50	29 48	11♒42	23 33	05♓25	17 22	29 28	11♈49	24♈29
1922	19 34	01♈23	13 17	25 20	07♉39	20 17	03♊16	16 37	00♋19	14 19	28 32	12♌52	27 15	11♍35
1923	23 56	07♌00	20 16	03♍44	17 25	01♎19	15 27	29 48	14♏19	28 55	13♐32	28 01	12♑15	26♑10
1924	22 43	07♑55	22 51	07♒24	21 30	05♓08	18 19	01♈05	13 33	25 45	07♉46	19 41	01♊33	13♊25
1925	07♉15	19 45	02♊04	14 13	26 13	08♋07	19 56	01♌43	13 30	25 21	07♍20	19 31	01♎58	14♎47
1926	08♍59	20 51	02♎52	15 04	27 32	10♏20	23 31	07♐03	20 58	05♑12	19 39	04♒16	18 55	03♓30
1927	14 52	28 16	11♒53	25 42	09♓41	23 48	08♈01	22 19	06♉37	20 53	05♊02	19 02	02♋49	16♋20
1928	13♊29	28 25	13♋09	27 36	11♌40	25 18	08♍30	21 18	03♎45	15 55	27 53	09♏44	21 31	03♐21
1929	28 11	10♏26	22 30	04♐27	16 19	28 09	09♑59	21 51	03♒47	15 49	27 58	10♓18	22 53	05♈45
1930	28 55	10♓48	22 48	04♈59	17 26	00♉13	13 26	27 06	11♊12	25 44	10♋33	25 33	10♌34	25♌25
1931	05♋54	19 44	03♌45	17 52	02♍03	16 13	00♎22	14 28	28 30	12♏27	16 18	10♐01	23 33	06♑51
1932	04♐29	19 18	03♑56	18 15	02♒11	15 40	28 42	11♓21	23 40	05♈43	17 37	29 27	11♉17	23♉12
1933	18 45	00♉54	12 55	24 50	06♊43	18 34	00♋27	12 21	24 20	06♌25	18 38	01♍02	13 40	26♍37
1934	18 43	00♍34	12 35	24 49	07♎23	20 20	03♏43	17 36	01♐55	16 38	01♑38	16 46	01♒52	16♒47
1935	26 53	10♑59	25 15	09♒38	24 03	08♓25	22 42	06♈51	20 50	04♉38	18 14	01♊36	14 45	27♊38
1936	26 06	10♊29	24 40	08♋35	22 11	05♌25	18 19	00♍54	13 13	25 19	07♎16	19 09	01♏03	13♏02
1937	09♎10	21 17	03♏13	15 03	26 51	08♐39	20 32	02♑31	14 39	26 57	09♒26	22 09	05♓06	18♓18
1938	08♒53	20 53	03♓02	15 24	28 03	11♈02	24 24	08♉13	22 28	07♊08	22 08	07♋20	22 34	07♌41
1939	17 18	01♋46	16 27	01♌15	15 02	00♍39	15 02	29 08	12♎55	26 26	09♏41	22 42	05♐30	18♐07
1940	17 22	01♐25	15 19	29 01	12♑27	25 34	08♒22	20 51	03♓04	15 04	26 56	08♈45	20 36	02♉34
1941	29 15	11♈14	23 05	04♉54	16 43	28 38	10♊40	22 53	05♋16	17 50	00♌35	13 32	26 40	10♍00
1942	29 20	11♌22	23 33	05♍56	18 36	01♎37	15 02	28 55	13♏16	28 02	13♐08	28 25	13♑41	28♑45
1943	08♐06	22 51	07♑48	22 48	07♒42	22 24	06♓48	20 53	04♈37	18 02	01♉09	14 01	26 39	09♊04
1944	09♉21	23 05	06♊39	19 57	02♋59	15 45	28 14	10♌30	22 33	04♍29	16 20	28 11	10♎08	22♎14
1945	18 54	00♎57	12 52	24 -45	06♏39	18 39	00♐47	13 06	25 39	08♑24	21 25	04♒39	18 07	01♓48
1946	19 42	01♒55	14 19	26 57	09♓52	23 05	06♈38	20 34	04♉50	19 26	04♊16	19 15	04♋15	19♋08
1947	28 33	13♊21	28 24	13♋34	28 41	13♌36	28 11	12♍23	16 09	09♎29	22 27	05♏05	17 27	29♏37
1948	01♏05	14 26	27 34	10♐31	23 15	05♑48	18 11	00♒23	12 25	24 22	06♓14	18 06	00♈02	12♈07
1949	08♓47	20 44	02♈35	14 24	26 16	08♉16	20 29	02♊58	15 46	28 53	12♋17	25 58	09♌50	23♌52
1950	10♋23	22 51	05♌29	18 19	01♍21	14 38	28 12	12♎03	26 13	10♏42	25 25	10♐17	25 11	09♑57
1951	19 09	04♐08	19 22	04♑43	19 57	04♒55	19 29	03♓35	17 14	00♈25	13 14	25 45	08♉00	20♉06
1952	22 45	05♉54	18 50	01♊33	14 04	26 24	08♋34	20 34	02♌27	14 15	26 01	07♍50	19 46	01♎53
1953	28 12	10♍07	21 58	03♎50	15 49	27 58	10♏23	23 06	06♐08	19 30	03♑10	17 07	01♒16	15♒34
1954	01♑00	13 39	26 31	09♒36	22 55	06♓28	20 15	04♈17	18 31	02♉56	17 27	02♊00	16 30	00♋50
1955	10♉25	25 15	10♊18	25 26	10♋30	25 22	09♌53	24 00	07♍41	20 55	03♎45	16 14	28 27	10♏28
1956	14 23	27 19	09♏58	22 23	04♐36	16 41	28 39	10♑33	22 24	04♒14	16 06	28 03	10♓07	22♓22
1957	17 57	29 53	11♓45	23 39	05♈38	17 47	00♉11	12 55	26 02	09♊34	23 29	07♋46	22 20	07♌03
1958	21 19	04♋20	17 36	01♌06	14 47	28 38	12♍36	26 39	10♎47	24 58	09♏11	23 23	07♐33	21♐35
1959	01♏26	16 09	01♐06	16 11	01♑14	16 05	00♒36	14 40	28 15	11♓22	24 04	06♈25	18 30	00♉24
1960	05♈33	18 17	00♉44	13 00	25 06	07♊06	19 02	00♋54	12 46	24 37	06♌31	18 29	00♍34	12♍50
1961	07♌47	19 35	01♍22	13 13	25 11	07♎23	19 54	02♏48	16 09	29 57	14♐10	28 46	13♑37	28♑34
1962	11♐55	25 13	08♑47	22 34	06♒31	20 35	04♓44	18 55	03♈07	17 18	01♉25	15 27	29 20	13♊02
1963	23 22	08♉00	22 46	07♊33	22 15	06♋44	20 54	04♌42	18 06	01♍06	13 45	26 06	08♎13	20♎11
1964	26 18	09♎01	21 26	03♏37	15 37	27 30	09♐19	21 07	02♑56	14 49	26 48	08♒55	21 12	03♓42
1965	27 36	09♒27	21 18	03♓15	15 21	27 40	10♈16	23 13	06♉35	20 23	04♊37	29 14	04♋10	19♋17
1966	01♊59	15 30	29 22	13♋32	27 54	12♌24	26 54	11♍21	25 39	09♎45	23 40	07♏21	20 50	04♐07
1967	15 25	29 45	14♏10	28 36	12♐58	27 12	11♑11	24 52	08♒11	21 08	03♓44	16 01	28 04	09♈58
1968	17 00	29 34	11♈49	23 59	05♉43	17 31	29 20	11♊11	23 07	05♋11	17 23	29 44	12♌15	24♌57
1969	17 52	29 43	11♌35	23 32	05♍37	17 55	00♎30	13 27	26 51	10♏44	25 07	09♐55	25 04	10♑23
1970	22 09	06♐02	20 17	04♑49	19 32	04♒17	18 58	03♓29	17 47	01♈49	15 35	29 07	12♉24	25♉28
1971	07♈38	21 53	06♉09	20 21	04♊26	18 20	01♋58	15 17	28 17	10♌58	23 21	05♍29	17 27	29♍19
1972	06♍54	19 26	01♎42	13 45	25 41	07♏33	19 26	01♐22	13 25	25 35	07♑56	20 27	03♒10	16♒06
1973	08♑03	19 54	01♒50	13 54	26 08	08♓37	21 24	04♈31	18 03	01♉59	16 20	01♊03	16 02	01♋10
1974	12♉31	26 27	10♊47	25 27	10♋20	25 19	10♌15	25 01	09♍30	23 39	07♎27	20 52	03♏58	16♏45
1975	00♎11	14 18	28 17	12♏06	25 44	09♐11	22 25	05♑26	18 13	00♒45	13 05	25 13	07♓12	19♓06
1976	26 59	09♓30	21 43	03♈43	15 34	27 22	09♉12	21 08	03♊15	15 34	28 09	11♋00	24 06	07♌27
1977	28 16	10♋17	22 24	04♌41	17 07	29 45	12♍37	25 46	09♎16	23 07	07♏21	21 57	06♐50	21♐56
1978	02♏36	16 40	01♐13	16 10	01♑22	16 38	01♒48	16 42	01♓14	15 19	28 57	12♈11	25 04	07♉39
1979	22 30	06♈27	20 12	03♉46	17 09	00♊20	13 20	26 06	08♋39	21 00	03♌08	15 06	26 56	08♍43
1980	16 45	29 06	11♍11	23 07	04♎58	16 50	28 47	10♏53	23 12	05♐47	18 39	01♑47	15 11	28♑49
1981	18 43	00♑50	13 06	25 31	08♒06	20 55	03♓59	17 20	00♈59	14 57	29 14	13♉48	28 33	13♊23
1982	23 30	07♉39	22 14	07♊08	22 16	07♋28	22 34	07♌26	21 57	06♍04	29 45	03♎00	15 53	28♎26
1983	14 30	28 30	12♎12	25 36	08♏44	21 36	04♐14	16 40	28 55	11♑01	23 00	04♒54	16 44	28♒34
1984	06♒25	18 44	00♓51	12 49	24 43	06♈37	18 35	00♉42	13 03	25 41	08♊39	21 59	05♋39	19♋38
1985	08♊42	20 59	03♋29	16 12	29 10	12♌21	25 45	09♍21	23 09	07♎08	21 18	05♏37	20 02	04♐32
1986	14 24	28 27	12♏55	27 45	12♐52	28 06	13♑17	28 15	12♒51	27 00	10♓39	23 48	06♈33	18♈55
1987	06♓33	20 26	03♈56	17 05	29 55	12♉31	24 56	07♊10	19 18	01♋19	13 15	25 08	06♌58	18♌49
1988	26 27	08♌37	20 35	02♍26	14 14	26 04	08♎01	20 11	02♏38	15 28	28 43	12♐23	26 26	10♑49
1989	28 51	11♐25	24 13	07♑16	20 31	03♒58	17 36	01♓23	16 18	29 21	13♈31	27 46	12♉04	26♉22
1990	05♈49	19 57	04♉26	19 14	04♊14	19 17	04♋15	18 57	03♌18	17 14	00♍43	13 47	26 28	08♎51
1991	27 38	11♍32	26 02	08♎09	20 57	03♏28	15 45	27 52	09♐50	21 43	03♑32	15 20	27 09	09♒01
1992	16 20	28 21	10♒16	22 06	03♓57	15 53	27 57	10♈14	22 48	05♉43	19 02	02♊46	16 54	01♋24
1993	18 50	01♊30	14 27	27 43	11♋16	25 05	09♌07	23 18	07♍33	21 50	06♎04	20 15	04♏19	18♏15
1994	27 47	11♎52	26 11	10♏43	25 23	10♐06	24 46	09♑16	23 30	07♒23	20 51	03♓55	16 35	28♓56
1995	18 48	02♓44	16 12	29 13	11♈50	24 09	06♉13	18 09	29 59	11♊47	23 37	05♋29	17 26	29♋29
1996	06♋28	18 26	00♌19	12 10	24♍00	05 55	17♎57	00 12	12 44	25♏39	09 01	22♐53	07 13	22♐00
1997	08♏29	21 23	04♐40	18 20	02♑20	16 35	01♒00	15 28	29 55	14♓15	28 27	12♈29	26 20	10♉02
1998	19 51	03♈54	18 08	02♉32	17 02	01♊33	15 58	00♋12	14 09	27 44	10♌57	23 46	06♍15	18♍27
1999	09♌23	23 10	06♍30	19 25	01♎59	14 16	26 21	08♏18	20 11	02♐03	13 57	25 54	07♑57	20♑06
2000	26 49	08♑39	20 27	02♒15	14 06	26 03	08♓11	20 33	03♈15	16 19	29 49	13♉47	28 11	12♊57

Moon

July

	1st	2nd	3rd	4th	5th	6th	7th	8th	9th	10th	11th	12th	13th	14th	15th	16th
1900	24♌35	06♍40	18 37	00♎30	12 23	23 22	06♏30	18 52	01♐36	14 36	28 02	11♑51	26 00	10♒25	25 00	09♓37
1901	27♐07	09♑45	22 37	05♒44	19 05	02♓38	16 21	00♈14	14 15	28 23	12♉37	26 55	11♊15	25 33	09♋44	23 44
1902	05♉02	19 26	04♊11	19 12	04♋21	19 28	04♌23	18 57	03♍04	16 42	29 51	12♎35	24 58	07♏05	19 00	00♐51
1903	26♍59	10♎28	23 35	06♏23	18 56	01♐16	13 27	25 32	07♑31	19 26	01♒18	13 10	25 03	06♓59	19 01	01♈14
1904	14♒36	26 33	08♓24	20 11	02♈01	13 59	26 09	08♉37	21 28	04♊44	18 27	02♋34	17 02	01♌45	16 34	01♍21
1905	17♊30	01♋23	13 32	26 56	10♌31	24 17	03♍12	22 13	06♎19	20 29	04♏42	18 55	03♐05	17 09	01♑02	14 42
1906	26♎36	11♏02	25 45	10♐38	25 35	10♑27	25 05	09♒23	23 17	06♓46	19 49	02♈31	14 54	27 02	09♉02	20 54
1907	18♓01	01♈32	14 39	27 25	09♉53	22 07	04♊09	16 04	27 54	09♋42	21 29	03♌19	15 13	27 14	09♍25	21 49
1908	04♌21	16 13	28 03	09♍54	21 49	03♎53	16 10	28 44	11♏40	25 00	08♐46	22 58	07♑32	22 25	07♒27	22 32
1909	07♐26	20 30	03♑54	17 38	01♒38	15 51	00♓12	14 35	28 57	13♈14	27 22	11♉21	25 09	08♊46	22 12	05♋25
1910	18♈51	03♉06	17 31	02♊03	16 36	01♋07	15 28	29 35	13♌22	26 46	09♍47	22 25	04♎45	16 49	28 43	10♏33
1911	08♍55	22 22	05♎23	17 59	00♏17	12 20	24 15	06♐05	17 54	29 44	11♑39	23 40	05♒28	18 04	00♓29	13 06
1912	24♑34	06♒27	18 18	00♓10	12 06	24 09	06♈25	18 58	01♉53	15 14	29 05	13♊25	28 11	13♋17	28 34	13♌49
1913	27♉22	10♊43	24 28	08♋34	22 57	07♌30	22 06	06♍39	21 05	05♎20	19 22	03♏11	16 48	00♐13	13 26	26 26
1914	10♎50	25 03	09♏22	23 45	08♐08	22 24	06♑30	20 19	03♒48	16 56	29 43	12♓10	24 22	06♈22	18 14	00♉05
1915	29♒18	23♓39	25 34	08♈08	20 25	02♉29	14 26	26 18	08♊09	20 03	02♋02	14 07	26 21	08♌44	21 19	04♍05
1916	14♋48	26 35	08♌23	20 15	02♍14	14 24	26 48	09♎31	22 36	06♏05	20 02	04♐24	19 09	04♑12	19 23	04♒34
1917	17♏32	01♐01	14 53	29 09	13♑43	28 30	13♒23	28 14	12♓55	27 22	11♈31	25 21	08♉50	22 01	02♊55	17 34
1918	03♈31	17 45	01♉56	16 00	29 58	13♊45	27 22	10♋25	23 53	06♌47	19 23	01♍46	13 56	25 57	07♎51	19 44
1919	19♌22	02♍41	15 37	28 10	10♎24	22 25	04♏17	16 06	27 55	09♐50	21 53	04♑08	16 37	29 20	12♒18	25 30
1920	04♑53	16 47	28 45	10♒49	23 01	05♓22	17 56	00♈44	13 50	27 17	11♉08	25 22	10♊00	24 56	10♋04	26 16
1921	07♉33	21 05	05♊05	19 34	04♋25	29 31	04♌43	19 48	04♍39	19 08	03♎13	16 53	00♏10	13 07	25 47	08♐14
1922	25♍49	09♎57	23 56	07♏47	21 28	05♐01	18 22	01♑31	14 27	27 09	09♒36	21 50	03♓52	15 45	27 33	09♈21
1923	09♒42	22 49	05♓33	17 57	00♈05	12 01	23 53	05♉43	17 38	29 41	11♊56	24 26	07♋10	20 10	03♌24	16 51
1924	25♊18	07♋15	19 17	01♌26	13 43	26 11	08♍52	21 49	05♎03	18 38	02♏35	16 54	01♐31	16 23	01♑22	16 20
1925	28♎01	11♏42	25 51	10♐25	25 21	10♑29	25 42	10♒48	25 40	10♓11	24 19	08♈36	21 18	04♉14	16 50	29 10
1926	17♓58	02♈13	16 15	00♉01	13 31	26 45	09♊45	22 31	05♋04	17 24	29 35	11♌36	23 31	05♍22	17 12	29 04
1927	29♋34	12♌29	25 06	07♍28	19 37	01♎36	13 30	25 23	07♏21	19 27	01♐45	14 20	27 13	10♑26	23 58	07♒48
1928	15♐15	27 17	09♑28	21 52	04♒28	17 18	00♓21	13 37	27 07	10♈51	24 49	09♉00	23 22	07♊53	22 30	07♋06
1929	18♈57	02♉34	16 37	01♊05	15 56	01♋03	16 18	01♌30	16 29	01♍06	15 16	28 56	12♎08	24 55	07♏21	19 31
1930	10♍01	24 17	08♎11	21 44	04♏58	17 55	00♐37	13 08	25 30	07♑43	19 49	01♒49	13 43	25 35	07♓26	19 19
1931	19♑54	02♒40	15 10	27 24	09♓26	21 18	03♈07	14 57	26 52	09♉00	21 25	04♊10	17 19	00♋51	14 46	28 59
1932	05♊15	17 30	29 57	12♋37	25 30	08♌35	21 52	05♍19	18 58	02♎47	16 46	00♏55	15 13	29 37	14♐04	28 27
1933	09♎55	23 37	07♏44	22 16	07♐09	22 15	07♑26	22 30	07♒19	21 46	05♓46	19 18	02♈25	15 08	27 33	09♉42
1934	01♓26	15 43	29 38	13♈10	26 20	09♉11	21 47	04♊08	16 19	28 20	10♋15	22 05	03♌52	15 39	27 18	09♍23
1935	10♋18	22 44	04♌58	17 01	28 57	10♍48	22 38	04♎32	16 35	28 50	11♏23	24 26	07♐32	21 13	05♑18	19 42
1936	25♏10	07♐30	20 05	02♑56	16 04	29 28	13♒07	26 59	11♓01	25 10	09♈23	23 37	07♉50	22 00	06♊03	19 59
1937	01♈48	15 35	29 40	14♉01	28 37	13♊23	28 13	13♋00	27 36	11♌55	25 52	09♍24	22 30	05♎13	17 36	29 42
1938	22♌30	06♍55	20 53	04♎22	17 25	00♏06	12 28	24 37	06♐36	18 29	00♑19	12 09	24 00	05♒55	17 56	00♓02
1939	00♑34	12 52	25 01	07♒03	18 59	00♓51	12 42	24 36	06♈37	18 50	01♉21	14 14	27 32	11♊20	25 36	10♋17
1940	14♉46	27 14	10♊02	23 11	06♋42	20 31	04♌36	18 50	03♍08	17 27	01♎43	15 53	29 56	13♏52	27 40	11♐20
1941	23♍33	07♎20	21 22	05♏39	20 07	04♐45	19 26	04♑02	18 27	02♒34	16 18	29 37	12♓32	25 05	07♈20	19 21
1942	13♒30	27 48	11♓38	25 00	07♈57	20 33	02♉52	14 58	26 56	08♊50	20 41	02♋33	14 27	26 25	08♌30	20 41
1943	21♊19	03♋24	15 22	27 13	09♌01	20 47	02♍35	14 30	26 34	08♎53	21 32	04♏34	18 03	02♐00	16 24	01♑11
1944	04♏34	17 13	00♐12	13 33	27 17	11♑20	25 39	10♒09	24 45	09♓20	23 49	08♈09	22 17	06♉11	19 50	03♊13
1945	15♓40	29 43	13♈53	28 10	12♉30	26 49	11♊05	25 13	09♋10	22 51	06♌15	19 21	02♍08	14 37	26 52	06♎15
1946	03♌45	18 00	01♍51	15 15	28 13	10♎49	23 06	05♏09	17 02	28 51	10♐39	22 30	04♑27	16 33	28 49	11♒18
1947	11♐38	23 33	05♑24	17 15	29 06	10♒59	22 57	05♓01	17 15	29 42	12♈25	25 27	08♉53	22 44	07♊02	21 44
1948	24♈26	07♉03	20 04	03♊31	17 25	01♋44	16 25	01♌19	16 18	01♍12	15 53	00♎17	14 20	28 03	11♏26	24 31
1949	07♍58	22 07	06♎16	20 23	04♏28	18 30	02♐28	16 18	29 59	13♑27	26 39	09♒35	22 14	04♓35	16 43	28 39
1950	24♑28	08♒36	22 18	05♓33	18 22	00♈49	12 59	24 57	06♉48	18 37	00♊29	12 28	24 36	06♋56	19 28	02♌12
1951	02♊04	13 58	25 49	07♋41	19 34	01♌30	13 30	25 37	07♍54	20 24	03♎11	16 18	29 49	13♏46	28 09	12♐54
1952	14♎18	27 04	10♏15	23 55	08♐02	22 35	07♑27	22 30	07♒36	22 36	07♓21	21 47	05♈51	19 33	02♉53	15 54
1953	29♒55	14♓16	28 35	12♈47	26 52	10♉47	24 30	08♊02	21 19	04♋23	17 11	29 46	12♌06	24 15	06♍15	18 08
1954	14♋56	28 43	12♌09	25 13	07♍58	20 23	02♎35	14 36	26 30	08♏23	20 19	02♐22	14 36	27 02	09♑43	22 41
1955	22♏20	04♐09	15 57	27 47	09♑42	21 44	03♒56	16 18	28 52	11♓40	24 44	08♈04	21 42	05♉39	19 55	04♊26
1956	04♈52	17 41	00♉53	14 29	28 33	13♊03	27 55	13♋03	28 17	13♌28	28 25	13♍01	27 10	10♎51	24 06	06♏57
1957	21♌48	06♍28	20 56	05♎09	19 05	02♏44	16 07	29 16	12♐13	24 58	07♑32	19 56	02♒11	14 17	26 16	08♓09
1958	05♑26	19 02	02♒20	15 18	27 57	10♓18	22 23	04♈18	16 08	27 57	09♉51	21 56	04♊15	16 53	29 52	13♋11
1959	12♉14	24 02	05♊54	17 52	29 58	12♋15	24 42	07♌19	20 08	03♍08	16 20	29 45	13♎25	27 20	11♏31	25 56
1960	25♍21	08♎11	21 25	05♏06	19 15	03♐52	18 51	04♑05	19 24	04♒35	19 29	03♓59	18 02	01♈36	14 44	27 29
1961	13♒29	28 15	12♓45	26 58	10♈51	24 25	07♉41	20 42	03♊27	16 00	28 21	10♋32	22 34	04♌29	16 18	28♍05
1962	26♊30	09♋42	22 38	05♌16	17 39	29 49	11♍48	23 41	05♎32	17 26	29 27	11♏40	24 10	06♐59	20 09	03♑41
1963	02♏05	13 58	25 54	07♐57	20 10	02♑34	15 12	28 03	11♒08	24 27	07♓59	21 44	05♈40	19 46	04♉01	18♉21
1964	16♓27	29 31	12♈55	26 40	10♉48	25 17	10♊03	25 01	10♋03	25 02	09♌48	24 15	08♍17	21 53	05♎03	17 49
1965	04♌25	19 25	04♍09	18 31	02♎28	15 59	29 07	11♏54	24 25	06♐41	18 47	00♑45	12 39	24 30	06♒21	18 13
1966	17♐12	00♑05	12 46	25 15	07♒33	19 40	01♓40	13 34	25 25	07♈19	19 19	01♉31	13 59	26 49	10♊03	23 44
1967	21♈46	03♉36	15 32	27 38	09♊59	22 36	05♋32	18 47	02♌17	16 01	29 56	13♍57	28 03	12♎10	26 18	10♏25
1968	07♍52	21 00	04♎25	18 07	02♏10	16 32	01♐11	16 03	01♑00	15 54	00♒34	14 55	28 50	12♓18	25 18	07♈55
1969	25♑41	10♒47	25 31	09♓49	23 40	07♈03	20 02	02♉40	15 03	27 13	09♊15	21 12	03♋04	14 56	25 48	08♌41
1970	08♊20	20 59	03♋26	15 41	27 47	09♌43	21 34	03♍20	15 07	26 59	09♎01	21 17	03♏53	16 52	00 19	28♐35
1971	11♎10	23 06	05♏10	17 27	00♐00	12 52	26 04	09♑34	23 20	07♒21	21 32	05♓49	20 08	04♈26	18 41	02♉50
1972	29♒16	12 40	26♓20	10 14	24♈23	08 45	23♉16	07 52	22♊27	06 55	21♋10	05 09	18♌46	02 02	14♍56	27 31
1073	16♋18	01♌17	15 58	00♍17	14 09	27 35	10♎36	23 14	06♏34	17 40	29 36	11♐26	23 14	05♑02	16 54	28 52
1974	29♏18	11♐38	23 48	05♑50	17 47	29 39	11♒30	23 21	05♓15	17 15	29 24	11♈46	24 26	07♉26	20 52	04♊43
1975	00♈59	12 54	24 58	07♉15	19 49	02♊44	16 03	29 47	13♋53	28 17	12♌54	27 36	12♍16	26 47	11♎06	25 09
1976	21♌00	04♍44	18 36	02♎35	16 41	00♏51	15 05	29 21	13♐36	27 46	11♑46	25 32	09♒01	22 10	04♓59	17 28
1977	07♑03	22 02	06♒44	21 01	04♓50	18 09	01♈02	13 31	25 43	07♉42	19 33	01♊21	13 11	25 06	07♋07	19 18
1978	20♉01	02♊13	14 17	26 15	08♋09	20 01	01♌52	13 44	25 39	07♍39	19 48	02♎11	14 52	27 54	11♏23	25 21
1979	20♍32	02♎25	14 31	26 53	09♏36	22 44	06♐20	20 21	04♑46	19 29	04♒22	19 16	04♓04	18 40	02♈59	17 01
1980	12♒38	26 36	10♓41	24 49	09♈01	23 12	07♉23	21 39	05♊30	19 20	02♋58	16 21	29 26	12♌14	24 46	07♍02
1981	28♊12	12♋50	27 11	11♌11	24 46	07♍57	20 46	03♎15	15 28	27 30	09♏25	21 17	03♐11	15 10	27 18	09♑25
1982	10♏44	22 49	04♐45	16 36	28 24	10♑12	22 03	03♒58	15 59	28 10	10♓32	23 09	06♈03	19 17	02 52	16 50
1983	10♓29	22 30	04♈43	17 10	29 57	13♉07	26 43	10♊45	25 12	10♋00	25 02	10♌09	25 12	10♍03	24 33	08♎41
1984	03♌53	18 16	02♍44	17 11	01♎31	15 43	29 44	13♏33	27 10	10♐35	23 48	06♑49	19 38	02♒15	14 40	26 53
1985	19♐00	03♑21	17 31	01♒22	14 53	28 02	10♓47	23 13	05♈22	17 19	29 09	10♉57	22 49	04♊50	17 03	29 31
1986	01♉03	12 59	24 49	06♊37	18 27	00♋20	12 20	24 26	06♌42	19 06	01♍40	14 27	27 27	10♎42	24 16	08♏10
1987	00♍43	12 43	24 54	07♎20	20 07	03♏19	16 59	01♐09	15 47	00♑48	16 04	01♒23	16 35	01♓28	15 58	30 00
1988	25♑25	10♒07	24 48	09♓21	23 43	07♈51	21 45	05♉24	18 50	02♊02	15 02	27 49	10♋24	22 46	04♌58	16 59
1989	10♊34	24 37	08♋25	21 56	05♌07	17 57	00♍29	12 44	24 47	06♎41	18 32	00♏25	12 25	24 35	07♐01	19 43
1990	21♎00	02♏59	14 52	26 44	08♐38	20 37	02♑42	14 56	27 20	09♒55	22 43	05♓44	18 59	02♈30	16 16	00♉19
1991	21♒00	03♓07	15 28	28 06	11♈03	24 24	08♉09	22 20	06♊55	21 48	06♋55	22 05	07♌09	21 59	06♍29	20 33
1992	16♋10	01♌05	16 02	00♍51	15 26	29 44	13♎41	27 16	10♏32	23 29	06♐10	18 37	00♑53	13 00	25 00	06♒55
1993	02♐01	15 37	29 00	12♑10	25 05	07♒46	20 13	02♓27	14 31	26 27	08♈19	20 13	02♉12	14 22	26 47	09♊32
1994	11♈01	22 55	04♉44	16 32	28 24	10♊25	22 37	05♋04	17 45	00♌42	13 53	27 18	10♍54	24 40	08♎34	22 36
1995	11♌39	23 59	06♍30	19 14	02♎14	15 33	29 14	13♏19	27 47	12♐36	27 39	12♑49	27 55	12♒46	27 16	11♓18
1996	07♑05	22 20	07♒32	22 33	07♓13	21 29	05♈19	18 43	01♉46	14 30	26 59	09♊15	21 24	03♋26	15 23	27 16
1997	23♉32	06♊52	20 00	02♋55	15 37	28 04	10♌19	22 22	04♍16	16 05	27 52	09♎43	21 42	03♏56	16 29	29 26
1998	00♎27	12 20	24 11	06♏05	18 06	00♐19	12 45	25 28	08♑26	21 41	05♒09	18 50	02♓41	16 40	00♈44	14 53
1999	02♒25	14 53	27 34	10♓28	23 39	07♈09	20 58	05♉08	19 36	04♊19	19 10	04♋03	18 49	03♌21	17 32	01♍20
2000	28♊00	13♋11	28 21	13♌20	28 00	12♍18	26 10	09♎36	22 39	05♏21	17 46	29 57	11♐58	23 51	05♑41	17 29

Year	17th	18th	19th	20th	21st	22nd	23rd	24th	25th	26th	27th	28th	29th	30th	31st
1900	24 12	08♈37	22 49	06♉28	20 32	04♊01	17 18	00♋22	13 14	25 55	08♌24	20 43	02♍52	14 53	26♍47
1901	07♌28	20 52	03♍56	16 38	29 02	11♎09	23 05	04♏55	16 44	28 38	10♐40	22 57	05♑30	18 23	01♒35
1902	12 39	24 31	06♑27	18 30	00♒42	13 03	25 35	08♓16	21 09	04♈15	17 35	01♉10	15 04	29 15	13♊43
1903	13 42	26 29	09♉41	23 20	07♊28	22 04	07♋03	22 17	07♌36	22 47	07♍42	22 12	06♎16	19 51	03♏00
1904	16 01	00♎27	14 38	28 32	12♏09	25 31	08♐38	21 31	04♑12	16 41	28 59	11♒05	23 05	04♓57	16♓45
1905	28 05	11♒10	23 56	06♓25	18 39	00♈40	12 35	24 36	06♉19	18 19	00♊30	12 56	25 41	08♋45	22♋10
1906	02♊46	14 40	26 40	08♋48	21 06	03♌35	16 17	29 12	12♍20	25 42	09♎18	23 08	07♏11	21 26	05♐51
1907	04♎29	17 28	00♏48	14 33	28 41	13♐13	28 04	13♑07	28 15	13♒19	28 10	12♓41	26 46	10♈25	23♈37
1908	07♓28	22 10	06♈31	20 29	04♉03	17 15	00♊06	12 41	25 03	07♋13	19 15	01♌11	13 03	24 53	06♍43
1909	18 26	01♌13	13 48	26 10	08♍20	20 21	02♎16	14 07	26 01	08♏00	20 10	02♐37	15 24	28 35	12♑12
1910	22 22	04♐16	16 20	18 37	11♑09	23 59	07♒04	20 26	04♓01	17 46	01♈40	15 40	29 44	13♉52	28♉02
1911	25 54	08♈58	22 19	06♉00	20 02	04♊25	19 08	04♋04	19 07	04♌06	18 53	03♍19	17 18	00♎49	13♎52
1912	28 52	13♍35	27 53	11♎44	25 09	08♏10	20 52	03♐19	15 33	27 39	09♑39	21 34	03♒27	15 19	27♒12
1913	09♑14	21 50	04♒12	16 24	28 24	10♓17	22 05	03♈53	15 44	27 44	09♉58	22 31	05♊28	18 51	02♋52
1914	12 00	24 02	06♊16	18 44	01♋30	14 34	27 55	11♌31	25 21	09♍21	23 27	07♎38	21 51	06♏04	20♏15
1915	17 06	00♎22	13 55	27 45	11♏54	26 18	10♐55	25 39	10♑25	25 04	09♒29	23 37	07♓22	20 43	03♈42
1916	19 35	04♓19	18 39	02♈33	16 01	29 03	11♉44	24 07	06♊15	18 13	00♋04	11 51	23 38	05♌27	17♌21
1917	00♋00	12 15	24 21	06♌20	18 14	00♍04	11 54	23 46	05♎43	17 50	00♏10	12 48	25 47	09♐11	23♐02
1918	01♏39	13 42	25 57	08♐29	21 21	04♑35	18 12	02♒10	16 25	00♓53	15 27	00♈01	14 28	28 45	12♉50
1919	08♓54	22 30	06♈17	20 13	04♉17	18 29	02♊48	17 10	01♋33	15 51	00♌00	13 55	27 31	10♍45	23♍38
1920	10♌18	25 03	09♍23	23 14	06♎35	19 31	02♏02	14 16	26 16	08♐09	19 58	01♑48	13 41	25 40	07♒47
1921	20 31	02♑40	14 42	26 40	08♒34	20 25	02♓17	14 10	26 08	08♈15	20 35	03♉13	16 13	29 39	13♊35
1922	21 15	03♉18	15 38	28 18	11♊22	24 52	08♋47	23 05	07♌39	22 24	07♍10	21 51	06♎21	20 38	04♏39
1923	00♍29	14 16	28 12	12♎14	26 22	10♏35	24 50	09♐04	23 14	07♑16	21 06	04♒39	17 55	00♓52	13♓30
1924	01♒07	15 36	29 42	13♓23	26 39	09♈30	22 01	04♉15	16 18	28 13	10♊05	21 57	03♋54	15 57	28♋08
1925	11♊19	23 17	05♋10	16 58	28 45	10♌33	22 24	04♍21	16 26	28 43	11♎14	24 03	07♏13	20 46	04♐45
1926	11♎04	23 14	05♏40	18 26	01♐34	15 08	29 08	13♑32	28 16	13♒13	28 16	13♓15	28 02	12♈32	26♈39
1927	21 53	06♓07	20 27	04♈48	19 06	03♉18	17 22	01♊17	15 02	28 36	11♋58	25 07	08♌04	20 46	03♍16
1928	21 35	05♌52	19 50	03♍26	16 38	29 27	11♎55	24 06	06♏04	17 55	29 43	11♐34	23 33	05♑43	18♑07
1929	01♐29	13 21	25 11	07♑00	18 53	00♒50	12 53	25 04	07♓23	19 52	02♈33	15 28	28 39	12♉10	26♉03
1930	01♈17	13 26	25 51	08♉35	21 44	05♊22	19 29	04♋04	19 03	04♌15	19 31	04♍40	19 32	04♎00	18♎02
1931	13♌25	27 58	12♍30	26 57	11♎15	25 22	09♏18	23 02	06♐34	19 55	03♑04	16 01	28 44	11♒15	23♒33
1932	12♑42	26 42	10♒23	23 43	06♓40	19 17	01♈36	13 40	25 36	07♉27	19 19	01♊17	13 25	25 46	08♋23
1933	21 42	03♊36	15 27	27 19	09♋15	21 16	03♌24	15 41	28 07	10♍46	23 37	06♎44	20 08	03♏49	17♏50
1934	21 27	03♎43	16 16	29 10	12♏29	26 13	10♐25	25 01	09♑57	25 06	10♒19	25 26	10♓18	24 48	08♈54
1935	04♒22	19 11	04♓00	18 45	03♈17	17 34	01♉32	15 11	28 31	11♊34	24 22	06♋56	19 17	01♌29	13♌32
1936	03♋44	17 16	00♌34	13 37	26 23	08♍54	21 10	03♎15	15 12	27 05	08♏58	20 57	03♐06	15 29	28♐11
1937	11♏37	23 27	05♐15	17 06	29 05	11♑13	23 34	06♒09	18 57	02♓00	15 16	28 44	12♈23	26 13	10♉13
1938	12 18	24 44	07♈24	20 21	03♉37	17 17	01♊22	15 50	00♋41	15 47	01♌00	16 09	01♍04	15 36	29♍40
1939	25 16	10♌25	25 32	10♍29	25 06	09♎21	23 11	06♏39	19 45	02♐34	15 08	27 31	09♑45	21 52	03♒52
1940	24 50	08♑08	21 13	04♒04	16 39	29 00	11♓07	23 04	04♈55	16 42	28 33	10♉31	22 43	05♊13	18♊06
1941	01♉14	13 05	24 57	06♊56	19 04	01♋26	14 01	26 52	09♌57	23 15	06♍44	20 25	04♎14	18 11	02♏16
1942	03♍02	15 35	28 22	11♎27	24 51	08♏38	22 48	07♐19	22 08	07♑07	22 08	07♒03	21 43	06♓02	19♓55
1943	16 14	01♒25	16 34	01♓33	16 13	00♈31	14 23	27 52	10♉57	23 42	06♊10	18 25	00♋28	12 24	24♋14
1944	16 22	29 17	11♋58	24 26	06♌42	18 49	00♍48	12 40	24 31	06♎22	18 17	00♏22	12 41	25 17	08♐14
1945	20 51	02♏44	14 39	26 40	08♐52	21 18	04♑01	17 03	00♒24	14 04	28 00	12♓06	26 21	10♈39	24♈57
1946	23 58	06♓53	20 00	03♈22	16 58	00♉49	14 54	29 13	13♊42	28 20	13♋00	27 36	12♌02	26 12	10♍00
1947	06♋46	22 00	07♌15	22 22	07♍09	21 31	05♎24	18 48	01♏46	14 21	26 38	08♐41	20 36	02♑27	14♑16
1948	07♐22	20 00	02♑28	14 47	26 57	09♒01	20 58	02♓51	14 42	26 33	08♈28	20 32	02♉48	15 22	28♉20
1949	10♈29	22 18	04♉10	16 12	28 28	11♊03	24 00	07♋21	21 04	05♌07	19 25	03♍52	18 21	02♎48	17♎09
1950	15 09	28 18	11♍37	25 08	08♎50	22 43	06♏48	21 04	05♐28	19 57	04♑26	18 48	02♒59	16 51	00♓23
1951	27 57	13♑09	28 19	13♒17	27 55	12♓08	25 53	09♈11	22 04	04♉37	16 52	18 56	10♊52	22 44	04♋36
1952	28 37	11♊06	23 23	05♋30	17 28	29 21	11♌09	22 56	04♍43	16 34	28 33	10♎42	23 07	05♏51	18♏58
1953	29 58	11♎50	23 49	05♏58	18 22	01♐05	14 10	27 39	11♑32	25 46	10♒17	25 00	09♓48	24 33	09♈09
1954	05 55	19 25	03♓08	17 03	01♈06	15 16	29 29	13♉43	27 56	12♊05	26 07	10♋00	23 42	07♌10	20♌22
1955	19 10	04♋02	18 54	03♌38	18 08	02♍16	16 00	29 19	12♎12	24 43	06♏56	18 56	00♐47	12 35	24♐24
1956	19 27	01♐43	13 46	25 42	07♑34	19 24	01♒15	13 08	25 05	07♓07	19 17	01♈36	14 08	26 56	10♉03
1957	20 00	01♈52	13 49	25 56	08♉18	21 00	04♊07	17 41	01♋44	16 14	01♌05	16 09	01♍16	16 16	01♎01
1958	26 50	10♌44	24 51	09♍05	23 21	07♐36	21 47	05♎54	19 54	03♏48	17 34	01♑12	14 39	27 53	10♒53
1959	10 33	25 17	09♑59	24 33	08♒51	22 48	06♓20	19 26	02♈09	14 32	26 39	08♉35	20 26	02♊17	14♊12
1960	09♉55	22 07	04♊09	16 05	27 57	09♋48	21 41	03♌36	15 36	27 42	09♍57	22 22	05♎00	17 55	01♏10
1961	09♍52	21 42	03♎41	15 53	28 22	11♏13	24 30	08♐14	22 27	07♑04	22 00	07♒09	22 19	07♓22	22 10
1962	17 33	01♒43	16 05	00♓36	15 09	29 39	14♈03	28 16	12♉16	26 03	09♊36	22 53	05♋57	18 47	01♌23
1963	02♊43	17 04	01♋20	15 25	29 17	12♌52	26 08	09♍04	21 42	04♎04	16 13	28 11	10♏05	21 58	03♐56
1964	00♏14	12 23	24 20	06♐10	17 58	29 47	12♑00	23 41	05♒51	18 11	00♓44	13 30	26 29	09♈42	23 10
1965	00♓08	12 08	24 16	06♈36	19 10	02♉03	18 18	28 57	12♊04	27 37	12♋31	27 42	12♌59	28 10	13♍07
1966	07♋51	22 21	07♌08	22 03	06♍58	21 43	06♎14	20 25	04♏17	17 49	01♐03	14 02	26 48	09♑23	21♑48
1967	24 31	08♐33	22 30	06♑19	19 57	03♒20	16 26	29 14	11♓44	23 58	05♈59	17 52	29 40	11♉30	23♉27
1968	20 12	02♉14	14 08	25 57	07♊48	19 43	01♋46	13 59	26 23	09♌00	21 48	04♍49	18 00	01♎23	14♎57
1969	20 38	02♍40	14 51	27 13	09♎51	22 48	06♏08	19 53	04♐05	18 42	03♑40	18 51	04♒04	19 10	03♓58
1970	28 35	13♑18	28 17	13♒21	28 22	13♓13	27 47	12♈00	25 51	09♉21	22 31	05♊23	18 00	00♋23	12♋36
1971	16 51	00♊42	14 22	27 48	11♋01	23 59	06♌42	19 11	01♍26	13 31	25 27	07♎18	19 10	01♏05	13♏08
1972	09♎48	21 54	03♏50	15 44	27 37	09♐36	21 43	04♑02	16 35	29 24	12♒28	25 47	09♓21	23 08	07♈05
1973	10♒58	23 13	05♓40	18 19	01♈14	14 25	27 54	11♉42	25 50	10♊16	24 57	09♋49	24 44	09♌35	24♌14
1974	19 02	03♋45	18 47	03♌59	19 12	04♍15	19 01	03♎21	17 15	00♏41	13 42	26 22	08♐44	20 54	02♑54
1975	08♏57	22 29	05♐46	18 51	01♑44	14 25	26 56	09♒17	21 28	03♓31	15 27	27 19	09♈09	21 03	03♉05
1976	29 40	11♈39	23 31	05♉19	17 10	29 09	11♊21	23 50	06♋37	19 45	03♌13	16 58	00♍57	15 04	29♍17
1977	01♌38	14 08	26 49	09♍41	22 45	06♎02	19 33	03♏21	17 25	01♐46	16 21	01♑05	15 52	00♒34	15♒03
1978	09♐46	24 38	09♑47	25 06	10♒22	25 25	10♓06	24 21	08♈07	21 26	04♉21	16 56	29 14	11♊21	23♊19
1979	00♉44	14 09	27 18	10♊12	22 52	05♋21	17 38	29 45	11♌44	23 36	05♍23	17 10	28 58	10♎52	22♎57
1980	19 06	01♎02	12 54	24 46	06♏43	18 50	01♐12	13 51	26 50	10♑11	23 52	07♒52	22 06	06♓31	21♓00
1981	22 04	04♒47	17 42	00♓52	14 16	27 52	11♈41	25 42	09♉53	24 12	08♊35	23 00	07♋22	21 36	05♌37
1982	01♊11	15 51	00♋46	15 50	00♌53	15 47	00♍24	14 39	28 27	11♎48	24 45	07♏18	19 34	01♐36	13♐29
1983	22 24	05♏42	18 39	01♐18	13 41	25 53	07♑56	19 53	01♒46	13 37	25 28	07♓20	19 17	01♈20	13♈34
1984	08♓57	20 53	02♈45	14 37	26 33	08♉39	20 59	03♊38	16 41	00♋09	14 04	28 23	13♌01	27 50	12♍43
1985	12♋17	25 21	08♌42	22 17	06♍03	19 59	04♎00	18 05	02♏12	16 20	00♐28	14 35	28 38	12♑34	26♑21
1986	22 24	06♐58	21 48	06♑46	21 45	06♒35	21 08	05♓16	18 56	02♈09	14 56	27 21	09♉30	21 27	03♊18
1987	13♈34	26 44	09♉32	22 02	04♊18	16 25	28 24	10♋19	22 11	04♌02	15 54	27 48	09♍46	21 51	04♎07
1988	28 52	10♍40	22 27	04♎16	16 12	28 21	10♏48	23 36	06♐51	20 33	04♑42	19 15	04♒06	19 07	04♓08
1989	02♑44	16 03	29 40	13♒31	27 35	11♓46	26 02	10♈19	24 34	08♉46	22 52	06♊49	20 37	04♋13	17♋35
1990	14 35	29 04	13♊41	28 20	12♋55	27 20	11♌29	25 19	08♍46	21 51	04♎34	17 00	29 10	11♏10	23♏04
1991	04♎10	17 22	00♏10	12 38	24 50	06♐51	18 43	00♑32	12 19	24 09	06♒03	18 04	00♓13	12 32	25♓04
1992	18 47	00♓37	12 29	24 26	06♈30	18 45	01♉16	14 07	27 20	11♊00	25 07	09♋40	24 34	09♌42	24♌56
1993	22 39	06♋10	20 04	04♌19	18 48	03♍25	18 04	02♎37	17 01	01♏10	15 05	28 45	12♐11	25 24	08♑25
1994	06♏45	20 59	05♐16	19 35	03♑51	18 00	01♒56	15 36	28 56	11♓56	24 34	06♈54	18 59	00♉53	12♉42
1995	24 50	07♈54	20 34	02♉53	14 57	26 51	08♊40	20 29	02♋21	14 18	26 23	08♌37	21 01	03♍35	16♍19
1996	09♌07	20 58	02♍50	14 47	26 50	09♎06	21 37	04♏29	17 46	01♐31	16 45	00♑26	15 30	00♒46	16♒05
1997	12♐48	26 37	10♑51	25 25	10♒11	25 03	09♓52	24 32	08♈57	23 06	06♉57	20 31	03♊49	16 51	29♊40
1998	29 05	13♉17	27 28	11♊34	25 33	09♋20	22 53	06♌09	19 07	01♍48	14 12	26 22	08♎22	20 15	02♏06
1999	14 43	27 42	10♎20	22 40	04♏46	16 44	28 37	10♐29	22 25	04♑28	16 39	29 01	11♒34	24 22	07♓22
2000	29 17	11♒09	23 06	05♓11	17 27	29 55	12♈40	25 43	09♉08	22 56	07♊08	21 41	06♋32	21 34	06♌40

Moon

August

Year	1st	2nd	3rd	4th	5th	6th	7th	8th	9th	10th	11th	12th	13th	14th	15th	16th
1900	08♎38	20 29	02♏25	14 31	26 51	09♐32	22 36	06♑07	20 07	04♒32	19 18	04♓16	19 19	04♈15	18 56	03♉19
1901	15♒05	28 51	12♓49	26 54	11♈03	25 13	09♉22	23 28	07♊32	21 31	05♋25	19 11	02♌47	16 10	29 18	12♍09
1902	28♊25	13♋15	28 05	12♌47	27 13	11♍16	24 53	08♎03	20 49	03♏13	15 21	27 19	09♐10	21 00	02♑54	14 55
1903	15♏48	28 16	10♐31	22 36	04♑34	16 28	28 21	10♒13	22 07	04♓04	16 07	28 17	10♈36	23 10	05♉59	19 10
1904	28♓32	10♈22	22 19	04♉29	16 55	29 44	12♊58	26 39	10♋49	25 23	10♌16	25 20	10♍26	25 25	10♎09	24 34
1905	05♌53	19 52	04♍04	18 24	02♎48	17 11	01♏30	15 43	29 46	13♐39	27 19	10♑47	24 01	07♒02	19 46	02♓18
1906	20♐20	04♑51	19 18	03♒35	17 37	01♓21	14 45	27 48	10♈30	22 55	05♉05	17 05	28 59	10♊52	22 48	04♋51
1907	06♉25	18 52	01♊03	13 01	24 52	06♋39	18 26	00♌17	12 13	24 17	06♍30	18 55	01♎32	14 22	27 28	10♏50
1908	18♍35	00♎32	12 37	24 53	07♏24	20 15	03♐28	17 07	01♑14	15 47	00♒42	15 53	01♓11	16 23	01♈21	15 55
1909	26♑13	10♒36	25 16	10♓04	24 52	09♈33	24 00	08♉12	22 05	05♊41	19 00	02♋06	14 58	27 39	10♌10	22 31
1910	12♊12	26 22	10♋27	24 25	08♌12	21 43	04♍56	17 50	00♎25	12 42	24 45	06♏38	18 27	00♐17	12 12	24 19
1911	26♎31	08♏50	20 53	02♐48	14 38	26 28	08♑21	20 22	02♒32	14 52	27 22	10♓03	22 51	05♈59	19 15	02♉43
1912	09♓06	21 06	03♈13	15 31	28 05	10♉58	24 15	07♊58	22 10	06♋47	21 47	07♌00	22 16	07♍24	22 14	06♎41
1913	16♋58	01♌36	16 27	01♍25	16 20	01♎06	15 36	29 47	13♏39	27 11	10♐26	23 24	06♑07	18 38	00♒56	13 05
1914	04♐21	18 20	02♑10	15 48	29 12	12♒21	25 13	07♓49	20 10	02♈18	14 17	26 10	08♉01	19 56	01♊58	14 13
1915	16♈19	28 39	10♉45	22 43	04♊35	16 28	28 25	10♋28	22 42	05♌08	17 48	00♍43	13 51	27 14	10♎49	24 37
1916	29♌21	11♍29	23 49	06♎21	19 09	02♏15	15 40	29 27	13♐36	28 05	12♑52	27 50	12♒52	27 50	12♓36	27 02
1917	07♑19	22 01	07♒01	22 11	07♓22	22 24	07♈08	21 29	05♉24	18 52	01♊56	14 40	27 06	09♋19	21 23	03♌19
1918	26♉41	10♊19	23 44	06♋56	19 56	02♌45	15 22	27 48	10♍03	22 08	04♎06	15 58	27 48	09♏41	21 42	03♐55
1919	06♎11	18 25	00♏26	12 18	24 07	05♐57	17 55	00♑04	12 29	25 11	08♒13	21 32	05♓08	18 57	02♈56	17 01
1920	20♒02	02♓27	15 01	27 46	10♈43	23 55	07♉22	21 06	05♊10	19 32	04♋11	19 01	03♌55	18 45	03♍21	17 36
1921	27♊59	12♋49	27 59	13♌17	28 33	13♍35	28 17	12♎32	26 19	09♏40	22 37	05♐14	17 35	29 45	11♑46	23 43
1922	18♏25	01♐54	15 10	28 11	11♑00	23 37	06♒01	18 15	00♓19	12 14	24 04	05♈51	17 38	29 32	11♉35	23 53
1923	25♓51	07♈58	19 55	01♉48	13 39	25 36	07♊41	20 00	02♋35	15 29	28 42	12♌15	26 05	10♍08	24 22	08♎42
1924	10♌30	23 04	05♍50	18 49	02♎02	15 30	29 12	13♏08	27 18	11♐40	26 10	10♑43	25 16	09♒41	23 53	07♓49
1925	19♐07	03♑51	18 51	04♒00	19 08	04♓06	18 47	03♈05	16 56	00♉20	13 18	25 54	08♊12	20 15	02♋09	13 57
1926	10♉24	23 46	06♊48	19 31	02♋00	14 16	26 23	08♌23	20 18	02♍09	13 59	25 49	07♎43	19 44	01♏54	14 17
1927	15♍32	27 38	09♎36	21 28	03♏20	15 16	27 20	09♐39	22 16	05♑15	18 39	02♒28	16 40	01♓11	15 53	00♈39
1928	00♒46	13 42	26 54	10♓20	23 57	07♈45	21 39	05♉40	19 46	03♊55	18 07	02♋20	16 31	00♌37	14 33	28 14
1929	10♊18	24 54	09♋48	24 51	09♌56	24 51	09♍29	23 41	07♎25	20 41	03♏30	15 57	28 07	10♐06	21 57	03♑46
1930	01♏38	14 50	27 41	10♐15	22 35	04♑46	16 49	28 47	10♒42	22 34	04♓26	16 18	28 14	10♈16	22 28	04♉53
1931	05♓39	17 36	29 26	11♈13	23 01	04♉57	17 04	29 28	12♊14	25 25	09♋02	23 06	07♌34	22 18	07♍12	22 07
1932	21♋16	04♌27	17 54	01♍35	15 27	29 27	13♎34	27 44	11♏57	26 09	10♐18	24 23	08♑20	22 07	05♒41	19 00
1933	02♐08	16 42	01♑26	16 15	01♒00	15 35	29 54	13♓51	27 24	10♈34	23 21	05♉49	18 01	00♊01	11 56	23 48
1934	22♈33	05♉47	18 37	01♊08	13 23	25 25	07♋19	19 08	00♌55	12 43	24 33	06♍29	18 32	00♎45	13 09	25 48
1935	25♌29	07♍21	19 11	01♎02	12 56	24 58	07♏11	19 40	02♐29	15 41	29 20	13♑25	27 56	12♒48	27 54	13♓05
1936	11♑13	24 38	08♒25	22 30	06♓50	21 19	05♈50	20 18	04♉39	18 49	02♊47	16 32	00♋05	13 25	26 34	09♌31
1937	24♉22	08♊39	23 03	07♋29	21 53	06♌11	20 15	04♍03	17 29	00♎33	13 15	25 38	07♏44	19 40	01♐29	13 18
1938	13♎15	26 21	09♏03	21 24	03♐30	15 25	27 16	09♑05	20 56	02♒52	14 54	27 04	09♓22	21 50	04♈27	17 17
1939	15♒48	27 41	09♓32	21 23	03♈18	15 20	27 32	10♉01	22 50	06♊04	19 47	03♋59	18 39	03♌41	18 57	04♍15
1940	01♋23	15 06	29 12	13♌38	28 16	12♍59	27 40	12♎14	26 35	10♏43	24 35	08♐13	21 36	04♑46	17 43	00♒28
1941	16♏27	00♐42	14 59	29 14	13♑24	27 23	11♒07	24 35	07♓42	20 30	02♈59	15 13	27 15	09♉09	21 01	02♊54
1942	03♈22	16 24	29 04	11♉26	23 33	05♊31	17 24	29 15	11♋09	23 08	05♌14	17 29	29 55	12♍33	25 24	08♎28
1943	06♌02	17 49	29 38	11♍31	23 31	05♎40	18 03	00♏43	13 43	27 05	10♐52	25 05	09♑41	24 36	09♒43	24 53
1944	21♐36	05♑24	19 36	04♒11	19 02	04♓01	19 01	03♈52	18 29	02♉45	16 40	00♊12	13 23	26 16	08♋53	21 16
1945	09♉12	23 20	07♊21	21 12	04♋54	18 25	01♌43	14 49	27 40	10♍17	22 41	04♎53	16 54	28 48	10♏40	22 33
1946	23♍24	06♎24	19 02	01♏20	13 23	25 16	07♐05	18 54	00♑48	12 52	25 08	07♒39	20 25	03♓27	16 44	00♈13
1947	26♑07	08♒02	20 01	02♓07	14 20	16 42	09♈16	22 02	05♉04	18 26	02♊08	16 14	00♋43	15 31	00♌34	15 41
1948	11♊45	25 39	10♋02	24 51	09♌57	25 12	10♍24	25 23	10♎01	24 14	08♏01	21 23	04♐24	17 06	29 33	11♑50
1949	01♏20	15 21	29 11	12♐51	26 19	09♑37	22 42	05♒34	18 13	00♓38	12 51	24 52	06♈45	18 33	00♉21	12 12
1950	13♓32	26 19	08♈46	20 57	02♉56	14 49	16 40	08♊35	20 37	02♋51	15 19	28 04	11♌05	24 22	07♍53	21 37
1951	16♋29	28 26	10♌29	22 40	05♍00	17 31	00♎14	13 11	26 25	09♏58	23 49	08♐01	22 29	07♑11	22 02	06♒52
1952	02♐30	16 30	00♑57	15 45	00♒50	16 02	01♓13	16 12	00♈52	15 09	29 00	12♉25	25 26	08♊05	20 27	02♋34
1953	23♈32	07♉38	21 26	04♊56	18 08	01♋04	13 46	26 16	08♌34	20 42	02♍43	14 38	26 29	08♎19	20 11	02♏08
1954	03♍18	15 57	28 21	10♎31	22 32	04♏26	16 19	28 14	10♐17	22 33	05♑05	17 57	01♒10	14 45	28 40	12♓51
1955	06♑19	18♒21	00 35	13 02	25♓42	08 35	21♈42	05 02	18♉33	02 16	16♊11	00 16	14 31	28♋54	13 22	27♌51
1956	23♉32	07♊26	21 45	06♋28	21 29	06♌42	21 55	06♍59	21 42	05♎59	19 47	03♏06	15 58	28 28	10♐40	22 40
1957	15♎25	29 25	13♏02	26 18	09♐16	21 58	04♑28	16 47	28 59	11♒03	23 02	04♓56	16 48	28 38	10♈30	22 27
1958	23♒38	06♓07	18 21	00♈23	12 16	24 04	05♉53	17 47	29 52	12♊13	24 55	08♋00	21 31	05♌25	19 41	04♍11
1959	26♊15	08♋30	20 57	03♌39	16 35	29 44	13♍05	26 37	10♎20	24 11	08♏11	22 19	06♐33	20 52	05♑11	19 27
1960	14♏46	28 46	13♐09	27 52	12♑50	27 54	12♒55	27 44	12♓14	26 20	10♈00	23 13	06♉03	18 32	00♊46	12 47
1961	05♈37	20 40	04♉19	17 35	00♊30	13 06	25 27	07♋36	19 36	01♌29	13 18	25 05	06♍52	18 42	00♎38	12 42
1962	13♌47	25 59	08♍02	19 58	01♎50	13 40	25 33	07♏33	19 45	02♐12	14 59	28 09	11♑45	25 46	10♒10	24 52
1963	15♐02	28 20	10♑54	23 46	06♒56	20 25	04♓10	18 09	02♈18	16 32	00♉49	15 04	29 15	13♊20	27 18	11♋07
1964	06♉53	20 51	05♊05	19 31	04♋08	18 51	03♌33	18 08	02♍28	16 28	00♎05	13 16	26 04	08♏30	20 39	02♐36
1965	27♍41	11♎46	25 23	08♏32	21 16	03♐41	15 51	27 50	09♑43	21 33	03♒23	15 15	27 11	09♓13	21 21	03♈37
1966	04♒04	16 12	28 13	10♓08	21 59	03♈50	15 42	27 40	09♉50	22 15	05♊02	18 14	01♋55	16 05	00♌43	15 42
1967	05♊36	18 01	00♋48	13 56	27 28	11♌20	25 29	09♍49	24 14	08♎40	23 01	07♏15	21 21	05♐17	19 03	02♑39
1968	28♎44	12♏43	26 55	11♐17	25 47	10♑20	24 50	09♒10	23 14	06♓57	20 18	03♈16	15 53	28 11	10♉15	22 10
1969	18♓23	02♈21	15 51	28 55	11♉36	23 59	06♊08	18 08	00♋01	11 53	23 44	05♌39	17 38	29 44	11♍57	24 20
1970	24♋39	06♌35	18 25	00♍12	11 59	23 47	05♎42	17 45	00♏01	12 36	25 32	08♐53	22 41	06♑56	21 35	06♒56
1971	25♏25	07♐59	20 53	04♑10	17 51	01♒54	16 16	00♓52	15 36	00♈20	14 59	29 27	13♉40	27 36	11♊15	24 36
1972	21♈10	05♉21	19 34	03♊49	18 02	02♋10	16 11	00♌02	13 40	27 02	10♍08	22 56	05♎28	17 45	29 50	11♏47
1973	08♍34	22 31	06♎01	19 06	01♏46	14 07	26 12	08♐07	19 55	01♑43	13 34	25 32	07♒39	19 58	02♓30	15 15
1974	14♑48	26 39	08♒30	20 21	02♓16	14 14	26 19	08♈33	20 57	03♉36	16 33	29 51	13♊34	27 42	12♋16	27 12
1975	15♉19	27 51	10♊46	24 08	07♋58	22 15	06♌56	21 54	06♍59	22 02	06♎52	21 24	05♏34	19 21	02♐47	15 53
1976	13♎30	27 41	11♏49	25 53	09♐52	23 44	07♑29	21 05	04♒28	17 38	00♓32	13 09	25 31	07♈39	19 36	01♉26
1977	29♒12	12♓56	26 15	09♈09	21 40	03♉54	15 54	27 47	09♊37	21 30	03♋29	15 37	27 57	10♌31	23 18	06♍18
1978	05♋13	17 04	28 56	10♌49	22 45	04♍47	16 56	29 14	11♎44	24 30	07♏34	21 00	04♐49	19 03	03♑39	18 33
1979	05♏18	17 59	01♐03	14 35	28 35	13♑02	27 50	12♒54	28 03	13♓09	28 03	12♈39	26 53	10♉42	24 08	07♊12
1980	05♈30	19 55	04♉12	18 19	02♊13	15 53	29 20	12♋33	25 31	08♌16	20 47	03♍07	15 15	27 15	09♎09	20 59
1981	19♌23	02♍50	15 57	28 44	11♎14	23 28	05♏31	17 27	29 19	11♐14	23 15	05♑27	17 52	00♒34	13 34	26 52
1982	25♐17	07♑05	18 55	00♒51	12 56	25 10	07♓35	20 12	03♈03	16 07	29 26	13♉01	26 52	10♊59	25 21	09♋56
1983	26♈00	08♉43	21 47	05♊16	19 11	03♋33	18 19	03♌24	18 40	03♍55	19 00	03♎44	18 02	01♏51	15 12	28 07
1984	27♍31	12♎07	26 26	10♏26	24 07	07♐30	20 37	03♑31	16 13	28 45	11♒07	23 20	05♓25	17 23	29 17	11♈07
1985	09♒54	23 11	06♓09	18 48	01♈10	13 17	25 13	07♉03	18 51	00♊44	12 47	25 04	07♋40	20 38	03♌57	17 38
1986	15♊07	26 59	08♋58	21 05	03♌23	15 52	28 32	11♍24	24 28	07♎42	21 09	04♏48	18 41	02♐47	17 06	01♑36
1987	16♎36	29 23	12♏31	26 05	10♐06	24 34	09♑24	24 32	09♒47	24 58	09♓56	24 32	08♈43	22 25	05♉40	18 32
1988	19♓03	03♈43	18 04	02♉05	15 44	29 04	12♊05	24 50	07♋20	19 39	01♌48	13 48	25 41	07♍30	19 16	01♎03
1989	00♌43	13 35	26 12	08♍35	20 45	02♎45	14 39	26 30	08♏23	20 22	02♐32	14 57	27 42	10♑48	24 17	08♒08
1990	04♐57	16 53	28 55	11♑07	23 32	06♒12	19 06	02♓16	15 40	29 18	13♈08	27 07	11♉14	25 26	09♊41	23 57
1991	07♈50	20 51	04♉11	17 50	01♊49	16 08	00♋45	15 35	00♌32	15 28	00♍15	14 46	28 55	12♎38	25 55	08♏46
1992	10♍04	24 57	09♎28	23 33	07♏11	20 23	03♐12	15 43	27 58	10♑03	22 01	03♒54	15 45	27 36	09♓29	21 24
1993	21♑14	03♒52	16 20	28 37	10♓44	22 44	04♈37	16 28	28 20	10♉17	22 24	04♊48	17 32	00♋41	14 18	28 22
1994	24♉31	06♊26	18 31	00♋51	13 28	26 26	09♌42	23 17	07♍07	21 07	05♎14	19 25	03♏35	17 44	01♐50	15 52
1995	29♍15	12♎23	25 46	09♏25	23 22	07♐37	22 08	06♑51	21 41	06♒29	21 08	05♓29	19 26	02♈58	16 03	28 44
1996	01♓15	16 06	00♈33	14 31	28 02	11♉08	23 51	06♊17	18 29	00♋31	12 27	24 20	06♌11	18 03	29 56	11♍54
1997	12♋16	24 40	06♌53	18 56	00♍52	12 42	24 28	06♎15	18 06	00♏05	12 18	24 49	07♐42	21 02	04♑49	19 04
1998	14♏01	26 03	08♐17	20 48	03♑37	16 46	00♒16	14 06	28 11	12♓28	26 53	11♈20	25 46	10♉06	24 17	08♊17
1999	20♓36	04♈04	17 46	01♉40	15 46	00♊02	14 25	28 52	13♋19	27 40	11♌51	25 47	09♍25	22 43	05♎41	18 19
2000	21♌41	06♍27	20 53	04♎54	18 27	01♏35	14 18	26 41	08♐49	20 46	02♑36	14 23	26 12	08♒04	20 03	02♓12

	17th	18th	19th	20th	21st	22nd	23rd	24th	25th	26th	27th	28th	29th	30th	31st
1900	17 20	01♊00	14 19	27 21	10♋08	22 43	05♌08	17 23	29 31	11♍32	23 28	05♎29	17 09	28 59	10♏54
1901	24 43	07♎02	19 06	01♏00	12 49	24 37	06♐30	18 34	00♑53	13 32	26 34	09♒59	23 48	07♓56	22♓19
1902	27 07	09♒30	22 06	04♓55	17 56	01♈08	14 32	28 06	11♉51	25 47	09♊52	24 08	08♋30	22 56	07♌21
1903	02♊43	16 42	01♋05	15 51	00♌52	16 01	01♍07	16 02	00♎36	14 45	28 27	11♏42	24 34	07♐05	19♐20
1904	08♏37	22 14	05♐35	18 34	01♑15	13 42	25 56	08♒01	19 59	01♓50	13 39	25 26	07♈15	19 08	01♉09
1905	14 37	26 44	08♈43	20 36	02♉27	14 20	26 19	08♊29	20 54	03♋39	16 46	00♌17	14 12	28 28	13♍03
1906	17 05	29 34	12♌18	25 29	08♍37	22 10	05♎58	19 55	04♏01	18 12	02♐25	16 38	00♑48	14 54	28♑53
1907	24 30	08♐27	22 43	07♑14	21 58	06♒49	21 40	06♓23	20 51	04♈59	18 41	01♉57	14 48	27 17	09♊28
1908	00♉03	13 41	26 53	09♊40	22 08	04♋20	16 21	28 15	10♌06	21 55	03♍46	15 39	27 36	09♎49	21♎50
1909	04♍42	16 46	28 43	10♎34	22 24	04♏15	16 12	28 20	10♐43	23 28	06♑38	20 16	04♒24	18 59	03♓55
1910	06♑42	19 24	02♒28	15 53	29 37	13♓37	27 48	12♈06	26 24	10♉41	24 52	08♊57	22 56	06♋47	20♋29
1911	16 25	00♊22	14 33	28 58	13♋33	28 14	12♌52	27 21	11♍34	25 25	08♎52	21 54	04♏34	16 54	29♏00
1912	20 40	04♏12	17 18	00♐01	12 26	24 37	06♑39	18 34	00♒26	12 18	24 12	06♓09	18 11	00♈20	12♈37
1913	25 06	07♓00	18 49	00♈36	12 24	24 16	06♉17	18 31	01♊02	13 55	27 14	11♋00	25 13	09♌51	24♌48
1914	26 44	09♋34	22 46	06♌20	20 15	04♍28	18 54	03♎28	18 03	02♏35	16 59	01♐11	15 10	28 54	12♑22
1915	08♏36	22 43	06♐57	21 16	05♑36	19 54	04♒06	18 08	01♓57	15 29	28 43	11♈38	24 15	06♉35	18♉43
1916	11♈03	24 37	07♉44	20 28	02♊50	14 57	26 52	08♋41	20 28	02♌17	14 11	26 13	08♍25	20 48	03♎24
1917	15 11	27 02	08♍52	20 43	02♎39	14 39	26 48	09♏08	21 44	04♐38	17 54	01♑36	15 45	00♒20	15♒18
1918	16 25	29 18	12♑37	26 23	10♒36	25 11	10♓03	25 03	10♈00	24 47	09♉17	23 26	07♊15	20 44	03♋55
1919	01♉08	15 16	29 23	13♊29	27 32	11♋31	25 24	09♌09	22 41	05♍59	19 01	01♎44	14 11	26 22	08♏20
1920	01♎27	14 50	27 46	10♏20	22 35	04♐37	16 30	28 20	10♑12	22 09	04♒15	16 32	29 00	11♓40	24♓33
1921	05♒36	17 28	29 20	11♓15	23 14	05♈18	17 31	29 56	12♉37	25 37	08♊59	22 46	07♋00	21 37	06♌34
1922	06♊31	19 33	03♋02	16 59	01♌22	16 07	01♍06	16 10	01♎12	16 02	00♏35	14 47	28 37	12♐05	25♐13
1923	23 03	07♏23	21 37	05♐45	19 44	03♑32	17 08	00♒32	13 41	26 35	09♓15	21 42	03♈56	15 59	27♈55
1924	21 24	04♈38	17 30	00♉03	12 20	24 24	06♊20	18 12	00♋06	12 05	24 13	06♌33	19 08	02♍00	15♍07
1925	25 44	07♌32	19 25	01♍24	13 31	25 49	08♎18	21 00	03♏57	17 10	00♐40	14 29	28 37	13♑03	27♑44
1926	26 58	10♐00	23 27	07♑22	21 44	06♒30	21 36	06♓51	22 07	07♈12	21 57	06♉16	20 07	03♊30	16♊28
1927	15 12	29 53	14♉10	28 11	11♊55	25 23	08♋37	21 37	04♌26	17 04	29 32	11♍49	23 58	05♎58	17♎52
1928	11♍38	24 43	07♎27	19 53	02♏02	14 00	25 50	07♐38	19 30	01♑31	13 46	26 19	09♒11	22 25	05♓58
1929	15 38	27 35	09♒39	21 53	04♓16	16 50	29 35	12♈30	25 38	08♉57	22 31	06♊20	20 26	04♋46	19♋20
1930	17 36	00♊41	14 12	28 12	12♋39	27 31	12♌40	27 57	13♍10	28 10	12♎48	27 00	10♏44	24 01	06♐54
1931	06♎55	21 31	05♏49	19 50	03♐31	16 54	00♑01	12 53	25 31	07♒56	20 11	02♓17	14 14	26 06	07♈53
1932	02♓02	14 47	27 17	09♈31	21 35	03♉30	15 22	27 14	09♊13	21 21	03♋43	16 24	29 25	12♌48	26♌32
1933	05♋41	17 41	29 49	12♌07	24 39	07♍24	20 23	03♎37	17 03	00♏43	14 35	28 37	12♐48	27 06	11♑27
1934	08♏44	22 00	05♐36	19 36	03♑57	18 38	03♒34	18 37	03♓40	18 34	03♈11	17 24	01♉11	14 30	27♉24
1935	28 11	13♈02	27 33	11♉39	25 18	08♊33	21 26	04♋01	16 21	28 29	10♌30	22 25	04♍17	16 07	27♍57
1936	22 16	04♍49	17 11	29 21	11♎23	23 17	05♏08	16 59	28 55	21♐02	23 23	06♑05	19 12	02♒45	16♒45
1937	25 12	07♑15	19 31	02♒04	14 55	28 04	11♓30	25 11	09♈02	23 01	07♉04	21 10	05♊17	19 24	03♋29
1938	00♉19	13 37	27 13	11♊08	25 23	09♋57	24 45	09♌41	24 37	09♍23	23 50	07♎54	21 30	04♏39	17♏23
1939	19 24	04♎15	18 42	02♏41	16 13	29 20	12♐06	24 35	06♑51	18 56	00♒55	12 50	24 43	06♓34	18♓27
1940	13 00	25 20	07♓30	19 30	01♈22	13 10	24 57	06♉46	18 44	00♊55	13 23	26 14	09♋31	23 15	07♌26
1941	14 55	27 07	09♋33	22 17	05♌20	18 42	02♍22	16 17	00♎23	14 37	28 55	13♏14	27 30	11♐41	25♐45
1942	21 46	05♏19	19 08	03♐12	17 29	01♑57	16 32	01♒09	15 41	00♓03	14 09	27 56	11♈21	24 25	07♉07
1943	09♓38	24 48	09♈17	23 20	06♉56	20 06	02♊51	15 17	27 26	09♋24	21 15	03♌02	14 49	26 39	08♍34
1944	03♌29	15 33	27 31	09♍24	21 15	03♎05	14 57	26 53	08♏58	21 14	03♐46	16 37	29 53	13♑35	27♑45
1945	04♐33	16 44	29 12	12♑00	25 12	08♒49	22 49	07♓09	21 44	06♈26	21 08	05♉43	20 05	04♊13	18♊05
1946	13 53	27 41	11♉38	25 40	09♊48	24 00	08♋15	22 31	06♌43	20 47	04♍39	18 14	01♎30	14 25	27♎00
1947	00♍44	15 32	29 57	13♎55	27 24	10♏24	23 01	05♐18	17 21	29 15	11♑05	22 55	04♒49	16 49	28♒57
1948	23 57	05♒59	17 55	29 48	11♓40	23 31	05♈24	17 22	29 28	11♉45	24 19	07♊13	20 32	04♋19	18♋35
1949	24 13	06♊29	19 04	02♋03	15 28	29 20	13♌36	28 12	13♍00	27 53	12♎43	27 23	11♏48	25 56	09♐46
1950	05♎31	19 32	03♏39	17 49	02♐01	16 13	00♑22	14 25	28 21	12♒04	25 33	08♓46	21 41	04♈19	16♈41
1951	21 36	06♓05	20 14	03♈59	17 20	00♉18	12 54	25 13	07♊18	19 15	01♋07	12 59	24 55	06♌58	19♌10
1952	14 33	26 24	08♌12	19 59	01♍47	13 40	25 38	07♎45	20 02	02♏32	15 19	28 24	11♐51	25 40	09♑52
1953	14 16	26 37	09♐16	22 17	05♑43	19 36	03♒56	18 39	03♓39	18 47	03♈55	18 53	03♉32	17 48	01♊39
1954	27 13	11♈41	26 08	10♉31	24 45	08♊48	22 40	06♋20	19 49	03♌06	16 11	29 05	11♍46	24 15	06♎32
1955	12♌16	26 30	10♍29	24 07	07♎23	20 15	02♏47	15 00	30 00	08♐51	20 40	02♑30	14 28	26 37	09♒02
1956	04♑33	16 23	28 13	10♒06	22 04	04♓09	16 22	28 43	11♈13	23 54	06♉48	19 57	03♊24	17 10	01♋17
1957	04♉34	16 54	29 33	12♊35	26 05	10♋04	24 33	09♌27	24 38	09♍56	25 10	10♎09	24 46	08♏57	22♏41
1958	18 50	03♎29	18 04	02♏30	16 43	00♐42	14 27	27 58	11♑16	24 22	07♒14	19 54	02♓22	14 38	26♓43
1959	03♒35	17 30	01♓08	14 27	27 25	10♈04	22 25	04♉32	16 30	28 22	10♊14	22 11	04♋17	16 36	29♋11
1960	24 42	06♋33	18 25	00♌21	12 22	24 32	06♍51	19 21	02♎03	14 58	28 07	11♏31	25 12	09♐08	23♐20
1961	24 57	07♏28	20 17	03♐29	17 05	01♑07	15 33	00♒21	15 25	00♓36	15 46	00♈44	15 23	19 38	13♉26
1962	09♓47	24 45	09♈39	24 21	08♉46	22 50	06♊32	19 53	02♋55	15 41	28 11	10♌30	22 40	04♍42	16♍38
1963	24 46	08♌14	21 28	04♍29	17 15	29 47	12♎05	24 11	06♏08	18 01	29 52	11♐48	23 54	06♑13	18♑51
1964	14 26	26 14	08♑05	20 04	02♒13	14 35	27 13	10♓05	23 13	06♈33	20 05	03♉47	17 37	01♊36	15♊41
1965	16 03	28 42	11♉35	24 46	08♊19	22 15	06♋34	21 16	06♌16	21 25	06♍33	21 30	06♎08	20 18	04♏00
1966	00♍54	16 07	01♎12	15 58	00♏21	14 19	27 52	11♐02	23 53	06♑28	18 50	01♒03	13 08	25 08	07♓03
1967	16 04	29 18	12♒19	25 07	07♓40	19 59	02♈07	14 04	25 54	07♉41	19 30	01♊26	13 34	26 00	08♋48
1968	04♊01	15 54	27 52	10♋00	22 20	04♌56	17 47	00♍55	14 17	27 52	11♎38	25 33	09♏35	23 42	07♐53
1969	06♎55	19 44	02♏48	16 11	29 53	13♐56	28 18	12♑56	27 46	12♒40	27 31	12♓09	26 30	10♈28	24♈01
1970	21 44	06♓57	22 02	06♈51	21 18	05♉21	18 57	02♊08	14 57	27 27	09♋41	21 44	03♌38	15 28	27♌15
1971	07♋42	20 32	03♌09	15 34	27 49	09♍54	21 53	03♎46	15 36	27 27	09♏21	21 23	03♐37	16 07	28♐58
1972	23 39	05♐33	17 31	29 40	12♑04	24 46	07♒48	21 11	04♓54	18 56	03♈10	17 33	01♉58	16 21	00♊38
1973	28 13	11♈24	24 47	08♉23	22 11	06♊11	20 22	04♋43	19 12	03♌45	18 16	02♍39	16 48	00♎38	14♎06
1974	12♌23	27 38	12♍48	27 42	12♎12	26 13	09♏44	22 48	05♐27	17 47	29 52	11♑48	23 39	05♒29	17♒20
1975	28 43	11♑20	23 46	06♒03	18 12	00♓14	12 11	24 04	05♈54	17 44	29 38	11♉39	23 51	06♊21	19♊12
1976	12 14	25 05	07♊04	19 17	01♋49	14 43	28 01	11♌44	25 48	10♍10	24 43	09♎20	23 54	08♏22	22♏39
1977	19 31	02♎55	16 29	00♏14	14 09	28 12	12♐24	26 43	11♑04	25 25	09♒41	23 46	07♓35	21 05	04♈15
1978	03♒37	18 43	03♓40	18 21	02♈39	16 32	29 57	12♉57	25 35	07♊56	20 02	02♋00	13 52	25 43	07♌36
1979	19 57	02♋26	14 41	26 46	08♌43	20 34	02♍22	14 09	25 57	07♎49	19 47	01♏56	14 18	26 58	09♐59
1980	02♏51	14 47	26 53	09♐12	21 50	04♑49	18 12	02♒01	16 14	00♓47	15 35	00♈31	15 25	00♉12	14♉43
1981	10♓27	24 17	08♈18	22 28	06♉41	20 56	05♊09	19 17	03♋20	17 16	01♌03	14 39	28 03	11♍13	24♍09
1982	24 40	09♌26	24 08	08♍38	22 50	06♎39	20 03	03♏01	15 37	27 53	09♐55	21 47	03♑35	15 24	27♑18
1983	10♐40	22 57	05♑01	16 57	28 48	10♒38	22 29	04♓23	16 21	28 25	10♈36	22 55	05♉26	18 10	01♊12
1984	22 57	04♉52	16 55	29 13	11♊49	24 49	08♋17	22 14	06♌40	21 30	06♍37	21 49	06♎57	21 51	06♏23
1985	01♍37	15 49	00♎10	14 33	28 54	13♏10	27 18	11♐19	25 11	08♑54	22 27	05♒49	18 59	01♓55	14♓37
1986	16 11	00♒46	15 15	29 29	13♓25	26 59	10♈08	22 55	05♉21	17 31	29 30	11♊23	23 14	05♋09	17♋11
1987	01♊03	13 18	25 21	07♋17	19 09	01♌00	12 53	24 49	06♍50	18 58	01♎14	13 42	26 21	09♏16	22♏29
1988	12 54	24 52	07♏01	19 27	02♐12	15 21	28 57	13♑00	27 30	12♒21	27 27	12♓40	27 49	12♈46	27♈23
1989	22 20	06♓48	21 26	06♈08	20 48	05♉19	19 38	03♊42	17 29	01♋00	14 14	27 13	09♌59	22 31	04♍53
1990	08♋10	22 18	06♌17	20 04	03♍37	16 53	29 51	12♎32	24 56	07♏07	19 07	01♐01	12 53	24 48	06♑52
1991	21 15	03♐26	15 25	27 16	09♑03	20 52	02♒46	14 48	27 00	09♓24	22 00	04♈50	17 52	01♉07	14♉35
1992	03♈25	15 33	27 51	10♉22	23 09	06♊17	19 48	03♋46	18 09	02♌57	18 04	03♍20	18 35	03♎37	18♎19
1993	12♌53	27 42	12♍43	27 46	12♎40	27 19	11♏38	25 34	09♐09	22 25	05♑24	18 08	00♒41	13 03	25♒17
1994	29 50	13♑41	27 25	10♒57	24 17	07♓20	20 07	02♈38	14 53	26 55	08♉47	20 36	02♊24	14 19	26♊25
1995	11♉06	23 12	05♊07	16 58	28 49	10♋44	22 47	05♌01	17 26	00♍05	12 57	26 01	09♎17	22 43	06♏21
1996	23 58	06♎10	18 32	01♏09	14 03	27 18	10♐57	25 00	09♑28	24 16	09♒19	24 27	09♓31	24 22	08♈52
1997	03♒43	18 40	03♓47	18 54	03♈53	18 37	03♉00	16 59	00♊36	13 50	26 44	09♋20	21 43	03♌53	15♌54
1998	22 05	05♋41	19 02	02♌10	15 04	27 44	10♍10	22 25	04♎30	16 27	28 19	10♏09	22 03	04♐04	16♐16
1999	00♏41	12 49	24 47	06♐40	18 33	00♑30	12 36	24 54	07♒27	20 17	03♓24	16 49	00♈29	14 22	28♈25
2000	14 30	26 59	09♈41	22 37	05♉47	19 13	02♊56	16 56	01♋12	15 44	00♌27	15 15	00♍03	14 42	29♍05

Moon

September

	1st	2nd	3rd	4th	5th	6th	7th	8th	9th	10th	11th	12th	13th	14th	15th	16th
1900	22♏57	05♐15	17 51	00♑51	14 19	28 17	12♒45	27 37	23♓48	28 06	13♈19	28 18	12♉56	27 07	10♊52	24 12
1901	06♈49	21 22	05♉51	20 12	04♊24	18 23	02♋11	15 47	29 12	12♌25	25 25	08♍13	20 27	03♎08	15 17	27 16
1902	21♌38	05♍43	19 30	02♎56	16 01	28 44	11♏08	23 18	05♐16	17 08	29 00	10♑56	23 00	05♒17	17 48	00♓36
1903	01♑23	13 19	25 11	07♒03	18 57	00♓57	13 02	25 16	07♈40	20 14	03♉01	16 03	29 20	12♊55	26 48	10♋59
1904	13♉20	25 47	08♊33	21 42	05♋16	19 17	03♌43	18 31	03♍36	18 47	03♎57	18 55	03♏35	17 50	01♐39	15 02
1905	27♍49	12♎39	27 26	12♏03	26 25	10♐29	24 15	07♑41	20 50	03♒43	16 22	28 48	11♓04	23 21	05♈12	17 07
1906	12♒43	26 21	09♓47	22 57	05♈51	18 28	00♉51	13 00	25 00	06♊53	18 45	00♋40	12 44	25 00	07♌34	20 28
1907	21♊26	03♋16	15 03	26 52	08♌47	20 51	03♍07	15 37	28♎20	11 17	24♏27	07 49	21 22	05♐06	19 01	03♑05
1908	02♏10	16 43	29 32	12♐40	26 10	10♑06	24 27	09♒12	24 16	09♓30	24 44	09♈47	24 29	08♉45	22 30	05♊46
1909	19♓03	04♈13	19 15	04♉00	18 22	02♊21	15 55	29 08	12♋03	24 42	07♌08	19 25	01♍34	13 36	25 32	07♎25
1910	04♌03	17 25	00♍35	13 30	26 10	08♎35	20 45	02♏45	14 36	26 23	08♐11	20 06	02♑13	14 37	27 21	10♒31
1911	10♐56	22 47	04♑39	16 36	28 41	10♒59	23 30	06♓16	19 16	02♈29	15 55	29 32	13♉18	27 13	11♊15	25 23
1912	25♈06	07♉48	20 46	04♊03	17 42	01♋43	16 06	00♌48	15 43	00♍43	15 40	00♎26	14 52	28 54	12♏31	25 42
1913	09♍56	25 06	10♎09	24 56	09♏22	23 24	07♐02	20 15	03♑07	15 41	28 00	10♒07	22 06	03♓58	15 47	27 35
1914	25♑37	08♒37	21 23	03♓56	16 18	28 29	10♈32	22 28	04♉19	16 10	28 04	10♊05	22 17	04♋45	17 33	00♌44
1915	00♊41	12 33	24 26	06♋24	18 30	00♌50	13 26	26 20	09♍34	23 07	06♎57	21 00	05♏12	19 28	03♐46	18 00
1916	16♎12	29 14	12♏29	25 58	09♐42	23 41	07♑53	22 19	06♒55	21 37	06♓18	20 51	05♈10	19 08	02♉43	15 52
1917	00♓31	15 50	01♈03	16 00	00♉32	14 36	28 10	11♊16	23 57	06♋19	18 26	00♌23	12 15	24 04	05♍54	17 47
1918	16♋50	29 32	12♌03	24 25	06♍28	18 44	00♎42	12 36	24 26	06♏15	18 06	00♐05	12 15	24 42	07♑30	20 45
1919	20♏11	01♐59	13 49	25 47	07♑59	20 28	03♒18	16 32	00♓08	14 06	28 20	12♈44	27 14	11♉42	26 05	10♊19
1920	07♈37	20 53	04♉19	17 57	01♊46	15 46	29 58	14♋19	28 46	13♌15	27 40	11♍55	25 53	09♎32	22 48	05♏42
1921	21♌42	06♍53	21 55	06♎40	21 01	04♏56	18 24	01♐26	14 06	26 27	08♑26	20 25	02♒28	14 20	26 12	08♓08
1922	08♑03	20 37	02♒58	15 08	27 10	09♓05	20 55	02♈43	14 30	26 20	08♉16	20 21	02♊40	15 16	28 14	11♋36
1923	09♉47	21 39	03♊34	15 39	27 56	10♋31	23 27	06♌46	20 29	04♍35	19 00	03♎39	18 26	03♏13	17 53	02♐21
1924	28♍31	12♎09	25 59	09♏59	24 06	08♐17	22 30	06♑42	20 52	04♒57	18 55	02♓42	16 17	29 37	12♈41	25 28
1925	12♒35	27 30	12♓20	26 58	11♈17	25 12	08♉41	21 43	04♊22	16 40	28 43	10♋36	22 23	04♌11	22 02	28 01
1926	29♊04	11♋23	23 30	05♌28	17 20	29 11	11♍01	22 52	04♎47	16 46	28 51	11♏06	23 31	06♐11	19 08	02♑28
1927	29♎42	11♏32	23 26	05♐27	17 43	00♑17	13 15	26 40	10♒35	24 57	09♓44	24 46	09♈55	24 59	09♉51	24♊22
1928	19♓48	03♈52	18 03	02♉19	16 34	00♊46	14 53	28 55	12♋51	26 40	10♌21	23 52	07♍10	20 15	03♎04	15 38
1929	04♌01	18 45	03♍22	17 46	01♎50	15 29	28 44	11♏34	24 03	06♐15	18 15	00♑08	11 59	23 52	05♒53	18 04
1930	19♐27	01♑44	13 50	26 48	07♒42	19 34	01♓26	13 20	25 19	07♈23	19 34	01♉55	14 28	27 17	10♊24	23 52
1931	19♈40	01♉29	13 25	25 32	07♊55	20 37	03♋44	17 17	01♌19	15 46	00♍35	15 39	00♎49	15 55	00♏49	15 25
1932	10♍35	24 53	09♎20	23 53	08♏24	22 51	07♐07	21 12	05♑04	18 41	02♒04	15 13	28 08	10♓49	23 19	05♈36
1933	25♑49	10♒08	24 18	08♓17	22 00	05♈25	18 30	01♉16	13 45	25 58	08♊00	19 54	01♋46	13 40	25 42	07♌54
1934	09♊56	22 09	04♋09	15 59	27 47	09♌34	21 25	03♍22	15 28	27 44	10♎12	22 52	05♏45	18 52	02♐12	15 48
1935	09♎50	21 47	03♏51	16 05	28 32	11♐16	24 21	07♑51	21 49	06♒13	21 02	06♓11	21 29	06♈47	21 52	06♉36
1936	01♓10	15 53	00♈48	15 45	00♉34	15 10	29 28	13♊26	27 03	10♋23	23 27	06♌17	18 55	01♍23	13 42	25 52
1937	17♋33	01♌32	15 25	29 07	12♍35	25 47	08♎40	21 16	03♏34	15 39	27 33	09♐21	21 10	03♑03	15 08	27 28
1938	29♏46	11♐53	23 49	05♑40	17 31	29 25	11♒26	23 36	05♓57	18 30	01♈15	14 11	27 18	10♉36	24 06	07♊48
1939	00♈23	12 23	25 30	06♉48	19 19	02♊09	15 20	28 56	12♋58	27 26	12♌16	27 22	12♍35	27 43	12♎38	27 11
1940	22♌01	06♍43	21 55	06♎57	21 51	06♏31	20 52	04♐51	18 29	01♑47	14 45	27 28	09♒56	22 12	04♓19	16 17
1941	09♑40	23 24	06♒57	20 15	03♓19	16 08	28 43	11♈04	23 13	05♉13	17 07	28 58	10♊51	22 51	05♋02	17 28
1942	19♉31	01♊41	13 40	25 33	07♋25	19 21	01♌23	13 37	26 03	08♍45	21 43	04♎57	18 25	02♏07	16 00	00♐01
1943	20♍36	02♎47	15 08	27 42	10♏30	23 34	06♐55	20 35	04♑34	18 53	03♒29	18 19	03♓16	18 11	02♈58	17 29
1944	12♒21	27 20	12♓32	27 49	12♈59	27 53	12♉23	26 26	10♊01	23 10	05♋55	18 23	00♌35	12 38	24 33	06♍25
1945	01♋41	15 03	28 12	11♌08	23 54	06♍28	18 52	01♎07	13 12	25 09	07♏01	18 50	00♐41	12 38	24 46	07♑11
1946	09♏16	21 19	03♐12	15 00	26 50	08♑46	20 54	03♒17	15 59	29 02	12♓24	26 07	09♈59	24 04	08♉14	22 27
1947	11♓14	23 41	06♈18	19 06	02♉05	15 16	28 42	12♊23	26 21	10♋35	25 05	09♌47	24 33	09♍17	23 51	08♎07
1948	03♌17	18 21	03♍36	18 53	04♎01	18 49	03♏13	17 09	00♐38	13 41	26 23	08♑47	20 59	03♒00	14 56	26 49
1949	23♐18	06♑33	19 33	02♒19	14 52	27 13	09♓25	21 27	03♈21	15 10	26 57	08♉45	20 37	02♊38	14 52	27 25
1950	28♈50	10♉50	22 43	04♊34	16 29	28 32	10♋47	23 19	06♌10	19 21	02♍54	26 46	00♎55	15 16	29 44	14♏14
1951	01♍34	14 10	27 01	10♎05	23 22	06♏54	20 38	04♐33	18 40	02♑55	17 17	01♒41	16 05	00♓23	14 31	28 24
1952	24♑26	09♒17	24 20	09♓27	24 27	09♈14	23 39	07♉39	21 11	04♊16	16 57	29 17	11♋23	23 17	05♌05	16 52
1953	15♊05	28 08	10♋51	23 18	05♌33	17 38	29 37	11♍31	23 22	05♎12	17 03	28 58	10♏57	23 05	05♐24	17 59
1954	18♎38	00♏35	12 28	24 18	06♐11	18 12	00♑26	12 58	25 52	09♒13	23 00	07♓12	21 46	06♈35	21 29	06♉20
1955	21♒43	04♓42	17 58	01♈29	15 12	29 04	13♉03	27 05	11♊10	25 17	09♋25	23 31	07♌36	21 35	05♍26	19 04
1956	15♋44	00♌29	15 25	00♍25	15 19	29 57	14♎14	28 03	11♏25	24 20	06♐52	19 06	01♑07	13 00	24 50	06♒42
1957	05♐59	18 54	01♑31	13 53	26 04	08♒06	20 03	01♓57	13 49	25 40	07♈34	19 30	01♉32	13 43	26 07	09♊46
1958	08♈39	20 29	02♉16	14 03	25 57	08♊01	20 20	03♋00	16 05	29 36	13♌35	27 40	12♍41	27 38	12♎24	26 52
1959	12♌03	25 15	08♍44	22 29	06♎28	20 35	04♏49	19 06	03♐22	17 35	01♑43	15 44	29 35	13♒16	26 44	09♓57
1960	07♑45	22 19	06♒58	21 36	06♓07	20 23	04♈22	17 59	01♉14	14 06	26 39	08♊54	20 58	02♋53	14 45	26 38
1961	26♉48	09♊44	22 18	04♋34	16 37	28 31	10♌19	22 06	03♍54	15 45	27 43	09♎48	22 03	04♏29	17 08	00♐03
1962	28♍30	10♎21	22 11	04♏05	16 05	28 14	10♐38	23 20	06♑24	19 54	03♒52	18 16	03♓06	18 13	03♈28	18 42
1963	01♒51	15 15	29 03	13♓13	27 39	12♈16	26 56	11♉31	25 58	10♊11	24 10	07♋54	21 24	04♌41	17 45	00♍38
1964	29♊52	14♋08	28 26	12♌44	26 56	10♍58	24 44	08♎11	21 17	04♏02	16 27	28 36	10♐33	22 22	04♑11	16 03
1965	17♏13	00♐00	12 26	24 34	06♑32	18 23	00♒13	12 05	24 01	06♓04	18 16	00♈36	13 06	25 46	08♉37	21 40
1966	18♓55	00♈46	12 37	24 31	06♉32	18 42	01♊07	13 51	26 58	10♋32	24 36	09♌07	24 03	09♍15	24 34	09♎47
1967	22♋01	05♌40	19 44	04♍10	18 51	03♎41	18 30	03♏13	17 43	01♐58	15 56	29 36	13♑00	26 08	09♒02	21 43
1968	22♐05	06♑18	20 26	04♒29	18 21	02♓00	15 23	28 29	11♈17	23 48	06♉03	18 07	00♊03	11 55	23 48	06♋46
1969	07♉10	19 56	02♊22	14 33	26 33	08♋27	20 18	02♌11	14 09	26 16	08♍33	21 01	03♎43	16 38	29 46	13♏09
1970	09♍02	20 52	02♎46	14 48	26 58	09♏21	21 58	04♐54	18 10	01♑48	15 50	00♒16	15 01	00♓02	15 09	00♈15
1971	12♑12	25 53	10♒00	24 33	09♓25	24 30	09♈38	24 39	09♉26	23 51	07♊53	21 30	04♋43	17 36	00♌11	12 33
1972	14♊46	28 44	12♋31	26 07	09♌32	22 46	05♍48	18 38	01♎15	13 38	25 50	07♏52	19 47	01♐37	13 28	25 25
1973	27♎10	09♏51	22 13	04♐18	16 12	28 01	09♑50	21 44	03♒47	16 03	28 35	11♓24	24 30	07♈51	21 26	05♉11
1974	29♒15	11♓16	23 24	05♈39	18 03	00♉37	13 22	26 22	09♊39	23 15	07♋13	21 32	06♌12	21 06	06♍08	21♍09
1975	02♋29	16 15	00♌32	15 15	00♍19	15 36	00♎52	15 58	00♏45	15 07	29 03	12♐32	25 37	08♑22	20 51	03♒08
1976	06♐44	20 36	04♑15	17 41	00♒55	13 56	26 44	09♓19	21 42	03♈53	15 54	27 47	09♉35	21 22	03♊12	15 10
1977	17♈04	29 33	11♉47	23 49	05♊43	17 35	29 29	11♋30	23 42	06♌08	18 51	01♍53	15 12	28 47	12♎37	26 37
1978	19♌34	01♍38	13 51	26 13	08♎47	21 34	04♏34	17 49	01♐20	15 08	29 13	13♑33	28 05	12♒45	27 28	12♓05
1979	23♐23	07♑14	21 30	06♒10	21 08	06♓18	21 30	06♈35	21 24	05♉51	19 51	03♊24	16 31	29 15	11♋39	23 48
1980	28♉56	12♊48	26 19	09♋30	22 24	05♌03	17 29	29 44	11♍51	23 51	05♎46	17 37	29 28	11♏19	23 15	05♐19
1981	06♎49	19 14	01♏26	13 27	25 22	07♐13	19 06	01♑06	13 18	25 47	08♒36	21 48	05♓24	19 22	03♈38	18 08
1982	08♒22	21 37	04♓06	16 49	29 47	12♈59	26 22	09♉57	23 41	07♊34	21 35	05♋44	19 59	04♌20	18 41	03♍00
1983	14♊34	28 19	12♋29	27 03	11♌57	27 05	12♍17	27 22	12♎11	26 35	10♏30	23 56	06♐54	19 29	01♑45	13 47
1984	20♏32	04♐15	17 35	00♑35	13 18	25 47	08♒05	20 15	02♓18	14 16	26 09	08♈01	19 51	01♉43	13 39	25 43
1985	27♓05	09♈19	02 21	03♉14	15 02	26 49	08♊41	20 44	03♋01	15 38	28 39	12♌05	25 57	10♍12	24 45	09♎30
1986	29♋25	11♌52	24 35	07♍33	20 45	04♎11	17 49	01♏37	15 33	29 36	13♐45	27 57	12♑11	26 23	10♒32	24 32
1987	06♐01	19 55	04♑09	18 42	03♒30	18 25	03♓21	18 08	02♈40	16 50	00♉36	13 56	26 52	09♊27	21 45	03♋49
1988	11♉36	25 24	08♊46	21 44	04♋23	16 18	28 06	09♌57	21 54	03♍59	16 18	28 06	09♎57	21 54	03♏59	16 15
1989	17♍04	29 06	11♎03	22 54	04♏45	16 37	28 34	10♐42	23 04	05♑44	18 47	02♒16	16 11	00♓32	15 15	00♈14
1990	19♑08	01♒40	14 31	27 43	11♓15	25 06	09♈12	23 28	07♉50	22 12	06♊30	20 41	04♋44	18 38	02♌21	15 54
1991	28♉15	12♊09	26 15	10♋33	25 01	09♌36	24 11	08♍42	23 02	07♎03	20 44	04♏00	16 52	29 22	11♐34	23 33
1992	02♏33	16 17	29 33	12♐22	24 50	07♑02	19 02	00♒55	12 45	24 36	06♓29	18 26	00♈29	12 39	24 57	07♉24
1993	07♓24	19 24	01♈19	13 10	24 59	06♉51	18 47	00♊53	13 14	25 54	08♋59	22 32	06♌35	21 07	06♍03	21 15
1994	08♋48	21 31	04♌37	18 08	02♍01	16 13	00♎38	15 11	29 45	14♏13	28 34	12♐44	26 41	10♑27	24 01	07♒23
1995	20♏09	04♐07	18 16	02♑32	16 55	01♒20	15 42	29 55	13♓55	27 37	10♈58	23 58	06♉38	18 59	01♊06	13 03
1996	22♈57	06♉34	19 46	02♊34	15 02	27 14	09♋15	21 10	03♌01	14 52	26 47	08♍46	20 53	03♎10	15 36	28 13
1997	27♌48	09♍38	21 25	03♎12	15 01	26 55	08♏58	21 13	03♐44	16 34	29 47	13♑26	27 31	12♒01	26 53	11♓59
1998	28♐45	11♑33	24 45	08♒21	22 22	06♓45	21 26	06♈17	21 10	05♉59	20 36	04♊57	18 57	02♋38	15 59	29 02
1999	12♉35	26 48	11♊00	25 11	09♋19	23 20	07♌14	20 58	04♍32	17 51	00♎56	13 45	26 19	08♏38	20 44	02♐41
2000	13♎06	26 43	09♏53	22 39	05♐04	17 11	29 07	10♑56	22 44	04♒35	16 33	28 41	11♓02	23 37	06♈26	19 29

Year	17th	18th	19th	20th	21st	22nd	23rd	24th	25th	26th	27th	28th	29th	30th
1900	07♋10	19 49	02♌14	14 28	26 33	08♍32	10 27	02♎19	14 09	26 00	07♏53	19 40	01♐57	14♐15
1901	09♏07	20 54	02♐41	14 33	26 35	08♑52	21 30	04♒32	18 00	01♓56	16 16	00♈56	15 49	00♉45
1902	13 42	27 03	10♈40	24 29	08♉27	22 32	06♊42	20 54	05♋06	19 16	30♌21	17 20	01♍10	14♍47
1903	25 27	10♌06	24 52	09♍38	24 17	08♎42	22 47	06♏30	19 48	02♐44	15 18	27 36	09♑40	21♑36
1904	28 21	10♑38	22 57	05♒04	17 00	28 51	10♓39	22 27	04♈17	16 12	28 13	10♉22	22 43	05♊16
1905	28 59	10♉49	22 42	04♊40	16 40	29 10	11♋49	24 51	08♌18	22 13	06♍34	21 19	06♎22	21♎33
1906	03♍45	17 23	01♎23	15 38	00♏04	14 34	29 03	13♐26	27 38	11♑39	25 28	09♒04	22 30	05♓44
1907	17 19	01♒41	16 07	00♓35	14 58	29 10	13♈06	26 43	09♉56	22 46	05♊16	17 27	29 26	11♋16
1908	18 36	01♋03	13 13	25 12	07♌03	18 52	00♍42	12 36	24 35	06♎41	18 55	01♏18	13 50	26♍32
1909	19 15	01♏04	12 56	24 52	07♐00	19 21	02♑01	15 06	28 38	12♒41	27 12	12♓09	17 23	12♈43
1910	24 06	08♓06	22 26	07♈01	21 43	06♉27	21 04	05♊30	19 43	03♋41	17 24	00♌52	14 06	27♌07
1911	09♋37	23 53	08♌08	22 19	06♍22	20 11	03♎43	16 57	29 51	12♏27	24 46	06♐52	18 48	00♑40
1912	08♐30	20 58	03♑11	15 12	27 06	08♒58	20 51	02♓47	14 51	27 03	09♈26	22 00	04♉47	17♉47
1913	09♈24	21 16	03♉13	15 20	27 38	10♊11	23 02	06♋15	19 51	03♌52	18 18	03♍05	18 08	03♎18
1914	14 21	18 24	12♍50	27 36	12♎34	27 35	12♏30	27 13	11♐37	25 39	09♑19	22 37	05♒35	10♒17
1915	02♑09	16 12	00♒06	13 52	27 27	10♓52	24 04	07♈03	19 47	02♉17	14 34	26 39	08♊36	20♊27
1916	28 38	11♊02	23 09	05♋04	16 53	28 41	10♌32	22 31	04♍43	17 08	29 48	12♎45	25 55	09♏19
1917	29 44	11♎46	23 55	06♏12	18 39	01♐19	14 13	27 25	10♑59	24 56	09♒17	24 00	09♓00	24♓09
1918	04♒30	18 44	03♓26	18 30	03♈45	19 00	04♉06	18 52	03♊15	17 11	00♋42	13 49	26 38	09♌10
1919	24 24	08♋18	22 01	05♌33	18 54	02♍03	14 59	27 42	10♎11	22 27	04♏31	16 25	28 14	10♐00
1920	18 16	00♐32	12 35	24 29	06♑21	18 14	00♒14	12 24	24 47	07♓26	20 22	03♈34	17 01	00♉41
1921	20 09	02♈18	14 35	27 02	09♉40	22 33	05♊41	19 06	02♋50	16 53	01♌14	15 50	00♍36	15♍26
1922	25 25	09♌40	24 20	09♍18	24 28	09♎40	24 45	09♏34	24 00	08♐01	21 36	04♑45	17 31	29♑59
1923	16 32	00♑26	14 02	27 20	10♒22	23 09	05♓43	18 06	00♈19	12 23	24 21	06♉15	18 06	29♉57
1924	07♉58	20 14	02♊18	14 14	26 06	07♋58	19 57	02♌06	14 31	27 15	10♍20	23 47	07♎35	21♎41
1925	10♍11	22 32	05♎07	17 55	00♏56	14 10	27 35	11♐12	25 00	09♑00	23 10	07♒30	21 57	06♓28
1926	16 12	00♒22	14 58	29 56	15♓08	00♈25	15 36	00♉29	14 58	28 57	12♊26	25 27	08♋04	20♋21
1927	08♊31	22 15	05♋38	18 41	01♌28	14 02	26 24	08♍38	20 44	02♎44	14 39	26 30	08♏20	20♏09
1928	27 56	10♏01	21 56	03♐44	15 32	27 23	09♑23	21 39	04♒13	17 11	00♓33	14 21	28 30	12♈56
1929	00♓28	13 05	25 56	09♈01	22 18	05♉47	19 25	03♊14	17 11	01♋15	15 27	29 43	14♌02	28♌18
1930	07♋43	21 57	06♌32	21 24	06♍25	21 27	06♎21	20 58	05♏14	19 03	02♐26	15 25	28 02	10♑21
1931	29 37	13♐25	26 49	09♑51	22 34	05♒00	17 13	29 16	11♓12	23 02	04♈50	16 38	28 28	10♉22
1932	17 44	29 43	11♉37	23 28	05♊20	17 17	29 23	11♋43	24 21	07♌21	20 45	04♍36	18 51	03♎27
1933	20 21	03♍06	16 09	29 31	13♎11	27 05	11♏10	25 22	09♐37	23 51	08♑03	22 09	06♒09	20♒01
1934	29 39	13♑46	28 08	12♒42	27 24	12♓09	26 50	11♈19	25 29	09♉17	22 38	05♊35	18 09	00♋23
1935	20 52	04♊39	17 57	00♋49	13 20	25 33	07♌35	19 29	01♍20	13 09	25 00	06♎54	18 53	00♏58
1936	07♎55	19 51	01♏43	13 31	25 21	07♐15	19 19	01♑37	14 15	27 17	10♒48	24 49	09♓20	24♓14
1937	10♒08	23 10	06♓35	20 21	04♈25	18 42	03♉07	17 33	01♊56	16 13	00♋21	14 20	28 09	11♌48
1938	21 42	05♋49	20 07	04♌34	19 06	03♍37	18 00	02♎09	16 00	29 29	12♏34	25 18	07♐42	19♐51
1939	11♏19	24 59	08♐12	21 02	03♑31	15 46	27 48	09♒44	21 36	03♓28	15 21	27 19	09♈22	21♈33
1940	28 10	09♈59	21 46	03♉34	15 26	27 26	09♊38	22 05	04♋52	18 02	01♌38	15 42	00♍11	15♍02
1941	00♌13	13 21	26 52	10♍46	25 01	09♎32	24 14	08♏59	23 40	08♐13	22 31	06♑33	20 17	03♒44
1942	14 09	28 21	12♑34	26 47	10♒57	25 01	08♓57	22 41	06♈11	19 25	02♉22	15 01	27 25	08♊34
1943	01♉36	15 18	28 32	11♊21	23 48	05♋58	17 54	29 43	11♌30	23 19	05♍13	17 17	29 32	11♎58
1944	18 15	00♎06	11 59	23 55	05♏56	18 04	00♐23	12 54	25 42	08♑51	22 23	06♒22	20 48	05♓38
1945	19 57	03♒10	16 51	01♓00	15 36	00♈31	15 36	00♉42	15 38	00♊17	14 35	28 29	12♋02	25♋14
1946	06♊38	20 47	04♋52	18 51	02♌46	16 33	00♍12	13 40	26 54	09♎54	22 36	05♏03	17 14	29♏14
1947	22 00	05♏27	18 29	01♐08	13 27	25 32	07♑27	19 19	01♒10	13 07	25 13	07♓29	19 58	02♈41
1948	08♓40	20 33	02♈28	14 28	26 34	08♉48	21 14	03♊54	16 50	00♋08	13 48	27 52	12♌19	27♌05
1949	10♋20	23 41	07♌29	21 45	06♍25	21 23	06♎30	21 38	06♏38	21 21	06♐44	19 43	03♑17	16♑30
1950	28 41	13♐01	27 11	11♑09	24 54	08♒26	21 44	04♓47	17 38	00♈15	12 40	24 53	06♉57	18♉54
1951	12♈00	25 17	08♉13	20 50	03♊10	15 17	27 14	09♋07	20 59	02♌56	15 02	27 21	09♍56	22♍49
1952	28 40	10♍34	22 34	04♎45	17 05	29 37	12♏22	25 20	08♐32	21 59	05♑41	19 41	03♒57	18♒27
1953	00♑54	14 13	27 57	12♒10	26 50	11♓51	27 07	12♈27	27 39	12♉33	27 02	11♊02	24 33	07♋36
1954	21 01	05♊25	19 31	03♋18	16 46	29 58	12♌56	25 42	08♍17	20 42	02♎58	15 05	27 05	08♏59
1955	02♎26	15 31	28 16	10♏43	22 54	04♐53	16 43	28 31	10♑22	22 20	04♒33	17 03	29 53	13♓06
1956	18 39	00♓44	12 59	25 24	08♈01	20 49	03♉48	16 58	00♊20	13 54	27 41	11♋42	25 56	10♌21
1957	21 46	05♋10	19 01	03♌18	18 01	03♍02	18 14	03♎27	18 30	03♏15	17 35	01♐27	14 52	27♐53
1958	12♏24	26 52	11♐01	24 48	08♑15	21 23	04♒13	16 49	29 12	11♓25	23 28	05♈24	17 14	29♈02
1959	22 56	05♈40	18 09	00♉24	12 29	24 25	06♊18	18 09	00♋05	12 10	24 29	07♌04	20 01	03♍20
1960	08♌36	20 43	03♍02	15 35	28 24	11♎27	24 46	08♏19	22 04	05♐59	20 02	04♑11	18 24	02♒39
1961	13 14	26 44	10♑35	24 46	09♒16	24 02	08♓59	23 58	08♈53	23 34	07♉54	21 48	05♊15	18♊16
1962	03♉43	18 24	02♊39	16 26	29 46	12♋42	25 17	07♌37	19 45	01♍44	13 38	25 29	07♎20	19♎11
1963	13 21	25 52	08♎12	20 23	02♏24	14 18	26 08	07♐58	19 51	01♑53	14 10	26 45	09♒45	23♒13
1964	28 05	10♒20	22 52	05♓44	18 55	02♈25	16 11	00♉08	14 13	28 22	12♊31	26 40	10♋46	24♋49
1965	04♊57	18 30	02♋19	16 27	00♌52	15 31	00♍19	15 08	29 51	14♎18	28 24	12♏04	25 18	08♐08
1966	24 45	09♏20	23 28	07♐09	20 24	03♑15	15 47	28 04	10♒11	22 09	04♓03	15 55	27 45	09♈40
1967	04♓12	16 29	28 37	10♈35	22 27	04♉15	16 02	27 51	09♊47	21 54	04♋18	17 02	00♌10	13♌46
1968	17 55	00♌18	12 59	26 00	09♍21	23 03	07♎02	21 15	05♏37	20 04	04♐30	18 52	03♑07	17♑11
1969	26 44	10♐33	24 34	08♑45	23 05	07♒31	21 58	06♓22	21 39	04♈42	18 29	01♉57	15 04	27♉51
1970	15 11	29 47	13♉59	27 44	11♊01	23 53	06♋22	18 34	00♌32	12 23	24 10	05♍57	17 47	29♍43
1971	24 43	06♍46	18 43	00♎36	12 27	24 17	06♏10	18 06	00♐08	12 21	24 47	07♑32	20 39	04♒12
1972	07♑32	19 55	02♒38	15 46	29 20	13♓20	27 43	12♈24	27 14	12♉05	26 48	11♊19	25 32	09♋27
1973	19 03	03♊02	17 04	01♋10	15 17	29 26	13♌35	27 40	11♍39	25 27	09♎00	22 15	05♏11	17♏47
1974	05♎58	20 26	04♏30	18 04	01♐12	13 54	26 16	08♑22	20 18	02♒09	13 59	25 53	07♓54	20♓02
1975	15 15	27 15	09♓10	21 03	02♈54	14 46	26 40	08♉38	20 43	02♊59	15 29	28 19	11♋31	25♋09
1976	27 22	09♋52	22 45	06♌04	19 49	04♍02	18 36	03♎27	18 25	03♏23	18 13	02♐48	17 05	01♑01
1977	10♏46	24 59	09♐13	23 27	07♑38	21 43	05♒41	19 30	03♓06	16 30	19 38	12♈31	25 09	07♉32
1978	26 32	10♈42	24 31	07♉57	21 00	03♊42	16 06	28 14	10♋12	22 05	03♌57	15 51	27 53	10♍05
1979	05♌45	17 36	29 23	11♍10	22 95	04♎53	16 53	29 02	11♏21	23 52	06♐38	19 39	03♑00	16♑40
1980	17 35	00♑08	13 01	26 19	10♒04	24 17	08♓56	23 55	09♈08	24 23	09♉30	24 20	08♊46	22♊45
1981	02♉44	17 20	01♊49	16 07	00♋12	14 03	27 40	11♌05	24 18	07♍19	20 09	02♎48	15 15	27♎32
1982	17 11	01♎08	14 46	28 04	11♏00	23 34	05♐51	17 52	29 45	11♑33	23 22	05♒19	17 27	29♒50
1983	25 41	07♒31	19 21	01♓15	13 14	25 20	07♈35	19 58	02♉31	15 14	28 09	11♊17	24 40	08♋21
1984	08♊00	20 34	03♋29	16 51	00♌42	15 02	29 48	14♍55	00♎12	15 29	00♏35	15 21	29 41	13♐34
1985	24 17	09♏01	23 35	04♐56	22 01	05♑49	19 22	02♒39	15 41	28 30	11♓06	23 30	05♈44	17♈47
1986	08♓21	21 55	05♈11	18 09	00♉49	13 13	25 23	07♊22	19 15	01♋07	13 02	25 06	07♌21	19♌53
1987	15 45	27 37	09♌28	21 23	03♍25	15 35	27 56	10♎30	23 16	06♏15	19 28	02♐56	16 36	00♑30
1988	28 44	11♐29	24 35	08♑02	21 54	06♒10	20 48	05♓44	20 51	06♈00	21 03	05♉50	20 14	04♊11
1989	15 20	00♉24	15 16	29 51	14♊02	27 50	11♋14	24 16	07♌00	19 29	01♍46	13 53	25 54	07♎49
1990	29 17	12♍27	25 25	08♎10	20 42	03♏01	15 08	27 06	08♐57	20 48	02♑41	14 42	26 57	09♒30
1991	05♑23	17 11	29 02	11♒00	23 09	05♓32	18 12	01♈08	14 19	27♉45	11 22	25 08	09♊01	23♊00
1992	20 02	02♊53	16 00	29 27	13♋14	27 25	11♌57	26 48	11♍50	26 55	11♎53	26 33	10♏50	24♏38
1993	06♎32	21 44	06♏39	21 12	05♐18	18 59	02♑14	15 09	27 46	10♒08	22 20	04♓24	16 23	28♓17
1994	20 32	03♓29	16 12	28 43	11♈01	23 07	05♉04	16 54	28 41	10♊29	22 23	04♋28	16 49	29♋30
1995	24 56	06♋48	18 45	00♌51	13 10	25 44	08♍35	21 44	05♎10	18 50	02♏43	16 45	00♐53	15♐06
1996	11♏05	24 11	07♐33	21 12	05♑09	19 22	03♒51	18 30	03♓15	17 58	02♈34	16 55	00♉56	14♉34
1997	27 12	12♈22	27 19	11♉57	26 09	09♊54	23 13	06♋06	18 39	00♌54	12 57	24 51	06♍39	18♍26
1998	11♌49	24 23	06♍45	18 57	01♎02	13 00	24 53	06♏44	18 34	00♐27	12 27	24 36	07♑01	19♑43
1999	14 34	26 25	08♑21	20 27	02♒47	15 25	28 26	11♓49	25 35	09♈42	24 03	08♉34	23 08	07♊38
2000	02♉44	16 10	29 47	13♊34	27 31	11♋34	25 50	10♌10	24 35	08♍59	23 17	07♎24	21 15	04♏45

Moon

October

	1st	2nd	3rd	4th	5th	6th	7th	8th	9th	10th	11th	12th	13th	14th	15th	16th
1900	26♐50	09♑46	23 07	06♒56	21 14	05♓58	21 02	06♈19	21 36	06♉44	21 32	05♊55	19 51	03♋18	16 21	29 01
1901	15♉38	00♊20	14 46	28 54	12♋42	26 12	09♌24	22 19	05♍01	17 30	29 47	11♎54	23 54	05♏46	17 34	29 20
1902	28♍10	11♎18	24 09	06♏43	19 03	01♐10	13 08	25 01	06♑52	18 48	00♒51	13 08	25 41	08♓34	21 49	05♈26
1903	03♒28	15 21	27 18	09♓22	21 37	04♈05	16 46	29 42	12♉51	26 14	09♊50	23 37	07♋35	21 41	05♌55	20 13
1904	18♊05	01♋12	14 39	28 28	12♌39	27 11	12♍00	27 01	12♎06	27 05	11♏50	26 13	10♐11	23 41	06♑44	19 23
1905	06♏42	21 40	06♐19	20 33	04♑22	17 45	00♒45	13 25	25 50	08♓03	20 07	02♈05	13 59	25 51	07♉42	19 35
1906	18♓47	01♈38	14 17	26 45	09♉00	21 06	03♊02	14 54	26 43	08♋35	29 37	02♌51	15 24	28 20	11♍42	25 33
1907	23♋04	04♌54	16 53	29 04	11♍31	24 15	07♎17	20 37	04♏11	17 58	01♐52	15 53	29 56	14♑01	28 07	12♒13
1908	09♐28	22 38	06♑05	19 52	04♒00	18 27	03♓12	18 08	03♈06	17 59	02♉35	16 50	00♊37	13 57	26 50	09♋21
1909	27♈58	12♉57	27 34	11♊44	25 27	08♋43	21 36	04♌11	16 30	28 39	10♍39	22 34	04♎26	16 17	28 08	10♏01
1910	09♍55	22 30	04♎54	17 06	29 08	11♏02	22 50	04♐36	16 24	28 17	10♑22	22 43	05♒25	18 31	02♓05	16 06
1911	12♑33	24 30	06♒37	18 58	01♓36	14 32	27 48	11♈22	25 13	09♉17	23, 30	07♊48	22 08	06♋26	20 39	04♌44
1912	01♊00	14 28	28 11	12♋08	26 19	10♌41	25 12	09♍47	24 20	08♎45	22 58	06♏52	20 27	03♐39	16 29	29 00
1913	18♎26	03♏24	18 02	02♐16	16 03	29 22	12♑16	24 48	07♒02	19 03	00♓56	12 44	24 31	06♈21	18 14	00♉15
1914	00♓45	13 02	25 10	07♈11	19 07	01♉00	12 51	24 43	06♊37	18 38	00♋48	13 12	25 54	08♌58	22 29	06♍27
1915	02♋18	14 14	26 19	08♌39	21 19	04♍21	17 48	01♎40	15 54	00♏25	15 05	29 47	14♐24	28 51	13♑03	26 59
1916	22♏53	06♐37	20 28	04♑27	18 31	02♒41	16 55	01♓12	15 27	29 36	13♈35	27 19	10♉44	23 48	06♊31	18 54
1917	09♈17	24 14	08♉50	22 59	06♊38	19 49	02♋34	14 58	27 05	09♌02	20 52	02♍42	14 33	26 30	08♎35	20 48
1918	21♌29	03♍39	15 42	27 39	09♎33	21 24	03♏13	15 04	26 58	08♐59	21 10	03♑36	16 21	29 30	13♒06	27 11
1919	21♐49	03♑46	15 56	28 23	11♒14	24 30	08♓12	22 21	06♈51	21 36	06♉30	21 23	06♊08	20 40	04♋56	18 53
1920	14♉32	28 31	12♊36	26 46	10♋57	25 09	09♌18	23 22	07♍19	21 05	04♎38	17 56	00♏57	13 41	26 09	08♐23
1921	00♎12	14 46	29 03	12♏58	26 29	09♐36	22 20	04♑45	16 55	28 54	10♒48	22 39	04♓33	16 33	28 42	11♈02
1922	12♒11	24 12	06♓06	17 55	29 42	11♈31	23 23	05♉19	17 24	29 37	12♊03	24 43	07♋40	20 56	04♌35	18 36
1923	11♊52	23 55	06♋09	18 39	01♌30	14 45	28 27	12♍36	27 10	12♎05	27 12	12♏23	27 26	12♐13	26 38	10♑38
1924	05♏59	20 25	04♐52	19 16	03♑32	17 38	01♒33	15 16	28 49	12♓11	25 22	08♈22	21 09	03♉44	16 07	28 18
1925	20♓57	05♈18	19 26	03♉14	16 40	29 41	12♊21	24 40	06♋44	18 37	00♌25	12 14	24 08	06♍12	18 30	01♎05
1926	02♌25	14 19	26 09	07♍58	19 50	01♎46	13 47	25 56	08♏13	20 38	03♐13	16 00	29 01	12♑19	25 56	09♒55
1927	02♐02	14 03	26 17	08♑47	21 40	04♒59	18 48	03♓07	17 54	03♈01	18 20	03♉38	18 45	03♊32	17 54	01♋49
1928	27♈34	12♉14	26 52	11♊22	25 40	09♋44	23 34	07♌10	20 32	03♍41	16 38	29 21	11♎52	24 11	06♏19	18 17
1929	12♍28	26 27	10♎11	23 36	06♏41	19 27	01♐54	14 06	26 07	08♑01	19 52	01♒47	13 49	26 03	08♓31	21 18
1930	22♑27	04♒24	16 16	28 07	10♓01	22 01	04♈07	16 23	28 50	11♉28	24 19	07♊23	20 42	04♋17	18 06	02♌10
1931	22♉23	04♊34	16 58	29 40	12♋42	26 07	09♌57	24 12	08♍51	23 48	08♎57	24 09	09♏13	24 02	08♐28	22 27
1932	18♎19	03♏18	18 15	03♐02	17 34	01♑45	15 35	29 03	12♒11	25 01	07♓37	20 00	02♈14	14 20	26 19	08♉14
1933	03♓44	17 17	00♈38	13 46	26 40	09♉18	21 42	03♊53	15 54	27 47	09♋38	21 30	03♌30	15 42	28 12	11♍03
1934	12♋23	24 14	06♌01	17 50	29 45	11♍49	24 07	06♎39	19 25	02♏27	15 42	29 08	12♐45	26 30	10♑23	24 24
1935	13♏09	25 30	08♐01	20 46	03♑49	17 12	00♒58	15 09	29 44	14♓39	29 47	14♈59	00♉04	14 52	29 15	13♊08
1936	09♈24	24 40	09♉50	24 44	09♊17	23 24	07♋06	20 24	03♌21	16 01	28 27	10♍42	22 49	04♎50	16 46	28 38
1937	25♌17	08♍34	21 39	04♎31	17 08	29 32	11♏43	23 42	05♐33	17 20	29 08	11♑00	23 03	05♒22	18 01	01♓05
1938	01♑49	13 42	25 33	07♒29	19 34	01♓50	14 20	27 06	10♈08	23 26	06♉57	20 40	04♊33	18 33	02♋38	16 48
1939	03♉53	16 24	29 08	12♊06	25 21	08♋56	22 50	07♌03	21 34	06♍19	21 10	06♎01	20 44	05♏12	19 20	03♐03
1940	00♎09	15 21	00♏30	15 27	00♐04	14 16	28 03	11♑23	24 20	06♒56	19 15	01♓21	13 19	25 10	06♈58	18 46
1941	16♒55	29 51	12♓33	25 03	07♈22	19 32	01♉34	13 30	25 22	07♊13	19 06	01♋04	13 12	25 34	08♌14	21 17
1942	21♊33	03♋26	15 18	27 13	09♌16	21 33	04♍06	17 00	00♎15	13 52	27 47	11♏58	26 18	10♐42	25 05	09♑23
1943	24♎37	07♏30	20 35	03♐52	17 21	01♑03	14 56	29 01	13♒18	27 44	12♓17	26 51	11♈20	25 38	09♉38	23 16
1944	20♓46	06♈04	21 20	06♉23	21 04	05♊17	18 59	02♋12	15 00	27 25	09♌35	21 33	03♍25	15 14	27 05	08♎58
1945	08♌10	20 51	03♍20	15 39	27 50	09♎54	21 52	03♏45	15 35	27 23	09♐14	21 10	03♑16	15 38	28 19	11♒26
1946	11♐05	22 53	04♑41	16 37	28 45	11♒10	23 57	07♓06	20 41	04♈39	18 56	03♉26	18 03	02♊40	17 11	01♋33
1947	15♈37	28 45	12♉05	25 37	09♊18	23 09	07♋09	21 17	05♌32	19 52	04♍12	18 29	02♎37	16 31	00♏08	13 25
1948	12♍05	27 10	12♎11	26 58	11♏25	25 28	09♐04	22 14	05♑00	17 27	29 39	11♓39	23 33	05♈24	17 16	29 12
1949	29♑21	11♒55	24 15	06♓23	18 23	00♈16	12 05	23 53	05♉41	17 32	29 29	11♊34	23 51	06♋23	19 14	02♌28
1950	00♊46	12 37	24 31	06♋32	18 45	01♌14	14 03	27 15	10♍53	24 56	09♎22	24 06	09♏01	23 58	08♐49	23 26
1951	06♎00	19 29	03♏14	17 12	01♐18	15 29	29 42	13♑54	28 03	12♒07	26 05	09♓55	23 36	07♈06	20 24	03♉27
1952	03♓09	17 57	02♈44	17 22	01♉44	15 44	29 18	12♊27	25 11	07♋34	19 40	01♌34	13 22	25 09	07♍00	18 59
1953	20♋16	02♌37	14 44	26 42	08♍34	20 24	02♎14	14 07	26 02	08♏03	20 10	02♐24	14 48	27 25	10♑18	23 30
1954	20♏48	02♐37	14 28	26 26	08♑37	21 05	03♒55	17 13	01♓00	15 18	00♈01	15 04	00♉18	15 30	00♊31	15 13
1955	26♓41	10♈35	24 44	09♉02	23 25	07♊47	22 05	06♋16	20 19	04♌13	17 59	01♍35	15 01	28 14	11♎15	24 01
1956	24♌54	09♍29	23 59	08♎19	22 22	06♏03	19 21	02♐15	14 49	27 04	09♑07	21 02	02♒53	14 47	26 46	08♓56
1957	10♑31	22 52	05♒00	16 59	28 52	10♓43	22 35	04♈30	16 29	28 35	10♉49	23 12	05♊47	18 37	01♋42	15 07
1958	10♉49	22 39	04♊34	16 39	28 58	11♋35	24 33	07♌58	21 49	06♍07	20 49	05♎50	21 00	06♏12	21 15	06♐01
1959	17♍02	01♎06	15 29	00♏04	14 46	29 27	14♐02	28 26	12♑35	26 28	10♒03	23 23	06♓27	19 17	01♈55	14 21
1960	16♒52	01♓02	15 05	28 59	12♈39	26 04	09♉11	22 00	04♊31	16 47	28 51	10♋46	22 37	04♌30	16 28	28 38
1961	00♋52	13 09	25 10	07♌02	18 49	00♍36	12 27	24 26	06♎34	18 53	01♏24	14 08	27 05	10♐14	23 35	07♑09
1962	01♏05	13 03	25 06	07♐18	19 42	02♑21	15 19	28 40	12♒27	26 41	11♓21	26 24	11♈40	27 00	12♉11	27 03
1963	07♓09	21 33	06♈18	21 18	06♉23	21 22	06♊08	20 34	04♋38	18 20	01♌42	14 46	27 35	10♍11	22 37	04♎53
1964	08♌48	22 41	06♍28	20 04	03♎28	16 37	29 30	12♏05	24 25	06♐30	18 25	00♑14	12 01	23 53	05♒54	18 11
1965	20♐36	02♑47	14 46	26 39	08♒30	20 23	02♓24	14 34	26 56	09♈30	22 18	05♉18	18 29	01♊52	15 26	19 10
1966	21♈36	03♉38	15 46	28 04	10♊36	23 23	06♋29	19 58	03♌51	18 09	02♍48	17 45	02♎51	17 56	02♏53	17 31
1967	27♌50	12♍19	27 09	12♎12	27 20	12♏23	27 14	11♐46	25 55	09♑40	23 03	06♒04	18 46	01♓13	13 27	25 32
1968	01♒03	14 42	28 09	11♓21	24 21	07♈06	19 39	01♉59	14 09	26 10	08♊04	19 55	01♋47	13 44	25 51	08♌11
1969	10♊20	22 32	04♋33	16 27	28 19	10♌13	22 13	04♍25	16 51	29 34	12♎35	25 53	09♏28	23 17	07♐17	21 23
1970	11♎48	24 02	06♏26	19 03	01♐52	14 55	28 13	11♑47	25 39	09♒48	24 13	08♓52	23 41	08♈32	23 18	07♉50
1971	18♒12	02♓40	17 34	02♈45	18 05	03♉21	18 25	03♊05	17 18	01♋01	14 16	27 06	09♌36	21 49	03♍51	15 17
1972	23♋03	06♌24	19 30	02♍23	15 06	27 37	09♎59	22 12	04♏17	16 14	28 05	09♐54	21 43	03♑37	15 40	27 59
1973	00♐06	12 10	24 04	05♑53	17 41	29 35	11♒41	24 02	06♓42	19 43	03♈06	16 49	00♉49	15 01	29 19	13♊38
1974	02♈21	14 51	27 31	10♉22	23 24	06♊38	20 04	03♋43	17 37	01♌45	16 06	00♍39	15 16	29 53	14♎22	29 36
1975	09♌15	23 48	08♍42	23 52	09♎07	24 17	09♏12	23 44	07♐49	21 27	04♑38	17 26	29 55	12♒09	24 11	06♓07
1976	14♑38	27 55	10♒54	23 38	06♓08	18 27	00♈35	12 36	24 29	06♉18	18 05	29 53	11♊45	23 44	05♋55	18 23
1977	19♉42	01♊43	13 37	25 29	07♋22	19 22	01♌33	14 00	26 46	09♍54	23 24	07♎17	21 29	05♏57	20 33	05♐13
1978	22♍30	05♎09	18 04	01♏13	14 37	28 13	12♐01	25 59	10♑04	24 15	08♒29	22 45	07♓00	21 09	05♈11	19 01
1979	00♒42	15 05	29 46	14♓41	29 42	14♈43	29 33	14♉04	28 12	11♊52	25 05	07♋52	20 17	02♌25	14 20	26 09
1980	06♋16	19 23	02♌08	14 35	26 49	08♍53	20 50	02♎43	14 34	26 25	08♏17	20 12	02♐12	14 18	26 35	09♑05
1981	09♏38	21 36	03♐27	15 16	27 07	09♑04	21 13	03♒39	16 27	29 42	13♓25	27 35	12♈10	27 03	12♉05	27 05
1982	12♓32	25 33	08♈52	22 27	06♉16	20 15	04♊19	18 26	02♋33	16 40	00♌45	14 47	28 45	12♍38	26 23	09♎56
1983	22♋21	06♌39	21 14	06♍02	20 54	05♎44	20 22	04♏40	18 34	02♐01	15 02	27 40	09♑59	22 03	03♒58	15 49
1984	27♐00	10♑02	22 42	05♒07	17 18	29 20	11♓17	23 10	05♈01	16 53	28 46	10♉44	22 47	04♊59	17 22	00 00
1985	29♈43	11♉33	23 19	05♊07	16 59	29 00	11♋15	23 49	06♌46	20 09	04♍00	18 17	02♎58	17 55	03♏01	18 06
1986	02♍43	15 54	29 24	13♎13	27 17	11♏33	25 55	10♐20	24 42	08♑59	23 08	07♒07	20 54	04♓28	17 50	00♈58
1987	14♑37	28 53	13♒18	27 48	12♓17	26 41	10♈54	24 52	08♉31	21 50	04♊47	17 25	29 44	11♋50	23 47	05♌39
1988	17♊41	00♋44	13 22	25 42	07♌46	19 40	01♍28	13 14	25 02	06♎55	18 54	01♏02	13 20	25 49	08♐30	21 24
1989	19♎42	01♏32	13 23	25 17	07♐15	19 22	01♑41	14 16	27 12	10♒32	24 20	08♓36	23 19	08♈24	23 41	09♉01
1990	22♒26	05♓47	19 34	03♈46	18 17	03♉01	17 50	02♊35	17 10	01♋29	15 32	29 17	12♌46	26 00	09♍01	21 51
1991	07♋03	21 10	05♌20	19 31	03♍41	17 47	01♎44	15 27	28 54	12♏01	24 48	07♐15	19 26	01♑24	13 14	25 02
1992	07♐58	20 51	03♑22	15 35	27 35	09♒27	21 18	03♓09	15 06	27 10	09♈23	21 45	04♉18	17 02	29 56	13♊01
1993	10♈09	21 59	03♉51	15 45	17 46	09♊55	22 17	04♋56	17 57	01♌23	15 17	29 38	14♍25	29 30	14♎45	00 00
1994	12♌37	26 10	10♍09	24 33	09♎16	24 10	09♏07	23 59	08♐40	23 04	07♑10	20 55	04♒22	17 30	00♓22	13 00
1995	29♐18	13♑31	27 39	11♒43	25 38	09♓23	22 56	06♈14	19 17	02♉04	14 35	26 53	08♊58	20 56	02♋48	14 40
1996	27♉49	10♊41	23 13	05♋28	17 30	29 25	11♌16	23 08	05♍05	17 12	29 29	12♎00	24 45	07♏45	20 59	04♐27
1997	00♎14	12 05	24 01	06♏04	18 17	00♐40	13 17	26 09	09♑20	22 50	06♒42	20 56	05♓30	20 22	05♈23	20 28
1998	02♒49	16 22	00♓22	14 49	29 40	14♈47	00♉02	15 13	00♊10	14 46	28 57	12♋41	25 58	08♌53	21 29	03♍49
1999	21♊59	06♋10	20 07	03♌52	17 24	00♍44	13 54	26 52	09♎38	22 13	04♏37	16 49	28 51	10♐45	22 35	04♑24
2000	17♏52	00♐37	13 01	25 09	07♑05	18 55	00♒43	12 35	24 37	06♓52	19 24	02♈14	15 23	28 49	12♉29	26 20

	17th	18th	19th	20th	21st	22nd	23rd	24th	25th	26th	27th	28th	29th	30th	31st
1900	11♌24	23 33	05♍33	17 27	29 18	11♎09	23 01	04♏56	16 57	29 04	11♐20	23 48	06♑29	19 28	02♒47
1901	11♐07	23 00	05♑01	17 17	29 51	12♒47	26 09	09♓59	24 16	08♈58	23 58	09♉08	24 19	09♊22	24♊08
1902	19 23	03♉38	18 04	02♊38	17 12	01♋42	16 03	00♌12	14 08	27 49	11♍15	24 27	07♎25	20 10	02♏43
1903	04♍33	18 51	03♎03	17 06	00♏56	14 28	27 42	10♐36	23 11	05♑30	17 35	29 31	11♒23	23 15	05♓12
1904	01♒42	13 46	25 39	07♓27	19 14	01♈04	13 00	25 03	07♉17	19 42	02♊19	15 07	28 09	11♋23	24♋51
1905	01♊30	13 31	25 40	08♋00	20 36	03♌30	16 49	00♍33	14 46	29 26	14♎28	29 45	15♏05	00♐17	15♐10
1906	09♎49	24 27	09♏18	24 15	09♐08	23 49	08♑13	22 17	06♒02	19 28	02♓37	15 33	28 16	10♈49	23♈12
1907	26 17	10♓19	24 16	08♈03	21 38	04♉58	17 59	00♊43	13 08	25 17	07♋15	19 05	00♌52	12 43	24♌42
1908	21 34	03♌34	15 26	27 16	09♍08	21 05	03♎11	15 27	27 55	10♏34	23 24	06♐26	19 39	03♑03	16♑39
1909	21 58	04♐01	16 13	28 38	11♑19	24 21	07♒46	21 37	05♓55	20 38	05♈39	20 50	06♉03	21 05	05♊49
1910	00♈33	15 20	00♉21	15 26	00♊26	15 14	29 45	13♋53	27 40	11♌05	24 10	06♍57	19 28	01♎47	13♎56
1911	18 41	02♍28	16 02	29 24	12♎32	25 26	08♏06	20 31	02♐45	14 48	26 44	08♑35	20 27	02♒23	14♒28
1912	11♑15	23 17	05♒12	17 03	28 57	10♓56	23 05	05♈27	18 04	00♉57	14 07	27 32	11♊11	25 01	08♋59
1913	12 24	24 42	07♊12	19 54	02♋51	16 04	29 34	13♌24	27 33	12♍01	25 44	11♎38	26 35	11♏27	25♏06
1914	20 53	05♎43	20 52	06♏09	21 24	06♐26	21 06	05♑20	19 05	02♒22	15 16	27 49	10♓07	22 13	04♈12
1915	10♒40	24 07	07♓21	20 22	03♈13	15 53	28 23	10♉42	22 51	04♊52	16 45	28 35	10♋24	22 17	04♌19
1916	01♋01	12 57	24 46	06♌34	18 26	00♍29	12 45	25 20	08♎14	21 29	05♏02	18 51	02♐52	17 00	01♑11
1917	03♏10	15 42	28 24	11♐17	24 22	07♑40	21 14	05♒04	19 12	03♓36	18 14	03♈00	17 47	02♉27	16♉51
1918	11♓45	26 42	11♈55	27 14	12♉28	27 26	12♊01	26 10	09♋50	23 03	05♌53	18 24	00♍40	12 44	24♍41
1919	02♌31	15 52	28 56	11♍46	24 22	06♎46	19 00	01♏04	13 00	24 50	06♐37	18 23	00♑13	12 09	24♑17
1920	20 26	02♑20	14 12	26 05	08♒04	20 14	02♓38	15 21	28 25	11♈50	25 36	09♉41	23 59	08♊28	24♊00
1921	23 34	06♉21	19 21	02♊35	16 02	29 42	13♋33	27 34	11♌44	26 01	10♍22	24 44	09♎03	23 14	07♏13
1922	02♍59	17 43	02♎41	17 47	02♏52	17 46	02♐21	16 32	00♑15	13 30	26 20	08♒48	20 58	02♓55	14♓45
1923	24 12	07♒22	20 12	02♓45	15 04	27 13	09♈14	21 11	03♉04	14 56	26 48	08♊41	20 38	02♋42	14♋55
1924	10♊19	22 13	04♋02	15 53	27 49	09♌56	22 19	05♍04	18 13	01♎50	15 53	00♏20	15 05	29 58	14♐51
1925	13 57	27 07	10♏32	24 10	07♐57	21 52	05♑52	19 55	03♒59	18 06	02♓13	16 19	00♈21	14 17	28♈01
1926	24 14	08♓54	23 48	08♈49	23 48	08♉35	23 02	07♊03	20 36	03♋42	16 23	28 44	10♌49	22 44	04♍35
1927	15 16	28 20	11♌03	23 30	05♍44	17 48	29 46	11♎40	23 31	05♏22	17 13	29 06	11♐05	23 11	05♑28
1928	00♐08	11 55	23 41	05♑31	17 30	29 43	12♒14	25 09	08♓29	22 18	06♈32	21 10	06♉04	21 07	06♊08
1929	04♈23	17 46	01♉27	15 22	29 28	13♊41	27 58	12♋16	26 30	10♌39	24 42	08♍35	22 17	05♎48	19♎05
1930	16 28	00♍57	15 33	00♎10	14 43	29 05	13♏11	26 58	10♐22	23 23	06♑04	18 26	00♒33	12 31	24♒23
1931	05♑58	19 03	01♒45	14 07	26 14	08♓10	20 00	01♈48	13 35	25 26	07♉23	19 26	01♊38	14 01	26♊35
1932	20 06	01♊57	13 50	25 46	07♋51	20 07	02♌40	15 33	28 51	12♍36	26 49	11♎29	26 31	11♏45	27♏02
1933	24 17	07♎57	21 59	06♏20	20 54	05♐34	20 11	04♑41	18 58	03♒01	16 50	00♓24	13 45	26 55	09♈53
1934	08♒32	22 46	07♓04	21 23	05♈39	19 47	03♉42	17 18	00♊34	13 28	26 01	08♋15	20 16	02♌07	13♌55
1935	26 32	09♋29	22 01	04♌16	16 17	28 09	09♍59	21 49	03♎43	15 43	27 51	10♏07	22 32	05♐07	17♐52
1936	10♏28	22 17	04♐09	16 05	28 10	10♑27	23 02	05♒59	19 22	03♓15	17 36	02♈24	17 32	02♉50	18♉08
1937	14 34	28 30	12♈49	27 27	12♉15	27 07	11♊54	26 31	10♋53	24 58	08♌45	22 15	05♍28	18 26	01♎10
1938	00♌59	15 11	29 20	13♍23	27 17	11♎00	24 28	07♏40	20 34	03♐11	15 32	27 40	09♑39	21 32	03♒24
1939	16 22	29 17	11♑51	24 07	06♒11	18 06	29 57	11♓49	23 45	05♈49	18 02	00♉27	13 04	25 56	09♊01
1940	00♉35	12 29	24 28	06♊36	18 54	01♋25	14 13	27 19	10♌46	24 37	08♍51	23 27	08♎21	23 25	08♏34
1941	04♍46	18 43	03♎05	17 51	02♏53	18 02	03♐08	18 02	02♑36	16 47	00♒33	13 54	26 53	09♓34	22♓00
1942	23 33	07♒33	21 24	05♓03	18 33	01♈52	15 00	27 56	10♉39	23 10	05♊27	17 33	29 30	11♋22	23♋11
1943	06♊30	19 21	01♋49	13 59	25 57	07♌46	19 34	01♍24	13 23	25 34	07♎59	20 42	03♏41	16 57	00♐26
1944	20 56	03♏00	15 11	27 30	09♐58	22 38	05♑30	18 38	02♒05	15 53	00♓04	14 36	29 27	14♈28	29♈32
1945	25 02	09♓07	23 42	08♈41	23 56	09♉15	24 28	09♊24	23 57	08♋04	21 43	04♌58	17 50	00♍25	12♍45
1946	15 43	29 40	13♌23	26 53	10♍10	23 15	06♎06	18 45	01♏12	13 26	25 29	07♐24	19 13	00♑59	12♑47
1947	26 21	08♐58	21 17	03♑23	15 20	27 12	09♒05	21 03	03♓10	15 31	28 08	11♈02	24 15	07♉45	21♉31
1948	11♈14	23 24	05♉43	18 14	00♊56	13 52	27 02	10♋27	24 07	08♌04	22 17	06♍42	21 17	05♎57	20♎35
1949	16 06	00♍10	14 39	29 30	14♎36	29 48	14♏58	29 55	14♐32	28 44	12♑28	25 45	08♒37	21 08	03♓21
1950	07♑46	21 45	05♒23	18 41	01♓40	14 24	26 55	09♈15	21 25	03♉29	15 27	27 21	09♊12	21 03	02♋57
1951	16 14	28 47	11♊04	23 10	05♋06	16 58	28 48	10♌44	22 49	05♍09	17 50	00♎52	14 19	28 09	12♏20
1952	01♎09	13 33	26 11	09♏03	22 09	05♐27	18 56	02♑35	16 23	00♒18	14 23	28 35	12♓54	27 16	11♈37
1953	07♒05	21 05	05♓30	20 19	05♈24	20 38	05♉49	20 47	05♊23	19 31	03♋08	16 17	29 00	11♌22	23♌29
1954	29 31	13♋24	26 52	09♌59	22 47	05♍20	17 42	29 54	11♎59	23 57	05♏51	17 42	29 31	11♐21	23♐13
1955	06♏33	18 52	00♐56	12 52	24 40	06♑27	18 16	00♒14	12 25	24 54	07♓45	21 02	04♈45	18 53	03♉21
1956	21 18	03♈56	16 48	29 56	13♉18	26 53	10♊38	24 32	08♋33	22 39	06♌50	21 02	05♍14	19 22	03♎24
1957	28 51	12♌56	27 20	12♍00	26 52	11♎47	26 37	11♏15	25 34	09♐30	23 02	06♑08	18 51	01♒16	13♒25
1958	20 25	04♑23	17 55	01♒03	13 48	26 15	08♓28	20 29	02♈23	14 13	26 00	07♉49	19 39	01♊35	13♊38
1959	26 37	08♉44	20 44	02♊38	14 30	26 21	08♋16	20 18	02♌33	15 04	27 55	11♍12	24 55	09♎06	23♎41
1960	11♍02	23 46	06♎49	20 14	03♏59	18 00	02♐13	16 33	00♑55	15 13	29 26	13♒31	27 25	11♓13	24♓50
1961	20 55	04♒54	19 07	03♓31	18 04	02♈41	17 16	01♉43	15 55	29 46	13♊13	26 15	08♋53	21 12	03♌14
1962	11♊29	25 25	08♋51	21 50	04♌25	16 41	28 44	10♍39	22 30	04♎19	16 11	28 06	10♏06	22 12	04♐26
1963	27 02	29 04	10♏59	22 50	04♐39	16 28	28 20	10♑20	22 34	05♒05	17 59	01♓21	15 13	29 35	14♈24
1964	00♓46	13 44	27 07	10♈53	24 59	09♉21	23 53	08♊28	23 00	07♋24	21 39	05♌41	19 31	03♍09	16♍34
1965	13♋04	27 08	11♌21	25 41	10♍04	24 26	08♎41	22 46	06♏34	20 02	03♐10	15 57	28 25	10♑38	22♑39
1966	01♐46	15 35	28 57	11♑54	24 30	06♒48	18 53	00♓49	12 41	24 32	06♈25	18 23	00♉28	12 41	25♉04
1967	07♈28	19 20	01♉08	12 56	24 47	06♊38	18 38	00♋48	13 11	25 53	08♌55	22 21	06♍14	20 32	05♎14
1968	20 50	03♍51	17 16	01♎07	15 22	00 00	14♏45	29 40	14♐33	29 15	13♑43	27 51	11♒38	25 05	08♓14
1969	05♑34	19 45	03♒55	18 03	02♓05	16 02	29 50	13♈29	16 56	10♉08	23 06	05♊47	18 12	00♋24	12♋24
1970	22 03	05♊51	19 13	02♋08	14 40	26 53	08♌52	20 42	02♍28	14 17	26 11	08♎15	20 31	03♏01	15♏44
1971	27 38	09♎28	21 19	03♏13	15 10	27 13	09♐22	21 39	04♑08	16 52	29 54	13♒17	27 06	11♓20	26♓00
1972	10♒39	23 43	07♓17	21 21	05♈52	20 47	05♉56	21 09	06♊14	21 04	05♋32	19 35	03♌14	16 31	29♌28
1973	27 56	12♋08	26 15	10♌14	24 05	07♍48	21 21	04♎44	17 53	00♏49	13 30	25 56	08♐07	20 08	01♑59
1974	12♏30	26 00	09♐06	21 50	04♑14	16 23	28 21	10♒13	22 05	04♓01	16 05	28 20	10♈49	23 32	06♉31
1975	17 59	29 50	11♈43	23 39	05♉40	17 48	00♊05	12 32	25 13	08♋09	21 23	04♌57	18 52	03♍08	17♍43
1976	01♌11	14 23	28 01	12♍07	26 39	11♎32	26 39	11♏52	26 59	11♐54	26 28	10♑38	24 21	07♒40	20♒34
1977	19 50	04♑18	18 33	02♒33	16 17	29 45	12♓58	25 57	08♈43	21 17	03♉39	15 52	27 56	09♊54	21♊46
1978	02♉36	15 54	28 53	11♊34	23 58	06♋07	18 06	29 58	11♌49	23 44	05♍47	18 03	00♎37	13 29	26♎43
1979	07♍55	19 44	01♎37	13 40	25 52	08♏16	20 52	03♐41	16 41	29 54	13♑19	26 58	10♒51	24 58	09♓18
1980	21 53	05♒02	18 37	02♓39	17 09	02♈04	17 16	02♉37	17 54	02♊56	17 35	01♋45	15 24	28 35	11♌20
1981	11♊56	26 29	10♋42	24 34	08♌05	21 18	04♍15	16 58	29 31	11♎53	24 07	06♏13	18 12	00♐06	11♐55
1982	23 15	06♏18	19 03	01♐32	13 44	25 44	07♑35	19 22	01♒11	13 08	25 16	07♓42	20 29	03♈39	17♈13
1983	27 41	09♓37	21 42	03♈57	16 24	29 03	11♉54	24 58	08♊13	21 38	05♋15	19 03	03♌01	17 10	01♍28
1984	12♋56	26 14	09♌55	24 02	08♍33	23 25	08♎29	23 38	08♏41	23 30	07♐57	21 59	05♑34	18 42	01♒28
1985	03♐02	17 42	02♑01	15 57	29 30	12♒41	25 32	08♓07	20 28	02♈38	14 39	26 33	08♉23	20 11	01♊59
1986	13 53	26 34	09♉01	21 17	03♊23	15 21	27 13	09♋05	20 59	03♌00	15 13	27 43	10♍32	23 46	07♎24
1987	17 31	29 27	11♍33	23 51	06♎24	19 15	02♏23	15 48	29 27	13♐19	27 20	11♑27	25 36	09♒46	23♒56
1988	04♑33	17 58	01♒41	15 42	00♓01	14 36	29 24	14♈17	29 09	13♉52	28 16	12♊17	25 52	09♋00	21♋42
1989	24 11	09♊02	23 28	07♋24	20 51	03♌52	16 31	28 51	10♍59	22 58	04♎51	16 42	28 33	10♏25	22♏20
1990	04♎29	16 58	29 17	11♏27	23 28	05♐22	17 11	29 00	10♑50	22 48	04♒59	17 28	00♓21	13 41	27♓30
1991	06♒53	18 53	01♓05	13 36	26 26	09♈38	23 10	07♉00	21 03	05♊15	19 31	03♋48	18 01	02♌09	16♌12
1992	26 19	09♋50	23 36	07♌37	21 54	06♍23	21 02	05♎43	20 19	04♏44	18 50	02♐33	15 52	28 47	11♑20
1993	15♏03	29 46	14♐04	27 54	11♑18	24 16	06♒54	19 14	01♓22	13 20	25 14	07♈05	18 56	00♉50	12♉47
1994	25 25	07♈40	19 45	01♉42	13 34	25 21	07♊08	18 57	00♋52	13 00	25 16	07♌53	20 54	04♍20	18♍13
1995	26 36	08♌42	21 00	03♍36	16 33	29 52	13♎32	27 34	11♏53	26 23	11♐00	25 36	10♑07	24 27	08♒34
1996	18 07	01♑58	15 58	00♒05	14 19	28 35	12♓53	27 08	11♈17	25 17	09♉02	22 31	05♊41	18 32	01♋04
1997	05♉26	20 08	04♊28	18 22	01♋47	14 46	27 20	09♌35	21 36	03♍27	15 14	27 00	08♎51	20 48	02♏55
1998	15 58	27 59	09♎55	21 48	03♏39	15 30	27 23	09♐19	21 21	03♑31	15 54	28 32	11♒31	24 53	08♓43
1999	16 18	28 20	10♒37	23 15	06♓16	19 45	03♈43	18 06	02♉50	17 47	02♊46	17 40	02♋20	16 41	00♌42
2000	10♊19	24 22	08♋26	20 32	08♌38	20 42	04♍48	18 43	02♎38	16 18	29 47	13♏00	25 56	08♐33	20♐54

Moon

November

Year	1st	2nd	3rd	4th	5th	6th	7th	8th	9th	10th	11th	12th	13th	14th	15th	16th
1900	16♒28	00♓32	14 58	29 43	14♈41	29 44	14♉43	29 29	13♊56	27 58	11♋34	24 44	07♌30	19 57	02♍07	14 06
1901	08♋32	22 31	06♌05	19 15	02♍04	14 34	26 50	08♎55	20 52	02♏43	14 31	26 18	08♐06	19 58	01♑55	14 02
1902	15♏05	27 16	09♐18	21 14	03♑06	14 56	26 50	08♒51	21 03	03♓32	16 22	29 36	13♈16	27 22	11♉52	26 42
1903	17♓20	29 41	12♈19	25 17	08♉34	22 09	06♊00	20 04	04♋15	18 29	02♌44	16 55	01♍01	15 01	28 54	12♎39
1904	08♌34	22 32	06♍45	21♎13	05♎51	20 35	05♏18	19 53	04♐12	18 10	01♑42	14 49	27 31	09♒52	21 56	03♓50
1905	29♐38	13♑36	27 05	10♒06	22 44	05♓03	17 10	29 07	10♈59	22 50	04♉41	16 35	28 33	10♊36	22 44	05♋01
1906	05♉27	17 33	29 32	11♊26	23 15	05♋03	16 55	28 53	11♌04	23 32	06♍23	19 42	03♎30	17 48	02♏33	17 38
1907	06♍55	19 27	02♎19	15 35	29 12	13♏10	27 22	11♐44	26 09	10♑34	24 53	09♒04	23 07	07♓00	20 43	04♈16
1908	00♒28	14 29	28 42	13♓06	27 36	12♈08	26 35	10♉51	24 51	08♊29	21 45	04♋38	17 11	29 26	11♌29	23 23
1909	20♊09	04♋02	17 27	00♌27	13 04	25 24	07♍31	19 28	01♎20	13 10	25 01	06♏55	18 55	01♐02	13 18	25 44
1910	25♎56	07♏49	19 38	01♐25	13 12	25 02	06♑58	19 04	01♒24	14 01	27 00	10♓25	24 16	08♈34	23 17	08♉19
1911	26♒47	09♓23	22 21	05♈43	19 29	03♉38	18 06	02♊47	17 34	02♋21	16 59	01♌24	15 33	29 23	12♍55	26 09
1912	23♋04	07♌13	21 24	05♍34	19 43	03♎47	17 45	01♏33	15 09	28 30	11♐34	24 21	06♑51	19 05	01♒07	13 02
1913	10♐24	24 17	07♑42	20 40	03♒15	15 30	27 31	09♓22	21 09	02♈57	14 49	26 50	09♉01	21 25	04♊01	16 50
1914	16♈06	27 57	09♉49	21 42	03♊37	15 37	27 42	09♋55	22 20	04♌59	17 57	01♍18	15 04	29 18	13♎58	28 59
1915	16♌35	29 12	12♍13	25 42	09♎40	24 06	08♏55	23 57	09♐04	24 05	08♑51	23 17	07♒21	21 02	04♓22	17 24
1916	15♑22	29 31	13♒37	27 38	11♓34	25 25	09♈08	22 41	06♉02	19 07	01♊57	14 30	26 48	08♋52	20 47	02♌35
1917	00♊54	14 33	27 46	10♋34	23 01	05♌12	17 10	29 03	10♍54	22 47	04♎48	16 59	29 22	11♏59	24 48	07♐51
1918	06♎33	18 23	00♏14	12 07	24 04	06♐06	18 16	00♑36	13 09	25 58	09♒06	22 36	06♓30	20 46	05♈25	20 19
1919	06♒41	19 27	02♓36	16 13	00♈18	14 49	29 41	14♉47	29 58	15♊05	29 58	14♋32	28 42	12♌28	25 49	08♍47
1920	07♋30	21 54	06♌08	20 10	03♍58	17 33	00♎54	14 01	26 54	09♏35	22 04	04♐22	16 30	28 29	10♑23	22 14
1921	20♏57	04♐22	17 27	00♑12	12 39	24 50	06♒50	18 43	00♓34	12 28	24 30	06♈43	19 12	01♉59	15 05	28 29
1922	26♓32	08♈20	20 12	02♉11	14 19	26 36	09♊05	21 46	04♋39	17 45	01♌04	14 39	28 29	12♍36	26 58	11♎34
1923	27♋22	10♌06	23 14	06♍46	20 46	05♎15	20 08	05♏20	20 40	05♐58	21 01	05♑41	19 53	03♒34	16 48	29 36
1924	29♐36	14♑07	28 19	12♒12	25 47	09♓05	22 08	04♈59	17 39	00♉08	12 29	24 40	06♊44	18 40	00♋31	12 20
1925	11♉32	24 44	07♊38	20 12	02♋29	14 32	26 25	08♌13	20 02	01♍56	14 02	26 24	09♎06	22 10	05♏35	19 22
1926	16♍25	28 19	10♎20	22 30	04♏51	17 22	00♐05	12 58	26 03	09♑19	22 47	06♒29	20 23	04♓31	18 52	03♈21
1927	18♑00	00♒51	14 04	27 43	11♓50	26 22	11♈17	26 26	11♉41	26 51	11♊45	26 17	10♋23	24 01	07♌12	20 00
1928	21♊01	05♋39	19 57	03♌54	17 29	00♍43	13 39	26 19	08♎45	20 59	03♏04	15 01	26 53	08♐41	20 27	02♑15
1929	02♏09	14 57	27 32	09♐52	22 01	04♑01	15 54	27 45	09♒39	21 39	03♓50	16 17	29 04	12♈14	25 47	09♉44
1930	06♓14	18 10	00♈13	12 27	24 56	07♉39	20 39	03♊54	17 24	01♋06	14 58	28 58	13♌04	27 14	11♍25	25 36
1931	09♋23	22 27	05♌47	19 27	03♍27	17 48	02♎26	17 18	02♏17	17 15	02♐03	16 33	00♑39	14 18	27 29	10♒15
1932	12♐11	27 01	11♑26	25 24	08♒54	21 58	04♓40	17 05	29 17	11♈20	23 17	05♉10	17 02	28 54	10♊48	22 44
1933	22♈41	05♉18	17 44	29 59	12♊04	24 02	05♋53	17 41	29 31	11♌28	23 37	06♍03	18 52	02♎08	15 52	00♏05
1934	25♌44	07♍41	19 50	02♎15	14 59	28 03	11♏25	25 04	08♐57	22 59	07♑06	21 15	05♒23	19 29	03♓33	17 33
1935	00♑48	13 58	27 23	11♒04	25 04	09♓22	23 56	08♈41	23 32	08♉19	22 54	07♊10	21 02	04♋28	17 28	00♌05
1936	03♊14	18 01	02♋21	16 14	29 40	12♌40	25 20	07♍42	19 52	01♎52	13 47	25 38	07♏28	19 19	01♐13	13 11
1937	13♎42	26 02	08♏11	20 12	02♐05	13 54	25 40	07♑27	19 20	01♒21	13 37	26 12	09♓10	22 33	06♈25	20 44
1938	15♒19	27 23	09♓40	22 13	05♈06	18 19	01♉54	15 48	29 58	14♊20	28 48	13♋17	27 43	12♌01	26 08	10♍03
1939	22♊19	05♋50	19 34	03♌29	17 35	01♍49	16 10	00♎34	14 58	29 16	13♏25	27 19	10♐55	24 12	07♑07	19 43
1940	23♏36	08♐22	22 45	06♑42	20 10	03♒11	15 48	28 06	10♓09	22 02	03♈49	15 36	27 25	09♉20	21 23	03♊34
1941	04♈15	16 21	28 21	10♉17	22 09	04♊01	15 53	27 48	09♋47	21 55	04♌14	16 49	29 44	13♍04	26 51	11♎07
1942	05♌04	17 04	29 19	11♍53	24 50	08♎13	22 04	06♏19	20 54	05♐42	20 34	05♑21	19 56	04♒16	18 17	02♓00
1943	14♐06	27 55	11♑50	25 49	09♒52	23 58	08♓06	22 15	06♈22	20 24	04♉18	17 58	01♊22	14 27	27 11	09♋37
1944	14♉28	29 07	13♊22	27 09	10♋28	23 20	05♌49	18 01	00♍01	11 53	23 43	05♎34	17 31	29 36	11♏50	24 14
1945	24♍54	06♎56	18 52	00♏45	12 35	24 25	06♐17	18 11	00♑12	12 23	24 46	07♒26	20 28	03♓55	17 49	02♈11
1946	24♑41	06♒46	19 08	01♓52	14 59	28 34	12♈37	27 03	11♉49	26 47	11♊49	26 45	11♋29	25 55	10♌01	23 46
1947	05♊30	19 37	03♋50	18 05	02♌20	16 32	00♍38	14 37	28 27	12♎06	25 33	08♏45	21 44	04♐27	16 55	29 11
1948	05♏06	19 23	03♐21	16 58	00♑11	13 02	25 32	07♒46	19 48	01♓42	13 33	25 25	07♈24	19 31	01♉52	14 26
1949	15♓22	27 15	09♈03	20 50	02♉39	14 32	26 31	08♊38	20 54	03♋21	16 00	28 54	12♌05	25 35	09♍26	23 37
1950	14♋57	27 07	09♌31	22 13	05♍19	18 51	02♎52	17 20	02♏12	17 22	02♐39	17 51	02♑50	17 27	01♒36	15 18
1951	26♏46	11♐21	25 57	10♑29	24 50	08♒59	22 54	06♓36	20 05	03♈22	16 29	29 24	12♉08	24 42	07♊04	19 15
1952	25♈53	09♉58	23 46	07♊14	20 19	03♋02	15 25	27 32	09♌27	21 15	03♍04	14 56	25 59	09♎15	21 49	04♏42
1953	05♍25	17 16	29 05	10♎57	22 53	04♏56	17 07	29 26	11♐54	24 31	07♑20	20 21	03♒37	17 09	01♓00	15 10
1954	05♑13	17 23	29 48	12♒34	25 45	09♓24	23 32	08♈09	23 09	08♉24	23 44	08♊57	23 54	08♋26	22 32	06♌10
1955	18♉03	02♊51	17 39	02♋19	16 47	00♌59	14 54	28 32	11♍54	25 01	07♎53	20 32	02♏59	15 15	27 21	09♐19
1956	17♎16	00♏54	14 16	27 21	10♐08	22 37	04♑52	16 56	28 51	10♒43	22 36	04♓35	16 45	29 10	11♈52	24 54
1957	25♒23	07♓16	19 07	01♈00	12 58	25 05	07♉23	19 53	02♊35	15 31	28 41	12♋03	25 39	09♌27	23 27	07♍38
1958	25♊49	08♋13	20 51	03♌47	17 04	00♍43	14 47	29 13	14♎01	29 04	14♏13	29 21	14♐16	28 52	13♑01	26 43
1959	08♏35	23 41	08♐48	23 47	08♑30	22 51	06♒47	20 19	03♓29	16 19	28 53	11♈14	23 25	05♉29	17 27	29 22
1960	08♈17	21 33	04♉38	17 30	00♊08	12 33	24 45	06♋46	18 40	00♌30	12 20	24 16	06♍23	18 47	01♎33	14 43
1961	15♌07	26 54	08♍43	20 37	02♎41	14 58	27 31	10♏21	23 27	06♐47	20 19	04♑01	17 50	01♒45	15 45	29 49
1962	16♐47	29 19	12♑03	25 02	08♒19	21 57	05♓57	20 21	05♈05	20 05	05♉12	20 15	05♊05	19 33	03♋34	17 06
1963	29♈33	14♉51	00♊07	15 11	29 55	14♋13	28 04	11♌30	24 32	07♍15	19 43	01♎58	14 04	26 03	07♏57	19 49
1964	29♍47	12♎47	25 34	08♏08	20 30	02♐39	14 39	26 30	08♑18	20 04	01♒55	13 54	26 08	08♓40	21 36	04♈58
1965	04♒32	16 24	28 19	10♓21	22 34	05♈02	17 47	00♉50	14 10	27 46	11♊36	25 36	09♋44	23 56	08♌10	22 23
1966	07♊38	20 25	03♋26	16 42	00♌14	14 02	28 08	12♍28	27 01	11♎41	26 24	11♏02	25 29	09♐39	23 27	06♑53
1967	20♎15	05♏26	20 39	05♐43	20 31	04♑55	18 52	02♒21	15 24	28 04	10♓26	22 32	04♈29	16 19	28 06	09♉54
1968	21♓06	03♈45	16 11	28 28	10♉36	22 38	04♊34	16 27	28 18	10♋10	22 06	04♌10	16 26	28 59	11♍53	25 12
1969	24♋17	06♌08	18 00	30 00	12♍12	24 42	07♎33	20 47	04♏25	18 25	02♐42	17 11	01♑44	16 16	00♒40	14 54
1970	28♏41	11♐51	25 12	08♑44	22 25	06♒15	20 15	04♓24	18 42	03♈05	17 30	01♉53	16 07	00♊06	13 46	27 04
1971	11♈00	26 14	11♉29	26 36	11♊24	25 45	09♋37	22 59	05♌53	18 25	00♍38	12 39	24 32	06♎21	18 11	00♏05
1972	12♍09	24 37	06♎55	19 04	01♏07	13 03	24 56	06♐45	18 34	00♑24	12 19	24 23	06♒40	19 15	02♓13	15 39
1973	13♑47	25 34	07♒27	19 31	01♓51	14 31	27 36	11♈06	25 01	09♉18	23 52	08♊36	23 23	08♋05	22 37	06♌55
1974	19♉44	03♊09	16 47	00♋34	14 29	28 32	12♌39	26 51	11♍05	25 17	09♎25	23 25	07♏13	20 46	04♐02	16 59
1975	02♎32	17 28	02♏24	17 11	01♐42	15 51	29 35	12♑53	25 47	08♒20	20 36	02♓39	14 34	26 24	08♈15	20 10
1976	03♓11	15 30	27 37	09♈35	21 27	03♉15	15 03	26 52	08♊44	20 42	02♋48	15 05	27 35	10♌21	23 27	06♍55
1977	03♋37	15 30	27 28	09♌36	21 58	04♍39	17 43	01♎14	15 11	29 35	14♏20	29 20	14♐26	29 29	14♑18	28 49
1978	10♏16	24 07	08♐13	22 27	06♑45	21 03	05♒18	19 26	03♓26	17 18	01♈02	14 36	28 01	11♉14	24 15	07♊02
1979	23♓49	08♈28	23 08	07♉43	22 06	06♊09	19 49	03♋03	15 53	28 21	10♌30	22 26	04♍15	16 02	27 53	09♎51
1980	23♌44	05♍54	17 52	29 45	11♎35	23 25	05♏18	17 15	29 17	11♐25	23 41	06♑06	18 42	01♒32	14 39	28 06
1981	23♐43	05♑33	17 28	29 34	11♒56	24 39	07♓48	21 26	05♈34	20 12	05♉12	20 27	05♊44	20 54	05♋47	20 16
1982	01♉08	15 21	29 46	14♊17	28 48	13♋14	27 32	11♌39	25 36	09♍20	22 53	06♎14	19 22	02♏18	15 01	27 30
1983	15♍52	00♎18	14 40	28 54	12♏53	26 33	09♐53	22 51	05♑29	17 49	29 55	11♒52	23 44	05♓37	17 34	29 42
1984	13♒54	26 04	08♓04	19 58	01♈48	13 40	25 34	07♉34	19 42	01♊58	14 25	27 04	09♋56	23 02	06♌25	20 04
1985	13♊49	25 44	07♋48	20 04	02♌36	15 28	28 42	12♍23	26 29	11♎01	25 55	11♏03	26 17	11♐27	26 23	10♑59
1986	21♎26	05♏51	20 32	05♐23	20 15	05♑01	19 35	03♒51	17 48	01♓24	14 43	27 44	10♈30	23 04	06♉27	17 41
1987	08♓02	22 04	05♈59	19 46	03♉22	16 44	29 51	12♊42	25 16	07♋35	19 41	01♌37	13 27	25 18	07♍13	19 19
1988	04♌03	16 08	28 01	09♍49	21 35	03♎26	15 25	27 34	09♏55	22 30	05♐19	18 20	01♑33	14 57	28 31	12♒15
1989	04♐19	16 23	28 35	10♑57	23 32	06♒23	19 36	03♓13	17 16	01♈45	16 38	01♉49	17 06	02♊20	17 18	01♋53
1990	11♈49	26 34	11♉36	26 47	11♊55	26 51	11♋28	25 42	09♌31	22 58	06♍08	18 54	01♎29	13 53	26 08	08♏14
1991	00♍08	13 57	27 37	11♎08	24 26	07♏32	20 22	02♐57	15 16	27 22	09♑18	21 07	02♒54	14 44	26 42	08♓53
1992	23♑36	05♒38	17 33	29 24	11♓17	23 17	05♈26	17 47	00♉22	13 11	26 15	09♊32	23 01	06♋40	20 29	04♌27
1993	24♉50	07♊01	19 21	01♋53	14 40	27 44	11♌07	24 52	08♍59	23 27	08♎12	23 08	08♏07	23 02	07♐43	22 04
1994	02♎34	17 17	02♏19	17 30	02♐40	17 41	02♑25	16 46	00♒41	14 11	27 17	10♓02	22 29	04♈42	16 44	28 39
1995	22♒26	06♓03	19 24	02♈32	15 26	28 07	10♉37	22 56	05♊06	17 07	29 02	10♋54	22 45	04♌40	16 42	28 57
1996	13♋20	25 23	07♌18	19 09	01♍01	12 59	25 08	07♎32	20 14	03♏16	16 39	00♐19	14 16	28 23	12♑37	26 54
1997	15♏12	27 40	10♐20	23 13	06♑17	19 34	03♒05	16 60	00♓50	15 05	29 34	14♈12	28 56	13♉37	28 09	12♊25
1998	23♓01	07♈46	22 52	08♉11	23 32	08♊43	23 33	07♋56	21 50	05♌13	18 09	00♍43	12 59	25 02	06♎58	18 49
1999	14♌23	27 44	10♍49	23 41	06♎20	18 49	01♏09	13 20	25 23	07♐20	19 11	00♑59	12 47	24 39	06♒39	18 52
2000	03♑00	14 54	26 43	08♒31	20 23	02♓25	14 42	27 19	20♈17	23 38	07♉22	21 25	05♊42	20 08	04♋37	19 03

	17th	18th	19th	20th	21st	22nd	23rd	24th	25th	26th	27th	28th	29th	30th
1900	25 59	07♎49	19 40	01♏36	13 38	25 49	08♐11	20 45	03♑31	16 30	29 43	13♒11	26 53	10♓50
1901	26 20	08♒53	21 45	04♓58	18 36	02♈39	17 07	01♉57	17 03	02♊17	17 28	02♋27	17 07	01♌20
1902	11♊42	26 44	11♋39	26 20	10♌40	24 38	08♍13	21 27	04♎23	17 02	29 29	11♏45	24 53	05♐54
1903	26 14	09♏40	22 53	05♐52	18 37	01♑07	13 23	25 27	07♒22	19 12	01♓02	12 57	25 03	07♈24
1904	15 38	27 25	09♈18	21 19	03♉32	16 00	28 42	11♊40	24 51	08♋14	23 47	05♌29	19 18	03♍14
1905	17 27	00♌06	12 59	26 12	09♍47	23 46	08♎10	22 56	07♏59	23 11	08♐19	23 15	07♑48	21♑54
1906	02♐53	18 06	03♑08	17 50	02♒08	16 00	29 28	12♓33	25 20	07♈52	20 12	02♉23	14 26	26♉24
1907	17 38	00♉48	13 45	26 49	08♊58	21 14	03♋18	15 13	27 01	08♌48	20 38	02♍36	14 47	27♍16
1908	05♍15	17 08	29 08	11♎18	23 41	06♏19	19 14	02♐25	15 50	29 29	13♑18	27 16	11♒20	25♒29
1909	08♑22	21 14	04♒22	17 48	01♓32	15 37	29 59	14♈37	29 25	14♉16	29 04	13♊40	27 59	11♋55
1910	23 31	08♊46	23 52	08♋40	23 06	07♌05	20 37	03♍43	16 26	28 50	10♎59	22 58	04♏50	16♏38
1911	09♎08	21 54	04♏27	16 49	29 02	11♐07	23 06	04♑59	16 50	28 41	10♒35	22 37	04♓51	17♓22
1912	24 52	06♓44	18 43	00♈53	13 19	26 05	09♉13	22 44	06♊34	20 42	05♋02	19 27	03♌52	18♌12
1913	29 51	13♋03	26 27	10♌02	23 49	07♍47	21 57	06♎18	20 47	05♏20	19 51	04♐14	18 22	02♑10
1914	14♏15	29 33	14♐43	29 34	13♑59	27 54	11♒19	24 16	06♓50	19 06	01♈08	13 03	24 53	06♉44
1915	00♈11	12 45	25 09	07♉24	19 31	01♊32	13 27	25 18	07♋06	18 55	00♌48	12 49	25 03	07♍35
1916	14 22	26 14	08♍16	20 33	03♎09	16 09	29 33	13♏21	27 30	11♐55	26 30	11♑08	25 43	10♒10
1917	21 06	04♑33	18 10	01♒57	15 53	29 58	14♓10	28 27	12♈47	27 05	11♉16	25 16	09♊00	22♊26
1918	05♉23	20 27	05♊22	20 00	04♋15	18 04	01♌26	14 24	26 59	09♍17	21 21	03♎16	15 06	26♎56
1919	21 27	03♎50	16 00	28 01	09♏55	21 45	03♐32	15 20	27 09	09♑03	21 04	03♒16	15 40	28♒22
1920	04♒05	16 02	28 08	10♓29	23 08	06♈09	19 36	03♉30	17 48	02♊28	17 22	02♋23	17 20	02♌07
1921	12♊11	26 06	10♋11	24 21	08♌34	22 46	06♍54	20 57	04♎55	18 46	02♏30	16 03	29 25	12♐34
1922	26 19	11♏06	25 49	10♐19	24 29	08♑15	21 35	04♒28	16 59	29 10	11♓08	22 58	04♈45	16♈34
1923	12♓03	24 16	06♈17	18 12	00♉04	11 55	23 47	05♊42	17 42	29 46	11♋57	24 17	06♌47	19♌32
1924	24 09	06♌03	18 06	00♍26	13 05	26 10	09♎45	23 49	08♏22	23 18	08♐28	23 42	08♑49	23♑40
1925	03♐25	17 40	02♑01	16 23	00♒43	14 57	29 03	13♓01	26 51	10♈31	24 00	07♉19	20 25	03♊17
1926	17 56	02♉29	16 54	01♊04	14 55	28 24	11♋29	24 12	06♌35	18 44	00♍42	12 34	24 26	06♎22
1927	02♍27	14 40	26 41	08♎35	20 25	02♏15	14 07	26 03	08♐05	20 15	02♑35	15 05	27 48	10♒46
1928	14 08	26 08	08♒20	20 48	03♓36	16 48	00♈27	14 32	29 04	13♉58	29 07	14♊22	29 33	14♋30
1929	24 02	08♊35	23 18	08♋04	22 45	07♌15	21 30	05♍29	19 10	02♎33	15 41	28 35	11♏15	23♏45
1930	09♎45	23 49	07♏46	21 31	05♐02	18 17	01♑14	13 53	26 15	08♒23	20 20	02♓12	14 02	25♓57
1931	22 38	04♓45	16 39	28 28	10♈14	22 04	04♉00	16 05	28 21	10♊49	23 30	06♋23	19 28	02♌44
1932	04♋45	16 53	29 11	11♌42	24 29	07♍39	21 13	05♎14	19 43	04♏37	19 48	05♐08	20 24	05♑26
1933	14 43	29 38	14♐43	29 45	14♑37	29 12	13♒25	27 16	10♓45	23 56	06♈51	19 33	02♉03	14♉23
1934	01♈29	15 19	29 00	12♉30	25 45	08♊45	21 28	03♋54	16 05	28 04	09♌55	21 42	03♍31	15♍28
1935	12 23	24 27	06♍21	18 12	00♎04	12 01	24 06	06♏22	18 50	01♐31	14 26	27 32	10♑51	24♑20
1936	25 16	07♑29	19 54	02♒34	15 32	28 50	12♓32	25 39	11♈08	25 57	11♉00	26 07	11♊09	25♊57
1937	05♉26	20 26	05♊35	20 44	05♋44	20 27	04♌47	18 44	02♍16	15 25	28 14	10♎45	23 02	05♏08
1938	23 46	07♎15	20 31	03♏33	16 23	28 59	11♐24	23 38	05♑42	17 39	29 31	11♒22	23 16	05♓17
1939	02♒02	14 07	26 03	07♓54	19 45	01♈42	13 49	26 09	08♉46	21 41	04♊55	18 26	02♋12	16♋10
1940	15 56	28 29	11♋14	24 11	07♌22	20 48	04♍30	18 29	02♎45	17 17	02♏01	16 51	01♐40	16♐19
1941	25 51	10♏56	26 14	11♐34	26 45	11♑37	26 01	09♒57	23 23	06♓22	18 59	01♈18	13 25	25♈23
1942	15 27	28 38	11♈37	24 24	07♉00	19 27	01♊45	13 53	25 53	07♋47	19 36	01♌24	13 15	25♌13
1943	21 47	03♌44	15 34	27 22	09♍13	21 13	03♎26	15 58	28 50	12♏04	25 39	09♐32	23 39	07♑54
1944	06♐49	19 35	02♑32	15 40	29 00	12♒33	26 20	10♓22	24 38	09♈05	23 41	08♉18	22 51	07♊12
1945	16 57	02♉01	17 16	02♊30	17 33	02♋17	16 36	00♌27	13 51	26 49	09♍26	21 45	03♎51	15♎48
1946	07♍10	20 16	03♎04	15 37	27 58	10♏09	22 11	04♐06	15 56	27 43	09♑30	21 19	03♒15	15♒20
1947	11♑15	23 12	05♒04	16 55	28 52	10♓57	23 16	05♈53	18 51	02♉12	15 56	00♊03	14 27	29♊04
1948	27 16	10♊22	23 42	07♋16	21 01	07♌55	18 56	03♍04	17 14	01♎27	15 39	29 49	13♏53	27♏47
1949	08♎09	22 57	07♏56	22 58	07♐54	22 36	06♑55	20 47	04♒11	17 07	29 42	11♓55	23 55	05♈45
1950	28 34	11♓26	24 00	06♈18	18 26	00♉26	12 22	24 15	06♊07	17 59	29 54	11♋51	23 55	06♌06
1951	01♋16	13 10	24 59	06♌48	18 41	00♍43	13 00	25 37	08♎40	22 10	06♏10	20 35	05♐22	20♐22
1952	17 54	01♐23	15 07	29 02	13♑03	27 09	11♒15	25 21	09♓26	23 29	07♈29	21 25	05♉13	16♉52
1953	29 39	14♈22	29 14	14♉06	18 50	13♊18	27 24	11♋03	24 16	07♌04	19 30	01♍40	13 39	25♍31
1954	19 22	02♍11	14 41	26 57	09♎02	20 59	02♏52	14 42	26 32	08♐24	20 19	02♑19	14 26	26♑44
1955	21 10	02♑57	14 43	26 33	08♒29	20 38	03♓03	15 49	29 00	12♈38	26 44	11♉16	26 08	11♊13
1956	08♉18	22 00	06♊01	20 15	04♋38	19 05	03♌30	17 51	02♍03	16 04	29 54	13♎31	26 55	10♏06
1957	21 57	06♎22	20 49	05♏13	19 30	03♐35	17 22	00♑50	13 57	26 43	09♒10	21 22	03♓21	15♓14
1958	09♒57	22 44	05♓10	17 19	29 16	11♈06	22 53	04♉40	16 32	28 30	10♊36	22 51	05♋17	17♋54
1959	11♊15	23 06	04♋59	16 55	28 58	11♌10	23 36	06♍21	19 29	03♎03	17 05	01♏37	16 34	01♐47
1960	28 20	12♏22	26 47	11♐28	26 16	11♑04	25 44	10♒09	24 17	08♓09	21 43	05♈03	18 10	01♉04
1961	13♓57	28 07	12♈18	26 27	10♉28	24 19	04♊54	21 10	04♋05	16 41	28 58	11♌01	22 54	04♍42
1962	00♌11	12 50	25 10	07♍15	19 10	01♎00	12 50	24 44	06♏44	18 52	01♐10	13 38	26 16	09♑05
1963	01♐38	13 28	25 20	07♑17	19 21	01♒37	14 08	26 59	10♓13	23 55	08♈04	22 40	07♉38	22♉50
1964	18 47	03♉02	17 37	02♊30	17 29	02♋27	17 15	01♌49	16 04	29 58	13♍32	26 47	09♎44	22♎26
1965	06♍32	20 36	04♎32	18 19	01♏54	15 17	28 24	11♐17	23 54	06♑17	18 28	00♒29	12 22	24♒14
1966	19 55	02♒35	14 57	27 04	09♓00	20 51	02♈43	14 37	26 39	08♉52	21 18	03♊59	16 55	00♋06
1967	21 44	03♊39	15 41	27 51	27♋51	10 11	22♌42	05 27	18♍29	01 49	29 32	13♎55	28 37	13♏34
1968	09♎00	23 15	07♏57	22 59	08♐14	23 29	08♑34	23 21	07♒42	21 37	05♓04	18 07	00♈49	13♈15
1969	28 55	12♓44	26 20	09♈45	22 59	06♉02	18 54	01♊35	14 04	26 22	08♋28	20 26	02♌17	14♌05
1970	09♋59	22 31	04♌45	16 45	28 36	10♍24	22 13	04♎10	16 19	28 44	11♏27	24 28	07♐47	21♐21
1971	12 03	24 10	06♐23	18 44	01♑15	13 57	26 49	09♒55	23 18	07♓00	21 01	05♈23	20 01	04♉53
1972	29 34	13♈58	28 49	13♉59	29 18	14♊36	29 40	14♋24	28 43	12♌33	25 57	08♍56	21 35	03♎58
1973	20 58	04♍44	18 15	01♎30	14 31	27 18	09♏53	22 16	04♐28	16 30	28 25	10♑14	22 00	03♒47
1974	29 38	12♑01	24 10	06♒09	18 02	29 54	11♓50	23 54	06♈10	18 43	01♉35	14 46	28 18	12♊08
1975	02♉12	14 23	26 45	09♊20	22 07	05♋07	18 21	01♌48	15 29	29 23	13♍28	27 44	12♎08	26♎37
1976	20 47	05♎04	19 43	04♏41	19 50	05♐01	20 05	04♑51	19 14	03♒09	16 35	29 35	12♓10	24♓27
1977	12♒56	26 39	09♓59	22 58	05♈41	18 09	00♉26	12 34	24 37	06♊34	18 28	00♋20	12 12	24♋05
1978	19 35	01♋54	14 01	25 58	07♌49	19 38	01♍31	13 32	25 47	08♎22	21 19	04♏43	18 32	02♐46
1979	22 01	04♏26	17 06	00♐02	13 13	25 37	10♑11	23 54	07♒44	21 40	05♓41	19 48	03♈59	18♈12
1980	11♓56	26 10	10♈47	25 42	10♉49	25 57	10♊56	25 37	09♋42	23 38	06♌56	19 47	02♍15	14♍26
1981	04♌19	17 56	01♍09	14 01	26 37	08♎58	21 09	03♏12	15 09	27 02	08♐52	20 42	02♑32	14♑25
1982	09♐46	21 51	03♑47	15 36	27 23	09♒11	21 06	03♓12	15 35	28 19	11♈28	25 04	09♉06	23♉32
1983	12♈01	24 37	07♉29	20 39	04♊05	17 46	01♋39	15 40	29 49	14♌00	28 12	12♍23	26 31	10♎33
1984	04♍01	16 16	02♎44	17 24	02♏09	16 53	01♐28	15 49	29 50	13♑28	26 42	09♒33	22 03	04♓16
1985	25 08	08♒50	22 05	04♓56	17 25	29 39	11♈40	23 33	05♉21	17 08	28 57	10♊49	22 47	04♋51
1986	29 47	11♊46	23 41	05♋33	17 24	29 18	11♌17	23 26	05♍50	18 34	01♎40	15 14	29 16	13♏46
1987	01♎40	14 19	27 22	10♏47	24 35	08♐42	23 03	07♑32	22 03	06♒28	20 46	04♓52	18 47	02♈30
1988	26 10	10♓15	24 30	08♈53	23 21	07♉49	22 11	06♊21	20 13	03♋43	16 50	29 33	11♌56	24♌02
1989	15 59	29 35	12♌41	25 23	07♍44	19 50	01♎46	13 37	25 27	07♏19	19 14	01♐16	13 24	25♐39
1990	20 14	02♐09	14 00	25 48	07♑37	19 29	01♒27	13 36	26 02	08♓49	22 01	05♈42	19 54	04♉33
1991	21 24	04♈16	17 33	01♉16	15 22	29 46	14♊24	29 08	13♋50	28 25	12♌49	26 58	10♍52	24♍31
1992	18 31	02♍41	16 55	01♎10	15 23	29 30	13♏27	27 10	10♐38	23 43	06♑34	19 06	01♒22	13♒26
1993	06♑01	19 32	02♒38	15 20	27 44	09♓52	21 50	03♈42	15 32	27 24	09♉21	21 27	03♊42	16♊08
1994	10♉29	22 17	04♊05	15 56	27 50	09♋51	22 01	04♌23	17 00	29 55	13♍12	26 53	10♎59	25♎29
1995	11♍29	24 21	07♎39	21 23	05♏34	20 09	05♐02	20 05	05♑08	20 03	04♒41	18 59	02♓52	16♓23
1996	11♒08	25 18	09♓22	23 19	07♈09	20 51	04♉23	17 45	00♊55	13 51	26 32	08♋59	21 13	03♌15
1997	26 18	09♋45	22 47	05♌25	17 42	29 44	11♍35	23 23	05♎10	17 04	29 08	11♏24	23 55	06♐42
1998	00♏39	12 30	24 25	06♐24	18 28	00♑38	12 56	25 25	08♒06	21 08	04♓20	17 59	02♈02	16♈30
1999	01♓24	14 20	27 45	11♈39	26 04	10♉54	26 03	11♊19	26 33	11♋33	26 13	10♌27	24 16	07♍40
2000	03♌23	17 23	01♍36	15 26	29 06	12♎35	25 52	08♏56	21 48	04♐25	16 49	29 01	11♑02	22♑54

Moon

December

	1st	2nd	3rd	4th	5th	6th	7th	8th	9th	10th	11th	12th	13th	14th	15th	16th
1900	25 ♓ 01	09 ♈ 23	23 55	08 ♉ 30	23 05	07 ♊ 33	21 47	05 ♋ 44	19 20	02 ♌ 33	15 24	27 55	10 ♍ 09	22 10	04 ♎ 03	15 53
1901	15 ♌ 04	28 21	11 ♍ 12	23 41	05 ♎ 52	17 51	29 41	11 ♏ 28	23 14	05 ♐ 03	16 57	28 58	11 ♑ 07	23 25	05 ♒ 54	18 36
1902	17 ♐ 51	29 44	11 ♑ 35	23 26	05 ♒ 20	17 19	29 29	11 ♓ 52	24 34	07 ♈ 39	21 11	05 ♉ 12	19 42	04 ♊ 37	29 50	05 ♋ 10
1903	20 ♈ 06	03 ♉ 11	16 42	00 ♊ 38	14 54	29 27	14 ♋ 07	28 48	13 ♌ 22	27 45	11 ♍ 54	25 48	09 ♎ 26	22 51	06 ♏ 05	19 06
1904	17 ♍ 17	01 ♎ 27	15 42	00 00	14 ♏ 16	28 27	12 ♐ 27	26 11	09 ♑ 35	22 37	05 ♒ 18	17 39	29 45	11 ♓ 39	23 27	05 ♈ 16
1905	05 ♒ 31	18 38	01 ♓ 20	13 42	25 48	07 ♈ 45	19 36	01 ♉ 26	13 19	25 17	07 ♊ 22	19 35	01 ♋ 57	14 28	27 10	10 ♌ 02
1906	08 ♊ 17	20 08	01 ♋ 58	13 48	25 42	07 ♌ 43	19 55	02 ♍ 22	15 08	28 19	11 ♎ 57	26 05	10 ♏ 40	25 38	10 ♐ 52	26 10
1907	10 ♎ 08	23 26	07 ♏ 09	21 18	05 ♐ 48	20 32	05 ♑ 24	20 14	04 ♒ 57	19 28	03 ♓ 41	17 37	01 ♈ 14	14 34	27 38	10 ♉ 27
1908	09 ♓ 40	23 51	08 ♈ 00	22 04	06 ♉ 01	19 48	03 ♊ 22	16 40	29 42	12 ♋ 27	24 56	07 ♌ 11	19 15	01 ♍ 10	13 02	24 55
1909	25 ♋ 26	08 ♌ 33	21 16	03 ♍ 40	15 49	27 47	09 ♎ 38	21 28	03 ♏ 20	15 19	27 27	09 ♐ 46	22 18	05 ♑ 05	18 05	01 ♒ 18
1910	28 ♏ 24	10 ♐ 13	22 04	04 ♑ 01	16 06	28 19	10 ♒ 44	23 24	06 ♓ 20	19 36	03 ♈ 14	17 16	01 ♉ 41	16 27	01 ♊ 29	16 38
1911	00 ♈ 13	13 30	27 15	11 ♉ 27	26 06	11 ♊ 04	26 15	11 ♋ 27	26 30	11 ♌ 26	25 38	09 ♍ 34	23 04	06 ♎ 11	18 58	01 ♏ 29
1912	02 ♍ 25	16 27	00 ♎ 19	14 02	27 34	10 ♏ 56	24 07	07 ♐ 08	19 56	02 ♑ 31	14 54	27 04	09 ♒ 04	20 56	02 ♓ 44	14 34
1913	15 ♑ 34	28 34	11 ♒ 10	23 27	05 ♓ 29	17 21	29 08	10 ♈ 57	22 52	04 ♉ 58	17 19	29 55	12 ♊ 49	26 00	09 ♋ 25	23 03
1914	18 ♉ 36	00 ♊ 33	12 36	24 45	07 ♋ 01	19 25	02 ♌ 00	14 46	27 47	11 ♍ 05	24 43	08 ♎ 42	23 04	07 ♏ 46	22 42	07 44
1915	20 ♍ 30	03 ♎ 52	17 44	02 ♏ 06	16 54	02 ♐ 02	17 20	02 ♑ 37	17 41	02 ♒ 25	16 44	00 ♓ 36	14 02	27 04	09 ♈ 46	22 13
1916	24 ♒ 25	08 ♓ 28	22 17	05 ♈ 53	19 15	02 ♉ 24	15 21	28 04	10 ♊ 35	22 54	05 ♋ 02	17 01	28 52	10 ♌ 40	22 27	04 ♍ 18
1917	05 ♋ 32	18 18	00 ♌ 45	12 58	24 59	06 ♍ 53	18 45	00 ♎ 39	12 41	24 54	07 ♏ 22	20 08	03 ♐ 12	16 35	00 ♑ 15	14 09
1918	08 ♏ 48	20 46	02 ♐ 52	15 07	27 33	10 ♑ 11	23 01	06 ♒ 06	19 24	02 ♓ 58	16 47	00 ♈ 51	15 09	29 39	14 ♉ 15	28 54
1919	11 ♓ 24	24 50	08 ♈ 41	22 59	07 ♉ 40	22 40	07 ♊ 52	23 07	08 ♋ 13	23 03	07 ♌ 29	21 27	04 ♍ 57	17 59	00 ♎ 38	12 57
1920	16 ♌ 36	00 ♍ 44	14 29	27 54	10 ♎ 58	23 46	06 ♏ 20	18 43	00 ♐ 56	13 02	25 02	06 ♑ 57	18 49	00 ♒ 40	12 32	24 28
1921	25 ♐ 28	08 ♑ 07	20 31	02 ♒ 41	14 40	26 32	08 ♓ 21	20 13	02 ♈ 12	14 25	26 57	09 ♉ 50	23 08	06 ♊ 50	20 55	05 ♋ 19
1922	28 ♈ 30	10 ♉ 36	22 56	05 ♊ 30	18 18	01 ♋ 20	14 35	28 00	11 ♌ 35	25 19	09 ♍ 10	23 10	07 ♎ 17	21 31	05 ♏ 50	20 11
1923	02 ♍ 34	15 58	29 46	13 ♎ 59	28 37	13 ♏ 35	28 46	13 ♐ 59	29 03	13 ♑ 49	28 09	11 ♒ 59	25 20	08 ♓ 14	20 45	02 ♈ 58
1924	08 ♒ 08	22 12	05 ♓ 50	19 06	02 ♈ 03	14 42	27 09	09 ♉ 25	21 32	03 ♊ 34	15 30	27 22	09 ♋ 11	21 01	02 ♌ 52	14 48
1925	15 ♊ 55	28 18	10 ♋ 29	22 28	04 ♌ 20	16 07	27 55	09 ♍ 48	21 53	04 ♎ 13	16 53	29 58	13 ♏ 29	27 25	11 ♐ 43	26 20
1926	18 ♎ 26	00 ♏ 42	13 11	25 57	08 ♐ 57	22 14	05 ♑ 43	19 25	03 ♒ 16	17 15	01 ♓ 20	15 29	92 41	13 ♈ 52	28 01	12 ♉ 04
1927	24 ♒ 02	07 ♓ 37	21 32	05 ♈ 47	20 19	05 ♉ 05	19 58	04 ♊ 51	19 36	04 ♋ 05	18 14	01 ♌ 58	15 17	28 12	10 ♍ 42	23 00
1928	29 ♋ 07	13 ♌ 18	27 03	10 ♍ 20	23 14	05 ♎ 47	18 03	00 ♏ 07	12 02	23 52	05 ♐ 39	17 26	29 16	11 ♑ 09	23 09	05 ♒ 17
1929	06 ♐ 04	18 15	00 ♑ 17	12 14	24 06	05 ♒ 57	17 49	29 46	11 ♓ 54	24 15	06 ♈ 56	20 00	03 ♉ 31	17 30	01 ♊ 57	16 46
1930	08 ♈ 01	20 18	02 ♉ 54	15 50	29 08	12 ♊ 48	26 45	10 ♋ 57	25 17	09 ♌ 40	24 01	08 ♍ 15	22 22	06 ♎ 20	20 08	03 ♏ 47
1931	16 ♌ 11	29 51	13 ♍ 43	27 47	12 ♎ 04	26 32	11 ♏ 07	25 43	10 ♐ 14	24 32	08 ♑ 32	22 10	05 ♒ 22	18 10	00 ♓ 35	12 44
1932	20 ♑ 04	04 ♒ 13	17 51	01 ♓ 00	13 45	26 09	08 ♈ 17	20 15	02 ♉ 08	13 58	25 49	07 ♊ 44	19 43	01 ♋ 47	13 58	26 17
1933	26 ♉ 36	08 ♊ 40	20 39	02 ♋ 32	14 21	26 09	07 ♌ 59	19 56	02 ♍ 02	14 25	27 08	10 ♎ 17	23 55	08 ♏ 03	22 40	07 ♐ 40
1934	27 ♍ 37	10 ♎ 03	22 51	06 ♏ 03	19 38	03 ♐ 36	17 52	02 ♑ 20	16 54	01 ♒ 29	15 58	00 ♓ 17	14 26	28 22	12 ♈ 05	25 35
1935	08 ♒ 00	21 50	05 ♓ 50	19 58	04 ♈ 15	18 36	02 ♉ 57	17 15	01 ♊ 24	15 19	28 56	12 ♋ 14	25 10	07 ♌ 48	20 08	02 ♍ 14
1936	10 ♋ 24	24 27	08 ♌ 02	21 11	03 ♍ 57	16 22	28 32	10 ♎ 31	22 23	04 ♏ 12	16 03	27 57	09 ♐ 58	22 07	04 ♑ 25	16 55
1937	17 ♏ 06	28 58	10 ♐ 47	22 34	04 ♑ 22	16 13	28 10	10 ♒ 15	22 32	05 ♓ 05	17 56	01 ♈ 10	14 49	28 55	13 ♉ 25	28 18
1938	17 ♓ 29	29 59	12 ♈ 49	26 03	09 ♉ 43	23 49	08 ♊ 18	23 05	08 ♋ 02	23 00	07 ♌ 50	22 27	06 ♍ 44	20 40	04 ♎ 14	17 28
1939	00 ♌ 15	14 25	28 36	12 ♍ 45	26 51	10 ♎ 53	24 50	08 ♏ 40	22 21	05 ♐ 52	19 11	02 ♑ 14	15 02	27 34	09 ♒ 51	21 56
1940	00 ♑ 41	14 41	28 13	11 ♒ 19	24 01	06 ♓ 20	18 24	00 ♈ 17	12 04	23 51	05 ♉ 43	17 44	29 56	12 ♊ 22	25 01	07 ♋ 54
1941	07 ♉ 16	19 08	00 ♊ 59	12 53	24 50	06 ♋ 50	18 57	01 ♌ 10	13 34	26 10	09 ♍ 02	22 15	05 ♎ 51	19 53	04 ♏ 21	19 12
1942	07 ♍ 24	19 53	02 ♎ 46	16 06	29 56	14 ♏ 16	29 02	14 ♐ 05	29 18	14 ♑ 28	29 25	14 ♒ 03	28 17	12 ♓ 07	25 34	08 ♈ 39
1943	22 ♑ 14	06 ♒ 33	20 48	04 ♓ 57	18 59	02 ♈ 53	16 40	00 ♉ 17	13 44	26 58	10 ♊ 00	22 47	05 ♋ 19	17 37	29 42	11 ♌ 37
1944	21 ♊ 15	04 ♋ 56	18 13	01 ♌ 07	13 41	25 ♍ 56	07 59	19 ♎ 53	01 45	13 38	25 ♏ 37	07 46	20 ♐ 08	02 44	15 35	28 ♑ 42
1945	27 ♎ 40	09 ♏ 30	21 20	03 ♐ 13	15 11	27 16	09 ♑ 29	21 52	04 ♒ 27	17 16	00 ♓ 22	13 46	27 31	11 ♈ 37	26 03	10 ♉ 44
1946	27 ♒ 39	10 ♓ 17	23 17	06 ♈ 43	20 36	04 ♉ 56	19 41	04 ♊ 44	19 57	05 ♋ 10	20 15	05 ♌ 01	19 25	03 ♍ 21	16 51	29 56
1947	13 ♋ 47	28 28	13 ♌ 02	27 24	11 ♍ 30	25 19	08 ♎ 52	22 09	05 ♏ 11	18 00	00 ♐ 37	13 03	25 19	07 ♑ 27	19 27	01 ♒ 21
1948	11 ♐ 28	24 53	08 ♑ 01	20 50	03 ♒ 21	15 35	27 38	09 ♓ 31	21 22	03 ♈ 13	15 11	27 21	09 ♉ 47	22 32	05 ♊ 39	19 06
1949	17 ♈ 32	29 20	11 ♉ 12	23 11	05 ♊ 21	17 42	00 ♋ 15	13 00	25 56	09 ♌ 04	22 24	05 ♍ 56	19 41	03 ♎ 40	17 52	02 ♏ 17
1950	18 ♌ 29	01 ♍ 04	14 06	27 27	11 ♎ 16	25 33	10 ♏ 17	25 22	10 ♐ 41	26 01	11 ♑ 11	26 01	10 ♒ 24	24 16	07 ♓ 39	20 34
1951	05 ♑ 24	20 20	05 ♒ 01	19 23	03 ♓ 24	17 03	00 ♈ 23	13 27	26 16	08 ♉ 53	21 20	03 ♊ 37	15 47	27 49	09 ♋ 45	21 36
1952	02 ♊ 17	15 27	28 20	10 ♋ 56	23 14	05 ♌ 19	17 14	29 02	10 ♍ 50	22 43	04 ♎ 45	17 02	29 39	12 ♏ 39	26 02	09 ♐ 47
1953	07 ♎ 21	19 15	01 ♏ 15	13 25	25 46	08 ♐ 19	21 05	04 ♑ 03	17 13	00 ♒ 34	14 07	27 50	11 ♓ 44	25 48	10 ♈ 02	24 23
1954	09 ♒ 15	22 02	05 ♓ 10	18 40	02 ♈ 36	16 55	01 ♉ 37	16 36	01 ♊ 43	16 50	01 ♋ 48	16 27	00 ♌ 42	14 31	27 52	10 ♍ 49
1955	26 ♊ 22	11 ♋ 26	26 15	10 ♌ 47	24 54	08 ♍ 38	21 58	04 ♎ 56	17 36	00 ♏ 00	12 12	24 15	06 ♐ 10	18 01	29 49	11 ♑ 36
1956	23 ♏ 05	05 ♐ 50	18 22	00 ♑ 43	12 53	24 54	06 ♒ 48	18 40	00 ♓ 31	12 28	24 35	06 ♈ 55	19 35	02 ♉ 36	16 04	29 56
1957	27 ♓ 04	08 ♈ 57	20 58	03 ♉ 11	15 38	28 23	11 ♊ 26	24 47	08 ♋ 23	22 13	06 ♌ 12	20 18	04 ♍ 26	18 35	02 ♎ 43	16 48
1958	00 ♌ 43	13 45	27 02	10 ♍ 35	24 26	08 ♎ 35	23 01	07 ♏ 42	22 32	07 ♐ 25	22 13	06 ♑ 46	20 59	04 ♒ 45	18 04	00 ♓ 57
1959	17 ♐ 09	02 ♑ 25	17 26	02 ♒ 03	16 12	29 51	13 ♓ 02	25 49	08 ♈ 17	20 30	02 ♉ 32	14 28	26 21	08 ♊ 12	20 05	01 ♋ 59
1960	13 ♉ 48	26 22	08 ♊ 45	20 59	03 ♋ 04	15 01	26 52	08 ♌ 40	20 29	02 ♍ 23	14 27	26 46	09 ♎ 27	22 34	06 ♏ 10	20 16
1961	16 ♍ 31	28 26	10 ♎ 31	22 54	05 ♏ 35	18 38	02 ♐ 01	15 44	29 42	13 ♑ 51	28 06	12 ♒ 23	26 38	10 ♓ 48	24 54	08 ♈ 53
1962	22 ♑ 05	05 ♒ 17	18 42	02 ♓ 21	16 15	00 ♈ 25	14 49	29 24	14 ♉ 04	28 42	13 ♊ 12	27 27	11 ♋ 21	27 51	07 ♌ 57	20 41
1963	08 ♊ 07	23 17	08 ♋ 11	22 42	06 ♌ 47	20 23	03 ♍ 33	16 20	28 47	10 ♎ 59	23 01	04 ♏ 55	16 45	28 34	10 ♐ 25	22 20
1964	04 ♏ 54	17 11	29 18	11 ♐ 17	23 09	04 ♑ 58	16 45	28 32	10 ♒ 24	22 24	04 ♓ 36	17 04	29 53	13 ♈ 06	26 46	10 ♉ 54
1965	06 ♓ 07	18 08	00 ♈ 19	12 47	25 34	08 ♉ 43	22 15	06 ♊ 09	20 24	04 ♋ 53	19 31	04 ♌ 12	18 48	03 ♍ 14	17 27	01 ♎ 25
1966	13 ♋ 30	27 07	10 ♌ 55	24 51	08 ♍ 55	23 04	07 ♎ 17	21 31	05 ♏ 45	19 55	03 ♐ 57	17 48	01 ♑ 24	14 43	27 42	10 ♒ 22
1967	28 ♏ 38	13 ♐ 41	28 32	13 ♑ 03	27 09	10 ♒ 47	23 57	06 ♓ 41	19 03	01 ♈ 08	13 02	24 50	06 ♉ 37	18 26	00 ♊ 21	12 25
1968	25 ♈ 29	07 ♉ 33	19 32	01 ♊ 26	13 19	25 11	07 ♋ 04	19 00	00 ♌ 59	13 05	25 21	07 ♍ 51	20 38	03 ♎ 48	17 24	01 ♏ 29
1969	25 ♌ 55	07 ♍ 52	20 01	02 ♎ 29	15 19	28 35	12 ♏ 21	26 33	11 ♐ 10	26 03	11 ♑ 03	26 00	10 ♒ 47	25 17	09 ♓ 26	23 15
1970	05 ♑ 08	19 03	03 ♒ 04	17 08	01 ♓ 13	15 18	29 23	13 ♈ 26	27 26	11 ♉ 21	25 08	08 ♊ 43	22 03	05 ♋ 07	17 52	00 ♌ 20
1971	19 ♉ 49	04 ♊ 40	19 49	03 ♋ 37	17 31	00 ♌ 57	13 56	26 33	08 ♍ 50	20 54	02 ♎ 48	14 39	26 31	08 ♏ 27	20 31	02 ♐ 45
1972	16 ♎ 08	28 09	10 ♏ 04	21 55	03 ♐ 45	15 35	27 28	09 ♑ 24	21 26	03 ♒ 37	16 00	28 38	11 ♓ 35	24 54	08 ♈ 38	22 47
1973	15 ♒ 40	27 42	09 ♓ 58	22 34	05 ♈ 33	18 58	02 ♉ 51	17 10	01 ♊ 52	16 51	01 ♋ 58	17 04	02 ♌ 01	16 40	00 ♍ 58	14 53
1974	26 ♊ 13	10 ♋ 30	24 53	09 ♌ 17	23 39	07 ♍ 54	22 01	05 ♎ 57	19 42	03 ♏ 14	16 34	29 41	12 ♐ 35	25 16	07 ♑ 44	20 00
1975	11 ♏ 06	25 30	09 ♐ 44	23 43	07 ♑ 23	20 41	03 ♒ 38	16 14	28 33	10 ♓ 38	22 33	04 ♈ 23	16 14	28 10	10 ♉ 16	22 35
1976	06 ♈ 29	18 22	00 ♉ 09	11 56	23 45	05 ♊ 39	17 40	29 49	12 ♋ 08	24 38	07 ♌ 19	20 13	03 ♍ 21	16 45	00 ♎ 27	14 28
1977	06 ♌ 04	18 10	00 ♍ 28	13 03	25 59	09 ♎ 21	23 10	07 ♏ 29	22 15	07 ♐ 22	22 41	08 ♑ 01	23 10	07 ♒ 59	22 20	06 ♓ 13
1978	17 ♐ 17	02 ♑ 01	16 47	01 ♒ 28	15 59	00 ♓ 14	14 13	27 56	11 ♈ 24	24 38	07 ♉ 40	20 31	03 ♊ 12	15 43	28 03	10 ♋ 13
1979	02 ♉ 25	16 34	00 ♊ 34	14 19	27 47	10 ♋ 54	23 40	06 ♌ 06	18 16	00 ♍ 14	12 03	23 51	05 ♎ 42	17 42	29 56	12 ♏ 27
1980	26 ♍ 25	08 ♎ 17	20 07	01 ♏ 59	13 55	25 58	08 ♐ 10	20 32	03 ♑ 03	15 44	28 36	11 ♒ 39	24 56	08 ♓ 27	22 13	06 ♈ 16
1981	26 ♑ 24	08 ♒ 33	20 55	03 ♓ 35	16 38	00 ♈ 06	14 03	28 28	13 ♉ 17	28 25	13 ♊ 41	28 57	14 ♋ 00	28 43	13 ♌ 00	26 49
1982	08 ♊ 16	23 10	08 ♋ 07	22 59	07 ♌ 39	22 02	06 ♍ 05	19 49	03 ♎ 13	16 20	29 10	11 ♏ 46	24 09	06 ♐ 22	18 26	00 ♑ 22
1983	24 ♎ 27	08 ♏ 10	21 42	05 ♐ 00	18 02	00 ♑ 49	13 20	25 37	07 ♒ 43	19 40	01 ♓ 32	13 25	25 21	07 ♈ 26	19 45	02 ♉ 22
1984	16 ♓ 17	28 10	10 ♈ 01	21 52	03 ♉ 50	15 56	28 15	10 ♊ 46	23 33	06 ♋ 34	19 50	03 ♌ 19	16 59	00 ♍ 49	14 48	28 54
1985	17 ♋ 05	29 29	12 ♌ 06	24 58	08 ♍ 08	21 38	05 ♎ 30	19 44	04 ♏ 20	19 12	04 ♐ 16	19 22	04 ♑ 21	19 04	03 ♒ 24	17 15
1986	17 ♏ 49	13 ♐ 49	29 04	14 ♑ 14	29 09	13 ♒ 42	27 48	11 ♓ 28	24 42	07 ♈ 34	20 08	02 ♉ 28	14 37	26 40	08 ♊ 37	20 31
1987	16 ♈ 02	29 24	12 ♉ 35	25 35	08 ♊ 24	21 01	03 ♋ 26	15 38	27 41	09 ♌ 35	21 24	03 ♍ 12	15 05	27 07	09 ♎ 25	22 04
1988	05 ♍ 56	17 45	29 32	11 ♎ 25	23 28	05 ♏ 44	18 17	01 ♐ 07	14 16	27 41	11 ♑ 19	25 07	09 ♒ 03	23 03	07 ♓ 06	21 10
1989	08 ♑ 04	20 37	03 ♒ 22	16 20	29 33	13 ♓ 05	26 57	11 ♈ 10	25 43	10 ♉ 31	25 29	10 ♊ 26	25 14	09 ♋ 45	23 52	07 ♌ 31
1990	19 ♉ 36	04 ♊ 52	20 12	05 ♋ 23	20 17	04 ♌ 47	18 50	02 ♍ 26	15 37	28 25	10 ♎ 56	23 12	05 ♏ 18	17 16	29 09	10 ♐ 59
1991	07 ♎ 54	21 04	03 ♏ 59	16 42	29 12	11 ♐ 31	23 39	05 ♑ 38	17 30	29 18	11 ♒ 04	22 54	04 ♓ 50	16 59	29 25	12 ♈ 12
1992	25 ♒ 21	07 ♓ 13	19 07	01 ♈ 06	13 16	25 40	08 ♉ 21	21 22	04 ♊ 42	18 21	02 ♋ 17	16 26	00 ♌ 44	15 05	29 27	13 ♍ 44
1993	28 ♊ 47	11 ♋ 39	24 44	08 ♌ 03	12 35	05 ♍ 21	19 20	03 ♎ 32	17 54	02 ♏ 34	16 55	01 ♐ 25	15 47	29 56	13 ♑ 48	27 19
1994	10 ♏ 20	25 26	10 ♐ 39	25 48	10 ♑ 44	25 19	09 ♒ 28	23 07	06 ♓ 19	19 05	01 ♈ 30	13 39	25 35	07 ♉ 25	19 12	00 ♊ 59
1995	29 ♓ 32	12 ♈ 23	24 59	07 ♉ 23	19 37	01 ♊ 43	13 44	25 40	07 ♋ 33	19 25	01 ♌ 17	13 12	25 14	07 ♍ 25	19 51	02 ♎ 36
1996	15 ♌ 08	26 57	08 ♍ 48	20 44	02 ♎ 51	15 16	28 02	11 ♏ 12	24 48	08 ♐ 49	23 11	07 ♑ 47	22 30	07 ♒ 12	21 46	06 ♓ 07
1997	19 ♐ 44	02 ♑ 59	16 25	00 ♒ 01	13 45	27 37	11 ♓ 34	25 39	09 ♈ 49	24 03	08 ♉ 20	22 34	06 ♊ 42	20 38	04 ♋ 17	17 36
1998	01 ♉ 19	16 24	01 ♊ 35	16 42	01 ♋ 33	16 02	00 ♌ 03	13 34	26 37	09 ♍ 15	21 34	03 ♎ 39	15 34	27 24	09 ♏ 14	21 08
1999	20 ♍ 42	03 ♎ 26	15 54	28 11	10 ♏ 18	22 19	04 ♐ 14	16 06	27 55	09 ♑ 44	21 35	03 ♒ 30	15 33	27 47	10 ♓ 18	23 09
2000	04 ♒ 41	16 28	28 19	10 ♓ 19	22 34	05 ♈ 07	18 04	01 ♉ 27	15 16	29 30	14 ♊ 04	28 53	13 ♋ 48	28 41	13 ♌ 25	27 55

	17th	18th	19th	20th	21st	22nd	23rd	24th	25th	26th	27th	28th	29th	30th	31st
1900	27 44	09♏42	21 50	04♐12	16 49	19 42	12♑52	26 17	09♒56	23 45	07♓42	21 45	05♈52	20 01	04♉11
1901	01♓31	14 43	28 12	12♈01	26 11	10♉40	25 26	10♊23	25 24	10♋19	25 00	09♌20	23 12	06♍36	19♍33
1902	20 26	05♌28	20 06	04♍17	17 59	01♎13	14 04	26 35	08♏51	20 56	02♐54	14 49	26 40	08♑32	20♑25
1903	01♐58	14 38	27 08	09♑27	21 36	03♒35	15 27	27 15	09♓03	20 56	02♈58	15 15	27 53	10♉56	24♉28
1904	17 09	29 13	11♉31	24 08	07♊04	20 21	03♋55	17 44	01♌43	15 50	29 59	14♍09	28 17	12♎22	26♎23
1905	23 06	06♍25	19 59	03♎50	17 59	02♏25	17 04	01♐51	16 38	01♑17	15 40	29 42	13♒19	26 30	09♓17
1906	11♑22	26 18	10♒51	24 57	08♓35	21 48	04♈37	17 07	29 22	11♉26	23 23	05♊15	17 05	28 55	10♋48
1907	23 03	05♊27	17 40	29 44	11♋41	23 32	50♌20	17 07	28 58	10♍55	23 05	05♎30	18 26	01♏26	15♏03
1908	06♎54	19 04	01♏28	14 10	27 13	10♐38	24 23	08♑27	22 46	07♒14	21 46	06♓15	20 38	04♈50	18♈50
1909	14 45	28 24	12♓14	26 14	10♈23	24 39	09♉00	23 23	07♊43	21 56	05♋58	19 43	03♌10	16 17	29♌03
1910	01♋46	16 43	01♌19	15 30	29 12	12♍26	25 13	07♎38	19 46	01♏41	13 29	25 15	07♐02	18 54	00♑53
1911	13 46	25 55	07♐56	19 53	01♑47	13 39	25 30	07♒23	19 19	01♓22	13 34	26 00	08♈44	21 51	05♉25
1912	26 29	08♈37	21 01	03♉48	17 00	00♊40	14 47	29 17	14♋02	28 56	13♌48	28 31	12♍58	27 08	10♎59
1913	06♌49	20 42	04♍40	18 41	02♎45	16 51	00♏58	15 05	29 09	13♐05	26 50	10♑20	23 31	06♒23	18♒56
1914	22 43	07♑29	21 55	05♒54	19 24	02♓28	15 07	27 27	09♈32	21 27	03♉18	15 09	27 04	09♊06	21♊16
1915	04♉27	16 31	28 29	10♊23	22 14	04♋04	15 55	27 49	09♌48	21 54	04♍12	16 45	29 37	12♎53	26♎33
1916	16 18	28 32	11♎05	24 00	07♏22	21 10	05♐25	20 02	04♑55	19 56	04♒57	19 49	04♓25	18 42	02♈38
1917	28 14	12♒27	17 43	10♓59	25 13	09♈21	23 22	07♉15	20 57	04♊27	17 45	00♋49	13 39	26 15	08♌37
1918	13♊28	27 52	12♋01	25 49	09♌14	22 16	04♍57	17 19	29 25	11♎21	23 12	05♏02	16 56	28 58	11♐11
1919	25 01	06♏55	18 44	00♐30	12 17	24 08	06♑05	18 08	00♒21	12 43	25 17	08♓04	21 06	04♈26	18♈05
1920	06♓32	18 47	01♈19	14 13	27 32	11♉19	25 36	10♊20	25 25	10♋43	26 01	11♌10	25 59	10♍22	24♍17
1921	19 53	04♌32	19 08	03♍34	17 49	01♎49	15 35	29 08	12♏29	25 38	08♐37	21 25	04♑03	16 29	28♑43
1922	04♐29	18 38	02♑33	16 09	29 23	12♒15	24 46	06♓59	18 58	00♈48	12 36	24 26	06♉24	18 35	01♊02
1923	14 59	26 52	08♉42	20 33	02♊28	14 29	26 37	08♋53	21 17	03♌52	16 36	29 32	12♍42	26 07	09 49
1924	26 53	09♍12	21 48	04♎47	18 12	02♏06	16 29	01♐18	16 26	01♑43	17 00	02♒04	16 48	01♓07	14♓58
1925	11♑06	25 56	10♒42	25 17	09♓37	23 41	07♈27	20 56	04♉09	17 06	29 50	12♊22	24 42	06♋51	18♋52
1926	25 59	09♊42	23 11	06♋23	19 18	01♌57	14 19	26 28	08♍28	02 21	02♎13	14 09	26 12	08♏28	21♏01
1927	05♎02	16 56	28 46	10♏36	22 30	04♐32	16 45	29 09	11♑47	24 38	07♒43	21 01	04♓32	18 15	02♈09
1928	17 35	00♓06	12 53	25 58	09♈26	23 16	07♉31	22 09	07♊05	22 14	07♋25	22 29	07♌17	21 42	05♍38
1929	01♋51	17 02	02♌09	17 02	01♍35	15 43	29 25	12♎43	25 39	08♏18	20 43	02♐57	15 03	27 03	08♑59
1930	17 17	00♐36	13 45	26 42	09♑26	21 56	04♒13	16 18	28 14	10♓03	21 52	03♈44	15 44	28 00	10♉35
1931	24 40	06♈29	18 16	00♉07	12 07	24 20	06♊47	19 32	02♋32	15 48	29 17	12♌56	26 43	10♍37	24♍35
1932	08♌44	21 22	04♍14	17 23	00♎50	14 40	28 52	13♏27	28 19	13♐22	28 26	13♑21	27 58	12♒11	25♒56
1933	22 54	08♑12	23 22	08♒16	22 46	06♓50	20 27	03♈41	16 33	29 07	11♉27	23 37	05♊39	17 35	29♊27
1934	08♉52	21 57	04♊49	17 28	29 54	12♋09	24 13	06♌08	17 57	29 44	11♍33	23 29	05♎35	17 58	00♏42
1935	14 11	26 04	07♎56	19 54	02♏01	14 21	26 57	09♐50	23 02	06♑31	20 16	04♒14	18 21	02♓33	16♓48
1936	29 38	12♒33	25 43	09♓08	22 48	06♈45	20 57	05♉23	19 58	04♊39	19 19	03♋52	18 10	02♌11	15♌48
1937	13♊27	28 42	13♋54	28 53	13♌31	27 43	11♍26	24 40	07♎30	19 58	02♏09	14 07	25 58	07♐45	19♐32
1938	00♏25	13 07	25 37	07♐56	20 07	02♑11	14 09	26 03	07♒55	19 46	01♓39	13 38	25 47	08♈10	20♈53
1939	03♓51	15 41	27 30	09♈25	21 31	03♉53	16 34	29 39	13♊09	27 02	11♋15	25 42	10♌17	24 52	08♍24
1940	21 00	04♌18	17 46	01♍23	15 09	29 04	13♎07	27 19	11♏39	26 02	10♐25	24 43	08♑48	22 36	06♒02
1941	04♐20	19 35	04♑46	19 43	04♒16	18 21	01♓56	15 02	27 43	10♈04	22 10	04♉06	15 58	27 48	09♊41
1942	21 28	04♉01	16 23	28 36	10♊41	22 40	04♋34	16 25	28 14	10♌03	21 56	03♍56	16 07	28 33	11♎21
1943	23 26	05♍13	17 04	29 02	11♎14	23 44	06♏37	19 54	03♐37	17 44	02♑11	16 51	01♒38	16 24	01♓03
1944	12♑02	25 36	09♒20	23 13	07♓13	21 19	05♈30	19 42	03♉54	18 03	02♊05	15 57	29 35	12♋58	26♋04
1945	25 37	10♊33	25 25	10♋05	24 25	08♌23	21 54	05♍01	17 44	00♎08	12 15	24 12	06♏03	17 52	29♏44
1946	12♎39	25 03	07♏13	19 12	01♐05	12 53	24 40	06♑28	18 19	00♒15	12 18	24 29	06♓53	19 31	02♈26
1947	13 12	25 03	06♓58	19 00	01♈14	13 44	26 37	09♉54	23 40	07♊53	22 31	07♋29	22 37	07♌45	22♌45
1948	02♋53	16 56	01♌09	15 29	29 49	14♍05	28 15	12♎17	26 11	09♏56	23 32	07♐00	20 17	03♑22	16♑15
1949	16 51	01♐30	16 08	00♑36	17 48	28 38	12♒03	25 03	07♓39	19 56	01♈57	13 48	25 36	07♉24	19♉19
1950	03♈07	15 23	27 26	09♉21	21 12	03♊03	14 56	26 52	08♋52	20 59	03♌12	15 33	28 04	10♍47	23♍46
1951	03♌24	15 13	27 05	09♍05	21 19	03♎52	16 48	00♏12	14 06	28 30	13♐20	18 19	13♑45	29 00	14♒01
1952	23 53	08♑13	22 43	07♒15	21 44	06♓07	20 20	04♈22	18 12	01♉50	15 15	28 28	11♊29	24 16	06♋51
1953	08♉47	23 10	07♊27	21 32	05♋20	18 49	01♌58	14 45	27 14	09♍27	21 28	03♎23	15 14	27 09	09♏11
1954	23 24	05♎40	17 44	29 39	11♏29	23 18	05♐09	17 06	29 09	11♑22	23 44	06♒18	19 05	02♓06	15♓22
1955	23 25	05♒18	17 18	29 28	11♓52	24 34	07♈37	21 03	04♉56	19 16	04♊00	19 02	04♋16	19 32	04♌38
1956	14♊14	28 51	13♋42	28 39	13♌32	28 14	12♍39	26 44	10♎29	23 53	06♏59	19 49	02♐26	14 52	27♐09
1957	00♏49	14 45	28 34	12♐13	26 41	08♑55	21 53	04♒34	16 59	29 09	11♓08	23 00	04♈49	16 41	28♈41
1958	13 27	25 37	07♈34	19 23	01♉10	12 59	24 55	07♊00	19 18	01♋49	14 34	27 31	10♌41	24 01	07♍31
1959	13 57	25 59	08♌08	20 25	02♍53	15 36	28 38	12♎03	25 53	10♏09	24 51	09♐54	25 09	10♑24	25♑30
1960	04♐49	19 45	04♑53	20 04	05♒06	19 52	04♓17	18 18	01♈55	15 11	28 08	10♉49	23 18	05♊36	17 46
1961	22 45	06♉29	20 03	03♊27	16 37	29 33	12♋14	24 40	06♌52	18 52	00♍44	12 32	24 21	06♎15	18♎20
1962	03♍04	15 13	27 11	09♎03	20 55	02♏50	14 64	27 08	09♐36	22 18	05♑15	18 26	01♒51	15 27	29♒13
1963	04♑20	16 27	28 43	11♒10	23 51	06♓47	20 02	03♈36	17 32	01♉50	16 25	01♊15	16 13	01♋10	15♋58
1964	25 27	10♊22	25 32	10♋46	25 55	10♌50	25 25	09♍34	23 16	06♎32	19 25	01♏58	14 15	26 20	08♐16
1965	14 06	28 31	11♏42	24 39	07♐24	19 57	02♑20	14 33	26 38	08♒36	20 29	02♓20	14 12	26 09	08♈17
1966	22 45	04♓53	16 50	28 42	10♈32	22 26	04♉29	16 46	29 21	12♊16	25 31	09♋07	23 00	07♌06	21♌20
1967	24 39	07♋04	19 41	02♌30	15 30	28 42	12♍06	25 44	09♎35	23 42	08♏02	22 35	07♐15	21 58	06♑34
1968	16 01	00♐58	16 13	01♑35	16 51	01♒52	16 28	00♓34	14 10	27 18	10♈01	22 25	04♉34	16 32	28♉26
1969	06♈45	19 57	02♉54	15 39	28 12	10♊36	22 51	04♋58	16 57	28 50	10♌40	22 27	04♍17	16 12	28♍19
1970	12 31	24 31	06♍22	18 10	29 59	11♎56	24 06	06♏33	19 20	02♐31	16 04	29 59	14♑10	28 33	13♒02
1971	15 11	27 48	10♑38	23 40	06♒53	20 17	03♓53	17 41	01♈40	15 50	00♉09	14 34	29 01	13♊24	27♊38
1972	07♉20	22 12	07♊18	22 28	07♋33	22 22	06♌50	20 52	07♍27	17 35	00♎20	12 45	24 54	06♏53	18♏44
1973	28 24	11♎32	24 21	06♏54	19 12	01♐20	13 20	25 13	07♑02	18 50	00♒38	12 28	24 24	06♓28	18♓45
1974	02♒06	14 04	25 57	07♓48	19 42	01♈43	13 56	26 25	09♉16	22 30	06♊10	20 15	04♋41	19 25	04♌17
1975	05♊10	18 03	01♋13	14 39	28 20	12♌13	26 13	10♍18	24 26	08♎34	22 41	06♏46	20 47	04♐42	18♐29
1976	28 47	13♏23	28 12	13♐08	28 02	12♑45	27 10	11♒10	24 45	07♓48	20 28	02♈47	14 50	26 42	08♉29
1977	19 36	02♈34	15 11	27 31	09♉38	21 38	03♊32	15 25	27 17	09♋10	21 05	03♌04	15 08	27 20	09♍41
1978	22 15	04♌09	15 58	27 43	09♍36	21 34	03♎45	16 16	29 10	12♏31	26 23	10♐44	25 29	10♑31	25♑40
1979	25 18	08♐30	22 02	05♑50	19 51	04♒01	18 14	02♓28	16 40	00♈47	14 49	28 46	12♉36	26 18	09♊50
1980	20 34	05♉06	19 47	04♊30	19 08	03♋33	17 39	01♌23	14 41	27 36	10♍09	22 25	04♎27	16 22	28♎13
1981	10♍12	23 09	05♎45	18 04	00♏11	12 08	24 00	05♐49	17 39	29 31	11♑27	23 29	05♒39	17 59	00♓31
1982	12 13	24 01	05♒48	17 37	29 32	11♓37	23 57	06♈35	19 37	03♉04	16 58	01♊20	16 05	01♋08	16♋21
1983	15 19	28 39	12♊22	26 25	10♋45	25 18	09♌55	24 32	09♍02	23 20	07♎25	21 14	04♏49	18 08	01♐14
1984	13♎06	27 21	11♏38	25 53	10♐02	24 02	07♑48	21 18	04♒28	17 19	29 51	12♓06	24 08	06♈01	17♈51
1985	00♓38	13 34	26 06	08♈19	20 17	02♉08	13 54	25 41	07♊33	19 31	01♋40	13 58	26 28	09♌08	22♌01
1986	02♋24	14 16	26 10	08♌06	20 08	02♍17	14 39	27 17	10♎16	23 39	07♏30	21 50	06♐38	21 46	07♑07
1987	05♏07	18 38	02♐38	17 02	01♑47	16 42	01♒40	16 30	01♓06	15 24	29 22	13♈01	26 22	09♉28	22♉20
1988	05♈15	19 20	03♉24	17 25	01♊19	15 03	28 34	11♋48	24 44	07♌21	19 41	01♍46	13 41	25 30	07♎18
1989	20 44	03♍31	15 57	28 07	10♎05	21 57	03♏48	15 41	27 41	09♐49	22 07	04♑37	17 19	00♒12	13♒17
1990	22 49	04♑39	16 32	28 30	10♒36	22 51	05♓21	18 07	01♈15	14 46	28 44	13♉07	27 52	12♊54	28♊05
1991	25 24	09♉04	23 10	07♊42	22 33	07♋36	22 42	07♌42	22 29	06♍57	21 02	04♎44	18 04	01♏02	13♏43
1992	27 55	11♎57	25 48	09♏29	22 57	06♐13	19 16	02♑05	14 41	27 05	09♒17	21 19	03♓14	15 06	26♓58
1993	10♒27	23 14	05♓41	17 52	29 51	11♈43	23 32	05♉25	17 25	29 37	12♊02	24 45	07♋44	21 01	04♌33
1994	12 50	24 47	06♋51	19 04	01♌27	14 00	26 46	09♍46	23 01	06♎33	20 25	04♏36	19 06	03♐52	18♐48
1995	15 46	29 21	13♏27	28 01	12♐59	28 14	13♑35	28 50	13♒48	28 22	12♓27	26 04	09♈13	22 00	04♉28
1996	20 13	04♈03	17 39	01♉01	14 11	27 10	09♊58	22 36	05♋03	17 19	29 26	11♌23	23 14	05♍02	16♍51
1997	00♌33	13 10	25 28	07♍31	19 23	01♎11	13 00	24 55	07♏02	19 24	02♐04	15 05	28 25	12♑03	25♑56
1998	03♐07	15 13	27 28	09♑53	22 27	05♒11	18 06	01♓14	14 37	28 15	12♈09	26 22	10♉49	25 29	10♊14
1999	06♈25	20 08	04♉20	18 59	04♊00	19 15	04♋32	19 42	04♌36	19 06	03♍08	16 43	29 52	12♎38	25♎05
2000	12♍07	26 00	09♎34	22 50	05♏49	18 33	01♐04	13 23	25 32	07♑33	19 27	01♒16	13 03	24 51	06♓43

Mercury

January

Year	1st	3rd	5th	7th	9th	11th	13th	15th	17th	19th	21st	23rd	25th	27th	29th	31st
1900	19♐00	21 36	24 18	27 03	29♑53	02 45	05 40	08 38	11 38	14 40	17 45	20 52	24 02	27 14	00♒28	03♒46
1901	27♐41	00♑44	03 49	06 56	10 04	13 14	16 26	19 39	22 55	26 13	29♒33	02 55	06 20	09 47	13 16	16♒48
1902	08♑55	12 08	15 23	18 39	21 57	25 17	28♒38	02 00	05 23	08 46	12 09	15 31	18 48	22 00	25 03	27♒53
1903	20♑40	23 54	27 07	00♒18	03 25	06 26	09 20	12♑01	14 25	16 26	17 58	18R55	19 09	18 38	17 22	15♒29
1904	28♑38	00♒32	01 59	02 52	03 03	02 28	01 06	29 05	26 38	24 01	21 35	19 34	18 07	17D17	17 00	17♑15
1905	09♑R06	06 27	04 09	02 25	01 19	00D53	01 03	01 42	02 48	04 14	05 56	07 53	10 01	12 18	14 43	17♑15
1906	17♐20	18 56	20 49	22 56	25 13	27 38	00♑10	02 48	05 30	08 17	11 07	14 01	16 58	19 57	22 59	26♑04
1907	21♐14	24 06	27 00	29♑57	02 56	05 57	08 59	12 04	15 11	18 20	21 31	24 45	28 01	01♒19	04 40	08♒03
1908	01♑18	04 26	07 36	10 46	13 59	17 13	20 29	23 46	27 06	00♒28	03 52	07 18	10 45	14 14	17 43	21♒12
1909	14♑33	17 49	21 06	24 24	27 43	01♒02	04 21	07 39	10 54	14 04	17 08	20 00	22 37	24 53	26 42	27♒57
1910	25♑42	28♒42	01 35	04 17	06 46	08 55	10 39	11 51	12R22	12 10	11 11	09 29	07 16	04 46	02 18	00♒07
1911	26♑R22	26 07	25 05	23 18	20 57	18 19	15 44	13 29	11 47	10 42	10D14	10 20	10 55	11 56	13 16	14♑54
1912	25♐R35	24 33	24D12	24 26	25 12	26 23	27 54	29♑42	01 44	03 56	06 17	08 46	11 20	14 00	16 45	19♑33
1913	17♐59	20 24	22 57	25 35	28 18	01♑05	03 55	06 50	09 46	12 45	15 46	18 50	21 56	25 05	28 16	01♒30
1914	25♐46	28♑47	01 49	04 54	08 00	11 07	14 17	17 28	20 41	23 57	27 14	00♒34	03 57	07 22	10 49	14♒19
1915	06♑45	09 57	13 10	16 25	19 42	23 00	26 20	29♒41	03 04	06 28	09 53	13 18	16 42	20 03	23 19	26♒27
1916	18♑32	21 48	25 03	28 18	01♒31	04 41	07 47	10 45	13 33	16 05	18 17	20 02	21 14	21R45	21 33	20♒35
1917	29♑10	01♒25	03 18	04 42	05R31	05 37	04 57	03 31	01 26	28♑58	26 23	24 01	22 04	20 40	19D53	19♑39
1918	15♑R20	12 45	10 04	07 36	05 38	04 17	03D35	03 30	03 57	04 52	06 09	07 44	09 34	11 37	13 49	16♑10
1919	18♐14	19 19	20 46	22 32	24 32	26 44	29♑04	01 33	04 08	06 48	09 32	12 20	15 12	18 07	21 06	24♑07
1920	19♐43	22 29	25 19	28 11	01♑06	04 04	07 04	10 06	13 10	16 16	19 24	22 35	25 48	29♒03	02 21	05♒42
1921	00♑49	03 56	07 04	10 14	13 25	16 38	19 53	23 10	26 29	29♒50	03 13	06 38	10 05	13 34	17 04	20♒35
1922	12♑21	15 36	18 53	22 10	25 29	28♒49	02 10	05 30	08 50	12 08	15 22	18 30	21 28	24 13	26 39	28♒40
1923	23♑51	26 58	00♒01	02 59	05 47	08 23	10 42	12 37	14 03	14R51	14 57	14 16	12 51	10 50	08 26	05♒57
1924	28♑05	28R50	28 53	28 09	26 39	24 31	21 58	19 20	16 57	15 01	13 41	12D58	12 50	13 13	14 03	15♑14
1925	29♐R40	28 01	27D04	26 46	27 03	27 50	29 02	00♑34	02 23	04 24	06 36	08 57	11 25	13 59	16 39	19♑23
1926	17♐18	19 29	21 50	24 19	26 54	29♑35	02 20	05 08	08 00	10 55	13 53	16 53	19 56	23 01	26 09	29♑20
1927	23♐54	26 53	29♑53	02 54	05 58	09 03	12 10	15 19	18 30	21 43	24 58	28 15	01♒35	04 58	08 22	11♒50
1928	04♑36	07 48	10 59	14 12	17 27	20 43	24 02	27 22	00♒44	04 08	07 33	10 59	14 25	17 51	21 15	24♒35
1929	17♑59	21 15	24 32	27 49	01♒05	04 19	07 31	10 37	13 36	16 24	18 55	21 06	22 48	23 56	24R23	24♒06
1930	28♑05	00♒43	03 07	05 10	06 47	07 51	08R15	07 53	06 45	04 55	02 35	00♑02	27 34	25 26	23 49	22♑47
1931	20♑R43	18 48	16 22	13 41	11 07	08 56	07 20	06 23	06D03	06 17	07 00	08 07	09 34	11 18	13 14	15♑22
1932	20♐06	20 29	21 22	22 39	24 17	26 10	28 16	00♑33	02 57	05 29	08 06	10 48	13 34	16 24	19 18	22♑14
1933	19♐41	22 22	25 08	27 57	00♑49	03 44	06 42	09 41	12 43	15 48	18 54	22 03	25 14	28♒28	01 44	05♒03
1934	28♐48	01♑53	04 59	08 07	11 16	14 27	17 40	20 55	24 12	27 31	00♒52	04 15	07 40	11 08	14 38	18♒09
1935	10♑10	13 24	16 39	19 56	23 14	26 34	29♒54	03 16	06 38	10 00	13 21	16 38	19 50	22 54	25 45	28♒20
1936	21♑51	25 03	28 12	01♒19	04 21	07 15	09 58	12 25	14 31	16 09	17 13	17R37	17 15	16 07	14 20	12♒05
1937	29♑29	00♒47	01R28	01 26	00♑37	29 03	26 51	24 18	21 42	19 22	17 30	16 14	15D34	15 28	15 53	16♑43
1938	05♑R28	03 04	01 11	29♐57	29D24	29 27	00♑02	01 03	02 26	04 07	06 02	08 09	10 26	12 50	15 21	17♑58
1939	17♐07	18 58	21 03	23 19	25 44	28 16	00♑53	03 36	06 22	09 12	12 06	15 02	18 01	21 03	24 07	27♑14
1940	22♐10	25 05	28 01	01♑00	04 01	07 04	10 08	13 15	16 23	19 33	22 46	26 01	29♒18	02 37	05 59	09♒24
1941	04♑05	07 14	10 25	13 37	16 52	20 07	23 25	26 44	00♒06	03 29	05 54	10 21	13 49	17 17	20 44	24♒09
1942	15♑48	19 04	22 21	25 39	28♒57	02 14	05 31	08 46	11 56	14 59	17 53	20 33	22 53	24 48	26 11	26♒55
1943	26♑37	29♒30	02 14	04 45	06 58	08 47	10 06	10R46	10 43	09 53	08 19	06 10	03 41	01♑10	28 54	27♑04
1944	24♑R42	23 50	22 12	19 57	17 20	14 42	12 21	10 30	09 18	08D43	08 43	09 14	10 11	11 29	13 05	14♑55
1945	22♐51	22R41	23D06	24 00	25 19	26 57	28 51	00♑57	03 13	05 37	08 08	10 45	13 27	16 13	19 03	21♑57
1946	18♐30	21 02	23 41	26 24	29♑11	02 01	04 55	07 51	10 49	13 50	16 54	19 59	23 07	26 18	29♒31	02♒47
1947	26♐52	29♑54	02 58	06 04	09 11	12 20	15 30	18 43	21 57	25 14	28♒33	01 54	05 17	08 43	12 11	15♒42
1948	08♑00	11 12	14 26	17 42	20 59	24 18	27 38	00♒59	04 22	07 46	11 09	14 32	17 52	21 08	24 17	27♒15
1949	21♑22	24 36	27 50	01♒01	04 09	07 11	10 05	12 58	15 14	17 18	18 54	19 54	20R13	19 46	18 35	16♒45
1950	29♑27	01♒24	02 55	03R51	04 07	03 36	02 19	00♑22	27 56	25 20	22 52	20 49	19 18	18D23	18 04	18♑15
1951	11♑R47	09 05	06 32	04 26	02 57	02D07	01 56	02 18	03 08	04 22	05 55	07 43	09 44	11 56	14 16	16♑44
1952	17♐34	18 58	20 41	22 40	24 51	27 11	29♑39	02 13	04 53	07 37	10 25	13 17	16 11	19 09	22 10	25♑13
1953	21♐58	24 49	27 43	00♑39	03 38	06 39	09 41	12 46	15 53	19 02	22 12	25 26	28♒41	01 59	05 20	08♒43
1954	02♑00	05 08	08 17	11 28	14 40	17 54	21 10	24 27	27 47	01♒09	04 32	07 58	11 26	14 54	18 24	21♒53
1955	13♑36	16 52	20 08	23 26	26 45	00♒04	03 23	06 42	09 59	13 13	16 21	19 21	22 08	24 37	26 43	28♒20
1956	24♑53	27 56	00♒54	03 43	06 21	08 43	10 43	12 15	13R11	13 26	12 55	11 38	09 43	07 21	04 50	02♒27
1957	27♑R24	27 14	26 16	24 34	22 16	19 39	17 03	14 45	12 59	11 50	11D18	11 21	11 53	12 51	14 10	15♑46
1958	26♐R47	25 41	25D15	25 26	26 08	27 17	28 46	00♑33	02 33	04 44	07 04	09 31	12 05	14 44	17 28	29♑16
1959	17♐37	19 57	22 25	25 00	27 40	00♑25	03 13	06 05	09 00	11 57	14 57	17 59	21 04	24 11	27 21	00♒34
1960	24♐58	27 58	01♑00	04 03	07 08	10 15	13 23	16 33	19 45	23 00	26 16	29♒35	02 56	06 19	09 45	13♒14
1961	07♑26	10 38	13 51	17 06	20 22	23 41	27 00	00♒22	03 45	07 09	10 34	13 59	17 23	20 45	24 02	27♒11
1962	19♑14	22 29	25 44	28♒59	02 13	05 24	08 30	11 30	14 19	16 53	19 08	20 56	22 11	22 47	22R39	21♒46
1963	28♑42	01♒08	03 15	04 57	06R08	06 41	06 29	05 30	03 47	01♑31	28 58	26 27	24 13	22 29	21 20	20♑46
1964	17♑43	15R22	12 42	10 04	07 47	06 03	04 58	04D31	04 39	05 18	06 22	07 46	09 27	11 23	13 29	15♑45
1965	19♐11	20 13	21 38	23 21	25 20	27 30	29♑50	02 18	04 52	07 31	10 15	13 03	15 55	18 49	21 47	24♑48
1966	20♐26	23 12	26 01	28♑53	01 48	04 45	07 45	10 47	13 51	16 57	20 05	23 15	26 28	29♒43	03 01	06♒21
1967	29♐57	03♑03	06 10	09 19	12 29	15 41	18 55	22 11	25 29	28♒48	02 10	05 34	09 01	12 29	15 58	19♒29
1968	11♑24	14 39	17 54	21 11	24 30	27 49	01♒10	04 31	07 51	11 11	14 28	17 40	20 44	23 38	26 16	28♒33
1969	24♑33	27 40	00♒44	03 43	06 33	09 10	11 31	13 29	14 58	15R51	16 01	15 25	14 05	12 07	09 45	07♒15
1970	29♑01	29 50	29R58	29 19	27 53	25 48	23 17	20 39	18 13	16 15	14 51	14 04	13D52	14 12	14 59	16♑09
1971	02♑00	29R59	28♐37	27 55	27D52	28 21	29 19	00♑39	02 18	04 12	06 17	08 33	10 57	13 27	16 04	18♑45
1972	17♐08	19 11	21 26	23 50	26 22	28♑59	01 41	04 28	07 18	10 11	13 07	16 05	19 07	22 11	25 17	28♑26
1973	24♐38	27 36	00♑36	03 37	06 41	09 46	12 53	16 01	19 12	22 25	25 40	28♒57	02 17	05 39	09 04	12♒31
1974	05♑18	08 29	11 40	14 53	18 08	21 25	24 43	28♒03	01 25	04 49	08 14	11 41	15 07	18 33	21 58	25♒18
1975	17♑03	20 18	23 35	26 52	00♒08	03 24	06 38	09 48	12 52	15 47	18 29	20 53	22 53	24 22	25R15	25♒25
1976	27♑27	00♒12	02 45	05 01	06 55	08 20	09R09	09 15	08 35	07 09	05 05	02 38	00♑05	27 43	25 47	24♑24
1977	21♑R55	20 05	17 41	15 01	12 25	10 11	08 31	07 30	07D06	07 17	07 57	09 02	10 27	12 08	14 03	16♑10
1978	21♐09	21 28	22 17	23 32	25 08	27♑00	29 05	01 20	03 43	06 14	08 50	11 32	14 18	17 07	20 00	22♑57
1979	19♐07	21 45	24 28	27♑15	00 05	02 59	05 54	08 53	11 53	14 56	18 01	21 09	24 19	27 31	00♒46	04♒03
1980	27♐57	01♑01	04 07	07 14	10 22	13 32	16 44	19 57	23 13	26 31	29♒50	03 12	06 37	10 03	13 32	17♒03
1981	10♑50	14 04	17 19	20 36	23 54	27 14	00♒34	03 56	07 19	10 41	14 02	17 19	20 32	23 37	26 31	29♒08
1982	22♑31	25 44	28♒54	02 01	05 04	07 59	10 43	13 12	15 21	17 03	18 11	18R38	18 21	17 18	15 35	13♒22
1983	29♑30	01♒06	02 10	02R34	02 14	01 07	29♑16	26 54	24 18	21 46	19 36	17 58	16 56	16D30	16 37	17♑12
1984	08♑R07	05 30	03 17	01 39	00 42	00D23	00 39	01 25	02 36	04 06	05 53	07 53	10 03	12 23	14 50	17♑23
1985	17♐58	19 48	21 51	24 06	26 30	29♑01	01 37	04 19	07 05	09 55	12 48	15 44	18 42	21 44	24 48	27♑55
1986	22♐53	25 47	28♑43	01 42	04 42	07 45	10 49	13 55	17 04	20 14	23 26	26 41	29♒58	03 17	06 39	10♒04
1987	03♑11	06 20	09 30	12 41	15 54	19 09	22 26	25 44	29♒05	02 27	05 51	09 17	12 45	16 13	19 41	23♒08
1988	14♑51	18 06	21 23	24 40	27 58	01♒17	04 34	07 51	11 04	14 12	17 12	20 01	22 34	24 45	26 28	27♒36
1989	27♑21	00♒15	03 01	05 33	07 49	09 41	11 02	11R47	11 49	11 04	09 34	07 28	05 01	02 29	00♑11	28♑18
1990	25♑R48	25 01	23 27	21 15	18 40	16 01	13 37	11 43	10 27	09D48	09 45	10 12	11 06	12 22	13 56	15♑45
1991	24♐R19	23D45	23 49	24 27	25 31	26 58	28 42	00♑41	02 51	05 10	07 37	10 11	12 50	15 33	18 21	21♑12
1992	18♐03	20 31	23 05	25 46	28 30	01♑18	04 10	07 04	10 01	13 01	16 03	19 07	22 14	25 23	28♒34	01♒49
1993	27♐33	00♑35	03 39	06 44	09 52	13 00	16 11	19 23	22 37	25 54	29♒12	02 33	05 57	09 23	12 51	16♒21
1994	08♑40	11 52	15 06	18 22	21 39	24 57	28 18	01♒39	05 02	08 26	11 50	15 13	18 34	21 50	25 00	28♒00
1995	20♑26	23 40	26 54	00♒07	03 17	06 23	09 23	12 14	14 51	17 09	19 03	20 25	21R10	21 11	20 26	18♒59
1996	29♑08	01♒19	03 07	04 24	05R05	05 03	04 14	02 40	00♑29	27 57	25 23	23 04	21 12	19 56	19D15	19♑08
1997	13♑R07	10 24	07 50	05 41	04 07	03D14	02 58	03 17	04 04	05 16	06 46	08 33	10 33	12 44	15 03	17♑30
1998	18♐29	19 50	21 32	23 28	25 38	27 57	00♑24	02 58	05 37	08 20	11 08	13 59	16 53	19 51	22 51	25♑54
1999	21♐16	24 05	26 58	29♑52	02 50	05 49	08 51	11 54	15 00	18 07	21 17	24 29	27♒43	01 00	04 19	07♒41
2000	01♑07	04 14	07 22	10 32	13 43	16 56	20 11	23 28	26 46	00♒07	03 30	06 54	10 21	13 49	17 18	20♒48

February

	1st	3rd	5th	7th	9th	11th	13th	15th	17th	19th	21st	23rd	25th	27th	29th
1900	05♒25	08 47	12 12	15 39	19 10	22 44	26 21	00♓00	03 42	07 26	11 10	14 52	18 32	22♓06	
1901	18♒34	22 07	25 41	29♓13	02 44	06 09	09 25	12 30	16 18	17 43	19 41	21 06	21 R55	22♓05	
1902	29♒11	01♓31	03 24	04 43	05 R24	05 22	04 38	03 16	01 23	29♒13	26 59	24 54	23 08	21♒48	
1903	14♒R22	11 58	09 33	07 23	05 37	04 23	03 D41	03 30	03 47	04 28	05 30	06 51	08 27	10♒16	
1904	17♑33	18 27	19 42	21 14	23 01	25 00	27 09	29♒27	01 53	04 25	07 04	09 47	12 36	15 30	18♒28
1905	18♑33	21 13	23 58	26 47	29 40	02♒37	05 37	08 41	11 49	15 00	18 15	21 34	24 57	28♓23	
1906	27♑38	00♒47	04 00	07 15	10 33	13 55	17 19	20 48	24 20	27 55	01♓34	05 16	09 01	12♓49	
1907	09♒46	13 14	16 44	20 18	23 53	27 31	01♓10	04 50	08 29	12 04	15 34	18 55	22 02	24♓52	
1908	22♒56	26 21	29♓42	02 55	05 55	08 39	11 01	12 55	14 15	14 R58	15 00	14 22	13 07	11 25	09♓24
1909	28♒R21	28 35	28 05	26 53	25 06	22 55	20 35	18 21	16 25	14 54	13 53	13 D22	13 19	13♒42	
1910	29♑R11	27 45	26 52	26 D32	26 42	27 18	28 17	29♒36	01 10	02 58	04 58	07 07	09 26	11♒52	
1911	15♑48	17 46	19 55	22 12	24 37	27 09	29♒46	02 29	05 17	08 09	11 06	14 07	17 11	20♒20	
1912	20♑59	23 53	26 50	29♒51	02 55	06 02	09 13	12 27	15 44	19 06	22 30	25 59	29♓31	03 07	06♓47
1913	03♒08	06 27	09 48	13 12	16 40	20 10	23 44	27 21	01♓01	04 44	08 28	12 14	15 59	19♓41	
1914	16♒04	19 37	23 12	26 47	00♓22	03 54	07 23	10 45	13 56	16 51	19 27	21 37	23 16	24♓20	
1915	27♒58	00♓46	03 15	05 20	06 54	07 R51	08 07	07 41	06 35	04 56	02 53	00♒41	28 33	26♒39	
1916	19♒R50	17 55	15 38	13 13	10 56	09 01	07 33	06 38	06 D13	06 18	06 48	07 40	08 52	10 21	12♒04
1917	19♑44	20 14	21 09	22 24	23 56	25 43	27 42	29♒51	02 09	04 34	07 06	09 45	12 29	15♒18	
1918	17♑23	19 55	22 32	25 14	28 01	00♒53	03 48	06 47	09 50	12 56	16 06	19 20	22 38	26♒00	
1919	25♑38	28♒44	01 53	05 04	08 18	11 36	14 57	18 21	21 49	25 21	28♓56	02 35	06 17	10♓02	
1920	07♒23	10 48	14 16	17 46	21 20	24 56	28♓34	02 15	05 56	09 37	13 15	16 49	20 15	23 29	26♓27
1921	22♒20	00 14	02♓20	04 25	06 28	08 29	10 29	12 26	14 22	16 16	18 R07	19 55	21 41	23♓24	
1922	29♒29	00♓41	01 13	01 02	00♒07	28 34	26 33	24 17	22 01	19 57	18 15	17 02	16 17	16♒D02	
1923	04♒R45	02 38	00 58	29♑51	29 D17	29 14	29♒39	00 28	01 37	03 04	04 45	06 39	08 44	10♒58	
1924	15♑57	17 35	19 27	21 30	23 43	26 04	28 33	01♒07	03 48	06 33	09 23	12 18	15 17	18 21	21♒28
1925	20 47	23 37	26 32	29 29	02 30	05 35	08 43	11 54	15 09	18 27	21 50	25 15	28♓45	02♓19	
1926	00♒56	04 11	07 29	10 49	14 13	17 40	21 11	24 45	28♓22	02 02	05 45	09 30	13 17	17♓04	
1927	13♒35	17 06	20 40	24 15	27 51	01♓28	05 04	08 36	12 02	15 19	18 22	21 06	23 27	25♓20	
1928	26♒12	29♓21	02 17	04 56	07 11	08 59	10 11	10 R45	10 36	09 47	08 23	06 31	04 23	02 14	00♓14
1929	23♒R40	00 25	02 29	04 32	06 33	08 32	10 30	12 25	14 18	16 D09	17 58	19 43	21 26	23♒05	
1930	22♑R28	22 D17	22 35	23 19	24 25	25 49	27 29	29♒22	01 26	03 39	06 01	08 30	11 06	13♒47	
1931	16♑29	18 50	21 18	23 52	26 32	19♒17	02 06	04 59	07 57	10 58	14 03	17 13	20 25	23♒42	
1932	23♑44	26 45	29♒50	02 57	06 08	09 22	12 39	15 59	19 23	22 50	26 21	29♓56	03 35	07 17	11♓03
1933	06♒43	10 07	13 33	17 02	20 34	24 09	27 47	01♓27	05 09	08 52	12 34	16 13	19 47	23♓13	
1934	19♒55	23 27	26 59	00♓29	03 54	07 12	10 18	13 09	15 39	17 43	19 15	20 R10	20 27	20♓04	
1935	29♒30	01♓28	02 55	03 R43	03 50	03 14	01 57	00♒08	27 58	25 42	23 33	21 42	20 16	19♒19	
1936	10♒R51	08 24	06 09	04 17	02 57	02 09	01 D53	02 05	02 43	03 43	05 02	06 36	08 24	10 24	12♒33
1937	17♑17	18 38	20 16	22 08	24♒11	26 24	28 45	01♒14	03 48	06 29	09 14	12 05	15 00	18♒00	
1938	19♑18	22 03	24 51	27 44	00 40	03 39	06 43	09 50	13 00	16 14	19 31	22 53	26 18	29♓47	
1939	28♑49	02♒00	05 14	08 31	11 52	15 15	18 42	22 12	25 46	29♓23	03 03	06 47	10 33	14♓20	
1940	11♒08	14 37	18 08	21 42	25 19	28♓56	02 35	06 12	09 48	13 18	16 40	19 50	22 43	25 14	27♓19
1941	25♒50	29♓07	02 16	05 11	07 49	10 03	11 47	12 56	13 R26	13 15	12 24	10 58	09 06	07♓01	
1942	27♒R01	26 04	25 35	23 53	21 44	19 23	17 05	15 04	13 28	12 21	11 D45	11 38	11 57	12♒40	
1943	26♑R22	25 22	24 D57	25 02	25 35	26 31	27 47	29♒19	01 06	03 05	05 13	07 31	09 56	12♒29	
1944	15♑55	18 02	20 19	22 43	25 14	27 51	00♒33	03 20	06 12	09 08	12 08	15 11	18 19	21 31	24♒47
1945	23♑25	26 23	29♒25	02 30	05 38	08 50	12 04	15 22	18 44	22 09	25 37	29♓10	02 46	06♓26	
1946	04♒26	07 46	11 09	14 35	18 04	21 36	25 11	28♓49	02 30	06 13	09 57	13 40	17 23	21♓00	
1947	17♒28	21 00	24 34	28 08	01♓40	05 09	08 31	11 43	14 42	17 21	19 36	21 22	22 33	23♓06	
1948	28♒39	01♓12	03 22	05 02	06 07	06 R31	06 13	05 13	03 37	01 37	29 24	27 12	25 14	23 37	22♓28
1949	15♒R40	13 17	10 51	08 39	06 51	05 33	04 48	04 D33	04 47	05 26	06 26	07 45	09 19	11♒07	
1950	18♑32	19 23	20 36	22 06	23 51	25 49	27 57	00♒01	02 39	05 10	07 48	10 31	13 20	16♒13	
1951	18♑00	20 37	23 19	26 05	28♒56	01 50	04 48	07 50	10 56	14 05	17 18	20 35	23 55	27♒19	
1952	26♑46	29♒57	03 04	06 18	09 34	12 54	16 17	19 43	23 13	26 46	00♓23	04 04	07 47	11 34	15♓23
1953	10♒26	13 54	17 24	20 57	24 33	28♓11	01 50	05 30	09 09	12 45	16 16	19 38	22 47	25♓39	
1954	23♒37	27 03	00♓25	03 38	06 41	09 27	11 51	13 48	15 12	15 R59	16 05	15 32	14 21	12♓41	
1955	28♒55	29 R35	29 32	28 45	27 19	25 20	23 04	20 45	28 37	16 50	15 31	14 42	14 D22	24♒30	
1956	01♒R23	29♑37	28 24	27 D44	27 36	27 57	28 43	29♒49	01 14	02 54	04 47	06 50	09 04	11 25	13♒54
1957	16♑39	18 36	20 43	23 00	25 24	27 55	00♒32	03 14	06 01	08 53	11 49	14 49	17 54	21♒02	
1958	21♑42	24 35	27 32	00♒33	03 37	06 44	09 54	13 08	16 25	19 46	23 10	26 38	00♓10	03♓46	
1959	02♒11	05 27	08 47	12 09	15 35	19 04	22 36	26 11	29♓50	03 31	07 15	11 00	14 45	18♓30	
1960	14♒59	18 31	22 05	25 40	29♓15	02 49	06 21	09 48	13 06	16 11	18 59	21 25	23 24	24 50	25♓39
1961	28♒42	01♓32	04 04	06 12	07 49	08 50	09 R11	08 49	07 47	06 11	04 11	02 00	29♒50	27♒55	
1962	21♒R03	19 12	16 56	14 31	12 13	10 15	08 45	07 46	07 18	07 D19	07 47	08 37	09 47	11♒14	
1963	20♑D41	20 55	21 35	22 38	24 00	25 39	27 30	29♒33	01 46	04 07	06 35	09 10	11 50	14♒36	
1964	16♑56	19 24	21 57	24 37	27 21	00♒09	03 02	05 59	09 00	12 04	15 12	18 24	21 40	24 59	28♒23
1965	26♑20	29♒25	02 33	05 44	08 58	12 16	15 37	19 01	22 28	26 00	29♓34	03 13	06 55	10♓41	
1966	08♒02	11 27	14 55	18 25	21 58	25 34	29♓13	02 53	06 35	10 16	13 55	17 29	20 56	24♓12	
1967	21♒15	24 45	28 14	01♓39	04 58	08 06	11 00	13 34	15 43	17 22	18 25	18 48	18 32	17♓38	
1968	29♒31	01♓05	02 R02	02 17	01 48	00♒38	28 53	26 44	24 26	22 14	20 18	18 47	17 45	17 D12	17♒07
1969	06♒03	03 53	02 10	01 00	00 D22	00 16	00 58	01 25	00 32	03 57	05 36	07 29	09 33	11♒46	
1970	16♑50	18 27	20 17	22 19	24 31	26 51	29♒19	01 53	04 33	07 18	10 07	13 02	16 00	19♒03	
1971	20♑08	22 56	25 48	28♒43	01 42	04 45	07 51	11 00	14 13	17 29	20 49	24 13	27 40	01♓12	
1972	00♒02	03 15	06 31	09 50	13 12	16 37	20 06	23 38	27 13	00♓52	04 33	08 12	12 04	15 51	19♓37
1973	14♒16	17 47	21 21	24 56	28♓33	02 10	05 45	09 18	12 45	16 03	19 08	21 55	24 18	26♓14	
1974	26♒56	00♓06	03 03	05 44	08 03	09 53	11 09	11 47	11 R43	10 58	09 37	07 48	05 42	03♓32	
1975	25♒R13	24 16	22 39	20 33	18 12	15 51	13 45	12 03	10 51	10 D09	09 58	10 13	10 53	11♒54	
1976	23♑R55	23 D24	23 24	23 53	24 46	25 59	27 30	29♒15	01 12	03 20	05 37	08 01	10 33	13 11	15♒54
1977	17♑17	19 36	22 04	24 37	27 16	00♒00	02 49	05 42	08 39	11 40	14 45	17 54	21 06	24♒23	
1978	24♑26	27 27	00♒31	03 39	05 49	10 02	13 19	16 39	20 03	23 30	27 01	00♓35	04 14	07♓56	
1979	05♒43	09 04	12 29	15 56	19 27	23 00	26 36	00♓15	03 57	07 39	11 22	15 03	18 41	22♓13	
1980	18♒48	22 21	25 53	29♓25	02 53	06 16	09 30	12 31	15 14	17 34	19 26	20 44	21 R25	21 26	20♓49
1981	00♓18	02 20	03 50	04 R43	04 54	04 22	03 10	01 24	29♒16	27 00	24 50	22 57	21 28	20♒28	
1982	12♒R09	09 42	07 25	05 31	04 06	03 15	02 D56	03 05	03 41	04 38	05 55	07 27	09 14	11♒12	
1983	17♑39	18 49	20 17	22 01	23 57	26 04	28 20	00♒44	03 15	05 52	08 34	11 22	14 14	17♒11	
1984	18♑42	21 23	24 09	26♒59	29 53	02 51	05 52	08 57	12 05	15 17	18 32	21 51	25 14	28♓41	02♓12
1985	29♑29	02♒41	05 54	09 11	12 31	15 55	19 21	22 51	26 25	00♓01	03 42	07 25	11 11	14♓59	
1986	11♒47	15 16	18 48	22 22	25 58	29♓36	03 14	06 52	10 28	13 59	17 22	20 34	23 29	26♓03	
1987	24♒50	28 11	01♓26	04 30	07 19	09 48	11 51	13 22	14 R16	14 30	14 02	12 57	11 20	09♓22	
1988	27♒R55	28 01	27 22	26 02	24 07	21 52	19 31	17 19	15 27	14 02	13 07	12 D43	12 46	13 15	14♒06
1989	27♑R34	26 31	26 D02	26 04	26 34	27 27	28 04	00♒12	01 57	03 54	06 02	08 18	10 43	13♒14	
1990	16♑44	18 50	21 06	23 29	25 59	28 36	01♒17	04 04	06 55	09 50	12 50	15 53	19 01	22♒12	
1991	22♑39	25 35	28♒35	01 38	04 44	07 54	11 07	14 23	17 42	21 05	24 32	28 02	01♓36	05♓14	
1992	03♒27	06 45	10 06	13 30	16 58	20 28	24 02	27 38	01♓18	05 00	08 43	12 28	16 11	19 52	23♓28
1993	18♒07	21 40	25 14	28♓48	02 20	05 49	09 13	12 27	15 27	18 09	20 27	22 16	23 31	24♓R09	
1994	29♒24	02♓00	04 13	05 57	07 05	07 R34	07 20	06 25	04 53	02 55	00♒43	28 30	26 30	24♒52	
1995	18♒R02	15 49	13 23	11 03	08 58	07 21	06 16	05 D43	05 39	06 03	06 51	07 58	09 23	11♒03	
1996	19♑16	19 53	20 53	22 12	23 49	25 39	27 41	29♒52	02 12	04 40	07 14	09 54	12 39	15 29	18♒24
1997	18♑46	21 22	24 03	26 49	29♒39	02 33	05 31	08 33	11 38	14 47	17 59	21 15	24 36	28♒00	
1998	27♒27	00 34	03 45	06 58	10 14	13 34	15 56	20 22	13 52	27 25	01 02	04 42	08 26	12♒12	
1999	09♒23	12 49	16 17	19 49	23 24	27 00	00♓39	04 19	07 59	11 37	15 12	18 40	21 57	25♓00	
2000	22♒33	26 01	29♓26	02 45	05 55	08 51	11 29	13 44	15 28	16 38	17 R09	17 00	16 11	14 49	13♓00

Mercury

March

	1st	3rd	5th	7th	9th	11th	13th	15th	17th	19th	21st	23rd	25th	27th	29th	31st
1900	25♓30	28♈41	01 34	04 04	06 08	07 41	08 42	09 R09	09 01	08 23	07 16	05 49	04 09	02 25	00 45	29♓16
1901	21♓R36	20 33	19 01	17 10	15 10	13 13	11 28	10 02	08 59	08 21	08 D08	08 18	08 50	09 42	10 51	12♓16
1902	20♒R56	20 D31	20 34	21 01	21 49	22 57	24 20	25 59	27 50	29♓52	02 04	04 25	06 54	09 31	12 15	15♓05
1903	12♒17	14 28	16 47	19 14	21 48	24 29	27 15	00♓08	03 06	06 09	09 17	12 31	15 49	19 14	22 43	26♓18
1904	19♒59	23 04	26 13	29♓27	02 45	06 08	09 35	13 08	16 44	20 26	24 13	28♈05	02 01	06 01	10 05	14♈11
1905	01♓54	05 29	09 08	12 52	16 39	20 31	24 26	28♈23	02 22	06 20	10 17	14 08	17 51	21 23	24 40	27♈39
1906	16♓38	20 28	24 16	28 00	01♈38	05 05	08 18	11 12	13 44	15 51	17 29	18 36	19 R13	19 18	18 54	18♈03
1907	27♓18	29♈18	00 45	01 38	01 55	01 37	00 45	29♓26	27 47	25 58	24 08	22 25	20 58	19 50	19 05	18♓D43
1908	08♓R21	06 17	04 23	02 49	01 39	00 55	00 D38	00 45	01 15	02 05	03 14	04 38	06 17	08 09	11 11	12♓24
1909	14♒27	15 33	16 55	18 32	20 22	22 24	24 35	26 55	29♓23	01 59	04 41	07 30	10 25	13 25	16 32	19♓44
1910	14♒25	17 05	19 50	22 40	25 36	28♓37	01 43	04 54	08 09	11 29	14 55	18 25	22 00	25 41	29♈27	03♈19
1911	23♒33	26 50	00♓12	03 37	07 07	10 42	14 21	18 05	21 53	25 46	29♈43	03 43	07 46	11 49	15 53	19♈53
1912	08♓39	12 25	16 14	20 06	24 01	27 56	01♈50	05 41	09 26	13 01	16 24	19 29	22 15	24 37	26 34	28♈04
1913	23♓19	26 48	00♈06	03 07	05 47	08 03	09 50	11 05	11 R47	11 56	11 33	10 41	09 26	07 53	06 12	04♈31
1914	24♓R47	24 36	23 49	22 31	20 49	18 54	16 57	15 07	13 33	12 19	11 29	11 D04	11 03	11 24	12 06	13♓06
1915	25♒R07	24 03	23 D26	23 16	23 32	24 10	25 08	26 24	27 55	29♓40	01 36	03 43	06 00	08 25	10 58	13♓39
1916	13♒00	15 01	17 11	19 30	21 58	24 32	27 13	00♓00	02 52	05 51	08 54	12 03	15 18	18 38	22 03	25♓34
1917	18♒12	21 11	24 14	27 22	00♓34	03 51	07 13	10 39	14 10	17 46	21 27	25 13	29♈04	02 59	06 59	11♈54
1918	29♒26	02♓56	06 30	10 09	13 52	17 39	21 30	25 25	29♈23	03 23	07 23	11 22	15 16	19 04	22 41	26♈05
1919	13♓51	17 41	21 32	25 23	29♈10	02 52	06 24	09 44	12 46	15 28	17 46	19 37	20 58	21 50	22 R10	22♈01
1920	27♓48	00♈13	02 10	03 35	04 R26	04 41	04 22	03 31	02 13	00♓36	28 49	27 01	25 21	23 55	22 48	22♓04
1921	14♓R03	12 04	10 00	08 03	06 20	05 00	04 04	03 D34	03 30	03 48	04 29	05 28	06 44	08 16	10 01	11♓58
1922	16♒13	16 48	17 44	18 58	20 28	22 12	24 07	26 14	28 29	00♓53	03 25	06 05	08 50	11 43	14 41	17♓45
1923	13♒21	15 50	18 27	21 09	23 58	26 51	29♓50	02 54	06 03	09 17	12 36	16 00	19 29	23 03	26 43	00♈28
1924	23♒04	26 17	29♓35	02 58	06 25	09 56	13 32	17 13	20 58	24 48	28♈43	02 41	06 43	10 47	14 53	18♈56
1925	05♓57	09 39	13 24	17 14	21 07	25 02	28♈58	02 54	06 48	10 36	14 17	17 45	20 58	23 53	26 25	28♈34
1926	20♓49	24 30	28 04	01♈28	04 36	07 26	09 52	11 52	13 22	14 19	14 R44	14 37	14 00	12 57	11 34	09♈59
1927	26♓39	27 R23	27 29	26 58	25 55	24 24	22 37	20 42	18 49	17 08	15 45	14 44	14 07	13 D54	14 04	14♓36
1928	29♒R21	27 51	26 48	26 D13	26 04	26 19	26 58	27 56	29 11	00♓42	02 26	04 23	06 30	08 46	11 12	13♓45
1929	13♒05	14 47	16 42	18 48	21 03	23 26	25 57	28 35	01♓19	04 09	07 05	10 07	13 14	16 27	19 45	23♓08
1930	16♒34	19 26	22 23	25 24	28♓31	01 41	04 57	08 17	11 42	15 12	18 47	22 27	26 12	00♈02	03 57	07♈57
1931	27♒03	00♓28	03 57	07 31	11 09	14 51	18 38	22 29	26 24	00♈22	04 23	08 25	12 25	16 23	20 14	23♈56
1932	12♓57	16 47	20 39	24 31	28♈23	02 11	05 53	09 25	12 43	15 44	18 25	20 41	22 30	23 50	24 41	25♈R02
1933	26♓27	29♈23	01 58	04 07	05 46	06 53	07 R24	07 21	06 46	05 41	04 15	02 34	00♓48	29 05	27 33	26♓17
1934	19♓05	17 36	15 45	13 44	11 44	09 56	08 25	07 18	06 37	06 D20	06 28	06 57	07 47	08 55	10 19	11♓57
1935	18♒R51	18 D50	19 14	20 00	21 05	22 27	24 04	25 54	27 55	00♓06	02 26	04 54	07 30	10 13	13 02	15♓58
1936	13♒41	16 04	18 34	21 10	23 53	26 41	29♓35	02 35	05 39	08 49	12 04	15 24	18 49	22 19	25 55	29♓36
1937	21♒03	24 12	27 24	00♓41	04 02	07 28	10 59	14 34	18 14	21 58	25 48	29♈42	03 40	07 42	11 47	15♈53
1938	03♓20	06 57	10 39	14 24	18 14	22 07	26 02	00♈00	03 58	07 54	11 45	15 30	19 04	22 24	25 27	28♈09
1939	18♓09	21 56	25 41	29♈19	02 48	06 04	09 02	11 38	13 50	15 33	16 45	17 R26	17 35	17 13	16 24	15♈12
1940	28♓10	29 27	00♈R08	00 12	29♓41	28 38	27 09	25 23	23 31	21 40	20 01	18 40	17 40	17 03	16 D50	17♓00
1941	04♓R54	02 56	01 18	00♒03	29 15	28 D54	28 58	29 25	00♓13	01 20	02 43	04 21	06 11	08 13	10 25	12♓45
1942	13♒43	15 03	16 39	18 28	20 28	22 38	24 58	27 25	29♓59	02 41	05 28	08 22	11 21	14 27	17 37	20♓53
1943	15♒07	17 52	20 41	23 36	26 36	29♓41	02 50	06 04	09 23	12 47	16 15	19 49	23 28	27 12	01♈01	04♈55
1944	26♒26	29♓48	03 15	06 45	10 20	14 00	17 44	21 32	25 25	29♈22	03 22	07 24	11 27	15 28	19 26	23♈17
1945	10♓10	13 58	17 48	21 41	25 35	29♈28	03 19	07 05	10 42	14 07	17 16	20 05	22 32	24 33	26 07	27♈12
1946	24♓31	27 50	00♈55	03 39	06 00	07 52	09 13	10 00	10 R13	09 54	09 04	07 49	06 16	04 34	02 50	01♈14
1947	23♓R01	22 19	21 03	19 23	17 27	15 28	13 35	11 56	10 39	09 46	09 17	09 D13	09 32	10 12	11 11	12♓26
1948	22♒R04	21 36	21 D36	22 01	22 47	23 52	25 14	26 51	28 40	00♓41	02 52	05 12	07 41	10 17	13 00	15♓49
1949	13♒07	15 16	17 35	20 01	22 34	25 14	28 00	00♓52	03 49	06 52	10 00	13 13	16 31	19 55	23 24	26♓58
1950	19♒11	22 13	25 20	28♓31	01 46	05 06	08 31	12 00	15 35	19 14	22 58	26 46	00♈40	04 38	08 40	12♈45
1951	00♓48	04 20	07 57	11 38	15 24	19 13	23 06	27 02	01♈00	05 00	08 58	12 53	16 41	21 20	23 47	26♈57
1952	17♓17	21 07	24 56	28♈41	02 20	05 48	09 03	11 59	14 34	16 43	18 25	19 36	20 R16	20 24	20 04	19♈16
1953	28♓08	00♈11	01 42	02 39	02 R59	02 45	01 57	00♓41	29 04	27 15	25 26	23 42	22 13	21 03	20 15	19♓51
1954	10♓R43	08 37	06 36	04 49	03 24	02 24	01 D51	01 43	01 59	02 37	03 34	04 49	06 19	08 03	09 59	12♓06
1955	15♒01	15 55	17 07	18 35	20 18	22 12	24 17	26 32	28♓55	01 27	04 05	06 49	09 41	12 38	15 41	18♓49
1956	15♒11	17 50	20 34	23 24	26 20	29♓20	02 25	05 36	08 51	12 10	15 35	19 05	22 40	26 21	00♈06	03♈57
1957	24♒15	27 32	00♓53	04 18	07 47	11 22	15 00	18 44	22 32	26 24	00♈21	04 21	08 24	12 28	16 31	20♈32
1958	07♓26	11 10	14 57	18 48	22 42	26 37	00♈32	04 25	08 14	11 56	15 27	18 43	21 41	24 18	26 31	28♈17
1959	22♓11	25 46	29♈11	02 23	05 16	07 47	09 52	11 27	12 30	12 R59	12 56	12 21	11 19	09 57	08 21	06♈39
1960	25♓50	25 R43	25 00	23 45	22 06	20 12	18 15	16 24	14 48	13 32	12 39	12 11	12 D07	12 26	13 05	14♓04
1961	26♒R21	25 13	24 33	24 D20	24 33	25 09	26 05	27 19	28 48	00♒31	02 26	04 32	06 48	09 12	11 44	14♒24
1962	12♒55	14 49	16 53	19 07	21 30	24 00	26 37	29♓20	02 09	05 04	08 05	11 10	14 22	17 38	21 00	24♓28
1963	17♒28	20 23	23 24	26 29	29♓39	02 53	06 12	09 35	13 04	16 37	20 15	23 58	27 46	01♈39	05 37	09♈39
1964	13♓40	17 54	22 02	26 04	29 58	03 44	07 24	10 55	14♈19	17 35	20 43	23 44	26 37	29 22	01 58	04 26
1965	14♓29	18 19	22 10	26 01	29♈49	03 32	07 05	10 27	13 31	16 16	18 36	20 30	21 55	22 50	23 R14	23♈09
1966	27♓12	29♈51	02 05	03 50	05 02	05 R39	05 42	05 09	04 07	02 41	01 00	29♓12	27 26	25 51	24 32	23♓34
1967	16♓R12	14 22	12 20	10 17	08 25	06 50	05 39	04 54	04 D34	04 38	05 06	05 54	07 00	08 22	09 59	11♓48
1968	17♒14	17 47	18 40	19 52	21 21	23 03	24 57	27 02	29♓17	01 40	04 11	06 50	09 35	12 26	15 24	18♓27
1969	14♒07	16 36	19 12	21 54	24 41	27 34	00♓33	03 36	06 45	09 58	13 16	16 40	20 09	23 42	27 22	01♈06
1970	22♒10	25 22	28♓37	01 57	05 21	08 50	12 24	16 02	19 44	23 32	27 24	01♈20	05 20	09 23	13 28	17♈33
1971	04♓48	08 27	12 11	15 58	19 49	23 43	27 39	01♈36	05 31	09 23	13 09	16 45	20 08	23 14	26 00	28♈24
1972	21♓30	25 12	28♈47	02 12	05 22	08 14	10 43	12 45	14 18	15 20	15 48	15 R45	15 11	14 11	12 51	11♈17
1973	27♓37	28 25	28 R34	28 08	27 08	25 41	23 55	22 01	20 08	18 25	17 00	15 57	15 17	15 D01	15 08	15♓37
1974	01♓R31	29♒48	28 29	27 36	27 11	27 D12	27 37	28 23	29 28	00 49	02 26	04 15	06 15	08 26	10 46	13♓15
1975	13♒13	14 47	16 34	18 33	20 43	23 01	25 27	28 01	00♓41	03 28	06 21	09 19	12 23	15 32	18 47	22♓07
1976	17♒18	20 09	23 06	26 07	29♓13	02 23	05 38	08 58	12 23	15♈52	19 27	23 06	26 51	00♈41	04 35	08♈35
1977	27♒43	01♓08	04 37	08 10	11 48	15 30	19 16	23 07	27 02	01 00	05 01	09 03	13 04	17 02	20 54	24♈37
1978	11♓41	15 30	19 21	23 13	27 06	00♈57	04 43	08 21	11 48	15 01	17 54	20 25	22 31	24 09	25 18	25♈58
1979	25♓34	28♈42	01 30	03 56	05 54	07 20	08 13	08 R31	08 16	07 28	06 15	04 42	02 59	01 13	29♓34	28♓07
1980	20♓R17	18 51	17 02	15 02	13 02	11 12	09 39	08 30	07 45	07 D26	07 30	07 58	08 45	09 51	11 13	12♓49
1981	19♒R57	19 D53	20 14	20 57	22 00	23 21	24 56	26 44	28 44	00♓54	03 13	05 40	08 15	10 57	13 46	16♓41
1982	13♒20	15 38	18 03	20 36	23 15	26 00	38♓50	01 46	04 48	07 55	11 06	14 23	17 45	21 12	24 45	28♓23
1983	20♒12	23 18	26 28	29♓42	03 01	06 24	09 52	13 24	17 01	20 43	24 30	28♈21	02 17	06 18	10 21	14♈27
1984	03♓59	07 36	11 17	15 02	18 52	22 44	26 40	00♈37	04 35	08 32	12 25	16 10	19 46	23 07	26 12	28♈57
1985	18♓47	22 35	26 20	29♈59	03 30	06 47	09 47	12 26	14 41	16 27	17 43	18 R27	18 39	18 21	17 36	16♈27
1986	28♓11	29♈48	00 51	01 R18	01 08	00♓24	29 10	27 34	25 45	23 52	22 06	20 33	19 20	18 29	18 D01	17♓57
1987	07♓R15	05 11	03 20	01 50	00 46	00♒D08	29♓57	00 10	00 46	01 42	02 55	04 24	06 06	08 01	10 07	12♓22
1988	14♒39	15 57	17 31	19 19	21 18	23 27	25 45	28 11	00♓45	03 26	06 13	09 06	12 05	15 09	18 19	21♓35
1989	15♒52	18 36	21 25	24 19	27 19	00♓23	03 32	06 45	10 04	13 27	16 55	20 29	24 07	27 51	01 40	05♈34
1990	25♒28	28♓47	02 11	05 39	09 12	12 48	16 30	20 16	24 06	28 01	01♈59	05 00	10 03	14 06	18 06	22♈02
1991	08♓56	12 41	16 30	20 22	24 16	28♈10	02 03	05 52	09 35	13 08	16 27	19 29	22 10	24 27	26 18	27♈40
1992	25♓12	28♈34	01 40	04 27	06 50	08 46	10 10	11 01	11 R19	11 03	10 16	09 05	07 34	05 53	04 09	02♈32
1993	24♓R08	23 29	22 18	20 40	18 46	16 46	14 52	13 12	11 52	10 56	10 D25	10 18	10 34	11 12	12 08	13♓22
1994	23♒R39	22 54	22 38	22 47	23 20	24 14	25 26	26 54	28 35	00♓29	02 34	04 49	07 12	09 43	12 22	15♓08
1995	12♒55	14 59	17 12	19 33	22 02	24 38	27 20	00♓09	03 03	06 02	09 07	12 17	15 32	18 52	22 18	25♓49
1996	19♒53	22 55	26 01	29♓12	02 27	05 47	09 11	12 40	16 14	19 53	23 36	27 25	01♈18	05 16	09 18	13♈23
1997	01♓28	05 00	08 36	12 17	16 02	19 51	23 44	27 40	01♈38	05 38	09 36	13 32	17 21	21 02	24 30	27♈42
1998	16♓01	19 51	23 41	27♈28	01 11	04 47	08 10	11 18	14 06	16 32	18 30	20 00	20 59	21 R27	21 25	20♈53
1999	27♓44	00♈03	01 54	03 12	03 R55	04 02	03 34	02 34	01 10	29♓28	27 38	25 50	24 11	22 49	21 47	21♓09
2000	12♓R00	09 55	07 53	06 04	04 37	03 34	02 D58	02 47	03 00	03 36	04 31	05 44	07 12	08 55	10 49	12♓54

April

	1st	3rd	5th	7th	9th	11th	13th	15th	17th	19th	21st	23rd	25th	27th	29th
1900	28♓R37	27 35	26 53	26 D33	26 36	26 59	27 41	28 42	29♈58	01 30	03 14	05 12	07 20	09 39	12♈07
1901	13♓04	14 50	16 47	18 55	21 14	23 41	26 16	29♈00	01 51	04 49	07 54	11 07	14 26	17 52	21♈25
1902	16♓33	19 33	22 39	25 51	29♈09	02 33	06 04	09 40	13 23	17 12	21 07	25 08	29♉15	03 27	07♉42
1903	28♓07	01♈50	05 39	09 33	13 33	17 37	21 46	25 58	00♉11	04 25	08 36	12 42	16 41	20 30	24♉07
1904	16♈15	20 22	24 26	28♉26	02 18	05 59	09 28	12 40	15 35	18 11	20 27	22 21	23 54	25 05	25♉53
1905	29♈01	01♉28	03 32	05 10	06 22	07 07	07 R26	07 20	06 50	06 01	04 55	03 38	02 17	00 57	29♈44
1906	17♈R30	16 09	14 38	13 02	11 30	10 08	09 00	08 11	07 D42	07 33	07 45	08 17	09 06	10 13	11♈35
1907	18♓41	18 53	19 26	20 17	21 27	22 51	24 30	26 22	28 25	00♈38	03 01	05 34	08 14	11 03	14♈00
1908	13♓34	16 00	18 35	21 17	24 06	27 02	00♈05	03 14	06 30	09 53	13 22	16 58	20 40	24 29	28♉25
1909	21♓22	24 42	28 08	01♈40	05 18	09 02	12 52	16 48	20 49	24 56	29♉07	03 22	07 39	11 56	16♉10
1910	05♈16	09 15	13 19	17 26	21 36	25 47	29♉58	04 05	08 06	11 59	15 41	19 10	22 24	25 21	28♉01
1911	21♈51	25 40	29♉20	02 46	05 56	08 47	11 18	13 27	15 13	16 36	17 34	18 R09	18 20	18 09	17♉37
1912	28♈39	29 26	29 R44	29 36	29 02	28 07	26 55	25 33	24 06	22 41	21 24	20 20	19 32	19 D03	18♈52
1913	03♈R43	02 15	01 04	00♓12	29 D41	29 32	29 44	00♈17	01 07	02 15	03 38	05 16	07 06	09 08	11♈22
1914	13♓43	15 07	16 46	18 37	20 40	22 53	25 16	27 47	00♈27	03 14	06 09	09 12	12 21	15 38	19♈02
1915	15♓02	17 52	20 50	23 53	27 03	00♈19	03 42	07 10	10 44	14 25	18 13	22 06	26♉06	00 12	04♉23
1916	27♓21	01 00	04♈45	08 35	12 31	16 32	20 38	24 49	29♉02	03 16	07 31	11 42	15 48	19 46	23♉34
1917	13♈06	17 14	21 22	25 29	29♉32	03 27	07 14	10 47	14 07	17 09	19 54	22 19	24 24	26 08	27♉31
1918	27♈41	00 38	03♉15	05 29	07 20	08 45	09 44	10 R17	10 25	10 09	09 32	08 36	07 27	06 10	04♉50
1919	21♈R46	20 58	19 49	18 24	16 52	15 19	13 53	12 38	11 40	11 00	10 D41	10 41	11 02	11 42	12♈39
1920	21♓R50	21 D39	21 51	22 23	23 14	24 22	25 46	27 24	29♈15	01 18	03 31	05 54	08 26	11 07	13♈56
1921	13♓00	15 13	17 35	20 05	22 44	25 30	28 23	01♈23	04 29	07 43	11 03	14 30	18 03	21 44	25♈31
1922	19♓19	22 32	25 51	29♈15	02 45	06 22	10 04	13 52	17 47	21 47	25 53	00♉04	04 18	08 35	12♉53
1923	02♈22	06 15	10 13	14 16	18 24	22 34	26 46	00♉58	05 07	09 12	13 09	16 55	20 30	23 50	26♉55
1924	20♈57	24 55	28♉44	02 23	05 47	08 56	11 46	14 16	16 24	18 10	19 33	20 33	21 09	21 R23	21♉14
1925	29♈29	00♉58	01 59	02 R33	02 39	02 19	01 37	00♈35	29 20	27 56	26 32	25 11	24 01	23 05	22♈25
1926	09♈R09	07 30	05 58	04 39	03 38	02 56	02 D36	02 37	02 58	03 39	04 37	05 52	07 22	09 05	11♈01
1927	14♓59	15 59	17 15	18 47	20 31	22 28	24 36	26 54	29♈21	01 56	04 40	07 32	10 31	13 37	16♈51
1928	15♓04	17 49	20 40	23 38	26 42	29♈52	03 09	06 32	10 02	13 38	17 20	21 09	25 04	29♉06	03♉13
1929	24♓52	28♈24	02 02	05 45	09 34	13 29	17 29	21 35	25 45	29♉58	04 13	08 29	12 42	16 50	20♉52
1930	09♈58	14 04	18 12	22 21	26 30	00♉35	04 34	08 25	12 04	15 30	18 40	21 32	24 06	26 21	28♉16
1931	25♈43	29♉06	02 11	04 57	07 22	09 23	11 01	12 13	13 00	13 R23	13 21	12 56	12 12	11 12	10♉01
1932	25♈R02	24 40	23 54	22 47	21 25	19 56	18 25	17 00	15 46	14 48	14 08	13 D47	13 47	14 06	14♈44
1933	25♓R47	25 03	24 D41	24 41	25 02	25 43	26 42	27 58	29♈28	01 12	03 08	05 16	07 34	10 02	12♈38
1934	12♓51	14 47	16 54	19 12	21 38	24 12	26 55	29♈45	02 42	05 46	08 57	12 14	15 39	19 10	22♈48
1935	17♓28	20 33	23 44	27 00	00♈23	03 51	07 26	11 07	14 54	18 47	22 46	26 51	01♉00	05 15	09♉32
1936	01♈29	05 18	09 13	13 13	17 17	21 26	25 38	29♉51	04 03	08 13	12 17	16 13	19 59	23 32	26♉51
1937	17♈56	22 01	26 01	29♉55	03 38	07 09	10 25	13 23	16 02	18 20	20 18	21 53	23 05	23 54	24♈21
1938	29♈22	01♉29	03 11	04 26	05 14	05 R35	05 30	05 01	04 11	03 05	01 47	00♈24	29 02	27 47	26♈44
1939	14♈R30	12 57	11 20	09 45	08 20	07 10	06 19	05 D48	05 37	05 48	06 18	07 07	08 12	09 34	11♈09
1940	17♓13	17 54	18 53	20 09	21 40	23 24	25 20	27 28	29♈45	02 12	04 48	07 32	10 24	13 23	16♈30
1941	13♓59	16 33	19 13	22 02	24 57	27 58	01♈06	04 21	07 42	11 09	14 43	18 23	22 11	26 04	00♉04
1942	22♓34	25 58	29♈28	03 04	06 46	10 34	14 28	18 27	22 32	26 41	00♉55	05 10	09 27	13 42	17♉53
1943	06♈55	10 56	15 02	19 10	23 20	27 30	01♉38	05 40	09 35	13 19	16 51	20 07	23 08	25 50	28♉15
1944	25♈09	28♉45	02 06	05 10	07 55	10 19	12 19	13 57	15 10	15 58	16 R22	16 22	16 01	15 19	14♉22
1945	27♈33	27 55	27 R48	27 15	26 20	25 08	23 44	22 15	20 49	19 30	18 23	17 34	17 03	16 D51	17♈00
1946	00♈30	29♓16	28 21	27 48	27 D37	27 47	28 18	29 07	00♈14	01 36	03 13	05 03	07 04	09 17	11♈39
1947	13♓10	14 48	16 38	18 40	20 52	23 13	25 44	28 23	01♈09	04 03	07 04	10 12	13 27	16 50	20♈19
1948	17♓17	20 16	23 22	26 33	29♈51	03 14	06 44	10 20	14 02	17 51	21 45	25 46	29♉53	04 04	08♉20
1949	29♓R47	02♈D30	06 18	10 12	14 11	18 15	22 24	26 36	00♉49	05 03	09 15	13 21	17 21	21 11	24♉50
1950	14♈49	18 56	23 02	27 05	01♉02	04 51	08 27	11 49	14 55	17 43	20 11	22 19	24 05	25 30	26♉32
1951	28♈25	01♉06	03 24	05 18	06 47	07 48	08 R24	08 33	08 18	07 41	06 45	05 35	04 16	02 55	01♉37
1952	18♈R44	17 26	15 56	14 21	12 48	11 24	10 15	09 24	08 52	08 D41	08 50	09 19	10 07	11 12	12♈32
1953	19♓D47	19 56	20 27	21 16	22 23	23 46	25 23	27 13	29♈15	01 27	03 49	06 21	09 00	11 49	14♈45
1954	13♓13	15 34	18 03	20 40	23 25	26 17	29♈16	02 21	05 33	08 52	12 17	15 49	19 27	23 13	27♈05
1955	20♓26	23 43	27 06	00♈34	04 09	07 49	11 35	15 28	19 26	23 30	27 38	01♉51	06 07	10 25	14♉41
1956	05♈55	09 53	13 56	18 04	22 14	26 25	00♉36	04 43	08 46	12 40	16 23	19 53	23 09	26 08	28♊50
1957	22♈30	26 21	00♉02	03 29	06 41	09 34	12 07	14 19	16 08	17 33	18 35	19 13	19 R27	19 18	18♉49
1958	29♈00	00♉05	00 R41	00 50	00 31	29♈49	28 48	27 31	26 06	24 40	23 18	22 05	21 07	20 26	20♈D04
1959	05♈R49	04 14	02 52	01 48	01 04	00 D42	00 41	01 01	01 40	02 37	03 51	05 20	07 02	08 57	11♈03
1960	14♓39	16 02	17 39	19 29	21 30	23 42	26 04	28 34	01♈13	04 00	06 54	09 56	13 04	16 20	19♈43
1961	15♓46	18 37	21 33	24 36	27 45	01♈01	04 22	07 50	11 24	15 05	18 52	22 45	26 44	00♉50	05♉00
1962	26♓14	29♈49	03 31	07 18	11 10	15 09	19 12	23 20	27 32	01♉46	06 01	10 14	14 24	18 27	22♉21
1963	11♈41	15 48	19 56	24 04	28♉10	02 10	06 02	09 44	13 12	16 25	19 21	21 58	24 15	26 13	27♉49
1964	28♈25	01♉24	04 04	06 20	08 13	09 41	10 44	11 20	11 R31	11 18	10 44	09 51	08 43	07 30	06♉07
1965	22♈R55	22 10	21 03	19 41	18 09	16 37	15 09	13 53	12 53	12 11	11 D49	11 47	12 05	12 42	13♈37
1966	23♓R13	22 D48	22 46	23 06	23 45	24 43	25 57	27 27	29♈10	01 05	03 12	05 29	07 55	10 31	13♈15
1967	12♓48	14 54	17 10	19 35	22 09	24 50	27 39	00♈35	03 38	06 47	10 03	13 26	16 56	20 32	24♈15
1968	20♓01	23 14	26 32	19 56	03♈25	07 01	10 43	14 31	18 25	22 25	26 30	00♉41	04 55	09 12	13♉30
1969	03♈01	06 53	10 51	14 54	19 01	23 11	27 23	01♉35	05 45	09 50	13 48	17 36	21 12	24 33	27♉40
1970	19♈35	23 36	27 31	01♉16	04 50	08 08	11 10	13 52	16 13	18 13	19 51	21 05	21 56	22 23	22♉R28
1971	29♈26	01♉12	02 30	03 21	03 44	03 R41	03 12	02 22	01 15	29♈56	28 32	27 08	25 51	24 46	23♈56
1972	10♈R27	08 48	07 15	05 55	04 51	04 07	03 44	03 D43	04 02	04 40	05 36	06 49	08 17	09 59	11♈53
1973	15♓59	16 57	18 12	19 41	21 25	23 20	25 26	27 43	00♈09	02 44	05 26	08 17	11 15	14 21	17♈34
1974	14♓32	17 12	19 59	22 52	25 53	29♈00	02 13	05 32	08 58	12 30	16 09	19 54	23 45	27 43	01♉47
1975	23♓49	27 18	00♈52	04 32	08 18	12 09	16 07	20 09	24 17	28♉28	02 43	06 59	11 13	15 25	19♉31
1976	10♈36	14 42	18 50	22 59	27 08	01♉14	05 14	09 06	12 46	16 13	19 25	22 20	24 56	27 13	29♊11
1977	26♈25	29♉49	02 56	05 45	08 12	10 16	11 56	13 12	14 02	14 R27	14 28	14 07	13 25	12 27	11♉18
1978	26♈R06	26 02	25 30	24 36	23 23	21 58	20 27	18 58	17 37	16 29	15 37	15 04	14 D52	14 59	15♈25
1979	27♓R31	26 33	25 57	25 D44	25 52	26 21	27 09	28 15	29♈36	01 12	03 00	05 01	07 12	09 34	12♈05
1980	13♓42	15 37	17 43	19 59	22 25	24 58	27 40	00♈29	03 25	06 28	09 39	12 56	16 19	19 50	23♈28
1981	18♓11	21 15	24 25	27 41	01♈03	04 31	08 05	11 45	15 32	19 24	23 23	27 27	01♉37	05 51	10♉08
1982	00♈14	04 00	07 52	11 49	15 51	19 58	24 08	28♉20	02 34	06 45	10 53	14 54	18 47	22 28	25♉55
1983	16♈30	20 36	24 39	28♉37	02 27	06 06	09 31	12 40	15 31	18 02	20 13	22 02	23 28	24 32	25♉13
1984	00♉11	02 21	04 06	05 24	06 15	06 R40	06 38	06 12	05 24	04 29	03 04	01 42	00♈20	29 03	27♈58
1985	15♈R45	14 14	12 37	11 02	09 36	08 24	07 30	06 56	06 D44	06 52	07 19	08 06	09 09	10 29	12♈03
1986	18♓03	18 32	19 20	20 25	21 47	23 23	25 12	27 13	29♈24	01 45	04 15	06 54	09 41	12 36	15♈39
1987	13♓33	16 01	18 38	21 22	24 12	27 10	00♈14	03 25	06 42	10 05	13 35	17 12	20 55	24 45	28♉42
1988	23♓15	26 39	00♈09	03 44	07 26	11 13	15 06	19 05	23 09	27 19	01♉32	05 47	10 04	14 19	18♉31
1989	07♈32	11 34	15 39	19 47	23 58	28♉08	02 16	06 19	10 15	14 00	17 33	20 52	23 54	26 39	29♊05
1990	23♈57	27 40	01♉10	04 25	07 22	09 59	12 14	14 05	15 34	16 37	17 16	17 R31	17 23	16 54	16♉07
1991	28♈11	38 R51	29 01	28 45	28 03	27 01	25 44	24 18	22 49	21 25	20 11	19 11	18 28	18 D04	18♈00
1992	01♈R47	00 31	29♓34	28 58	28 D44	28 52	29 20	00♈07	01 12	02 32	04 07	05 55	07 55	10 06	12♈28
1993	14♓04	15 40	17 29	19 29	21 40	24 01	26 30	29♈08	01 54	04 47	07 47	10 54	14 09	17 30	20♈58
1994	16♓33	19 28	22 30	25 38	28♈52	02 12	05 38	09 10	12 49	16 34	20 25	24 22	28♉25	02 34	06♉47
1995	27♓37	01♈16	05 01	08 52	12 48	16 49	20 55	25 05	29♉18	03 32	07 46	11 56	16 00	19 57	23♉42
1996	15♈26	19 34	23 40	27 44	01♉42	05 31	09 09	12 33	15 41	18 30	21 01	23 11	25 00	26 27	27♉33
1997	29♈11	01♉54	04 15	06 12	07 43	08 48	09 27	09 39	09 27	08 53	07 59	06 51	05 33	04 12	02♉54
1998	20♈R28	19 22	17 59	16 26	14 51	13 21	12 03	11 00	10 16	09 D52	09 49	10 06	10 42	11 36	12♈46
1999	20♓R58	20 D53	21 11	21 49	22 45	23 58	25 27	27 09	29♈03	01 09	03 25	05 51	08 25	11 09	14♈00
2000	14♓01	16 21	18 49	21 26	24 10	27 01	29♈59	03 04	06 15	09 33	12 58	16 29	20 07	23 52	27♈43

Mercury

May

	1st	3rd	5th	7th	9th	11th	13th	15th	17th	19th	21st	23rd	25th	27th	29th	31st
1900	14♈45	17 31	20 26	23 29	26 40	29♉59	03 26	07 01	10 45	14 36	18 34	22 41	26 43	01♊11	05 33	09♊57
1901	25♈05	28♉53	02 47	06 28	10 55	15 08	19 47	23 48	28 10	02 32	06 50	11 04	15 10	19 08	22 57	25♊35
1902	12♉01	16 20	20 37	24 51	28♊59	02 58	06 47	10 25	13 51	17 04	20 04	22 49	25 21	27 38	29♋40	01♋27
1903	27♉31	00♊40	03 33	06 09	08 28	10 30	12 14	13 38	14 44	15 31	15 R58	16 06	15 54	15 27	14 44	13♊50
1904	26♉R19	26 23	26 07	25 32	24 43	23 41	22 32	21 21	20 13	19 11	18 21	17 45	17 D26	17 24	17 39	18♉13
1905	28♈R42	27 54	27 24	27 D13	27 20	27 46	28 29	29♉30	00 46	02 18	04 03	06 02	08 13	10 36	13 10	15♉55
1906	13♈12	15 01	17 03	19 16	21 40	24 13	26 56	29♉48	02 50	06 00	09 19	12 46	16 23	20 08	24 01	28♉03
1907	17♈05	20 17	23 37	27 04	00♉39	04 21	08 12	12 09	16 14	20 25	24 41	29♊02	03 25	07 48	12 10	16♊28
1908	02♉27	06 35	10 49	15 07	19 27	23 48	28♊08	02 24	06 35	10 37	14 31	18 14	21 46	25 06	28 14	01♋10
1909	20♉20	24 24	28♊17	02 00	05 31	08 49	11 52	14 40	17 14	19 32	21 34	23 19	24 48	25 59	26 51	27♊25
1910	00♊23	02 26	04 09	05 32	06 36	07 18	07 R41	07 43	07 25	06 53	06 04	05 05	04 00	02 51	01 46	00♊47
1911	16♉R48	15 45	14 34	13 19	12 06	11 00	10 04	09 23	08 D58	08 51	09 02	09 32	10 19	11 22	12 42	14♉17
1912	19♈02	19 30	20 16	21 20	22 29	24 13	26 00	28 00	00♉12	02 35	05 08	07 52	10 46	13 50	17 03	20♉26
1913	13♈45	16 18	19 00	21 51	24 50	27 58	01♉13	04 37	08 10	11 50	15 38	19 35	23 39	27 50	02♊06	06♊27
1914	22♈32	26 10	29♉55	03 48	07 47	11 53	16 05	20 22	24 42	29♊05	03 27	07 28	12 03	16 12	20 13	24♊05
1915	08♉38	12 57	17 17	21 35	25 51	00♊01	04 04	07 57	11 40	15 11	18 29	21 35	24 27	27 06	29♋30	01♋40
1916	27♉10	00♊32	03 40	06 32	09 08	11 27	13 30	15 14	16 40	17 48	18 37	19 06	19 R17	19 08	18 43	18♊03
1917	28♉32	29 11	29 R29	29 25	29 02	28 23	27 29	26 25	25 16	24 06	23 00	22 04	21 19	20 49	21 D36	20♉40
1918	03♉R34	02 26	01 30	00 50	00 D28	00 24	00 39	01 12	02 03	03 10	04 32	06 09	08 00	10 04	12 21	14♉49
1919	13♈52	15 21	17 03	18 58	21 05	23 23	25 51	28 29	01♉17	04 14	07 20	10 35	13 59	17 32	21 14	25♉05
1920	23♈13	25 40	28 07	00 34	03♉01	05 28	07 56	10 23	12 50	15 17	17 44	20 11	22♊38	25 06	27 33	30♊00
1921	29♈25	03♉26	07 33	11 45	16 02	20 23	24 44	29♊05	03 23	07 36	11 41	15 38	19 25	23 03	26 27	29♊40
1922	17♉09	21 22	25 28	29♊26	03 13	06 49	10 12	13 22	16 17	18 58	21 24	23 34	25 29	27 07	28 28	29♊32
1923	29♉43	02♊13	04 25	06 19	07 54	09 09	10 03	10 38	10 R53	10 49	10 26	09 47	08 56	07 54	06 48	05♊40
1924	20♉R45	19 59	18 59	17 50	16 37	15 25	14 18	13 22	12 40	12 13	12 D04	12 13	12 40	13 25	14 26	15♉44
1925	22♈R04	22 D02	22 20	22 56	23 49	24 59	26 24	28 04	29♉56	02 01	04 18	06 46	09 25	12 14	15 13	18♉22
1926	13♈08	15 26	17 54	20 31	23 18	26 13	19♉17	02 29	05 50	09 19	12 57	16 42	20 36	24 38	28♊47	03♊02
1927	20♈12	23 40	27 16	00♉59	04 49	08 46	12 51	17 01	21 17	25 37	29♊30	04 23	08 44	13 01	17 13	21♊17
1928	07♉26	11 43	16 02	20 22	24 41	28♊56	03 08	07 07	10 59	14 41	18 10	21 28	24 33	27 25	00♋30	02♋28
1929	23♉54	23♊08	22 31	22 04	21 47	21 39	21 41	21 52	22 11	22 39	23 15	23 58	24 48	25 R44	26 49	27♊58
1930	29♉51	01♊04	01 56	02 R26	02 36	02 25	01 56	01 12	00♉15	29 09	28 00	26 52	25 50	24 58	24 18	23♉55
1931	08♉R44	07 26	06 14	05 12	04 23	03 D50	03 36	03 39	04 01	04 41	05 38	06 51	08 20	10 03	11 59	14♉09
1932	15♈40	16 52	18 20	20 01	21 55	24 01	26 18	28♉46	01 24	04 12	07 09	10 16	13 31	16 56	20 30	24♉14
1933	15♈23	18 17	21 18	24 28	27 45	01♉11	04 44	08 25	12 14	16 11	20 15	24 25	28♊42	03 03	07 26	11♊50
1934	26♈34	00♉26	04 25	08 30	12 41	16 58	21 18	25 40	00♊01	04 21	08 36	12 44	16 45	20 35	24 16	27♊45
1935	13♉50	18 08	22 23	26 32	00♊33	04 25	08 05	11 34	14 49	17 51	20 38	23 12	25 30	27 34	29♋21	00♋52
1936	29♉55	02♊42	05 12	07 24	09 19	10 54	12 11	13 07	13 45	14 R02	14 00	13 40	13 04	12 15	11 15	10♊09
1937	24♉R26	24 09	23 34	22 44	21 41	20 31	19 19	18 10	17 08	16 17	15 41	15 D21	15 19	15 34	16 08	16♉59
1938	25♈R55	25 24	25 D11	25 17	25 42	26 25	27 26	28 42	00♉13	01 58	03 56	06 06	08 28	11 01	13 45	16♉39
1939	12♈58	14 59	17 11	19 34	22 06	24 48	27 39	00♉39	03 48	07 05	10 31	14 05	17 48	21 40	25 39	29♉46
1940	19♈45	23 07	26 36	00♉13	03 57	07 49	11 48	15 53	20 05	24 23	28♊44	03 07	07 30	11 51	16 07	20♊17
1941	04♉11	08 22	12 38	16 58	21 18	25♊38	29 56	04 07	08 12	12 08	15 53	19 28	22 50	26 00	28♋58	01♋43
1942	21♉57	25 53	29♊39	03 12	06 32	09 38	12 29	15 04	17 24	19 28	21 14	22 43	23 55	24 48	25 22	25♊R37
1943	00♊20	02 05	03 30	04 34	05 17	05 R40	05 42	05 25	04 51	04 02	03 02	01 56	00 47	29♉42	28 43	27♉55
1944	13♉R14	11 58	10 42	09 31	08 28	07 39	07 05	06 D48	06 50	07 10	07 48	08 43	09 54	11 21	13 03	14♉58
1945	17♈27	18 13	19 16	20 34	22 07	23 54	26 54	28 05	00♉27	03 00	05 42	08 35	11 37	14 49	18 10	21♉41
1946	14♈11	16 52	19 42	22 40	25 46	29♉01	02 23	05 53	09 32	13 18	17 12	21 14	25 23	29♊38	03 58	08♊21
1947	23♈55	27 38	01♉28	05 25	09 29	13 39	17 54	22 14	26 36	00♊58	05 19	09 36	13 47	17 50	21 44	25♊28
1948	12♉38	16 57	21 15	25 29	29♊37	03 38	07 28	11 07	14 34	17 29	20 50	23 37	26 10	28 29	00♋33	02♋21
1949	28♉15	01♊25	04 19	06 58	09 19	11 23	13 09	14 36	15 44	16 33	17 02	17 R13	17 05	16 39	15 58	15♊05
1950	27♉12	27 R30	27 27	27 04	26 23	25 29	24 24	23 14	22 03	20 57	20 00	29 15	18 45	18 D31	18 36	18♉58
1951	00♉R27	29♈30	28 49	28 D26	28 21	28 36	29 08	29♉58	01 05	02 27	04 03	05 54	07 57	10 13	12 40	15♉18
1952	14♈06	15 54	17 55	20 06	22 28	25 01	27 43	00♉34	03 34	06 43	10 01	13 28	17 03	20 48	24 40	28♉41
1953	17♈48	21 00	24 19	27 45	01♉19	05 01	08 51	12 47	16 51	21 02	25 18	29♊38	04 01	08 25	12 47	17♊05
1954	01♉03	05 08	09 19	13 34	17 53	22 14	26 35	00♊54	05 08	09 15	13 15	17 04	20 43	24 10	27 26	00♋29
1955	18♉54	23 02	27 02	00♊51	04 30	07 55	11 07	14 05	16 48	19 15	21 27	23 23	25 03	26 25	27 29	28♊15
1956	01♊14	03 19	05 05	06 31	07 37	08 22	08 R47	08 52	08 38	08 07	07 20	06 23	05 18	04 10	03 04	02♊04
1957	18♉R03	17 02	15 52	14 37	13 24	12 16	11 19	10 36	10 09	09 D59	10 08	10 35	11 20	12 21	13 39	15♉11
1958	20♈01	20 17	20 53	21 45	22 55	24 19	25 58	27 50	29♉55	02 11	04 38	07 16	10 03	13 01	16 09	19♉26
1959	13♈21	15 48	18 24	21 10	24 04	27 06	00♉17	03 36	07 03	10 39	14 23	18 14	22 14	26 21	00♊34	04♊53
1960	23♈13	16 51	00♉35	04 27	08 26	12 31	16 42	20 59	25 20	29♊42	04 05	08 25	12 41	16 51	20 53	24♊46
1961	09♉15	13 37	17 53	22 12	26 28	00♊39	04 43	08 37	12 21	15 53	19 13	22 20	25 13	27 53	00♋20	02♋32
1962	26♉04	29♊35	02 52	05 53	08 39	11 09	13 22	16 17	16 55	18 15	19 15	19 57	20 19	20 R23	20 08	19♊37
1963	29♉03	29♊36	00 28	00 R37	00 27	29♉57	29 12	28 14	27 08	25 58	24 50	23 47	22 54	22 15	21 51	21♉44
1964	04♉R51	03 41	02 44	02 02	01 38	01 D31	01 44	02 15	03 03	04 08	05 28	07 04	08 53	10 55	13 10	15♉36
1965	14♈49	16 15	17 56	19 49	21 54	24 11	26 38	29♉15	02 01	04 57	08 02	11 17	14 40	18 12	21 53	25♉43
1966	16♈08	19 08	22 16	25 32	28♉56	02 27	06 06	09 53	13 48	17 50	21 58	26 13	00♊33	04 55	09 19	13♊42
1967	28♈05	02♉02	06 05	10 15	14 29	18 48	23 09	27 31	01♊51	06 07	10 17	14 19	18 13	21 55	25 27	28♊48
1968	27♉11	29 39	02 06	04♊34	07 01	09 29	11 56	14 23	16 51	19 18	21 46	24 13	26 40	29 08	01♋35	04♋24
1969	00♊30	03 02	05 17	07 13	08 50	10 07	11 04	11 42	11 R59	11 57	11 37	11 01	10 11	09 11	08 04	06♊57
1970	22♉R12	21 37	20 45	19 42	18 31	17 17	16 07	15 04	14 13	13 36	13 16	13 D13	13 29	14 02	14 53	16♉01
1971	23♈R23	23 D09	23 15	23 39	24 22	25 21	26 37	28 08	29 52	01♉49	03 59	06 20	08 52	11 35	14 28	17♉31
1972	13♈59	16 15	18 42	21 19	24 04	26 59	00♉02	03 13	06 33	10 01	13 37	17 23	21 16	25 17	29♊25	03♊40
1973	20♈55	24 22	27 57	01♉39	05 29	09 26	13 29	17 39	21 55	26 15	00♊37	05 00	09 22	13 40	17 52	21♊56
1974	05♉57	10 12	14 30	18 50	23 10	27 28	01♊41	05 47	09 45	13 33	17 10	20 35	23 47	26 47	29♋34	02♋07
1975	23♉29	27 17	00♊53	04 16	07 24	10 17	12 55	15 17	17 22	19 09	20 40	21 52	22 45	23 19	23 R35	23♊32
1976	00♊48	02 04	02 58	03 32	03 R44	03 36	03 10	02 27	01 32	00♉28	29 19	28 11	27 07	26 14	25 32	25♉06
1977	10♉R01	08 44	07 31	06 27	05 36	05 02	04 D45	04 46	05 05	05 43	06 38	07 49	09 15	10 56	12 51	14♉59
1978	16♈10	17 12	18 30	20 02	21 49	23 47	25 58	28 19	00♉51	03 32	06 24	09 25	12 35	15 53	19 23	23♉00
1979	14♈45	17 34	20 30	23 35	26 48	00♉08	03 37	07 13	10 57	14 50	18 49	22 56	27 10	01♊28	05 50	10♊14
1980	22♈12	18♉04	05 02	09 07	13 18	17 34	21 54	26 16	00♊38	04 57	09 13	13 22	17 23	21 15	24 56	28♊27
1981	14♉26	18 44	22 59	17 09	01♊11	05 04	08 46	12 15	15 32	18 36	21 25	24 00	26 20	28 25	00♋15	01♋48
1982	29♉09	02♊06	04 47	07 10	09 16	11 03	12 32	13 41	14 30	15 00	15 R11	15 02	14 36	13 55	13 02	11♊59
1983	25♉R32	25 29	25 05	24 24	23 29	22 23	21 12	20 01	18 54	17 55	17 10	16 39	16 D26	16 30	16 52	17♉32
1984	27♈R08	26 24	26 D19	26 23	26 46	27 26	28 24	29♉38	01 07	02 50	04 47	06 56	09 16	11 48	14 30	17♉23
1985	13♈50	15 49	18 00	20 21	22 53	25 34	28 24	01♉23	04 30	07 47	11 11	14 45	18 27	22 17	26 16	00♊22
1986	18♈49	22 06	25 31	29♉03	02 43	06 30	10 25	14 27	18 35	22 50	27 09	01♊31	05 54	10 17	14 36	18♊50
1987	02♉44	06 53	11 07	15 24	19 45	24 05	28♊25	02 40	06 49	10 50	14 42	18 23	21 53	25 11	28 16	01♋09
1988	22♉36	26 33	00♊20	03 55	07 16	10 23	13 16	15 53	18 15	20 21	22 09	23 41	24 55	25 50	26 27	26♊R45
1989	01♊12	03 00	04 27	05 34	06 21	06 R46	06 51	06 36	06 04	05 18	04 19	03 13	02 05	00 59	29♉59	29♉09
1990	15♉R05	13 54	12 38	11 23	10 15	09 17	08 33	08 05	07 D55	08 03	08 30	09 14	10 16	11 33	13 05	14♉52
1991	18♈15	18 50	19 42	20 51	22 15	23 53	25 45	27 48	00♉04	02 30	05 06	07 53	10 49	13 55	17 11	20♉36
1992	14♈59	17 39	20 27	23 24	26 29	29♉43	03 04	06 34	10 11	13 57	17 51	21 52	26 00	00♊15	04 34	08♊57
1993	24♈34	28♉16	02 06	06 02	10 06	14 15	18 30	22 49	27 11	01♊34	05 55	10 12	14 24	18 28	22 23	26♊08
1994	11♉04	15 23	19 42	12 59	18♊11	02 16	06 13	09 59	13 34	16 56	20 05	23 01	25 43	28 11	00♋24	02♋23
1995	27♉16	00♊35	03 40	06 28	08 50	11 15	13 12	14 51	16 11	17 13	17 55	18 R17	18 21	18 06	17 35	16♊49
1996	28♉15	28 R36	28 36	28 15	27 37	26 44	25 41	24 31	23 21	22 14	21 15	20 28	19 56	19 D40	19 42	20♉02
1997	01♉R43	00 44	00♈01	29 36	29 D29	29 40	00♉10	00 58	02 02	03 23	04 57	06 46	08 48	11 01	13 27	16♉04
1998	14♈12	15 52	17 45	19 49	22 05	24 31	27 07	29♉52	02 47	05 51	09 03	12 25	15 55	19 34	23 22	27♉18
1999	16♈59	20 06	23 20	26 42	00♉12	03 49	07 34	11 26	15 26	19 33	13 04	28♊04	02 26	06 49	11 12	15♊33
2000	17♉54	16 49	15 37	14 23	13 11	12 07	11 16	10♊40	10 24	10 29	10 56	11 46	13 00	14 36	16 34	18♋54

June

	1st	3rd	5th	7th	9th	11th	13th	15th	17th	19th	21st	23rd	25th	27th	29th
1900	12♊09	16 32	20 51	25 05	29♋13	03 12	07 03	10 44	14 16	17 39	20 51	23 54	26 47	29♌30	02♌02
1901	28♊20	01♋41	04 52	07 50	10 38	13 13	15 36	17 46	19 42	21 25	22 53	24 04	25 00	25 37	25♋R57
1902	02♋14	03 36	04 41	05 28	05 58	06R09	06 01	05 37	04 57	04 04	03 01	01 52	00 43	29♊37	28♊39
1903	13♊R19	12 13	11 06	10 02	09 06	08 20	07 49	07D34	07 36	07 57	08 36	09 34	10 50	12 23	14♊14
1904	18♉36	19 36	20 52	22 24	24 11	26 12	28 28	00♊56	03 38	06 32	09 39	12 57	16 28	20 11	24♊03
1905	17♉21	20 22	23 34	26 55	00♊27	04 09	08 00	12 01	16 09	20 24	24 43	29♋06	03 29	07 50	12♋07
1906	00♊06	04 18	08 36	12 58	17 22	21 46	26 07	00♋25	04 36	08 40	12 37	16 25	20 05	23 35	26♋57
1907	18♊34	22 43	26 43	00♋35	04 16	07 48	11 10	14 22	17 23	20 13	22 52	25 20	27 36	29♌40	01♌31
1908	02♋33	05 10	07 34	09 44	11 40	13 21	14 47	15 56	16 49	17 23	17R40	17 39	17 19	16 43	15♋52
1909	27♊R35	27 41	27 29	27 01	26 18	25 22	24 19	23 12	22 05	21 03	20 11	19 31	19D07	19 01	19♊13
1910	00♊R22	29♉41	29 15	29D05	29 14	29 40	00♊24	01 26	02 45	04 20	06 12	08 19	10 40	13 17	16♊07
1911	15♉09	17 05	19 14	21 36	24 11	26 57	29♊55	03 04	06 25	09 57	13 40	17 32	21 34	25 44	00♋00
1912	22♉11	25 49	29♊35	03 31	07 34	11 46	16 03	20 24	24 48	29♋11	03 32	07 49	12 00	16 05	20♋02
1913	08♊39	13 03	17 27	21 47	26 03	00♋13	04 15	08 08	11 53	15 28	18 55	22 11	25 18	28 16	01♌03
1914	25♊57	29 34	03♋00	06 15	09 19	12 12	14 53	17 22	19 39	21 43	23 34	25 10	26 31	27 36	28♋24
1915	02♋40	04 27	05 59	07 15	08 13	08 53	09R15	09 19	09 06	08 35	07 49	06 52	05 45	04 35	03♋25
1916	17♊R38	16 40	15 35	14 28	13 23	12 25	11 38	11 04	10D46	10 45	11 03	11 40	12 36	13 50	15♊22
1917	20♉49	21 21	22 09	23 15	24 38	26 16	28 09	00♊16	02 37	05 12	08 01	11 02	14 15	17 41	21♊19
1918	16♉07	18 52	21 48	24 54	28 12	01♊39	05 17	09 05	13 03	17 09	21 21	25 40	00♋01	04 23	08♋45
1919	27♉03	01♊06	05 16	09 33	13 54	18 17	22 41	27 03	01♋22	05 35	09 41	13 40	17 31	21 14	24♋47
1920	17♊26	21 39	25 46	29♋45	03 35	07 16	10 46	14 07	17 18	20 18	23 08	25 47	28 15	00♌32	02♌36
1921	01♋12	04 07	06 50	09 21	11 38	13 42	15 32	17 07	18 26	19 29	20 14	20 42	20R51	20 42	20♋16
1922	29♊57	00♋33	00R51	00 51	00 33	29♊59	29 10	28 11	27 06	25 57	24 51	23 52	23 03	22 28	22♊D10
1923	05♊R08	04 08	03 19	02 43	02D22	02 19	02 33	03 06	03 57	05 05	06 31	08 13	10 11	12 25	14♊54
1924	16♉29	18 10	20 04	22 13	24 34	27 08	29♊54	02 52	06 02	09 24	12 57	16 41	20 35	24 38	28♋49
1925	20♉00	23 24	26 58	00♊41	04 33	08 34	12 43	16 59	21 19	25 42	00♋05	04 27	08 45	12 58	17♋04
1926	05♊12	09 34	13 57	18 21	22 43	27 00	01♋12	05 16	09 13	13 01	16 39	20 09	23 29	26 40	29♌42
1927	23♊16	27 06	00♋47	04 17	07 37	10 46	13 43	16 30	19 05	21 28	23 39	25 37	27 22	28 52	00♌06
1928	03♋35	05 39	07 27	09 00	10 17	11 17	11 59	12R24	12 30	12 18	11 49	11 05	10 08	09 02	07♋51
1929	21♊R58	21 20	20 28	19 28	18 22	17 15	16 12	15 17	14 33	14 04	13D52	13 58	14 23	15 07	16♊10
1930	23♉D49	23 51	24 11	24 49	25 44	26 56	28 25	00♊09	02 08	04 22	06 50	09 32	12 27	15 35	18♊56
1931	15♉18	17 45	20 25	23 15	26 17	29♊29	02 53	06 27	10 11	14 05	18 08	22 19	26 35	00♋56	05♋18
1932	26♉08	00♊05	04 09	08 21	12 38	16 59	21 23	25 47	00♋08	04 26	08 37	12 42	16 40	20 29	24♋10
1933	14♊01	18 22	22 38	26 47	00♋49	04 42	08 26	12 00	15 24	18 39	21 44	24 38	27 23	29♌56	02♌19
1934	29♊26	02♋38	05 39	08 28	11 05	13 29	15 40	17 38	19 21	20 50	22 02	22 58	23 36	23R57	23♋59
1935	01♋32	02 37	03 25	03 54	04R05	03 58	03 34	02 54	02 02	00 59	29♊51	28 42	27 37	26 40	25♊56
1936	09♊R36	08 30	07 29	06 38	05 59	05D36	05 30	05 42	06 12	07 00	08 07	09 31	11 12	13 09	15♊22
1937	17♉31	18 47	20 18	22 05	24 05	26 19	28♊47	01 27	04 19	07 24	10 41	14 09	17 49	21 40	25♊40
1938	18♉10	21 20	24 39	28 09	01♊49	05 38	09 36	13 42	17 56	22 14	26 36	01♋00	05 22	09 41	13♋55
1939	01♊52	06 08	10 29	14 52	19 16	23 39	27♋58	02 11	05 18	10 17	14 07	17 49	21 22	24 46	28♋00
1940	22♊20	26 18	00♋07	03 46	07 16	10 34	13 42	16 40	19 26	22 01	24 25	26 36	28 35	00♌20	01♌51
1941	03♋01	05 26	07 37	09 34	11 16	12 43	13 53	14 46	15 21	15R38	15 37	15 19	14 43	13 53	12♋52
1942	25♊R38	25 26	24 58	24 15	23 19	22 16	21 09	20 03	19 02	18 10	17 31	17D07	17 01	17 14	17♊46
1943	27♉R36	27 10	27D01	27 09	27 36	28 20	29 22	00♊40	02 15	04 06	06 11	08 32	11 06	13 55	16♊57
1944	16♉01	18 15	20 42	23 21	26 12	29♊14	02 27	05 51	09 26	13 12	17 07	21 12	25 23	29♋40	04♋01
1945	23♉30	27 14	01♊08	05 09	09 19	13 34	17 55	22 18	26 42	01♋04	05 23	09 36	13 43	17 42	21♋34
1946	10♊33	14 57	19 19	23 36	27 48	01♋52	05 48	09 35	13 12	16 41	19 59	23 08	26 07	28♌56	01♌35
1947	27♊16	00♋45	04 02	07 08	10 02	12 45	15 15	17 33	19 38	21 30	23 07	24 29	25 35	26 23	26♋55
1948	03♋10	04 34	05 41	06 31	07 02	07R16	07 11	06 49	06 11	05 19	04 17	03 09	01 59	00 52	29♊53
1949	14♊R35	13 30	12 23	11 18	10 21	09 33	09 00	08 42	08D42	09 01	09 38	10 33	11 46	13 17	15♊06
1950	19♉16	20 04	21 10	22 32	24 10	26 02	28 09	00♊29	03 02	05 49	08 48	11 59	15 23	18 58	22♊45
1951	16♉41	19 36	22 41	25 56	29♊22	02 57	06 43	10 38	14 42	18 53	23 10	27 31	01♋54	06 16	10♋36
1952	00♊44	04 56	09 13	13 35	17 59	22 23	26 44	01♋02	05 14	09 19	13 17	17 05	20 46	24 17	27♋40
1953	19♊12	23 21	27 22	01♋15	04 57	08 30	11 53	15 06	18 08	20 59	23 40	26 09	28 27	00♌33	02♌25
1954	01♋56	04 41	07 13	09 31	11 36	13 27	15 03	16 22	17 26	18 12	18 40	18R50	18 42	18 16	17♋34
1955	28♊31	28R49	28 48	28 30	27 56	27 08	26 09	25 04	23 56	22 51	21 52	21 03	20 29	20D11	20♊12
1956	01♊R38	00 55	00 26	00D14	00 20	00 44	01 26	02 25	03 42	05 15	07 04	09 09	11 29	14 04	16♊53
1957	16♉03	17 57	20 05	22 25	24 58	27 43	00♊39	03 47	07 07	10 38	14 19	18 11	22 12	26 22	00♋37
1958	21♉08	24 40	28♊21	02 11	06 10	10 17	14 31	18 50	23 12	27 36	01♋58	06 18	10 33	14 41	18♋43
1959	07♊04	11 27	15 51	20 14	24 33	28♋46	02 53	06 52	10 42	14 23	17 54	21 17	24 30	27 33	00♌26
1960	26♊38	00♋16	03 43	07 00	10 05	12 59	15 41	18 11	20 30	22 35	24 28	26 06	27 29	28 36	29♋27
1961	03♋32	05 22	06 55	08 13	09 13	09 56	10 21	10R27	10 16	09 47	09 03	08 07	07 02	05 51	04♋41
1962	19♊R16	18 25	17 24	16 18	15 12	14 09	13 14	12 31	12 02	11D51	11 57	12 22	13 06	14 08	15♊29
1963	21♉D47	22 07	22 45	23 40	24 52	26 20	28 04	00♊02	02 15	04 41	07 21	10 15	13 21	16 39	20♊10
1964	16♉54	19 38	22 32	25 38	28♊54	02 21	05 58	09 45	13 41	17 46	21 59	26 16	00♋38	05 00	09♋22
1965	27♉41	01♊43	05 53	10 08	14 29	18 52	23 16	27 39	01♋58	06 12	10 19	14 18	18 10	21 53	25♋28
1966	15♊52	20 10	24 21	28♋25	02 20	06 06	09 43	13 10	16 27	19 33	22 30	25 15	27 50	00♌14	02♌26
1967	00♋24	03 26	06 17	08 55	11 21	13 33	15 32	17 16	18 45	19 59	20 55	21 34	21R55	21 58	21♋42
1968	00♋59	01 38	01R58	02 00	01 45	01 12	00♊26	29 28	28 23	27 15	26 08	25 07	24 16	23 39	23♊D19
1969	06♊R24	05 24	04 33	03 54	03D32	03 26	03 38	04 08	04 56	06 03	07 26	09 06	11 02	13 14	15♊41
1970	16♉41	18 12	19 58	21 58	24 11	26 38	29♊16	02 07	05 10	08 25	11 51	15 29	19 17	23 15	27♊21
1971	19♉06	22 24	25 52	29♊29	03 16	07 12	11 17	15 29	19 46	24 08	28♋31	02 54	07 14	11 30	15♋41
1972	05♊49	10 11	14 35	18 59	23 21	27 39	01♋51	05 56	09 53	13 41	17 21	20 51	24 13	27 25	00♌27
1973	23♊56	27 47	01♋29	05 00	08 21	11 31	14 30	17 17	19 54	22 19	24 31	26 31	28 17	29♌49	01♌05
1974	03♋19	05 31	07 29	09 12	10 39	11 50	12 43	13 19	13 37	13R36	13 18	12 43	11 54	10 53	09♋45
1975	23♊R24	22 55	22 12	21 17	20 14	19 07	18 01	17 00	16 09	15 30	15D07	15 01	15 14	15 46	16♊36
1976	24♉R59	24D59	25 16	25 52	26 45	27 54	29♊21	01 03	03 00	05 12	07 38	10 18	13 12	16 19	19♊38
1977	16♉07	18 33	21 11	24 00	27 01	00♊12	03 34	07 07	10 50	14 44	18 46	22 56	27 12	01♋32	05♋54
1978	24♉53	28♊44	02 44	06 51	11 05	15 24	19 47	24 11	28♋34	02 54	07 09	11 18	15 20	19 14	23♋00
1979	12♊26	16 49	21 07	25 21	29♋27	03 25	07 15	10 55	14 25	17 46	20 57	23 58	26 48	29♌28	01♌58
1980	00♋08	03 22	06 24	09 14	11 52	14 18	16 31	18 30	20 15	21 46	23 01	23 59	24 39	25R02	25♋07
1981	02♋29	03 37	04 27	04 59	05R12	05 07	04 46	04 08	03 17	02 15	01♊08	29 58	28 52	27 54	27♊07
1982	11♊R26	10 19	09 14	08 17	07 30	06 56	06D39	06 39	06 58	07 35	08 30	09 43	11 13	13 00	15♊04
1983	17♉59	19 04	20 26	22 03	23 55	26 01	28 20	00♊52	03 37	06 34	09 43	13 05	16 38	20 22	24♊16
1984	18♉54	22 02	25 21	28♊49	02 28	06 16	10 14	14 19	18 32	22 50	27 12	01♋35	05 57	10 17	14♋31
1985	02♊28	06 44	11 04	15 28	19 52	24 15	28♋34	02 48	06 55	10 55	14 46	18 29	22 03	25 27	28♌43
1986	20♊55	24 58	28♋53	02 38	06 13	09 38	12 53	15 57	18 50	21 32	24 03	26 22	28 28	00♌22	02♌02
1987	02♋31	05 04	07 24	09 30	11 22	12 58	14 19	15 23	16 09	16 38	16R49	16 41	16 16	15 35	14♋40
1988	26♊R47	26 38	26 11	25 30	24 36	23 34	22 27	21 20	20 18	19 25	18 44	18D18	18 09	18 19	18D48
1989	28♉R50	28 21	28D10	28 16	28 39	29 21	00♊21	01 37	03 10	04 58	07 02	09 20	11 53	14 40	17♊41
1990	15♉50	17 57	20 16	22 48	25 31	28 26	01♊33	04 50	08 19	11 58	15 48	19 47	23 55	28♋09	02♋27
1991	22♉22	26 00	29♊48	03 45	07 50	12 02	16 20	20 42	25 06	29♋29	03 50	08 07	12 17	16 21	20♋18
1992	11♊09	15 33	19 55	24 13	28♋25	02 30	06 27	10 15	13 53	17 22	20 42	23 52	26 52	29♌42	02♌22
1993	27♊57	01♋26	04 45	07 52	10 48	13 32	16 04	18 23	20 30	22 23	24 02	25 26	26 34	27 26	27♋59
1994	03♋16	04 51	06 09	07 10	07 53	08R18	08 25	08 13	07 45	07 02	06 06	05 01	03 52	02 42	01♋38
1995	16♊R22	15 21	14 15	13 08	12 06	11 11	10 29	10 00	09D49	09 55	10 20	11 04	12 06	13 26	15♊03
1996	20♉19	21 05	22 09	23 28	25 04	26 54	28♊59	01 17	03 49	06 34	09 32	12 42	16 05	19 39	23♊24
1997	17♉27	20 20	23 24	26 38	00♊03	03 37	07 22	11 16	15 19	19 30	23 46	28♋07	02 30	06 52	11♋12
1999	17♉42	21♊55	26 01	29 59	03 47	07 26	10 55	14♋14	17 22	20 20	23 08	25 44	28 09	00 22	02♋23
2000	02♋42	05 28	08 01	10 22	12 28	14 21	15 58	17 20	18 26	19 14	19 45	19 57	19 52	19 28	18♋48

Mercury

July

Year	1st	3rd	5th	7th	9th	11th	13th	15th	17th	19th	21st	23rd	25th	27th	29th	31st
1900	04♌24	06 33	08 31	10 16	11 47	13 03	14 03	14 45	15R09	15 15	15 00	14 27	13 34	12 26	11 06	09♌37
1901	25♋R58	25 41	25 06	24 16	23 12	21 59	20 41	19 24	18 13	17 12	16 28	16D02	15 58	16 18	17 01	18♋10
1902	27♊R53	27 23	27D11	27 19	27 46	28 35	29♋44	01 14	03 04	05 13	07 42	10 29	13 34	16 54	20 29	24♋16
1903	16♊20	18 43	21 22	24 16	27 24	00♋47	04 23	08 11	12 09	16 15	20 26	24 40	28♌55	03 09	07 19	11♌25
1904	28♊05	02♋15	06 30	10 49	15 09	19 28	23 43	27 54	02♌00	05 59	09 52	13 37	17 16	20 48	24 12	27♌30
1905	16♋19	20 25	24 17	28♌16	02 00	05 36	09 04	12 24	15 37	18 42	21 38	24 27	27 07	29♍39	02 02	04♍15
1906	00♌10	03 14	06 08	08 54	11 29	13 55	16 10	18 13	20 05	21 44	23 09	24 18	25 11	25 46	26R03	25♌59
1907	03♌09	04 31	05 38	06 28	07 01	07R15	07 09	06 45	06 03	05 05	03 53	02 32	01 07	29♋44	28 29	27♋28
1908	14♋R50	13 39	12 25	11 13	10 07	09 13	08 33	08D13	08 13	08 35	09 19	10 27	11 57	13 49	16 04	18♋38
1909	19♊45	20 37	21 48	23 19	25 08	27 15	29♋40	02 23	05 22	08 37	12 07	15 49	19 42	23 44	27 52	02♌02
1910	19♊12	22 30	26 01	29♋44	03 37	07 40	11 50	16 05	20 22	24 39	28♌54	03 05	07 11	11 12	15 07	18♌55
1911	04♋20	08 41	13 02	17 20	21 33	25 42	29♌44	03 38	07 26	11 07	14 40	18 06	21 25	24 36	27 41	00♍37
1912	23♋52	27 33	01♌06	04 30	07 47	10 55	13 55	16 46	19 29	22 03	24 27	26 41	28 44	00♍35	02 14	03♍40
1913	03♌40	06 07	08 23	10 27	12 19	13 58	15 22	16 31	17 24	17 59	18R14	18 11	17 47	17 04	16 03	14♌48
1914	28♋55	29R07	29 00	28 35	27 53	26 56	25 47	24 30	23 10	21 53	20 44	19 48	19 10	18D53	18 59	19♋29
1915	17♋R11	19 17	21 40	24D19	27 14	00 23	03 47	07 25	11 14	15 12	19 19	23 30	27 44	01 58	06 10	10♋19
1916	25♊08	29 07	03 14	07 27	11 45	16♋04	20 22	24 38	28 50	02 57	06 58	10 52	14 39	18♌20	21 54	25♌20
1917	02♊21	01 26	00♋45	00 21	00 15	00 30	01 06	02 03	03♌22	05 01	07 01	09 21	12 00	14 57	18 11	21♌41
1918	13♋03	17 17	21 24	25 25	29♌19	03 05	06 43	10 14	13 37	16 53	20 00	23 00	25 52	28 36	01♍12	03♍39
1919	28♋13	01 29	04 36	07 35	10 24	13 04	15 35	17 55	20 05	22 03	23 49	25 21	26 39	27 41	28 26	28♌53
1920	04♌28	06 06	07 29	08 37	09 29	10 02	10R17	10 13	09 50	09 09	08 10	06 58	05 36	04 09	02 44	01♌27
1921	19♋R33	18 36	17 29	16 15	15 00	13 48	12 45	11 55	11 22	11D09	11 18	11 49	12 44	14 02	15 44	17♋48
1922	22♊10	22 30	23 09	24 09	25 28	27 07	29♋05	01 22	03 56	06 48	09 57	13 20	16 58	20 47	24 45	28♋51
1923	17♊38	20 36	23 48	27 14	00♋52	04 42	08 41	12 49	17 02	21 17	25 34	29♌49	04 01	08 08	12 10	16♌05
1924	03♋05	07 25	11 46	16 06	20 22	24 35	28♌41	02 41	06 34	10 20	13 59	17 31	20 56	24 13	27 24	00♍27
1925	21♋03	24 55	28♌39	02 15	05 42	09 02	12 13	15 16	18 11	20 58	23 35	26 04	28 23	00♍32	02 30	04♍16
1926	02♌34	05 16	07 48	10 09	12 20	14 18	16 04	17 37	18 55	19 56	20 41	21R08	21 15	21 02	20 29	19♌36
1927	01♌05	01 46	02R08	02 13	01 58	01 25	00 36	29♋32	28 18	26 57	25 36	24 20	23 14	22 24	21D54	21♋46
1928	06♋R39	05 33	04 36	03 52	03D25	03 16	03 29	04 03	04 59	06 16	07 55	09 55	12 16	14 56	17 54	21♋10
1929	17♊31	19 11	21 08	23 23	25 54	28♋41	01 45	05 03	08 35	12 19	16 15	20 18	24 27	28♌40	02 53	07♌05
1930	22♊29	26 14	00♋09	02 13	08 24	12 40	16 59	21 17	25 33	29♌46	03 54	07 55	11 51	15 40	19 22	22♌58
1931	09♋39	13 58	18 13	22 22	26 24	00♌20	04 08	07 49	11 22	14 47	18 06	21 16	24 19	27 15	00♍02	02♍42
1932	27♋42	01 06	04 21	07 28	10 26	13 15	15 54	18 25	20 45	22 55	24 53	26 39	28 12	29♍31	00 34	01♍20
1933	04♌30	06 29	08 14	09 46	11 03	12 04	12 48	13R13	13 20	13 07	12 35	11 45	10 39	09 20	07 54	06♌25
1934	23♋R42	23 09	22 19	21 17	20 05	18 49	17 33	16 23	15 23	14 39	14D13	14 08	14 26	15 08	16 14	17♋44
1935	25♊R26	25 14	25 21	25 49	26 36	27 44	29♋12	01 00	03 07	05 33	08 18	11 19	14 37	18 09	21 53	25♋48
1936	17♊51	20 35	23 34	26 47	00♋14	03 54	07 45	11 45	15 53	20 06	24 22	28♌37	02 51	07 01	11 06	15♌06
1937	29♊48	04♋02	08 21	12 41	17 01	21 18	25 31	29♌39	03 40	07 35	11 23	15 04	18 38	22 05	25 24	28♌37
1938	18♋03	22 05	25 58	29♌45	03 23	06 53	10 15	13 30	16 36	19 35	22 25	25 06	27 39	00♍03	02 17	04♍21
1939	01♌06	04 02	06 49	09 26	11 52	14 09	16 13	18 06	19 46	21 12	22 23	23 17	23 54	24R12	24 10	23♌47
1940	03♌06	04 06	04 48	05R13	05 18	05 05	04 33	03 44	02 40	01 25	00♋03	28 40	27 21	26 13	25 12	24♋48
1941	11♋R42	10 29	09 18	08 13	07 19	06 41	06D20	06 20	06 41	07 24	08 29	09 57	11 47	13 58	16 30	19♋20
1942	18♊37	19 47	21 16	23 04	25 10	27 33	00♋13	03 09	06 21	09 48	13 28	17 19	21 19	25 26	29♌37	03♌49
1943	20♊13	23 41	27 22	01♋13	05 14	09 23	13 37	17 54	22 12	26 28	00♌41	04 50	08 53	12 50	16 40	20♌24
1944	08♋23	12 43	17 01	21 14	25 21	29♌22	03 16	07 02	10 42	14 13	17 38	20 54	24 04	27 06	00♍01	02♍48
1945	25♋17	28♌53	02 19	05 38	08 48	11 49	14 42	17 26	20 01	22 26	24 41	26 46	28 38	00♍19	01 45	02♍56
1946	04♌03	06 20	08 25	10 18	11 58	13 23	14 33	15 27	16 03	16 20	16R18	15 56	15 15	14 16	13 03	11♌38
1947	27♋R07	27 02	26 38	25 57	25 01	23 53	22 37	21 19	20 03	18 55	18 00	17 22	17 04	17D08	17 37	18♋30
1948	29♊R06	28 33	28 18	28D23	28 48	29♋34	00 40	02 08	03 55	06 03	08 29	11 15	14 17	17 36	21 10	24♋56
1949	17♊11	19 32	22 08	25 01	28 08	01♋29	05 04	08 51	12 48	16 53	21 04	25 18	29♌33	03 46	07 57	12♌03
1950	26♊42	00♋47	04 59	09 16	13 35	17 55	22 13	26 26	00♌35	04 38	08 35	12 24	16 07	19 43	23 12	26♌34
1951	14♋51	19 01	23 04	27 00	00♌49	04 29	08 02	11 27	14 44	17 54	20 55	23 49	26 36	29♍12	01 40	03♍59
1952	00♌54	03 59	06 54	09 40	12 17	14 44	17 00	19 05	20 58	22 39	24 05	25 17	26 12	26 50	27R08	27♌07
1953	04♌05	05 29	06 38	07 30	08 05	08R21	08 19	07 57	07 17	06 20	05 10	03 50	02 25	01 01	29♋45	28♋41
1954	16♋R39	15 33	14 20	13 06	11 55	10 53	10 04	09 31	09D17	09 25	09 55	10 49	12 05	13 43	15 44	18♋07
1955	21♊31	21 10	22 09	23 28	25 05	27 01	29♋15	01 47	04 36	07 42	11 03	14 37	18 24	22 21	26 26	00♌35
1956	19♊56	23 12	26 42	00♋24	04 16	08 18	12 28	16 42	20 59	25 15	29♌31	03 42	07 49	11 50	15 45	19♌34
1957	04♋56	09 17	13 38	17 56	22 10	26 19	00♌22	04 17	08 06	11 47	15 21	18 47	22 07	25 19	28 24	01♍22
1958	22♋37	26 23	00♌01	03 31	06 52	10 05	13 10	16 07	18 55	21 34	24 04	26 24	28 34	00♍33	02 20	03♍54
1959	03♌10	05 43	08 06	10 18	12 18	14 05	15 38	16 57	18 00	18 46	19R14	19 22	19 11	18 40	17 50	16♌43
1960	29♋59	00♌14	00R10	29♋47	29 07	28 11	27 03	25 47	24 27	23 08	21 58	21 00	20 19	19 59	20D02	20♋30
1961	03♋R35	02 39	01 56	01 29	01D21	01 33	02 06	03 01	04 17	05 54	07 52	10 09	12 46	15 41	18 54	22♋22
1962	17♊07	19 03	21 16	23 45	26 30	29♋31	02 46	06 16	09 58	13 51	17 53	22 02	26 14	00♌28	04 42	08♌52
1963	23♊53	27 46	01♋48	05 58	10 13	14 31	18 50	23 08	27 23	01♌32	05 37	09 34	13 26	17 10	20 48	24♌19
1964	13♋40	17 54	22 02	26 04	29♌58	03 44	07 24	10 55	14 19	17 35	20 43	23 44	26 37	29♍22	01 58	04♍26
1965	28♋54	02♌11	05 19	08 19	11 09	13 50	16 22	18 44	20 54	22 54	24 41	26 16	27 35	28 40	29 27	29♌56
1966	04♌26	06 13	07 46	09 04	10 05	10 50	11R17	11 25	11 14	10 44	09 56	08 52	07 35	06 10	04 43	03♌20
1967	21♋R10	20 21	19 20	18 10	16 55	15 40	14 31	13 32	12 48	12D22	12 16	12 33	13 13	14 17	15 44	17♋34
1968	23♊16	23 33	24 10	25 07	26 24	28 01	29♋56	02 11	04 43	07 33	10 40	14 02	17 38	21 26	25 24	29♋28
1969	18♊23	21 20	24 31	27 55	01♋32	05 21	09 19	13 26	17 38	21 54	26 10	00♌26	04 37	08 45	12 47	16♌44
1970	01♋36	05 53	10 13	14 34	18 52	23 07	27 17	01♌21	05 18	09 08	12 51	16 27	19 56	23 18	26 32	29♌40
1971	19♋44	23 40	27 29	01♌09	04 42	08 06	11 22	14 30	17 30	20 22	23 05	25 39	28 04	00♍19	02 24	04♍17
1972	03♌20	06 03	08 36	10 59	13 11	15 11	16 59	18 33	19 52	20 56	21 43	22 12	22R21	22 11	21 40	20♌50
1973	02♌05	02 49	03 14	03R21	03 08	02 38	01 50	00 48	29♋34	28 14	26 52	25 35	24 28	23 35	23 02	22♋52
1974	08♋R33	07 22	06 18	05 25	04 47	04 27	04D26	04 46	05 28	06 32	07 58	09 45	11 54	14 22	17 09	20♋15
1975	17♊46	19 14	21 00	23 04	25 25	28 03	00♋56	04 05	07 29	11 07	14 56	18 54	23 00	27 11	01♌24	05♌37
1976	23♊10	26 54	00♋48	04 52	09 02	13 17	17 36	21 54	26 10	00♌23	04 31	08 34	12 30	16 19	20 02	23♌38
1977	10♋15	14 35	18 50	22 59	27 02	00♌58	04 47	08 29	12 02	15 29	18 48	21 59	25 03	27 59	00♍47	03♍28
1978	26♋38	00♌07	03 27	06 39	09 42	12 37	15 22	17 58	20 25	22 41	24 47	26 41	28 22	29♍50	01 03	01♍59
1979	04♌16	06 23	08 17	09 57	11 24	12 35	13 29	14 07	14R25	14 25	14 05	13 26	12 29	11 18	09 55	08♌27
1980	24♋R53	24 21	23 33	22 32	21 22	20 05	18 49	17 37	16 36	15 49	15D20	15 13	15 28	16 07	17 10	18♋37
1981	26♊R35	26D21	26 25	26 50	27 35	28 40	00♋06	01 51	03 56	06 20	09 02	12 02	15 18	18 49	22 32	26♋26
1982	17♊23	19 58	22 47	25 52	29♋11	02 43	06 27	10 22	14 26	18 36	22 50	27 06	01♌21	05 33	09 41	13♌44
1983	28♊20	02♋31	06 47	11 07	15 27	19 46	24 01	28♌12	02 18	06 16	10 08	13 53	17 31	21 02	24 26	27♌43
1984	18♋40	22 42	26 37	00♌24	04 03	07 34	10 57	14 12	17 19	20 18	23 09	25 52	28 26	00♍51	03 06	05♍11
1985	01♌49	04 47	07 34	10 12	12 40	14 58	17 04	18 58	20 40	22 08	23 21	24 17	24 56	25R16	25 17	24♌57
1986	03♌27	04 37	05 31	06R06	06 24	06 22	06 02	05 24	04 29	03 20	02 01	00♋38	29 16	28 00	26 57	26♋11
1987	13♋35	12 24	11 11	10 01	08 59	08 11	07 38	07D25	07 32	08 01	08 52	10 06	11 43	13 41	16 00	18♋39
1988	19♊37	20 45	22 11	23 57	26 00	28 21	00♋59	03 54	07 04	10 29	14 08	17 58	21 57	26 04	00♌14	04♌26
1989	20♊55	24 23	28 02	01♋52	05 52	10 00	14 14	18 31	22 49	27 05	01♌18	05 27	09 31	13 28	17 19	21♌04
1990	06♋49	11 10	15 30	19 46	23 56	28♌01	01 59	05 50	09 33	13 09	16 38	19 59	23 13	26 20	29♍19	02♍11
1991	24♋06	27 46	01♌18	04 42	07 57	11 03	14 02	16 51	19 32	22 03	24 24	26 35	28 36	00♍24	01 59	03♍20
1992	04♌52	07 10	09 17	11 12	12 53	14 20	15 32	16 28	17R06	17 26	17 26	17 07	16 28	15 32	14 20	12♌56
1993	28♋R15	28 11	27 50	27 11	26 17	25 10	23 55	22 36	21 19	20 10	19 13	18 32	18D11	18 13	18 38	19♋28
1994	00♋R42	00♊00	29 33	29 25	29 37	00♋10	01 03	02 17	03 52	05 47	08 02	10 36	13 28	16 37	20 02	23♋41
1995	16♊58	19 09	21 36	24 18	27 16	00♋29	03 56	07 35	11 26	15 27	19 35	23 47	28♌02	02 16	06 28	10♌37
1996	27♊20	01 24	05♋36	09 53	14 12	18 31	22 49	27 03	01♌12	05 16	09 13	13 03	16 47	20 23	23 53	27♌15
1997	15♋28	19 38	23 42	27 39	01♌28	05 09	08 43	12 08	15 26	18 37	21 39	24 33	27 20	29♍58	02 27	04♍47
1998	00♌01	03 11	06 12	09 04	11 47	14 19	16 42	18 54	20 55	22 44	24 19	25 40	26 46	27 34	28 05	28♌R16
1999	04♌11	05 45	07 03	08 06	08R52	09 20	09 29	09 20	08 51	08 05	07 02	05 47	04 25	02 59	01 37	00♌25
2000	17♋R54	16 49	15 37	14 23	13 11	12 07	11 16	10 40	10D24	10 29	10 56	11 46	13 00	14 36	16 34	18♋54

August

	1st	3rd	5th	7th	9th	11th	13th	15th	17th	19th	21st	23rd	25th	27th	29th	31st
1900	08♌R52	07 23	06 03	04 57	04 11	03 D 50	03 55	04 29	05 32	07 03	09 02	11 27	14 14	17 21	20 44	24♌19
1901	18♋53	20 38	22 47	25 17	28 08	01♌18	04 44	08 23	12 12	16 08	20 08	24 09	28♍09	02 06	06 01	09♍51
1902	26♋13	00♌13	04 19	08 27	12 36	16 43	20 46	24 46	28♍40	02 30	06 13	09 52	13 25	16 52	20 14	23♍31
1903	13♌26	17 24	21 15	25 01	28♍40	02 13	05 40	09 01	12 16	15 25	18 29	21 26	24 18	27 03	29♎42	02♎14
1904	29♌07	02♍15	05 16	08 10	10 57	13 36	16 08	18 32	20 47	22 53	24 48	26 31	28 02	29 18	00♎18	00♎59
1905	05♍17	07 14	08 59	10 31	11 48	12 50	13 34	13 R 59	14 03	13 44	13 03	11 59	10 35	08 54	07 05	05♍13
1906	25♌49	25 14	24 19	23 06	21 40	20 04	18 26	16 53	15 33	14 33	13 D 57	13 50	14 14	15 09	16 36	18♌32
1907	27♋R04	26 D 33	26 25	26 43	27 27	28 39	00♌18	02 22	04 50	07 40	10 49	14 14	17 52	21 38	25 31	29♌26
1908	20♋03	23 06	26 27	00♌01	03 47	07 42	11 43	15 47	19 51	23 54	27 54	01♍50	05 42	09 28	13 10	16♍47
1909	04♌08	08 19	12 28	16 33	20 34	24 29	28♍19	02 03	05 41	09 13	12 40	16 01	19 17	22 27	25 32	28♍32
1910	20♌46	24 25	27 57	01♍22	04 41	07 54	11 01	14 01	16 55	19 43	22 23	24 57	27 23	29♎41	01 51	03♎50
1911	02♍03	04 49	07 27	09 56	12 17	14 29	16 30	18 21	19 59	21 23	22 32	23 25	23 58	24 R 10	24 00	23♍25
1912	04♍17	05 19	06 03	06 R 29	06 35	06 19	05 42	04 43	03 25	01 51	00♌07	28 22	26 42	25 17	24 15	23♌41
1913	14♌R05	12 35	11 03	09 36	08 20	07 22	06 D 46	06 36	06 56	07 44	09 03	10 50	13 04	15 42	18 42	21♌58
1914	19♋54	21 02	22 35	24 33	26 54	29♌37	02 39	05 59	09 33	13 18	17 10	21 08	25 07	29♍07	03 04	06♍58
1915	23♋30	27 18	01♌15	05 18	09 25	13 32	17 39	21 43	25 42	29♍38	03 28	07 12	10 52	14 26	17 54	21♍18
1916	12♌21	16 23	20 18	24 08	27 52	01♍30	05 01	08 27	11 46	15 00	18 09	21 11	24 08	26 59	29♎44	02♎22
1917	27♌01	00♍18	03 28	06 32	09 28	12 18	15 01	17 37	20 04	22 24	24 34	26 35	28 25	00♎02	01 26	02♎34
1918	04♍49	07 02	09 04	10 56	12 35	14 00	15 10	16 04	16 39	16 R 53	16 46	16 16	15 22	14 06	12 32	10♍44
1919	28♌R59	28 55	28 31	27 46	26 41	25 20	23 46	22 07	20 28	18 59	17 46	16 56	16 D 34	16 43	17 24	18♌37
1920	00♌R53	29♋58	29 D 25	29 15	29 32	00♌17	01 29	03 09	05 15	07 45	10 36	13 47	17 13	20 52	24 38	28♌30
1921	18♋58	21 34	24 30	27 44	01♌13	04 54	08 46	12 44	16 46	20 49	24 51	28♍51	02 48	06 40	10 27	14♍09
1922	00♌55	05 05	09 15	13 24	17 30	21 31	25 27	29♍17	03 03	06 42	10 16	13 44	17 06	20 24	23 36	26♍42
1923	18♌01	21 47	25 27	29♍01	02 28	05 49	09 04	12 13	15 15	18 12	21 02	23 46	26 23	28♎52	01 15	03♎28
1924	01♍56	04 49	07 34	10 11	12 41	15 01	17 13	19 15	21 05	22 43	24 08	25 18	26 10	26 43	26 R 56	26♍45
1925	05♍04	06 29	07 40	08 34	09 10	09 R 26	09 22	08 55	08 06	06 56	05 28	03 47	01 59	00♌14	28 39	27♌23
1926	19♌R04	17 47	16 19	14 45	13 12	11 48	10 38	09 49	09 D 25	09 29	10 03	11 08	12 43	14 46	17 14	20♌05
1927	21♋51	22 21	23 16	24 37	26 23	28 34	01♌08	04 02	07 15	10 43	14 24	18 13	22 08	26 06	00♍04	04♍01
1928	22♋54	26 31	00♌19	04 17	08 20	12 26	16 32	20 37	24 39	28♍37	02 30	06 18	10 01	13 39	17 11	20♍39
1929	09♌10	13 17	17 19	21 16	25 07	28♍52	02 31	06 04	09 31	12 52	16 08	19 18	22 23	25 21	28 15	01♎02
1930	24♌43	28 09	01♍28	04 40	07 46	10 45	13 38	16 24	19 03	21 34	23 58	26 13	28 18	00♎14	01 58	03♎29
1931	03♍58	06 25	08 42	10 50	12 47	14 33	16 05	17 24	18 26	19 11	19 R 36	19 40	19 21	18 39	17 33	16♍05
1932	01♍36	01 R 53	01 50	01 26	00 41	29♌36	28 13	26 38	24 56	23 16	21 44	20 30	19 39	19 D 17	19 26	20♌09
1933	05♌R42	04 23	03 17	02 30	02 D 06	02 09	02 40	03 39	05 06	07 00	09 20	12 03	15 07	18 27	22 00	25♌43
1934	18♋38	20 42	23 09	25 57	29♌03	02 26	06 03	09 51	13 46	17 46	21 48	25 49	29♍49	03 45	07 37	11♍25
1935	27♋49	01♌54	06 03	10 12	14 21	18 26	22 28	26 25	00♍16	04 02	07 42	11 17	14 47	18 11	21 29	24♍43
1936	17♌04	20 55	24 39	28♍18	01 50	05 16	08 35	11 49	14 57	17 59	20 54	23 44	26 27	29♎04	01 34	03♎56
1937	00♍11	03 14	06 09	08 58	11 39	14 12	16 37	18 53	21 00	22 56	24 41	26 13	27 30	28 32	29 15	29♍38
1938	05♍18	07 05	08 38	09 57	11 00	11 46	12 R 13	12 19	12 03	11 25	10 24	09 04	07 27	05 39	03 49	02♍06
1939	23♌R28	22 36	21 26	20 01	18 28	16 52	15 20	14 00	12 58	12 D 20	12 09	12 29	13 19	14 41	16 32	18♌50
1940	24♋D40	24 43	25 12	26 07	27 28	29♌16	01 28	04 03	06 59	10 14	13 43	17 24	21 14	25 08	29♍05	03♍02
1941	20♋53	24 10	27 41	01♌26	05 20	09 20	13 24	17 29	21 34	25 36	29♍34	03 28	07 17	11 01	14 39	18♍13
1942	05♌55	10 06	14 13	18 16	22 13	26 05	29♍52	03 32	07 06	10 35	13 58	17 15	20 27	23 33	26 34	29♍30
1943	22♌14	25 48	29♍15	02 36	05 51	08 59	12 01	14 56	17 45	20 27	23 02	25 29	27 48	29♎58	01 59	03♎49
1944	04♍09	06 44	09 10	11 28	13 35	15 33	17 18	18 51	20 10	21 13	21 58	22 R 23	22 27	22 08	21 25	20♍17
1945	03♍26	04 13	04 40	04 R 48	04 35	04 00	03 04	01 49	00♌18	28 37	26 53	25 13	23 48	22 43	22 06	22♌D00
1946	10♌R54	09 23	07 57	06 41	05 42	05 05	04 D 53	05 09	05 54	07 08	08 51	11 00	13 34	16 29	19 43	23♌12
1947	19♋06	20 36	22 30	24 48	27 26	00♌25	03 42	07 14	10 57	14 49	18 47	22 47	26 48	00♍47	04 43	08♍35
1948	26♋52	00♌52	04 57	09 05	13 14	17 21	21 24	25 24	29♍19	03 09	06 53	10 31	14 05	17 32	20 55	24♍13
1949	14♌04	18 02	21 54	25 40	29♍20	02 54	06 21	09 43	12 58	16 08	19 12	22 10	25 02	27 48	00♎27	03♎00
1950	28♌12	01♍24	04 29	07 27	10 19	13 03	15 40	18 09	20 29	22 41	24 42	26 33	28 12	29♎38	00 48	01♎40
1951	05♍04	07 08	09 01	10 41	12 07	13 19	14 14	14 51	15 R 08	15 04	14 36	13 46	12 34	11 03	09 18	07♏26
1952	26♌R58	26 26	25 33	24 22	22 57	21 22	19 43	18 09	16 47	15 43	15 D 04	14 54	15 14	16 06	17 30	19♌23
1953	28♋R16	27 D 41	27 30	27 45	28 26	29♌35	01 10	03 12	05 37	08 25	11 32	14 56	18 33	22 18	26 10	00♍05
1954	19♋26	22 18	25 28	28♌54	02 34	06 24	10 21	14 23	18 27	22 31	26 33	00♍31	04 25	08 15	11 59	15♍39
1955	02♌40	06 52	11 02	15 09	19 12	23 11	27 04	00♍51	04 33	08 08	11 38	15 03	18 22	21 35	24 43	27♍46
1956	21♌26	25 05	28♍37	02 03	05 23	08 37	11 44	14 45	17 39	20 28	23 09	25 44	28 11	00♎30	02 40	04♎41
1957	02♍48	05 34	08 13	10 44	13 05	15 18	17 21	19 13	20 52	22 19	23 30	24 24	25 00	25 R 15	25 07	24♍35
1958	04♍36	05 48	06 44	07 22	07 R 40	07 38	07 14	06 28	05 21	03 56	02 18	00♌32	28 47	27 12	25 55	25♌03
1959	16♌R04	14 38	13 06	11 35	10 11	09 01	08 10	07 D 44	07 45	08 16	09 16	10 46	12 44	15 08	17 55	21♌01
1960	20♋53	21 58	23 28	25 23	27 42	00♌22	03 23	06 41	10 13	13 58	17 50	21 47	25 46	29♍45	03 42	07♍37
1961	24♋11	27 58	01♌54	05 57	10 03	14 10	18 17	22 21	26 21	00♍16	04 07	07 52	11 31	15 06	18 35	21♍59
1962	10♌56	15 01	19 00	22 53	26 40	00♍21	03 56	07 25	10 49	14 06	17 17	20 23	23 23	26 18	29♎06	01♎49
1963	26♌02	29♍22	02 36	05 44	08 45	11 39	14 26	17 06	19 38	22 03	24 19	26 26	28 22	00♎07	01 40	02♎58
1964	05♍37	07 51	09 55	11 47	13 28	14 55	16 07	17 02	17 40	17 57	17 R 52	17 24	16 33	15 20	13 47	12♍00
1965	00♍R03	00♌02	29 40	28 58	27 55	26 36	25 03	23 23	21 44	20 13	18 57	18 04	17 D 39	17 44	18 21	19♌31
1966	02♌R42	01 36	00 49	00 D 23	00 24	00 51	01 46	03 09	04 59	07 15	09 54	12 53	16 10	19 42	23 24	27♌13
1967	18♋38	21 01	23 45	26 48	00♌08	03 42	07 28	11 23	15 23	19 25	23 28	27 29	01♍28	05 22	09 12	12♍57
1968	01♌32	05 42	09 52	14 01	18 07	22 08	26 05	29♍56	03 41	07 21	10 55	14 24	17 47	21 04	24 17	27♍24
1969	18♌39	22 26	26 07	29♍41	03 09	05 30	09 46	12 55	15 58	18 56	21 46	24 31	27 09	29♎39	02 02	04♎17
1970	01♍11	04 08	06 58	09 40	12 14	14 41	16 58	19 06	21 03	22 49	24 22	25 42	26 45	27 30	27 56	27♍R59
1971	05♍09	06 44	08 04	09 09	09 56	10 25	10 R 33	10 20	09 45	08 48	07 30	05 56	04 11	02 23	00♌40	29♌12
1972	20♌18	19 03	17 36	16 02	14 29	13 02	11 50	10 58	10 31	10 32	11 03	12 04	13 36	15 36	18 02	20 51
1973	22♋55	23 22	24 14	25 52	27 15	29♌24	01 55	04 47	07 58	11 26	15 05	18 58	22 49	26 46	00♏44	04♏41
1974	21♋54	25 23	29♌05	02 57	06 57	11 02	15 08	19 14	23 18	27 18	01♍14	05 05	08 51	12 32	16 07	19♍37
1975	04♌43	11 52	15 57	19 57	23 51	27 39	01♍22	04 58	08 29	11 54	15 13	18 26	21 34	24 36	27 32	00♎23
1976	25♌24	28♍50	02 09	05 23	08 29	11 29	14 22	17 09	19 48	22 21	24 45	27 01	29♎08	01 05	02 50	04♎23
1977	04♍45	07 13	09 31	11 40	13 39	15 26	17 00	18 20	19 25	20 12	20 R 40	20 46	20 30	19 50	18 47	17♍22
1978	02♍21	02 R 51	03 01	02 50	02 18	01 24	00♌12	28 44	27 05	25 23	23 45	22 18	21 12	20 D 31	20 21	20♌43
1979	07♌R43	06 17	05 02	04 02	03 24	03 D 10	03 23	04 04	05 14	06 52	08 56	11 26	14 17	17 28	20 53	24♌31
1980	19♋29	21 31	23 56	26 41	29♌46	03 07	06 43	10 29	14 24	18 23	22 25	26 26	00♍26	04 22	08 15	12♍03
1981	28♋26	02♌31	06 39	10 49	14 57	19 03	23 05	27 02	00♍54	04 40	08 21	11 56	15 26	18 51	22 10	25♍24
1982	15♌44	19 38	23 26	27 08	00♍44	04 13	07 37	10 54	14 05	17 11	20 10	23 04	25 51	28 31	01♎05	03♎32
1983	29♌19	02♍26	05 25	08 18	11 04	13 42	16 12	18 33	20 46	22 49	24 41	26 21	27 48	29 00	29♎54	00♎30
1984	06♍09	07 57	09 32	10 53	11 58	12 46	13 R 15	13 24	13 10	12 35	11 37	10 18	08 43	06 56	05 06	03♍21
1985	24♌R39	23 49	22 41	21 18	19 45	18 08	16 35	15 13	14 08	13 D 27	13 13	13 29	14 16	15 34	17 22	19♌38
1986	25♋R56	25 D 44	25 56	26 35	27 40	29♌12	01 09	03 30	06 14	09 18	12 38	16 13	19 57	23 49	27 45	01♍41
1987	20♋05	23 12	26 35	00♌12	04 01	07 58	12♍00	16 04	20 09	24 13	28♍13	02 10	06 01	09 48	13 29	17♍06
1988	06♌32	10 43	14 50	18 53	22 51	26 44	00 30	04 11	07 46	11 15	14 39	17 56	21 09	24 16	27 17	00♎13
1989	22♌54	26 28	29♍56	03 18	06 33	09 42	12 44	15 40	18 30	21 12	23 48	26 16	28 36	00♎48	02 50	04♎41
1990	03♍34	06 14	08 46	11 09	13 23	15 27	17 20	19 01	20 29	21 41	22 38	23 16	23 R 33	23 28	23 00	22♍07
1991	03♍55	04 52	05 32	05 R 52	05 52	05 30	04 47	03 44	02 22	00♌46	29 03	27 19	25 44	24 25	23 31	23♌D05
1992	12♌R11	10 41	09 13	07 55	06 54	06 13	05 D 58	06 11	06 52	08 03	09 42	11 49	14 20	17 14	20 26	23♌52
1993	20♋03	21 30	23 21	25 36	28 12	01♌09	04 24	07 54	11 36	15 27	19 24	23 24	27 25	01♍24	05 20	09♍13
1994	25♋35	29♌29	03 31	07 38	11 46	15 54	20 00	24 02	27 59	01♍52	05 39	09 21	12 58	16 29	19 54	23♍15
1995	12♌40	16 41	20 37	24 26	28 10	01♍47	05 18	08 43	12 02	15 15	18 22	21 24	24 20	27 09	29♎53	02♎30
1996	28♌54	02♍06	05 12	08 11	11 03	13 48	16 26	18 55	21 17	23 30	25 33	27 25	29 05	00♎32	01 44	02♎39
1997	05♍53	07 58	09 52	11 34	13 02	14 16	15 13	15 53	16 R 12	16 10	15 46	14 58	13 48	12 19	10 35	08♍43
1998	28♌R14	27 54	27 14	26 14	24 57	23 27	21 50	20 12	18 41	17 25	16 30	16 D 01	16 02	16 35	17 39	19♌14
1999	29♋R54	29 06	28 D 39	28 37	29 02	29♌54	01 13	02 59	05 10	07 44	10 40	13 54	17 23	21 04	24 52	28♌45
2000	20♋12	23 02	26 10	29♌35	03 13	07 02	10 59	15 01	19 04	23 08	27 10	01♍08	05 03	08 53	12 37	16♍17

Mercury

September

	1st	3rd	5th	7th	9th	11th	13th	15th	17th	19th	21st	23rd	25th	27th	29th
1900	26♌10	29♍57	03 48	07 39	11 31	15 20	19 06	22 49	26 28	00♎03	03 34	07 01	10 24	13 44	16♎59
1901	11♍44	15 28	19 06	22 40	26 09	29♎33	02 53	06 09	09 20	12 28	15 31	18 30	21 25	24 16	27♎03
1902	25♍08	28 18	01♎22	04 22	07 16	10 06	12 50	15 29	18 02	20 28	22 48	24 59	27 02	28 53	00♏33
1903	03♎27	05 49	08 01	10 05	11 58	13 40	15 09	16 22	17 17	17 52	18 04	17 49	17 07	15 55	14♎15
1904	01♎R11	01 20	01 05	00♍25	29 19	27 49	25 59	23 56	21 51	19R56	18 22	17 19	16D53	17 08	18♍02
1905	04♍R20	02 45	01 31	00D46	00 35	01 00	02 01	03 36	05 41	08 13	11 06	14 15	17 36	21 05	24♍39
1906	19♌41	22 16	25 13	28♍27	01 54	05 31	09 14	12 59	16 46	20 31	24 15	27 55	01♎33	05 07	08♎37
1907	01♍24	05 19	09 13	13 03	16 50	20 32	24 11	27 45	01♎14	04 39	08 00	11 18	14 31	17 41	20♎47
1908	18♍33	22 02	25 26	28♎46	02 00	05 10	08 16	11 17	14 14	17 06	19 54	22 37	25 15	27♏47	00♏13
1909	00♍00	02♎51	05 37	08 17	10 51	13 19	15 39	17 51	19 54	21 47	23 28	24 55	26 06	26 58	27♎R28
1910	04♎46	06 29	07 59	09 14	10 12	10 50	11R06	10 58	10 23	09 20	07 51	05 58	03 50	01♍38	29♍34
1911	22♍R59	21 47	20 15	18 25	16 26	14 28	12 42	11 17	10D23	10 05	10 26	11 25	12 59	15 04	17♍35
1912	23♌D36	23 52	24 42	26 05	28 00	00♍22	03 08	06 12	09 32	13 01	16 37	20 16	23 56	27♎37	01♎15
1913	23♌42	27 18	01♍01	04 50	08 40	12 30	16 19	20 05	23 48	27 27	01♎02	04 34	08 01	11 25	14♎45
1914	08♍54	12 42	16 26	20 05	23 40	27 10	00♎35	03 56	07 13	10 25	13 34	16 38	19 39	22 36	25♎29
1915	22♍58	26 14	29♎25	02 31	05 32	08 29	11 21	14 07	16 49	19 24	21 54	24 17	26 33	28♏40	00♏38
1916	03♎39	06 08	08 29	10 42	12 45	14 39	16 21	17 49	19 03	19 58	20R32	20 43	20 27	19 43	18♎28
1917	03♎02	03 43	04R03	04 00	03 31	02 36	01 16	29♍33	27 33	25 26	23 23	21 37	20 19	19 36	19♍34
1918	09♍R47	07 54	06 09	04 43	03 43	03D16	03 25	04 11	05 32	07 25	09 47	12 31	15 34	18 50	22♍15
1919	19♌25	21 24	23 49	26 38	29♍45	03 07	06 40	10 19	14 03	17 47	21 32	25 15	28♎55	02 33	06♎07
1920	00♍27	04 21	08 15	12 07	15 55	19 40	23 21	26 57	00♎30	03 58	07 22	10 42	13 58	17 11	20♎19
1921	15♍59	19 34	23 04	26 29	29♎49	03 05	06 17	09 24	12 27	15 25	18 19	21 09	23 54	26 34	29♏10
1922	28♍14	01♎13	04 06	06 55	09 37	12 14	14 45	17 09	19 25	21 33	23 31	25 18	26 53	28 12	29♎14
1923	04♎32	06 32	08 20	09 57	11 20	12 26	13 15	13R42	13 46	13 23	12 33	11 14	09 30	07 26	05♎12
1924	26♍R30	25 42	24 29	22 55	21 03	19 02	17 02	15 15	13 51	12D58	12 43	13 07	14 09	15 46	17♍54
1925	26♌R55	26 22	26 21	26 56	28 05	29 47	01♍59	04 35	07 33	10 46	14 11	17 43	21 20	24 59	28♎38
1926	21♌38	24 56	28♍27	02 07	05 52	09 41	13 30	17 18	21 04	24 46	28♎26	02 01	05 33	09 01	12♎25
1927	05♍59	09 51	13 40	17 24	21 04	24 39	28 09	01♎36	04 57	08 15	11 29	14 38	17 44	20 46	23♎45
1928	22♍20	25 40	28♎55	02 05	05 10	08 11	11 07	13 58	16 45	19 26	22 02	24 32	26 55	29♏11	01♏18
1929	02♎24	05 02	07 34	09 58	12 16	14 24	16 23	18 11	19 47	21 08	22 13	22 57	23R20	23 17	22♎45
1930	04♎09	05 17	06 08	06R39	06 47	06 30	05 48	04 38	03 03	01 09	29♍02	26 54	24 57	23 24	22♍D25
1931	15♍R15	13 25	11 29	09 37	07 59	06 45	06D02	05 55	06 25	07 31	09 12	11 23	13 59	16 54	20♍05
1932	20♌42	22 14	24 15	26 42	29♍32	02 41	06 04	09 36	13 15	16 57	20 41	24 24	28 05	01♎43	05♎19
1933	27♌37	01♍28	05 21	09 14	13 05	16 53	20 38	24 19	27 56	01♎29	04 58	08 23	11 43	15 00	18♎14
1934	13♍17	16 58	20 33	24 04	27 31	00♎52	04 09	07 22	10 30	13 35	16 35	19 31	22 22	25 10	27♎52
1935	26♍18	29♎24	02 25	05 20	08 11	10 56	13 36	16 09	18 36	20 57	23 09	25 12	27 05	28 47	00♏14
1936	05♎04	07 13	09 13	11 02	12 39	14 01	15 08	15 56	16R23	16 26	16 02	15 10	13 49	12 02	09♎55
1937	29♍R41	29 30	28 53	27 52	26 26	24 40	22 40	20 36	18 40	17 03	15 55	15D22	15 29	16 16	17♍39
1938	01♍R20	00♌04	29D15	28 59	29 18	00♍12	01 41	03 40	06 07	08 57	12 03	15 23	18 52	22 26	26♍03
1939	20♌08	23 01	26 13	29♍38	03 14	06 57	10 43	14 31	18 18	22 03	25 45	29♎25	03 00	06 33	10♎01
1940	04♍59	08 53	12 44	16 31	20 13	23 51	27 25	00♎54	04 19	07 39	10 56	14 09	17 17	20 23	23♎24
1941	19♍57	23 23	26 44	00♎00	03 12	06 19	09 21	12 19	15 12	18 00	20 44	23 23	25 55	28 22	00♏42
1942	00♎55	03 42	06 23	08 58	11 26	13 47	16 01	18 05	19 59	21 41	23 10	24 23	25 17	25R51	26♎00
1943	04♎40	06 11	07 28	08 28	09 09	09R28	09 24	08 53	07 55	06 30	04 42	02 38	00♍27	28 22	26♍36
1944	19♍R35	17 57	16 05	14 07	12 13	10 35	09 21	08D39	08 33	09 06	10 16	12 00	14 13	16 51	19♍48
1945	22♌10	22 54	24 11	26 00	28 18	00♍59	04 01	07 18	10 46	14 22	18 02	21 44	25 25	29♎06	02♎44
1946	25 00	28♍43	02 31	06 23	10 14	14 05	17 53	21 38	25 19	28♎56	02 29	05 58	09 24	12 45	16 03
1947	10♍30	14 16	17 57	21 33	25 05	28♎32	01 55	05 13	08 27	11 36	14 42	17 44	20 41	23 35	26♎24
1948	25♍49	28♎59	02 04	05 05	08 00	10 50	13 35	16 14	18 48	21 15	23 35	25 48	27 51	29♏44	01♏25
1949	04♎14	06 36	08 50	10 55	12 49	14 33	16 03	17 18	18 15	18 53	19R07	18 56	18 16	17 07	15♎30
1950	02♎00	02R22	02 22	01 58	01 07	29♍51	28 13	26 17	24 12	22 09	20 20	18 57	18D08	17 58	18♍28
1951	06♍R31	04 46	03 17	02 14	01D42	01 45	02 24	03 38	05 26	07 42	10 23	13 23	16 37	20 02	23♍33
1952	20♌30	23 02	25 57	29♍09	02 36	06 12	09 54	13 39	17 25	21 10	24 54	28♎35	02 12	05 46	09♎17
1953	02♍03	05 58	09 52	13 42	17 29	21 12	24 50	28♎24	01 54	05 20	08 41	11 59	15 13	18 22	21♎29
1954	17♍27	20 59	24 25	27 48	01♎05	04 18	07 26	10 30	13 29	16 24	19 15	22 01	24 42	27 18	29♏48
1955	29♍15	02♎10	05 00	07 43	10 21	12 52	15 17	17 34	19 43	21 42	23 31	25 07	26 28	27 32	28♎16
1956	05♎38	07 22	08 53	10 10	11 10	11 51	12R10	12 05	11 33	10 33	09 06	07 16	05 09	02 56	00♍50
1957	24♍R10	23 01	21 31	19 42	17 44	15 45	13 56	12 29	11 31	11D09	11 26	12 21	13 51	15 53	18♍21
1958	24♌R48	24D43	25 12	26 15	27 51	29♍57	02 29	05 23	08 33	11 57	15 29	19 06	22 46	26 23	00♎06
1959	22♌41	26 10	29♍49	03 34	07 23	11 14	15 03	18 51	22 35	26 17	29♎54	03 28	06 57	10 23	13♎45
1960	09♍33	13 21	17 05	20 45	24 20	27 50	01♎15	04 37	07 54	11 06	14 15	17 20	20 21	23 18	26♎12
1961	23♍39	26 55	00♎06	03 13	06 15	09 12	12 04	14 51	17 33	20 10	22 40	25 04	27 21	29♏29	01♏28
1962	03♎08	05 40	08 06	10 24	12 34	14 34	16 23	18 00	19 23	20 29	21 17	21 43	21R44	21 17	20♍20
1963	03♎31	04 24	04 57	05R08	04 55	04 17	03 12	01 42	29♍51	27 47	25 40	23 42	22 05	21 00	20♍D33
1964	11♍R03	09 10	07 23	05 54	04 51	04 20	04D25	05 07	06 24	08 15	10 34	13 16	16 17	19 32	22♍56
1965	20♌17	22 13	24 36	27 22	00♍27	03 48	07 19	10 58	14 41	18 26	22 10	25 53	29♎34	03 11	06♎45
1966	29♌09	03♍02	06 57	10 49	14 40	18 27	22 10	25 49	29♎23	02 54	06 20	09 42	13 01	16 15	19♎26
1967	14♍48	18 26	21 59	25 26	28♎50	02 08	05 22	08 32	11 37	14 38	17 35	20 28	23 16	25 59	28♎37
1968	28♍56	01♎55	04 50	07 39	10 22	12 59	15 31	17 55	20 13	22 22	24 21	26 10	27 46	29 07	00♏11
1969	05♎21	07 22	09 12	10 51	12 15	13 24	14 14	14 44	14R51	14 31	13 44	12 28	10 47	08 44	06♎30
1970	27♍R52	27 19	26 22	25 00	23 18	21 21	19 19	17 23	15 43	14 30	13 51	13D51	14 30	15 47	17♍37
1971	28♌R35	27 43	27D22	27 35	28 24	29♍46	01 40	04 02	06 48	09 52	13 10	16 38	20 12	23 50	27♍29
1972	22♌23	25 39	29♍08	02 48	06 33	10 21	14 10	17 58	21 43	25 26	29♎06	02 41	06 13	09 42	13♎06
1973	06♍38	10 31	14 19	18 04	21 44	25 19	28♎50	02 17	05 39	08 57	12 11	15 21	18 27	21 29	24♎28
1974	21♍20	24 43	28 00	01♎13	04 21	07 25	10 24	13 18	16 07	18 52	21 31	24 04	26 32	28♏52	01♏05
1975	01♎47	04 29	07 05	09 34	11 56	14 10	16 15	18 10	19 53	21 24	22 39	23 36	24R13	24 25	24♎11
1976	05♎04	06 14	07 07	07R41	07 51	07 38	06 58	05 51	04 19	02 26	00♍20	28 11	26 12	24 36	23♍33
1977	16♍R32	14 43	12 47	10 54	09 14	07 56	07D09	06 58	07 24	08 26	10 04	12 12	14 45	17 39	20♍47
1978	26♌45	29 33	02 18	04 58	07♍34	10 04	12 26	14 40	16 41	18 28	19 56	21 00	21 34	21♎32	20♎48
1979	26♌23	00♍11	04 03	07 56	11 48	15 38	19 25	23 08	26 47	00♎22	03 53	07 20	10 43	14 03	17♎18
1980	13♍55	17 36	21 12	24 44	28 10	01♎32	04 49	08 03	11 11	14 16	17 17	20 13	23 05	25 53	28♎36
1981	26♍59	00♎05	03 06	06 03	08 54	11 40	14 20	16 54	19 22	21 43	23 57	26 01	27 56	29 38	01♏07
1982	04♎43	06 57	09 03	10 59	12 44	14 15	15 32	16 32	17 13	17R31	17 23	16 49	15 45	14 13	12♎18
1983	00♎R40	00 43	00 22	29♍36	28 25	26 50	24 58	22 55	20 53	19 02	17 35	16D40	16 23	16 46	17♍47
1984	02♍R34	01 15	00 22	00D02	00 17	01 07	02 32	04 29	06 53	09 40	12 46	16 04	19 32	23 06	26♍42
1985	20♌55	23 45	26 55	00♍19	03 54	07 36	11 22	15 09	18 56	22 41	26 24	00♎04	03 39	07 12	10♎40
1986	03♍40	07 35	11 27	15 16	19 01	22 42	26 18	29♎49	03 17	06 40	09 58	13 13	16 24	19 32	22♎36
1987	18♍52	22 21	25 45	29♎03	02 18	05 27	08 32	11 33	14 29	17 20	20 07	22 48	25 25	27 55	00♏20
1988	01♎39	04 26	07 08	09 44	12 13	14 35	16 49	18 54	20 49	22 33	24 04	25 19	26 16	26R52	27♎04
1989	05♎32	07 05	08 24	09 26	10 09	10R31	10 30	10 02	09 07	07 45	05 59	03 56	01 45	29♍39	27♍50
1990	21♍R32	20 05	18 21	16 25	14 27	12 37	11 07	10 05	09D37	09 46	10 34	11 57	13 54	16 17	19♍03
1991	23♌04	23 27	24 25	25 55	27 55	00♍22	03 12	06 20	09 42	13 14	16 51	20 32	24 13	27 54	01♎34
1992	25♌40	29♍22	03 10	07 01	10 52	14 43	18 31	22 16	25 57	29♎35	03 08	06 38	10 03	13 25	16♎43
1993	11♍08	14 54	18 36	22 12	25 44	29♎12	02 35	05 53	09 07	12 18	15 24	18 26	21 24	24 18	27♎07
1994	24♍53	28 06	01♎14	04 17	07 15	10 09	12 57	15 40	18 17	20 48	23 13	25 30	27 39	29♏39	01♏28
1995	03♎46	06 13	08 32	10 42	12 43	14 34	16 12	17 37	18 46	19 36	20R05	20 10	19 48	18 57	17♎37
1996	03♎00	03R25	03 28	03 06	02 18	01 05	29♍29	27 34	25 29	23 25	21 34	20 08	19D15	19 00	19♍26
1997	07♍R47	06 01	04 30	03 23	02D47	02 46	03 21	04 32	06 16	08 30	11 08	14 06	17 19	20 42	24♍13
1998	20♌13	22 31	25 12	28 15	01♍33	05 03	08 42	12 25	16 11	19 57	23 41	27 23	01♎03	04 39	08♎11
1999	00♍43	04 38	08 33	12 25	16 14	19 59	23 40	27 17	00♎49	04 17	07 41	11 00	14 16	17 28	20♎37
2000	18♍05	21 37	25 05	28♎27	01 45	04 58	08 07	11 11	14 11	17 07	19 58	22 44	25 26	28 02	00♏33

October

Year	1st	3rd	5th	7th	9th	11th	13th	15th	17th	19th	21st	23rd	25th	27th	29th	31st
1900	20♎12	23 21	26 26	29♏29	02 28	05 24	08 17	11 06	13 52	16 34	19 12	21 44	24 11	26 31	28 42	00♐43
1901	29♎45	02♏22	04 54	07 20	09 39	11 50	13 51	15 41	17 18	18 39	19 39	20R16	20 23	19 58	18 57	17♏18
1902	01♏58	03 07	03 55	04R20	04 17	03 44	02 38	00♎59	28 53	26 28	24 01	21 47	20 04	19D01	18 44	19♎11
1903	12♎R12	09 57	07 40	05 38	04 04	03D08	02 55	03 24	04 34	06 17	08 29	11 01	13 50	16 49	19 57	23♎09
1904	19♍33	21 34	24 02	26 50	29♎53	03 06	06 26	09 50	13 15	16 42	20 07	23 32	26 55	00♏16	03 35	06♏52
1905	28♍15	01♎51	05 27	09 00	12 32	16 01	19 27	22 50	26 10	29♏28	02 44	05 57	09 07	12 16	15 23	18♏27
1906	12♎04	15 27	18 47	22 03	25 17	28♏27	01 35	04 40	07 42	10 42	13 39	16 33	19 24	22 12	24 57	27♏37
1907	23♎49	26 48	29♏43	02 35	05 23	08 07	10 47	13 22	15 51	18 14	20 29	22 36	24 31	26 14	27 39	28♏45
1908	02♏32	04 44	06 46	08 37	10 15	11 38	12 43	13 26	13R42	13 28	12 41	11 18	09 22	07 00	04 27	02♏00
1909	27♎R33	27 09	26 14	24 48	22 54	20 39	18 15	15 58	14 03	12 44	12D08	12 17	13 08	14 35	16 32	18♎52
1910	27♍R52	26 43	26D14	26 27	27 21	28 51	00♎53	03 19	06 04	09 02	12 11	15 25	18 43	22 03	25 24	28♎44
1911	20♍26	23 33	26 50	00♎14	03 42	07 12	10 42	14 12	17 40	21 07	24 31	27 53	01♏12	04 30	07 45	10♏58
1912	04♎52	08 25	11 56	15 24	18 48	22 09	25 28	28♏43	01 56	05 07	08 15	11 20	14 24	17 25	20 24	23♏21
1913	18♎02	21 15	24 24	27 31	00♏35	03 35	06 33	09 27	12 18	15 06	17 50	20 31	23 06	25 36	28 00	00♐16
1914	28♎17	01♏02	03 41	06 16	08 45	11 08	13 23	15 30	17 26	19 10	20 39	21 50	22 38	22R58	22 48	22♏01
1915	02♏24	03 57	05 14	06 12	06R48	06 58	06 39	05 47	04 21	02 24	00♎04	27 34	25 11	23 13	21 53	21♎D18
1916	16♎R46	14 41	12 23	10 06	08 04	06 32	05D39	05 30	06 04	07 17	09 04	11 17	13 50	16 39	19 38	22♎45
1917	20♍12	21 28	23 18	25 36	28 16	01♎12	04 21	07 37	10 58	14 22	17 46	21 11	24 35	27 57	01♏18	04♏37
1918	25♍46	29♎20	02 55	06 29	10 02	13 33	17 02	20 28	23 51	27 12	00♏30	03 45	06 59	10 10	13 19	16♏26
1919	09♎37	13 04	16 28	19 48	23 05	26 20	29♏31	02 39	05 45	08 48	11 49	14 47	17 43	20 36	23 26	26♏13
1920	23♎25	26 27	29♏25	02 20	05 12	08 00	10 44	13 24	15 59	18 29	20 52	23 08	25 15	27 11	28 53	00♐19
1921	01♏39	04 02	06 17	08 25	10 22	12 07	13 38	14 52	15 45	16 14	16 14	15 41	14 32	12 48	10 34	08♏03
1922	29♎55	00♏R12	00♎01	29 20	28 07	26 23	24 14	21 50	19 26	17 20	15 45	14D51	14 42	15 17	16 30	18♎16
1923	03♎R01	01 07	29♍42	28D55	28 51	29♎29	00 45	02 35	04 52	07 29	10 22	13 26	16 37	19 52	23 10	26♎29
1924	20♍26	23 19	26 26	29♎42	03 06	06 33	10 01	13 30	16 58	20 25	23 50	27 13	00♏33	03 52	07 08	10♏23
1925	02♎16	05 52	09 25	12 56	16 23	19 48	23 09	26 28	29♏44	02 58	06 09	09 17	12 24	15 28	18 30	21♏30
1926	15♎46	19 03	22 17	25 27	28♏35	01 40	04 42	07 40	10 36	13 29	16 19	19 05	21 48	24 26	26 59	29♏27
1927	26♎39	29♏30	02 16	04 58	07 36	10 08	12 34	14 54	17 06	19 08	20 58	22 35	23 55	24 53	25R27	25♏30
1928	03♏16	05 02	06 35	07 52	08 50	09R25	09 33	09 12	08 17	06 47	04 47	02 24	29♎53	27 31	25 36	24♎20
1929	21♎R43	20 11	18 14	15 58	13 37	11 26	09 39	08 30	08D02	08 19	09 18	10 51	12 54	15 20	18 02	20♎56
1930	22♍06	22 27	23 29	25 06	27 13	29♎44	02 34	05 37	08 49	12 07	15 28	18 51	22 15	25 37	28♏59	02♏19
1931	23♍26	26 53	00♎25	03 58	07 31	11 03	14 33	18 02	21 28	24 51	28 12	01♏30	04 46	08 00	11 11	14♏21
1932	08♎51	12 20	15 46	19 09	22 28	25 44	28♏57	02 08	05 16	08 21	11 24	14 25	17 23	20 19	23 12	26♏02
1933	21♎24	24 30	27 33	00♏33	03 30	06 23	09 13	11 59	14 42	17 19	19 52	22 19	24 40	26 52	28 54	00♐43
1934	00♏30	03 02	05 29	07 48	10 00	12 03	13 54	15 33	16 56	17 59	18R40	18 53	18 34	17 40	16 09	14♏05
1935	01♏24	02 16	02R44	02 47	02 19	01 19	29♎47	27 46	25 25	22 58	20 41	18 51	17 40	17D13	17 31	18♎30
1936	07♎R39	05 27	03 34	02 11	01D28	01 28	02 10	03 30	05 22	07 41	10 19	13 13	16 16	19 26	22 40	25♎57
1937	19♍35	21 59	24 43	27 44	00♎56	04 16	07 41	11 07	14 35	18 02	21 28	24 52	28 14	01♏35	04 53	08♏10
1938	29♍41	03♎17	06 53	10 26	13 56	17 24	20 49	24 10	27 30	00♏46	04 00	07 11	10 21	13 28	16 33	19♏36
1939	13♎26	16 47	20 05	23 19	26 31	29♏39	02 45	05 48	08 48	11 45	14 39	17 31	20 19	23 04	25 45	28♏22
1940	26♎22	29♏16	02 07	04 53	07 35	10 13	12 46	15 12	17 32	19 44	21 46	23 37	25 14	26 33	27 31	28♏03
1941	02♏54	04 57	06 49	08 29	09 54	11 02	11 48	12R09	12 01	11 20	10 04	08 15	05 59	03 28	00♎59	28♎50
1942	25♎R41	24 52	23 32	21 44	19 33	17 11	14 52	12 53	11 27	10D42	10 41	11 24	12 44	14 36	16 52	19♎27
1943	25♍R21	24D44	24 49	25 35	26 58	28♎54	01 16	03 58	06 55	10 03	13 17	16 36	19 57	23 19	26 41	00♏02
1944	22♍58	26 19	29♎46	03 16	06 48	10 19	13 50	17 19	20 45	24 10	27 32	00♏52	04 09	07 24	10 37	13♏48
1945	06♎19	09 52	13 21	16 47	20 10	23 29	26 46	00♏00	03 11	06 20	09 26	12 30	15 31	18 31	21 28	24♏22
1946	19♎17	22 28	25 36	28♏40	01 41	04 39	07 34	10 25	13 13	15 58	18 38	21 14	23 45	26 09	28 26	00♐33
1947	29♎09	01♏49	04 24	06 54	09 17	11 33	13 41	15 38	17 24	18 54	20 08	20 59	21 25	21R20	20 41	19♏24
1948	02♏53	04 03	04 54	05 21	05R22	04 52	03 49	02 14	00♎10	27 46	25 18	23 02	21 15	20 08	19D46	20♎09
1949	13♎30	11R14	08 57	06 53	06 15	04 15	03D57	04 22	05 28	07 08	09 17	11 47	14 34	17 33	20D39	23♎51
1950	19♍37	21 21	23 34	26 10	29♎04	02 11	05 27	08 49	12 13	15 39	19 05	22 30	25 54	29♏16	02 36	05♏54
1951	27♍07	00♎43	04 19	07 54	11 26	14 56	18 24	21 49	25 11	28♏30	01 47	05 01	08 13	11 23	14 31	17♏37
1952	12♎44	16 07	19 27	22 44	25 58	29 09	02♏16	05 22	08 24	11 24	14 21	17 16	20 07	22 56	25 41	28♏23
1953	24♎32	27 31	00♏27	03 19	06 07	08 52	11 32	14 08	16 38	19 01	21 18	23 26	25 23	27 07	28 34	29♏43
1954	02♏11	04 27	06 35	08 33	10 20	11 53	13 09	14 06	14R39	14 44	14 17	13 16	11 39	09 32	07 03	04♏30
1955	28♎R37	28 31	27 55	26 48	25 11	23 07	20 46	18 23	16 13	14 31	13D28	13 10	13 36	14 42	16 22	18♎28
1956	29♍R05	27 52	27D19	27 27	28 17	29♎44	01 42	04 06	06 49	09 46	12 54	16 07	19 25	22 45	26 05	29♎25
1957	21♍11	24 16	27 32	00♎55	04 23	07 52	11 23	14 52	18 21	21 47	25 11	28♏33	01 53	05 10	08 26	11♏39
1958	03♎43	07 18	10 51	14 20	17 46	21 09	24 29	27 47	01♏01	04 13	07 22	10 29	13 34	16 36	19 37	22♏35
1959	17♎04	20 19	23 31	26 39	29♏45	02 47	05 46	08 43	11 36	14 26	17 12	19 55	22 34	25 07	27 35	29♏56
1960	29♎01	01♏46	04 26	07 01	09 31	11 55	14 11	16 19	18 17	20 02	21 33	22 45	23 36	24 00	23R53	23♏10
1961	03♏15	04 50	06 09	07 10	07 48	08R02	07 45	06 57	05 34	03 40	01 22	28♎52	26 28	24 27	23 02	22♎22
1962	18♎R55	17 02	14 50	12 31	10 18	08 26	07 09	06 33	06D01	07 31	08 58	10 56	13 18	15 58	18 52	21♎54
1963	20♍47	21 41	23 11	25 13	27 40	00♎27	03 28	06 40	09 58	13 21	16 45	20 09	23 33	26 56	00♏18	03♏38
1964	20♍26	00♎00	03 34	07 09	10 42	14 13	17 41	21 07	24 31	27 52	01♏10	04 26	07 39	10 51	14 00	17♏07
1965	10♎16	13 43	17 07	20 28	23 45	26 59	00♏11	03 20	06 26	09 29	12 30	15 29	18 24	21 18	24 08	26♏56
1966	22♎34	25 38	28♏38	01 35	04 29	07 20	10 06	12 49	15 27	18 00	20 28	22 48	25 01	27 04	28 55	00♐31
1967	01♏10	03 37	05 57	08 10	10 14	12 06	13 47	15 11	16 18	17 02	17R20	17 08	16 21	14 58	13 01	10♏38
1968	00♏55	01 14	01 07	00♎29	29 19	27 38	25 32	23 08	20 44	18 35	16 56	15D57	15 44	16 14	17 24	19♎06
1969	04♎R18	02 21	00 53	00♍D02	29♎53	00 27	01 39	03 26	05 40	08 15	11 06	14 09	17 19	20 34	23 52	27♎10
1970	19♍55	22 37	25 35	28♎46	02 06	05 31	08 59	12 27	15 56	19 23	22 49	26 13	29♏35	02 54	06 12	09♏27
1971	01♎08	04 45	08 19	11 51	15 21	18 47	22 10	25 31	28♏48	02 03	05 15	08 25	11 33	14 39	17 42	20♏43
1972	16♎27	19 44	22 59	26 09	29♏17	02 22	05 24	08 23	11 20	14 13	17 03	19 50	22 33	25 12	27 56	00♐14
1973	27♎23	00♏14	03 01	05 44	08 22	10 55	13 22	15 42	17 55	19 58	21 50	23 28	24 50	25 51	26 28	26♏R35
1974	03♏09	05 02	06 44	08 11	09 21	10 10	10 35	10R33	09 58	08 49	07 07	04 56	02 28	29♎58	27 44	26♎04
1975	23♎R28	22 14	20 32	18 25	16 06	13 47	11 43	10 10	09D17	09 07	09 41	10 54	12 40	14 52	17 25	20♎12
1976	23♍D09	23 26	24 24	25 57	28 01	00♎30	03 18	06 20	09 31	12 48	16 09	19 32	22 55	26 18	29♏39	03♏00
1977	24♍07	27 34	01♎05	04 38	08 11	11 43	15 13	18 42	22 08	25 31	28♏52	02 10	05 27	08 40	11 52	15♏02
1978	19♎21	17 14	14 38	11 53	09 21	07 19	05 59	05♏24	05 30	06 13	07 25	09 00	10 54	13 02	15 22	17♏50
1979	20♎30	23 38	26 44	29♏45	02 44	05 39	08 31	11 20	14 05	16 45	10 21	21 52	24 18	27 34	28 43	00♐40
1980	01♏14	03 47	06 15	08 35	10 48	12 52	14 45	16 25	17 50	18 56	19 39	19R55	19 40	18 50	17 23	15♏22
1981	02♏20	03 14	03R45	03 50	03 26	02 30	01 01	29♎03	26 44	24 16	21 57	20 04	18 48	18D16	18 30	19♎25
1982	10♎R06	07 49	05 43	04 00	02 52	02D26	02 42	03 40	05 13	07 17	09 44	12 29	15 26	18 32	21 44	24♎59
1983	19♍24	21 32	24 04	26 55	00♎01	03 17	06 38	10 04	13 31	16 58	20 24	23 49	27 13	00♏34	03 54	07♏11
1984	00♎19	03 56	07 32	11 05	14 35	18 03	21 28	24 50	28 09	01♏26	04 40	07 51	11 01	14 08	17 13	20♏17
1985	14♎05	17 27	20 45	24 00	27 11	00♏20	03 26	06 29	09 29	12 27	15 22	18 14	21 02	23 48	26 29	29♏00
1986	25♎36	28 32	01♏25	04 14	06 59	09 39	12 15	14 46	17 10	19 27	21 35	23 34	25 19	26 49	28 01	28♏49
1987	02♏37	04 45	06 45	08 33	10 07	11 26	12 25	13R02	13 12	12 52	11 57	10 28	08 27	06 03	03 30	01♏07
1988	26♎R48	26 02	24 46	23 00	20 51	18 29	16 09	14 07	12 37	11D47	11 42	12 20	13 37	15 26	17 40	20♎13
1989	26♍R31	25D50	25 50	26 31	27 51	29♎43	02 03	04 43	07 39	10 45	13 59	17 18	20 38	24 00	27 21	00♏42
1990	22♍05	25 20	28♎44	02 12	05 43	09 14	12 45	16 15	19 43	23 08	26 32	29♏53	03 11	06 28	09 42	12♏54
1991	05♎11	08 45	12 16	15 44	19 08	22 30	25 48	29♏03	02 16	05 26	08 34	11 39	14 42	17 43	20 41	23♏37
1992	19♎58	23 09	26 17	29♏21	02 23	05 21	08 16	11 08	13 57	16 42	19 23	21 59	24 30	26 55	29♐13	01♐22
1993	29♎53	02♏34	05 09	07 40	10 04	12 21	14 30	16 29	18 16	19 49	21 04	21 58	22R27	22 26	21 51	20♏38
1994	03♏04	04 25	05 29	06 11	06R29	06 18	05 36	04 20	02 32	00♎19	27 51	25 26	23 19	21 46	20D57	20♎53
1995	15♎R49	13 42	11 24	09 10	07 14	05 50	05D06	05 05	05 47	07 07	08 59	11 17	13 54	16 46	19 48	22♎56
1996	20♍31	22 12	24 21	26 55	29♎48	02 54	06 09	09 30	12 54	16 19	19 45	23 10	26 34	29♏56	03 16	06♏34
1997	27♍47	01♎23	04 58	08 33	12 06	15 36	19 03	22 28	25 51	29♏10	02 27	05 41	08 54	12 04	15 11	18♏17
1998	11♎40	15 06	18 28	21 46	25 02	28 14	01♏24	04 30	07 34	10 36	13 35	16 31	19 24	22 15	25 02	27♏46
1999	23♎42	26 43	29♏41	02 35	05 26	08 13	10 56	13 35	16 08	18 36	20 57	23 10	25 14	27 07	28 45	00♐06
2000	02♏57	05 14	07 23	09 23	11 11	12 46	14 04	15 03	15R39	15 47	15 24	14 26	12 53	10 49	08 22	05♏48

Mercury

November

	1st	3rd	5th	7th	9th	11th	13th	15th	17th	19th	21st	23rd	25th	27th	29th
1900	01♐38	03 19	04 41	05 41	06 13	06 13	05 34	04 15	02 17	29♏49	27 07	24 31	22 23	20 54	20♏D12
1901	16♏R16	13 53	11 17	08 46	06 40	05 12	04 D 30	04 34	05 19	06 38	08 25	10 34	12 58	15 34	18♏18
1902	19♎40	21 03	22 57	25 13	27 46	00♏31	03 25	06 25	09 29	12 36	15 44	18 53	22 02	25 11	28♏20
1903	24♎46	28 02	01♏18	04 35	07 51	11 07	14 21	17 35	20 47	23 58	27 09	00♐18	03 27	06 36	09♐43
1904	08♏30	11 45	14 57	18 08	21 18	24 26	27 34	00♐40	03 44	06 48	09 51	12 54	15 55	18 54	21♐53
1905	19♏59	23 01	26 01	28♐59	01 56	04 50	07 42	10 31	13 18	15 59	18 36	21 07	23 28	25 39	27♐35
1906	28♏57	01♐31	03 58	06 19	08 30	10 30	12 16	13 43	14 47	15 R 23	15 24	14 45	13 24	11 22	08♐50
1907	29♏09	29 R 36	29 30	28 48	27 27	25 28	23 01	20 20	17 47	15 41	14 15	13 D 35	13 40	14 25	15♏44
1908	00♏R54	29♎10	28 D 08	27 52	28 20	29♏27	01 05	03 08	05 29	08 04	10 49	13 42	16 39	19 39	22♏42
1909	20♎09	22 53	25 48	28♏50	01 57	05 06	08 17	11 29	14 41	17 53	21 05	24 16	27 26	00♐36	03♐45
1910	00♏24	03 43	07 01	10 18	13 33	16 46	19 58	23 09	26 19	29♐28	02 36	05 43	08 50	11 56	15♐01
1911	12♏34	15 44	18 53	22 00	25 05	28 10	01♐13	04 14	07 14	10 13	13 11	16 06	19 00	21 50	24♐37
1912	24♏48	27 42	00♐33	03 21	06 05	08 46	11 21	13 51	16 12	18 24	20 22	22 04	23 25	24 19	24♐R39
1913	01♐21	03 22	05 10	06 41	07 52	08 R 37	08 51	08 28	07 25	05 41	03 22	00♏43	28 01	25 40	23♏55
1914	21♏R24	19 41	17 27	14 53	12 16	09 58	08 13	07 D 13	06 59	07 29	08 35	10 12	12 11	14 28	16♏59
1915	21♎17	21 49	22 59	24 41	26 48	29♏14	01 54	04 44	07 40	10 41	13 46	16 52	19 59	23 07	26♏15
1916	24♎20	27 33	00♏47	04 02	07 18	10 33	13 47	17 01	20 13	23 25	26 36	29♐46	02 55	06 04	09♐12
1917	06♏15	09 32	12 46	15 59	19 10	22 20	25 29	28♐36	01 43	04 49	07 53	10 57	14 00	17 02	20♐04
1918	17♏59	21 04	24 06	27 08	00♐07	03 05	06 01	08 55	11 46	14 34	17 19	20 00	22 34	25 01	27♐18
1919	27♏35	00♐16	02 53	05 25	07 50	10 06	12 13	14 06	15 42	16 57	17 R 46	18 02	17 40	16 35	14♐47
1920	00♐54	01 46	02 11	02 03	01 17	29♏51	27 48	25 17	22 36	20 05	18 02	16 41	16 D 07	16 16	17♏05
1921	06♏R45	04 19	02 19	00 59	00 D 26	00 37	01 29	02 55	04 48	07 02	09 31	12 11	14 59	17 53	20♏51
1922	19♎19	21 40	24 18	27 08	00 06	03 09	06 16	09 26	12 36	15 47	18 58	22 09	25 19	28♐29	01♐38
1923	28♎09	01♏38	04 46	08 04	11 20	14 34	17 48	21 00	24 11	27 21	00♐30	03 38	06 46	09 53	12♐59
1924	11♏59	15 11	18 21	21 29	24 36	27 41	00♐46	03 49	06 51	09 51	12 51	15 49	18 45	21 39	24♐31
1925	23♏00	25 57	28♐52	01 44	04 34	07 21	10 05	12 43	15 17	17 43	20 00	22 06	23 56	25 27	26♐33
1926	00♐38	02 55	05 02	06 57	08 36	09 57	10 54	11 R 22	11 15	10 28	09 00	06 53	04 18	01 35	29♏03
1927	25♏R19	24 29	23 01	20 58	18 28	15 49	13 21	11 21	10 03	09 D 31	09 44	10 37	12 01	13 52	16♏01
1928	23♎R59	23 D 51	24 27	25 41	27 25	29♏34	02 00	04 40	07 29	10 25	13 25	16 28	19 33	22 39	25♏46
1929	22♎27	25 32	28♏42	01 55	05 08	08 23	11 37	14 50	18 03	21 15	24 27	27 37	00♐47	03 56	07♐05
1930	03♏59	07 17	10 33	13 47	17 00	20 12	23 22	26 31	29♐39	02 45	05 52	08 57	12 02	15 06	18♐09
1931	15♏55	19 02	22 07	25 11	28 13	01♐13	04 12	07 10	10 05	12 59	15 49	18 37	21 20	23 59	26♐30
1932	27♏26	00♐12	02 54	05 32	08 04	10 29	12 46	14 53	16 46	18 22	19 36	20 R 22	20 35	20 08	18♐59
1933	01♐32	02 57	04 01	04 38	04 44	04 14	03 04	01 14	28♏52	26 12	23 33	21 18	19 40	18 47	18♏40
1934	12♏R54	10 20	07 47	05 34	03 58	03 D 06	03 00	03 37	04 50	06 33	08 38	11 00	13 35	16 19	19♏09
1935	19♎13	21 01	23 14	25 45	28 29	01♏23	04 23	07 27	10 35	13 43	16 53	20 03	23 13	26 23	29♐32
1936	27♎36	00♏54	04 11	07 28	10 45	13 59	17 13	20 26	23 37	26 48	29♐57	03 06	06 14	09 22	12♐29
1937	09♏47	13 01	16 13	19 23	22 32	25 39	28♐45	01 50	04 54	07 57	10 58	13 59	16 58	19 56	22♐53
1938	21♏07	24 07	27♐05	00 02	02 56	05 48	08 37	11 23	14 05	16 41	19 12	21 35	23 47	25 45	27♐26
1939	29♏38	02♐06	04 27	06 39	08 41	10 28	11 59	13 07	13 R 48	13 56	13 26	12 14	10 20	07 54	05♐11
1940	28♏R07	27 51	26 57	25 25	23 17	20 45	18 05	15 38	13 43	12 30	12 D 03	12 21	13 16	14 43	16♏35
1941	27♎R59	26 47	26 D 22	26 41	27 40	29♏13	01 12	03 31	06 04	08 49	11 41	14 38	17 39	20 42	23♏47
1942	20♎50	23 44	26 46	29♏53	03 03	06 15	09 28	12 41	15 54	19 06	22 28	25 29	28♐39	01 49	04♐58
1943	01♏42	05 01	08 18	11 34	14 48	18 01	21 13	24 23	27 32	00♐41	03 48	06 54	10 00	13 06	16♐10
1944	15♏23	18 31	21 38	24 43	27 46	00♐59	03 50	06 48	09 47	12 43	15 37	18 29	21 17	24 01	26♐41
1945	25♏49	28♐40	01 27	04 12	06 52	09 28	11 58	14 20	16 32	18 32	20 17	21 41	22 40	23 R 07	22♐57
1946	01♐33	03 22	04 56	06 10	06 59	07 R 20	07 05	06 10	04 35	02 23	29♏47	27 05	24 38	22 44	21♏34
1947	18♏R33	16 25	13 54	11 18	08 54	07 02	05 52	05 D 28	05 49	06 49	08 20	10 16	12 31	15 00	17♏40
1948	20♎35	21 56	23 47	26 01	28 32	01♏16	04 09	07 09	10 12	13 18	16 26	19 34	22 43	25 52	29♐01
1949	25♎28	28♏43	02 00	05 16	08 33	11 48	15 02	18 16	21 28	24 40	27 50	01♐00	04 09	07 17	10♐25
1950	07♏33	10 48	14 02	17 14	20 24	23 33	26 41	29♐48	02 53	05 58	09 02	12 04	15 06	18 07	21♐06
1951	19♏09	22 12	25 13	28 13	01♐10	04 06	06 59	09 51	12 39	15 24	18 04	20 38	23 06	25 24	27♐29
1952	29♏42	02♐16	04 45	07 D 07	09 19	11 21	13 08	14 38	15 45	16 R 24	16 29	15 54	14 37	12 39	10♐09
1953	00♐08	00 38	00 36	29♏58	28 41	26 46	24 20	21 40	19 06	16 56	15 25	14 D 40	14 41	15 22	16♏37
1954	03♏R18	01 12	29♎43	28 D 59	29 01	29♏46	01 05	02 54	05 05	07 32	10 11	12 59	15 53	18 52	21♏53
1955	19♎40	22 16	25 04	28 02	01♏06	04 14	07 24	10 35	13 47	16 59	20 10	23 21	26 32	29♐42	02♎51
1956	01♏05	04 24	07 42	10 59	14 13	17 27	20 39	23 50	27 00	00♐09	03 17	06 24	09 31	12 37	15♐43
1957	13♏15	16 25	19 34	22 41	25 47	28♐51	01 54	04 56	07 57	01 56	13 53	16 49	19 43	22 34	25♐21
1958	24♏03	26 58	29♐51	02 41	05 27	08 11	10 50	13 23	15 50	18 08	20 15	22 07	23 42	24 53	25♐34
1959	01♐04	03 12	05 08	06 50	08 14	09 15	09 R 49	09 49	09 11	07 51	05 52	03 23	00♏40	28 04	25♏56
1960	22♏R35	20 56	18 45	16 11	13 34	11 13	09 24	08 19	08 D 01	08 26	09 29	11 03	13 00	15 16	17♏44
1961	22♎D19	22 46	23 53	25 32	27 37	00♏01	02 39	05 28	08 24	11 24	14 28	17 34	20 41	23 49	26♏57
1962	23♎27	26 38	29♏51	03 06	06 21	09 36	12 51	16 05	19 18	22 30	25 41	28♐52	02 01	05 10	08♐19
1963	05♏17	08 34	11 50	15 03	18 16	21 26	24 36	27 44	00♐51	03 57	07 02	10 07	13 10	16 13	19♐15
1964	18♏40	21 45	24 48	27 49	00 49	03 47	06 43	09 37	12 29	15♐18	18 04	20 45	23 20	25 48	28♐06
1965	28♏18	01♐00	03 38	06 10	08 36	10 54	13 01	14 56	16 35	17 52	18 44	19 R 04	18 46	17 46	16♐02
1966	01♐12	02 20	03 R 02	03 15	02 52	01 50	00♏09	27 53	25 16	22 36	20 14	18 27	17 24	17 08	17♏33
1967	09♏R21	06 47	04 30	02 45	01 D 43	01 27	01 56	03 02	04 40	06 41	09 01	11 35	14 D 18	17 09	20♏04
1968	20♎08	22 27	25 03	27 52	00♏49	03 52	06 58	10 07	13 17	16 28	19 39	22 49	26 00	29♐10	02♐19
1969	28♎50	02♏09	05 27	08 44	12 00	15 15	18 29	21 41	24 52	28 02	01♐11	04 19	07 27	10 34	13♐40
1970	11♏04	14 17	17 28	20 37	23 45	26 51	29♐56	03 00	06 02	09 04	12 04	15 03	18 01	20 56	23♐49
1971	22♏13	25 12	28 08	01♐02	03 54	06 43	09 28	12 10	14 47	17 18	19 41	21 54	23 54	25 38	27♐00
1972	01♐26	03 44	05 52	07 48	09 30	10 53	11 53	12 24	12 R 21	11 39	10 14	08 11	05 38	02 54	00♏20
1973	26♏R26	25 40	24 15	22 15	19 47	17 08	14 38	12 34	11 12	10 35	10 D 44	11 33	12 54	14 42	16♏50
1974	25♎R29	24 53	25 D 04	25 55	27 22	29♏17	01 33	04 05	06 49	09 41	12 38	15 40	18 44	21 49	24♏56
1975	21♎40	24 42	27 49	01♏00	04 13	07 27	10 41	13 55	17 08	20 20	23 32	26 43	29♐53	03 03	06♐12
1976	04♏39	07 57	11 13	14 28	17 41	20 52	24 02	27 11	00♐19	03 26	06 33	09 38	12 43	15 47	18♐50
1977	16♏36	19 43	22 48	25 52	28♐55	01 55	04 55	07 52	10 48	13 42	16 33	19 21	22 05	24 44	27♐17
1978	26♏45	29 33	02♐18	04 58	07 34	10 04	12 26	14 40	16 41	18 28	19 56	21 00	21 R 34	21 32	20♐48
1979	01♐34	03 10	04 27	05 21	05 R 47	05 40	04 54	03 27	01 23	28♏52	26 10	23 38	21 36	20 15	19♏D41
1980	14♏R12	11 39	09 05	06 49	05 08	04 D 11	04 01	04 33	05 43	07 23	09 26	11 46	14 20	17 03	19♏52
1981	20♎06	21 51	24 01	26 30	29♏13	02 06	05 05	08 09	11 16	14 24	17 34	20 44	23 53	27 03	00♐12
1982	26♎38	29♏55	03 13	06 30	09 47	13 02	16 17	19 30	22 42	25 53	29♐03	02 12	05 21	08 29	11♐36
1983	08♏49	12 04	15 17	18 28	21 38	24 46	27 53	00♐58	04 03	07 06	10 09	13 10	16 10	19 09	22♐07
1984	21♏48	24 48	27 47	00♐43	03 38	06 30	09 20	12 06	14 49	17 26	19 58	22 21	24 35	26 35	28♐18
1985	00♐23	02 52	05 14	07 28	09 30	11 20	12 52	14 03	14 R 48	15 00	14 34	13 26	11 36	09 13	06♐30
1986	29♏R03	29 08	28 37	27 28	25 41	23 21	20 44	18 07	15 50	14 11	13 D 16	13 07	13 41	14 50	16♏30
1987	00♏R05	28♎28	27 34	27 27	28 03	29♏16	01 00	03 07	05 32	08 11	10 58	13 52	16 51	19 53	22♏57
1988	21♎35	24 28	27 29	00♏36	03 45	06 57	10 10	13 23	16 35	19 47	22 59	26 10	29♐20	02 30	05♐39
1989	02♏22	05 41	08 59	12 15	15 29	18 42	21 54	25 04	28 13	01♐22	04 29	07 36	10 42	13 47	16♐52
1990	14♏29	17 38	20 46	23 52	26 57	00♐00	03 01	06 02	09 01	11 58	14 53	17 47	20 37	23 24	26♐07
1991	25♏05	27 57	00♐47	03 34	06 17	08 56	11 29	13 56	16 15	18 23	20 18	21 55	23 10	23 R 58	24♐11
1992	02♐22	04 13	05 49	07 06	07 58	08 R 22	08 11	07 21	05 50	03 42	01♏07	28 24	25 55	23 57	22♏42
1993	19♏R48	17 44	15 15	12 38	10 12	08 15	07 01	06 D 32	06 49	07 44	09 13	11 06	13 19	15 47	18♏25
1994	21♎07	22 06	23 39	25 40	28 01	00♏38	03 26	06 21	09 22	12 27	15 33	18 41	21 50	24 59	28♏07
1995	24♎32	27 46	01♏02	04 18	07 35	10 50	14 05	17 19	20 32	23 44	26 55	00♐05	03 14	06 23	09♐31
1996	08♏13	11 28	14 42	17 54	21 05	24 14	27 22	00♐29	03 34	06 39	09 43	12 46	15 48	18 49	21♐49
1997	19♏50	22 53	25 54	28♐54	01 52	04 48	07 42	10 34	13 22	16 07	18 48	21 24	23 52	26 12	28♐19
1998	29♏07	01♐44	04 17	06 43	09 02	11 10	13 07	14 48	16 09	17 06	17 R 32	17 22	16 31	14 57	12♐45
1999	00♐38	01 25	01 44	01 28	00♏34	29 02	26 53	24 20	21 39	19 12	17 16	16 04	15 D 38	15 55	16♏50
2000	04♏R34	02 25	00 52	00♎D03	00♏01	00 41	01 58	03 43	05 52	08 17	10 55	13 42	16 36	19 34	22♏34

December

Year	1st	3rd	5th	7th	9th	11th	13th	15th	17th	19th	21st	23rd	25th	27th	29th	31st
1900	20♏14	20 55	22 08	23 48	25 47	28 02	00♐28	03 03	05 44	08 31	11 21	14 15	17 11	20 09	23 08	26♐10
1901	21♏18	27 23	29 26	01♐27	03 27	05 25	07 21	09 15	11 07	12 56	14 43	16 27	18 08	19♑45	21 19	22♑49
1902	01♐29	04 37	07 46	10 54	14 02	17 11	20 19	23 28	26 38	29♑48	02 59	05 10	09 23	12 36	15 49	19♑03
1903	12♐51	15 58	19 05	22 12	25 19	28 26	01♑32	04 39	07 44	10 48	13 50	16 49	19 43	22 30	25 08	27♑32
1904	24♐50	27 44	00♑35	03 21	06 02	08 34	10 55	13 02	14 48	16 09	16R57	17 06	16 29	15 06	13 01	10♑28
1905	29♐13	00♑26	01R09	01 15	00 37	29♐15	27 10	24 36	21 50	19 16	17 11	15 46	15D04	15 03	15 37	16♐39
1906	06♐R05	03 30	01 23	29♏58	29D17	29 20	00♐00	01 12	02 47	04 42	06 52	09 14	11 44	14 21	17 03	19♐49
1907	17♏28	19 32	21 52	24 23	27 02	29 47	02 38	05 31	08 27	11 26	14 26	17 27	20 30	23 34	26 39	29♐45
1908	25♏46	28♐51	01 57	05 03	08 09	11♐16	14 23	17 31	20 38	23 47	26 56	00♑06	03 17	06 29	09 41	12♑56
1909	06♐54	10 02	13 11	15 19	19 28	22 36	25 45	28♑55	02 04	05 15	08 25	11 36	14 46	17 56	21 04	24♑10
1910	18♐06	21 11	24 15	27 19	00♑21	03 22	06 22	09 18	12 10	14 56	17 33	19 59	22 11	24 01	25 24	26♑13
1911	27♐19	29♑55	02 22	04 38	06 39	08 20	09 37	10R21	10 26	09 47	08 21	06 14	03 39	00♐55	28 23	26♐22
1912	24♐R20	23 18	21 32	19 10	16 27	13 45	11 24	09 40	08D40	08 22	08 44	09 38	10 58	12 40	14 38	16♐49
1913	22♏R55	22D40	23 06	24 07	25 36	27 27	29♐35	01 56	04 26	07 04	09 47	12 35	15 27	18 21	21 17	24♐16
1914	19♏38	22 25	25 17	28 13	01♐11	04 12	07 13	10 16	13 20	16 24	19 30	22 36	25 43	28♑51	01 59	05♑09
1915	29♏24	02♐32	05 40	08 48	11 56	15 04	18 13	21 22	24 31	27 40	00♑51	04 02	07 14	10 27	13 40	16♑55
1916	12♐20	15 28	18 35	21 43	24 50	27 58	01♑06	04 13	07 20	10 27	13 32	16 35	19 35	22 30	25 18	27♑56
1917	23♐04	26 02	28♑58	01 52	04 42	07 26	10 04	12 31	14 45	16 42	18 14	19 17	19R42	19 24	18 19	16♑29
1918	29♐22	01♑08	02 33	03 29	03R51	03 31	02 26	00♐37	28 12	25 28	22 47	20 29	18 48	17D50	17 32	17♐52
1919	12♐R25	09 42	07 01	04 41	02 59	02D01	01 47	02 13	03 12	04 38	06 24	08 28	10 43	13 09	15 42	18♐21
1920	18♏25	20 11	22 16	24 35	27 06	29♐44	02 29	05 19	08 12	11 07	14 05	17 04	20 05	23 08	26 11	29♐16
1921	23♏52	26 54	29♐58	03 03	06 08	09 14	12 20	15 27	18 34	21 41	24 50	27 59	01♑08	04 19	07 31	10♑44
1922	04♐47	07 56	11 05	14 13	17 22	20 30	23 39	26 48	29♑58	03 09	06 19	09 31	12 42	15 54	19 05	22♑16
1923	16♐05	19 11	22 17	25 22	28 27	01♑31	04 34	07 35	10 34	13 29	16 19	19 02	21 35	23 54	25 54	27♑29
1924	27♐18	00♑01	02 37	05 05	07 21	09 22	11 02	12 16	12R57	12 58	12 13	10 42	08 31	05 54	03 11	00♑43
1925	27♐R08	27 06	26 21	24 51	22 41	20 04	17 18	14 48	12 48	11 31	10D57	11 03	11 44	12 54	14 27	16♐17
1926	27♏R03	25 45	25D12	25 23	26 10	27 28	29♐10	01 11	03 25	05 51	08 25	11 05	13 50	16 39	19 31	22♐26
1927	18♏26	21 01	23 44	26 33	29♐26	02 22	05 20	08 21	11 22	14 25	17 29	20 33	23 39	26 45	29♑53	03♑02
1928	18♏54	02♐01	05 09	08 17	11 24	14 32	17 40	20 49	23 58	27 07	00♑17	03 28	06 40	09 53	13 07	16♑22
1929	10♐13	13 22	16 30	19 38	22 46	25 54	29♑02	02 11	05 19	08 28	11 36	14 43	17 48	20 51	23 50	26♑42
1930	21♐11	24 13	27 13	00♑11	03 07	06 00	08 48	11 30	14 04	16 25	18 30	20 14	21 30	22R11	22 11	21♑24
1931	28♐53	01♑04	02 59	04 34	05 44	06R20	06 17	05 30	03 57	01 44	29♐05	26 21	23 53	21 57	20 42	20♐D08
1932	17♐R06	14 40	11 56	09 16	07 00	06 23	04D30	04 21	04 50	05 51	07 18	09 05	11 09	13 24	15 50	18♐22
1933	19♏14	20 22	21 57	23 54	26 07	28 32	01♐06	03 48	06 34	09 25	12 18	15 15	18 13	21 12	24 14	27♐16
1934	22♏04	25 03	28 04	01♐06	04 09	07 14	10 19	13 24	16 30	19 37	22 44	25 52	29♑01	02 11	05 21	08♑33
1935	02♐41	05 50	08 59	12 07	15 15	18 24	21 33	24 42	27 51	01♑02	04 12	07 24	10 36	13 49	17 02	20♑14
1936	15♐36	18 43	21 49	24 55	28 01	01♑07	04 12	07 16	10 18	13 18	16 15	19 06	21 49	24 22	26 41	28♑39
1937	25♐46	28♑37	01 23	04 04	06 37	08 59	11 08	12 58	14 24	15R19	15 37	15 10	13 57	12 00	09 31	06♑48
1938	28♐43	29R32	29 46	29 18	28 05	26 09	23 40	20 55	18 17	16 04	14 30	13D39	13 30	13 57	14 55	16♐18
1939	02♐R32	00♏17	28 42	27D52	27 46	28 20	29♐26	00 58	02 50	04 59	07 19	09 48	12 25	15 07	17 54	20♐44
1940	18♏45	21 09	23 44	26 27	29♐15	02 07	05 02	08 00	11 00	14 01	17 03	20 06	23 11	26 16	29♑23	02♑30
1941	26♏53	29♐59	03 06	06 13	09 20	12 27	15 35	18 43	21 51	25 00	28 10	01♑20	04 31	07 43	10 56	14♑11
1942	08♐07	11 15	14 24	17 32	20 40	23 49	26 58	00♑07	03 16	06 25	09 35	12 44	15 53	19 01	22 06	25♑08
1943	19♐15	22 18	25 21	28 23	01♑23	04 22	07 17	10 09	12 55	15 34	18 01	20 15	22 09	23 38	24R34	24♑50
1944	29♐13	01♑36	03 47	05 41	07 15	08 22	08R55	08 48	07 55	06 17	04 01	01♐20	28 37	26 13	24 21	23♐10
1945	22♐04	20R27	18 12	15 33	12 48	10 21	08 28	07 18	06 52	07 06	07 55	09 11	10 50	12 46	14 56	17♐17
1946	21♏09	21 28	22 23	23 47	25 35	27 41	00♐00	02 30	05 08	07 51	10 39	13 31	16 25	19 22	22 21	25♐21
1947	20♏27	23 19	26 15	29♐14	02 15	05 17	08 20	11 24	14 29	17 35	20 41	23 48	26 55	00♑04	03 13	06♑24
1948	02♐10	05 19	08 27	11 35	14 44	17 52	21 01	24 10	27 19	00♑30	03 40	06 52	10 04	13 17	16 31	19♑45
1949	13♐32	16 40	19 47	22 54	26 01	29♑08	02 15	05 21	08 27	11 31	14 33	17 33	20 27	23 16	25 55	28♑21
1950	24♐04	27 00	29♑53	02 43	05 27	08 05	10 33	12 49	14 49	16 26	17 35	18R09	18 00	17 05	05 24	13♑05
1951	29♐19	00♑48	01 50	02R19	02 08	01 13	29♐32	27 14	24 33	21 49	19 25	17 35	16 27	16D02	16 15	17♐01
1952	07♐R24	04 48	02 37	01 07	00D22	00 21	00♐57	02 06	03 39	05 32	07 40	10 00	12 30	15 06	17 47	20♐33
1953	18♏19	20 21	22 39	25 09	27 47	00♐32	03 22	06 15	09 11	12 09	15 08	18 10	21 12	24 16	27 20	00♑26
1954	24♏56	28 00	01♐06	04 11	07 18	10 24	13 31	16 38	19 46	22 54	26 02	29♑12	02 22	05 33	08 46	11♑59
1955	06♐00	09 09	12 18	15 26	18 34	21 43	24 52	28 01	01♑11	04 21	07 31	10 42	13 52	17 03	20 12	23♑20
1956	18♐48	21 53	24 57	28 01	01♑04	04 05	07 05	10 02	12 54	15 41	18 20	20 48	23 01	24 54	26 20	27♑13
1957	28♐04	00♑41	03 09	05 27	07 30	09 14	10 33	11R21	11 30	10 56	09 35	07 31	04 58	02 14	29♐41	27♐35
1958	25♐R40	25 04	23 44	21 42	19 09	16 24	13 48	11 41	10 14	09D30	09 29	10 04	11 09	12 38	14 27	16♐30
1959	24♏R28	23D46	23 48	24 29	25 42	27 20	29♐18	01 31	03 56	06 29	09 09	11 54	14 44	17 36	20 31	23♐28
1960	20♏23	23 10	26 01	28♐56	01 54	04 54	07 55	10 58	14 02	17 06	20 11	23 17	26 24	29♑32	02 41	05♑51
1961	00♐05	03 13	06 21	09 29	12 37	15 46	18 54	22 03	25 12	28 21	01♑32	04 43	07 55	11 08	14 21	17♑36
1962	11♐27	14 35	17 42	20 50	23 58	27 05	00♑13	03 21	06 28	09 35	12 42	15 46	18 48	21 47	24 39	27 24
1963	22♐16	25 15	28 13	01♑09	04 01	06 49	09 31	12 05	14 28	16 36	18 24	19 45	20 34	20R42	20 05	18♑42
1964	00♑11	02 00	03 28	04 27	04R53	04 37	03 37	01 52	29♐29	26 47	24 05	21 44	19 59	18 56	18 35	18♐51
1965	13♐R43	11 01	08 19	05 56	04 09	03D07	02 49	03 10	04 06	05 29	07 14	09 15	11 30	13 54	16 27	19♐05
1966	18♏35	20 06	22 00	24 11	26 35	29♐09	01 50	04 37	07 27	10 21	13 18	16 16	19 16	22 17	25 20	28♐24
1967	23♏03	26 05	29♐08	02 12	05 17	08 22	11 28	14 34	17 41	20 48	23 56	27 04	00♑14	03 24	06 35	09♑48
1968	05♐28	08 37	11 45	14 54	18 02	21 11	24 20	27 29	00♑39	03 49	07 00	10 12	13 23	16 35	19 47	22♑58
1969	16♐47	19 53	22 58	26 04	29♑09	02 13	05 16	08 18	11 17	14 13	17 04	19 48	22 22	24 43	26 45	28♑23
1970	26♐40	29♑26	02 06	04 40	07 04	09 14	11 07	12 38	13 40	14R05	13 48	12 45	10 57	08 33	05 51	03♑12
1971	27♐55	28R16	27 57	26 54	25 07	22 44	20 01	17 19	14 59	13 15	12 15	11D58	12 19	13 12	14 31	16♐11
1972	28♏R16	26 54	26 17	26D23	27 07	28 22	00♐02	02 00	04 14	06 38	09 11	11 50	14 35	17 24	20 15	23♐10
1973	19♏13	21 47	24 29	27 17	00♐10	03 06	06 04	09 04	12 05	15 08	18 11	21 16	24 21	27 28	00♑35	03♑44
1974	28♏03	01♐10	04 17	07 25	10 32	13 40	16 48	19 56	23 05	26 14	29♑24	02 35	05 46	08 58	12 12	15♑26
1975	09♐20	12 29	15 37	18 45	21 53	25 01	28 09	01♑18	04 27	07 35	10 44	13 52	16 58	20 03	23 05	26♑01
1976	21♐53	24 55	27 55	00♑54	03 51	06 44	09 33	12 16	14 50	17 13	19 21	21 07	22 26	23R12	23 16	22♑33
1977	29♐41	01♑53	03 50	05 28	06 41	07R21	07 23	06 40	05 12	03 02	00♐25	27 41	25 10	23 10	21 50	21♐D13
1978	07♐R45	11 16	14 43	18 08	21 29	24 47	28 02	01D14	04 23	07 30	10 34	13 36	16 36	19 33	22 28	25♐20
1979	19♏51	20 39	21 58	23 43	25 46	28 04	00♐33	03 10	05 54	08 42	11 34	14 28	17 25	20 24	23 24	26♐26
1980	22♏47	25 45	28♐45	01 47	04 51	07 55	11 00	14 05	17 11	20 18	23 25	26 33	29♑41	02 51	06 02	09♑13
1981	03♐21	06 30	09 39	12 47	15 56	19 04	22 13	25 22	28♑32	01 42	04 53	08 04	11 16	14 29	17 42	20♑55
1982	14♐43	17 50	20 57	24 03	27 09	00♑15	03 21	06 26	09 29	12 31	15 30	18 24	21 13	23 53	26 21	28♑32
1983	25♐02	27 55	00♑44	03 29	06 07	08 36	10 54	12 56	14 38	15 52	16R33	16 34	15 49	14 18	12 06	09♑29
1984	29♐38	00♑R31	00 49	00♐25	29 17	27 25	24 59	22 14	19 34	17 18	15 40	14D44	14 31	14 55	15 50	17♐10
1985	03♐R50	01 32	29♏52	28D58	28 47	29 17	00♐20	01 49	03 40	05 46	08 05	10 34	13 10	15 51	18 37	21♐27
1986	18♏26	20 43	23 11	25 49	28 34	01♐23	04 17	07 13	10 12	13 12	16 13	19 16	22 19	25 24	28♑30	01♑37
1987	26♏02	29♐07	02 14	05 21	08 27	11 35	14 42	17 50	20 58	24 06	27 15	00♑25	03 36	06 47	10 00	13♑14
1988	08♐48	11 56	15 05	18 13	21 21	24 30	27 39	00♑48	03 57	07 07	10 17	13 26	16 35	19 43	22 49	25♑52
1989	19♐56	23 00	26 03	29♑05	02 06	05 05	08 01	10 53	13 40	16 20	18 49	21 05	23 01	24 33	25R33	25♑54
1990	28♐44	01♑13	03 32	05 37	07 24	08 48	09R43	10 01	09 36	08 25	06 30	04 02	01♐18	28 40	26 27	24♐51
1991	23♐R44	22 34	20 41	18 14	15 30	12 50	10 35	08 58	08D06	07 56	08 24	09 25	10 50	12 36	14 38	16♐52
1992	22♏D13	22 27	23 18	24 40	26 25	28 29	00♐47	03 16	05 52	08 35	11 23	14 14	17 08	20 04	23 02	26♐02
1993	21♏11	24 02	26 58	29♐56	02 56	05 58	09 01	12 05	15 10	18 15	21 21	24 28	27 36	00♑44	03 54	07♑04
1994	01♐16	04 25	07 33	10 41	13 50	16 58	20 07	23 15	26 25	29♑35	02 45	05 56	09 08	12 21	15 35	18♑49
1995	12♐39	15 46	18 54	22 01	25 08	28 15	01♑22	04 29	07 35	10 40	13 44	16 46	19 44	22 37	25 22	27♑56
1996	24♐47	27 43	00♑37	03 27	06 12	08 51	11 21	13 39	15 40	17 20	18 32	19R10	19 06	18 15	16 39	14♑24
1997	00♑10	01 42	02 47	03R20	03 13	02 23	00♐47	28 32	25 52	23 08	20 41	18 47	17 34	17D05	17 14	17♐57
1998	10♐R07	07 22	04 54	02 58	01D46	01 19	01 33	02 23	03 42	05 23	07 23	09 36	12 00	14 31	17 10	19♐53
1999	18♏16	20 07	22 16	24 38	27 12	29♐53	02 39	05 30	08 24	11 21	14 20	17 20	20 22	23 24	26 28	29♐34
2000	25♏37	28♐41	01 46	04 52	07 58	11 05	14 11	17 18	20 26	23 34	26 43	29♑52	03 02	06 13	09 26	12♑39

Venus

January

Year	1st	3rd	5th	7th	9th	11th	13th	15th	17th	19th	21st	23rd	25th	27th	29th	31st
1900	06♒23	08 52	11 21	13 50	16 19	18 48	21 16	23 45	26 13	28 41	01♓09	03 37	06 05	08 32	11 00	13♓27
1901	10♐45	13 14	15 43	18 12	20 42	23 11	25 40	28 10	00♑39	03 09	05 38	08 08	10 37	13 07	15 36	18♑06
1902	23♑33	24 56	26 15	27 28	28 37	29 39	00♒34	01 23	02 04	02 37	03 01	03 16	03 21	03 17	03 03	02♒38
1903	17♑19	19 50	22 21	24 51	27 22	29♒53	02 23	04 54	07 25	09 55	12 26	14 56	17 27	19 57	22 27	24♒57
1904	25♏10	27 29	29♐49	02 10	04 30	06 52	09 14	11 36	13 58	16 21	18 44	21 08	23 31	25 55	28 19	00♑44
1905	22♒14	24 36	26 57	29♓17	01 37	03 57	06 16	08 34	10 51	13 08	15 24	17 40	19 54	22 08	24 20	26♓32
1906	29♐02	01♑33	04 04	06 35	09 06	11 37	14 07	16 38	19 09	21 40	24 11	26 42	29♒12	01 43	04 14	06♒44
1907	01♐51	02 43	03 42	04 48	05 59	07 15	08 36	10 02	11 32	13 06	14 43	16 23	18 07	19 53	21 42	23♐33
1908	05♒46	08 15	10 44	13 13	15 41	18 10	20 39	23 07	25 35	28 03	00♓31	02 59	05 26	07 54	10 21	12♓49
1909	11♐22	13 51	16 21	18 50	21 19	23 48	26 18	28♑47	01 17	03 47	06 16	08 46	11 15	13 45	16 15	18♑44
1910	22♒47	24 05	25 18	26 24	27 25	28 19	29 06	29♓45	00 17	00 39	00 52	00 56	00 49	00 33	00♒06	29♒30
1911	17♑59	20 30	23 01	25 32	28 02	00♒33	03 04	05 34	08 05	10 35	13 06	15 36	18 07	20 37	23 07	25♒37
1912	25♏35	27 55	00♐16	02 37	04 58	07 20	09 42	12 05	14 28	16 51	19 15	21 39	24 03	26 27	28♑51	01♑16
1913	22♒43	25 04	27 24	29♓44	02 04	04 22	06 41	08 58	11 15	13 31	15 46	18 01	20 14	22 26	24 38	26♓48
1914	29♐43	02♑14	04 45	07 16	09 47	12 17	14 48	17 19	19 50	22 21	24 52	27 22	29♒53	02 24	04 55	07♒25
1915	00♐29	01 29	02 36	03 48	05 05	06 28	07 55	09 26	11 00	12 38	14 20	16 04	17 51	19 40	21 32	23♐26
1916	06♒24	08 53	11 22	13 51	16 20	18 48	21 17	23 45	26 13	28 41	01♓09	03 36	06 04	08 31	10 58	13♓25
1917	12♐01	14 30	16 59	19 29	21 58	24 27	26 57	29♑27	01 56	04 26	06 55	09 25	11 55	14 25	16 54	19♑24
1918	21♒56	23 07	24 13	25 12	26 04	26 50	27 27	27 57	28 17	28 R 29	28 30	28 22	28 03	27 35	26 56	26♒09
1919	18♑40	21 11	23 42	26 13	28 43	01♒14	03 45	06 15	08 46	11 16	13 46	16 17	18 47	21 17	23 48	26♒18
1920	26♏02	28 22	00♐43	03 05	05 27	07 49	10 12	12 35	14 58	17 22	19 46	22 10	24 35	26 59	29♑24	01♑49
1921	23♒11	25 31	27 51	00♓10	02 29	04 47	07 04	09 21	11 37	13 52	16 06	18 20	20 32	22 44	24 54	27♓03
1922	00♑24	02 55	05 25	07 56	10 27	12 58	15 28	18 00	20 31	23 01	25 32	28 03	00♒34	03 05	05 35	08♒06
1923	29♏16	00♐24	01 38	02 56	04 20	05 47	07 19	08 55	10 34	12 16	14 01	15 49	17 39	19 31	21 26	23♐23
1924	07♒02	09 31	12 00	14 28	16 57	19 25	21 54	24 22	26 50	29♓18	01 45	04 13	06 40	09 07	11 34	14♓01
1925	12♐38	15 08	17 37	20 06	22 36	25 06	27 35	00♑05	02 35	05 04	07 34	10 04	12 34	15 03	17 33	20♑03
1926	20♒56	22 00	22 58	23 49	24 32	25 08	25 36	25 54	26 R 04	26 03	25 53	25 32	25 02	24 21	23 32	22♒34
1927	19♑20	21 51	24 22	26 52	29♒23	01 54	04 24	06 55	09 25	11 56	14 26	16 56	19 27	21 57	24 27	26♒57
1928	26♏28	28 49	01♐11	03 33	05 55	08 18	10 41	13 04	15 28	17 52	20 17	22 41	25 06	27 31	29♑56	02♑22
1929	23♒37	25 57	28 16	00♓35	02 53	05 10	07 27	09 42	11 58	14 12	16 25	18 37	20 49	22 59	25 08	27♓16
1930	01♑04	03 35	06 06	08 37	11 08	13 38	16 09	18 40	21 11	23 42	26 13	28 44	01♒14	03 45	06 16	08♒47
1931	28♏13	29♐27	00 47	02 12	03 40	05 13	06 49	08 29	10 12	11 58	13 46	15 37	17 30	19 25	21 23	23♐21
1932	07♒40	10 09	12 37	15 06	17 34	20 03	22 31	24 59	27 27	29♓54	02 22	04 49	07 16	09 43	12 10	14♓36
1933	13♐17	15 46	18 16	20 45	23 15	25 45	28 14	00♑44	03 14	05 43	08 13	10 43	13 13	15 43	18 13	20♑43
1934	19♒47	20 44	21 33	22 15	22 49	23 15	23 31	23 R 38	23 36	23 23	23 01	22 28	21 46	20 55	19 55	18♒50
1935	20♑01	22 32	25 03	27 33	01♒04	02 35	05 05	07 36	10 06	12 37	15 07	17 37	20 07	22 37	25 08	27♒38
1936	26♏56	29 18	01♐40	04 02	06 25	08 49	11 12	13 36	16 00	18 25	20 49	23 14	25 40	28 05	00♑30	02♑56
1937	24♒04	26 23	28 42	00♓59	03 17	05 33	07 59	10 04	12 18	14 31	16 44	18 55	21 05	23 14	25 21	27♓28
1938	01♑45	04 16	06 47	09 18	11 49	14 20	16 50	19 21	21 52	24 23	26 54	29♒25	01 55	04 26	06 57	09♒28
1939	27♏18	28 39	00♐04	01 34	03 07	04 45	06 25	08 09	09 55	11 44	13 36	15 30	17 26	19 23	21 22	23♐24
1940	08♒18	10 46	13 15	15 43	18 12	20 40	23 08	25 36	28 03	00♓31	02 58	05 25	07 52	10 19	12 45	15♓11
1941	13♐55	16 25	18 54	21 24	23 54	26 23	28♑53	01 23	03 53	06 22	08 52	11 22	13 52	16 22	18 52	21♑22
1942	18♒28	19 16	19 56	20 28	20 52	21 06	21 R 11	21 07	20 52	20 27	19 52	19 08	18 15	17 15	16 08	14♒57
1943	20♑41	23 12	25 43	28 13	00♒44	03 14	05 45	08 15	10 46	13 16	15 46	18 17	20 47	23 17	25 47	28♒17
1944	27♏24	29 46	02♐09	04 32	06 55	09 19	11 43	14 07	16 31	18 56	21 21	23 46	26 12	28 37	01♑03	03♑29
1945	24♒29	26 48	29♓05	01 22	03 39	05 54	08 09	10 23	12 36	14 48	17 00	19 10	21 18	23 26	25 32	27♓37
1946	02♑26	04 57	07♐28	09 59	12 30	15 01	17 31	20 02	22 33	25 04	27 35	00♒06	02 36	05 07	07 38	10♒09
1947	26♏31	27 57	29 28	01 02	02 40	04 21	06 06	07 53	09 43	11 35	13 29	15 25	17 24	19 24	21 25	23♏28
1948	08♒56	11 24	13 53	16 21	18 49	21 17	23 45	26 13	28 40	01♓07	03 35	06 01	08 28	10 55	13 21	15♓47
1949	14♐34	17 04	19 33	22 03	24 33	27 03	29♑33	02 03	04 32	07 02	09 32	12 02	14 32	17 02	19 32	22♑02
1950	16♒59	17 37	18 08	18 29	18 R 41	18 44	18 37	18 20	17 53	17 16	16 30	15 36	14 34	13 26	12 14	11♒00
1951	21♑22	23 52	26 23	28♒54	01 24	03 55	06 25	08 56	11 26	13 56	16 27	18 57	21 27	23 57	26 27	28♒57
1952	27♏53	00♐16	02 39	05 02	07 26	09 50	12 14	14 39	17 04	19 29	21 54	24 20	26 46	29♑11	01 38	04♑04
1953	24♒54	27 11	29♓28	01 45	04 00	06 15	08 29	10 42	12 54	15 05	17 14	19 23	21 30	23 36	25 41	27♓44
1954	03♑06	05 37	08 08	10 39	13 10	15 41	18 12	20 43	23 14	25 44	28 15	00♒46	03 17	05 48	08 18	10♒49
1955	25♏50	27 22	28 57	00♐36	02 18	04 03	05 51	07 41	09 34	11 28	13 25	15 24	17 24	19 26	21 30	23♐35
1956	09♒33	12 01	14 30	16 58	19 26	21 53	24 21	26 49	29♓16	01 43	04 10	05 37	09 03	11 29	13 55	16♓21
1957	15♐13	17 42	20 59	17 08	18 18	19 28	20♑39	21 51	23 01	24 13	25 25	26 37	27 59	29 02	00 15	01♑28
1958	15♒18	15 47	16 06	16 R 16	16 17	16 08	15 48	15 19	14 40	13 52	12 56	11 53	10 44	09 32	08 18	07♒04
1959	22♑02	24 33	27 04	29♒34	02 05	04 35	07 06	09 36	12 06	14 37	17 07	19 37	22 07	24 37	27 07	29♒37
1960	28♏23	00♐46	03 10	05 33	07 57	10 22	12 47	15 12	17 37	20 02	22 28	24 54	27 20	29♑46	02 12	04♑35
1961	25♒17	27 34	29♓50	02 06	04 20	06 34	08 47	10 59	13 09	15 19	17 28	19 35	21 41	23 45	25 48	27♓49
1962	03♑47	06 18	08 49	11 20	13 51	16 22	18 53	21 24	23 55	26 25	28♒56	01 27	03 58	06 29	08 59	11♒30
1963	25♏16	26 51	28 31	00♐14	02 00	03 48	05 39	07 32	09 27	11 25	13 24	15 25	17 27	19 31	21 37	23♐43
1964	10♒10	12 38	15 06	17 34	20 02	22 30	24 57	27 25	29♓52	02 19	04 45	07 12	09 38	12 04	14 30	16♓55
1965	15♐50	18 20	20 50	23 20	25 50	28 20	00♑50	03 20	05 50	08 20	10♒50	13 20	15 50	18 20	20 51	23♑21
1966	13♒24	13 41	13 R 49	13 48	13 36	13 15	12 43	12 02	11 12	10 14	09 09	08 00	06 47	05 33	04 20	03♒10
1967	22♑42	25 13	27 43	00♒14	02 44	05 15	07 45	10 16	12 46	15 16	17 46	20 16	22 46	25 16	27 46	00♓16
1968	28♏52	01♐16	03 40	06 04	08 29	10 53	13 19	15 44	18 09	20 35	23 01	25 27	27 53	00♑20	02 46	05♑13
1969	25♒40	27 56	00♓11	02 25	04 39	06 52	09 03	11 14	13 23	15 32	17 39	19 44	21 49	23 51	25 52	27♓51
1970	04♑28	06 59	09 30	12 01	14 32	17 03	19 34	22 05	24 36	27 07	29♒37	02 08	04 39	07 10	09 40	12♒11
1971	24♏48	26 28	28 12	29♐58	01 47	03 38	05 32	07 28	09 25	11 26	13 27	15 30	17 34	19 40	21 47	23♐55
1972	10♒48	13 16	15 44	18 12	20 39	23 07	25 34	28 01	00♓28	02 55	05 21	07 47	10 13	12 39	15 05	17♓30
1973	16♐30	19 00	21 30	24 00	26 30	29♑00	01 31	04 01	06 31	09 01	11 31	14 01	16 31	19 01	21 32	24♑02
1974	11♒16	11 R 22	11 19	11 05	10 41	10 07	09 24	08 32	07 32	06 26	05 16	04 03	02 49	01 37	00♑27	29♑23
1975	23♑23	25 53	28 24	00♒54	03 25	05 55	08 26	10 56	13 26	15 56	18 27	20 57	23 27	25 56	28 26	00♓56
1976	29♏23	01♐47	04 12	06 36	09 01	11 26	13 52	16 17	18 43	21 09	23 35	26 01	28 28	00♑55	03 21	05♑48
1977	26♒01	28 16	00♓31	02 44	04 57	07 08	09 19	11 28	13 36	15 43	17 48	19 52	21 55	23 55	25 54	27♓51
1978	05♑08	07 39	10 10	12 41	15 12	17 43	20 14	22 45	25 16	27 47	00♒17	02 48	05 19	07 50	10 20	12♒51
1979	24♏24	26 08	27 55	29♐45	01 37	03 31	05 27	07 25	09 25	11 27	13 30	15 35	17 41	19 49	21 57	24♐07
1980	11♒24	13 52	16 19	18 47	21 14	23 42	26 09	28 36	01♓02	03 29	05 55	08 21	10 47	13 12	15 37	18♓02
1981	17♐08	19 38	22 08	24 39	27 09	29♑39	02 09	04 39	07 09	09 39	12 09	14 40	17 10	19 40	22 10	24♑40
1982	08♒54	08 48	08 32	08 06	07 30	06 45	05 51	04 50	03 43	02 32	01 18	00♑05	28 53	27 45	26 42	25♑46
1983	24♑03	26 33	29♒04	01 34	04 05	06 35	09 05	11 36	14 06	16 36	19 06	21 36	24 06	26 36	29♓05	01♓35
1984	29♏54	02♐18	04 43	07 08	09 33	11 59	14 25	16 50	19 16	21 43	24 09	26 34	29♑02	01 29	03 56	06♑23
1985	26♒21	28 36	00♓49	03 01	05 13	07 23	09 32	11 40	13 47	15 52	17 56	19 58	21 58	23 57	25 54	27♓48
1986	05♑48	08 19	10 50	13 21	15 52	18 23	20 54	23 25	25 56	28 27	00♒58	03 29	05 59	08 30	11 01	13♒32
1987	24♏05	25 53	27 43	29♐36	01 30	03 27	05 26	07 26	09 28	11 32	13 37	15 43	17 51	20 00	22 10	24♐21
1988	12♒01	14 28	16 56	19 23	21 50	24 17	26 44	29♓11	01 37	04 04	06 30	08 55	11 21	13 46	16 11	18♓35
1989	17♐48	20 18	22 48	25 18	27 48	00♑18	02 49	05 19	07 49	10 19	12 49	15 20	17 50	20 20	22 50	25♑21
1990	06♒R17	05 59	05 31	04 53	04 05	03 10	02 07	00 59	29♑47	28 33	27 20	26 09	25 02	24 01	23 07	22♑22
1991	24♑43	27 14	29♒44	02 15	04 45	07 15	09 46	12 16	14 46	17 16	19 46	22 16	24 46	27 16	29♓45	02♓15
1992	00♐26	02 51	05 16	07 41	10 07	12 33	14 59	17 25	19 51	22 18	24 44	27 11	29♑38	02 05	04 32	06♑59
1993	26♒41	28♓54	01 06	03 18	05 28	07 37	09 44	11 51	13 56	15 59	18 01	20 01	22 00	23 56	25 50	27♓42
1994	06♑30	09 01	11 32	14 03	16 34	19 05	21 36	24 07	26 37	29♒08	01 39	04 10	06 41	09 11	11 42	14♒13
1995	23♏51	25 42	27 35	29♐31	01 28	03 27	05 28	07 30	09 34	11 40	13 46	15 54	18 04	20 14	22 25	24♐37
1996	12♒37	15 05	17 32	19 59	22 26	24 53	27 20	29 46	02♑13	04 38	07 04	09 30	11 55	14 20	16 44	19♑09
1997	18♐27	20 57	23 27	25 57	28 28	00♑58	03 29	05 59	08 29	10 59	13 29	15 59	18 30	21 00	23 30	26♑01
1998	03♒R24	02 54	02 14	01 25	00♑27	29 23	28 14	27 02	25 48	24 35	23 24	22 19	21 19	20 28	19 45	19♑11
1999	25♑23	27 53	00♒24	02 54	05 24	07 55	10 25	12 55	15 25	17 35	20 25	22 55	25 25	27 54	00♓24	02♒54
2000	00♐58	03 23	05 48	08 14	10 40	13 06	15 32	17 58	20 25	22 52	25 19	27 46	00♑13	02 40	05 07	07♑35

February

	1st	3rd	5th	7th	9th	11th	13th	15th	17th	19th	21st	23rd	25th	27th	29th
1900	14 ♓ 40	17 07	19 34	22 00	24 26	26 52	29 ♈ 17	01 43	04 08	06 32	08 56	11 20	13 44	16 ♈ 07	
1901	19 ♑ 21	21 50	24 20	16 50	29 ♒ 19	01 49	04 18	06 48	09 18	11 47	14 17	16 47	19 16	21 ♒ 46	
1902	02 ♓ R 22	01 43	00 55	29 ♒ 59	28 55	27 46	26 34	25 19	24 05	22 53	21 45	20 42	19 47	19 ♒ 01	
1903	26 ♒ 12	28 43	01 ♓ 13	03 43	06 12	08 42	11 12	13 41	16 11	18 40	21 09	23 38	26 07	28 ♓ 36	
1904	01 ♑ 56	04 21	06 46	09 11	11 36	14 02	16 27	18 53	21 19	23 45	26 11	28 37	01 ♒ 04	03 30	05 ♑ 56
1905	27 ♓ 37	29 ♈ 47	01 56	04 03	06 10	08 15	10 18	12 20	14 20	16 18	18 14	20 08	21 59	23 ♈ 48	
1906	08 ♒ 00	10 30	13 01	15 32	18 02	20 32	23 03	25 33	28 04	00 ♓ 34	03 04	05 34	08 04	10 ♓ 34	
1907	24 ♐ 29	26 24	28 20	00 ♑ 19	02 19	04 21	06 24	08 28	10 34	12 41	14 48	16 57	19 07	21 ♑ 18	
1908	14 ♓ 02	16 29	18 55	21 21	23 48	26 13	28 39	01 ♈ 04	03 29	05 53	08 17	10 41	13 04	15 ♈ 27	17 ♑ 50
1909	19 ♑ 59	22 29	24 59	27 28	29 ♒ 58	02 28	04 57	07 27	09 57	12 26	14 56	17 26	19 55	22 ♒ 25	
1910	29 ♒ R 08	28 18	27 20	26 15	25 05	23 52	22 38	21 24	20 13	19 06	18 05	17 12	16 28	15 ♒ 53	
1911	26 ♒ 52	29 ♓ 22	01 52	04 22	06 52	09 22	11 51	14 21	16 50	19 19	21 48	24 18	26 46	29 ♈ 15	
1912	02 ♑ 29	04 54	07 19	09 44	12 10	14 36	17 02	19 28	21 54	24 20	26 46	29 ♒ 13	01 39	04 06	06 ♒ 47
1913	27 ♓ 53	00 ♈ 02	02 09	04 15	06 20	08 23	10 25	12 24	14 22	16 18	18 12	20 03	21 52	23 ♈ 39	
1914	08 ♒ 41	11 11	13 42	16 13	18 43	21 14	23 44	26 14	28 45	01 ♓ 15	03 45	06 15	08 45	22 ♒ 16	
1915	24 ♐ 24	26 21	28 20	00 ♑ 20	02 22	04 26	06 31	08 37	10 44	12 53	15 02	17 12	19 23	21 ♑ 35	
1916	14 ♓ 38	17 05	19 31	21 57	24 23	26 48	29 ♈ 14	01 38	04 03	06 27	08 51	11 14	13 37	16 00	18 ♈ 22
1917	20 ♑ 39	23 09	25 39	28 08	00 ♒ 38	03 08	05 37	08 07	10 37	13 07	15 36	18 06	20 36	23 ♒ 05	
1918	25 ♒ R 42	24 42	23 36	22 25	21 11	29 57	18 44	17 34	16 28	15 29	14 38	13 56	13 23	13 ♒ 00	
1919	27 ♒ 33	00 ♓ 03	02 33	05 03	07 32	10 02	12 31	15 01	17 30	19 59	22 28	24 57	27 26	29 ♓ 55	
1920	03 ♑ 02	05 27	07 53	10 18	12 44	15 10	17 36	20 02	22 29	24 55	27 22	29 ♒ 48	02 15	04 42	07 ♒ 09
1921	28 ♓ 07	00 ♈ 14	02 20	04 25	06 28	08 29	10 29	12 26	14 22	16 16	18 07	19 55	21 41	23 ♈ 24	
1922	09 ♒ 21	11 52	14 23	16 53	19 24	21 54	24 25	26 55	29 ♓ 25	01 56	04 26	06 56	09 26	11 ♓ 56	
1923	24 ♐ 21	26 21	28 22	00 ♑ 24	02 28	04 34	06 40	08 48	10 56	13 06	15 17	17 28	19 40	21 ♑ 53	
1924	15 ♓ 14	17 40	20 06	22 32	24 57	27 23	29 ♈ 48	02 12	04 36	07 00	09 24	11 47	14 09	16 31	18 ♈ 53
1925	21 ♑ 18	23 48	26 18	28 ♒ 47	01 17	03 47	06 17	08 47	11 16	13 46	16 16	18 46	21 15	23 45	
1926	22 ♒ R 03	20 55	19 44	18 30	17 15	16 03	14 54	13 50	12 53	12 04	11 24	10 53	10 33	10 ♒ D 22	
1927	28 ♒ 12	00 ♓ 42	03 12	05 42	08 11	10 41	13 10	15 04	18 09	20 38	23 07	25 36	28 05	00 ♈ 33	
1928	03 ♑ 34	06 00	08 26	10 52	13 18	15 44	18 10	20 37	23 03	25 30	27 57	00 ♒ 24	02 51	05 18	07 45
1929	28 ♓ 19	00 ♈ 25	02 29	04 32	06 33	08 32	10 30	12 25	14 18	16 09	17 58	19 43	21 26	23 05	
1930	10 ♒ 02	12 33	15 03	17 34	20 04	22 35	25 05	27 35	00 ♓ 06	02 36	05 06	07 36	10 06	12 ♓ 36	
1931	24 ♐ 22	26 23	28 26	00 ♑ 30	02 36	04 43	06 51	09 00	11 10	13 21	15 33	17 45	19 59	22 ♑ 13	
1932	15 ♓ 49	18 15	20 41	23 06	25 32	27 57	00 ♈ 21	02 45	05 09	07 33	09 56	12 19	14 41	17 03	19 ♈ 24
1933	21 ♑ 58	24 28	26 57	29 ♒ 27	01 57	04 27	06 57	09 27	11 56	14 26	16 56	19 26	21 55	24 ♒ 25	
1934	18 ♒ R 15	17 03	15 48	14 34	13 22	12 14	11 12	10 17	09 30	08 52	08 24	08 05	07 D 57	07 ♒ 58	
1935	28 ♒ 53	01 ♓ 22	03 52	06 22	08 52	11 21	13 51	16 20	18 49	21 18	23 47	26 16	28 44	01 ♈ 13	
1936	04 ♑ 09	06 35	09 01	11 27	13 53	16 20	18 46	21 13	23 40	26 07	28 34	01 ♒ 01	03 28	05 55	08 ♒ 22
1937	28 ♓ 30	00 ♈ 34	02 37	04 38	06 37	08 34	10 29	12 22	14 13	16 01	17 46	19 29	21 08	22 ♈ 44	
1938	10 ♒ 43	13 14	15 44	18 15	20 45	23 16	25 46	28 17	00 ♓ 47	03 17	05 47	08 18	10 48	13 ♓ 18	
1939	24 ♐ 25	26 28	28 33	00 ♑ 39	02 46	04 54	07 04	09 14	11 25	13 38	15 50	18 04	20 18	22 ♑ 33	
1940	16 ♓ 24	18 50	21 15	23 41	26 06	28 30	00 ♈ 55	03 19	05 42	08 05	10 28	12 50	15 12	17 33	19 ♈ 54
1941	22 ♑ 37	25 07	27 37	00 ♒ 07	02 37	05 07	07 37	10 06	12 36	15 06	17 36	20 06	22 35	25 ♒ 05	
1942	14 ♒ R 20	13 05	11 51	10 40	09 33	08 32	07 39	06 54	06 19	05 53	05 D 37	05 31	05 35	05 ♒ 48	
1943	29 ♒ 32	02 ♓ 02	04 31	07 01	09 31	12 00	14 30	16 59	19 28	21 57	24 26	26 ♈ 54	29 23	01 ♈ 51	
1944	04 ♑ 42	07 08	09 35	12 01	14 28	16 54	19 21	21 48	24 15	26 42	29 ♒ 09	01 36	04 03	06 31	08 ♒ 58
1945	28 ♓ 38	00 ♈ 41	02 41	04 40	06 37	08 32	10 25	12 15	14 03	15 48	17 30	19 08	20 43	22 ♈ 15	
1946	11 ♒ 24	13 55	16 25	18 56	21 26	23 57	26 27	28 ♓ 58	01 28	03 58	06 28	08 58	11 28	13 ♓ 58	
1947	24 ♐ 30	26 35	28 42	00 ♑ 49	02 58	05 08	07 18	09 30	11 42	13 56	16 09	18 24	20 39	22 ♑ 55	
1948	16 ♓ 59	19 25	21 50	24 15	26 40	29 ♈ 04	01 28	03 52	06 15	08 38	11 00	13 22	15 43	18 04	20 ♈ 24
1949	23 ♑ 27	25 47	28 17	00 47	03 17	05 47	08 17	10 47	13 17	15 47	18 17	20 47	23 16	25 ♑ 46	
1950	10 ♒ R 23	09 09	07 59	06 53	05 54	05 03	04 20	03 47	03 23	03 D 10	03 06	03 12	03 27	03 ♒ 51	
1951	00 ♓ 12	02 42	05 11	07 41	10 10	12 40	15 09	17 38	20 07	22 36	25 05	27 33	00 ♈ 02	02 ♈ 30	
1952	05 ♑ 17	07 43	10 10	12 36	15 03	17 30	19 57	22 24	24 51	27 18	29 ♒ 46	02 13	04 40	07 08	09 ♒ 35
1953	28 ♓ 45	00 ♈ 45	02 44	04 40	06 35	08 27	10 17	12 05	13 49	15 31	17 09	18 44	20 15	21 ♈ 42	
1954	12 ♒ 44	14 35	17 06	19 ♒ 36	22 07	24 37	27 08	29 ♓ 38	02 08	04 39	07 09	09 39	12 09	14 ♓ 39	
1955	24 ♐ 38	26 44	28 52	01 ♑ 01	03 11	05 22	07 34	09 47	12 00	14 15	16 30	18 45	21 01	23 ♑ 18	
1956	17 ♓ 34	19 59	22 24	24 48	27 13	29 ♈ 37	02 00	04 24	06 46	09 09	11 31	13 52	16 13	18 34	20 ♈ 53
1957	23 ♑ 57	26 27	28 ♒ 57	01 27	03 57	06 27	08 57	11 27	13 56	16 26	18 56	21 26	23 56	26 ♒ 26	
1958	06 ♒ R 28	05 18	04 14	03 16	02 27	01 46	01 15	00 54	00 D 43	00 42	00 50	01 07	01 33	02 ♒ 08	
1959	00 ♓ 52	03 21	05 51	08 20	10 50	13 19	15 48	18 17	20 46	23 15	25 44	28 12	00 ♈ 41	03 ♈ 09	
1960	05 ♑ 52	08 19	10 45	13 12	15 39	18 06	20 33	23 01	25 28	27 55	00 ♒ 23	02 50	05 18	07 45	10 ♒ 13
1961	28 ♓ 49	00 ♈ 47	02 44	04 38	06 30	08 20	10 06	11 51	13 32	15 10	16 44	18 14	19 41	21 ♈ 02	
1962	12 ♒ 45	15 16	17 47	20 17	22 48	25 18	27 49	00 ♓ 19	02 49	05 20	07 50	10 20	12 50	15 ♓ 20	
1963	24 ♐ 50	26 55	29 ♑ 04	01 15	03 26	05 38	07 51	10 05	12 19	14 35	16 50	19 07	21 24	23 ♑ 41	
1964	18 ♓ 08	20 33	22 57	25 21	27 45	00 ♈ 09	02 32	04 55	07 17	09 39	12 01	14 22	16 42	19 02	21 ♈ 22
1965	24 ♑ 36	27 06	29 ♒ 36	02 06	04 36	07 06	09 36	12 06	14 36	17 06	19 36	22 06	24 36	27 ♒ 06	
1966	02 ♒ R 36	01 33	00 37	29 ♑ 50	29 11	28 43	28 24	28 D 15	28 16	28 27	28 46	29 14	29 ♒ 51	00 ♒ 35	
1967	01 ♓ 31	04 00	06 30	08 59	11 29	13 58	16 27	18 56	21 25	23 54	26 22	28 ♈ 51	01 19	03 ♈ 47	
1968	06 ♑ 26	08 53	11 20	13 47	16 14	18 42	21 09	23 36	26 04	28 31	00 ♒ 59	03 26	05 54	10 ♒ 50	
1969	28 ♓ 50	00 ♈ 46	02 40	04 32	06 21	08 08	09 51	11 32	13 09	14 43	16 13	17 38	18 59	20 ♈ 16	
1970	13 ♒ 26	15 57	18 28	20 58	23 29	25 59	28 30	01 ♓ 00	03 30	06 00	08 31	11 01	13 31	16 ♓ 01	
1971	24 ♐ 59	27 09	29 ♑ 19	01 31	03 43	05 57	08 11	10 25	12 41	14 57	17 13	19 31	21 48	24 ♑ 06	
1972	18 ♓ 42	21 07	23 31	25 55	28 19	00 ♈ 42	03 05	05 27	07 49	10 11	12 32	14 52	17 12	19 31	21 ♈ 50
1973	25 ♑ 17	27 47	00 ♒ 17	02 47	05 17	07 48	10 18	12 48	15 18	17 48	20 18	22 47	25 17	27 ♒ 47	
1974	28 ♑ R 53	27 59	27 14	26 38	26 11	25 55	25 D 48	25 52	26 05	26 26	26 57	27 35	28 21	29 ♑ 13	
1975	02 ♓ 11	04 40	07 10	09 39	12 08	14 38	17 07	19 35	22 04	24 33	27 01	29 ♈ 30	01 58	04 ♈ 26	
1976	07 ♑ 02	09 29	11 56	14 23	16 51	19 18	21 45	24 13	26 41	29 ♒ 08	01 36	04 04	06 32	08 59	11 ♒ 27
1977	28 ♓ 49	00 ♈ 43	02 34	04 23	06 09	07 52	09 32	11 09	12 42	14 11	15 36	16 56	18 12	19 ♈ 22	
1978	14 ♒ 06	16 37	19 08	21 38	24 09	26 39	29 ♓ 10	01 40	04 10	06 40	09 10	11 41	14 10	16 ♓ 40	
1979	25 ♐ 12	27 23	29 ♑ 35	01 47	04 01	06 15	08 30	10 45	13 02	15 19	17 36	19 54	22 12	24 ♑ 31	
1980	19 ♓ 15	21 39	24 03	26 26	28 ♈ 50	01 12	03 35	05 57	08 18	10 39	13 00	15 20	17 39	19 58	22 ♈ 16
1981	25 ♑ 56	28 26	00 ♒ 56	03 26	05 56	08 26	10 57	13 27	15 57	18 26	20 57	23 26	25 56	28 ♒ 26	
1982	25 ♑ R 21	24 38	24 04	23 40	23 D 26	23 22	23 27	23 42	24 06	24 38	25 18	26 06	27 00	28 ♑ 01	
1983	02 ♓ 50	05 19	07 49	10 18	12 47	15 16	17 45	20 14	22 43	25 11	27 39	00 ♈ 08	02 35	05 ♈ 03	
1984	07 ♑ 37	10 04	12 32	14 59	17 27	19 54	22 22	24 49	27 17	29 ♒ 45	02 13	04 41	07 09	09 37	12 ♒ 05
1985	28 ♓ 45	00 ♈ 36	02 24	04 10	05 53	07 32	09 08	10 41	12 09	13 34	14 53	16 08	17 17	18 ♈ 20	
1986	14 ♒ 50	17 18	19 48	22 19	24 49	27 20	29 ♓ 50	02 20	04 51	07 21	09 51	12 21	14 51	17 ♓ 21	
1987	25 ♐ 26	27 39	29 ♑ 52	02 05	04 20	06 35	08 51	11 07	13 24	15 42	18 00	20 19	22 38	24 ♑ 57	
1988	19 ♓ 48	22 12	24 35	26 58	29 ♈ 21	01 44	04 06	06 27	08 48	11 09	13 29	15 48	18 07	20 25	22 ♈ 43
1989	26 ♑ 36	29 ♒ 06	01 36	04 07	06 37	09 07	11 37	14 07	16 37	19 07	21 37	24 07	26 37	29 ♓ 07	
1990	22 ♑ R 03	21 31	21 09	20 D 58	20 56	21 04	21 21	21 46	22 21	23 03	23 52	24 48	25 50	26 ♑ 58	
1991	03 ♓ 30	05 59	08 28	10 57	13 26	15 55	18 24	20 53	23 22	25 50	28 18	00 ♈ 46	03 14	05 ♈ 42	
1992	08 ♑ 13	10 41	13 08	15 36	18 03	20 31	22 59	25 27	27 55	00 ♒ 23	02 51	05 19	07 47	10 15	12 ♒ 43
1993	28 ♓ 37	00 ♈ 25	02 11	03 53	05 32	07 08	08 40	10 07	11 31	12 50	14 03	15 11	16 14	17 ♈ 10	
1994	15 ♒ 28	17 59	20 29	23 00	25 30	28 01	00 ♓ 31	03 01	05 32	08 02	10 32	13 02	15 32	18 ♓ 02	
1995	25 ♐ 43	27 57	00 ♑ 11	02 25	04 41	06 57	09 14	11 31	13 49	16 07	18 26	20 45	23 04	25 ♑ 24	
1996	20 ♓ 20	22 44	25 07	27 30	29 ♈ 53	02 15	04 36	06 57	09 18	11 38	13 57	16 16	18 34	20 52	23 ♈ 09
1997	27 ♑ 16	29 ♒ 46	02 16	04 47	07 17	09 47	12 17	14 47	17 18	19 48	22 18	24 48	27 18	29 ♓ 47	
1998	18 ♑ R 57	18 38	18 D 29	18 30	18 40	18 59	19 27	20 03	20 47	21 37	22 35	23 39	24 48	26 ♑ 03	
1999	04 ♓ 08	06 38	09 07	11 36	14 05	16 34	19 02	21 31	23 59	26 28	28 ♈ 56	01 24	03 52	06 ♈ 19	
2000	08 ♑ 49	11 16	13 44	16 12	18 40	21 08	23 35	26 03	28 31	00 ♒ 59	03 28	05 56	08 24	10 52	13 ♒ 20

Venus

March

	1st	3rd	5th	7th	9th	11th	13th	15th	17th	19th	21st	23rd	25th	27th	29th	31st
1900	18♈30	20 52	23 14	25 36	27 57	00♉17	02 37	04 57	07 16	09 34	11 52	14 09	16 25	18 41	20 56	23♈10
1901	24♒15	26 44	29♓14	01 43	04 13	06 42	09 11	11 40	14 10	16 39	19 08	21 37	24 06	26 35	29♈04	01♈33
1902	18♒R24	17 57	17 39	17 D32	17 34	17 46	18 06	18 35	19 12	19 56	20 48	21 45	22 49	23 58	25 13	26♒32
1903	01♈05	03 34	06 02	08 30	10 58	13 26	15 54	18 22	20 49	23 16	25 43	28 10	00♉37	03 04	05 30	07♉56
1904	07♒10	09 36	12 03	14 30	16 56	19 23	21 50	24 17	26 44	29♓11	01 38	04 05	06 32	08 59	11 26	13♓53
1905	25♈35	27 19	29 00	00♉37	02 12	03 42	05 08	06 30	07 47	08 59	10 06	11 06	12 00	12 47	13 27	13♉59
1906	13♓04	15 34	18 04	20 34	23 04	25 33	28 03	00♈32	03 01	05 31	08 00	10 29	12 58	15 27	17 56	20♈25
1907	23♑30	25 42	27 55	00♒09	02 24	04 39	06 55	09 11	11 28	13 45	16 02	18 20	20 39	22 58	25 17	27♒36
1908	19♈01	21 23	23 45	26 06	28 26	00♉46	03 06	05 25	07 43	10 01	12 18	14 35	16 50	19 05	21 20	23♉33
1909	24♒54	27 24	29♓53	02 23	04 52	07 21	09 51	12 20	14 49	17 18	19 48	22 17	24 46	27 15	29♈44	02♈13
1910	15♒R28	15 13	15 D07	15 12	15 25	15 48	16 19	16 58	17 44	18 37	19 36	20 41	21 52	23 07	24 28	25♒52
1911	01♈44	04 12	06 41	09 09	11 37	14 05	16 32	19 00	21 27	23 54	26 21	28♉48	01 15	03 41	06 07	08♉33
1912	07♒46	10 13	12 40	16 06	17 33	20 00	22 27	24 54	27 21	29♓48	02 16	04 42	07 10	09 37	12 04	14♓31
1913	25♈22	27 02	28 40	00♉13	01 43	03 09	04 30	05 47	06 58	08 03	09 03	09 56	10 42	11 20	11 51	12♉13
1914	13♓46	16 15	18 45	21 15	23 45	26 14	28 44	01♈13	03 43	06 12	08 41	11 10	13 39	16 08	18 37	21♈06
1915	23♑48	26 01	28 16	00♒30	02 46	05 02	07 18	09 35	11 53	14 11	16 29	18 47	21 06	23 26	25 45	28♒05
1916	19♈33	21 55	24 16	26 36	28♉57	01 16	03 35	05 54	08 11	10 28	12 45	15 01	17 16	19 30	21 43	23♉56
1917	25♒35	28 04	00♓34	03 03	05 33	08 02	10 31	13 01	15 30	17 59	20 28	22 58	25 27	27 56	00♈25	02♈54
1918	12♒R47	12 D44	12 51	13 06	13 31	14 04	14 45	15 32	16 30	17 28	18 34	19 46	21 03	22 24	23 50	25♒19
1919	02♓23	04 52	07 20	09♈48	12 16	14 44	17 11	19 39	22 06	24 33	27 00	29 26	01 52	04 19	06 45	09♈10
1920	08♒22	10 49	13 16	15 43	18 10	20 37	23 04	25 32	27 59	00♓26	02 53	05 21	07 48	10 15	12 43	15♓10
1921	25♈04	26 41	28 14	29♉43	01 08	02 29	03 45	04 55	06 00	06 59	07 51	08 35	09 13	09 42	10 02	10♉14
1922	14♓26	16 56	19 26	21 56	24 25	26 55	29♈24	01 54	04 23	06 52	09 21	11 50	14 19	16 48	19 17	21♈46
1923	24♑07	26 21	28 36	00♒52	03 08	05 25	07 42	10 00	12 18	14 36	16 55	19 14	21 34	23 54	25 14	28♒34
1924	20♈04	22 25	24 46	27♉06	29 25	02 54	07 03	06 21	08 38	10 54	13 10	15 25	17 39	19 53	22 05	24♉17
1925	26♒15	28 44	01♓14	03 43	06 13	08 42	11 11	13 41	16 10	18 39	21 09	23 38	26 07	28 36	01♈05	03♈34
1926	10♒21	10 29	10 47	11 14	11 48	12 31	13 20	14 17	15 19	16 27	17 40	18 58	20 20	21 57	11 34	09♒59
1927	03♈02	05 30	07 58	10 26	12 54	15 22	17 49	20 16	22 43	25 10	27 37	00♉03	02 29	04 55	07 21	09♉47
1928	08♒58	11 25	13 52	16 19	18 47	21 14	23 41	26 08	28 36	01♓03	03 31	05 58	08 25	10 53	13 20	15♓48
1929	24♈42	26 14	27 43	29 07	00♉27	01 42	02 52	03 55	04 53	05 44	06 28	07 04	07 32	07 51	08 R01	08♉02
1930	15♓06	17 36	20 06	22 36	25 06	27 35	00♈05	02 34	05 03	07 32	10 01	12 30	14 59	17 28	19 57	22♈26
1931	24♑27	26 42	28♒58	01 15	03 32	05 49	08 07	10 25	12 44	15 03	17 23	19 42	22 02	24 23	26 43	29♒04
1932	20♈35	22 55	25 15	27 35	29♉54	02 12	04 30	06 47	09 04	11 20	13 35	15 49	18 02	20 15	22 26	24♉37
1933	26♒55	29 24	01♓54	04 24	06 53	09 23	11 52	14 21	16 51	19 20	21 49	24 18	26 48	29♈17	01 46	04♈15
1934	08♒09	08 29	08 57	09 34	10 18	11 09	12 07	13 10	14 20	15 34	16 53	18 17	19 44	21 16	22 50	24♒28
1935	03♈41	06 09	08 37	11 05	13 33	16 00	18 28	20 55	23 22	25 48	28 15	00♉41	03 07	05 33	07 59	10♉24
1936	09♒36	12 03	14 30	16 57	19 25	21 52	24 19	26 47	29♓14	01 42	04 09	06 37	09 04	11 32	13 59	16♓27
1937	24♈16	25 44	27 07	28♉26	29 40	00 49	01 52	02 49	03 39	04 21	04 56	05 23	05 41	05 R49	05 48	05♉37
1938	15♓48	18 18	20 47	23 17	25 47	28 16	00♈46	03 15	05 44	08 13	10 43	13 11	15 40	18 09	20 38	23♈06
1939	24♑49	27 05	29♒22	01 39	03 56	06 14	08 33	10 52	13 11	15 31	17 51	20 11	22 32	24 52	27 14	29♒35
1940	21♈05	23 25	25 44	28 03	00♉22	02 40	04 57	07 13	09 29	11 44	13 59	16 12	18 24	20 36	22 47	24♉56
1941	27♒35	00♓05	02 34	05 04	07 33	10 03	12 32	15 02	17 31	20 00	22 30	24 59	27 28	29♈57	02 26	04♈55
1942	06♒10	06 40	07 18	08 04	08 57	09 56	11 01	12 12	13 28	14 48	16 13	17 41	19 13	20 49	22 28	24♒09
1943	04♈19	06 47	09 15	11 43	14 11	16 38	19 05	21 32	23 59	26 26	28♉52	01 18	03 44	06 09	08 35	11♉00
1944	10♒12	12 39	15 06	17 34	20 01	22 29	24 56	27 24	29♓52	02 19	04 47	07 14	09 42	12 10	14 37	17♓05
1945	23♈42	25 05	26 24	27 37	28 45	29♉47	00 42	01 31	02 12	02 46	03 11	03 28	03 R35	03 32	03 20	02♉57
1946	16♓28	18 58	21 28	23 58	26 27	28♈57	01 26	03 56	06 25	08 54	11 23	13 52	16 21	18 50	21 18	23♈47
1947	25♑11	27 28	29♒46	02 04	04 22	06 41	09 00	11 19	13 39	15 59	18 20	20 40	23 01	25 23	27 44	00♓06
1948	21♈34	23 54	26 13	28 31	00♉49	03 06	05 23	07 39	09 54	12 08	14 21	16 34	18 45	20 56	23 05	25♉14
1949	28♒16	00 46	03♓15	05 45	08 14	10 44	13 13	15 43	18 12	20 42	23 11	25 40	28 09	00♈38	03 08	05♓37
1950	04♒24	05 04	05 51	06 45	07 46	08 53	10 05	11 22	12 43	14 09	15 39	17 12	18 48	20 28	22 10	23♒55
1951	04♈58	07 26	09 54	12 22	14 49	17 16	19 43	22 10	24 37	27 03	29♉29	01 55	04 21	06 46	09 12	11♉36
1952	10♒49	13 17	15 44	18 12	20 39	23 07	25 35	28 02	00♓30	02 58	05 25	07 53	10 21	12 49	15 16	17♓44
1953	23♈04	24 22	25 34	26 41	27 42	28 36	29 24	00♉04	00 36	01 00	01 15	01 R21	01 16	01 02	00 38	00♉04
1954	17♓09	19 39	22 08	24 38	27 08	29♈37	02 07	04 36	07 05	09 34	12 03	14 32	17 01	19 29	21 58	24♈27
1955	25♑35	27 52	00♒11	02 29	04 48	07 07	09 27	11 47	14 07	16 28	18 49	21 10	23 31	25 53	28 15	00♓37
1956	22♈03	24 22	26 41	28♉58	01 16	03 32	05 48	08 03	10 17	12 31	14 43	16 55	19 05	21 15	23 23	25♉30
1957	28♒56	01♓25	03 55	06 25	08 54	11 24	13 53	16 23	18 52	21 22	23 51	26 20	28♈49	01 18	03 48	06♈17
1958	02♒50	03 39	04 35	05 37	06 44	07 58	09 16	10 38	12 05	13 36	15 10	16 48	18 28	20 11	21 57	23♒45
1959	05♈37	08 05	10 32	13 00	15 27	17 54	20 21	22 48	25 14	27 40	00♉06	02 32	04 58	07 23	09 48	12♉12
1960	11♒27	13 55	16 22	18 50	21 18	23 45	26 13	28 41	01♓09	03 36	06 04	08 32	11 00	13 28	15 56	18♓23
1961	22♈19	23 31	24 37	25 37	26 30	27 16	27 55	28 26	28 48	29 02	20 R06	29 00	28 44	28 19	27 43	26♈58
1962	17♓50	20 19	22 49	25 19	27 48	00♈18	02 47	05 17	07 46	10 15	12 44	15 13	17 41	20 10	22 39	25♈07
1963	25♑59	28 17	00♒36	02 55	05 15	07 34	09 55	12 15	14 36	16 57	19 18	21 40	24 02	26 24	28 46	01♓09
1964	22♈31	24 49	27 07	29♉24	01 41	03 57	06 12	08 26	10 39	12 52	15 03	17 14	19 23	21 32	23 39	25♉45
1965	29♒35	02♓05	04 35	07 05	09 34	12 04	14 33	17 03	19 32	22 01	24 31	27 00	29♈29	01 58	04 28	06♈57
1966	01♒25	02 23	03 26	04 36	05 50	07 09	08 33	10 01	11 32	13 08	14 46	16 27	18 11	19 57	21 46	23♒37
1967	06♈15	08 42	11 10	13 37	16 04	18 31	20 58	23 25	25 51	28 17	00♉43	03 08	05 34	07 59	10 23	12♉48
1968	12♒03	14 31	16 59	19 27	21 55	24 23	26 51	29♓18	01 46	04 14	06 42	09 10	11 38	14 06	16 34	19♓02
1969	21♈26	22 32	23 30	24 23	25 08	25 45	26 14	26 35	26 47	26 R49	26 42	26 25	25 57	25 20	24 34	23♈29
1970	18♓30	21 00	23 30	26 00	28 29	00♈59	03 28	05 57	08 26	10 55	13 24	15 53	18 22	20 60	23 19	25♈47
1971	26♑25	28 44	01♒03	03 23	05 43	08 03	10 24	12 45	15 06	17 28	19 49	22 11	24 34	26 56	29♓19	01♓42
1972	22♈59	25 17	27 34	29♉51	02 06	04 21	06 35	08 49	11 01	13 13	15 23	17 33	19 41	21 48	23 54	25♉59
1973	00♓17	02 47	05 17	07 46	10 16	12 46	15 15	17 45	20 14	22 44	25 13	27 42	00♈11	02 41	05 10	07♈39
1974	00♒12	01 17	02 28	03 44	05 04	06 29	07 58	09 30	11 06	12 45	14 27	16 12	17 59	19 49	21 40	23♒34
1975	06♈53	09 21	11 48	14 15	16 42	19 09	21 36	24 02	26 28	28♉54	01 20	03 45	06 10	08 35	11 00	13♉24
1976	12♒41	15 09	17 37	20 05	22 33	25 01	27 29	29♓57	02 25	04 53	07 21	09 49	12 17	14 45	17 13	19♓41
1977	20♈26	21 24	22 15	22 59	23 35	24 03	24 22	24 R32	24 33	24 23	24 04	23 35	22 57	22 09	21 13	20♈09
1978	19♓10	21 40	24 10	26 39	29♈09	01 38	04 07	06 37	09 06	11 35	14 04	16 32	19 01	21 30	23 58	26♈26
1979	26♑50	29♒10	01 30	03 50	06 10	08 31	10 52	13 14	15 35	17 57	20 19	22 42	25 04	27 27	29♓50	02♒13
1980	23♈25	25 42	27 59	00♉14	02 29	04 43	05 57	09 09	11 21	13 31	15 40	17 49	19 56	22 02	24 06	26♉09
1981	00♓56	03 26	05 56	08 26	10 55	13 25	15 54	18 24	20 53	23 23	25 52	28 21	00♈51	03 20	05 49	08♈18
1982	29♑07	00♒19	01 36	02 58	04 24	05 53	07 27	09 04	10 43	12 26	14 12	16 00	17 50	19 42	21 36	23♒32
1983	07♈31	09 58	12 25	14 53	17 19	19 46	22 12	24 39	27 04	29♉30	01 56	04 21	06 46	09 10	11 34	13♉58
1984	13♒19	15 47	18 15	20 43	23 11	25 39	28 07	00♓35	03 03	05 31	07 59	10 28	12 56	15 24	17 52	20♓20
1985	19♈17	20 07	20 50	21 25	21 51	22 09	22 R17	22 16	22 05	21 44	21 13	20 33	19 44	18 46	17 42	16♈32
1986	19♓51	22 20	24 50	27 20	29♈49	02 18	04 48	07 17	09 46	12 15	14 44	17 13	19 41	22 10	24 38	27♈06
1987	27♑17	29♒37	01 57	04 18	06 39	09 00	11 22	13 44	16 06	18 28	20 51	23 14	25 37	28 00	00♓23	02♓46
1988	23♈51	26 08	28 23	00♉38	02 52	05 06	07 18	09 29	11 40	13 49	15 57	18 04	20 10	22 15	24 18	26♉19
1989	01♓37	04 07	06 37	09 06	11 36	14 06	16 35	19 05	21 34	24 04	26 33	29♈02	01 32	04 01	06 30	08♈59
1990	28♑12	29♒30	00 52	02 19	03 50	05 24	07 02	08 43	10 26	12 12	14 01	15 52	17 44	19 39	21 36	23♒34
1991	08♈09	10 36	13 04	15 30	17 57	20 23	22 50	25 16	27♉41	00 07	02 32	04 57	07 22	09 46	12 10	14♉34
1992	13♒57	16 25	18 53	21 22	23 50	26 18	28♓46	01 14	03 42	06 11	08 39	11 07	13 35	16 03	18 31	20♓59
1993	17♈58	18 40	19 13	19 38	19 55	20 R01	19 58	19 45	19 23	18 50	18 08	17 17	16 18	15 13	14 02	12♈48
1994	20♓31	23 01	25 31	28 00	00♈30	02 59	05 28	07 57	10 27	12 55	15 24	17 53	20 21	22 50	25 18	27♈46
1995	27♑45	00♒05	02 26	04 48	07 09	09 31	11 53	14 15	16 38	19 00	21 23	23 46	26 09	28 33	00♓56	03♓20
1996	24♈17	26 32	28 47	01♉01	03 15	05 27	07 38	09 48	11 58	14 06	16 13	18 18	20 23	22 26	24 27	26♉27
1997	02♓17	04 47	07 17	09 47	12 17	14 46	17 16	19 46	22 15	24 44	27 14	29♈43	02 12	04 42	07 11	09♈40
1998	27♑23	28 47	00♒15	01 46	03 22	05 00	06 41	08 26	10 12	12 02	13 53	15 46	17 42	19 39	21 37	23♒37
1999	08♈46	11 14	13 40	16 07	18 34	21 00	23 26	25 52	28 17	00♉42	03 07	05 32	07 57	10 21	12 44	15♉08
2000	14♒34	17 03	19 31	21 59	24 28	26 56	29♓24	01 52	04 21	06 49	09 17	11 45	14 14	16 42	17 10	21♓38

April

Year	1st	3rd	5th	7th	9th	11th	13th	15th	17th	19th	21st	23rd	25th	27th	29th
1900	24♉17	26 30	28 43	00♊54	03 04	05 14	07 22	09 29	11 35	13 40	15 44	17 46	19 46	21 45	23♊43
1901	02♈47	05 16	07 45	10 14	12 42	15 11	17 39	20 08	22 36	25 05	27 33	00♉01	02 30	04 58	07♉26
1902	27♒13	28 39	00♓09	01 42	03 18	04 57	06 39	08 24	10 11	12 00	13 52	15 45	17 40	19 37	21♓35
1903	09♉09	11 35	14 00	16 26	18 51	21 15	23 40	25 04	28 28	00♊52	03 15	05 38	08 01	10 24	12♊46
1904	15♓07	17 34	20 01	22 28	24 55	27 22	29♈49	02 17	04 44	07 11	09 38	12 05	14 32	16 59	19♈26
1905	14♉12	14 31	14 R41	14 42	14 33	14 14	13 45	13 07	12 19	11 23	10 20	09 11	07 58	06 43	05♉27
1906	21♈39	24 08	26 36	29♉04	01 33	04 01	06 29	08 57	11 25	13 52	16 20	18 48	21 15	23 42	26♉10
1907	28♒46	01♓06	03 26	05 47	08 07	10 28	12 49	15 11	17 33	19 54	22 16	24 38	27 01	29♈23	01♈46
1908	24♉39	26 52	29♊03	01 13	03 23	05 31	07 38	09 44	11 49	13 52	15 54	17 55	19 53	21 51	23♊46
1909	03♈27	05 56	08 25	10 54	13 22	15 51	18 19	20 48	23 16	25 45	28 13	00♉42	03 10	05 38	08♉06
1910	26♒36	28 06	29♓40	01 17	02 58	04 41	06 26	08 14	10 04	11 55	13 49	15 45	17 42	19 40	21♓41
1911	09♉46	12 11	14 37	17 02	19 27	21 51	24 16	26 40	29♊03	01 27	03 50	06 13	08 36	10 58	13♊20
1912	15♓45	18 12	20 39	23 07	25 34	28 01	00♈28	02 55	05 23	07 50	10 17	12 44	15 11	17 39	20♈06
1913	12♉21	12 R29	12 28	12 18	11 57	11 27	10 47	09 58	09 01	07 57	06 47	05 34	04 18	03 03	01♉49
1914	22♈20	24 48	27 17	29♉45	02 13	04 42	07 09	09 37	12 05	14 33	17 00	19 28	21 55	24 23	26♉50
1915	29♒15	01♓36	03 56	06 17	08 38	11 00	13 21	15 43	18 05	20 27	22 50	25 12	27 35	29♈57	02♈20
1916	25♉02	27 13	29 24	01♊33	03 41	05 48	07 54	09 59	12 02	14 04	16 04	18 03	20 00	21 55	23♊48
1917	04♈08	06 37	09 06	11 35	14 03	16 32	19 00	21 29	23 57	26 26	28♉54	01 23	03 51	06 19	08♉47
1918	26♒05	27 40	29♓18	00 59	02 42	04 29	06 17	08 07	10 00	11 54	13 50	15 48	17 47	19 47	21♓49
1919	10♉23	12 49	15 14	17 39	20 03	22 28	24 52	27 16	29♊39	02 02	04 25	06 48	09 10	11 32	13♊54
1920	16♓23	18 51	21 18	23 45	26 13	28 40	01♈07	03 35	06 02	08 29	10 56	13 24	15 51	18 18	20♈45
1921	10♉R16	10 14	10 01	09 39	09 07	08 26	07 36	06 37	05 32	04 22	03 08	01 52	00♈37	29 24	28♉15
1922	23♈00	25 29	27 57	00♉25	02 53	05 21	07 49	10 17	12 45	15 13	17 40	20 07	22 35	25 02	27♉29
1923	29♒45	02♓05	04 26	06 48	09 09	11 31	13 53	16 15	18 37	21 00	23 22	25 45	28 08	00 31	02♓54
1924	25♉22	27 33	29♊42	01 50	03 57	06 03	08 07	10 11	12 12	14 13	16♉11	18 08	20 03	21 56	23♉47
1925	04♈48	07 17	09 46	12 15	14 44	17 12	19 41	22 09	24 38	27 06	29♉35	02 03	04 31	06 59	09♉28
1926	25♒39	27 18	29 00	00♓44	02 31	04 20	06 11	08 04	09 59	11 55	13 53	15 53	17 54	19 56	21♓59
1927	11♉00	13 25	15 50	18 14	20 39	23 03	25 27	27 50	00♊14	02 37	04 59	07 22	09 44	12 05	24♊26
1928	17♓01	19 29	21 56	24 24	26 51	29♈18	01 46	04 13	06 41	09 08	11 35	14 03	16 30	18 57	21♈25
1929	07♉R58	07 44	07 20	06 47	06 04	05 12	04 13	03 07	01 56	00 41	29♈25	28 10	26 58	25 50	24♈48
1930	23♈40	26 08	28 37	01♉05	03 33	06 01	08 29	10 57	13 24	15 52	18 19	20 47	23 14	25 41	28♉08
1931	00♓15	02 36	04 57	07 19	09 41	12 03	14 25	16 48	19 10	21 33	23 56	26 19	28 42	01♈05	03♈29
1932	25♉42	27 51	29♊59	02 06	04 12	06 16	08 19	10 21	12 21	14 19	16 16	18 11	20 04	21 54	23♊43
1933	05♈29	07 58	10 27	12 56	15 24	17 53	20 22	22 50	25 19	27 47	00♉15	02 44	05 12	07 40	10♉08
1934	25♒18	27 01	28 46	00♓33	02 23	04 14	06 08	08 03	10 00	11 59	13 59	16 00	18 03	20 07	22♓11
1935	11♉37	14 02	16 26	18 51	21 15	23 39	26 03	28 26	00♊49	03 11	05 34	07 56	10 17	12 39	15♊00
1936	17♓41	20 08	22 36	25 03	27 31	29♈58	02 25	04 53	07 20	09 48	12 15	14 43	17 10	19 37	22♈05
1937	05♉R28	05 03	04 27	03 43	02 50	01 49	00 42	29♈30	28 16	27 00	25 45	24 33	23 26	22 26	21♈33
1938	24♈21	26 49	29♉18	01 46	04 14	06 42	09 10	11 37	14 05	16 32	19 00	21 27	23 54	26 21	28♊48
1939	00♓46	03 07	05 29	07 51	10 13	12 36	14 58	17 21	19 44	22 07	24 30	26 53	29♈17	01 40	04♈04
1940	26♉01	28 09	00♊15	02 21	04 25	06 28	08 30	10 30	12 28	14 25	16 19	18 12	20 02	21 50	23♊36
1941	06♈10	08 39	11 07	13 36	16 05	18 34	21 02	23 31	25 59	28 28	00♉56	03 24	05 53	08 21	10♉49
1942	25♒01	26 47	28 35	00♓25	02 17	04 11	06 07	08 05	10 04	12 04	14 06	16 09	18 13	20 18	22♓25
1943	12♉12	14 37	17 02	19 26	21 50	24 14	26 37	28♊00	01 23	03 45	06 07	08 29	10 50	13 11	15♊31
1944	18♓19	20 46	23 14	25 41	28 09	00♈36	03 04	05 32	07 59	10 27	12 54	15 22	17 49	20 16	22♈44
1945	02♉R42	02 05	01 19	00♈24	29 22	28 14	27 02	25 47	24 32	23 17	22 07	21 01	20 01	19 10	18♈27
1946	25♈01	27 29	29♉58	02 26	04 54	07 22	09 50	12 17	14 45	17 12	19 39	22 06	24 34	27 00	29♊27
1947	01♓17	03 39	06 01	08 23	10 46	13 08	15 31	17 54	20 18	22 41	25 04	27 28	29♈52	02 15	04♈39
1948	26♉18	28 24	00♊30	02 34	04 37	06 38	08 38	10 36	12 33	14 27	16 19	18 09	19 57	21 43	23♊25
1949	06♈51	09 20	11 49	14 18	16 46	19 15	21 44	24 12	26 41	29♉09	01 37	04 06	06 34	09 02	11♉30
1950	24♒49	26 37	28 28	00♓21	02 15	04 12	06 10	08 10	10 10	12 13	14 16	16 21	18 26	20 33	22♓40
1951	12♉49	15 13	17 38	20 02	22 25	24 49	27 12	29♊35	01 57	04 19	06 41	09 02	11 23	13 44	26♊04
1952	18♓58	21 26	23 53	26 21	28♈48	01 16	03 44	06 11	08 39	11 06	13 34	16 02	18 29	20 57	23♈24
1953	29♈R43	28 56	28 00	26 56	25 47	24 34	23 19	22 04	20 50	19 40	18 36	17 38	16 48	16 07	15♈35
1954	25♈41	28 09	00♉37	03 05	05 33	08 01	10 29	12 57	15 24	17 51	20 19	22 46	25 13	29 39	00♊06
1955	01♓48	04 10	06 33	08 56	11 19	13 42	16 05	18 28	20 51	23 15	25 39	28 02	00♈26	02 50	05♈14
1956	26♉33	28 39	00♊43	02 46	04 47	06 46	08 44	10 40	12 35	14 27	16 17	18 04	19 49	21 32	23♊11
1957	07♈31	10 00	12 29	14 58	17 27	19 55	22 24	24 52	27 21	19♉49	02 18	04 46	07 14	09 42	12♉11
1958	24♒40	26 31	28 24	00♓19	02 16	04 15	06 15	08 16	10 19	12 23	14 27	16 33	18 40	20 48	22♓57
1959	13♉25	15 49	18 13	20 37	23 00	25 23	27 46	00♊09	02 31	04 52	07 14	09 35	11 55	14 15	16♊35
1960	19♓37	22 05	24 33	27 01	29♈28	01 56	04 24	06 51	09 19	11 47	14 14	16 42	19 09	21 37	24♈04
1961	26♈R32	25 35	24 30	23 20	22 07	20 51	19 36	18 23	17 14	16 11	15 14	14 26	13 47	13 17	23♈56
1962	26♈21	28♉49	01 18	03 46	06 14	08 41	11 09	13 37	16 04	18 31	20 58	23 25	25 52	28 19	00♊45
1963	02♓20	04 43	07 06	09 29	11 52	14 15	16 38	19 02	21 26	23 50	26 13	28 38	01♈02	03 26	05♈50
1964	26♉47	28 51	00♊54	02 55	04 54	06 52	08 48	10 42	12 34	14 23	16 11	17 56	19 38	21 17	22♊52
1965	08♈11	10 40	13 10	15 38	18 07	20 35	23 04	25 32	28 01	00♉29	02 58	05 26	07 54	10 22	12♉51
1966	24♒33	26 27	28 23	00♓20	02 19	04 19	06 21	08 24	10 28	12 34	14 40	16 47	18 55	21 04	23♓14
1967	14♉00	16 24	18 48	21 11	23 34	25 57	28 20	00♊42	03 04	05 25	07 46	10 06	12 27	14 46	17♊06
1968	20♓26	22 43	25 11	27 39	00♈07	02 35	05 02	07 30	09 58	12 25	14 53	17 21	19 48	22 16	24♈44
1969	23♈R09	22 03	20 52	19 38	18 22	17 07	15 55	14 47	13 44	12 50	12 03	11 26	10 57	10 39	10♈D30
1970	27♈01	29♉30	01 58	04 26	06 54	09 21	11 49	14 16	16 44	19 11	21 38	24 05	26 31	28♊58	01♊24
1971	02♓53	05 16	07 39	10 02	12 26	14 49	17 13	19 37	22 01	24 25	26 49	29♈13	01 38	04 02	06♈26
1972	27♉00	29♊03	01 04	03 03	05 00	06 56	08 50	10 41	12 31	14 18	16 03	17 44	19 23	20 58	22♊30
1973	08♈53	11 22	13 51	16 20	18 49	21 18	23 46	26 15	28 43	01♉12	03 40	06 08	08 36	11 05	13♉33
1974	24♒31	26 27	28 25	00♓24	02 25	04 27	06 31	08 35	10 41	12 48	14 55	17 04	19 13	21 23	23♓34
1975	14♉36	17 00	19 23	21 46	24 09	26 32	28♊54	01 16	03 37	05 58	08 19	10 39	12 59	15 18	17♊37
1976	20♓55	23 23	25 51	28 19	00♈46	03 14	05 42	08 10	10 38	13 05	15 33	18 01	20 28	22 56	25♈24
1977	19♈R35	18 23	17 09	15 53	14 38	13 26	12 19	11 18	10 25	09 40	09 04	08 38	08 22	08 D15	08♈18
1978	27♈40	00♉09	02 37	05 05	07 32	10 00	12 27	14 55	17 22	19 49	22 16	24 43	27 09	29 36	02♊02
1979	03♓25	05 48	08 12	10 35	12 59	15 23	17 47	20 11	22 35	24 59	27 23	29♈48	02 12	04 37	07♈02
1980	27♉10	29♊11	01 10	03 07	05 03	06 56	08 48	10 37	12 24	14 08	15 49	17 28	19 03	20 34	22♊02
1981	09♈33	12 02	14 30	16 59	19 28	21 57	24 25	26 54	29♉23	01 51	04 19	06 48	09 16	11 44	14♉12
1982	24♒30	26 29	28 28	00♓30	02 32	04 36	06 41	08 47	10 54	13 02	15 11	17 20	19 31	21 42	23♓53
1983	15♉10	17 34	19 57	22 20	24 42	27 04	29♊26	01 48	04 09	06 29	08 50	11 09	13 29	15 48	18♊06
1984	21♓34	24 02	26 30	28♈58	01 26	03 54	06 21	08 49	11 17	13 45	16 13	18 40	21 08	23 36	26♈03
1985	15♈R55	14 40	13 24	12 10	10 58	09 52	08 52	08 01	07 17	06 44	06 19	06 05	06 D00	06 05	06♈18
1986	28♈20	00♉48	03 16	05 44	08 12	10 39	13 07	15 34	18 01	20 28	22 55	25 22	27 48	00♊15	02♊41
1987	03♓58	06 22	08 45	11 09	13 33	15 57	18 22	20 46	23 10	25 35	27 59	00♈24	02 49	05 13	07♈38
1988	27♉19	29♊18	01 15	03 10	05 04	06 55	08 44	10 30	12 14	13 55	15 33	17 08	18 39	20 06	21♊30
1989	10♈14	12 43	15 11	17 40	20 09	22 38	25 06	27 35	00♉04	02 32	05 00	07 29	09 57	12 25	14♉53
1990	24♒33	26 33	28 35	00♓38	02 42	04 47	06 54	09 01	11 09	13 18	15 28	17 39	19 50	22 02	24♒15
1991	15♉45	18 09	20 32	22 54	25 16	27 38	00♊00	02 21	04 41	07 01	09 21	11 41	13 59	16 18	18♊36
1992	22♓13	24 42	27 10	29♈38	02 06	04 34	07 02	09 29	11 57	14 25	16 53	19 21	21 49	24 16	26♈44
1993	12♈R10	10 55	09 40	08 30	07 25	06 26	05 36	04 54	04 22	04 00	03 D48	03 45	03 51	04 07	04♈31
1994	29♈00	01♉28	03 56	06 24	08 52	11 19	13 46	16 14	18 41	21 08	23 34	26 01	28 27	00♊54	03♊20
1995	04♓32	06 56	09 20	11 44	14 08	16 32	18 57	21 21	23 46	26 10	28 35	01♈00	03 25	05 50	08♈15
1996	27♉26	29♊23	01 18	03 11	05 02	06 50	08 36	10 20	12 01	13 38	15 12	16 43	18 10	19 33	20♊51
1997	10♈54	13 23	15 52	18 21	20 50	23 19	25 47	28 16	00♉44	03 13	05 41	08 09	10 37	13 05	15♉34
1998	24♒38	26 40	28 43	00♓48	02 53	05 00	07 08	09 16	11 26	13 36	15 47	17 59	20 11	22 24	24♓37
1999	16♉19	18 42	21 05	23 27	25 49	28 10	00♊31	02 52	05 12	07 32	09 52	12 10	14 29	16 47	29♊04
2000	22♓52	25 20	27 49	00♈17	02 45	05 13	07 41	10 09	12 37	15 04	17 32	20 00	22 28	24 56	27♈24

Venus

May

	1st	3rd	5th	7th	9th	11th	13th	15th	17th	19th	21st	23rd	25th	27th	29th	31st
1900	25♊38	27 32	29♋24	01 13	03 01	04 45	06 47	08 06	09 42	11 15	12 44	14 09	15 31	16 47	17 59	19♋06
1901	09♉54	12 22	14 50	17 18	19 46	22 14	24 41	27 09	29♊37	02 04	04 32	07 00	09 27	11 55	14 22	16♊50
1902	23♓35	25 36	27 38	29♈42	01 46	03 52	05 59	08 06	10 14	12 23	14 33	16 44	18 55	21 07	23 19	25♈32
1903	15♊08	17 30	19 51	22 12	24 33	26 53	29♋12	01 32	03 51	06 09	08 27	10 45	13 02	15 18	17 34	19♋50
1904	21♈53	24 20	26 47	29♉14	01 42	04 09	06 36	09 03	11 30	13 57	15 24	18 51	21 18	23 45	26 12	18♉39
1905	04♉R14	03 03	01 59	01 00	00♈10	29 28	28 56	28 33	28 D20	28 16	28 22	28 37	29 00	29 32	00♉11	00♉57
1906	28♉37	01♊04	03 30	05 57	08 24	10 50	13 16	15 43	18 09	20 35	23 01	25 26	27 52	00♋17	02 43	05♋08
1907	04♈08	06 31	08 54	11 17	13 41	16 04	18 27	20 51	23 15	25 38	28 02	00♉26	02 50	05 14	07 38	10♉03
1908	25♊39	27 31	29♋20	01 07	02 52	04 33	06 12	07 48	09 20	10 49	12 13	13 34	14 50	16 01	17 07	18♋07
1909	10♉34	13 02	15♊30	17 58	20 26	22 54	25 21	27 49	00 17	02 45	05 12	07 40	10 07	12 35	15 02	17♊30
1910	23♓42	25 45	27 49	29♈54	01 59	04 07	06 14	08 23	10 32	12 42	14 53	17 05	19 17	21 29	23 43	25♈56
1911	15♊42	18 03	20 24	22 44	25 04	27 24	29♋44	02 02	04 21	06 39	08 56	11 13	13 30	15 46	18 01	20♋16
1912	22♈33	25 00	27 27	29♉54	02 21	04 48	07 15	09 43	12 10	14 37	17 04	19 31	20 58	24 25	26 52	29♉19
1913	00♉40	29♈36	28 39	27 50	27 10	26 40	26 19	26 D07	26 05	26 12	26 29	26 54	27 27	28 07	28 54	29♈48
1914	29♉17	01♊44	04 10	06 37	09 03	11 30	13 56	16 22	18 48	21 14	23 40	26 05	28 31	00♋56	03 21	05♋46
1915	04♈43	07 06	09 29	11 53	14 16	16 40	19 04	21 27	23 51	26 15	28 39	01♉03	03 27	05 52	08 16	10♉40
1916	25♊39	27 28	29♋15	00 59	02 41	04 19	05 54	07 26	08 54	10 18	11 38	12 53	14 04	15 09	16 08	17♋01
1917	11♉15	13 43	16 11	18 39	21 07	23 35	26 02	28 30	00♊58	03 26	05 53	08 21	10 48	13 16	15 43	18♊11
1918	23♓52	25 56	28 02	00♈08	02 15	04 23	06 32	08 42	10 52	13 03	15 15	17 27	19 40	21 54	24 08	26♈22
1919	16♊15	18 36	20 56	23 17	25 36	27 56	00♋15	02 33	04 51	07 08	09 25	11 42	13 58	16 13	18 28	20♋42
1920	23♈13	25 40	28 07	00♉34	03 01	05 28	07 56	10 23	12 50	15 17	17 44	20 11	22 38	25 06	27 33	30♉00
1921	27♈R12	26 17	25 29	24 51	24 22	24 03	23 D53	23 53	24 02	24 20	24 47	25 21	26 02	26 51	27 46	28♈47
1922	29♉56	02♊23	04 49	07 16	09 42	12 09	14 35	17 01	19 26	21 52	24 18	26♋43	29 08	01 34	03 59	06♋23
1923	05♈17	07 41	10 04	12 28	14 51	17 15	19 39	22 03	24 27	26 51	19♉15	01 40	04 04	06 28	08 53	11♉18
1924	25♊35	27 22	29 05	00♋46	02 24	03 59	05 31	06 58	08 22	09 41	10 56	12 05	13 09	14 08	15 00	15♋45
1925	11♉56	14 24	16 52	19 20	21 47	24 15	26 43	29♊11	01 38	04 06	06 33	09 01	11 28	13 56	16 23	18♊51
1926	24♓04	26 09	28 16	00♈23	02 32	04 41	06 51	09 02	11 13	13 25	15 37	17 50	20 04	22 18	24 33	26♈48
1927	16♊47	19 08	21 28	23 48	26 07	28 26	00♋45	03 02	05 20	07 37	09 53	12 09	14 24	16 39	18 53	21♋06
1928	23♈52	26 19	28 46	01♉13	03 41	06 08	08 35	11 02	13 30	15 57	18 24	20 51	23 18	25 56	28 13	00♊40
1929	23♈R54	23 08	22 31	22 04	21 47	21 D39	21 41	21 52	22 11	22 39	23 15	23 58	24 48	25 44	26 46	27♈53
1930	00♊35	03 02	05 28	07 55	10 21	12 47	15 13	17 39	20 05	22 30	24 56	27♋21	29 46	02 11	04 36	07♋01
1931	05♈52	08 16	10 39	13 03	15 27	17 51	20 15	22 39	25 03	27 28	29♉52	02 17	04 41	07 06	09 30	11♉55
1932	25♊29	27 12	28 52	00♋30	02 04	03 35	05 03	06 26	07 44	08 58	10 06	11 10	12 08	12 69	13 43	14♋20
1933	12♉37	15 05	17 33	20 00	22 28	24 56	27 24	29♊51	02 19	04 47	07 14	09 42	12 09	14 37	17 04	19♊32
1934	24♓17	26 24	28 32	00♈41	02 50	05 00	07 11	09 23	11 35	13 48	16 01	18 15	20 29	22 44	24 59	27♈15
1935	17♊20	19 40	22 00	24 19	26 38	28♋57	01 15	03 32	05 49	08 05	10 21	12 36	14 51	17 05	19 18	21♋30
1936	24♈32	26 59	29♉27	01 43	04 21	06 48	09 16	11 43	14 10	16 37	19 05	21 32	23 59	26 26	28♊54	01♊21
1937	20♈R49	20 13	19 48	19 32	19 D27	19 30	19 43	20 04	20 33	21 10	21 54	22 45	23 53	24 46	25 54	27♈08
1938	01♊15	03 41	06 08	08 34	11 00	13 26	15 52	18 18	20 44	24 09	25 34	27 59	00♋24	02 49	05 14	07♋39
1939	06♈28	08 51	11 15	13 39	16 03	18 27	20 52	23 16	25 40	28 05	00♉30	02 54	05 19	07 44	10 08	12♉33
1940	25♊19	26 59	28 36	00♋10	01 41	03 07	04 30	05 48	07 01	08 09	09 12	10 08	10 58	11 41	12 17	12♋45
1941	13♉17	15 45	18 13	20 41	13 09	25 37	28 04	00♊32	02 59	05 27	07 55	10 22	12 50	15 17	17 44	20♊12
1942	24♓32	26 40	28 49	00♈58	03 09	05 20	07 32	09 44	11 57	14 11	16 25	18 40	20 55	23 10	25 26	27♈42
1943	17♊52	20 11	22 31	24 49	27 08	29♋26	01 43	04 00	06 16	08 32	10 47	13 02	15 16	17 29	19 41	21♋53
1944	10♈05	12 32	15♉00	17 27	19 55	22 22	24 50	27 18	29 45	02 13	04 41	07 09	09 36	12 04	14♊32	17♊00
1945	17♈R54	17 30	17 16	17 D12	17 17	17 31	17 54	18 25	19 04	19 49	20 42	21 40	22 44	23 54	25 08	26♈27
1946	01♊54	04 20	06 47	09 13	11 39	14 05	16 31	18 56	21 22	23 47	26 12	28 37	01♋02	03 27	05 51	08♋16
1947	07♈03	09 27	11 51	14 15	16 39	19 04	21 28	23 53	26 17	28 42	01♉07	03 32	05 58	08 21	10 46	13♉11
1948	25♊05	26 42	28 15	19♋45	01 11	02 33	03 50	05 03	06 10	07 12	08 08	08 57	09 39	10 13	10 40	10♋58
1949	13♉59	16 27	18 55	21 22	23 50	26 18	28 46	01♊12	03 41	06 08	08 36	11 03	13 31	15 58	18 26	20♊53
1950	24♓48	26 58	29♈08	01 18	03 30	05 42	07 54	10 08	12 21	14 36	16 40	19 06	21 21	23 37	25 54	28♈11
1951	18♊23	20 43	23 01	25 20	27 38	29♋55	02 12	04 28	06 44	08 59	11 14	13 27	15 40	17 53	20 04	22♋15
1952	25♈52	28 19	00♉46	03 14	05 41	08 08	10 36	13 03	15 30	17 57	20 25	22 52	25 20	27 47	00♊14	02♊42
1953	15♈R13	15 D01	14 58	15 05	15 21	15 46	16 18	16 58	17 45	18 39	19 39	20 44	21 54	23 09	24 29	25♈53
1954	02♊33	04 59	07 25	09 51	12 17	14 43	17 09	19 34	22 00	24 25	26 50	29♋15	01 39	04 04	06 28	08♋52
1955	07♈39	10 03	12 47	14 51	17 16	19 40	22 05	24 30	26 54	29♉19	01 44	04 09	06 34	08 59	11 24	13♉49
1956	24♊47	26 20	27 50	29 15	00♋36	01 53	03 05	04 12	05 13	06 07	06 55	07 37	08 10	08 35	08 52	09♋R00
1957	14♉39	17 07	19 35	22 03	24 30	26 58	29♊26	01 53	04 21	06 49	09 16	11 43	14 11	16 38	19 05	21♊33
1958	25♓06	27 16	19♈17	01 39	03 51	06 04	08 18	10 32	12 46	15 01	17 16	19 32	21 49	24 05	26 22	28♓39
1959	18♊54	21 13	23 31	25 49	28 07	00♋24	02 40	04 56	07 11	09 25	11 39	13 52	16 04	18 16	20 26	22♋36
1960	26♈32	28♉59	01 27	03 54	06 22	08 49	11 17	13 44	16 11	18 39	21 06	23 33	26 01	28 28	00♊55	03♊23
1961	12♈R46	12 D45	12 54	13 11	13 37	14 11	14 53	15 41	16 36	17 37	18 43	19 54	21 11	22 31	23 56	25♈24
1962	03♊12	05 38	08 04	10 30	12 56	15 22	17 47	20 13	22 38	25 03	27♋28	29 52	02 17	04 41	07 05	09♋29
1963	08♈14	10 39	13 03	15 28	17 52	20 17	22 42	25 07	27 32	29♉57	02 22	04 47	07 12	09 37	12 02	14♉27
1964	24♊25	25 54	27 18	28 39	29♋55	01 06	02 12	03 12	04 06	04 53	05 33	06 06	06 30	06 46	06 R52	06♋50
1965	15♉19	17 47	20 15	22 43	25 10	27 38	00♊06	02 33	05 01	07 28	09 56	12 23	14 51	17 18	19 45	22♊12
1966	25♓24	27 36	29♈48	02 00	04 13	06 27	08 41	10 56	13 11	15 27	17 43	19 59	22 16	24 33	26 50	29♈08
1967	19♊24	21 43	24 00	26 18	28 35	00♋51	03 07	05 22	07 36	09 50	12 03	14 15	16 26	18 37	20 47	22♋56
1968	27♈11	29♉39	02 06	04 34	07 01	09 29	11 56	14 23	16 51	19 18	21 46	24 13	26 40	29♊08	01 35	04♊02
1969	10♈31	10 42	11 01	11 28	12 04	12 46	13 36	14 32	15 34	16 42	17 43	19 12	20 33	21 58	23 28	25♈00
1970	03♊51	06 17	08 43	11 09	13 34	16 00	18 25	20 51	23 16	25 51	28 05	00♋30	02 54	05 18	07 42	10♋06
1971	08♈51	11 16	13 40	16 05	18 30	20 55	23 19	25 44	18 09	00♉35	03 00	05 25	07 50	10 15	12 41	15♉06
1972	23♊59	25 23	26 43	27 58	29 08	00♋13	01 12	02 05	02 52	03 31	04 02	04 25	04 39	04 R45	04 40	04♋27
1973	16♉01	18 29	20 57	23 25	25 52	28 20	00♊48	03 15	05 43	08 10	10 37	13 05	15 32	18 00	20 27	22♊54
1974	25♓46	27 58	00♈10	02 24	04 38	06 52	09 07	11 22	13 38	15 54	18 11	20 28	22 45	25 03	27 21	29♈39
1975	19♊55	22 13	24 30	26♋47	29 03	01 19	03 34	05 48	08 02	10 15	12 28	14 38	16 49	18 58	21 07	23♋15
1976	27♈51	00♉19	02 47	05 14	07 42	10 09	12 37	15 07	17 32	19 59	22 26	24 54	27 21	29♊49	02 16	04♊43
1977	08♈30	08 50	09 19	09 56	10 40	11 31	12 29	13 32	14 41	15 54	17 12	18 35	20 01	21 31	23 04	24♈41
1978	04♊28	06 55	09 20	11 46	14 12	16 37	19 02	21 28	23 52	26 17	28♋42	01 06	03 30	05 54	08 18	10♋41
1979	09♈26	11 51	14 16	16 41	19 06	21 31	23 56	26 21	28 46	01♉11	03 36	06 02	08 27	10 53	13 18	15♉44
1980	23♊26	24 45	25 59	27 09	28 13	29 11	00♋03	00 48	01 26	01 56	02 18	02 R31	02 35	02 30	02 14	01♋49
1981	16♉40	19 08	21 36	24 04	26 32	28♊59	01 27	03 54	06 22	08 49	11 17	13 44	16 11	18 38	21 06	23♊33
1982	26♓06	28 19	00♈32	02 46	05 01	07 16	09 32	11 47	14 04	16 21	18 38	20 55	23 13	25 31	27 50	00♉09
1983	20♊24	22 41	24 58	27 14	29♋29	01 44	03 58	06 12	08 25	10 37	12 48	14 59	17 09	19 17	21 25	23♋31
1984	28♈31	00♉59	03 26	05 54	08 22	10 49	13 17	15 44	18 12	20 39	23 06	25 34	28 01	00♊29	02 56	05♊24
1985	06♈41	07 11	07 49	08 35	09 27	10 26	11 30	12 40	13 54	15 13	16 37	18 04	19 34	21 08	22 45	24♈25
1986	05♊07	07 33	09 59	12 24	14 50	17 15	19 40	22 05	24 30	26 54	29♋19	01 43	04 07	06 30	08 54	11♋17
1987	10♈03	12 28	14 53	17 18	19 43	22 08	24 33	26 59	29♉24	01 29	04 15	06 40	09 06	11 31	13 57	16♉22
1988	22♊48	24 02	25 11	26 14	27 12	28 02	28 46	29♋23	29 52	00 13	00 R24	00 27	00 20	00♊04	29 37	29♊01
1989	17♉21	19 49	22 17	24 45	27 13	29♊40	02 07	04 35	07 03	09 30	11 57	14 25	16 52	19 19	21 46	24♊13
1990	26♓28	28 42	00♈57	03 11	05 26	07 42	09 58	12 15	14 32	16 49	19 07	21 25	23 43	26 01	28 21	00♉40
1991	20♊53	23 09	25 26	27 41	19♋56	02 10	04 24	06 26	08 49	11 00	13 10	15 20	17 28	19 36	21 42	23♋48
1992	29♈12	01♉39	04 07	06 35	09 02	11 30	13 57	16 25	18 52	21 20	23 27	26 15	28 42	01♊10	03 37	06♊05
1993	05♈03	05 43	06 29	07 23	08 23	09 28	10 39	11 54	13 14	14 38	16 06	17 38	19 13	20 50	22 31	24♈14
1994	05♊46	08 11	10 37	13 03	15 28	17 53	20 18	22 43	25 07	27 32	29♋56	02 20	04 43	07 07	09 30	11♋53
1995	10♈40	13 05	15 30	17 55	20 21	22 46	25 11	27 37	00♉02	02 27	04 53	07 18	09 44	12 10	14 35	17♉01
1996	22♊04	23 12	24 15	25 11	26 01	26 43	27 19	27 46	28 06	28 R16	28 17	28 09	27 51	27 23	26 46	26♊00
1997	18♉02	20 29	22 57	25 25	27 53	00♊21	02 48	05 16	07 43	10 10	12 38	15 05	17 32	19 59	22 26	24♊53
1998	26♓51	29♈06	01 21	03 36	05 52	08 09	10 25	12 42	15 00	17 18	19 36	21 54	24 13	26 32	28♉52	01♉11
1999	21♊21	23 37	25 52	28 07	00♋21	02 34	04 47	06 59	09 10	11 21	13 30	15 39	17 46	19 53	21 58	24♋02
2000	29♈51	02♉19	04 47	07 15	09 42	12 10	14 37	17 05	19 32	22 00	24 27	26 55	29♊22	01 58	04 17	06♊45

June

	1st	3rd	5th	7th	9th	11th	13th	15th	17th	19th	21st	23rd	25th	27th	29th
1900	19♋37	20 36	21 27	22 13	22 50	23 21	23 43	23R56	24 00	23 55	23 41	23 17	22 43	22 01	21♋10
1901	18♊03	20 31	22 58	25 25	27 52	00♋20	02 47	05 14	07 41	10 08	12 35	15 02	17 29	19 56	22♋R23
1902	26♈39	28♉53	01 07	03 22	05♌38	07 53	10 09	12 26	14 43	17 00	19 18	21 36	23 54	26 13	28♉32
1903	20♋57	23 12	25 26	27 39	29 51	02 03	04 14	06 24	08 34	10 42	12 50	14 57	17 02	19 07	21♌10
1904	29♉53	02♊20	04 47	07 14	09 41	12 08	14 35	17 02	19 30	21 57	24 24	26 51	29♋19	01 46	04♋13
1905	01♉23	02 19	03 21	04 28	05♊40	06 57	08 18	09 43	11 12	12 44	14 20	15♋58	17 39	19 23	21♋09
1906	06♋20	08 45	11 10	13 35	15 59	18 23	20 47	23 11	25 35	27 59	00♌22	02 45	05 08	07 31	09♌54
1907	11♉15	13 39	16 04	18 28	20 53	23 18	25 43	28 08	00♊33	03 58	05 23	07 48	10 13	12 39	15♊04
1908	18♋35	19 26	20 10	20 47	21 16	21 36	21R48	21 51	21 45	21 29	21 03	20 28	19 44	18 51	17♋52
1909	18♊43	21 11	23 38	26 05	28 32	00♋59	03 27	05 54	08 21	10 48	13 15	15 42	18 09	20 36	23♋03
1910	27♈03	29♉18	01 33	03 49	06 04	08 21	10 37	12 55	15 12	17 30	19 48	22 06	24 25	26 44	29♊03
1911	21♋23	23 37	25 50	28 03	00♌14	02 25	04 35	06 45	08 53	11 00	13 07	15 12	17 16	19 19	21♌21
1912	00♊33	03 00	05 27	07 54	10 21	12 48	15 16	17 43	20 10	22 37	25 05	27 32	29 59	02 27	04♊54
1913	00♉18	01 20	02 29	03 42	05 00	06 22	07 47	09 17	10 50	12 26	14 05	15 46	17♋30	19 17	21♋05
1914	06♋59	09 23	11 48	14 12	16 37	19 01	21 25	23 48	26 12	28 35	00♌58	03 21	05 44	08 07	10♌29
1915	11♉53	14 17	16 42	19 07	21 31	23 56	26 21	28 46	01♊12	03 37	06 02	08 27	10 53	13 18	15♊44
1916	17♋25	18 08	18 44	19 12	19 31	19R42	19 43	19 35	19 18	18 51	18 14	17 28	16 35	15 34	14♋27
1917	19♊24	21 52	24 19	26 46	29♋13	01 40	04 08	06 35	09 02	11 29	13 56	16 23	18 49	21 16	23♋43
1918	27♈29	29♉45	02 00	04 16	05 33	08 50	11 07	13 25	15 42	18 01	20 19	22 38	24 57	27 16	29♊36
1919	21♋48	24 02	26 14	28 26	00♌37	02 47	04 56	07 04	09 11	11 17	13 23	15 27	17 29	19 31	21♌31
1920	01♊13	03 40	06 08	08 35	11 02	13 29	15 56	18 24	20 51	23 18	25 46	28 13	00♋40	03 08	05♋35
1921	29♈20	00♉29	01 43	03 02	04 25	05 51	07 21	08 55	10 31	12 11	13 53	15 37	17 24	19 13	21♉04
1922	07♋36	10 00	12 25	14 49	17 13	19 37	22 01	24 24	26 48	29♌11	01 34	03 56	06 19	08 41	11♌03
1923	12♉30	14 55	17 19	19 44	22 09	24 34	26 59	29♊24	01 50	04 15	06 40	09 06	11 31	13 57	16♊23
1924	16♋05	16 40	17 06	17 24	17R34	17 34	17 25	17 06	16 37	15 59	15 12	14 17	13 15	12 07	10♋55
1925	20♊04	22 32	24 59	27 26	29♋53	02 20	04 47	07 14	09 41	12 08	14 35	17 02	19 29	21 56	24♋22
1926	27♈56	00♉11	02 28	04 44	07 01	09 19	11 36	13 54	16 13	18 31	20 50	23 09	25 29	27♊49	00♊09
1927	22♋13	24 25	26 36	28 47	00♌57	03 06	05 14	07 21	09 27	11 32	13 36	15 39	17 40	19 40	21♌39
1928	01♊53	04 21	06 48	09 15	11 42	14 09	16 37	19 04	21 31	23 59	26 26	28♋53	01 21	03 48	06♋16
1929	28♈29	29♉44	01 04	02 27	03 55	05 26	07 00	08 37	10 17	12 00	13 45	15 32	17 21	19 13	21♉06
1930	08♋13	10 37	13 02	15 26	17 50	20 13	22 37	25 00	27 23	29♌46	02 09	04 31	06 54	09 16	11♌37
1931	13♉07	15 32	17 57	20 22	22 47	25 12	27 38	00♊03	02 28	04 54	07 19	09 45	12 10	14 36	17♊02
1932	14♋36	15 01	15 18	15R26	15 24	15 14	14 53	14 23	13 44	12 55	11 59	10 56	09 47	08 34	07♋20
1933	20♊45	23 12	25 39	28 07	00♋34	03 01	05 28	07 55	10 22	12 49	15 15	17 42	20 09	22 36	25♋02
1934	28♈23	00♉39	02 56	05 13	07 31	09 49	12 07	14 25	16 44	19 03	21 22	23 42	26 02	28♊22	00♊42
1935	22♋36	24 48	26 59	29♌08	01 17	03 25	05 32	07 38	09 43	11 47	13 49	15 50	17 50	19 48	21♌45
1936	02♊34	05 02	07 29	09 56	12 23	14 51	17 18	19 45	22 12	24 40	27 07	29♋35	02 02	04 29	06♋57
1937	27♈46	29 07	00♉31	01 59	03 31	05 06	06 43	08 24	10 07	11 52	13 40	15 30	17 22	19 15	21♉10
1938	08♋51	11 15	13 39	16 03	18 27	20 50	23 13	25 36	27 59	00♌22	02 44	05 07	07 29	09 50	12♌12
1939	13♉46	16 11	18 36	21 01	23 26	25 51	28 17	00♊42	03 07	05 33	07 59	10 24	12 50	15 16	17♊42
1940	12♋56	13 12	13R18	13 15	13 03	12 41	12 10	11 29	10 39	09 42	08 38	07 28	06 15	05 00	03♋45
1941	21♊25	23 53	26 20	28♋47	01 14	03 41	06 08	08 35	11 02	13 28	15 55	18 22	20 49	23 15	25♋42
1942	28♈50	01♉07	03 25	05 42	08 00	10 18	12 37	14 56	17 15	19 34	21 54	24 14	26♊34	28 55	01♊15
1943	22♋58	25 09	27 19	29♌28	01 35	03 42	05 48	07 53	09 56	11 59	13 59	15 59	17 57	19 53	21♌48
1944	03♊14	05 42	08 09	10 36	13 03	15 31	17 58	20 25	22 53	25 20	27 47	00♋15	02 42	05 10	07♋37
1945	27♈08	28 33	00♉02	01 35	03 10	04 49	06 30	08 13	09 59	11 47	13 38	15 30	17 24	19 19	21♉16
1946	09♋28	11 52	14 16	16 39	19 03	21 26	23 49	26 12	28 35	00♌57	03 19	05 41	08 03	10 24	12♌45
1947	14♉24	16 49	19 14	21 39	24 04	26 30	28♊55	01 21	03 46	06 12	08 38	11 04	13 30	15 56	18♊22
1948	11♋04	11R09	11 05	10 51	10 28	09 55	09 13	08 22	07 23	06 18	05 08	03 54	02 39	01 24	00♊12
1949	22♊06	24 34	27 01	29♋28	01 55	04 22	06 49	09 15	11 42	14 09	16 36	19 02	21 29	23 56	26♋22
1950	29♈19	01♉36	03 54	06 12	08 31	10 49	13 08	15 28	17 47	20 07	22 27	24 47	27♊08	29 29	01♊49
1951	23♋20	25 30	27 39	29♌46	01 53	03 59	06 03	08 07	10 09	12 09	14 09	16 06	18 02	19 57	21♌49
1952	03♊55	06 23	08 50	11 17	13 45	16 12	18 39	21 06	23 34	26 01	28 29	00♋56	03 23	05 51	08♋18
1953	26♈37	28 06	29♉39	01 15	02 54	04 36	06 20	08 07	09 55	11 46	13 38	15 33	17 28	19 26	21♉25
1954	10♋04	12 28	14 52	17 15	19 39	22 02	24 25	26 47	29♌09	01 32	03 53	06 15	08 36	10 57	13♌18
1955	15♉02	17 27	19 52	22 17	24 43	27 08	29♊34	01 59	04 25	06 51	09 17	11 43	14 09	16 35	19♊01
1956	09♋R01	08 55	08 40	08 15	07 40	06 57	06 05	05 05	03 59	02 48	01 34	00♊19	29 05	27 53	26♊45
1957	22♊46	25 13	27 40	00♋07	02 34	05 01	07 28	09 55	12 22	14 48	17 15	19 42	22 08	24 35	27♋01
1958	29♈48	02♉06	04 24	06 43	09 02	11 21	13 40	16 00	18 20	20 40	23 00	25 21	27♊42	00 03	02♊24
1959	23♋41	25 49	27 57	00♌03	02 09	04 13	06 17	08 18	10 19	12 18	14 15	16 11	18 05	19 57	21♌48
1960	04♊36	07 04	09 31	11 58	14 26	16 53	19 20	21 48	24 15	26 42	29♋10	01 37	04 05	06 32	09♋00
1961	26♈10	27 43	29♉20	01 00	02 42	04 27	06 14	08 03	09 54	11 47	13 41	15 38	17 35	19 34	21♉35
1962	10♋41	13 05	15 28	17 51	20 14	22 37	25 00	27 22	29♌44	02 06	04 28	06 49	09 10	11 31	13♌51
1963	15♉40	18 05	20 31	22 56	25 22	27 47	00♊13	02 39	05 04	07 30	09 56	12 22	14 48	17 15	19♊41
1964	06♋R45	06 28	06 01	05 25	04 40	03 47	02 46	01 39	00♊28	29 14	27 58	26 44	25 33	24 26	23♊25
1965	23♊26	25 53	28 20	00♋47	03 14	05 41	08 08	10 34	13 01	15 28	17 54	20 21	22 47	25 14	27♋40
1966	00♉17	02 36	04 54	07 13	09 32	11 52	14 12	16 32	18 52	21 12	23 33	25 54	28♊15	00 36	02♊58
1967	24♋00	26 07	28 13	00♌19	02 23	04 26	06 28	08 28	10 27	12 24	14 20	16 14	18 05	19 55	21♌43
1968	05♊16	07 44	10 11	12 38	15 06	17 33	20 00	22 28	24 55	27 22	29♋50	02 17	04 45	07 12	09♋40
1969	25♈48	27 25	29 05	00♉48	02 33	04 21	06 10	08 02	09 55	11 50	13 46	15 44	17 44	19 44	21♈46
1970	11♋18	13 41	16 04	18 27	20 50	23 13	25 35	27 57	00♌19	02 40	05 01	07 22	09 43	12 03	14♌23
1971	16♉19	18 44	21 10	23 35	26 01	28 27	00♊52	03 18	05 44	08 10	10 36	13 02	15 28	17 55	20♊21
1972	04♋R16	03 48	03 10	02 24	01 29	00♊28	29 20	28 08	26 54	25 39	24 25	23 14	22 08	21 09	20♊17
1973	24♊07	26 34	29♋01	01 28	03 55	06 22	08 49	11 15	13 42	16 09	18 35	21 01	23 28	25 54	28♋20
1974	00♉49	03 07	05 26	07 46	10 05	12 25	14 45	17 05	19 26	21 47	24 08	26 29	28♊51	01 12	03♊34
1975	24♋18	26 25	28 30	00♌34	02 37	04 38	06 38	08 37	10 34	12 29	14 23	16 14	18 04	19 51	21♋36
1976	05♊57	08 25	10 52	13 19	15 47	18 14	20 41	23 09	25 36	28 04	00♋31	02 58	05 26	07 53	10♋21
1977	25♈30	27 11	28 54	00♉40	02 28	04 18	06 09	08 03	09 59	11 55	13 54	15 54	17 54	19 57	22♉00
1978	11♋53	14 16	16 39	19 02	21 24	23 47	26 09	28 31	00♌52	03 13	05 34	07 55	10 15	12 35	14♌55
1979	16♉56	19 22	21 48	24 13	26 39	29♊05	01 31	03 56	06 22	08 48	11 15	13 41	16 07	18 33	21♊00
1980	01♋R33	00 54	00♊06	29 10	28 08	26 59	25 47	24 32	23 17	22 04	20 54	19 49	18 50	18 00	17♊18
1981	24♊46	27 13	29♋40	02 07	04 34	07 01	09 27	11 54	14 20	16 47	19 13	21 40	24 06	26 32	28♌58
1982	01♉18	03 37	05 57	08 16	10 36	12 56	15 17	17 37	19 58	22 19	24 41	27♊02	29 24	01 46	04♊08
1983	24♋34	26 39	28 43	00♌46	02 47	04 47	06 45	08 42	10 37	12 30	14 22	16 11	17 58	19 43	21♌25
1984	06♊37	09 05	11 32	14 00	16 27	18 54	21 22	23 49	26 16	28 44	01♋11	03 39	06 06	08 34	11♋01
1985	25♈16	27 00	28 46	00♉34	02 25	04 17	06 11	08 07	10 04	12 03	14 03	16 04	18 07	20 10	22♉15
1986	12♋29	14 52	17 14	19 37	21 59	24 21	26 43	29♌05	01 26	03 47	06 07	08 27	10 47	13 07	15♌26
1987	17♉35	20 01	22 27	24 52	27 18	29♊44	02 10	04 36	07 02	09 28	11 54	14 21	16 47	19 13	21♊40
1988	28♊R40	27 51	26 53	25 49	24 40	23 27	22 12	20 57	19 45	18 35	17 31	16 34	15 45	15 04	14♊33
1989	25♊27	27 54	00♋21	02 47	05 14	07 41	10 07	12 34	15 00	17 27	19 53	22 19	24 46	27 12	29♌38
1990	01♉50	04 09	06 29	08 49	11 09	13 30	15 50	18 11	20 33	22 54	25 16	27 37	29 59	02 21	04♊44
1991	24♋50	26 54	28 56	00♌57	02 57	04 55	06 51	08 46	10 39	12 30	14 19	16 06	17 50	19 32	21♌11
1992	07♊18	09 46	12 13	14 41	17 08	19 36	22 03	24 30	26 58	29♋25	01 53	04 20	06 47	09 15	11♋42
1993	25♈06	26 53	28 42	00♉32	02 25	04 20	06 16	08 13	10 12	12 13	14 14	16 17	18 21	20 26	22♉32
1994	13♋05	15 27	17 50	20 12	22 34	24 56	27 17	29♌38	01 59	04 20	06 40	09 00	11 19	13 38	15♌57
1995	18♉14	20 40	23 06	25 32	27 57	00♊23	02 49	05 15	07 42	10 08	12 34	15 00	17 27	19 53	22♊20
1996	25♊R33	24 35	23 30	22 19	21 06	19 51	18 36	17 24	16 15	15 13	14 17	13 29	12 50	12 20	11♊59
1997	26♊07	28 33	01♋00	03 27	05 64	08 20	10 47	13 13	15 40	18 06	20 32	22 58	25 24	27 50	00♌16
1998	02♉21	04 41	07 01	09 21	11 42	14 03	16 24	18 45	21 07	23 28	25 50	28 12	00♊34	02 57	05♊19
1999	25♋04	27 06	29♌07	01 06	03 04	05 00	06 55	08 47	10 38	12 27	14 13	15 57	17 38	19 16	20♌52
2000	07♊59	10 26	12 53	15 21	17 48	20 16	22 43	25 11	27♋38	00 05	02 33	05 00	07 28	09 55	12♋23

Venus

July

	1st	3rd	5th	7th	9th	11th	13th	15th	17th	19th	21st	23rd	25th	27th	29th	31st
1900	20♋R11	19 06	17 56	16 42	15 27	14 13	13 00	11 52	10 50	09 55	09 08	08 30	08 01	07 41	07 D 31	07♋31
1901	24♋50	27 17	29♌44	02 10	04 37	07 04	09 30	11 57	14 24	16 50	19 16	21 43	24 09	26 35	29♍02	01♍28
1902	00♊51	03 11	05 30	07 51	10 11	12 32	14 53	17 14	19 35	21 57	24 19	26 41	29♋04	01 26	03 49	06♋13
1903	23♌12	25 13	27 12	29♍10	01 06	03 01	04 53	06 44	08 33	10 19	12 04	13 45	15 24	17 00	18 33	20♍03
1904	06♋41	09 08	11 36	14 03	16 31	18 58	21 26	23 54	26 21	28♌49	01 17	03 45	06 13	08 41	11 08	13♌36
1905	22♉57	24 47	26 40	28 34	00♊29	02 26	04 25	06 25	08 26	10 28	12 32	14 37	16 43	18 00	20 58	23♊06
1906	12♌16	14 38	17 00	19 22	21 43	24 05	26 25	28 46	01♍06	03 26	05 46	08 06	10 25	12 43	15 02	17♍20
1907	17♊30	19 56	22 22	24 47	27 13	29♋40	02 06	04 34	06 59	09 25	11 52	14 19	16 45	19 12	21 39	24♋07
1908	16♋R46	15 35	14 21	13 06	11 52	10 40	09 33	08 32	07 38	06 52	06 15	05 47	05 30	05 D 21	05 22	05♋33
1909	25♋29	27 56	00♌23	02 50	05 16	07 43	10 09	12 36	15 02	17 29	19 55	22 21	24 47	27 14	29♍40	02♍06
1910	01♊23	03 43	06 03	08 24	10 44	13 05	15 27	17 48	20 10	22 32	24 54	27 16	29♋39	02 02	04 25	06♋49
1911	23♌22	25 21	27 18	29♍14	01 09	03 01	04 51	06 40	08 26	10 09	11 51	13 29	15 04	16 37	18 05	19♍30
1912	07♋22	09 49	12 17	14 44	17 12	19 39	22 07	24 35	27 02	29♌30	01 58	04 26	06 54	09 21	11 49	14♌17
1913	22♉56	24 49	26 43	28 39	00♊36	02 35	04 35	06 37	08 39	10 43	12 48	14 54	17 01	19 09	21 18	23♊28
1914	12♌51	15 13	17 35	19 56	22 17	24 38	26 58	29♍19	01 39	03 58	06 18	08 36	10 55	13 13	15 31	17♍49
1915	18♊10	20 36	23 01	25 27	27 54	00♋20	02 46	05 13	07 39	10 06	12 32	14 59	17 26	19 53	22 20	24♋47
1916	13♋R16	12 02	10 47	09 33	08 22	07 15	06 15	05 22	04 38	04 02	03 36	03 20	03 D 13	03 15	03 27	03♋47
1917	26♋10	28 37	01♌03	03 30	05 56	08 23	10 49	13 16	15 42	18 08	20 34	23 01	25 27	27 53	00♍19	02♍45
1918	01♊56	04 16	06 37	08 58	11 19	13 40	16 02	18 24	20 45	23 08	25 30	27 53	00♋16	02 39	05 02	07♋26
1919	23♌30	25 27	27 23	29♍17	01 09	02 59	04 47	06 33	08 16	09 57	11 34	13 09	14 41	16 09	17 33	18♍53
1920	08♋03	10 30	12 57	15 25	17 53	20 20	22 48	25 16	27 43	00♌11	02 39	05 07	07 34	10 02	12 30	14♌58
1921	22♉57	24 52	26 48	28 46	00♊45	02 45	04 47	06 50	08 54	10 59	13 05	15 12	17 20	19 29	21 39	23♊50
1922	13♌25	15 47	18 08	20 29	22 50	25 10	27 30	29♍50	02 10	04 29	06 48	09 06	11 24	13 42	15 59	18♍16
1923	18♊49	21 15	23 41	26 07	28 33	00♋59	03 26	05 52	08 19	10 45	13 12	15 39	18 06	20 33	23 00	25♋28
1924	09♋R40	08 26	07 12	06 02	04 56	03 57	03 06	02 23	01 49	01 24	01 09	01 D 04	01 07	01 20	01 42	02♋11
1925	26♋49	29♌16	01 42	04 09	06 35	09 02	11 28	13 54	16 20	18 47	21 13	23 39	26 05	28 31	00♍57	03♍22
1926	02♊29	04 50	07 10	09 31	11 53	14 14	16 36	18 58	21 20	23 43	26 06	28 29	00♋52	03 15	05 39	08♋02
1927	23♌26	25 31	27 25	29♍17	01 06	02 54	04 39	06 22	08 02	09 39	11 13	12 44	14 11	15 34	16 54	18♍09
1928	08♋43	11 11	13 38	16 06	18 33	21 01	23 28	25 56	28 24	00♌52	03 19	05 47	08 15	10 43	13 11	15♌39
1929	23♉01	24 57	26 55	28 55	00♊56	02 58	05 01	07 05	09 10	11 16	13 24	15 32	17 41	19 51	22 01	24♊13
1930	13♌59	16 20	18 41	21 02	23 22	25 42	28 02	00♍22	02 41	04 59	07 18	09 36	11 53	14 11	16 27	18♍44
1931	19♊28	21 54	24 20	26 46	29♋13	01 39	04 05	06 32	08 59	11 26	13 52	16 19	18 46	21 14	23 41	26♋08
1932	06♋R05	04 52	03 42	02 38	01 40	00 50	00♊08	29 35	29 12	28 D 59	28 55	29 00	29 14	29 37	00♋08	00♋47
1933	27♋29	29 56	02 22	04 48	07 15	09 41	12 07	14 33	17 00	19 26	21 52	24 18	26 43	19 09	01♍35	04♍00
1934	08♊03	05 24	07 45	10 06	12 28	14 50	17 12	19 34	21 57	24 19	26 42	29♋05	01 29	03 52	06 16	08♋40
1935	23♌40	25 33	27 25	29♍14	01 01	02 46	04 28	06 08	07 44	09 18	10 48	12 14	13 37	14 55	16 09	17♍18
1936	09♋24	11 52	14 19	16 47	19 14	21 42	24 10	26 37	29♌05	01 33	04 01	06 28	08 56	11 24	13 52	16♌20
1937	23♉07	25 05	27 05	29♊06	01 08	03 12	05 16	07 22	09 28	11 35	13 44	15 53	18 03	20 13	22 25	24♊37
1938	14♌33	16 54	19 15	21 35	23 55	26 15	28 34	00♍53	03 11	05 30	07 48	10 05	12 22	14 39	16 55	19♍11
1939	20♊08	22 34	25 00	27 26	29♋53	02 19	04 46	07 12	09 39	12 06	14 33	17 00	19 27	21 54	24 22	26♋49
1940	02♋R32	01 24	00♊20	29 23	28 35	27 55	27 24	27 02	26 D 50	26 47	26 54	27 10	27 34	28 06	28 45	29♋32
1941	28♋09	00♌35	03 01	05 28	07 54	10 20	12 46	15 12	17 38	20 04	22 30	24 56	27 22	29♍47	02 13	04♍38
1942	03♊36	05 57	08 19	10 41	13 02	15 25	17 47	20 09	22 32	24 55	27 18	29♋42	02 05	04 29	06 53	09♋17
1943	23♌41	25 32	27 21	29♍08	00 52	02 34	04 13	05 49	07 22	08 51	10 17	11 39	12 56	14 09	15 17	16♍20
1944	10♋05	12 32	15 00	17 27	19 55	22 22	24 50	27 18	29♌45	02 13	04 41	07 09	09 36	12 04	14 32	17♌00
1945	23♉15	25 15	27 16	29♊18	01 22	03 27	05 32	07 39	09 47	11 55	14 04	16 14	18 25	20 37	22 49	25♊02
1946	15♌06	17 27	19 47	22 07	24 26	26 46	29♍05	01 23	03 41	05 59	08 16	10 33	12 50	15 06	17 21	19♍36
1947	20♊48	23 14	25 40	28 06	00♋33	02 59	05 26	07 53	10 20	12 47	15 14	17 41	20 08	22 35	25 02	27♋30
1948	29♊R04	28 01	27 06	26 18	25 40	25 10	24 51	24 D 40	24 39	24 47	25 04	25 29	26 02	26 43	27 31	28♊25
1949	28♋49	01♌15	03 41	06 07	08 34	11 00	13 26	15 52	18 18	20 43	23 09	25 35	28 00	00♍26	02 51	05♍16
1950	04♊11	06 32	08 54	11 16	13 38	16 00	18 23	20 45	23 08	25 32	27 55	00♋19	02 42	05 06	07 30	09♋55
1951	23♌40	25 28	27 15	28 59	00♍40	02 19	03 54	05 26	06 55	08 20	09 41	10 58	12 10	13 17	14 18	15♍14
1952	10♋46	13 13	15 41	18 08	20 36	23 04	25 31	27 59	00♌27	02 54	05 22	07 50	10 18	12 45	15 13	17♌41
1953	23♉25	25 26	27 29	29♊33	01 38	03 44	05 50	07 58	10 07	12 16	14 26	16 37	18 49	21 01	23 14	25♊28
1954	15♌39	17 59	20 19	22 38	24 58	27 16	29♍35	01 53	04 11	06 28	08 45	11 01	13 17	15 32	17 47	20♍01
1955	21♊27	23 53	26 20	28 46	01♋13	03 39	06 06	08 33	11 00	13 27	15 54	18 21	20 48	23 15	25 43	28♋10
1956	25♊R43	24 49	24 03	23 26	22 58	22 40	22 D 31	22 32	22 41	23 00	23 26	24 00	24 42	25 31	26 26	27♊27
1957	29♋27	01♌54	04 20	06 46	09 12	11 38	14 04	16 30	18 56	21 21	23 47	26 12	28 38	01♍03	03 28	05♍53
1958	04♊45	07 07	09 29	11 51	14 13	16 36	18 59	21 22	23 45	26 08	28 32	00♋56	03 20	05 44	08 08	10♋33
1959	23♌36	25 22	27 05	28 46	00♍24	01 59	03 31	04 59	06 23	07 44	08 59	10 10	11 16	12 16	13 11	13♍59
1960	11♋27	13 55	16 22	18 50	21 17	23 45	26 13	28 40	01♌08	03 36	06 03	08 31	10 59	13 27	15 54	18♌22
1961	23♉36	25 39	27 43	29♊48	01 55	04 02	06 09	08 18	10 28	12 38	14 49	17 01	19 13	21 26	23 40	25♊54
1962	16♌11	18 31	20 50	23 09	25 28	27 47	00♍05	02 22	04 39	06 56	09 12	11 28	13 43	15 58	18 12	20♍25
1963	22♊07	24 33	27 00	29♋26	01 53	04 19	06 46	09 13	11 40	14 07	16 34	19 01	21 29	23 56	26 24	28♋51
1964	22♊R32	21 47	21 12	20 46	20 29	20 22	20 D 24	20 35	20 55	21 22	21 58	22 41	23 30	24 26	25 28	26♊35
1965	00♌06	02 32	04 59	07 25	09 51	12 16	14 42	17 08	19 34	21 59	24 24	26 50	29♍15	01 40	04 05	06♍30
1966	05♊20	07 42	10 04	12 26	14 49	17 12	19 35	21 58	24 21	26 45	29♋09	01 32	03 57	06 21	08 45	11♋10
1967	23♌28	25 11	26 52	28 29	00♍04	01 35	03 02	04 26	05 45	07 00	08 11	09 15	10 15	11 08	11 54	12♍34
1968	12♋07	14 35	17 02	19 30	21 57	24 25	26 52	29♌20	01 48	04 15	06 43	09 11	11 39	14 06	16 34	19♌02
1969	23♉49	25 54	27 59	00♊05	02 12	04 20	06 29	08 39	10 50	13 01	15 13	17 25	19 38	21 52	24 06	26♊21
1970	16♌43	19 03	21 22	23 40	25 59	28 16	00♍34	02 51	05 08	07 24	09 39	11 54	14 09	16 23	18 38	20♍49
1971	22♊47	25 14	27 40	00♋07	02 33	05 00	07 27	09 54	12 21	14 48	17 15	19 42	22 10	24 37	27 05	29♋32
1972	19♊R33	18 59	18 34	18 19	18 D 13	18 17	18 29	18 51	19 20	19 56	20 40	21 31	22 28	23 30	24 38	25♊52
1973	00♌47	03 13	05 39	08 05	10 30	12 56	15 22	17 48	20 13	22 38	25 04	27 29	29♍54	02 19	04 44	07♍09
1974	05♊56	08 18	10 41	13 03	15 26	17 49	20 12	22 36	24 59	27 23	29♋47	02 11	04 35	07 00	09 24	11♋49
1975	23♌19	24 58	26 35	28 09	29♍40	01 07	02 29	03 48	05 02	06 12	07 16	08 14	09 06	09 51	10 29	11♍00
1976	12♋48	15 16	17 43	20 11	22 39	25 06	27 34	00♌01	02 29	04 57	07 24	09 52	12 20	14 47	17 15	19♌43
1977	24♉04	26 10	28 16	00♊24	02 32	04 41	06 51	09 01	11 13	13 25	15 37	17 51	20 04	22 19	24 34	26♊49
1978	17♌14	19 33	21 52	24 10	26 28	28 45	01♍02	03 19	05 35	07 50	10 05	12 19	14 33	16 46	18 59	21♍11
1979	23♊26	25 53	28 19	00♋46	03 12	05 39	08 06	10 33	13 00	15 27	17 55	20 22	22 49	25 17	27 44	00♌12
1980	16♊R45	16 21	16 D 08	16 03	16 09	16 23	16 45	17 16	17 54	18 39	19 30	20 28	21 32	22 40	23 54	25♊13
1981	01♌24	03 50	06 16	08 42	11 08	13 33	15 59	18 24	20 50	23 15	25 40	28 05	00♍30	02 55	05 20	07♍44
1982	06♊30	08 53	11 15	13 38	16 01	18 24	20 48	23 11	25 35	27 59	00♋23	02 47	05 12	07 36	10 01	12♋26
1983	23♌04	24 40	26 13	27 43	29 09	00♍31	01 49	03 03	04 11	05 14	06 11	07 02	07 46	08 23	08 52	09♍13
1984	13♋29	15 56	18 24	20 51	23 19	25 46	28 14	00♌42	03 09	05 37	08 04	10 32	13 00	15 27	17 55	20♌23
1985	24♉20	26 27	28 35	00♊43	02 52	05 02	07 13	09 24	11 36	13 49	16 02	18 16	20 31	22 46	25 01	27♊17
1986	17♌45	20 03	22 22	24 39	26 57	29♍13	01 30	03 46	06 01	08 16	10 30	12 44	14 57	17 09	19 21	21♍32
1987	24♊06	26 33	28♋59	01 26	03 53	06 20	08 47	11 14	13 41	16 08	18 35	21 03	23 30	25 58	28 25	00♌53
1988	14♊R11	13 D 59	13 56	14 02	14 18	14 42	15 13	15 53	16 39	17 32	18 30	19 35	20 44	21 59	23 18	24♊41
1989	02♌04	04 30	06 55	09 21	11 46	14 12	16 38	19 03	21 28	23 53	26 18	28 43	01♍08	03 32	05 57	08♍21
1990	07♊06	09 29	11 52	14 15	16 38	19 01	21 25	23 49	26 13	28 37	01♋01	03 26	05 50	08 15	10 40	13♋05
1991	22♌46	24 19	25 48	27 14	28 35	29♍52	01 05	02 12	03 14	04 10	05 00	05 43	06 19	06 46	07 06	07♍17
1992	14♋10	16 37	19 05	21 33	24 00	26 28	28♌55	01 23	03 50	06 18	08 45	11 13	13 41	16 08	18 36	21♌04
1993	24♉38	26 46	28 55	01♊04	03 14	05 25	07 36	09 49	12 01	14 15	16 29	18 43	20 59	23 14	25 30	27♊47
1994	18♌16	20 34	22 51	25 08	27 25	29♍41	01 57	04 13	06 27	08 41	10 55	13 08	15 20	17 32	19 43	21♍53
1995	24♊46	27 13	29♋40	02 06	04 33	07 00	09 27	11 54	14 21	16 49	19 16	21 43	24 11	26 38	29♌06	01♌34
1996	11♊R49	11 D 47	11 55	12 12	12 37	13 10	13 50	14 38	15 32	16 31	17 37	18 47	20 02	21 22	22 46	24♊14
1997	02♌42	05 08	07 34	09 59	12 25	14 50	17 15	19 41	22 06	24 31	26 55	29♍20	01 45	04 09	06 33	08♍58
1998	07♊42	10 05	12 28	14 51	17 14	19 38	22 02	24 26	26 50	29♋14	01 39	04 03	06 28	08 53	11 18	13♋44
1999	22♌24	23 52	25 17	26 37	27 54	29 05	00♍12	01 13	02 08	02 56	03 38	04 12	04 39	04 57	05 R 07	05♍07
2000	14♋50	17 18	19 45	22 13	24 40	27 03	29♌35	02 03	04 30	06 58	09 25	11 53	14 21	16 48	19 16	21♌43

August

	1st	3rd	5th	7th	9th	11th	13th	15th	17th	19th	21st	23rd	25th	27th	29th	31st
1900	07♋34	07 47	08 09	08 38	09 16	10 00	10 51	11 49	12 52	14 01	15 15	16 33	17 56	19 23	20 54	22♋27
1901	02♍41	05 07	07 33	09 58	12 24	14 50	17 15	19 41	22 06	24 32	26 57	29♎22	01 47	04 12	06 37	09♎01
1902	07♋24	09 48	12 12	14 36	17 00	19 24	21 49	24 14	26 39	29♌04	01 30	03 55	06 21	08 47	11 14	13♌40
1903	20♍46	22 10	23 30	24 45	25 55	27 01	28 00	28 54	29♎41	00 21	00 54	01 19	01 36	01 R 44	01 42	01♎32
1904	14♌50	17 18	19 46	22 14	24 43	27 11	29♍39	02 07	04 35	07 03	09 32	12 00	14 28	16 56	19 24	21♍53
1905	24♊11	26 21	28 32	00♋43	02 55	05 08	07 22	09 36	11 51	14 07	16 23	18 39	20 57	23 14	25 33	27♋52
1906	18♍28	20 46	23 03	25 19	27 35	29♎51	02 06	04 20	06 34	08 47	11 00	13 12	15 24	17 35	19 45	21♎54
1907	25♋20	27 48	00♌15	02 43	05 10	07 38	10 06	12 34	15 02	17 30	19 58	22 27	24 55	27 24	29 52	02♌21
1908	05♋41	06 04	06 35	07 13	07 59	08 51	09 49	10 53	12 03	13 17	14 37	16 00	17 27	18 58	20 33	22♋10
1909	03♍19	05 44	08 10	10 36	13 01	15 27	17 52	20 18	22 43	25 08	27 33	29♎58	02 23	04 48	07 12	09♎37
1910	08♋00	10 24	12 48	15 12	17 37	20 02	22 26	24 51	27 17	29♌42	02 08	04 34	07 00	09 26	11 52	14♌19
1911	20♍11	21 30	22 45	23 54	24 58	25 57	26 49	27 35	28 13	28 44	29 08	29 23	29 R 29	29 25	29 13	28♍51
1912	15♌31	17 59	20 27	22 55	25 23	27 51	00♍19	02 48	05 16	07 44	10 12	12 40	15 08	17 37	20 05	22♍33
1913	24♊33	26 44	28♋55	01 08	03 21	05 34	07 48	10 03	12 19	14 35	16 52	19 09	21 27	23 45	26 04	28♋23
1914	18♍57	21 14	23 30	25 46	28 02	00♎16	02 31	04 44	06 58	09 10	11 22	13 33	15 44	17 54	20 03	22♎11
1915	26♋01	28 29	00♌56	03 24	05 51	08 19	10 47	13 15	15 43	18 12	20 40	23 08	25 37	28 05	00♍34	03♍03
1916	04♋00	04 32	05 12	05 59	06 52	07 51	08 56	10 06	11 21	12 41	14 05	15 33	17 05	18 39	20 18	21♋58
1917	03♍57	06 23	08 49	11 14	13 40	16 05	18 30	20 56	23 21	25 46	28 11	00♎35	03 00	05 24	07 49	10♎13
1918	08 38	11 02	13 26	15 50	18 15	20 40	23 05	25 30	27 55	00♌21	02 47	05 13	07 39	10 05	12 32	14♌59
1919	19♍31	20 45	21 53	22 56	23 54	24 45	25 29	26 06	26 36	26 57	27 R 10	27 14	27 09	26 55	26 31	25♍57
1920	16♌12	18 40	21 08	23 36	26 04	28 32	01♍00	03 28	05 66	08 25	10 53	13 21	15 49	18 17	20 45	23♍13
1921	24♊55	27 07	29♋19	01 32	03 46	06 00	08 15	10 31	12 47	15 04	17 21	19 39	21 57	24 16	26 35	28♋55
1922	19♍25	21 41	23 57	26 12	28 26	00♎41	02 54	05 07	07 19	09 31	11 42	13 52	16 Q2	18♍11	20 18	22♍25
1923	26♋41	29♌09	01 36	04 04	06 32	09 00	11 28	13 56	16 24	18 52	21 20	23 49	26 17	28 46	01 14	03♌43
1924	02♋29	03 10	03 58	04 52	05 52	06 58	08 09	09 25	10 45	12 09	13 38	15 10	16 45	18 23	20 05	21♋49
1925	04♍35	07 01	09 26	11 51	14 17	16 42	19 07	21 32	23 57	26 22	28 46	01♎11	03 35	06 00	08 24	10♎48
1926	09♋14	11 39	14 03	16 27	18 52	21 17	23 42	26 08	28 33	00♌59	03 25	06 51	08 17	10 44	13 11	15♌38
1927	18♍44	19 52	20 54	21 50	22 40	23 23	23 58	24 26	24 46	24 R 57	25 00	24 53	24 36	24 10	23 35	22♍51
1928	16♌53	19 20	21 48	24 16	26 44	29♍12	01 40	04 08	06 36	09 05	11 33	14 01	16 29	18 57	21 25	23♍53
1929	25♊19	27 31	29♋44	01 58	04 13	06 28	08 43	10 59	13 16	15 33	17 51	20 09	22 28	24 47	27 07	29♋27
1930	19♍52	22 07	24 22	26 37	28 51	01♎04	03 17	05 29	07 40	09 51	12 01	14 10	16 19	18 26	20 33	22♎39
1931	27♋22	29♌49	02 17	04 45	07 12	09 40	12 08	14 37	17 05	19 33	22 01	24 30	26 58	29♍27	01 56	04♍24
1932	01♋08	01 57	02 53	03 54	05 00	06 12	07 29	08 49	10 14	11 43	13 16	14 51	16 30	18 12	19 66	21♋43
1933	05♍13	07 39	10 04	12 29	14 54	17 19	19 44	22 09	24 34	26 58	29♎23	01 47	04 11	06 35	08 59	11♎23
1934	09♋52	12 16	14 41	17 06	19 31	21 56	24 21	26 47	29♌12	01 38	04 04	06 30	08 57	11 24	13 50	16♌17
1935	17♍50	18 51	19 46	20 35	21 17	21 51	22 17	22 35	22 R 45	22 45	22 36	22 18	21 50	21 13	20 27	19♍33
1936	17♌34	20 02	22 30	24 57	27 25	29♍53	02 21	04 49	07 17	09 45	12 13	14 41	17 09	19 37	22 05	24♍33
1937	25♊43	27 57	00♋11	02 25	04 40	06 56	09 12	11 29	13 46	16 03	18 22	20 40	22 59	25 19	27 39	00♋00
1938	20♍18	22 33	24 48	27 01	29♎15	01 27	03 39	05 50	08 01	10 10	12 19	14 27	16 35	18 41	20 46	22♎51
1939	28♋03	00♌30	02 58	05 26	07 53	10 21	12 49	15 18	17 46	20 14	22 42	25 11	27 39	00♍08	02 37	05♍06
1940	29♊57	00♋54	01 56	03 03	04 16	05 33	06 54	08 20	09 49	11 22	12 58	14 37	16 19	18 04	19 51	21♋40
1941	05♍51	08 16	10 41	13 06	15 31	17 56	20 21	22 46	25 10	27 34	29♎59	02 23	04 47	07 10	09 34	11♎58
1942	10♋29	12 54	15 18	17 43	20 08	22 34	24 59	27 25	29♌51	02 17	04 43	07 09	09 36	12 03	14 30	16♌58
1943	16♍49	17 43	18 30	19 10	19 43	20 08	20 25	20 R 33	20 31	20 20	20 00	19 30	18 51	18 04	17 08	16♍06
1944	18♌14	20 42	23 10	26 37	28 05	00♍33	03 01	05 29	07 57	10 25	12 53	15 21	17 49	20 17	22 45	25♍13
1945	26♊09	28 22	00♋37	02 52	05 08	07 24	09 41	11 58	14 16	16 34	18 53	21 12	23 31	25 51	28 12	00♋33
1946	20♍44	22 58	25 11	27 25	29♎39	01 49	04 00	06 10	08 19	10 28	12 37	14 43	16 49	18 54	20 57	23♎00
1947	28♋44	01♌11	03 39	06 07	08 35	11 03	13 31	15 59	18 27	20 55	23 24	25 52	28 21	00♍50	03 18	05♍47
1948	28♊54	29♋57	01 06	02 19	03 37	04 59	06 25	07 55	09 28	11 05	12 44	14 27	16 11	17 59	19 48	21♋40
1949	06♍29	08 54	11 19	13 44	16 09	18 33	20 58	23 22	25 47	28 11	00♎35	02 59	05 22	07 46	10 09	12♎33
1950	11♋07	13 32	15 56	18 21	20 47	23 12	25 38	28 04	00♌30	02 56	05 22	07 49	10 15	12 42	15 09	17♌36
1951	15♍39	16 25	17 04	17 35	17 59	18 14	18 R 20	18 17	18 04	17 42	17 10	16 29	15 40	14 43	13 40	12♍31
1952	18♌55	21 23	23 51	26 18	28♍46	01 14	03 42	06 10	08 38	11 06	13 34	16 01	18 29	20 57	23 25	25♍52
1953	26♊35	28 49	01♋04	03 20	05 36	07 53	10 10	12 28	14 46	17 05	19 24	21 44	24 04	26 24	28 45	01♌06
1954	21♍08	23 22	25 35	27 47	29♎59	02 09	04 19	06 29	08 37	10 44	12 51	14 57	17 01	19 05	21 07	23♎08
1955	29♋24	01♌52	04 19	06 47	09 15	11 43	14 11	16 39	19 08	21 36	24 05	26 33	29♍02	01 30	03 59	06♍28
1956	27♊59	29 08	00♋22	01 41	03 04	04 31	06 01	07 35	09 12	10 52	12 34	14 19	16 07	17 57	19 49	21♋43
1957	07♍06	09 31	11 56	14 21	16 45	19 10	21 34	23 58	26 22	28 46	01♎10	03 33	05 57	08 20	10 43	13♎06
1958	11♋45	14 10	16 35	19 00	21 25	23 51	26 17	28 43	01♌09	03 35	06 01	08 28	10 55	13 22	15 40	19♌16
1959	14♍20	14 58	15 28	15 49	16 R 03	16 07	16 02	15 48	15 24	14 51	14 08	13 17	12 19	11 14	10 04	08♍51
1960	19♌36	22 04	24 32	26 59	29♍27	01 55	04 23	06 51	09 18	11 46	14 14	16 42	19 10	21 37	24 05	26♍33
1961	27♊02	29♋17	01 33	03 49	06 06	08 23	10 41	12 59	15 18	17 37	19 56	22 16	24 36	26 57	29♌18	01♌40
1962	21♍32	23 45	25 57	28 08	00♎19	02 29	04 38	06 46	08 53	10 59	13 05	15 09	17 12	19 14	21 15	23♎14
1963	00♌05	02 33	05 00	07 28	09 56	12 24	14 52	17 20	19 49	22 17	24 46	27 14	29♍43	02 11	04 40	07♍09
1964	27♊11	28 26	29♋45	01 09	02 36	04 07	05 41	07 18	08 59	10 42	12 27	14 15	16 05	17 57	19 51	21♋47
1965	07♍43	10 08	12 32	14 57	17 21	19 45	22 09	24 33	26 57	29♎21	01 44	04 08	06 31	08 54	11 17	13♎39
1966	12♋22	14 47	17 13	19 38	22 03	24 29	26 55	29♌21	01 47	04 14	06 40	09 07	11 34	14 01	16 28	18♌56
1967	12♍51	13 20	13 40	13 R 52	13 54	13 48	13 32	13 06	12 31	11 47	10 54	09 54	08 49	07 38	06 25	05♍10
1968	20♌16	22 43	25 11	27 39	00♍07	02 35	05 02	07 30	09 58	12 26	14 53	17 21	19 49	22 17	24 44	27♍12
1969	27♊29	29 44	02♋01	04 18	06 35	08 53	11 11	13 30	15 49	18 08	20 28	22 48	25 09	27 30	29♌51	02♌11
1970	21♍56	24 07	26 18	28 28	00♎38	02 47	04 55	07 02	09 08	10 10	12 15	14 18	16 20	18 21	20 21	23♎18
1971	00♌46	03 14	05 42	08 09	10 37	13 05	15 34	18 02	20 30	22 59	25 27	27 56	00♍24	02 53	05 22	07♍50
1972	26♊30	27 49	29 14	00♋42	02 13	03 48	05 26	07 07	08 50	10 36	12 24	14 14	16 07	18 01	19 57	21♋55
1973	08♍21	10 46	13 10	15 34	17 58	20 23	22 46	25 10	27 34	29♎57	02 20	04 43	07 06	09 29	11 52	14♎14
1974	13♋02	15 27	17 52	20 18	22 43	25 09	27 35	00♌01	02 28	04 54	07 21	09 48	12 15	14 42	17 09	19♌37
1975	11♍13	11 31	11 R 41	11 42	11 34	11 16	10 49	10 12	09 26	08 33	07 32	06 25	05 13	03 59	02 45	01♍32
1976	20♌57	23 24	25 52	28 20	00♍47	03 15	05 43	08 10	10 38	13 06	15 34	18 01	20 29	22 57	25 24	27♍52
1977	27♊57	00♋13	02 30	04 48	07 05	09 24	11 42	14 01	16 21	18 41	21 01	23 22	25 43	28 04	00♌26	02♌48
1978	22♍17	24 28	26 38	28 47	00♎56	03 04	05 10	07 16	09 21	11 24	13 27	15 28	17 28	19 26	21 23	23♎19
1979	01♌26	03 54	06 21	08 49	11 17	13 45	16 14	18 42	21 10	23 39	26 07	28 36	01 04	03 33	06 02	08♌30
1980	25♊53	27 18	28 47	00♋19	01 54	03 32	05 13	06 57	08 43	10 32	12 22	14 15	16 09	18 06	20 04	22♋03
1981	08♍56	11 21	13 45	16 09	18 33	20 57	23 21	25 44	28 07	00♎31	02 54	05 16	07 39	10 01	12 24	14♎46
1982	13♋39	16 04	18 29	20 55	23 21	25 47	28 13	00♌39	03 06	05 32	07 59	10 26	12 53	15 21	17 48	20♌16
1983	09♍21	09 R 29	09 28	09 18	08 59	08 29	07 51	07 04	06 09	05 07	03 59	02 47	01 33	00♌18	29 05	27♌56
1984	21♌37	24 04	26 32	28♍59	01 27	03 55	06 22	08 50	11 18	13 45	16 13	18 40	21 08	23 36	26 03	28♍31
1985	28♊26	00♋42	03 00	05 17	07 36	09 54	12 13	14 33	16 53	19 13	21 34	23 55	26 16	28 38	01♌00	03♌23
1986	22♍37	24 47	26 56	29♎05	01 12	03 19	05 24	07 29	09 32	11 34	13 35	15♍34	17 32	19 29	21 24	23♍17
1987	02♌07	04 35	07 02	09 30	11 58	14 26	16 55	19 23	21 51	24 20	26 48	29 17	01 45	04 14	06 43	09♌12
1988	25♊24	26 53	28 26	00♋01	01 40	03 22	05 06	06 52	08 41	10 32	12 24	14 19	16 16	18 14	20 13	22♋15
1989	09♍33	11 58	14 22	16 46	19 09	21 33	23 56	26 20	28 43	01♎06	03 28	05 51	08 13	10 35	12 57	15♎19
1990	14♋18	16 43	19 09	21 34	24 00	26 26	28♌53	01 19	03 46	06 13	08 39	11 07	13 34	16 01	18 29	20♌56
1991	07♍R19	07 17	07 05	06 43	06 13	05 33	04 44	03 48	02 44	01 36	00♌23	29 09	27 55	26 42	25 33	24♌30
1992	22♌17	24 45	27 13	29♍40	02 08	04 35	07 03	09 31	11 58	14 26	16 53	19 21	21 48	24 16	26 43	29♍10
1993	28♊55	01♋13	03 30	05 49	08 07	10 26	12 46	15 06	17 26	19 47	22 08	24 29	26 51	29♌13	01 36	03♌58
1994	22♍57	25 06	27 14	29♎22	01 28	03 33	05 37	07 40	09 42	11 42	13 42	15 39	17 35	19 30	21 22	23♎13
1995	02♌48	05 16	07 43	10 11	12 39	15 08	17 36	20 04	22 32	25 01	27 29	29♍58	02 26	04 55	07 24	09♍53
1996	24♊59	26 32	28 08	29♋47	01 29	03 13	05 00	06 49	08 40	10 33	12 28	14 25	16 23	18 23	20 24	22♋27
1997	10♍10	12 34	14 57	17 21	19 45	22 08	24 31	26 54	29♎17	01 39	04 02	06 24	08 46	11 08	13 29	15♎51
1998	14♋56	17 22	19 47	22 13	24 39	27 05	29♌32	01 58	04 25	06 52	09 19	11 46	14 13	16 41	19 08	21♌36
1999	05♍R03	04 50	04 26	03 54	03 12	02 22	01 24	00♌20	29 11	27 58	26 43	25 29	24 17	23 09	22 07	21♌12
2000	22♌57	25 25	27 52	00♍20	02 47	05 15	07 42	10 10	12 37	15 05	17 32	20 00	22 27	24 54	27 22	29♍49

Venus

September

	1st	3rd	5th	7th	9th	11th	13th	15th	17th	19th	21st	23rd	25th	27th	29th
1900	23♋16	24 54	26 36	28 20	00♌07	01 56	03 48	05 41	07 37	09 34	11 33	13 34	15 36	17 40	19♌45
1901	10♎14	12 38	15 02	17 27	19 51	22 15	24 39	27 02	29♏26	01 49	04 12	06 35	08 58	11 21	13♏43
1902	14♌54	17 21	19 48	22 15	24 42	27 10	29♍38	02 05	04 34	07 02	09 30	11 59	14 27	16 56	19♍25
1903	01♎R23	00 58	00 23	29♍39	28 47	27 48	26 43	25 33	24 20	23 06	21 53	20 43	19 37	18 37	17♍45
1904	23♍07	25 35	28 03	00♎31	03 00	05 28	07 56	10 24	12 53	15 21	17 49	20 17	22 45	25 13	27♎41
1905	29♋01	01♌21	03 41	06 01	08 22	10 43	13 05	15 27	17 50	20 12	22 36	24 59	27 24	29♍48	02♍13
1906	22♎58	24 02	26 10	28♏17	00 22	02 27	04 30	06 32	08 33	10 33	12 31	14 28	16 23	18 17	20♏08
1907	03♍35	06 04	08 33	11 02	13 31	16 00	18 30	20 59	23 28	25 58	28 27	00♎57	03 26	05 56	08♎25
1908	23♋00	24 42	26 27	28 14	00♌03	01 55	03 49	05 44	07 42	09 41	11 42	13 44	15 48	17 53	20♌00
1909	10♎49	13 13	15 37	18 01	20 25	22 49	25 12	27 36	29♏59	02 22	04 45	07 08	09 30	11 53	14♏15
1910	15♌33	18 00	20 27	22 54	25 22	27 49	00♍17	02 45	05 13	07 41	10 10	12 38	15 07	17 36	20♍05
1911	28♍R36	28 00	27 15	26 21	25 20	24 14	23 03	21 49	20 35	19 23	18 13	17 09	16 10	15 20	14♍37
1912	23♍47	26 15	28 43	01♎11	03 40	06 08	08 36	11 04	13 32	16 00	18 28	20 56	23 24	25 52	28♎20
1913	29♋33	01♌53	04 13	06 34	08 55	11 17	13 39	16 01	18 24	20 47	23 11	25 35	27 59	00♍24	02♍49
1914	23♎15	25 21	27 27	29♏32	01 35	03 38	05 39	07 39	09 37	11 34	13 30	15 23	17 15	19 05	20♏52
1915	04♍17	06 46	09 15	11 44	14 13	16 42	19 11	21 41	24 10	26 39	29♎09	01 38	04 08	06 37	09♎10
1916	22♋50	24 35	26 22	28 12	00♌04	01 58	03 53	05 51	07 50	09 51	11 54	13 58	16 03	18 09	20♌17
1917	11♎25	13 49	16 13	18 37	21 00	23 24	25 47	28 10	00♏33	02 56	05 18	07 41	10 03	12 25	14♏46
1918	16♌12	18 39	21 07	23 34	26 02	28 29	00♍57	03 25	05 54	08 22	10 11	13 19	15 48	18 17	20♍46
1919	25♍R37	24 51	23 56	22 54	21 46	20 34	19 20	18 06	16 54	15 45	14 42	13 45	12 55	12 15	11♍44
1920	24♍27	26 55	29♎23	01 51	04 20	06 48	09 16	11 44	14 12	16 40	19 08	21 36	24 04	26 31	28♏59
1921	00♌05	02 25	04 46	07 07	09 29	11 51	14 13	16 36	18 59	21 22	23 46	26 11	28 35	01♍00	03♍25
1922	23♎28	25 34	27 38	29♏42	01 44	03 44	05 44	07 42	09 38	11 33	13 26	15 17	17 06	18 53	20♏38
1923	04♍58	07 26	09 55	12 24	14 53	17 23	19 52	22 21	24 50	27 20	29♎49	02 19	04 48	07 18	09♎47
1924	22♋42	24 29	26 19	28 11	00♌06	02 01	03 59	05 59	08 00	10 02	12 06	14 11	16 18	18 26	20♌35
1925	12♎00	14 23	16 47	19 10	21 34	24 00	26 20	28 43	01♏05	03 28	05 50	08 12	10 34	12 55	15♏17
1926	16♌51	19 18	21 46	24 13	26 41	29♍09	01 37	04 05	06 33	09 02	11 30	13 59	16 28	18 57	21♍26
1927	22♍R26	21 29	20 26	91 18	18 06	16 51	15 37	14 25	13 17	12 14	11 19	10 31	09 52	09 23	09♍03
1928	25♍07	27 35	00♎03	02 31	04 59	07 27	09 55	12 23	14 51	17 19	19 46	22 14	24 42	27♏10	29♏38
1929	00♌37	02 58	05 19	07 40	10 02	12 25	14 47	17 11	19 34	21 58	24 22	26 46	29♍11	01 36	04♍02
1930	23♎41	25 45	27 48	29♏50	01 50	03 49	05 46	07 42	09 37	11 29	13 19	15 08	16 54	18 38	20♏19
1931	05♍39	08 08	10 37	13 06	15 35	18 04	20 33	23 02	25 32	28 01	00♎30	03 00	05 29	07 59	10♎28
1932	22♋37	24 28	26 20	28 14	00 10	02 08	04 08	06 09	08 11	10 15	12 21	14 27	16 35	18 44	20♋54
1933	12♎35	14 58	17 22	19 45	22♌08	24 31	26 53	29♏16	01 38	04 00	06 22	08 44	11 05	13 26	15♏47
1934	17♌31	19 58	22 26	24 53	27 21	29♍49	02 17	04 46	07 14	09 42	12 11	14 40	17 09	19 38	22♍07
1935	19♍R03	17 59	16 50	15 37	14 23	13 09	11 58	10 50	09 49	08 54	08 08	07 31	07 03	06 45	06♍D37
1936	25♍47	28 15	00♎43	03 11	05 39	08 07	10 35	13 03	15 30	17 58	20 26	22 54	25 21	27 49	00♏17
1937	01♌10	03 31	05 53	08 15	10 37	13 00	15 23	17 46	20 10	22 34	24 58	27 23	29♍48	02 13	04♍39
1938	23♎52	25 55	27 56	29♏56	01 55	03 52	05 47	07 41	09 32	11 22	13 10	14 55	16 38	18 19	19♏56
1939	06♍20	08 49	11 18	13 47	16 16	18 46	21 14	23 43	26 13	28 42	01♎12	03 41	06 10	08 40	11♎09
1940	22♋36	24 29	26 23	28 19	00♌17	02 17	04 18	06 21	08 25	10 30	12 37	14 45	16 54	19 04	21♌15
1941	13♎09	15 33	17 56	20 19	22 41	25 04	27 26	29♏48	02 10	04 32	06 53	09 15	11 36	13 56	16♏17
1942	18♌10	20 38	23 05	25 33	28 01	00♍29	02 57	05 25	07 54	10 23	12 51	15 20	17 49	20 18	22♍47
1943	15♍R33	14 23	13 10	11 55	10 42	09 31	08 24	07 24	06 31	05 46	05 10	04 44	04 28	04 D21	04♍24
1944	26♍27	28♎55	01 22	03 50	06 18	08 46	11 14	13 41	16 09	18 37	21 04	23 32	26 00	28 27	00♏55
1945	01♌43	04 06	06 27	08 49	11 12	13 35	15 58	18 22	20 46	23 10	25 34	27 59	00♍26	02 50	05♍16
1946	24♎01	26 02	28 02	00♏00	01 56	03 51	05 44	07 35	09 25	11 12	12 56	14 38	16 18	17 55	19♏28
1947	07♍01	09 30	11 59	14 28	16 57	19 26	21 56	24 25	26 54	29♎23	01 53	04 22	06 52	09 21	11♎51
1948	22♋37	24 32	26 28	28 26	00♌26	02 28	04 30	06 34	08 40	10 47	12 54	15 03	17 13	19 24	21♌36
1949	13♎44	16 07	18 30	20 52	23 15	25 37	27 59	00♏21	02 42	05 04	07 25	09 45	12 06	14 26	16♏47
1950	18♌50	21 18	23 45	26 13	28 41	01♍09	03 37	06 06	08 34	11 03	13 32	16 01	18 30	20 59	23♍28
1951	11♍R55	10 42	09 28	08 15	07 04	05 59	05 00	04 08	03 25	02 50	02 26	02 11	02 D06	02 11	02♍25
1952	27♍07	29♎35	02 02	04 30	06 58	09 25	11 53	14 21	16 48	19 16	21 44	24 11	26 39	29♏06	01♏33
1953	02♌17	04 39	07 01	09 23	11 46	14 10	16 33	18 57	21 21	23 46	26 11	28 36	01♍01	03 27	05♍53
1954	24♎08	26 08	28 05	00♏01	01 66	03 48	05 39	07 27	09 14	10 58	12 39	14 18	15 53	17 26	18♏55
1955	07♍42	10 11	12 40	15 09	17 38	20 07	22 36	25 06	27 35	00♎04	02 34	05 03	07 32	10 02	12♎31
1956	22♋41	24 37	26 36	28 36	00♌37	02 40	04 44	06 50	08 56	11 04	13 13	15 23	17 34	19 46	21♌59
1957	14♎18	16 40	19 03	21 25	23 47	26 09	28 31	00♏52	03 13	05 34	07 55	10 15	12 35	14 55	17♏15
1958	19♌30	21 58	24 25	26 53	29 21	01♍49	04 18	06 46	09 15	11 44	14 12	16 41	19 10	21 40	24♍09
1959	08♍R14	07 00	05 48	04 38	03 34	02 36	01 46	01 04	00 32	00 09	29♌D56	29 52	29♍58	00 13	00♍37
1960	27♍47	00♎15	02 42	05 10	07 37	10 05	12 33	15 00	17 28	19 55	22 23	24 50	27 17	29♏45	02♏12
1961	02♌51	05 13	07 36	09 58	12 22	14 45	17 09	19 33	21 58	24 22	26 48	29♍13	01 39	04 04	06♍31
1962	24♎13	26 10	28 06	00♏00	01 52	03 42	05 30	07 16	08 59	10 39	12 17	13 52	15 23	16 51	18♏15
1963	08♍32	10 52	13 21	15 50	18 19	20 48	23 17	25 47	28 16	00♎45	03 15	05 44	08 13	10 43	13♎12
1964	22♋46	24 45	26 45	28 46	00♌49	02 54	04 59	07 06	09 14	11 23	13 33	15 44	17 56	20 09	22♌23
1965	14♎51	17 13	19 35	21 57	24 19	26 40	29♏02	01 23	03 43	06 04	08 24	11 44	13 04	15 23	17♏42
1966	20♌10	22 37	25 05	27 33	00♍01	02 29	04 58	07 26	09 55	12 24	14 53	17 22	19 51	22 20	24♍49
1967	04♍R33	03 21	02 13	01 10	00♌13	29 24	28 44	28 13	27 52	27 D41	27 39	27 46	28 03	28 28	29♌01
1968	28♍26	00♎53	03 21	05 49	08 16	10 44	13 11	15 38	18 06	20 33	23 00	25 28	27 55	00♏22	02♏49
1969	03♌25	05 47	08 10	10 33	12 57	15 20	17 45	20 09	22 34	24 59	27 24	29♍50	02 15	04 42	07♍08
1970	24♎16	26 11	28 04	29♏56	01 45	03 33	05 18	07 00	08 40	10 17	11 51	13 21	14 48	16 11	17♏29
1971	09♍05	11 34	14 03	16 32	19 01	21 30	23 59	26 28	28♎57	01 26	03 56	06 25	08 54	11 24	13♎53
1972	22♋55	24 55	26 57	29♌00	01 04	03 10	05 17	07 25	09 34	11 44	13 55	16 06	18 19	20 33	22♌48
1973	15♎25	17 47	20 09	22 30	24 52	27 13	29♏34	01 54	04 15	06 35	08 55	11 14	13 33	15 52	18♏11
1974	20♌51	23 18	25 46	28 14	00♍43	03 11	05 39	08 08	10 37	13 06	15 35	18 04	20 33	23 02	25♍31
1975	00♍R56	29 49	28 46	27 51	27 04	26 26	25 57	25 37	25 D27	25 27	25 36	25 54	26 20	26 55	27♌37
1976	29♍05	01♎33	04 01	06 28	08 55	11 23	13 50	16 17	18 45	21 12	23 39	26 06	28 33	01♏00	03♏27
1977	04♌00	06 22	08 45	11 09	13 33	15 57	18 21	20 46	23 11	25 36	28 01	00♍27	02 53	05 19	07♍46
1978	19♎05	18 01	16 52	15♏40	14 27	13 15	12 06	11 01	10 03	09 13	08 31	07 58	07 36	07 23	07♏20
1979	09♍45	12 14	14 43	17 12	19 41	22 10	24 39	27 08	29♎37	02 06	04 36	07 05	09 34	12 04	14♎33
1980	23♋04	25 05	27 09	29♌13	02 19	03 26	05 34	07 43	09 53	12 04	14 16	16 29	18 42	20 57	23♌12
1981	15♎57	18 18	20 40	23 01	25 22	27 43	00♏03	02 24	04 43	07 03	09 22	11 41	14 00	16 18	18♏36
1982	21♌29	23 57	26 25	28 53	01♍22	03 50	06 18	08 47	11 16	13 45	16 14	18 43	21 12	23 42	26♍11
1983	27♌R23	26 22	25 28	24 42	24 06	23 38	23 21	23 D12	23 14	23 24	23 44	24 11	24 47	25 31	26♌21
1984	29♍44	02♎12	04 39	07 07	09 34	12 01	14 28	16 55	19 23	21 50	24 17	26 44	29♏11	01 38	04♏05
1985	04♌34	06 57	09 21	11 44	14 08	16 32	18 57	21 22	23 47	26 13	28 38	01♍04	03 30	05 57	08♍24
1986	24♎13	26 03	27 52	29♏38	01 21	03 03	04 41	06 16	07 48	09 17	10 41	12 02	13 18	14 29	15♏35
1987	10♍26	12 55	15 24	17 53	20 22	22 51	25 20	27 49	00♎18	02 47	05 17	07 46	10 15	12 44	15♎14
1988	23♋16	25 19	27 24	29♌29	01 36	03 44	05 54	08 04	10 15	12 27	14 40	16 53	19 08	21 23	23♌39
1989	16♎30	18 51	21 12	23 33	25 54	28 14	00♏34	02 54	05 13	07 32	09 51	12 09	14 27	16 45	19♏02
1990	22♌10	24 38	27 06	29♍34	02 03	04 31	07 00	09 28	11 57	14 26	16 55	19 24	21 54	24 23	26♍52
1991	24♌R01	23 08	22 24	21 49	21 23	21 07	21 D01	21 04	21 16	21 36	22 05	22 43	23 27	24 18	25♌16
1992	00♎24	02 52	05 19	07 46	10 13	12 40	15 08	17 35	20 02	22 29	24 56	27 22	29♏49	02 16	04♏43
1993	05♌10	07 33	09 57	12 21	14 45	17 09	19 34	21 59	24 25	26 50	29♍16	01 42	04 09	06 35	09♍02
1994	24♎08	25 55	27 41	29♏24	01 04	02 42	04 16	05 47	07 15	08 39	09 58	11 13	12 23	13 28	14♏27
1995	11♍07	13 36	16 05	18 34	21 03	23 32	26 01	28 30	00♎59	03 28	05 57	08 27	10 56	13 25	15♎55
1996	23♋29	25 34	27 39	29♌46	01 55	04 04	06 14	08 25	10 37	12 50	15 04	17 18	19 33	21 49	24♌06
1997	17♎01	19 22	21 43	24 03	26 24	28 44	01♏03	03 22	05 41	08 00	10 18	12 36	14 53	17 11	19♏27
1998	22♌50	25 18	27 46	00♍14	02 43	05 11	07 40	10 08	12 37	15 06	17 35	20 05	22 34	25 03	27♍33
1999	20♌R47	20 04	19 31	19 07	18 52	18 D47	18 52	19 05	19 28	19 58	20 36	21 22	22 14	23 13	24♌18
2000	02♎03	03 30	05 57	08 24	10 51	13 18	15 45	18 12	20 39	23 06	25 33	28 00	00♏26	02 53	05♏19

October

	1st	3rd	5th	7th	9th	11th	13th	15th	17th	19th	21st	23rd	25th	27th	29th	31st
1900	21♌51	23 59	26 08	28 18	00♍29	02 40	04 53	07 07	09 22	11 38	13 54	16 11	18 29	20 47	23 06	25♍26
1901	16♏05	18 27	20 49	23 11	25 32	27 53	00♐14	02 35	04 55	07 15	09 35	11 54	14 13	16 31	18 49	21♐07
1902	21♍54	24 24	26 53	29♎22	01 52	04 22	06 51	09 21	11 51	14 21	16 51	19 21	21 52	24 22	26 52	29♎23
1903	17♍R01	16 26	16 01	15 45	15 D 40	15 43	15 57	16 19	16 49	17 28	18 14	19 07	20 07	21 12	22 23	23♍40
1904	00♏09	02 37	05 05	07 33	01 01	12 29	14 57	17 24	19 52	22 20	24 48	27 15	29♐43	02 10	04 38	07♐05
1905	04♍38	07 03	09 29	11 54	14 21	16 47	19 14	21 41	24 08	26 35	29♎03	01 31	03 59	06 27	08 56	11♎25
1906	22♏51	24 37	26 20	28 01	29♐39	01 14	02 45	04 13	05 37	06 56	08 11	09 21	10 25	11 24	12 16	13♐01
1907	10♎55	13 25	15 54	18 24	20 54	23 24	25 54	28 24	00♏53	03 23	06 53	08 23	10 53	13 23	15 53	18♏23
1908	22♌08	24 16	26 26	28 37	00♍49	03 02	05 16	07 30	09 56	12 02	14 19	16 37	18 56	21 15	23 34	25♍55
1909	16♏36	18 58	21 19	23 41	26 02	28 22	00♐43	03 03	05 22	07 42	10 01	12 20	14 38	16 56	19 14	21♐31
1910	22♍34	25 04	27 33	00♎03	02 32	05 02	07 32	10 02	12 32	15 02	17 32	20 02	22 32	25 03	27 33	00♏04
1911	14♍R04	13 41	13 27	13 D 23	13 28	13 43	14 07	14 39	15 19	16 06	17 00	18 01	19 07	20 19	21 37	22♍59
1912	00♏48	03 16	05 44	08 12	10 39	13 07	15 35	18 03	20 30	22 58	25 25	27 53	00♐20	02 48	05 15	07♐42
1913	05♍14	07 40	10 06	12 32	14 58	17 25	19 52	22 19	24 46	27 14	29♎41	02 10	04 38	07 06	09 35	12♎04
1914	22♏38	24 20	26 00	27 37	29 11	00♐41	02 08	03 31	04 49	06 02	07 11	08 14	09 10	10 01	10 44	11♐19
1915	11♎36	14 06	16 36	19 06	21 35	24 05	26 35	29♏05	01 35	04 04	06 34	09 04	11 34	14 04	16 34	19♏04
1916	22♌26	24 36	26 47	28♍59	01 12	03 25	05 40	07 55	10 12	12 29	14 47	17 05	19 24	21 44	24 04	26♍25
1917	17♏08	19 29	21 50	24 11	26 31	28♐51	01 11	03 31	05 50	08 09	10 28	12 46	15 03	17 21	19 37	21♐54
1918	23♍15	25 45	28 14	00♎44	03 13	05 43	08 13	10 43	13 13	15 43	18 13	20 43	23 14	25 44	28 14	00♏45
1919	11♍R22	11 D 10	11 08	11 15	11 31	11 56	12 29	13 10	13 59	14 54	15 56	17 03	18 16	19 34	20 57	22♍24
1920	01♏27	03 55	06 23	08 50	11 18	13 46	16 13	18 41	21 08	23 36	26 03	28 30	00♐58	03 25	05 52	08♐19
1921	05♍51	08 17	10 43	13 09	15 35	18 02	21 29	22 57	25 24	27 52	00♎20	02 48	05 16	07 45	10 14	12♎43
1922	22♏20	23 59	25 35	27 08	28 37	00♐03	01 24	02 41	03 53	05 00	06 01	06 56	07 45	08 26	09 00	09♐25
1923	12♎17	14 46	17 16	19 46	22 16	24 45	27 15	29♏45	02 15	04 45	07 15	09 44	12 14	14 44	17 14	19♏44
1924	22♌45	24 56	27 08	29♍20	01 34	03 49	06 04	08 20	10 37	12 55	15 13	17 32	19 52	22 12	24 33	26♍55
1925	17♏38	19 58	22 19	24 39	26 59	29♐19	01 38	03 57	06 16	08 34	10 52	13 10	15 27	17 43	19 59	22♐15
1926	15♍55	26 25	28♎54	01 24	03 54	06 23	08 53	11 23	13 53	16 23	18 53	21 24	23 54	26 24	28♏55	01♏25
1927	08♍R53	08 D 52	09 01	09 19	09 45	10 20	11 02	11 52	12 48	13 51	14 59	16 13	17 32	18 55	20 23	21♍55
1928	02♏05	04 33	07 00	09 28	11 56	14 23	16 51	19 18	21 45	24 13	26 40	29♐07	01 34	04 02	06 29	08♐55
1929	06♍27	08 53	11 20	13 46	16 13	18 40	21 07	23 34	26 02	28 30	00♎58	03 26	05 55	08 24	10 52	13♎21
1930	21♏57	23 33	25 05	26 33	27 57	29 17	00♐33	01 44	02 49	03 48	04 42	05 28	06 08	06 40	07 03	07♐18
1931	12♎58	15 28	17 57	20 27	22 57	25 26	27 56	00♏26	02 56	05 25	07 55	10 25	12 55	15 25	18 54	20♏24
1932	23♌05	25 17	27 30	29♍44	01 59	04 14	06 30	08 47	11 05	13 23	15 42	18 02	20 22	22 43	25 04	27♍26
1933	18♏08	20 28	22 49	25 08	27 28	29♐47	02 06	04 24	06 42	09 00	11 17	13 34	15 50	18 06	20 21	22♐36
1934	24♍36	27 06	29♎35	02 05	04 35	07 05	09 34	12 04	14 35	17 05	19 35	22 05	24 35	27 06	29♏36	02♏07
1935	06♍38	06 48	07 R 08	07 36	08 11	08 55	09 46	10 43	11 46	12 56	14 10	15 30	16 54	18 23	19 55	21♍31
1936	02♏44	05 12	07 39	10 07	12 34	15 01	17 29	19 56	22 23	24 50	27 18	29♐45	02 12	04 39	07 05	09♐32
1937	07♍05	09 31	11 57	14 24	16 51	19 18	21 46	24 13	26 41	29♎09	01 37	04 06	06 34	09 03	11 32	14♎01
1938	21♏30	23 01	24 29	25 52	27 11	28 25	29♐34	00 38	01 36	02 28	03 12	03 50	04 19	04 41	04 R 53	04♐56
1939	13♎39	16 08	18 38	21 08	23 37	26 07	28 37	01♏07	03 36	06 06	08 36	11 06	13 35	16 05	18 35	21♏04
1940	23♌27	25 40	27 53	00♍08	02 23	04 40	06 56	09 14	11 32	13 51	16 11	18 31	20 52	23 13	25 35	27♍57
1941	18♏37	20 57	23 17	25 36	27 55	00♐13	02 32	04 49	07 07	09 24	11 40	13 56	16 12	18 27	20 41	22♐55
1942	25♍17	27 46	00♎16	02 45	05 15	07 45	10 15	12 45	15 15	17 45	20 15	22 46	25 16	27 46	00♏17	02♏47
1943	04♍36	04 57	05 27	06 04	06 48	07 40	08 38	09 43	10 53	12 08	13 28	14 53	16 22	17 55	19 32	21♍12
1944	03♏22	05 50	08 17	10 44	13 11	15 39	18 06	20 33	23 00	25 27	27 54	00♐21	02 48	05 15	07 41	10♐08
1945	07♍42	10 08	12 35	15 02	17 29	19 56	22 24	24 52	27 20	29♎48	02 16	04 45	07 13	09 42	12 11	14♎41
1946	20♏58	22 24	23 46	25 04	26 17	27 25	28 27	29 24	00♐13	00 56	01 32	01 59	02 18	02 28	02 R 29	02♐21
1947	14♎20	16 50	19 19	21 49	24 18	26 48	29♏18	01 47	04 17	06 47	09 17	11 46	14 16	16 46	19 15	21♏45
1948	23♌49	26 03	28 18	00♍33	02 49	05 06	07 24	09 42	12 01	14 20	16 40	19 01	21 22	23 44	26 06	28♍29
1949	19♏06	21 26	23 45	26 04	28 22	00♐40	02 57	05 15	07 31	09 48	12 03	14 19	16 33	18 47	21 01	23♐14
1950	25♍58	28 27	00♎57	03 26	05 56	08 26	10 56	13 26	15 56	18 26	20 57	23 27	25 57	28 27	00♏58	03♏28
1951	02♍47	03♎18	03 56	04 42	05 35	06 34	07 40	08 50	10 07	11♏27	12 53	14 22	15 56	17 33	19 13	20♏57
1952	04♏01	06 28	08 55	11 22	13 50	16 17	18 44	21 11	23 38	26 04	28 31	00♐58	03 25	05 51	08 18	10♐44
1953	08♍19	10 46	13 13	15 40	18 07	20 35	23 02	25 30	27 58	00♎26	02 55	05 24	07 52	10 21	12 50	15♎20
1954	20♏20	21 41	22 58	24 09	25 16	26 16	27 11	27 59	28 40	29 13	29 39	29♐55	00 R 03	00♏02	29 51	29♏30
1955	15♎01	17 30	20 00	22 29	24 59	27 28	29♏58	02 28	04 57	07 27	09 57	12 26	14 56	17 26	19 55	22♏25
1956	24♌13	26 28	28 43	00♍59	03 16	05 34	07 52	10 11	12 30	14 50	17 11	19 32	21 53	24 16	26 38	29♍01
1957	19♏34	21 53	24 12	26 30	28 48	01♐05	03 22	05 38	07 54	10 10	12 25	14 39	16 53	19 06	21 19	23♐31
1958	26♍38	29♎08	01 38	04 07	06 37	09 07	11 37	14 07	16 37	19 07	21 38	24 08	26 38	29♏09	01 39	04♏09
1959	01♍09	01 49	02 36	03 30	04 31	05 37	06 48	08 05	09 27	10 53	12 23	13 57	15 34	17 15	18 59	20♍45
1960	04♏39	07 06	09 33	12 00	14 27	16 54	19 21	21 48	24 15	26 41	29♐08	01 35	04 01	06 28	08 54	11♐20
1961	08♍57	11 24	13 51	16 18	18 45	21 13	23 41	26 09	28 37	01♎06	03 34	06 03	08 32	11 01	13 30	16♎00
1962	19♏35	20 50	22 01	23 06	24 05	24 58	25 44	26 23	26 55	27 18	27 32	27 R 38	27 34	27 20	26 57	26♏24
1963	15♎42	18 11	20 41	23 10	25 40	28 09	00♏39	03 08	05 38	08 07	10 37	13 07	15 36	18 06	20 35	23♏48
1964	24♌37	26 53	29♍09	01 25	03 43	06 01	08 20	10 39	12 59	15 20	17 41	20 03	22 25	24 47	27 10	29♍34
1965	20♏01	22 20	24 38	26 55	29♐12	01 29	03 45	06 01	08 16	10 31	12 45	14 58	17 11	19 23	21 35	23♐45
1966	27♍19	29♎48	02 18	04 48	07 18	09 48	12 18	14 48	17 18	19 48	22 18	24 48	27 19	29♏49	02 20	04♏50
1967	29♌43	00♍31	01 26	02 27	03 34	04 47	06 04	07 27	08 53	10 24	11 58	13 36	15 17	17 01	18 48	20♍38
1968	05♏46	07 44	10 10	12 37	15 04	17 31	19 58	22 24	24 51	27 17	29♐44	02 10	04 37	07 03	09 29	11♐55
1969	09♍35	12 01	14 29	16 56	19 24	21 51	24 19	26 47	29♎16	01 44	04 13	06 42	09 11	11 40	14 09	16♎39
1970	18♏43	19 52	20 56	21 54	22 45	23 30	24 07	24 36	24 57	25 10	25 R 13	25 06	24 50	24 25	23 50	23♏06
1971	16♎23	18 52	21 22	23 51	26 20	28♏50	01 19	03 49	06 19	08 48	11 18	13 47	16 17	18 46	21 16	23♏45
1972	25♌03	27 19	29♍36	01 53	04 12	06 30	08 50	11 10	13 30	15 51	18 13	20 35	22 57	25 20	27 44	00♎08
1973	20♏29	22 47	25 04	27 21	29♐37	01 53	04 09	06 24	08 38	10 52	13 05	15 17	17 29	19 40	21 51	24♐00
1974	28♍01	00♎30	03 00	05 30	08 00	10 30	13 00	15 30	18 00	20 30	23 00	25 31	28 01	00♏31	03 02	05♏32
1975	28♌27	29 23	00♍25	01 33	02 46	04 05	05 27	06 55	08 26	10 00	11 39	13 20	15 04	16 52	18 42	20♍34
1976	05♏54	08 21	10 48	13 15	15 42	18 08	20 35	23 01	25 28	27 54	00♐20	02 46	05 13	07 39	10 05	12♐30
1977	10♍13	12 40	15 07	17 34	20 02	22 30	24 58	27 27	29♎55	02 24	04 52	07 21	09 50	12 20	14 49	17♎19
1978	07♏27	07 44	08 09	08 42	09 24	10 13	11 09	12 11	13 R 20	14 34	15 53	17 17	18 45	20 17	21 54	23♏33
1979	17♎02	19 32	22 01	24 31	27 00	29♏30	01 59	04 28	06 58	09 27	11 57	14 26	16 56	19 25	21 55	24♏24
1980	25♌28	27 45	00♍03	02 21	04 39	06 59	09 19	11 39	14 00	16 22	18 44	21 06	23 29	25 52	28 16	00♎40
1981	20♏54	23 11	25 28	27 44	00♐00	02 15	04 30	06 44	08 57	11 10	13 22	15 34	17 45	19 54	22 03	24♐12
1982	28♍40	01♎10	03 40	06 09	08 39	11 09	13 39	16 09	18 40	21 10	23 40	26 10	28 41	01♏11	03 42	06♏12
1983	27♌18	28 22	29♍30	00 45	02 04	03 27	04 55	06 26	08 02	09 40	11 22	13 07	14 54	16 45	18 37	20♍32
1984	06♏31	08 58	11 25	13 51	16 18	18 44	21 11	23 37	26 03	28 29	00♐56	03 22	05 47	08 13	10 39	13♐05
1985	10♍51	13 18	15 45	18 13	20 41	23 09	25 37	28 05	00♎34	03 03	05 32	08 01	10 30	12 59	15 29	17♎58
1986	16♏36	17 31	18 19	19 00	19 33	19 59	20 15	20 R 23	20 22	20 11	19 50	19 20	18 40	17 52	16 56	15♏53
1987	17♎43	20 13	22 42	25 11	27 41	00♏10	02 39	05 09	07 38	10 08	12 37	15 06	17 36	20 05	22 35	25♏04
1988	25♌56	28 13	00♍31	02 50	05 09	07 29	09 49	12 10	14 31	16 54	19 16	21 39	24 02	26 26	28♎50	01♎14
1989	21♏19	23 36	25 52	28 07	00♐23	02 37	04 51	07 04	09 17	11 28	13 40	15 50	17 59	20 08	22 16	24♐22
1990	29♍22	01♎52	04 21	06 51	09 21	11 51	14 21	16 51	19 21	21 51	24 22	26 52	29♏22	01 53	04 23	06♏54
1991	26♌20	27 30	28 45	00♍05	01 29	02 57	04 29	06 05	07 44	09 26	11 11	12 59	14 49	16 42	18 37	20♍34
1992	07♏09	09 36	12 03	14 29	16 55	19 22	21 48	24 14	26 40	29♐06	01 32	03 58	06 23	08 49	11 15	13♐40
1993	11♍29	13 57	16 24	18 52	21 20	23 48	26 16	28 45	01♎14	03 43	06 12	08 41	11 10	13 39	16 09	18♎38
1994	15♏20	16 06	16 45	17 17	17 40	17 55	18 R 01	17 57	17 44	17 21	16 48	16 06	15 16	14 18	13 14	12♏05
1995	18♎23	20 53	23 22	25 52	28 21	00♏50	03 20	05 49	08 18	10 48	13 17	15 47	18 16	20 45	23 15	25♏44
1996	26♌23	28 41	01♍00	03 19	05 39	07 59	10 20	12 42	15 03	17 26	19 49	22 12	24 35	26 59	29 24	01♎49
1997	21♏43	23 59	26 15	28 29	00♐44	02 57	05 10	07 22	09 34	11 45	13 55	16 04	18 12	20 19	22 25	24♐30
1998	00♎02	02 32	05 02	07 32	10 01	12 31	15 01	17 32	20 02	22 32	25 02	27 32	00♏03	02 33	05 04	07♏34
1999	25♌28	26 44	28 04	29♍29	00 58	02 31	04 07	05 47	07 29	09 15	11 03	12 53	14 46	16 41	18 38	20♍37
2000	07♏46	10 12	12 39	15 05	17 31	19 57	22 23	27 49	27 15	29♐41	02 07	04 32	06 58	09 23	11 48	14♐13

Venus

November

Year	1st	3rd	5th	7th	9th	11th	13th	15th	17th	19th	21st	23rd	25th	27th	29th
1900	26♍36	28♎57	01 18	03 40	06 02	08 24	10 48	13 11	15 35	17 59	20 24	22 49	25 15	27 40	00♏06
1901	22♐16	24 33	26 49	29♑05	01 21	03 35	05 50	08 03	10 16	12 28	14 39	16 49	18 53	21 06	23♑13
1902	00♏38	03 09	05 39	08 10	10 41	13 11	15 42	18 13	20 44	23 14	25 45	28 16	00♐47	03 18	05♐49
1903	24♍20	25 43	27 11	28 43	00♎19	01 58	03 40	05 26	07 14	09 05	10 58	12 53	14 51	16 50	18♎51
1904	08♐19	10 46	13 13	15 41	18 08	20 35	23 02	25 29	27 56	00♑22	02 49	05 16	07 42	10 08	12♑34
1905	12♎39	15 08	17 37	20 06	22 35	25 05	27 34	00♏04	02 34	05 04	07 34	10 04	12 34	15 05	17♏35
1906	13♐21	13 54	14 20	14 36	14 R44	14 42	14 31	14 10	13 39	12 59	12 11	11 14	10 11	09 02	07♐51
1907	19♏38	22 08	24 38	27 08	29♐38	02 08	04 38	07 08	09 38	12 08	14 38	17 07	19 37	22 07	24♐37
1908	27♍05	29♎26	01 48	04 10	06 33	08 56	11 19	13 43	16 07	18 32	20 57	23 23	25 48	28 14	00♏41
1909	22♐39	24 55	27 11	29♑26	01 40	03 54	06 07	08 20	10 31	12 42	14 52	17 01	19 08	21 15	23♑20
1910	01♏19	03 49	06 20	08 51	11 21	13 52	16 23	18 53	21 24	23 55	26 26	28♐57	01 28	03 58	06♐29
1911	23♍41	25 10	26 42	28 18	29♎58	01 41	03 27	05 15	07 07	09 00	10 56	12 53	14 53	16 55	18♎58
1912	08♐56	11 23	13 50	16 17	18 44	21 11	23 38	26 05	28 31	00♑58	03 24	05 51	08 17	10 43	13♑09
1913	13♎18	15 47	18 16	20 46	23 15	25 45	28 14	00♏44	03 14	05 44	08 14	10 44	13 15	15 45	18♏15
1914	11♐34	11 57	12 12	12 R17	12 13	11 59	11 36	11 03	10 20	09 30	08 31	07 27	06 18	05 06	03♐53
1915	20♏19	22 49	25 19	27 49	00♐18	02 48	05 18	07 48	10 18	12 48	15 18	17 48	20 18	22 47	25♐17
1916	27♍36	29♎57	02 19	04 42	07 05	09 28	11 52	14 16	16 41	19 06	21 32	23 57	26 23	28♏50	01♏16
1917	23♐02	25 27	27 32	29♑46	02 00	04 12	06 25	08 36	10 46	12 56	15 04	17 12	19 18	21 23	23♑26
1918	02♏00	04 31	07 01	09 32	12 03	14 33	17 04	19 35	22 06	24 36	27 07	29♐38	02 09	04 40	07♐11
1919	23♍09	24 42	26 19	27 59	29♎42	01 29	03 17	05 09	07 03	08 59	10 57	12 57	14 58	17 02	19♎06
1920	09♐33	12 00	14 27	16 54	19 20	21 47	24 14	26 40	29 07	01♑33	03 59	06 25	08 51	11 17	13♑43
1921	06♎45	04 19	02 19	01 00	00 26	00 37	01♏29	02 55	04 48	07 02	09 31	12 11	14 59	17 53	20♏51
1922	09♐35	09 R47	09 50	09 44	09 27	09 01	08 26	07 16	06 19	05 16	04 08	02 57	01 44	00 32	29♏23
1923	20♏59	23 28	25 58	28 28	00♐58	03 28	05 58	08 28	10 58	13 28	15 57	18 27	20 57	23 27	25♐56
1924	28♍05	00♎28	02 50	05 13	07 36	10 00	12 25	14 49	17 14	19 40	22 05	24 31	26 57	29♏24	01♏51
1925	23♐22	25 37	27 51	00♑04	02 16	04 28	06 39	08 49	10 58	13 07	15 14	17 19	19 24	21 27	23♑29
1926	02♏40	05 11	07 42	10 12	12 43	15 14	17 44	20 15	22 46	25 16	27 47	00♐18	02 49	05 20	07♐51
1927	22♍42	24 11	26 00	27 43	29♎30	01 19	03 11	05 05	07 01	08 59	10 59	13 01	15 05	17 10	19♎16
1928	10♐09	12 36	15 02	17 29	19 56	22 22	24 49	27 15	29♑41	02 07	04 33	06 59	09 25	11 50	14♑16
1929	14♎36	17 05	19 35	22 04	24 34	27 03	29♏33	02 03	04 33	07 03	09 34	12 04	14 34	17 05	19♏35
1930	07♐R22	07 22	07 14	06 55	06 26	05 48	05 02	04 07	03 05	01 59	00 48	29♏35	28 23	27 13	26♏06
1931	21♏39	24 09	26 39	29♐08	01 38	04 08	06 38	09 08	11 38	14 07	16 37	19 07	21 37	24 06	26♐36
1932	28♍37	00♎59	03 22	05 44	08 10	10 34	12 58	15 23	17 49	20 14	22 40	25 07	27 33	00♏00	02♏27
1933	23♐43	25 57	28 10	00♑22	02 33	04 44	06 54	09 02	11 10	13 17	15 22	17 26	19 29	21 30	23♑30
1934	03♏22	05 52	08 23	10 54	13 24	15 55	18 26	20 57	23 27	25 58	28 29	01♐00	03 31	06 01	08♐32
1935	22♍20	24 01	25 45	27 32	29♎22	01 14	03 08	05 04	07 03	09 03	11 05	13 09	15 14	17 21	19♎29
1936	10♎46	13♏12	15 39	18 05	20 32	22 58	25 24	27 50	00 16	02 42	05♐08	07 34	09 59	12 24	14♐50
1937	15♎16	17 45	20 14	22 44	25 14	27 44	00♏13	02 43	05 14	07 44	10 14	12 44	15 15	17 45	20♏16
1938	04♐R54	04 43	04 22	03 51	03 11	02 22	01 26	00♏22	29 14	28 03	26 50	25 38	24 29	23 24	22♏25
1939	22♏19	24 49	27 19	29♐49	02 18	04 48	07 18	09 48	12 17	14 47	17 17	19 46	22 16	24 46	27♐15
1940	29♍08	01♎31	03 55	06 18	08 43	11 07	13 32	15 57	18 23	20 49	23 15	25 41	28 08	00♏35	03♏02
1941	24♐02	26 14	28 26	00♑37	02 48	04 57	07 05	09 13	11 19	13 24	15 28	17 30	19 31	21 30	23♑27
1942	04♏02	06 33	09 04	11 34	14 05	16 36	19 06	21 37	24 08	26 39	29♐09	01 40	04 11	06 42	09♐13
1943	22♍03	23 47	25 34	27 24	29♎16	01 11	03 08	05 06	07 07	09 09	11 13	13 18	15 25	17 33	19♎43
1944	11♐21	13 48	16 14	18 40	21 07	23 33	25 59	28 25	00♑50	03 16	05 42	08 07	10 32	12 57	15♑22
1945	15♎55	18 25	20 54	23 24	25 54	28 24	00 54	03♏24	05 54	08 24	10 54	13 25	15 55	18 26	20♏56
1946	02♐R13	01 49	01 16	00 34	29♏43	28 45	27 40	26 31	25 19	24 06	22 55	21 46	20 42	19 45	18♏56
1947	23♏00	25 30	27 59	00♐29	02 59	05 28	07 58	10 28	12 57	15 27	17 57	20 26	22 56	25 25	27♐55
1948	29♍41	02♎04	04 28	06 52	09 16	11 41	14 07	16 32	18 58	21 24	23 51	26 17	28 44	01♏12	03♏39
1949	24♐20	26 31	28 42	00♑52	03 01	05 09	07 16	09 22	11 26	13 29	15 31	17 32	19 30	21 27	23♑22
1950	04♏44	07 14	09 45	12 15	14 46	17 17	19 47	22 18	24 49	27 20	29♐50	02 21	04 52	07 23	09♐54
1951	21♍50	23 37	25 27	27 20	29♎15	01 11	03 10	05 11	07 13	09 17	11 23	13 30	15 38	17 48	19♎59
1952	11♐57	14 24	16 50	19 16	21 42	24 08	26 34	28♑59	01 25	03 50	06 15	08 41	11 05	13 30	15♑55
1953	16♎34	19 04	21 34	24 03	26 33	29♏03	01 33	04 03	06 34	09 04	11 34	14 05	16 35	19 06	21♏36
1954	29♏R16	28 41	27 57	27 04	26 04	24 58	23 48	22 35	21 22	20 11	19 03	18 01	17 06	16 18	15♏30
1955	23♏40	26 09	28 39	01♐09	03 38	06 08	08 37	11 07	13 37	15 06	18 36	21 05	23 35	26 04	28♐34
1956	00♎13	02 37	05 01	07 25	09 50	12 15	14 41	17 07	19 33	21 59	24 26	26 53	29♏20	01 48	04♏15
1957	24♐36	26 47	28♑56	01 05	03 12	05 19	07 24	09 28	11 31	13 33	15 32	17 31	19 27	21 21	23♑14
1958	05♏25	07 55	10 26	12 56	15 27	17 58	20 28	22 59	25 30	28 01	00♐31	03 02	05 33	08 04	10♐35
1959	21♍40	23 30	25 23	27 18	29♎15	01 14	03 15	05 18	07 22	09 27	11 35	13 43	15 53	18 04	20♎15
1960	12♐33	14 59	17 25	19 51	22 17	24 43	27 08	29♑33	01 59	04 24	06 49	09 14	11 38	14 03	16♑27
1961	17♎14	19 44	22 14	24 43	27 13	29 43	02♏13	04 44	07 14	09 44	12 15	14 45	17 16	19 46	22♏17
1962	26♏R05	25 18	24 24	23 23	22 16	21 05	19 52	18 39	17 28	16 21	15 20	14 27	13 42	13 04	12♏38
1963	24♏20	25 49	29♐19	01 48	04 18	06 48	09 17	11 47	14 16	16 46	19 15	21 45	24 14	26 43	29♑13
1964	00♎46	03 10	05 34	07 59	10 24	12 50	15 16	17 42	20 08	22 35	25 02	27 29	29♏56	02 24	04♏52
1965	24♐50	27 00	29♑08	01 15	03 21	05 26	07 30	09 32	11 33	13 32	15 30	17 26	19 20	21 11	23♑01
1966	06♏05	08 36	11 06	13 37	16 08	18 38	21 09	23 40	26 10	28 41	01♐12	03 43	06 13	08 44	11♐15
1967	21♍33	23 27	25 22	27 19	29♎19	01 20	03 22	05 27	07 32	09 40	11 48	13 58	16 09	18 21	20♎34
1968	13♐08	15 34	18 00	20 25	22 51	25 16	27 42	00♑07	02 32	04 57	07 21	09 46	12 10	14 34	16♑58
1969	17♎54	20 23	22 53	25 23	27 53	00♏23	02 53	05 23	07 54	10 24	12 55	15 25	17 56	20 26	22♏57
1970	22♏R41	21 45	20 42	19 34	18 23	17 10	15 57	14 47	13 41	12 42	11 49	11 06	10 31	10 07	09♏52
1971	25♏00	27 30	29♐59	02 29	04 58	07 28	09 57	12 26	14 56	17 25	19 55	22 24	24 54	27 23	29♑52
1972	01♎20	03 44	06 09	08 34	10 59	13 25	15 51	18 18	20 44	23 11	25 38	28 06	00♏33	03 01	05♏29
1973	25♐04	27 12	29♑19	01 25	03 29	05 33	07 34	09 35	11 34	13 31	15 26	17 19	19 10	20 59	22♑45
1974	06♏47	09 18	11 49	14 19	16 50	19 20	21 51	24 22	26 52	29♐23	01 54	04 25	06 55	09 26	11♐57
1975	21♍31	23 26	25 24	27 23	29♎25	01 28	03 32	05 38	07 45	09 54	12 04	14 15	16 27	18 40	20♎54
1976	13♐43	16 09	18 35	21 00	23 25	25 50	28 15	00♑40	03 05	05 29	07 54	10 18	12 42	15 06	17♑29
1977	18♎33	21 03	23 33	26 03	28 33	01♏03	03 33	06 04	08 36	11 04	13 35	16 05	18 36	21 07	23♏37
1978	19♏R05	18 01	16 52	15 40	14 27	13 15	12 06	11 01	10 03	09 13	08 31	07 58	07 36	07 D23	07♏20
1979	25♏39	28 08	00♐38	03 07	05 37	08 06	10 36	13 05	15 34	18 04	20 33	23 02	25 32	28 01	00♑30
1980	01♎52	04 17	06 42	09 08	11 34	14 00	16 26	18 53	21 19	23 46	26 14	28 41	01♏09	03 37	06♏05
1981	25♐15	27 22	29♑27	01 31	03 34	05 36	07 35	09 34	11 30	13 25	15 17	17 08	18 56	20 41	22♑24
1982	07♏27	09 58	12 28	14 59	17 29	20 00	22 31	25 01	27 32	00♐03	02 34	05 04	07 35	10 06	12♐36
1983	21♍30	23 28	25 27	27 29	29♎32	01 37	03 43	05 50	07 59	10 09	12 20	14 32	16 45	18 59	21♎14
1984	14♐17	16 43	19 08	21 33	23 58	26 23	28 48	01♑13	03 37	06 01	08 25	10 49	13 13	15 36	17♑59
1985	19♎13	21 43	24 13	26 43	29♏13	01 43	04 13	06 44	09 14	11 44	14 15	16 46	19 16	21 47	24♏18
1986	15♏R20	14 10	12 58	11 45	10 33	09 25	08 22	07 25	06 36	05 57	05 26	05 06	04 D55	04 55	05♏04
1987	26♏19	28♐48	01 18	03 47	06 16	08 46	11 15	13 44	16 13	18 43	21 12	23 41	26 11	28 40	01♑09
1988	02♎27	04 52	07 17	09 43	12 09	14 35	17 02	19 29	21 56	24 23	26 51	29♏18	01 46	04 14	06♏43
1989	25♐25	27 30	29♑34	01 36	03 37	05 37	07 34	09 30	11 24	13 16	15 06	16 53	18 38	20 19	21♑58
1990	08♏09	10 39	13 10	15 40	18 11	20 41	23 12	25 43	28 13	00♐44	03 15	05 45	08 16	10 47	13♐18
1991	21♍33	23 33	25 35	27 38	29 43	01♎49	03 56	06 05	08 15	10 26	12 39	14 52	17 06	19 21	21♎37
1992	14♐53	17 18	19 43	22 08	24 33	26 57	29♑22	01 46	04 10	06 34	08 57	11 21	13 44	16 07	18♑30
1993	19♎53	22 23	24 53	27 23	29♏53	02 24	04 54	07 24	09 55	12 25	14 56	17 27	19 57	22 28	24♏59
1994	11♏R30	10 17	09 04	07 53	06 46	05 44	04 50	04 03	03 25	02 56	02 38	02 D29	02 31	02 42	03♏02
1995	26♏59	29♐28	01 57	04 27	06 56	09 25	11 54	14 23	16 53	19 22	21 51	24 20	26 49	29♑18	01♑48
1996	03♎01	05 26	07 52	10 18	12 44	15 11	17 38	20 05	22 32	24 59	27 27	29♏55	02 23	04 52	07♏20
1997	25♐33	27 36	29♑38	01 38	03 37	05 34	07 30	09 23	11 14	13 03	14 50	16 34	18 14	19 52	21♑27
1998	08♏49	11 20	13 50	16 21	18 51	21 22	23 53	26 23	28♐54	01 24	03 55	06 26	08 57	11 27	13♐58
1999	21♍38	23 39	25 43	27 48	29♎54	02 02	04 10	06 21	08 32	10 44	12 57	15 11	17 27	19 43	21♎59
2000	15♐26	17 51	20 16	22 40	25 05	27 29	29♑53	02 17	04 41	07 04	09 28	11 51	14 14	16 36	18♑58

December

	1st	3rd	5th	7th	9th	11th	13th	15th	17th	19th	21st	23rd	25th	27th	29th	31st
1900	02♏33	04 59	07 26	09 53	12 20	14 48	17 15	19 43	22 11	24 39	27 07	29♐36	02 04	04 33	07 02	09♐31
1901	25♑18	27 23	29♒26	01 27	30 27	05 25	07 21	09 15	11 07	12 56	14 43	16 27	18 08	19 45	21 19	22♒49
1902	08♐20	10 51	13 22	15 53	18 23	20 54	23 25	25 56	28 27	00♑58	03 29	06 00	08 31	11 02	13 33	16♑04
1903	20≏54	22 59	25 04	27 12	29♏20	01 30	03 41	05 53	08 06	10 20	12 35	14 51	17 07	19 24	21 42	24♏01
1904	15♑00	17 26	19 52	22 17	24 42	27 08	29♒33	01 57	04 22	06 46	09 09	11 33	13 56	16 19	18 41	21♒03
1905	20♏06	22 36	25 07	27 37	00♐08	02 38	05 09	07 40	10 11	12 41	15 12	17 43	20 14	22 45	25 16	27♐47
1906	06♐R38	05 25	04 16	03 11	02 13	01 22	00 39	00♏07	29 44	29 D 30	29 27	29 33	29♐49	00 14	00 47	01♐28
1907	27♐07	29 37	02♑07	04 37	07 06	09 36	12 06	14 36	17 05	19 35	22 04	24 34	27 03	29♒32	02 02	04♒31
1908	03♏07	05 34	08 01	10 28	12 55	15 23	17 51	20 19	22 47	25 15	27 44	00♐12	02 11	05 10	07 39	10♐08
1909	25♑24	27 27	29♒28	01 27	03 24	05 20	07 13	09 05	10 53	12 40	14 23	16 03	17 40	19 13	20 42	22♒07
1910	09♐01	11 31	14 02	16 33	19 04	21 35	24 06	26 37	29♑08	01 39	04 10	06 40	09 11	11 42	14 13	16♑44
1911	21≏02	23 08	25 16	27 25	29♏35	01 46	03 58	06 11	08 25	10 40	12 56	15 13	17 30	19 48	22 07	24♏26
1912	15♑34	18 00	20 25	22 50	25 15	27 40	00♒05	02 29	04 53	07 17	09 41	12 04	14 26	16 49	19 11	21♒32
1913	20♏46	23 16	25 47	28 18	00♐48	03 19	05 50	08 20	10 51	13 22	15 53	18 24	20 55	23 26	25 57	28♐28
1914	02♐R41	01 32	00♏29	29 32	28 43	28 02	27 32	27 11	27 D 00	26 59	27 08	27 26	27 53	28 28	29 11	00♏01
1915	27♐47	00♑17	02 47	05 16	07 46	10 16	12 45	15 15	17 45	20 14	22 44	25 13	27 42	00♒11	02 41	05♒10
1916	08♏43	06 10	08 37	11 04	13 32	16 00	18 28	20 56	23 24	25 53	28 21	00♐50	03 19	05 48	08 17	10♐46
1917	25♑28	27 29	29♒28	01 25	03 20	05 13	07 03	08 51	10 37	12 20	13 59	15 35	17 07	18 36	19 59	21♒18
1918	09♐41	12 12	14 43	17 14	19 45	22 16	24 47	27 18	29♑49	02 20	04 51	07 21	09 52	12 23	14 54	17♑25
1919	21≏13	23 20	25 29	27 39	29♏50	02 03	04 16	06 30	08 46	11 01	13 18	15 36	17 54	20 12	22 32	24♏51
1920	16♑08	18 33	20 58	23 23	25 48	28 13	00♒37	03 01	05 24	07 48	10 11	12 34	14 56	17 18	19 39	22♒00
1921	21♏26	23 57	26 27	28♐58	01 29	03 59	06 30	09 01	11 32	14 03	16 33	19 04	21 35	24 06	26 37	29♐08
1922	28♏R49	27 47	26 52	26 05	25 26	24 58	24 40	24 D 31	24 32	24 43	25 03	25 32	26 09	26 54	27 46	28♏45
1923	28♐26	00♑56	03 25	05 55	08 25	10 53	13 24	15 54	18 23	20 53	23 22	25 51	28 20	00♒50	03 19	05♒48
1924	04♏18	06 45	09 12	11 40	14 08	16 36	19 04	21 32	24 01	26 29	28♐58	01 27	03 56	06 25	08 54	11♐24
1925	25♑29	27 27	29♒24	01 18	03 10	05 01	06 48	08 33	10 15	11 54	13 29	15 00	16 28	17 51	19 09	20♒21
1926	10♐22	12 53	15 24	17 54	20 25	22 56	25 27	27 58	00♑29	03 00	05 31	08 01	10 32	13 03	15 34	18♑05
1927	21≏24	23 33	25 43	27 55	00♏07	02 21	04 35	06 50	09 06	11 23	13 41	15 59	18 18	20 37	22 57	25♏17
1928	16♑41	19 06	21 31	23 55	26 20	28 44	01♒08	03 31	05 55	08 18	10 40	13 02	15 24	17 46	20 07	22♒27
1929	22♏06	24 36	27 07	29♐38	02 09	04 39	07 10	09 41	12 12	14 43	17 14	19 44	22 15	24 46	27 17	29♐48
1930	25♏R06	24 12	23 27	22 51	22 25	22 08	22 D 02	22 06	22 19	22 41	23 12	23 51	24 37	25 31	26 31	27♏37
1931	29♐06	01♑35	04 05	06 34	09 04	11 34	14 03	16 32	19 02	21 31	24 00	26 30	28♒59	01 28	03 57	06♒26
1932	04♏54	07 21	09 49	12 17	14 45	17 13	19 41	22 10	24 38	27 07	29♐36	02 05	04 34	07 03	09 33	12♐02
1933	25♑28	27 24	29♒18	01 10	02 59	04 46	06 30	08 11	09 49	11 23	12 54	14 20	15 42	16 59	18 11	19♒17
1934	11♐03	13 34	16 05	18 36	21 07	23 38	26 09	28 39	01♑10	03 41	06 12	08 43	11 14	13 44	16 15	18♑46
1935	21≏38	23 49	26 00	28 13	00♏26	02 41	04 56	07 12	09 29	11 47	14 05	16 24	18 44	21 04	23 24	25♏45
1936	17♑14	19 39	22 04	24 28	26 52	29♒16	01 39	04 02	06 25	08 48	11 10	13 32	15 53	18 14	20 34	22♒54
1937	22♏46	25 17	27 48	00♐19	02 49	05 20	07 51	10 22	12 53	15 24	17 54	20 25	22 56	25 27	27 58	00♑29
1938	21♏R33	20 60	20 16	19 53	19 D 38	19 34	19 40	19 55	20 19	20 52	21 33	22 21	23 16	24 18	25 26	26♏39
1939	29♐45	02♑14	04 44	07 13	09 43	12 12	14 42	17 11	19 40	22 10	24 39	27 08	29♒37	02 06	04 35	07♒04
1940	05♏30	07 58	10 25	12 53	15 22	17 50	20 18	22 47	25 16	27 45	00♐14	02 43	05 12	07 41	10 11	12♐40
1941	25♑23	27 16	29♒07	00 56	02 42	04 26	06 06	07 43	09 16	10 46	12 11	13 32	14 84	15 59	17 03	18♒02
1942	11♐43	14 14	16 45	19 16	21 47	24 18	26 49	29♑20	01 50	04 21	06 52	09 23	11 54	14 24	16 55	19♑26
1943	21≏53	24 05	26 18	28 31	00♏46	03 01	05 17	07 34	09 52	12 10	14 29	16 49	19 09	21 30	23 51	26♏13
1944	17♑46	20 11	22 35	24 59	27 22	29♒46	02 09	04 32	06 54	09 16	11 38	13 59	16 20	18 40	21 00	23♒19
1945	23♏27	25 58	28 29	00♐59	03 30	06 01	08 32	11 03	13 34	16 05	18 35	21 06	23 37	26 08	28 39	01♑10
1946	18♏R15	17 43	17 21	17 10	17 D 08	17 15	17 33	17 59	18 33	19 16	20 06	21 03	22 06	23 15	24 30	25♏49
1947	00♑25	02 54	05 23	07 53	10 22	12 52	15 21	17 50	20 19	22 49	25 18	27 47	00 16	02♒44	05 13	07♒42
1948	06♏07	08 35	11 03	13 31	15 59	18 28	20 56	23 25	25 54	28 23	00♐52	03 21	05 51	08 20	10 50	13♐19
1949	25♑15	27 06	28 54	00♒39	02 22	04 01	05 38	07 10	08 39	10 03	11 23	12 47	13 47	14 50	15 47	16♒37
1950	12♐24	14 55	17 26	19 57	22 28	24 59	27 30	00♑00	02 31	05 02	07 33	10 04	12 34	15 05	17 36	20♑06
1951	22≏10	24 23	26 37	28 52	01♏07	03 23	05 40	07 58	10 17	12 36	14 55	17 16	19 37	21 58	24 20	26♏42
1952	18♑19	20 43	23 07	25 30	27 53	00♒16	02 39	05 01	07 23	09 45	12 06	14 27	16 47	19 07	21 26	23♒45
1953	24♏07	26 38	29♐09	01 39	04 10	06 41	09 12	11 43	14 14	16 45	19 16	21 47	24 18	26 49	29♑19	01♑50
1954	15♏R10	14 51	14 D 41	14 41	14 51	15 10	15 38	16 15	16 59	17 51	18 49	19 54	21 04	22 20	23 41	25♏06
1955	01♑03	03 33	06 02	08 31	11 01	13 30	15 59	18 28	20 57	23 26	25 55	28 24	00♒53	03 22	05 50	08♒19
1956	06♏43	09 11	11 39	14 08	16 36	19 05	21 34	24 02	26 32	29♐01	01 30	03 59	06 29	08 58	11 28	13♐57
1957	25♑04	26 51	28 36	00♒18	01 57	03 32	05 04	06 31	07 54	09 13	10 26	11 34	12 36	13 32	14 20	15♒01
1958	13♐05	15 36	18 07	20 38	23 09	25 39	28 10	00♑41	03 12	05 43	08 14	11 44	13 15	15 46	18 16	20♑47
1959	22≏28	24 42	26 57	29♏13	01 29	03 46	06 04	08 23	10 42	13 02	15 22	17 43	20 04	22 26	24 48	27♏11
1960	18♑51	21 14	23 38	26 01	28 24	00♒46	03 08	05 30	07 52	10 13	12 33	14 54	17 13	19 32	21 51	24♒09
1961	24♏48	27 18	29♐49	02 20	04 51	07 22	09 53	12 24	14 55	17 26	19 57	22 27	24 58	27 29	00♑00	02♑31
1962	12♏R20	12 13	12 D 16	12 28	12 49	13 19	13 57	14 43	15 36	16 35	17 41	18 53	20 10	21 32	22 58	24♏29
1963	01♑42	04 12	06 41	09 10	11 39	14 08	16 37	19 06	21 35	24 04	26 33	29♒02	01 31	03 59	06 28	08♒56
1964	04♏20	09 48	12 16	14 45	17 14	19 42	22 11	24 40	27 09	29♐39	02 08	04 38	07 07	09 37	12 06	14♐36
1965	24♑48	26 32	28 13	29♒51	01 25	02 56	04 22	05 44	07 02	08 14	09 20	10 21	11 15	12 01	12 40	13♒11
1966	13♐46	16 16	18 47	21 18	23 49	26 20	28♑50	01 21	03 52	06 23	08 54	11 24	13 55	16 26	18 56	21♑27
1967	22≏48	25 03	27 18	29♏35	01 52	04 10	06 29	08 48	11 08	13 28	15 49	18 11	20 32	22 55	25 18	27♏41
1968	19♑22	21 45	24 08	26 31	28♒53	01 16	03 37	05 58	08 19	10 39	12 59	15 19	17 38	19 56	22 14.	24♒31
1969	25♏28	27 59	00♐29	03 00	05 31	08 02	10 33	13 04	15 35	18 06	20 37	23 08	25 39	28 10	00♑41	03♑12
1970	09♏D47	09 52	10 06	10 29	11 01	11 40	12 28	13 22	14 23	15 31	16 44	18 02	19 25	20 52	22 24	23♏59
1971	02♑22	04 51	07 20	09 49	12 18	14 47	17 16	19 45	22 14	24 43	27 12	29♒40	02 09	04 37	07 06	09♒34
1972	07♏57	10 26	12 54	15 23	17 52	20 21	22 50	25 19	27 48	00♐18	02 47	05 17	07 46	10 16	12 46	15♐15
1973	24♑28	26 09	27 46	29♒19	00 49	02 14	03 35	04 51	06 02	07 07	08 06	08 58	09 43	10 20	10 49	11♒10
1974	14♐28	16 58	19 29	22 00	24 31	27 01	29♑32	02 03	04 34	07 04	09 35	12 06	14 36	17 07	19 38	22♑08
1975	23≏09	25 25	27 41	29♏59	02 17	04 35	06 55	09 15	11 35	13 56	16 17	18 39	21 02	23 25	25 48	28♏11
1976	19♑52	22 15	24 38	27 00	29♒22	01 44	04 05	06 25	08 46	11 06	13 25	15 44	18 02	20 20	22 37	24♒53
1977	26♏08	28 39	01♐10	03 41	06 12	08 43	11 13	13 44	16 15	18 46	21 17	23 48	26 19	28♑50	01 21	03♑52
1978	17♏44	18 46	19 42	20 32	21 15	21 50	22 18	22 37	22 47	22 48	22 39	22 20	21 52	21 15	20 29	19♏35
1979	02♑59	05 28	07 57	10 27	12 55	15 24	17 53	20 22	22 51	25 20	27 48	00♒17	02 45	05 14	07 42	10♒10
1980	08♏34	11 02	13 31	16 00	18 29	20 58	23 27	25 56	28 26	00♐55	03 25	05 54	08 24	10 54	13 24	15♐53
1981	24♑03	25 39	27 12	28 41	00♒05	01 25	02 40	03 49	04 53	05 50	06 41	07 24	07 59	08 26	08 44	08♒R53
1982	15♐07	17 38	20 09	22 39	25 10	27 41	00♑12	02 42	05 13	07 44	10 14	12 45	15 16	17 46	20 17	22♑47
1983	23≏30	25 47	28 04	00♏22	02 41	05 01	07 21	09 41	12 02	14 24	16 46	19 08	21 31	23 54	26 18	28♏42
1984	20♑22	22 44	25 07	27 28	29♒50	02 11	04 32	06 52	09 12	11 31	13 49	16 08	18 25	20 42	22 58	25♒14
1985	26♏48	29♐19	01 50	04 21	06 52	09 23	11 54	14 25	16 56	19 27	21 58	24 29	27 00	29♑31	02 02	04♑33
1986	05♏22	05 49	06 25	07 08	07 58	08 56	10 00	11 09	12 24	13 44	15 09	16 39	18 12	19 49	21 29	23♏12
1987	03♑38	06 07	08 36	11 05	13 34	16 03	18 31	21 00	23 29	25 57	28 26	00♒54	03 23	05 51	08 19	10♒47
1988	09♏11	11 40	14 09	16 38	19 07	21 36	24 05	26 35	29 04	01♐34	04 03	06 33	09 03	11 33	14 03	16♐33
1989	23♑33	25 05	26 33	27 56	29 15	00♒29	01 37	02 39	03 35	04 23	05 05	05 38	06 03	06 19	06 R 25	06♒22
1990	15♐48	18 19	20 50	23 20	25 51	28 22	00♑52	03 23	05 54	08 25	10 55	13 26	15 56	18 27	20 58	23♑28
1991	23≏54	26 11	28 29	00♏48	03 08	05 28	07 48	10 10	12 31	14 53	17 16	19 39	22 02	24 25	26 50	29♏14
1992	20♑52	23 14	25 36	27 57	00♒18	02 39	04 59	07 18	09 37	11 56	14 14	16 31	18 48	21 04	23 19	25♒34
1993	27♏30	00♐00	02 31	05 02	07 33	10 04	12 35	15 06	17 37	20 08	22 39	25 10	27 41	00♑12	02 43	05♑14
1994	03♏31	04 08	04 53	05 45	06 44	07 49	09 00	10 16	11 38	13 03	14 33	16 07	17 45	19 26	21 10	22♏57
1995	04♑17	06 45	09 14	11 43	14 12	16 41	19 09	21 38	24 06	26 35	29♒03	01 32	03 59	05 28	08 56	11♒23
1996	09♏49	12 18	14 46	17 16	19 45	22 14	24 44	27 13	29♐43	02 12	04 42	07 12	09 42	12 12	14 42	17♐12
1997	22♑57	24 24	25 46	27 04	28 16	29 23	00♒24	01 18	02 05	02 44	03 16	03 38	03 R 52	03 56	03 51	03♒35
1998	16♐29	18 59	21 30	24 00	26 31	29♑02	01 32	04 03	06 34	09 04	11 35	14 06	16 36	19 07	21 37	24♑08
1999	24≏17	26 35	28♏54	01 14	03 34	05 55	08 16	10 37	12 59	15 22	17 45	20 08	22 32	24 56	27 21	29♏45
2000	21♑20	23 42	26 03	28 24	00♒44	03 04	05 24	07 43	10 01	12 19	14 36	16 53	19 09	21 24	23 38	25♒52

Mars

January

Year	1st	3rd	5th	7th	9th	11th	13th	15th	17th	19th	21st	23rd	25th	27th	29th
1900	13♑52 15	25 16	58 18	30 20	03 21	36 23	10 24	43 26	16 27	50 29	24 00♒	57 02	31 04	05 05	39 07♒13
1901	11♍39 11	54 12	08 12	18 12	26 12	31 12R	33 12	32 12	28 12	20 12	10 11	56 11	39 11	19 10	56 10♍R29
1902	29♑13 00♒	47 02	22 03	56 05	30 07	05 08	40 10	14 11	49 13	24 14	59 16	33 18	08 19	43 21	18 22♒53
1903	05♎02 05	50 06	36 07	21 08	04 08	46 09	27 10	07 10	44 11	21 11	55 12	28 12	59 13	28 13	55 14♎20
1904	15♒20 16	54 18	29 20	03 21	37 23	12 24	46 26	20 27	55 29	29 01♓	03 02	37 04	12 05	46 07	20 08♓54
1905	23♎23 24	27 25	30 26	32 27	34 28	35 29	36 00♏	36 01	35 02	34 03	32 04	30 05	27 06	23 07	19 08♏13
1906	03♓23 04	55 06	27 07	59 09	30 11	02 12	34 14	05 15	36 17	08 18	39 20	10 21	41 23	12 24	43 26♓14
1907	08♏52 10	05 11	17 12	30 13	43 14	55 16	07 17	20 18	32 19	43 20	55 22	06 23	18 24	29 25	40 26♏50
1908	22♓50 24	14 25	39 27	03 28	28 29	52 01♈	16 02	41 04	05 05	29 06	53 08	18 09	42 11	06 12	30 13♈54
1909	23♏56 25	15 26	35 27	54 29	14 00♐	33 01	53 03	13 04	33 05	52 07	12 08	32 09	52 11	12 12	32 13♐52
1910	17♈52 18	55 19	59 21	03 22	08 23	14 24	20 25	26 26	33 27	41 28	49 29	57 01♉	06 02	15 03	25 04♉34
1911	08♐02 09	26 10	51 12	15 13	40 15	05 16	30 17	35 19	20 20	46 22	11 23	37 25	03 26	29 27	55 29♐21
1912	24♉20 24	25 24	34 24	44 24	58 25	14 25	33 25	55 26	18 26	44 27	12 27	43 28	15 28	49 29	25 00♊02
1913	22♐56 24	24 25	52 27	21 28	50 00♑	19 01	48 03	18 04	47 06	17 07	47 09	17 10	47 12	17 13	47 15♑18
1914	16♋R31 15	43 14	55 14	08 13	20 12	34 11	49 11	06 10	24 09	45 09	08 08	33 08	02 07	34 07	09 06♋R46
1915	07♑27 08	59 10	31 12	02 13	34 15	06 16	39 18	11 19	44 21	16 22	49 24	22 25	55 27	28 29	01 00♒35
1916	29♌R49 29	48 29	43 29	35 29	24 29	09 28	51 28	30 28	06 27	39 27	09 26	36 26	00 25	21 24	41 23♌R58
1917	23♑19 24	53 26	27 28	01 29	35 01♒	09 02	43 04	17 05	52 07	26 09	01 10	35 12	10 13	45 15	19 16♒54
1918	27♍04 27	41 28	17 28	52 29	24 29	55 00♎	23 00	50 01	14 01	36 01	56 02	14 02	29 02	41 02	51 02♎58
1919	09♒07 10	42 12	16 13	51 15	26 17	00 18	35 20	10 21	44 23	19 24	54 26	28 28	03 29	38 01♓	12 02♓50
1920	16♎30 17	29 18	26 19	23 20	19 21	15 22	10 23	03 23	56 24	48 25	39 26	29 27	18 28	06 28	53 29♎38
1921	26♒39 28	12 29	45 01♓	18 02	52 04	25 05	58 07	31 09	04 10	37 12	09 13	42 15	15 16	47 18	20 19♓52
1922	03♏13 04	23 05	32 06	41 07	50 08	59 10	07 11	16 12	23 13	31 14	38 15	45 16	52 17	58 19	04 20♏10
1923	15♓02 16	30 17	58 19	26 20	54 22	22 23	50 25	18 26	46 28	14 29	42 01♈	09 02	37 04	04 05	32 06♈59
1924	17♏55 19	13 20	30 21	47 23	04 24	21 25	38 26	55 28	12 29	29 00♐	46 02	03 03	20 04	37 05	54 07♐11
1925	07♈37 08	51 10	06 11	20 12	36 13	51 15	06 16	22 17	37 18	53 20	09 21	25 22	42 23	58 25	15 26♈31
1926	02♐44 04	06 05	29 06	52 08	15 09	38 11	01 12	24 13	47 15	11 16	34 17	58 19	22 20	46 22	10 23♐34
1927	08♉11 08	45 09	20 09	58 10	37 11	18 12	00 12	44 13	29 14	16 15	03 15	53 16	43 17	34 18	26 19♉20
1928	16♐49 18	16 19	43 21	10 22	37 24	05 25	32 27	00 28	28 29	56 01♑	25 02	53 04	22 05	50 07	19 08♑48
1929	25♊R37 24	58 24	21 23	47 23	16 22	48 22	23 22	01 21	43 21	28 21	16 21	07 21	02 20D	59 21	00 21♊04
1930	01♑55 03	25 04	56 06	27 07	57 09	28 10	59 12	31 14	02 15	34 17	06 18	38 20	10 21	42 23	14 24♑47
1931	15♌35 15	12 14	45 14	15 13	43 13	07 12	29 11	49 11	06 10	22 09	36 08	49 08	01 07	13 06	25 06♌37
1932	16♑45 18	18 19	51 21	24 22	57 24	31 26	04 27	38 29	12 00♒	46 02	20 03	54 05	28 07	02 08	37 10♒11
1993	18♍00 18	24 18	47 19	07 19	25 19	41 19	53 20	04 20	11 20	15 20R	17 20	16 20	11 20	03 29	53 19♍R39
1934	03♒01 04	35 06	10 07	44 09	19 10	54 12	28 14	03 15	38 17	13 18	48 20	22 21	57 23	32 25	07 26♒42
1935	09♎42 10	34 11	25 12	15 13	03 13	51 14	37 15	23 16	07 16	49 17	31 18	11 18	49 19	26 20	01 20♎35
1936	19♒22 20	56 22	30 24	04 25	38 27	12 28	46 00♓	20 01	54 03	27 05	01 06	35 08	09 09	43 11	16 12♓50
1937	27♎21 28	27 29	32 00♏	37 01	42 02	46 03	50 04	53 05	56 07	58 08	00 09	02 10	02 11	03 12	02 13♏01
1938	07♓46 09	17 10	48 12	18 13	49 15	20 16	50 18	21 19	51 21	21 22	52 24	22 25	52 27	22 28	51 00♈21
1939	12♏30 13	44 14	59 16	13 17	27 18	41 19	56 21	10 22	24 23	38 24	51 26	05 27	18 28	32 29	45 00♐58
1940	27♓58 29	19 00♈	41 02	02 03	24 04	45 06	07 07	29 08	51 10	12 11	34 12	56 14	18 15	40 17	01 18♈23
1941	27♏26 28	47 00♐	07 01	28 02	49 04	10 05	31 06	52 08	13 09	34 10	55 12	17 13	38 15	00 16	21 17♐43
1942	24♈50 25	45 26	40 27	37 28	34 29	33 00♉	32 01	32 02	32 03	34 04	36 05	38 06	41 07	45 08	50 09♉54
1943	11♐29 12	54 14	20 15	45 17	11 18	37 20	03 21	29 22	55 24	22 25	48 27	15 28	42 00♑	09 01	36 03♑03
1944	05♊R25 05	12 05	02 04	55 04	52 04D	52 04	54 05	00 05	09 05	20 05	34 05	51 06	10 06	32 06	56 07♊22
1945	26♐26 27	55 29	24 00♑	54 02	23 03	53 05	23 06	53 08	23 09	54 11	24 12	55 14	26 15	57 17	28 18♑59
1946	28♋R16 27	34 26	49 26	03 25	16 24	28 23	40 22	52 22	05 21	18 20	33 19	49 19	06 18	26 17	48 17♋R13
1947	11♑05 12	37 14	09 15	41 17	13 18	46 20	19 21	52 23	25 24	58 26	31 28	04 29	38 01♒	11 02	45 04♒19
1948	07♍15 07	25 07	32 07	36 07R	37 07	34 07	29 07	20 07	09 06	54 06	35 06	14 05	50 05	22 04	52 04♍R18
1949	27♑05 28	39 00♒	13 01	47 03	21 04	56 06	30 08	05 09	39 11	14 12	49 14	23 15	58 17	33 19	08 20♒43
1950	02♎13 02	56 03	38 04	19 04	58 05	36 06	12 06	46 07	19 07	50 08	18 08	45 09	10 09	32 09	52 10♎10
1951	13♒02 14	36 16	11 17	45 19	20 20	54 22	29 24	03 25	38 27	13 28	47 00♓	22 01	56 03	30 05	05 06♓39
1952	20♎40 21	41 22	42 23	42 24	42 25	41 26	39 27	37 28	34 29	30 00♏	26 01	21 02	15 03	08 04	00 04♏51
1953	00♓51 02	23 03	56 05	28 07	01 08	33 10	05 11	38 13	10 14	42 16	14 17	46 19	18 20	50 22	21 23♓53
1954	06♏55 08	07 09	18 10	30 11	41 12	51 14	02 15	13 16	23 17	33 18	43 19	52 21	02 22	11 23	20 24♏28
1955	19♓49 21	15 22	41 24	07 25	34 27	00 28	26 29	52 01♈	18 02	44 04	10 05	36 07	01 08	27 09	53 11♈19
1956	21♍26 22	44 24	03 25	21 26	40 27	58 29	17 00♐	35 01	54 03	13 04	31 05	50 07	08 08	27 09	46 11♐05
1957	13♈41 14	50 15	59 17	08 18	18 19	28 20	39 21	50 23	01 24	13 25	25 26	37 27	49 29	02 00♉	15 01♉28
1958	06♐12 07	35 08	59 10	23 11	47 13	11 14	35 15	59 17	24 18	48 20	13 21	38 23	03 24	28 25	53 27♐18
1959	17♉26 17	44 18	05 18	28 18	54 19	22 19	52 20	24 20	58 21	33 22	11 22	51 23	31 24	13 24	57 25♉42
1960	20♐19 21	47 23	14 24	42 26	10 27	39 29	07 00♑	36 02	04 03	33 05	02 06	32 08	01 09	31 11	00 12♑30
1961	08♋R07 07	21 06	35 05	50 05	08 04	27 03	48 03	13 02	39 02	09 01	42 01	18 00	57 00	39 00	25 00♋R14
1962	05♑29 07	00 08	31 10	03 11	34 13	06 14	37 16	09 17	41 19	13 20	46 22	18 23	51 25	24 26	56 28♑29
1963	24♌R35 24	24 24	10 23	53 23	32 23	08 22	41 22	11 21	39 21	03 20	25 19	44 19	02 18	17 17	31 16♌R45
1964	20♑27 22	00 23	34 25	07 26	41 28	15 29	48 01♒	22 02	57 04	31 06	05 07	39 09	14 10	48 12	23 13♒58
1965	23♍49 24	22 24	52 25	21 27	48 26	12 26	35 26	55 27	12 27	27 27	40 27	50 27	57 28	01 28R	03 28♍R01
1966	06♒53 08	27 10	02 11	36 13	11 14	46 16	20 17	55 19	30 21	05 22	40 24	14 25	50 27	24 28	59 00♓34
1967	14♎07 15	03 15	58 16	52 17	45 18	37 19	29 20	19 21	08 21	57 22	44 23	30 24	14 24	58 25	40 26♎21
1968	23♒26 25	00 26	34 28	07 29	41 01♓	14 02	48 04	22 05	55 07	28 09	02 10	35 12	08 13	42 15	15 16♓48
1969	01♏11 02	19 03	27 04	34 05	42 06	48 07	55 09	01 10	07 11	12 12	18 13	22 14	26 15	30 16	33 17♏36
1970	12♓15 13	44 15	14 16	43 18	12 19	42 21	11 22	40 24	09 25	38 27	07 28	36 00♈	05 01	34 03	02 04♈31
1971	16♏04 17	20 18	36 19	52 21	08 22	24 23	39 24	55 26	11 27	27 28	42 29	58 01♐	13 02	29 03	44 05♐00
1972	03♈23 04	41 05	59 07	16 08	35 09	53 11	11 12	30 13	48 15	07 16	26 17	45 19	04 20	23 21	42 23♈01
1973	00♐55 02	16 03	38 05	00 06	22 07	44 09	06 10	28 11	51 13	13 14	36 15	58 17	21 18	44 20	07 21♐30
1974	02♉33 03	17 04	02 04	49 05	37 06	26 07	16 08	08 09	00 09	54 10	49 11	44 12	41 13	38 14	36 15♉35
1975	14♐58 16	24 17	50 19	16 20	43 22	10 23	37 25	04 26	31 27	58 29	26 00♑	53 02	21 03	49 05	17 06♑45
1976	17♊R22 16	52 16	25 16	01 15	40 15	23 15	08 14	57 14	50 14	45 14D	44 14	45 14	50 14	58 15	08 15♊21
1977	29♐59 01♑	28 02	58 04	28 05	59 07	29 09	00 10	31 12	01 13	33 15	04 16	35 18	07 19	38 21	10 22♑42
1978	09♌R03 08	31 07	55 07	17 06	37 05	54 05	10 04	24 03	37 02	49 02	01 01	13 00	26 29♋	39 28	53 28♋08
1979	14♑42 16	15 17	47 19	20 20	53 22	26 23	59 27	33 27	06 28	40 00♒	13 01	47 03	21 04	55 06	29 08♒03
1980	13♍58 14	18 14	35 14	49 15	01 15	10 15	17 15	20 15R	21 15	18 15	12 15	03 14	51 14	36 14	17 13♍R56
1981	00♒50 02	24 03	59 05	33 07	07 08	42 10	17 11	51 13	26 15	01 16	36 18	10 19	45 21	20 22	55 24♒30
1982	07♎03 07	52 08	39 09	25 10	10 10	54 11	37 12	17 12	57 13	35 14	11 14	46 15	19 15	50 16	19 16♎46
1983	17♒00 18	34 20	09 21	43 23	17 24	51 26	26 28	00 29	34 01♓	08 02	43 04	17 05	51 07	25 08	59 10♓33
1984	24♎40 25	44 26	48 27	51 28	54 29	36 00♏	57 01	59 02	59 03	59 04	59 05	58 06	56 07	53 08	50 09♏46
1985	05♓08 06	40 08	12 09	43 11	15 12	46 14	18 15	49 17	20 18	52 20	23 21	54 23	25 24	56 26	26 27♓57
1986	10♏34 11	48 13	01 14	14 15	27 16	40 17	52 19	05 20	17 21	29 22	41 23	53 25	05 26	17 27	28 28♏39
1987	24♓45 26	09 27	33 28	57 00♈	20 01	44 03	08 04	32 05	56 07	20 08	44 10	07 11	31 12	55 14	18 15♈42
1988	24♏56 26	15 27	35 28	55 00♐	14 01	34 02	54 04	14 05	34 06	54 08	14 09	35 10	55 12	15 13	35 14♐56
1989	20♈12 21	14 22	16 23	19 24	22 25	26 26	31 27	36 28	42 29	49 00♉	55 02	03 03	10 04	18 05	27 06♉36
1990	09♐39 11	03 12	28 13	53 15	18 16	43 18	08 19	33 20	59 22	24 23	50 25	16 26	42 28	08 29	35 01♑01
1991	27♉D45 27	46 27	50 27	57 28	06 28	19 28	34 28	51 29	12 29	34 29	59 00♊	26 00	56 01	27 01	27 02♊18
1992	23♐47 25	16 26	44 28	13 29	42 01♑	11 02	40 04	10 05	39 07	09 08	39 10	08 11	39 13	09 14	39 16♑10
1993	20♋R25 19	38 18	50 18	03 17	15 16	27 15	41 14	56 14	12 13	30 12	50 12	13 11	38 11	07 10	38 10♋R12
1994	09♑04 10	36 12	07 13	39 15	11 16	43 18	16 19	48 21	21 22	53 24	26 25	59 27	32 29	05 00♒	39 02♒12
1995	02♍39 02R	40 02	38 02	34 02	26 02	14 02	00 01	42 01	21 00	57 00	30 00♌	00 29	27 28	51 28	13 27♌32
1996	24♑10 25	44 27	18 28	51 00♒	25 02	00 03	34 05	08 06	42 08	17 09	51 11	26 13	01 14	35 16	10 17♒45
1997	29♍14 29	54 00♎	31 01	07 01	41 02	14 02	45 03	13 03	40 04	04 04	27 04	47 05	04 05	19 05	32 05♎42
1998	10♒46 12	20 13	55 15	30 17	04 18	39 20	13 21	48 23	23 24	57 26	32 28	07 29	41 01♓	16 02	51 04♓25
1999	18♎23 19	22 20	21 21	18 22	15 23	12 24	07 25	02 25	56 26	49 27	42 28	33 29	23 00♏	12 01	00 01♏47
2000	27♒35 29	08 00♓	41 02	14 03	47 05	20 06	53 08	26 09	59 11	31 13	04 14	37 16	09 17	42 19	14 20♓46

February

Year	1st	3rd	5th	7th	9th	11th	13th	15th	17th	19th	21st	23rd	25th	27th	29th
1900	08♒00	09 35	11 09	12 43	14 18	15 52	17 27	19 01	20 36	22 11	23 45	25 20	26 54	28♒29	
1901	10♍R15	09 44	09 11	08 34	07 56	07 15	06 32	05 48	05 02	04 15	03 28	02 40	01 52	01♍05	
1902	23♒41	25 15	26 50	28 25	00♓00	01 35	03 10	04 45	06 20	07 54	09 29	11 03	12 38	14♓12	
1903	14♎32	14 54	15 13	15 30	15 44	15 56	16 06	16 12	16R16	16 17	16 15	16 10	16 02	15 51	
1904	09♓41	11 15	12 49	14 22	15 56	17 29	19 03	20 36	22 10	23 43	25 16	26 49	28 21	29♈54	01♈26
1905	08♏40	09 34	10 26	11 18	12 08	12 58	13 46	14 33	15 19	16 04	16 48	17 30	18 11	18♏51	
1906	26♓59	28 30	00♈01	01 31	03 01	04 31	06 01	07 31	09 01	10 30	11 59	13 28	14 57	16♈26	
1907	27♏26	28 36	29♐46	00 56	02 06	03 15	04 25	05 33	06 42	07 50	08 58	10 06	11 13	12♐20	
1908	14♈36	16 00	17 23	18 47	20 11	21 35	22 58	24 21	25 45	27 08	28 31	29♉54	01 17	02 40	04♉03
1909	14♐32	15 53	17 13	18 33	19 53	21 14	22 34	23 54	25 15	26 35	27 56	29 16	00♑37	01♑57	
1910	05♉09	06 20	07 30	08 41	09 52	11 03	12 15	13 26	14 38	15 50	17 02	18 15	19 27	20♉40	
1911	00♑05	01 31	02 58	04 24	05 51	07 18	08 45	10 12	11 39	13 07	14 34	16 02	17 30	18♑58	
1912	00♊22	01 02	01 43	02 26	03 10	03 56	04 43	05 31	06 20	07 10	08 01	08 53	09 46	10 40	11♊35
1913	16♑03	17 34	19 05	20 36	22 07	23 39	25 10	26 41	28 13	29♒45	01 17	02 48	04 21	05♒53	
1914	06♋R36	06 19	06 05	05 54	05 46	05D42	05 40	05 42	05 46	05 53	06 03	06 16	06 31	06♋49	
1915	01♒21	02 55	04 28	06 02	07 36	09 10	10 44	12 18	13 52	15 26	17 00	18 34	20 09	21♒43	
1916	23♌R36	22 51	22 04	21 17	20 29	19 41	18 53	18 06	17 20	16 35	15 52	15 10	14 31	13 54	13♌19
1917	17♒42	19 17	20 51	22 26	24 01	25 36	27 11	28 46	00♓21	01 56	03 30	05 05	06 40	08♓15	
1918	03♎01	03R04	03 04	03 00	02 54	02 45	02 33	02 17	01 58	01 36	01 11	00 44	00♍13	29♍40	
1919	03♓34	05 09	06 43	08 18	09 52	11 26	13 01	14 35	16 09	17 43	19 16	20 50	22 24	23♓57	
1920	00♏01	00 44	01 27	02 08	02 47	03 25	04 02	04 37	05 10	05 41	06 11	06 38	07 03	07 27	07♏48
1921	20♓38	22 11	23 43	25 15	26 47	28 18	29♈50	01 21	02 53	04 24	05 55	07 26	08 56	10♈27	
1922	20♏42	21 47	22 52	23 56	24 59	26 02	27 05	28 07	29 09	00♐10	01 10	02 10	03 10	04♐08	
1923	07♈43	09 10	10 37	12 03	13 30	14 57	16 23	17 50	19 16	20 42	22 08	23 34	25 00	26♈25	
1924	07♐50	09 07	10 24	11 41	12 57	14 14	15 31	16 47	18 04	19 20	20 37	21 53	23 09	24 26	25♐42
1925	27♈10	28 27	29♉44	01 01	02 18	03 35	04 52	06 09	07 26	08 43	10 01	11 18	12 35	13♉53	
1926	24♐16	25 40	27 05	28 29	29♑54	01 18	02 43	04 08	05 33	06 58	08 23	09 49	11 14	12♑40	
1927	19♉47	20 41	21 37	22 33	23 31	24 29	25 27	26 27	27 27	28 27	29 28	00♊30	01 32	02 35	
1928	09♑33	11 02	12 31	14 01	15 30	17 00	18 30	20 00	21 30	23 00	24 31	26 01	27 32	29♑02	00♒33
1929	21♊07	21 15	21 26	21 39	21 55	22 14	22 35	22 58	23 23	23 51	24 20	24 52	25 25	26♊00	
1930	25♑33	27 05	28 38	00♒11	01 44	03 17	04 50	06 23	07 56	09 30	11 03	12 37	14 10	15♒44	
1931	05♌R14	04 28	03 42	02 59	02 17	01 38	01 00	00 26	29♋54	29 25	28 59	28 36	28 17	28♋01	
1932	10♒58	12 33	14 08	15 42	17 17	18 52	20 26	22 01	23 36	25 11	26 45	28 20	29♓55	01 30	03♓04
1933	19♍R30	19 12	18 50	18 25	17 57	17 26	16 52	16 16	15 38	14 57	14 14	13 30	12 44	11♍57	
1934	27♒29	29 04	00♓39	02 14	03 49	05 24	06 58	08 33	10 07	11 42	13 16	14 51	16 25	17♓59	
1935	20♎51	21 21	21 50	22 17	22 42	23 04	23 25	23 43	23 58	24 11	24 22	24 30	24 35	24♎R37	
1936	13♓37	15 10	16 43	18 17	19 50	21 23	22 56	24 28	26 01	27 34	29 06	00♈38	02 10	03 42	05♈14
1937	13♏31	14 29	15 26	16 23	17 19	18 14	19 08	20 01	20 54	21 45	22 36	23 26	24 14	25♏01	
1938	01♈06	02 35	04 05	05 34	07 03	08 32	10 01	11 30	12 58	14 27	15 55	17 23	18 51	20♈19	
1939	01♐35	02 48	04 00	05 13	06 26	07 38	08 50	10 02	11 14	12 26	13 37	14 48	15 59	17♐10	
1940	19♈04	20 26	21 47	23 09	24 31	25 52	27 14	28 35	29♉57	01 18	02 40	04 01	05 22	06 43	08♉04
1941	18♐24	19 46	21 07	22 29	23 51	25 13	26 35	27 57	29♑20	00 42	02 04	03 27	04 49	05♑12	
1942	10♉27	11 33	12 39	13 45	14 52	15 59	17 06	18 14	19 22	20 31	21 40	22 49	23 58	25♉08	
1943	03♑47	05 15	06 42	08 10	09 38	11 06	12 34	14 02	15 31	16 59	18 28	19 57	21 25	22♑54	
1944	07♊36	08 05	08 37	09 10	09 45	10 22	11 00	11 40	12 21	13 03	13 47	14 33	15 19	16 07	16♊56
1945	19♑45	21 16	22 48	24 20	25 51	27 23	28♒55	00 28	02 00	03 32	05 05	06 37	08 10	09♒43	
1946	16♋R56	16 25	15 57	15 32	15 10	14 52	14 37	14 24	14 15	14 10	14 07	14D07	14 10	14♋16	
1947	05♒06	06 40	08 14	09 48	11 22	12 56	14 30	16 05	17 39	19 13	20 48	22 22	23 57	25♒31	
1948	04♍R01	03 23	02 44	02 02	01 18	00♌33	29 47	28 59	28 12	27 24	26 36	25 49	25 03	24 18	23♌35
1949	21♒30	23 05	24 40	26 15	27♓50	29 25	01 00	02 35	04 10	05 44	07 19	08 54	10 28	12♓03	
1950	10♎18	10 32	10 44	10 52	10 59	11R02	11 02	11 00	10 54	10 45	10 33	10 18	10 00	09♎39	
1951	07♓26	09 00	10 35	12 09	13 43	15 17	16 51	18 24	19 58	21 32	23 05	24 38	26 11	27♓44	
1952	05♏16	06 06	06 55	07 42	08 29	09 14	09 58	10 41	11 22	12 02	12 40	13 17	13 52	14 26	14♏58
1953	24♓39	26 10	27 41	29 12	00♈43	02 14	03 45	05 16	06 46	08 16	09 47	11 17	12 47	14♈16	
1954	25♏02	26 11	27 18	28 26	29♐33	00 40	01 46	02 53	03 58	05 04	06 09	07 13	08 17	09♐21	
1955	12♈01	13 27	14 52	16 17	17 42	19 08	20 32	21 57	23 22	24 47	26 11	27 35	29 00	00♉24	
1956	11♐44	13 03	14 21	15 40	16 59	18 18	19 37	20 55	22 14	23 33	24 52	26 10	27 29	28 48	00♑06
1957	02♉04	03 18	04 31	05 45	06 59	08 13	09 27	10 42	11 56	13 11	14 25	15 40	16 55	18♉10	
1958	28♐01	29♑26	00 52	02 18	03 43	05 09	06 35	08 02	09 28	10 54	12 21	13 48	15 14	16♑41	
1959	26♉05	26 52	27 40	28 29	29 19	00♊11	01 03	01 57	02 51	03 46	04 42	05 39	06 36	07♊34	
1960	13♑15	14 45	16 15	17 46	19 16	20 47	22 17	23 48	25 19	26 50	28 21	29♒53	01 24	02 55	04♒27
1961	00♋R10	00 03	00♊00	00 00	00♋D03	00 08	00 17	00 28	00 42	00 58	01 17	01 39	02 02	02♋28	
1962	29♑16	00♒49	02 22	03 56	05 29	07 02	08 36	10 10	11 43	13 17	14 51	16 25	17 59	19♒33	
1963	16♌R21	15 33	14 45	13 57	13 10	12 23	11 38	10 55	10 13	09 33	08 56	08 22	07 50	07♌21	
1964	14♒45	16 20	17 54	19 29	21 04	22 39	24 14	25 49	27 23	28 58	00♓33	02 08	03 43	05 18	06♓52
1965	27♍R59	27 53	27 44	27 31	27 16	26 57	26 35	26 10	25 42	25 11	24 38	24 02	23 23	22♍42	
1966	01♓21	02 56	04 30	06 05	07 40	09 14	10 48	12 23	13 57	15 31	17 06	18 40	20 14	21♓48	
1967	26♎41	27 19	27 56	28 32	29 05	29 37	00♏07	00 35	01 01	01 25	01 47	02 06	02 23	02♏38	
1968	17♓34	19 07	20 40	22 12	23 45	25 17	26 50	28 22	29♈54	01 26	02 57	04 29	06 00	07 32	09♈03
1969	18♏07	19 10	20 11	21 12	22 13	23 13	24 12	25 11	26 09	27 06	28 02	28 58	29♐53	00♐47	
1970	05♈15	06 43	08 11	09 39	11 07	12 35	14 03	15 31	16 58	18 25	19 52	21 19	22 46	24♈13	
1971	05♐37	06 53	08 08	09 23	10 38	11 52	13 08	14 22	15 37	16 51	18 06	19 20	20 34	21♐48	
1972	23♈41	25 00	26 19	27 38	28 58	00♉17	01 36	02 55	04 14	05 34	06 53	08 12	09 31	10 51	12♉10
1973	22♐12	23 35	24 58	26 22	27 45	29 08	00♑32	01 56	03 20	04 43	06 07	07 31	08 56	10♑20	
1974	16♉05	17 04	18 05	19 06	20 08	21 10	22 13	23 17	24 20	25 25	26 29	27 35	28 40	29♊46	
1975	07♑29	08 58	10 27	11 55	13 24	14 53	16 22	17 52	19 21	20 50	22 20	23 50	25 19	26♑49	
1976	15♊29	15 46	16 05	16 27	16 51	17 17	17 46	18 16	18 48	19 22	19 58	20 35	21 14	21 54	22♊36
1977	23♑28	25 00	26 32	28 05	29♒37	01 10	02 42	04 15	05 48	07 21	08 54	10 27	12 00	13♒33	
1978	27♋R47	27 05	26 26	25 49	25 14	24 42	24 14	23 48	23 26	23 06	22 50	22 37	22 28	22♋21	
1979	08♒51	10 25	11 59	13 34	15 08	16 43	18 17	19 52	21 26	23 01	24 36	26 10	27 45	29♓20	
1980	13♍R44	13 18	12 48	12 16	11 41	11 04	10 24	09 42	08 59	08 13	07 27	06 40	05 52	05 05	04♍17
1981	25♒18	26 53	28 27	00♓02	01 37	03 12	04 47	06 22	07 57	09 31	11 06	12 40	14 15	15♓49	
1982	16♎59	17 23	17 45	18 05	18 22	18 37	18 49	18 59	19 06	19R10	19 11	19 09	19 04	18♎56	
1983	11♓20	12 54	14 27	16 01	17 35	19 08	20 42	22 15	23 48	25 21	26 54	28 27	29♈59	01♈32	
1984	10♏14	11 09	12 03	12 56	13 48	14 40	15 30	16 20	17 08	17 55	18 41	19 26	20 09	20 52	21♏32
1985	28♓42	00♈13	01 43	03 13	04 43	06 13	07 43	09 12	10 42	12 11	13 40	15 10	16 38	18♈07	
1986	29♏15	00♐26	01 37	02 47	03 58	05 08	06 18	07 27	08 37	09 45	10 54	12 03	13 11	14♐19	
1987	16♈24	17 47	19 11	20 34	21 58	23 21	24 44	26 07	27 30	28 53	00♉16	01 39	03 01	04♉24	
1988	15♐36	16 56	18 17	19 37	20 58	22 19	23 39	25 00	26 21	27 42	29 02	00♑23	01 44	03 05	04♑26
1989	07♉10	08 19	09 29	10 39	11 49	13 00	14 10	15 21	16 33	17 44	18 55	20 07	21 19	22♉31	
1990	01♑44	03 11	04 38	06 04	07 31	08 59	10 26	11 53	13 21	14 48	16 16	17 44	19 12	20♑40	
1991	02♊54	03 31	04 10	04 51	05 33	06 17	07 02	07 48	08 35	09 24	10 13	11 04	11 55	12♊48	
1992	16♑55	18 26	19 57	21 28	22 59	24 31	26 02	27 34	29 05	00♒37	02 09	03 41	05 13	06 45	08♒18
1993	10♋R00	09 39	09 22	09 07	08 56	08 48	08 43	08D41	08 42	08 46	08 52	09 02	09 14	09♋29	
1994	02♒59	04 32	06 06	07 40	09 14	10 48	12 22	13 56	15 30	17 04	18 38	20 12	21 47	23♒21	
1995	27♌R11	26 27	25 42	24 56	24 09	23 21	22 33	21 45	20 58	20 12	19 27	18 43	18 02	17♌22	
1996	18♒32	20 07	21 42	23 17	24 52	26 27	28 02	29♓37	01 12	02 46	04 21	05 56	07 31	09 06	10♓40
1997	05♎46	05 52	05R55	05 55	05 52	05 46	05 37	05 25	05 09	04 51	04 29	04 05	03 37	03♎06	
1998	05♓13	06 47	08 22	09 56	11 30	13 05	14 39	16 13	17 47	19 21	20 54	22 28	24 02	25♓35	
1999	02♏11	02 56	03 40	04 23	05 04	05 44	06 22	06 59	07 35	08 08	08 40	09 10	09 37	10♏03	
2000	21♓33	23 05	24 37	26 09	27 41	29 12	00♈44	02 15	03 46	05 18	06 48	08 19	09 50	11 20	12♈51

Mars
March

Year	1st	3rd	5th	7th	9th	11th	13th	15th	17th	19th	21st	23rd	25th	27th	29th	31st
1900	00♓03	01 38	03 13	04 47	06 22	07 56	09 31	11 05	12 40	14 14	15 48	17 22	18 56	20 30	22 04	23♓38
1901	00♍R19	29♌33	28 50	28 08	27 28	26 50	26 15	25 42	25 13	24 46	24 22	24 02	23 44	23 30	23 19	23♌11
1902	15♓47	17 21	18 55	20 29	22 03	23 37	25 11	26 44	28 18	29♈51	01 24	02 58	04 30	06 03	07 36	09♈08
1903	15♎R36	15 19	14 58	14 34	14 08	13 38	13 06	12 31	11 54	11 15	10 33	09 50	09 06	08 20	07 34	06♎47
1904	02♈12	03 45	05 17	06 49	08 20	09 52	11 23	12 55	14 26	15 57	17 27	18 58	20 28	21 59	23 29	24♈58
1905	19♏29	20 06	20 40	21 13	21 44	22 14	22 41	23 06	23 29	23 50	24 09	24 25	24 38	24 50	24 58	25♏04
1906	17♈55	19 24	20 52	22 20	23 48	25 16	26 44	28 11	29♉38	01 06	02 33	03 59	05 26	06 52	08 19	09♉45
1907	13♐27	14 33	15 39	16 44	17 49	18 54	19 58	21 02	22 05	23 07	24 09	25 10	26 11	27 11	28 10	29♐09
1908	04♉44	06 07	07 29	08 51	10 14	11 36	12 58	14 20	15 41	17 03	18 25	19 46	21 07	22 29	23 50	25♉11
1909	03♑18	04 38	05 59	07 19	08 40	10 00	11 21	12 41	14 02	15 22	16 43	18 03	19 24	20 44	22 05	23♑25
1910	21♉53	23 06	24 19	25 32	26 45	27 59	29 12	00♊26	01 39	02 53	04 07	05 21	06 35	07 48	09 02	10♊16
1911	20♑26	21 54	23 22	24 50	26 19	27 47	29 16	00♒44	02 13	03 42	05 11	06 40	08 09	09 38	11 07	12♒36
1912	12♊02	12 58	13 55	14 52	15 50	16 49	17 48	18 48	19 48	20 49	21 50	22 52	23 54	24 57	26 00	27♊04
1913	07♒25	08 57	10 30	12 02	13 35	15 07	16 40	18 12	19 45	21 18	22 51	24 24	25 56	27 29	29 02	00♓35
1914	07♋09	07 31	07 56	08 22	08 51	09 21	09 54	10 28	11 03	11 41	12 19	12 59	13 41	14 24	15 08	15♋53
1915	23♒17	24 52	26 26	28 00	29♓35	01 09	02 43	04 18	05 52	07 26	09 01	10 35	12 09	13 43	15 17	16♓51
1916	13♌R03	12 33	12 06	11 41	11 20	11 02	10 48	10 36	10 28	10 22	10D20	10 20	10 24	10 30	10 39	10♌50
1917	09♓49	11 24	12 58	14 33	16 07	17 42	19 16	20 50	22 24	23 58	25 32	27 05	28 39	00♈12	01 46	03♈19
1918	29♍R04	28 25	27 45	27 02	26 18	25 33	24 46	23 59	23 12	22 25	21 39	20 53	20 08	19 25	18 44	18♍05
1919	25♓31	27 04	28 37	00♈10	01 43	03 16	04 48	06 21	07 53	09 25	10 57	12 29	14 00	15 32	17 03	18♈34
1920	07♏57	08 15	08 30	08 42	08 52	09 00	09 04	09R06	09 05	09 00	08 53	08 43	08 29	08 12	07 53	07♏30
1921	11♈57	13 27	14 57	16♉27	17 57	19 27	20 56	22 25	23 54	25 23	26 52	28 20	29 48	01 16	02 44	04♉12
1922	05♐06	06 03	06 59	07 55	08 50	09 44	10 37	11 29	12 20	13 10	13 59	14 47	15 34	16 19	17 03	17♐45
1923	27♈51	29 16	00♉41	02 06	03 31	04 56	06 20	07 45	09 09	10 33	11 57	13 21	14 45	16 08	17 32	18♉55
1924	26♐20	27 36	28 52	00♑08	01 24	02 39	03 55	05 10	06 25	07 40	08 55	10 10	11 25	12 39	13 53	15♑08
1925	15♉10	16 27	17 45	19 02	20 20	21 37	22 54	24 11	25 29	26 46	28 03	29 20	00♊38	01 55	03 12	04♊29
1926	14♑05	15 31	16 56	18 22	19 48	21 14	22 40	24 06	25 33	26 59	28 25	29♒52	01 18	02 45	04 11	05♒38
1927	03♊38	04 42	05 26	06 50	07 55	09 01	10 06	11 12	12 19	13 25	14 32	15 39	16 47	17 54	19 02	20♊10
1928	01♒19	02 50	04 21	05 52	07 23	08 54	10 26	11 57	13 29	15 00	16 32	18 04	19 35	21 07	22 39	24♒11
1929	26♊36	27 14	27 54	28 35	29 17	00♋01	00 46	01 32	02 19	03 07	03 57	04 47	05 38	06 30	07 23	08♋17
1930	17♒18	18 52	20 25	21 59	23 33	25 07	26 41	28 15	29♓48	01 22	02 56	04 30	06 04	07 38	09 12	10♓46
1931	27♋R47	27 37	27 31	27D27	27 26	27 28	27 33	27 41	27 51	28 04	28 19	28 37	28 58	29 20	29 45	00♌12
1932	03♓52	05 27	07 01	08 36	10 10	11 45	13 19	14 54	16 28	18 02	19 37	21 11	22 45	24 19	25 52	27♓26
1933	11♍R10	10 22	09 35	08 48	08 02	07 17	06 33	05 52	05 12	04 34	04 00	03 27	02 58	02 31	02 08	01♍48
1934	19♓33	21 07	22 41	24 15	25 49	27 22	28 56	00♈29	02 02	03 35	05 08	06 41	08 13	09 46	11 18	12♈50
1935	24♎R36	24 32	24 26	24 16	24 03	23 47	23 27	23 05	22 40	22 12	21 41	21 07	20 31	19 53	19 13	18♎30
1936	06♈00	07 32	09 03	10 34	12 05	13 36	15 07	16 38	18 08	19 38	21 08	22 38	24 08	25 37	27 07	28♈36
1937	25♏48	26 33	27 17	27 59	28 40	29 20	29♐58	00 34	01 09	01 41	02 13	02 42	03 09	03 34	03 57	04♐18
1938	21♈47	23 14	24 42	26 09	27 36	29 03	00♉29	01 56	03 22	04 48	06 14	07 40	09 06	10 31	11 56	13♉21
1939	18♐20	19 31	20 41	21 50	23 00	24 09	25 18	26 26	27 34	28 43	29♑50	00 57	02 03	03 09	04 15	05♑20
1940	08♉44	10 06	11 26	12 47	14 08	15 28	16 49	18 09	19 30	20 50	22 10	23 30	24 50	26 10	27 30	28♉49
1941	07♑34	08 57	10 19	11 42	13 05	14 28	15 50	17 13	18 36	19 59	21 22	22 45	24 08	25 31	26 54	28♑17
1942	26♉18	27 28	28 38	29♊48	00 59	02 10	03 20	04 32	05 43	06 54	08 06	09 18	10 29	11 41	12 53	14♊06
1943	24♑24	25 53	27 22	28 52	00♒21	01 51	03 20	04 50	06 20	07 50	09 20	10 51	12 20	13 50	15 21	16♒51
1944	17♊20	18 11	19 02	19 54	20 47	21 41	22 36	23 31	24 27	25 24	26 22	27 20	28 18	29 18	00♋18	01♋18
1945	11♒15	12 48	14 21	15 54	17 27	19 01	20 34	22 07	23 40	25 13	26 47	28 20	29♓53	01 27	03 00	04♓33
1946	14♋25	14 36	14 50	15 07	15 26	15 47	16 10	16 36	17 03	17 33	18 04	18 37	19 12	19 48	20 26	21♋05
1947	27♒06	28♓40	00 15	01 49	03 24	04 58	06 33	08 07	09 42	11 16	12 50	14 25	15 59	17 33	19 07	20♓41
1948	23♌R14	22 34	21 56	21 21	20 48	20 18	19 51	19 27	19 06	18 48	18 33	18 22	18 14	18 09	18 06	18♌D07
1949	13♓38	15 12	16 47	18 21	19 55	21 29	23 03	24 37	26 11	27 44	29♈18	00 51	02 25	03 58	05 31	07♈04
1950	09♎R14	08 47	08 17	07 44	07 09	06 31	05 51	05 09	04 25	03 40	02 54	02 08	01 21	00 34	29♍48	29♍02
1951	29♓17	00♈50	02 23	03 55	05 28	07 00	08 32	10 04	11 36	13 07	14 39	16 10	17 41	19 11	20 42	22♈13
1952	15♏13	15 41	16 08	16 33	16 56	17 16	17 34	17 50	18 03	18 13	18 21	18 26	18R28	18 28	18 24	18♏17
1953	15♈46	17 15	18 44	20 13	21 42	23 11	24 39	26 07	27 36	29 03	00♉31	01 15	02 43	04 10	06 20	07♉47
1954	10♐24	11 27	12 29	13 30	14 31	15 31	16 31	17 30	18 28	19 26	20 22	21 18	22 14	23 08	24 01	24♐54
1955	01♉48	03 12	04 36	05 59	07 23	08 46	10 09	11 32	12 55	14 18	15 41	17 04	18 26	19 48	21 11	22♉33
1956	00♑46	02 04	03 23	04 42	06 00	07 19	08 37	09 56	11 14	12 32	13 51	15 09	16 27	17 45	19 03	20♑21
1957	19♉25	20 40	21 55	23 10	24 25	25 40	26 56	28 11	29♊26	00 42	01 57	03 12	04 28	05 43	06 59	08♊14
1958	18♑08	19 35	21 02	22 29	23 57	25 24	26 52	28 19	29♒47	01 15	02 43	04 10	05 38	07 06	08 34	10♒03
1959	08♊33	09 32	10 32	11 32	12 33	13 35	14 37	15 39	16 42	17 46	18 50	19 54	20 58	22 03	23 09	24♊14
1960	05♒13	06 45	08 16	09 48	11 20	12 52	14 24	15 37	17 29	19 01	20 33	22 06	23 38	25 11	26 43	28♒16
1961	02♋55	03 25	03 56	04 30	05 04	05 41	06 19	06 59	07 40	08 22	09 06	09 50	10 37	11 24	12 12	13♋01
1962	21♒07	22 41	24 15	25 50	27 24	28 58	00♓32	02 06	03D40	05 15	06 49	08 23	09 57	11 31	13 05	14♓39
1963	06♌R55	06 32	06 12	05 56	05 43	05 32	05 25	05 21	05 20	05 22	05 27	05 34	05 44	05 57	06 13	06♌30
1964	07♓40	09 14	10 49	12 23	13 58	15 32	17 07	18 41	20 15	21 49	23 24	24 57	26 31	28 05	29♈38	01♈12
1965	22♍R00	21 15	20 30	19 43	18 56	18 09	17 22	16 35	15 49	15 04	14 21	13 40	13 00	12 23	11 48	11♍16
1966	23♓21	24 55	26 28	28 02	29♈35	01 08	02 41	04 14	05 47	07 19	08 51	10 24	11 56	13 28	14 59	16♈31
1967	02♏50	03 00	03 07	03R11	03 12	03 10	03 05	02 57	02 46	02 32	02 15	01 54	01 31	01 05	00 36	00♏04
1968	09♈48	11 19	12 50	14 21	15 51	17 21	18 51	20 21	21 51	23 20	24 49	26 19	27 48	29♉16	00 45	02♉13
1969	01♐40	02 32	03 24	04 14	05 03	05 52	06 39	07 25	08 09	08 52	09 34	10 15	10 53	11 31	12 06	12♐40
1970	25♈39	27 05	28 32	29♉58	01 24	02 50	04 15	05 41	07 06	08 31	09 56	11 21	12 45	14 10	15 34	16♈58
1971	23♐02	24 15	25 29	26 42	27 55	29 08	00 21	01 34	02 46	03 58	05 10	06 22	07 34	08 45	09 56	11♐06
1972	12♉49	14 08	15 27	16 46	18 05	19 24	20 43	22 02	23 20	24 39	25 58	27 16	28 35	29♊53	01 11	02♊30
1973	11♑44	13 08	14 33	15 57	17 22	18 47	20 11	21 36	23 01	24 26	25 51	27 16	28 41	00♒06	01 31	02♒56
1974	00♊53	01 59	03 06	04 14	05 21	06 29	07 37	08 45	09 54	11 03	12 12	13 21	14 31	15 40	16 50	18♊00
1975	28♑19	29♒50	01 20	02 50	04 21	05 51	07 22	08 53	10 24	11 54	13 25	14 56	16 27	17 59	19 30	21♒01
1976	22♊58	23 41	24 26	25 12	26 00	26 48	27 38	28 28	29 20	00♋12	01 05	01 59	02 53	03 49	04 45	05♋42
1977	15♒07	16 40	18 14	19 47	21 21	22 54	24 28	26 01	27 34	29 09	00♓42	02 16	03 50	05 23	06 57	08♓31
1978	22♋R17	22D17	22 19	22 24	22 32	22 43	22 56	23 12	23 30	23 51	24 14	24 38	25 05	25 34	26 05	26♋37
1979	00♓54	02 29	04 04	05 38	07 13	08 48	10 22	11 57	13 31	15 05	16 40	18 14	19 48	21 22	22 56	24♓30
1980	03♍R54	03 08	02 22	01 39	00 57	00♌17	29 39	29 04	28 31	28 01	27 35	27 11	26 50	26 33	26 19	26♌07
1981	17♓24	18 58	20 32	22 06	23 40	25 14	26 48	28 21	29♈55	01 28	03 01	04 34	06 07	07 40	09 13	10♈45
1982	18♎R45	18 31	18 14	17 54	17 30	17 04	16 35	16 03	15 29	14 52	14 12	13 31	12 48	12 04	11 18	10♎32
1983	03♈04	04 36	06 09	07 40	09 12	10 44	12 15	13 47	15 18	16 49	18 19	19 50	21 20	22 50	24 20	25♈50
1984	21♏52	22 31	23 08	23 43	24 17	24 38	25 18	25 46	26 12	26 36	26 58	27 17	27 34	27 49	28 01	28♏10
1985	19♈36	21 04	22 32	24 00	25 28	26 56	28 23	29♉51	01 18	02 45	04 12	05 38	07 05	08 31	09 57	11♉23
1986	15♐26	16 33	17 40	18 46	19 52	20 58	22 03	23 08	24 12	25 16	26 19	27 21	28 23	29 25	00♑26	01♑26
1987	05♉46	07 09	08 31	09 53	11 15	12 37	13 59	15 21	16 42	18 04	19 25	20 47	22 08	23 29	24 50	26♉11
1988	05♑06	06 27	07 48	09 09	10 30	11 51	13 12	14 33	15 54	17 15	18 36	19 57	21 18	22 39	24 00	25♑21
1989	23♉43	24 56	26 08	27 21	28 34	29♊47	01 00	02 13	03 26	04 39	05 53	07 06	08 19	09 33	10 47	12♊00
1990	22♑08	23 37	25 05	26 33	28 02	29♒31	00 59	02 28	03 57	05 26	06 55	08 25	09 54	11 23	12 53	14♒22
1991	13♊41	14 36	15 31	16 26	17 23	18 20	19 18	20 16	21 15	22 15	23 15	24 16	25 18	26 19	27 22	28♊24
1992	09♒04	10 36	12 09	13 41	15 14	16 46	18 19	19 52	21 25	22 58	24 31	26 04	27 37	29 10	00♓43	02♓16
1993	09♋46	10 06	10 28	10 52	11 18	11 47	12 17	12 49	13 22	13 58	14 35	15 13	15 53	16 34	17 17	18♋01
1994	24♒55	26 30	28 04	29♓38	01 13	02 47	04 22	05 56	07 30	09 05	10 39	12 13	13 47	15 21	16 55	18♓29
1995	16♌R45	16 11	15 39	15 10	14 44	14 22	14 02	13 46	13 32	13 22	13 15	13D11	13 10	13 12	13 17	13♌24
1996	11♓28	13 02	14 37	16 11	17 46	19 20	20 54	22 28	24 02	25 36	27 10	28 44	00♈17	01 51	03 24	04♈57
1997	02♎R33	01 57	01 19	00 39	29♍56	29 12	28 27	27 41	26 54	26 07	25 20	24 33	23 48	23 03	22 20	21♍39
1998	27♓09	28 42	00♈15	01 48	03 21	04 53	06 26	07 58	09 30	11 02	12 34	14 06	15 38	17 09	18 40	20♈11
1999	10♏27	10 49	11 08	11 25	11 40	11 52	12 01	12 08	12 11	12 12	12 10	12 05	11 57	11 46	11 31	11♏14
2000	13♈36	15 06	16 36	18 06	19 35	21 05	22 34	24 03	25 32	27 01	28 29	29♉57	01 26	02 53	04 21	05♉49

April

	1st	3rd	5th	7th	9th	11th	13th	15th	17th	19th	21st	23rd	25th	27th	29th
1900	24♓25	25 59	27 32	29 06	00♈39	02 12	03 45	05 18	06 51	08 24	09 56	11 28	13 01	14 33	16♈04
1901	23♌R08	23 D 04	23 04	23 07	23 12	23 20	23 31	23 44	24 00	24 18	24 39	25 02	25 27	25 54	26♌23
1902	09♈55	11 27	12 59	14 31	16 03	17 34	19 05	20 37	22 08	23 39	25 09	26 40	28 10	29♉40	01♉10
1903	06♎R24	05 37	04 52	04 07	03 23	02 41	02 01	01 23	00 47	00♍14	29 43	29 15	28 51	28 29	28♍11
1904	25♈43	27 13	28 42	00♉11	01 40	03 09	04 37	06 06	07 34	09 02	10 29	11 57	13 24	14 51	16♉18
1905	25♏05	25 R 07	25 05	25 00	24 52	24 42	24 28	24 11	23 51	23 28	23 02	22 34	22 03	21 29	20♏53
1906	10♉28	11 53	13 19	14 44	16 10	17 35	19 00	20 24	21 49	23 13	24 37	26 01	27 25	28 49	00♊12
1907	29♐38	00♑35	01 32	02 28	03 23	04 17	05 10	06 02	06 53	07 42	08 31	09 18	10 04	10 49	11♑32
1908	25♉51	27 12	28 33	29♊53	01 14	02 34	03 54	05 14	06 34	07 54	09 14	10 33	11 53	13 12	14♊32
1909	24♑05	25 25	26 46	28 06	29♒26	00 46	02 06	03 26	04 45	06 05	07 24	08 44	10 03	11 22	12♒41
1910	10♊54	12 08	13 22	14 36	15 50	17 04	18 19	19 33	20 47	22 02	23 16	24 30	25 45	26 59	28♊13
1911	13♒21	14 50	16 19	17 49	19 18	20 47	22 17	23 46	26 16	26 45	28 15	29♓44	01 14	02 43	04♓13
1912	27♊36	28 40	29♋45	00 49	01 55	03 00	04 06	05 12	06 18	07 25	08 32	09 39	10 46	11 54	13♋02
1913	01♓22	02 55	04 27	06 00	07 33	09 06	10 39	12 12	13 45	15 17	06 50	18 22	19 55	21 27	23♓00
1914	16♋16	17 03	17 51	18 41	19 31	20 22	21 14	22 06	23 00	23 54	24 49	25 45	26 41	27 39	28♋36
1915	17♓38	19 12	20 46	22 19	23 53	25 26	27 00	28 33	00♈06	01 40	03 13	04 45	06 18	07 51	09♈23
1916	10♌57	11 13	11 30	11 51	12 13	12 38	13 04	13 33	14 04	14 36	15 10	15 46	16 23	17 02	17♌42
1917	04♈05	05 38	07 11	08 44	10 16	11 49	13 21	14 53	16 25	17 56	19 28	20 59	22 31	24 01	25♈32
1918	17♍R46	17 10	16 37	16 07	15 39	15 15	14 53	14 35	14 20	14 08	13 59	13 54	13 D 51	13 52	13♍55
1919	19♈19	20 50	22 21	23 51	25 21	26 51	28 22	29♉51	01 20	02 49	04 18	05 47	07 16	08 44	10♉56
1920	07♏R18	06 51	06 21	05 48	05 13	04 36	03 57	03 16	02 33	01 49	01 04	00♎19	29 34	28 49	28♎05
1921	04♉56	06 23	07 50	09 17	10 44	12 11	13 37	15 03	16 29	17 55	19 21	20 46	22 11	23 36	25♉01
1922	18♐07	18 47	19 26	20 04	20 39	21 13	21 45	22 16	22 44	23 10	23 34	23 56	24 15	24 32	24♐46
1923	19♉36	20 59	22 22	23 45	25 07	26 30	27 52	29 14	00♊36	01 58	03 20	04 41	06 02	07 24	08♊45
1924	15♑45	16 58	18 12	19 25	20 38	21 51	23 03	24 16	25 28	26 39	27 60	29 01	00♒12	01 22	02♒32
1925	05♊07	06 24	07 41	08 58	10 15	11 32	12 49	14 06	15 22	16 39	17 56	19 12	20 29	21 46	23♊02
1926	06♒21	07 48	09 15	10 41	12 08	13 35	15 02	16 29	17 55	19 22	20 49	22 16	23 43	25 09	26♒36
1927	20♊44	21 53	23 02	24 11	25 20	26 29	27 38	28 48	29 58	01 08	02 18	03 28	04 38	05 49	07♊00
1928	24♒57	26 29	28 00	29♓32	01 04	02 36	04 08	05 40	07♋12	08 44	10 16	11 48	13 20	14 51	16♋23
1929	08♋44	09 39	10 35	11 31	12 28	13 25	14 24	15 23	16 22	17 22	18 22	19 23	20 25	21 27	22♋29
1930	11♓33	13 06	14 40	16 14	17 47	19 21	20 54	22 27	24 01	25 34	27 07	28 40	00♈13	01 45	03♈18
1931	00♌26	00 55	01 27	02 00	02 35	03 11	03 49	04 28	05 09	05 51	06 35	07 20	08 06	08 53	09♌41
1932	28♓13	29♈46	01 20	02 53	04 26	05 59	07 32	09 05	10 37	12 10	13 42	15 14	16 46	18 17	19♈49
1933	01♍R39	01 23	01 11	01 01	00 55	00 D 52	00 52	00 55	01 00	01 09	01 20	01 33	01 50	02 08	02♍29
1934	13♈36	15 08	16 39	18 11	19 42	21 13	22 44	24 15	25 45	27 16	28 46	00♉16	01 45	03 15	04♉44
1935	18♎R09	17 24	16 39	15 53	15 07	14 21	13 35	12 50	12 07	11 25	10 44	10 06	09 29	08 56	08♎25
1936	29♈20	00♉49	02 18	03 46	05 14	06 42	08 10	09 38	11 05	12 32	13 59	15 26	16 53	18 19	19♉46
1937	04♐27	04 44	04 59	05 11	05 21	05 27	05 R 31	05 32	05 30	05 25	05 17	05 06	04 42	04 35	04♐15
1938	14♉04	15 29	16 53	18 18	19 42	21 06	22 30	23 54	25 18	26 41	28 50	29♊28	00 51	02 14	03♊36
1939	05♑53	06 57	08 01	09 05	10 07	11 10	12 11	13 12	14 12	15 12	16 10	17 08	18 05	19 01	19♑56
1940	29♉29	00♊49	02 08	03 27	04 47	06 06	07 25	08 44	10 03	11 22	12 41	13 59	15 18	16 36	17♊54
1941	28♑58	00♒21	01 44	03 07	04 30	05 53	07 16	08 39	10 01	11 24	12 47	14 10	15 32	16 55	18♒17
1942	14♊42	15 54	17 06	18 19	19 31	20 44	21 56	23 09	24 22	25 35	26 48	28 01	29 14	00♋27	01♋40
1943	17♒36	19 07	20 37	22 08	23 38	25 09	26 39	28 10	29♓40	01 11	02 41	04 12	05 43	07 13	08♓44
1944	01♋49	02 50	03 51	04 53	05 56	06 59	08 02	09 06	10 10	11 14	12 19	13 24	14 30	15 36	16♋42
1945	05♓20	06 53	08 27	10 00	11 33	13 06	14 40	16 13	17 46	19 19	20 52	22 25	23 57	25 30	27♓03
1946	21♋26	22 07	22 50	23 34	24 19	25 06	25 53	26 42	27 31	28 22	29 13	00♌05	00 58	01 52	02♌47
1947	21♓28	23 02	24 35	26 09	27 42	29♈16	00 49	02 22	03 55	05 28	07 01	08 34	10 06	11 39	13♈11
1948	18♌08	18 13	18 21	18 32	18 45	19 00	19 18	19 39	20 01	20 26	20 52	21 22	21 52	22 25	22♌59
1949	07♈50	09 23	10 55	12 27	13 59	15 31	17 03	18 35	20 06	21 37	23 08	24 39	26 10	27 41	29♈11
1950	28♍R40	27 56	27 14	26 34	25 56	25 20	24 45	24 16	23 49	23 24	23 03	22 44	22 29	22 17	22♍R09
1951	22♈58	24 28	25 58	27 28	28 57	00♉27	01 56	03 25	04 54	06 22	07 51	09 19	10 48	12 15	13♉42
1952	18♏R13	18 01	17 47	17 29	17 09	16 45	16 19	15 50	15 18	14 44	14 07	13 28	12 48	12 06	11♏R23
1953	08♉31	09 57	11 24	12 50	14 16	15 41	17 07	18 33	19 58	21 23	22 48	24 12	25 37	27 01	28♉25
1954	25♐20	26 10	27 00	27 49	28 36	29 22	00♑07	00 50	01 32	02 13	02 52	03 29	04 05	04 39	05♑11
1955	23♉14	24 35	25 57	27 19	28 40	00♊01	01 23	02 44	04 05	05 25	06 46	08 07	09 27	10 47	12♊08
1956	21♑00	22 17	23 35	24 52	26 10	27 27	28 44	00♒01	01 17	02 34	03 50	05 06	06 22	07 37	08♒53
1957	08♊52	10 07	11 23	12 38	13 54	15 09	16 24	17 40	18 55	20 11	21 26	22 41	23 57	25 12	26♊28
1958	10♒47	12 15	13 43	15 11	16 40	18 08	19 36	21 05	22 33	24 02	25 30	26 59	28 27	29 55	01♓24
1959	24♊47	25 53	26 59	28 06	29 13	00♋20	01 27	02 35	03 43	04 51	05 59	07 08	08 17	09 25	10♋34
1960	29♒02	00♓34	02 07	03 39	05 12	06 44	08 17	09 49	11 22	12 54	14 27	15 59	17 31	19 04	20♓36
1961	13♋26	14 17	15 08	16 01	16 54	17 48	18 43	19 38	20 34	21 31	22 29	23 27	24 26	25 25	26♋25
1962	15♓26	17 00	18 33	20 07	21 41	23 14	24 48	26 21	27 54	29 28	01♈01	02 34	04 07	05 39	07♈12
1963	06♌40	07 01	07 25	07 50	08 18	08 47	09 19	09 52	10 26	11 03	11 41	12 20	13 01	13 43	14♌27
1964	01♈59	03 32	05 50	06 38	08 11	09 43	11 16	12 48	14 21	15 53	17 25	18 56	20 28	21 59	23♈30
1965	11♍R01	10 33	10 09	09 47	09 29	09 13	09 01	08 52	08 46	08 D 44	08 44	08 47	08 53	09 01	09♍13
1966	17♈17	18 48	20 19	21 50	23 21	24 51	26 21	27 52	29 22	00♉51	02 21	03 50	05 19	06 48	08♉17
1967	29♎R47	29 12	28 34	27 54	27 12	26 29	25 45	25 00	24 14	23 28	22 43	21 58	21 14	20 32	19♎R51
1968	02♉57	04 25	05 53	07 21	08 48	10 16	11 43	13 10	14 36	16 03	17 29	18 55	20 21	21 47	23♉12
1969	12♐56	13 28	13 57	14 24	14 49	15 12	15 33	15 51	16 07	16 20	16 31	16 38	16 43	16 R 46	16♐R45
1970	17♉40	19 04	20 28	21 51	23 15	24 38	26 01	27 24	28 47	00♊09	01 32	02 54	04 16	05 38	07♊00
1971	11♑42	12 52	14 02	15 11	16 20	17 29	18 37	19 45	20 53	22 00	23 06	24 12	25 17	26 22	27♑26
1972	03♊09	04 27	05 45	07 03	08 21	09 39	10 57	12 15	13 33	14 50	16 08	17 26	18 43	20 01	21♊18
1973	03♒39	05 04	06 29	07 54	09 19	10 45	12 10	13 35	15 00	16 26	17 51	19 16	20 41	22 06	23♒31
1974	18♊35	19 46	20 56	22 06	23 17	24 28	25 39	26 50	28 01	29 12	00♋24	01 35	02 47	03 59	05♋10
1975	21♒47	23 18	24 49	26 21	27 52	29 23	00♓55	02 26	03 58	05 28	07 00	08 32	10 03	11 34	13♓06
1976	06♋10	07 08	08 07	09 06	10 05	11 05	12 06	13 07	14 09	15 11	16 13	17 16	18 19	19 23	20♋27
1977	09♓17	10 51	12 25	13 58	15 31	17 05	18 38	20 12	21 45	23 18	24 51	26 24	27 57	29 30	01♈02
1978	26♋54	27 29	28 06	28 44	29 24	00♌05	00 47	01 31	02 15	03 01	03 49	04 37	05 26	06 16	07♌07
1979	25♓17	26 51	28 24	29 58	01♈31	03 04	04 38	06 11	07 43	09 16	10 49	12 21	13 53	15 26	16♈58
1980	26♌R03	25 56	25 53	25 52	25 55	26 00	26 08	26 19	26 32	26 48	27 06	27 27	27 50	28 15	28♌R42
1981	11♈31	13 04	14 36	16 08	17 39	19 11	20 42	22 13	23 44	25 15	26 46	28 16	29 46	01♉16	02♉46
1982	10♎R09	09 23	08 36	07 50	07 06	06 22	05 40	04 59	04 21	03 45	03 12	02 41	02 13	01 48	01♎R27
1983	26♈35	28 05	29 34	01♉03	02 32	04 01	05 29	06 58	08 26	09 54	11 22	12 49	14 17	15 44	17♉11
1984	28♏13	28 19	28 21	28 20	28 16	28 10	28 00	27 47	27 32	27 13	26 51	26 26	25 59	25 28	24♏55
1985	12♉06	13 32	14 57	16 23	17 48	19 13	20 37	22 02	23 26	24 51	26 15	27 38	29 02	00♊26	01♊49
1986	01♑56	02 55	03 53	04 51	05 48	06 44	07 38	08 33	09 26	10 18	11 09	11 58	12 47	13 35	14♑21
1987	26♉51	28 12	29 32	00♊53	02 13	03 33	04 53	06 13	07 33	08 53	10 12	11 32	12 51	14 11	15♊30
1988	26♑01	27 22	28 43	00♒04	01 25	02 45	04 06	05 26	06 47	08 07	09 27	10 47	12 07	13 27	14♒47
1989	12♊37	13 51	15 05	16 18	17 32	18 46	20 00	21 14	22 28	23 42	24 56	26 11	27 25	28 39	29♋53
1990	15♒07	16 36	18 06	19 36	21 05	22 35	24 05	25 34	26 04	28 34	00♓04	01 33	03 03	04 33	06♓02
1991	28♊56	29 59	01♋03	02 07	03 11	04 16	05 12	06 26	07 32	08 38	09 44	10 51	11 58	13 05	14♋12
1992	03♓02	04 35	06 08	07 41	09 14	10 47	12 20	13 53	15 26	16 59	18 31	20 04	21 37	23 09	24♓42
1993	18♋23	19 09	19 56	20 44	21 32	22 22	23 13	24 05	24 57	25 51	26 45	27 40	28 36	29 32	00♌29
1994	19♓16	20 50	22 24	23 58	25 31	27 05	28 38	00♈12	01 45	03 18	04 51	06 24	07 56	09 29	11♈01
1995	13♌29	13 40	13 54	14 11	14 30	14 51	15 15	15 40	16 08	16 37	17 09	17 42	18 17	18 53	19♌31
1996	05♈44	07 16	08 49	10 22	11 54	13 27	14 59	16 31	18 03	19 34	21 06	22 37	24 08	25 39	27♈10
1997	21♍R19	20 41	20 05	19 31	19 01	18 33	18 09	17 47	17 29	17 14	17 02	16 53	16 47	16 D 45	16♍45
1998	20♈57	22 27	23 58	25 28	26 58	28 28	29 58	01♉28	02 57	04 26	05 55	07 24	08 52	10 21	11♉49
1999	11♏R04	10 42	10 18	09 50	09 19	08 46	08 11	07 33	06 53	06 11	05 29	04 45	04 00	03 15	02♏R30
2000	06♉33	08 00	09 27	10 54	12 21	13 47	15 13	16 40	18 05	19 31	20 57	22 22	23 47	25 12	26♉37

Mars

May

Year	1st	3rd	5th	7th	9th	11th	13th	15th	17th	19th	21st	23rd	25th	27th	29th	31st
1900	17♈36	19 08	20 39	22 10	23 41	25 12	26 42	28 13	29♉43	01 13	02 43	04 12	05 42	07 11	08 40	10♉09
1901	26♌54	27 27	28 01	28 38	29 15	29♍55	00 36	01 18	02 02	02 47	03 33	04 21	05 09	05 59	06 50	07♍42
1902	02♉39	04 09	05 38	07 07	08 36	10 05	11 33	13 01	14 29	15 57	17 24	18 52	20 19	21 46	23 12	24♉39
1903	27♍R55	27 43	27 35	27 29	27 D26	27 27	27 30	27 37	27 46	27 58	28 13	28 30	28 50	29 12	29 40	00♎04
1904	17♉45	19 11	20 38	22 04	23 30	24 55	26 21	27 46	29 11	00♊36	02 01	03 25	04 50	06 14	07 38	09♊01
1905	20♏R15	19 35	18 54	18 12	17 29	16 45	16 01	15 18	14 36	13 54	13 14	12 35	11 58	11 24	10 52	10♏23
1906	01♊36	02 58	04 22	05 44	07 07	08 29	09 52	11 14	12 36	13 57	15 19	16 41	18 02	19 23	20 44	22♊05
1907	12♑14	12 54	13 33	14 10	14 45	15 18	15 49	16 18	16 44	17 09	17 31	17 51	18 08	18 22	18 34	18♑44
1908	15♊51	17 10	18 29	19 48	21 07	22 26	23 44	25 03	26 21	27 40	28 58	00♋16	01 34	02 52	04 10	05♋28
1909	13♒59	15 18	16 36	17 54	19 12	20 30	21 47	23 04	24 21	25 37	26 53	28 09	29♓24	00 39	01 54	03♓07
1910	29♊28	00♋42	01 57	03 11	04 26	05 40	06 55	08 09	09 24	10 38	11 53	13 07	14 22	15 36	16 51	18♋05
1911	05♓42	07 11	08 41	10 10	11 39	13 08	14 37	16 06	17 35	19 03	20 32	22 00	23 29	24 57	26 25	27♓53
1912	14♋10	15 18	16 27	17 36	18 44	19 54	21 03	22 12	23 22	24 32	25 42	26 52	28 02	29 13	00♌23	01♌34
1913	24♓32	26 04	27 36	29 08	00♈40	02 12	03 44	05 15	06 46	08 18	09 49	11 19	12 50	14 21	15 51	17♈21
1914	29♋35	00♌34	01 34	02 34	03 34	04 36	05 37	06 39	07 42	08 45	09 48	10 52	11 57	13 01	14 06	15♌12
1915	10♈55	12 27	13 59	15 31	17 03	18 34	20 05	21 37	23 08	24 38	26 09	27 39	29 09	00♉39	02 09	03♉38
1916	18♌23	19 07	19 51	20 36	21 23	22 11	23 00	23 50	24 41	25 33	26 26	27 20	28 15	29 10	00♍06	01♍03
1917	27♈03	28 33	00♉03	01 33	03 03	04 33	06 02	07 31	09 00	10 29	11 57	13 26	14 54	16 22	17 49	19♉17
1918	14♍01	14 10	14 22	14 36	14 53	15 13	15 34	15 38	16 25	16 53	17 24	17 56	18 30	19 06	19 44	20♍23
1919	11♉40	13 08	14 36	16 03	17 30	18 57	20 24	21 51	23 17	24 43	26 09	27 35	29 00	00♊26	01 51	03♊16
1920	27♎R22	26 40	25 59	25 21	24 44	24 10	23 39	23 10	22 45	22 22	22 03	21 47	21 34	21 24	21 18	21♎D15
1921	26♉26	27 51	29 15	00♊39	02 03	03 27	04 50	06 14	07 37	09 00	10 23	11 46	13 08	14 30	15 53	17♊15
1922	24♐58	25 06	25 13	25 R16	25 16	25 14	25 08	25 00	24 48	24 33	24 16	23 55	23 32	23 05	22 37	22♐06
1923	10♊06	11 26	12 47	14 08	15 28	16 48	18 09	19 29	20 48	22 08	23 28	24 47	26 07	27 26	28 45	00♋04
1924	03♒41	04 50	05 58	07 06	08 13	09 19	10 25	11 30	12 35	13 39	14 42	15 44	16 46	17 47	18 46	19♒45
1925	24♊19	25 35	26 51	28 08	29♋24	00 40	01 56	03 13	04 28	05 45	07 01	08 17	09 33	10 49	12 05	13♋21
1926	28♒03	29♓29	00 56	02 22	03 49	05 15	06 41	08 07	09 33	10 59	12 25	13 50	15 16	16 41	18 06	19♓31
1927	08♋10	09 21	10 32	11 43	12 55	14 06	15 18	16 29	17 40	18 52	20 04	21 16	22 28	23 41	24 53	26♋05
1928	17♓55	19 26	20 58	22 30	24 00	25 32	27 03	28 34	00♈05	01 35	03 06	04 36	06 07	07 37	09 07	10♈37
1929	23♋32	24 35	25 39	26 42	27 47	28 52	29♌57	01 02	02 08	03 14	04 20	05 27	06 34	07 41	08 48	09♌56
1930	04♈51	06 23	07 55	09 27	10 59	12 31	14 03	15 34	17 05	18 37	20 07	21 38	23 09	24 39	26 09	27♈39
1931	10♌30	11 20	12 11	13 03	13 56	14 50	15 45	16 40	17 36	18 33	19 31	20 29	21 28	22 27	23 28	24♌28
1932	21♈20	22 52	24 23	25 53	27 24	28 54	00♉25	01 55	03 24	04 54	06 23	07 53	09 22	10 50	12 19	13♉47
1933	02♍52	03 18	03 45	04 15	04 46	05 20	05 55	06 31	07 10	07 50	08 31	09 14	09 58	10 44	11 30	12♍19
1934	06♉13	07 42	09 11	10 39	12 08	13 36	15 04	16 31	17 59	19 26	20 53	22 20	23 47	25 13	26 39	28♉05
1935	07♎R56	07 31	07 09	06 50	06 34	06 22	06 13	06 06	06 03	06 04	06 07	06 13	06 22	06 34	06 48	07♎06
1936	21♉12	22 38	24 03	25 29	26 54	28 19	29♊44	01 08	02 33	03 57	05 21	06 45	08 09	09 32	10 56	12♊19
1937	03♐51	03 26	02 57	02 26	01 52	01 16	00 38	29♏59	29 18	28 37	27 55	27 12	26 30	26 48	26 07	24♏28
1938	04♊59	06 21	07 43	09 05	10 27	11 49	13 10	14 32	15 53	17 14	18 35	19 56	21 16	22 37	23 57	25♊18
1939	20♑50	21 43	22 35	23 26	24 16	25 04	25 51	26 36	27 20	28 03	28 44	29 23	30♒00	00 35	01 08	01♒40
1940	19♊13	20 31	21 49	23 07	24 25	25 43	27 01	28 19	29♋36	00 54	02 11	03 29	04 46	06 03	07 20	08♋38
1941	19♒39	21 01	22 23	23 45	25 07	26 28	26 50	29 11	00♓32	01 53	03 13	04 34	05 54	07 13	08 33	09♓52
1942	02♋53	04 07	05 20	06 33	07 47	09 00	10 13	11 27	12 40	13 54	15 08	16 21	17 35	18 49	20 03	21♋16
1943	10♓14	11 45	13 15	14 45	16 15	17 45	19 16	20 45	22 15	23 45	25 15	26 44	28 13	29♈43	01 12	02♈40
1944	23♋15	24 28	25 40	26 53	28 06	29 19	00 32	01 46	02 59	04 13	05 27	06♌41	07 55	09 10	10 24	11♌39
1945	28♓35	00♈07	01 40	03 12	04 44	05 16	07 48	09 19	10 51	12 22	13 53	15 24	16 55	18 25	19 56	21♈26
1946	03♌42	04 38	05 35	06 33	07 31	08 30	09 29	10 29	11 30	12 31	13 32	14 34	15 37	16 40	17 43	18♌47
1947	14♈43	16 15	17 47	19 18	20 49	22 21	23 52	25 22	26 53	28 24	29♉54	01 24	02 54	04 23	05 53	07♉22
1948	23♌35	24 13	24 52	25 32	26 14	26 57	27 42	28 28	29 15	00♍03	00 53	01 43	02 35	03 27	04 20	05♍15
1949	00♉41	02 11	03 41	05 10	06 39	08 08	09 37	11 06	12 34	14 03	15 31	16 58	18 26	19 53	21 21	22♉48
1950	22♍R03	22 00	22 01	22 05	22 11	22 20	22 32	22 46	23 04	23 23	23 45	24 10	24 36	25 05	25 36	26♍09
1951	15♉10	16 37	18 04	19 31	20 57	22 24	23 50	25 16	26 42	28 07	29♊32	00 58	02 23	03 47	05 12	06♊36
1952	10♏R39	09 55	09 10	08 26	07 43	07 00	06 19	05 40	05 02	04 26	03 53	03 23	02 56	02 31	02 10	01♏52
1953	29♉49	01♊13	02 37	04 00	05 23	06 46	08 09	09 32	10 55	12 17	13 39	15 01	16 23	17 45	19 07	20♊28
1954	05♑40	06 08	06 34	06 57	07 18	07 36	07 52	08 06	08 16	08 24	08 30	08 32	08 31	08 27	08 21	08♑11
1955	13♊28	14 48	16 07	17 27	18 47	20 06	21 25	22 45	24 04	25 23	26 42	28 01	29 19	00♋38	01 57	03♋15
1956	10♒08	11 23	12 37	13 51	15 05	16 19	17 32	18 44	19 57	21 08	22 20	23 30	24 41	25 50	26 59	28♒08
1957	27♊43	28 58	00♋14	01 29	02 44	03 59	05 15	06 30	07 45	09 00	10 16	11 31	12 46	14 01	15 16	16♋32
1958	02♓52	04 20	05 49	07 17	08 45	10 13	11 41	13 09	14 37	16 04	17 32	18 59	20 26	21 53	23 20	24♓47
1959	11♋44	12 53	14 03	15 12	16 22	17 32	18 43	19 53	21 04	22 14	23 25	24 36	25 47	26 58	28 09	29♋21
1960	22♓08	23 40	25 12	26 43	28 15	29♈47	01 18	02 49	04 21	05 52	07 23	08 53	10 24	11 54	13 25	14♈55
1961	27♋26	28 26	29 28	00♌30	01 32	02 35	03 38	04 42	05 46	06 50	07 55	09 00	10 06	11 11	12 18	13♌24
1962	08♈44	10 17	11 49	13 21	14 53	16 24	17 56	19 27	20 58	22 29	24 00	25 30	27 01	28 31	00♉01	01♉31
1963	15♌11	15 57	16 45	17 33	18 22	19 12	20 04	20 56	21 49	22 43	23 37	24 33	25 29	26 27	27 24	28♌23
1964	25♈01	26 32	28 03	29♉33	01 03	02 33	04 03	05 33	07 02	08 31	10 00	11 29	12 57	14 26	15 54	17♉22
1965	09♍27	09 43	10 02	10 24	10 47	11 13	11 41	12 11	12 43	13 17	13 52	17 30	15 08	15 49	16 31	17♍14
1966	09♉46	11 14	12 42	14 10	15 37	17 05	18 33	20 00	21 26	22 53	24 20	25 56	27 12	28 38	00♊03	01♊29
1967	19♎R12	18 35	18 01	17 29	17 00	16 34	16 11	15 51	15 34	15 21	15 11	15 04	15 D00	14 59	15 02	15♎07
1968	24♉38	26 03	27 28	28 53	00♊17	01 42	03 06	04 30	05 54	07 17	08 41	10 04	11 27	12 50	14 13	15♊35
1969	16♐R41	16 34	16 25	16 12	15 56	15 37	15 15	14 51	14 23	13 53	13 21	12 47	12 11	11 32	10 53	10♐13
1970	08♊21	09 43	11 04	12 26	13 47	15 08	16 29	17 49	19 10	20 30	21 50	23 10	24 30	25 50	27 10	28♊30
1971	28♑30	29♒33	00 35	01 37	02 37	03 37	04 36	05 34	06 31	07 28	08 23	09 17	10 09	11 01	11 51	12♒40
1972	22♊35	23 52	25 10	26 27	27 44	29 01	00♋18	01 35	02 52	04 08	05 25	06 42	07 58	09 15	10 31	11♋48
1973	24♒56	26 21	27 46	29 11	00♓35	02 00	03 24	04 48	06 12	07 36	09 00	10 24	11 47	13 11	14 34	15♓56
1974	06♋22	07 34	08 46	09 59	11 11	12 23	13 35	14 48	16 00	17 13	18 26	19 38	20 51	22 04	23 17	24♋30
1975	14♓37	16 08	17 39	19 10	20 41	22 12	23 43	25 13	26 44	28 13	29♈45	01 15	02 45	04 15	05 44	07♈14
1976	21♋31	22 36	23 41	24 46	25 52	26 58	28 04	29 11	00♌18	01 25	02 32	03 40	04 48	05 56	07 04	08♌13
1977	02♈35	04 07	05 39	07 12	08 44	10 16	11 47	13 19	14 50	16 22	17 52	19 23	20 54	22 25	23 55	25♈25
1978	07♌59	08 52	09 46	10 40	11 36	12 32	13 29	14 26	15 24	16 23	17 22	18 22	19 23	20 24	21 26	22♌28
1979	18♈29	20 01	21 32	23 04	24 35	26 05	27 36	29 07	00♉37	02 07	03 37	05 07	06 36	08 05	09 34	11♉03
1980	29♌11	29 42	00♍15	00 50	01 26	02 04	02 43	03 24	04 06	04 50	05 35	06 22	07 09	07 58	08 48	09♍39
1981	04♉16	05 45	07 15	08 44	10 12	11 41	13 09	14 38	16 05	17 33	19 01	20 28	21 55	23 22	24 49	26♉15
1982	01♎R08	00 53	00 41	00 32	00 26	00 D23	00 23	00 27	00 33	00 42	00 54	01 09	01 26	01 46	02 08	02♎33
1983	18♉37	20 04	21 30	22 56	24 22	25 48	27 14	28 39	00♊04	01 29	02 54	04 18	05 43	07 07	08 31	09♊54
1984	24♏R20	23 43	23 04	22 23	21 41	20 59	20 15	29 32	18 49	18 06	17 25	16 44	16 05	15 28	14 53	14♏20
1985	03♊12	04 35	05 58	07 21	08 43	10 06	11 28	12 50	14 12	15 33	16 55	18 16	19 38	20 59	22 20	23♊40
1986	15♑05	15 49	16 30	17 11	17 49	18 26	29 00	19 33	20 04	20 33	21 00	21 24	21 46	22 06	22 23	22♑37
1987	16♊49	18 08	19 27	20 46	22 05	23 23	24 42	26 00	27 19	28 37	29♋55	01 13	02 31	03 49	05 07	06♋25
1988	16♒06	17 25	18 44	20 03	21 22	22 41	23 59	25 17	26 35	27 52	29 09	00♓26	01 42	02 58	04 14	05♓29
1989	01♋07	02 21	03 36	04 50	06 04	07 18	08 33	09 47	11 01	12 16	13 30	14 44	15 59	17 13	18 27	19♋42
1990	07♓32	09 02	10 31	12 01	13 30	14 59	16 29	17 58	19 47	40 56	22 25	23 54	25 22	26 51	28 19	29♓47
1991	15♋20	16 28	17 36	18 44	19 52	21 01	22 10	23 19	24 28	25 38	26 47	27 57	29 09	00♌17	01 27	02♌38
1992	26♓14	27 46	29♈19	00 51	02 23	03 54	05 26	06 58	08 29	10 00	11 32	13 02	14 33	16 04	17 34	19♈05
1993	01♌27	02 25	03 24	04 24	05 24	06 24	07 25	08 27	09 29	10 31	11 34	12 38	13 42	14 46	15 51	16♌56
1994	12♈34	14 06	15 38	17 10	18 41	20 13	21 44	23 15	24 46	26 17	27 47	29♉18	00 48	02 18	03 47	05♉17
1995	20♌11	20 52	21 34	22 18	23 03	23 49	24 36	25 25	26 14	27 05	27 56	28 49	29♍42	00 36	01 31	02♍27
1996	28♈40	00♉11	01 41	03 11	04 41	06 10	07 40	09 09	10 38	12 06	13 35	15 03	16 31	17 59	19 47	40♉54
1997	16♍48	16 54	17 03	17 15	17 29	17 46	18 05	18 27	18 51	19 18	19 46	20 16	20 49	21 23	21 59	22♍37
1998	13♉17	14 45	16 12	17 40	19 07	20 34	22 00	23 27	24 53	26 19	27 45	29 11	00♊36	02 01	03 27	04♊51
1999	01♏R46	01 02	00♎19	29 37	28 58	28 20	27 44	27 11	26 41	26 13	25 49	25 27	25 09	24 54	24 43	24♎34
2000	28♉02	29 26	00♊50	02 14	03 38	05 02	06 26	07 49	09 12	10 35	11 58	13 20	14 43	16 05	17 27	18♊49

June

	1st	3rd	5th	7th	9th	11th	13th	15th	17th	19th	21st	23rd	25th	27th	29th
1900	10♉53	12 21	13 49	15 17	16 45	18 12	19 40	21 07	22 33	24 00	25 26	26 52	28 18	29♊43	01♊09
1901	08♍08	09 02	09 56	10 51	11 47	12 44	13 42	14 40	15 40	16 40	17 41	18 42	19 44	20 47	21♍51
1902	25♉22	26 48	28 14	29♊40	01 05	02 31	03 56	05 21	06 45	08 10	09 34	10 58	12 21	13 45	15♊08
1903	00♎18	00 48	01 21	01 55	02 31	03 09	03 49	04 30	05 13	05 57	06 43	07 31	08 20	09 10	10♎02
1904	09♊43	11 07	12 30	13 53	15 16	16 38	18 01	19 23	20 45	22 07	23 29	24 51	26 12	27 33	28♊54
1905	10♏R09	09 44	09 22	09 03	08 48	08 36	08 27	08 22	08 D20	08 21	08 22	08 28	08 37	08 49	09♏04
1906	22♊45	24 06	25 27	26 47	28 07	29♋27	00 47	02 07	03 27	04 46	06 06	07 25	08 44	10 04	11♋23
1907	18♑47	18 52	18 R54	18 53	18 49	18 41	18 31	18 18	18 02	17 43	17 22	16 58	16 31	16 03	15♑32
1908	06♋07	07 24	08 42	10 00	11 17	12 34	13 52	15 09	16 26	17 43	19 01	20 18	21 35	22 51	24♋08
1909	03♓44	04 57	06 10	07 22	08 34	09 45	10 55	12 04	13 13	14 21	15 28	16 34	17 39	18 43	19♓46
1910	18♋43	19 57	21 12	22 26	23 41	24 56	26 10	27 25	28 40	29♌55	01 09	02 24	03 39	04 54	06♌09
1911	28♓37	00♈04	01 31	02 58	04 25	05 52	07 18	08 44	10 10	11 36	13 01	14 26	15 50	17 15	18♈39
1912	02♌09	03 20	04 31	05 43	06 54	08 06	09 17	10 29	11 41	12 53	14 05	15 18	16 30	17 43	18♌55
1913	18♈06	19 36	21 06	22 35	24 04	25 33	27 02	28 31	29♉59	01 27	02 55	04 22	05 49	07 16	08♉43
1914	15♌45	16 51	17 57	19 04	20 11	21 18	22 26	23 34	24 42	25 51	27 00	28 09	29 18	00♍28	01♍38
1915	04♉23	05 52	07 21	08 50	10 18	11 47	13 15	14 42	16 10	17 37	19 04	20 31	21 58	23 24	24♉50
1916	01♍32	02 30	03 29	04 29	05 29	06 30	07 32	08 34	09 37	10 40	11 44	12 48	13 53	14 59	16♍05
1917	20♉00	21 28	22 54	24 21	25 48	27 14	28 40	00♊05	01 31	02 56	04 21	05 46	07 11	08 35	09♊59
1918	20♍44	21 26	22 09	22 54	23 40	24 27	25 16	26 06	26 57	27 50	28 43	29♎38	00 33	01 30	02♎27
1919	03♊58	05 23	06 47	08 11	09 35	10 59	12 22	13 46	15 09	16 32	17 55	19 17	20 40	22 02	23♊24
1920	21♎15	21 16	21 21	21 29	21 40	21 53	22 09	22 29	22 50	23 15	23 41	24 11	24 42	25 16	25♎51
1921	17♊56	19 17	20 39	22 00	23 22	24 43	26 04	27 25	28 45	00♋06	01 26	02 46	04 06	05 26	06♋46
1922	21♐R49	21 15	20 40	20 02	19 24	18 45	18 06	17 27	16 48	16 09	15 32	14 56	14 22	13 50	13♐20
1923	00♋44	02 03	03 22	04 40	05 59	07 17	08 36	09 54	11 13	12 31	13 49	15 07	16 25	17 42	19♋00
1924	20♒14	21 11	22 06	23 01	23 54	24 46	25 37	26 26	27 13	27 59	28 43	29 26	00♓06	00 45	01♓21
1925	13♋59	15 15	16 30	17 46	19 02	20 18	21 34	22 49	24 05	25 21	26 36	27 52	29 08	00♌23	01♌39
1926	20♓13	21 38	23 02	24 26	25 49	27 13	28 36	29♈59	01 21	02 43	04 04	05 26	06 46	08 07	09♈26
1927	26♋41	27 54	29 06	00♌19	01 32	02 44	03 57	05 10	06 23	07 36	08 50	10 03	11 16	12 30	13♌43
1928	11♈21	12 51	14 20	15 49	17 18	18 47	20 15	21 44	23 11	24 39	26 07	27 34	29 00	00♉27	01♉53
1929	10♌30	11 38	12 47	13 55	15 04	16 13	17 23	18 33	19 42	20 53	22 03	23 13	24 24	25 35	26♌46
1930	28♈24	29♉54	01 23	02 53	04 22	05 50	07 19	08 47	10 15	11 43	13 10	14 38	16 05	17 32	18♉58
1931	24♌59	26 00	27 03	28 05	29 08	00♍12	01 16	02 21	03 26	04 32	05 38	06 44	07 51	08 58	10♍06
1932	14♉31	15 59	17 27	18 55	20 22	21 49	23 16	24 42	26 09	27 35	29 01	00♊26	01 52	03 17	04♊42
1933	12♍43	13 33	14 24	15 16	16 09	17 03	17 58	18 54	19 51	20 48	21 47	22 46	23 46	24 47	25♍49
1934	28♉48	00♊14	01 39	03 04	04 29	05 54	07 19	08 43	10 07	11 31	12 55	14 18	15 42	17 05	18♊28
1935	07♎15	07 36	08 00	08 26	08 54	09 24	09 57	10 32	11 08	11 46	12 27	13 08	13 52	14 37	15♎24
1936	13♊00	14 23	15 46	17 08	18 31	19 53	21 15	22 37	23 58	25 20	26 41	28 02	29♋23	00 44	02♋05
1937	24♏R08	23 31	22 55	22 22	21 51	21 23	20 58	20 36	20 17	20 01	19 49	19 40	19 34	19 D32	19♏33
1938	25♊58	27 18	28 38	29♋58	01 17	02 37	03 56	05 16	06 35	07 54	09 13	10 32	11 50	13 09	14♋28
1939	01♒55	02 23	02 49	03 12	03 33	03 51	04 07	04 20	04 30	04 37	04 41	04 42	04 41	04 36	04♒28
1940	09♋16	10 33	11 50	13 07	14 24	15 41	16 58	18 15	19 31	20 48	22 05	23 21	24 38	25 54	27♋10
1941	10♓31	11 50	13 08	14 26	15 43	17 00	18 16	19 32	20 48	22 03	23 17	24 30	25 43	26 56	28♓07
1942	21♋53	23 07	24 21	25 35	26 49	28 03	29 17	00♌31	01 45	02 59	04 14	05 28	06 42	07 57	09♌11
1943	03♈25	04 53	06 22	07 50	09 18	10 46	12 13	13 40	15 07	16 34	18 00	19 27	20 52	22 18	23♈43
1944	05♌27	06 37	07 47	08 57	10 08	11 19	12 30	13 41	14 52	15 03	17 15	18 27	19 38	20 50	22♌03
1945	22♈11	23 41	25 11	26 40	28 09	29 39	01♉07	02 36	04 04	05 32	07 00	08 28	09 55	11 22	12♉49
1946	19♌19	20 24	21 29	22 34	23 40	24 46	25 53	27 00	28 07	29 14	00♍22	01 31	02 39	03 48	04♍57
1947	08♉06	09 35	11 04	12 32	14 00	15 28	16 56	18 23	19 51	21 18	22 44	24 11	25 37	27 03	28♉29
1948	05♍42	06 38	07 34	08 31	09 29	10 28	11 27	12 28	13 29	14 30	15 32	16 35	17 39	18 43	19♍47
1949	23♉31	24 58	26 24	27 50	29 16	00♊42	02 07	03 33	04 58	06 22	07 47	09 11	10 36	12 00	13♊23
1950	26♍26	27 02	27 39	28 18	28 59	29♎42	00 25	01 11	01 58	02 46	03 36	04 26	05 19	06 12	07♎06
1951	07♊18	08 42	10 06	11 30	12 53	14 17	15 40	17 02	18 25	19 48	21 10	22 32	23 54	25 16	26♊37
1952	01♏R44	01 30	01 20	01 14	01 D10	01 10	01 13	01 19	01 28	01 41	01 56	02 13	02 34	02 57	03♏23
1953	21♊09	22 30	23 51	25 12	26 32	27 53	29 13	00♋34	01 54	03 14	04 34	05 54	07 13	08 33	09♋52
1954	08♑R05	07 50	07 33	07 13	06 50	06 25	05 57	05 27	04 55	04 21	03 46	03 10	02 33	01 56	01♑19
1955	03♋54	05 12	06 31	07 49	09 07	10 25	11 42	13 00	14 18	15 36	16 53	18 11	19 28	20 45	22♋03
1956	28♒42	29♓49	00 56	02 02	03 07	04 11	05 14	06 16	07 17	08 17	09 16	10 14	11 10	12 05	12♓59
1957	17♋09	18 24	19 40	20 55	22 10	23 25	24 40	25 55	27 10	28 26	29♌41	00 56	02 11	03 26	04♌42
1958	25♓30	26 56	28 23	29♈49	01 14	02 40	04 05	05 30	06 55	08 19	09 43	11 07	12 30	13 53	15♈15
1959	29♍56	01 08	02 20	03 32	04 44	05 56	07 08	08 20	09 32	10 45	11 58	13 10	14 23	15 36	16♎49
1960	15♈40	17 10	18 39	20 08	21 38	23 06	24 35	26 04	27 32	29 00	00♉28	01 55	03 22	04 49	06♉16
1961	13♌57	15 04	16 12	17 19	18 27	19 35	20 44	21 52	23 01	24 11	25 20	26 30	27 40	28 50	00♍01
1962	02♉16	03 45	05 14	06 43	08 12	09 41	11 09	12 37	14 05	15 32	17 00	18 27	19 53	21 20	22♉46
1963	28♌53	29♍52	00 52	01 53	02 55	03 57	04 59	06 02	07 06	08 10	09 15	10 20	11 25	12 32	13♍38
1964	18♉06	19 33	21 00	22 28	23 54	25 21	26 48	28 14	29♊40	01 05	02 31	03 56	05 21	06 46	08♊10
1965	17♊37	18 22	19 09	19 57	20 47	21 37	22 29	23 22	24 16	25 10	26 06	27 03	28 01	28 59	29♊59
1966	02♎11	03 36	05 01	06 26	07 50	09 15	10 39	12 03	13 26	14 50	16 13	17 36	18 59	20 22	21♎44
1967	15♊11	15 21	15 34	15 49	16 07	16 28	16 52	17 18	17 46	18 16	18♋49	19 24	20 00	20 39	21♋20
1968	16♐R16	17 39	19 01	20 23	21 44	23 06	24 27	25 49	27 10	28 31	29 52	01 12	02 33	03 53	05♐13
1969	09♈53	09 12	08 31	07 51	07 11	06 32	05 54	05 18	04 45	04 13	03 44	03 18	02 55	02 35	02♈18
1970	29♊09	00 29	01 48	03 08	04 27	05 46	07 05	08 23	09 42	11 01	12 19	13 37	14 56	16 14	17♊32
1971	13♒03	13 50	14 35	15 18	16 00	16 40	17 18	17 54	18 28	19 00	19 29	19 56	20 20	20 42	21♒01
1972	12♋26	13 43	14 59	16 15	17 32	18 48	20 04	21 20	22 37	23 53	25 09	26 25	27 41	28 57	00♌13
1973	16♓38	18 00	19 22	20 44	22 05	23 26	24 47	26 07	27 27	28 46	00♈05	01 24	02 42	03 59	05♈16
1974	25♋06	26 19	27 33	28 46	29♌59	01 12	02 26	03 39	04 53	06 06	07 20	08 34	09 48	11 02	12♌16
1975	07♈59	09 28	10 57	12 26	13 55	15 23	16 51	18 19	19 47	21 14	22 42	24 08	25 35	27 01	28♈27
1976	08♌48	09 57	11 06	12 15	13 25	14 35	15 45	16 55	18 06	19 16	20 27	21 38	22 49	24 01	25♌13
1977	26♈10	27 40	29 10	00♉39	02 08	03 37	05 06	06 35	08 03	09 31	10 59	12 26	13 53	15 20	16♉47
1978	22♌59	24 02	25 05	26 09	27 14	28 18	29 24	00♍29	01 35	02 42	03 49	04 56	06 04	07 11	08♍20
1979	11♉47	13 16	14 44	16 12	17 40	19 07	20 35	22 02	23 29	24 55	26 22	27 48	29 14	00♊39	02♊05
1980	10♍05	10 57	11 51	12 45	13 40	14 36	15 33	16 31	17 30	18 30	19 30	20 31	21 32	22 35	23♍38
1981	26♉58	28 24	29♊50	01 16	02 41	04 07	05 32	06 57	08 21	09 46	11 10	12 34	13 57	15 21	16♊44
1982	02♎46	03 14	03 44	04 16	04 51	05 27	06 05	06 44	07 26	08 09	08 53	09 39	10 27	11 16	12♎06
1983	10♊36	12 00	13 23	14 46	16 09	17 32	18 54	20 17	21 39	23 01	24 23	25 44	27 06	28 27	29♋48
1984	14♏R05	13 37	13 11	12 49	12 29	12 13	12 01	11 51	11 45	11 D42	11 43	11 46	11 53	12 03	12♏16
1985	24♊21	25 41	27 02	28 22	29♋42	01 02	02 22	03 42	05 02	06 21	07 41	09 00	10 19	11 38	12♋57
1986	22♑43	22 53	23 01	23 R05	23 07	23 05	23 01	22 53	22 43	22 29	22 13	21 54	21 32	21 08	20♑42
1987	07♋04	08 21	09 39	10 56	12 14	13 31	14 48	16 06	17 23	18 40	19 57	21 14	22 31	23 48	25♋05
1988	06♓07	07 21	08 35	09 49	11 02	12 14	13 26	14 37	15 47	16 57	18 06	19 14	20 21	21 27	22♓32
1989	20♋19	21 34	22 48	24 03	25 17	26 32	27 46	29 01	00♌15	01 30	02 45	03 59	05 14	06 29	07♌43
1990	00♈31	01 59	03 26	04 54	06 21	07 48	09 14	10 41	12 07	13 33	14 59	16 24	17 49	19 14	20♈38
1991	03♌13	04 24	05 35	06 45	07 57	09 08	10 19	11 31	12 43	13 54	15 06	16 19	17 31	18 43	19♌56
1992	19♈50	21 20	22 50	24 19	25 48	27 17	28 46	00♉15	01 43	03 11	04 39	06 07	07 34	09 01	10♉28
1993	17♌28	18 34	19 40	20 46	21 53	23 00	24 07	25 15	26 23	27 31	28 40	29♍49	00 58	02 08	03♍17
1994	06♉02	07 31	09 00	10 28	11 57	13 25	14 53	16 21	17 49	19 16	20 43	22 10	23 36	25 03	26♉29
1995	02♍56	03 53	04 51	05 49	06 49	07 49	08 49	09 51	10 53	11 55	12 58	14 02	15 06	16 11	17♍16
1996	21♉38	23 05	24 32	25 58	27 25	28 51	00♊17	01 42	03 08	04 33	05 58	07 23	08 48	10 12	11♊36
1997	22♍56	23 36	24 18	25 02	25 47	26 33	27 20	28 09	28 59	29♎51	00 43	01 37	02 32	03 27	04♎24
1998	05♊34	06 58	08 23	09 47	11 11	12 34	13 58	15 21	16 44	18 07	19 30	20 53	22 15	23 37	24♊59
1999	24♎R31	24 D28	24 27	24 30	24 36	24 44	24 56	25 11	25 28	25 49	26 11	26 37	27 05	27 35	28♎07
2000	19♊30	20 52	22 13	23 35	24 56	26 17	27 38	28 59	00♋19	01 40	03 00	04 20	05 40	07 00	03♋20

Mars

July

	1st	3rd	5th	7th	9th	11th	13th	15th	17th	19th	21st	23rd	25th	27th	29th	31st
1900	02♊34	03 58	05 23	06 47	08 11	09 35	10 58	12 22	13 44	15 07	16 29	17 52	19 13	20 35	21 56	23♊17
1901	22♍55	24 00	25 05	26 11	27 17	28 24	29♎32	00 40	01 48	02 58	04 07	05 17	06 28	07 39	08 50	10♎02
1902	16♊31	17 54	19 17	20 39	22 02	23 24	24 46	26 07	27 29	28 50	00♋11	01 31	02 52	04 12	05 32	06♋52
1903	10♎54	11 48	12 44	13 40	14 37	15 36	16 35	17 35	18 37	19 39	20 42	21 46	22 51	23 56	25 03	26♎10
1904	00♋15	01 36	02 57	04 17	05 37	06 57	08 17	09 37	10 57	12 16	13 36	14 55	16 14	17 33	18 51	20♋10
1905	09♏32	09 54	10 19	10 46	11 16	11 48	12 23	13 00	13 39	14 20	15 02	15 47	16 34	17♌22	18 12	19♌04
1906	12♋41	14 00	15 19	16 37	17 56	19 14	20 32	21 50	23 08	24 26	25 44	27 02	28 20	29 37	00 55	02♑12
1907	15♑R00	14 27	13 52	13 17	12 42	12 06	11 31	10 57	10 24	09 53	09 24	08 57	08 32	08 10	07 50	07♑34
1908	25♋25	26 42	27 59	29 15	00♌32	01 49	03 05	04 22	05 38	06 55	08 11	09 28	10 44	12 01	13 17	14♌33
1909	20♓48	21 49	22 49	23 47	24 44	25 39	26 33	27 26	28 16	29 05	29♈52	00 37	01 20	02 00	02 39	03♈15
1910	07♌23	08 38	09 53	11 08	12 23	13 38	14 54	16 09	17 24	18 39	19 54	21 10	22 25	23 41	24 56	25♌12
1911	20♈02	21 25	22 47	24 10	25 31	26 52	28 13	29♉33	00 53	02 12	03 31	04 49	06 06	07 23	08 38	09♉54
1912	20♌08	21 21	22 34	23 48	25 01	26 14	27 28	28 42	29♍56	01 10	02 24	03 38	04 53	06 07	07 22	08♍37
1913	10♉09	11 35	13 01	14 27	15 52	17 16	18 41	20 05	21 28	22 52	24 15	25 37	26 59	28 21	29♊42	01♊03
1914	02♍48	03 59	05 10	06 21	07 32	08 44	09 55	11 08	12 20	13 32	14 45	15 58	17 12	18 25	19 39	20♍53
1915	26♉16	27 41	29♊06	00 31	01 56	03 20	04 44	05 08	07 32	08 55	10 18	11 40	13 03	14 25	15 47	17♊08
1916	17♍11	18 18	19 26	20 33	21 42	22 51	24 00	25 09	26 20	27 30	28 41	29♎52	01 04	02 16	03 28	04♎41
1917	11♊23	12 47	14 10	15 34	16 57	18 19	19 42	21 04	22 26	23 48	25 10	26 31	27 52	29 13	00♋34	01♋54
1918	03♎26	04 25	05 26	06 27	07 29	08 31	09 35	10 39	11 44	12 50	13 56	15 04	16 11	17 20	18 29	19♎38
1919	24♊46	26 08	27 29	28 50	00♋11	01 32	02 53	04 14	05 34	06 54	08 14	09 34	10 54	12 13	13 33	14♋52
1920	26♎29	27 09	27 50	28 34	29 19	00♏06	00 54	01 44	02 36	03 29	04 23	05 19	06 16	07 14	08 13	09♏14
1921	08♋06	09 26	10 45	12 04	13 23	14 42	16 01	17 20	18 38	19 57	21 15	22 34	23 52	25 10	26 28	27♋46
1922	12♐R53	12 28	12 07	11 49	11 33	11 22	11 13	11D08	11 06	11 08	11 13	11 21	11 32	11 47	12 04	12♐25
1923	20♋18	21 35	22 53	24 10	25 27	26 45	28 02	29 19	00♌36	01 53	03 10	04 27	05 44	07 01	08 18	09♌35
1924	01♓55	02 27	02 56	03 23	03 47	04 09	04 28	04 44	04 57	05 07	05 14	05R18	05 19	05 16	05 10	05♓02
1925	02♌55	04 11	05 26	06 42	07 57	09 13	10 29	11 45	13 00	14 16	15 32	16 47	18 03	19 19	20 35	21♌51
1926	10♈46	12 05	13 23	14 40	15 57	17 14	18 29	19 44	20 58	22 12	23 24	24 36	25 47	26 57	28 06	29♈14
1927	14♌57	16 11	17 25	18 38	19 53	21 07	22 21	23 35	24 49	26 04	27 18	28 33	29♍48	01 03	02 18	03♍33
1928	03♉19	04 45	06 10	07 35	08 59	10 23	11 47	13 10	14 33	15 56	17 18	18 40	20 01	21 22	22 42	24♉01
1929	27♌57	29 09	00♍21	01 33	02 45	03 58	05 10	06 23	07 36	08 49	10 03	11 16	12 30	13 44	14 58	16♍12
1930	20♉24	21 50	23 16	24 41	26 06	27 31	28 55	00♊19	01 43	03 07	04 30	05 53	07 16	08 38	10 00	11♊21
1931	11♍14	12 22	13 31	14 40	15 50	17 00	18 10	19 21	20 32	21 43	22 55	24 07	25 19	26 32	27 45	28♍38
1932	06♊06	07 31	08 55	10 19	11 43	13 06	14 29	15 52	17 15	18 37	19 59	21 21	22 43	24 04	25 25	27♊35
1933	26♍51	27 55	28 58	00♎03	01 08	02 13	03 20	04 27	05 34	06 42	07 51	09 00	10 09	11 20	12 30	13♎42
1934	19♊50	21 13	22 35	23 57	25 19	26 41	28 02	29♋24	00 45	02 06	03 26	04 47	06 07	07 27	08 47	10♋06
1935	16♎12	17 02	17 53	18 45	19 39	20 34	21 30	22 27	23 25	24 25	25 25	26 26	27 29	28 32	29♏36	00♏42
1936	03♋25	04 45	06 06	07 26	08 45	10 05	11 25	12 44	14 04	15 23	16 42	18 01	19 19	20 38	21 56	23♋15
1937	19♏37	19 44	19 55	20 09	20 25	20 45	21 07	21 32	22 00	22 31	23 04	23 39	24 16	24 56	25 38	26♏22
1938	15♋46	17 04	18 23	19 41	20 59	22 17	23 34	24 52	26 10	27 28	28 45	00♌03	01 20	02 37	03 55	05♌12
1939	04♒R17	04 04	03 47	03 28	03 06	02 42	02 16	01 47	01 17	00 46	00♑13	29 40	29 07	28 34	28 01	27♑30
1940	28♋27	29♌43	01 00	02 16	03 32	04 49	06 05	07 21	08 37	09 54	11 10	12 26	13 42	14 58	16 14	17♌31
1941	29♓17	00♈27	01 36	02 44	03 51	04 57	06 02	07 06	08 08	09 09	10 09	11 08	12 05	13 00	13 54	14♈46
1942	10♌25	11 40	12 54	14 09	15 24	16 38	17 53	19 08	20 23	21 38	22 53	24 08	25 23	26 38	27 54	29♌09
1943	25♈08	26 32	27 56	29♉20	00 43	02 06	03 28	04 50	06 12	07 32	08 53	10 13	11 32	12 51	14 09	15♉27
1944	23♌15	24 28	25 40	26 53	28 06	29 19	00♍32	01 46	02 59	04 13	05 27	06 41	07 55	09 10	10 24	11♍39
1945	14♉15	15 41	17 07	18 33	19 58	21 23	22 47	24 12	25 36	26 59	28 22	29♊45	01 07	02 30	03 51	05♊13
1946	06♍07	07 17	08 27	09 37	10 48	11 59	13 10	14 22	15 34	16 46	17 58	19 11	20 14	21 37	22 51	24♍05
1947	29♉54	01♊19	02 44	04 09	05 33	06 58	08 22	09 45	11 09	12 32	13 54	15 17	16 39	18 01	19 23	20♊44
1948	20♍52	21 58	23 04	24 11	25 18	26 26	27 35	28 43	29♎53	01 02	02 12	03 23	04 34	05 45	06 57	08♎10
1949	14♊47	16 10	17 33	18 56	20 19	21 41	23 03	24 25	25 47	27 08	28 30	29♋51	01 12	02 32	03 53	05♋13
1950	08♎02	08 58	09 56	10 54	11 54	12 54	13 55	14 57	16 00	17 04	18 09	19 14	20 21	21 28	22 35	23♎44
1951	27♊59	29♋20	00 41	02 02	03 23	04 43	06 04	07 24	08 44	10 04	11 23	12 43	14 02	15 21	16 40	17♋59
1952	03♏52	04 22	04 56	05 31	06 08	06 48	07 29	08 12	08 57	09 44	10 33	11 23	12 15	13 08	14 04	14♏59
1953	11♋11	12 30	13 49	15 08	16 27	17 46	19 04	20 23	21 41	22 59	24 17	25 35	26 53	28 11	29♌29	00♋46
1954	00♑R42	00♐06	29 30	28 57	28 25	27 55	27 28	27 04	26 42	26 23	26 07	25 54	25 45	25 38	25D36	25♐36
1955	23♋20	24 37	25 54	27 11	28 28	29♌45	01 02	02 19	03 36	04 52	06 09	07 26	08 42	09 59	11 16	12♌32
1956	13♓51	14 42	15 31	16 18	17 03	17 47	18 28	19 07	19 44	20 19	20 51	21 21	21 48	22 13	22 34	22♓53
1957	05♌57	07 12	08 27	09 43	10 58	12 13	13 29	14 44	15 59	17 15	18 30	19 46	21 01	22 17	23 33	24♌48
1958	16♈37	17 59	19 20	20 40	22 00	23 20	24 39	25 57	27 15	28 32	29♉49	01 05	02 20	03 34	04 47	06♉00
1959	18♌02	19 15	20 29	21 42	22 56	24 10	25 24	26 38	27 52	29 06	00♍20	01 34	02 49	04 04	05 18	06♍33
1960	07♉42	09 08	10 33	11 59	13 24	14 48	16 12	17 36	19 00	20 23	21 46	23 08	24 30	25 51	27 12	28♉33
1961	01♍11	02 22	03 34	04 45	05 47	07 09	08 21	09 33	10 46	11 59	13 12	14 25	15 39	16 52	18 06	19♍20
1962	24♉12	25 38	27 04	28 29	29♊54	01 18	02 43	04 07	05 30	06 54	08 17	09 40	11 02	12 24	13 46	15♊08
1963	14♍45	15 53	17 01	18 09	19 18	20 27	21 36	22 46	23 57	25 07	26 18	27 30	28 42	29♎54	01 07	02♎19
1964	09♊35	10 59	12 22	13 46	15 09	16 33	17 55	19 18	20 40	22 02	23 24	24 46	26 07	27 28	28 49	00♋10
1965	00♎59	02 00	03 02	04 05	05 08	06 12	07 17	08 22	09 28	10 35	11 43	12 51	13 59	15 08	16 18	17♎29
1966	23♊06	24 28	25 50	27 12	28 33	29♋55	01 16	02 37	03 57	05 18	06 38	07 58	09 18	10 38	11 58	13♋17
1967	22♎02	22 46	23 31	24 19	25 08	25 58	26 50	27 43	28 37	29♏33	00 30	01 28	02 27	03 28	04 29	05♏32
1968	06♋33	07 54	09 13	10 33	11 52	13 11	14 31	15 50	17 09	18 27	19 46	21 05	22 23	23 41	25 00	26♋18
1969	02♐R04	01 53	01 46	01D43	01 42	01 45	01 51	02 01	02 13	02 29	02 48	03 10	03 34	04 02	04 32	05♐04
1970	18♋50	20 08	21 26	22 43	24 01	25 19	26 36	27 54	29 11	00♌28	01 46	03 03	04 20	05 37	06 54	08♌11
1971	21♒18	21 32	21 43	21 51	21 55	21 57	21 56	21 52	21 45	21 34	21 21	21 05	20 46	20 24	20 00	19♒35
1972	01♌29	02 45	04 01	05 17	06 33	07 49	09 05	10 21	11 37	12 53	14 09	15 25	16 41	17 56	19 12	20♌28
1973	06♈33	07 48	09 03	10 17	11 31	12 44	13 56	15 07	16 19	17 26	18 35	19 42	20 48	21 53	22 57	23♈59
1974	13♌30	14 44	15 58	17 12	18 26	19 41	20 55	22 10	23 24	24 39	25 54	27 09	28 24	29♍39	00 54	02♍09
1975	29♈53	01♉18	02 44	04 08	05 32	06 56	08 20	09 43	11 05	12 27	13 49	15 10	16 31	17 51	19 11	20♈30
1976	26♌24	27 36	28 49	00♍01	01 13	02 26	03 39	04 52	06 05	07 19	08 32	09 46	11 00	12 14	13 28	14♍43
1977	18♉13	19 39	21 05	22 30	23 56	25 21	26 45	28 10	29♊34	00 57	02 20	03 43	05 06	06 28	07 50	09♊11
1978	09♍28	10 38	11 47	12 57	14 07	15 17	16 28	17 39	18 50	20 02	21 14	22 26	23 39	24 52	26 05	27♍18
1979	03♊30	04 55	06 19	07 44	09 08	10 32	11 55	13 19	14 42	16 05	17 27	18 49	20 11	21 33	22 55	24♊16
1980	24♍41	25 46	26 50	27 56	29 02	00♎08	01 16	02 23	03 32	04 40	05 50	06 59	08 10	09 21	10 32	11♎43
1981	18♊07	19 30	20 53	22 15	23 38	25 00	26 21	27 43	29 04	00♋26	01 47	03 07	04 28	05 48	07 08	08♋28
1982	12♎58	13 51	14 45	15 40	16 37	17 34	18 33	19 32	20 33	21 34	22 37	23 40	24 44	25 49	26 55	28♎02
1983	01♋09	02 30	03 51	05 11	06 32	07 52	09 12	10 32	11 51	13 11	14 30	15 49	17 09	18 27	19 46	21♋05
1984	12♏32	12 50	13 12	13 37	14 04	14 33	15 05	15 39	16 16	16 54	17 35	18 18	19 02	19 49	20 37	21♏27
1985	14♋16	15 34	16 53	18 11	19 30	20 48	22 06	23 24	24 42	26 00	27 18	28 36	29♌53	01 11	02 28	03♌46
1986	20♑R13	19 42	19 10	18 37	18 02	17 27	16 52	16 18	15 43	15 10	14 38	14 08	13 39	13 13	12 49	12♑28
1987	26♋21	27 38	28 55	00♌12	01 28	02 45	04 01	05 18	06 34	07 51	09 07	10 24	11 40	12 56	14 13	15♌29
1988	23♓36	24 39	25 42	26 42	27 42	28 40	29♈37	00 32	01 26	02 18	03 08	03 56	04 43	05 28	06 10	06♈50
1989	08♌58	10 13	11 28	12 43	13 58	15 13	16 28	17 43	18 58	20 13	21 28	22 44	23 59	25 14	26 30	27♌45
1990	22♈02	23 25	24 48	26 11	27 33	28 54	00♉16	01 36	02 57	04 16	05 36	06 54	08 12	09 29	10 46	12♉02
1991	21♌08	22 21	23 34	24 47	26 00	27 14	28 27	29♍41	00 54	02 08	03 22	04 36	05 51	07 05	08 20	09♍34
1992	11♉55	13 21	14 47	16 12	17 37	19 02	20 27	21 51	23 15	24 38	26 01	27 24	28 47	00♊09	01 30	02♊51
1993	04♍28	05 38	06 48	07 59	09 10	10 22	11 33	12 45	13 58	15 10	16 23	17 36	18 49	20 02	21 16	22♍30
1994	27♉54	29♊20	00 46	02 10	03 35	04 59	06 24	07 48	09 11	10 34	11 57	13 20	14 42	16 05	17 26	18♉48
1995	18♍22	19 28	20 36	21 43	22 50	23 59	25 07	26 16	27 26	28 36	29♎46	00 57	02 08	03 20	04 32	05♎44
1996	13♊00	14 24	15 47	17 10	18 33	19 56	21 19	22 42	24 03	25 25	26 46	28 08	29♋29	00 50	02 10	03♋31
1997	05♎22	06 20	07 20	08 20	09 21	10 24	11 27	12 30	13 35	14 40	15 46	16 52	18 00	19 08	20 16	21♎25
1998	26♊21	27 43	29 04	00♋25	01 46	03 07	04 28	05 49	07 09	08 29	09 49	11 09	12 29	13 48	15 07	16♋27
1999	28♎42	29 18	29♏57	00 37	01 20	02 04	02 50	03 37	04 27	05 17	06 10	07 04	07 59	08 55	09 53	10♏52
2000	09♋40	10 59	12 18	13 38	14 57	16 16	17 35	18 53	20 12	21 30	22 49	24 07	25 25	26 43	28 01	29♋19

August

Year	1st	3rd	5th	7th	9th	11th	13th	15th	17th	19th	21st	23rd	25th	27th	29th	31st
1900	23♊58	25 18	26 39	27 59	29 18	00♋38	01 57	03 16	04 34	05 52	07 10	08 28	09 45	11 02	12 19	13♋35
1901	10♎38	11 51	13 04	14 17	15 31	16 46	18 00	19 15	20 31	21 47	23 03	24 20	25 37	26 54	28 12	29♎30
1902	04♋32	08 52	10 11	11 30	12 49	14 08	15 27	16 45	18 03	19 21	20 39	21 56	23 13	24 30	25 47	27♋04
1903	26♎44	27 52	29 01	00♏11	01 21	02 33	03 44	04 57	06 10	07 23	08 37	09 52	11 07	12 23	13 40	14♏57
1904	20♋49	22 07	23 26	24 44	26 02	27 19	28 37	29♌55	01 12	02 29	03 46	05 03	06 20	07 37	08 53	10♌10
1905	19♏31	20 25	21 21	22 18	23 16	24 16	25 17	26 19	27 23	28 27	29♐33	00 40	01 47	02 56	04 06	05♐17
1906	02♌51	04 08	05 25	06 42	07 59	09 16	10 33	11 50	13 07	14 24	15 40	16 57	18 13	19 30	20 46	22♌03
1907	07♑R27	07 15	07 06	07 01	06 D59	07 00	07 05	07 13	07 25	07 40	07 57	08 18	08 42	09 09	09 38	10♑10
1908	15♌12	16 28	17 44	19 01	20 17	21 33	22 50	24 06	25 22	26 38	27 55	29 11	00♍28	01 44	03 00	04♍17
1909	03♈32	04 04	04 34	05 01	05 26	05 47	06 05	06 20	06 32	06 41	06 46	06 R48	06 46	06 41	06 33	06♈22
1910	26♌49	28 05	29 21	00♍36	01 52	03 08	04 24	05 40	06 56	08 12	09 28	10 45	12 01	13 18	14 34	15♍51
1911	10♉31	11 45	12 58	14 10	15 22	16 33	17 42	18 51	19 59	21 06	22 11	23 16	24 19	25 21	26 21	27♉21
1912	15♍31	17 59	20 27	22 55	25 23	27 51	00 19	02 48	05 16	07 44	10 12	12 40	15 08	17 37	20 05	22♍33
1913	01♊44	03 04	04 24	05 48	07 02	08 20	09 38	10 55	12 19	13 28	14 44	15 59	17 14	18 47	19 41	20♊54
1914	21♍30	22 45	23 59	25 14	26 29	27 44	29 00	00♌16	01 32	02 48	04 04	05 21	06 38	07 55	09 13	10♌30
1915	17♊49	19 10	02 30	21 50	23 10	24 30	25 49	27 08	28 27	29♋45	01 03	02 21	03 38	04 54	06 11	07♋27
1916	05♎18	06 31	07 45	08 59	10 13	11 28	12 43	13 59	15 14	16 31	17 47	19 04	20 21	21 39	22 57	24♎15
1917	02♋34	03 54	05 14	06 33	07 53	09 12	10 31	11 49	13 08	14 26	15 44	17 01	18 19	19 36	20 53	22♋09
1918	20♎13	21 24	22 35	23 47	24 59	26 12	27 25	28 39	29♏53	01 08	02 24	03 40	04 56	06 13	07 30	08♏48
1919	15♋31	16 50	18 09	19 27	20 46	22 04	23 22	24 40	25 58	27 15	28 33	29♌50	01 07	02 24	03 41	04♌57
1920	09♏45	10 47	11 50	12 55	14 00	15 06	16 13	17 22	18 31	19 40	20 51	22 03	23 15	24 28	25 42	26♏57
1921	28♋25	29♌42	01 00	02 17	03 35	04 52	06 09	07 26	08 43	10 00	11 17	12 34	13 50	15 07	16 23	17♌40
1922	12♐37	13 02	13 30	14 00	14 34	15 09	15 47	16 28	17 10	17 55	18 41	19 30	20 21	21 13	22 07	23♐03
1923	10♌13	11 30	12 46	14 03	15 19	16 36	17 53	19 09	20 26	21 42	22 59	24 15	25 31	26 48	28 04	29♌20
1924	04♓R56	04 43	04 26	04 07	03 46	03 22	02 56	02 29	02 00	01 29	00 58	00 26	29♒54	29 23	28 52	28♒22
1925	22♌29	23 45	25 00	26 16	27 32	28 48	00♍04	01 21	02 37	03 53	05 09	06 26	07 42	08 58	10 15	11♍31
1926	29♈47	00♉53	01 59	03 02	04 05	05 06	06 06	07 04	08 01	08 56	09 50	10 41	11 31	12 20	13 06	13♉50
1927	04♍10	05 26	06 41	07 56	09 12	10 28	11 43	12 59	14 15	15 31	16 48	18 04	19 21	20 37	21 54	23♍11
1928	24♉41	26 00	27 18	28 36	29♊53	01 10	02 26	03 42	04 56	06 10	07 24	08 36	09 48	10 59	12 10	13♊19
1929	16♍50	18 04	19 19	20 34	21 50	23 05	24 21	25 37	26 53	28 09	29♎25	00 42	01 59	03 16	04 33	05♎50
1930	12♊02	13 23	14 43	16 03	17 23	18 43	20 02	21 21	22 39	23 57	25 14	26 31	27 48	29 04	00♋20	01♋35
1931	29♍35	00♎48	02 02	03 17	04 31	05 46	07 01	08 17	09 33	10 49	12 06	13 22	14 39	15 57	17 14	18♎32
1932	27♊26	28 47	00♋07	01 27	02 46	04 06	05 25	06 44	08 02	09 20	10 38	11 56	13 13	14 30	15 47	17♋03
1933	14♎17	15 29	16 42	17 55	19 08	20 22	21 36	22 51	24 06	25 22	26 38	27 54	29 11	00♏28	01 46	03♏04
1934	10♋46	12 06	13 25	14 44	16 03	17 21	18 40	19 58	21 16	22 34	23 51	25 09	26 26	27 43	29 00	00♌16
1935	01♏14	02 21	03 28	04 36	05 45	06 55	08 05	09 16	10 28	11 40	12 54	14 07	15 22	16 37	17 52	19♏09
1936	23♋54	25 12	26 30	27 48	29 06	00♌23	01 41	02 58	04 15	05 33	06 50	08 06	09 23	10 40	11 56	13♌13
1937	26♏44	27 31	28 20	29 10	00♐02	00 56	01 51	02 48	03 46	04 46	05 47	06 49	07 53	08 58	10 40	11♐11
1938	05♌50	07 07	08 24	09 41	10 58	12 15	13 32	14 49	16 05	17 22	18 38	19 55	21 11	22 28	23 44	25♌01
1939	27♑R14	26 44	26 16	25 50	25 26	25 04	24 45	24 29	24 15	24 06	23 59	23 56	23 D56	23 59	24 05	24♑15
1940	18♌09	19 25	20 41	21 57	23 14	24 30	25 46	27 02	28 18	29♍35	00 51	02 07	03 24	04 40	05 56	07♍13
1941	15♈11	16 01	16 48	17 34	18 17	18 58	19 37	20 13	20 47	21 18	21 47	22 12	22 35	22 54	23 11	23♈24
1942	29♌47	01♍02	02 18	03 33	04 49	06 05	07 21	08 37	09 53	11 09	12 25	13 41	14 58	16 14	17 31	18♍48
1943	16♉05	17 22	18 38	19 53	21 07	22 21	23 34	24 46	25 57	27 08	28 18	29♊26	00 34	01 40	02 46	03♊50
1944	12♍16	13 31	14 46	16 01	17 17	18 32	19 48	21 04	22 20	23 36	24 52	26 09	27 26	28 42	29♎59	01♎17
1945	05♊53	07 14	08 34	09 54	11 13	12 32	13 51	15 09	16 26	17 43	19 00	20 16	21 32	22 47	24 01	25♊15
1946	24♍42	25 56	27 10	28 25	29♎40	00 55	02 10	03 26	04 42	05 58	07 15	08 31	09 48	11 05	12 23	13♎41
1947	21♊24	22 45	24 06	25 26	26 46	28 06	29♋25	00 44	02 03	03 21	04 39	05 57	07 14	08 31	09 48	11♋04
1948	08♎46	09 59	11 12	12 26	13 40	14 54	16 09	17 25	18 40	19 56	21 13	22 29	23 46	25 04	26 22	27♎40
1949	05♋53	07 13	08 32	09 51	11 11	12 30	13 48	15 07	18 25	17 43	19 01	20 19	21 36	22 53	24 10	25♋27
1950	24♎18	25 27	26 37	27 48	28 59	00♏11	01 23	02 36	03 50	05 04	06 19	07 34	08 50	10 06	11 23	12♏40
1951	18♋39	19 57	21 16	22 34	32 52	25 11	26 28	27 46	29 04	00♌21	01 38	02 56	04 13	05 29	06 46	08♌03
1952	15♏28	16 26	17 26	18 26	19 28	20 31	21 35	22 40	23 46	24 54	26 02	27 11	28 21	29♐32	00 44	01♐56
1953	01♌25	02 42	04 00	05 17	06 34	07 52	09 09	10 26	11 43	12 59	14 16	15 33	16 49	18 06	19 22	20♌39
1954	25♐38	25 43	25 53	26 05	26 20	26 39	27 01	27 25	27 53	28 23	28 56	29 31	00♑09	00 49	01 31	02♑16
1955	13♌10	14 27	15 43	17 00	18 16	19 33	20 49	22 06	23 22	24 38	25 55	27 11	28 27	29♍44	01 00	02♍16
1956	23♓01	23 15	23 26	23 34	23 38	23 39	23 37	23 32	23 23	23 12	22 57	22 39	22 19	21 56	21 30	21♓03
1957	25♌26	26 42	27 58	29 14	00♍29	01 45	03 01	04 17	05 33	07 50	08 06	09 22	10 38	11 55	13 11	14♍28
1958	06♉36	07 47	08 58	10 07	11 16	12 23	13 30	14 35	15 39	16 42	17 43	18 43	19 42	20 39	21 34	22♉28
1959	07♍11	08 26	09 41	10 56	12 12	13 27	14 43	15 59	17 15	18 31	19 47	21 04	22 20	23 37	24 53	26♍10
1960	29♉13	00♊33	01 52	03 11	04 29	05 47	07 04	08 21	09 37	10 53	12 08	13 22	14 36	15 49	17 01	18♊12
1961	19♍58	21 12	22 27	23 42	24 57	26 12	27 28	28 43	29♎59	01 16	02 32	03 49	05 06	06 23	07 40	08♎57
1962	15♊48	17 10	18 30	19 51	21 11	22 30	23 49	25 08	26 27	27 45	29 03	00♋20	01 37	02 54	04 10	05♋26
1963	02♎56	04 09	05 23	06 37	07 52	09 06	10 21	11 37	12 53	14 09	15 25	16 42	17 59	19 16	20 34	21♎51
1964	00♋50	02 10	03 30	04 50	06 10	07 29	08 48	10 07	11 25	12 43	14 01	15 19	16 36	17 53	19 10	20♋27
1965	18♎04	19 15	20 27	21 39	22 52	24 05	25 19	26 33	27 48	29 03	00♏19	01 35	02 51	04 08	05 26	06♏44
1966	13♋57	15 16	16 35	17 54	19 12	20 31	21 49	23 07	24 25	25 43	27 00	28 17	29♌35	00 51	02 08	03♌25
1967	06♏03	07 07	08 12	09 18	10 25	11 33	12 41	13 50	15 01	16 12	17 23	18 36	19 49	21 02	22 17	23♏32
1968	26♋57	28 15	29♌32	00 50	02 08	03 25	04 42	06 00	07 17	08 34	09 51	11 07	12 24	13 41	14 57	16♌14
1969	05♐22	05 58	06 36	07 17	08 00	08 45	09 32	10 20	11 11	12 04	12 58	13 54	14 51	15 50	16 50	17♐52
1970	08♌49	10 06	11 23	12 40	13 57	15 13	16 30	17 47	19 03	20 20	21 36	22 53	24 09	25 25	26 42	27♌58
1971	19♒R21	18 53	18 23	17 52	17 21	16 49	16 17	15 46	15 15	14 45	14 17	13 51	13 27	13 05	12 46	12♒30
1972	21♌06	22 22	23 38	24 54	26 11	27 27	28 43	29♍59	01 15	02 31	03 48	05 04	06 20	07 37	08 53	10♍10
1973	24♈30	25 31	26 30	27 27	28 23	29 17	00♉10	01 01	01 50	02 37	03 22	04 04	04 45	05 23	05 58	06♉31
1974	02♍46	04 02	05 17	06 33	07 48	09 04	10 20	11 36	12 52	14 08	15 24	16 40	17 57	19 13	20 30	21♍47
1975	21♉10	22 28	23 46	25 03	26 20	27 35	28 51	00♊05	01 19	02 32	03 44	04 56	06 06	07 16	08 25	09♊33
1976	15♍21	16 35	17 50	19 05	20 20	21 36	22 51	24 07	25 23	26 39	27 56	29 12	00♎29	01 46	03 03	04♎20
1977	09♊52	11 13	12 34	13 54	15 14	16 33	17 52	19 11	20 29	21 46	23 03	24 20	25 36	26 52	28 08	29♊22
1978	27♍55	29 09	00♎23	01 38	02 52	04 07	05 23	06 38	07 54	09 10	10 27	11 43	13 00	14 17	15 35	16♎53
1979	24♊54	25 17	27 37	28 58	00♋18	01 37	02 56	04 15	05 34	06 53	08 11	09 29	10 46	12 03	13 20	14♋37
1980	12♎19	13 32	14 44	15 58	17 11	18 25	19 40	20 55	22 10	23 26	24 42	25 59	27 16	28 33	29♏51	01♏09
1981	09♋08	10 28	11 47	13 06	14 25	15 44	17 03	18 21	19 39	20 57	22 15	23 32	24 50	26 07	27 24	28♋41
1982	28♎36	29♏43	00 52	02 01	03 11	04 22	05 33	06 45	07 58	09 11	10 25	11 39	12 54	14 10	15 26	16♏43
1983	21♋44	23 03	24 21	25 39	26 57	28 15	29♌33	00 50	02 08	03 25	04 42	05 59	07 16	08 33	09 50	11♌06
1984	21♏53	22 46	23 40	24 35	25 32	26 31	27 31	28 32	29♐34	00 37	01 42	02 48	03 55	05 02	06 11	07♐21
1985	04♌24	05 42	06 59	08 16	09 33	10 50	12 07	13 24	14 41	15 57	17 14	18 31	19 47	21 04	22 20	23♌36
1986	12♑R18	12 02	11 48	11 37	11 30	11 D26	11 25	11 28	11 34	11 44	11 56	12 12	12 31	12 53	13 18	13♑45
1987	16♌07	17 24	18 40	19 56	21 13	22 29	23 45	25 01	26 18	27 34	28 50	00♍07	02 23	02 39	03 56	05♍12
1988	07♈10	07 47	08 21	08 53	09 22	09 48	10 12	10 32	10 50	11 04	11 15	11 22	11 R27	11 28	11 25	11♈20
1989	28♌23	29♍39	00 54	02 10	03 26	04 42	05 58	07 13	08 30	09 46	11 02	12 18	13 34	14 51	16 07	17♍24
1990	12♉39	13 54	15 08	16 21	17 34	18 45	19 56	21 06	22 15	23 23	24 29	25 35	26 39	27 43	28 45	29♉45
1991	10♍12	11 27	12 42	13 57	15 12	16 28	17 43	18 59	20 15	21 31	22 47	24 04	25 20	26 37	27 54	29♍11
1992	03♊32	04 52	06 12	07 32	08 51	10 09	11 28	12 45	14 02	15 19	16 35	17 51	19 06	20 20	21 34	22♊47
1993	23♍07	24 21	25 36	26 50	28 05	29♎21	00 36	01 52	03 08	04 24	05 40	06 57	08 14	09 31	10 48	12♎06
1994	19♊29	20 50	22 10	23 31	24 51	26 11	27 30	28 49	00♋08	01 26	02 44	04 02	05 19	06 36	07 53	09♋09
1995	06♎21	07 34	08 47	10 01	11 15	12 29	13 44	14 59	16 15	17 31	18 47	20 04	21 21	22 38	23 55	25♎13
1996	04♋11	05 31	06 51	08 10	09 30	10 49	12 08	13 26	14 45	16 03	17 21	18 39	19 56	21 13	22 30	23♋47
1997	22♎00	23 10	24 21	25 32	26 44	27 57	29 10	00 24	01♏38	02 52	04 07	05 23	06 39	07 56	09 13	10♏30
1998	17♋06	18 25	19 44	21 02	22 21	23 39	24 57	26 15	27 33	28 50	00♌08	01 25	02 42	03 59	05 16	06♌32
1999	11♏22	12 22	13 24	14 27	15 31	16 36	17 42	18 49	19 57	21 05	22 15	23 26	24 37	25 49	27 02	28♏15
2000	29♋58	01♌16	02 33	03 51	05 08	06 25	07 42	08 59	10 16	11 33	12 50	14 07	15 24	16 40	17 57	19♌13

Mars

September

	1st	3rd	5th	7th	9th	11th	13th	15th	17th	19th	21st	23rd	25th	27th	29th
1900	14♋13	15 29	16 44	17 59	19 14	20 28	21 42	22 55	24 09	25 22	26 34	27 46	28 58	00♌09	01♌19
1901	00♏10	01 28	02 47	04 07	05 26	06 47	08 07	09 28	10 49	12 11	13 33	14 55	16 17	17 40	19♏03
1902	27♋42	28 59	00♌15	01 30	02 46	04 01	05 17	06 32	07 46	09 01	10 15	11 29	12 43	13 56	15♌09
1903	15♏36	16 53	18 12	19 30	20 50	22 09	23 30	24 50	26 11	27 33	28 55	00♐17	01 40	03 04	04♐27
1904	10♌48	12 04	13 20	14 37	15 52	17 08	18 24	19 39	20 55	22 10	23 25	24 40	25 55	27 10	28♌24
1905	05♐52	07 04	08 17	09 31	10 45	12 01	13 17	14 33	15 51	17 09	18 27	19 47	21 07	22 27	23♐48
1906	22♌41	23 57	25 13	26 29	27 46	29 02	00♍18	01 34	02 50	04 06	05 21	06 37	07 53	09 09	10♍24
1907	10♑27	11 03	11 42	12 22	13 05	13 51	14 38	15 27	16 18	17 11	18 06	19 02	20 00	20 59	22♑00
1908	04♍55	06 11	07 28	08 44	10 01	11 17	12 34	13 50	15 07	16 23	17 40	18 57	20 14	21 30	22♍47
1909	06♈R15	05 59	05 39	05 17	04 52	04 25	03 56	03 24	02 51	02 17	01 43	01 08	00 33	29♓58	29♓25
1910	16♍29	17 46	19 03	20 20	21 37	22 54	24 11	25 28	26 46	28 03	29 21	00♎39	01 56	03 14	04♎32
1911	27♉50	28 47	29♊43	00 37	01 29	02 20	03 09	03 56	04 41	05 24	06 05	06 44	07 20	07 54	08♊25
1912	28♍54	00♎11	01 29	02 46	04 04	05 22	06 40	07 59	09 17	10 36	11 55	13 14	14 33	15 52	17♎12
1913	21♊30	22 41	23 52	25 03	26 12	27 21	28 29	29♋36	00 42	01 48	02 53	03 56	04 59	06 01	07♋01
1914	11♎09	12 27	13 45	15 04	16 22	17 41	19 00	20 20	21 39	22 59	24 19	25 40	27 00	28 21	29♏42
1915	08♋05	09 20	10 35	11 50	13 04	14 18	15 31	16 44	17 56	19 08	20 19	21 30	22 40	23 50	25♋00
1916	24♎54	26 13	27 32	28 51	00♏10	01 30	02 51	04 11	05 32	06 53	08 15	09 36	10 58	12 21	13♏43
1917	22♋47	24 04	25 19	26 35	27 51	29 06	00♌21	01 35	02 49	04 03	05 17	06 30	07 44	08 56	10♌09
1918	09♏27	10 45	12 04	13 23	14 43	16 03	17 24	18 45	20 06	21 28	22 50	24 13	25 36	26 59	28♏23
1919	05♌36	06 52	08 08	09 24	10 40	11 56	13 11	14 26	15 42	16 57	18 12	19 26	20 41	21 55	23♌09
1920	27♏34	28 50	00♐06	01 23	02 40	03 58	05 17	06 36	07 56	09 16	10 37	11 59	13 21	14 43	16♐06
1921	18♌18	19 34	20 51	22 07	23 23	24 39	25 55	27 10	28 26	29♍42	00 57	02 13	03 28	04 44	05♍59
1922	23♐32	24 30	25 30	26 31	27 33	28 37	29♑42	00 48	01 56	03 04	04 14	05 24	06 36	07 48	09♑02
1923	29♌59	01♍15	02 31	03 48	05 04	06 20	07 37	08 53	10 09	11 26	12 42	13 58	15 14	16 31	17♍47
1924	28♒R07	27 40	27 14	26 50	26 29	26 10	25 54	25 41	25 31	25 24	25 D 21	25 20	25 23	25 28	25♒37
1925	12♍10	13 26	14 43	15 59	17 16	18 33	19 50	21 07	22 24	23 41	24 58	26 16	27 33	28 51	00♎08
1926	14♉11	14 51	15 30	16 05	16 38	17 09	17 37	18 02	18 23	18 42	18 58	19 10	19 20	19 25	19♉R27
1927	23♍49	25 06	26 23	27 41	28 58	00♎16	01 33	02 51	04 09	05 27	06 46	08 04	09 23	10 41	12♎00
1928	13♊54	15 02	16 09	17 16	18 21	19 26	20 29	21 32	22 33	23 33	24 32	25 29	26 25	27 20	28♊14
1929	06♎29	07 47	09 05	10 23	11 41	13 00	14 18	15 37	16 57	18 16	19 35	20 55	22 15	23 35	24♎56
1930	02♋12	03 27	04 41	05 54	07 07	08 20	09 32	10 43	11 54	13 04	14 14	15 23	16 31	17 39	18♋46
1931	19♎11	20 29	21 48	23 07	24 26	25 45	27 05	28 25	29♏45	01 06	02 27	03 48	05 09	06 31	07♏53
1932	17♋42	18 58	20 13	21 29	22 44	23 58	25 13	26 27	27 40	28 54	00♌07	01 19	02 31	03 43	04♌55
1933	03♏43	05 02	06 21	07 40	09 00	10 20	11 41	13 01	14 23	15 44	17 06	18 29	19 51	21 14	22♏38
1934	00♌55	02 11	03 27	04 43	05 59	07 15	08 30	09 45	11 00	12 15	13 29	14 43	15 57	17 11	18♌25
1935	19♏47	21 04	22 22	23 40	24 59	26 18	27 38	28 58	00♐19	01 40	03 01	04 24	05 46	07 09	08♐33
1936	13♌51	15 07	16 24	17 40	18 56	20 11	21 27	22 43	23 58	25 14	26 29	27 44	28 59	00♍14	01♍29
1937	11♐44	12 53	14 03	15 13	16 25	17 37	18 51	20 05	21 20	22 36	23 52	25 09	26 27	27 46	29♐05
1938	25♌39	26 55	28 11	29♍28	00 44	02 00	03 16	04 32	05 48	07 04	08 21	09 37	10 53	12 09	13♍24
1939	24♑21	24 36	24 54	25 14	25 38	26 04	26 33	27 05	27 39	28 16	28 56	29 37	00♒21	01 07	01♒55
1940	07♍51	09 08	10 24	11 41	12 57	14 14	15 30	16 47	18 04	19 21	20 37	21 54	23 11	24 28	25♍45
1941	23♈29	23 37	23 42	23 43	23 41	23 35	23 26	23 14	22 58	22 39	22 16	21 51	21 23	20 52	20♈20
1942	19♍26	20 43	22 00	23 17	24 34	25 51	27 09	28 26	29♎44	01 01	02 19	03 37	04 55	06 13	07♎31
1943	04♊22	05 25	06 26	07 27	08 25	09 23	10 19	11 14	12 07	12 58	13 48	14 36	15 22	16 06	16♊48
1944	01♎55	03 13	04 30	05 48	07 06	08 24	09 43	11 01	12 20	13 39	14 58	16 17	17 36	18 56	20♎16
1945	25♊52	27 05	28 17	29♋29	00 40	01 51	03 01	04 10	05 18	06 26	07 33	08 39	09 44	10 48	11♋51
1946	14♎20	15 38	16 56	18 15	19 34	20 53	22 12	23 31	24 51	16 11	27 32	28 52	00♏13	01 34	02♏56
1947	11♋42	12 58	14 14	15 29	16 43	17 58	19 12	20 25	21 38	22 51	24 03	25 15	26 26	27 37	28♋47
1948	28♎19	29♏38	00 57	02 16	03 36	04 56	06 16	07 37	08 58	10 19	11 41	13 03	14 25	15 47	17♏10
1949	26♋05	27 21	28 37	29♌53	01 08	02 24	03 39	04 54	06 08	07 23	08 37	09 50	11 04	12 17	13♌30
1950	13♏19	14 37	15 56	17 15	18 34	19 54	21 15	22 35	23 57	25 18	26 40	28 03	29♐26	00 49	02♐13
1951	08♌41	09 57	11 14	12 30	13 46	15 01	16 17	17 33	18 48	20 03	21 18	22 33	23 48	25 03	26♌17
1952	02♐33	03 47	05 01	06 16	07 32	08 49	10 06	11 24	12 43	14 02	15 22	16 42	18 03	19 25	20♐47
1953	21♌17	22 33	23 49	25 05	26 22	27 38	28 54	00♍10	01 25	02 41	03 57	05 13	06 28	07 44	08♍59
1954	02♑39	03 27	04 16	05 08	06 01	06 56	07 53	08 51	09 51	10 52	11 55	12 59	14 04	15 10	16♑17
1955	02♍55	04 11	05 27	06 44	08 00	09 17	10 33	11 49	13 06	14 22	15 39	16 55	18 12	19 29	20♍45
1956	20♓R48	20 18	19 46	19 14	18 41	18 07	17 34	17 02	16 31	16 01	15 33	15 06	14 42	14 20	14♓01
1957	15♍06	16 23	17 40	18 56	20 13	21 30	22 47	24 04	25 22	26 39	27 56	29 14	00♎32	01 49	03♎07
1958	22♉55	23 46	24 36	25 24	26 09	26 53	27 35	28 14	28 51	29 25	29♊57	00 26	00 52	01 16	01♊36
1959	26♍49	28 06	29♎23	00 41	01 58	03 16	04 34	05 52	07 10	08 28	09 47	11 06	12 24	13 43	15♎02
1960	18♊48	19 58	21 08	22 17	23 25	24 32	25 39	26 44	27 49	28 52	29♋55	00 56	01 57	02 56	03♋54
1961	09♎36	10 54	12 12	13 30	14 49	16 08	17 26	18 46	20 05	21 25	22 44	24 04	25 25	26 45	28♎06
1962	06♋04	07 19	08 33	09 48	11 01	12 15	13 27	14 40	15 52	17 03	18 14	19 24	20 34	21 43	22♋51
1963	22♎31	23 49	25 08	26 27	27 46	29 05	00♏25	01 45	03 06	04 27	05 48	07 09	08 31	09 53	11♏15
1964	21♋05	22 21	23 37	24 53	26 08	27 23	28 38	29♌52	01 06	02 20	03 33	04 46	05 59	07 12	08♌24
1965	07♏23	08 41	10 00	11 20	12 39	13 59	15 20	16 41	18 02	19 24	20 46	22 08	23 31	24 54	26♏18
1966	04♌03	05 20	06 36	07 52	09 08	10 23	11 39	12 54	14 09	15 24	16 39	17 54	19 08	20 22	21♌36
1967	24♏10	25 26	26 43	28 00	29 18	00♐37	01 56	03 15	04 35	05 56	07 17	08 39	10 01	11 24	12♐47
1968	16♌52	18 08	19 24	20 41	21 57	23 12	24 28	25 44	27 00	28 15	29♍31	00 46	02 01	03 17	04♍32
1969	18♐23	19 27	20 32	21 38	22 45	23 53	25 03	26 13	27 24	28 37	29♑50	01 04	02 19	03 35	04♑51
1970	28♌36	29♍53	01 09	02 25	03 42	04 58	06 14	07 30	08 46	10 03	11 19	12 35	13 51	15 07	16♍24
1971	12♒R22	12 11	12 02	11 56	11 54	11 D 54	11 58	12 05	12 15	12 29	12 45	13 05	13 27	13 53	14♒21
1972	10♍48	12 04	13 21	14 38	15 54	17 11	18 28	19 45	21 01	22 18	23 36	24 53	26 10	27 27	28♍44
1973	06♉47	07 16	07 41	08 04	08 24	08 41	08 55	09 05	09 12	09 16	09 R 16	09 12	09 05	08 54	08♉40
1974	22♍25	23 42	24 59	26 16	27 34	28 51	00♎08	01 26	02 44	04 02	05 20	06 38	07 56	09 15	10♎33
1975	10♊07	11 14	12 19	13 24	14 27	15 29	16 31	17 30	18 29	19 26	20 22	21 17	22 10	23 02	23♊52
1976	04♎59	06 17	07 34	08 52	10 10	11 29	12 47	14 06	15 25	16 44	18 03	19 23	20 43	22 03	23♎23
1977	00♊00	01♋14	02 27	03 40	04 52	06 04	07 15	08 26	09 36	10 45	11 54	13 02	14 09	15 16	16♋21
1978	17♎32	18 50	20 08	21 27	22 46	24 05	25 25	26 45	28 05	29 25	00♏45	02 06	03 27	04 49	06♏10
1979	15♋15	16 31	17 47	19 02	20 17	21 32	22 46	24 00	25 14	26 27	27 40	28 52	00♌04	01 16	02♌27
1980	01♏48	03 06	04 25	05 45	07 04	08 24	09 45	11 06	12 27	13 48	15 10	16 32	17 55	19 17	20♏41
1981	29♋19	00♌35	01 51	03 07	04 23	05 38	06 54	08 09	09 24	10 38	11 52	13 07	14 21	15 34	16♌48
1982	17♏21	18 39	19 57	21 15	22 34	23 54	25 14	26 34	27 55	29 17	00♐39	02 01	03 24	04 47	06♐11
1983	11♌45	13 01	14 17	15 33	16 49	18 05	19 21	20 37	21 52	23 07	24 23	25 38	26 53	28 08	29♌22
1984	07♐56	09 08	10 20	11 33	12 47	14 01	15 17	16 33	17 49	19 07	20 25	21 44	23 03	24 24	25♐44
1985	24♌15	25 31	26 47	28 03	29 20	00♍36	01 52	03 08	04 24	05 40	06 56	08 12	09 27	10 43	11♍59
1986	14♑00	14 32	15 06	15 43	16 22	17 04	17 48	18 34	19 22	20 12	21 03	21 57	22 52	23 49	24♑47
1987	05♍50	07 07	08 23	09 40	10 56	12 13	13 29	14 46	16 02	17 19	18 36	19 52	21 09	22 26	23♍43
1988	11♈R16	11 05	10 51	10 33	10 13	09 50	09 24	08 55	08 25	07 53	07 19	06 45	06 09	05 34	04♈59
1989	18♍02	19 19	20 36	21 53	23 10	24 27	25 44	27 02	28 19	29♎36	00 54	02 12	03 30	04 48	06♎06
1990	00♊15	01 14	02 11	03 07	04 02	04 54	05 45	06 35	07 22	08 07	08 51	09 32	10 11	10 48	11♊22
1991	29♍49	01♎07	02 24	03 42	04 59	06 17	07 35	08 53	10 12	11 30	12 49	14 08	15 27	16 46	18♎06
1992	23♊23	24 35	25 47	26 58	28 08	29 17	00♋26	01 33	02 40	03 47	04 52	05 57	07 00	08 03	09♋04
1993	12♎45	14 03	15 21	16 39	17 58	19 17	20 36	21 55	23 15	24 35	25 55	27 15	28 35	29♏56	01♏17
1994	09♋47	11 03	12 18	13 33	14 47	16 01	17 14	18 27	19 40	20 52	22 04	23 15	24 26	25 36	26♋46
1995	25♎52	27 11	28 29	29♏48	01 08	02 28	03 47	05 08	06 28	07 49	09 11	10 32	11 54	13 16	14♏39
1996	24♋25	25 41	26 57	28 13	29♌29	00 44	01 59	03 14	04 28	05 42	06 56	08 09	09 23	10 36	11♌48
1997	11♏09	12 27	13 46	15 05	16 25	17 45	19 05	20 26	21 47	23 09	24 31	25 53	27 16	28 39	00♐03
1998	07♌11	08 27	09 43	10 59	12 15	13 31	14 47	16 02	17 17	18 33	19 47	21 02	22 17	23 31	24♌46
1999	28♏52	00♐07	01 22	02 39	03 55	05 13	06 31	07 49	09 09	10 28	11 49	13 10	14 31	15 53	17♐15
2000	19♌51	21 08	22 24	23 40	24 56	26 12	27 28	28 44	00♍00	01 15	02 31	03 46	05 02	06 17	07♍33

October

Year	1st	3rd	5th	7th	9th	11th	13th	15th	17th	19th	21st	23rd	25th	27th	29th	31st
1900	02♌30	03 39	04 49	05 58	07 06	08 14	09 21	10 28	11 34	12 40	13 45	14 49	15 53	16 56	17 59	19♌00
1901	20♏27	21 51	23 15	24 39	28 04	27 29	26 54	00♐20	01 46	03 12	04 39	06 06	07 33	09 00	10 29	11♐56
1902	16♌22	17 35	18 48	19 59	21 12	22 23	23 35	24 46	25 56	27 07	28 17	29♍27	00 36	01 45	02 54	04♍03
1903	05♐52	07 16	08 41	10 06	11 32	12 58	14 24	15 51	17 18	18 45	20 13	21 40	23 09	24 37	26 06	27♐35
1904	29♌39	00♍53	02 07	03 21	04 35	05 49	07 03	08 16	09 29	10 43	11 56	13 08	14 21	15 34	16 46	17♍58
1905	25♐10	26 32	27 55	29 18	00♑42	02 06	03 30	04 55	06 21	07 47	09 13	10 39	12 06	13 34	15 01	16♑29
1906	11♍40	12 56	14 11	15 27	16 42	17 58	19 13	20 29	21 44	22 59	24 15	25 30	26 45	28 00	29 16	00♎31
1907	23♑02	24 05	25 10	26 15	27 22	28 30	29♒39	00 49	02 00	03 12	04 24	05 37	06 51	08 06	09 21	10♒37
1908	24♍04	25 21	26 38	27 55	29 12	00♎29	01 46	03 03	04 20	05 38	06 55	08 12	09 30	10 47	12 05	13♎22
1909	28♓R52	28 21	27 52	27 25	27 00	26 38	26 18	26 02	25 49	25 38	25 31	25 D28	25 27	25 30	25 36	25♓45
1910	05♎50	07 09	08 27	09 46	11 04	12 23	13 42	15 01	16 20	17 39	18 58	20 18	21 37	22 57	24 17	25♎37
1911	08♊54	09 20	09 43	10 03	10 20	10 34	10 45	10 53	10 R57	10 58	10 55	10 48	10 38	10 24	10 07	09♊46
1912	18♎31	19 51	21 11	22 31	23 52	25 12	26 33	27 54	29 15	00♏36	01 58	03 19	04 41	06 03	07 25	08♏48
1913	08♋01	09 00	09 57	10 53	11 48	12 41	13 34	14 24	15 14	16 02	16 48	17 32	18 15	18 56	19 35	20♋12
1914	01♏03	02 25	03 46	05 08	06 31	07 53	09 16	10 39	12 02	13 25	14 49	16 13	17 37	19 01	20 26	21♏50
1915	26♋08	27 17	28 24	29♌31	00 38	01 44	02 48	03 53	04 56	05 59	07 02	08 03	09 04	10 03	11 02	12♌00
1916	15♏06	16 30	17 53	19 17	20 41	22 06	23 30	24 55	26 20	27 46	29 12	00♐38	02 04	03 31	04 58	06♐25
1917	11♌21	12 33	13 44	14 55	16 06	17 17	18 27	19 36	20 46	21 55	23 03	24 11	25 19	26 26	27 33	28♌39
1918	29♏47	01♐11	02 36	04 01	05 26	06 52	08 18	09 45	11 11	12 39	14 06	15 34	17 02	18 30	19 58	21♐27
1919	24♌23	25 37	26 51	28 04	29 18	00♍31	01 44	02 56	04 09	05 21	06 33	07 45	08 57	10 08	11 19	12♍30
1920	17♐30	18 53	20 18	21 42	23 08	24 33	25 59	27 26	28 52	00♑19	01 47	03 15	04 43	06 11	07 40	09♑09
1921	07♍14	08 29	09 44	10 59	12 14	13 29	14 44	15 59	17 13	18 28	19 42	20 57	22 11	23 25	24 39	25♍53
1922	10♑16	11 31	12 47	14 03	15 21	16 39	17 57	19 16	20 36	21 56	23 17	24 39	26 00	27 23	28 46	00♒09
1923	19♍03	20 20	21 36	22 53	24 09	25 26	26 42	27 58	29 15	00♎31	01 48	03 04	04 21	05 38	06 54	08♎11
1924	25♒49	26 04	26 23	26 44	27 08	27 34	28 03	28 35	29 09	29♓45	00 24	01 04	01 47	02 31	03 18	04♓06
1925	01♎26	02 43	04 01	05 19	06 37	07 55	09 13	10 31	11 50	13 08	14 27	15 45	17 04	18 23	19 42	21♎01
1926	19♉R26	19 21	19 12	19 00	18 44	18 25	18 03	17 37	17 08	16 37	16 03	15 26	14 48	14 08	13 27	12♉46
1927	13♎19	14 38	15 58	17 17	18 37	19 56	21 16	22 36	23 56	25 17	26 37	27 58	29 19	00♏40	02 01	03♏23
1928	29♊06	29♋56	00 45	01 32	02 18	03 01	03 43	04 23	05 00	05 36	06 09	06 39	07 08	07 34	07 57	08♋17
1929	26♎16	27 37	28 58	00♏20	01 41	03 03	04 25	05 47	07 09	08 32	09 54	11 17	12 41	14 04	15 28	16♏52
1930	19♋52	20 58	22 03	23 07	24 10	25 12	26 14	27 15	28 14	29 13	00♌11	01 08	02 04	02 58	03 52	04♌44
1931	09♏15	10 38	12 00	13 23	14 47	16 10	17 34	18 58	20 22	21 47	23 12	24 37	26 03	27 28	28 54	00♐20
1932	06♌06	07 16	08 27	09 37	10 46	11 55	13 03	14 11	15 19	16 26	17 32	18 38	19 44	20 48	21 53	22♌56
1933	24♏02	25 26	26 50	28 15	29♐40	01 05	02 30	03 56	05 23	05 49	08 16	09 43	11 11	12 38	14 06	15♐34
1934	19♌38	20 52	22 05	23 17	24 30	25 43	26 54	28 06	29 17	00♍28	01 39	02 50	04 00	05 10	06 20	07♍29
1935	09♐57	11 21	12 46	14 11	15 36	17 02	18 28	19 55	21 22	22 49	24 17	25 45	27 13	28 42	00♑10	01♑40
1936	02♍44	03 59	05 13	06 27	07 42	08 56	10 10	11 24	12 38	13 52	15 05	16 19	17 32	18 45	19 58	21♍11
1937	00♑25	01 45	03 06	04 28	05 50	07 13	08 36	10 00	11 24	12 48	14 13	15 38	17 04	18 30	19 57	21♑23
1938	14♍40	15 56	17 12	18 28	19 44	21 00	22 15	23 31	24 47	26 03	27 19	28 34	29♎50	01 06	02 21	03♎37
1939	02♒44	03 36	04 29	05 23	06 20	07 17	08 17	09 17	10 19	11 22	12 26	13 32	14 38	15 45	16 54	18♒03
1940	27♍03	28 20	29♎37	00 54	02 12	03 29	04 46	06 04	07 22	08 39	09 57	11 15	12 33	13 51	15 09	16♎27
1941	19♈R46	19 10	18 33	17 56	17 18	16 40	16 03	15 27	14 52	14 18	13 47	13 17	12 51	12 27	12 05	11♈47
1942	08♎50	10 08	11 27	12 46	14 05	15 24	16 43	18 02	19 22	20 41	22 01	23 21	24 41	26 01	27 21	28♎42
1943	17♊28	18 06	18 41	19 15	19 45	20 13	20 39	21 01	21 21	21 38	21 52	22 02	22 09	22 R13	22 14	22♊11
1944	21♎36	22 56	24 16	25 37	26 57	28 18	29♏39	01 01	02 22	03 44	05 06	06 28	07 50	09 13	10 35	11♏58
1945	12♋55	13 56	14 57	15 57	16 56	17 53	18 49	19 45	20 39	21 31	22 23	23 13	24 01	24 48	25 34	26♋18
1946	04♏17	05 39	07 01	08 23	09 46	11 09	12 32	13 55	15 19	16 42	18 07	19 31	20 55	22 20	23 45	25♏10
1947	29♋57	01♌06	02 15	03 23	04 31	05 38	06 45	07 51	08 57	10 01	11 05	12 09	13 12	14 14	15 15	16♌15
1948	18♏34	19 57	21 21	22 45	24 10	25 34	26 59	28 25	29♐50	01 16	02 42	04 09	05 36	07 03	08 30	09♐58
1949	14♌43	15 55	17 07	18 19	19 31	20 42	21 53	23 03	24 13	25 23	26 33	27 42	28 51	29♍59	01 07	02♍15
1950	03♐37	05 01	06 26	07 51	09 16	10 42	12 09	13 35	15 02	16 29	17 57	19 25	20 53	22 21	23 50	25♐19
1951	27♌31	28 46	00♍00	01 13	02 27	03 41	04 54	06 07	07 20	08 33	09 46	10 58	12 11	13 23	14 35	15♍47
1952	22♐09	23 32	24 56	26 20	27 44	29 09	00♑34	02 00	03 26	04 52	06 19	07 47	09 14	10 42	12 10	13♑39
1953	10♍15	11 30	12 46	14 01	15 16	16 31	17 47	19 02	20 17	21 32	22 47	24 02	25 16	26 31	27 46	29♍00
1954	17♑26	18 36	19 46	20 58	22 10	23 23	24 37	25 52	27 08	28 24	29♒41	00 58	02 16	03 35	04 54	06♒14
1955	22♍02	23 18	24 35	25 52	27 08	28 25	29♎42	00 59	02 16	03 33	04 49	06 06	07 23	08 40	09 58	11♎15
1956	13♓R45	13 31	13 21	13 14	13 D10	13 09	13 12	13 18	13 26	13 38	13 53	14 11	14 31	14 55	15 20	15♓49
1957	04♎25	05 43	07 01	08 19	09 37	10 56	12 14	13 33	14 52	16 10	17 29	18 48	20 08	21 27	22 46	24♎06
1958	01♊54	02 08	02 19	02 27	02 R31	02 32	02 29	02 23	02 13	01 59	01 42	01 21	00 57	00 30	00♉00	29♉27
1959	16♎22	17 41	19 01	20 21	21 41	23 01	24 21	25 41	27 02	28 23	29♏44	01 05	02 26	03 48	05 09	06♏31
1960	04♋51	05 46	06 41	07 34	08 25	09 15	10 03	10 50	11 35	12 18	13 00	13 39	14 17	14 52	15 25	15♋56
1961	29♎27	00♏48	02 09	03 31	04 53	06 15	07 37	09 00	10 22	11 45	13 09	14 32	15 56	17 91	18 43	20♏08
1962	23♋59	25 06	26 13	27 19	28 24	29♌28	00 32	01 35	02 37	03 39	04 39	05 39	06 38	07 36	08 33	09♌29
1963	12♏37	14 00	15 23	16 47	18 10	19 34	20 58	22 23	23 47	25 12	26 38	28 03	29♐29	00 55	02 22	03♐48
1964	09♌36	10 47	11 58	13 09	14 19	15 29	16 38	17 47	18 56	20 04	21 12	22 19	23 26	24 32	25 38	26♌43
1965	27♏42	29 06	00♐30	01 55	03 21	04 46	06 12	07 38	09 05	10 31	11 59	13 26	14 54	16 22	17 50	19♐19
1966	22♌50	24 03	25 17	26 30	27 43	28 56	00♍08	01 20	02 33	03 44	04 56	06 07	07 19	08 29	09 40	10♍50
1967	14♐10	15 34	16 59	18 24	19 49	21 14	22 40	24 07	25 34	27 01	28 28	29 56	01♑24	02 52	04 21	05♑50
1968	05♍47	07 02	08 17	09 31	10 46	12 00	13 15	14 29	15 44	16 58	18 12	19 26	20 40	21 54	23 07	24♍21
1969	06♑08	07 26	08 44	10 04	11 23	12 44	14 05	15 26	16 48	18 11	19 34	20 57	22 21	23 46	25 10	26♑35
1970	17♍40	18 56	20 12	21 28	22 44	24 01	25 17	26 33	27 49	29 05	00♎21	01 37	02 54	04 10	05 26	06♎42
1971	14♒51	15 25	16 00	16 38	17 18	18 00	18 45	19 31	20 19	21 09	22 00	22 53	23 48	24 44	25 42	26♒40
1972	00♎02	01 19	02 37	03 54	05 12	06 30	07 47	09 05	10 23	11 41	12 59	14 18	15 36	16 54	18 13	19♎31
1973	08♉R22	08 01	07 36	07 09	06 39	06 07	05 32	04 56	04 18	03 38	02 58	02 18	01 37	00 57	00♈18	29♈40
1974	11♎52	13 11	14 30	15 49	17 08	18 28	19 47	21 07	22 27	23 47	25 07	26 27	27 48	29 08	00♏29	01♏50
1975	24♊40	25 26	26 11	26 53	27 34	28 12	28 49	29 23	29♋55	00 24	00 51	01 15	01 36	01 54	02 10	02♋22
1976	24♎43	26 03	27 24	28 45	00♏06	01 27	02 49	04 11	05 33	06 55	08 17	09 40	11 02	12 25	13 49	15♏12
1977	17♋26	18 30	19 34	20 36	21 38	22 39	23 38	24 37	25 34	26 31	27 26	28 21	29 14	00♌05	00 56	01♌45
1978	07♏32	08 54	10 17	11 40	13 03	14 26	15 49	17 13	18 37	20 01	21 25	22 08	23 33	24 58	26 23	27♏49
1979	03♌37	04 48	05 58	07 07	08 16	09 24	10 32	11 40	12 47	13 53	14 59	16 04	17 08	18 12	19 16	20♌18
1980	22♏04	23 28	24 52	26 16	27 41	29 06	00♐31	01 57	03 23	04 49	06 16	07 42	09 10	10 37	12 05	13♐32
1981	18♌01	19 14	20 26	21 39	22 51	24 02	25 14	26 25	27 36	28 47	29♍57	01 07	02 17	03 26	04 36	05♍44
1982	07♐35	08 59	10 24	11 49	13 14	14 40	16 06	17 33	18 59	20 27	21 55	23 22	24 51	26 19	27 48	29♐17
1983	00♍37	01 52	03 06	04 20	05 34	06 48	08 02	09 16	10 29	11 43	12 56	14 09	15 22	16 35	17 47	19♍00
1984	27♐05	28 27	29♑50	01 12	02 26	04 00	05 24	06 48	08 14	09 39	11 05	12 31	13 58	15 25	16 52	18♑20
1985	13♍15	14 30	15 46	17 02	18 17	19 33	20 48	22 04	23 19	24 35	25 50	27 06	28 21	29♎36	00 51	02♎07
1986	25♑46	26 48	27 50	28 54	29♒59	01 05	02 12	03 20	04 29	05 39	06 50	08 02	09 15	10 28	11 42	12♒57
1987	25♍00	26 16	27 33	28 50	00♎07	01 24	02 42	03 59	05 16	06 33	07 51	09 08	10 26	11 43	13 01	14♎18
1988	04♈R24	03 50	03 17	02 45	02 16	01 49	01 24	01 02	00 43	00 26	00 13	00♓04	29 57	29 D53	29 53	29♓56
1989	07♎24	08 42	10 00	11 19	12 38	13 56	15 15	16 34	17 53	19 12	20 32	21 51	23 11	24 31	25 50	27♎10
1990	11♊54	12 23	12 50	13 14	13 35	13 53	14 08	14 19	14 28	14 R32	14 34	14 34	14 26	14 17	14 04	13♊48
1991	19♎25	20 45	22 05	23 25	24 45	26 06	27 26	28 47	00♏08	01 30	02 51	04 12	05 34	06 56	08 18	09♏41
1992	10♋05	11 04	12 03	13 00	13 56	14 51	15 44	16 36	17 27	18 16	19 04	19 50	20 35	21 17	21 58	22♋37
1993	02♏38	04 00	05 22	06 44	08 06	09 28	10 51	12 14	13 37	15 00	16 24	17 48	19 12	20 36	22 01	23♏26
1994	27♋55	29 04	00♌12	01 19	02 26	03 32	04 38	05 43	06 47	07 50	08 53	09 55	10 56	11 57	12 57	13♌55
1995	16♏02	17 25	18 48	20 12	21 36	23 00	24 24	25 49	27 14	28 40	00♐05	01 31	02 58	04 24	05 51	07♐18
1996	13♌01	14 13	15 24	16 36	17 47	18 58	20 08	21 18	22 27	23 37	24 45	25 54	27 02	28 09	29 17	00♌23
1997	01♐27	02 51	04 16	05 41	07 06	08 32	09 58	11 24	12 51	14 18	15 45	17 13	18 41	20 09	21 38	23♐06
1998	26♌00	27 14	28 27	29♍41	00 54	02 08	03 21	04 34	05 46	06 59	08 11	09 23	10 35	11 47	12 58	14♍09
1999	18♐38	20 02	21 25	22 49	24 14	25 39	27 05	28 31	29 57	01♑24	02 51	04 18	05 46	07 14	08 42	10♑11
2000	08♍48	10 03	11 18	12 33	13 48	15 03	16 18	17 33	18 48	20 02	21 17	22 31	23 46	25 00	26 15	27♍39

Mars

November

	1st	3rd	5th	7th	9th	11th	13th	15th	17th	19th	21st	23rd	25th	27th	29th
1900	19♌31	20 31	21 31	22 31	23 29	24 26	25 23	26 18	27 13	28 07	28 59	29♍51	00 41	01 30	02♍18
1901	12♐40	14 08	15 37	17 06	18 35	20 04	21 34	23 04	24 34	26 04	27 35	29 06	00♑37	02 08	03♑39
1902	04♍37	05 45	06 52	07 59	09 06	10 12	11 18	12 23	13 28	14 33	15 37	16 40	17 43	18 46	19♍47
1903	28♐20	29♑50	01 20	02 50	04 20	05 51	07 21	08 52	10 24	11 55	13 27	14 59	16 31	18 03	19♑36
1904	18♍34	19 46	20 58	22 10	23 21	24 33	25 44	26 55	28 05	29 16	00♎26	01 36	02 46	03 55	05♎04
1905	17♑13	18 41	20 10	21 39	23 08	24 38	26 07	27 37	29 07	00♒37	02 08	03 38	05 09	06 40	08♒11
1906	01♎08	02 23	03 38	04 53	06 08	07 23	08 38	09 53	11 07	12 22	13 37	14 51	16 06	17 20	18♎35
1907	11♒15	12 32	13 50	15 08	16 26	17 45	19 05	20 24	21 45	23 05	24 26	25 47	27 09	28 30	29♓52
1908	14♎01	15 19	16 36	17 54	19 12	20 30	21 48	23 06	24 24	25 42	27 00	28 18	29♏37	00 55	02♏14
1909	25♓50	26 03	26 20	26 39	27 00	27 25	27 52	28 21	28 53	29 26	00♈03	00 41	01 21	02 02	02♈46
1910	26♎17	27 37	28 57	00♏17	01 38	02 59	04 19	05 40	07 01	08 22	09 44	11 05	12 27	13 49	15♏11
1911	09♊R35	09 09	08 40	08 08	07 34	06 57	06 17	05 36	04 53	04 09	03 24	02 39	01 54	01 09	00♊25
1912	09♏29	10 52	12 15	13 38	15 01	16 24	17 48	19 12	20 36	22 00	23 24	24 49	26 14	27 39	29♏04
1913	20♋30	21 04	21 36	22 05	22 32	22 57	23 19	23 38	23 55	24 09	24 20	24 28	24 R32	24 34	24♋32
1914	22♏33	23 58	25 23	26 49	28 15	29♐41	01 07	02 33	04 00	05 27	06 54	08 22	09 49	11 17	12♐45
1915	12♌29	13 26	14 21	15 16	16 09	17 02	17 53	18 43	19 32	20 19	21 05	21 50	22 33	23 14	23♌54
1916	07♐09	08 36	10 04	11 32	13 00	14 29	15 58	17 27	18 56	20 26	21 55	23 25	24 56	26 26	27♐57
1917	29♌12	00♍18	01 23	02 27	03 32	04 35	05 38	06 40	07 42	08 43	09 43	10 43	11 42	12 40	13♍38
1918	22♐12	23 41	25 11	26 40	28 10	29♑41	01 11	02 42	04 13	05 44	07 16	08 47	10 19	11 52	13♑24
1919	13♍06	14 16	15 27	16 37	17 47	18 56	20 06	21 15	22 24	23 32	24 40	25 48	26 56	28 03	29♍10
1920	09♑53	11 23	12 52	14 22	15 53	17 23	18 54	20 25	21 56	23 27	24 59	26 30	28 02	29♒34	01♒06
1921	26♍30	27 44	28 58	00♎12	01 26	02 39	03 53	05 06	06 19	07 32	08 46	09 59	11 11	12 24	13♎37
1922	00♒51	02 14	03 39	05 03	06 28	07 53	09 18	10 44	12 10	13 36	15 03	16 29	17 56	19 23	20♒50
1923	08♎49	10 06	11 22	12 29	13 56	15 13	16 29	17 46	19 03	20 20	21 37	22 53	24 10	25 27	26♎44
1924	04♓31	05 21	06 13	07 07	08 02	08 58	09 56	10 54	11 54	12 55	13 57	15 00	16 03	17 08	18♓13
1925	21♎40	22 59	24 19	25 38	26 57	28 17	29♏37	00 57	02 16	03 36	04 57	06 17	07 37	08 58	10♏18
1926	12♉R24	11 42	11 00	10 19	09 38	08 59	08 22	07 47	07 14	06 44	06 17	05 53	05 31	05 13	04♉58
1927	04♏03	05 25	06 47	08 09	09 31	10 53	12 15	13 38	15 01	16 24	17 47	19 10	20 34	21 57	23♏21
1928	08♋27	08 43	08 56	09 06	09 13	09 R17	09 17	09 14	09 07	08 57	08 44	08 27	08 06	07 43	07♋16
1929	17♏34	18 58	20 22	21 47	23 12	24 37	26 02	27 27	28 53	00♐19	01 45	03 11	04 38	06 05	07♐32
1930	05♌10	06 00	06 49	07 37	08 23	09 08	09 51	10 32	11 12	11 50	12 26	13 00	13 33	14 03	14♌30
1931	01♐03	02 30	03 57	05 24	06 51	08 19	09 46	11 15	12 43	14 11	15 40	17 09	18 38	20 08	21♐37
1932	23♌28	24 31	25 33	26 34	27 35	28 35	29♍34	00 32	01 30	02 27	03 23	04 18	05 12	06 05	06♍57
1933	16♐19	17 48	19 17	20 46	22 15	23 45	25 15	26 45	28 16	29♑46	01 17	02 48	04 20	05 51	07♑23
1934	08♍04	09 13	10 22	11 30	12 38	13 46	14 53	16 00	17 06	18 12	19 18	20 23	21 28	22 32	23♍36
1935	02♑24	03 54	05 24	06 54	08 24	09 55	11 26	12 57	14 28	16 00	17 31	19 03	20 35	22 07	23♑40
1936	21♍48	23 00	24 13	25 25	26 38	27 50	29 02	00♎14	01 25	02 37	03 48	04 59	06 10	07 21	08♎31
1937	22♑07	23 34	25 02	26 29	27 58	29♒26	00 55	02 23	03 52	05 22	06 51	08 20	09 50	11 20	12♒50
1938	04♎15	05 31	06 46	08 02	09 17	10 33	11 48	13 04	14 19	15 35	16 50	18 06	19 21	20 37	21♎52
1939	18♒37	19 48	20 59	22 11	23 23	24 36	25 50	27 04	28 19	29♓35	00 51	02 07	03♐24	04 41	05♐59
1940	17♎06	18 24	19 42	21 01	22 19	23 38	24 56	26 15	27 33	28 52	00♏11	01 30	02 49	04 08	05♏28
1941	11♈R39	11 26	11 16	11 09	11 D05	11 05	11 07	11 13	11 22	11 33	11 48	12 06	12 26	12 49	13♈14
1942	29♎22	01♏43	02 04	03 24	04 46	06 07	07 28	08 50	10 11	11 33	12 55	14 17	15 39	17 02	18♏24
1943	22♊R08	21 59	21 47	21 32	21 13	20 50	20 25	19 56	19 24	18 49	18 12	17 32	16 50	16 06	15♊21
1944	12♏40	14 03	15 26	16 50	18 14	19 38	21 02	22 26	23 51	25 16	26 41	28 06	29 31	00 57	02♏23
1945	26♋39	27 20	28 00	28 37	29 13	29♌46	00 17	00 46	01 13	01 38	01 59	02 19	02 35	02 49	03♌00
1946	25♏53	27 19	28 45	00♐11	01 37	03 04	04 30	05 57	07 25	08 52	10 20	11 48	13 16	14 45	16♐13
1947	16♌45	17 45	18 43	19 41	20 38	21 34	22 28	23 22	24 15	25 06	25 57	26 46	27 34	28 20	29♌06
1948	10♐41	12 09	13 38	15 06	16 35	18 04	19 33	21 03	22 32	24 02	25 33	27 03	28 34	00♑05	01♑36
1949	02♍48	03 55	05 02	06 08	07 13	08 19	09 23	10 28	11 31	12 34	13 37	14 39	15 40	16 41	17♍41
1950	26♐03	27 33	29 03	00♑33	02 03	03 33	05 04	06 35	08 06	09 38	11 09	12 41	14 13	15 45	17♑18
1951	16♍22	17 34	18 45	10 56	21 07	22 18	23 28	24 38	25 48	26 58	28 07	29 17	00♎26	01 34	02♎43
1952	14♑23	15 52	17 21	18 50	20 20	21 50	23 20	24 50	26 21	27 52	29♒23	00 54	02 25	03 57	05♒28
1953	29♍38	00♎52	02 07	03 21	04 36	05 50	07 04	08 18	09 33	10 47	12 01	13 14	14 28	15 42	16♎56
1954	06♒54	08 15	09 36	10 57	12 19	13 41	15 04	16 26	17 49	19 13	20 37	22 00	23 25	24 49	26♒14
1955	11♎53	13 10	14 28	15 45	17 02	18 20	19 37	20 54	22 12	23 29	24 47	26 05	27 22	28 40	29♏58
1956	16♓04	16 36	17 10	17 47	18 25	19 06	19 48	20 33	21 19	22 06	22 55	23 46	24 38	25 31	26♓26
1957	24♎46	26 05	27 25	28 45	00♏05	01 25	02 45	04 06	05 26	06 47	08 08	09 29	10 50	12 11	13♏32
1958	29♉R10	28 33	27 54	27 13	26 31	25 48	25 04	24 20	23 36	22 52	22 10	21 29	20 50	20 13	19♉39
1959	07♏12	08 34	09 57	11 19	12 42	14 47	15 28	16 51	18 14	19 38	21 02	22 25	23 50	25 14	26♏38
1960	16♑11	16 38	17 03	17 25	17 45	18 01	18 15	18 26	18 34	18 38	18 39	18 37	18 31	18 23	18♑10
1961	20♑50	22 15	23♒40	25 05	26 30	27 56	29 22	00 48	02 14	03 40	05 07	06 34	08 01	09 28	10♒56
1962	09♓56	10 50	11 43	12 35	13 26	14 15	15 04	15 50	16 36	17 20	18 02	18 43	19 22	19 59	20♓34
1963	04♐32	05 59	07 26	08 53	10 21	11 49	13 17	14 46	16 15	17 44	19 13	20 42	22 12	23 42	25♐12
1964	27♌16	28 20	29 24	00♍28	01 30	02 32	03 34	04 34	05 35	06 34	07 33	08 30	09 28	10 24	11♍19
1965	20♐03	21 32	23 01	24 31	26 01	27 31	29 01	00♑32	02 02	03 33	05 04	06 36	08 08	09 39	11♑12
1966	11♍25	12 35	13 45	14 55	16 04	17 13	18 21	19 29	20 37	21 45	22 52	23 58	25 05	26 11	27♍17
1967	06♑35	08 04	09 34	11 04	12 34	14 05	15 36	17 07	18 38	20 09	21 41	23 12	24 44	26 16	27♑49
1968	24♍58	26 11	27 24	28 38	29♎51	01 04	02 17	03 29	04 42	05 54	07 07	08 19	09 31	10 43	11♎55
1969	27♑18	28 43	00♒09	01 35	03 02	04 29	05 56	07 23	08 51	10 19	11 47	13 15	14 43	16 12	17♒40
1970	07♎20	08 37	09 53	11 09	12 25	13 41	14 58	16 14	17 30	18 46	20 02	21 19	22 35	23 51	25♎07
1971	27♒10	28 11	29 12	00♓15	01 19	02 24	03 29	04 36	05 43	06 51	08 00	09 10	10 20	11 31	12♓43
1972	20♎11	21 30	22 48	24 07	25 26	26 45	28 04	29♏24	00 43	02 03	03 22	04 42	06 01	07 21	08♏41
1973	29♈R22	28 47	28 14	27 43	27 15	26 49	26 27	26 08	25 51	25 38	25 28	25 22	25 19	25 D19	25♈22
1974	02♏30	03 52	05 13	06 34	07 56	09 18	10 40	12 02	13 24	14 47	16 09	17 32	18 55	20 18	21♏41
1975	02♋27	02 35	02 R39	02 40	02 37	02 31	02 22	02 09	01 52	01 32	01 09	00 42	00♊12	29 39	29♊04
1976	15♏54	17 18	18 41	20 06	21 30	22 54	24 19	25 44	27 09	28 35	00♐00	01 26	02 52	04 18	05♐45
1977	02♌09	02 56	03 42	04 25	05 08	05 48	06 27	07 04	07 38	08 11	08 42	09 10	09 37	10 00	10♌22
1978	29♏15	00♐41	02 07	03 34	05 01	06 28	07 55	09 23	10 50	12 18	13 47	15 15	16 44	18 13	19♐42
1979	20♌49	21 51	22 52	23 52	24 51	25 50	26 38	27 45	28 41	29♍36	00 30	01 23	02 15	03 05	03♍55
1980	14♐17	15 45	17 13	18 42	20 11	21 41	23 11	24 40	26 11	27 41	29 11	00♑42	02 13	03 44	05♑16
1981	06♍18	07 27	08 34	09 42	10 49	11 56	13 02	14 08	15 13	16 18	17 22	18 26	19 30	20 33	21♍35
1982	00♑02	01 31	03 01	04 31	06 01	07 32	09 03	10 34	12 05	13 36	15 08	16 40	18 12	19 44	21♑17
1983	19♍36	20 48	22 01	23 12	24 24	25 36	26 47	27 58	29 09	00♎20	01 31	02 41	03 51	05 01	06♎11
1984	19♑04	20 32	22 00	23 29	24 58	26 27	27 57	29♒26	00 56	02 26	03 56	05 27	06 57	08 28	09♒59
1985	02♎44	03 59	05 14	06 30	07 45	09 00	10 15	11 30	12 45	13 59	15 14	16 29	17 44	18 58	20♎13
1986	13♒34	14 50	16 06	17 23	18 40	19 58	21 17	22 36	23 55	25 14	26 34	27 55	29 15	00♓36	01♓57
1987	14♎57	16 15	17 33	18 50	20 08	21 26	22 44	24 02	25 21	26 39	27 57	29 15	00♏34	01 52	03♏11
1988	29♓58	00♈06	00 16	00 30	00 46	01 05	01 27	01 52	02 19	02 48	03 20	03 54	04 30	05 08	05♈48
1989	27♎51	29 11	00♏31	01 51	03 12	04 33	05 54	07 15	08 36	09 57	11 18	12 40	14 02	15 24	16♏46
1990	13♊R38	13 17	12 52	12 24	11 53	11 19	10 43	10 03	09 22	08 40	07 56	07 11	06 25	05 40	04♊55
1991	10♏22	11 45	13 07	14 30	15 54	17 17	18 41	20 04	21 28	22 52	24 17	25 41	27 06	28 31	29♐56
1992	22♋56	23 32	24 06	24 38	25 07	25 35	25 59	26 22	26 41	26 58	27 12	27 23	27 31	27 R36	27♋37
1993	24♏08	25 33	26 59	28 24	29♐50	01 16	02 43	04 09	05 36	07 03	08 30	09 58	11 25	12 53	14♐21
1994	14♌25	15 22	16 18	17 14	18 08	19 02	19 54	20 45	21 35	22 24	23 11	23 57	24 41	25 25	26♌06
1995	08♐02	09 29	10 57	12 25	13 53	15 21	16 50	18 19	19 48	21 18	22 47	24 17	25 47	27 18	28♐48
1996	00♍57	02 03	03 08	04 13	05 18	06 22	07 25	08 28	09 30	10 32	11 33	12 33	13 33	14 32	15♍30
1997	23♐51	25 20	26 50	28 20	29♑50	01 20	02 50	04 21	05 52	07 23	08 55	10 26	11 58	13 30	15♑03
1998	14♍45	15 56	17 06	18 17	19 27	20 37	21 46	22 56	24 05	25 14	26 22	27 30	28 38	29♎46	00♎53
1999	10♑56	12 25	13 54	15 24	16 54	18 24	19 54	21 25	22 56	24 27	25 58	27 29	29 01	00♒33	02♒05
2000	28♍06	29 20	00♎34	01 48	03 02	04 15	05 29	06 43	07 56	09 09	10 23	11 36	12 49	14 02	15♎15

December

Year	1st	3rd	5th	7th	9th	11th	13th	15th	17th	19th	21st	23rd	25th	27th	29th	31st
1900	03♍05	03 51	04 35	05 17	05 58	06 38	07 16	07 52	08 26	08 59	09 29	09 58	10 24	10 48	11 10	11♍30
1901	05♑11	06 43	08 15	09 47	11 19	12 52	14 25	15 58	17 31	19 04	20 37	22 11	23 45	25 18	26 52	28♑26
1902	20♍49	21 49	22 49	23 48	24 47	25 45	26 42	27 39	28 34	29 29	00♎23	01 16	02 08	02 59	03 49	04♎38
1903	21♑09	22 41	24 14	25 47	27 21	28 54	00♒27	02 01	03 35	05 09	06 42	08 16	09 51	11 25	12 59	14♒33
1904	06♎13	07 22	08 31	09 39	10 47	11 54	13 02	14 09	15 15	16 22	17 28	18 33	19 38	20 43	21 48	22♎52
1905	09♒42	11 13	12 45	14 16	15 48	17 19	18 51	20 23	21 54	23 26	24 58	26 30	28 02	29♓34	01 05	02♓37
1906	19♎49	21 03	22 18	23 32	24 46	26 00	27 14	28 28	29♏41	00 55	02 09	03 22	04 36	06 49	07 02	08♏15
1907	01♓15	02 37	04 00	05 23	06 46	08 09	09 33	10 56	12 20	13 44	15 08	16 32	17 56	19 20	20 44	22♓08
1908	03♏32	04 50	06 09	07 28	08 46	10 05	11 24	12 43	14 02	15 21	16 40	17 59	19 18	20 37	21 57	23♏16
1909	03♈31	04 18	05 06	05 56	06 47	07 39	08 33	09 27	10 23	11 20	12 18	13 17	14 17	15 17	16 18	17♈20
1910	16♐33	17 55	19 17	20 40	22 02	23 25	24 48	26 11	27♑34	28 57	00 20	01 44	03 08	04 32	05 56	07♑20
1911	29♉R43	29 02	28 23	27 46	27 12	26 41	26 12	25 47	25 24	25 05	24 49	24 36	24 27	24 21	24 18	24♉19
1912	00♐29	01 55	03 20	04 46	06 12	07 39	09 05	10 32	11 59	13 26	14 53	16 20	17 48	19 15	20 43	22♐11
1913	24♋R27	24 18	24 06	23 51	23 32	23 10	22 45	22 16	21 44	21 10	20 33	19 53	19 11	18 27	17 41	16♋55
1914	14♐14	15 42	17 11	18 40	20 09	21 38	23 08	24 37	26 07	27 37	29 08	00♑38	02 09	03 40	05 11	06♑42
1915	24♌33	25 09	25 44	26 17	26 48	27 16	27 43	28 07	28 29	28 48	29 05	29 20	29 31	29 40	29 46	29♌R49
1916	29♐28	00♑59	02 30	04 01	05 33	07 05	08 37	10 09	11 41	13 14	14 47	16 20	17 53	19 26	20 59	22♑33
1917	14♍35	15 31	16 26	17 20	18 13	19 05	19 57	20 47	21 36	22 24	23 10	23 56	24 40	25 23	26 04	26♍44
1918	14♑56	16 29	18 02	19 35	21 08	22 41	24 14	25 48	27 22	28 55	00♒29	02 03	03 37	05 11	06 46	08♒20
1919	00♎16	01 22	02 28	03 34	04 39	05 43	06 47	07 51	08 54	09 57	10 59	12 00	13 01	14 02	15 02	16♎01
1920	02♒38	04 11	05 43	07 16	08 48	10 21	11 54	13 27	15 00	16 33	18 06	19 39	21 13	22 46	24 19	25♒52
1921	14♎49	16 02	17 14	18 26	19 38	20 50	22 01	23 13	24 24	25 35	26 46	27 57	29 07	00♏18	01 28	02♏38
1922	22♒18	23 45	25 13	26 40	28 08	29 36	01♓04	02 32	04 00	05 28	06 56	08 25	09 53	11 21	12 49	14♓18
1923	28♎01	29 18	00♏35	01 52	03 09	04 26	05 43	07 00	08 17	09 34	10 51	12 08	13 26	14 43	16 00	17♏17
1924	19♓19	20 26	21 34	22 42	23 51	25 00	26 11	27 21	28 32	29♈43	00 55	02 07	03 20	04 33	05 47	07♈00
1925	11♏39	13 00	14 20	15 41	17 03	18 24	19 45	21 07	22 28	23 50	25 12	26 34	27 56	29 18	00♐40	02♐03
1926	04♉R47	04 38	04 33	04 D31	04 33	04 37	04 45	04 56	05 09	05 26	05 44	06 06	06 30	06 56	07 24	07♉55
1927	24♏45	26 09	27 34	28 58	00♐23	01 48	03 13	04 38	06 03	07 29	08 55	10 21	11 47	13 13	14 39	16♐06
1928	06♋R46	06 12	05 36	04 58	04 17	03 34	02 49	02 03	01 16	00 29	29♊42	28 55	28 08	27 23	26 39	25♊57
1929	08♐59	10 26	11 54	13 21	14 49	16 18	17 46	19 15	20 43	22 12	23 41	25 11	26 40	28 10	29♑40	01♑10
1930	14♌56	15 19	15 40	15 58	16 14	16 27	16 37	16 44	16 R48	16 49	16 46	16 41	16 32	16 20	16 05	15♌46
1931	23♐07	24 37	26 07	27 38	29 09	00♑40	02 11	03 42	05 13	06 45	08 17	09 49	11 21	12 53	14 26	15♑59
1932	07♍48	08 37	09 26	10 13	11 00	11 44	12 28	13 10	13 50	14 29	15 07	15 43	16 16	16 48	17 18	17♍46
1933	08♑55	10 27	11 59	13 32	15 05	16 37	18 10	19 44	21 17	22 50	24 24	25 58	27 32	29 06	00♒40	02♒14
1934	24♍39	25 42	26 45	27 46	28 48	29♎48	00 48	01 47	02 46	03 44	04 41	05 38	06 34	07 28	08 23	09♎16
1935	25♑13	26 45	28 18	29♒51	01 24	02 58	04 31	06 04	07 38	09 12	10 45	12 19	13 53	15 27	17 01	18♒35
1936	09♎42	10 52	12 02	13 12	14 21	15 30	16 39	17 48	18 57	20 05	21 13	22 20	23 28	24 35	25 41	26♎48
1937	14♒20	15 50	17 21	18 51	20 22	21 53	23 23	24 54	26 25	27 56	29♓26	00 57	02 28	03 59	05 30	07♓01
1938	23♎07	24 23	25 38	26 53	28 08	29♏23	00 39	01 54	03 09	04 24	05 39	06 53	08 08	09 23	10 38	11♏52
1939	07♓17	08 35	09 54	11 13	12 32	13 52	15 11	16 31	17 51	19 12	20 32	21 53	23 14	24 35	25 56	27♓17
1940	06♏47	08 06	09 26	10 45	12 05	13 24	14 44	16 04	17 24	18 44	20 04	21 24	22 44	24 05	25 25	26♏46
1941	13♈42	14 12	14 45	15 19	15 55	16 34	17 14	17 55	18 39	19 24	20 11	20 59	21 48	22 39	23 30	24♈23
1942	19♏47	21 10	22 33	23 56	25 20	26 43	28 07	29♐31	00 55	02 19	03 43	05 07	06 32	07 57	09 21	10♐46
1943	14♊R36	13 50	13 03	12 17	11 32	10 48	10 06	09 25	08 46	08 10	07 36	07 06	06 38	06 13	05 51	05♊33
1944	03♐48	05 15	06 41	08 08	09 34	11 01	12 28	13 56	15 23	16 51	18 19	19 47	21 15	22 44	24 12	25♐41
1945	03♌08	03 12	03 R14	03 12	03 07	02 59	02 47	02 32	02 13	01 52	01 27	00 59	00♋27	29 53	29 16	28♋37
1946	17♐42	19 11	20 40	22 10	23 39	25 09	26 39	28 10	29♑40	01 11	02 42	04 13	05 44	07 15	08 47	10♑19
1947	29♌50	00♍32	01 13	01 52	02 30	03 06	03 40	04 12	04 42	05 10	05 36	05 59	06 20	06 39	06 56	07♍09
1948	03♑07	04 38	06 10	07 42	09 14	10 46	12 19	13 51	15 24	16 57	18 30	20 03	21 37	23 10	24 44	26♑18
1949	18♍41	19 39	20 37	21 35	22 31	23 27	24 22	25 16	26 09	27 01	27 52	28 42	29 31	00♎19	01 05	01♎51
1950	18♑50	20 23	21 56	23 29	25 02	26 35	28 09	29♒43	01 16	02 50	04 24	05 58	07 32	09 06	10 41	12♒15
1951	03♐51	04 58	06 06	07 13	08 20	09 26	10 32	11 38	12 43	13 48	14 53	15 57	17 01	18 04	19 06	20♎09
1952	07♒00	08 32	10 04	11 36	13 08	14 40	16 12	17 45	19 17	20 49	22 22	23 55	25 27	27 00	28 32	00♓05
1953	18♎09	19 23	20 36	21 49	23 02	24 16	25 29	26 41	27 54	29 07	00♏19	01 32	02 44	03 56	05 08	06♏20
1954	27♒39	29 04	00♓29	01 54	03 20	04 45	06 11	07 37	09 03	10 29	11 55	13 21	14 47	16 13	17 39	19♓06
1955	01♏15	02 33	03 51	05 09	06 27	07 45	09 03	10 21	11 39	12 57	14 15	15 33	16 52	18 10	19 28	20♏47
1956	27♓22	28 19	29 17	00♈16	01 16	02 17	03 19	04 21	05 25	06 29	07 34	08 39	09 45	10 52	11 59	13♈07
1957	14♏54	16 15	17 37	18 58	20 20	21 42	23 05	24 27	25 49	27 12	28 35	29♐57	01 20	02 44	04 07	05♐30
1958	19♉R06	18 37	18 11	17 47	17 27	17 10	16 56	16 46	16 39	16 35	16 35	16 38	16 43	16 52	17 04	17♉18
1959	28♏03	29♐28	00 53	02 18	03 44	05 09	06 35	08 01	09 27	10 53	12 20	13 46	15 13	16 40	18 07	19♐35
1960	17♋R54	17 35	17 13	16 47	16 18	15 46	15 11	14 33	13 53	13 10	12 26	11 41	10 54	10 06	09 19	08♋31
1961	12♐23	13 51	15 20	16 48	18 16	19 45	21 14	22 44	24 13	25 42	27 12	28 42	00♑12	01 43	03 13	04♑44
1962	21♌08	21 39	22 08	22 36	23 00	23 23	23 43	24 01	24 16	24 28	24 37	24 44	24 47	24 R48	24 45	24♌39
1963	26♐42	28 13	29♑43	01 14	02 46	04 17	05 48	07 20	08 52	10 24	11 57	13 29	15 02	16 34	18 07	19♑40
1964	12♍14	13 07	14 00	14 51	15 42	16 31	17 19	18 06	18 52	19 36	20 19	21 01	21 41	22 20	22 57	23♍32
1965	12♑44	14 16	15 49	17 22	18 54	20 28	22 01	23 34	25 08	26 41	28 15	29♒49	01 23	02 57	04 31	06♒06
1966	28♍22	29 27	00♎31	01 35	02 38	03 41	04 44	05 46	06 47	07 48	08 49	09 47	10 46	11 45	12 42	13♎39
1967	29♑21	00♒54	02 26	03 59	05 32	07 05	08 38	10 12	11 45	13 18	14 52	16 25	17 59	19 32	21 06	22♒39
1968	13♎06	14 17	15 29	16 40	17 51	19 01	20 12	21 22	22 32	23 42	24 52	26 02	27 11	28 20	29♏28	00♏37
1969	19♒09	20 38	22 07	23 36	25 05	26 34	28 04	29♓33	01 03	02 32	04 02	05 31	07 01	08 30	10 00	11♓29
1970	26♎24	27 40	28 56	00♏12	01 28	02 45	04 01	05 17	06 33	07 49	09 05	10 22	11 38	12 54	14 10	15♏26
1971	13♓55	15 08	16 21	17 34	18 48	20 02	21 17	22 32	23 48	25 04	26 20	27 36	28 53	00♈10	01 27	02♈44
1972	10♏01	11 21	12 42	14 02	15 22	16 43	18 04	19 24	20 45	22 06	23 27	24 48	26 09	27 31	28 52	00♐14
1973	25♈28	25 38	25 50	26 05	26 23	26 44	27 07	27 32	28 00	28 30	29 02	29 36	00♉12	00 50	01 30	02♉11
1974	23♏04	24 28	25 51	27 16	28 40	00♐04	01 28	02 53	04 18	05 43	07 08	08 33	09 58	11 24	12 49	14♐15
1975	28♊R25	27 45	27 02	26 18	25 32	24 46	23 59	23 12	22 25	21 39	20 55	20 11	19 30	18 50	18 13	17♊39
1976	07♐11	08 38	10 05	11 32	13 00	14 27	15 55	17 23	18 51	20 20	21 48	23 17	24 46	26 15	27 44	29♐14
1977	10♌41	10 57	11 10	11 21	11 28	11 32	11 34	11 32	11 27	11 18	11 06	10 51	10 33	10 11	09 46	09♌18
1978	21♐11	22 41	24 11	25 41	27 11	28 41	00♑12	01 43	03 14	04 45	06 16	07 48	09 20	10 52	12 24	13♑56
1979	04♍44	05 31	06 17	07 02	07 45	08 27	09 07	09 46	10 23	10 58	11 31	12 03	12 32	12 59	13 25	13♍48
1980	06♑48	08 19	09 51	11 24	12 56	14 29	16 01	17 34	19 08	20 41	22 14	23 48	25 21	26 55	28 29	00♒03
1981	22♍37	23 38	24 38	25 38	26 38	27 36	28 34	29 31	00♎28	01 24	02 18	03 12	04 05	04 58	05 49	06♎39
1982	22♑49	24 22	25 55	27 28	29 01	00♒35	02 08	03 42	05 15	06 49	08 23	09 57	11 31	13 05	14 39	16♒13
1983	07♎20	08 30	09 39	10 47	11 56	13 04	14 12	15 19	16 26	17 33	18 40	19 46	20 52	21 58	23 03	24♎08
1984	11♒30	13 01	14 32	16 03	17 35	19 06	20 37	22 09	23 41	25 12	26 44	28 16	29 47	01♓19	02 51	04♓23
1985	21♎27	22 42	23 56	25 11	26 25	27 39	28 54	00♏08	01 22	02 36	03 50	05 03	06 17	07 31	08 44	09♏58
1986	03♓19	04 41	06 03	07 25	08 47	10 10	11 33	12 56	14 19	15 42	17 05	18 29	19 52	21 16	22 39	24♓03
1987	04♏29	05 48	07 07	08 25	09 44	11 03	12 22	13 41	15 00	16 20	17 39	18 58	20 17	21 37	22 56	24♏16
1988	06♈30	07 13	07 58	08 45	09 33	10 22	11 13	12 06	12 59	13 54	14 49	15 46	16 44	17 42	18 42	19♈42
1989	18♏08	19 30	20 52	22 15	23 38	25 00	26 23	27 47	29 10	00♐33	01 57	03 20	04 44	06 08	07 32	08♐57
1990	04♊R11	03 28	02 46	02 06	01 28	00 53	00 20	29♉50	29 23	29 00	28 39	28 22	28 08	27 57	27 50	27♉46
1991	01♐21	02 47	03 30	04 55	06 21	07 48	09 14	10 40	12 07	13 34	15 01	16 28	17 56	19 23	20 51	23♐03
1992	27♋R36	27 31	27 22	27 11	26 56	26 37	26 15	25 50	25 22	24 50	24 16	23 39	22 59	22 17	21 34	20♋48
1993	15♐50	17 18	18 47	20 16	21 45	23 14	24 44	26 14	27 44	29 14	00♑44	02 15	03 45	05 16	06 47	08♑19
1994	26♌46	27 24	28 01	28 35	29 08	29 39	00♍07	00 34	00 58	01 20	01 39	01 56	02 11	02 22	02 31	02♍37
1995	00♑19	01 50	03 21	04 53	06 24	07 56	09 28	11 00	12 32	14 05	15 38	17 11	18 44	20 17	21 50	23♑23
1996	16♍28	17 24	18 20	19 15	20 09	21 03	21 55	22 46	23 36	24 25	25 13	26 00	26 45	27 30	28 13	28♍54
1997	16♑35	18 08	19 40	21 13	22 46	24 20	25 53	27 27	29 00	00♒34	02 08	03 42	05 16	06 50	08 24	09♒59
1998	02♎00	03 06	04 13	05 18	06 24	07 29	08 34	09 38	10 41	11 45	12 47	13 50	14 51	15 53	16 53	17♎53
1999	03♒37	50 09	06 41	08 13	09 46	11 19	12 51	14 24	15 57	17 30	19 03	20 36	22 09	23 42	25 15	26♒48
2000	16♎27	17 40	18 52	20 05	21 17	22 29	23 41	24 53	26 04	27 16	28 27	29♏38	00 49	02 00	03 11	04♏21

Jupiter

	January 1st	5th	9th	13th	17th	21st	25th	29th	February 1st	5th	9th	13th	17th	21st	25th	29th
1900	01♐08	01 55	02 40	03 24	04 06	04 47	05 27	06♐04	06♐31	07 06	07 38	08 08	08 36	09 02	09♐25	
1901	25♐58	26 51	27 45	28 37	29 ♑30	00 21	01 12	02♑02	02♑38	03 26	04 13	04 58	05 42	06 25	07♑06	
1902	21♑24	22 19	23 16	24 12	25 08	26 05	27 0q	27♑57	28♑39	29♒35	00 30	01 25	02 19	03 13	04♒05	
1903	18♒20	19 12	20 04	20 58	21 52	22 47	23 43	24♒39	25♒22	26 19	27 16	28 14	29 12	00♓09	01♓07	
1904	17♓46	18 24	19 04	19 46	20 30	21 16	22 03	22♓51	23♓29	24 19	25 11	26 04	26 58	27 53	28 48	29♓44
1905	20♈41	20 56	21 14	21 35	21 59	22 25	22 54	23♈25	23♈50	24 26	25 03	25 43	26 24	27 07	27♈52	
1906	27♉R11	26 56	26 44	26 35	26 30	26 D28	26 29	26♉33	26♉39	26 49	27 02	27 18	27 37	27 59	28♉24	
1907	05♋R33	05 01	04 30	03 59	03 30	03 04	02 39	02♋16	02♋R01	01 43	01 28	01 17	01 08	01 02	01♋D00	
1908	12♌R05	14 41	11 15	10 47	10 17	09 47	09 15	08♌43	08♌19	07 48	07 16	06 46	06 17	05 50	05 24	05♌01
1909	14♍R31	14 29	14 23	14 14	14 02	13 48	13 30	13♍10	12♍R53	12 29	12 03	11 35	11 06	10 36	10♍05	
1910	13♎17	13 36	13 53	14 07	14 18	14 26	14 31	14♎33	14♎R33	14 29	14 23	14 14	14 01	13 46	13♎29	
1911	09♏32	10 08	10 42	11 15	11 45	12 14	12 40	13♏03	13♏19	13 38	13 55	14 08	14 19	14 27	14♏31	
1912	04♐32	05 20	06 07	06 53	07 37	08 20	09 02	09♐42	10♐11	10 48	11 23	11 58	12 28	12 57	13 23	13♐48
1913	29♐35	09 ♑30	01 24	02 17	03 10	04 03	04 55	05♑46	06♑23	07 13	08 01	08 48	09 34	10 18	11♑02	
1914	25♑10	26 06	27 02	27 58	28 54	29♒51	00 48	01♒44	02♒27	03 23	04 19	05 14	06 09	07 04	07♒58	
1915	22♒22	23 13	24 04	24 57	25 50	26 44	27 39	28♒35	29♒17	00♓14	01 11	02 08	03 06	04 04	05♓02	
1916	22♓12	22 48	23 25	24 05	24 47	25 30	26 15	27♓02	27♓38	28 27	29 18	00♈09	01 02	01 55	02 50	03♈45
1917	25♈38	25 49	26 03	26 20	26 40	27 03	27 28	27♈56	28♈19	28 52	29 26	00♉03	00 42	01 23	02♉05	
1918	02♊R34	02 15	02 00	01 47	01 38	01 31	01 D28	01♊29	01♊31	01 37	01 47	01 59	02 14	02 33	02♊54	
1919	10♋R56	19 24	09 52	09 20	08 50	08 21	07 53	07♋28	07♋R11	06 50	06 32	06 16	06 04	05 55	05♋49	
1920	17♌R00	16 39	16 15	15 50	15 22	14 53	14 22	13♌51	13♌R27	12 55	12 23	11 52	11 22	10 52	10 25	09♌59
1921	18♏54	18 R55	18 52	18 47	18 38	18 27	18 12	17♏55	17♏R40	17 19	16 55	16 29	16 01	15 32	15♏02	
1922	17♎14	17 36	17 56	18 12	18 27	18 38	18 46	18♎51	18♎R53	18 53	18 50	18 44	18 35	18 23	18♎08	
1923	13♏13	13 51	14 28	15 03	15 35	16 06	16 34	17♏01	17♏19	17 41	18 00	18 16	18 30	18 41	18♏49	
1924	08♐06	08 55	09 43	10 30	11 16	12 01	12 45	13♐26	13♐57	14 36	15 13	15 49	16 22	16 53	17 23	17♐50
1925	03♑09	04 04	04 58	05 53	06 47	07 40	08 33	09♑24	10♑03	10 54	11 43	12 32	13 19	14 05	14♑50	
1926	28♑50	29♒46	00 41	01 38	02 34	03 31	04 27	05♒24	06♒07	07 03	08 00	08 56	09 52	10 47	11♒42	
1927	26♒18	27 06	27 57	28 48	29♓40	00 34	01 28	02♓23	03♓05	04 01	04 57	05 54	06 52	07 49	08♓47	
1928	26♓32	27 05	27 40	28 17	28 56	29♈37	00 21	01♈05	01♈40	02 27	03 16	04 06	04 58	05 50	06 43	07♈38
1929	00♉30	00 36	00 46	01 00	01 16	01 35	01 57	02♉22	02♉43	03 12	03 44	04 18	04 54	05 33	06♉13	
1930	07♊R53	07 31	07 12	06 56	06 42	06 32	06 25	06♊D22	06♊21	06 23	06 29	06 37	06 49	07 04	07♊21	
1931	16♋R14	15 42	15 10	14 38	14 06	13 35	13 06	12♋39	12♋R19	11 56	11 34	11 16	11 00	10 47	10♋38	
1932	21♌R50	21 32	21 11	20 47	20 22	19 54	19 25	18♌55	18♌R31	18 00	17 28	16 56	16 25	15 55	15 25	14♌58
1933	23♍11	23 R15	23 16	23 14	23 08	23 00	22 49	22♍34	22♍R22	22 03	21 41	21 18	20 52	20 24	19♍55	
1934	21♎06	21 31	21 53	22 13	22 30	22 44	22 55	23♎04	23♎08	23 11	23 11	23 09	23 03	22 54	22♎42	
1935	16♏51	17 31	18 09	18 46	19 21	19 54	20 25	20♏53	21♏13	21 38	22 00	22 20	22 36	22 50	23♏02	
1936	11♐39	12 29	13 19	14 07	14 54	15 41	16 26	17♐09	17♐41	18 22	19 02	19 39	20 15	20 49	21 21	21♐51
1937	06♑46	07 41	08 36	09 31	10 25	11 20	12 13	13♑06	13♑46	14 37	15 28	16 18	17 07	17 55	18♑42	
1938	02♒38	03 33	04 29	05 25	06 21	07 18	08 14	09♒11	09♒54	10 51	11 48	12 45	13 41	14 37	15♒33	
1939	00♓26	01 13	02 02	02 52	03 43	04 35	05 28	06♓23	07♓04	07 59	08 55	09 52	10 49	11 46	12♓44	
1940	01♈09	01 39	02 11	02 45	03 22	04 01	04 42	05♈24	05♈57	06 43	07 30	08 18	09 08	09 59	10 51	11♈44
1941	05♉41	05 43	05 49	05 58	06 10	06 26	06 44	07♉05	07♉23	07 49	08 18	08 49	09 22	09 58	10♉35	
1942	13♊R26	13 01	12 38	12 18	12 01	11 47	11 36	11♊29	11♊R25	11 D23	11 24	11 29	11 37	11 48	12♊02	
1943	21♋R34	21 03	20 30	19 58	19 26	18 54	18 24	17♋54	17♋R33	17 07	16 43	16 21	16 02	15 46	15♋23	
1944	26♌R32	26 17	25 58	25 38	25 15	24 49	24 22	23♌53	23♌R30	23 00	22 28	21 56	21 25	20 53	20 23	19♌54
1945	27♍18	27 25	27 29	27 R30	27 28	27 22	27 14	27♍03	26♍R52	26 36	26 17	25 56	25 32	25 06	24♍39	
1946	24♎49	25 16	25 41	26 03	26 23	26 40	26 54	27♎05	27♎12	27 18	27 R22	27 22	27 19	27 13	27♎05	
1947	20♏22	21 04	21 44	22 23	23 00	23 35	24 08	24♏39	25♏00	25 28	25 52	26 15	26 34	26 51	27♏06	
1948	15♐09	16 00	16 50	17 40	18 29	19 17	20 03	20♐48	21♐21	22 04	22 46	23 26	24 04	24 40	25 14	25♐46
1949	10♑23	11 19	12 14	13 09	14 05	15 00	15 54	16♑48	17♑28	18 21	19 13	20 04	20 55	21 44	22♑33	
1950	06♒30	07 25	08 20	09 15	10 12	11 08	12 05	13♒02	13♒45	14 42	15 40	16 38	17 34	18 30	19♒27	
1951	04♓42	05 27	06 14	07 03	07 52	08 43	09 36	10♓29	11♓09	12 04	12 59	13 55	14 52	15 49	16♓46	
1952	05♈57	06 23	06 52	07 23	07 57	08 33	09 11	09♈51	10♈22	11 06	11 51	12 37	13 26	14 15	15 05	15♈57
1953	11♉R01	10 D59	11 00	11 05	11 13	11 24	11 38	11♉56	12♉11	12 33	12 58	13 26	13 56	14 29	15♉03	
1954	19♊R01	18 34	18 08	17 45	17 25	17 07	16 52	16♊40	16♊R34	16 28	16 25	16 26	16 29	16 36	16♊46	
1955	26♋R51	26 21	25 49	25 17	24 45	24 13	23 41	23♋10	22♋R48	22 20	21 53	21 29	21 07	20 48	20♋31	
1956	01♍R12	01 00	00 45	00 27	00♌06	29 43	29 18	28♌51	28♌R29	28 00	27 29	26 58	26 26	25 54	25 23	24♌53
1957	01♎26	01 36	01 43	01 47	01 48	01 46	01 41	01♎33	01♎R25	01 11	00 55	00 37	00♍15	29 52	29♍26	
1958	28♎35	39 05	29 32	29♏57	00 19	00 39	00 56	01♏11	01♏20	01 29	01 36	01 R39	01 40	01 37	01♏32	
1959	23♏58	24 42	25 24	26 04	26 43	27 20	27 56	28♏29	28♏53	29 22	29♐50	00 15	00 38	00 58	01♐15	
1960	18♐45	19 37	20 28	21 19	22 09	22 58	23 46	24♐33	25♐08	25 52	26 36	27 17	27 58	28 36	29 13	29♐47
1961	14♑06	15 02	15 58	16 54	17 49	18 45	19 40	20♑35	21♑15	22 09	23 03	23 55	24 47	25 38	26♑28	
1962	10♒28	11 22	12 16	13 11	14 07	16 03	16 00	16♒57	17♒40	18 37	19 35	20 32	21 30	22 27	23♒24	
1963	09♓01	09 44	10 29	11 16	12 04	12 54	13 44	14♓36	15♓16	16 10	17 04	17 59	18 55	19 52	20♓49	
1964	10♈44	11 07	11 32	12 00	12 31	13 04	13 39	14♈17	14♈46	15 27	16 10	16 54	17 40	18 27	19 16	20♈06
1965	16♉R15	16 09	16 D06	16 07	16 11	16 18	16 28	16♉42	16♉54	17 12	17 34	17 58	18 25	18 54	19♉26	
1966	24♊R26	23 57	23 29	23 03	22 39	22 18	22 00	21♊45	21♊R36	21 26	21 19	21 15	21 15	21 18	21♊24	
1967	01♌R55	01 27	00 56	00 25	29♋53	29 21	28 49	28♋17	27♋R54	27 24	26 56	26 29	26 05	25 42	25♋23	
1968	05♍R42	05 32	05 20	05 05	04 48	04 27	04 05	03♍40	03♍R20	02 51	02 22	01 51	01 20	00 48	00♌17	29♌46
1969	05♎27	05 41	05 51	05 58	06 02	06 03	06 02	05♎57	05♎R51	05 41	05 28	05 12	04 53	04 32	04♎09	
1970	02♏20	02 52	03 21	03 49	04 14	04 36	04 56	05♏14	05♏25	05 37	05 47	05 54	05 57	05 R58	05♏56	
1971	27♏35	28 20	29♐04	29 46	00 27	01 06	01 44	02♐19	02♐45	03 17	03 47	04 14	04 40	05 03	05♐23	
1972	22♐21	23 14	24 07	24 59	25 50	26 40	27 30	28♐18	28♐53	29♑40	00 25	01 09	01 51	02 31	03 10	03♑47
1973	17♑49	18 45	19 42	20 38	21 34	22 30	23 25	24♑21	25♑02	25 57	26 51	27 45	28 38	29♒30	00♒21	
1974	14♒25	15 18	16 12	17 06	18 01	18 57	19 53	20♒50	21♒33	22 30	23 28	24 25	25 23	26 20	27♒18	
1975	13♓19	14 00	14 43	15 28	16 14	17 02	17 51	18♓42	19♓20	20 13	21 06	22 00	22 56	23 51	24♓48	
1976	15♈32	15 51	16 13	16 37	17 05	17 34	18 07	18♈41	19♈08	19 47	20 27	21 09	21 53	22 39	23 25	24♈14
1977	21♉32	21 22	21 15	21 11	21 11	21 14	21 20	21♉29	21♉38	21 53	22 11	22 32	22 55	23 22	23♉50	
1978	29♊R52	29 21	28 51	28 23	27 57	27 33	27 12	26♊53	26♊R41	26 27	26 17	26 09	26 05	26 05	26♊07	
1979	07♌R00	06 33	06 04	05 34	05 03	04 32	04 00	03♌27	03♌R04	02 33	02 03	01 34	01 07	00 37	00♌20	
1980	10♍R12	10 06	09 57	09 46	09 31	09 13	08 53	08♍31	08♍R12	07 46	07 18	06 49	06 18	05 47	05 15	04♍44
1981	09♎30	09 47	10 00	10 10	10 18	10 R22	10 23	10♎22	10♎R18	10 11	10 01	09 48	09 33	09 14	08♎48	
1982	06♏04	06 38	07 10	07 40	08 08	08 33	08 56	09♏16	09♏30	09 45	09 58	10 08	10 15	10 R19	10♏20	
1983	01♐11	01 57	02 42	03 26	04 09	04 50	05 29	06♐07	06♐34	07 03	07 41	08 11	08 39	09 05	09♐28	
1984	25♐55	26 48	27 42	28 34	29♑26	00 18	01 08	01♑58	02♑34	03 22	04 09	04 54	05 38	06 21	07 02	07♑41
1985	21♑27	22 23	23 19	24 16	25 12	26 08	27 04	28♑00	28♑42	29♒37	00 32	01 27	02 21	03 14	04♒06	
1986	18♒15	19 07	20 00	20 53	21 48	22 43	23 39	24♒35	25♒18	26 15	27 12	28 09	29 07	00♓05	01♓02	
1987	17♓31	18 09	18 50	19 33	20 17	21 03	21 51	22♓40	23♓18	24 09	25 01	25 54	26 48	27 43	28♓39	
1988	20♈14	20 29	20 47	21 08	21 32	21 59	22 28	23♈00	23♈25	24 01	24 38	25 18	26 00	26 43	27 28	28♈15
1989	26♉R44	26 30	26 19	26 11	26 D07	26 06	26 08	26♉13	26♉20	26 31	26 45	27 02	27 22	27 45	28♉10	
1990	05♋R13	04 41	04 10	03 40	03 12	02 45	02 21	01♋59	01♋R44	01 27	01 13	01 02	00 55	00 D50	00♋49	
1991	11♌R59	11 35	11 08	10 40	10 10	09 39	09 07	08♌35	08♌R11	07 40	07 08	06 38	06 10	05 43	05♌18	
1992	14♍R38	14 35	14 30	14 21	14 09	13 55	13 38	13♍18	13♍R01	12 37	12 11	11 43	11 14	10 44	10 13	09♍41
1993	13♎29	13 48	14 04	14 18	14 28	14 36	14 R40	14♎42	14♎R41	14 37	14 30	14 20	14 08	13 52	13♎34	
1994	09♏46	10 22	10 56	11 28	11 58	12 26	12 51	13♏14	13♏30	13 48	14 04	14 17	14 27	14 34	14♏R38	
1995	04♐44	05 32	06 18	07 04	07 48	08 30	09 12	09♐51	10♐20	10 57	11 31	12 04	12 35	13 03	13♐29	
1996	29♐29	00♑23	01 17	02 10	03 03	03 56	04 47	05♑38	06♑16	07 05	07 53	08 40	09 26	10 10	10 53	11♑34
1997	25♑10	26 06	27 02	27 58	28 55	29♒51	00 48	01♒44	02♒26	03 22	04 18	05 13	06 08	07 02	07♒56	
1998	22♒15	23 05	23 57	24 50	25 43	26 38	27 33	28♒29	29♒11	00♓08	01 05	02 02	03 00	03 58	04♓56	
1999	21♓56	22 33	23 11	23 51	24 34	25 18	26 03	26♓51	27♓27	28 17	29 07	29♈59	00 52	01 46	02♈41	
2000	25♈14	25 25	25 39	25 56	26 17	26 40	27 06	27♈34	27♈57	28 30	29 05	29♉42	00 21	01 02	01 45	02♉29

	March								April							
	1st	5th	9th	13th	17th	21st	25th	29th	1st	5th	9th	13th	17th	21st	25th	29th
1900	09♐46	10 04	10 19	10 31	10 41	10 48	10 R51	10♐52	10♐R51	10 46	10 38	10 28	10 15	09 59	09 40	09♐19
1901	07♑45	08 23	08 59	09 32	10 04	10 33	11 00	11♑25	11♑42	12 02	12 19	12 34	12 46	12 54	13 00	13♑R03
1902	04♒57	05 48	06 38	07 27	08 14	09 01	09 46	10♒29	11♒00	11 41	12 19	12 56	13 31	14 03	04 34	15♒02
1903	02♓05	03 02	03 59	04 56	05 53	06 49	07 44	08♓39	09♓19	10 12	11 04	11 56	12 46	13 35	14 23	15♓09
1904	29♓♈58	00 55	01 52	02 50	03 47	04 45	05 44	06♈42	07♈25	08 23	09 21	10 19	11 16	12 13	13 09	14♈05
1905	28♈39	29♉26	00 15	01 05	01 57	02 49	03 42	04♉36	05♉17	06 12	07 08	08 04	09 00	09 57	10 54	11♉51
1906	28♉51	29 21	29♊52	00 27	01 03	01 41	02 21	03♊02	03♊35	04 19	05 05	05 52	06 40	07 29	08 19	09♊10
1907	01♋01	01 05	01 12	01 22	01 35	01 51	02 10	02♋32	02♋49	03 15	03 44	04 14	04 47	05 21	05 58	06♋36
1908	04♌R56	04 35	04 18	04 03	03 51	03 43	03 37	03♌D34	03♌34	03 37	03 42	03 51	04 02	04 17	04 34	04♌53
1909	09♍R33	09 02	08 31	08 00	07 31	07 03	06 37	06♍13	05♍R56	05 36	05 19	05 04	04 52	04 42	04 36	04♍32
1910	13♎R09	12 46	12 21	11 55	11 27	10 58	10 27	09♎57	09♎R34	09 03	08 32	08 03	07 34	07 07	06 41	06♎17
1911	14♏R33	14 32	14 28	14 20	14 10	13 57	13 42	13♏23	13♏R08	12 46	12 21	11 55	11 27	10 58	10 28	09♏58
1912	13♐53	14 14	14 33	14 49	15 01	15 11	15 19	15♐23	15♐R24	15 23	15 19	15 12	15 02	14 49	14 33	14♐15
1913	11♑43	12 23	13 01	13 37	14 11	14 43	15 13	15♑41	16♑00	16 23	06 44	17 02	17 17	17 30	17 39	17♑46
1914	08♒51	09 43	10 34	11 25	12 14	13 02	13 49	14♒34	15♒07	15 50	16 31	17 10	17 47	18 23	18 56	19♒27
1915	06♓00	06 57	07 55	08 52	09 49	10 46	11 42	12♓38	13♓19	14 13	15 07	15 59	16 51	17 42	18 31	19♓19
1916	03♈59	04 55	05 51	06 48	07 46	08 43	09 41	10♈39	11♈23	12 21	13 19	14 17	15 14	16 11	17 08	18♈05
1917	02♉50	03 36	04 23	05 11	06 01	06 52	07 44	08♉36	09♉16	10 10	11 05	12 00	12 56	13 52	14 49	15♉46
1918	03♊18	03 44	04 13	04 44	06 18	05 53	06 31	07♊10	07♊40	08 23	09 06	09 51	10 38	11 26	12 14	13♊04
1919	05♋R46	05 46	05 50	05 56	06 06	06 18	06 34	06♋52	07♋07	07 30	07 55	08 23	08 53	09 25	09 59	10♋25
1920	09♌R53	09 30	09 10	08 62	08 37	08 25	08 16	08♌10	08♌R07	08 06	08 09	08 14	08 22	08 33	08 47	09♌03
1921	14♍R31	13 59	13 28	12 57	12 26	11 58	11 30	11♍04	10♍R45	10 22	10 02	09 44	09 29	09 17	09 07	09♍00
1922	17♎R51	17 31	17 09	16 44	16 18	15 50	15 21	14♎51	14♎R28	13 57	13 26	12 56	12 26	11 57	11 30	11♎04
1923	18♏54	18 56	18 55	18 51	18 45	18 35	18 22	18♏07	17♏R53	17 33	17 11	16 47	16 20	15 53	15 24	14♏55
1924	17♐56	18 20	18 42	19 01	19 17	19 30	19 40	19♐48	19♐51	19 54	19 53	19 50	19 43	19 33	19 31	19♐06
1925	15♑34	16 15	16 56	17 34	18 11	18 45	19 18	19♑48	20♑09	20 36	20 59	21 21	21 39	21 55	22 08	22♑19
1926	12♒36	13 29	14 22	15 13	16 04	16 53	17 42	18♒29	19♒03	19 48	20 31	21 12	21 52	22 30	29 06	23♒40
1927	09♓45	10 43	11 41	12 39	13 36	14 33	15 30	16♓37	17♓08	18 04	18 58	19 52	20 45	21 37	22 28	23♓18
1928	07♈51	08 47	09 42	10 39	11 36	12 33	13 30	14♈28	15♈12	16 10	17 08	18 05	19 03	20 01	20 58	21♈55
1929	06♉55	07 39	08 24	09 11	09 59	10 48	11 39	12♉30	13♉09	14 02	14 56	15 51	16 46	17 41	18 37	19♉33
1930	07♊42	08 06	08 31	08 59	09 30	10 02	10 37	11♊14	11♊43	12 23	13 05	13 48	14 33	15 19	16 06	16♊54
1931	10♋R31	10 28	10 27	10 30	10 36	10 45	10 57	11♋12	11♋25	11 45	12 07	12 32	12 59	13 28	13 59	14♋33
1932	14♌R51	14 26	14 03	13 42	13 24	13 09	12 56	12♌47	12♌R42	12 37	12 36	12 38	12 43	12 51	13 01	13♌15
1933	19♍R25	18 54	18 23	17 52	17 21	16 51	16 21	15♍53	15♍R34	15 09	14 46	14 25	14 07	13 52	13 39	13♍29
1934	22♎R27	22 10	21 50	21 28	21 04	20 38	20 10	19♎41	19♎R19	18 48	18 18	17 47	17 16	16 47	16 18	15♎50
1935	23♏10	23 15	23 18	23 17	23 13	23 07	22 57	22♏45	22♏R34	22 17	21 57	21 35	21 11	20 45	20 18	19♏49
1936	21♐58	22 24	22 49	23 10	23 30	23 46	24 00	24♐11	24♐17	24 23	24 26	24 26	24 22	24 16	24 07	23♐55
1937	19♑27	20 11	20 53	21 34	22 12	22 50	23 25	23♑58	24♑21	24 50	25 17	25 42	26 04	26 23	26 40	26♑53
1938	16♒28	17 22	18 16	19 09	20 01	20 52	21 42	22♒21	23♒07	23 53	24 38	25 22	26 04	26 44	27 23	27♒59
1939	13♓42	14 40	15 38	16 36	17 34	18 32	19 29	20♓26	21♓09	22 05	23 00	23 55	24 49	25 42	26 35	27♓26
1940	11♈57	12 52	13 47	14 42	15 38	16 35	17 32	18♈29	19♈13	20 10	21 08	22 06	23 04	24 01	24 59	25♈57
1941	11♉15	11 56	12 39	13 24	14 10	14 58	15 47	16♉37	17♉15	18 06	18 59	19 52	20 46	21 41	22 36	23♉18
1942	12♊18	12 38	13 00	13 25	13 53	14 23	14 55	15♊29	15♊56	16 34	17 13	17 54	18 37	19 21	20 06	20♊53
1943	15♋R22	15 15	15 11	15 10	15 13	15 18	15 26	15♋38	15♋48	16 04	16 23	16 45	17 09	17 36	18 04	18♋35
1944	19♌R47	19 19	18 54	18 31	18 10	17 52	17 36	17♌23	17♌R16	17 08	17 04	17 02	17 03	17 08	17 15	17♌25
1945	24♍R10	23 40	23 09	22 38	22 04	21 36	21 06	20♍37	20♍16	19 49	19 24	19 01	18 40	18 22	18 07	17♍54
1946	26♎53	26 R38	26 21	26 01	25 39	25 15	24 49	24♎21	24♎00	23 R30	23 00	22 29	21 58	21 28	20 58	20♎29
1947	27♏17	27 25	27 31	27 R34	27 33	27 30	27 23	27♏14	27♏05	26 R51	26 34	26 14	25 53	25 29	25 03	24♏36
1948	25♐54	26 23	26 51	27 15	27 38	27 57	28 14	28♐28	28♐37	28 47	28 53	28 56	28 56	28 53	28 48	28♐39
1949	23♑20	24 05	24 50	25 32	26 14	26 53	27 31	28♑07	28♑32	29 04	29 34	00♒02	00 27	00 49	01 09	01♒27
1950	20♒23	21 18	22 13	23 07	24 00	24 53	25 44	26♒35	27♒12	28 01	28 48	29♓34	00 18	01 01	01 42	02♓21
1951	17♓44	18 42	19 40	20 39	21 37	22 35	23 32	24♓30	25♓13	26 10	27 06	28 02	28 57	29♈52	00 45	01♈38
1952	16♈10	17 03	17 56	18 51	19 46	20 42	21 39	22♈35	23♈18	24 16	25 13	26 11	27 09	28 07	29♉04	29♉48
1953	15♉40	16 19	17 00	17 42	18 26	19 12	19 59	20♉47	21♉24	22 14	23 05	23 57	24 50	25 43	26 38	27♉32
1954	16♊59	17 15	17 34	17 56	18 20	18 47	19 15	19♊47	20♊12	20 47	21 24	22 02	22 43	23 25	24 08	24♊53
1955	20♋R17	20 07	19 59	19 54	19 53	19 55	19 59	20♋07	20♋15	20 28	20 43	21 02	21 23	21 46	22 12	22♋40
1956	24♌R45	24 17	23 49	23 24	23 00	22 39	22 21	22♌04	21♌R55	21 44	21 36	21 31	21 29	21 30	21 34	21♌41
1957	28♍R59	28 30	28 01	27 30	26 59	26 28	25 57	25♍27	25♍R05	24 36	24 10	23 45	23 22	23 01	22 42	22♍27
1958	01♏R23	01 12	00 57	00 40	00 21	29♎59	29 35	29♎09	28♎R49	28 20	27 51	27 20	26 50	26 19	25 49	25♎19
1959	01♐30	01 41	01 50	01 56	01 59	01 59	01 56	01♐50	01♐R44	01 32	01 18	01 02	00 43	00 21	29♏58	29♏32
1960	29♐♑56	00 28	00 58	01 25	01 51	02 14	02 34	02♑51	03♑03	03 15	03 25	03 32	03 36	03 37	03 35	03♑30
1961	27♑16	28 04	28 50	29♒35	00 18	01 00	01 40	02♒18	02♒46	03 12	03 46	04 17	04 46	05 12	05 36	05♒58
1962	24♒20	25 17	26 12	27 07	28 02	28 56	29♓48	00♓40	01♓31	02 21	03 10	03 57	04 43	05 28	06 11	06♓52
1963	21♓46	22 44	23 42	24 40	25 38	26 36	27 34	28♓32	29♓15	00♈13	01 10	02 06	03 02	03 58	04 52	05♈46
1964	20♈19	21 10	22 00	22 56	23 50	24 45	25 41	26♈37	27♈19	28 16	29 13	00♉11	01 08	02 06	03 04	04♉01
1965	20♉00	20 36	21 14	21 54	22 36	23 20	24 04	24♉51	25♉26	26 15	27 04	27 55	28 46	29♊39	00 32	01♊26
1966	21♊34	21 46	22 01	22 19	22 40	23 04	23 30	23♊58	24♊21	24 53	25 28	26 04	26 42	27 22	28 03	28♊46
1967	25♋R06	24 52	24 41	24 32	24 27	24 26	24 27	24♋31	24♋36	24 46	24 58	25 13	25 31	25 52	26 15	26♋40
1968	29♌R38	29 08	28 39	28 12	27 46	27 23	27 01	26♌43	26♌R30	26 16	26 05	25 57	25 52	25 50	25 51	25♌54
1969	03♎R43	03 16	02 48	02 18	01 47	01 16	00 45	00♍14	29♍R52	29 22	28 54	28 27	28 02	27 39	27 18	27♍00
1970	05♏R50	05 42	05 31	05 17	05 00	04 41	04 19	03♏55	03♏R36	03 09	02 41	02 11	01 41	01 11	00 40	00♏09
1971	05♐41	05 56	06 08	06 17	06 23	06 27	06 R27	06♐25	06♐R21	06 13	06 02	05 48	05 32	05 13	04 52	04♐29
1972	03♑56	04 31	05 04	05 34	06 02	06 28	06 51	07♑12	07♑26	07 42	07 56	08 06	08 13	08 18	08 R19	08♑18
1973	01♒11	02 00	02 48	03 35	04 20	05 04	05 46	06♒27	06♒56	07 34	08 09	08 43	09 14	09 43	10 10	10♒34
1974	28♒15	29 12	00♓08	01 04	01 59	02 54	03 48	04♓41	05♓21	06 12	07 03	07 52	08 40	09 27	10 12	10♓56
1975	25♓45	26 42	27 39	28 37	29♈35	00 33	01 32	02♈30	03♈13	04 11	05 08	06 05	07 02	07 58	08 54	09♈49
1976	24♈26	25 16	26 07	26 59	27 52	28 46	29♉40	00♉36	01♉17	02 13	03 10	04 07	05 04	06 01	06 59	07♉56
1977	24♉21	24 55	25 30	26 07	26 47	27 28	28 11	28♉55	29♉♊29	00 16	01 04	01 53	02 43	03 34	04 26	05♊19
1978	26♊12	26 21	26 33	26 47	27 05	27 25	27 48	28♊13	28♊34	29 03	29 35	00♋09	00 44	01 22	02 01	02♋42
1979	00♋R00	29 43	29 28	29 17	29 08	29 03	29 D00	29♋01	29♋04	29 10	29 19	29 31	29 46	00♌03	00 23	00♌46
1980	04♍R36	04 05	03 35	03 06	02 39	02 13	01 49	01♍28	01♍R14	00 57	00 42	00 31	00 23	00 17	00 15	00♍15
1981	08♎R30	08 05	07 38	07 10	06 40	06 07	05 39	05♎08	04♎R45	04 14	03 45	03 16	02 50	02 24	02 01	01♎40
1982	10♏R18	10 13	10 04	09 54	09 40	09 23	09 04	08♏43	08♏R25	08 00	07 33	07 05	06 36	06 06	05 35	05♏05
1983	09♐49	10 07	10 22	10 35	10 44	10 51	10 55	10♐55	10♐R54	10 49	10 42	10 32	10 18	10 03	09 44	09♐23
1984	07♑50	08 27	09 03	09 36	10 06	10 35	11 01	11♑25	11♑42	12 01	12 18	12 31	12 42	12 50	12 56	12♑R58
1985	04♒58	05 48	06 38	07 26	08 13	08 59	09 43	10♒26	10♒57	11 36	12 14	12 50	13 24	13 56	14 26	14♒53
1986	02♓00	02 57	03 54	04 51	05 47	06 43	07 38	08♓32	09♓12	10 05	10 57	11 48	12 37	13 26	14 13	14♓59
1987	29♓♈35	00 32	01 29	02 26	03 24	04 22	05 20	06♈18	07♈02	08 00	08 58	09 55	10 52	11 49	12 45	13♈41
1988	28♈27	29 15	00♉04	00 55	01 47	02 39	03 33	04♉27	05♉08	06 04	07 00	07 56	08 53	09 50	10 47	11♉44
1989	28♉38	29 09	29♊42	00 17	00 53	01 32	02 13	02♊55	03♊28	04 13	04 59	05 46	06 35	07 25	08 15	09♊07
1990	00♋50	00 55	01 03	01 14	01 28	01 45	02 05	02♋27	02♋46	03 12	03 41	04 12	04 46	05 21	05 58	06♋37
1991	04♌R55	04 35	04 17	04 02	03 51	03 42	03 36	03♌33	03♌33	03 36	03 41	03 50	04 01	04 16	04 33	04♌52
1992	09♍R33	09 02	08 31	08 01	07 32	07 04	06 39	06♍15	05♍R58	05 39	05 22	05 07	04 56	04 47	04 41	04♍D38
1993	13♎R13	12 50	12 25	11 58	11 30	11 01	10 30	10♎00	09♎R36	09 06	08 35	08 06	07 37	07 04	06 45	06♎16
1994	14♏R39	14 38	14 33	14 25	14 14	14 01	13 44	13♏25	13♏R10	12 47	12 22	11 55	11 27	10 58	10 28	09♏58
1995	13♐53	14 14	14 32	14 48	15 01	15 11	15 18	15♐22	15♐R23	15 22	15 18	15 11	15 01	14 48	14 32	14♐14
1996	11♑44	12 24	13 01	13 37	14 10	14 42	15 11	15♑38	15♑56	16 19	16 39	16 56	17 10	17 22	17 31	17♑36
1997	08♒48	09 40	10 31	11 21	12 10	12 57	13 43	14♒28	15♒01	15 43	16 23	17 02	17 38	18 13	18 46	19♒16
1998	05♓53	06 51	07 49	08 46	09 43	10 39	11 35	12♓30	13♓11	14 05	14 58	15 51	16 42	17 32	18 21	19♓09
1999	03♈36	04 32	05 29	06 26	07 23	08 21	09 19	10♈17	11♈01	11 59	12 57	13 55	14 52	15 50	16 46	17♈43
2000	02♉40	02 27	04 14	05 03	05 54	06 45	07 37	08♉30	09♉11	10 05	11 00	11 56	12 52	13 48	14 45	15♉42

Jupiter

	May 1st	May 5th	May 9th	May 13th	May 17th	May 21st	May 25th	May 29th	June 1st	June 5th	June 9th	June 13th	June 17th	June 21st	June 25th	June 29th
1900	09♐R08	08 44	08 18	07 50	07 22	06 52	06 22	05♐51	05♐R28	04 58	04 28	04 00	03 33	03 07	02 43	02♐21
1901	13♑R04	13 02	12 57	12 50	12 39	12 26	12 10	11♑51	11♑R35	11 R13	10 48	10 21	09 53	09 24	08 54	08♑23
1902	15♒R15	15 40	16 01	16 21	16 40	16 51	17 01	17♒09	17♒13	17 15	17 15	17 11	17 04	16 55	16 42	16♒26
1903	15♓32	16 16	16 59	17 39	18 18	18 56	19 31	20♓04	20♓27	20 56	21 23	21 47	22 08	22 27	22 43	22♓56
1904	14♈32	15 27	16 21	17 14	18 06	18 57	19 47	20♈36	21♈12	21 58	22 44	23 27	24 09	24 49	25 28	26♈04
1905	12♉20	13 17	14 14	15 11	16 08	17 05	18 01	18♉56	19♉38	20 33	21 27	22 21	23 14	24 06	24 57	25♉47
1906	09♊36	10 28	11 21	12 15	13 09	14 04	14 58	15♊54	16♊35	17 30	18 26	19 21	20 17	21 12	22 07	23♊02
1907	06♋55	07 36	08 18	09 02	09 46	10 32	11 19	12♋07	12♋44	13 34	14 24	15 15	16 07	16 59	17 51	18♋44
1908	05♌04	05 27	05 53	06 21	06 51	07 23	07 57	08♌32	09♌00	09 39	10 19	11 00	11 43	12 27	13 12	13♌58
1909	04♍D32	04 33	04 37	04 44	04 53	05 06	05 21	05♍38	05♍53	06 15	06 39	07 06	07 34	08 05	08 38	09♍12
1910	06♎R06	05 56	05 28	05 12	05 00	04 50	04 42	04♎38	04♎D37	04 38	04 41	04 48	04 57	05 09	05 24	05♎41
1911	09♏R43	09 12	08 42	08 12	07 43	07 16	07 50	06♏26	06♏R09	05 49	05 31	05 16	05 02	04 53	04 46	04♏41
1912	14♐R05	13 43	13 19	12 54	12 26	11 58	11 28	10♐58	10♐R35	10 05	09 34	09 05	08 36	08 08	07 43	07♐18
1913	14♑48	17 R50	17 49	17 45	17 39	17 29	17 16	17♑01	16♑R47	16 27	16 05	15 41	15 14	14 47	14 18	13♑48
1914	19♒42	20 09	20 34	20 57	21 17	21 35	21 49	22♒01	22♒07	22 14	22 17	22 17	22 15	22 09	22 00	21♒48
1915	19♓43	20 29	21 14	21 57	22 38	23 18	23 56	24♓32	24♓57	25 29	25 59	26 26	26 51	27 14	27 34	27♓50
1916	18♈33	19 28	20 23	21 17	22 10	23 03	23 54	24♈45	25♈22	26 09	26 57	27 42	28 26	29 09	29♉50	00♉28
1917	16♉14	17 11	18 08	19 05	20 02	20 59	21 55	22♉51	23♉33	24 28	25 23	26 18	27 11	28 04	28 56	29♊47
1918	13♊29	14 20	15 12	16 05	16 58	17 52	18 46	19♊40	20♊22	21 16	22 12	23 07	24 02	24 57	25 52	26♊47
1919	10♋53	11 32	12 12	12 53	13 36	14 21	15 06	15♋53	16♋29	17 17	18 06	18 56	19 45	20 38	21 30	22♋22
1920	09♌13	09 33	09 56	10 21	10 48	11 18	11 50	12♌23	12♌49	13 26	14 04	14 44	15 25	16 08	16 51	17♌36
1921	08♍R58	08 56	08 57	09 00	09 07	09 16	09 28	09♍43	09♍56	10 15	10 36	11 00	11 27	11 55	12 25	12♍58
1922	10♎R52	10 29	10 09	09 51	09 35	09 22	09 12	09♎04	09♎R01	08 D58	08 59	09 02	09 09	09 18	09 29	09♎44
1923	14♏R40	14 09	13 39	13 08	12 38	12 10	11 42	11♏16	10♏58	10 35	10 14	09 56	09 41	09 28	09 17	09♏10
1924	18♐R57	18 38	18 17	17 53	17 28	17 01	16 32	16♐03	15♐40	15 10	14 39	14 09	13 39	13 10	12 43	12♐16
1925	22♑22	22 28	22 R31	22 31	22 27	22 21	22 12	22♑00	21♑R49	21 32	21 12	20 50	20 26	20 00	19 33	19♑04
1926	23♒56	24 26	24 55	25 21	25 44	26 05	26 23	26♒38	25♒48	26♈58	27 05	27 R09	27 10	27 08	27 03	26♒55
1927	23♓42	24 30	25 17	26 02	26 45	27 27	28 07	28♓46	29♓13	29♉48	00 21	00 51	01 19	01 45	02 08	02♓29
1928	22♈23	23 19	24 15	25 10	26 04	26 58	27 50	28♈42	29♈20	00 10	00 58	01 46	02 32	03 16	03 59	04♈40
1929	20♉02	20 58	21 55	22 52	23 49	24 45	25 42	26♉38	27♉21	28 16	29 12	00♊07	01 01	01 55	02 48	03♊40
1930	17♊19	18 09	19 00	19 51	20 43	21 36	22 29	23♊23	24♊04	24 59	25 53	26 48	27 43	28 38	29♋33	00♋28
1931	14♋50	15 27	16 05	16 44	17 26	18 08	18 52	19♋37	20♋12	20 59	21 47	22 36	23 26	24 16	25 07	25♋59
1932	13♌22	13 40	14 00	14 22	14 47	15 14	15 43	16♌14	16♌39	17 14	17 50	18 28	19 07	19 48	20 30	21♌14
1933	13♍R26	13 20	13 18	13 18	13 21	13 28	13 37	13♍48	13♍59	14 15	14 34	14 56	15 19	15 45	16 13	16♍43
1934	15♎R37	15 12	14 49	14 29	14 10	13 54	13 41	13♎31	13♎R25	13 19	13 17	13 17	13 20	13 26	13 35	13♎47
1935	19♏R34	19 04	18 34	18 03	17 33	17 03	16 34	16♏06	15♏R45	15 22	14 59	14 38	14 20	14 04	13 50	13♏40
1936	23♐R48	23 32	23 13	22 52	22 29	22 04	21 37	21♐09	20♐R47	20 17	19 47	19 16	18 45	18 15	17 46	17♐19
1937	26♑59	27 09	27 15	27 R18	27 19	27 16	27 11	27♑02	26♑R54	26 40	26 24	26 05	25 43	25 20	24 54	24♓27
1938	28♒17	28 51	29 22	29 51	00 18	00 42	01 03	01♓22	01♓35	01 49	02 00	02 08	02 13	02 15	02 14	02♓10
1939	27♓51	28 41	29♈29	00 17	01 02	01 46	02 29	03♈10	03♈39	04 27	04 52	05 26	05 57	06 26	06 53	07♈17
1940	26♈25	27 22	28 18	29 14	00♉09	01 04	01 57	02♉50	03♉29	04 20	05 10	05 59	06 47	07 33	08 18	09♉01
1941	24♉00	24 56	25 52	26 49	27 45	28 42	29 38	00♉35	01♉17	02 13	03 09	04 04	04 59	05 53	06♊47	07♊40
1942	21♊16	22 05	22 54	23 44	24 35	25 27	26 20	27♊13	27♊53	28 46	29♋40	00 35	01 29	02 24	03 19	04♋14
1943	18♋52	19 25	20 01	20 39	21 18	21 59	22 41	23♋24	23♋57	24 43	25 30	26 17	27 06	27 55	28 45	29♋36
1944	25♌10	25 54	26 38	27 24	28 11	28 59	29 47	00♌36	01♌14	02 04	02 55	03 46	04 37	05 29	06 21	07♌13
1945	17♍R49	17 40	17 35	17 D32	17 32	17 35	17 41	17♍50	17♍58	18 12	18 28	18 47	19 08	19 31	19 57	20♍25
1946	20♎R16	19 49	19 24	19 01	18 40	18 22	18 06	17♎52	17♎R44	17 36	17 30	17 D27	17 28	17 31	17 37	17♎45
1947	24♏R21	23 52	23 22	22 52	22 21	21 51	21 21	20♏52	20♏R31	20 05	19 40	19 17	18 56	18 37	18 21	18♏07
1948	28♐R34	28 21	28 05	27 47	27 26	27 03	26 38	26♐12	25♐R51	25 22	24 52	24 21	23 51	23 20	22 50	22♐21
1949	01♒34	01 47	01 58	02 05	02 09	02 R10	02 09	02♒04	01♒R58	01 48	01 35	01 19	01 01	00 40	00♑17	29♑52
1950	02♓40	03 16	03 51	04 23	04 53	05 20	05 45	06♓08	06♓23	06 41	06 56	07 08	07 18	07 24	07 27	07♓27
1951	02♈04	02 55	03 45	04 34	05 22	06 08	06 53	07♈26	08♈07	08 48	09 26	10 03	10 37	11 09	11 39	12♈07
1952	00♉31	01 28	02 24	03 21	04 17	05 12	06 06	07♉00	07♉40	08 32	09 24	10 14	11 03	11 51	12 38	13♉23
1953	28♉00	28 55	29♊51	00 47	01 43	02 40	03 36	04♊32	05♊14	06 11	07 06	08 02	08 57	09 52	10 46	11♊40
1954	25♊16	26 02	26 50	27 39	28 29	29 19	00♋10	01♋02	01♋42	02 35	03 28	04 22	05 16	06 10	07 04	07♋59
1955	22♋55	23 27	24 00	24 35	25 12	25 51	26 31	27♋13	27 45	28 29	29 14	30♌00	00 47	01 35	02 24	03♌14
1956	21♌46	21 57	22 28	22 28	22 47	23 08	23 32	23♌59	24 20	24 50	25 22	25 55	26 31	27 08	27 47	28♌27
1957	22♍R20	22 08	22 00	21 54	21 51	21 51	21 53	21♍59	22♍05	22 16	22 29	22 45	23 03	23 24	23 48	24♍13
1958	25♎R04	24 36	24 09	23 44	23 21	23 00	22 41	22♎25	22♎R15	22 03	21 55	21 49	21 46	21 46	21 49	21♎54
1959	29♏R19	28 51	28 22	27 52	27 22	26 51	26 21	25 51	25♏R29	25 01	24 34	24 08	23 45	23 24	23 05	22♏49
1960	03♑R26	03 16	03 04	02 49	02 31	02 11	01 48	01♑24	01♑R04	00 37	00 08	29 38	29 08	28 37	28 06	27♑36
1961	06♒12	06 29	06 43	06 54	07 02	07 07	07 R09	07♒08	07♒R06	06 59	06 50	06 38	06 23	06 05	05 45	05♒23
1962	07♓02	07 41	08 18	08 53	09 26	09 57	10 25	10♓51	11♓09	11 31	11 50	12 06	12 19	12 29	12 36	12♓40
1963	06♈13	07 05	07 57	08 47	09 37	10 25	11 11	11♈57	12♈30	13 12	13 53	14 32	15 09	15 44	16 17	16♈48
1964	04♉30	05 27	06 24	07 21	08 17	09 13	10 08	11♉03	11♉43	12 36	13 29	14 20	15 11	16 00	16 48	17♉35
1965	01♊53	02 47	03 42	04 38	05 33	06 29	07 25	08♊21	09♊03	09 59	10 55	11 51	12 46	13 41	14 36	15♊30
1966	29♊08	29♋53	00 39	01 26	02 15	03 04	03 54	04♋45	05♋24	06 16	07 08	08 01	08 54	09 48	10 42	11♋36
1967	26♋54	27 23	27 54	28 26	29 01	29 38	00♌16	00♌56	01♌27	02 09	02 52	03 37	04 23	05 10	05 58	06♌46
1968	25♌57	24 05	26 16	26 30	26 46	27 05	27 26	27♌50	28♌09	28 37	29 07	29♍38	00 12	00 47	01 24	02♍03
1969	26♍R51	26 37	26 25	26 16	26 10	26 D07	26 06	26♍09	26♍13	26 21	26 31	26 44	27 00	27 18	27 39	28♍02
1970	29♎R54	29 25	28 57	28 30	28 05	27 41	27 20	27♎01	26♎R49	26 34	26 23	26 14	26 08	26 D05	26 05	26♎07
1971	04♐R16	03 50	03 22	02 54	02 24	01 53	01 23	00♐52	00♐R30	00♏01	29 32	29 05	28 40	28 16	27 54	27♏35
1972	08♑R16	08 10	08 01	07 49	07 35	07 17	06 58	06♑35	06♑R18	05 52	05 25	04 56	04 27	03 56	03 26	02♑55
1973	10♒45	11 05	11 23	11 38	11 49	11 58	12 04	12♒07	12♒R08	12 05	12 00	11 51	11 40	11 26	11 09	10♒49
1974	11♓17	11 59	12 39	13 16	13 52	14 26	14 58	15♓27	15♓47	16 12	16 35	16 54	17 11	17 25	17 37	17♓45
1975	10♈16	11 09	12 02	12 54	13 45	14 45	15 23	16♈10	16♈44	17 29	18 12	18 53	19 33	20 11	20 46	21♈20
1976	08♉25	09 22	10 20	11 16	12 13	13 09	14 05	15♉00	15♉41	16 36	17 29	18 21	19 13	20 04	20 53	21♉42
1977	05♊45	06 39	07 33	08 28	09 23	10 18	11 14	12♊10	12♊51	13 47	14 43	15 39	16 34	17 29	18 24	19♊19
1978	03♋03	03 46	04 30	05 16	06 03	06 51	07 40	08♋29	09♋07	09 58	10 50	11 42	12 35	13 28	14 21	15♋15
1979	00♌58	01 24	01 52	02 23	02 55	03 29	04 06	04♌43	05♌13	05 53	06 35	07 18	08 03	08 48	09 25	10♌22
1980	00♍16	00 21	00 29	00 40	00 53	01 09	01 27	01♍48	02♍06	02 31	02 58	03 27	03 59	04 32	05 07	05♍44
1981	01♎R30	01 13	00 58	00 46	00 37	00 31	00 27	00♎D27	00♎28	00 33	00 40	00 50	01 03	01 19	01 37	01♎57
1982	04♏R49	04 19	03 50	03 22	02 54	02 29	02 06	01♏44	01♏R30	01 12	00 58	00 46	00 37	00 30	00 27	00♏26
1983	09♐R12	08 48	08 22	07 55	07 26	06 56	06 26	05♐55	05♐R33	05 02	04 33	04 04	03 37	03 11	02 47	02♐26
1984	12♑R58	12 55	12 50	12 41	12 30	12 16	11 59	11♑40	11♑R24	11 01	10 35	10 08	09 40	09 11	08 40	08♑10
1985	15♒R06	15 29	15 50	16 09	16 24	16 37	16 47	16♒53	16♒R56	16 58	16 56	16 52	16 44	16 33	16 20	16♒03
1986	15♓21	16 05	16 47	17 27	18 05	18 42	19 16	19♓48	20♓11	20 39	21 05	21 28	21 48	22 06	22 21	22♓33
1987	14♈09	15 03	15 57	16 50	17 42	18 33	19 23	20♈12	20♈48	21 34	22 19	23 02	23 44	24 24	25 03	25♈39
1988	12♉13	13 10	14 07	15 04	16 01	16 58	17 54	18♉50	19♉31	20 26	21 20	22 14	23 06	23 58	24 49	25♉39
1989	09♊33	10 26	11 19	12 13	13 07	14 02	14 57	15♊53	16♊34	17 30	18 25	19 21	20 17	21 12	22 07	23♊02
1990	06♋57	07 38	08 20	09 04	09 50	10 36	11 24	12♋12	12♋49	13 39	14 30	15 21	16 13	17 05	17 58	18♋51
1991	05♌03	05 26	05 52	06 20	06 50	07 22	07 56	08♌32	09♌00	09 38	10 19	11 00	11 43	12 27	13 12	13♌59
1992	04♍38	04 40	04 44	04 52	05 02	05 15	05 30	05♍49	06♍04	06 25	06 51	07 18	07 47	08 18	08 51	09♍26
1993	06♎R11	05 51	05 33	05 18	05 06	04 57	04 50	04♎46	04♎D45	04 47	04 51	04 58	05 08	05 21	05 36	05♎54
1994	09♏R42	09 12	08 42	08 12	07 44	07 17	06 51	06♏27	06♏R11	05 51	05 34	05 19	05 07	04 57	04 51	04♏47
1995	14♐R04	13 43	13 19	12 53	12 26	11 57	11 28	10♐58	10♐R35	10 04	09 34	09 04	08 35	08 08	07 42	07♐18
1996	17♑R38	17 39	17 38	17 33	17 25	17 14	17 01	16♑44	16♑R31	16 10	15 47	15 22	14 56	14 27	13 58	13♑28
1997	19♒30	19 57	20 21	20 43	21 02	21 19	21 32	21♒43	21♒49	21 54	12 R56	21 56	21 52	21 45	21 35	21♒22
1998	19♓32	20 18	21 02	21 44	22 25	23 04	23 41	24♓17	24♓41	25 13	25 42	26 08	26 32	26 54	27 13	27♓29
1999	18♈11	19 06	20 01	20 55	21 49	22 41	23 32	24♈23	25♈00	25 48	26 35	27 20	28 04	28 46	29 27	00♉06
2000	16♉10	17 07	18 04	19 02	19 59	20 55	21 52	22♉48	23♉30	24 25	25 20	26 14	27 08	28 01	28 53	29♉43

Year	July 1st	July 5th	July 9th	July 13th	July 17th	July 21st	July 25th	July 29th	August 1st	August 5th	August 9th	August 13th	August 17th	August 21st	August 25th	August 29th
1900	02♐R11	01 53	01 38	01 25	01 14	01 07	01 02	01♐D01	01♐02	01 05	01 12	01 21	01 33	01 48	02 06	02♐26
1901	08♑R08	07 37	07 07	06 37	06 09	05 41	05 16	04♑52	04♑R36	04 16	03 58	03 44	03 32	03 23	03 17	03♑D14
1902	16♒R18	15 58	15 36	15 12	14 46	14 19	13 49	13♒19	12♒R56	12 25	11 54	11 23	10 53	10 23	09 55	09♒29
1903	23♓02	23 10	23 16	23 R18	23 18	23 14	23 07	22♓57	22♓R48	22 32	22 14	21 54	21 31	21 06	20 38	20♓10
1904	26♈22	26 55	27 26	27 55	28 21	28 45	29 06	29♈25	29♈37	29 50	00♉00	00 08	00 R12	00 13	00 11	00♉05
1905	26♉12	27 00	27 47	28 33	29 17	00♊00	00 41	01♊21	01♊49	02 25	02 59	03 31	04 01	04 28	04 53	05♊15
1906	23♊29	24 23	25 17	26 10	27 03	27 54	28 46	29♋36	00♋13	01 01	01 49	02 35	03 20	04 03	04 45	05♋25
1907	19♋11	20 04	20 58	21 52	22 45	23 39	24 33	25♋26	26♋06	26 59	27 51	28 43	29♌35	00 26	01 16	02♌05
1908	14♌22	15 09	15 58	16 47	17 37	18 27	19 18	20♌09	20♌48	21 40	22 32	23 25	24 17	25 10	26 02	26♌54
1909	09♍30	10 07	10 45	11 25	12 06	12 49	13 33	14♍17	14♍52	15 38	16 26	17 14	18 03	18 53	19 43	20♍33
1910	05♎51	06 12	06 35	07 01	07 29	07 58	08 30	09♎04	09♎30	10 07	10 45	11 25	12 06	12 48	13 32	14♎17
1911	04♏R40	04 40	04 43	04 49	04 58	05 09	05 23	05♏40	05♏54	06 15	06 39	07 05	07 33	08 03	08 35	09♏09
1912	07♐R07	06 46	06 28	06 12	05 58	05 47	05 40	05♐35	05♐R33	05 D33	05 37	05 43	05 52	06 04	06 18	06♐36
1913	13♑R32	13 02	12 31	12 00	11 31	11 01	10 34	10♑08	09♑R49	09 27	09 06	08 48	08 33	08 21	08 11	08♑05
1914	21♒R41	21 25	21 06	20 45	20 22	19 56	19 29	19♒00	18♒R38	18 07	17 36	17 04	16 33	16 03	15 33	15♒05
1915	27♓58	28 11	28 20	28 27	28 30	28 31	28 28	28♓22	28♓R15	28 04	27 50	27 33	27 13	26 50	26 26	25♓59
1916	00♉47	01 23	01 57	02 29	02 58	03 26	03 50	04♉12	04♉27	04 44	04 58	05 09	05 18	05 23	05 R25	05♉23
1917	00♊13	01 02	01 51	02 38	03 24	04 09	04 52	05♊33	06♊03	06 42	07 18	07 53	08 25	08 56	09 23	09♊49
1918	27♊15	38 09	29 03	29♋57	00 50	01 42	02 34	03♋25	04♋03	04 52	05 41	06 28	07 15	07 59	08 43	09♋25
1919	22♋49	23 42	24 35	25 28	26 22	27 15	28 09	29♋02	29♋42	00♌35	01 28	02 20	03 12	04 04	04 55	05♌45
1920	17♌59	18 45	19 33	20 21	21 10	21 59	22 50	23♌40	24♌19	25 10	26 02	26 54	27 46	28 39	29 31	00♍23
1921	13♍14	13 49	14 26	15 04	15 44	16 25	17 07	17♍51	18♍24	19 10	19 56	20 44	21 31	22 21	23 10	24♏00
1922	09♎52	10 10	10 31	10 54	11 19	11 47	12 17	12♎48	13♎13	13 48	14 24	15 02	15 42	16 23	17 05	17♎49
1923	09♏07	09 04	09 04	09 07	09 12	09 20	09 32	09♏45	09♏57	10 16	10 37	11 00	11 26	11 53	12 23	12♏55
1924	12♐R04	11 41	11 19	11 00	10 44	10 30	10 19	10♐11	10♐R07	10 04	10 04	10 07	10 12	10 21	10 33	10♐47
1925	18♑R49	18 19	17 48	17 17	16 47	16 17	15 47	15♑19	14♑R59	14 34	14 11	13 50	13 32	13 16	13 03	12♑53
1926	26♒R50	26 37	26 22	26 04	25 43	25 20	24 55	24♒28	24♒R06	23 37	23 06	22 35	22 04	21 33	21 02	20♒32
1927	02♈38	02 54	03 08	03 18	03 26	03 30	03 31	03♈29	03♈R26	03 18	03 08	02 54	02 38	02 19	01 57	01♈33
1928	05♉00	05 38	06 15	06 50	07 22	07 52	08 20	08♉45	09♉02	09 23	09 41	09 56	10 08	10 17	10 22	10♉R25
1929	04♊06	04 56	05 46	06 35	07 22	08 09	08 53	09♊37	10♊08	10 49	11 28	12 05	12 39	13 12	13 43	14♊11
1930	00♋56	01 50	02 45	03 39	04 32	05 25	06 18	07♋09	07♋48	08 38	09 28	10 16	11 04	11 50	12 36	13♋19
1931	26♋25	27 17	28 10	29 03	29♌56	00 49	01 42	02♌36	03♌16	04 09	05 02	05 55	06 47	07 39	08 30	09♌21
1932	21♌36	22 21	23 07	23 54	24 42	25 21	26 20	27♌10	27♌48	28 39	29♍30	00 22	01 14	02 06	02 58	03♍50
1933	16♍59	17 32	18 07	18 43	19 21	20 01	20 42	21♍24	21♍56	22 41	23 26	24 12	24 59	25 48	26 36	27♍26
1934	13♎53	14 09	14 27	14 48	15 10	15 36	16 03	16♎32	16♎56	17 29	18 03	18 40	19 18	19 57	20 38	21♎21
1935	13♏36	13 29	13 26	13 26	13 28	13 33	13 41	13♏52	14♏02	14 18	14 36	14 57	15 20	15 45	16 13	16♏43
1936	17♐R05	16 40	16 16	15 54	15 35	15 18	15 04	14♐52	14♐R46	14 39	14 36	14 36	14 38	14 44	14 52	15♐03
1937	24♑R13	24 44	23 14	22 43	22 12	21 41	21 11	20♑41	20♑R20	19 53	19 27	19 04	18 42	18 23	18 07	17♑53
1938	02♓R07	01 58	01 46	01 32	01 14	00 54	00 32	00♒07	29♒R48	29 20	28 51	28 20	27 49	27 18	26 46	26♒15
1939	07♈28	07 48	08 05	08 20	08 31	08 40	08 45	08♈R48	08♈R47	08 44	08 37	08 28	08 15	08 00	07 42	07♈26
1940	09♉23	10 03	10 42	11 20	11 55	12 28	12 58	13♉27	13♉27	14 11	14 32	14 51	15 07	15 20	15 30	15♉37
1941	08♊06	08 58	09 49	10 39	11 28	12 15	13 02	13♊47	14♊20	15 02	15 43	16 22	16 59	17 35	18 08	18♊39
1942	04♋41	05 36	06 30	07 24	08 18	09 12	10 04	10♋57	11♋36	12 27	13 17	14 07	14 55	15 43	16 29	17♋14
1943	00♌01	00 53	01 45	02 37	03 30	04 23	05 16	06♌09	06♌49	07 42	08 35	09 27	10 20	11 12	12 04	12♌55
1944	25♌10	25 54	26 38	27 24	28 11	28 59	29♍47	00♍36	01♍14	02 04	02 55	03 46	04 37	05 29	06 21	07♍13
1945	20♍40	21 11	21 43	22 18	22 54	23 32	24 11	24♍52	25♍24	26 07	26 51	27 36	28 22	29 09	29 57	00♍26
1946	17♎51	18 03	18 19	18 37	18 57	19 20	19 45	20♎12	20♎34	21 05	21 38	22 13	22 49	23 27	24 06	24♎47
1947	18♏02	17 52	17 46	17 42	17 D42	17 44	17 49	17♏57	18♏05	18 18	18 33	18 51	19 12	19 36	20 01	20♏28
1948	22♐R07	21 39	21 13	20 49	20 27	20 08	19 51	19♐36	19♐R27	19 17	19 11	19 07	19 06	19 08	19 14	19♐22
1949	29♑R39	29 11	28 42	28 12	27 41	27 10	26 39	26♑09	25♑R46	25 17	24 50	24 24	24 00	23 38	23 18	23♑01
1950	07♓R26	07 21	07 13	07 03	06 49	06 32	06 13	05♓52	05♓R34	05 08	04 41	04 12	03 42	03 11	02 39	02♓08
1951	12♈19	12 43	13 04	13 23	13 38	13 51	14 00	14♈07	14♈10	14 11	14 09	14 03	13 55	13 43	13 29	13♈11
1952	13♉45	14 28	15 10	15 49	16 27	17 03	17 36	18♉08	18♉30	18 57	19 22	19 45	20 04	20 31	20 35	20♉46
1953	12♊06	12 59	13 51	14 42	15 32	16 21	17 08	17♊55	18♊29	19 13	19 56	20 37	21 16	21 54	22 30	23♊03
1954	08♋26	09 21	10 15	11 09	12 03	12 57	13 50	14♋43	15♋22	16 14	17 05	17 55	18 45	19 33	20 21	21♋07
1955	03♌39	04 30	05 21	06 12	07 04	07 57	08 49	09♌42	10♌22	11 15	12 08	13 01	13 53	14 46	15 38	16♌29
1956	28♌48	29♍30	00 13	00 58	01 44	02 30	03 18	04♍06	04♍42	05 32	06 22	07 13	08 04	08 55	09 47	10♍38
1957	24♍27	24 55	25 26	25 58	26 33	27 09	27 47	28♍26	28♍56	29♎38	00 21	01 05	01 50	02 36	03 23	04♎11
1958	21♎58	22 08	22 20	22 36	22 53	23 14	23 36	24♎01	24♎21	24 50	25 21	25 54	26 28	27 05	27 42	28♎22
1959	22♏R41	22 29	22 19	22 12	22 D09	22 08	22 09	22♏14	22♏20	22 30	22 42	22 57	23 15	23 36	23 59	24♏24
1960	27♐R21	26 52	26 25	25 58	25 34	25 12	24 52	24♐34	24♐R22	24 09	23 59	23 52	23 48	23 D47	23 48	23♐53
1961	05♒R11	04 45	04 18	03 49	03 19	02 48	02 17	01♒46	01♒R23	00 53	00 24	29♑56	29 29	29 04	28 42	28♑22
1962	12♓41	12 41	12 37	12 30	12 21	12 08	11 52	11♓34	11♓R18	10 56	10 31	10 04	09 35	09 06	08 35	08♓03
1963	17♈02	17 29	17 54	18 16	18 35	18 52	19 05	19♈16	19♈22	19 27	19 R29	19 28	19 24	19 16	19 05	18♈52
1964	17♉58	18 43	19 27	20 08	20 48	21 26	22 03	22♉37	23♉01	23 31	23 59	24 25	24 48	25 08	25 25	25♉40
1965	15♊57	16 50	17 43	18 34	19 25	26 15	21 04	21♊52	22♊27	23 13	23 57	24 40	25 21	26 01	26 39	27♊15
1966	12♋03	12 58	13 52	14 46	15 40	16 34	17 27	18♋20	19♋00	19 52	20 44	21 35	22 25	23 14	24 03	24♋50
1967	07♌11	08 01	08 51	09 42	10 33	11 25	12 17	13♌10	13♌49	14 42	15 35	16 27	17 20	18 13	19 05	19♌57
1968	02♍22	03 03	03 45	04 28	05 13	05 58	06 45	07♍32	08♍08	08 57	09 46	10 36	11 26	12 17	13 09	14♍00
1969	28♍14	28 40	29 09	29♎39	00 12	00 46	01 22	02♎00	02♎29	03 09	03 51	04 34	05 18	06 03	06 49	07♎36
1970	26♎09	26 16	26 26	26 38	26 54	27 11	27 31	27♎54	28♎12	18 39	19 07	29♏38	00 11	00 45	01 21	01♏59
1971	27♏R27	27 11	26 58	26 48	26 41	26 37	26 D36	26♏37	26♏41	26 47	26 57	27 09	27 24	27 42	28 02	28♏25
1972	02♑R40	02 10	01 40	01 12	00 46	00 21	29 58	29♑38	29♐R24	29 08	28 54	28 43	28 36	28 31	28 D29	28♐31
1973	10♒R39	10 16	09 50	09 24	08 55	08 26	07 55	07♒24	07♒R01	06 30	05 59	05 29	05 01	04 34	04 09	03♒43
1974	17♓48	17 51	17 52	17 49	17 43	17 35	17 23	17♓08	16♓R55	16 36	16 14	15 49	15 23	14 55	14 25	13♓54
1975	21♈36	22 06	22 34	23 00	23 22	23 43	24 00	24♈15	24♈23	24 33	24 39	24 R42	24 42	24 38	24 32	24♈22
1976	22♉06	22 52	23 37	24 21	25 03	25 53	26 22	27♉07	27♉25	26 47	26 57	27 09	27 24	27♊42	28 02	28♊25
1977	19♊46	20 40	21 33	22 25	23 17	24 08	24 58	25♊47	26♊23	27 10	27 56	28 40	29 23	00♋05	00 45	01♋23
1978	15♋41	16 36	17 30	18 24	19 18	20 12	21 05	21♋59	22♋38	23 31	24 23	25 15	26 06	26 56	27 43	28♋34
1979	10♌46	11 35	12 25	13 15	14 06	14 57	15 48	16♌40	17♌20	18 12	19 04	19 57	20 50	21 42	22 48	23♌27
1980	06♍03	06 42	07 22	08 04	08 50	09 31	10 16	11♍03	11♍38	12 26	13 14	14 04	14 53	15 44	16 35	17♍26
1981	02♎08	02 32	02 58	03 26	03 57	04 29	05 03	05♎39	06♎07	06 46	07 26	08 07	08 50	09 34	10 19	11♎05
1982	00♏27	00 31	00 38	00 47	00 59	01 14	01 31	01♏51	02♏08	02 32	02 58	03 26	03 57	04 30	05 04	05♏40
1983	02♐R16	01 57	01 41	01 28	01 18	01 10	01 06	01♐04	01♐05	01 08	01 15	01 24	01 36	01 51	02 08	02♐28
1984	07♑R54	07 24	06 54	06 24	05 56	05 29	05 04	04♑40	04♑R24	04 05	03 49	03 35	03 23	03 15	03 10	03♑D08
1985	15♒R54	15 34	15 12	14 47	14 20	13 52	13 23	12♒52	12♒R29	11 38	11 27	10 56	10 26	09 57	09 30	09♒04
1986	22♓38	22 46	22 50	22 51	22 50	22 45	22 37	22♓26	22♓R16	21 59	21 41	21 19	20 55	20 29	20 02	19♓32
1987	25♈56	26 29	27 00	27 29	27 55	28 18	28 39	28♈57	29♈09	29 22	29 32	29 39	29 43	29 44	29 42	29♈36
1988	26♉03	26 51	27 38	28 23	29 07	29♊50	00 30	01♊09	01♊37	02 13	02 46	03 18	03 47	04 14	04 38	04♊59
1989	23♊29	24 23	25 17	26 10	27 03	27 54	28 45	29♋35	00♋12	01 01	01 48	02 34	03 18	04 02	04 43	05♋23
1990	19♋18	20 12	21 06	21 59	22 53	23 47	24 41	25♋34	26♋14	27 07	28 00	28 52	29♌43	00 34	01 24	02♌14
1991	14♌22	15 10	15 58	16 48	17 38	18 28	19 19	20♌10	20♌49	21 41	22 34	23 26	24 19	25 24	26 04	26♌56
1992	09♍44	10 21	11 00	11 40	12 22	13 05	13 49	14♍34	15♍08	15 55	16 43	17 31	18 20	19 10	20 00	20♍51
1993	06♎03	06 25	06 49	07 15	07 43	08 13	08 45	09♎19	09♎46	10 22	11 01	11 41	12 22	13 05	13 49	14♎34
1994	04♏R46	04 47	04 50	04 57	05 06	05 18	05 32	05♏50	06♏04	06 26	06 50	07 16	07 44	08 15	08 47	09♏21
1995	07♐R07	06 46	06 27	06 11	05 57	05 47	05 39	05♐34	05♐32	05 R32	05 36	05 42	05 51	06 02	06 17	06♐34
1996	13♑R13	12 42	12 11	11 41	11 11	10 43	10 15	09♑60	09♑R32	09 10	08 50	08 33	08 18	08 07	07 58	07♑52
1997	21♒R15	20 58	20 38	20 16	19 52	19 26	18 58	18♒29	18♒R07	17 36	17 04	16 33	16 02	15 32	15 03	14♒35
1998	27♓35	27 47	27 56	28 01	28 04	28 03	27 59	27♓52	27♓R45	27 32	27 17	26 59	26 38	26 15	25 50	25♓22
1999	00♉24	01 00	01 34	02 06	02 35	03 02	03 26	03♉48	04♉03	04 20	04 34	04 45	04 53	04 58	04 59	04♉58
2000	00♊09	00 58	01 46	02 33	03 19	04 03	04 46	05♊27	05♊57	06 35	07 11	07 45	08 17	08 46	09 13	09♊38

Jupiter

	September								October							
	1st	5th	9th	13th	17th	21st	25th	29th	1st	5th	9th	13th	17th	21st	25th	29th
1900	02 ♐ 43	03 07	03 34	04 03	04 35	05 08	05 43	06 ♐ 20	06 ♐ 40	07 19	08 01	08 44	09 28	10 13	11 00	11 ♐ 48
1901	03 ♑ 14	03 16	03 21	03 30	03 41	03 55	04 12	04 ♑ 32	04 ♑ 43	05 07	05 33	06 02	06 33	07 06	07 41	08 ♑ 19
1902	09 ♒ R11	08 48	08 27	08 10	07 55	07 43	07 34	07 ♒ 28	07 ♒ R26	07 D 25	07 27	07 32	07 40	07 52	08 06	08 ♒ 24
1903	19 ♓ R47	19 16	18 45	18 13	17 41	17 10	16 39	16 ♓ 10	15 ♓ R56	15 29	15 04	14 42	14 22	14 04	13 50	13 ♓ 39
1904	29 ♈ R59	29 48	29 34	29 17	28 58	28 35	28 11	27 ♈ 44	27 ♈ R30	27 00	26 29	25 58	25 25	24 53	24 21	23 ♈ 49
1905	05 ♊ 30	05 48	06 02	06 14	06 23	06 28	06 R 30	06 ♊ 29	06 ♊ R28	06 22	06 13	06 01	05 45	05 27	05 06	04 ♊ 43
1906	05 ♋ 55	06 32	07 07	07 41	08 12	08 41	09 08	09 ♋ 32	09 ♋ 43	10 03	10 21	10 36	10 47	10 56	11 02	11 ♋ R04
1907	02 ♌ 42	03 30	04 17	05 02	05 47	06 30	07 12	07 ♌ 52	08 ♌ 12	08 49	09 25	09 59	10 31	11 01	11 29	11 ♌ 54
1908	27 ♌ 33	28 25	29 16	00 ♍ 07	00 58	01 48	02 37	03 ♍ 26	03 ♍ 50	04 37	05 23	06 08	06 52	07 34	08 15	08 ♍ 55
1909	21 ♍ 12	22 03	22 55	23 46	24 38	25 30	26 22	27 ♍ 14	27 ♍ 40	28 31	29 ♎ 22	00 13	01 03	01 53	02 42	03 ♎ 30
1910	14 ♎ 51	15 38	16 25	17 13	18 03	18 52	19 43	20 ♎ 34	20 ♎ 59	21 51	22 42	23 34	24 27	25 19	26 11	27 ♎ 03
1911	09 ♏ 36	10 13	10 51	11 32	12 14	12 57	13 41	14 ♏ 27	14 ♏ 50	15 37	16 25	17 15	18 04	18 55	19 46	20 ♏ 38
1912	06 ♐ 51	07 12	07 37	08 03	08 32	09 04	09 37	10 ♐ 12	10 ♐ 31	11 08	11 48	12 29	13 12	13 57	14 42	15 ♐ 29
1913	08 ♑ R02	08 D 00	08 02	08 07	08 15	08 26	08 40	08 ♑ 56	09 ♑ 06	09 26	09 50	10 16	10 44	11 15	11 48	12 ♑ 23
1914	14 ♒ R44	14 19	13 56	13 34	13 16	13 00	12 47	12 ♒ 38	12 ♒ R34	12 29	12 27	12 28	12 33	12 40	12 51	13 ♒ 05
1915	25 ♓ R38	25 08	24 38	24 06	23 34	23 02	22 31	22 ♓ 00	21 ♓ R45	21 16	20 48	20 23	19 59	19 39	19 21	19 ♓ 06
1916	05 ♉ R20	05 13	05 03	04 50	04 34	04 15	03 53	03 ♉ 29	03 ♉ R16	02 49	02 20	01 50	01 18	00 46	00 ♈ 13	29 ♈ 41
1917	10 ♊ 06	10 27	10 45	11 00	11 13	11 22	11 28	11 ♊ R31	11 ♊ R31	11 29	11 24	11 16	11 04	10 50	10 32	10 ♊ 12
1918	09 ♋ 56	10 35	11 13	11 48	12 22	12 53	13 23	13 ♋ 50	14 ♋ 02	14 26	14 46	15 04	15 19	15 31	15 41	15 ♋ 47
1919	06 ♌ 22	07 11	07 59	08 45	09 31	10 16	10 59	11 ♌ 41	12 ♌ 01	12 41	13 18	13 54	14 29	15 01	15 31	15 ♌ 59
1920	01 ♍ 02	01 54	02 46	03 38	04 29	05 19	06 09	06 ♍ 58	07 ♍ 22	08 11	08 58	09 44	10 29	11 13	11 55	12 ♍ 37
1921	24 ♍ 38	25 29	26 20	27 12	28 04	28 56	29 ♎ 48	00 ♎ 39	01 ♎ 05	01 57	02 49	03 40	04 31	05 21	06 11	07 ♎ 00
1922	18 ♎ 23	19 08	19 55	20 42	21 31	22 20	23 10	24 ♎ 00	24 ♎ 25	25 16	26 08	27 00	27 52	28 44	29 ♏ 36	00 ♏ 29
1923	13 ♏ 21	13 56	14 33	15 12	15 52	16 34	17 17	18 ♏ 01	18 ♏ 24	19 10	19 58	20 46	21 35	22 25	23 16	24 ♏ 07
1924	11 ♐ 00	11 19	11 40	12 04	12 31	13 00	13 31	14 ♐ 04	14 ♐ 21	14 57	15 35	16 15	16 56	17 39	18 23	19 ♐ 09
1925	12 ♑ R48	12 43	12 41	12 42	12 47	12 54	13 05	13 ♑ 18	13 ♑ 26	13 44	14 04	14 27	14 53	15 21	15 51	16 ♑ 24
1926	20 ♒ R10	19 42	19 16	18 52	18 31	18 12	17 55	17 ♒ 42	17 ♒ 36	17 R 27	17 22	17 19	17 20	17 23	17 31	17 ♒ 41
1927	01 ♈ R13	00 46	00 ♓ 16	29 46	29 14	28 43	28 10	27 ♓ 39	27 ♓ R23	26 52	26 23	25 55	25 29	25 05	24 43	24 ♓ 25
1928	10 ♉ R25	10 22	10 16	10 07	09 54	09 39	09 21	09 ♉ 00	08 ♉ R48	08 23	07 57	07 28	06 58	06 26	05 54	05 ♉ 21
1929	14 ♊ 31	14 55	15 16	15 35	15 51	16 04	16 13	16 ♊ 20	16 ♊ 22	16 R 24	16 23	16 19	16 11	16 00	15 46	15 ♊ 29
1930	13 ♋ 51	14 32	15 11	15 49	16 25	16 59	17 31	18 ♋ 00	18 ♋ 14	18 41	19 04	19 25	19 43	19 59	20 11	20 ♋ 21
1931	09 ♌ 59	10 48	11 37	12 25	13 12	13 58	14 42	15 ♌ 15	15 ♌ 47	16 28	17 07	17 45	18 22	18 56	19 28	19 ♌ 58
1932	04 ♍ 30	05 22	06 14	07 05	07 57	08 48	09 38	10 ♍ 28	10 ♍ 53	11 42	12 30	13 17	14 03	14 48	15 32	16 ♍ 15
1933	28 ♍ 03	28 54	29 ♎ 45	00 36	01 27	02 19	03 11	04 ♎ 03	04 ♎ 29	05 21	06 12	07 04	07 55	08 46	09 36	10 ♎ 26
1934	21 ♎ 53	22 38	23 23	24 10	24 57	25 46	26 35	27 ♎ 25	27 ♎ 50	28 40	29 32	00 ♏ 23	01 15	02 07	03 00	03 ♏ 52
1935	17 ♏ 07	17 40	18 15	18 52	19 31	20 11	20 53	21 ♏ 36	21 ♏ 58	22 43	23 30	24 17	25 05	25 55	26 45	27 ♏ 36
1936	15 ♐ 14	15 30	15 48	16 10	16 34	17 00	17 29	18 ♐ 00	18 ♐ 16	18 50	19 26	20 04	20 44	21 25	22 08	22 ♐ 52
1937	17 ♑ R45	17 37	17 31	17 29	17 30	17 34	17 41	17 ♑ 51	17 ♑ 57	18 11	18 28	18 48	19 11	19 37	20 04	20 ♑ 35
1938	25 ♒ R52	25 23	24 54	24 28	24 03	23 41	23 21	23 ♒ 04	22 ♒ R57	22 44	22 34	22 28	22 24	22 24	22 27	22 ♒ 33
1939	07 ♈ R03	06 38	06 11	05 42	05 12	04 40	04 09	03 ♈ 36	03 ♈ R20	02 49	02 17	01 47	01 19	00 52	00 28	00 ♓ 05
1940	15 ♉ 40	15 R 41	15 39	15 34	15 25	15 14	14 59	14 ♉ 42	14 ♉ R32	14 10	13 46	13 20	12 52	12 22	11 51	11 ♉ 19
1941	19 ♊ 01	19 28	19 52	20 14	20 34	20 50	21 04	21 ♊ 14	21 ♊ 18	21 24	21 R 27	21 26	21 22	21 15	21 05	20 ♊ 52
1942	17 ♋ 47	18 30	19 11	19 51	20 29	21 05	21 39	22 ♋ 11	22 ♋ 26	22 55	23 21	23 45	24 06	24 25	24 40	24 ♋ 53
1943	13 ♌ 33	14 23	15 13	16 02	16 49	17 36	18 22	19 ♌ 06	19 ♌ 28	20 11	20 52	21 32	22 10	22 46	23 20	23 ♌ 52
1944	07 ♍ 52	08 44	09 36	10 28	11 20	12 11	13 02	13 ♍ 52	14 ♍ 17	15 07	15 56	16 44	17 31	18 17	19 02	19 ♍ 46
1945	01 ♎ 23	02 13	03 03	03 54	04 45	05 37	06 29	07 ♎ 20	07 ♎ 46	08 38	09 30	10 22	11 13	12 05	12 55	13 ♎ 46
1946	25 ♎ 19	26 02	26 47	27 33	28 19	29 07	29 ♏ 55	00 ♏ 44	01 ♏ 09	02 00	02 50	03 42	04 33	05 25	06 18	07 ♏ 10
1947	20 ♏ 50	21 22	21 55	22 31	23 08	23 46	24 27	25 ♏ 09	25 ♏ 30	26 14	26 59	27 46	28 33	29 22	00 ♐ 11	01 ♐ 02
1948	19 ♐ 30	19 43	19 59	20 17	20 39	21 03	21 29	21 ♐ 58	22 ♐ 13	22 45	23 19	23 55	24 33	25 12	25 54	26 ♐ 37
1949	22 ♑ R50	22 38	22 29	22 23	22 D 21	22 21	22 24	22 ♑ 30	22 ♑ 35	22 46	23 00	23 17	23 36	23 59	24 24	24 ♑ 52
1950	01 ♓ R44	01 13	00 43	00 ♒ 15	29 47	29 22	28 59	28 ♒ 38	28 ♒ R29	28 13	27 59	27 48	27 41	27 36	27 35	27 ♒ 38
1951	12 ♈ R57	12 34	12 10	11 43	11 15	10 45	10 14	09 ♈ 42	09 ♈ R26	08 54	08 22	07 50	07 20	06 51	06 23	05 ♈ 58
1952	20 ♉ 52	20 57	20 R 59	20 58	20 54	20 47	20 36	20 ♉ 23	20 ♉ R15	19 57	19 36	19 12	18 47	18 19	17 49	17 ♉ 18
1953	23 ♊ 27	23 57	24 25	24 50	25 12	25 32	25 49	26 ♊ 03	26 ♊ 09	26 18	26 25	26 R 28	26 28	26 25	26 19	26 ♊ 09
1954	21 ♋ 41	22 25	23 08	23 49	24 29	25 07	25 43	26 ♋ 17	26 ♋ 34	27 05	27 34	28 00	28 25	28 46	29 05	29 ♋ 21
1955	17 ♌ 08	17 58	18 48	19 38	20 27	21 14	22 01	22 ♌ 47	23 ♌ 09	23 53	24 36	25 17	25 56	26 34	27 11	27 ♌ 45
1956	11 ♍ 17	12 09	13 01	13 53	14 45	15 37	16 28	17 ♍ 19	17 ♍ 44	18 34	19 24	20 12	21 00	21 48	22 34	23 ♍ 19
1957	04 ♎ 47	05 37	06 26	07 17	08 08	08 59	09 50	10 ♎ 42	11 ♎ 08	12 00	12 52	13 44	14 36	15 27	16 19	17 ♎ 09
1958	28 ♎ 53	29 ♏ 35	00 18	01 02	01 48	02 35	03 22	04 ♏ 11	04 ♏ 35	05 25	06 15	07 06	07 58	08 50	09 42	10 ♏ 34
1959	24 ♏ 45	25 14	25 45	26 18	26 54	27 31	28 10	28 ♏ 50	29 ♏ 11	29 ♐ 53	00 37	01 23	02 09	02 57	03 46	04 ♐ 35
1960	23 ♐ 59	24 09	24 21	24 37	24 55	25 16	25 40	26 ♐ 06	26 ♐ 20	26 50	27 21	27 55	28 31	29 09	29 49	00 ♑ 30
1961	28 ♑ 08	27 R 53	27 40	27 30	27 23	27 20	27 D 19	27 ♑ 22	27 ♑ 24	27 32	27 42	27 55	28 12	28 31	28 53	29 ♑ 18
1962	07 ♓ R39	07 08	06 37	06 06	05 37	05 09	04 43	04 ♓ 19	04 ♓ R08	03 48	03 31	03 16	03 05	02 56	02 51	02 ♓ D49
1963	18 ♈ R40	18 21	18 00	17 36	17 10	16 42	16 13	15 ♈ 42	15 ♈ R26	14 54	14 22	13 50	13 18	12 47	12 17	11 ♈ 49
1964	25 ♉ 49	25 58	26 04	26 R 07	26 07	26 04	25 57	25 ♉ 47	25 ♉ R41	25 27	25 10	24 49	24 27	24 01	23 34	23 ♉ 05
1965	27 ♊ 40	28 13	28 43	29 11	29 36	29 ♋ 59	00 19	00 ♋ 37	00 ♋ 44	00 57	01 07	01 14	01 R 18	01 19	01 16	01 ♋ 10
1966	25 ♋ 25	26 10	26 55	27 37	28 19	28 59	29 37	00 ♌ 13	00 ♌ 30	01 04	01 35	02 04	02 31	02 55	03 17	03 ♌ 36
1967	20 ♌ 36	21 27	22 17	23 07	23 57	24 45	25 33	26 ♌ 20	26 ♌ 43	27 28	28 12	28 54	29 ♍ 36	00 15	00 53	01 ♍ 30
1968	14 ♍ 39	15 31	16 23	17 15	18 07	18 59	19 50	20 ♍ 41	21 ♍ 07	21 58	22 48	23 37	24 26	25 14	26 01	26 ♍ 47
1969	08 12	09 00	09 49	10 39	11 30	12 21	13 12	14 03	14 29	15 21	16 13	17 05	17 57	18 49	19 41	20 32
1970	02 ♏ 29	03 10	03 52	04 35	05 20	06 05	06 52	07 ♏ 40	08 ♏ 04	08 53	09 43	10 33	11 24	12 16	13 08	14 ♏ 00
1971	28 ♏ 44	29 11	29 ♐ 40	00 11	00 44	01 20	01 57	02 ♐ 35	02 ♐ 55	03 37	04 19	05 03	05 49	06 36	07 23	08 ♐ 12
1972	28 ♐ 34	28 40	28 50	29 02	29 17	29 35	29 56	00 ♑ 19	00 ♑ 32	00 59	01 28	02 00	02 34	03 09	03 47	04 ♑ 27
1973	03 ♒ R30	03 11	02 54	02 41	02 30	02 23	02 19	02 ♒ D17	02 ♒ 18	02 22	02 28	02 38	02 51	03 06	03 25	03 ♒ 47
1974	13 ♓ R31	12 59	12 28	11 56	11 25	10 56	10 27	10 ♓ 01	09 ♓ R48	09 25	09 04	08 46	08 30	08 18	08 08	08 ♓ 02
1975	24 ♈ R13	23 58	23 40	23 20	22 57	22 31	22 04	21 ♈ 35	21 ♈ R20	20 49	20 09	19 44	19 04	18 40	18 09	17 ♈ 39
1976	00 ♊ 38	09 51	01 01	01 08	01 R 12	01 12	01 10	01 ♊ 04	01 ♊ R00	00 49	00 35	00 19	29 ♉ 59	29 37	29 12	28 ♉ 46
1977	01 ♋ 50	02 25	02 57	03 28	03 56	04 22	04 45	05 ♋ 06	05 ♋ 15	05 31	05 45	05 56	06 03	06 R 07	06 09	06 ♋ 06
1978	08 ♋ 04	08 ♌ 22	08 36	08 47	08 56	09 01	09 04	09 ♌ 03	09 ♌ 01	08 55	08 46	08 35	08 20	08 02	07 41	07 ♌ 18
1979	24 ♌ 06	24 57	25 49	26 39	27 29	28 19	29 07	29 ♍ 55	00 ♍ 18	01 05	01 50	02 34	03 16	03 58	04 37	05 ♍ 15
1980	18 ♍ 04	18 56	19 48	20 40	21 32	22 24	23 16	24 ♍ 07	24 ♍ 33	25 24	26 15	27 05	27 54	28 43	29 ♎ 31	00 ♎ 19
1981	11 ♎ 40	12 28	13 16	14 06	14 65	15 46	16 37	17 ♎ 28	17 ♎ 54	18 46	19 37	20 30	21 22	22 14	23 06	23 ♎ 58
1982	06 ♏ 08	06 47	07 28	08 10	08 53	09 38	10 24	11 ♏ 10	11 ♏ 34	12 22	13 11	14 01	14 52	15 43	16 35	17 ♏ 27
1983	02 ♐ 45	03 09	03 36	04 05	04 36	05 09	05 44	06 ♐ 21	06 ♐ 40	07 20	08 01	08 44	09 28	10 13	11 00	11 ♐ 48
1984	03 ♑ 08	03 11	03 17	03 26	03 38	03 53	04 11	04 ♑ 31	04 ♑ 42	05 07	05 33	06 02	06 34	07 07	07 43	08 ♑ 21
1985	08 ♒ R46	08 24	08 04	07 48	07 33	07 22	07 14	07 ♒ 09	07 ♒ R08	07 D 08	07 10	07 17	07 26	07 38	07 53	08 ♒ 11
1986	19 ♓ R10	18 38	18 07	17 35	17 03	16 32	16 02	15 ♓ 33	15 ♓ R20	14 53	14 29	14 08	13 49	13 33	13 19	13 ♓ 09
1987	29 ♈ R29	29 18	29 04	28 47	28 27	28 04	27 39	27 ♈ 12	26 ♈ R58	26 28	25 58	25 26	24 54	24 12	23 49	25 ♈ 17
1988	05 ♊ 13	05 30	05 44	05 55	06 02	06 R 07	06 08	06 ♊ 06	06 ♊ R04	05 57	05 47	05 34	05 18	04 59	04 37	04 ♊ 13
1989	05 ♋ 52	06 29	07 04	07 37	08 08	08 36	09 02	09 ♋ 26	09 ♋ 37	09 57	10 13	10 27	10 38	10 46	10 51	10 ♋ R53
1990	02 ♌ 50	03 38	04 25	05 10	05 54	06 37	07 19	07 ♌ 59	08 ♌ 18	08 56	09 31	10 05	10 37	11 06	11 33	11 ♌ 58
1991	27 ♌ 35	28 27	29 ♍ 18	00 10	01 00	01 50	02 40	03 ♍ 28	03 ♍ 52	04 39	05 26	06 11	06 54	07 37	08 11	08 ♍ 59
1992	21 ♍ 30	22 21	23 13	24 04	24 56	25 48	26 40	27 ♍ 32	27 ♍ 58	28 49	29 ♎ 40	00 31	01 21	02 11	03 00	03 ♎ 48
1993	15 ♎ 08	15 55	16 43	17 31	18 20	19 10	20 01	20 ♎ 52	21 ♎ 17	22 09	23 00	23 52	24 45	25 37	26 29	27 ♎ 21
1994	09 ♏ 48	10 26	11 05	11 45	12 27	13 11	13 55	14 ♏ 41	15 ♏ 04	15 52	16 40	17 29	18 19	19 10	20 01	20 ♏ 53
1995	06 ♐ 49	07 10	07 35	08 01	08 30	09 01	09 34	10 ♐ 09	10 ♐ 28	11 05	11 45	12 26	13 09	13 53	14 38	15 ♐ 25
1996	07 ♑ R50	07 D 49	07 52	07 58	08 06	08 18	08 32	08 ♑ 50	08 ♑ 59	09 21	09 45	10 11	01 40	11 12	11 45	12 ♑ 21
1997	14 ♒ R15	13 50	13 27	13 07	12 50	12 35	12 23	12 ♒ 14	12 ♒ R11	12 D 07	12 06	12 08	12 13	12 22	12 33	12 ♒ 48
1998	25 ♓ R01	24 31	24 00	23 28	22 56	22 24	21 53	21 ♓ 23	21 ♓ R08	20 39	20 12	19 48	19 25	19 05	18 48	18 ♓ 34
1999	04 ♉ R55	04 47	04 37	04 24	04 07	03 48	03 27	03 ♉ 02	02 ♉ R49	02 22	01 53	01 22	00 51	00 ♈ 18	29 46	29 ♈ 13
2000	09 ♊ 55	10 15	10 33	10 47	10 58	11 07	11 12	11 ♊ R14	11 ♊ R14	11 11	11 05	10 56	10 44	10 28	10 10	09 ♊ 49

November | December

Year	Nov 1st	Nov 5th	Nov 9th	Nov 13th	Nov 17th	Nov 21st	Nov 25th	Nov 29th	Dec 1st	Dec 5th	Dec 9th	Dec 13th	Dec 17th	Dec 21st	Dec 25th	Dec 29th
1900	12♐25	13 15	14 05	14 57	15 49	16 41	17 35	18♐28	18♐55	19 50	20 44	21 39	22 33	23 28	24 23	25♐17
1901	08♑48	09 28	10 10	10 54	11 40	12 26	13 15	14♑04	14♑29	15 20	16 11	17 04	17 58	18 52	19 47	20♑42
1902	08♒39	09 01	09 27	09 54	10 24	10 56	11 31	12♒08	12♒27	13 07	13 49	14 33	15 18	16 05	16 53	17♒42
1903	13♓R33	13 27	13 R25	13 26	13 30	13 38	13 49	14♓03	14♓11	14 30	14 51	15 15	15 42	16 12	16 44	17♓18
1904	23♈R26	22 56	22 28	22 02	21 39	21 18	20 59	20♈44	20♈R37	20 27	20 19	20 15	20 15	20 17	20 23	20♈32
1905	04♊24	03 R57	03 27	02 57	02 25	01 53	01 20	00♊47	00♊R31	00 ♉00	29 29	29 00	28 32	28 04	27 44	27♉24
1906	11♋04	11 R01	10 54	10 45	10 32	10 16	09 58	09♋36	09♋R25	09 00	08 33	08 04	07 34	07 02	06 30	05♋57
1907	12♌11	12 32	12 50	13 05	13 17	13 27	13 33	13♌36	13♌R37	13 35	13 30	13 23	13 12	12 58	12 41	12♌21
1908	09♍24	10 00	10 35	11 08	11 39	12 08	12 34	12♍58	13♍09	13 29	13 47	14 02	14 14	14 22	14 28	14♍31
1909	04♎06	04 53	05 38	06 23	07 06	07 48	08 29	09♎08	09♎27	10 03	10 38	11 11	11 42	12 10	12 36	13♎00
1910	27♎42	28 34	29♏25	00 16	01 07	01 57	02 46	03♏35	03♏58	04 46	05 32	06 17	07 00	07 43	08 24	09♏03
1911	21♏17	22 10	23 03	23 56	24 49	25 42	26 36	27♏29	27♏55	28 48	29 ♐41	00 33	01 24	02 15	03 06	03♐55
1912	16♐05	16 54	17 44	18 35	19 26	20 18	21 11	22♐05	22♐32	23 26	24 20	25 16	26 10	27 05	27 59	28♐54
1913	12♑51	13 29	14 10	14 52	15 36	16 21	17 08	17♑56	18♑20	19 10	20 01	20 53	21 46	22 39	23 33	24♑28
1914	13♒17	13 36	13 58	14 22	14 50	15 19	15 51	16♒26	16♒44	17 22	18 01	18 43	19 26	20 11	20 58	21♒46
1915	18♓R56	18 47	18 40	18 D37	18 37	18 41	18 47	18♓56	19♓03	19 R18	19 36	19 57	20 20	20 47	21 15	21♓47
1916	29♈R17	28 46	28 16	27 47	27 21	26 56	26 34	26♈15	26♈07	25 52	25 40	25 32	25 D27	25 26	25 27	25♈32
1917	09♊R55	09 30	09 04	08 35	08 04	07 33	07 01	06♊28	06♊12	05 39	05 07	04 36	04 07	03 39	03 13	02♊50
1918	15♋R49	15 50	15 47	15 41	15 32	15 19	15 04	14♋46	14♋36	14 14	13 49	13 23	12 54	12 24	11 53	11♋21
1919	16♌17	16 41	17 02	17 Q0	17 36	17 48	17 58	18♌05	18♌07	18 R09	18 07	18 03	17 55	17 45	17 31	17♌14
1920	13♍07	13 45	14 22	14 57	15 30	16 01	16 30	16♍56	17♍09	17 32	17 52	18 10	18 24	18 36	18 45	18♍52
1921	07♎36	08 24	09 11	09 56	10 41	11 24	12 07	12♎47	13♎07	13 45	14 22	14 57	15 30	16 01	16 29	16♎56
1922	01♏08	02 00	02 52	03 43	04 35	05 25	06 15	07♏05	07♏29	08 17	09 04	09 51	10 36	11 20	12 02	12♏43
1923	24♏46	25 38	26 31	27 24	28 17	29 10	00 ♐03	00♐57	01♐24	02 17	03 10	04 03	04 55	05 57	06 38	07♐29
1924	19♐44	20 32	21 21	22 11	23 01	23 53	24 45	25♐38	26♐05	26 59	27 53	28 48	29 ♑43	00 38	01 33	02♑28
1925	16♑50	17 27	18 05	18 45	19 27	20 11	20 56	21♑43	22♑07	22 56	23 45	24 36	25 28	26 21	27 15	28♑09
1926	17♒50	18 06	18 24	18 46	19 10	19 37	20 06	20♒38	20♒55	21 30	22 07	22 46	23 28	24 11	24 56	25♒42
1927	24♓R13	23 59	23 49	23 41	23 D37	23 37	23 39	23♓45	23♓50	24 01	24 15	24 32	24 52	25 15	25 40	26♓09
1928	04♉R57	04 25	03 53	03 23	02 54	02 27	02 02	01♉39	01♉R29	01 11	00 55	00 45	00 34	00 28	00 26	00♉27
1929	15♊R14	14 53	14 28	14 02	13 33	13 03	21 32	12♊00	11♊R44	11 11	10 38	10 06	09 35	09 05	08 37	08♊11
1930	20♋26	20 30	20 31	20 29	20 23	20 14	20 03	19♋48	19♋R39	19 20	18 58	18 34	18 08	17 39	17 09	16♋38
1931	20♌19	20 45	21 09	21 30	21 49	22 04	22 17	22♌27	22♌31	22 36	22 38	22 37	22 33	22 26	22 15	22♌02
1932	16♍46	17 26	18 05	18 42	19 17	19 50	20 21	20♍50	21♍03	21 29	21 52	22 12	22 30	22 45	22 57	23♍06
1933	11♎03	11 52	12 39	13 26	14 12	14 57	15 40	16♎23	16♎43	17 23	18 02	18 38	19 13	19 46	20 17	20♎46
1934	04♏31	05 24	06 16	07 08	08 00	08 51	09 42	10♏32	10♏57	11 46	12 34	13 21	14 08	14 53	15 37	16♏20
1935	28♏14	29 06	29 ♐58	00 51	01 44	02 38	03 31	04♐25	04♐52	05 45	06 39	07 32	08 25	09 17	10 09	11♐01
1936	23♐26	24 13	25 01	25 50	26 40	27 31	28 23	29♐15	29♐42	00 ♑35	01 29	01 24	03 19	04 14	05 09	06♑04
1937	20♑59	21 33	22 09	22 48	23 28	24 10	24 54	25♑39	26♑02	26 49	27 38	28 28	29 19	00♒11	01 04	01♒58
1938	22♒40	22 52	23 07	23 25	23 45	24 09	24 35	25♒04	25♒19	25 52	26 27	27 04	27 43	28 24	29 07	29♓51
1939	29♓50	29 33	29 18	29 07	28 58	28 54	28 52	28♓54	28♓56	29 03	29 13	29 26	29 42	00♈02	00 24	00♈49
1940	10♉R54	10 22	09 49	09 17	08 46	08 17	07 49	07♉24	07♉R12	06 50	06 31	06 14	06 01	05 51	05 44	05♉D41
1941	20♊R40	20 21	20 00	19 36	19 10	18 42	18 13	17♊42	17♊R26	16 53	16 21	15 48	15 16	14 44	14 14	13♊46
1942	25♋01	25 09	25 R13	25 14	25 12	25 07	24 59	24♋48	24♋R41	24 25	24 06	23 45	23 21	22 55	22 27	21♋57
1943	24♌15	24 44	25 10	25 34	25 55	26 13	26 29	26♌42	26♌47	26 56	27 01	27 04	27 03	26 59	26 52	26♌42
1944	20♍18	21 00	21 40	22 18	22 55	23 30	24 03	24♍34	24♍49	25 17	25 42	26 05	26 26	26 43	26 58	27♍11
1945	14♎23	15 13	16 01	16 49	17 36	18 22	19 06	19♎50	20♎11	20 53	21 33	22 11	22 48	23 23	23 56	24♎27
1946	07♏50	08 42	09 35	10 27	11 19	12 11	13 02	13♏53	14♏18	15 08	15 58	16 46	17 34	18 20	19 06	19♏50
1947	01♐40	02 31	03 23	04 16	05 09	06 02	06 56	07♐50	08♐17	09 11	10 04	10 58	11 52	12 45	13 38	14♐30
1948	27♐10	27 57	28 42	29 ♑31	00 20	01 10	02 01	02♑53	03♑19	04 13	05 06	06 01	06 55	07 50	08 46	09♑41
1949	25♑14	25 46	26 20	26 57	27 34	28 14	28 56	29♑40	00♒02	00 48	01 36	02 24	03 14	04 05	04 57	05♒51
1950	27♒41	27 49	28 00	28 14	28 32	28 52	29 15	29♒40	29♒54	00 ♓24	00 56	01 30	02 07	02 45	03 26	04♓09
1951	05♈R40	05 19	05 01	04 45	04 33	04 24	04 18	04♈D15	04♈15	04 17	04 23	04 32	04 44	04 59	05 18	05♈39
1952	16♉R55	16 22	15 50	15 17	14 45	14 14	13 44	13♉16	13♉R02	12 37	12 14	11 54	11 37	11 23	11 12	11♉04
1953	26♊R00	25 45	25 27	25 07	24 43	24 18	23 50	23♊21	23♊R06	22 34	22 02	21 30	20 57	20 25	19 53	19♊23
1954	29♋31	29 42	29 50	29 55	29 R57	29 55	29 50	29♋43	29♋R37	29 25	29 09	28 51	28 30	28 06	27 41	27♋13
1955	28♌09	28 40	29 09	29 35	29 ♍59	00 20	00 39	00♍55	01♍02	01 14	01 22	01 28	01 30	01 30	01 26	01♍19
1956	23♍52	24 35	25 16	25 57	26 35	27 12	27 47	28♍20	28♍36	29 06	29 34	29 ♎59	00 23	00 43	01 01	01♎16
1957	17♎47	18 37	19 27	20 15	21 03	21 50	22 36	23♎21	23♎43	24 26	25 08	25 48	26 27	27 04	27 39	28♎12
1958	11♏14	12 06	12 59	13 52	14 44	15 37	16 29	17♏20	17♏46	18 37	19 27	20 16	21 05	21 41	22 39	23♏25
1959	05♐13	06 04	06 56	07 48	08 41	09 34	10 27	11♐21	11♐48	12 42	13 37	14 31	15 25	16 18	17 12	18♐05
1960	01♑02	01 47	02 32	03 19	04 07	04 57	05 47	06♑38	07♑04	04 57	08 50	09 44	10 38	11 33	12 29	13♑24
1961	29♑38	00 07	00 38	01 12	01 48	02 26	03 06	03♑48	04♒09	04 53	05 39	06 27	07 15	08 05	08 56	09♒48
1962	02♓50	02 53	03 00	03 11	03 24	03 40	04 00	04♓22	04♓34	05 01	05 30	06 01	06 35	07 11	07 49	08♓29
1963	11♈29	11 05	10 43	10 24	10 07	09 54	09 43	09♈37	09♈R34	09 D32	09 34	09 36	09 46	09 57	10 12	10♈29
1964	22♉R42	22 11	21 39	21 06	20 33	20 01	19 30	18♉59	18♉R45	18 17	17 51	17 28	17 07	16 49	16 34	16♉22
1965	01♋R04	00 53	00 38	00 21	00 ♊01	29 38	29 13	28♊46	28♊31	28 01	27 30	26 58	26 26	25 53	25 21	24♊49
1966	03♌48	04 03	04 14	04 22	04 27	04 R29	04 28	04♌24	04♌R20	04 11	03 59	03 43	03 25	03 05	02 41	02♌16
1967	01♍55	02 28	02 59	03 28	03 54	04 18	04 40	04♍58	05♍07	05 21	05 33	05 42	05 48	05 R50	05 50	05♍46
1968	27♍21	28 06	28 49	29 ♎30	00 10	00 49	01 26	02♎01	02♎18	02 50	03 20	03 48	04 14	04 37	04 58	05♎16
1969	21♎11	22 01	22 51	23 41	24 30	25 18	26 05	26♎51	27♎14	27 58	28 41	29 23	00 ♏03	00 42	01 19	01♏54
1970	14♏40	15 31	16 25	17 18	18 11	19 04	19 56	20♏48	21♏14	22 06	22 57	23 47	24 37	25 26	26 14	27♏01
1971	08♐49	09 40	10 31	11 23	12 15	13 08	14 02	14♐55	15♐22	16 16	17 11	18 05	18 59	19 54	20 48	21♐41
1972	04♑58	05 40	06 24	07 10	07 57	08 45	09 35	10♑25	10♑51	11 42	12 35	13 29	14 23	15 17	16 12	17♑08
1973	04♒05	04 31	04 59	05 30	05 04	06 39	07 17	07♒57	08♒17	09 00	09 44	10 30	11 17	12 05	12 55	13♒46
1974	08♓R00	07 D59	08 02	08 08	08 18	08 30	08 46	09♓05	09♓15	09 38	10 04	10 32	11 03	11 36	12 12	12♓50
1975	17♈R17	16 50	16 D25	16 02	15 42	15 24	15 10	14♈59	14♈R54	14 48	14 45	14 45	14 49	14 56	15 07	15♈20
1976	28♉R24	27 54	27 23	26 51	26 18	25 46	25 13	24♉42	24♉R26	23 56	23 28	23 02	22 38	22 16	21 58	21♉42
1977	06♋R03	05 55	05 44	05 30	05 13	04 54	04 31	04♋07	03♋R54	03 26	02 56	02 25	01 53	01 21	00 48	00♊16
1978	29♌09	29 56	00 41	01 26	02 09	02 50	03 R30	04♌08	04♌R27	05 02	05 35	06 07	06 36	07 03	07 28	07♌50
1979	05♍43	06 18	06 51	07 22	07 51	08 23	08 41	09♍08	09♍13	09 30	09 45	09 57	10 06	10 12	10 14	10♍14
1980	00♎53	01 39	02 23	03 06	03 48	04 28	05 07	05♎44	06♎02	06 36	07 09	07 39	08 07	08 33	08 56	09♎17
1981	24♎36	25 27	26 18	27 08	27 58	28 47	29 35	00♏22	00♏46	01 31	02 16	02 59	03 41	04 22	05 01	05♏38
1982	18♏06	18 59	19 51	20 44	21 38	22 31	23 23	24♏16	24♏42	25 34	26 26	27 17	28 08	28 58	29 ♐47	00♐35
1983	12♐24	13 14	14 04	14 56	15 47	16 40	17 33	18♐27	18♐54	19 48	20 42	21 37	22 31	23 26	24 20	25♐14
1984	08♑50	09 31	10 14	10 58	11 43	12 30	13 18	14♑08	14♑33	15 24	16 16	17 08	18 02	18 56	19 51	20♑46
1985	08♒27	08 50	09 16	09 44	10 15	10 48	11 23	12♒01	12♒20	13 00	13 43	14 27	15 12	15 59	16 48	17♒37
1986	13♓R04	12 59	12 D58	13 00	13 06	13 14	13 26	13♓41	13♓50	14 09	14 32	14 57	15 25	15 55	16 28	17♓03
1987	22♈54	22 25	21 57	21 32	21 08	20 47	20 29	20♈14	20♈R08	19 57	19 50	19 D47	19 46	19 49	19 55	20♈05
1988	03♊R53	03 25	02 56	02 25	01 53	01 20	00 48	00♊15	29♉R59	29 28	28 57	28 29	28 02	27 37	27 16	26♉56
1989	10♋R52	10 48	10 41	10 30	10 17	10 00	09 41	09♋19	09♋R07	08 41	08 14	07 45	07 14	06 42	06 10	05♋37
1990	12♌15	12 35	12 52	13 07	13 19	13 28	13 33	13♌R36	13♌R36	13 34	13 28	13 20	13 08	12 53	12 36	12♌16
1991	09♍27	10 04	10 39	11 12	11 43	12 12	12 39	13♍03	13♍14	13 35	13 52	14 07	14 19	14 28	14 34	14♍R37
1992	04♎23	05 10	05 55	06 40	07 23	08 05	08 45	09♎24	09♎43	10 19	10 53	11 26	11 56	12 24	12 50	13♎13
1993	28♎00	28 52	29 ♏43	00 34	01 24	02 14	03 03	03♏51	04♏15	05 02	05 48	06 32	07 16	07 58	08 38	09♏17
1994	21♏32	22 24	25 17	24 10	25 03	25 56	26 50	27♏43	28♏09	29 02	29 ♐54	00 46	01 37	02 28	03 18	04♐08
1995	16♐01	16 50	17 39	18 30	19 21	20 13	21 06	21♐59	22♐26	23 20	24 15	25 09	26 04	26 58	27 53	28♐48
1996	12♑48	13 27	14 08	14 51	15 35	16 20	17 07	17♑56	18♑20	19 10	20 01	20 53	21 46	22 40	23 34	24♑29
1997	13♒01	13 21	13 43	14 09	14 37	15 07	15 40	16♒15	16♒33	17 11	17 51	18 33	19 17	20 03	20 49	21♒38
1998	18♓R26	18 17	18 12	18 10	18 11	18 15	18 23	18♊34	18♓41	18 57	19 15	19 37	20 02	20 29	20 59	21♓31
1999	28♈R49	28 18	27 48	27 20	26 54	26 29	26 08	25♈53	25♈R41	25 26	25 15	25 07	25 02	25 01	25 03	25♈08
2000	09♊R31	09 06	08 39	08 09	07 39	07 07	06 34	06♊02	05♊R45	05 13	04 41	04 11	03 42	03 14	02 49	02♊27

Saturn

	January								February							
	1st	5th	9th	13th	17th	21st	25th	29th	1st	5th	9th	13th	17th	21st	25th	29th
1900	27♐43	28 11	28 38	29 05	29 32	29♑58	00 23	00♑48	01♑06	01 29	01 52	02 13	02 34	02 53	03♑11	
1901	07♑42	08 10	08 39	09 07	09 34	10 02	10 29	10♑55	11♑15	11 40	12 05	12 29	12 52	13 15	13♑36	
1902	17♑42	18 10	18 39	19 07	19 35	20 04	20 32	20♑59	21♑20	21 47	22 14	22 40	23 05	23 30	23♑54	
1903	27♑47	28 14	28 42	29 11	29♒39	00 08	00 36	01♒05	01♒26	01 54	02 22	02 50	03 17	03 43	04♒10	
1904	08♒00	08 27	08 54	09 22	09 50	10 18	10 46	11♒15	11♒37	12 05	12 34	13 02	13 31	13 59	14 27	14♒54
1905	18♒33	18 58	19 24	19 50	20 17	20 45	21 13	21♒41	22♒03	22 31	23 00	23 29	23 58	24 27	24♒56	
1906	29♒16	29 39	00♓03	00 27	00 53	01 19	01 45	02♓13	02♓34	03 02	03 30	03 59	04 28	04 57	05♓26	
1907	10♓21	10 41	11 02	11 24	11 47	12 10	12 35	13♓01	13♓20	13 47	14 15	14 43	15 11	15 40	16♓09	
1908	21♓52	22 08	22 25	22 44	23 03	23 24	23 46	24♓09	24♓27	24 52	25 18	25 44	26 11	26 39	27 07	27♓35
1909	03♈56	04 08	04 21	04 36	04 52	05 09	05 28	05♈48	06♈04	06 26	06 49	07 13	07 38	08 04	08♈31	
1910	16♈31	16 37	16 45	16 54	17 06	17 18	17 33	17♈49	18♈02	18 20	18 39	19 00	19 22	19 45	20♈10	
1911	29♈R42	29 D42	29 44	29 48	29 54	00♉01	00 10	00♉21	00♉30	00 44	00 59	01 16	01 34	01 53	02♉14	
1912	13♉R31	13 25	13 21	13 D19	13 18	13 20	13 23	13♉28	13♉33	13 41	13 51	14 02	14 16	14 30	14 46	15♉04
1913	27♉R52	27 41	27 32	27 24	27 18	27 13	27 D11	27♉10	27♉11	27 13	27 17	27 23	27 31	27 40	27♉51	
1914	12♊R46	12 30	12 15	12 02	11 50	11 39	11 31	11♊24	11♊R19	11 15	11 D13	11 13	11 14	11 17	11♊22	
1915	27♊R59	27 40	27 22	27 04	26 48	26 33	26 18	26♊06	25♊R57	25 47	25 39	25 32	25 27	25 24	25♊D22	
1916	13♋R20	13 00	12 40	12 21	12 02	11 43	11 25	11♋08	10♋R56	10 41	10 27	10 14	10 03	09 54	09 46	09♋40
1917	28♋R29	28 11	27 52	27 32	27 13	26 53	26 33	26♋14	26♋R00	25 41	25 24	25 07	24 52	24 38	24♋25	
1918	13♌R24	13 09	12 52	12 35	12 17	11 58	11 39	11♌20	11♌R05	10 45	10 26	10 07	09 48	09 31	09♌14	
1919	27♌R48	27 38	27 26	27 13	26 59	26 43	26 26	26♌09	25♌R55	25 36	25 17	24 58	24 38	24 19	24♌00	
1920	11♍R37	11 32	11 26	11 18	11 08	10 57	10 44	10♍30	10♍R19	10 03	09 46	09 29	09 10	08 52	08 32	08♍13
1921	24♍R47	24 48	24 47	24 44	24 39	24 33	24 25	24♍16	24♍R08	23 56	23 42	23 28	23 12	22 55	22♍38	
1922	07♎22	07 28	07 33	07 35	07 R36	07 36	07 33	07♎29	07♎R25	07 18	07 09	06 59	06 47	06 34	06♎20	
1923	19♎23	19 34	19 44	19 52	19 58	20 03	20 05	20♎R07	20♎R06	20 05	20 01	19 56	19 49	19 41	19♎31	
1924	00♏54	01 09	01 23	01 36	01 47	01 57	02 05	02♏11	02♏15	02 18	02 R20	02 20	02 18	02 15	02 10	02♏04
1925	12♏04	12 23	12 41	12 57	13 12	13 26	13 38	13♏49	13♏56	14 04	14 10	14 14	14 17	14 R19	14♏18	
1926	22♏48	23 10	23 31	23 51	24 10	24 28	24 44	24♏59	25♏09	25 21	25 32	25 42	25 50	25 56	26♏00	
1927	03♐16	03 40	04 04	04 27	04 48	05 09	05 29	05♐47	06♐01	06 17	06 32	06 46	06 58	07 09	07♐18	
1928	13♐30	13 56	14 22	14 47	15 11	15 35	15 57	16♐19	16♐34	16 54	17 13	17 30	17 46	18 01	18 15	18♐27
1929	23♐42	24 10	24 37	25 03	25 29	25 55	26 19	26♐43	27♐01	27 23	27 44	28 05	28 24	28 42	28♐59	
1930	03♑43	04 11	04 39	05 07	05 34	06 01	06 28	06♑53	07♑13	07 37	08 01	08 24	08 47	09 08	09♑28	
1931	13♑42	14 11	14 39	15 08	15 36	16 04	16 32	16♑59	17♑19	17 46	18 12	18 37	19 02	19 26	19♑49	
1932	23♑45	24 13	24 42	25 10	25 39	26 07	26 36	27♑04	27♑25	27 53	28 20	28 48	29 14	29 40	00♒06	00♒30
1933	04♒02	04 29	04 57	05 25	05 54	06 22	06 51	07♒19	07♒41	08 09	08 38	09 06	09 34	10 02	10♒29	
1934	14♒23	14 49	15 16	15 43	16 10	16 38	17 06	17♒35	17♒56	18 25	18 54	19 23	19 52	20 20	20♒49	
1935	25♒00	25 24	25 48	26 13	26 40	27 06	27 33	28♒01	28♒22	28 51	29 20	29♓48	00 18	00 47	01♓16	
1936	05♒56	06 17	06 39	07 02	07 26	07 51	08 16	08♒43	09♒03	09 30	09 58	10 27	10 55	11 24	11 54	12♒23
1937	17♓21	17 39	17 58	18 18	18 39	19 02	19 25	19♓49	20♓08	20 34	21 01	21 28	21 55	22 24	22♓52	
1938	29♓09	29 23	29 38	29♈54	00 12	00 30	00 51	01♈12	01♈29	01 52	02 16	02 41	03 07	03 34	04♈01	
1939	11♈30	11 38	11 48	12 00	12 13	12 28	12 44	13♈01	13♈15	13 35	13 56	14 19	14 42	15 06	15♈31	
1940	24♈26	24 28	24 33	24 39	24 47	24 57	25 08	25♈21	25♈31	25 47	26 04	26 22	26 42	27 03	27 25	27♈48
1941	07♉R58	07 55	07 54	07 54	07 57	08 01	08 07	08♉15	08♉22	08 33	08 45	08 59	09 14	09 31	09♉49	
1942	22♉R06	21 57	21 50	21 44	21 40	21 D38	21 38	21♉40	21♉42	21 47	21 54	22 02	22 12	22 24	22♉37	
1943	06♊R46	06 32	06 19	06 08	05 58	05 50	05 44	05♊39	05♊R37	05 35	05 36	05 38	05 42	05 47	05♊55	
1944	21♊R51	21 33	21 16	21 00	20 45	20 32	20 20	20♊09	20♊R02	19 D54	19 48	19 44	19 42	19 41	19 42	19♊45
1945	07♋R04	06 44	06 25	06 06	05 48	05 31	05 14	04♋59	04♋R48	04 36	04 24	04 14	04 06	03 59	03♋54	
1946	22♋R21	22 02	21 42	21 22	21 02	20 43	20 24	20♋05	19♋R52	19 35	19 19	19 04	18 50	18 38	18♋27	
1947	07♌R23	07 06	06 49	06 30	06 11	05 52	05 32	05♌13	04♌R58	04 39	05 20	05 01	03 44	03 27	03♌12	
1948	21♌R59	21 47	21 33	21 18	21 02	20 45	02 27	20♌08	19♌54	19 34	19 15	18 55	18 36	18 17	17 59	17♌41
1949	06♍R00	05 52	05 43	05 33	05 21	05 07	04 52	04♍37	04♍24	04 06	03 48	03 30	03 10	02 51	02♍32	
1950	19♍R26	19 25	19 21	19 16	19 09	19 01	18 51	18♍39	18♍R30	18 16	18 01	17 45	17 28	17 10	16♍52	
1951	02♎15	02 19	02 R21	02 22	02 21	02 18	02 13	02♎07	02♎R01	01 52	01 41	01 29	01 15	01 01	00♎45	
1952	14♎29	14 38	14 45	14 51	14 56	14 R58	14 59	14♎58	14♎R56	14 52	14 46	14 39	14 30	14 20	14 08	13♎55
1953	26♎14	26 27	26 39	26 50	26 59	27 06	27 11	27♎15	27♎17	27 R18	27 17	27 15	27 10	27 05	26♎57	
1954	07♏29	07 46	08 03	08 17	08 31	08 43	08 53	09 02	09♏07	09 13	09 18	09 20	09 R21	09 20	09♏18	
1955	18♏20	18 41	19 01	19 20	19 37	19 53	20 08	20♏21	20♏30	20 40	20 50	20 57	21 04	21 07	21♏10	
1956	28♏53	29 17	29 40	00♐01	00 22	00 41	01 00	01♐17	01♐29	01 44	01 57	02 09	02 19	02 28	02 36	02♐41
1957	09♐18	09 44	10 08	10 32	10 55	11 18	11 39	11♐59	12♐13	12 31	12 48	13 04	13 18	13 31	13♐42	
1958	19♐26	19 53	20 20	20 46	21 11	21 36	22 00	22♐22	22♐39	23 00	23 20	23 39	23 57	24 14	24♐29	
1959	29♐28	29♑56	00 24	00 51	01 18	01 44	02 10	02♑35	02♑53	03 17	03 40	04 02	04 23	04 43	05♑02	
1960	09♑28	09 56	10 24	10 53	11 20	11 48	12 15	12♑42	13♑02	13 28	13 53	14 17	14 41	15 04	15 26	15♑47
1961	19♑35	20 04	20 32	21 01	21 29	21 57	22 25	22♑53	23♑14	23 41	24 08	24 34	25 00	25 25	25♑49	
1962	29♑41	00♒09	00 37	01 05	01 34	02 02	02 31	02♒59	03♒20	03 49	04 17	04 45	05 12	05 39	06♒05	
1963	09♒56	10 23	10 50	11 17	11 45	12 14	12 42	13♒11	13♒32	14 01	14 30	14 58	15 34	15 55	16♒30	
1964	20♒25	20 50	21 15	21 42	22 08	22 36	23 03	23♒31	23♒53	24 21	24 50	25 19	25 48	26 17	26 46	27♒15
1965	01♓17	01 40	02 03	02 27	02 53	03 18	03 45	04♓12	04♓33	05 01	05 29	05 58	06 27	06 56	07♓25	
1966	12♓26	12 45	13 05	13 27	13 49	14 13	14 38	15♓03	15♓22	15 49	16 16	16 44	17 12	17 41	18♓10	
1967	24♓01	24 16	24 33	24 51	25 10	25 30	25 52	26♓15	26♓32	26 57	27 22	27 48	28 15	28 43	29♓11	
1968	06♈06	06 17	06 29	06 43	06 58	07 15	07 33	07♈52	08♈07	08 28	08 51	09 15	09 39	10 04	10 31	10♈58
1969	18♈48	18 53	19 01	19 10	19 20	19 33	19 46	20♈02	20♈14	20 32	20 51	21 11	21 33	21 56	22♈19	
1970	02♉R04	02 D03	02 05	02 08	02 13	02 20	02 28	02♉39	02♉47	03 00	03 15	03 31	03 48	04 07	04♉27	
1971	15♉R57	15 51	15 46	15 43	15 D42	15 43	15 45	15♉49	15♉54	16 01	16 10	16 21	16 34	16 48	17♉03	
1972	00♊R25	00 13	00♉03	29 54	29 46	29 41	29 37	29♉35	29♉D35	29 36	29 39	29 44	29 50	29♊59	00 09	00♊20
1973	15♊R18	15 02	14 46	14 32	14 20	14 09	13 59	13♊52	13♊R47	13 42	13 39	13 D38	13 39	13 41	13♊45	
1974	00♋R32	00 13	29♊55	29 37	29 20	29 04	28 49	28♊36	28♊R27	28 16	28 07	27 59	27 54	27 50	27♊47	
1975	15♋R52	15 33	15 13	14 53	14 34	14 15	13 57	13♋39	13♋R27	13 11	12 57	12 44	12 32	12 21	12♋13	
1976	01♌R04	00 46	00 27	00♋08	29 48	29 28	29 09	28♋49	28♋R35	28 16	27 58	27 41	27 25	27 09	26♋56	26♋43
1977	15♌R50	15 35	15 19	15 03	14 45	14 26	14 07	13♌48	13♌R33	13 14	12 54	12 35	12 16	11 58	11♌41	
1978	00♍R10	00♌00	29 49	29 36	29 22	29 07	28 51	28♌34	28♌R20	28 02	27 43	27 23	27 04	26 45	26♌25	
1979	13♍R54	13 49	13 44	13 36	13 27	13 17	13 05	12♍51	12♍R40	12 25	12 08	11 51	11 33	11 15	10♍56	
1980	26♍59	27 R01	27 01	26 59	26 56	26 50	26 44	26♍35	26♍R28	26 17	26 04	25 50	25 35	25 19	25 02	24♍45
1981	09♎30	09 37	09 42	09 45	09 R47	09 47	09 45	09♎41	09♎R38	09 31	09 23	09 13	09 02	08 50	08♎36	
1982	21♎27	21 39	21 49	21 57	22 04	22 09	22 13	22♎R15	22♎R15	22 14	22 11	22 06	22 00	21 52	21♎43	
1983	02♏54	03 10	03 25	03 38	03 50	04 00	04 08	04♏15	04♏19	04 23	04 R26	04 26	04 25	04 22	04♏18	
1984	13♏56	14 16	14 35	14 51	15 08	15 22	15 35	15♏47	15♏54	16 03	16 10	16 16	16 20	16 R22	16 23	16♏22
1985	24♏44	25 06	25 28	25 48	26 07	26 25	26 42	26♏57	27♏08	27 20	27 32	27 42	27 50	27 57	28♏02	
1986	05♐10	05 34	05 58	06 21	06 44	07 05	07 25	07♐44	07♐57	08 14	08 29	08 43	08 56	09 07	09♐17	
1987	15♐23	15 49	16 15	16 41	17 05	17 29	17 52	18♐14	18♐29	18 50	19 09	19 26	19 43	19 58	20♐12	
1988	25♐28	25 56	26 23	26 50	27 16	27 42	28 07	28♐31	28♐49	29 12	29 34	29♑55	00 15	00 34	00 51	01♑08
1989	05♑36	06 04	06 32	07 00	07 27	07 55	08 21	08♑47	09♑06	09 31	09 56	10 19	10 42	11 03	11♑24	
1990	15♑36	16 04	16 33	17 01	17 29	17 58	18 26	18♑53	19♑13	19 40	20 06	20 32	20 57	21 21	21♑45	
1991	25♑40	26 08	26 36	27 04	27 33	28 02	28 30	28♑58	29♑20	29 48	00 15	00 43	01 09	01 36	02♑01	
1992	05♒51	06 18	06 46	07 14	07 42	08 10	08 39	09♒08	09♒29	09♒58	10 27	10 55	11 23	11 51	12 18	12♒45
1993	16♒21	16 47	17 13	17 40	18 07	18 35	19 03	19♒32	19♒53	20 22	20 51	21 20	21 49	22 18	22♒46	
1994	27♒00	27 23	27 48	28 13	28 39	29 05	29 32	00♓00	00♓21	00 49	01 18	01 47	02 16	02 45	03♓15	
1995	07♓59	08 20	08 42	09 04	09 28	09 52	10 18	10♓44	11♓04	11 31	11 59	12 27	12 56	13 25	13♓54	
1996	19♓24	19 41	19 59	20 18	20 39	21 01	21 23	21♓47	22♓06	22 31	22 57	23 24	23 52	24 20	24 48	25♓17
1997	01♈20	01 33	01 47	02 03	02 20	02 39	02 59	03♈20	03♈36	03 58	04 23	04 48	05 13	05 40	06♈07	
1998	13♈45	13 53	14 02	14 13	14 26	14 40	14 56	15♈13	15♈26	15 46	16 06	16 28	16 51	17 15	17♈40	
1999	26♈46	26 48	26 52	26 57	27 05	27 14	27 24	27♈36	27♈47	28 02	28 18	28 36	28 55	29 15	29♈37	
2000	10♉R24	10 20	10 18	10 D17	10 19	10 22	10 27	10♉33	10♉39	10 49	11 00	11 13	11 27	11 43	12 01	12♉20

	March								April							
	1st	5th	9th	13th	17th	21st	25th	29th	1st	5th	9th	13th	17th	21st	25th	29th
1900	03♑28	03 44	03 58	04 11	04 23	04 33	04 42	04♑49	04♑54	04 58	04 01	05R02	05 02	05 00	04 57	04♑52
1901	13♑56	14 15	14 34	14 50	15 06	15 20	15 33	15♑45	15♑53	16 02	16 09	16 15	16 19	16 22	16R24	16♑23
1902	24♑17	24 39	25 01	25 21	25 40	25 58	26 15	26♑31	26♑42	26 55	27 07	27 17	27 26	27 34	27 40	27♑44
1903	04♒35	05 00	05 24	05 47	06 10	06 31	06 51	07♒10	07♒24	07 41	07 57	08 12	08 25	08 37	08 48	08♒57
1904	15♒01	15 27	15 54	16 19	16 44	17 08	17 31	17♒53	18♒09	18 30	18 49	19 07	19 24	19 40	19 55	20♒08
1905	25♒24	25 52	26 20	26 48	27 15	27 41	28 07	28♒32	28♒50	29 14	29 37	29♓58	00 19	00 39	00 57	01♒14
1906	05♓56	06 25	06 54	07 23	07 51	08 19	08 47	09♓14	09♓34	10 00	10 26	10 51	11 15	11 38	12 00	12♓21
1907	16♓38	17 08	17 37	18 07	18 36	19 06	19 35	20♓03	20♓25	20 53	21 21	21 48	22 15	22 41	23 06	23♓30
1908	27♓43	28 12	28 41	29 11	29♈41	00 11	00 40	01♈10	01♈32	02 02	02 31	03 00	03 29	03 57	04 24	04♈51
1909	08♈58	09 26	09 54	10 23	10 53	11 22	11 52	12♈22	12♈45	13 15	13 45	14 15	14 45	15 15	15 44	16♈13
1910	20♈35	21 01	21 27	21 55	22 23	22 51	23 20	23♈50	24♈12	24 42	25 13	25 43	26 14	26 44	27 15	27♈45
1911	02♉36	02 59	03 23	03 48	04 13	04 40	05 07	05♉35	05♉57	06 26	06 55	07 25	07 56	08 26	08 57	09♉27
1912	15♉08	15 28	15 48	16 10	16 33	16 57	17 22	17♉47	18♉07	18 35	19 03	19 31	20 00	20 30	21 00	21♉30
1913	02♉04	28 19	28 34	28 52	29 10	29 30	29♊52	00♊14	00♊31	00 56	01 21	01 47	02 14	02 41	03 10	03♊39
1914	11♊29	11 38	11 48	12 00	12 13	12 28	12 45	13♊03	13♊17	13 37	13 59	14 21	14 45	16 10	15 35	16♊02
1915	25♊23	25 25	25 29	25 34	25 42	25 51	26 02	26♊15	26♊25	26 40	26 57	27 15	27 34	27 55	28 17	28♊39
1916	09♋R39	09 35	09 33	09 33	09 34	09 38	09 43	09♋50	09♋56	10 06	10 17	10 30	10 44	11 00	11 18	11♋37
1917	24♋R13	24 04	23 55	23 49	23 44	23 41	23 D39	23♋40	23♋41	23 45	23 50	23 57	24 06	24 16	24 28	24♋41
1918	08♌R58	08 43	08 29	08 17	08 07	07 57	07 50	07♌44	07♌R41	07 38	07 D37	07 38	07 40	07 44	07 50	07♌57
1919	23♌R41	23 23	23 06	22 50	22 34	22 20	22 08	21♌56	21♌R49	21 40	21 33	21 27	21 24	21 D22	21 21	21♌23
1920	08♍R08	07 49	07 30	07 12	06 54	06 37	06 20	06♍05	05♍R54	05 41	05 29	05 19	05 10	05 02	04 56	04♍52
1921	22♍R20	22 01	21 43	21 24	21 05	20 46	20 27	20♍09	19♍R56	19 40	19 24	19 09	18 56	18 43	18 32	18♍23
1922	06♎R05	05 49	05 32	05 14	04 56	04 37	04 19	04♎00	03♎R46	03 27	03 09	02 52	02 35	02 19	02 04	01♎50
1923	19♎R20	19 07	18 54	18 39	18 23	18 06	17 49	17♎31	17♎R17	16 59	16 40	16 22	16 04	15 46	15 28	15♎11
1924	02♏R02	01 53	01 43	01 32	01 20	01 06	00 51	00♏35	00♏R23	00♎06	29 48	29 30	29 12	28 54	28 36	28♎17
1925	14♏R16	14 13	14 08	14 01	13 53	13 43	13 32	13♏20	13♏R10	12 55	12 40	12 24	12 07	11 50	11 32	11♏14
1926	26♏03	26R05	26 04	26 02	25 59	25 54	25 47	25♏39	25♏R32	25 21	25 09	24 56	24 42	24 27	24 11	23♏55
1927	07♐25	07 31	07 36	07 39	07R40	07 40	07 38	07♐34	07♐R30	07 24	07 16	07 07	06 57	06 45	06 32	06♐18
1928	18♐29	18 40	18 48	18 55	19 01	19 05	19R07	19♐08	19♐R07	19 05	19 02	18 57	18 50	18 42	18 32	18♐22
1929	29♐15	29 29	29 42	29♑53	00 03	00 12	00 19	00♑24	00♑27	00 30	00R31	00 31	00 29	00 25	00 20	00♑13
1930	09♑47	10 05	10 22	10 38	10 52	11 04	11 16	11♑26	11♑32	11 39	11 45	11 49	11 52	11R53	11 52	11♑50
1931	20♑11	20 32	20 52	21 12	21 29	21 46	22 02	22♑16	22♑25	22 37	22 47	22 56	23 03	23 09	23 13	23♑16
1932	00♒36	01 00	01 23	01 45	02 06	02 26	02 45	03♒02	03♒15	03 30	03 44	03 57	04 08	04 18	04 27	04♒34
1933	10♒55	11 21	11 47	12 11	12 35	12 58	13 20	13♒41	13♒56	14 15	14 33	14 50	15 06	15 20	15 33	15♒44
1934	21♒17	21 45	22 12	22 39	23 05	23 30	23 55	24♒19	24♒37	24 59	25 21	25 41	26 01	26 19	26 36	26♒52
1935	01♓45	02 14	02 42	03 11	03 39	04 06	04 33	05♓00	05♓19	05 44	06 09	06 33	06 55	07 17	07 38	07♓58
1936	12♓30	13 00	13 29	13 58	14 27	14 56	15 25	15♓53	16♓14	16 41	17 08	17 34	18 00	18 25	18 49	19♓11
1937	23♓22	23 51	24 20	24 50	26 20	25 50	26 19	26♓49	27♓11	27 40	28 08	28 37	29 04	29 32	29♈58	00♈24
1938	04♈29	04 58	05 27	05 56	06 26	06 55	07 25	07♈55	08♈18	08 48	09 18	09 48	10 17	10 46	11 15	11♈43
1939	15♈57	16 24	16 51	17 20	17 48	18 17	18 47	19♈17	19♈39	20 09	20 40	21 10	21 40	22 10	22 41	23♈10
1940	27♈54	28 18	28 43	29 10	29 37	00♉04	00 32	01♉01	01♉23	01 53	02 23	02 53	03 23	03 54	04 25	04♉55
1941	10♉09	10 30	10 52	11 15	11 39	12 04	12 30	12♉57	13♉18	13 46	14 14	14 43	15 13	15 43	16 13	16♉44
1942	22♉52	23 08	23 26	23 45	24 05	24 27	24 50	25♉14	25♉32	25 58	26 24	26 51	27 19	27 47	28 16	28♉46
1943	06♊04	06 15	06 27	06 42	06 57	07 14	07 33	07♊52	08♊08	08 30	08 53	09 17	09 42	10 08	10 34	11♊02
1944	19♊46	19 51	19 58	20 07	20 17	20 29	20 42	20♊58	21♊10	21 27	21 46	22 07	22 28	22 50	23 14	23♊39
1945	03♋R51	03 50	03 50	03 53	03 57	04 03	04 10	04♋20	04♋28	04 40	04 53	05 09	05 25	05 43	06 03	06♋23
1946	18♋R18	18 10	18 04	18 00	17 58	17 57	17 58	18♋01	18♋05	18 11	18 18	18 28	18 39	18 51	19 06	19♋21
1947	02♌R57	02 44	02 33	02 23	02 14	02 07	02 02	01♌59	01♌R57	01 D57	01 58	02 02	02 07	02 13	02 21	02♌31
1948	17♌R36	17 20	17 04	16 49	16 36	16 24	16 14	16♌05	15♌R59	15 53	15 49	15 46	15 D45	15 46	15 49	15♌53
1949	02♍R13	01 54	01 35	01 17	01 00	00 44	00 29	00♍16	00♍R06	29♌55	29 45	29 36	29 30	29 24	29 21	29♌19
1950	16♍R33	16 14	15 55	15 35	15 17	14 58	14 40	14♍23	14♍R11	13 55	13 41	13 28	13 16	13 05	12 56	12♍49
1951	00♎R29	00♍11	29 53	29 35	29 16	28 57	28 38	28♍20	28♍R06	27 48	27 30	27 14	26 58	26 43	26 30	26♍18
1952	13♎R52	13 37	13 22	13 06	12 48	12 31	12 12	11♎54	11♎R40	11 21	11 03	10 44	10 27	10 09	09 53	09♎37
1953	26♎R48	26 38	26 26	26 14	25 59	25 44	25 28	25♎11	24♎R58	24 40	24 22	24 04	23 45	23 27	23 09	22♎51
1954	09♏R14	09 08	09 01	08 53	08 42	08 31	08 18	08♏05	07♏R53	07 38	07 22	07 04	06 47	06 29	06 11	05♏53
1955	21♏R11	21 10	21 08	21 04	20 58	20 51	20 43	20♏33	20♏R24	20 12	19 59	19 44	19 29	19 13	18 56	18♏39
1956	02♐43	02 46	02 48	02R49	02 48	02 45	02 41	02♐35	02♐R29	02 21	02 11	02 00	01 48	01 34	01 20	01♐04
1957	13♐52	14 00	14 07	14 12	14 16	14R18	14 18	14♐17	14♐R15	14 11	14 06	13 59	13 50	13 41	13 30	13♐17
1958	24♐43	24 56	25 07	25 17	25 25	25 32	25 37	25♐40	25♐R42	25 43	25 42	25 39	25 35	25 30	25 23	25♐14
1959	05♑20	05 36	05 52	06 06	06 18	06 29	06 39	06♑47	06♑52	06 57	07 01	07R03	07 04	07 03	07 00	06♑57
1960	15♑52	16 11	16 30	16 47	17 03	17 18	17 31	17♑43	17♑51	18 01	18 09	18 15	18 20	18 24	18 25	18♑R26
1961	26♑13	26 35	26 57	27 17	27 37	27 55	28 13	28♑29	28♑40	28 50	29 03	29 14	29 24	29 33	29 39	29♑45
1962	06♒31	06 56	07 20	07 44	08 06	08 28	08 49	09♒08	09♒27	09 44	10 00	10 15	10 29	10 41	10 51	11♒01
1963	16♒50	17 17	17 44	18 10	18 35	18 59	19 23	19♒46	20♒02	02 24	20 44	21 03	21 20	21 37	21 52	05♒46
1964	27♒22	27 50	28 18	28 46	29 13	29 40	00♓06	00♓31	00♓49	01 13	01 36	01 59	02 20	02 40	02 59	03♓17
1965	07♓55	08 24	08 53	09 22	09 51	10 19	10 47	11♓14	11♓35	12 01	12 27	12 52	13 16	13 40	14 02	14♓24
1966	18♓39	19 09	19 38	20 08	20 37	21 07	21 36	22♓05	22♓27	22 55	23 2e	23 51	24 18	24 44	25 09	25♓34
1967	29♓39	00♈08	00 37	01 07	01 37	02 07	02 36	03♈06	03♈29	03 58	04 28	04 57	05 26	05 54	06 22	06♈50
1968	11♈04	11 32	12 01	12 29	12 59	13 28	13 58	14♈28	14♈51	15 21	15 51	16 21	16 51	17 21	18 06	18♈20
1969	22♈44	23 10	23 36	24 03	24 31	25 00	25 29	25♈58	26♈20	26 50	27 21	27 51	28 21	28 52	29 23	29♉53
1970	04♉49	05 11	05 35	05 59	06 25	06 51	07 18	07♉46	08♉08	08 36	09 06	09 36	10 06	10 36	11 07	11♉37
1971	17♉20	17 39	17 58	18 19	18 41	19 05	19 29	19♉54	20♉14	20 40	21 08	21 36	22 05	22 34	23 04	23♉34
1972	00♊24	00 37	00 53	01 09	01 27	01 47	02 07	02♊29	02♊47	03 10	03 35	04 01	04 27	04 55	05 23	05♊52
1973	13♊52	13 59	14 09	14 20	14 33	14 47	15 03	15♊20	15♊34	15 54	16 15	16 37	17 00	17 24	17 50	18♊16
1974	27♊D47	27 49	27 52	27 57	28 04	28 12	28 22	28♊34	28♊44	28 58	29 15	29 32	29 51	00 11	00 32	00♊54
1975	12♋R07	12 02	11 58	11 D57	11 57	11 59	12 03	12♋09	12♋14	12 23	12 33	12 45	12 58	13 13	13 30	13♋47
1976	26♋R40	26 30	26 21	26 14	26 08	26 04	26 D02	26♋02	26♋03	26 05	26 10	26 16	26 24	26 33	26 45	26♋57
1977	11♌R24	11 09	10 55	10 42	10 31	10 21	10 13	10♌07	10♌R03	09 59	09 D57	09 57	09 59	10 02	10 07	10♌14
1978	26♌R07	25 48	25 31	25 14	24 58	24 44	24 31	24♌19	24♌R11	24 01	23 54	23 47	23 43	23 40	23 D39	23♌40
1979	10♍R36	10 17	09 58	09 39	09 21	09 03	08 46	08♍30	08♍R19	08 05	07 52	07 41	07 31	07 23	07 16	07♍10
1980	24♍R40	24 22	24 03	23 44	23 25	23 06	22 48	22♍30	22♍R16	21 59	21 43	21 28	21 14	21 01	20 50	20♍40
1981	08♎R21	08 06	07 49	07 32	07 14	06 55	06 36	06♎18	06♎R04	05 45	05 27	05 09	04 52	04 36	04 21	04♎07
1982	21♎R32	21 20	21 07	20 52	20 37	20 21	20 04	19♎46	19♎R32	19 14	18 56	18 37	18 19	18 01	17 43	17♎26
1983	04♏R12	04 05	03 56	03 45	03 33	03 20	03 06	02♏51	02♏R39	02 22	02 05	01 47	01 29	01 11	00 53	00♎35
1984	16♏R22	16 19	16 14	16 08	16 00	15 51	15 40	15♏28	15♏R18	15 05	14 50	14 34	14 17	14 00	13 43	13♏25
1985	28♏05	28R07	28 07	28 06	28 03	27 58	27 52	27♏45	27♏R38	27 28	27 16	27 04	26 50	26 35	26 20	26♏03
1986	09♐25	09 32	09 37	09 40	09R42	09 42	09 41	09♐38	09♐R34	09 29	09 21	09 13	09 03	08 51	08 39	08♐25
1987	20♐25	20 36	20 45	20 53	21 00	21 05	21 08	21♐R10	21♐R10	21 09	21 06	21 02	20 56	20 49	20 40	20♐30
1988	01♑12	01 26	01 40	01 52	02 02	02 11	02 19	02♑25	02♑28	02 31	02R33	02 33	02 32	02 28	02 24	02♑18
1989	11♑43	12 02	12 19	12 35	12 50	13 03	13 15	13♑25	13♑32	13 40	13 46	13 51	13 54	13 55	13 55	13♑54
1990	22♑07	22 29	22 49	23 09	23 27	23 44	24 00	24♑15	24♑25	24 37	24 47	24 57	25 05	25 11	25 15	25♑19
1991	02♒26	02 51	03 14	03 36	03 58	04 19	04 38	04♒56	06♒09	05 26	05 41	05 54	06 06	06 17	06 27	06♒34
1992	12♒52	13 18	13 44	14 09	14 33	14 56	15 18	15♒40	15♒55	16 15	16 33	16 51	17 07	17 21	17 35	17♒47
1993	23♒14	23 42	24 10	24 37	25 03	25 29	25 54	26♒18	26♒36	26 59	27 21	27 42	28 02	28 20	28 38	28♒54
1994	03♓44	04 13	04 41	05 10	05 38	06 06	06 33	07♓00	07♓20	07 45	08 10	08 34	08 57	09 19	09 41	10♓01
1995	14♓23	14 53	15 22	15 52	16 21	16 50	17 19	17♓48	18♓09	18 36	19 04	19 30	19 56	20 22	20 46	21♓10
1996	25♓24	25 54	26 23	26 53	27 22	27 52	28 22	28♓52	29♈14	29 43	00 12	00 40	01 08	01 36	02 03	02♈29
1997	06♈35	07 03	07 32	08 01	08 31	09 00	09 30	10♈00	10♈23	10 53	11 23	11 53	12 23	12 52	13 21	13♈49
1998	18♈06	18 32	18 59	19 27	19 56	20 25	20 54	21♈24	21♈46	22 16	22 47	23 17	23 47	24 18	24 48	25♈18
1999	00♈00	00♉23	00 48	01 14	01 40	02 08	02 35	03♉04	03♉26	03 55	04 25	04 55	05 25	05 56	06 26	06♉57
2000	12♉24	12 45	13 06	13 29	13 53	14 18	14 43	15♉10	15♉30	15 58	16 26	16 55	17 25	17 55	18 25	18♉55

Saturn

	May 1st	May 5th	May 9th	May 13th	May 17th	May 21st	May 25th	May 29th	June 1st	June 5th	June 9th	June 13th	June 17th	June 21st	June 25th	June 29th
1900	04♑R49	04 42	04 33	04 23	04 12	04 00	03 47	03♑32	03♑R21	03 05	02 49	02 32	02 14	01 67	01 39	01♑22
1901	16♑R22	16 20	16 17	16 10	16 03	15 54	15 45	15♑33	15♑R24	15 11	14 57	14 42	14 27	14 10	13 53	13♑36
1902	27♑46	27 48	27 48	27 47	27 44	27 40	27 35	27♑28	27♑R21	27 12	27 01	26 49	26 36	26 22	26 07	25♑51
1903	09♒01	09 08	09 13	09 17	09 19	09 R 19	09 18	09♒16	09♒R13	09 08	09 01	08 53	08 44	08 33	08 21	08♒08
1904	20♒14	20 25	20 35	20 43	20 49	20 55	20 58	21♒R00	21♒R00	21 00	20 57	20 53	20 48	20 42	20 33	20♒23
1905	01♓23	01 38	01 52	02 05	02 16	02 26	02 35	02♓42	02♓46	02 50	02 53	02 R 54	02 53	02 51	02 48	02♓42
1906	12♓31	12 51	13 09	13 26	13 42	13 57	14 10	14♓22	14♓30	14 39	14 47	14 53	14 58	15 01	15 R 02	15♓02
1907	23♓42	24 05	24 27	24 49	25 09	25 27	25 45	26♓02	26♓13	26 27	26 40	26 51	27 01	27 09	27 16	27♓21
1908	05♈04	05 30	05 56	06 20	06 43	07 06	07 27	07♈48	08♈02	08 21	08 38	08 54	09 08	09 21	09 33	09♈42
1909	16♈28	16 56	17 24	17 51	18 18	18 43	19 08	19♈33	19♈50	20 12	20 34	20 54	21 13	21 31	21 48	22♈03
1910	28♈00	28 30	29 00	29 29	29 ♉ 58	00 26	00 54	01♉21	01♉41	02 07	02 32	02 56	03 19	03 42	04 03	04♉23
1911	09♉43	10 14	10 44	11 15	11 45	12 15	12 45	13♉15	13♉36	14 05	14 33	15 00	15 27	15 53	16 18	16♉42
1912	21♉45	22 16	22 47	23 18	23 49	24 20	24 51	25♉22	25♉45	26 15	26 45	27 14	27 43	28 12	28 39	29♉07
1913	03♊53	04 23	04 53	05 24	05 54	06 25	06 56	07♊28	07♊51	08 22	08 53	09 24	09 55	10 25	10 55	11♊24
1914	16♊15	16 43	17 11	17 40	18 09	18 39	19 10	19♊40	20♊03	20 34	21 06	21 37	22 08	22 39	23 10	23♊42
1915	28♊51	29 16	29 ♋ 41	00 04	00 34	01 02	02 31	02♋00	02♋22	02 52	03 22	03 53	04 23	04 55	05 26	05♋57
1916	11♋46	12 07	12 29	12 52	13 15	13 40	14 06	14♋33	14♋53	15 21	15 50	16 19	16 48	17 18	17 49	18♋19
1917	24♋48	25 04	25 21	25 39	25 59	26 20	26 42	27♋05	27♋23	27 47	28 13	28 40	29 07	29 35	00♌03	00♌32
1918	08♌02	08 12	08 23	08 36	08 51	09 07	09 24	09♌43	09♌57	10 18	10 40	11 03	11 27	11 52	12 17	12♌43
1919	21♌24	21 28	21 33	21 41	21 49	22 00	22 12	22♌25	22♌36	22 52	23 10	23 28	23 48	24 09	24 31	24♌54
1920	04♍R51	04 D 49	04 49	04 51	04 54	04 59	05 06	05♍14	05♍21	05 32	05 45	05 59	06 14	06 31	06 48	07♍08
1921	18♍R19	18 11	18 06	18 01	17 D 59	17 58	17 59	18♍02	18♍05	18 10	18 17	18 25	18 36	18 47	19 00	19♍15
1922	01♎R44	01 32	01 21	01 12	01 04	00 58	00 53	00♎50	00♎R49	00 D 59	00 50	00 53	00 58	01 04	01 12	01♎21
1923	15♎R03	14 48	14 33	14 20	17 08	13 57	13 47	13♎39	13♎R34	13 28	13 25	13 D 22	13 21	13 22	13 25	13♎29
1924	28♎R09	27 51	27 34	27 18	24 03	26 48	26 35	26♎23	26♎R15	26 05	25 57	25 49	25 44	25 40	25 38	25♎D37
1925	11♏R05	10 47	10 29	10 11	09 54	09 37	09 21	09♏05	08♏R54	08 41	08 28	08 17	08 07	07 59	07 51	07♏46
1926	23♏R46	23 29	23 11	22 53	22 35	22 17	21 59	21♏42	21♏R30	21 13	20 58	20 43	20 30	20 17	20 06	29♏56
1927	06♐R11	05 55	05 39	05 22	05 05	04 48	04 30	04♐12	03♐R59	03 41	03 24	03 07	02 51	02 35	02 21	02♐07
1928	18♐R16	18 03	17 50	17 35	17 20	17 03	16 47	16♐29	16♐R16	15 58	15 41	15 23	15 06	14 48	14 32	14♐16
1929	00♑R09	00 ♐ 00	29 50	29 39	29 26	29 13	28 58	28♑43	28♑R31	28 14	27 57	27 40	27 22	27 04	26 47	26♑29
1930	11♑R49	11 44	11 38	11 31	11 22	11 12	11 01	10♑48	10♑R38	10 24	10 09	09 53	09 36	09 19	09 02	08♑44
1931	23♑R16	23 17	23 15	23 12	23 08	23 02	22 55	22♑46	22♑R39	22 28	22 15	22 02	21 48	21 33	21 17	21♑00
1932	04♒36	04 41	04 44	04 R 45	04 45	04 44	04 41	04♒36	04♒R31	04 24	04 15	04 05	03 54	03 42	03 28	03♒14
1933	15♒50	15 59	16 07	16 13	16 18	16 21	16 R 23	16♒23	16♒R22	16 19	16 15	16 09	16 02	15 53	15 43	15♒32
1934	26♒59	27 13	27 25	27 36	27 46	27 54	28 01	28♒06	28♒08	28 R 10	28 11	28 10	28 08	28 04	27 58	27♒51
1935	08♓07	08 25	08 42	08 58	09 12	09 25	09 36	09♓46	09♓53	10 00	10 06	10 10	10 12	10 R 13	10 13	10♓11
1936	19♓23	19 44	20 05	20 24	20 42	20 59	21 15	21♓29	21♓39	21 51	22 01	22 10	22 18	22 24	22 28	22♓31
1937	00♈37	01 02	01 26	01 49	02 11	02 32	02 52	03♈11	03♈24	03 41	03 56	04 10	04 22	04 54	04 43	04♈51
1938	11♈57	12 25	12 51	13 18	13 43	14 08	14 31	14♈54	15♈10	15 31	15 51	16 10	16 27	16 43	16 58	17♈11
1939	23♈25	23 55	24 24	24 52	25 20	25 48	26 14	26♈40	26♈59	27 24	27 48	28 10	28 32	28 53	29 12	29♈30
1940	05♉10	05 41	06 11	06 41	07 11	07 41	08 09	08♉38	08♉59	09 26	09 53	10 19	10 44	11 08	11 32	11♉54
1941	16♉59	17 30	18 01	18 32	19 03	19 33	20 04	20♉34	20♉57	21 26	21 55	22 24	22 52	23 19	23 46	24♉12
1942	29♉01	29 31	00 ♊ 01	00 32	01 03	01 34	02 05	02♊36	02♊59	03 30	04 01	04 31	05 01	05 31	06 00	06♊29
1943	11♊16	11 44	12 13	12 43	13 13	13 43	14 14	14♊45	15♊08	15 39	16 11	16 42	17 13	17 44	18 14	18♊45
1944	23♊51	24 17	24 44	25 12	25 40	26 09	26 38	27♊08	27♊31	28 01	28 32	29 03	29 34	00 ♋ 05	00 37	01♋08
1945	06♋34	06 56	07 20	07 44	08 09	08 36	09 03	09♋30	09♋52	10 20	10 50	11 19	11 50	12 20	12 51	13♋22
1946	19♋29	19 47	20 06	20 26	20 48	21 10	21 34	21♋58	22♋17	22 44	23 10	23 38	24 06	24 35	25 04	25♋34
1947	02♌37	02 49	03 03	03 18	03 35	03 53	04 12	04♌33	04♌49	05 11	05 35	05 59	06 24	06 50	07 17	07♌45
1948	15♌56	16 03	16 11	16 21	16 33	16 46	17 00	17♌16	17♌29	17 47	18 07	18 26	18 49	19 12	19 36	20♌00
1949	29♌D19	29 19	29 22	29 26	29 32	29 39	29 48	29♍59	00♍08	00 21	00 35	00 51	01 09	01 27	01 47	02♍08
1950	12♍R46	12 40	12 47	12 35	12 35	12 36	12 40	12♍44	12♍49	12 57	13 06	13 17	13 29	13 43	13 58	14♍14
1951	26♍R12	26 02	25 53	25 46	25 40	25 36	25 34	25♍D33	25♍33	25 35	25 39	25 44	25 51	25 59	26 09	26♍20
1952	09♎R30	09 16	09 03	08 52	08 41	08 33	08 25	08♎19	08♎R16	08 13	08 D 12	08 12	08 14	08 17	08 22	08♎29
1953	22♎R43	22 26	22 10	21 55	21 41	21 28	21 16	21♎05	20♎R58	20 59	20 44	20 39	20 35	20 D 34	20 33	20♎35
1954	05♏R43	05 26	05 08	04 50	04 34	04 18	04 02	03♏48	03♏R38	03 26	03 15	03 06	02 57	02 51	02 45	02♏42
1955	18♏R30	18 12	17 54	17 36	17 18	17 00	16 43	16♏26	16♏R14	15 59	15 45	15 31	15 19	15 08	14 58	14♏50
1956	00♐R56	00 40	00 23	00 ♏ 05	29 47	29 29	29 12	28♏54	28♏R41	28 24	28 07	27 51	27 36	27 22	27 09	26♏57
1957	13♐R11	12 57	12 42	12 26	12 10	11 53	11 36	11♐18	11♐R05	10 47	10 29	10 12	09 55	09 39	09 23	09♐08
1958	25♐R10	24 59	24 48	24 35	24 21	24 06	23 51	23♐34	23♐R22	23 05	22 47	22 30	22 12	21 54	21 37	21♐20
1959	06♑R54	06 48	06 40	06 31	06 21	06 09	05 56	05♑42	05♑R32	05 16	05 00	04 43	04 26	04 09	03 51	03♑34
1960	18♑R25	18 23	18 19	18 14	18 08	17 59	17 50	17♑40	17♑R31	17 18	17 04	16 49	16 34	16 18	16 01	15♑44
1961	29♑48	29 50	29 R 51	29 51	29 49	29 45	29 40	29♑33	29♑R27	29 18	29 08	18 57	28 44	28 30	28 15	28♑00
1962	11♒R03	11 10	11 16	11 20	11 23	11 R 24	11 23	11♒21	11♒R19	11 14	11 08	11 01	10 52	10 41	10 30	10♒17
1963	22♒13	22 25	22 35	22 44	22 52	22 58	23 02	23♒05	23♒06	23 R 07	23 05	23 02	22 58	22 52	22 44	22♒35
1964	03♓25	03 41	03 56	04 09	04 21	04 31	04 40	04♓48	04♓52	04 57	05 01	05 02	05 R 02	05 01	04 58	04♓53
1965	14♓34	14 54	15 13	15 31	15 47	16 02	16 16	16♓28	16♓37	16 47	16 55	17 02	17 07	17 11	17 13	17♓13
1966	25♓46	26 10	26 32	26 54	27 14	27 34	27 52	28♓09	28♓21	18 36	28 49	29 01	29 11	29 20	29 28	29♓33
1967	07♈03	07 30	07 55	08 20	08 44	09 07	09 30	09♈51	10♈06	10 25	10 43	11 00	11 15	11 29	11 42	11♈53
1968	18♈35	19 03	19 31	19 59	20 25	20 52	21 17	21♈42	21♈59	22 22	22 44	23 05	23 25	23 43	24 00	24♈16
1969	00♉08	00 38	01 08	01 38	02 07	02 35	03 03	03♉31	03♉51	04 17	04 43	05 07	05 31	05 54	06 15	06♉36
1970	11♉53	12 24	12 54	13 25	13 56	14 26	14 56	15♉26	15♉47	16 16	16 45	17 12	17 39	18 05	18 31	18♉55
1971	23♉49	24 20	24 51	25 22	25 53	26 24	26 55	27♉26	27♉49	28 19	28 49	29 19	29 ♊ 48	00 17	00 45	01♊13
1972	06♊06	06 36	07 06	07 36	08 07	08 37	09 08	09♊40	10♊03	10 34	11 05	11 36	12 07	12 37	13 08	13♊37
1973	18♋29	18 56	19 24	19 53	20 22	20 52	21 22	21♋52	22♋16	22 46	23 18	23 49	24 20	24 51	25 22	25♋53
1974	01♋06	01 30	01 55	02 21	02 48	03 15	03 43	04♋12	04♋34	05 04	05 34	06 04	06 35	07 06	07 37	08♋08
1975	13♋57	14 17	14 38	15 00	15 23	15 47	16 12	16♋38	16♋58	17 26	17 54	18 22	18 51	19 21	19 51	20♋22
1976	27♋04	27 19	27 36	27 53	28 13	28 33	28 54	29♋17	29♋34	29 ♌ 59	00 24	00 50	01 17	01 44	02 13	02♌41
1977	10♌18	10 27	10 38	10 51	11 05	11 20	11 37	11♌54	12♌09	12 29	12 51	13 13	13 36	14 01	14 26	14♌52
1978	23♌41	23 44	23 49	23 55	24 04	24 13	24 25	24♌37	24♌48	25 03	25 20	25 38	25 57	26 18	26 39	27♌02
1979	07♍R08	07 06	07 D 05	07 05	07 08	07 11	07 17	07♍24	07♍31	07 41	07 52	08 05	08 19	08 35	08 52	09♍10
1980	20♍R35	20 27	20 21	20 16	20 13	20 D 12	20 12	20♍14	20♍16	20 21	20 27	20 35	20 45	20 56	21 08	21♍22
1981	04♎R00	03 47	03 36	03 26	03 18	03 11	03 06	03♎02	03♎R01	03 D 00	03 01	03 03	03 07	03 13	03 20	03♎28
1982	17♎R18	17 02	16 47	16 33	16 21	16 09	15 59	15♎50	15♎R45	15 39	15 34	15 31	15 D 30	15 30	15 32	15♎35
1983	00♏R26	00 ♎ 08	29 51	29 34	29 18	29 03	28 49	28♎37	28♎R28	28 17	28 08	28 00	27 54	27 49	27 45	27♎44
1984	13♏R16	12 57	12 39	12 22	12 04	11 47	11 31	11♏15	11♏R04	10 50	10 37	10 25	10 15	10 06	09 58	09♏52
1985	25♏R55	25 38	25 20	25 02	24 44	24 26	24 09	23♏51	23♏R38	23 22	23 06	22 51	22 37	22 24	22 13	22♏02
1986	08♐R18	08 03	07 47	07 31	07 13	06 56	06 38	06♐20	06♐R07	05 49	05 32	05 15	04 59	04 43	04 28	04♐14
1987	20♐R25	20 13	20 00	19 46	19 31	19 15	18 59	18♐42	18♐R29	18 11	17 53	17 35	17 18	17 01	16 44	16♐27
1988	02♑R14	02 06	01 56	01 45	01 33	01 20	01 06	00♑50	00♑R39	00 ♐ 22	00 05	29 48	29 30	29 13	28 55	28♐37
1989	13♑R53	13 49	13 43	13 36	13 28	13 18	13 08	12♑55	12♑R46	12 32	12 17	12 01	11 45	11 28	11 11	10♑53
1990	25♑R20	25 20	25 20	25 17	25 13	25 08	25 01	24♑53	24♑R46	24 35	24 23	24 11	23 57	23 42	23 26	23♑10
1991	06♒38	06 43	06 47	06 50	06 R 51	06 50	06 48	06♒44	06♒R40	06 33	06 26	06 16	06 06	05 54	05 41	05♒27
1992	17♒52	18 02	18 11	18 17	18 23	18 27	18 29	18♒R29	18♒R29	18 27	18 23	18 18	18 11	18 03	17 54	17♒43
1993	29♒02	29 16	29 29	29 41	29 51	30 ♓ 00	00 07	00♓12	00♓15	00 18	00 R 20	00 19	00 17	00 14	00 09	00♓03
1994	10♓11	10 29	10 46	11 02	11 17	11 31	11 43	11♓53	12♓00	12 08	12 14	12 19	12 22	12 R 24	12 24	12♓23
1995	21♓21	21 43	22 04	22 25	22 44	23 01	23 18	23♓33	23♓44	23 57	24 08	24 18	24 26	24 33	24 39	24♓42
1996	02♈42	03 07	03 31	03 55	04 17	04 39	04 59	05♈19	05♈32	05 50	06 06	06 20	06 33	06 45	06 55	07♈04
1997	14♈03	14 31	14 58	15 25	15 51	16 15	16 40	17♈03	17♈20	17 41	18 01	18 20	18 38	18 55	19 10	19♈24
1998	25♈33	26 03	26 32	27 01	27 29	27 57	28 24	28♈50	29♈09	29 34	29 ♉ 59	00 22	00 44	01 05	01 25	01♉44
1999	07♉12	07 43	08 13	08 44	09 14	09 43	10 13	10♉42	11♉03	11 31	11 58	12 25	12 50	13 15	13 39	14♉02
2000	19♉11	19 41	20 12	20 43	21 14	21 45	22 15	22♉46	23♉08	23 38	24 08	24 36	25 05	25 32	25 59	26♉26

	July								August							
	1st	5th	9th	13th	17th	21st	25th	29th	1st	5th	9th	13th	17th	21st	25th	29th
1900	01♑R13	00 56	00 39	00 22	00♐07	29 52	29 38	29♐25	29♐R16	29 05	28 55	28 46	28 D39	28 34	28 30	28♐27
1901	13♑R27	13 09	12 52	12 34	12 17	12 00	11 44	11♑28	11♑R17	11 02	10 49	10 37	10 26	10 16	10 07	10♑00
1902	25♑R43	26 26	25 09	24 52	24 34	24 26	23 59	23♑41	23♑R29	23 12	22 56	22 41	22 26	22 13	22 01	21♑50
1903	08♒R01	07 47	07 31	07 15	06 58	06 41	06 23	06♒06	05♒R52	05 35	05 17	05 00	04 43	04 27	04 12	03♒57
1904	20♒R18	20 06	19 53	19 40	19 25	19 09	18 53	18♒36	18♒R23	18 05	17 47	17 29	17 12	16 54	16 37	16♒20
1905	02♓R39	02 32	02 23	02 13	02 01	01 49	01 35	01♓20	01♓R09	00 52	00 35	00 18	00♒00	29 42	29 24	29♒06
1906	15♓R01	14 59	14 55	14 49	14 42	14 33	14 23	14♓12	14♓R03	13 49	13 35	13 19	13 03	12 46	12 29	12♓11
1907	27♓R23	27 26	27 R27	27 27	27 25	27 21	27 16	27♓09	27♓R03	26 54	26 43	26 31	26 18	26 04	25 48	25♓32
1908	09♈48	09 55	10 02	10 06	10 09	10 R11	10 11	10♈09	10♈R06	10 02	09 56	09 48	09 39	09 28	09 16	09♈03
1909	22♈10	22 24	22 35	22 46	22 54	23 01	23 07	23♈11	23♈13	23 R14	23 13	23 11	23 07	23 01	22 54	22♈45
1910	04♉32	04 51	05 07	05 23	05 37	05 50	06 01	06♉11	06♉17	06 24	06 29	06 33	06 R35	06 35	06 33	06♉30
1911	16♉53	17 16	17 37	17 58	18 17	18 35	18 51	19♉07	19♉17	19 30	19 41	19 50	19 58	20 05	20 09	20♉12
1912	29♉20	29♊46	00 11	00 35	00 58	01 20	01 41	02♊01	02♊15	02 33	02 49	03 04	03 18	03 29	03 40	03♊48
1913	11♊39	12 08	12 36	13 03	13 30	13 56	14 21	14♊45	15♊02	15 25	15 46	16 06	16 24	16 42	16 58	17♊12
1914	23♊57	24 27	24 57	25 27	25 56	26 25	26 53	27♊20	27♊40	28 06	28 31	28 55	29 19	29 41	00♋01	00♋22
1915	06♋13	06 44	07 15	07 46	08 17	08 47	09 17	09♋47	10♋09	10 37	11 05	11 33	11 59	12 25	12 50	13♋14
1916	18♋35	19 06	19 37	20 08	20 39	21 10	21 41	22♋12	22♋35	23 05	23 35	24 04	24 33	25 01	25 29	25♋56
1917	00♌47	01 17	01 47	02 17	02 48	03 19	03 49	04♌20	04♌44	05 15	05 45	06 16	06 46	07 16	07 46	08♌15
1918	12♌57	13 25	13 53	14 21	14 51	15 20	15 50	16♌20	16♌43	17 14	17 45	18 15	18 46	19 17	19 47	20♌18
1919	25♌06	25 30	25 55	26 21	26 48	27 16	27 44	28♌12	28♌34	29 04	29 33	00♍03	00 33	01 04	01 34	02♍05
1920	07♍18	07 38	08 00	08 23	08 47	09 12	09 37	10♍04	10♍24	10 51	11 19	11 48	12 17	12 46	13 16	13♍46
1921	19♍22	19 39	19 56	20 15	20 35	20 57	21 19	21♍42	22♍00	22 24	22 50	23 16	23 43	24 10	24 38	25♍07
1922	01♎27	01 38	01 51	02 05	02 21	02 38	02 56	03♎16	03♎31	03 52	04 14	04 38	05 02	05 26	05 52	06♎18
1923	13♎31	13 38	13 46	13 55	14 06	14 18	14 32	14♎47	14♎59	15 17	15 35	15 55	16 15	16 37	17 00	17♎23
1924	25♎37	25 39	25 43	25 47	25 53	26 01	26 10	26♎21	26♎30	26 43	26 58	27 14	27 31	27 49	28 08	28♎29
1925	07♏R43	07 40	07 38	07 38	07 39	07 42	07 46	07♏52	07♏57	08 06	08 16	08 27	08 40	08 54	09 10	09♏27
1926	19♏R51	19 43	19 36	19 31	19 28	19 25	19 25	19♏26	19♏28	19 31	19 37	19 43	19 52	20 02	20 13	20♏25
1927	02♐R01	01 49	01 38	01 28	01 20	01 13	01 08	01♐04	01♐R03	01 D01	01 02	01 04	01 07	01 13	01 19	01♐27
1928	14♐R08	13 53	13 39	13 26	13 15	13 04	12 55	12♐47	12♐R42	12 37	12 33	12 31	12 D30	12 31	12 33	12♐37
1929	26♐R21	26 04	25 48	25 32	25 17	25 03	24 50	24♐39	24♐R31	24 21	24 13	24 06	24 01	23 57	23 54	23♐D54
1930	08♑R35	08 18	08 00	07 43	07 26	07 10	06 54	06♑39	06♑R29	06 15	06 03	05 52	05 43	05 35	05 28	05♑22
1931	20♑R52	20 34	20 17	19 59	19 41	19 24	19 06	18♑50	18♑R37	18 21	18 06	17 52	17 39	17 27	17 16	17♑06
1932	03♒R06	02 50	02 34	02 17	01 59	01 42	01 24	01♒06	00♒R53	00 35	00 18	00♑02	29 46	29 31	29 17	29♑04
1933	15♒R26	15 13	14 59	14 44	14 28	14 12	13 55	13♒37	13♒R24	13 06	12 48	12 30	12 13	11 56	11 39	11♒23
1934	27♒R47	27 38	27 28	27 16	27 03	26 49	26 34	26♒18	26♒R06	25 49	25 32	25 14	24 56	24 38	24 20	24♒01
1935	10♓R09	10 05	09 59	09 51	09 42	09 32	09 20	09♓08	08♓R57	08 43	08 27	08 11	07 54	07 36	07 18	07♓00
1936	22♓R32	22 32	22 31	22 28	22 23	22 17	22 10	22♓01	21♓R53	21 42	21 29	21 15	21 01	20 45	20 28	20♓11
1937	04♈55	05 01	05 05	05 07	05 R08	05 07	05 05	05♈01	04♈R57	04 50	04 42	04 33	04 22	04 09	30 56	03♈41
1938	17♈17	17 29	17 38	17 46	17 53	17 58	18 01	18♈R03	18♈R03	18 02	17 59	17 54	17 48	17 41	17 31	17♈21
1939	29♈39	29♉55	00 10	00 24	00 36	00 46	00 55	01♉03	01♉07	01 12	01 15	01 R16	01 16	01 14	01 10	01♉05
1940	12♉05	12 25	12 45	13 03	13 20	13 35	13 50	14♉02	14♉11	14 21	14 29	14 36	14 41	14 45	14 R47	14♉47
1941	24♉24	24 49	25 13	25 35	25 57	26 17	26 36	26♉54	27♉07	27 23	27 37	27 49	28 01	28 10	28 18	28♉24
1942	06♊43	07 11	07 38	08 04	08 29	08 54	09 17	09♊40	09♊56	10 16	10 36	10 54	11 10	11 25	11 39	11♊52
1943	19♊00	19 30	19 59	20 28	20 56	21 24	21 51	22♊17	22♊36	23 01	23 24	23 47	24 08	24 29	24 48	25♊05
1944	01♋23	01 54	02 25	02 55	03 26	03 55	04 24	04♋53	05♋14	05 42	06 08	06 34	06 59	07 24	07 47	08♋09
1945	13♋37	14 09	14 40	15 11	15 42	15 13	16 43	17♋14	17♋36	18 06	18 35	19 04	19 32	19 59	20 25	20♋51
1946	25♋49	25 20	26 50	27 21	27 52	28 23	28 54	29♋25	29♋48	00♌19	00 49	01 19	01 49	02 19	02 48	03♌16
1947	07♌59	08 27	08 56	09 26	09 56	10 26	10 56	11♌27	11♌50	12 21	12 52	13 23	13 53	14 24	14 54	15♌24
1948	20♌13	20 39	21 06	21 33	22 01	22 30	22 59	23♌28	23♌51	24 21	24 51	25 21	25 52	26 23	26 53	27♌24
1949	02♍R19	02 41	03 05	03 29	03 54	04 20	04 47	05♍14	05♍35	06 04	06 32	07 02	07 31	08 01	08 31	09♍01
1950	14♍25	14 41	15 01	15 21	15 43	16 06	16 29	16♍54	17♍13	17 38	18 05	18 32	19 00	19 28	19 57	20♍26
1951	26♍27	26 40	26 55	27 12	27 29	27 48	28 07	28♍28	28♍45	29 08	29 31	29♎56	00 21	00 47	01 14	01♍41
1952	08♎32	08 41	08 52	09 04	09 17	09 31	09 47	10♎04	10♎18	10 37	10 58	11 19	11 41	12 05	12 29	12♎54
1953	20♎36	20 40	20 45	20 51	21 00	21 10	21 21	21♎34	21♎44	21 59	22 15	22 33	22 52	23 11	23 32	23♎54
1954	02♏R40	02 D39	02 39	02 41	02 44	02 49	02 55	03♏03	03♏10	03 20	03 32	03 46	04 00	04 16	04 33	04♏52
1955	14♏R46	14 40	14 35	14 32	14 D30	14 30	14 32	14♏35	14♏38	14 44	14 51	15 00	15 10	15 21	15 34	15♏49
1956	26♏R51	26 41	26 32	26 25	26 19	26 15	26 12	26♏D10	26♏10	26 11	26 14	26 19	26 24	26 32	26 41	26♏51
1957	09♐R01	08 47	08 34	08 23	08 13	08 04	07 56	07♐50	07♐R47	07 43	07 D41	07 41	07 42	07 45	07 49	07♐55
1958	21♐R12	20 56	20 40	20 26	20 12	19 59	19 48	19♐38	19♐R31	19 23	19 17	19 12	19 08	19 D06	19 06	19♐07
1959	03♑R25	03 07	02 50	02 33	02 17	02 02	01 47	01♑34	01♑R24	01 12	01 02	00 53	00 45	00 38	00 33	00♑30
1960	15♑R35	15 17	15 00	14 42	14 25	14 08	13 51	13♑35	13♑R24	13 09	12 55	12 43	12 31	12 21	12 12	12♑05
1961	27♑R52	27 35	27 18	27 01	26 43	26 25	26 08	25♑50	25♑R37	25 21	25 04	24 49	24 34	24 20	24 08	23♑56
1962	10♒R10	09 56	09 41	09 25	09 09	08 51	08 34	08♒16	08♒R03	07 45	07 27	07 10	06 53	06 37	06 21	06♒06
1963	22♒R30	22 20	22 08	21 54	21 40	21 25	21 09	20♒52	20♒R40	20 22	20 04	19 46	19 28	19 11	18 53	18♒36
1964	04♓R50	04 43	04 35	04 25	04 14	04 02	03 49	03♓34	03♓R23	03 07	02 50	02 33	02 15	01 57	01 39	01♓21
1965	17♓R13	17 11	17 07	17 02	16 56	16 48	16 38	16♓28	16♓R19	16 06	15 52	15 37	15 21	15 04	14 47	14♓29
1966	29♓36	29 39	29 R41	29 41	29 40	29 37	29 32	29♓26	29♓R20	29 12	29 02	28 50	28 37	28 23	28 08	27♓53
1967	11♈58	12 07	12 14	12 20	12 24	12 27	12 R28	12♈27	12♈R25	12 22	12 17	12 10	12 02	11 52	11 41	11♈28
1968	24♈24	24 38	24 50	25 01	25 10	25 18	25 24	25♈29	25♈31	25 R33	25 33	25 31	25 28	25 23	25 17	25♈09
1969	06♉46	07 05	47 22	07 38	07 53	08 06	08 18	08♉29	08♉35	08 43	08 49	08 53	08 56	08 R57	08 56	08♉54
1970	19♉07	19 30	19 52	20 13	20 33	20 51	21 08	21♉24	21♉35	21 48	22 00	22 10	22 19	22 26	22 31	22♉35
1971	01♊27	01 53	02 19	02 44	03 08	03 30	03 52	04♊13	04♊28	04 46	05 03	05 19	05 34	05 47	05 58	06♊08
1972	13♊52	14 21	14 49	15 17	15 44	16 10	16 36	17♊00	17♊18	17 41	18 02	18 23	18 42	19 00	19 16	19♊32
1973	26♊09	26 39	27 10	27 40	28 09	28 38	29 06	28♊34	29♊54	00♋21	00 46	01 10	01 34	01 57	02 18	02♋38
1974	08♋24	08 55	09 26	09 57	10 28	10 59	11 29	11♋59	12♋21	12 50	13 18	13 46	14 12	14 39	15 04	15♋28
1975	20♋37	21 08	21 39	22 10	22 41	23 12	23 43	24♋14	24♋37	25 07	25 38	26 07	26 36	27 05	27 33	28♋00
1976	02♌56	03 25	03 55	04 26	04 56	05 27	05 58	06♌29	06♌52	07 23	07 54	08 24	08 55	09 25	09 54	10♌24
1977	15♌05	15 33	16 00	16 29	16 58	17 27	17 57	18♌27	18♌50	19 20	19 51	20 22	20 52	21 23	21 54	22♌24
1978	27♌13	27 37	28 02	28 28	28 55	29 22	29♍49	00♍18	00♍39	01 09	01 38	02 08	02 38	03 08	03 39	04♍09
1979	09♍20	09 40	10 01	10 24	10 47	11 11	11 36	12♍02	12♍21	12 48	13 16	13 44	14 20	14 42	15 11	15♍41
1980	21♍29	21 45	22 02	22 21	22 40	23 01	23 23	23♍46	24♍03	24 27	24 53	25 18	25 45	26 12	26 40	27♍08
1981	03♎33	03 44	03 57	04 11	04 26	04 42	05 00	05♎19	05♎34	05 54	06 16	06 39	07 03	07 27	07 53	08♎19
1982	15♎38	15 44	15 51	16 00	16 10	16 22	16 35	16♎50	17♎01	17 18	17 36	17 55	18 16	18 37	18 59	19♎22
1983	27♎D43	27 44	27 46	27 50	27 55	28 02	28 10	28♎20	28♎29	28 41	28 55	29 10	29 26	29 44	00♏02	00♏22
1984	09♏R49	09 45	09 43	09 D42	09 43	09 45	09 49	09♏54	09♏59	10 07	10 17	10 28	10 40	10 54	10 09	11♏25
1985	21♏R57	21 49	21 42	21 36	21 32	21 29	21 D28	21♏28	21♏30	21 33	21 38	21 44	21 52	22 01	22 12	22♏24
1986	04♐R07	03 55	03 44	03 34	03 25	03 18	03 12	03♐08	03♐R06	03 D04	03 04	03 05	03 09	03 13	03 19	03♐29
1987	16♐R19	16 04	15 49	15 36	15 24	15 12	15 02	14♐54	14♐R48	14 42	14 37	14 34	14 D32	14 32	14 34	14♐37
1988	28♐R29	28 12	27 55	27 39	27 24	27 10	26 57	26♐45	26♐R36	26 26	26 18	26 10	26 04	26 00	25 57	25♐D56
1989	10♑R44	10 26	10 09	09 51	09 34	09 18	09 02	08♑47	08♑R36	08 22	08 10	07 59	07 49	07 40	07 33	07♑27
1990	23♑R01	22 44	22 27	22 09	21 51	21 33	21 16	20♑59	20♑R46	20 30	20 15	20 00	19 47	19 34	19 23	19♑13
1991	05♒R20	05 05	04 49	04 32	04 15	03 57	03 39	03♒22	03♒R08	02 51	02 33	02 17	02 00	01 45	01 30	01♒16
1992	17♒R37	17 24	17 11	16 56	16 41	16 24	16 08	15♒50	15♒R37	15 19	15 01	14 43	14 26	14 08	13 51	13♒35
1993	29♒R59	29 50	29 40	29 29	29 16	29 03	28 48	28♒33	28♒R21	28 04	27 47	27 29	27 11	26 53	26 35	26♒17
1994	12♓R21	12 17	12 12	12 05	11 57	11 47	11 36	11♓23	11♓R13	10 59	10 44	10 28	10 11	09 54	09 36	09♓18
1995	24♓44	24 R45	24 45	24 43	24 39	24 34	24 28	24♓20	24♓R13	24 02	23 51	23 38	23 23	23 97	22 52	22♓35
1996	07♈08	07 14	07 19	07 22	07 R24	07 24	07 22	07♈19	07♈R15	07 09	07 02	06 53	06 42	06 30	06 17	06♈03
1997	19♈31	19 43	19 53	20 02	20 09	20 15	20 19	20♈21	20♈R22	20 21	20 19	20 15	20 10	20 03	19 54	19♈44
1998	01♉53	02 10	02 25	02 39	02 52	03 03	03 13	03♉21	03♉26	03 32	03 35	03 R37	03 38	03 36	03 33	03♉29
1999	14♉13	14 35	14 55	15 14	15 32	15 49	16 04	16♉17	16♉27	16 38	16 48	16 55	17 02	17 07	17 10	17♉R11
2000	26♉39	27 04	27 28	27 51	28 13	28 34	28 54	29♉12	29♉25	29 41	29♊56	00 10	00 21	00 32	00 40	00♊47

Saturn

Year	Sep 1st	Sep 5th	Sep 9th	Sep 13th	Sep 17th	Sep 21st	Sep 25th	Sep 29th	Oct 1st	Oct 5th	Oct 9th	Oct 13th	Oct 17th	Oct 21st	Oct 25th	Oct 29th
1900	28♐D26	28 26	28 28	28 31	28 36	28 42	28 50	29♐00	29♐05	29 16	29 29	29 44	29♑59	00 16	00 34	00♑53
1901	09♑R56	09 52	09 49	09 D47	09 47	09 49	09 53	09♑57	10♑00	10 08	10 16	10 27	10 38	10 51	11 06	11♑21
1902	21♑R42	21 33	21 26	21 20	21 16	21 13	21 D11	21♑11	21♑12	21 15	21 19	21 25	21 32	21 41	21 51	22♑03
1903	03♒R47	03 34	03 23	03 12	03 04	02 56	02 50	02♒46	02♒R44	02 D42	02 41	02 42	02 45	02 49	02 55	03♒03
1904	16♒R08	15 52	15 37	15 24	15 11	15 00	14 59	14♒41	14♒R37	14 31	14 26	14 23	14 D21	14 21	14 22	14♒27
1905	28♒R52	28 35	28 18	28 01	27 45	27 31	27 17	27♒04	26♒R58	26 47	26 37	26 29	26 23	26 18	26 14	26♒D12
1906	11♓R57	11 39	11 21	11 02	10 44	10 27	10 10	09♓54	09♓R46	09 32	09 18	09 06	08 54	08 45	08 36	08♓29
1907	25♓R19	25 02	24 44	24 26	24 07	23 49	23 30	23♓12	23♓R03	22 46	22 29	22 13	21 58	21 49	21 31	21♓19
1908	08♈R52	08 47	08 21	08 04	07 46	07 28	07 09	06♈50	06♈R41	06 22	06 04	05 45	05 28	05 11	04 54	04♈39
1909	22♈R38	22 27	22 14	22 00	21 45	21 29	21 12	20♈55	20♈R46	20 27	20 08	19 49	19 30	19 11	18 53	18♈35
1910	06♉R27	06 21	06 13	06 04	05 53	05 41	05 28	05♉13	05♉R06	04 49	04 32	04 14	03 56	03 37	03 18	02♉58
1911	20♉R13	20 13	20 12	20 08	20 03	19 56	19 48	19♉38	19♉R32	19 20	19 07	18 52	18 36	18 19	18 01	17♉43
1912	03♊54	04 00	04 04	04 R06	04 07	04 06	04 03	03♊58	03♊R55	03 48	03 39	03 29	03 17	03 04	02 49	02♊34
1913	17♊22	17 34	17 44	17 53	18 00	18 05	18 09	18♊R10	18♊R10	18 10	18 07	18 02	17 56	17 48	17 39	17♊28
1914	00♋35	00 52	01 08	01 23	01 36	01 47	01 57	02♋05	02♋08	02 14	02 18	02 R20	02 20	02 18	02 15	02♋10
1915	13♋31	13 53	14 14	14 33	14 52	15 09	15 24	15♋38	15♋44	15 56	16 06	16 14	16 21	16 26	16 29	16♋R30
1916	26♋15	26 41	27 05	27 29	27 51	28 12	28 33	28♋51	29♋00	29 17	29 32	29 46	29♌58	00 09	00 18	00♌25
1917	08♌36	09 04	09 32	09 58	10 24	10 49	11 13	11♌36	11♌47	12 09	12 29	12 47	13 05	13 21	13 35	13♌48
1918	20♌40	21 10	21 39	22 08	22 36	23 04	23 30	23♌57	24♌09	24 34	24 58	25 21	25 43	26 03	26 22	26♌40
1919	02♍28	02 58	03 28	03 58	04 28	04 57	05 26	05♍54	06♍08	06 35	07 02	07 28	07 53	08 17	08 40	09♍02
1920	14♍08	14 38	15 08	15 38	16 09	16 38	17 08	17♍37	17♍52	18 21	18 49	19 17	19 44	20 11	20 36	21♍01
1921	25♍28	25 57	26 27	26 56	27 26	27 56	28 26	28♍56	29♍10	29♎40	00 09	00 38	01 07	01 35	02 03	02♎30
1922	06♎39	07 06	07 34	08 02	08 31	09 00	09 29	09♎58	10♎13	10 43	12 12	11 42	12 11	12 40	13 09	13♎37
1923	17♎41	18 06	18 32	18 59	19 25	19 53	20 21	20♎49	21♎03	21 32	22 01	22 30	23 00	23 29	23 58	24♎27
1924	28♎45	29 07	29 30	29♏54	00 19	00 45	01 11	01♏38	01♏51	02 19	02 47	03 15	03 43	04 12	04 41	05♏10
1925	09♏40	09 59	10 19	10 40	11 02	11 25	11 48	12♏13	12♏25	12 51	13 17	13 44	14 11	14 39	15 07	15♏35
1926	20♏56	20 51	21 07	21 24	21 43	22 03	22 23	22♏45	22♏56	23 19	23 43	24 08	24 33	24 59	25 26	25♏53
1927	01♐34	01 45	01 57	02 11	02 26	02 42	02 59	03♐17	03♐27	03 47	04 08	04 30	04 53	05 17	05 42	06♐07
1928	12♐41	12 48	12 56	13 05	13 16	13 29	13 42	13♐57	14♐05	14 22	14 41	15 00	15 20	15 42	16 04	16♐27
1929	23♐54	23 56	23 59	24 05	24 11	24 19	24 29	24♐40	24♐46	24 59	25 14	25 29	25 46	26 05	26 24	26♐44
1930	05♑R19	05 17	05 D16	05 16	05 18	05 21	05 27	05♑33	05♑37	05 46	05 56	06 08	06 22	06 36	06 52	07♑09
1931	17♑R00	16 53	16 47	16 43	16 40	16 D39	16 39	16♑41	16♑43	16 47	16 53	17 01	17 10	17 21	17 33	17♑46
1932	28♑R55	28 44	28 34	28 26	28 19	28 14	28 10	28♑08	28♑R07	28 D07	28 09	28 12	28 17	28 24	28 32	28♑41
1933	11♒R12	10 57	10 44	10 32	10 20	10 11	10 02	09♒55	09♒R52	09 48	09 45	09 D43	09 43	09 45	09 48	09♒53
1934	23♒R49	23 32	23 16	23 00	22 45	22 32	22 19	22♒08	22♒R03	21 54	21 46	21 39	21 35	21 22	21 D30	21♒30
1935	06♓R46	06 28	06 10	05 52	05 35	05 19	05 03	04♓48	04♓R41	04 27	04 15	04 04	03 55	03 47	03 40	03♓36
1936	19♓R58	19 40	19 22	19 03	18 45	18 26	18 09	17♓51	17♓R43	17 26	17 11	16 56	16 43	16 31	16 20	16♓11
1937	03♈R30	03 13	02 56	02 39	02 20	02 02	01 43	01♈25	01♈R15	00 57	00 39	00 21	00♓05	29 49	29 34	29♈20
1938	17♈R12	16 59	16 45	16 30	16 14	15 57	15 39	15♈21	15♈R12	14 53	14 34	14 15	13 56	13 38	13 20	13♈03
1939	01♉R00	00 51	00 42	00 31	00 18	00♈04	29 50	29♈34	29♈R25	29 08	28 50	28 32	28 13	27 54	27 35	27♈15
1940	14♉R46	14 43	14 38	14 32	14 24	14 15	14 04	13♉52	13♉R45	13 31	13 16	12 59	12 42	12 24	12 06	11♉47
1941	28♉28	28 31	28 R33	28 33	28 31	28 27	28 22	28♉15	28♉R11	28 02	27 51	27 39	27 25	27 10	26 54	26♉37
1942	12♊00	12 09	12 17	12 23	12 28	12 30	12 R31	12♊31	12♊R30	12 26	12 21	12 14	12 06	11 56	11 44	11♊31
1943	25♊18	25 33	25 47	25 59	26 10	26 19	26 26	26♊32	26♊34	26 37	26 R38	26 37	26 35	26 31	26 25	26♊18
1944	08♋24	08 44	09 03	09 20	09 36	09 51	10 04	10♋15	10♋20	10 29	10 36	10 41	10 45	10 R47	10 47	10♋45
1945	21♋10	21 34	21 57	22 19	22 39	22 59	23 17	23♋34	23♋42	23 56	24 09	24 21	24 31	24 39	24 45	24♋50
1946	03♌37	04 04	04 30	04 56	05 20	05 44	06 06	06♌28	06♌38	06 57	07 16	07 33	07 48	08 02	08 14	08♌25
1947	15♌46	16 15	16 44	17 12	17 39	18 06	18 32	18♌57	19♌09	19 32	19 55	20 16	20 36	20 55	21 12	21♌28
1948	27♌46	28 16	28 46	29 16	29♍45	00 13	00 41	01♍09	01♍22	01 48	02 14	02 38	03 02	03 24	03 46	04♍06
1949	09♍24	09 54	10 25	10 55	11 25	11 54	12 24	12♍53	13♍07	13 35	14 03	14 30	14 56	15 22	15 46	16♍10
1950	20♍48	21 18	21 48	22 18	22 48	23 17	23 47	24♍17	24♍32	25 01	25 30	25 59	26 27	26 55	27 22	27♍48
1951	02♎02	02 30	02 58	03 27	03 57	04 26	04 56	05♎25	05♎40	06 10	06 39	07 09	07 38	08 07	08 35	09♎03
1952	13♎13	13 39	14 06	14 33	15 01	15 30	15 58	16♎27	16♎42	17 11	17 40	18 09	18 39	19 08	19 37	20♎06
1953	24♎11	24 35	24 59	26 24	25 50	26 16	26 43	27♎11	27♎25	27 53	28 21	28 50	29 19	29♏48	00 17	00♏46
1954	05♏06	05 26	05 48	06 10	06 33	06 57	07 22	07♏47	08♏00	08 27	08 54	09 21	09 49	10 17	10 46	11♏14
1955	16♏00	16 17	16 35	16 54	17 14	17 35	17 56	18♏20	18♏31	18 55	19 20	19 46	20 12	20 39	21 06	21♏34
1956	27♏00	27 13	27 27	27 42	27 59	28 17	28 36	28♏56	29♏06	29 28	29♐51	00 14	00 38	01 03	01 29	01♐55
1957	08♐00	08 09	08 19	08 30	08 43	08 57	09 12	09♐29	09♐38	09 56	10 16	10 36	10 58	11 20	11 44	12♐08
1958	19♐09	19 13	19 18	19 25	19 33	19 43	19 55	20♐07	20♐14	20 29	20 45	21 02	21 21	21 40	22 01	22♐23
1959	00♑R28	00 28	00 28	00 31	00 35	00 40	00 47	00♑55	01♑00	01 11	01 23	01 37	01 51	02 08	02 25	02♑43
1960	12♑R00	11 55	11 52	11 50	11 D49	11 51	11 53	11♑58	12♑01	12 07	12 15	12 25	12 36	12 49	13 03	13♑18
1961	23♑R48	23 39	23 31	23 25	23 20	23 16	23 15	23♑D14	23♑15	23 17	23 20	23 26	23 33	23 41	23 51	24♑02
1962	05♒R56	05 43	05 31	05 20	05 11	05 03	04 56	04♒51	04♒R49	04 47	04 D46	04 46	04 48	04 52	04 58	05♒05
1963	18♒R23	18 07	17 52	17 38	17 25	17 13	17 02	16♒52	16♒R48	16 41	16 35	16 31	16 28	16 D27	16 27	16♒30
1964	01♓R07	00 50	00 32	00 15	29♒59	29 44	29 30	29♒17	29♒R10	28 59	28 49	28 40	28 33	28 28	28 24	28♒21
1965	14♓R15	13 57	13 39	13 20	13 02	12 45	12 28	12♓11	12♓R03	11 48	11 34	11 21	11 09	10 59	10 50	10♓43
1966	27♓R40	27 23	27 05	26 47	26 28	26 10	25 51	25♓33	25♓R24	25 06	24 49	24 33	24 17	24 03	23 49	23♓37
1967	11♈R18	11 04	10 48	10 32	10 14	09 56	09 38	09♈19	09♈R10	08 51	08 32	08 14	07 56	07 38	07 21	07♈06
1968	25♈R01	24 51	24 39	24 25	24 11	23 55	23 39	23♈21	23♈R13	22 54	22 36	22 17	21 57	21 38	21 20	21♈01
1969	08♉R51	08 45	08 39	08 30	08 20	08 08	07 56	07♉41	07♉R34	07 18	07 01	06 44	06 25	06 07	05 48	05♉28
1970	22♉37	22 R37	22 36	22 34	22 29	22 23	22 15	22♉06	22♉R01	21 49	21 36	21 22	21 06	20 50	20 32	20♉14
1971	06♊14	06 21	06 26	06 30	06 R31	06 32	06 30	06♊26	06♊R24	06 18	06 10	06 01	05 50	05 38	05 24	05♊09
1972	19♊42	19 55	20 05	20 15	20 22	20 28	20 33	20♊35	20♊R36	20 36	20 34	20 30	20 25	20 17	20 09	19♊58
1973	02♋52	03 10	03 27	03 42	03 56	04 08	04 18	04♋27	04♋31	04 37	04 42	04 44	04 R45	04 44	04 42	04♋37
1974	15♋46	16 08	16 29	16 49	17 08	17 26	17 42	17♋56	18♋03	18 16	18 26	18 35	18 43	18 48	18 52	18♋54
1975	28♋21	28 47	29 12	29 36	29♌59	00 21	00 42	00♌57	01♌11	01 28	01 45	01 59	02 13	02 24	02 34	02♌43
1976	10♌45	11 14	11 41	12 08	12 34	13 00	13 24	13♌47	13♌59	14 20	14 41	15 00	15 18	15 35	15 50	16♌04
1977	22♌47	23 16	23 46	24 15	24 43	25 11	25 38	26♌05	26♌17	26 43	27 07	27 30	27 52	28 13	28 33	28♌51
1978	11♍25	11 46	12 05	12 23	12 39	12 54	13 08	13♍20	13♍25	13 35	13 42	13 48	13 53	13 56	13 56	13♍55
1979	16♍03	16 33	17 03	17 33	18 04	18 34	19 03	19♍33	19♍47	20 16	20 45	21 13	21 41	22 08	22 34	22♍59
1980	27♍30	27 59	28 28	28 57	29 27	29♎57	00 26	00♎56	01♎11	01 41	02 10	02 39	03 08	03 36	04 04	04♎31
1981	08♎39	09 06	09 33	10 01	10 30	10 59	11 28	11♎57	12♎12	12 41	13 11	13 40	14 10	14 39	15 08	15♎36
1982	19♎40	20 05	20 30	20 57	21 23	21 50	22 18	22♎46	23♎01	23 29	23 58	24 27	24 56	25 26	25 55	26♎23
1983	00♏38	00 59	01 22	01 46	02 10	02 35	03 01	03♏27	03♏40	04 08	04 35	05 03	05 32	06 00	06 29	06♏58
1984	11♏38	11 56	12 16	12 37	12 58	13 21	13 44	14♏08	14♏21	14 46	15 12	15 38	16 06	16 33	17 01	17♏29
1985	22♏34	22 48	23 04	23 21	23 40	23 59	24 19	24♏40	24♏51	25 14	25 38	26 02	26 28	26 53	27 20	27♏47
1986	03♐34	03 44	03 55	04 08	04 23	04 38	04 55	05♐13	05♐23	05 43	06 03	06 25	06 48	07 11	07 36	08♐01
1987	14♐40	14 46	14 53	15 01	15 12	15 23	15 36	15♐50	15♐58	16 14	16 32	16 50	17 10	17 31	17 53	18♐16
1988	25♐56	26 47	26 00	26 05	26 11	26 18	26 28	26♐38	26♐44	26 57	27 11	27 26	27 43	28 01	28 20	28♐40
1989	07♑R23	07 20	07 D18	07 18	07 20	07 23	07 27	07♑33	07♑37	07 45	07 55	08 07	08 20	08 34	08 49	09♑06
1990	19♑R06	18 58	18 52	18 47	18 44	18 43	18 D42	18♑44	18♑45	18 49	18 55	19 02	19 10	19 20	19 32	19♑45
1991	01♒R07	00 55	00 45	00 36	00 28	00 22	00 17	00♒14	00♒R12	00 D12	00 12	00 15	00 19	00 24	00 31	00♒40
1992	13♒R23	13 09	12 55	12 42	12 30	12 20	12 11	12♒04	12♒R01	11 55	11 52	11 D50	11 49	11 50	11 53	11♒58
1993	26♒R04	25 46	25 30	25 14	24 59	24 45	24 32	24♒20	24♒R15	24 05	23 57	23 50	23 44	23 41	23 D39	23♒38
1994	09♓R04	08 46	08 27	08 09	07 52	07 35	07 19	07♓04	06♓R56	06 43	06 30	06 19	06 09	06 00	05 53	05♓48
1995	22♓R22	22 05	21 46	21 28	21 09	20 51	20 33	20♓16	20♓R06	19 50	19 33	19 18	19 04	18 51	18 39	18♓29
1996	05♈R52	05 36	05 19	05 02	04 43	04 25	04 06	03♈48	03♈R38	03 20	03 02	02 44	02 27	02 11	01 55	01♈41
1997	19♈R36	19 23	19 10	18 55	18 39	18 22	18 05	17♈47	17♈R38	17 19	17 00	16 41	16 22	16 04	15 46	15♈28
1998	03♉R24	03 16	03 07	02 57	02 45	02 32	02 17	02♉02	01♉R54	01 37	01 19	01 01	00 42	00 23	00♈04	29♈45
1999	17♉R11	17 09	17 06	17 01	16 54	16 46	16 36	16♉24	16♉R18	16 05	15 50	15 35	15 18	15 00	14 42	14♉23
2000	00♊52	00 56	00 58	00 R59	00 58	00 55	00 50	00♊44	00♊R40	00 32	00 21	00 10	29 57	29 42	29 27	29♊10

Saturn

Year	November 1st	5th	9th	13th	17th	21st	25th	29th	December 1st	5th	9th	13th	17th	21st	25th	29th
1900	01♑08	01 29	01 51	02 14	02 38	03 03	03 28	03♑54	04♑07	04 34	05 01	05 28	05 56	06 24	06 53	07♑21
1901	11♑34	11 52	12 11	12 31	12 53	13 15	13 38	14♑02	14♑14	14 39	15 05	15 31	15 58	16 25	16 53	17♑21
1902	22♑13	22 27	22 43	23 00	23 18	23 37	23 58	24♑19	24♑30	24 53	25 17	25 41	26 07	26 33	26 59	27♑26
1903	03♒09	03 20	03 31	03 44	03 59	04 15	04 32	04♒50	05♒00	05 20	05 41	06 03	06 26	06 50	07 15	07♒41
1904	14♒29	14 36	14 43	14 52	15 02	15 15	15 28	15♒43	15♒51	16 08	16 27	16 46	17 07	17 29	17 51	18♒15
1905	26♒12	26 13	26 16	26 20	26 26	26 34	26 43	26♒54	27♒00	27 13	27 28	27 44	28 01	28 20	28 39	29♒00
1906	08♓R25	08 21	08 D19	08 18	08 19	08 22	08 26	08♓32	08♓36	08 44	08 55	09 06	09 19	09 34	09 50	10♓07
1907	21♓R11	21 02	20 55	20 49	20 45	20 42	20 D41	20♓42	20♓43	20 46	20 51	20 58	21 07	21 17	21 28	21♓41
1908	04♈R28	04 15	04 03	03 52	03 43	03 36	03 30	03♈26	03♈R24	03 D22	03 22	03 24	03 28	03 33	03 40	03♈49
1909	18♈R21	18 04	17 48	17 33	17 20	17 07	16 56	16♈46	16♈R42	16 35	16 29	16 25	16 D23	16 23	16 24	16♈27
1910	02♉R44	02 25	02 06	01 48	01 31	01 14	00 58	00♉44	00♉R37	00 25	00 14	00♈04	29 56	29 50	29 45	29♈43
1911	17♉R29	17 10	16 50	16 31	16 11	15 52	15 34	15♉16	15♉R07	14 50	14 35	14 20	14 07	13 55	13 45	13♉36
1912	02♊R21	02 04	01 46	01 27	01 07	00 48	00 28	00♊09	29♉R58	29 40	29 21	29 03	28 46	28 30	28 15	28♉02
1913	17♊R19	17 05	16 50	16 34	16 17	16 00	15 41	15♊22	15♊R12	14 52	14 32	14 13	13 53	13 34	13 16	12♊58
1914	02♋R05	01 57	01 47	01 36	01 23	01 09	00 54	00♋37	00♋R28	00♊11	29 52	29 33	29 13	28 53	28 33	28♊14
1915	16♋R30	16 28	16 25	16 19	16 12	16 03	15 53	15♋41	15♋R35	15 21	15 05	14 49	14 31	14 13	13 54	13♋35
1916	00♌29	00 33	00 R36	00 36	00 35	00 32	00 27	00♌20	00♌R17	00 07	29♋57	29 45	29 31	29 16	29 00	28♋43
1917	13♌57	14 07	14 16	14 23	14 28	14 31	14 R32	14♌32	14♌R31	14 28	14 23	14 17	14 09	13 59	13 47	13♌34
1918	26♌53	27 09	27 23	27 35	27 46	27 55	28 03	28♌08	28♌11	28 14	28 R15	28 15	28 12	28 08	28 02	27♌55
1919	09♍18	09 38	09 56	10 14	10 29	10 44	10 57	11♍08	11♍13	11 22	11 29	11 35	11 39	11 R41	11 41	11♍39
1920	21♍19	21 42	22 04	22 26	22 45	23 04	23 21	23♍37	23♍44	23 58	24 10	24 21	24 29	24 37	24 42	24♍46
1921	02♎50	03 16	03 41	04 05	04 28	04 50	05 11	05♎31	05♎41	05 59	06 15	06 31	06 44	06 57	07 07	07♎16
1922	13♎58	14 26	14 53	15 19	15 45	16 10	16 34	16♎57	17♎08	17 30	17 50	18 10	18 28	18 44	19 00	19♎13
1923	24♎49	25 17	25 46	26 14	26 41	27 08	27 34	28♎00	28♎12	28 36	29 00	29 22	29 44	00♏04	00 23	00♏41
1924	05♏32	06 01	06 30	06 58	07 27	07 55	08 22	08♏49	09♏03	09 29	09 54	10 19	10 43	11 06	11 28	11♏49
1925	15♏57	16 25	16 54	17 23	17 51	18 20	18 48	19♏17	19♏31	19 58	20 25	20 52	21 18	21 43	22 08	22♏31
1926	26♏14	26 41	27 10	27 38	28 06	28 35	29 04	29♏32	29♏46	00♐15	00 43	01 10	01 38	02 05	02 31	02♐57
1927	06♐27	06 53	07 20	07 47	08 15	08 43	09 11	09♐39	09♐54	10 22	10 51	11 19	11 47	12 15	12 43	13♐10
1928	16♐45	17 10	17 35	18 01	18 27	18 54	19 22	19♐50	20♐04	20 32	21 00	21 28	21 57	22 25	22 53	23♐21
1929	27♐00	27 23	27 46	28 10	28 34	29 00	29 26	29♐52	00♑05	00 33	01 00	01 28	01 56	02 25	02 53	03♑22
1930	07♑23	07 42	08 03	08 24	08 46	09 09	09 33	09♑58	10♑11	10 37	11 03	11 30	11 57	12 25	12 53	13♑21
1931	17♑57	18 13	18 30	18 48	19 07	19 28	19 49	20♑12	20♑24	20 47	21 12	21 37	22 03	22 30	22 57	23♑24
1932	20♑43	20 34	20 25	20 17	20 09	20♒02	19 55	19♒49	00♒53	01 15	01 37	02 01	02 25	02 50	03 16	03♒42
1933	09♒58	10 06	10 15	10 26	10 39	10 52	11 08	11♒24	11♒33	11 51	12 11	12 32	12 53	13 16	13 40	17♒04
1934	21♒31	21 34	21 39	21 45	21 53	22 03	22 14	22♒26	22♒33	22 48	23 04	23 21	23 40	24 00	24 21	24♒43
1935	03♓R33	03 D31	03 31	03 32	03 35	03 39	03 46	03♓54	03♓58	04 09	04 21	04 34	04 49	05 05	05 22	05♓41
1936	16♓R05	15 58	15 53	15 49	15 D47	15 47	15 49	15♓52	15♓54	16 00	16 08	16 17	16 27	16 40	16 54	17♓09
1937	29♓R11	28 59	28 49	28 40	28 33	28 28	28 24	28♓22	28♓D21	28 22	28 24	28 28	28 33	28 41	28 50	29♓00
1938	12♈R51	12 35	12 20	21 07	11 55	11 44	11 35	11♈27	11♈R24	11 19	11 16	11 D14	11 14	11 16	11 19	11♈25
1939	27♈R01	26 43	26 25	26 08	25 52	25 37	25 23	25♈10	25♈R04	24 54	24 45	24 37	24 32	24 28	24 D25	24♈25
1940	11♉R32	11 13	10 53	10 34	10 16	09 58	09 40	09♉24	09♉R16	09 01	08 47	08 35	08 24	08 15	08 07	08♉01
1941	26♉R24	26 05	25 57	25 27	25 08	24 48	24 29	24♉10	24♉R00	23 42	23 25	23 08	22 52	22 38	22 25	22♉13
1942	11♊R21	11 05	10 49	10 32	10 14	09 55	09 36	09♊16	09♊R06	08 47	08 27	08 08	07 49	07 31	07 14	06♊58
1943	26♊R11	26 01	25 49	25 35	25 21	25 05	24 48	24♊30	24♊R21	24 02	23 43	23 23	23 04	22 44	22 24	22♊05
1944	10♋R43	10 38	10 32	10 24	10 14	10 02	09 49	09♋35	09♋R28	09 12	08 55	08 37	08 18	07 59	07 39	07♋19
1945	24♋52	24 R54	24 54	24 52	24 48	24 42	24 35	24♋26	24♋R21	24 10	23 57	23 43	23 27	23 11	22 53	22♋35
1946	08♌32	08 40	08 46	08 50	08 53	08 R53	08 52	08♌49	08♌R47	08 42	08 35	08 26	08 15	08 03	07 50	07♌35
1947	21♌39	21 53	22 05	22 15	22 24	22 31	22 36	22♌39	22♌40	22 R41	22 40	22 36	22 32	22 25	22 17	22♌07
1948	04♍20	04 38	04 55	05 10	05 23	05 35	05 46	05♍55	05♍58	06 04	06 09	06 11	06 R12	06 12	06 09	06♍04
1949	16♍27	16 49	17 10	17 29	17 48	18 04	18 20	18♍34	18♍40	13 52	19 02	19 10	19 17	19 22	19 25	19♍R26
1950	28♍07	28 32	28 56	29 19	29 41	00♎02	00 21	00♎40	00♎48	01 05	01 20	01 33	01 45	01 55	02 04	02♎11
1951	09♎24	09 51	10 17	10 43	11 07	11 31	11 54	12♎16	12♎27	12 47	13 06	13 24	13 40	13 55	14 09	14♎21
1952	20♎27	20 56	21 23	21 51	22 17	22 43	23 09	23♎33	23♎45	24 08	24 30	24 51	25 11	25 29	25 47	26♎03
1953	01♏08	01 37	02 05	02 34	03 02	03 29	03 56	04♏23	04♏36	05 01	05 26	05 50	06 12	06 34	06 55	07♏15
1954	11♏36	12 05	12 33	13 02	13 31	13 59	14 27	14♏55	15♏09	15 36	16 02	16 28	16 54	17 18	17 42	18♏04
1955	21♏55	22 23	22 51	23 20	23 49	24 17	24 46	25♏14	25♏28	25 56	26 24	26 51	27 18	27 45	28 10	28♏35
1956	02♐15	02 42	03 10	03 37	04 06	04 34	05 02	05♐31	05♐45	06 13	06 42	07 10	07 38	08 05	08 32	08♐59
1957	12♐26	12 52	13 18	13 44	14 11	14 39	15 07	15♐35	15♐49	16 17	16 45	17 14	17 42	18 10	18 38	19♐06
1958	22♐39	23 03	23 27	23 51	24 17	24 43	25 10	25♐37	25♐50	26 18	26 46	27 14	27 42	28 11	28 39	29♐07
1959	02♑58	03 19	03 40	04 03	04 26	04 50	05 15	05♑40	05♑53	06 20	06 47	07 14	07 42	08 10	08 38	09♑06
1960	13♑31	13 48	14 07	14 27	14 48	15 10	15 33	15♑56	16♑08	16 33	16 59	17 25	17 52	18 19	18 46	19♑14
1961	24♑12	24 26	24 41	24 57	25 15	25 34	25 54	26♑15	26♑26	26 49	27 12	27 37	28 02	28 27	28 54	29♑21
1962	05♒11	05 21	05 32	05 44	05 58	06 14	06 31	06♒48	06♒58	07 18	07 39	08 01	08 23	08 47	09 12	09♒37
1963	16♒32	16 37	16 44	16 52	17 02	17 14	17 26	17♒41	17♒48	18 05	18 22	18 41	19 01	19 22	19 44	20♒07
1964	28♒21	28 D21	28 23	28 27	28 33	28 40	28 49	28♒59	29♒05	29 17	29 31	29 47	00♓04	00 22	00 41	01♓02
1965	10♓R38	10 34	10 31	10 D29	10 30	10 32	10 35	10♓41	10♓44	10 52	11 02	11 13	11 26	11 40	11 55	12♓12
1966	23♓R29	23 19	23 11	23 05	23 00	22 57	22 D55	22♓55	22♓56	22 59	23 03	23 09	23 17	23 26	23 38	23♓50
1967	06♈R54	06 40	06 27	06 16	06 06	05 57	05 50	05♈45	05♈R43	05 40	05 D39	05 40	05 42	05 46	05 52	06♈00
1968	20♈R48	20 31	20 14	19 59	19 44	19 31	19 19	19♈09	19♈R05	18 57	18 50	18 46	18 43	81 D42	18 42	81♈45
1969	05♉R14	04 55	04 36	04 17	03 59	03 42	03 26	03♉12	03♉R04	02 51	02 40	02 30	02 21	02 14	02 09	02♉50
1970	20♉R00	19 41	19 22	19 02	18 43	18 24	18 05	17♉46	17♉R38	17 20	17 04	16 49	16 36	16 23	16 12	16♉03
1971	04♊R57	04 40	04 23	04 04	03 45	03 36	03 06	02♊46	02♊R37	02 17	01 58	01 40	01 22	01 05	00 50	00♊36
1972	19♊R49	19 37	19 22	19 07	18 50	18 33	18 14	17♊55	17♊R45	17 26	17 06	16 46	16 27	16 07	15 49	15♊31
1973	04♋R33	04 26	04 16	04 06	03 54	03 40	03 25	03♋09	03♋R01	02 43	02 25	02 06	01 46	01 27	01 07	00♋47
1974	18♋R54	18 53	18 51	18 46	18 39	18 31	18 22	18♋10	18♋R04	17 51	17 36	17 20	17 03	16 45	16 26	16♋07
1975	02♌48	02 53	02 57	02 R58	02 58	02 56	02 53	02♌47	02♌R44	02 36	02 26	02 15	02 02	01 48	01 33	01♌21
1976	16♌13	16 24	16 33	16 40	16 46	16 50	16 R52	16♌53	16♌R52	16 50	16 46	16 40	16 30	16 23	16 12	16♌00
1977	29♌04	29 21	29 35	29 48	00♍00	00 10	00 18	00♍24	00♍27	00 31	00 R33	00 33	00 31	00 27	00 23	00♍16
1978	04♍32	05 02	05 33	06 03	06 32	07 02	07 30	07♍59	08♍13	08 41	09 07	09 34	09 59	10 R23	10 47	11♍09
1979	23♍18	23 41	24 04	24 26	24 46	25 06	26 24	25♍40	25♍48	26 03	26 16	26 27	26 37	26 46	26 52	26♍57
1980	04♎51	05 17	05 43	06 07	06 31	06 53	07 15	07♎35	07♎45	08 03	08 20	08 36	08 50	09 03	09 14	09♎22
1981	15♎57	16 25	16 52	17 19	17 45	18 10	18 34	18♎58	19♎09	19 31	19 51	20 11	20 29	20 47	21 03	21♎17
1982	26♎45	27 14	27 43	28 11	28 38	29 05	29 32	29♏57	00♏10	00 34	00 58	01 21	01 43	02 03	02 23	02♏41
1983	07♏20	07 49	08 17	08 46	09 15	09 43	10 11	10♏38	10♏51	11 18	11 44	12 09	12 33	12 57	13 19	13♏41
1984	17♏51	18 19	18 48	19 17	19 45	20 14	20 42	21♏11	21♏24	21 52	22 19	22 46	23 12	23 38	24 03	24♏26
1985	28♏07	28 35	29 03	29 31	29♐59	00 28	00 56	01♐25	01♐39	02 08	02 36	03 04	03 31	03 58	04 25	04♐51
1986	08♐20	08 46	09 13	09 40	10 08	10 36	11 04	11♐32	11♐46	12 15	12 45	13 12	13 40	14 08	14 35	15♐03
1987	18♐33	18 57	19 22	19 48	20 14	20 41	21 08	21♐35	21♐49	22 17	22 45	23 14	23 42	24 11	24 39	25♐07
1988	28♐55	29 17	29 40	00♑04	00 28	00 53	01 19	01♑45	01♑59	02 26	02 53	03 21	03 49	04 18	04 46	05♑14
1989	09♑19	09 38	09 58	10 19	10 41	11 04	11 28	11♑53	12♑05	12 31	12 57	13 24	13 51	14 19	14 46	15♑15
1990	19♑55	20 11	20 27	20 45	21 05	21 24	21 46	22♑08	22♑19	22 43	23 07	23 32	23 58	24 25	24 52	25♑19
1991	00♒48	00 59	01 12	01 26	01 42	01 59	02 16	02♒31	02♒46	03 07	03 29	03 52	04 15	04 40	05 05	05♒31
1992	12♒02	12 09	12 18	12 29	12 40	12 54	13 08	13♒25	13♒33	13 51	14 10	14 31	14 52	15 15	15 38	16♒02
1993	23♒39	23 41	23 45	23 51	23 58	24 07	24 18	24♒30	24♒36	24 51	25 06	25 23	25 41	26 01	26 21	26♒43
1994	05♓R44	05 42	05 D41	05 41	05 44	05 48	05 54	06♓01	06♓05	06 15	06 26	06 39	06 54	07 09	07 26	07♓45
1995	18♓R22	18 15	18 08	18 04	18 01	18 D00	18 00	18♓03	18♓R04	18 09	18 16	18 24	18 33	18 45	18 58	19♓12
1996	01♈R31	01 19	01 08	00 59	00 51	00 45	00 40	00♈38	00♈R37	00 D37	00 38	00 41	00 46	00 53	01 02	01♈12
1997	15♈R16	14 59	14 44	14 31	14 18	14 07	13 57	13♈49	13♈R45	13 39	13 35	13 D33	13 33	13 33	13 36	13♈41
1998	29♈R30	29 12	28 54	28 36	28 20	28 04	27 50	27♈36	27♈R30	27 19	27 09	27 01	26 55	26 50	26 47	26♈D46
1999	14♉R09	13 50	13 30	13 11	12 52	12 33	12 16	11♉58	11♉R50	11 34	11 20	11 07	10 55	10 45	10 36	10♉29
2000	28♉R57	28 39	28 20	28 01	27 42	27 22	27 03	26♉43	26♉R34	26 15	25 58	25 41	25 24	25 10	24 56	24♉41

Uranus

	January					February					March				
	1st	7th	13th	19th	25th	1st	7th	13th	19th	25th	1st	7th	13th	19th	25th
1900	10♐08	10 28	10 46	11 04	11 20	11 37	11 49	12 00	12 10	12 17	12 21	12 26	12 R 28	12 29	12♐R 28
1901	14♐19	14 39	14 58	15 16	15 33	15 51	16 05	16 17	16 28	16 37	15 42	16 48	16 52	16 R 54	16♐R 54
1902	18♐26	18 47	19 07	19 26	19 43	20 03	20 18	20 31	20 43	20 53	20 59	21 06	21 12	21 15	21♐R 17
1903	22♐32	22 53	23 14	23 33	23 52	24 12	24 28	24 42	24 55	25 07	25 14	25 22	25 29	25 34	25♐R 37
1904	26♐36	26 57	27 18	27 38	27 57	28 18	28 35	28 51	29 05	29 18	29 27	29 37	29 44	29 50	29♐55
1905	00♑41	01 R 03	01 24	01 44	02 04	02 25	02 43	02 59	03 14	03 28	00 36	03 47	03 56	04 03	04♑09
1906	04♑41	05 03	05 R 24	05 45	06 05	06 27	06 45	07 03	07 18	07 33	07 42	07 54	08 04	08 13	08♑20
1907	08♑39	09 01	09 R 22	09 43	10 04	10 27	10 46	11 04	11 20	11 36	11 45	11 59	12 10	12 20	12♑28
1908	12♑36	12 58	13 19	13 R 40	14 01	14 25	14 44	15 03	15 20	15 36	15 49	16 03	16 15	16 25	16♑35
1909	16♑35	16 57	17 18	17 39	18 00	18 24	18 44	19 03	19 21	19 38	19 48	20 03	20 17	20 29	20♑39
1910	20♑30	20 51	21 12	21 33	21 54	22 19	22 39	22 58	23 17	23 35	23 46	24 02	24 16	24 29	24♑41
1911	24♑23	24 44	25 05	25 26	25 47	26 12	26 32	26 52	27 11	27 30	27 41	27 58	28 13	28 27	28♑40
1912	28♑15	28 36	28 57	29 18	29♒39	00 04	00 24	00 44	01 04	01 23	01 38	01 56	02 12	02 26	02♒40
1913	02♒10	02 31	02 51	03 12	03 33	03 58	04 19	04 39	04 59	05 19	05 31	05 49	06 06	06 21	05♒36
1914	06♒01	06 21	06 41	07 02	07 23	07 48	08 09	08 29	08 50	09 09	09 22	09 41	09 58	10 14	10♒30
1915	09♒52	10 11	10 31	10 51	11 12	11 36	11 57	12 18	12 39	12 59	13 12	13 31	13 49	14 06	14♒22
1916	13♒41	14 00	14 19	14 39	15 00	15 24	15 45	16 06	16 26	16 47	17 03	17 23	17 41	17 59	18♒16
1917	17♒33	17 51	18 10	18 30	18 50	19 14	19 35	19 56	20 17	20 37	20 51	21 10	21 29	21 48	22♒05
1918	21♒22	21 39	21 57	22 17	22 36	23 00	23 21	23 41	24 02	24 23	24 36	24 57	25 16	25 35	25♒53
1919	25♒10	25 27	25 44	26 03	26 22	26 45	27 05	27 26	27 47	28 08	28 21	28 42	29 02	29 21	29♒39
1920	28♒58	29 14	29 31	29♓48	00 07	00 30	00 50	01 10	01 31	01 52	02 09	02 29	02 49	03 09	03♓28
1921	02♓48	03 03	03 20	03 37	03 55	04 17	04 37	04 57	05 18	05 39	05 52	06 13	06 33	06 53	07♓13
1922	06♓37	06 51	07 06	07 23	07 40	08 02	08 21	08 41	09 01	09 22	09 36	09 56	10 17	10 37	10♓57
1923	10♓25	10 38	10 53	11 08	11 25	11 46	12 05	12 24	12 44	13 05	13 19	13 39	14 00	14 20	14♓40
1924	14♓15	14 27	14 40	14 55	15 11	15 31	15 49	16 08	16 28	16 48	17 05	17 25	17 46	18 07	18♓27
1925	18♓06	18 18	18 30	18 44	19 00	19 19	19 37	19 55	20 15	20 35	20 48	21 09	21 29	21 50	22♓10
1926	21♓57	22 07	22 19	22 32	22 47	23 05	23 22	23 40	23 59	24 18	24 32	24 52	25 12	25 33	25♓53
1927	25♓49	25 58	26 09	26 21	26 34	26 52	27 08	27 25	27 44	28 03	28 16	28 36	28 56	29 17	29♓37
1928	29♓42	29 50	29♈59	00 10	00 23	00 39	00 55	01 12	01 29	01 48	02 04	02 23	02 43	03 04	03♈24
1929	03♈38	03 44	03 53	04 03	04 15	04 30	04 45	05 01	05 18	05 36	05 49	06 08	06 28	06 48	07♈09
1930	07♈33	07 38	07 46	07 55	08 05	08 20	08 34	08 49	09 05	09 23	09 35	09 54	10 13	10 33	10♈53
1931	11♈29	11 34	11 40	11 48	11 57	12 10	12 23	12 37	12 53	13 10	13 21	13 40	13 59	14 18	14♈38
1932	15♈27	15 30	15 35	15 42	15 50	16 02	16 14	16 27	16 42	16 58	17 12	17 30	17 48	18 08	18♈28
1933	19♈27	19 29	19 33	19 38	19 46	19 57	20 08	20 20	20 34	20 49	21 00	21 18	21 36	21 54	22♈14
1934	23 RD 28	23 28	23 31	23 35	23 41	23 51	24 01	24 12	24 25	24 40	24 50	25 07	25 24	25 42	26♈01
1935	27♈R 31	27 D 30	27 31	27 34	27 39	27 50	27 56	28 06	28 18	28 32	28 41	28 57	29 14	29 31	29♈50
1936	01♉R 35	01 D 33	01 33	01 35	01 38	01 45	01 52	02 02	02 13	02 25	02 36	02 51	03 08	03 35	03♉43
1937	05♉R 42	05 38	05 D 37	05 38	05 40	05 46	05 52	06 01	06 11	06 22	06 31	06 45	07 00	07 17	07♉35
1938	09♉R 51	09 46	09 D 44	09 43	09 44	09 48	09 53	10 00	10 09	10 20	10 28	10 41	10 55	11 11	11♉28
1939	14♉R 02	13 56	13 52	13 D 50	13 50	13 52	13 56	14 02	14 10	14 19	14 26	14 38	14 52	15 07	15♉23
1940	18♉R 16	18 09	18 04	18 00	17 D 59	17 59	18 02	18 07	18 13	18 21	18 29	18 40	18 53	19 07	19♉23
1941	22♉R 31	22 23	22 17	22 12	22 D 10	22 09	22 11	22 14	22 19	22 27	22 32	22 42	22 54	23 07	23♉22
1942	26♉R 50	26 41	26 33	26 27	26 23	26 RD 21	26 21	26 23	26 27	26 33	26 38	26 47	26 57	27 09	27♉23
1943	01♊R 11	01 01	00 52	00 45	00 40	00 36	00 D 34	00 35	00 38	00 42	00 46	00 54	01 03	01 14	01♊26
1944	05♊R 34	05 23	05 13	05 05	04 58	04 53	04 D 50	04 50	04 51	04 54	04 58	05 04	05 12	05 22	05♊34
1945	09♊R 58	09 46	09 35	09 26	09 19	09 12	09 08	09 D 06	09 06	09 08	09 11	09 16	09 23	09 32	09♊42
1946	14♊R 26	14 13	14 02	13 51	13 43	13 34	13 29	13 26	13 D 25	13 25	13 27	13 30	13 36	13 43	13♊53
1947	18♊R 57	18 43	18 31	18 19	18 09	18 00	17 53	17 48	17 46	17 D 45	17 45	17 47	17 52	17 58	18♊06
1948	23♊R 30	23 16	23 02	22 50	22 39	22 28	22 20	22 14	22 10	22 07	22 D 07	22 08	22 11	22 16	22♊23
1949	28♊R 03	27 48	27 34	27 21	27 09	26 57	26 48	26 41	26 36	26 32	26 R 31	26 D 31	26 32	26 36	26♊41
1950	02♋R 41	02 26	02 12	01 57	01 44	01 31	01 21	01 12	01 06	01 01	00 58	00 D 57	00 57	00 59	01♋02
1951	07♋R 21	07 06	06 51	06 36	06 22	06 08	05 57	05 47	05 39	05 32	05 29	05 26	05 D 24	05 25	05♋27
1952	12♋R 03	11 48	11 32	11 17	11 03	10 47	10 35	10 24	10 15	10 07	10 02	09 57	09 D 55	09 54	09♋55
1953	16♋R 45	16 30	16 14	15 59	15 44	15 28	15 15	15 03	14 53	14 44	14 39	14 33	14 29	14 D 26	14♋26
1954	21♋R 32	21 16	21 01	20 45	20 30	20 13	19 59	19 46	19 35	19 25	19 19	19 11	19 06	19 02	19♋00
1955	26♋R 20	26 05	25 49	25 34	25 18	25 00	24 46	24 32	24 20	24 08	24 02	23 53	23 46	23 41	23♋37
1956	01♌R 09	00 55	00 39	00 24	00 08	29 50	29 35	29 21	29 07	28 55	28 46	28 36	28 28	28 21	28♋R 17
1957	05♌R 57	05 43	05 28	05 13	04 57	04 39	04 24	04 09	03 55	03 41	03 33	03 22	03 13	03 05	02♌R 59
1958	10♌R 49	10 35	10 21	10 06	09 50	09 32	09 16	09 01	08 46	08 32	08 24	08 12	08 01	07 52	07♌R 44
1959	15♌R 40	15 28	15 14	15 00	14 45	14 27	14 11	13 55	13 40	13 25	13 16	13 03	12 51	12 41	12♌R 32
1960	20♌R 32	20 21	20 08	19 54	19 40	19 22	19 06	18 50	18 35	18 20	18 07	17 54	17 41	17 30	17♌R 20
1961	25♌R 23	25 12	25 00	24 47	24 33	24 16	24 00	23 44	23 29	23 13	23 03	22 49	22 35	22 22	22♌R 11
1962	00♍R 15	00 ♌ 05	29 55	29 43	29 29	29 13	28 57	28 42	28 26	28 10	28 00	27 45	27 31	27 17	27♌R 05
1963	05♍R 06	04 58	04 49	04 38	04 26	04 10	03 55	03 40	03 25	03 09	02 58	02 43	02 28	02 14	01♍R 58
1964	09♍R 57	09 51	09 43	09 33	09 22	09 07	08 54	08 39	08 24	08 08	07 55	07 39	07 24	07 09	06♍R 55
1965	14♍R 47	14 42	14 35	14 27	14 17	14 03	13 50	13 36	13 21	13 06	12 55	12 39	12 24	12 08	11♍R 54
1966	19♍R 37	19 34	19 28	19 21	19 12	19 00	18 48	18 35	18 21	18 06	17 55	17 40	17 24	17 09	16♍R 53
1967	24♍R 25	24 24	24 20	24 15	24 07	23 57	23 46	23 34	23 20	23 06	22 56	22 41	22 25	22 09	21♍R 54
1968	29♍R 13	29 13	29 11	29 07	29 01	28 52	28 43	28 32	28 19	28 06	27 54	27 39	27 23	27 08	26♍R 52
1969	03♎59	04 R 01	04 00	03 57	03 53	03 45	03 37	03 27	03 15	03 02	02 53	02 39	02 24	02 08	01♎R 53
1970	08♎43	08 46	08 R 48	08 47	08 44	08 38	08 31	08 22	08 12	08 00	07 51	07 38	07 23	07 08	06♎R 53
1971	13♎26	13 30	13 33	13 R 34	13 33	13 29	13 23	13 16	13 07	12 56	12 48	12 36	12 22	12 07	11♎R 52
1972	18♎06	18 12	18 17	18 19	18 R 19	18 17	18 12	18 06	17 58	17 49	17 42	17 30	17 17	17 03	16♎R 48
1973	22♎45	22 52	22 58	23 02	23 R 04	23 03	23 00	22 56	22 49	22 41	22 35	22 24	22 12	21 59	21♎R 45
1974	27♎20	27 29	27 37	27 42	27 45	27 R 47	27 46	27 43	27 38	27 31	27 26	27 16	27 05	26 53	26♎R 40
1975	01♏53	02 03	02 12	02 19	02 24	02 R 28	02 29	02 27	02 24	02 19	02 14	02 06	01 56	01 45	01♏R 33
1976	06♏23	06 35	06 46	06 54	07 01	07 06	07 R 08	07 09	07 07	07 03	06 59	06 52	06 43	06 33	06♏R 21
1977	10♏53	11 06	11 18	11 27	11 35	11 42	11 46	11 R 47	11 47	11 44	11 42	11 36	11 29	11 20	11♏R 10
1978	15♏19	15 33	15 46	15 57	16 06	16 15	16 20	16 23	16 R 24	16 24	16 22	16 18	16 12	16 05	15♏R 56
1979	19♏42	19 57	20 12	20 24	20 35	20 45	20 52	20 56	20 59	21 R 00	21 00	20 57	20 53	20 47	20♏R 39
1980	24♏03	24 20	24 35	24 49	25 01	25 12	25 21	25 27	25 31	25 R 34	25 34	25 33	25 30	25 25	25♏R 18
1981	28♏25	28 42	28 58	29 13	29 26	29 39	29 48	29 56	00♐01	00 05	00 R 06	00 07	00 05	00 02	29♐R 56
1982	02♐41	03 00	03 17	03 32	03 49	04 01	04 12	04 21	04 28	04 33	04 35	04 R 37	04 37	04 35	04♐R 32
1983	06♐56	07 15	07 33	07 50	08 05	08 21	08 33	08 43	08 52	08 58	09 02	09 05	09 R 07	09 06	09♐R 04
1984	11♐08	11 28	11 47	12 04	12 21	12 38	12 51	13 03	13 13	13 21	13 26	13 30	13 R 33	13 34	13♐R 33
1985	15♐22	15 42	16 01	16 20	16 37	16 55	17 09	17 21	17 32	17 41	17 46	17 52	17 57	17 R 59	17♐R 59
1986	19♐30	19 51	20 10	20 29	20 47	21 07	21 22	21 35	21 47	21 58	22 04	22 11	22 17	22 R 21	22♐R 22
1987	23♐36	23 57	24 17	24 37	24 55	25 16	25 32	25 47	26 00	26 11	26 18	26 27	26 34	26 39	26♐R 42
1988	27♐40	28 01	28 22	28 42	29 01	29 22	29 39	29♑55	00 09	00 22	00 32	00 41	00 49	00 56	01♑00
1989	01♑45	02 07	02 28	02 48	03 08	03 30	03 47	04 04	04 19	04 32	04 40	04 51	05 01	05 08	05♑14
1990	05♑45	06 07	06 28	06 49	07 09	07 32	07 50	08 07	08 23	08 38	08 47	08 59	09 09	09 18	09♑25
1991	09♑44	10 05	10 27	10 48	11 08	11 31	11 50	12 08	12 25	12 41	12 50	13 04	13 15	13 25	13♑34
1992	13♑41	14 02	14 24	14 45	15 06	15 29	15 49	16 08	16 25	16 42	16 54	17 08	17 21	17 32	17♑41
1993	17♑40	18 02	18 23	18 44	19 05	19 29	19 49	20 08	20 26	20 43	20 54	21 09	21 22	21 35	21♑45
1994	21♑35	21 56	22 17	22 38	23 00	23 24	23 44	24 04	24 23	24 40	24 52	25 07	25 22	25 35	25♑47
1995	25♑28	25 49	26 10	26 32	26 53	27 17	27 38	27 58	28 17	28 36	28 47	29 04	29 19	29 34	29♑46
1996	29♑21	29 42	00♒02	00 24	00 45	01 09	01 30	01 50	02 10	02 29	02 44	03 02	03 18	03 33	03♒46
1997	03♒16	03 36	03 57	04 18	04 39	05 04	05 25	05 45	06 05	06 24	06 37	06 55	07 12	07 27	07♒42
1998	07♒07	07 27	07 47	08 08	08 29	08 53	09 14	09 35	09 55	10 15	10 28	10 46	11 04	11 21	11♒36
1999	10♒57	11 17	11 36	11 57	12 17	12 42	13 03	13 24	13 44	14 04	14 18	14 37	14 55	15 12	15♒28
2000	14♒47	15 06	15 25	15 45	16 05	16 29	16 50	17 11	17 32	17 52	18 09	18 28	18 47	19 05	19♒21

	April 1st	April 7th	April 13th	April 19th	April 25th	May 1st	May 7th	May 13th	May 19th	May 25th	June 1st	June 7th	June 13th	June 19th	June 25th
1900	12♐R 24	12 18	12 12	12 03	11 53	11 42	11 29	11 16	11 02	10 48	10 30	10 15	10 01	09 47	09♐R 33
1901	16♐R 52	16 48	16 42	16 35	16 26	16 16	16 04	15 52	15 39	15 24	15 08	14 53	14 38	14 23	14♐R 09
1902	21♐R 17	21 14	21 10	21 04	20 56	20 47	20 37	20 25	20 12	19 58	19 42	19 27	19 13	18 58	18♐R 44
1903	25♐R 38	25 37	25 34	25 30	25 24	25 16	25 06	24 56	24 44	24 31	24 15	24 01	23 46	23 31	23♐R 17
1904	29♐R 57	29 57	29 55	29 52	29 47	29 40	29 31	29 21	92 10	28 58	28 43	28 29	28 14	28 00	27♐R 45
1905	04♑ 13	04 R 14	04 14	04 12	04 08	04 02	03 55	03 46	03 36	03 25	03 10	02 57	02 43	02 28	02♑R 14
1906	08♑ 26	08 28	08 R 30	08 29	08 26	08 21	08 16	08 08	07 59	07 49	07 35	07 22	07 09	06 55	06♑R 40
1907	12♑ 35	12 40	12 R 42	12 43	12 42	12 39	12 34	12 27	12 19	12 10	11 58	11 46	11 33	11 19	11♑R 05
1908	16♑ 44	16 49	16 53	16 R 54	16 54	16 52	16 49	16 43	16 36	16 28	16 16	16 05	15 52	15 39	15♑R 25
1909	20♑ 49	20 56	21 00	21 04	21 R05	21 04	21 02	20 58	20 52	20 44	20 34	20 24	20 12	20 00	19♑R 46
1910	24♑ 52	25 00	25 06	25 10	25 R13	25 14	25 15	25 10	25 05	24 59	24 50	24 40	24 30	24 18	24♑R 05
1911	28♑ 53	29 02	29 09	29 15	29 19	29 R21	29 21	29 20	29 16	29 11	29 04	28 55	28 46	28 35	28♑R 23
1912	02♒ 53	03 03	03 12	03 18	03 23	03 26	03 R 27	03 27	03 25	03 21	03 14	03 07	02 58	02 48	02♒R 36
1913	06♒ 50	07 02	07 11	07 19	07 25	07 30	07 R 32	07 33	07 32	07 29	07 24	07 18	07 10	07 01	06♒R 50
1914	10♒ 46	10 58	11 09	11 18	11 25	11 31	11 35	11 R 37	11 37	11 36	11 32	11 27	11 20	11 12	11♒R 02
1915	14♒ 39	14 52	15 04	15 14	15 23	15 30	15 35	15 38	15 R 40	15 40	15 38	15 34	15 28	15 21	15♒R 13
1916	18♒ 33	18 47	19 00	19 11	19 20	19 28	19 34	19 39	19 R 41	19 42	19 41	19 38	19 33	19 27	19♒R 20
1917	22♒ 24	22 39	22 52	23 04	23 15	23 24	23 31	23 37	23 41	23 R 43	23 43	23 41	23 38	23 33	23♒R 26
1918	26♒ 12	26 28	26 43	26 56	27 07	27 17	27 26	27 33	27 38	27 R 41	27 43	27 43	27 40	27 37	27♒R 31
1919	00♒ 00	00♓ 16	00 32	00 46	00 58	01 09	01 19	01 27	01 33	01 38	01 41	01 R 42	01 41	01 39	01♓R 34
1920	03♓ 48	04 06	04 22	04 37	04 50	05 02	05 12	05 21	05 29	05 34	05 38	05 R 40	05 40	05 39	05♓R 35
1921	07♓ 34	07 52	08 09	08 24	08 38	08 51	08 05	09 13	09 21	09 28	09 34	09 37	09 R 38	09 38	09♓R 36
1922	11♓ 18	11 37	11 54	12 11	12 26	12 40	12 52	13 03	13 13	13 21	13 28	13 33	13 35	13 R 36	13♓R 35
1923	15♓ 03	15 22	15 40	15 57	16 13	16 27	16 41	16 53	17 04	17 13	17 21	17 27	17 31	17 R 33	17♓R 33
1924	18♓ 50	19 09	19 27	19 45	20 01	20 17	20 31	20 44	20 56	21 06	21 15	21 22	21 25	21 28	21♓R 31
1925	22♓ 34	22 53	23 12	23 30	23 47	24 04	24 19	24 33	24 45	24 56	25 07	25 15	25 21	25 25	25♓R 27
1926	26♓ 17	26 37	26 56	27 15	27 33	27 50	28 06	28 21	28 34	28 46	28 59	29 07	29 15	29 20	29♓ 34
1927	00♈ 01	00 21	00 41	01 00	01 19	01 36	01 53	02 09	02 23	02 36	02 50	03 00	03 08	03 15	03♈ 20
1928	03♈ 48	04 09	04 29	04 48	06 07	05 25	05 42	05 59	06 14	06 28	06 42	06 53	07 02	07 10	07♈ 16
1929	07♈ 33	07 53	08 13	08 33	08 53	09 11	09 29	09 46	10 02	10 17	10 33	10 44	10 55	11 04	11♈ 11,
1930	11♈ 17	11 38	11 58	12 18	12 38	12 57	13 16	13 36	13 50	14 06	14 23	04 36	14 47	14 57	15♈ 05
1931	15♈ 02	15 23	15 43	16 04	16 24	16 44	17 03	17 21	17 38	17 55	18 12	18 26	18 39	18 50	19♈ 00
1932	18♈ 51	19 12	19 32	19 53	20 13	20 33	20 52	21 11	21 29	21 46	22 05	22 19	22 33	22 45	22♈ 55
1933	22♈ 37	22 58	23 18	23 39	24 00	24 20	24 40	24 59	25 17	25 35	25 55	26 10	26 24	26 37	26♈ 49
1934	26♈ 25	26 45	27 05	27 26	27 47	28 07	28 27	28 47	29 06	29 24	29 45	00♉ 01	00 26	00 40	00♉ 43
1935	00♉ 13	00 33	00 53	01 14	01 34	01 55	02 15	02 35	02 55	03 14	03 35	03 52	04 08	04 23	04♉ 37
1936	04♉ 05	04 25	04 45	05 06	05 26	05 47	06 08	06 28	06 48	07 07	07 29	07 47	08 03	08 19	08♉ 34
1937	07♉ 56	08 15	08 35	08 56	09 16	09 37	09 58	10 18	10 39	10 58	11 21	11 39	11 57	12 13	12♉ 29
1938	11♉ 49	12 07	12 27	12 47	13 07	13 28	13 49	14 10	14 30	14 51	15 13	15 32	15 51	16 08	16♉ 24
1939	15♉ 43	16 01	16 20	16 40	17 00	17 21	17 42	18 02	18 23	18 44	19 07	19 27	19 46	20 04	20♉ 21
1940	19♉ 42	20 00	20 18	20 38	20 58	21 18	21 39	22 00	22 21	22 42	23 05	23 25	23 45	24 03	24♉ 21
1941	23♉ 40	23 57	24 15	24 34	24 54	25 14	25 35	25 55	26 16	26 37	27 02	27 22	27 42	28 01	28♉ 20
1942	27♉ 40	27 57	28 14	28 32	28 52	29 11	29 32	29♊ 52	00 13	00 34	00 59	01 20	01 40	02 00	02♊ 19
1943	01♊ 43	01 58	02 15	02 32	02 51	03 10	03 30	03 51	04 12	04 33	04 58	05 18	05 39	05 59	06♊ 19
1944	05♊ 49	06 04	06 20	06 37	06 56	07 15	07 34	07 55	08 15	08 26	09 01	09 22	09 43	10 04	10♊ 24
1945	09♊ 56	10 10	10 25	10 42	10 59	11 18	11 37	11 57	12 17	12 38	13 03	13 24	13 45	14 06	14♊ 27
1946	14♊ 05	14 18	14 32	14 48	15 04	15 22	15 41	16 00	16 21	16 41	17 06	17 27	17 48	18 09	18♊ 30
1947	18♊ 17	18 29	18 42	18 56	19 12	19 29	19 47	20 06	20 29	20 53	21 10	21 32	21 53	22 14	22♊ 36
1948	22♊ 33	22 43	22 56	23 09	23 24	23 41	23 58	24 17	24 36	24 56	25 20	25 41	26 03	26 24	26♊ 45
1949	26♊ 50	26 59	27 10	27 23	27 37	27 52	28 09	28 26	28 45	29 05	29 28	29♋ 49	00 10	00 32	00♋ 54
1950	01♋ 09	01 17	01 27	01 38	01 51	02 06	02 21	02 38	02 56	03 15	03 38	03 59	04 20	04 41	05♋ 03
1951	05♋ 32	05 39	05 47	05 57	06 07	06 22	06 37	06 53	07 10	07 28	07 51	08 11	08 32	08 53	09♋ 14
1952	09♋ 59	10 05	10 12	10 21	10 32	10 44	10 58	11 13	11 30	11 47	12 09	12 29	12 49	03 10	03♋ 31
1953	14♋ 28	14 32	14 38	14 46	14 55	15 06	15 19	15 33	15 48	16 05	16 26	16 45	17 05	17 25	17♋ 47
1954	19♋ 00	19 03	19 07	19 13	19 21	19 31	19 42	19 55	20 10	20 26	20 46	21 04	21 23	21 43	22♋ 04
1955	23♋D 36	23 37	23 39	23 44	23 50	23 59	24 09	24 21	24 34	24 49	25 08	25 25	25 44	26 03	26♋ 23
1956	28♋D 14	28 13	28 15	28 18	28 23	28 30	28 39	28 50	29 02	29 16	29 34	29♌ 51	00 09	00 28	00♌ 48
1957	02♌R 54	02 D 52	02 52	02 54	02 58	03 03	03 11	03 20	03 31	03 44	04 01	04 16	04 33	04 51	05♌ 10
1958	07♌R 38	07 34	07 D 32	07 32	07 35	07 39	07 45	07 52	08 02	08 13	08 29	08 43	08 59	09 16	09♌ 35
1959	12♌R 23	12 18	12 15	12 D 13	12 14	12 16	12 21	12 27	12 35	12 45	12 59	13 12	13 27	13 43	14♌ 01
1960	17♌ 10	17 04	16 59	16 57	16 56	16 57	17 00	17 05	17 12	17 21	17 33	17 46	18 00	18 15	18♌ 32
1961	22♌R 00	21 52	21 46	21 42	21 D40	21 39	21 41	21 44	21 50	21 57	22 08	22 19	22 32	22 46	23♌ 01
1962	26♌R 52	26 43	26 36	26 30	26 26	26 24	26 D 24	26 26	26 30	26 35	26 44	26 54	27 05	27 18	27♌ 32
1963	01♍R 46	01 36	01 27	01 20	01 14	01 11	01 D 09	01 09	01 11	01 15	01 23	01 31	01 41	01 52	02♍ 05
1964	06♍R 40	06 29	06 19	06 11	06 04	05 59	05 56	05 D 55	05 56	05 59	06 04	06 11	06 20	06 30	06♍ 42
1965	11♍R 38	11 25	11 14	11 05	10 56	10 50	10 45	10 43	10 D 42	10 43	10 47	10 52	10 59	11 08	11♍ 18
1966	16♍R 37	16 23	16 11	16 00	15 50	15 43	15 36	15 32	15 D 30	15 29	15 31	15 35	15 40	15 47	15♍ 57
1967	21♍R 36	21 22	21 09	20 57	20 46	20 37	20 29	20 23	20 19	20 D 17	20 17	20 19	20 23	20 29	20♍ 36
1968	26♍R 34	26 19	26 06	25 53	25 41	25 31	25 22	25 15	25 10	25 06	25 05	25 D 05	25 08	26 12	25♍ 19
1969	01♎R 35	01 19	01 05	00 51	00 39	00 27	00 17	00 09	00♍ 02	29 57	29 R 53	29 D 52	29 53	29 56	00♎ 01
1970	06♎R 35	06 19	06 04	05 50	05 36	05 24	05 13	05 03	04 55	04 48	04 43	04 40	04 D 39	04 41	04♎ 44
1971	11♎R 34	11 19	11 03	10 48	10 34	10 21	10 09	09 58	09 48	09 40	09 33	09 29	09 26	09 D 26	09♎ 27
1972	16♎R 30	16 15	15 59	15 44	15 29	15 15	15 02	14 51	14 40	14 31	14 23	14 17	14 14	14 12	14♎D 12
1973	21♎R 28	21 12	20 57	20 41	20 26	20 12	19 58	19 45	19 34	19 22	19 13	19 06	19 01	18 58	18♎D 56
1974	26♎R 23	26 08	25 53	25 38	25 22	25 07	24 53	24 39	24 27	24 15	24 04	23 55	23 49	23 44	23♎D 41
1975	01♏R 17	01 03	00 48	00 33	00 17	00 02	29♎ 47	29 33	29 22	29 07	28 54	28 44	28 36	28 30	28♎ 25
1976	06♏R 06	05 53	05 38	05 23	05 08	04 52	04 37	04 23	04 09	03 56	03 42	03 31	03 22	03 15	03♏R 09
1977	10♏R 56	10 43	10 29	10 14	09 59	09 44	09 29	09 14	08 59	08 46	08 31	08 19	08 09	08 00	07♏R 52
1978	15♏R 43	15 31	15 18	15 04	14 49	14 34	14 19	14 04	13 49	13 35	13 19	13 06	12 55	12 45	12♏R 37
1979	20♏R 28	20 17	20 04	19 51	19 37	19 22	19 07	18 52	18 37	18 23	18 06	17 53	17 41	17 30	17♏R 20
1980	25♏R 08	24 58	24 47	24 34	24 21	24 06	23 52	23 37	23 22	23 07	22 50	22 36	22 23	22 11	22♏R 01
1981	29♏R 48	29 39	29 29	29 17	29 04	28 51	28 37	28 22	28 07	27 52	27 35	27 20	27 07	26 54	26♏R 43
1982	04♐R 25	04 17	04 08	03 58	03 46	03 33	03 19	03 05	02 50	02 35	02 18	02 03	01 49	01 36	01♐R 23
1983	08♐R 59	08 52	08 45	08 35	08 24	08 12	08 00	07 46	07 31	07 17	06 59	06 44	06 30	06 16	06♐R 03
1984	13♐R 29	13 24	18 17	13 09	12 59	12 47	12 35	12 22	12 08	11 54	11 36	11 21	11 07	10 53	10♐R 37
1985	17♐R 57	17 53	17 48	17 41	17 32	17 22	17 10	16 58	16 45	16 31	16 14	15 59	15 44	15 27	15♐R 15
1986	22♐R 22	22 20	22 16	22 19	22 02	21 53	21 43	21 31	21 19	21 05	20 49	20 34	20 19	20 05	19♐R 50
1987	26♐R 44	26 43	26 40	26 36	26 29	26 22	26 12	26 02	25 50	25 37	25 21	25 07	24 52	24 38	24♐R 23
1988	01♑R 02	01 03	01 01	00 68	00 53	00 46	00 37	00 28	00 17	00 04	29 49	29 35	29 21	29 06	28♑R 52
1989	05♑ 18	05 R 20	05 20	05 18	05 14	05 08	05 01	04 52	04 42	04 31	04 17	04 03	03 49	03 35	03♑R 20
1990	09♑ 31	09 34	09 R 35	09 35	09 32	09 28	09 22	09 15	09 06	08 56	08 42	08 29	08 16	08 02	07♑R 47
1991	13♑ 41	13 46	13 48	13 R 49	13 48	13 45	13 40	13 34	13 26	13 17	13 05	12 53	12 40	12 26	12♑R 12
1992	17♑ 50	17 55	17 59	18 R 01	18 01	17 59	17 55	17 50	17 43	17 35	17 23	17 12	17 00	16 47	16♑R 33
1993	21♑ 55	22 02	22 07	22 10	22 R 11	22 11	22 09	22 05	21 59	21 52	21 41	21 31	21 20	21 07	20♑R 54
1994	25♑ 58	26 06	26 13	26 17	26 R 20	26 21	26 20	26 17	26 13	26 06	25 57	25 48	25 38	25 26	25♑R 13
1995	29♑ 59	00♒ 08	00 16	00 22	00 26	00 R 28	00 28	00 27	00 24	00 19	00 11	00♑ 03	29 54	29 43	29♑ 31
1996	04♒ 00	04 10	04 18	04 25	04 30	04 34	04 R 35	04 35	04 32	04 29	04 22	04 15	04 06	03 56	03♒R 45
1997	07♒ 57	08 08	08 18	08 26	08 32	04 34	04 35	04 R 35	04 32	04 29	08 32	08 26	08 18	08 09	07♒R 59
1998	11♒ 52	12 04	12 15	12 24	12 32	08 37	08 39	08 R 40	08 40	08 47	12 40	12 35	12 28	12 20	12♒R 10
1999	15♒ 45	15 59	16 11	16 21	16 30	12 38	12 42	12 44	12 R 45	12 43	16 46	16 41	16 36	16 29	16♒R 21
2000	19♒ 39	19 54	20 06	20 17	20 27	20 35	20 41	20 46	20 48	20 R 49	20 48	20 46	20 41	20 35	20♒R 27

Uranus

Year	July 1st	July 7th	July 13th	July 19th	July 25th	August 1st	August 7th	August 13th	August 19th	August 25th	September 1st	September 7th	September 13th	September 19th	September 25th
1900	09♐R20	09 09	08 59	08 49	08 41	08 34	08 30	08 D28	08 27	08 29	08 32	08 38	08 45	08 54	09♐04
1901	13♐R56	13 43	13 32	13 22	13 13	13 04	12 59	12 55	12 D53	12 53	12 55	12 59	13 04	13 12	13♐21
1902	18♐R30	18 17	18 05	17 53	17 43	17 34	17 27	17 22	17 18	17 16	17 D17	17 19	17 23	17 29	17♐37
1903	23♐R36	03 49	04 02	04 15	04 28	22 02	21 54	21 47	21 42	21 39	21 D38	21 39	21 41	21 46	21♐52
1904	27♐R31	27 17	27 03	26 50	26 39	26 27	26 18	26 10	26 04	26 00	25 58	25 D57	25 59	26 02	26♐08
1905	01♑R59	01 45	01 31	01 18	01 05	00 52	00 42	00 33	00 26	00 21	00 17	00 D15	00 15	00 17	00♑21
1906	06♑R26	06 11	05 57	05 43	05 30	05 16	05 05	04 55	04 47	04 40	04 35	04 32	04 D30	04 31	04♑33
1907	10♑R51	10 36	10 21	10 07	09 54	09 39	09 27	09 16	09 07	08 59	08 52	03 48	08 45	08 D44	08♑45
1908	15♑R21	14 57	14 42	14 28	14 14	13 58	13 46	13 35	13 25	13 16	13 08	13 02	12 58	12 D56	12♑56
1909	19♑R32	19 18	19 04	18 49	18 35	18 19	18 06	17 54	17 43	17 33	17 23	17 17	17 12	17 08	17♑D07
1910	23♑R52	23 38	23 24	23 09	22 55	22 38	22 25	22 12	22 00	21 50	21 39	21 31	21 25	21 20	21♑R17
1911	28♑R10	27 56	27 42	27 28	27 13	26 57	26 43	26 30	26 17	26 06	25 54	25 45	25 37	25 31	25♑R27
1912	02♒R24	02 11	01 57	01 43	01 28	01 12	00 58	00 44	00 31	00 19	00 06	29♑57	29 48	29 41	29♑36
1913	06♒R39	06 26	06 13	05 59	05 45	05 28	05 14	04 59	04 46	04 33	04 20	04 09	04 00	03 52	03♒R46
1914	10♒R51	10 40	10 27	10 14	10 00	09 43	09 29	09 14	09 00	08 47	08 33	08 21	08 11	08 02	07♒R55
1915	15♒R03	14 52	14 40	14 27	14 13	13 57	13 42	13 28	13 14	13 00	12 50	12 33	12 22	12 12	12♒R03
1916	02♒R58	03 07	03 15	03 24	03 32	03 41	03 48	03 55	04 01	04 07	16 54	16 42	16 30	16 19	16♒R10
1917	23♒R18	23 09	22 58	22 46	22 34	22 18	22 04	21 50	21 35	21 21	21 05	20 52	20 39	20 28	20♒R18
1918	27♒R24	27 16	27 06	26 55	26 43	26 28	26 14	26 00	25 46	25 31	25 15	25 01	24 48	24 36	24♒R25
1919	01♓R28	01 21	01 12	01 02	00 51	00 36	00 23	00 09	29♒55	29 41	29 24	29 10	28 56	28 44	28♒32
1920	05♓R30	05 24	05 16	05 06	04 55	04 42	04 29	04 15	04 01	03 47	03 30	03 16	03 02	02 49	02♓R37
1921	09♓R32	09 26	09 19	09 11	09 01	08 48	08 36	08 23	08 09	07 55	05 48	05 45	05 43	05 43	05♓R45
1922	13♓R32	13 28	13 22	13 15	13 06	12 54	12 42	12 30	12 17	12 03	11 46	11 32	11 18	11 04	10♓R50
1923	17♓R32	17 29	17 24	17 18	17 10	16 59	16 48	16 37	16 24	16 10	15 54	15 40	15 25	15 11	14♓R57
1924	21♓R30	21 28	21 24	21 19	21 12	21 02	20 52	20 41	20 28	20 15	19 59	19 45	91 31	19 17	19♓R02
1925	25♓R29	25 28	25 25	25 21	25 15	25 06	24 57	24 47	24 35	24 23	24 07	23 54	23 39	23 24	23♓R10
1926	29♓R26	29 26	29 25	29 22	29 17	29 10	29 02	28 52	28 41	28 30	28 15	28 01	27 47	27 33	27♓R18
1927	03♈23	03 R25	03 25	03 23	03 19	03 13	03 06	02 57	02 48	02 37	02 22	02 09	01 56	01 41	01♈R27
1928	07♈20	07 R23	07 24	07 23	07 20	07 15	07 09	07 01	06 52	06 42	06 28	06 15	06 02	05 48	05♈R34
1929	11♈17	11 20	11 R23	11 23	11 22	11 18	11 13	11 06	10 58	10 48	10 36	10 24	10 11	09 57	09♈R43
1930	15♈12	15 17	15 21	15 R22	15 22	15 20	15 16	15 11	15 04	14 55	14 43	14 32	14 20	14 07	13♈R53
1931	19♈08	19 14	19 19	19 22	19 R23	19 22	19 19	19 15	19 09	19 02	18 51	18 41	18 29	18 16	18♈R03
1932	23♈04	23 11	23 17	23 21	23 R23	23 23	23 22	23 18	23 13	23 07	22 57	22 47	22 36	22 24	22♈R11
1933	26♈59	27 08	27 15	27 20	27 23	27 25	27 R25	27 23	27 19	27 13	27 05	26 56	26 46	26 34	26♈R22
1934	00♉54	01 04	01 12	01 18	01 23	01 26	01 R27	01 27	01 24	01 20	01 13	01 05	00 56	00 45	00♉R33
1935	04♉49	05 00	05 09	05 17	05 23	05 28	05 R30	05 31	05 30	05 27	05 21	05 14	05 06	04 56	04♉R45
1936	08♉47	08 59	09 09	09 18	09 25	09 31	09 34	09 R35	09 35	09 33	09 29	09 23	09 15	09 07	08♉R56
1937	12♉43	12 56	13 07	13 17	13 25	13 33	13 38	13 40	13 R42	13 41	13 38	13 33	13 27	13 19	13♉R10
1938	16♉40	16 53	17 06	17 17	17 27	17 36	17 42	17 46	17 R48	17 49	17 47	17 44	17 39	17 33	17♉R24
1939	20♉37	20 52	21 06	21 18	21 29	21 39	21 46	21 52	21 56	21 R58	21 58	21 56	21 52	21 47	21♉R40
1940	24♉38	24 54	25 08	25 21	25 33	25 45	25 53	26 00	26 04	26 08	26 R09	26 08	26 05	26 01	25♉R55
1941	28♉37	28 54	29 09	29 23	29 36	29 50	29♊59	00 07	00 13	00 18	00 21	00 21	00 20	00 17	00♊R12
1942	02♊37	02 55	03 11	03 26	03 40	03 55	04 06	04 15	04 23	04 28	04 33	04 R35	04 35	04 33	04♊R30
1943	06♊38	06 57	07 14	07 30	07 45	08 01	08 13	08 24	08 33	08 40	08 46	08 49	08 R51	08 51	08♊R48
1944	10♊43	11 02	11 20	11 37	11 53	12 10	12 23	12 25	12 44	12 53	13 00	13 05	13 07	13 R08	13♊R07
1945	14♊47	15 06	15 25	15 43	15 59	16 18	16 32	16 45	16 56	17 06	17 15	17 21	17 25	17 27	17♊R27
1946	18♊51	19 11	19 31	19 49	20 07	20 26	20 41	20 55	21 08	21 19	21 29	21 37	21 42	21 46	21♊R48
1947	22♊59	23 17	23 37	23 56	24 15	24 35	24 52	25 07	25 20	25 33	25 45	25 54	26 01	26 06	26♊09
1948	27♊07	27 28	27 48	28 08	28 27	28 48	29 05	29 21	29 36	29 51	00 03	00 13	00 21	00 27	00♋31
1949	01♋15	01 36	01 57	02 18	02 38	03 00	03 18	03 35	03 50	04 05	04 20	04 31	04 40	04 48	04♋54
1950	05♋24	05 46	06 07	06 28	06 49	07 12	07 31	07 49	08 05	08 21	08 37	08 50	09 01	09 10	09♋18
1951	09♋36	09 58	10 19	10 41	11 02	11 25	11 45	12 04	12 22	12 38	12 56	13 10	13 22	13 33	13♋42
1952	13♋53	14 15	14 37	14 58	15 20	15 44	16 04	16 24	16 42	17 00	17 18	17 33	17 47	17 58	18♋09
1953	18♋08	18 30	18 52	19 14	19 36	20 00	20 21	20 41	21 01	21 19	21 39	21 55	22 10	22 23	22♋35
1954	22♋25	22 47	23 09	23 31	23 53	24 18	24 39	25 00	25 20	25 40	26 01	26 18	26 34	26 48	27♋01
1955	26♋44	27 06	27 27	27 49	28 11	28 37	28 55	29 20	29 41	00♌01	00 23	00 41	00 58	01 14	01♌28
1956	01♌08	01 29	01 51	02 13	02 35	03 01	03 23	03 44	04 06	04 26	06 56	06 59	06 59	06 58	06♌55
1957	05♌30	05 51	06 12	06 34	06 56	07 22	07 44	08 06	08 28	08 49	11 33	11 37	11 40	11 40	11♌38
1958	09♌54	10 14	10 35	10 57	11 18	11 44	12 07	12 29	12 51	13 13	16 09	16 15	16 19	16 22	16♌22
1959	14♌19	14 39	14 59	15 20	15 42	16 08	16 30	16 52	17 14	17 37	20 46	20 53	20 59	21 03	21♌05
1960	18♌50	19 09	19 29	19 49	20 10	20 36	20 58	21 21	21 43	22 05	22 31	22 52	23 13	23 33	23♌53
1961	23♌18	23 36	23 55	24 15	24 36	25 01	25 23	25 46	26 08	26 30	26 56	27 18	27 40	28 01	28♌21
1962	27♌48	28 05	28 24	28 43	29 03	29 28	29♍49	00 11	00 34	00 56	01 22	01 45	02 07	02 28	02♍49
1963	02♍20	02 36	02 53	03 12	03 31	03 55	04 16	04 38	05 00	05 23	05 49	06 11	06 34	06 56	07♍17
1964	06♍56	07 11	07 27	07 45	08 04	08 27	08 48	09 09	09 31	09 53	10 20	10 42	11 05	11 27	11♍49
1965	11♍31	11 45	12 00	12 16	12 34	12 57	13 17	13 37	13 59	14 21	18 19	18 35	18 49	19 02	19♍12
1966	16♍07	16 20	16 34	16 49	17 06	17 27	17 47	18 07	18 28	18 49	22 52	23 09	23 24	23 38	23♍51
1967	20♍46	20 57	21 09	21 24	21 39	21 59	22 18	22 37	22 57	23 19	27 24	27 42	27 59	28 14	28♍28
1968	25♍27	25 37	25 48	26 01	26 16	26 35	26 53	27 11	27 31	27 51	01 59	02 18	02 35	02 52	03♎07
1969	00♎07	00 16	00 26	00 37	00 51	01 08	01 25	01 43	02 01	02 21	06 30	06 49	07 08	07 25	07♎41
1970	04♎49	04 55	05 04	05 15	05 29	05 43	05 58	06 15	06 33	06 55	07 15	07 36	07 57	08 20	08♎42
1971	09♎31	09 36	09 43	09 52	10 03	10 17	10 31	10 49	11 04	11 22	11 44	12 04	12 25	12 47	13♎09
1972	14♎14	14 18	14 24	14 31	14 41	14 54	15 07	15 21	15 37	15 54	16 16	16 36	16 56	17 21	17♎39
1973	18♎57	18 59	19 03	19 09	19 17	19 28	19 40	19 53	20 08	20 24	20 44	21 03	21 23	21 43	22♎05
1974	23♎D40	23 40	23 43	23 47	23 53	24 03	24 13	24 25	24 38	24 53	25 12	25 30	25 49	26 09	26♎30
1975	28♎R23	28 D22	28 22	28 25	28 30	28 38	28 46	28 57	29 09	29 22	03 09	03♏31	03 53	04 15	04♏36
1976	03♏R05	03 D03	03 02	03 04	03 07	03 13	03 21	03 30	03 41	03 53	07 33	07 56	08 18	08 40	09♏02
1977	07♏R47	07 44	07 D42	07 41	07 43	07 48	07 53	08 01	08 10	08 22	11 53	12 16	12 38	13 00	13♏22
1978	12♏R30	12 24	12 21	12 D19	12 19	12 22	12 26	12 32	12 40	12 50	16 12	16 34	16 56	17 19	17♏41
1979	17♏R12	17 05	17 00	16 57	16 55	16 56	16 59	17 03	17 10	17 18	20 29	20 51	21 13	21 36	21♏58
1980	21♏R52	21 44	21 38	21 33	21 31	21 D30	21 31	21 35	21 40	21 47	24 49	25 11	25 33	25 55	26♏17
1981	26♏R32	26 23	26 16	26 10	26 06	26 03	26 D03	26 05	26 09	26 14	29 04	29 25	29 47	00 09	00♏32
1982	01♐R12	01 02	00 53	00 46	00 41	00 36	00 D35	00 35	00 37	00 41	03 18	03 39	04 00	04 22	04♐44
1983	05♐R51	05 40	05 30	05 21	05 15	05 09	05 06	05 D04	05 05	05 07	07 30	07 51	08 12	08 33	08♐55
1984	10♐R26	10 14	10 04	09 54	09 47	09 39	09 35	09 33	09 D32	09 34	11 45	12 05	12 25	21 47	13♐08
1985	15♐R02	14 49	14 38	14 27	14 18	14 10	14 04	14 00	13 D58	13 58	15 55	16 14	16 34	16 55	17♐16
1986	19♐R36	19 23	19 11	18 59	18 49	18 39	18 32	18 27	18 23	18 D22	20 04	20 23	20 42	21 02	21♐22
1987	24♑R09	23 55	23 42	23 30	23 19	23 07	22 59	22 53	22 48	22 45	24 D12	24 29	24 48	25 07	25♐27
1988	28♑R37	28 23	28 09	27 57	27 45	27 33	27 24	27 16	27 10	27 06	28 22	28 D38	28 56	29 14	29♐34
1989	03♑R06	02 51	02 37	02 24	02 12	01 58	01 48	01 40	01 32	01 27	02 27	02 D43	02 59	03 17	03♑36
1990	07♑R33	07 18	07 04	06 50	06 37	06 23	06 12	06 02	05 54	05 47	06 32	06 46	07 D02	07 19	07♑37
1991	11♑R58	11 43	11 29	11 15	11 01	10 46	10 34	10 23	10 14	10 06	10 36	10 49	11 04	11 D20	11♑37
1992	16♑R19	16 04	15 50	15 35	15 21	15 06	14 53	14 42	14 32	14 22	14 41	14 53	15 07	15 D22	15♑39
1993	20♑R40	20 26	20 11	19 57	19 43	19 27	19 14	19 02	18 51	18 41	18 44	18 55	19 08	19 22	19♑D37
1994	25♑R00	24 46	24 32	24 17	24 03	23 47	23 33	23 20	23 08	22 58	22 46	22 56	23 07	23 20	23♑35
1995	29♑R18	29 05	28 51	28 36	28 19	28 05	27 51	27 38	27 25	27 14	26 48	26 57	27 07	27 19	27♑32
1996	03♒R32	03 19	03 06	02 51	02 37	02 20	02 06	01 52	01 39	01 27	00 51	00 58	01 08	01 19	01♒R31
1997	07♒R47	07 35	07 21	07 07	06 53	06 37	06 22	06 08	05 55	05 42	04 52	04 58	05 06	05 16	05♒R27
1998	12♒R00	11 48	11 35	11 22	11 08	10 51	10 37	10 23	10 09	09 56	08 53	08 58	09 05	09 13	09♒R23
1999	16♒R11	16 00	15 48	15 35	15 21	15 05	14 51	14 36	14 22	14 09	12 54	12 57	13 03	13 10	13♒R19
2000	20♒R18	20 08	19 57	19 44	19 31	19 15	19 01	18 46	18 32	18 18	16 54	16 57	17 01	17 08	17♒R16

Uranus

	October					November					December				
	1st	7th	13th	19th	25th	1st	7th	13th	19th	25th	1st	7th	13th	19th	25th
1900	09♐17	09 30	09 45	10 02	10 20	10 42	11 02	11 22	11 43	12 05	12 27	12 49	13 11	13 33	13♐54
1901	13♐32	13 45	13 59	14 14	14 31	14 52	15 11	15 31	15 51	16 13	16 34	16 56	17 18	17 40	18♐02
1902	17♐47	17 58	18 11	18 25	18 41	19 01	19 19	19 38	19 58	20 19	20 40	21 02	21 24	21 46	22♐07
1903	22♐00	22 10	22 22	22 35	22 49	23 08	23 26	23 44	24 03	24 23	24 44	25 06	25 27	25 49	26♐11
1904	26♐15	26 23	26 34	26 46	26 59	27 17	27 34	27 52	28 10	28 30	28 50	29 11	29 33	29♑54	00♑16
1905	00♑26	00 34	00 43	00 54	01 04	01 23	01 38	01 55	02 13	02 32	02 52	03 12	03 33	03 54	04♑20
1906	04♑37	04 43	04 51	05 01	05 12	05 27	05 41	05 57	06 14	06 32	06 51	07 11	07 32	07 63	08♑14
1907	08♑48	08 52	08 59	09 07	09 17	09 30	09 44	09 59	10 15	10 32	10 50	11 10	11 30	11 50	12♑11
1908	12♑58	13 01	13 07	13 14	13 23	13 35	13 48	14 02	14 17	14 34	14 51	15 10	15 30	15 50	16♑11
1909	17♑07	17 09	17 13	17 19	17 27	17 38	17 49	18 02	18 16	18 32	18 48	19 06	19 25	19 45	20♑05
1910	21♑D16	21 17	21 20	21 24	21 30	21 40	21 50	22 01	22 14	22 29	22 45	23 02	23 20	23 39	23♑59
1911	25♑R25	25 D24	25 25	25 29	25 33	25 41	25 50	26 01	26 13	26 26	26 41	26 57	27 14	27 33	27♑52
1912	29♑R33	29 D31	29 31	29 33	29 37	29 44	29 52	00♒01	00 12	00 25	00 39	00 54	01 11	01 29	01♒44
1913	03♒R41	03 38	03 D37	03 37	03 40	03 45	03 51	03 59	04 10	04 21	04 34	04 49	05 04	05 21	05♒39
1914	07♒R49	07 44	07 42	07 D42	07 42	07 46	07 51	07 58	08 07	08 17	08♑29	08 42	08 57	09 13	09♑30
1915	11♒R56	11 51	11 47	11 D45	11 45	11 47	11 50	11 56	12 03	12 12	12 23	12 36	12 49	13 04	13♒21
1916	16♒R02	15 55	15 51	15 48	15 D47	15 47	15 50	15 55	16 01	16 09	16 19	16 31	16 44	16 58	17♒14
1917	20♒R09	20 01	19 55	19 51	19 D48	19 48	19 49	19 52	19 57	20 04	20 13	20 23	20 35	20 48	21♒03
1918	24♒R15	24 06	23 59	23 54	23 50	23 48	23 D48	23 50	23 53	23 59	24 06	24 16	24 26	24 39	24♒52
1919	28♒R21	28 11	28 03	27 57	27 52	27 48	27 D47	27 47	27 50	27 54	28 00	28 08	28 18	28 29	28♒41
1920	02♓R25	02 15	02 06	01 58	01 53	01 48	01 D45	01 45	01 47	01 50	01 55	02 02	02 11	02 21	02♓33
1921	06♓R31	06 20	06 10	06 02	05 54	05 48	05 45	05 D43	05 43	05 45	05 49	05 55	06 02	06 11	06♓22
1922	10♓R37	10 26	10 15	10 05	09 57	09 49	09 45	09 42	09 D41	09 41	09 44	09 48	09 54	10 02	10♓12
1923	14♓R44	14 31	14 20	14 09	14 00	13 51	13 45	13 41	13 D39	13 38	13 39	13 42	13 47	13 54	14♓03
1924	18♓R49	18 36	18 23	18 12	18 02	17 53	17 46	17 41	17 37	17 D36	17 36	17 38	17 42	17 48	17♓55
1925	22♓R56	22 43	22 30	22 18	22 07	21 56	21 48	21 42	21 37	21 34	21 D33	21 34	21 37	21 41	21♓48
1926	27♓R04	26 50	26 37	26 24	26 13	26 00	25 52	25 44	25 38	25 34	25 D32	25 31	25 33	25 36	25♓41
1927	01♈R13	00 58	00 44	00 31	00 19	00 06	29♓56	29 47	29 41	29 35	29 32	29 D30	29 30	29 32	29♓36
1928	05♈R19	05 05	04 51	04 37	04 24	04 10	04 00	03 51	03 43	03 36	03 32	03 29	03 D28	03 29	03♈32
1929	09♈R29	09 14	09 00	08 46	08 32	08 18	08 06	07 56	07 47	07 40	07 34	07 30	07 D28	07 27	07♈29
1930	13♈R39	13 24	18 09	12 55	12 41	12 26	12 14	12 02	11 53	11 44	11 37	11 32	11 28	11 D27	11♈27
1931	17♈R49	17 34	17 20	17 05	16 51	16 35	16 22	16 10	15 59	15 50	15 42	15 35	15 30	15 28	15♈D26
1932	21♈R57	21 43	21 28	21 14	20 59	20 43	20 29	20 17	20 05	19 55	19 46	19 39	19 33	19 29	19♈D27
1933	26♈R09	25 55	25 40	25 26	25 11	24 54	24 40	24 27	24 15	24 04	23 54	23 45	23 38	23 33	23♈30
1934	00♉R21	00♈07	29 53	29 38	29 24	29 07	28 52	28 38	28 25	28 13	28 03	27 53	27 45	27 39	27♈34
1935	04♉R33	04 20	04 07	03 52	03 38	03 20	03 06	02 51	02 38	02 25	02 13	02 03	01 54	01 46	01♉R40
1936	08♉R45	08 32	08 19	08 05	07 50	07 33	07 18	07 04	06 50	06 36	06 24	06 13	06 03	05 54	05♉R47
1937	12♉R59	12 48	12 35	12 21	12 07	11 50	11 35	11 20	11 06	10 52	10 39	10 26	10 16	10 06	09♉R58
1938	17♉R15	17 04	16 52	16 39	16 25	16 08	15 53	15 38	15 23	15 09	14 55	14 42	14 31	14 20	14♉R11
1939	21♉R31	21 21	21 10	20 57	20 44	20 28	20 13	19 58	19 43	19 28	19 14	19 00	18 48	18 36	18♉R26
1940	25♉R47	25 38	25 27	25 15	25 02	24 46	24 32	24 17	24 02	23 47	23 32	23 18	23 05	22 53	22♉R42
1941	00♊R05	29♉57	29 48	29 37	29 24	29 09	28 55	28 40	28 25	28 10	27 55	27 41	27 27	27 14	27♉R02
1942	04♊R25	04 18	04 09	03 59	03 48	03 33	03 19	03 05	02 50	02 38	02 20	02 05	01 51	01 37	01♊R24
1943	08♊R44	08 39	08 31	08 22	08 12	07 58	07 45	07 31	07 17	07 02	06 47	06 32	06 17	06 03	05♊R49
1944	13♊R04	12 59	12 53	12 45	12 36	12 23	12 10	11 57	11 43	11 28	11 13	10 57	10 42	10 28	10 14
1945	17♊R26	17 22	17 17	17 10	17 02	16 50	16 38	16 26	16 12	15 58	15 43	15 27	15 12	14 57	14♊R42
1946	21♊R48	21 46	21 42	21 36	21 28	21 19	21 10	20 56	20 43	20 29	20 15	19 59	19 44	19 29	19♊R14
1947	26♊R10	26 10	26 08	26 03	25 57	25 48	25 39	25 28	25 16	25 02	24 48	24 33	24 18	24 03	23♊R47
1948	00♋34	00 R35	00 34	00 31	00 26	00 18	00 09	29♊59	29 48	29 35	29 R21	29 07	28 52	28 36	28♊R21
1949	04♋58	05 01	05 R01	04 59	04 56	04 50	04 42	04 33	04 23	04 11	03 58	03 44	03 29	03 14	02♋R59
1950	09♋23	09 27	09 R29	09 29	09 27	09 23	09 17	09 09	09 00	08 49	08 37	08 24	08 09	07 55	07♋R39
1951	13♋49	13 55	13 58	13 R59	13 59	13 56	13 52	13 45	13 37	13 28	13 17	13 04	12 51	12 36	12♋R21
1952	18♋17	18 24	18 28	18 R31	18 32	18 31	18 27	18 22	18 15	18 06	17 56	17 45	17 32	17 18	17♋R03
1953	22♋44	22 53	22 59	23 03	23 R06	23 06	23 04	23 01	22 55	22 48	22 39	22 28	22 16	22 03	21♋R49
1954	27♋12	27 22	27 30	27 36	27 40	27 R42	27 42	27 40	27 36	27 30	27 22	27 13	27 02	26 50	26♋R37
1955	01♌41	01 52	02 01	02 09	02 15	02 19	02 R20	02 20	02 17	02 13	02 06	01 58	01 49	01 38	01♌R25
1956	06♌50	06 43	06 34	06 24	06 12	06 56	06 59	06 R59	06 58	06 55	06 50	06 43	06 34	05 24	06♌R12
1957	10♌41	10 54	11 06	11 17	11 25	11 33	11 37	11 R40	11 40	11 38	11 34	11 29	11 22	11 13	11♌R03
1958	15♌10	15 25	15 38	15 50	16 00	16 09	16 15	16 19	16 R22	16 22	16 20	16 16	16 10	16 02	15♌R53
1959	19♌39	19 55	20 10	20 23	20 34	20 46	20 54	21 00	21 03	21 R05	21 04	21 02	20 58	20 52	20♌R44
1960	24♌11	24 28	24 44	24 58	25 11	25 23	25 32	25 39	25 44	25 47	25 R48	25 47	25 44	25 39	25♌R33
1961	28♌40	28 58	29 15	29 31	29 45	29 59	00 09	00 18	00 25	00 29	00 32	00 R33	00 32	00 28	00♌R23
1962	03♍09	03 28	03 46	04 03	04 18	04 34	04 46	04 50	05 05	05 11	05 15	05 18	05 R18	05 16	05♍R13
1963	07♍38	07 58	08 17	08 35	08 51	09 09	09 22	09 34	09 44	09 52	09 58	10 02	10 04	10 R04	10♍R02
1964	12♍10	12 31	12 51	13 09	13 27	18 45	13 59	14 13	14 24	14 33	14 41	14 46	14 49	14 R51	14♍R50
1965	16♍39	17 00	17 21	17 40	17 59	18 19	18 35	18 49	19 02	19 12	19 21	19 29	19 34	19 37	19♍R38
1966	21♍08	21 30	21 51	22 11	22 31	22 52	23 07	23 24	23 38	23 51	24 01	24 10	24 17	24 22	24♍R25
1967	25♍37	25 59	26 21	26 42	27 02	27 24	27 42	27 59	28 14	28 28	28 40	28 51	28 59	29 06	29♍10
1968	00♎09	00 31	00 53	01 15	01 36	01 59	02 18	02 35	02 52	03 07	03 20	03 31	03 41	03 49	03♎55
1969	04♎37	05 00	05 22	05 44	06 05	06 30	06 49	07 08	07 25	07 41	07 56	08 09	08 20	08 30	08♎37
1970	09♎05	09 28	09 50	10 12	10 34	10 59	11 20	11 39	11 58	12 15	12 31	12 45	12 57	13 08	13♎17
1971	13♎32	13 54	14 17	14 40	15 02	15 27	15 48	16 09	16 28	16 46	17 03	17 19	17 33	17 45	17♎56
1972	18♎01	18 24	18 47	19 09	19 32	19 58	20 19	20 40	21 00	21 19	21 37	21 53	22 08	22 22	22♎33
1973	22♎27	22 49	23 12	23 34	23 57	24 23	24 45	25 06	25 27	25 47	26 05	26 23	26 39	26 54	27♎07
1974	26♎51	27 13	27 35	27 58	28 20	28 47	29 09	29 31	29♏52	00 13	00 32	00 51	01 08	01 24	01♏38
1975	01♏14	01 35	01 57	02 20	02 42	03 09	03 35	03 57	04 19	04 40	04 56	05 16	05 34	05 51	06♏07
1976	05♏40	06 01	06 23	06 45	07 07	07 33	07 56	08 18	08 40	09 02	09 23	09 42	10 01	10 19	10♏36
1977	10♏02	10 22	10 43	11 05	11 27	11 53	12 16	12 38	13 00	13 22	13 43	14 04	14 24	14 42	15♏00
1978	14♏23	14 43	15 03	15 24	15 46	16 12	16 34	16 56	17 19	17 41	18 03	18 24	18 44	19 04	19♏22
1979	18♏44	19 02	19 22	19 42	20 03	20 29	20 51	21 13	21 36	21 58	22 20	22 42	23 03	23 23	23♏42
1980	23♏06	23 24	23 43	24 03	24 24	24 49	25 11	25 33	25 55	26 17	26 40	27 01	27 23	27 43	28♏03
1981	27♏25	27 42	28 00	28 19	28 39	29 04	29 25	29♐47	00 09	00 32	00 54	01 16	01 37	01 58	02♐19
1982	01♐44	02 00	02 17	02 35	02 54	03 18	03 39	04 00	04 22	04 44	05 06	05 28	05 50	06 12	06♐33
1983	06♐01	06 16	06 32	06 49	07 11	07 30	07 51	08 12	08 33	08 55	09 17	09 39	10 01	10 23	10♐44
1984	10♐20	10 34	10 49	11 06	11 23	11 45	12 05	12 25	12 47	13 08	13 30	13 52	14 14	14 40	15♐01
1985	14♐36	14 49	15 03	15 18	15 35	15 55	16 14	16 34	16 55	17 16	17 38	18 00	18 22	18 44	19♐05
1986	18♐51	19 02	19 15	19 29	19 45	20 04	20 23	20 42	21 02	21 22	21 44	22 05	22 27	22 49	23♐11
1987	23♐05	23 15	23 26	23 39	23 54	24 12	24 29	24 48	25 07	25 27	25 48	26 09	26 31	26 53	27♐15
1988	27♐19	27 28	27 38	27 50	28 06	28 22	28 38	28 56	29 14	29 34	29 54	00♑15	00 37	00 58	01♑20
1989	01♑31	01 39	01 48	01 58	02 11	02 27	02 43	02 59	03 17	03 36	03 56	04 16	04 37	04 58	05♑20
1990	05♑43	05 49	05 56	06 06	06 17	06 32	06 46	07 02	07 19	07 37	07 56	08 16	08 36	08 57	09♑19
1991	09♑54	09 58	10 04	10 12	10 22	10 36	10 49	11 04	11 20	11 37	11 55	12 14	12 34	12 55	13♑16
1992	14♑42	14 08	14 13	14 20	14 29	14 41	14 53	15 07	15 22	15 39	15 56	16 15	16 35	16 55	17♑15
1993	18♑14	18 16	18 20	18 25	18 33	18 44	18 55	19 08	19 22	19 37	19 54	20 12	20 31	20 50	21♑10
1994	22♑R23	22 D24	22 26	22 31	22 37	22 46	22 56	23 07	23 20	23 35	23 51	24 08	24 26	24 45	25♑05
1995	26♑R32	26 D32	26 33	26 36	26 40	26 48	26 57	27 07	27 19	27 32	27 47	28 03	28 20	28 39	28♑58
1996	00♒R41	00 D39	00 39	00 41	00 44	00 51	00 58	01 08	01 19	01 31	01 45	02 01	02 17	02 35	02♒53
1997	04♒R49	04 46	04 D44	04 45	04 47	04 52	04 58	05 06	05 16	05 27	05 40	05 55	06 10	06 27	06♒45
1998	08♒R56	08 52	08 D49	08 49	08 50	08 53	08 58	09 05	09 13	09 23	09 35	09 48	10 03	10 19	10♒36
1999	13♒R04	12 58	12 54	12 D52	12 52	12 54	12 57	13 03	13 10	13 19	13 29	13 42	13 55	14 10	14♒27
2000	17♒R10	17 03	16 58	16 55	16 D54	16 54	16 57	17 02	17 08	17 16	17 25	17 37	17 49	18 04	18♒19

Neptune

	January					February					March				
	1st	7th	13th	19th	25th	1st	7th	13th	19th	25th	1st	7th	13th	19th	25th
1900	25♊R13	25 04	24 54	24 46	24 38	24 30	24 25	24 20	24 16	24 14	24 13	24D13	24 14	24 15	24♊19
1901	27♊R31	27 21	27 12	27 03	26 55	26 47	26 41	26 36	26 32	26 29	26 28	26D27	26 27	26 29	26♊31
1902	29♊R49	29 39	29 30	29 21	29 12	29 04	28 57	28 52	28 47	28 44	28 42	28 41	28D41	28 42	28♊44
1903	02♋R07	01 57	01 47	01 38	01 30	01 20	01 14	01 08	01 03	00 59	00 57	00 55	00D54	00 55	00♋57
1904	04♋R25	04 15	04 05	03 56	03 47	03 37	03 30	03 24	03 18	03 14	03 11	03 09	03D08	03 09	03♋10
1905	06♋R42	06 32	06 22	06 12	06 03	05 53	05 46	05 39	05 34	05 29	05 27	05 24	05 23	05D22	05♋23
1906	09♋R00	08 50	08 40	08 30	08 21	08 11	08 03	07 56	07 50	07 45	07 42	07 39	07 37	07D36	07♋37
1907	11♋R18	11 08	10 58	10 48	10 39	10 28	10 20	10 13	10 06	10 01	09 58	09 54	09 52	09 51	09♋D51
1908	13♋R36	13 26	13 16	13 06	12 56	12 46	12 37	12 30	12 23	12 16	12 13	12 09	12 06	12 05	12♋D05
1909	15♋R53	15 43	15 32	15 22	15 13	15 02	14 53	14 45	14 38	14 32	14 29	14 25	14 21	14 19	14♋D18
1910	18♋R11	18 01	17 50	17 40	17 30	17 19	17 11	17 02	16 55	16 49	16 45	16 40	16 36	16 34	16♋D33
1911	20♋R28	20 18	20 08	19 58	19 48	19 37	19 28	19 19	19 12	19 06	19 01	18 56	18 51	18 48	18♋D47
1912	22♋R46	22 36	22 26	22 16	22 06	21 54	21 45	21 36	21 28	21 21	21 16	21 10	21 06	21 02	21♋R00
1913	25♋R02	24 52	24 42	24 31	24 21	24 10	24 00	23 52	23 43	23 36	23 31	23 26	23 21	23 17	23♋R14
1914	27♋R19	27 09	26 59	26 49	26 39	26 27	26 17	26 08	26 00	25 52	25 47	25 41	25 36	25 32	25♋R29
1915	29♋R36	29 26	29 16	29 06	28 56	28 44	28 34	28 25	28 16	28 08	28 03	27 56	27 51	27 46	27 43
1916	01♌R53	01 43	01 33	01 23	01 13	01 01	00 51	00 42	00 33	00 25	00 18	00 11	00 05	00♋05	00♋01
1917	04♌R08	03 58	03 49	03 39	03 29	03 17	03 07	02 57	02 48	02 40	02 34	02 27	02 21	02 16	02♌R11
1918	06♌R25	06 15	06 06	05 56	05 46	05 34	05 24	05 14	05 05	04 56	04 51	04 43	04 37	04 31	04♌R26
1919	08♌R41	08 32	08 23	08 13	08 03	07 51	07 41	07 31	07 22	07 13	07 07	06 59	06 52	06 46	06♌R40
1920	10♌R58	10 49	10 40	10 30	10 20	10 09	09 58	09 49	09 39	09 30	09 22	09 14	09 07	09 01	08♌R55
1921	13♌R13	13 04	12 55	12 46	12 36	12 24	12 14	12 04	11 56	11 45	11 39	11 31	11 23	11 16	11♌R10
1922	15♌R29	15 20	15 12	15 02	14 53	14 41	14 31	14 21	14 11	14 01	13 55	13 47	13 39	13 32	13♌R25
1923	17♌R44	17 36	17 28	17 19	17 09	16 58	16 47	16 37	16 27	16 18	16 12	16 03	15 55	15 47	15♌R40
1924	20♌R00	19 52	19 44	19 35	19 25	19 14	19 04	18 54	18 44	18 34	18 26	18 17	18 09	18 01	17♌R54
1925	22♌R13	22 06	21 58	21 49	21 40	21 29	21 19	21 08	20 58	20 49	20 42	20 33	20 24	20 16	20♌R09
1926	24♌R28	24 21	24 13	24 05	23 56	23 45	23 35	23 25	23 14	23 05	22 58	22 49	22 40	22 32	22♌R24
1927	26♌R43	26 36	26 29	26 20	26 11	26 00	25 51	25 41	25 31	25 20	25 14	25 04	24 55	24 47	24♌R39
1928	28♌R57	28 51	28 44	28 36	28 27	28 16	28 07	27 57	27 46	27 36	27 28	27 19	27 09	27 01	26♌R53
1929	01♍R10	01 04	00 57	00 49	00 41	00 30	00 21	00 11	00♌01	29 51	29♌R44	29 34	29 25	29 16	29♌R08
1930	03♍R24	03 19	03 12	03 05	02 57	02 46	02 37	02 27	02 17	02 04	02 00	01 50	01 41	01 32	01♍R26
1931	05♍R38	05 33	05 27	05 20	05 12	05 02	04 53	04 43	04 33	04 23	04 16	04 06	03 57	03 48	03♍R39
1932	07♍R52	07 47	07 42	07 35	07 27	07 18	07 09	06 59	06 49	06 39	06 31	06 21	06 11	06 02	05♍R53
1933	10♍R05	10 01	09 55	09 49	09 41	09 32	09 23	09 13	09 04	08 54	08 47	08 37	08 27	08 18	08♍R09
1934	12♍R18	12 14	12 09	12 03	11 56	11 47	11 38	11 29	11 20	11 10	11 03	10 53	10 43	10 34	10♍R24
1935	14♍R32	14 28	14 23	14 18	14 11	14 02	13 54	13 45	13 35	13 26	13 19	13 09	12 59	12 49	12♍R40
1936	16♍R44	16 41	16 37	16 32	16 25	16 17	16 09	16 00	15 51	15 41	15 33	15 23	15 13	15 03	14♍R54
1937	18♍R56	18 53	18 49	18 44	18 38	18 30	18 24	18 14	18 05	17 55	17 48	17 38	17 28	17 19	17♍R09
1938	21♍R08	21 06	21 02	20 58	20 52	20 44	20 37	20 28	20 19	20 10	20 04	19 54	19 44	19 34	19♍R24
1939	23♍R20	23 18	23 15	23 11	23 05	22 58	22 51	22 43	22 34	22 25	22 18	22 09	21 59	21 49	21♍R39
1940	25♍R31	25 30	25 27	25 23	25 19	25 12	25 05	24 57	24 49	24 40	24 32	24 22	24 12	24 02	23♍R52
1941	27♍R42	27 41	27 39	27 35	27 31	27 24	27 17	27 10	27 01	26 53	26 46	26 37	26 27	26 17	26♍R07
1942	29♍R53	29 52	29 51	29 48	29 43	29 37	29 31	29 24	29 16	29 07	29 01	28 52	28 42	28 32	28♍R22
1943	02♎R04	02 04	02 02	02 00	01 56	01 51	01 45	01 38	01 30	01 22	01 16	01 07	00 57	00 47	00♎R37
1944	04♎14	04R15	04 14	04 12	04 09	04 04	03 58	03 52	03 45	03 36	03 29	03 20	03 10	03 01	02♎R51
1945	06♎25	08R26	06 26	06 24	06 21	06 16	06 11	06D04	05 57	05 49	05 44	05 35	05 25	05 16	05♎06
1946	08♎36	08 47	08R37	08 36	08 33	08 29	08 24	08 18	08D12	08 04	07 58	07 50	07 39	07 31	07♎21
1947	10♎46	10 48	10R48	10 48	10 46	10 42	10 38	10 32	10 26	10 18	10 13	10 04	09 55	09 46	09♎R36
1948	12♎56	12 59	13 00	12R59	12 58	12 55	12 51	12 46	12 38	12 32	12 26	12 18	12 09	11 59	11♎R50
1949	15♎07	15 09	15 10	15R10	15 09	15 06	15 03	14 58	14 52	14 45	14 40	14 32	14 23	14 14	14♎R05
1950	17♎16	17 19	17 21	17R21	17 21	16 08	15 59	15 49	15 39	15 29	16 54	16 47	16 38	16 29	16♎R20
1951	19♎25	19 23	19 16	19R08	13 00	19 30	19 27	18 33	18 24	18 16	19 08	19 01	18 52	18 44	18♎R34
1952	21♎34	21 38	21 41	21R42	21 43	21 42	21 39	21 36	21 31	21 26	21 20	21 13	21 05	20 56	20♎R47
1953	23♎43	23 48	23 51	23 53	23R53	23 52	23 50	23 47	23 43	23 38	23 34	23 27	23 19	23 11	23♎R01
1954	25♎51	26 57	26 00	26 03	26R04	26 04	26 02	25 59	25 55	25 50	25 47	25 40	25 33	25 25	25♎R16
1955	28♎00	28 06	28 10	28 13	28 14	28R14	28 13	28 11	28 08	28 03	28 00	27 54	27 46	27 39	27♎R30
1956	00♏09	00 14	00 19	00 22	00 24	00 25	00 25	00 23	00 20	00 16	00 12	00 06	29♎59	29 51	29♎43
1957	02♏18	02 24	02 29	02 32	02 35	02R36	02 36	02 34	02 32	02 28	02 25	02 19	02 13	02 05	01♏R57
1958	04♏26	04 32	04 38	04 42	04 45	04 47	04R47	04 46	04 44	04 40	04 37	04 32	04 26	04 19	04♏R11
1959	06♏34	06 41	06 47	06 51	06 54	06 57	06R58	06 57	06 55	06 53	06 50	06 45	06 40	06 33	06♏R26
1960	08♏42	08 49	08 55	09 00	09 04	09 07	09 08	09R08	09 07	09 04	09 02	08 57	08 52	08 45	08♏R38
1961	10♏51	10 58	11 05	11 10	11 14	11 17	11 19	11R19	11 18	11 16	11 14	11 10	11 05	10 59	10♏R52
1962	12♏58	13 06	13 13	13 18	13 23	13 27	13 29	13R30	13 29	13 27	13 26	13 22	13 17	13 12	13♏R05
1963	15♏05	15 13	15 20	15 27	15 32	15 36	15 39	15 40	15R40	15 39	15 37	15 34	15 30	15 24	15♏R17
1964	17♏11	17 20	17 28	17 35	17 40	17 45	17 48	17 50	17R50	17 50	17 48	17 45	17 41	17 36	17♏R30
1965	19♏19	19 28	19 36	19 43	19 49	19 54	19 58	20 00	20R01	20 00	19 59	19 57	19 53	19 49	19♏R43
1966	21♏26	21 35	21 43	21 51	21 57	22 03	22 07	22 09	22R11	22 11	22 10	22 08	22 05	22 01	21♏R56
1967	23♏32	23 42	23 51	23 58	24 05	24 12	24 16	24 19	24R21	24 21	24 21	24 20	24 17	24 13	24♏R09
1968	25♏39	25 49	25 58	26 06	26 13	26 20	26 25	26 28	26 31	26R32	26 32	26 31	26 28	26 25	26♏R20
1969	27♏47	27 57	28 06	28 15	28 22	28 30	28 35	08 38	28 41	28R42	28 43	28 42	28 40	28 37	28♏R33
1970	29♏54	00♐04	00 14	00 23	00 30	00 38	00 44	00 48	00 51	00 53	00R53	00 53	00 52	00 49	00♐R46
1971	02♏00	02 11	02 21	02 30	02 38	02 47	02 52	02 57	03 01	03 03	03 04	03R04	03 04	03 01	02♐R58
1972	04♐06	04 18	04 28	04 38	04 46	04 55	05 02	05 07	05 11	05 14	05 15	05R15	05 15	05 13	05♐R10
1973	06♐15	06 26	06 36	06 46	06 55	07 04	07 11	07 16	07 21	07 24	07 25	07 26	07R26	07 25	07♐R22
1974	08♐21	08 32	08 43	08 53	09 02	09 12	09 19	09 24	09 30	09 33	09 35	09 37	09R37	09 36	09♐R34
1975	10♐26	10 38	10 49	11 00	11 09	11 19	11 27	11 33	11 39	11 43	11 45	11 47	11R48	11 48	11♐R46
1976	12♐23	12 44	12 55	13 06	13 16	13 27	13 35	13 41	13 47	13 52	13 55	13 57	13R58	13 58	13♐R57
1977	14♐39	14 52	15 03	15 14	15 24	15 35	15 43	15 50	15 56	16 02	16 04	16 07	16 08	16R09	16♐R08
1978	16♐45	16 57	17 09	17 20	17 31	17 42	17 51	17 58	18 05	18 10	18 13	18 16	18 18	18R19	18♐R19
1979	18♐50	19 03	19 15	19 26	19 37	19 49	19 58	20 06	20 13	20 18	20 22	20 26	20 28	20R30	21♐R30
1980	20♐56	21 08	21 21	21 43	21 44	21 56	22 05	22 13	22 21	22 27	24 40	24 45	24 48	24R51	24♐R52
1981	23♐03	23 16	23 29	23 41	23 52	24 04	24 14	24 22	24 30	24 36	24 40	24 45	24 48	24 51	24♐R52
1982	25♐09	25 22	25 35	25 47	25 59	26 11	26 21	26 30	26 38	26 45	26 49	26 54	26 58	27 01	27♐R02
1983	27♐15	27 28	27 41	27 53	28 05	28 18	28 28	28 38	28 46	28 54	28 58	29 04	29 08	29 11	29♐13
1984	29♐21	29 34	29 47	00♑00	00 12	00 25	00 36	00 46	00 54	01 02	01 08	01 14	01 19	01 22	01♑24
1985	01♑29	01 43	01 56	02 09	02 21	02 34	02 45	02 55	03 04	03 12	03 17	03 23	03 28	03 32	03♑35
1986	03♑35	03 49	04 02	04 15	04 27	04 41	04 52	05 03	05 12	05 20	05 26	05 32	05 38	05 42	05♑46
1987	05♑41	05 55	06 08	06 21	06 34	06 48	06 59	07 10	07 20	07 29	07 34	07 41	07 47	07 52	07♑56
1988	07♑47	08 01	08 14	08 28	08 40	08 55	09 06	09 17	09 27	09 37	09 44	09 51	09 57	10 03	10♑07
1989	09♑56	10 09	10 23	10 36	10 49	11 03	11 15	11 26	11 36	11 46	11 52	11 59	12 06	12 12	12♑17
1990	12♑01	12 15	12 29	12 42	12 55	13 10	13 22	13 33	13 44	13 54	14 00	14 08	14 15	14 21	14♑26
1991	14♑07	14 21	14 34	14 48	15 01	15 16	15 28	15 40	15 51	16 01	16 07	16 16	16 24	16 30	16♑36
1992	16♑13	16 27	16 40	16 54	17 07	17 22	17 35	17 47	17 58	18 10	18 17	18 26	18 34	18 40	18♑46
1993	18♑22	18 35	18 49	19 02	19 16	19 31	19 44	19 56	20 07	20 18	20 24	20 34	20 42	20 49	20♑56
1994	20♑28	20 41	20 55	21 09	21 22	21 38	21 50	22 03	22 14	22 25	22 32	22 42	22 51	22 58	23♑05
1995	22♑34	22 48	23 01	23 15	23 29	23 44	23 57	24 10	24 22	24 33	24 40	24 50	24 59	25 07	25♑14
1996	24♑41	24 54	25 08	25 22	25 35	25 51	26 04	26 17	26 29	26 40	26 50	27 00	27 09	27 18	27♑25
1997	26♑50	27 03	27 17	27 31	27 44	28 00	28 13	28 26	28 38	28 50	28 57	29 08	29 18	29 26	29♑34
1998	28♑57	29 10	29 24	29 37	29 51	00♒07	00 20	00 33	00 46	00 58	01 05	01 16	01 26	01 35	01♒43
1999	01♒04	01 17	01 30	01 44	01 58	02 14	02 27	02 40	02 53	03 06	03 13	03 24	03 34	03 44	03♒52
2000	03♒11	03 24	03 37	03 51	04 04	04 20	04 34	04 47	05 00	05 12	05 22	05 34	05 44	05 54	06♒03

	April					May					June				
	1st	7th	13th	19th	25th	1st	7th	13th	19th	25th	1st	7th	13th	19th	25th
1900	24♊24	24 30	24 37	24 45	24 54	25 04	25 14	25 25	25 37	25 50	26 05	26 28	26 31	26 44	26♊58
1901	26♊36	26 42	26 48	26 56	27 04	27 43	27 24	27 35	27 46	27 58	28 13	28 26	28 39	28 53	29♊06
1902	28♊48	28 53	28 59	29 06	29 14	29 23	29 33	29 44	29♋56	00 07	00 21	00 34	00 47	01 01	01♋14
1903	01♋00	01 05	01 10	01 17	01 25	01 33	01 43	01 53	02 04	02 16	02 30	02 43	02 56	03 09	03♋22
1904	03♋13	03 18	03 23	03 29	03 37	03 45	03 54	04 04	04 15	04 27	04 41	04 53	05 06	05 19	05♋33
1905	05♋26	05 30	05 34	05 40	05 47	05 55	06 04	06 14	06 24	06 36	06 50	07 02	07 15	07 28	07♋41
1906	07♋39	07 42	07 46	07 52	07 58	08 06	08 14	08 24	08 34	08 45	08 58	09 11	09 23	09 36	09♋50
1907	09♋52	09 55	09 59	10 03	10 10	10 17	10 25	10 34	10 44	10 54	11 08	11 20	11 32	11 45	11♋58
1908	12♋06	12 08	12 12	12 16	12 22	12 29	12 37	12 45	12 55	13 06	13 19	13 30	13 43	13 56	14♋09
1909	14♋19	14 21	14 24	14 28	14 33	14 40	14 47	14 56	15 05	15 12	15 28	15 39	15 51	16 04	16♋17
1910	16♋32	16 34	16 36	16 40	16 45	16 51	16 58	17 06	17 15	17 24	17 37	17 48	18 00	18 12	18♋25
1911	18♋46	18 47	18 49	18 52	18 56	19 02	19 08	19 16	19 24	19 34	19 46	19 57	20 09	20 21	20♋33
1912	20♋D59	21 00	21 02	21 04	21 08	21 14	21 20	21 27	21 36	21 45	21 57	22 07	22 19	22 31	22♋43
1913	23♋R13	23 D 13	23 14	23 16	23 20	23 25	23 30	23 37	23 45	23 54	24 05	24 16	24 27	24 39	24♋51
1914	25♋R26	25 D 26	25 27	25 28	25 31	25 36	25 41	25 48	25 55	26 03	26 14	26 25	26 36	26 47	26♋59
1915	27♋R40	27 D 39	27 39	27 41	27 43	27 47	27 52	27 58	28 05	28 13	28 23	28 33	28 44	28 55	29♋07
1916	29♋R54	29 53	29 D 52	29 53	29 56	29 59	00 04	00 09	00 16	00 24	00 34	00 44	00 54	01 06	01♌17
1917	02♌R08	02 06	02 D 05	02 06	02 08	02 11	02 15	02 20	02 26	02 34	02 44	02 53	03 03	03 14	03♌25
1918	04♌R22	04 20	04 D 19	04 19	04 20	04 22	04 26	04 31	04 37	04 44	04 53	05 02	05 12	05 22	05♌34
1919	06♌R36	06 34	06 32	06 D 32	06 32	06 34	06 38	06 42	06 47	06 54	07 03	07 11	07 21	07 31	07♌42
1920	08♌R50	08 47	08 45	08 D 45	08 45	08 47	08 50	08 54	08 59	09 05	09 14	09 22	09 31	09 41	09♌52
1921	11♌R05	11 01	10 59	10 D 58	10 D 58	10 59	11 01	11 05	11 10	11 15	11 23	11 31	11 40	11 50	12♌01
1922	13♌R19	13 16	13 13	13 11	13 D 10	13 11	13 13	13 16	13 20	13 26	13 33	13 41	13 49	13 59	14♌09
1923	15♌R34	15 30	15 26	15 24	15 D 22	15 23	15 25	15 27	15 31	15 36	15 43	15 50	15 58	16 07	15♌17
1924	17♌R48	17 43	17 39	17 37	17 D 36	17 35	17 37	17 39	17 42	17 47	17 54	18 00	18 08	18 17	18♌27
1925	20♌R02	19 57	19 53	19 50	19 48	19 D 48	19 48	19 50	19 53	19 57	20 03	20 10	20 17	20 25	20♌35
1926	22♌R16	22 11	22 06	22 03	22 01	22 00	22 D 00	22 01	22 03	22 07	22 13	22 19	22 26	22 34	22♌43
1927	24♌R31	24 25	24 20	24 16	24 14	24 12	24 D 12	24 12	24 14	24 17	24 22	24 28	24 35	24 42	24♌51
1928	26♌R44	26 38	26 33	26 29	26 26	26 24	26 D 23	26 24	26 26	26 28	26 33	26 38	26 45	26 52	27♌01
1929	28♌R59	28 53	28 47	28 43	28 39	28 37	28 D 36	28 36	28 37	28 39	28 43	28 48	28 54	29 01	29♌09
1930	01♍R14	01 07	01 01	00 56	00 52	00 50	00 48	00 D 48	00 48	00 50	00 54	00 58	01 04	01 10	01♍18
1931	03♍R29	03 22	03 16	03 10	03 06	03 03	03 01	03 D 00	03 00	03 01	03 04	03 08	03 13	03 19	03♍26
1932	05♍R43	05 36	05 29	05 24	05 19	05 16	05 13	05 D 12	05 12	05 13	05 16	05 19	05 24	05 30	05♍37
1933	07♍R59	07 51	07 44	07 38	07 33	07 29	07 26	07 24	07 D 24	07 24	07 27	07 30	07 34	07 39	07♍46
1934	10♍R14	10 06	09 59	09 52	09 47	09 43	09 39	09 37	09 D 36	09 36	09 38	09 40	09 44	09 49	09♍55
1935	12♍R29	12 21	12 14	12 07	12 01	11 56	11 52	11 50	11 D 48	11 48	11 49	11 51	11 54	11 59	12♍04
1936	14♍R43	14 .35	14 27	14 20	14 14	14 09	14 05	14 02	14 00	13 D 59	14 00	14 02	14 05	14 09	14♍14
1937	16♍R58	16 49	16 41	16 34	16 28	16 22	16 18	16 14	16 12	16 D 11	16 11	16 12	16 15	16 18	16♍23
1938	19♍R13	19 04	18 56	18 48	18 41	18 35	18 30	18 27	18 24	18 D 22	18 22	18 23	18 25	28 28	28♍32
1939	21♍R28	21 19	21 10	21 02	20 55	20 49	20 43	20 39	20 36	20 34	20 D 33	20 33	20 35	20 37	20♍41
1940	23♍R41	23 32	23 23	23 15	23 08	23 01	22 55	22 51	22 47	22 45	22 44	22 D 44	22 45	22 48	22♍51
1941	25♍R56	25 46	25 37	25 29	25 21	25 15	25 09	25 04	25 00	24 57	24 55	24 D 55	24 55	24 57	25♍00
1942	28♍R11	28 01	27 52	27 43	27 35	29 28	27 22	27 17	27 12	27 09	27 06	27 D 06	27 06	27 07	27♍10
1943	00♎R26	00 16	00 07	29♍58	29 50	29 R 42	29 36	29 30	29 25	29 21	29 18	29 D 17	29 17	92 18	29♍20
1944	02♎R39	02 29	02 20	02 11	02 03	01 55	01 48	01 42	01 37	01 33	01 .30	01 28	01 D 28	01 29	01♎30
1945	04♎R54	04 44	04 35	04 26	04 17	04 09	04 02	03 56	03 50	03 46	03 42	03 40	03 D 39	03 39	03♎41
1946	07♎R09	07 00	06 50	06 41	06 32	06 24	06 16	06 10	06 04	05 59	05 44	05 52	05 51	05 D 50	05♎51
1947	09♎R25	09 15	09 05	08 56	08 47	08 38	08 30	08 23	08 16	08 10	08 07	08 04	08 02	08 D 02	08♎02
1948	11♎R38	11 28	11 19	11 09	11 00	10 51	10 43	10 36	10 30	10 24	10 19	10 16	10 14	10 D 13	10♎13
1949	13♎R53	13 43	13 34	13 24	13 15	13 06	12 58	12 50	12 43	12 37	12 32	12 28	12 26	12 24	12♎D24
1950	16♎R08	15 59	15 49	15 39	15 29	15 20	15 12	15 04	14 57	14 51	14 45	14 41	14 37	14 35	14♎D35
1951	18♎R23	18 13	18 03	17 54	17 44	17 35	17 26	17 18	17 11	17 04	16 57	16 53	16 49	16 47	16♎D46
1952	20♎R36	20 26	20 16	20 07	19 57	19 48	19 39	19 31	19 23	19 16	19 09	19 04	19 02	18 58	18♎D56
1953	22♎R51	22 41	22 31	22 21	22 11	22 02	21 53	21 44	21 37	21 29	21 22	21 17	21 13	21 10	21♎D08
1954	25♎R50	24 55	24 46	24 36	24 26	24 16	24 07	23 59	23 50	23 43	23 35	23 30	23 25	23 21	23♎R19
1955	27♎R20	27 10	27 00	26 51	26 41	26 31	26 22	26 13	26 04	25 57	25 49	25 43	25 38	25 34	25♎R31
1956	29♎R33	29 23	29 14	29 04	28 54	28 44	28 35	28 26	28 17	28 09	28 01	27 55	27 49	27 45	27♎R42
1957	01♏R47	01 38	01 28	01 19	01 09	00 59	00 49	00 40	00 31	00 23	00 15	00 08	00 02	29 58	29♏R54
1958	04♏R02	03 53	03 43	03 33	03 24	03 14	03 04	02 55	02 46	02 37	02 28	02 22	02 15	02 10	02♏R06
1959	06♏R16	06 07	05 58	05 48	05 38	05 29	05 19	05 09	05 00	04 52	04 42	04 35	04 29	04 23	04♏R19
1960	08♏R28	08 20	08 11	08 01	07 51	07 41	07 32	07 22	07 13	07 04	06 55	06 47	06 41	06 35	06♏R30
1961	10♏R42	10 34	10 25	10 16	10 06	09 56	09 46	09 37	09 27	09 18	09 09	09 01	08 54	08 48	08♏R43
1962	12♏R56	12 48	12 39	12 30	12 20	12 11	12 01	11 51	11 42	11 33	11 23	11 15	11 07	11 01	10♏R55
1963	15♏R10	15 02	14 53	14 44	14 35	14 25	14 15	14 06	13 56	13 47	13 36	13 28	13 21	13 14	13♏R08
1964	17♏R22	17 14	17 06	16 57	16 47	16 38	16 28	16 18	16 09	15 59	15 49	15 40	15 33	15 26	15♏R19
1965	19♏R35	19 28	19 20	19 11	19 02	18 52	18 43	18 33	18 23	18 14	18 03	17 54	17 46	17 39	17♏R32
1966	21♏R49	21 42	21 34	21 25	21 16	21 07	20 57	20 47	20 37	20 28	20 17	20 08	20 00	19 52	19♏R45
1967	24♏R02	23 55	23 47	23 39	23 30	23 21	23 12	23 02	22 52	22 42	22 31	22 22	22 14	22 06	21♏R59
1968	26♏R14	26 07	26 00	25 52	25 43	25 34	25 25	25 15	25 05	24 55	24 44	24 35	24 27	24 18	24♏R11
1969	28♏R27	28 21	28 14	28 06	27 58	27 49	27 39	27 30	27 20	27 10	26 59	26 50	26 41	26 33	26♏R25
1970	00♐R40	00 34	00 27	00 20	00 12	00 03	29♏54	29 44	29 34	29 25	29 R 13	29 04	28 55	28 47	28♏R39
1971	02♐R53	02 48	02 41	02 34	02 26	02 18	02 09	01 59	01 49	01 40	01 28	01 19	01 10	01 01	00♐R53
1972	05♐R05	05 00	04 54	04 47	04 39	04 31	04 22	04 12	04 03	03 53	03 42	03 32	03 23	03 14	03♐R06
1973	07♐R18	07 13	07 07	07 01	06 53	06 45	06 36	06 27	06 18	06 06	05 57	05 47	05 38	05 29	05♐R20
1974	09♐R31	09 26	09 21	09 14	09 07	08 59	08 51	08 42	08 32	08 23	08 11	08 02	07 52	07 43	07♐R34
1975	11♐R43	11 39	11 34	11 28	11 21	11 14	11 05	10 57	10 47	10 38	10 27	10 17	10 07	09 58	09♐R49
1976	13♐R54	13 51	13 46	13 40	13 33	13 26	13 18	13 09	13 00	12 51	12 39	12 30	12 20	12 11	12♐R01
1977	16♐R06	16 03	15 58	15 53	15 47	15 40	15 32	15 23	15 14	15 05	14 54	14 44	14 35	14 25	14♐R16
1978	18♐R17	18 15	18 11	18 06	18 00	17 53	17 46	17 37	17 29	17 20	17 08	16 59	16 49	16 39	16♐R30
1979	20♐R29	20 26	20 23	20 19	20 13	20 07	19 59	19 52	19 43	19 34	19 23	19 13	19 04	18 54	18♐R44
1980	22♐R40	22 38	22 35	22 30	22 25	22 19	22 12	22 04	21 56	21 47	21 36	21 27	21 17	21 07	20♐R58
1981	24♐R51	24 50	24 47	24 43	24 38	24 33	24 26	24 19	24 10	24 02	23 51	23 42	23 32	23 22	23♐R13
1982	27♐R03	27 02	26 59	26 56	26 52	26 46	26 40	26 33	26 25	26 17	26 06	25 57	25 47	25 37	25♐R28
1983	29♐R14	29 14	29 12	29 09	29 05	29 00	28 54	28 47	28 40	28 32	28 21	28 12	28 02	27 53	27♐R43
1984	01♑R26	01 25	01 24	01 21	01 18	01 13	01 07	01 01	00 53	00 45	00 35	00 26	00 16	00 07	29♑R57
1985	03♑37	03 R 37	03 36	03 34	03 31	03 27	03 21	03 15	03 08	03 00	02 50	02 41	02 32	02 21	02♑R11
1986	05♑48	05 R 49	05 48	05 47	05 44	05 40	05 35	05 29	05 23	05 15	05 06	04 57	04 47	04 38	04♑R28
1987	07♑59	08 R 00	08 00	07 59	07 57	07 53	07 49	07 43	07 37	07 30	07 21	07 12	07 03	06 53	06♑R44
1988	10♑10	10 12	10 R 12	10 11	10 09	10 06	10 02	09 56	09 50	09 43	09 34	09 26	09 17	09 07	08♑R58
1989	12♑20	12 22	12 R 23	12 23	12 21	12 19	12 15	12 10	12 04	11 58	11 49	11 41	11 32	11 23	11♑R13
1990	14♑31	14 33	14 R 34	14 35	14 34	14 31	14 28	14 24	14 18	14 12	14 03	13 56	13 47	13 38	13♑R29
1991	16♑41	16 44	16 46	16 R 46	16 46	16 44	16 41	16 37	16 32	16 26	16 18	16 10	16 02	15 53	15♑R44
1992	18♑51	18 55	18 57	18 R 58	18 57	18 56	18 53	18 50	18 45	18 39	18 31	18 24	18 16	18 07	17♑R58
1993	21♑01	21 05	21 08	21 R 09	21 09	21 08	21 06	21 03	20 59	20 53	20 46	20 39	20 31	20 22	20♑R13
1994	23♑11	23 16	23 19	23 21	23 R 21	23 21	23 19	23 16	23 12	23 08	23 01	22 54	22 46	22 38	22♑R29
1995	25♑21	25 26	25 30	25 32	25 R 33	25 33	25 32	25 30	25 26	25 22	25 15	25 09	25 02	24 54	24♑R45
1996	27♑32	27 37	27 41	27 44	27 R 45	27 45	27 45	27 42	27 39	27 35	27 29	27 23	27 16	27 08	26♑R59
1997	29♑42	29 47	29 52	29 55	29 57	29 R 58	29 57	29 56	29 53	29 49	29 44	29 38	29 31	29 23	29♑R15
1998	01♒52	01 58	02 02	02 06	02 09	02 R 10	02 10	02 09	02 07	02 03	01 58	01 53	01 46	01 39	01♒R31
1999	04♒01	04 08	04 13	04 17	04 20	04 22	04 R 22	04 22	04 20	04 17	04 12	04 07	04 01	03 54	03♒R47
2000	06♒12	06 18	06 24	06 28	06 32	06 34	06 R 35	06 34	06 33	06 30	06 26	06 21	06 15	06 09	06♒R01

Neptune

July

Year	1st	7th	13th	19th	25th
1900	27♊11	27 24	27 37	27 49	28 01
1901	29♊19	29 33	29 45	29♋58	00 10
1902	01♋28	01 41	01 54	02 07	02 19
1903	03♋36	03 49	04 02	04 15	04 28
1904	05♋46	05 59	06 13	06 26	06 38
1905	07♋55	08 08	08 21	08 34	08 47
1906	10♋03	10 16	10 30	10 43	10 56
1907	12♋11	12 25	12 38	12 51	13 04
1908	14♋22	14 35	14 49	15 02	15 15
1909	16♋30	16 44	16 57	17 10	17 23
1910	18♋38	18 52	19 05	19 18	19 32
1911	20♋46	20 59	21 13	21 26	21 40
1912	22♋56	23 10	23 23	23 36	23 50
1913	25♋04	25 17	25 30	25 44	25 57
1914	27♋12	27 25	27 38	27 51	28 05
1915	29♋20	29 32	29 46	29♌59	00 12
1916	01♋30	01 42	01 55	02 09	02 22
1917	03♌38	03 50	04 03	04 16	04 29
1918	05♌46	05 58	06 11	06 24	06 37
1919	07♌54	08 06	08 18	08 31	08 44
1920	10♌04	10 16	10 28	10 41	10 54
1921	12♌12	12 23	12 36	12 48	13 01
1922	14♌20	14 31	14 43	14 56	15 09
1923	16♌28	16 39	16 51	17 03	17 16
1924	18♌37	18 48	19 00	19 12	19 25
1925	20♌45	20 56	21 07	21 19	21 32
1926	22♌52	23 03	23 14	23 26	23 38
1927	25♌00	25 10	25 21	25 33	25 45
1928	27♌10	27 10	27 30	27 42	27 54
1929	29♌18	29 27	29 38	29♍49	00 01
1930	01♍26	01 35	01 46	01 56	02 08
1931	03♍35	03 44	03 53	04 04	04 15
1932	05♍45	05 53	06 03	06 13	06 24
1933	07♍53	08 02	08 11	08 21	08 32
1934	10♍02	10 10	10 19	10 29	10 39
1935	12♍11	12 18	12 27	12 36	12 46
1936	14♍21	14 28	14 36	14 45	14 55
1937	16♍29	16 36	16 44	16 53	17 02
1938	18♍38	18 44	18 52	19 00	19 09
1939	20♍46	20 52	20 59	21 07	21 16
1940	22♍56	23 02	23 08	23 16	23 25
1941	25♍05	25 10	25 16	25 24	25 32
1942	27♍14	27 19	27 25	27 32	27 40
1943	29♍23	29 28	29 33	29 40	29 47
1944	01♎33	01 38	01 43	01 49	01 57
1945	03♎43	03 47	03 52	03 58	04 05
1946	05♎54	05 57	06 01	06 07	06 13
1947	08♎04	08 06	08 10	08 15	08 21
1948	10♎14	10 17	10 20	10 25	10 31
1949	12♎25	12 27	12 30	12 34	12 39
1950	14♎35	14 36	14 39	14 43	14 48
1951	16♎45	16 46	16 49	16 52	16 56
1952	18♎56	18 57	18 59	19 02	19 06
1953	21♎R07	21 D07	21 08	21 11	21 14
1954	23♎R18	23 D17	23 18	23 20	23 23
1955	25♎R29	25 D28	25 28	25 30	25 33
1956	27♎R40	27 D39	27 39	27 40	27 43
1957	29♎R51	29 50	29 D50	29 50	29 52
1958	02♏R03	02 01	02 D00	02 01	02 02
1959	04♏R15	04 13	04 D11	04 11	04 12
1960	06♏R27	06 24	06 22	06 D22	06 23
1961	08♏R39	08 35	08 33	08 D33	08 33
1962	10♏R51	10 47	10 45	10 D43	10 43
1963	13♏R03	12 59	12 56	12 54	12 D53
1964	15♏R14	15 10	15 07	15 05	15 D04
1965	17♏R27	17 22	17 18	17 16	17 D14
1966	19♏R39	19 34	19 30	19 27	19 25
1967	21♏R52	21 47	21 42	21 39	21 36
1968	24♏R05	23 59	23 54	23 50	23 48
1969	26♏R18	26 12	26 07	26 03	25 59
1970	28♏R31	28 25	28 19	28 15	28 11
1971	00♐R45	00 39	00 33	00 28	00 24
1972	02♐R58	02 51	02 45	02 40	02 36
1973	05♐R12	05 05	04 58	04 53	04 48
1974	07♐R26	07 18	07 12	07 06	07 01
1975	09♐R40	09 32	09 25	09 19	09 13
1976	11♐R53	11 45	11 38	11 31	11 25
1977	14♐R07	13 59	13 51	13 44	13 38
1978	16♐R21	16 12	16 04	15 57	15 51
1979	18♐R35	18 26	18 18	18 11	18 04
1980	20♐R48	20 39	20 31	02 23	20 16
1981	23♐R03	22 54	22 45	22 37	22 30
1982	25♐R18	25 09	25 00	24 52	24 44
1983	27♐R34	27 24	27 15	27 07	26 59
1984	29♐R47	29 38	29 29	29 20	29 12
1985	02♐R03	01 53	01 44	01 35	01 27
1986	04♑R19	04 09	04 00	03 51	03 42
1987	06♑R34	06 24	06 15	06 06	05 57
1988	08♑R48	08 38	08 29	08 19	08 11
1989	11♑R03	10 54	10 44	10 35	10 24
1990	13♑R19	13 09	13 00	12 50	12 41
1991	15♑R34	15 25	15 15	15 05	14 56
1992	17♑R48	17 39	17 29	17 19	17 10
1993	20♑R04	19 55	19 45	19 35	19 26
1994	22♑R20	22 10	22 01	21 51	21 41
1995	24♑R36	24 26	24 17	24 07	23 56
1996	26♑R50	26 41	26 31	26 22	26 12
1997	29♑R06	28 57	28 48	28 38	28 28
1998	01♒R23	01 13	01 04	00 54	00 45
1999	03♒R38	03 30	03 20	03 11	03 01
2000	05♒R53	05 44	05 35	05 26	05 16

August

Year	1st	7th	13th	19th	25th
1900	28 14	28 25	28 34	28 43	28 51
1901	00 23	00 34	00 44	00 54	01 02
1902	02 33	02 44	02 54	03 04	03 12
1903	04 42	04 53	05 04	05 13	05 23
1904	06 52	07 04	07 15	07 25	07 33
1905	09 01	09 13	09 24	09 35	09 44
1906	11 10	11 22	11 34	11 44	11 54
1907	13 19	13 31	13 43	13 54	14 04
1908	15 30	15 42	15 54	16 05	16 16
1909	17 38	17 51	18 03	18 14	18 25
1910	19 47	19 59	20 12	20 23	20 34
1911	21 55	22 08	22 20	22 52	22 43
1912	24 05	24 18	24 30	24 42	24 54
1913	26 13	26 26	26 38	26 51	27 02
1914	28 20	28 33	28 46	28 59	29 11
1915	000 28	00 41	00 54	01 06	01 19
1916	02 37	02 51	03 04	03 16	03 29
1917	04 45	04 58	05 11	05 24	05 37
1918	06 52	07 06	07 19	07 32	07 45
1919	09 00	09 13	09 27	09 40	09 53
1920	11 10	11 23	11 36	11 49	12 02
1921	13 17	13 30	13 44	13 57	14 10
1922	15 24	15 37	15 51	16 04	16 17
1923	17 31	17 44	17 58	18 11	18 24
1924	19 40	19 53	20 09	20 20	20 33
1925	21 47	22 00	22 13	22 26	22 40
1926	23 53	24 06	24 19	24 33	24 46
1927	26 00	26 13	26 26	26 39	26 52
1928	28 08	28 21	28 34	28 48	29 01
1929	00 15	00 28	00 41	00 54	01 07
1930	02 22	02 35	02 47	03 01	03 14
1931	04 29	04 41	04 54	05 07	05 21
1932	06 38	06 50	07 03	07 16	07 29
1933	08 45	08 57	09 10	09 23	09 36
1934	10 52	11 06	11 19	11 29	11 42
1935	12 59	13 11	13 23	13 36	13 48
1936	15 08	15 19	15 31	15 44	15 57
1937	17 15	17 26	17 38	17 50	18 03
1938	19 21	19 32	19 44	19 56	20 08
1939	21 28	21 38	21 50	22 02	22 14
1940	23 36	23 47	23 58	24 10	24 22
1941	25 43	25 53	26 04	26 16	26 28
1942	27 50	28 00	28 10	28 22	28 34
1943	29♎57	00 07	00 17	00 28	00 40
1944	02 06	02 16	02 26	02 37	02 48
1945	04 14	04 23	04 33	04 44	04 55
1946	06 22	06 31	06 40	06 50	07 01
1947	08 30	08 38	08 47	08 57	09 08
1948	10 39	10 47	10 56	11 06	11 16
1949	12 47	12 55	13 03	13 13	13 23
1950	14 55	15 02	15 10	15 19	15 29
1951	17 03	17 10	17 17	17 26	17 35
1952	19 12	19 18	19 26	19 34	19 44
1953	21 20	21 26	21 33	21 41	21 50
1954	23 29	23 34	23 41	23 49	23 57
1955	25 37	25 43	25 49	25 56	26 04
1956	27 47	27 52	27 58	28 05	28 13
1957	29 56	00♏01	00 06	00 13	00 20
1958	02 06	02 09	02 15	02 21	02 28
1959	04 15	04 18	04 23	04 29	04 36
1960	06 25	06 28	06 33	06 38	06 45
1961	08 35	08 37	08 41	08 46	08 53
1962	10 44	10 47	10 50	10 55	11 00
1963	12 54	12 56	12 59	13 03	13 08
1964	15 04	15 06	15 08	15 12	15 17
1965	17 14	17 15	17 17	17 21	17 25
1966	19 D24	19 25	19 27	19 30	19 34
1967	21 D35	21 D35	21 36	21 39	21 42
1968	23 46	23 D46	23 47	23 49	23 52
1969	25 57	25 D56	25 57	25 59	26 01
1970	28 09	28 D08	28 08	28 09	28 12
1971	00 20	00 D19	00 18	00 19	00 21
1972	02 32	02 30	02 D29	02 30	02 31
1973	04 44	04 42	04 D40	04 40	04 41
1974	06 56	06 53	06 51	06 D51	06 51
1975	09 08	09 05	09 03	09 D02	09 02
1976	11 20	11 16	11 14	11 D12	11 12
1977	13 32	13 28	13 25	13 23	13 D22
1978	15 44	15 40	15 37	15 34	15 D33
1979	17 57	17 52	17 48	17 46	17 D44
1980	20 09	20 04	20 00	19 57	19 D55
1981	22 23	22 17	22 13	22 09	22 07
1982	24 36	24 31	24 26	24 22	24 19
1983	26 50	26 44	26 39	26 35	26 31
1984	29 04	28 57	28 52	28 47	28 44
1985	01♑R18	01 11	01 05	01 00	00 56
1986	03 33	03 26	03 19	03 14	03 09
1987	05 47	05 40	05 33	05 28	05 23
1988	08 01	07 53	07 46	07 40	07 35
1989	10 16	10 08	10 00	09 54	09 49
1990	12 30	12 22	12 15	12 08	12 02
1991	14 46	14 37	14 29	14 22	14 16
1992	16 59	16 51	16 43	16 35	16 29
1993	19 15	19 06	18 58	18 50	18 43
1994	21 30	21 21	21 13	21 05	20 58
1995	23 46	23 37	23 28	23 20	23 13
1996	26 01	25 52	25 43	25 34	25 27
1997	28 17	28 08	27 59	27 50	27 42
1998	00 33	00 24	00 15	00 06	29 58
1999	02 50	02 40	02 31	02 22	02 13
2000	05 04	04 55	04 45	04 36	04 28

September

Year	1st	7th	13th	19th	25th
1900	28 59	29 05	29 09	29 13	29♊15
1901	01 10	01 16	01 21	01 25	01♋28
1902	03 21	03 28	03 33	03 38	03♋41
1903	05 32	05 39	05 45	05 50	05♋53
1904	07 44	07 51	07 57	08 02	08♋06
1905	09 54	10 02	10 09	10 14	10♋19
1906	12 05	12 13	12 20	12 26	12♋31
1907	14 15	14 24	14 31	14 38	14♋43
1908	16 27	16 36	16 43	16 50	16♋56
1909	18 37	18 46	18 54	19 01	19♋07
1910	20 46	20 56	21 05	21 12	21♋19
1911	22 56	23 06	23 15	23 23	23♋30
1912	25 07	25 17	25 26	25 34	25♋41
1913	27 15	27 26	27 35	27 44	27♋52
1914	29 24	29 35	29 44	29♌55	00♌02
1915	01 32	01 43	01 53	02 01	02♌11
1916	03 42	03 54	04 04	04 14	04♌22
1917	05 51	06 02	06 13	06 23	06♌32
1918	07 59	08 11	08 22	08 32	08♌41
1919	10 07	10 19	10 31	10 41	10♌51
1920	12 17	12 29	12 40	12 51	13♌01
1921	15 53	15 56	15 58	15 59	15♌58
1922	16 32	16 44	16 56	17 08	17♌18
1923	18 39	18 52	19 04	19 15	19♌26
1924	20 48	21 01	21 13	21 25	21♌36
1925	22 55	23 08	23 20	23 32	23♌44
1926	25 01	25 14	25 27	25 39	25♌51
1927	27 08	27 21	27 34	27 46	27♌58
1928	29 17	29 30	29 42	29♍55	00♍07
1929	01 23	01 36	01 49	02 02	02♍14
1930	03 30	03 43	03 56	04 09	04♍21
1931	05 36	05 49	06 03	06 16	06♍28
1932	07 45	07 58	08 11	08 24	08♍37
1933	09 51	10 05	10 18	10 31	10♍44
1934	11 58	12 11	12 24	12 38	12♍51
1935	14 04	14 17	14 31	14 44	14♍57
1936	16 12	16 25	16 39	16 52	17♍05
1937	18 18	18 31	18 45	18 58	19♍11
1938	20 24	20 37	20 50	21 03	21♍17
1939	22 29	22 42	22 55	23 09	23♍22
1940	24 37	24 50	25 03	25 16	25♍30
1941	26 42	26 55	27 08	27 22	27♍35
1942	28 48	29 01	29 14	29 27	29♍41
1943	00 54	01 07	01 20	01 33	01♎46
1944	03 02	03 15	03 28	03 41	03♎54
1945	05 09	05 19	05 34	05 47	06♎00
1946	07 15	07 27	07 40	07 53	08♎06
1947	09 21	09 33	09 46	09 59	10♎12
1948	11 29	11 41	11 54	12 07	12♎20
1949	13 36	13 47	14 00	14 12	14♎25
1950	15 41	15 53	16 05	16 17	16♎30
1951	17 48	17 59	18 11	18 23	18♎36
1952	19 56	20 07	20 18	20 30	20♎43
1953	22 02	22 13	22 24	22 36	22♎48
1954	24 08	24 19	24 30	24 42	24♎54
1955	26 15	26 25	26 36	26 47	27♎00
1956	28 23	28 33	28 44	28 55	29♎07
1957	00 30	00 40	00 50	01 01	01♏13
1958	02 38	02 47	02 57	03 08	03♏19
1959	04 45	04 54	05 03	05 14	05♏25
1960	06 54	07 02	07 12	07 22	07♏33
1961	09 01	09 09	09 18	09 28	09♏39
1962	11 08	11 16	11 25	11 35	11♏45
1963	13 16	13 23	13 32	13 41	13♏51
1964	15 24	15 32	15 40	15 49	15♏59
1965	17 32	17 39	17 46	17 55	18♏05
1966	19 40	19 46	19 53	20 02	20♏11
1967	21 49	21 54	22 01	22 09	22♏18
1968	23 57	24 03	24 10	24 18	24♏26
1969	26 06	26 11	26 18	26 25	26♏33
1970	28 15	28 20	28 26	28 33	28♏41
1971	00 24	00 29	00 34	00 41	00♏48
1972	02 35	02 39	02 44	02 50	02♏57
1973	04 44	04 48	04 52	04 58	05♏05
1974	06 54	06 57	07 01	07 06	07♏13
1975	09 03	09 06	09 10	09 15	09♐21
1976	11 13	11 16	11 19	11 24	11♐29
1977	13 23	13 25	13 28	13 32	13♐37
1978	15 33	15 35	15 37	15 42	15♐47
1979	17 44	17 44	17 47	17 50	17♐55
1980	19 54	19 55	19 57	20 00	20♐04
1981	22 05	22 D06	22 07	22 09	22♐13
1982	24 17	24 D17	24 17	24 19	24♐23
1983	26 29	26 D28	26 28	26 30	26♐32
1984	28 41	28 D40	28 40	28 41	28♐43
1985	00 53	00 51	00 D51	00 52	00♑54
1986	03 06	03 04	03 D03	03 03	03♑04
1987	05 18	05 16	05 D14	05 14	05♑15
1988	07 31	07 28	07 26	07 D25	07♑26
1989	09 43	09 40	09 38	09 D37	09♑37
1990	11 56	11 53	11 50	11 D48	11♑48
1991	14 10	14 06	14 02	14 00	14♑D00
1992	16 22	16 18	16 15	16 12	16♑D11
1993	18 36	18 31	18 27	18 25	18♑D23
1994	20 51	20 45	20 41	20 38	20♑36
1995	23 05	22 59	22 55	22 51	22♑R48
1996	25 19	25 13	25 08	25 04	25♑R01
1997	27 34	27 27	27 22	27 18	27♑R14
1998	29 49	29 42	29 36	29 32	29♑R28
1999	02 04	01 57	01 51	01 46	01♒R42
2000	04 18	04 11	04 05	03 59	03♒R55

	October					November					December				
	1st	7th	13th	19th	25th	1st	7th	13th	19th	25th	1st	7th	13th	19th	25th
1900	29♊R16	29 15	29 14	29 11	29 08	29 02	28 56	28 49	28 41	28 32	28 23	28 13	28 03	27 53	27♊R43
1901	01♋R29	01 30	01 29	01 26	01 23	01 18	01 12	01 05	00 58	00 50	00 41	00 31	00 21	00♊11	00♊R01
1902	03♋R43	03 43	03 43	03 41	03 38	03 34	03 28	03 22	03 15	03 07	02 58	02 49	02 39	02 29	02♋R19
1903	05♋R56	05 57	05 57	05 56	05 54	05 49	05 45	05 39	05 32	05 24	05 16	05 07	04 57	04 47	04♋R37
1904	08♋R09	08 11	08 11	08 10	08 08	08 04	08 00	07 54	07 48	07 40	07 32	07 23	07 13	07 04	06♋R54
1905	10♋R22	10 24	10 25	10 25	10 23	10 20	10 16	10 11	10 04	09 57	09 49	09 41	09 31	09 22	09♋R12
1906	12♋R35	12 37	12 39	12 39	12 38	12 35	12 32	12 27	12 21	12 14	12 07	11 58	11 49	11 40	11♋R30
1907	14♋R47	14 51	14 52	14 53	14 53	14 50	14 47	14 43	14 38	14 31	14 24	14 16	14 07	13 58	13♋R48
1908	17♋R04	17 04	17 06	17 07	17 07	17 05	17 02	16 58	16 53	16 47	16 40	16 32	16 23	16 14	16♋R04
1909	19♋R13	19 16	19 19	19 21	19 21	19 20	19 17	19 14	19 09	19 03	18 57	18 49	18 41	18 32	18♋R22
1910	21♋R24	21 29	21 32	21 34	21 34	21 34	21 32	21 29	21 25	21 19	21 13	21 06	20 58	20 49	20♋R40
1911	23♋R36	23 40	23 44	23 47	23 48	23 48	23 46	23 44	23 40	23 35	23 29	23 22	23 15	23 06	22♋R57
1912	25♋R47	25 53	25 57	25 59	26 01	26 01	26 00	25 58	25 54	25 50	25 44	25 37	25 30	25 22	25♋R13
1913	27♋58	28 04	28 08	28 11	28 14	28 14	28 14	28 12	28 09	28 05	28 00	27 53	27 46	27 38	27♋R30
1914	00♌09	00 15	00 20	00 23	00 26	00 27	00 27	00 26	00 23	00 20	00 15	00 09	00♋02	29 55	29♋R46
1915	02♌19	02 25	02 31	02 35	02 38	02 40	02 40	02 40	02 38	02 34	02 30	02 25	02 18	02 11	02♌R03
1916	04♌30	04 37	04 43	04 47	04 50	04 53	04 54	04 53	04 51	04 48	04 44	04 39	04 33	04 26	04♌R18
1917	06♌40	06 47	06 53	06 58	07 02	07 05	07 06	07 06	07 05	07 03	06 59	06 54	06 49	06 42	06♌R34
1918	08♌50	08 58	09 04	09 10	09 14	09 18	09 19	09 20	09 19	09 17	09 14	09 10	09 04	08 58	08♌R51
1919	11♌00	11 08	11 15	11 21	11 25	11 29	11 32	11 33	11 33	11 31	11 28	11 25	11 20	11 14	11♌R07
1920	13♌10	13 19	13 26	13 32	13 37	13 42	13 44	13 46	13 46	13 44	13 42	13 39	13 34	13 28	13♌R22
1921	15♌56	15 53	15 49	15 43	15 37	14 25	14 37	14 48	15 00	15 10	15 19	15 28	15 36	15 42	15♌R48
1922	17♌28	17 37	17 45	17 52	17 58	18 04	18 08	18 10	18 11	18 11	18 09	18 07	18 03	17 58	17♌R52
1923	19♌37	19 46	19 55	20 02	20 09	20 15	20 19	20 22	20 23	20 23	20 23	20 20	20 17	20 13	20♌R07
1924	21♌46	21 56	22 05	22 13	22 19	22 26	22 30	22 33	22 35	22 36	22 35	22 33	22 30	22 26	22♌R21
1925	23♌54	24 04	24 13	24 21	24 29	24 36	24 40	24 44	24 46	24 47	24 47	24 46	24 44	24 40	24♌R35
1926	26♌02	26 12	26 22	26 30	26 38	26 45	26 51	26 55	26 57	26 59	27 00	26 59	26 57	26 53	26♌R49
1927	28♌09	28 20	28 30	28 39	28 47	28 55	29 00	29 05	29 08	29 10	29 11	29 11	29 09	29 07	29♌R03
1928	00♍18	00 29	00 49	00 48	00 57	01 05	01 11	01 16	01 19	01 22	01 23	01 23	01 22	01 19	01♍R16
1929	02♍26	02 37	02 47	02 57	03 50	03 14	03 21	03 26	03 30	03 33	03 35	03 35	03 34	03 32	03♍R29
1930	04♍33	04 44	04 55	05 05	05 14	05 23	05 30	05 36	05 41	05 44	05 46	05 47	05 47	05 45	05♍R43
1931	06♍40	06 52	07 03	07 13	07 22	07 32	07 40	07 46	07 51	07 55	07 58	07 59	07 59	07 58	07♍R56
1932	08♍49	09 01	09 12	09 23	09 32	09 42	09 50	10 56	10 02	10 06	10 09	10 11	10 11	10 11	10♍R09
1933	10♍56	11 08	11 20	11 30	11 40	11 51	11 59	12 06	12 12	12 16	12 20	12 22	12 23	12 23	12♍R22
1934	13♍03	13 15	13 27	13 38	13 48	13 59	14 08	14 15	14 21	14 26	14 30	14 33	14 35	14 35	14♍R34
1935	15♍10	15 22	15 34	15 45	15 56	16 07	16 16	16 24	16 30	16 36	16 41	16 44	16 46	16 47	16♍R46
1836	17♍18	17 31	17 43	18 54	18 05	18 16	18 25	18 33	18 40	18 46	18 51	18 55	18 57	18 58	18♍R58
1937	19♍24	19 37	19 49	20 01	20 12	20 24	20 33	20 41	20 49	20 55	21 00	21 04	21 07	21 09	21♍R09
1938	21♍30	21 43	21 55	22 07	22 18	22 31	22 40	22 49	23 57	23 04	23 09	23 14	23 17	23 19	23♍R20
1939	23♍35	23 48	24 01	24 13	24 23	24 37	24 47	24 56	25 05	25 12	25 18	25 23	25 27	25 30	25♍R31
1940	25♍43	25 56	26 09	26 21	26 33	26 46	26 56	27 05	27 14	27 21	27 28	27 33	27 37	27 40	27♍R41
1941	27♍49	28 02	28 14	28 27	28 39	28 52	29 03	29 12	29 21	29 29	29 36	29 42	29 46	29 50	29♍52
1942	29♍54	00♎07	00 20	00 33	00 45	00 59	01 09	01 20	01 29	01 37	01 44	01 51	01 56	01 59	02♎02
1943	02♎00	02 13	02 26	02 39	02 51	03 05	03 16	03 27	03 36	03 45	03 53	04 59	04 05	04 09	04♎12
1944	04♎08	04 21	04 34	04 47	04 59	05 13	05 25	05 35	05 45	05 54	06 02	06 09	06 15	06 19	06♎23
1945	06♎14	06 27	06 40	07 53	07 06	07 20	07 32	07 43	08 53	08 02	08 10	08 18	08 24	08 29	08♎33
1946	08♎20	08 33	08 46	09 59	09 14	09 27	09 38	10 50	10 00	10 10	10 18	10 26	10 33	10 38	10♎43
1947	10♎25	10 39	11 52	11 05	11 18	11 33	11 45	12 56	12 07	12 17	12 26	12 34	12 41	12 47	12♎52
1948	12♎33	13 46	13 00	13 13	13 26	13 41	14 53	14 05	14 16	14 26	14 35	14 43	14 51	14 57	15♎02
1949	14♎38	15 52	15 05	15 19	15 32	15 47	16 59	16 11	16 22	16 33	16 42	16 51	17 59	17 06	17♎11
1950	16♎43	17 57	17 10	17 24	17 37	17 52	18 04	18 17	18 28	18 39	18 49	19 58	19 06	19 13	19♎20
1951	18♎49	19 02	19 15	19 29	19 42	19 57	20 10	20 22	20 34	20 45	20 56	21 05	21 14	21 21	21♎28
1952	20♎56	21 09	21 23	21 36	21 49	22 05	22 18	22 30	22 42	22 53	23 04	23 13	23 22	23 30	23♎37
1953	23♎01	23 14	23 28	23 41	23 55	24 10	24 55	24 58	25 00	25 01	25 01	25 00	24 57	24 54	24♎50
1954	25♎07	25 20	25 33	25 46	26 00	26 15	26 28	26 41	26 54	27 05	27 17	27 27	27 36	27 45	27♎53
1955	27♎12	27 25	27 38	27 52	28 05	28 21	28 34	28 47	28 59	29 11	29 23	29 34	29 43	29♏52	00♏01
1956	29♎20	29 33	29 46	29♏59	00 13	00 28	00 42	00 55	01 07	01 19	01 31	01 42	01 52	02 01	02♏10
1957	01♏25	01 38	01 51	02 05	02 18	02 34	02 47	03 00	03 13	03 25	03 37	03 48	03 59	04 08	04♏17
1958	03♏31	03 44	03 57	04 10	04 23	04 39	04 52	05 06	05 19	05 31	05 43	05 55	06 05	06 15	06♏23
1959	05♏37	05 49	06 02	06 15	06 29	06 44	06 58	07 11	07 24	07 37	07 49	08 01	08 12	08 22	08♏32
1960	07♏45	07 57	08 10	08 23	08 36	08 52	09 06	09 19	09 32	09 45	09 57	10 09	10 20	10 31	10♏40
1961	09♏51	10 03	10 15	10 28	10 42	10 57	11 11	11 24	11 37	11 50	12 03	12 15	12 27	12 37	12♏47
1962	11♏56	12 08	12 21	12 33	12 47	13 02	13 16	13 29	13 43	13 56	14 08	14 21	14 32	14 43	14♏54
1963	14♏02	14 14	14 26	14 39	14 52	15 07	15 21	15 34	16 47	16 01	16 14	16 26	16 38	16 49	17♏00
1964	16♏10	16 21	16 33	16 46	16 59	17 14	17 28	17 41	18 55	18 08	18 21	18 33	18 46	18 57	19♏08
1965	18♏15	18 26	18 38	19 51	19 03	19 19	19 32	19 46	20 59	20 10	20 26	20 38	21 51	21 03	21♏14
1966	20♏21	20 32	20 44	21 56	21 09	21 24	21 37	22 51	22 04	22 18	22 31	22 44	23 56	23 08	24♏25
1967	22♏28	22 38	23 50	23 01	23 14	23 29	23 42	24 56	24 09	24 23	24 36	25 49	25 02	25 14	25♏26
1968	24♏36	24 46	25 57	25 09	25 22	25 37	26 50	26 03	26 17	26 30	26 44	27 57	27 10	27 22	27♏34
1969	26♏43	27 53	27 04	27 15	27 27	27 42	28 55	28 09	28 22	28 36	28 49	29 02	29 15	29 28	29♏40
1970	28♏50	29 00	29 10	29 22	29 34	29 48	00♐01	00 14	00 28	00 41	00 55	01 08	01 21	01 34	01♐46
1971	00♐57	01 07	01 17	01 28	01 40	01 54	02 07	02 20	02 33	02 47	03 00	03 14	03 27	03 40	03♐53
1972	03♐06	03 15	03 25	03 36	03 48	04 02	04 15	04 28	04 41	04 55	05 08	05 22	05 35	05 48	06♐00
1973	05♐13	05 22	05 32	05 42	05 54	06 08	06 20	06 33	07 46	07 00	07 13	07 27	07 40	07 54	08♐06
1974	07♐20	07 29	07 38	08 49	08 00	08 13	08 26	08 39	09 52	09 05	09 19	09 32	09 46	09 59	10♐12
1975	09♐28	09 36	09 45	10 55	10 05	10 19	10 31	10 44	11 57	11 12	11 23	11 37	12 51	12 04	12♐17
1976	11♐36	11 44	12 53	12 03	12 13	12 26	12 38	13 51	13 04	13 17	13 31	13 44	14 58	14 11	14♐24
1977	13♐44	14 51	14 00	14 09	14 21	14 32	14 44	15 56	15 09	15 22	15 36	16 49	16 03	16 16	16♐30
1978	15♐52	16 59	16 07	16 16	16 26	16 38	17 50	17 02	17 14	17 27	17 41	18 54	18 08	18 21	18♐47
1979	18♐00	18 06	18 14	18 23	18 32	17 44	17 44	17 47	17 50	17 55	18 00	18 06	18 14	18 23	18♐32
1980	20♐09	20 15	20 23	20 31	20 41	20 53	21 04	21 15	21 28	21 43	21 54	22 07	22 21	22 34	22♐48
1981	22♐18	22 24	22 31	22 39	22 48	22 59	23 10	23 22	23 34	23 46	23 59	24 13	24 26	24 40	24♐53
1982	24♐27	24 32	24 39	24 47	24 55	25 06	25 17	25 28	25 40	25 52	26 05	26 19	26 32	26 46	26♐59
1983	26♐36	26 41	26 47	27 55	27 03	27 14	27 24	27 35	27 46	27 59	28 11	28 25	28 38	28 52	29♐05
1984	28♐48	28 52	29 57	29 04	29 12	29 23	29 33	29 44	29♑55	00 07	00 20	00 33	01 46	00 00	01♑16
1985	00♑57	01 01	01 06	01 13	01 20	01 31	01 40	10 51	02 02	02 14	02 26	02 39	03 52	03 06	03♑19
1986	03♑07	03 11	03 16	03 22	03 29	03 38	03 48	04 58	04 09	04 20	04 33	04 45	05 59	05 12	05♑26
1987	05♑17	05 20	05 25	05 30	05 37	05 46	06 55	06 05	06 16	06 27	06 39	07 52	07 05	07 18	07♑31
1988	07♑28	07 31	07 35	07 40	07 48	08 56	08 04	08 14	08 24	08 36	08 48	09 00	09 13	09 26	09♑40
1989	09♑38	09 41	09 45	09 49	09 55	10 04	10 12	10 21	10 31	10 42	10 54	11 06	11 19	11 32	11♑45
1990	11♑49	11 51	11 54	12 59	12 04	12 12	12 20	12 29	12 39	12 49	13 01	13 13	13 25	13 38	13♑51
1991	14♑00	14 01	14 04	14 08	14 13	14 21	14 28	14 37	14 46	14 56	15 07	15 19	15 31	15 44	15♑57
1992	16♑11	16 13	16 15	16 19	16 23	16 30	16 38	16 46	17 55	17 05	17 16	17 28	17 40	17 53	18♑06
1993	18♑23	18 24	18 26	18 29	18 33	18 40	18 46	19 54	19 03	19 13	19 23	19 35	19 47	19 59	20♑12
1994	20♑R35	20 D35	20 36	20 39	20 43	20 49	21 55	21 03	21 11	21 21	21 31	21 42	22 54	22 06	22♑19
1995	22♑R47	22 D47	22 48	22 50	22 53	23 59	23 05	23 12	23 20	23 29	23 39	24 49	24 01	24 13	24♑26
1996	24♑R59	25 D59	25 00	25 01	25 05	25 10	25 15	25 22	25 30	25 39	25 48	26 59	26 10	26 22	26♑35
1997	27♑R12	27 D11	27 11	27 13	27 15	27 20	27 25	27 31	27 39	27 47	28 56	28 07	28 18	28 30	28♑42
1998	29♑R25	29 24	29 D23	29 24	29 26	29 30	29 35	29 41	29 48	29♒56	00 05	00 15	00 25	00 37	00♒R49
1999	01♒R38	01 36	01 D36	01 36	01 38	01 41	01 45	01 51	02 57	02 50	02 13	02 23	02 33	02 44	02♒R56
2000	03♒R51	03 49	03 D48	03 48	03 49	03 52	03 56	04 01	04 08	04 15	04 23	04 33	04 43	04 54	05♒R05

Pluto

January

Year	1st	7th	13th	19th	25th
1900	15♊R15	15 09	15 03	14 58	14 54
1901	16♊R16	16 10	16 04	15 59	15 54
1902	17♊R17	17 10	17 05	16 59	16 55
1903	18♊R18	18 12	18 06	18 00	17 55
1904	19♊R20	19 13	19 07	19 02	18 57
1905	20♊R21	20 14	20 08	20 03	19 58
1906	21♊R23	21 17	21 11	21 05	21 00
1907	22♊R26	22 20	22 13	22 08	22 02
1908	23♊R30	23 23	23 17	23 11	23 05
1909	24♊R32	24 26	24 19	24 13	24 08
1910	25♊R36	25 36	25 23	26 17	25 11
1911	26♊R41	26 34	26 27	26 19	26 13
1912	27♊R46	27 39	27 32	27 26	27 20
1913	28♊R50	28 43	28 36	28 30	28 24
1914	29♊R55	29 48	29 42	29 35	29 29
1915	01♋R02	00 55	00 48	00 41	00 35
1916	02♋R09	02 01	01 55	01 48	01 42
1917	03♋R15	03 08	03 01	02 54	02 48
1918	04♋R23	04 16	04 09	04 02	03 56
1919	05♋R32	05 24	05 16	05 10	05 04
1920	06♋R41	06 33	06 26	06 19	06 13
1921	07♋R49	07 42	07 35	07 27	07 21
1922	08♋R59	08 52	08 45	08 38	08 31
1923	10♋R10	10 03	09 55	09 48	09 41
1924	11♋R22	11 14	11 07	10 59	10 52
1925	12♋R32	12 25	12 17	12 10	12 03
1926	13♋R45	13 38	13 30	13 23	13 16
1927	14♋R59	14 51	14 43	14 36	14 29
1928	16♋R13	16 05	15 58	15 50	15 43
1929	17♋R27	17 20	17 12	17 04	16 57
1930	18♋R44	18 36	18 28	18 21	18 13
1931	20♋R01	19 53	19 45	19 38	19 30
1932	21♋R19	21 11	21 04	20 56	20 48
1933	22♋R37	22 29	22 21	22 14	22 06
1934	23♋R57	23 49	23 41	23 33	23 26
1935	25♋R18	25 10	25 02	24 54	24 46
1936	26♋R39	26 32	26 24	26 16	26 08
1937	28♋R01	27 53	27 45	27 37	27 29
1938	29♋R25	29 17	29 09	29 01	28 53
1939	00♌R49	00 42	00 34	00 26	00 18
1940	02♌R15	02 08	02 00	01 52	01 44
1941	03♌R42	03 34	03 26	03 18	03 10
1942	05♌R10	05 03	04 55	04 47	04 39
1943	06♌R40	06 33	06 25	06 17	06 09
1944	08♌R12	08 05	07 57	07 49	07 41
1945	09♌R43	09 36	09 28	09 20	09 12
1946	11♌R18	11 10	11 03	10 55	10 46
1947	12♌R53	12 46	12 39	12 31	12 22
1948	14♌R30	14 23	14 16	14 08	13 59
1949	16♌R08	16 01	15 53	15 45	15 37
1950	17♌R48	17 41	17 34	17 26	17 18
1951	19♌R29	19 23	19 16	19 08	19 00
1952	21♌R13	21 06	20 59	20 52	20 44
1953	22♌R57	22 50	22 43	22 36	22 28
1954	24♌R44	24 37	24 31	24 23	24 15
1955	26♌R32	26 26	26 20	26 12	26 05
1956	28♌R23	28 17	28 11	28 04	27 57
1957	00♍R14	00 09	00♌02	29 55	29 48
1958	02♍R08	02 03	01 57	01 50	01 43
1959	04♍R04	03 59	03 53	03 47	03 39
1960	06♍R02	05 57	05 51	05 45	05 38
1961	08♍R01	07 56	07 51	07 44	07 37
1962	10♍R02	09 58	09 53	09 46	09 40
1963	12♍R05	12 01	11 56	11 51	11 44
1964	14♍R10	14 07	14 02	13 57	13 51
1965	16♍R17	16 14	16 10	16 04	15 58
1966	18♍R26	18 24	18 20	18 15	18 09
1967	20♍R38	20 35	20 32	20 28	20 22
1968	22♍R51	22 49	22 46	22 42	22 37
1969	25♍R06	25 05	25 02	24 58	24 54
1970	27♍R24	27 23	27 20	27 17	27 13
1971	29♍R42	29 42	29 40	29 38	29 34
1972	02♎03	02 R03	02 02	01 59	01 56
1973	04♎25	04 R26	04 25	04 23	04 20
1974	06♎49	06 R50	06 49	06 48	06 45
1975	09♎13	09 R15	09 15	09 14	09 12
1976	11♎39	11 42	11 R43	11 42	11 41
1977	14♎07	14 10	14 R11	14 11	14 10
1978	16♎36	16 39	16 41	16 R42	16 41
1979	19♎06	19 10	19 12	19 R14	19 13
1980	21♎37	21 41	21 44	21 46	21 R47
1981	24♎09	24 14	24 18	24 20	24 R21
1982	26♎42	26 47	26 51	26 54	26 R56
1983	29♎14	29 20	29 25	29 29	29 31
1984	01♏48	01 54	01 59	02 04	02 07
1985	04♏22	04 29	04 35	04 39	04 43
1986	06♏55	07 03	07 09	07 14	07 18
1987	09♏28	09 36	09 43	09 49	09 53
1988	12♏00	12 10	12 13	12 23	12 28
1989	14♏34	14 43	14 51	14 57	15 03
1990	17♏05	17 15	17 23	17 30	17 36
1991	19♏36	19 46	19 55	20 03	20 09
1992	22♏06	22 16	22 27	22 34	22 41
1993	24♏37	24 48	24 57	25 06	25 13
1994	27♏05	27 16	27 26	27 35	27 43
1995	29♏32	29 44	29♐54	00 03	00 12
1996	01♐58	02 10	02 20	02 30	02 39
1997	04♐24	04 36	04 47	04 57	05 06
1998	06♐47	06 59	07 10	07 21	07 30
1999	09♐08	09 20	09 32	09 42	09 52
2000	11♐27	11 40	11 52	12 03	12 13

February

Year	1st	7th	13th	19th	25th
1900	14 49	14 46	14 44	14 42	14 D42
1901	15 49	15 46	15 44	15 42	15 D41
1902	16 50	16 46	16 44	16 42	16 41
1903	17 15	17 47	17 44	17 42	17 41
1904	18 52	18 48	18 45	18 43	18 41
1905	19 52	19 49	19 46	19 44	19 42
1906	20 54	20 51	20 48	20 45	20 44
1907	21 57	21 53	21 50	21 47	21 45
1908	23 00	22 56	22 52	22 49	22 48
1909	24 02	23 58	23 54	23 52	23 50
1910	25 06	25 01	24 58	24 55	24 53
1911	26 10	26 05	26 01	25 58	25 56
1912	27 14	27 09	27 05	27 02	26 59
1913	28 18	28 13	28 09	28 06	28 03
1914	29 23	29 18	29 14	29 10	29 08
1915	00 29	00 24	00 19	00 16	00 13
1916	01 35	01 30	01 25	01 22	01 19
1917	02 41	02 36	02 31	02 28	02 24
1918	03 49	03 43	03 39	03 35	03 31
1919	04 57	04 51	04 47	04 42	04 39
1920	06 06	06 00	05 55	05 51	05 47
1921	07 14	07 08	07 03	06 59	06 55
1922	08 24	08 18	08 13	08 08	08 04
1923	09 34	09 28	09 23	09 18	09 14
1924	10 45	10 39	10 33	10 28	10 24
1925	11 55	11 49	11 44	11 39	11 35
1926	13 08	13 02	12 56	12 50	12 46
1927	14 21	14 14	14 08	14 03	13 58
1928	15 35	15 28	15 22	15 17	15 12
1929	16 49	16 42	16 36	16 30	16 25
1930	18 05	17 58	17 52	17 46	17 41
1931	19 22	19 15	19 08	19 02	18 57
1932	20 40	20 33	20 26	20 20	20 14
1933	21 57	21 50	21 43	21 37	21 32
1934	23 17	23 10	23 03	22 56	22 50
1935	24 37	24 30	24 23	24 17	24 11
1936	25 59	25 52	25 44	25 38	25 32
1937	27 20	27 13	27 05	26 59	26 52
1938	28 44	28 36	28 29	28 22	28 15
1939	00 09	00♋01	29 53	29 46	29 40
1940	01 35	01 27	01 19	01 12	01 05
1941	03 00	02 52	02 45	02 38	02 31
1942	04 29	04 21	04 13	04 03	03 55
1943	05 59	05 51	05 43	05 36	05 28
1944	07 31	07 23	07 15	07 07	06 59
1945	09 02	08 54	08 46	08 38	08 30
1946	10 37	10 28	10 20	10 12	10 04
1947	12 12	12 04	11 56	11 48	11 40
1948	13 50	13 41	13 33	13 25	13 17
1949	15 27	15 19	15 10	15 02	14 54
1950	17 08	17 59	16 51	16 42	16 34
1951	18 50	18 41	18 33	18 24	18 16
1952	20 34	20 25	20 16	20 08	19 59
1953	22 18	22 09	22 00	21 52	21 43
1954	24 05	23 57	23 48	23 39	23 30
1955	25 55	25 46	25 37	25 28	25 20
1956	27 46	27 38	27 29	27 20	27 11
1957	29 R38	29 29	29 20	29 11	29 02
1958	01 33	01 24	01 16	01 06	00 57
1959	03 30	03 21	03 13	03 04	02 54
1960	05 29	05 20	05 11	05 02	04 53
1961	07 28	07 20	07 11	07 02	06 52
1962	09 31	09 22	09 14	09 05	08 55
1963	11 35	11 27	11 19	11 10	11 00
1964	13 42	13 34	13 26	13 17	13 08
1965	15 50	15 42	15 34	15 25	15 16
1966	18 01	17 54	17 45	17 37	17 27
1967	20 15	20 07	19 59	19 51	19 42
1968	22 30	22 23	22 15	22 07	21 58
1969	24 47	24 40	24 32	24 24	24 18
1970	27 06	26 59	26 52	26 44	26 35
1971	29 27	29 21	29 14	29 06	28 58
1972	01 51	01 44	01 37	01 29	01 21
1973	04 14	04 09	04 02	03 55	03 47
1974	06 41	06 35	06 29	06 22	06 14
1975	09 08	09 R04	08 58	08 51	08 44
1976	11 37	11 R33	11 28	11 22	11 14
1977	14 07	14 R03	13 58	13 52	13 45
1978	16 39	16 36	16 31	16 26	16 19
1979	19 12	19 09	19 05	19 00	18 54
1980	21 46	21 44	21 40	21 36	21 30
1981	24 20	24 19	24 16	24 11	24 06
1982	26 56	26 55	26 52	26 49	26 44
1983	29 R33	29 31	29 30	29 26	29 22
1984	02 R08	02 08	02 07	02 05	02 01
1985	04 45	04 R45	04 44	04 42	04 39
1986	07 21	07 R22	07 22	07 20	07 18
1987	09 57	09 R59	09 59	09 58	09 56
1988	12 32	12 35	12 R36	12 35	12 34
1989	15 08	15 10	15 R12	15 12	15 11
1990	17 42	17 45	17 47	17 R48	17 47
1991	20 15	20 19	20 22	20 R23	20 23
1992	22 48	22 52	22 56	22 58	22 R58
1993	25 20	25 25	25 29	25 31	25 R32
1994	27 51	27 56	28 00	28 03	28 05
1995	00 20	00 26	00 31	00 34	00 36
1996	02 48	02 54	02 59	03 04	03 06
1997	05 15	05 22	05 28	05 32	05 35
1998	07 40	07 47	07 53	07 58	08 01
1999	10 03	10 10	10 17	10 22	10 26
2000	12 23	12 32	12 38	21 44	12 49

March

Year	1st	7th	13th	19th	25th
1900	14♊42	14 42	14 44	14 46	14♊49
1901	15 41	15 41	15 43	15 45	14♊47
1902	16 42	16 D42	16 42	16 44	16♊46
1903	17 41	17 D41	17 42	17 43	17♊46
1904	18 41	18 D41	18 42	18 43	18♊46
1905	19 42	19 D42	19 42	19 44	19♊46
1906	20 43	20 D43	20 43	20 45	20♊47
1907	21 45	21 D44	21 45	21 46	21♊48
1908	22 46	22 D46	22 46	22 47	22♊49
1909	23 49	23 D48	23 48	23 49	23♊51
1910	24 52	24 D51	24 51	24 52	24♊53
1911	25 55	25 D54	25 54	25 54	25♊56
1912	26 58	26 D57	26 57	26 59	26♊59
1913	28 02	28 01	28 D00	28 01	28♊02
1914	29 06	29 05	29 D04	29 05	29♊06
1915	00 11	00 10	00 D09	00 09	00♋10
1916	01 17	01 15	01 D14	01 14	01♋15
1917	02 23	02 21	02 D20	02 20	02♋21
1918	03 30	03 28	03 26	03 D26	03♋27
1919	04 37	04 35	04 33	04 D33	04♋33
1920	05 44	05 42	05 41	05 D40	05♋41
1921	06 53	06 50	06 49	06 D48	06♋48
1922	08 02	07 59	07 57	07 D56	07♋56
1923	09 11	09 09	09 07	09 05	09♋D05
1924	10 21	10 18	10 16	10 15	10♋D14
1925	11 32	11 29	11 26	11 25	11♋D24
1926	12 43	12 40	12 38	12 36	12♋D35
1927	13 56	13 52	13 50	13 48	18♋D47
1928	15 08	15 05	15 02	15 00	14♋D59
1929	16 23	16 19	16 16	16 14	16♋D13
1930	17 38	17 34	17 31	17 28	17♋D27
1931	18 54	18 50	18 47	18 44	18♋R42
1932	20 10	20 06	20 03	20 00	19♋R58
1933	21 28	21 24	21 20	21 17	21♋R15
1934	22 47	22 43	22 39	22 36	22♋R34
1935	24 07	24 02	23 58	23 55	23♋R52
1936	25 27	25 22	25 18	25 14	25♋R12
1937	26 49	26 44	26 39	26 36	26♋R33
1938	28 11	28 06	28 02	27 59	27♋R55
1939	29 35	29 30	29 25	29 21	29♋R18
1940	01 00	00 54	00 49	00 45	00♌R42
1941	02 26	02 20	02 15	02 11	02♌R07
1942	03 54	03 48	03 43	03 38	03♌R33
1943	05 24	05 18	05 12	05 04	05♌R03
1944	06 54	06 47	06 42	06 36	06♌R32
1945	08 26	08 19	08 12	08 08	08♌R03
1946	10 00	09 53	09 47	09 41	09♌R36
1947	11 35	11 28	11 21	11 16	11♌R11
1948	13 10	13 03	12 57	12 51	12♌R46
1949	14 48	14 41	14 34	14 28	14♌R23
1950	16 29	16 21	16 14	16 08	16♌R02
1951	18 10	18 02	17 55	17 48	17♌R42
1952	19 52	19 44	19 37	19 30	19♌R24
1953	21 37	21 29	21 22	21 15	21♌R08
1954	23 25	23 16	23 08	23 01	22♌R55
1955	25 14	25 05	24 57	24 50	24♌R43
1956	27 03	26 55	26 47	26 39	26♌R32
1957	28 56	28 48	28 39	28 31	28♌R24
1958	00 51	00 42	00 34	00 26	00♍R18
1959	02 48	02 39	02 30	02 22	02♍R14
1960	04 45	04 36	04 27	04 19	04♍R11
1961	06 46	06 37	06 28	06 19	06♍R11
1962	08 49	08 40	08 31	08 22	08♍R13
1963	10 54	10 45	10 35	10 26	10♍R16
1964	13 00	12 50	12 41	12 32	12♍R23
1965	15 09	15 00	14 50	14 41	14♍R32
1966	17 21	17 12	17 02	16 53	16♍R43
1967	19 35	19 26	19 16	19 07	18♍R57
1968	21 50	21 41	21 31	21 21	21♍R12
1969	24 09	23 59	23 50	23 40	23♍R30
1970	26 29	26 20	26 10	26 00	25♍R51
1971	28 52	28 42	28 33	28 23	28♍R13
1972	01 15	01 05	00 56	00 46	00♎R36
1973	03 41	03 32	03 22	03 12	03♎R02
1974	06 09	06 00	05 50	05 41	05♎R31
1975	08 38	08 30	08 20	08 10	08♎R01
1976	11 08	10 59	10 50	10 41	10♎R31
1977	13 40	13 32	13 23	13 14	13♎R04
1978	16 14	16 06	15 58	15 48	15♎R39
1979	18 49	18 42	18 33	18 24	18♎R15
1980	21 25	21 17	21 09	20 59	20♎R49
1981	24 02	23 55	23 47	23 39	23♎R29
1982	26 40	26 34	26 26	26 18	26♎R09
1983	29 29	29 13	29 06	28 58	28♎R49
1984	01 57	01 51	01 44	01 37	01♏R28
1985	04 36	04 31	04 24	04 17	04♏R09
1986	07 15	07 10	07 04	06 58	06♏R50
1987	09 54	09 50	09 44	09 38	09♏R31
1988	12 31	12 28	12 23	12 17	12♏R10
1989	15 09	15 06	15 01	14 56	14♏R49
1990	17 46	17 44	17 40	17 35	17♏R29
1991	20 22	20 20	20 17	20 13	20♏R07
1992	22 58	22 56	22 53	22 49	22♏R44
1993	25 32	25 32	25 29	25 25	25♏R20
1994	28 R05	28 05	28 03	28 00	27♏R56
1995	00 37	00 37	00 34	00 33	00♐30
1996	03 08	03 08	03 07	03 05	03♐02
1997	05 36	05 R37	05 37	05 35	05♐R33
1998	08 03	08 05	08 R05	08 04	08♐R02
1999	10 28	10 30	10 R31	10 31	10♐R29
2000	12 52	12 54	12 R55	12 55	12♐R54

	April					May					June				
	1st	7th	13th	19th	25th	1st	7th	13th	19th	25th	1st	7th	13th	19th	25th
1900	14♊53	14 58	15 03	15 08	15 15	15 21	15 29	15 36	15 44	15 52	16 02	16 10	16 18	16 27	16♊35
1901	15♊52	15 56	16 01	16 07	16 13	16 19	16 27	16 34	16 42	16 50	16 59	17 08	17 16	17 24	17♊33
1902	16♊50	16 55	16 59	17 05	17 11	17 18	17 25	17 32	17 40	17 48	17 58	18 06	18 14	18 23	18♊31
1903	17♊50	17 54	17 58	18 04	18 10	18 16	18 23	18 31	18 38	18 46	18 56	19 04	19 13	19 21	19♊29
1904	18♊50	18 54	18 59	19 04	19 10	19 16	19 23	19 31	19 39	19 47	19 56	20 04	20 13	20 21	20♊30
1905	19♊50	19 54	19 58	20 04	20 09	20 16	20 23	20 30	20 38	20 46	20 55	21 04	21 12	21 21	21♊29
1906	20♊50	20 54	20 58	21 04	21 09	21 16	21 22	21 30	21 37	21 45	21 55	22 03	22 12	22 20	22♊29
1907	21♊51	21 55	21 59	22 04	22 10	22 16	22 23	22 30	22 37	22 45	22 55	23 03	23 12	23 20	23♊29
1908	22♊53	22 56	23 01	23 06	23 11	23 18	23 24	23 31	23 39	23 47	23 57	24 05	24 13	24 22	24♊30
1909	23♊54	23 58	24 02	24 07	24 12	24 18	24 25	24 32	24 40	24 48	24 57	25 06	25 14	25 23	25♊31
1910	24♊56	24 59	25 04	25 08	25 14	25 20	25 26	25 33	25 41	25 49	25 58	26 06	26 15	26 24	26♊32
1911	25♊58	26 02	26 05	26 10	26 15	26 21	26 28	26 35	26 42	26 50	26 59	27 08	27 16	27 25	27♊33
1912	27♊01	27 05	27 09	27 13	27 18	27 24	27 31	27 38	27 45	27 33	28 02	28 11	28 19	28 28	28♊37
1913	28♊05	28 08	28 11	28 16	28 21	28 27	28 33	28 40	28 47	28 55	29 04	29 13	29 21	29 30	29♊39
1914	29♊08	29 11	29 15	29 19	29 24	29 30	29 36	29 43	29 50	29♋58	00 07	00 15	00 24	00 33	00♋41
1915	00♋12	00 15	00 18	00 22	00 27	00 33	00 39	00 46	00 53	01 01	01 10	01 18	01 27	01 36	01♋44
1916	01♋17	01 20	01 23	01 27	01 33	01 38	01 44	01 51	01 58	02 06	02 15	02 23	02 32	02 41	02♋49
1917	02♋22	02 25	02 28	02 32	02 37	02 43	02 48	02 55	03 02	03 10	03 19	03 27	03 36	03 45	03♋54
1918	03♋28	03 31	03 34	03 38	03 42	03 47	03 53	04 00	04 07	04 15	04 24	04 32	04 41	04 49	04♋58
1919	04♋34	04 37	04 40	04 44	04 48	04 53	04 59	05 05	05 12	05 20	05 29	05 37	05 46	05 55	06♋03
1920	05♋42	05 44	05 47	05 51	05 55	06 00	06 06	06 12	06 19	06 27	06 36	06 44	06 53	07 02	07♋11
1921	06♋49	06 51	06 54	06 58	07 02	07 07	07 13	07 19	07 26	07 33	07 42	07 50	07 59	08 08	08♋17
1922	07♋57	07 59	08 02	08 05	08 09	08 14	08 20	08 26	08 32	08 40	08 49	08 57	09 06	09 14	09♋23
1923	09♋06	09 07	09 10	09 13	09 17	09 22	09 27	09 33	09 40	09 47	09 56	10 04	10 13	10 21	10♋30
1924	10♋15	10 17	10 19	10 22	10 26	10 31	10 36	10 42	10 49	10 56	11 05	11 13	11 22	11 31	11♋40
1925	11♋25	11 26	11 28	11 31	11 35	11 40	11 45	11 51	11 57	12 05	12 14	12 22	12 30	12 39	12♋48
1926	12♋35	12 36	12 38	12 41	12 45	12 49	12 54	13 00	13 07	13 14	13 23	13 31	13 39	13 48	13♋57
1927	18♋47	13 48	13 49	13 52	13 55	14 00	14 05	14 10	14 17	14 24	14 32	14 41	14 49	14 58	15♋07
1928	14♋59	15 00	15 02	15 04	15 08	15 12	15 17	15 22	15 29	15 36	15 45	15 53	16 01	16 10	16♋19
1929	16♋12	16 13	16 14	16 17	16 20	16 24	16 29	16 34	16 41	16 47	16 56	17 04	17 13	17 21	17♋30
1930	17♋R26	17 D 27	17 28	17 30	17 33	17 37	17 42	17 47	17 53	18 00	18 09	18 17	18 25	18 34	18♋43
1931	18♋R41	18 D 42	18 43	18 45	18 48	18 51	18 56	19 01	19 07	19 14	19 22	19 30	19 38	19 47	19♋56
1932	19♋R57	19 D 58	19 59	20 01	20 03	20 07	20 11	20 17	20 23	20 29	20 38	20 46	20 54	21 03	21♋12
1933	21♋R14	21 D 14	21 15	21 17	21 19	21 23	21 27	21 32	21 38	21 44	21 53	22 01	22 09	22 18	22♋27
1934	22♋R32	22 D 32	22 32	22 34	22 36	22 40	22 44	22 49	22 54	23 01	23 09	23 16	23 25	23 33	23♋42
1935	23♋R51	23 D 50	23 51	23 52	23 54	23 57	24 01	24 06	24 11	24 17	24 26	24 33	24 41	24 50	24♋59
1936	25♋R10	25 D 09	25 10	25 11	25 13	25 16	25 20	25 25	25 30	25 36	25 44	25 52	26 00	26 09	26♋18
1937	26♋R31	26 D 30	26 30	26 31	26 33	26 36	26 39	26 44	26 49	26 55	27 03	27 10	27 19	27 27	27♋36
1938	27♋R52	27 D 51	27 51	27 52	27 53	27 56	28 00	28 04	28 09	28 15	28 23	28 30	28 38	28 46	28♋55
1939	29♋R15	29 D 14	29 13	29 14	29 15	29 18	29 21	29 25	29 30	29 36	29 43	29 51	29♌58	00 07	00♌16
1940	00♌R39	00 37	00 D 37	00 37	00 39	00 41	00 44	00 48	00 53	00 59	01 06	01 14	01 21	01 30	01♌39
1941	02♌R04	02 03	02 D 02	02 02	02 03	02 05	02 08	02 12	02 17	02 22	02 30	02 27	02 44	02 53	03♌02
1942	03♌R31	03 29	03 D 28	03 28	03 29	03 31	03 33	03 37	03 42	03 47	03 54	04 01	04 09	04 17	04♌26
1943	04♌R59	04 47	04 D 56	04 55	04 56	04 58	05 00	05 04	05 08	05 13	05 20	05 27	05 34	05 43	05♌51
1944	06♌R28	06 26	06 D 25	06 24	06 25	06 26	06 29	06 32	06 36	06 41	06 48	06 55	07 03	07 11	07♌19
1945	07♌R59	07 57	07 55	07 D 54	07 55	07 56	07 58	08 01	08 05	08 10	08 17	08 24	08 31	08 39	08♌49
1946	09♌R32	09 29	09 27	09 D 26	09 26	09 27	09 29	09 32	09 36	09 40	09 47	09 54	10 01	10 09	10♌17
1947	11♌R06	11 03	11 00	10 59	10 D 59	11 00	11 01	11 04	11 08	11 14	11 18	11 25	11 32	11 39	11♌48
1948	12♌R41	12 37	12 35	12 34	12 D 33	12 34	12 35	12 38	12 41	12 46	12 52	12 48	13 05	13 13	13♌21
1949	14♌R18	14 14	14 11	14 10	14 D 09	14 09	14 10	14 13	14 16	14 20	14 26	14 32	14 39	14 47	14♌55
1950	15♌R56	15 52	15 49	15 47	15 D 46	15 46	15 47	15 49	15 52	15 56	16 02	16 07	16 14	16 21	16♌30
1951	17♌R37	17 32	17 29	17 27	17 D 25	17 25	17 26	17 27	17 30	17 34	17 39	17 45	17 51	17 58	18♌06
1952	19♌R18	19 13	19 10	19 08	19 D 06	19 05	19 06	19 08	19 10	19 14	19 19	19 24	19 31	19 38	19♌48
1953	21♌R02	20 57	20 54	20 51	20 49	20 48	20 D 48	20 49	20 51	20 55	21 00	21 05	21 11	21 18	21♌26
1954	22♌R48	22 43	22 39	22 36	22 33	22 32	22 D 32	22 35	22 38	22 40	22 42	22 47	22 53	23 00	23♌08
1955	24♌R36	24 30	24 26	24 22	24 20	24 18	24 D 18	24 19	24 20	24 23	24 27	24 32	24 38	24 44	24♌52
1956	26♌R25	26 19	26 14	26 11	26 08	26 06	26 D 06	26 06	26 08	26 10	26 14	26 19	26 24	26 31	26♌38
1957	28♌R16	28 11	28 06	28 02	27 59	27 57	27 D 56	27 56	27 57	27 59	28 03	28 07	28 12	28 18	28♌26
1958	00♍R10	00♌04	29 59	29 54	29 51	29 49	29 D 47	29 47	29 48	29 49	29 53	29♍57	00 02	00 08	00♍15
1959	02♍R06	01 59	01 54	01 49	01 45	01 43	01 41	01 D 40	01 41	01 42	01 45	01 49	01 53	01 59	02♍06
1960	04♍R02	03 56	03 50	03 45	03 41	03 38	03 36	03 D 35	03 36	03 37	03 40	03 43	03 48	03 54	04♍00
1961	06♍R02	05 55	05 49	05 44	05 39	05 36	05 34	05 33	05 D 32	05 33	05 36	05 39	05 43	05 48	05♍55
1962	08♍R04	07 57	07 50	07 45	07 40	07 36	07 34	07 32	07 D 32	07 32	07 34	07 37	07 41	07 45	07♍51
1963	10♍R08	10 01	09 54	09 48	09 43	09 39	09 35	09 34	09 D 32	09 32	09 34	09 36	09 40	09 45	09♍50
1964	12♍R13	12 05	11 58	11 52	11 47	11 43	11 39	11 37	11 36	11 D 35	11 37	11 39	11 42	11 47	11♍52
1965	14♍R22	14 14	14 07	14 00	13 54	13 50	13 46	13 43	13 41	13 D 41	13 41	13 43	13 46	13 50	13♍55
1966	16♍R33	16 25	16 17	16 10	16 06	15 59	15 55	15 52	15 49	15 D 48	15 49	15 50	15 53	15 56	16♍01
1967	18♍R47	18 38	18 30	18 23	18 16	18 10	18 06	18 03	18 00	17 D 59	17 58	17 59	18 01	18 05	18♍09
1968	21♍R01	20 52	20 44	20 37	20 30	20 24	20 19	20 15	20 13	20 D 11	20 10	20 11	20 13	20 16	20♍20
1969	23♍R19	23 10	23 02	22 54	22 47	22 41	22 35	22 31	22 28	22 D 26	22 24	22 25	22 26	22 29	22♍32
1970	25♍R39	25 29	25 22	25 13	25 06	24 59	24 54	24 49	24 45	24 43	24 41	24 D 41	24 42	24 44	24♍R47
1971	28♍R02	27 52	27 44	27 35	27 27	27 20	27 14	27 09	27 05	27 02	26 59	26 D 59	26 59	27 01	27♍R04
1972	00♎R25	00 15	00 06	29 57	29 49	29 42	29 36	29 30	29 26	29 22	29 20	29 D 19	29 19	29 20	29♍R23
1973	02♎R51	02 41	02 32	02 23	02 15	02 07	02 00	01 54	01 19	01 45	01 42	01 41	01 D 40	01 41	01♎R43
1974	05♎R19	05 09	05 00	04 50	04 42	04 34	04 27	04 20	04 15	04 10	04 05	04 05	04 D 04	04 04	04♎R06
1975	07♎R49	07 39	07 29	07 20	07 11	07 03	06 55	06 48	06 42	06 37	06 33	06 31	06 D 29	06 29	06♎30
1976	10♎R19	10 09	09 59	09 50	09 40	09 32	09 24	09 17	09 11	09 07	09 01	08 58	08 D 56	08 56	08♎56
1977	12♎R52	12 42	12 32	12 22	12 13	12 04	11 56	11 49	11 42	11 36	11 31	11 27	11 25	11 D 24	11♎24
1978	15♎R27	15 17	15 07	14 57	14 46	14 38	14 30	14 22	14 15	14 09	14 03	13 59	13 56	13 D 54	13♎54
1979	18♎R03	17 53	17 43	17 33	17 23	17 14	17 05	16 57	16 50	16 43	16 36	16 32	16 29	16 26	16♎R25
1980	20♎R39	20 29	20 19	20 09	19 59	19 50	19 41	19 32	19 25	19 18	19 11	19 06	19 02	19 00	18♎R58
1981	23♎R18	23 08	22 58	22 48	22 38	22 28	22 19	22 10	22 02	21 54	21 47	21 42	21 38	21 35	21♎R33
1982	25♎R58	25 48	25 38	25 28	25 18	25 08	24 58	24 49	24 41	24 33	24 25	24 20	24 15	24 11	24♎R09
1983	28♎R38	28 29	28 19	28 09	27 58	27 48	27 39	27 29	27 21	27 13	27 04	26 58	26 53	26 49	26♎R45
1984	01♏R18	01 08	00 58	00 48	00 38	00 28	00 18	00 09	00♎00	29 51	29♎R43	29 36	29 31	29 26	29♎R23
1985	03♏R59	03 50	03 40	03 30	03 20	03 09	03 00	02 50	02 41	02 32	02 23	02 16	02 10	02 05	02♏R00
1986	06♏R40	06 31	06 21	06 11	06 01	05 51	05 41	05 31	05 22	05 13	05 03	04 56	04 49	04 44	04♏R39
1987	09♏R21	09 12	09 03	08 53	08 43	08 33	08 23	08 13	08 03	07 53	07 44	07 36	07 29	07 23	07♏R18
1988	12♏R00	11 52	11 43	11 33	11 23	11 13	11 03	10 53	10 43	10 34	10 23	10 15	10 08	10 02	09♏R56
1989	14♏R41	14 32	14 23	14 14	14 04	13 54	13 44	13 34	13 24	13 15	13 04	12 56	12 48	12 41	12♏R36
1990	17♏R20	17 12	17 04	16 55	16 45	16 35	16 25	16 15	16 05	15 55	15 44	15 36	15 28	15 21	15♏R14
1991	19♏R59	19 52	19 44	19 35	19 25	19 15	19 05	18 55	18 45	18 35	18 24	18 16	18 07	18 00	17♏R53
1992	22♏R36	22 29	22 21	22 12	22 03	21 53	21 44	21 33	21 23	21 14	21 02	20 53	20 45	20 37	20♏R30
1993	25♏R14	25 07	24 59	24 51	24 42	24 32	24 23	24 13	24 03	23 53	23 41	23 32	23 23	23 15	23♏R08
1994	27♏R50	27 43	27 36	27 28	27 19	27 10	27 00	26 51	26 41	26 31	26 19	26 10	26 01	25 52	25♏R45
1995	00♐R24	00 18	00 12	00♏04	19 56	29 47	29 37	29 27	29 18	29 08	28 56	28 46	28 37	28 29	28♐R21
1996	02♐R57	02 51	02 44	02 37	02 29	02 20	02 11	02 01	01 51	01 42	01 30	01 20	01 11	01 02	00♐R54
1997	05♐R28	05 23	05 17	05 10	05 02	04 54	04 45	04 33	04 26	04 16	04 04	03 54	03 45	03 36	03♐R28
1998	07♐R58	07 53	07 47	07 41	07 34	07 25	07 17	07 07	06 58	06 48	06 37	06 27	06 17	06 08	05♐R59
1999	10♐R26	10 21	10 16	10 10	10 03	09 55	09 47	09 38	09 29	09 17	09 08	08 58	08 48	08 39	08♐R30
2000	12♐R51	12 47	12 42	12 36	12 30	12 22	12 14	12 05	11 56	11 46	11 35	11 25	11 16	11 06	10♐R57

Pluto

July

Year	1st	7th	13th	19th	25th
1900	16♊43	16 50	16 58	17 05	17 11
1901	17♊41	17 48	17 56	18 17	18 22
1902	18♊39	18 47	18 54	19 02	19 08
1903	19♊38	19 45	19 53	20 00	20 07
1904	20♊38	20 46	20 54	21 01	21 08
1905	21♊37	21 46	21 53	22 00	22 07
1906	22♊37	22 45	22 53	23 00	23 08
1907	23♊37	23 45	23 53	24 01	24 08
1908	24♊39	24 47	24 55	25 03	25 10
1909	25♊40	25 48	25 56	26 04	26 11
1910	26♊41	26 49	26 57	27 05	27 13
1911	27♊42	27 50	27 58	28 07	28 14
1912	28♊45	28 54	29 02	29 10	29 18
1913	29♊47	29 56	00♋04	00 12	00 20
1914	00♋50	00 59	01 07	01 15	01 23
1915	01♋53	02 02	02 10	02 19	02 27
1916	02♋58	03 07	03 15	03 24	03 32
1917	04♋02	04 11	04 20	04 28	04 35
1918	05♋07	05 16	05 25	05 33	05 41
1919	06♋12	06 21	06 30	06 39	06 47
1920	07♋20	07 28	07 37	07 46	07 54
1921	08♋26	08 35	08 44	08 52	09 01
1922	09♋32	09 41	09 50	09 59	10 08
1923	10♋39	10 49	10 58	11 07	11 15
1924	11♋49	11 58	12 07	12 16	12 25
1925	12♋57	13 06	13 15	13 24	13 33
1926	14♋06	14 15	14 24	14 34	14 43
1927	15♋16	15 25	15 34	15 44	15 53
1928	16♋28	16 37	16 47	16 56	17 05
1929	17♋40	17 49	17 58	18 08	18 17
1930	18♋52	19 01	19 11	19 20	19 30
1931	20♋05	20 15	02 24	20 34	20 43
1932	21♋21	21 30	21 40	21 50	21 59
1933	22♋36	22 45	22 55	23 05	23 14
1934	23♋52	24 01	24 11	24 20	24 30
1935	25♋08	25 18	25 27	25 37	25 47
1936	26♋27	26 37	26 46	26 56	27 06
1937	27♋45	27 55	28 05	28 15	28 24
1938	29♋05	29 14	29 24	29 34	29 44
1939	00♌25	00 34	00 44	00 54	01 04
1940	01♌48	01 58	02 08	02 18	02 28
1941	03♌11	03 20	03 30	03 40	03 51
1942	04♌35	04 45	04 54	05 05	05 15
1943	06♌00	06 10	06 20	06 30	06 40
1944	07♌29	07 38	07 48	07 58	08 09
1945	08♌57	09 07	09 16	09 27	09 37
1946	10♌26	10 36	10 46	10 56	11 06
1947	11♌57	12 06	12 16	12 26	12 37
1948	13♌30	13 40	13 50	14 00	14 11
1949	15♌04	15 13	15 23	15 33	15 44
1950	16♌38	16 48	16 58	17 06	17 18
1951	18♌15	18 24	18 34	18 44	18 55
1952	19♌54	20 04	20 13	20 24	20 34
1953	21♌34	21 44	21 55	22 03	22 14
1954	23♌16	23 25	23 35	23 45	23 55
1955	24♌59	25 09	25 18	25 28	25 39
1956	26♌46	26 55	27 05	27 15	27 25
1957	28♌34	28 42	28 52	29 02	29 12
1958	00♍22	00 31	00 40	00 50	01 00
1959	02♍13	02 22	02 31	02 40	02 51
1960	04♍07	04 16	04 25	04 34	04 45
1961	06♍02	06 10	06 19	06 28	06 39
1962	07♍58	08 06	08 15	08 24	08 34
1963	09♍57	10 04	10 13	10 22	10 32
1964	11♍59	12 06	12 14	12 24	12 33
1965	14♍01	14 09	14 17	14 25	14 35
1966	16♍07	16 13	16 21	16 31	16 39
1967	18♍14	18 21	18 28	18 36	18 46
1968	20♍25	20 31	20 39	20 47	20 56
1969	22♍37	22 43	22 50	22 58	23 07
1970	24♍52	24 57	25 04	25 11	25 20
1971	27♍08	27 13	27 19	27 26	27 34
1972	29♎27	29 31	29 37	29 44	29 52
1973	01♎47	01 51	01 56	02 03	02 10
1974	04♎08	04 12	04 17	04 23	04 31
1975	06♎32	06 35	06 40	06 46	06 52
1976	08♎58	09 01	09 05	09 11	09 17
1977	11♎25	11 28	11 32	11 37	11 41
1978	13♎55	13 57	14 00	14 04	14 11
1979	16♎26	16 27	16 30	16 33	16 38
1980	18♎58	18 59	19 02	19 05	19 10
1981	21♎32	21 33	21 35	21 37	21 41
1982	24♎R07	24 07	24 08	24 11	24 14
1983	26♎R44	26 43	26 43	26 45	26 48
1984	29♎R20	29 19	29 19	29 21	29 23
1985	01♏R58	01 56	01 56	01 57	01 59
1986	04♏R36	04 34	04 33	04 33	04 34
1987	07♏R14	07 11	07 10	07 09	07 10
1988	09♏R52	09 49	09 47	09 46	09 46
1989	12♏R31	12 27	12 24	12 23	12 23
1990	15♏R09	15 05	15 02	15 00	14 59
1991	17♏R47	17 43	17 39	17 36	17 35
1992	20♏R24	20 19	20 15	20 12	20 D10
1993	23♏R01	22 56	22 51	22 48	22 45
1994	25♏R38	25 32	25 27	25 23	25 20
1995	28♏R13	28 07	28 01	27 57	27 54
1996	00♐R47	00 40	00 34	00 29	00 26
1997	03♐R20	03 13	03 06	03 01	02 57
1998	05♐R51	05 44	05 37	05 32	05 27
1999	08♐R22	08 14	08 07	08 01	07 56
2000	10♐R49	10 40	10 34	10 27	10 22

August

Year	1st	7th	13th	19th	25th
1900	17 18	17 24	17 28	17 32	17 36
1901	18 17	18 22	18- 27	18 31	18 35
1902	19 16	19 21	19 26	19 31	19 34
1903	20 15	20 20	20 26	20 30	20 34
1904	21 15	21 21	21 26	21 31	21 35
1905	22 15	22 21	22 26	22 31	22 35
1906	23 15	23 21	23 27	23 32	23 36
1907	24 16	24 22	24 28	24 33	24 37
1908	25 18	25 24	25 30	25 35	25 40
1909	26 19	26 26	26 32	26 37	26 41
1910	27 21	27 27	27 33	27 39	27 44
1911	28 23	28 29	28 36	28 41	28 46
1912	29 26	29 33	29 39	29 45	29 50
1913	00 29	00 36	00 42	00 48	00 53
1914	01 32	01 39	01 45	01 51	01 57
1915	02 35	02 43	02 49	02 55	03 01
1916	03 41	03 48	03 55	04 01	04 07
1917	04 46	04 53	05 00	05 06	05 12
1918	05 51	05 58	06 05	06 12	06 18
1919	06 56	07 04	07 11	07 18	07 24
1920	08 04	08 12	08 19	08 26	08 32
1921	09 11	09 18	09 26	09 33	09 39
1922	10 18	10 25	10 33	10 40	10 47
1923	11 25	11 33	11 41	11 48	11 55
1924	12 35	12 43	12 51	12 58	13 05
1925	13 43	13 52	14 00	14 07	14 14
1926	14 53	15 01	15 09	15 17	15 24
1927	16 03	16 12	16 20	16 28	16 35
1928	17 16	17 24	17 33	17 41	17 48
1929	18 28	18 36	18 45	18 53	19 00
1930	19 40	19 49	19 58	20 06	20 14
1931	20 54	21 03	21 12	21 20	21 28
1932	22 10	22 19	22 28	22 37	22 45
1933	23 25	23 35	23 44	23 52	24 00
1934	24 41	24 51	25 00	25 09	25 17
1935	25 58	26 08	26 17	26 26	26 35
1936	27 17	27 27	27 36	27 45	27 54
1937	28 36	28 46	28 55	29 04	29 13
1938	29 56	00♌05	00 15	00 24	00 33
1939	01 16	01 26	01 36	01 45	01 55
1940	02 40	02 50	02 59	03 09	03 19
1941	04 03	04 13	04 23	04 33	04 42
1942	05 27	05 37	05 47	05 57	06 07
1943	06 52	07 03	07 13	07 23	07 33
1944	08 21	08 31	08 42	08 52	09 02
1945	09 49	10 00	10 11	10 21	10 31
1946	11 19	11 30	11 40	11 51	12 01
1947	12 49	13 00	13 11	13 23	13 34
1948	14 23	14 34	14 45	14 56	15 06
1949	15 59	16 08	16 19	16 29	16 40
1950	17 31	17 42	17 53	18 04	18 15
1951	19 07	19 18	19 30	19 41	19 52
1952	20 47	20 58	21 10	21 21	21 32
1953	22 27	22 38	22 49	23 01	23 12
1954	24 08	24 20	24 31	24 42	24 54
1955	25 51	26 03	26 14	26 26	26 37
1956	27 38	27 50	28 01	28 13	28 25
1957	29 25	29 36	29 48	00♍00	00 11
1958	01 13	01 25	01 36	01 48	02 00
1959	03 03	03 15	03 26	03 38	03 50
1960	04 57	05 09	05 21	05 33	05 45
1961	06 51	07 02	07 14	07 26	07 38
1962	08 47	08 58	09 10	09 22	09 34
1963	10 44	10 55	11 07	11 19	11 31
1964	12 46	12 57	13 09	13 21	13 33
1965	14 47	14 58	15 10	15 20	15 34
1966	16 51	17 02	17 14	17 26	17 38
1967	18 57	19 08	19 19	19 32	19 44
1968	21 07	21 18	21 29	21 41	21 54
1969	23 18	23 28	23 39	23 51	24 04
1970	25 31	25 41	25 52	26 04	26 18
1971	27 45	27 55	28 06	28 17	28 29
1972	00 03	00 13	00 23	00 35	00 47
1973	02 21	02 30	02 41	02 52	03 04
1974	04 40	04 50	04 59	05 11	05 22
1975	07 01	07 12	07 20	07 31	07 40
1976	09 26	09 25	09 44	09 55	10 06
1977	11 51	11 59	12 08	12 19	12 29
1978	14 17	14 25	14 34	14 44	14 55
1979	16 46	16 53	17 03	17 13	17 23
1980	19 17	19 24	19 32	19 41	19 51
1981	21 48	21 54	22 02	22 11	22 20
1982	24 20	24 26	24 33	24 41	24 51
1983	26 53	26 59	27 05	27 13	27 22
1984	29 28	29 33	29 39	29 47	29 55
1985	02 02	02 07	02 13	02 20	02 28
1986	04 37	04 41	04 47	04 53	05 00
1987	07 13	07 16	07 21	07 27	07 33
1988	09 48	09 51	09 56	10 01	10 08
1989	12 24	12 26	12 30	12 35	12 41
1990	14 59	15 01	15 04	15 09	15 14
1991	17 35	17 36	17 38	17 42	17 47
1992	20 10	20 10	20 13	20 16	20 21
1993	22 R44	22 D44	22 46	22 48	22 52
1994	25 R18	25 D18	25 28	25 21	25 24
1995	27 51	27 50	27 50	27 52	27 54
1996	00 23	00 D21	00 21	00 22	00 25
1997	02 53	02 51	02 D51	02 51	02 53
1998	05 23	05 20	05 D19	05 19	05 20
1999	07 51	07 48	07 46	07 D45	07 46
2000	10 17	10 14	10 11	10 D10	10 11

September

Year	1st	7th	13th	19th	25th
1900	17 39	17 41	17 42	17 42	17♊41
1901	18 38	18 40	18 41	18 42	18♊41
1902	19 38	19 40	19 41	19 42	19♊42
1903	20 38	20 40	20 41	20 42	20♊42
1904	21 38	21 41	21 42	21 43	21♊43
1905	22 39	22 42	22 43	22 44	22♊44
1906	23 40	23 43	23 46	23 46	23♊46
1907	24 42	24 44	24 47	24 48	24♊48
1908	25 44	25 47	25 49	25 50	25♊51
1909	26 46	26 49	26 51	26 53	26♊54
1910	27 48	27 52	27 54	27 56	27♊57
1911	28 51	28 54	28 57	28 59	29♊00
1912	29 55	29 58	00 01	00 03	00♊04
1913	00 58	01 02	01 05	01 07	01♋08
1914	02 02	02 06	02 09	02 11	02♋13
1915	03 07	03 11	03 14	03 16	03♋18
1916	04 12	04 16	04 20	04 22	04♋24
1917	05 18	05 22	05 26	05 28	05♋30
1918	06 24	06 28	06 32	06 35	06♋37
1919	07 30	07 35	07 39	07 42	07♋45
1920	08 38	08 43	08 48	08 50	08♋53
1921	09 59	09 56	09 52	09 47	09♋42
1922	10 54	10 59	11 03	11 07	11♋10
1923	12 02	12 07	12 12	12 16	12♋19
1924	13 12	13 17	13 22	13 26	13♋29
1925	14 21	14 27	14 32	14 36	14♋40
1926	15 32	15 39	15 43	15 48	15♋51
1927	16 43	16 49	16 54	16 59	17♋03
1928	17 56	18 02	18 07	18 12	18♋16
1929	19 09	19 15	19 21	19 26	19♋29
1930	20 22	20 29	20 35	20 40	20♋44
1931	21 37	21 44	21 50	21 55	22♋00
1932	22 53	23 00	23 06	23 12	23♋17
1933	24 09	24 16	24 23	24 29	24♋34
1934	25 26	25 34	25 40	25 46	25♋51
1935	26 44	26 51	26 58	27 04	27♋10
1936	28 04	28 11	28 18	28 25	28♋30
1937	29 23	29 31	29 38	29 45	29♋50
1938	00 43	00 51	00 59	01 06	01♌12
1939	02 05	02 13	02 21	02 28	02♌34
1940	03 29	03 37	03 45	03 52	03♌59
1941	04 53	05 01	05 09	05 17	05♌24
1942	06 18	06 27	06 35	06 43	06♌50
1943	07 44	07 53	08 02	08 10	08♌17
1944	09 13	09 23	09 31	09 39	09♌47
1945	10 43	10 52	11 01	11 09	11♌17
1946	12 13	12 22	12 31	12 40	12♌48
1947	13 44	13 54	14 03	14 12	14♌20
1948	15 18	15 28	15 38	15 47	15♌55
1949	16 53	17 03	17 12	17 22	17♌30
1950	18 28	18 38	18 48	18 58	19♌06
1951	20 05	20 15	20 25	20 35	20♌45
1952	21 45	21 56	22 06	22 16	22♌26
1953	23 25	23 36	23 47	23 57	24♌07
1954	25 07	25 18	25 29	25 40	25♌50
1955	26 51	27 02	27 13	27 24	27♌34
1956	28 38	28 50	29 01	29 12	29♌22
1957	00 25	00 37	00 48	01 00	01♍10
1958	02 14	02 26	02 38	02 49	03♍00
1959	04 04	04 16	04 28	04 40	04♍51
1960	05 59	06 11	06 23	06 35	06♍46
1961	07 53	08 05	08 17	08 29	08♍41
1962	09 48	10 01	10 13	10 26	10♍38
1963	11 46	11 59	12 11	12 24	12♍36
1964	13 48	14 00	14 13	14 26	14♍38
1965	15 49	16 02	16 15	10 27	16♍40
1966	17 53	18 06	18 19	18 31	18♍44
1967	19 59	20 11	20 25	20 38	20♍51
1968	22 09	22 22	22 35	22 48	23♍01
1969	24 18	24 31	24 45	24 58	24♍11
1970	26 31	26 43	26 57	27 10	27♍24
1971	28 44	28 57	29 10	29 24	29♍37
1972	01 01	01 14	01 28	01 41	01♎55
1973	03 18	03 31	03 44	03 58	04♎12
1974	05 37	05 49	06 03	06 16	06♎30
1975	07 56	08 09	08 22	08 36	08♎49
1976	10 20	10 33	10 46	10 59	11♎13
1977	12 43	12 57	13 09	13 22	13♎38
1978	15 08	15 20	15 33	15 46	16♎00
1979	17 34	17 46	17 59	18 12	18♎26
1980	20 04	20 16	20 28	20 41	20♎55
1981	22 33	22 44	22 57	23 09	23♎23
1982	25 03	25 14	25 24	25 41	25♎R52
1983	27 33	27 44	27 56	28 08	28♎R21
1984	00 07	00 17	00 28	00 41	00♏R53
1985	02 38	02 49	03 00	03 11	03♏R24
1986	05 11	05 20	05 31	05 42	05♏R55
1987	07 43	07 52	08 02	08 13	08♏R25
1988	10 17	10 26	10 36	10 47	10♏R58
1989	12 49	12 58	13 07	13 18	13♏R29
1990	15 22	15 30	15 39	15 49	15♏R59
1991	17 54	18 01	18 10	18 19	18♏R30
1992	20 27	20 34	20 42	20 51	21♏R01
1993	22 58	23 05	23 12	23 21	23♏R31
1994	25 29	25 35	25 42	25 50	25♏R59
1995	27 59	28 05	28 11	28 18	28♏R27
1996	00 29	00 34	00 40	00 47	00♐55
1997	02 57	03 01	03 06	03 13	03♐21
1998	05 23	05 27	05 32	05 38	05♐45
1999	07 48	07 51	07 56	08 01	08♐08
2000	10 12	10 15	10 19	10 24	10♐31

	October					November					December				
	1st	7th	13th	19th	25th	1st	7th	13th	19th	25th	1st	7th	13th	19th	25th
1900	17♊R40	17 38	17 35	17 32	17 28	17 22	17 16	17 10	17 04	16 58	16 51	16 44	16 37	16 30	16♊R23
1901	18♊R40	18 38	18 35	18 32	18 28	18 23	18 17	18 11	18 05	17 59	17 52	17 45	17 38	17 31	17♊R24
1902	19♊R41	19 39	19 36	19 33	19 29	19 24	19 18	19 13	19 07	19 00	18 53	18 46	18 39	18 33	18♊R26
1903	20♊R41	20 40	20 37	20 34	20 30	20 25	20 20	20 14	20 08	20 02	19 55	19 48	19 41	19 34	19♊R27
1904	21♊R42	21 41	21 38	21 35	21 33	21 26	21 21	21 16	21 10	21 03	20 56	20 49	20 42	20 35	20♊R29
1905	22♊R44	22 42	22 40	22 37	22 34	22 29	22 24	22 18	22 12	22 06	21 59	21 52	21 45	21 38	21♊R31
1906	23♊R46	23 45	23 43	23 40	23 36	23 31	23 26	23 21	23 15	23 09	23 02	22 55	22 48	22 41	22♊R34
1907	24♊R48	24 47	24 45	24 43	24 39	24 34	24 30	24 24	24 18	24 12	24 06	23 59	23 52	23 45	23♊R38
1908	25♊R51	25 50	25 48	25 45	25 42	25 37	25 32	25 27	25 21	25 15	25 08	25 01	24 54	24 47	24♊R40
1909	26♊R54	26 53	26 51	26 49	26 45	26 41	26 36	26 31	26 25	26 19	26 13	26 06	25 59	25 52	25♊R44
1910	27♊R57	27 56	27 55	27 52	27 49	27 45	27 40	27 35	27 30	27 24	27 17	27 10	27 03	26 56	26♊R49
1911	29♊R00	29 00	28 59	28 57	28 54	28 49	28 45	28 40	28 34	28 28	28 22	28 15	28 08	28 01	27♊R54
1912	00♋R04	00 04	00 03	00♊01	29 58	29 54	29 49	29 44	29 39	29 33	29 26	29 19	29 12	29 05	28♊R58
1913	01♋R09	01 09	01 07	01 06	01 03	00 59	00 55	00 50	00 44	00 38	00 32	00 25	00 18	00 11	00♋R04
1914	02♋R14	02 14	02 13	02 11	02 08	02 05	02 00	01 56	01 50	01 44	01 38	01 31	01 25	01 17	01♋R10
1915	03♋R19	03 19	03 18	03 17	03 14	03 11	03 07	03 02	02 57	02 51	02 45	02 38	02 31	02 24	02♋R17
1916	04♋R25	04 25	04 25	04 23	04 21	04 17	04 13	04 09	04 03	03 58	03 51	03 45	03 38	03 31	03♋R23
1917	05♋32	05R32	05 31	05 30	05 28	05 24	05 21	05 16	05 11	05 05	04 59	04 53	04 46	04 39	04♋R31
1918	06♋39	06R39	06 39	06 38	06 36	06 32	06 29	06 25	06 20	06 14	06 08	06 01	05 55	05 47	05♋R40
1919	07♋46	07R47	07 47	07 46	07 44	07 41	07 37	07 33	07 28	07 23	07 17	07 11	07 04	06 57	06♋R49
1920	08♋54	08R55	08 55	08 54	08 52	08 49	08 46	08 42	08 37	08 32	08 26	08 19	08 12	08 05	07♋R58
1921	10♋03	10R04	10 04	10 03	10 02	09 46	09 51	09 55	09 58	10 01	10 03	10 04	10 04	10 03	10♋R02
1922	11♋12	11R13	11 13	11 13	11 11	11 09	11 06	11 02	10 57	10 52	10 46	10 40	10 33	10 26	10♋R19
1923	12♋21	12 23	12R23	12 23	12 22	12 19	12 16	12 13	12 08	12 03	11 57	11 51	11 45	11 38	11♋R30
1924	13♋31	13 33	13R34	13 33	13 32	13 30	13 27	13 23	13 19	13 14	13 08	13 02	12 55	12 48	12♋R41
1925	14♋41	14 44	14R45	14 45	14 44	14 42	14 39	14 35	14 31	14 26	14 21	14 15	14 08	14 01	13♋R54
1926	15♋53	15 55	15R56	15 57	15 56	15 54	15 52	15 48	15 44	15 39	15 34	15 28	15 21	15 15	15♋R07
1927	17♋06	17 08	17 09	17R10	17 09	17 07	17 05	17 02	16 58	16 53	16 48	16 42	16 36	16 29	16♋R22
1928	18♋19	18 21	18 23	18R23	18 23	18 21	18 19	18 16	18 12	18 08	18 02	17 56	17 50	17 43	17♋R36
1929	19♋33	19 35	19 37	19R38	19 38	19 36	19 34	19 32	19 28	19 23	19 18	19 12	19 06	18 59	18♋R53
1930	20♋48	20 51	20 52	20R53	20 53	20 52	20 51	20 48	20 44	20 40	20 35	20 30	20 23	20 17	20♋R09
1931	22♋03	22 06	22 08	22R10	22 10	22 09	22 08	22 05	22 02	21 58	21 53	21 47	21 41	21 35	21♋R28
1932	23♋20	23 24	23 26	23R27	23 27	23 27	23 25	23 23	23 20	23 16	23 11	23 05	22 59	22 53	22♋R45
1933	24♋38	24 41	24 43	24 45	24R46	24 45	24 44	24 42	24 39	24 35	24 30	24 25	24 19	24 12	24♋R05
1934	25♋56	25 59	26 02	26 04	26R05	26 05	26 04	26 02	25 59	25 55	25 51	25 45	25 40	25 33	25♋R26
1935	27♋15	27 18	27 21	27 23	27R25	27 25	27 24	27 22	27 20	27 16	27 02	27 07	27 01	26 55	26♋R48
1936	28♋35	28 39	28 42	28 44	28R45	28 46	28 45	28 43	28 41	28 37	28 33	28 28	28 22	28 16	28♋R09
1937	29♋56	29♌59	00 03	00 06	00 07	00 08	00 07	00 06	00 03	00 00	29 56	29 51	29 46	29 40	29♋R33
1938	01♌17	01 22	01 25	01 28	01 30	01R31	01 30	01 29	01 27	01 24	01 20	01 16	01 10	01 04	00♌R58
1939	02♌40	02R45	02 48	02 51	02 54	02 55	02 55	02 54	02 52	02 49	02 46	02 41	02 36	02 30	02♌R24
1940	04♌04	04 09	04 13	04 17	04 19	04R20	04 20	04 20	04 18	04 15	04 12	04 07	04 02	03 56	03♌R50
1941	05♌30	05 35	05 39	05 43	05 45	05R47	05 47	05 47	05 45	05 43	05 40	05 35	05 30	05 25	05♌R18
1942	06♌56	07 01	07 06	07 10	07 13	07 15	07R15	07 15	07 14	07 12	07 09	07 05	07 00	06 55	06♌R48
1943	08♌24	08 29	08 34	08 38	08 41	08 44	08R45	08 45	08 44	08 42	08 39	08 36	08 31	08 26	08♌R20
1944	09♌53	09 59	10 05	10 09	10 12	10 15	10R16	10 16	10 15	10 14	10 11	10 07	10 03	09 57	09♌R51
1946	11♌24	11 30	11 35	11 40	11 44	11 46	11 48	11R48	11 48	11 46	11 44	11 41	11 36	11 31	11♌R25
1946	12♌55	13 02	13 07	13 12	13 17	13 20	13 21	13R22	13 22	13 21	13 19	13 15	13 11	13 06	13♌R01
1947	14♌28	14 35	14 41	14 46	14 50	14 54	14 56	14 57	14R57	14 56	14 54	14 52	14 48	14 43	14♌R38
1948	16♌03	16 10	16 16	16 22	16 26	16 30	16 32	16 34	16R34	16 33	16 31	16 29	16 25	16 20	16♌R15
1949	17♌38	17 46	17 52	17 58	18 03	18 07	18 10	18 11	18R12	18 12	18 10	18 08	18 04	18 00	17♌R55
1950	19♌15	19 23	19 29	19 36	19 40	19 45	19 49	19 51	19 52	19 51	19 50	19 48	19 45	19 41	19♌R36
1951	20♌53	21 01	21 08	21 15	21 20	21 26	21 29	21 31	21 33	21 33	21 32	21 30	21 28	21 24	21♌R19
1952	22♌35	22 43	22 50	22 57	23 02	23 08	23 12	23 14	23 16	23 16	23 16	23 14	23 11	23 08	23♌R03
1953	24♌16	24 25	24 32	24 39	24 45	24 51	24 55	24 58	25 00	25 R01	25 01	25 00	24 57	24 54	24♌R50
1954	25♌59	26 08	26 16	26 24	26 30	26 36	26 41	26 44	26 47	26 R48	26 48	26 47	26 45	26 42	26♌R38
1955	27♌44	27 53	28 02	28 10	28 16	28 23	28 28	28 32	28 35	28 36	28R37	28 26	28 35	28 32	28♌R28
1956	29♌32	29 42	29 50	29♍58	00 05	00 13	00 18	00 22	00♍25	00 26	00R27	00 27	00 26	00 23	00♍R20
1957	01♍21	01 30	01 39	01 48	01 55	02 03	02 08	02 13	02 16	02 18	02R19	02 20	02 19	02 16	02♍R13
1958	03♍11	03 21	03 30	03 39	03 46	03 55	04 00	04 05	04 09	04 12	04R13	04 14	04 13	04 12	04♍R09
1959	05♍02	05 12	05 22	05 31	05 39	05 48	05 54	06 00	06 04	06 07	06 09	06R10	06 10	06 08	06♍R06
1960	06♍58	07 08	07 18	07 27	07 36	07 44	07 51	07 57	08 01	08 04	08 07	08R08	08 08	08 07	08♍R04
1961	08♍52	09 03	09 14	09 23	09 32	09 41	09 48	09 54	09 59	10 03	10 06	10 07	10R08	10 07	10♍R05
1962	10♍49	11 00	11 11	11 21	11 30	11 40	11 47	11 54	11 59	12 04	12 07	12 09	12R10	12 09	12♍R08
1963	12♍48	12 59	13 10	13 21	13 30	13 40	13 48	13 55	14 01	14 06	14 10	14 12	14 13	14R14	14♍R13
1964	14♍50	15 02	15 13	15 24	15 34	15 44	15 52	15 59	16 06	16 11	16 15	16 18	16 19	16R20	16♍R19
1965	16♍52	17 04	17 16	17 27	17 37	17 48	17 57	18 05	18 11	18 17	18 21	18 25	18 27	18 28	18♍R28
1966	18♍57	19 09	19 21	19 32	19 43	19 55	20 04	20 12	20 19	20 25	20 30	20 34	20 37	20 38	20♍R39
1967	21♍03	21 16	21 28	21 40	21 51	22 03	22 13	22 21	22 29	22 35	22 41	22 45	22 49	22 51	22♍R52
1968	23♍14	23 27	23 39	23 51	24 03	24 15	24 25	24 34	24 42	24 50	24 54	24 59	25 03	25 05	25♍R06
1969	25♍24	25 37	25 50	26 02	26 14	26 27	26 37	26 47	26 55	27 02	27 09	27 14	27 18	27 21	27♍R23
1970	27♍37	27 50	28 03	28 16	28 28	28 41	28 52	29 01	29 10	29 18	29 25	29 31	29 36	29 39	29♍R41
1971	29♍51	00♎04	00 17	00 30	00 43	00 56	01 07	01 18	01 27	01 35	01 43	01 49	01 54	01 58	02♎01
1972	02♎09	02 22	02 35	02 48	03 01	03 15	03 26	03 37	03 47	03 55	04 03	04 10	04 16	04 20	04♎23
1973	04♎25	04 39	04 53	05 06	05 19	05 33	05 45	05 56	06 06	06 15	06 24	06 31	06 37	06 42	06♎46
1974	06♎44	06 58	07 11	07 25	07 38	07 53	08 05	08 16	08 27	08 37	08 46	08 53	09 00	09 06	09♎10
1975	09♎03	09 17	09 31	09 45	09 58	10 14	10 26	10 38	10 49	10 59	11 09	11 17	11 24	11 30	11♎35
1976	11♎27	11 41	11 55	12 09	12 23	12 38	12 51	13 03	13 14	13 25	13 35	13 43	13 51	13 57	14♎03
1977	13♎50	14 04	14 18	14 32	14 46	15 02	15 15	15 27	15 39	15 50	16 00	16 09	16 18	16 25	16♎31
1978	16♎14	16 28	16 43	16 57	17 11	17 27	17 40	17 53	18 05	18 17	18 27	18 37	18 46	18 53	19♎01
1979	18♎40	18 54	19 08	19 22	19 37	19 53	20 06	20 20	20 32	20 44	20 55	21 05	21 15	21 23	21♎30
1980	21♎09	21 23	21 37	21 52	22 06	22 22	22 36	22 50	23 02	23 14	23 26	23 36	23 46	23 54	24♎02
1981	23♎37	23 51	24 05	24 19	24 34	24 50	25 04	25 18	25 31	25 44	25 55	26 06	26 17	26 26	25♎34
1982	26♎05	26 19	26 34	26 48	27 03	27 19	27 33	27 47	28 01	28 14	28 26	28 37	28 48	28 57	29♎06
1983	28♎35	28 49	29 03	29 20	29 34	29 49	00 03	00 17	00 31	00 44	00 56	01 08	01 19	01 29	01♏38
1984	01♏07	01 21	01 35	01 49	02 40	02 21	02 35	02 49	03 03	03 16	03 29	03 41	03 53	04 05	04♏12
1985	03♏37	03 51	04 05	04 19	04 34	04 51	05 05	05 19	05 33	05 47	06 00	06 12	06 24	06 35	06♏45
1986	06♏07	06 21	06 35	06 49	07 03	07 20	07 35	07 49	08 04	08 17	08 31	08 43	08 56	09 07	09♏17
1987	08♏38	08 51	09 05	09 19	09 33	09 50	10 05	10 19	10 34	10 48	11 01	11 14	11 27	11 38	11♏49
1988	11♏10	11 23	11 37	11 53	12 08	12 22	12 37	12 51	13 06	13 20	13 33	13 47	13 59	14 11	14♏22
1989	13♏41	13 53	14 07	14 20	14 35	14 51	15 06	15 21	15 35	15 49	16 03	16 17	16 29	16 42	16♏53
1990	16♏11	16 23	16 36	16 50	17 04	17 20	17 35	17 49	18 04	18 18	18 32	18 46	18 59	19 12	19♏23
1991	18♏41	18 53	19 05	19 19	19 32	19 49	20 03	20 18	20 32	20 47	21 10	21 15	21 18	21 41	21♏53
1992	21♏12	21 24	21 36	21 49	22 03	22 19	22 34	22 48	23 02	23 17	23 31	23 45	23 59	24 11	24♏24
1993	23♏41	23 52	24 04	24 17	24 30	24 47	25 01	25 15	25 29	25 44	25 58	26 12	26 26	26 39	26♏52
1994	26♏09	26 20	26 32	26 44	26 57	27 13	27 27	27 41	27 55	28 10	28 24	28 38	28 52	29 05	29♏18
1995	28♏36	28 47	28 58	29 10	29 23	29 38	29♐52	00 06	00 20	00 35	00 49	01 03	01 17	01 31	01♐44
1996	01♐04	01 14	01 25	01 37	01 50	02 05	02 18	02 32	02 46	03 01	03 15	03 29	03 43	03 57	04♐10
1997	03♐29	03 39	03 51	04 01	04 13	04 28	04 41	04 55	05 09	05 23	05 37	05 51	06 05	06 19	06♐32
1998	05♐53	06 02	06 12	06 23	06 35	06 50	07 03	07 16	07 30	07 44	07 58	08 12	08 26	08 40	08♐53
1999	08♐16	08 24	08 34	08 44	08 56	09 10	09 22	09 36	09 49	10 03	10 17	10 31	10 45	10 59	11♐12
2000	12♐37	12 51	13 05	13 19	13 32	10 12	10 15	10 19	10 24	10 31	10 38	10 46	10 56	11 06	11♐17

Moon's Node

	Jan 1st	Feb 1st	Mar 1st	Apr 1st	May 1st	Jun 1st	Jul 1st	Aug 1st	Sept 1st	Oct 1st	Nov 1st	Dec 1st
1900	19♐09	17♐31	16♐02	14♐24	12♐48	11♐10	09♐34	07♐56	06♐17	04♐42	03♐04	01♐28
1901	29♏50	28♏11	26♏42	25♏04	23♏29	21♏50	20♏15	18♏36	16♏58	15♏22	13♏44	12♏09
1902	10♏30	08♏52	07♏23	55♏44	04♏09	02♏30	00♏55	29♎17	27♎38	26♎03	24♎24	22♎49
1903	21♎10	19♎32	18♎03	16♎24	14♎49	13♎11	11♎35	09♎57	08♎18	06♎43	05♎05	03♎29
1904	01♎51	00♎12	28♍48	27♍02	25♍26	23♍48	22♍12	20♍34	18♍55	17♍20	15♍42	14♍06
1905	12♍28	10♍49	09♍20	07♍42	06♍07	04♍28	02♍53	01♍14	29♌36	28♌00	26♌22	24♌47
1906	23♌08	21♌30	20♌01	18♌22	16♌47	15♌08	13♌33	11♌55	07♌02	05♌27	10♌16	08♌41
1907	03♌48	02♌10	00♌41	29♋03	27♋27	25♋49	24♋13	22♋35	20♋56	19♋21	17♋43	16♋07
1908	14♋29	12♋50	11♋18	09♋40	08♋04	06♋26	04♋51	03♋12	01♋34	29♊58	28♊20	26♊44
1909	25♊06	23♊27	21♊58	20♊20	18♊45	17♊06	15♊31	13♊52	12♊14	10♊39	09♊00	07♊25
1910	05♊46	04♊08	02♊39	01♊00	29♉25	27♉46	26♉11	24♉33	22♉54	21♉19	19♉40	18♉05
1911	16♉27	14♉48	13♉19	11♉41	10♉05	08♉27	06♉51	05♉13	03♉34	01♉59	00♉21	28♈45
1912	27♈07	25♈28	23♈56	22♈18	20♈42	19♈04	17♈29	15♈50	14♈12	12♈36	10♈58	09♈22
1913	07♈44	06♈05	04♈37	02♈58	01♈23	29♓44	28♓09	26♓30	24♓52	23♓17	21♓38	20♓03
1914	18♓24	16♓46	15♓17	13♓38	12♓03	10♓25	08♓49	07♓11	05♓32	03♓57	02♓18	00♓43
1915	29♒05	27♒26	25♒57	24♒19	22♒43	21♒05	19♒30	17♒51	16♒13	14♒37	12♒59	11♒23
1916	09♒45	08♒06	06♒34	04♒56	03♒20	01♒42	00♒07	28♑28	26♑50	25♑14	23♑36	22♑01
1917	20♑22	18♑44	17♑15	15♑36	14♑01	12♑22	10♑47	09♑08	07♑30	05♑55	04♑16	02♑41
1918	01♑02	29♐24	27♐55	26♐16	24♐41	23♐03	21♐27	19♐49	18♐10	16♐35	14♐56	13♐21
1919	11♐43	10♐04	08♐35	06♐57	05♐21	03♐43	02♐08	00♐29	28♏51	27♏15	25♏37	24♏01
1920	22♏23	20♏44	19♏12	17♏34	15♏59	14♏20	12♏55	11♏06	09♏28	07♏52	06♏14	04♏39
1921	03♏00	01♏22	29♎53	28♎14	26♎39	25♎00	23♎25	21♎47	20♎08	18♎33	16♎54	15♎19
1922	13♎40	12♎02	10♎33	08♎54	07♎19	05♎41	04♎05	02♎27	00♎48	29♍13	27♍35	25♍59
1923	24♍21	22♍42	21♍13	19♍35	17♍59	16♍21	14♍46	13♍07	11♍29	09♍53	08♍15	06♍40
1924	05♍01	03♍23	01♍50	00♍12	28♌37	26♌58	25♌23	23♌44	22♌06	20♌30	18♌52	17♌17
1925	15♌38	14♌00	12♌31	10♌52	09♌17	07♌38	06♌03	04♌25	02♌46	01♌11	29♋32	27♋57
1926	26♋18	24♋40	23♋11	21♋33	19♋57	18♋19	16♋43	15♋05	13♋26	11♋51	10♋13	08♋37
1927	06♋59	05♋20	03♋51	02♋13	00♋38	28♊59	27♊24	25♊45	24♊07	22♊31	20♊53	19♊18
1928	17♊39	16♊01	14♊28	12♊50	11♊15	09♊36	08♊01	06♊22	04♊44	03♊09	01♊30	29♉55
1929	28♉16	26♉38	25♉09	23♉30	21♉55	20♉16	18♉41	17♉03	15♉24	13♉49	12♉10	10♉35
1930	08♉57	07♉18	05♉49	04♉11	02♉35	00♉57	29♈21	27♈43	26♈04	24♈29	22♈51	21♈15
1931	19♈37	17♈58	16♈29	14♈51	13♈16	11♈37	10♈02	08♈23	06♈45	05♈09	03♈31	01♈56
1932	00♈17	28♓39	27♓07	25♓28	23♓53	22♓14	20♓39	19♓00	17♓22	15♓47	14♓08	12♓33
1933	10♓54	09♓16	07♓47	06♓08	04♓33	02♓55	01♓19	29♒41	28♒02	26♒27	24♒48	23♒13
1934	21♒35	19♒56	18♒27	16♒49	15♒13	13♒35	12♒00	10♒21	08♒43	07♒07	05♒29	03♒53
1935	02♒15	00♒36	29♑04	27♑29	25♑54	24♑15	22♑40	21♑01	19♑23	17♑48	16♑09	14♑34
1936	12♑55	11♑17	09♑45	08♑06	06♑31	04♑52	03♑17	01♑38	00♐00	28♐25	26♐46	25♐11
1937	23♐32	21♐54	20♐25	18♐46	17♐11	15♐33	13♐57	12♐19	10♐40	09♐05	07♐26	05♐51
1938	04♐13	02♐34	01♐05	29♏27	27♏51	26♏13	24♏38	22♏59	21♏21	19♏45	18♏07	16♏31
1939	14♏53	13♏14	11♏46	10♏07	08♏32	06♏53	05♏18	03♏39	02♏01	00♏26	28♎47	27♎12
1940	25♎33	23♎55	22♎23	20♎44	19♎09	17♎30	15♎55	14♎17	12♎38	11♎03	09♎24	07♎49
1941	06♎10	04♎32	03♎03	01♎24	29♍49	28♍11	26♍35	24♍57	23♍18	21♍43	20♍05	18♍29
1942	16♍51	15♍12	13♍43	12♍05	10♍29	08♍51	07♍16	05♍37	03♍59	02♍23	00♍45	29♌10
1943	27♌21	25♌53	24♌24	22♌45	21♌10	19♌31	17♌56	16♌17	14♌39	13♌04	11♌25	09♌50
1944	08♌11	06♌33	05♌01	03♌22	01♌47	00♌08	28♋33	26♋55	25♋16	23♋41	22♋02	20♋27
1945	18♋48	17♋10	15♋41	14♋03	12♋27	10♋49	09♋13	07♋35	05♋56	04♋21	02♋43	01♋07
1946	29♊29	27♊50	26♊21	24♊43	23♊08	21♊29	19♊54	18♊15	16♊37	15♊14	13♊23	11♊48
1947	10♊09	08♊31	07♊02	05♊23	03♊48	02♊09	00♊34	28♉56	27♉17	25♉42	24♉03	22♉28
1948	20♉49	19♉11	17♉39	16♉00	14♉25	12♉46	11♉11	09♉33	07♉54	06♉19	04♉40	03♉05
1949	01♉27	29♈48	28♈19	26♈41	25♈05	23♈27	21♈51	20♈13	18♈34	16♈59	15♈21	13♈45
1950	12♈07	10♈28	08♈59	07♈21	05♈46	04♈07	02♈32	00♈53	29♓15	27♓39	26♓01	24♓26
1951	22♓47	21♓09	19♓40	18♓01	16♓26	14♓47	13♓12	11♓34	09♓55	08♓20	06♓41	05♓06
1952	03♓27	01♓49	00♓17	28♒38	27♒03	25♒25	23♒49	22♒11	20♒32	18♒57	17♒18	15♒43
1953	14♒05	12♒26	10♒57	09♒19	07♒43	06♒05	04♒30	02♒51	01♒13	29♑37	27♑59	26♑23
1954	24♑45	23♑06	21♑37	19♑59	18♑24	16♑45	15♑10	13♑31	11♑53	10♑18	08♑39	07♑04
1955	05♑25	03♑47	02♑18	00♑39	29♐04	27♐25	25♐50	24♐12	22♐33	20♐58	19♐19	17♐44
1956	16♐06	14♐27	12♐55	11♐16	09♐41	08♐03	06♐27	04♐49	03♐10	01♐35	29♏56	28♏21
1957	26♏43	25♏04	23♏35	21♏57	20♏21	18♏43	17♏08	15♏29	13♏51	12♏15	10♏37	09♏01
1958	07♏23	05♏44	04♏16	02♏47	01♏02	29♎23	27♎48	26♎09	24♎31	22♎56	21♎17	19♎42
1959	18♎03	16♎25	14♎56	13♎17	11♎42	10♎04	08♎28	06♎50	05♎11	03♎36	01♎57	00♎22
1960	28♍44	27♍05	25♍33	23♍54	22♍19	20♍41	19♍05	17♍27	15♍48	14♍13	12♍35	10♍59
1961	09♍21	07♍42	06♍13	04♍35	02♍59	01♍21	29♌46	28♌07	26♌29	24♌53	23♌15	21♌40
1962	20♌01	18♌23	16♌54	15♌15	13♌40	12♌01	10♌26	08♌47	07♌09	05♌34	03♌55	02♌20
1963	00♌42	29♋03	27♋34	25♋56	24♋20	22♋42	21♋06	19♋28	17♋49	16♋14	14♋35	13♋00
1964	11♋22	09♋43	08♋11	06♋33	04♋57	03♋19	01♋43	00♋05	28♊26	26♊51	25♊13	23♊27
1965	21♊59	20♊20	18♊51	17♊13	15♊38	13♊59	12♊24	10♊45	09♊07	07♊31	05♊53	04♊18
1966	02♊39	01♊01	29♉32	27♉53	26♉18	24♉39	23♉04	21♉26	19♉47	18♉12	16♉33	14♉58
1967	13♉19	11♉41	10♉12	08♉33	06♉58	05♉20	03♉44	02♉06	00♉27	28♈52	27♈14	25♈38
1968	24♈00	22♈21	20♈49	19♈11	17♈35	15♈57	14♈21	12♈43	11♈04	09♈29	07♈51	16♈56
1969	04♈37	02♈58	01♈29	29♓51	28♓16	26♓37	25♓02	23♓23	21♓45	20♓09	18♓31	16♓56
1970	15♓17	13♓39	12♓10	10♓31	08♓56	07♓17	05♓42	04♓04	02♓25	00♓50	29♓11	27♒36
1971	25♒57	24♒19	22♒50	21♒12	19♒36	17♒58	16♒22	14♒44	13♒05	11♒30	09♒52	08♒16
1972	06♒38	04♒59	03♒27	01♒49	00♒13	28♑35	27♑00	25♑21	23♑43	22♑07	20♑29	18♑53
1973	17♑15	15♑36	14♑07	12♑29	10♑54	09♑15	07♑40	06♑01	04♑23	02♑48	01♑09	29♐34
1974	27♐55	26♐17	24♐48	23♐09	21♐34	19♐55	18♐20	16♐42	15♐03	13♐28	11♐49	10♐14
1975	08♐36	06♐57	05♐28	03♐50	02♐14	00♐36	29♏00	27♏22	25♏43	24♏08	22♏30	20♏54
1976	19♏16	17♏37	16♏05	14♏27	12♏51	11♏13	09♏38	07♏59	06♏21	04♏45	03♏07	01♏31
1977	29♎53	28♎14	26♎46	25♎07	23♎32	21♎53	20♎18	18♎39	17♎01	15♎26	13♎47	12♎12
1978	10♎33	08♎55	07♎26	05♎47	04♎12	02♎34	00♎58	29♍20	27♍41	26♍06	24♍27	22♍52
1979	21♍14	19♍35	18♍06	16♍28	14♍52	13♍14	11♍39	10♍00	08♍22	06♍46	05♍08	03♍32
1980	01♍54	00♍15	28♌43	27♌05	25♌29	23♌51	22♌16	20♌37	18♌59	17♌23	15♌45	14♌10
1981	12♌31	10♌53	09♌24	07♌45	06♌10	04♌31	02♌56	01♌17	29♋39	28♋04	26♋25	24♋50
1982	23♋11	21♋33	20♋04	18♋25	16♋50	15♋12	13♋36	11♋58	10♋19	08♋44	07♋05	05♋30
1983	03♋52	02♋13	00♋44	29♊06	27♊30	25♊52	24♊17	22♊38	21♊00	19♊24	17♊46	16♊10
1984	14♊32	12♊53	11♊21	09♊43	08♊08	06♊29	04♊54	03♊15	01♊37	00♊01	28♉23	26♉48
1985	25♉09	23♉31	22♉02	20♉23	18♉48	17♉09	15♉34	13♉56	12♉17	10♉42	09♉03	07♉28
1986	05♉49	04♉11	02♉42	01♉03	29♈28	27♈50	26♈14	24♈36	22♈57	21♈22	19♈44	18♈08
1987	16♈30	14♈51	13♈22	11♈44	10♈08	08♈30	06♈55	05♈16	03♈38	02♈02	00♈24	28♓49
1988	27♓10	25♓32	23♓59	22♓21	20♓46	19♓07	17♓32	15♓53	14♓15	12♓39	11♓01	09♓26
1989	07♓47	06♓09	04♓40	03♓01	01♓26	29♒47	28♒12	26♒34	24♒55	23♒20	21♒41	20♒06
1990	18♒27	16♒49	15♒20	13♒42	12♒06	10♒28	08♒52	07♒14	05♒35	04♒00	02♒22	00♒46
1991	29♑08	27♑29	26♑00	24♑22	22♑47	21♑08	19♑33	17♑54	16♑16	14♑40	13♑02	11♑27
1992	09♑48	08♑10	06♑37	04♑59	03♑24	01♑45	00♑10	28♐31	26♐53	25♐18	23♐39	22♐04
1993	20♐25	18♐47	17♐18	15♐39	14♐04	12♐25	10♐50	09♐12	07♐33	05♐58	04♐19	02♐44
1994	01♐06	29♏27	27♏58	26♏20	24♏44	23♏06	21♏30	19♏52	18♏13	16♏38	15♏00	13♏24
1995	11♏46	10♏07	08♏38	07♏00	05♏25	03♏46	02♏11	00♏32	28♎54	27♎18	25♎40	24♎05
1996	22♎26	20♎48	19♎16	17♎37	16♎02	14♎23	12♎48	11♎09	09♎31	07♎56	06♎17	04♎42
1997	03♎03	01♎25	29♍56	28♍17	26♍42	25♍04	23♍28	21♍50	20♍11	18♍36	16♍57	15♍22
1998	13♍44	12♍05	10♍36	08♍58	07♍22	05♍44	04♍09	02♍30	00♍52	29♌16	27♌38	26♌02
1999	24♌24	22♌45	21♌16	19♌38	18♌03	16♌24	14♌49	13♌10	11♌32	09♌57	08♌18	06♌43
2000	05♌05	03♌26	01♌54	00♌15	28♋40	27♋01	25♋26	23♋47	22♋09	20♋34	18♋55	17♋20

INDEX

Page references to illustrations appear in italics.

INDEX